Access™ 2007 Bible

Michael R. Groh, Joseph C. Stockman,

Gavin Powell, Cary N. Prague,

Michael R. Irwin, and Jennifer Reardon

Wiley Publishing, Inc.

Access™ 2007 Bible

Published by
Wiley Publishing, Inc.
10475 Crosspoint Boulevard
Indianapolis, IN 46256
www.wiley.com

Published simultaneously in Canada

Library of Congress Control Number: 2006936763

ISBN-13: 978-0-470-04673-9
ISBN-10: 0-470-04673-2

Manufactured in the United States of America

10 9 8 7 6 5 4 3 2

1B/TR/QT/QW/IN

For general information on our other products and services or to obtain technical support, please contact our Customer Care Department within the U.S. at (800) 762-2974, outside the U.S. at (317) 572-3993 or fax (317) 572-4002.

Wiley also publishes its books in a variety of electronic formats. Some content that appears in print may not be available in electronic books.

About the Authors

Michael R. Groh is a well-known author, writer, and consultant specializing in Windows database systems. His company, PC Productivity Solutions, provides information-management applications to companies across the country. Over the last 25 years, Mike has worked with a wide variety of programming languages, operating systems, and computer hardware, ranging from programming a DEC PDP-8A using the Focal interpreted language to building distributed applications under Visual Studio .NET and Microsoft SharePoint.

Mike was one of the first people outside of Microsoft to see Access in action. He was among a select group of journalists and publishers invited to preview the Access 1.0 beta (then called Cirrus) at the 1992 Windows World Conference in Chicago. Since then, Mike has been involved in every Microsoft Access beta program, as an insider and as a journalist and reporter documenting the evolution of this fascinating product.

Mike has authored parts of more than 20 different computer books and is a frequent contributor to computer magazines and journals. Mike has written more than 200 articles and editorials over the last 15 years, mostly for Advisor Media (San Diego, CA). He frequently speaks at computer conferences virtually everywhere in the world, and is technical editor and contributor to periodicals and publications produced by Advisor Media.

Mike holds a master's degree in Clinical Chemistry from the University of Iowa (Iowa City, IA) and an MBA from Northeastern University (Boston, MA).

Mike can be reached at `AccessBible@mikegroh.com`. Please prefix the e-mail subject line with "AccessBible:" to get past the spam blocker on this account.

Joseph C. Stockman is an independent consultant, software designer, and author who has been using Microsoft Access since its initial release. He has also developed courseware and taught classes in Access and VBA. Joe developed his first application in Access, and then migrated into Visual Basic and Visual Basic .NET, where he specializes in creating applications for the Windows Mobile platform. He worked for several software companies before forming his consulting business in 2002, where he deals with all types of clients including healthcare, financial, government, manufacturing, and small business. His ability to turn his customers' wishes into working applications keeps them satisfied. Joe is also writing the fundamentals column for the *Advisor Guide to Microsoft Access* magazine.

Gavin Powell is a computer consultant and a writer, with over 20 years of IT experience and over 10 titles to his credit. He has worked as a programmer, analyst, data modeler, database administrator, and Unix administrator. Gavin is also a semiprofessional musician, songwriter, and recording engineer, playing multiple instruments and writing prolifically. Gavin can be reached by e-mail at `info@oracledbaexpert.com` or `ezpowell@ezpowell.com`.

Cary N. Prague is an internationally best-selling author and lecturer in the database industry. He owns Database Creations, Inc., the world's largest Microsoft Access add-on company. Their products include a line of financial software; Business! for Microsoft Office, a mid-range accounting system, POSitively Business! Point of Sale software, the Inventory Barcode manager for mobile data collection, and the Check Writer and General Ledger. Database Creations also produces a line of developer tools including the appBuilder, an application generator for Microsoft Access, the EZ Access Developer Tools for building great user interfaces, appWatcher for maintaining code bases among several developers, and Surgical Strike, the only Patch Manager for Microsoft Access.

Cary also owns Database Creations Consulting, LLC., a successful consulting firm specializing in Microsoft Access and SQL Server applications. Local and national clients include many Fortune 100 companies including manufacturers, defense contractors, insurance, health-care, and software industry companies. His client list includes Microsoft, United Technologies, ABB, Smith & Wesson Firearms, Pratt and Whitney Aircraft, ProHealth, OfficeMax, Continental Airlines, and other Fortune 500 companies.

Formerly, he has held numerous management positions in corporate information systems, including Director of Managed Care Reporting for MetraHealth, Director of Corporate Finance and Software Productivity at Travelers Insurance where he was responsible for software support for 35,000 end users, and Manager of Information Systems support for Northeast Utilities.

He is one of the top best-selling authors in the computer database management market, having written over 40 books that have sold over one million copies on software including Microsoft Access, Borland (Ashton-Tate) dBASE, Paradox, R:Base, Framework, and graphics. Cary's books include 11 books in the *Access Bible* series (recently number one on the Ingram Bestselling Database Titles list and in the Amazon.com top 100), *Access 97 Secrets, dBASE for Windows Handbook, dBASE IV Programming* (winner of the Computer Press Association's Book of the Year award for Best Software Specific Book), and *Everyman's Database Primer Featuring dBASE IV.* He recently completed several books for Access 2003 including *Weekend Crash Course in Office Access 2003 Programming*. Cary recently sold a product line named eTools for Microsoft Access to MightyWords, a division of FatBrain.com and Barnes and Noble.

Cary is certified in Access as a Microsoft Certified Professional and has passed the MOUS test in Access and Word. He is a frequent speaker at seminars and conferences around the country. He is on the exclusive Microsoft Access Insider Advisory Board and makes frequent trips to Microsoft headquarters in Redmond, WA. He has been voted the best speaker by the attendees of several national conferences. Recently, he was a speaker for Microsoft sponsored conferences in New Orleans, Hawaii, Phoenix, Chicago, Toronto, Palm Springs, Boston, and Orlando. He has also spoken at Borland's Database Conference, Digital Consulting's Database World, Microsoft's Developer Days, Computerland's Technomics Conference, COMDEX, and COMPAQ Computer's Innovate. He was a contributing editor to *Access Advisor* magazine and has written for the *Microsoft Office Developer's* journal.

He is active in local town politics serving on the South Windsor, Connecticut Board of Education, Parks and Recreation Commission, and the Board of Assessment Appeals.

Cary holds a master's degree in computer science from Rensselaer Polytechnic Institute, and an M.B.A and Bachelor of Accounting from the University of Connecticut. He is also a Certified Data Processor.

Michael R. Irwin is considered one of the leading authorities on automated database and Internet management systems today. He is a noted worldwide lecturer, a winner of national and international awards, best-selling author, and developer of client/server, Internet, Intranet, and PC-based database management systems.

Michael has extensive database knowledge, gained by working with the Metropolitan Police Department in Washington, D.C. as a developer and analyst for the Information Systems Division for over 20 years and assorted Federal Agencies of the United States Government. Since retiring in June 1992, he runs his own consulting firm, named The Irwin Group, and is principal partner in the company - IT in Asia, LLC, specializing in Internet database integration and emphasizing Client/Server and net solutions. With consulting offices in Cincinnati, Ohio, Bangkok, Thailand, and Manila, Philippines, his companies offer training and development of Internet and database applications. His company has the distinction of being one of the first Microsoft Solution's Providers (in 1992). His local, national, and international clients include many software companies, manufacturers, government agencies, and international companies.

His range of expertise includes database processing and integration between mainframe, minicomputer, and PC-based database systems, as well as B-2-B and B-2-C integration between back-end databases; he is a leading authority on PC-based databases.

He is one of the top best-selling authors in the computer database management market, having authored numerous database books, with several of them consistently on the best-sellers lists. His books, combined, have sold nearly a million copies worldwide. His most recent works include *The OOPs Primer* (Borland Press), *dBASE 5.5 for Windows Programming* (Prentice Hall), *Microsoft Access 2002 Bible*, *Microsoft Access 2002 Bible Gold Edition* (co-authored), and *Working with the Internet*. The *Access Bible* series have constantly been number one on the Ingram Best-selling Database Titles list and is consistently in the Amazon.com and Buy.com top 10. He has also written several books on customs and cultures of the countries of Asia (including China, Japan, Thailand, and India). Two of his books have won international acclaim. His books are published in over 24 languages worldwide. He has been a contributing editor and author to many well-known magazines and journals.

He is a frequent speaker at seminars and conferences around the world and has been voted the best speaker by the attendees of several international conferences.

Michael has developed and markets several add-on software products for the Internet and productivity related applications. Many of his productivity applications can be obtained from several of his Internet sites or on many common download sites. Many of his application and systems are distributed as freeware and careware. He has also developed and distributes several development tools and add-ins for a wide range of developer applications.

Jennifer Reardon is considered a leading developer of custom database applications. She has over ten years' experience developing client/server and PC-based applications. She has accumulated much of her application development experience working as lead developer for Database Creations. She has partnered with Cary Prague developing applications for many Fortune 500 companies.

Her most significant projects include a spare parts inventory control system for Pratt & Whitney's F22 program, an engineering specifications system for ABB-Combustion Engineering, and an emergency event tracking system for the State of Connecticut. She was also the lead developer of many of the Database Creations add-on software products including Business, Yes! I Can Run My Business, Check Writer, and the User Interface Construction Kit.

She has co-authored *Access 2003 Bible, Access 2002 Bible,* and *Access 2000 Weekend Crash Course*. She has also written chapters in other books on subjects including Data Access Pages, the Microsoft Database Engine, the VBA programming environment, creating help systems, and using Microsoft Office 2000 Developer. She has authored chapters in *Microsoft Access 97 Bible* and *Access 97 Secrets*.

Jennifer owns her own consulting firm, Advanced Software Concepts, providing custom applications to both the public and private sectors. She specializes in developing client information systems for state-managed and privately-held healthcare organizations. She has also developed a job costing and project management system for an international construction company. Her corporate experience includes seven years with The Travelers where she was an Associate Software Engineer serving on numerous mission-critical client/server software development projects using Easel, C, SQL Server, and DB2. She has contributed several chapters for books on dBase and Microsoft Access.

Jennifer holds a Bachelor of Science degree from the University of Massachusetts.

Credits

Acquisitions Manager
Greg Croy

Project Editor
Elizabeth Kuball

Technical Editor
Vincent McCune

Copy Editor
Elizabeth Kuball

Editorial Manager
Jodi Jensen

Vice President & Executive Group Publisher
Richard Swadley

Vice President and Publisher
Andy Cummings

Editorial Director
Mary C. Corder

Project Coordinator
Heather Kolter

Graphics and Production Specialists
Carrie A. Foster
Brooke Graczyk
Denny Hager
Joyce Haughey
Jennifer Mayberry

Quality Control Technicians
Laura Albert
Jessica Kramer
Christine Pingleton

Media Development Project Supervisor
Laura Moss

Media Development Specialist
Kit Malone

Proofreading and Indexing
Techbooks

Contents
at a Glance

Part IV: Professional Database Development 821

Part V: Access as an Enterprise Platform 1163

Part VI: Appendixes 1265

Part IV: Professional Database Development 821

Part V: Access as an Enterprise Platform 1163

When we first saw Access in July of 1992, we were instantly sold on this new-generation database management and access tool. We've all spent the last 15 years using Access daily. In fact, we eat, breathe, live, and sleep Access!

The fact that we can earn a living from our work with principally one product is a tribute to the Microsoft Access designers. This product has changed the productivity of corporations and private citizens of the world. More people use this product to run their businesses, manage their affairs, track the most important things in their lives, and manage data in their work and play than any other product ever written. It is indeed a privilege to be part of this worldwide community.

Now we have completely rewritten this book for Access 2007, with new examples and more in-depth coverage. We've covered every new feature we could think of for the beginning and intermediate users and especially enhanced our programming section. Over 500,000 copies of our *Access Bible*s have been sold for all versions of Microsoft Access; for this we thank all of our loyal readers.

Our first acknowledgment is to all the users of Access who have profited and benefited beyond everyone's wildest dreams.

There are many people who assisted us in writing this book. We'd like to recognize each of them.

To Greg Croy, whom we complain to each day. Thanks for listening, Pilgrim.

To Carole McClendon, the very best literary agent in the business, and all the folks at Waterside Productions for being our agents.

A special thank you to Erik Rucker, Clint Covington, Michael McCormack, Jensen Harris, Shavaj Dhanial, and the rest of the Microsoft Access 2007 Team! You've built a terrific product, and we thank you!

> Also, thanks to the Fixed Income–IT group at Raymond James Financial: Julie Valdez, Marek Pokropinski, Aalan Elliot, Aly Fernandez, Bernard Brown, Coni Brown, Lilly Dejesus-Normand, Mae Mello, Michel Thiran, Nancy Hawkins, Renee Crumity, and Steven Twors. Thanks so much for your patience during my many absences during this project!
>
> Thanks to these wonderful people, we were able to deliver a quality book to our readers.
>
> For Pam. You are the one.

—Mike Groh

Acknowledgments

This book is dedicated to my mom, who sadly passed away a few days after I finished the project. She has always supported me and encouraged me in everything that I've done. She may not have known what Access is or does, but she knew I loved working with it. I'm sure she's looking into bookstores everywhere and is proud to see her son's name. I miss you, mom, and you'll always be with me. Also, a big thanks to my family and friends, who supported me during this project and the difficult time afterwards.

—Joe Stockman

This book is dedicated to anyone and everyone using Access 2007. My hope is that readers have as much fun exploring the interface and features as I did during the process of working on parts of this book.

—Gavin Powell

Introduction

Welcome to the *Access 2007 Bible,* your personal guide to a powerful, easy-to-use database-management system. This book is in its tenth revision and has been totally rewritten for Microsoft Access 2007 with new text, new pictures, and a completely new and improved set of example files.

This book examines Access 2007 with more examples than any other Access 2007 book. We strongly believe that Microsoft Access is an excellent database manager and the best desktop and workgroup database-development system available today. Our goal with this book is to share what we know about Access and, in the process, to help make your work and your life easier.

This book contains everything you need in order to learn Microsoft Access to a mid-advanced level. The book starts off with database basics and builds, chapter by chapter, on topics previously covered. In places where it is essential that you understand previously covered topics, we present the concepts again and review how to perform specific tasks before moving on. Although each chapter is an integral part of the book as a whole, each chapter can also stand on its own and has its own example files. You can read the book in any order you want, skipping from chapter to chapter and from topic to topic. (Note that this book's index is particularly thorough; you can refer to the index to find the location of a particular topic you're interested in.)

The examples in this book have been well thought out to simulate the types of tables, queries, forms, and reports most people need to create when performing common business activities. There are many notes, tips, and techniques (and even a few secrets) to help you better understand Microsoft Access.

This book easily substitutes for the online help included with Access. This book guides you through each task you need to perform with Access. This book follows a much more structured approach than the Microsoft Access online help, going into more depth on almost every topic and showing many different types of examples. You're also going to find much more detail than in most other books on Microsoft Access.

Is This Book for You?

We wrote this book for beginning, intermediate, and even advanced users of Microsoft Access 2007. With any product, most users start at the beginning. If, however, you're already familiar with Microsoft Access and you've worked with the sample files or other Access applications, you may want to start with the later parts of this book. Note, however, that starting at the beginning of a book is usually a good idea so you don't miss out on the secrets and tips in the early chapters.

We think this book covers Microsoft Access 2007 in detail better than any other book currently on the market. We hope you'll find this book helpful while working with Access, and that you enjoy the innovative style of a Wiley book.

Yes — If you have no database experience

If you're new to the world of database management, this book has everything you need to get started with Microsoft Access 2007. It then offers advanced topics for reference and learning. Beginning developers should pay particular attention to Part I, where we cover the essential skills necessary for building successful and efficient databases. Your ability as a database designer is constantly judged by how well the applications you build perform, and how well they handle data entrusted to them by their users. The chapters in Part I won't necessarily make you an expert database designer, but we guarantee you'll be a better developer if you carefully read this material.

Yes — If you've used other database managers like Filemaker

If you're abandoning another database (such as Filemaker, Paradox, or FoxPro) or even upgrading from an earlier version of Access, this book is for you. You'll have a head start because you're already familiar with database managers and how to use them. With Microsoft Access, you will be able to do all the tasks you've performed with other database systems — without programming or getting lost. This book will take you through each subject step by step.

Yes — If you want to learn the basics of Visual Basic for Applications (VBA) programming

We understand that a very large book is needed to properly cover VBA, but we took the time to put together many chapters that build on what you learn in the forms chapters of this book. The VBA programming chapters use the same examples you'll be familiar with by the end of the book. Part II of this book explains the nuts and bolts — with lots of gritty technical details — of writing VBA procedures and building Access applications around the code you add to your databases. Part II provides everything you need (other than a lot of practice!) to become a bona-fide VBA programmer.

Conventions Used in This Book

The following conventions are used in this book:

- When you're instructed to press a key combination (press and hold down one key while pressing another key), the key combination is separated by a plus sign. Ctrl+Esc, for example, indicates that you must hold down the Ctrl key and press the Esc key; then release both keys.

- *Point the mouse* refers to moving the mouse so that the mouse pointer is on a specific item. *Click* refers to pressing the left mouse button once and releasing it. *Double-click* refers to pressing the left mouse button twice in rapid succession and then releasing it. *Right-click* refers to pressing the right mouse button once and releasing it. *Drag* refers to pressing and holding down the left mouse button while moving the mouse.
- *Italic type* is used for new terms and for emphasis.
- **Bold type** is used for material you need to type directly into the computer.
- A `special typeface` is used for information you see on-screen — error messages, expressions, and formulas, for example.

Icons and Alerts

You'll notice special graphic symbols, or icons, used in the margins throughout this book. These icons are intended to alert you to points that are particularly important or noteworthy. The following icons are used in this book:

This icon highlights a special point of interest about the topic under discussion.

This icon points to a useful hint that may save you time or trouble.

This icon alerts you that the operation being described can cause problems if you're not careful.

CROSS-REF **This icon points to a more complete discussion in another chapter of the book.**

ON the CD-ROM **This icon highlights information for readers who are following the examples and using the sample files included on the disc accompanying this book.**

NEW FEATURE **This icon calls attention to new features of Access 2007.**

Sidebars

In addition to noticing the icons used throughout this book, you'll also notice material placed in gray boxes. This material offers background information, an expanded discussion, or a deeper insight about the topic under discussion. Some sidebars offer nuts-and-bolts technical explanations, and others provide useful anecdotal material.

How This Book Is Organized

This book contains 41 chapters divided into five parts. In addition, the book contains a sixth part containing three appendixes.

Part I: Access Building Blocks

Part I consists of nine chapters that cover virtually every aspect of Access development. For many Access developers, these chapters are all that you'll ever need. The chapters in this part cover basic database design, referential integrity, constructing tables and queries, building forms and reports, and using the new features in Access 2007.

Chapters 1 through 3 contains great conceptual material on understanding the basic elements of data, introduces you to the buzzwords of database management, and teaches you how to plan tables and work with Access data types. Chapter 4 through 6 teaches you Access queries, expressions, and working with Datasheet view. Much has changed in Access 2007, and even experienced Access users are easily confused by the new user interface.

Chapters 7 through 9 take you on a tour of various types of forms and get a complete understanding of form controls. These chapters drill into the process of creating great-looking and effective forms and reports. You'll learn how to take best advantage of the new features in Access 2007.

Part II: Programming Microsoft Access

Virtually every serious Access application uses VBA code to perform operations not possible with macros, or to make using the application easier and more reliable. Learning VBA programming is often a daunting task, so the six chapters in this part take extra care to explain the principles behind VBA programming, and show you how to take advantage of this powerful programming language.

In these chapters, you'll learn not only the fundamental skills required to become proficient in VBA, you'll also learn many "inside" tricks and techniques to apply to your Access application development projects. You'll come to understand and appreciate the complex object and event models that drive Access applications, and how to construct the VBA code necessary to take advantage of this rich programming environment.

Part III: More Advanced Access Techniques

One you've gotten through the basics of building Access applications, you'll want your database development skills to extend and enhance your Access applications. Part III includes ten chapters that cover virtually every aspect of advanced Access development, including importing and exporting data, exchanging data with other Windows applications, and integrating Access with Microsoft SharePoint.

The techniques in Part III would normally take most Access developers several years to master. We've carefully selected a potpourri of techniques that have proven valuable to each of us in relevant development efforts. Each chapter is accompanied by an example database that demonstrates the techniques documented in the chapter.

Part IV: Professional Database Development

Over the years, Access has grown in its features and capabilities. Although most Access developers never have to use the techniques and features documented in Part IV, we've included these techniques to make the *Microsoft Access 2007 Bible* the most comprehensive reference possible.

Part IV includes 11 chapters covering a wide range of professional-level Access techniques. In these chapters, you'll read about advanced features such as database replication, object-oriented programming in Access, using the Windows API, creating Access libraries as a way to reuse your VBA code, and customizing the Access 2007 ribbons. Almost all of the information in Part IV has been added for this edition of the *Microsoft Access Bible,* and reflects the growth and expansion of Access's capabilities.

Part V: Access as an Enterprise Platform

Access is often employed in "enterprise" environments as a front-end to data stored in a variety of server database systems, such as Microsoft SQL Server and Oracle. In addition, Microsoft has improved SharePoint Services, and has added seamless integration and data sharing between Access and SharePoint. The five chapters in Part V cover a variety of topics that are of interest to developers working in enterprise environments. In these chapters, you'll see how XML is often used as a data exchange medium, and how Access integrates with server database engines such as SQL Server and Oracle.

You'll also learn how to upsize Access applications to SQL Server. Access 2007 seamlessly integrates with SQL Server, as either a simple consumer of SQL Server data, or as a direct interface to a SQL Server database. The chapters in Part V cover this important technology in detail.

Part VI: Appendixes

The last part contains three appendixes. Appendix A presents a series of tables listing Access specifications, including maximum and minimum sizes of many of the controls in Access. Appendix B describes the contents of the CD-ROM. And Appendix C tells you what's new with Access 2007.

Pardon Our Dust!

It almost goes without saying that this book was written during the Access 2007 beta testing phase. It's possible that a few of the figures in this book don't exactly match what you see when you open Access 2007, or that the terminology will have changed between the time we wrote our chapters and the time you installed Access 2007 on your computer. Please bear with us — Microsoft has done a great job of documenting its plans and expectations for Access 2007 and we authors have done our best to explain the many changes. We hope that any differences you encounter between our descriptions and explanations and your experience with Access 2007 are minor and do not impact your workflow.

Please feel free to drop us an e-mail at `AccessBible@mikegroh.com` if you have a question or comment about the material in the Access 2007 Bible. Also, contact us if you have a more general question about development with Access or SQL Server, and we will try to help you out. Before to prefix the subject line of your e-mail with AccessBible: or you won't get past the spam blocker on this account.

Guide to the Examples

The examples in *Access 2007 Bible* are specially designed to maximize your learning experience. Throughout this book, you'll see many examples of good business table design and implementation, form and report creation, and module coding in Visual Basic. You'll see examples that use both Jet (the internal database of Microsoft Access) as well as examples that connect to SQL Server databases. You'll also see forms that work with SharePoint data located in remote locations on the Internet.

As every developer knows, it's important to understand what you're creating and programming from the application standpoint. This is sometimes called "the business of business," and in this book we have chosen a simple example that we hope any business or developer can relate to. More importantly, in this or any book you must relate to it successfully in order to learn. When developing systems, you often find yourself analyzing applications that you don't have a lot of experience with. Obviously an aerospace engineer makes a better analyst when developing a system to track airplane engines, but any good developer can develop any system as long as he's willing to work with the business experts. In this book, the authors and their words will serve as the business experts.

The examples in this book use a fictitious company named Access Auto Auctions, or AA Auctions for short. AA Auctions buys and sells cars, trucks, and other vehicles. They directly sell these vehicles and also offer them for sale through auctions both at their equally fictitious showroom and on the Internet. The example database contains the necessary tables, queries, forms, reports, and module code to facilitate their business needs.

NOTE **Within this guide we use some terms that have not been thoroughly explained yet. Feel free to skip over them and return to this guide often as you start new chapters that use these forms and reports.**

TIP **While professional developers will always split program and data objects into two separate database files, it is acceptable during development to combine all of the objects into one database and split them when development is complete. When you're working in a program database and you're linked to your data file, you must load the data database file before you can make changes to the table design. You'll learn more about this throughout the book.**

The Main Menu Switchboard

When you load the completed example file (`Access Auto Auctions.mdb`), you'll see the main menu (known as a Switchboard) shown in Figure FM-1. This Switchboard contains buttons that display the main areas of the system.

FIGURE FM-1

The Access Auto Auctions main Switchboard that allows the user to open various forms and reports

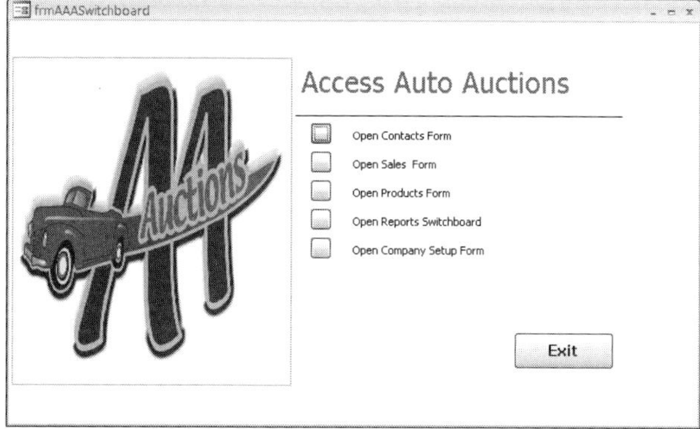

These main areas include

- **Contacts:** Buyers and Sellers of vehicles and parts that AA Auctions deal with. Rather than traditionally separate Customer and Supplier tables, the Contacts table provides a single source of all people working with AA Auctions.
- **Sales:** This button displays an invoice form that lets AA Auctions enter information about the buyer (which comes from the Contacts information). Sales allows for an unlimited number of line items on the Invoice, and each item is selected from information stored in the Products system.
- **Products:** Lists of everything that AA Auctions sells or offers for auctions These include vehicles, parts, and anything that needs to be tracked for sales or inventory purposes including descriptions, costs, selling prices, and even pictures of each vehicle or part.
- **Reports:** Any good application contains reports at many levels. This button actually does nothing. Normally, it would be used to display a generic report manager that displays reports while allowing specifications of the report name and parameters that only shows data between certain dates or for certain vehicle types.

- **Company Setup:** This displays a form that contains information used by the entire system. This is used when you need global values such as your company name (Access Auto Auctions in this example) or other information that can be used by the entire application.

Understanding the Data Tables

Data is the most important part of any system and in Access (as well as every other database management system), data is arranged into logical groupings known as *tables.* Tables help define the structure of the data, as well as hold the data itself. Tables are related to each other in order to pass data back and forth and to help assemble the chaos of data into well-defined and well-formatted information.

The diagram in Figure FM-2 displays the table schema in the Access Auto Auctions example. As you will learn in Part I of this book, the lines, arrows, and symbols between the tables mean something important and communicate to the developer how the data interacts. You'll learn terms like *table, field, record, relationship, referential integrity, normalization, primary keys,* and *foreign keys* as you begin to understand how tables work within a database.

FIGURE FM-2

The Access Auto Auctions relationship diagram

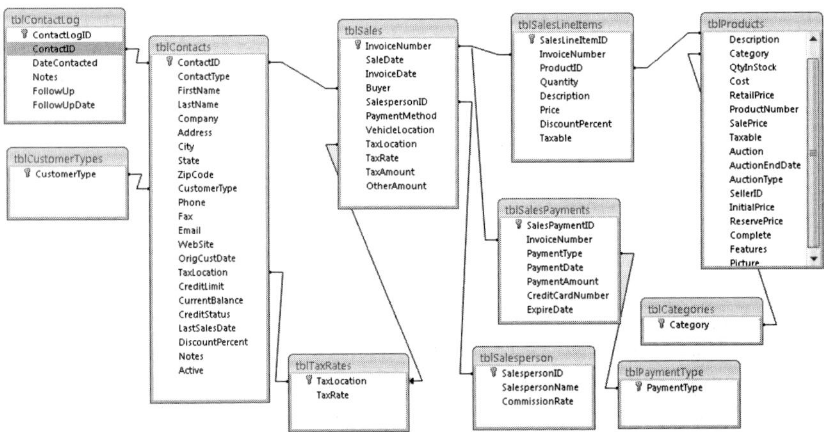

The example database consists of the 11 core tables shown in Figure FM-2. Many of the smaller tables are *lookup* tables whose sole purpose is to provide a list of valid selections. The larger tables hold data used by the database application itself. All of these tables include a number of data fields that are used as the definitions of the data. The lines between the tables show how tables are related:

- **`tblSales`:** Contains fields for the main part of the sale. This includes information that occurs once for each sale, such as the invoice number, dates of the sale, the buyer ID (which links to the `tblContacts`_table to retrieve information about the buyer including taxing information), the salesperson ID (which links to the `tblSalesperson` table), the taxing location (which links to the `tblTaxRates` table), and various other financial information.

- **`tblSalesPerson`:** Contains salespeople that sell products for Access Auto Auctions along with their commission rates. It is linked to the sales invoice and is used when a salesperson is selected in the invoice form.
- **`tblTaxRates`**: Contains a list of taxing locations and tax rates and is used by the sales invoice when the buyer is selected in the form. The taxing location is retrieved from `tblTaxRates`, and then the tax rate used by the invoice to calculate taxes owed.
- **`tblSalesLineItems`:** Contains fields for the individual line items that will make up the sale. The sale may contain a variety of items. Several vehicles may be sold to a single buyer at one time. The buyer may buy parts, accessories, or services. You'll see a form created later that allows for the data entry of an invoice and an unlimited number of line items that will be stored in this table.

  The data fields in the `tblSalesLineItems` table include the invoice number, which is used to link the main invoice table to the invoice line items table as well as the quantity purchased. The product ID field (which links to the `tblProducts` table) is used to retrieve information about the product including the item description, price, and taxability status. A discount field allows a discount to be entered.

  The way this table is used violates true relational database theory. Rather than simply link from the `tblSalesLineItems` table to the `tblProducts` table by the product ID field, data values from the `tblProducts` table are copied to the `tblSalesLineItems`. This is often done with time-dependent data. If a customer bought a part today with a price of $10 and next week the price goes up to $15 as stored in the `tblProducts` table, it would be wrong if the invoice then showed the price of $15.

CROSS-REF **You learn more about relational database theory and how to build tables in Part I of this book**

- **`tblSalesPayments`:** Contains fields for the individual payment lines. The invoice may be paid for by a variety of methods. The customer may make a deposit for the sale with a check, and then split the remaining amount owed with a variety of credit cards. By having unlimited payment lines in the invoice form you can do this.

  The data fields in `tblSalesPayments` include the invoice number which is used to link the main invoice table. There is a field for the payment type (which links to `tblPaymentType`) to only allow entry of valid payment types, as well as the payment date, payment amount, and any check or credit-card number and the credit-card expiration date.
- **`tblPaymentType`:** Is simply a lookup table with valid values for types of payments. Only valid payment types can be chosen for a payment.
- **`tblContacts`:** Contains information about all the people and companies that Access Auto Auctions works with. This data includes customers, suppliers, buyers, and sellers. Names, physical addresses, phone and fax numbers, e-mail addresses, and Web sites and all the financial information about the contact is stored in this table. Unlike the `tblSalesLineitems` table information, this data is linked from an invoice form and,

with the exception of some changing financial data, is never copied to any other table. This way if a customer changes his address or phone number, any invoice that is related to the contact data, instantly shows the updated information.

- **tblContactLog:** Contains zero or more entries for each contact in tblContacts. This information includes the contact date, notes or items discussed, and follow-up information. The contacts form manages all of this information.
- **tblCustomerTypes:** Simply contains a list of valid customer types that can be selected through the Contacts form. It is important in all applications that certain data be limited to valid values. In this example, each valid value triggers certain business rules. Therefore, data entry must be limited to those values.
- **tblProducts:** Contains information about the items sold or auctioned by Access Auto Auctions. This table contains information used by the invoices line items.

  tblProducts will be one of the main tables used in this book. The frmProducts form is used to teach nearly all form development lessons in the book so you should pay particular attention to it.
- **tblCategories:** Is used to lookup a list of valid categories.

Understanding the Products Form

frmProducts, shown in Figure FM-3, is the first form that shows how to build Access forms. It is also one of the forms that you'll use frequently through the book. The Products form was developed with most of the form control types used in Microsoft Access to handle data types such as text, currency, date, yes/no, memo, and OLE pictures.

It is important to have a good understanding of the use of the form as well as the technical details of building it. The form contains information about each product and is bound (tied) to tblProducts. As you enter information into the frmProducts form, it is stored in the tblProducts table.

The top of the frmProducts form contains a control that allows you to quickly find a record. This *Quick Find* is programmed using VBA code behind a combo box selection. The bottom of the form contains a series of command buttons that will be used to demonstrate how to create new records, delete existing records, and display a custom search and custom print dialog box.

Understanding the Product Form Subform

frmProducts is a great example of how a form works. It displays many records at once but only selected fields. There is also a button alongside each record to delete any records that are no longer needed. Each of the column headers is actually a button with code behind it that can be clicked on to sort the records displayed by the form. One click and the data in that column is used to sort the records in ascending order. The next click sorts the records in descending order.

FIGURE FM-3

The Access Auto Auctions Products form, which allows data entry for all vehicles and parts sold or auctioned

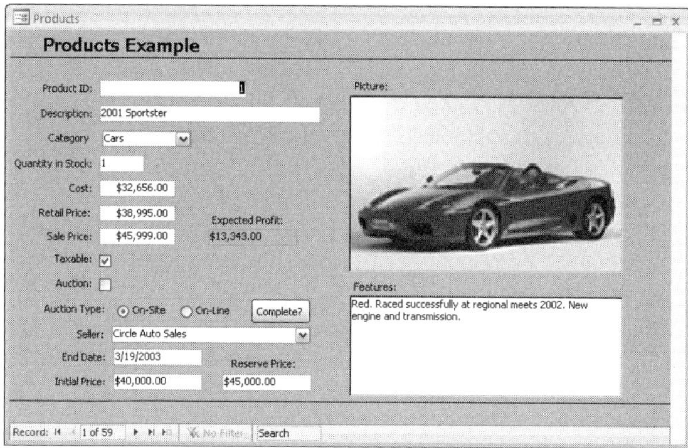

Understanding the Contacts Form

`frmContacts`, shown in Figure FM-4, is used to maintain information about the various Access Auto Auctions contacts. This includes the contact's name and address, whether they are a buyer, seller, or both. This form includes information if the buyer or seller is a car dealer or parts store that they regularly do business with or someone who just once came to an auction, bid on a car, and won.

The Contact form, like the Products form, contains a tab control. This allows you to show several screens within one form. The Contacts form is used in later chapters to illustrate how to display objects within a form based on certain conditions and to show how to use a calendar to store and display data as well.

FIGURE FM-4

The Access Auto Auctions `frmContacts` form showing a tabbed dialog box and values used with the `tblContacts` table

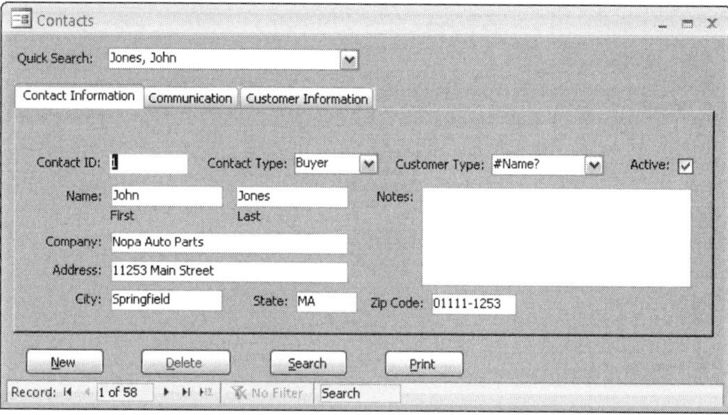

Using the Sales Form

`frmSales`, shown in Figure FM-5, demonstrates some more advanced form concepts. Unlike all the other forms, the Invoice form contains two subforms, each of which uses a relationship known as *one-to-many.* This means that there may be one or more records in each subform that relate to (use the same key as) the main form. In this example, each invoice is used to sell one or more products to a buyer. After all the products are selected for the invoice and a total price is calculated, you enter one or more payments to pay for the vehicle. The buyer may make a deposit with a check, and then pay the remaining balance with two different credit cards.

This form also demonstrates simple and complex calculations. The calculation of the Amount column in the invoice line items is Qty x Price x (1-Discount%) for example. All of the amount records have to be totaled to calculate the subtotal field. Then a tax rate is retrieved and calculated to get the tax amount. This plus the other amount must be summed to get the total. All this is happening using fields in the Invoice Line items (`fsubSalesLineitems`) subform.

`fsubSalesPayments` subform also shows how to calculate a total in one subform (the total of all payments) and use that total with controls in other parts of the form. This is how the amount due is calculated, using data from the main form and both subforms.

The invoice form also shows several other important techniques, including displaying values in other forms. Each line item and payment can also be deleted by using a button and the code will be explained here as well. The bottom of the invoice form also contains buttons to create a new record to fill in any defaults, as well as to delete an unneeded invoice and to display search and print dialog boxes.

FIGURE FM-5

The Access Auto Auctions Sales Invoice form used to show multiple linked subforms and totals

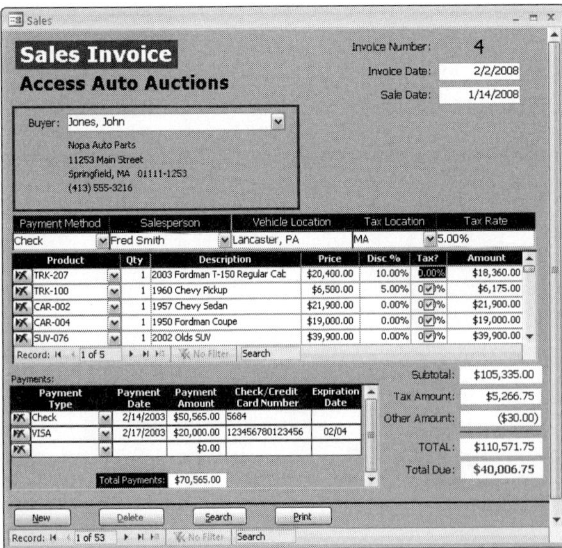

Part I

Access Building Blocks

Each part of this book builds on previous parts, and the chapters in each part contain examples that draw on techniques explained in previous parts and chapters. As a developer, your applications will benefit from the skills you acquire by reading the chapters and practicing the examples contained in this book.

But everyone has to start somewhere when they approach a new discipline, and Part I of this book presents the fundamental skills necessary for anyone to succeed at database development with Microsoft Access. The topics covered in this part explain the skills and techniques that are necessary to successfully use the Microsoft Access capabilities documented in the remaining parts of this book.

The chapters in this part provide the information that you'll need to build strong applications with Microsoft Access. These chapters go well beyond simply describing how to build tables, forms, and reports with Access. They give you the essential skills necessary to normalize data and plan and implement effective tables. Not the least of these essential skills is choosing the data types for the fields in your tables and providing strong, descriptive names for these important database objects. You'll also examine the steps necessary to properly create relationships between tables and specify the characteristics that govern those relationships.

If you're already familiar with the steps involved in database design, you may want to skim these chapters to learn how to perform these operations with Access 2007. Even if you're familiar with earlier versions of Access, you have a lot to learn from these chapters because so much has changed in the Access developer environment. And if you're new to Access, you'll want to read carefully the chapters in this part and spend enough time working through the examples to gain a thorough understanding of these important topics.

IN THIS PART

Chapter 1

An Introduction to Database Development

In this chapter, you learn the concepts and terminology of databases and how to design the tables that your forms and reports will use. Finally, you build the actual tables used by this book's Access Auto Auctions example database.

The fundamental concept underlying Access databases is that data is stored in tables. Tables are comprised of rows and columns of data, much like an Excel worksheet. Each table represents a single entity, such as a person or product.

As you work with Access, you'll spend considerable time designing and refining the tables in your Access applications. Table design and implementation are two characteristics that distinguish database development from most other activities you may pursue.

After you understand the basic concepts and terminology, the next important lesson to learn is good database design. Without a good design, you constantly rework your tables, and you may not be able to extract the information you want from your database. Throughout this book, you learn how to use the basic components of Access applications, including queries, forms, and reports. You also learn how to design and implement each of these objects. The Access Auto Auctions case study provides invented examples, but the concepts are not fictitious.

This chapter is not easy to understand; some of its concepts are complex. If your goal is to get right into Access, you may want to skip to Chapter 2 and read about the process of building tables. If you're fairly familiar with Access but new to designing and creating tables, you may want to read this chapter before starting to create tables.

IN THIS CHAPTER

Understanding what a database is

Examining the differences between databases, tables, records, fields, and values

Learning why multiple tables are used in a database

Looking at database objects

Learning a five-step design method

Creating the overall design of a database system

Designing database tables and relationships

Designing input forms

Designing menus

To jump right into using Access, skip to Chapter 2.

The Database Terminology of Access

Before examining the actual table examples in this book, it's a good idea to have a firm understanding of the terminology that is used when working with databases — especially Access databases. Microsoft Access follows traditional database terminology. The terms *database, table, record, field,* and *value* indicate a hierarchy from largest to smallest.

Databases

Generally, the word *database* is a computer term for a collection of information concerning a certain topic or business application. Databases help you organize this related information in a logical fashion for easy access and retrieval.

Databases aren't only for computers. There are also manual databases; we simply refer to these as *manual filing systems* or *manual database systems.* These filing systems usually consist of people, papers, folders, and filing cabinets — paper is the key to a manual database system. In a real manual database system, you probably have in/out baskets and some type of formal filing method. You access information manually by opening a file cabinet, taking out a file folder, and finding the correct piece of paper. You use paper forms for input, perhaps by using a typewriter. You find information by manually sorting the papers or by copying information from many papers to another piece of paper (or even into an Excel spreadsheet). You may use a spreadsheet or calculator to analyze the data or display it in new and interesting ways.

An Access database is nothing more than an automated version of the filing and retrieval functions of a paper filing system. Access databases store information in a carefully defined structure. Access tables store data in a variety of forms, from simple lines of text (such as name and address) to complex data such as pictures, sounds, or video images. Storing data in a precise, known format enables a database management system (DBMS) like Access to turn data into useful information.

Tables serve as the primary data repository in an Access database. Queries, forms, and reports provide access to the data, enabling a user to add or extract data, and presenting the data in useful ways. Most developers add macros or Visual Basic for Applications (VBA) code to forms and reports to make their applications easier to use.

A relational database management system (RDBMS), such as Access, stores data in related tables. For instance, a table containing employee data (names and addresses) may be related to a table containing payroll data (pay date, pay amount, and check number). Queries allow the user to ask complex questions (such as "What is the sum of all paychecks issued to Jane Doe in 2007?") from these related tables, with the answers displayed as on-screen forms and printed reports.

In Access, a *database* is the overall container for the data and associated objects. It is more than the collection of tables, however — a database includes many types of objects, including queries, forms, reports, macros, and code modules.

Access works a single database at a time. As you open Access, a single database is presented for you to use. You may open several copies of Access at the same time and simultaneously work with more than one database.

Many Access databases contain hundreds, or even thousands, of tables, forms, queries, reports, macros, and modules. With a few exceptions, all of the objects in an Access 2007 database reside within a single file with an extension of `accdb`, `.accde`, or `.adp`.

The `.adp` file format is a special database format used by Access to act as a front end to work with SQL Server data.

Tables

A table is just a container for raw information (called *data*), similar to a folder in a manual filing system. Each table in an Access database contains information about a single entity, such as a person or product, and the data is organized into rows and columns.

In the section titled "A Five-Step Design Method" later in this chapter, you learn a successful technique for planning Access tables. In Chapters 2 and 3, you learn the very important rules governing relational table design and how to incorporate those rules into your Access databases. These rules and guidelines ensure your applications perform with the very best performance while protecting the integrity of the data contained within your tables.

In fact, it is very important that you begin to think of the objects managed by your applications in abstract terms. Because each Access table defines an entity, you must learn to think of the table *as* the entity. As you design and build Access databases, or even when working with an existing application, you must think of how the tables and other database objects represent the physical entities managed by your database.

After you create a table, you view the table in a spreadsheet-like form, called a *datasheet,* comprising rows and columns (known as *records* and *fields,* respectively — see the following section, "Records and fields"). Figure 1-1 shows the datasheet view of the Contacts table in the Access Auto Auction application.

The Contacts table represents people who work with the Auto Auction. Notice how the table is divided into horizontal (left-to-right) rows, and vertical (top-to-bottom) columns of data. Each row (or record) defines a single contact, while each column (or field) represents one type of information known about a contact entity.

FIGURE 1-1

A table displayed as a datasheet

tblContacts : Table

Contact ID	Contact Type	First Name	Last Name	Company	Address	City	
1	Buyer	John	Jones	Nopa Auto Par	11253 Main St	Springfield	MA
2	Seller	Hank	Masters	Jiffy Auto Sale	623 Field Road	Springfield	MO
3	Both	Larry	Minkler	All Start Autos	971 E Main St	Detroit	MI
11	Both	Joe	Hammerman	Columbia Chev	105 Main Stree	Columbia	MA
12	Buyer	Cary	James	James Auto Pa	59 South Stree	Portland	CT
13	Buyer	Mark	Uno	Fillion Sales Ar	8908 North Pa	South Windsor	CT
14	Buyer	Brandon	Aley	Tip Top Chevy	1916 Erickson	Fairbanks	MA
15	Both	Michael	Dennis	Newbury Auto	75 Main Street	Bedford	NY
16	Both	Mark	Martin	Peekskill Sales	51 Tolland Tnp	Lake Peekskill	NY
17	Both	Karl	Johnson	KJ Auto Repair	350 Broadway	Rye	NY
18	Both	William	Gleason	R & G Monda Ir	196 East Street	Derby	CT
19	Both	Alex	Tomaso	Tires National	46 School Stre	Oneco	CT
20	Both	Karla	Hayes	Hayes Auction	54 E Center Str	Granby	CT
21	Seller	Teresa	Aikins	Middletown A	100 Northfield	Middletown	CT
22	Both	John	Marino	Bill Thomas Sal	986 Buckingha	Brewster	NY
23	Both	Donald	Peterson	Yantic Auto Pa	8 Oak Street	Yantic	CT
24	Seller	Dennie	Parkson	ACC Car Sales	963 New Engla	Peekskill	NY
25	Buyer	Ann	Bond	A-1 Auto Sales	54 South Main	Colchester	CT
26	Seller	Joe	Crook	Main Street Us	61 North Main	Windsor	CT
27	Both	Jeffrey	Lan	LAN Trucking	108 Thomas Rc	North Branch	NJ
28	Buyer	Matt	Smith	ABC Trucking	7 Depot Rd	Stratford	CT
29	Both	David	Smith	Fordman Color	123 Federal St	Quincy	MA
30	Both	Cindy	Casey	Circle Auto Sal	123 South Stre	Newington	NH
31	Both	Karen	Bailey	Sammy Fordm	59 West Churc	Westbourgh	MA
32	Both	Alvin	Schindler	Pine Plains RM	Rt 9	Pine Plains	NY

Record: 5 of 58 No Filter Search

For instance, the top row in tblContacts contains data describing John Jones, including his first name and last name, his address, and the company he works for. Each bit of information describing Mr. Jones is a field (`FirstName`, `LastName`, `Address`, `Company`, and so on). Fields are combined to form a record, and records are grouped to build the table.

Each field in an Access table includes many properties that specify the type of data contained within the field, and how Access should handle the field's data. These properties include the name of the field (`LastName`) and the type of data in the field (`Text`). A field may include other properties as well. For instance, the Size property tells Access how many characters to allow for a person's last name. (You learn much more about fields and field properties in Chapter 2.)

Records and fields

As Figure 1-1 shows, the datasheet is divided into rows (called *records*) and columns (called *fields*), with the first row (the heading on top of each column) containing the names of the fields in the database. Each row is a single record containing fields that are related to that record. In a manual system, the rows are individual forms (sheets of paper), and the fields are equivalent to the blank areas on a printed form that you fill in.

Values

At the intersection of a row (record) and a column (field) is a *value* — the actual data element. For example, John, the name in the first record, represents one data value. You may have a couple questions, such as: What makes this row different from other rows in the table? Is it possible to have another John Jones in the same table? If there is more than one John Jones, how does the database tell them apart?

Relational Databases

Microsoft Access is a relational database development system. Access data is stored in related tables, where data in one table (such as customers) is related to data in another table (such as orders). Access maintains the relationships between related tables, making it easy to extract a customer and all of the customer's orders, without losing any data or pulling order records not owned by the customer.

Working with multiple tables

Multiple tables simplify data entry and reporting by decreasing the input of redundant data. By defining two tables for an application that uses customer information, for example, you don't need to store the customer's name and address every time the customer purchases an item.

After you've created the tables, they need to be related to each other. For example, if you have a Contacts table and a Sales table, you must relate the Contacts table to the Sales table in order to see all the sales records for a Contact. If you had only one table, you would have to repeat the Contact name and address for each sale record. Two tables let you look up information in the Contact table for each sale by using the related fields Contact ID (in Contacts) and Buyer ID (in Sales). This way, when a customer changes address, for example, the address changes only in one record in the Contact table; when the Sales information is on-screen, the correct contact address is always visible.

Separating data into multiple tables within a database makes the system easier to maintain because all records of a given type are within the same table. By taking the time to segment data properly into multiple tables, you experience a significant reduction in design and work time. This process is known as *normalization*. (You can read about normalization in Chapter 2.)

Later in this chapter in the section titled "A Five-Step Design Method," you have the opportunity to work through a case study for the Access Auto Auctions that consists of five tables.

Knowing why you should create multiple tables

The prospect of creating multiple tables always intimidates beginning database users. Most often, they want to create one huge table that contains all of the information they need — in this case, a Customer table with all the sales performed by the customer and all the items sold or bought for each customer.

So, they create a single table containing a lot of fields, including fields for customer information (contact), sales information (date of sale, salesperson, amount paid, discounts, and so on), and the product information (quantity sold, product description, individual prices, and so on) for each sale. Such a table quickly grows to an unmanageable number of fields and continues growing as new items are added.

As you can see, the table design begins to take on a life of its own. After you've created the single table, it becomes even more difficult to maintain. You begin to realize that you have to input the customer information for every sale a customer makes (repeating the information over and over). The same is true for the items purchased for each sale, which is multiple items for each sale (thus, duplicating information again). This makes the system more inefficient and prone to data-entry mistakes. The information stored in the table becomes inefficiently maintained — many fields may not be appropriate for each record, and the table ends up with a lot of empty fields.

It's important to create tables that hold the minimum of information while still making the system easy to use and flexible enough to grow. To accomplish this, you need to consider making more than one table, with each table containing records with fields that are related only to the focus of that table. Then, after you create the tables, you link them so that you're able to glean useful information from them. Although this process sounds extremely complex, the actual implementation is relatively easy. Again, this process of creating multiple tables from a single table is known as *normalization* (or normalizing your tables).

Access Database Objects and Views

If you're new to databases (or even if you're an experienced database user), you need to understand some key concepts before starting to build Access databases. The Access database contains seven types of top-level objects, which consist of the data and tools that you need to use Access:

- **Table:** Holds the actual data
- **Query:** Searches for, sorts, and retrieves specific data
- **Form:** Lets you enter and display data in a customized format
- **Report:** Displays and prints formatted data
- **Pages:** Publishes data to a corporate intranet
- **Macro:** Automates tasks without programming
- **Module:** Contains programs written in the Visual Basic for Applications (VBA) programming language

Datasheets

Datasheets are one of the many ways by which you can view data in Access. Although not a database object, a datasheet displays a list of records from a table in a format similar to an accounting spreadsheet or Excel worksheet. A datasheet displays data as a series of rows and columns (comparable to an Excel spreadsheet). A datasheet displays a table's information in its raw form. The datasheet view is the default mode for displaying all fields for all records.

You scroll through the datasheet using the directional keys on your keyboard. You can also display related records in other tables while in a datasheet. In addition, you can make changes to the displayed data.

CAUTION Use caution when making changes or allowing a user to modify data in datasheet format. When a datasheet record is updated, the data in the underlying table is permanently changed.

Queries

Queries extract information from a database. A query selects and defines a group of records that fulfill a certain condition. Many forms and most reports are based on queries that pre-filter data before it is displayed. Queries are often called from VBA procedures to change, add, or delete database records.

An example of a query is when a person at the Auto Sales office tells the database, "Show me all customers, in alphabetical order by name, who live in Massachusetts and bought something over the past six months, and display them sorted by Customer name," or "Show me all customers who bought cars for a value of $35,000 or more for the past six months and display them sorted by customer name and then by value of the car."

Instead of asking the question in English words, the person uses the query by example (QBE) method. When you enter instructions into the QBE Design window, the query translates the instructions into Structured Query Language (SQL) and retrieves the desired data. Chapter 4 discusses the QBE Design window and building queries.

In the first example, the query first combines data from both the Sales and Contact tables, using the related field Contact ID (the common link between the tables). Next, it retrieves the first name, last name, and any other data you want to see. Access then filters the records, selecting only those in which the value of the sales date is within six months of the current date. The query sorts the resulting records first by contact's last and first names. Finally, the records appear on-screen in a datasheet.

A similar action takes place for the second example — using sales, contacts, invoice items, and products and the criteria applied to the search is where the `Description` field has a car bought whose value in the `Price` field is greater than or equal to $35,000.

After you run a query, the resulting set of records may be used in a form that is displayed on-screen or printed on a report. In this way, user access is limited to the data that meets the criteria in the returned records.

Data-entry and display forms

Data-entry forms help users get information into a database table quickly, easily, and accurately. Data-entry and display forms provide a more structured view of the data than what a datasheet provides. From this structured view, database records can be viewed, added, changed, or deleted. Entering data through the data-entry forms is the most common way to get the data into the database table.

Data-entry forms restrict access to certain fields within the table. Forms also check the validity of your data before it is added to the database table.

Most users prefer to enter information into data-entry forms rather than datasheet views of tables. Data-entry forms often resemble familiar paper documents and can aid the user with data-entry tasks. Forms make data entry self-explanatory by guiding the user through the fields of the table being updated.

Display-only screens and forms are solely for inquiry purposes. These forms allow for the selective display of certain fields within a given table. Displaying some fields and not others means that you can limit a user's access to sensitive data while allowing inquiry into other fields.

Reports

Reports present your data in printed format. Access supports several different types of reports. A report may list all records in a given table (such as a customer table) or may list only the records meeting a certain criterion, such as all customers living in the State of Washington. You do this by basing the report on a query that selects only the records needed by the report.

Your reports can combine multiple tables to present complex relationships among different sets of data. An example is printing an invoice. You access the customer table to obtain the customer's name and address (and other relevant data) and related records in the sales table to print the individual line-item information for the products ordered. You then instruct Access to calculate the totals and print them in a specific format on the form. Additionally, you can have Access output records into an *invoice report,* a printed document that summarizes the invoice.

TIP **When you design your database tables, keep in mind all the types of information that you want to print. Doing so ensures that the information you require in your various reports is available from within your database tables.**

Designing the system's objects

To create database objects, such as tables, forms, and reports, you first complete a series of tasks known as *design*. The better your design is, the better your application will be. The more you think through your design, the faster you can complete any system. The design process is not some necessary evil, nor is its intent to produce voluminous amounts of documentation. The sole intent of designing an object is to produce a clear-cut path to follow as you implement it.

A Five-Step Design Method

Figure 1-2 is a version of the design method that is modified especially for use with Access. This is a top-down approach, starting with the overall system design and ending with the forms design, and it consists of five steps.

FIGURE 1-2

The five-step design flowchart. This design methodology is particularly well-suited for Access databases.

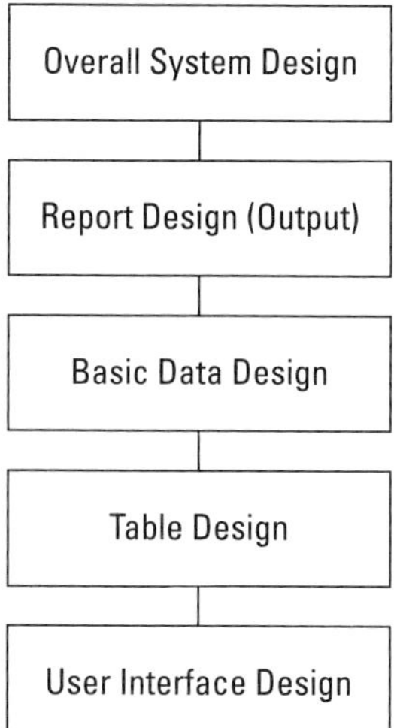

These five design steps, along with the database system illustrated by the examples in this book, teach a great deal about Access and provide a great foundation for creating database applications — including tables, queries, forms, data pages, reports, macros, and simple VBA (Visual Basic for Applications) modules.

The time you spend on each step depends entirely on the circumstances of the database you're building. For example, sometimes the users give you an example of a report they want printed from their Access database, and the sources of data on the report are so obvious that designing the report takes a few minutes. Other times, particularly when the users' requirements are complex, or the business processes supported by the application require a great deal of research, you may spend many days on Step 1.

As you read through each step of the design process, *always* look at the design in terms of outputs and inputs. Although you see actual components of the system (cars, buyers, sellers, and transactions), remember that the focus of this chapter is how to design each step. As you watch the Access Auto Auctions system being designed, pay attention to the design process, not the actual system.

Step 1: The overall design — from concept to reality

All software developers face similar problems, the first of which is determining how to meet the needs of the end user. It's important to understand the overall requirements before zeroing in on the details.

The five-step design method shown in Figure 1-2 helps you to create the system that you need, at an affordable price (measured in time or dollars). The Access Auto Auctions database, for example, allows the client to sell items (vehicles and parts) to customers. The Access Auto Auctions database automates the following tasks:

- Entering and maintaining contact information for customers and sellers (name, address, and financial history)
- Entering and maintaining sales information (sales date; payment method; total amount, including tax; buyer ID; and other fields)
- Entering and maintaining sales line item information (details of items actually purchased)
- Viewing information from all the tables (sales, contacts, sales line items purchased, and payment information)
- Asking all types of questions about the information in the database
- Producing a current contacts directory
- Producing a monthly invoice report
- Producing a customer sales history
- Producing mailing labels and mail-merge reports

These nine tasks that the Access Auto Auctions automates have been expressed by the client. You may need to consider other tasks as you start the design process.

Most of the information that is necessary to build the system comes from the eventual users. This means that you need to sit down with them and learn how the existing process works. To accomplish this you need to do a thorough *needs analysis* of the existing system and how you might automate it.

One way to accomplish this is to prepare a series of questions that give insight to the client's business and how the client uses his data. For example, when considering automating an auto auction business, you may consider asking these questions:

- What reports and forms are currently used?
- How are sales, customer, contacts, and other records currently stored?
- How are billings processed?

As you ask these questions and others, the client will probably remember other things about his business that you should know.

A walkthrough of the existing process is also necessary to get a "feel" for the business. Most likely, you'll have to go back several times to observe the existing process and how the employees work.

When you prepare to follow the remaining steps, keep the client involved — let him know what you're doing and ask for his input as to what you want to accomplish, making sure it is within the scope of his needs.

Step 2: Report design

Although it may seem odd to start with reports, in many cases users are more interested in the printed output from a database than they are in any other aspect of the application. Reports often include virtually every bit of data managed by an application. Because reports tend to be comprehensive, reports are often the best way to gather important information about a database's requirements. In the case of the Access Auto Auctions database, the printed reports contain detailed and summarized versions of most all the data in the database.

After you've defined the Access Auto Auctions' overall systems in terms of what must be accomplished, you can begin report design.

When you see the reports that you will create in this section, you may wonder, "Which comes first — the chicken or the egg?" Does the report layout come first, or do you first determine the data items and text that make up the report? Actually, these items are considered at the same time.

It isn't important how you lay out the fields in a report. The more time you take now, however, the easier it will be to construct the report. Some people go so far as to place gridlines on the report so that they will know the exact location they want each bit of data to occupy. In this example, you can just do it visually.

The reports in Figures 1-3 and 1-4 were created with two different purposes. The report in Figure 1-3 displays information about an individual contact (buyer, seller, or both). In contrast, the report in Figure 1-4 is an invoice with billing and customer information. Both of these reports were based on the type of information they use. The design and layout of each report is driven by the report's purpose and the data it contains.

FIGURE 1-3

A contact information report

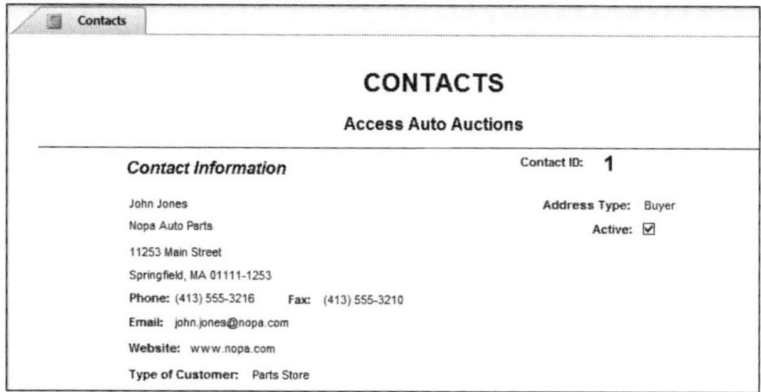

FIGURE 1-4

A sales invoice report containing sales information

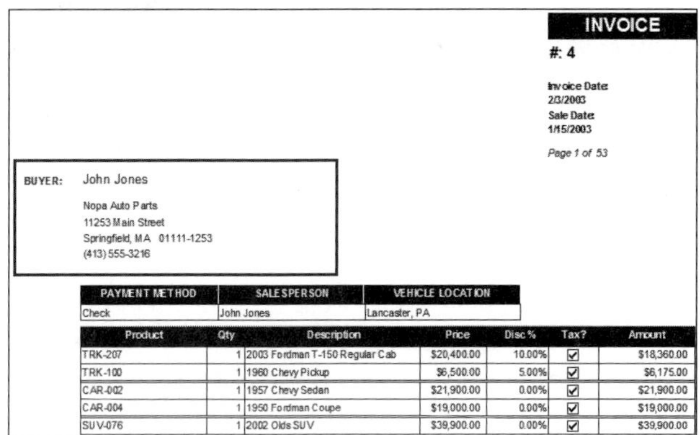

INVOICE

#: 4

Invoice Date:
2/3/2003
Sale Date:
1/15/2003

Page 1 of 53

BUYER: John Jones
Nopa Auto Parts
11253 Main Street
Springfield, MA 01111-1253
(413) 555-3216

PAYMENT METHOD	SALESPERSON	VEHICLE LOCATION
Check	John Jones	Lancaster, PA

Product	Qty	Description	Price	Disc %	Tax?	Amount
TRK-207	1	2003 Fordman T-150 Regular Cab	$20,400.00	10.00%	☑	$18,360.00
TRK-100	1	1960 Chevy Pickup	$6,500.00	5.00%	☑	$6,175.00
CAR-002	1	1957 Chevy Sedan	$21,900.00	0.00%	☑	$21,900.00
CAR-004	1	1950 Fordman Coupe	$19,000.00	0.00%	☑	$19,000.00
SUV-076	1	2002 Olds SUV	$39,900.00	0.00%	☑	$39,900.00

CROSS-REF **You can read more about the reports for the Access Auto Auctions system in Chapters 9 and 20.**

Step 3: Data design: What fields are required?

The next step in the design phase is to take an inventory of all the information or data fields that are needed by the reports. One of the best methods is to list the data items in each report. As you do so, take careful note of items that are included in more than one report. Make sure that you keep the same name for a data item that is in more than one report because the data item is really the same item.

Another method is to see whether you can separate the data items into some logical arrangement. Later, these data items are grouped into table structures and then mapped onto data-entry screens (forms). You should enter customer data (buyers and sellers), for example, as part of a contact table process, not as part of a sales entry.

Determining contact information

First, look at each report you have reviewed or attempted to make for the Access Auto Auctions system. For this system, start with the customer data and list the data items, as shown in Table 1-1.

TABLE 1-1

Customer-Related Data Items Found in the Reports

Contacts Report	Invoice Report
Customer Name	Customer Name
Street	Street
City	City
State	State
ZIP Code	ZIP Code
Phone Numbers	Phone Number
Type of Customer	
E-Mail Address	
Web Site Information	
Contact Log Information (four fields)	
Discount Rate	
Customer Since	
Last Sales Date	
Sales Tax Rate	
Credit Information (four fields)	

As you can see by comparing the type of contact (customer) information needed for each report, there are many common fields. Most of the data fields pertaining to the customer are found in both reports. Table 1-1 shows only some of the fields that are used in each report — those related to customer information. Fields appearing on both reports appear on the same rows in the table, which allows you to see more easily which items are in which reports. You can look across a row instead of looking for the same names in both reports. Because the related row and the field names are the same, you can easily make sure that you have all the data items. Although locating items easily is not critical for this small database, it becomes very important when you have to deal with large tables containing many fields.

Determining sales information

After extracting the customer data, you can move on to the sales data. In this case, you need to analyze only the Invoice report for data items that are specific to the sales. Table 1-2 lists the fields in the report that contain information about the sales.

TABLE 1-2

Sales Data Items Found in the Reports

Individual Invoice Report	Line Item Data
Invoice Number	
Sales Date	
Invoice Date	
Payment Method	
Payment Salesperson	
Discount (overall for sale)	
Tax Location	
Tax Rate	
Product Purchased (multiple lines)	Product Purchased
Quantity Purchased (multiple lines)	Quantity Purchased
Description of Item Purchased (multiple lines)	Description of Item Purchased
Price of Item (multiple lines)	Price of Item
Discount for each item (multiple lines)	Discount for Each Item
Taxable? (multiple lines)	Taxable?
Payment Type (multiple lines)	
Payment Date (multiple lines)	
Payment Amount (multiple lines)	
Credit Card Number (multiple lines)	
Expiration Date (multiple lines)	

As you can see when you examine the type of sales information needed for the report, a couple of items (fields) are repeating (for example, the `Product Purchased`, `Number of Items Purchased`, and `Price of Item` fields). Each invoice can have multiple items, and each of these items needs the same type of information — number ordered and price per item. Each sales invoice will probably have more than one item that is sold and being invoiced. Also, each invoice may include partial payments, and it is possible that this payment information will have multiple lines of payment information, so these repeating items can be put into their own grouping.

Determining line item information

You can take all the individual items that you found in the sales information group in the preceding section and extract them to their own group for the invoice report. Table 1-2 shows the information related to each line item.

Looking back at the report in Figure 1-4, you can see that the data from Table 1-2 doesn't list the calculated field amount, but you can re-create it easily in the report.

TIP **Unless a numeric field needs to be specifically stored in a table, simply recalculate it when you run the report (or form). You should avoid creating fields in your tables that can be created based on other fields — these calculation fields can be easily created and displayed in a form or report. As you'll read in Chapter 2, storing calculated values in database tables leads to data maintenance problems.**

Step 4: Table design

Now for the difficult part: You must determine what fields are needed for the tables that make up the reports. When you examine the multitude of fields and calculations that make up the many documents you have, you begin to see which fields belong to the various tables in the database. (You already did much of the preliminary work by arranging the fields into logical groups.) For now, include every field you extracted. You will need to add others later (for various reasons), although certain fields won't appear in any table.

It is important to understand that it isn't necessary to add every little bit of data into the database's tables. For instance, users may express a desire to add vacation and other out-of-office days to the database to make it easy to know which employees are available on a particular day. However, it is very easy to burden an application's initial design by incorporating too many ideas during the initial development phases. Because Access tables are so easy to modify later on, it is probably best to put aside noncritical items until the initial design is complete. Generally speaking, it's not difficult to accommodate user requests after the database development project is under way.

After you've used each report to display all the data, it's time to consolidate the data by purpose (for example, grouped into logical groups) and then compare the data across those functions. To do this step, first you look at the contact information and combine all of its different fields to create one set of data items. Then you do the same thing for the sales information and the line item information. Table 1-3 compares data items from these three groups of information.

TABLE 1-3

Comparing the Data Items from the Contact Information, Sales Information, and Line Item Information

Contacts Data	Invoice Data	Line Items
Customer Name	Invoice Number	Product Purchased
Street	Sales Date	Quantity Purchased
City	Invoice Date	Description of Item Purchased
State	Payment Method	Price of Item

continued

TABLE 1-3 *(continued)*

Contacts Data	Invoice Data	Line Items
ZIP Code	Payment Salesperson	Discount for Each Item
Phone Numbers (two fields)	Discount (overall for this sale)	Taxable?
Type of Customer	Tax Location	
E-Mail Address	Tax Rate	
Web Site Information	Payment Type (multiple lines)	
Contact Log Information (four fields)	Payment Date (multiple lines)	
Discount Rate	Payment Amount (multiple lines)	
Customer Since	Credit Card Number (multiple lines)	
Last Sales Date	Expiration Date (multiple lines)	
Sales Tax Rate		
Credit Information (four fields)		

Consolidating and comparing data is a good way to start creating the individual table definitions for Access Auto Auctions, but you have much more to do.

As you learn more about how to perform a data design, you also learn that the contacts data must be split into two groups. Some of these items are used only once for a contact while other items may have multiple entries. An example is the Contact Log information. Each contact may have multiple log items recorded in the database. This is also true for the Sales column — the payment information can have multiple lines of information.

It is necessary to further break these types of information into their own columns, thus separating all related types of items into their own columns — an example of the *normalization* part of the design process. For example, one customer can have multiple contacts with the company. One customer may make multiple payments toward a single sale. Of course, we've already broken the data into three categories above: contacts, invoices, and sales line items.

Keep in mind that one customer may have multiple invoices, and each invoice may have multiple line items on it. The contact category represents customer (buyer or seller) information, the invoice category contains information about individual sales, and the line items category contains information about each invoice. Notice that these three columns are all related; for example, one customer can have multiple invoices and each invoice may require multiple detail lines (line items).

The relationships between tables can be different. For example, each sales invoice has one and only one customer, while each customer may have multiple sales. A similar relationship exists between the sales invoice and the line items of the invoice.

CROSS-REF **We cover creating and understanding relationships and the normalization process in Chapter 2.**

Assuming that the three groupings represent the main three tables of your system, less additional fields, you need to link tables together. This step, of course, means adding table relationships to the database design.

Database table relationships require a unique field in both tables involved in a relationship. Without a unique identifier in each table, the database engine is unable to properly join and extract related data.

None of the tables in our design has a unique identifier, which means that you need to add at least one more field to each table to serve as the anchor for a relationship to other tables. For example, you could add a `ContactID` field to the Contacts table, then add the same field to the Invoice table, and establish a relationship between the tables through the `ContactID` field in each table. (Creating relationships is explained in Chapter 3.) The database engine uses the relationship between the Contacts and Invoices table to link customers with their invoices. Linking tables is done through special fields, known as *key* fields.

With an understanding of the need for linking one group of fields to another group, you can add the required key fields to each group. Table 1-4 shows two new groups and link fields created for each group of fields. These linking fields, known as *primary keys* and *foreign keys,* are used to link these tables together.

The field that uniquely identifies each row in a table is called the *primary key.* The corresponding field in a related table is called the *foreign key.* In our example, the `ContactID` field in the Contacts table is a primary key, while the `ContactID` field in the Invoices table is a foreign key.

Let's assume a certain record in the Contacts table has 12 in its `ContactID` field. Any records in the Invoices table with 12 in its `ContactID` field is "owned" by contact number 12. As you'll see in Chapters 2 and 3, special rules apply to choosing and managing primary and foreign keys. The notion of primary and foreign keys is the single most important concept behind relational databases. You can read much more about this important concept in Chapters 2 and 3.

TABLE 1-4

Main Tables with Keys

Contacts Data	Invoice Data	Line Items Data	Contact Log Data	Sales Payment Data
ContactID	InvoiceID	InvoiceID	ContactLogID	InvoiceID
Customer Name	ContactID	Line Number	ContactID	Payment Type
Street	Invoice Number	Product Purchased	Contact Date	Payment Date
City	Sales Date	Quantity Purchased	Contact Notes	Payment Amount

continued

TABLE 1-4 *(continued)*

Contacts Data	Invoice Data	Line Items Data	Contact Log Data	Sales Payment Data
State	Invoice Date	Description of Item Purchased	Follow Up?	Credit Card Number
ZIP Code	Payment Method	Price of Item	Follow-Up Date	Expiration Date
Phone Numbers (two fields)	Payment Salesperson	Discount for Each Item		
Type of Customer	Discount (overall for this sale)	Taxable?		
E-Mail Address	Tax Location			
Web Site Information	Tax Rate			
Discount Rate				
Customer Since				
Last Sales Date				
Sales Tax Rate				

With the key fields added to each table, you can now find a field in each table that links it to other tables in the database. For example, Table 1-4 shows a `ContactID` field in both the Contacts table (where it is the table's primary key) and the Invoice table (where it is a foreign key).

You have identified the core of the three primary tables for your system, as reflected by the first three columns in Table 1-4. This is the general, or first, cut toward the final table designs. You have also created two additional tables (columns) from fields shown in Table 1-3.

Taking time to properly design your database and the tables contained within it is arguably the most important step in developing a database-oriented application. By designing your database efficiently, you maintain control of the data — eliminating costly data-entry mistakes and limiting your data entry to essential fields.

Although this book is not geared toward teaching database theory and all of its nuances, this is a good point to briefly describe the art of database normalization. You'll read the details of normalization in Chapter 3, but in the meantime you should know that normalization is the process of breaking data down into constituent tables. Earlier in this chapter you read about how many Access developers add dissimilar information, such as contacts, invoice data, and invoice line items, into one large table. A large table containing dissimilar data quickly becomes unwieldy and hard to keep updated. Because a contact's phone number appears in every row containing that customer's data, multiple updates must be made when the contact's phone number changes.

Normalization is the process of breaking data into smaller, more manageable tables. Each table defines one and only one *entity*, such as a contact or an invoice, but not both. The contact and invoice tables are related through a primary key (`ContactID` in the customers table) and a foreign key (also named `ContactID`) in the invoices table.

There is much more involved in the normalization process, but, in the meantime, we'll leave that for Chapter 3.

Step 5: Form design: Input

After you've created the data and established table relationships, it's time to design your forms. *Forms* are made up of the fields that can be entered or viewed in Edit mode. If at all possible, your screens should look much like the forms that you use in a manual system. This setup makes for the most user-friendly system.

When you're designing forms, you need to place three types of objects on-screen:

- Labels and text box data-entry fields (the fields on Access forms and reports are usually called *controls*)
- Special controls (multiple-line text boxes, option buttons, list boxes, check boxes, business graphs, and pictures)
- Graphical objects to visually enhance them (colors, lines, rectangles, and three-dimensional effects)

When designing a form, place your fields (text boxes, check boxes, list boxes, and radio buttons) just where you want them on the form. Ideally, if the form is being developed from an existing printed form, the Access data-entry form should resemble the printed form. The fields should be in the same relative place on the screen as they are in the printed counterpart.

Labels display messages, titles, or captions. Text boxes provide an area where you can type or display text or numbers that are contained in your database. Check boxes indicate a condition and are either unchecked or checked (selected). Other types of controls available with Access include list boxes, combo boxes, option buttons, toggle buttons, and option groups.

CROSS-REF **Chapter 7 covers the various types of controls available in Access.**

In this book, you create several basic data-entry forms:

- **Contact Log:** A simple data-entry form
- **Contacts:** A slightly more complex data-entry form, containing several different types of controls
- **Sales:** Combines data from multiple tables
- **Products:** Data-entry form for adding products to the Access Auto Auction database.

You'll encounter each of these forms as you read through the following chapters. Although the Access Auto Auction is but one type of database application built with Microsoft Access, the principles you learn building the Access Auto Auction tables, queries, forms, reports, and other database objects are applicable to virtually any other Access project.

Summary

This chapter introduces the concepts and considerations driving database development. There is no question that data is important to users. Most companies simply cannot operate without their customer and product lists, accounts receivable and accounts payable, and payroll information. Even very small companies must efficiently manage their business data.

Good database design means much more than sitting down and knocking together a few tables. Very often, poor database design habits come back to haunt developers and users in the form of missing or erroneous information on screens and printed reports. Users quickly tire of re-entering the same information over and over again, and business managers and owners expect database applications to *save* time and money, not contribute to a business's overhead.

Chapter 2

Creating Access Tables

In this chapter, you learn how to create a new Access database and its tables. You establish the database container to hold your tables, forms, queries, reports, and code that you build as you learn Access. Finally, you create the actual tables used by the Access Auto Auctions database.

ON the CD-ROM This chapter uses the `Chapter02.accdb` database. If you have not already copied these files onto your machine from the CD, you'll need to do so now.

IN THIS CHAPTER

- Creating a new Access database
- Creating a table
- Navigating in the Table window
- Entering field names and descriptions
- Selecting a field data type
- Entering field properties
- Changing a table design
- Creating a primary key
- Saving a table's design
- Renaming, copying, and deleting tables

Getting Started with Access 2007

As you open Access 2007, the default environment (see Figure 2-1) is revealed. We'll examine the Access environment in more detail later in this chapter, but you should understand the major components of the user interface as you get started using Access 2007. Even experienced Access developers are surprised at how different Access 2007 looks from previous versions.

Each time you open Access, the welcome screen may or may not look different, depending on whether you have elected to have Office Online periodically updated. In an effort to provide a high level of support for Microsoft Office users, Microsoft has equipped each of the Office applications with the ability to communicate directly with Microsoft's Web servers and download new content to the user's desktop. Notice the Automatically Update This Content from Office Online button in the Office Online box near the bottom-center of this main screen. This button configures Microsoft Access to look for new Office Online content each time you open Access. In fact, your Access Welcome Screen will likely look quite different from Figure 2-1 because of the content continuously released by Microsoft Office Online.

FIGURE 2-1

The Access 2007 welcome screen provides a wealth of information.

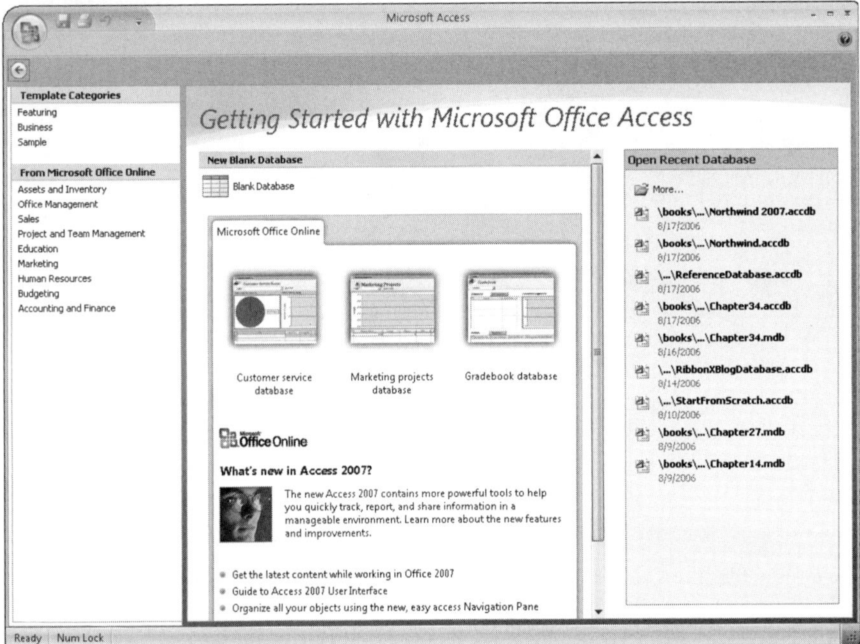

The center of the screen is dominated by the Microsoft Office Online "templates," which are described in the next section. The right side of the screen contains a list of recently opened databases, while the left side of the screen contains a navigation bar for templates.

The Templates section

When you start Microsoft Access, you see the initial welcome screen (refer to Figure 2-1). For online users of Microsoft Access 2007, the content of the welcome screen changes from time to time as Microsoft updates the online templates available on the Microsoft Web site.

We'll take a look at creating a new database in the "Creating a Database" section of this chapter. In the meantime, let's take a look at the purpose of online templates. Microsoft has long been concerned that building Access databases is too difficult for most people. Not everyone takes the time to understand the rules governing database design, or to learn the intricacies of building tables, queries, forms, and reports.

Microsoft established the online templates repository as a way to provide beginners and other busy people the opportunity to download partially or completely built Access applications. The template databases cover many common business requirements such as inventory control and sales management. You may want to take a moment to explore the online templates, but they aren't covered in this book.

The File menu

Our main interest at the moment is the large round button in the upper-left corner of the main Access screen. This button opens the File menu (see Figure 2-2), which is the gateway to a large number of options for creating, opening, or configuring Access databases. Notice that a list of recently opened databases appears to the right of the buttons in the File menu.

FIGURE 2-2

The File menu contains many important commands.

Rather than discuss each of these commands at the moment, we'll cover each command in detail as we work through the Access user interface. For the moment, notice the `New` command at the very top of the File menu. We'll use this button to create a new Access database in the next section.

NOTE **Some confusion exists over the name of the large, round button you see in the upper-left corner of the main Access window. Most users call this button the File button and the drop-down that appears as this button is clicked the File menu. However, Microsoft refers to the round button as the Microsoft Office Button and its drop-down as the Office menu. You'll see both expressions used in this book, but in all cases we're referring to the large, round button in the upper left corner of the main Access 2007 screen.**

Creating a Database

There are many ways to create a new database file. You may have noticed the Blank Database button in the upper-left corner of the Office Online area in the main Access screen. This button and the New button in the File menu both reveal the Blank Database area in the right section of the main screen. Clicking either of these buttons transforms the main screen, as shown in Figure 2-3. The Blank Database area replaces the list of recently opened databases on the main screen.

FIGURE 2-3

Enter the name of the new database in the File Name box in the Blank Database area.

Enter the name of the new database in the File Name box in the Blank Database area. By default, Access creates the new database file in whichever Windows folder you most recently opened from within Access. If you want to use a different folder, use the folder icon to the right of the File Name box to browse to the location you want to use.

Access provides a default name of Database1.accdb for new databases. Be sure to provide a name that you'll recognize. In Figure 2-4, the new database is named MyAccessAutoAuctions.accdb. (Entering the extension .accdb is optional because Access automatically supplies it if you do not.)

When the new database is created, Access automatically opens it for you.

FIGURE 2-4

The new MyAccessAutoAuctions database is created.

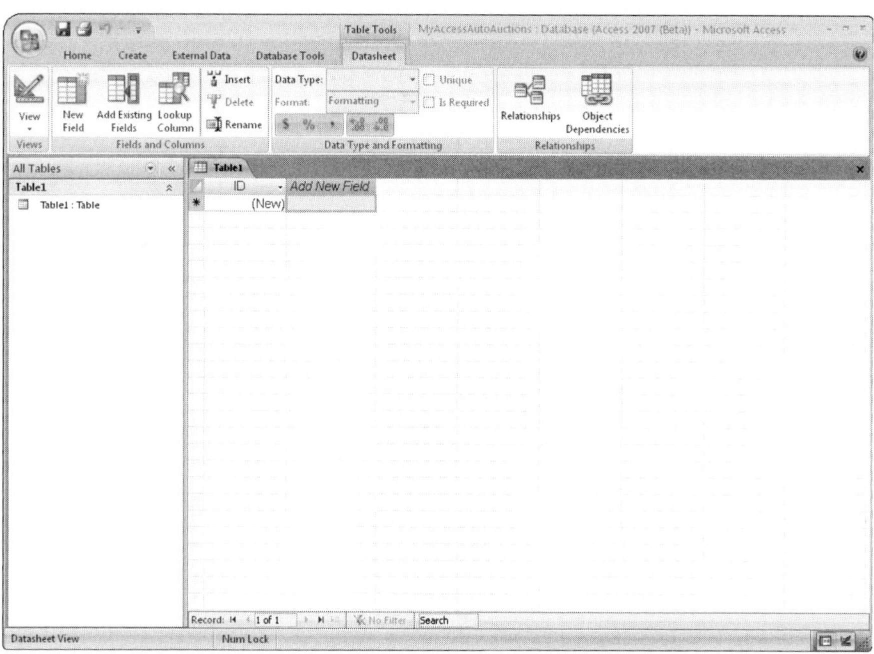

NOTE **Access 2007 recognizes all previous versions of Access database files. By default, the 2007 format (with the `.accdb` extension) is used, but you can specify either Access 2000, 2002–2003, or Access 2007 as the default format. Choose File ➪ Access Options ➪ Personalize, select the Default File Format option, and choose whichever format you prefer. For instance, if much of your Access 2007 work is performed on Access 2000 databases, you should choose the 2000 format to preserve backward compatibility. Users still working with Access 2000 are not able to open Access files created in the `.accdb` format.**

This book uses a mix of Access file formats for its examples. All of the Access Auto Auctions files on your disc are in Access 2007 format, but other examples may be in Access 2000 or 2002–2003 formats.

Access 2007 works directly with Access 2000, 2002–2003, and 2007 databases. Earlier Access database files (such as Access 97 or 95) must be converted to 2000, 2002–2003, or 2007 before they can be used in Access 2007. Access examines the database file you're opening and, if it determines the file must be converted, presents you with the Database Enhancement dialog box shown in Figure 2-5.

Understanding How Access Works with Data

There are many ways that Microsoft Access works with data. For simplicity, most of the examples in this book use data stored in local tables. A *local table* is contained within the Access `.accdb` file that is open in front of you. This is how you've seen examples so far.

In many professionally developed Microsoft Access applications, the actual tables are kept in a database (usually called the *back end*) separate from the other interface objects (forms, reports, queries, pages, macros, and modules). The back-end data file stays on a file server on the network, and each user has a copy of the front-end database (containing the forms and reports) on his computer. This is done to make the application more maintainable. By separating the data and their tables into another database, maintenance work (building new indexes, repairing the tables, and so on) is more easily done without affecting the remainder of the system.

For example, you may be working with a multiuser system and find a problem with a form or report in the database. If all the data and interface objects are in the same database, you have to shut down the system while repairing the broken form or report — other users could not work with the application while you repair the form or report.

By separating data from other objects, you can fix the erring object while others are still working with the data. After you've fixed the problem, you deliver the new changes to the others, and they import the form or report into their local databases.

In addition, there is a more critical reason to separate your data from the interface objects: security. By maintaining the data in its own database, you maintain better control over the information. The back-end database is physically separated from users, and it is unlikely a user can accidentally or intentionally delete or modify the back-end database files. Also, the back-end database is easily backed up and maintained without affecting users.

While you may want to first develop your application with the tables within the `.accdb` database, later you can use the Database Splitter wizard to automatically move the tables in your `.accdb` file to a separate Access `.accdb` file. This process is explained in Chapter 16.

FIGURE 2-5

Opening an obsolete Access data file invokes the Database Enhancement dialog box.

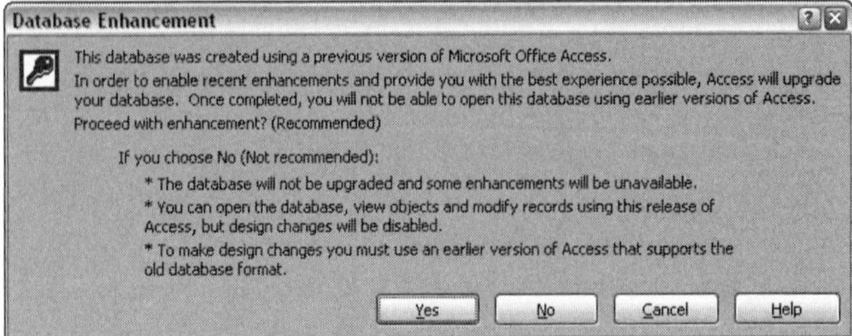

Responding Yes to the Database Enhancement dialog box opens a second dialog box (not shown) asking for the name of the converted database. Selecting No opens the obsolete database in read-only mode, enabling you to view, but not modify, objects in the database. This process is sometimes referred to as *enabling* the obsolete database.

Choosing to enable an obsolete database is sometimes necessary when you must understand the design of an old database, but if users are still working with the old database and it cannot be upgraded to Access 2007 format.

If you're following the examples in this book, note that we have chosen `MyAccessAutoAuctions.accdb` as the name of the database file you create as you complete this chapter. This database is for our hypothetical business, Access Auto Auctions. After you enter the filename, Access creates the empty database.

ON the CD-ROM **The CD-ROM that comes with this book contains multiple database files. The completed file containing all the data is named *AccessAutoAuctionsData.accdb,* and the Access 2007 database file containing the completed objects (forms, queries, reports, macros, and modules) is *AccessAutoAuctions.accdb.***

The CD-ROM contains a single example database file for most chapters in this book. The example file for a chapter is named `ChapterXX.accdb (and, sometimes ChapterXX.mdb)`, where `xx` is a chapter number. If a chapter uses files where the data is split from the other objects, the names are ChapterXXFrontEnd.accdb and ChapterXXBackEnd.accdb. This chapter describes building a single database file named `MyAccessAutoAuctions.accdb`.

The Access 2007 Environment

The initial Access screen, after creating a new database, is shown in Figure 2-6. Along the top of the screen is the Access *ribbon*, which replaces the toolbars and menus seen in previous versions of Access. The ribbon is divided into a number of groups. We'll be looking at each of the groups and the controls in each group as we work our way through the next several chapters.

At the left side of the screen is the *Navigation Pane* containing the names of all of the different types of objects in the Access database. In Figure 2-6, the Navigation Pane displays the names of tables in the database, but could just as easily show queries, forms, reports, and other Access object types. The Navigation Pane can even display a combination of different types of objects.

The right side of the screen shows a blank table, ready to be filled in with the details necessary for the table to be used in the new Access database.

FIGURE 2-6

The main Access interface when working with a new database

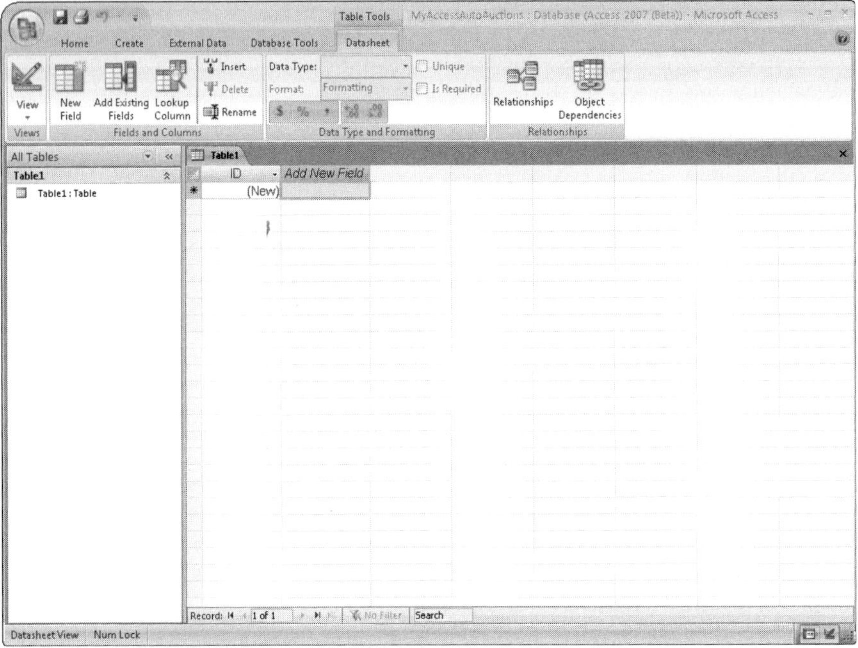

The Navigation Pane

The Navigation Pane, at the left of the screen, is your primary navigation aid when working with Access. By default, the list is filled with the names of tables in the current database but can also display other types of objects by clicking on the drop-down list in the Navigation Pane's title bar to reveal the navigation options (see Figure 2-7).

FIGURE 2-7

Choosing an alternate display for the Navigation pane

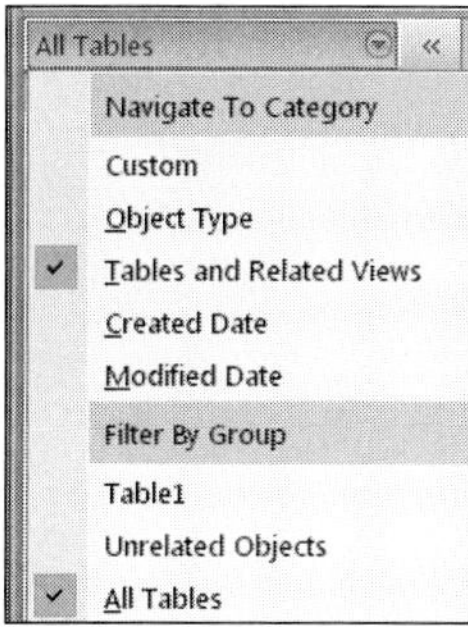

The navigation options are:

- **Custom:** The `Custom` option creates a new tab in the Navigation pane. This new tab is titled `Custom Group 1` by default and contains objects that you drag and drop into the tab's area. Items added to a custom group still appear in their respective "object type" view, as described next.
- **Object Type:** The `Object Type` setting is most similar to previous versions of Access. When selected, `Object Type` transforms the selection list to display the usual Access object types: tables, queries, forms, reports, and so on.
- **Tables and Related Views:** The `Tables and Related Views` setting requires a bit of explanation. Access 2007 tries very hard to keep the developer informed of the hidden connections between objects in the database. For instance, a particular table may be used in a number of queries, or referenced from a form or report. In previous versions of Access, these relationships were very difficult to determine, and, before Access 2007, no effective tool was built into Access to help you understand these relationships.

  Figure 2-8 shows how the `Tables and Related Views` works. The Shippers table has been expanded to show that it is related to six other objects in the Northwind Traders database. This information helps a developer to understand that changing the Shippers table affects a number of other objects in the database.

FIGURE 2-8

The Tables and Related Views setting is a powerful tool for analyzing an Access database.

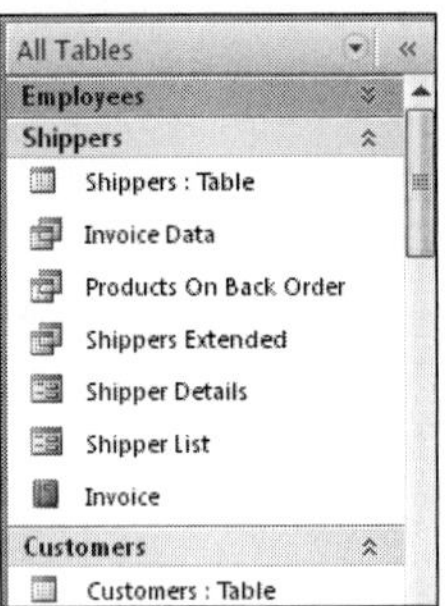

- **Created Date, Modified Date:** These options group the database objects by either the created date or the modified date. These settings are useful when you need to know when an object was either created or last modified.
- **Filter By Group:** The `Filter By Group` option filters the selected object type (tables, forms, and so on) by a number of grouping options. The grouping option is determined by the navigation category chosen in `Navigate To Category` selected at the top of the Navigation pane. For instance, selecting `Created Date` changes the options under the `Filter By Group` to the following options: `Today`, `Yesterday`, `Last Week`, `Two Weeks Ago`, and so on.

  The `Filter By Group` option is really only helpful when you have a fairly large number of objects in your Access database. If you have an Access database containing several hundred different forms, you'll find it very useful to filter by forms that were modified within the last week or so. But when there are only a few objects in a database, the Filter By Group option has little effect.
- **Unrelated Objects, All Tables:** These options appear in Figure 2-7 because the `Tables and Related Views` is selected as the primary navigation option. The `Unrelated Objects` is the opposite of the `Tables and Related Views`. When selected, the `Unrelated Objects` option shows you all of the objects that are not related to the selected table, query, or other Access object.

The `All Tables` setting is the default when choosing to view tables in the database.

The ribbon

The Access ribbon occupies the top portion of the main access screen. The ribbon replaces the menus and toolbars seen in previous versions of Access. The ribbon's appearance changes depending on what task you're working on in the Access environment. Figure 2-9 shows the Datasheet ribbon seen when you're working with Access tables. A very different ribbon appears when working with forms or reports.

FIGURE 2-9

The Access 2007 ribbon

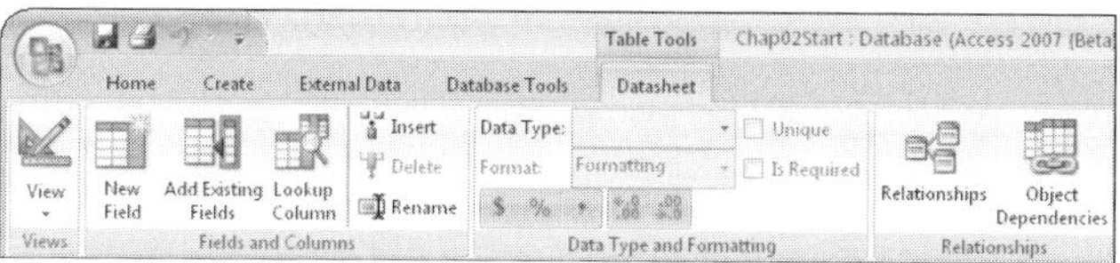

The ribbon is divided into a number of groups, each containing any number of controls. In Figure 2-9, the `Data Type and Formatting` group is selected. The `Data Type and Formatting group` includes options for selecting how a datasheet appears on the screen, while the `Fields and Columns` group contains commands for modifying and specifying the fields within the table.

The other groups on the Datasheet tab (`Views`, `Fields and Columns`, and `Relationships`) contain controls that perform other tasks commonly associated with Access datasheets. For instance, The `View` control in the `Views` group changes the datasheet view of the table to design view, making it easy to update the table's design.

Instead of explaining each of the groups and controls within groups on the ribbon, we will study each relevant ribbon command in the proper context in this chapter and chapters that follow.

Other relevant features of the Access environment

The Access environment includes a number of other important features. In the far-right lower corner are two buttons that enable you to quickly change the selected objects in the middle of the screen from Design view to the object's Normal view. For instance, in the case of an Access table, the Normal view is to display the table as a datasheet, while a report's Normal view is to display the report in Print Preview.

Figure 2-10 illustrates one of the more interesting changes for Access 2007. A common complaint among some developers with earlier versions of Access was the fact that, when multiple objects were simultaneously opened in the Access environment, the objects would often overlap and obscure each other, making it more difficult to navigate between the objects. For instance, in Access 2000 you might have a form open in Design view and a table open in Datasheet view at the same time. Invariably, one of these objects would overlap the other and, depending on how large the object was, might completely obscure the other object.

Microsoft has added a tabbed user interface to Access, preventing objects from obscuring other objects that are open at the same time. In Figure 2-10, the contacts (tblContacts) table is currently in use. Two other database objects (frmIndexTest and tblZipCodesIndexed) are also opened in the Access work area. Clicking on a tab associated with an object, such as `frmIndexTest`, instantly brings that object to the top.

FIGURE 2-10

The tabbed interface is a welcome addition to Access 2007.

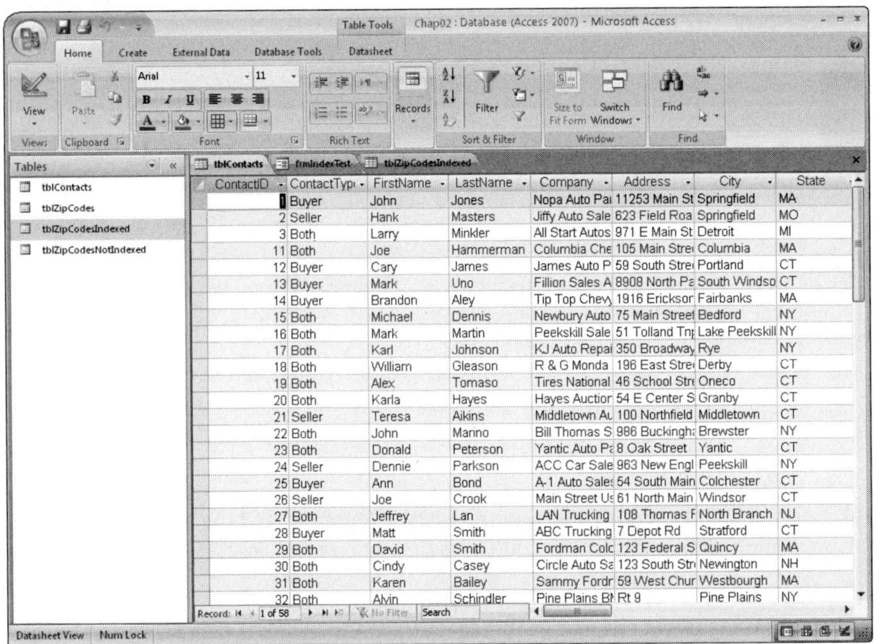

When an object such as `tblContacts` is put into Design view (by clicking to the last word, right-clicking the tab, and selecting `Design View`) the data sheet is replaced with the Table Designer (see Figure 2-11). The Access 2007 environment is highly adaptable to whichever tasks you are currently performing in your database.

TIP **If you decide you don't care for the tabbed interface, select the Office button, and click the Access Options button in the lower-right corner of the Office menu. Then, select the Current Database tab, and change the Document Window Options from Tabbed Documents to Overlapping Windows.**

FIGURE 2-11

The Access environment adapts to your workflow.

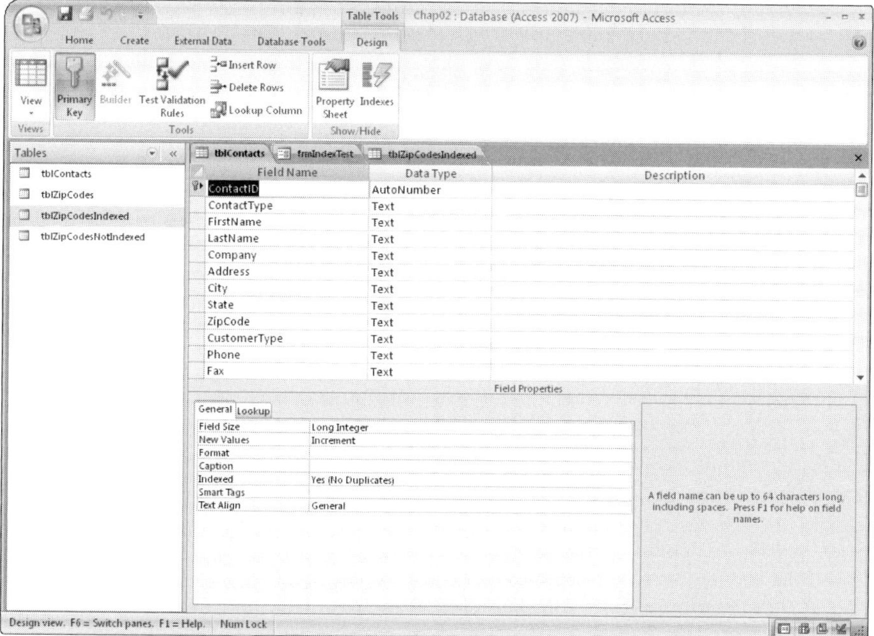

Creating a New Table

Creating database tables is as much art as it is science. A good working knowledge of the user's requirements is a primary requirement for any new database project. Chapter 3 covers the details of applying database design rules to the creation of Access tables. In the meantime, let's take a look at the steps required to create basic Access tables. In the following sections, you'll study the process of adding tables to an Access database, including the relatively complex subject of choosing the proper data type to assign to each field in a table.

It is always a good idea to plan tables on paper first, before sitting down at Access and using the Access tools to add tables to the database. Many tables, especially small ones, really don't require a lot of forethought before adding them to the database. After all, not much planning is required to design a table holding lookup information such as the names of cities and states. However, more complex entities such as customers and products usually require considerable thought and effort to properly implement.

Although you can create the table interactively without any forethought, carefully planning a database system is a good idea. You can make any changes later, but doing so wastes time; generally, the result is a system that is harder to maintain than one that is well planned from the beginning. Before you get started, you should understand the table design process.

In the following sections, we'll be exploring the new, blank table added by Access as the new database was created. It's important to understand the steps required to add new tables to an Access database. Because the steps required to add tables have changed so dramatically from earlier versions of Access, even experienced Access developers will want to read the following sections.

The importance of naming conventions

As your databases grow in size and complexity, the need to establish a naming convention for the objects in your databases increases. As you already know, changes to the name of an object are not propagated throughout the database. Even with the `Name AutoCorrect` option turned on (Office button ➪ Access Options ➪ Current Database ➪ Name AutoCorrect Options), Access only corrects the most obvious name changes. Changing the name of a table breaks virtually every query, form, and report that uses the information from that table. Your best defense is to adopt reasonable object names and use a naming convention early on as you begin building Access databases and to stick with the naming convention throughout the project.

Access imposes very few restrictions on the names assigned to database objects. Therefore, it is entirely possible to have two distinctly different objects (for instance, a form and a report, or a table and a macro) with the same name. (You can't, however, have a table and a query with the same name, because tables and queries occupy the same namespace in the database.)

Although simple names like Contacts and Orders are adequate, as a database grows in size and complexity you may become confused about which object a particular name refers to. For instance, later in this book, you'll read about manipulating database objects through code and macros. When working with Visual Basic for Applications (VBA), the programming language built into Access 2007, there must be no ambiguity or confusion between referenced objects. Having both a form and a report named Contacts might be confusing to you *or* your code.

The simplest naming convention is to prefix object names with a three- or four-character string indicating the type of object carrying the name. Using this convention, tables are prefixed with `tbl` and queries with `qry`. The prefix for forms, reports, macros, and modules are `frm`, `rpt`, `mcr`, and `bas` or `mod`, respectively.

In this book, most compound object names appear in mixed case: `tblBookOrders`, `tblBookOrderDetails`, and so on. Most people find mixed-case names easier to read and remember than names that appear in all-uppercase or all-lowercase characters (such as `TBLBOOKORDERS` or `tblbookorderdetails`).

Also, at times, we'll use informal references for database objects. For instance, the formal name of the table containing contact information in the previous examples is `tblContacts`. An informal reference to this table might be "the contacts table."

In most instances, your users never see the formal names of database objects. One of your challenges as an application developer is to provide a seamless user interface that hides all data-management and data-storage entities that support the user interface. You can easily control the text that appears in the title bars and surfaces of the forms, reports, and other user interface components to hide the actual names of the data structures and interface constituents.

Take advantage of the long object names that Access permits to give your tables, queries, forms, and reports descriptive, informative names. There is no reason why you should confine a table name to `ConInfo` when `ContactInformation` is handled just as easily and is much easier to understand.

Descriptive names can be carried to an extreme, of course. There's no point in naming a form `frmUpdateContactInformation` if `frmUpdateInfo` does just as well. Long names are more easily misspelled or misread than shorter names, so use your judgment.

Finally, although Access lets you use spaces in database object names, you should avoid spaces at all costs. Spaces do not add to readability and can cause major headaches, particularly when upsizing to client-server environments or using OLE automation with other applications. Even if you don't anticipate extending your Access applications to client-server or incorporating OLE or DDE automation into your applications, get into the habit of not using spaces in object names.

The table design process

Creating a table design is a multistep process. By following the steps in order, your table design can be created readily and with minimal effort:

1. **Create a new table.**
2. **Enter field names, data types, and (optionally) descriptions.**
3. **Enter properties for the fields.**
4. **Set the table's primary key.**
5. **Create indexes for necessary fields.**
6. **Save the table's design.**

Generally speaking, some tables are never really finished. As users' needs change, or the business rules governing the application change, you may find it necessary to open an existing table in Design view. This book, like most books on Access, describes the process of creating tables as if every table you ever work on is brand new. The truth is, however, that most of the work that you do on an Access application is performed on existing objects in the database. Some of those objects you have added yourself, while other objects may have been added by another developer at some time in the past. However, the process of maintaining an existing database component is exactly the same as creating the same object from scratch.

Just a quick note about modifying tables once they're built: Adding a *new* field to a table almost never causes problems. Existing queries, forms, and reports, and even VBA code, will continue using the table as before. After all, these object won't reference the new field because the field was added after their creation. Therefore, you can add a new field and incorporate the field where needed in your application, and everything works as expected.

The trouble comes from removing or renaming a field in a table. Even with AutoCorrect turned on, Access will not update field name references in VBA code, in control properties, and in expressions throughout the database. *Changing* an existing field (or any other database object, for that matter) is always a bad idea. You should always strive to provide your tables, fields, and other database objects with good, strong, descriptive names at the time you add them to the database, rather than planning to go back later and fix them.

Adding a new table to the database

Begin by selecting the Create tab on the ribbon at the top of the Access screen. The Create tab (see Figure 2-12) contains all of the tools necessary to create not only tables, but also forms, reports, and other database objects. The following examples use the `Chapter02.accdb` database found on this book's CD.

FIGURE 2-12

The Create tab contains tools necessary for adding new objects to your Access database.

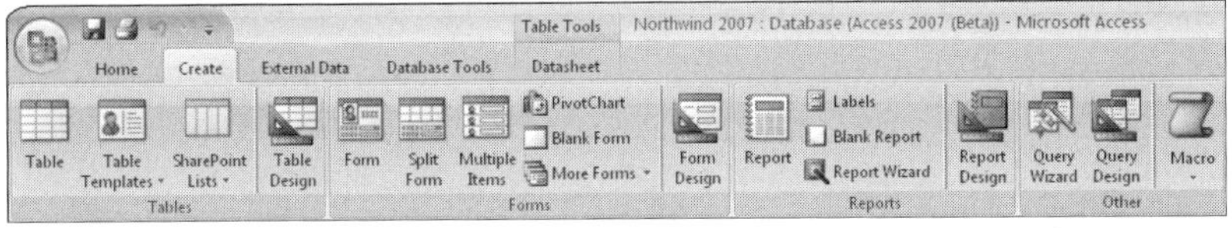

There are two main ways to add new tables to an Access database, both of which are invoked from the Tables group on the Create tab:

- **Clicking on the Table button:** Adds a complete new table to the database.
- **Clicking on the Table Design button:** Adds a table in Design view to the database.

For our example, we'll be using the Table Design button, but first, let's take a look at the Table button.

Begin by clicking on the `Table` button to add a new table to the Access environment. The new table appears in Datasheet view in the tabbed region of the Access screen. A portion of the new table is shown in Figure 2-13. Notice that the new table appears in Datasheet view, with an ID column already inserted, and an Add New Field column to the right of the ID field.

FIGURE 2-13

A portion of the new table in Datasheet view in the Access environment

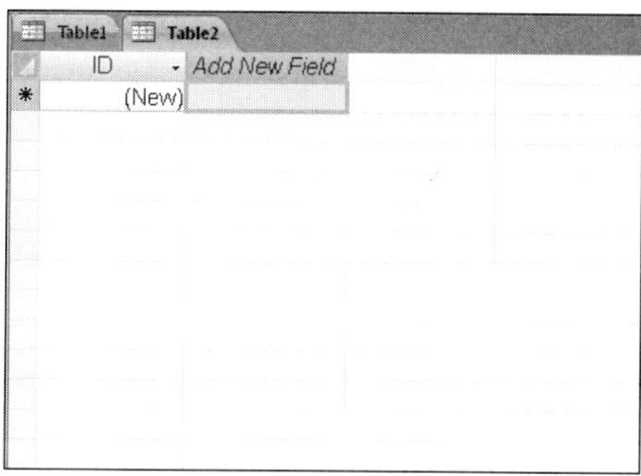

The `Add New Field` column is intended to permit users to quickly add tables to an Access database. All that is needed is to simply begin entering data into the `Add New Field` column. You assign the field a name by right-clicking the field's heading, selecting Rename Column, and entering a name for the field. In other words, building an Access table can be very much like creating a spreadsheet in Microsoft Excel. This approach was usually referred to as "creating a table in Datasheet view" in previous versions of Microsoft Access.

Although it is entirely possible to build an access table without ever switching to Design view, we believe that this is a terrible idea. Building tables by entering data and casually providing names for the table's fields circumvents one of the most critical steps in building in the serious database system.

Relational database systems such as Access are constructed by breaking data into constituent entities, and then building a table for each entity. The tables in an Access database should carefully and accurately reflect the entities they describe. Seemingly small issues, such as deciding which data type to assign to a field, has a dramatic impact on the utility, performance, and integrity of the database and its data.

Each table added to an Access database, and each field added to every table, should have a purpose in the overall database design. Even when adding tables using the Table button, it is far too easy to add tables that do not conform to the rules described in Chapter 3, and which do not fit well into the database's design.

The second approach to add new tables is to use the Table Design button, located on the right side of the Tables grouping on the Create tab. Access opens a new table in Design view, as shown in Figure 2-14.

FIGURE 2-14

A new table added in Design view

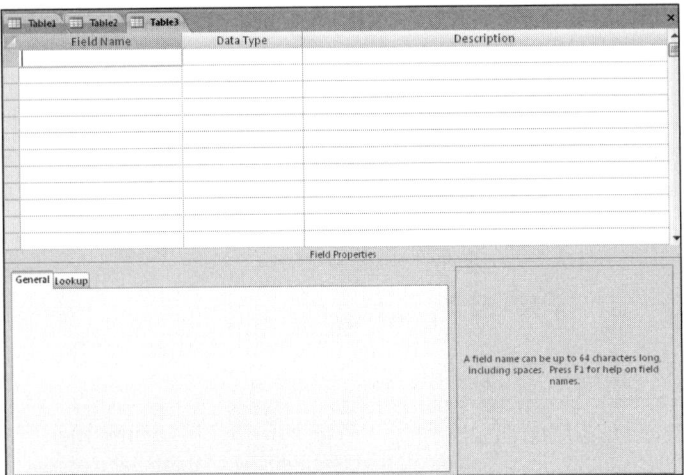

The table designer is quite easy to understand, and each column is clearly labeled. At the far left is the `Field Name` column, where you input the names of fields you add to the table. You assign a data type to each field in the table, and (optionally) provide a description for the field.

For this exercise, we'll create the Contacts table for the Access Auto Auctions application. The basic design of this table is outlined in Table 2-1.

TABLE 2-1

The Access Auto Auctions Contacts Table Design

Field Name	Data Type	Description
`ContactID`	AutoNumber	Primary key
`ContactType`	Text 50	Type of contact (Wholesaler, dealer, parts store, other)
`FirstName`	Text 50	Contact's first name
`LastName`	Text 50	Contact's last name
`Company`	Text 50	The Contact's employer or other affiliation
`Address`	Text 50	Contact's address
`City`	Text 50	Contact's city
`State`	Text 50	Contact's state

Field Name	Data Type	Description
ZipCode	Text 50	Contact's zip code
Phone	Text 50	Contact's phone
Fax	Text 50	Contact's fax
E-Mail	Text 100	Contact's e-mail address
WebSite	Text 100	Contact's Web address
OrigCustDate	DateTime	The date the contact first purchased something from Access Auto Auctions
TaxLocation	Text 50	Used to determine the applicable sales tax
CreditLimit	Currency	Customer's credit limit in dollars
CurrentBalance	Currency	Customer's current balance in dollars
CreditStatus	Text	A description of the customer's credit status
LastSalesDate	DateTime	The most recent date the customer purchased something from Access Auto Auctions
DiscountPercent	Double	The customary discount provided to the customer
Notes	Memo	Notes and observations regarding this customer
Active	Yes/No	A yes/no value, indicating whether the customer is still buying or selling to Access Auto Auctions

Some of the fields in the preceding table are rather generous in the amount of space allocated for the field's data. For instance, it is unlikely that anyone's name occupies 50 characters, but there is no harm in providing for very long names. Access only stores as many characters as are actually entered into a text field. Therefore, allocating 50 characters does not actually use 50 characters for every name in the database.

The design spelled out in Table 2-1 is a good starting point for the Contacts table.

Looking once again at Figure 2-14, you see that the Table Design window consists of two areas:

- **The field entry area (top):** Use the field entry area to enter each field's name and data type. You can also enter an optional description.
- **The field properties area (bottom):** The property area at the bottom of the window is for entering more different specifications, called *properties,* for each field. These properties include field size, format, input mask, and default value, among others. The actual properties displayed in the properties area depend upon the data type of the field. You learn much more about these properties later in this book.

You can switch between the upper and lower areas of the table designer by clicking the mouse when the pointer is in the desired pane or by pressing F6.

Using the Design ribbon tab

The Design tab on the Access ribbon, shown in Figure 2-15, contains many controls that assist in creating a new table definition.

FIGURE 2-15

The Design tab of the ribbon

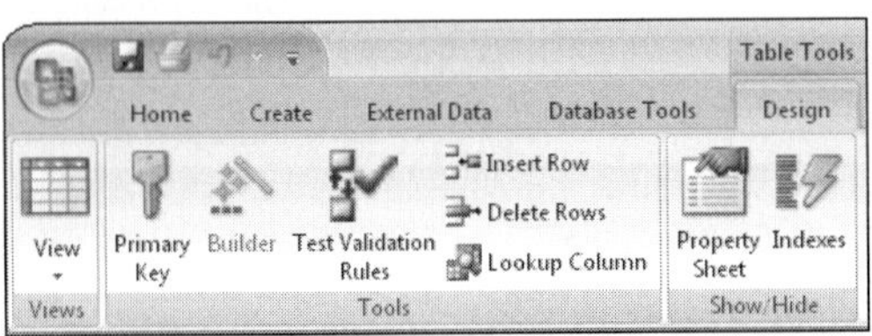

We will only mention a few of these buttons at this time. You'll learn much more about the other buttons later in this chapter and in subsequent chapters of this book.

Primary Key

Use this button to designate which of the fields in the table you want to use as the table's primary key. By tradition, the primary key appears at the top of the list of fields in the table. Moving a field is easy: Simply left-click on the gray selector to the left of the field's name to highlight the field in the Table Designer, and drag the field to its new position.

Insert Rows

Although it makes very little difference to the database engine, many developers are fussy about the sequence of fields in a table. Also, particularly when assigning an index or composite index to a table, you want the fields to be next to each other in the table's field list (composite keys, consisting of multiple fields combined as a single key, are discussed in detail in Chapter 3). The `Insert Row` button inserts a blank row just above the position occupied by the mouse cursor. For instance, if the cursor is currently in the second row of the Table Designer, clicking the `Insert Row` button inserts an empty row in the second position, moving the existing second row to the third position.

Delete Rows

Conversely, the `Delete Rows` button removes a row from the table's design. Be careful, however, because Access does not ask you to confirm the deletion before actually removing the row.

Property Sheet

The `Property Sheet` button opens the Properties window (see Figure 2-16) for the table. These properties enable you to specify important table characteristics such as a validation rule to apply to the entire table, or an alternate sort order for the table's data.

FIGURE 2-16

The Table properties window

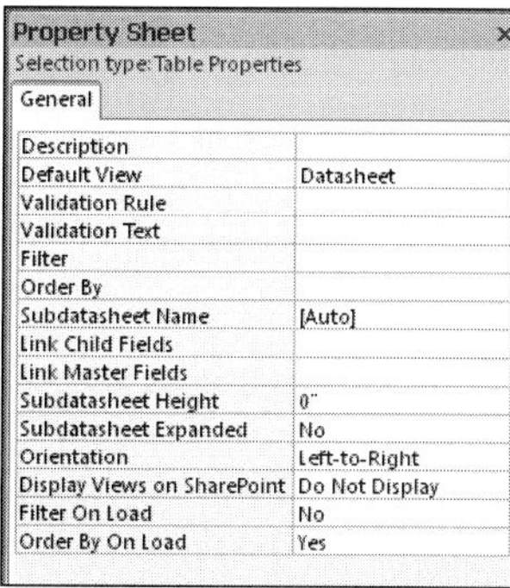

Indexes

Indexes are discussed in much more detail later in this chapter. Clicking the Indexes button opens the Indexes dialog box (shown in Figure 2-25 in the "Multiple-field indexes" section, later in this chapter), enabling you to specify the details of indexes on the fields in your table.

Working with fields

Fields are created by entering a field name and a field data type in each row of the field entry area of the Table Design window. The field description is an option to identify the field's purpose. The description appears in the status bar at the bottom of the screen during data entry. After entering each field's name and data type, you can further specify how each field is used by entering properties in the property area.

Naming a field

A field name should be descriptive enough to identify the field to you as the developer, to the user of the system, and to Access. Field names should be long enough to quickly identify the purpose of the field, but not overly long. (Later, as you enter validation rules or use the field name in a calculation, you'll want to save yourself from typing long field names.)

To enter a field name, position the pointer in the first row of the Table Design window under the `Field Name` column. Then type a valid field name, observing these rules:

- Field names can be from 1 to 64 characters.
- Field names can include letters, numbers, and many special characters.
- Field names cannot include a period (.), exclamation point (!), brackets ([ ]), or accent grave (`).

- You can't use low-order ASCII characters, for example Ctrl+J or Ctrl+L (ASCII values 0 to 31).
- You can't start with a blank space.
- You can't use a double quotation mark (") in the name of a Microsoft Access project file.

You can enter field names in upper-, lower-, or mixed case. If you make a mistake while typing the field name, position the cursor where you want to make a correction and type the change. You can change a field name at any time — even if it's in a table and the field contains data — for any reason.

NOTE **Access is not case sensitive, so the database itself doesn't care whether you name a table `tblContacts` or `TblContacts`. The selection of upper-, lower-, or mixed case is entirely your decision and should be aimed at making your table names descriptive and easy to read.**

CAUTION **After your table is saved, if you change a field name that is also used in queries, forms, or reports, you have to change it in those objects as well. One of the leading causes of errors in Access applications stems from changing the names of fundamental database objects such as tables and fields, but neglecting to make all of the changes required throughout the database. Overlooking a field name reference in the control source of a control on the form or report, or deeply embedded in VBA code somewhere in the application, is far too easy.**

Specifying a data type

The next step is to actually create your tables and define your fields for those tables. You must also decide what type of data each of your fields will hold. In Access, you can choose any of several data types (these data types are detailed later in this chapter):

- **Text:** Alphanumeric characters, up to 255 characters
- **Memo:** Alphanumeric characters, very long strings up to 65,538 (64K) characters
- **Number:** Numeric values of many types and formats
- **Date/Time:** Date and time data
- **Currency:** Monetary data
- **AutoNumber:** Automatically incremented numeric counter
- **Yes/No:** Logical values, Yes/No, True/False
- **OLE Object:** Pictures, graphs, sound, video, word processing, and spreadsheet files
- **Hyperlink:** A field that links to a picture, graph, sound, video, and word processing and spreadsheet files

One of these data types must be assigned to each of your fields. You must also specify the length of the Text fields, or accept the default of 50 characters for Text fields.

Designing data-entry rules

The last major design decision concerns data validation, which becomes important as users enter data. You want to make sure that only good data (data that passes certain defined tests) gets into your system. You have to deal with several types of data validation. You can test for known individual items, stipulating that the `Gender` field can accept only the values `Male`, `Female`, or `Unknown`, for example. Or you can test for ranges, specifying that the value of `Weight` must be between `0` and `1,500` pounds.

Designing lookup tables

Sometimes you need to design entire tables to perform data validation or just to make it easier to create your system; these are called *lookup tables*. For example, because Access Auto Auctions needs a field to determine the customer's tax rate, you may decide to use a lookup table that contains the tax location, and tax rate. Another example is when a customer pays an invoice using some specific method — cash, credit card, money order, and on and on.

Because the tax rate can change, storing tax rates makes much more sense than hard-coding tax rates into the application. Using lookup tables, Access looks up the current tax rate in `tblTaxRates` whenever an invoice is created. The tax rate applied to an invoice is stored along with the other invoice data in the Invoice/Sales table because it is time-dependent data, and the value stored in `tblTaxRates` may be different in the future.

Another purpose of a lookup table is to limit data entry in a field to a specific value. For example, you can use a table containing payment types (cash, check, MasterCard, and so on). The payment types table (`tblPaymentTypes`) can be used as a lookup table to ensure only approved payment methods can be entered in the Invoice table.

TIP **When you create a field in a table, you can use the data type Lookup Wizard. It is not an actual data type, but is instead a way of storing a field one way and displaying it another way.**

Although you can create a field on a data-entry form that limits the entry of valid contact types to seller, buyer, or both, you create a table with only one field — ContactType — and use the ContactType field in tblContacts to link to this field in the ContactType lookup table.

NOTE **You create a lookup table in exactly the same way as you create any other table, and it behaves in the same way. The only difference is in the way you use the table's data.**

Several lookup tables are included in the Access Auto Auctions application: `tblPaymentType`, `tblTaxRates`, and `tblCategories`.

Assigning field data types

After you name a field, you must decide what type of data the field holds. Before you begin entering data, you should have a good grasp of the data types that your system will use. Ten basic types of data are shown in Table 2-2; some data types (such as numbers) have several options.

TABLE 2-2

Data Types Available in Microsoft Access

Data Type	Type of Data Stored	Storage Size
Text	Alphanumeric characters	0–255 characters
Memo	Alphanumeric characters	0–65,536 characters
Number	Numeric values	1, 2, 4, or 8 bytes, 16 bytes for Replication ID (GUID)
Date/Time	Date and time data	8 bytes
Currency	Monetary data	8 bytes
AutoNumber	Automatic number increments	4 bytes, 16 bytes for Replication ID (GUID)
Yes/No	Logical values: Yes/No, True/False	1 bit (0 or –1)
OLE Object	Pictures, graphs, sound, video	Up to 1GB (disk space limitation)
Hyperlink	Link to an Internet resource	0–64,000 characters
Attachment	A special field (new in Access 2007) that enables you to attach external files to an Access database	Varies by attachment
Lookup Wizard	Displays data from another table	Generally 4 bytes

Figure 2-17 shows the Data Type drop-down list used to select the data type for the field you just created.

FIGURE 2-17

The Data Type drop-down list

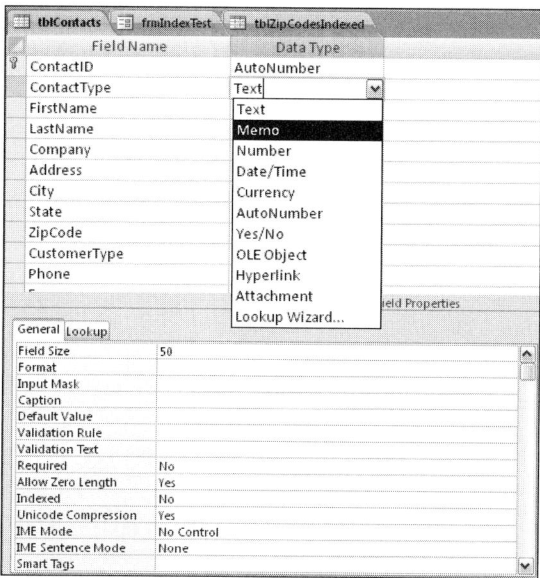

Here are the basic rules to consider when choosing the data type for new fields in your tables:

- **The data type should reflect the data stored in the field.** For instance, you should select one of the numeric data types to store numbers like quantities and prices. Do not store data like phone numbers or Social Security numbers in numeric fields, however. Your application will not be performing numeric operations like addition or multiplication on phone numbers, and this data should not be stored in numeric fields. Instead, use text fields for common data such as Social Security numbers and phone numbers.

  Also, numeric fields never store leading zeros. Putting a zip code such as 02173 into a numeric field means only the last four digits (2173) are actually stored.
- **Consider the storage requirements of the data type you've selected.** Although you can use a long integer data type in place of a simple integer or byte value, the storage requirements of a long integer (4 bytes) is twice that of a simple integer. This means that twice as much memory is required to use and manipulate the number and twice as much disk space is required to store its value. Whenever possible, use byte or integer data types for simple numeric data.
- **Will you want to sort or index the field?** Because of their binary nature, memo and OLE object fields cannot be sorted or indexed. Use memo fields sparingly. The overhead required to store and work with memo fields is considerable.

- **Consider the impact of data type on sorting requirements.** Numeric data sort differently than text data. Using the numeric data type, a sequence of numbers will sort as expected: 1, 2, 3, 4, 5, 10, 100. The same sequence stored as text data will sort like this: 1, 10, 100, 2, 3, 4, 5. If it's important to sort text data in a numeric sequence, you'll have to first apply a conversion function to the data before sorting.

NOTE **If it's important to have text data representing numbers to sort in the proper order, you may want to prefix the numerals with zeros (001, 002, and so on). Then the text values will sort in the expected order: 001, 002, 003, 004, 005, 010, 100.**

- **Is the data text or date data?** When working with dates, you're almost always better off storing the data in a `Date/Time` field than as a `Text` field. Text values sort differently than date data (dates are stored internally as numeric values), which can upset reports and other output that rely on chronological order.
- **Keep in mind the reports that will be needed.** You won't be able to sort or group memo or OLE data on a report. If it's important to prepare a report based on memo or OLE data, add a Tag field like a date or sequence number, which can be used to provide a sorting key, to the table.

Text data type

Any type of data that is simply characters (letters, numbers, punctuation). Names, addresses, and descriptions are all text data, as are numeric data that are not used in a calculation (such as telephone numbers, Social Security numbers, and zip codes).

Although you specify the size of each `Text` field in the property area, you can enter no more than 255 characters of data in any `Text` field. Access uses variable length fields to store text data. If you designate a field to be 25 characters wide and you use only 5 characters for each record, then only enough room to store 5 characters is used in your database.

You will find that the `.accdb` database file may quickly grow quite large, but text fields are not the usual cause. However, it is good practice to limit text field widths to the maximum you believe they will be used for. Names are tricky because some cultures have long names. However, it is a safe bet that a postal code might be less than 12 characters wide while a U.S. state abbreviation is always 2 characters wide. By limiting the size of the text width, you also limit the number of characters that users can enter when the field is used in a form.

Memo data type

The `Memo` data type holds a variable amount of data from 0 to 65,536 characters for each record. Therefore, if one record uses 100 characters, another requires only 10, and yet another needs 3,000, you use only as much space as each record requires.

Notice that you did not specify a field size for the `Memo` data type. Access allocates as much space is necessary for the memo data.

Number data type

The `Number` data type enables you to enter *numeric* data; that is, numbers that will be used in mathematical calculations. (If you have data that will be used in monetary calculations, you should use the `Currency` data type, which performs calculations without rounding errors.)

The exact type of numeric data stored in a number field is determined by the `Field Size` property. Table 2-3 lists the various numeric data types, their maximum and minimum ranges, the decimal points supported by each numeric data type, and the storage (bytes) required by each numeric data type.

TABLE 2-3

Numeric Field Settings

Field Size Setting	Range	Decimal Places	Storage Size
Byte	0 to 255	None	1 byte
Integer	–32,768 to 32,767	None	2 bytes
Long Integer	–2,147,483,648 to 2,147,483,647	None	4 bytes
Double	-1.797×10^{308} to 1.797×10^{308}	15	8 bytes
Single	-3.4×10^{38} to 3.4×10^{38}	7	4 bytes
Replication ID	N/A	N/A	16 bytes
Decimal	1–28 precision	15	8 bytes

Many errors are caused by choosing the wrong numeric type for number fields. For instance, notice that the maximum value for the `Integer` data type is 32,767. We once saw a database that ran perfectly for several years and then started crashing with overflow errors. It turned out that the overflow was caused by a particular field being set to the Integer data type, and when the company occasionally processed very large orders, the 32,767 maximum was exceeded.

It is best to design your tables very conservatively and allow for larger values than you ever expect to see in your database. This is not to say that it is a good idea to use the `Double` data type for all numeric fields. The `Double` data type is very large (8 bytes) and is quite slow when used in calculations for another numeric operation. Instead, the `Single` data type is probably best for most floating-point calculations, and the `Long Integer` is best for most data where decimal points are irrelevant.

Date/Time data type

The `Date/Time` data type is a specialized number field for holding dates or times (or dates *and* times). When dates are stored in a `Date/Time` field, it is easy to calculate days between dates and other calendar operations. Date data stored in `Date/Time` fields sort and filter properly as well.

Currency

The `Currency` data type is another specialized number field. `Currency` numbers are not rounded during calculations and preserve 15 digits of precision to the left of the decimal point and 4 digits to the right. Because the `Currency` data type uses a fixed-decimal-point position, they are faster in numeric calculations than doubles.

AutoNumber

The `AutoNumber` field is another specialized `Number` data type. When an `AutoNumber` field is added to a table, Access automatically assigns an integer value to the field (beginning at 1) and increments the value each time a record is added to the table. Alternatively (determined by the `New Values` property), the value of the `AutoNumber` field is a random integer that is automatically inserted into new records.

Only one `AutoNumber` field can appear in a table. Once assigned to a record, the value of an `AutoNumber` field cannot be changed programmatically or by the user. `AutoNumber` fields are equivalent to the `Long Integer` data type and occupy 4 bytes, but display only positive values. The range of possible values for `AutoNumber` fields, then, range from 1 to 4,294,967,296 — more than adequate to use as the primary key for most tables.

Yes/No

`Yes/No` fields accept only one of two possible values. Internally stored as a 1 or 0 bit, the `Yes/No` field is used to indicate yes/no, on/off, or true/false. A `Yes/No` field occupies a single bit of storage.

OLE Object

The `OLE Object` field stores OLE data, highly specialized binary objects such as Microsoft Word documents, Excel worksheets, sound or video clips, and images. The OLE object is created by an OLE server application and can be linked to the parent application or embedded in the Access table. OLE objects can only be displayed in bound object frames in Access forms and reports. OLE objects can be as large as 1GB or more in size. OLE fields cannot be indexed.

Attachment

The `Attachment` data type is new for Access 2007. In fact, the `Attachment` data type is one of the reasons Microsoft changed the format of the Access data file. The older MDB format is unable to accommodate attachments.

The Attachment data type is relatively complex, compared to the other type of Access fields. Please see the section titled "Understanding the Attachment Data Type" later in this chapter for details on this interesting type of field.

Hyperlink data type

The `Hyperlink` data type field holds combinations of text and numbers stored as text and used as a hyperlink address. It can have up to three parts:

- The visual text that appears in a field (usually underlined).
- The Internet address — the path to a file (UNC, or Universal Naming Convention, path) or page (URL or Uniform Resource Locator).
- Any sub-address within the file or page. An example of a sub-address is the name of an Access 2000 form or report. Each part is separated by the pound symbol (#).

Lookup Wizard

The `Lookup Wizard` data type inserts a field that enables the end user to choose a value from another table or from the results of an SQL statement. The values may also be presented as a combo box or list box. At design time, the `Lookup Wizard` leads the developer through the process of defining the lookup characteristics when this data is assigned to a field.

Dragging a field created by the `Lookup Wizard` from the field list as you design a form, a combo box or list box is automatically created on the form. The list box or combo box also appears on a query datasheet that contains the field.

Entering a field description

The field description is completely optional; you use it only to help you remember a field's uses or to let another developer understand the field's purpose. Often you don't use the description column at all, or you use it only for fields whose purpose is not obvious. If you enter a field description, it appears in the status bar whenever you use that field in Access — in the datasheet or in a form. The field description can help clarify a field whose purpose is ambiguous or give the user a fuller explanation of the values valid for the field during data entry.

Creating tblContacts

Working with the different data types (plus the Lookup Wizard), you should be ready to create the final working copy of `tblContacts`. When creating the table, you must add a field that is used to link this table to two other tables (`tblSales` and `tblContactLog`) in the Access Auto Auctions application.

AutoNumber fields and Access

Access gives special considerations to AutoNumber fields and assigning values to AutoNumber fields. You cannot change a previously defined field from another type to AutoNumber. If you try to change an existing field in a table to the AutoNumber field type, Access displays a `Control can't be edited: It's bound to AutoNumber field "ContactID"` error in the status bar (the exact error you see will differ, of course, depending on which field is designated as the AutoNumber).

Completing tblContacts

With tblContacts in Design view, you're now ready to create or modify all the fields of `tblContacts`. Table 2-1, earlier in this chapter, shows the completed field definitions for `tblContacts`. If you're following the examples, you should be able to complete the table design. Enter the field names and data types exactly as shown. You may also need to rearrange some of the fields. The next few pages explain how to change existing fields (which includes rearranging the field order, changing a field name, and deleting a field).

Here are the steps for adding fields to a table structure:

1. **Place the cursor in the Field Name column in the row where you want the field to appear.**
2. **Enter the field name and press Enter or Tab.**
3. **In the Data Type column, click the down arrow and select the data type.**
4. **Place the pointer in the Description column and type a description (optional).**

Repeat each of these steps to create each of the data entry fields for `tblContacts`. You can press the down-arrow (↓) key to move between rows, or simply use the mouse and click on any row. Remember that F6 moves you from the top to the bottom of the Table Design window and back.

Changing a Table Design

As you create your table, you should be following a well-planned design. Yet changes are sometimes necessary, even with a plan. You may find that you want to add another field, remove a field, change a field name or data type, or simply rearrange the order of the field names. You can make these changes to your table at any time. After you enter data into your table, however, things get a bit more complicated. You have to make sure that any changes made don't affect the data entered previously.

NEW FEATURE **In previous versions of Access, changing a field name usually meant that any queries, forms, reports, macros, or modules that referenced that field name would no longer work and had to be manually found and changed. Since Access 2002, the AutoCorrect feature automatically seeks out most occurrences of the name and changes it for you.**

Inserting a new field

To insert a new field, in the Table Design window, place your cursor on an existing field and choose Insert ➪ Rows or click the Insert Rows button in the toolbar. A new row is added to the table, and existing fields are pushed down. You can then enter a new field definition. Inserting a field does not disturb other fields or existing data. If you have queries, forms, or reports that use the table, you may need to add the field to those objects as well.

Deleting a field

There are three ways to delete a field. While the table is in Design View:

- Select the field by clicking the row selector and pressing the Delete key.
- Right-click on the selected field and choose Delete Rows from the shortcut menu.
- Select the field and click the Delete Rows button from the Tools group on the ribbon's Design tab.

When you delete a field containing data, you'll see a warning that you will lose data in the table for the selected field. If the table is empty, you won't care. If your table contains data, however, make sure that you want to eliminate the data for that field (column). You will also have to delete the same field from queries, forms, reports, macros, and VBA code that use the field name.

TIP **When you delete a field, you can immediately select the Undo button and return the field to the table. But you must do this step before you save the changed table's definition or make any other changes to the table's design.**

TIP **If you attempt to delete a field that is part of a relationship (primary or secondary key field), Access informs you that you cannot delete it until you delete the reference in the Relationships window.**

If you delete a field, you must also delete all references to that field throughout Access. Because you can use a field name in forms, queries, reports, and even table-data validation, you must examine your system carefully to find any instances where you may have used the specific field name.

Changing a field location

One of the easiest changes to make is to move a field's location. The order of your fields, as entered in the table's Design View, determines the initial display sequence in the datasheet that displays your data. If you decide that your fields should be rearranged, click on a field selector and use the mouse to drag the field to its new location.

Changing a field name

You change a field's name by selecting an existing field name in the Table Design screen and entering a new name; Access updates the table design automatically. As long as you are creating a new table, this process is easy.

CAUTION **If you used the field name in any forms, queries, or reports, however, you must also change the field's name in each object that references the field. (Remember that you can also use a field name in validation rules and calculated fields in queries, as well as in macros and module expressions — all of which must be changed.) Even with AutoCorrect turned on, Access only catches the most obvious references to the changed field names, and fails to update references in validation rules, expressions, `ControlSource` properties, and many other places. As you can see, it's a good idea not to change a field name because it creates more work.**

Changing a field size

Making a field size larger is simple in a table design. However, only text and number fields can be increased in size. You simply increase the Field Size property for text fields or specify a different field size for number fields. You must pay attention to the decimal-point property in number fields to make sure that you don't select a new size that supports fewer decimal places than you currently have.

When you want to make a field size smaller, make sure that none of the data in the table is larger than the new field width. (If it is, the existing data will be truncated.) Text data types should be made as small as practical to limit the amount of data entered by the user.

TIP **Remember that each text field uses only the number of characters actually entered in the field. You should still try to make your fields only as large as the largest value so that Access can stop someone from entering a value that may not fit on a form or report.**

Data conversion issues

If, in spite of your best efforts, it becomes necessary to change the data type of a field containing data, you may suffer data loss as the data-type conversion occurs. You should be aware of the effects of a data-type conversion on existing data:

- **Any data type to AutoNumber:** Can't be done. The AutoNumber field type must be created fresh in a new field.
- **Text to Number, Currency, Date/Time, or Yes/No:** In most cases, the conversion will be made without damaging the data. Inappropriate values are automatically deleted. For instance, a text field containing "January 28, 2007" will be faithfully converted to a Date/Time field. If, however, you change a field containing "January 28, 2007" to a Yes/No data type, its value will be deleted.
- **Memo to Text:** A straightforward conversion with no loss or corruption of data. Any text longer than the field size specified for the Text field is truncated and lost.
- **Number to Text:** No loss of information. The number value is converted to text using the General Number format.
- **Number to Currency:** Because the Currency data type uses a fixed decimal point, some precision may be lost as the number is truncated.
- **Date/Time to Text:** No loss of information. Date and time data are converted to text with the General Date format.
- **Currency to Text:** No loss of information. The currency value is converted to text without the currency symbol.
- **Currency to Number:** Simple, straightforward conversion. Some data may be lost as the currency value is converted to fit the new number field. For instance, when converting Currency to Long Integer, the decimal portion is truncated (cut off).

- **AutoNumber to Text:** Conversion occurs without loss of data, except in a case where the width of the text field is inadequate to hold the entire AutoNumber value. In this case, the number is truncated.
- **AutoNumber to Number:** Simple, straightforward conversion. Some data may be lost as the AutoNumber value is converted to fit the new number field. For instance, an AutoNumber larger than 32,767 will be truncated if it is converted to an Integer field.
- **Yes/No to Text:** Simple conversion of Yes/No value to text. No loss of information.
- **OLE Data Type:** Cannot be converted to any other type of data.

Assigning field properties

The field properties built into Access tables are powerful allies that can help you manage the data in your tables. In most cases, the field property is enforced by the database engine, which means the property is consistently applied throughout the application. For instance, if you've set the Default Value property in the table design, the default value is available in the table's Datasheet view, on forms, and in queries.

Each field data type has its own set of properties. For instance, numeric fields have a Decimal Places property, and Text fields have a Text Align property. Although many data types share a number of properties (such as Name) in common, there are enough different field properties to make it easy to become confused or to improperly use the properties. The following sections discuss some of the more important and frequently used field properties.

NOTE **The following sections include many references to properties, and property settings in the Access table designer. The formal name for a property (such as `DefaultValue`) never contains a space, while the property's expression in the table designer usually contains a space for readabilty (Default Value). These relative minor differences become important when referencing properties in expressions, VBA code, and macros. When making a formal reference to a property in code or a macro, always use the "spaceless" version of the property's name, not the property reference you see in the Access user interface.**

Common properties

Here is a list of all the general properties (note that they may not all be displayed, depending on which data type you chose):

- **Field Size:** When applied to Text fields, limits size of the field to the specified number of characters (1–255). The default is 50.
- **New Values:** Applies to AutoNumber fields. Allows specification of increment or random type.
- **Format:** Changes the way data appears after you enter it (uppercase, dates, and so on). There are many different types of formats that may be applied to Access data. Many of these differences are explained later in this chapter.

- **Input Mask:** Used for data entry into a predefined format (phone numbers, zip codes, Social Security numbers, dates, customer IDs). Applicable to both numeric and text data types.
- **Decimal Places:** Specifies number of decimal places for Numeric and Currency data types.
- **Caption:** Optional label for form and report fields. Access uses the Caption property instead of the field name in these situations.
- **Default Value:** The value automatically provided for new data entry into the field. This value can be any value appropriate for the field's data type. A default is no more than an initial value; you can change it during data entry. To specify a default value, simply enter the desired value into the Default Value property setting. A default value can be an expression, as well as a number or a text string.

NOTE **Because the Default Value for Number and Currency data types is set to 0 (zero), by default, these fields are set automatically to 0 when you add a new record. In many situations, such as medical test results and many financial applications, zero is not an appropriate default value for numeric fields. Be sure to verify that zero is an appropriate default value in your Access applications.**

- **Validation Rule:** Ensures that data entered into the field conforms to some business rule, such as "greater than zero," "date must occur after January 1, 2000," and so on.
- **Validation Text:** Displays a message when data fails validation.
- **Required:** Specifies whether you must enter a value into a field.
- **Allow Zero Length:** Determines whether you may enter an empty string (`" "`) into a text field type to distinguish it from a null value.
- **Indexed:** Speeds up data access and (if desired) limits data to unique values. Indexing is explained in greater detail later in this chapter.
- **Unicode Compression:** Used for multilanguage applications. Requires about twice the data storage but enables Office documents including Access reports to be displayed correctly no matter what language or symbols are used. Generally speaking, Unicode is of no value unless the application is likely to be used in Asian environments.
- **IME Mode:** Also known as the Kanji Conversion Mode property, this mode is used to show whether the Kanji mode is maintained when the control is lost. The setting has no relevance in English or European-language applications.
- **IME Sentence Mode:** Used to determine the Sequence mode of fields of a table or controls of a form that switch when the focus moves in or out of the field. The setting has no relevance in English or European-language applications.
- **Smart Tags:** Used to assign a specific action to obtain data in this field. For example, the Financial Symbol Smart Tag obtains recent stock quotes on MSN Money Central.

NOTE **IME Mode and IME Sequence Mode are available only if international support for Simplified Chinese, Traditional Chinese, or Japanese is enabled through Microsoft Office Language Settings. *IME* stands for Input Method Editor.**

Format

The Format property specifies how the data contained in table fields appears whenever the data is displayed or printed. When set at the table level, the format is in effect throughout the application. There are different format specifiers for each data type.

Access provides built-in format specifiers for most field data types. The exact format used to display field values is influenced by the Regional Settings in the Windows Control Panel.

The Format property affects only the way a value is displayed and not the value itself or how the value is stored in the database.

If you elect to build a custom format, construct a string in the field's Format property box. There are a number of different symbols you use for each data type. Access provides global format specifications to use in any custom format specifier:

- **(space):** Display spaces as characters.
- `"SomeText"`: Display the text between the quotes as literal text.
- `!` **(exclamation mark):** Left-aligns the display.
- `*` **(asterisk):** Fills empty space with the next character.
- \ **(backslash):** Displays the next character as literal text. Use the backslash to display characters that otherwise have special meaning to Access.
- **[color]:** Displays the output in the color (black, blue, green, cyan, red, magenta, yellow, white) indicated between the brackets.

The Format property takes precedence when both a format specifier and input mask have been defined.

Number and Currency field formats

There is a wide variety of valid formats for Number and Currency fields. You can use one of the built-in formats or construct a custom format of your own:

- **General Number:** The number is displayed in the format in which it was entered (this is the default format for numeric data fields).
- **Currency:** Add a thousands separator (usually a comma), use a decimal point with two digits to the right of the decimal, and enclose negative numbers in parentheses.
- **Fixed:** Always display at least one digit with two digits to the right of the decimal point.
- **Standard:** Use the thousands separator with two digits to the right of the decimal point.
- **Percent:** The number value is multiplied by 100 and a percent sign is added to the right. Percent values are displayed with two decimal places to the right of the decimal point.

- **Scientific:** Scientific notation is used to display the number.
- **Euro:** Prepends the Euro currency symbol to the number and uses spaces instead of commas as the thousands delimiter.

The built-in numeric formats are summarized in Table 2-4.

TABLE 2-4

Numeric Format Examples

Format Type	Number as Entered	Number as Displayed	Format Defined
General	987654.321	987654.3	######.#
Currency	987654.321	$987,654.32	$###,##0.00
Euro	987654.321	€987,654.32	€###,##0.00
Fixed	987654.321	987654.32	######.##
Standard	987654.321	987,654.32	###,###.##
Percent	.987	98.7%	###.##%
Scientific	987654.321	9.88E+05	###E+00

All the formats above are the default formats based on setting the Decimal places property to AUTO.

Custom numeric formats

Custom formats are created by combining a number of symbols to form a format specifier. The symbols used with Number and Currency fields are listed below:

- `.` **(period):** Specifies where the decimal point should appear.
- `,` **(comma):** The thousands separator.
- `0` **(zero):** A placeholder for zero or a digit.
- `#` **(pound sign):** A placeholder for nothing or a digit.
- `$` **(dollar sign):** Display the dollar sign character.
- `%` **(percent sign):** Multiply the value by 100 and add a percent sign.
- `E-` **or** `e-`**:** Use scientific notation to display the number. Use a minus sign to indicate a negative exponent and no sign for positive exponents.
- `E+` **or** `e+`**:** Same as previous, but use a plus sign to indicate positive exponents.

You create custom formats by composing a string made up of one to four sections separated by semicolons. Each section has a different meaning to Access:

- **First section:** The format specifier for positive values.

- **Second section:** The format specifier for negative values.
- **Third section:** The format specifier for zero (0) values.
- **Fourth section:** The format specifier for null values.

Each section is a combination of a numeric formatting string and an optional color specification. Here's an example of a custom format:

```
0,000.00[Green];(0,000.00)[Red];"Zero";"—"
```

This format specifies showing the number with zeros in all positions (even if the number is less than 1,000), using the comma thousands separator, enclosing negative numbers in parentheses, using three pound signs to indicate a zero value, and using three dashes for null values.

Date/Time field formats

Access includes a wide variety of built-in and custom formats applicable to Date/Time fields. You are able to create a custom format to display date and time data in virtually any format imaginable.

Built-in Date/Time formats

The following are the built-in Date/Time formats:

- **General Date:** If the value contains a date only, do not display a time value and vice versa. Dates are displayed in the built-in Short Date format, while time data is displayed in the Long Time format.
- **Long Date:** Sunday, May 13, 2007
- **Medium Date:** 13-May-07
- **Short Date:** 5/13/07
- **Long Time:** 9:21:17 AM
- **Medium Time:** 09:21 AM
- **Short Time:** 9:21:17

Date and time formats are influenced by the Regional Settings in the Windows Control Panel.

Custom Date/Time formats

Custom formats are created by constructing the specifier as a string containing the following symbols:

- **: (colon):** Separates time elements (hours, minutes, seconds).
- **/ (forward slash):** Separates date elements (days, months, years).
- `c` **(lowercase c):** Instructs Access to use the built-in General Date format.
- `d` **(lowercase d):** Displays the day of the month as one or two digits, as necessary.
- `dd`: Displays the day of the month using two digits ("9" displays as "09").

- ddd: Displays the first three letters of the day of the week (Sun, Mon, Tue, Wed, Thu, Fri, Sat).
- dddd: Uses the full name of the day of the week (Sunday, Monday, Tuesday, Wednesday, Thursday, Friday, Saturday).
- ddddd: Uses the built-in Short Date format.
- dddddd: Uses the built-in Long Date format.
- w: Uses a number to indicate the day of the week.
- ww: Shows the week of the year (1 to 53).
- m: Displays the month of the year using one or two digits.
- mm: Displays the month of the year using two digits (with leading zero if necessary).
- mmm: Uses the first three characters of the month (Jan, Feb, Mar, Apr, May, Jun, Jul, Aug, Sep, Oct, Nov, Dec).
- mmmm: Displays the full name of the month (for example, January).
- q: Displays the date as the quarter of the year.
- y: Displays the day of the year (1 through 366).
- yy: Uses the last two digits of the year (for example, 07).
- yyyy: Uses the full four-digit year (2007).
- h: Displays the hour using one or two digits.
- hh: Displays the hour using two digits.
- n: Displays the minutes using one or two digits.
- nn: Displays the minutes using two digits.
- s: Displays the seconds using one or two digits.
- ss: Displays the seconds using two digits.
- tttt: Uses the built-in Long Time format.
- AM/PM: Uses a 12-hour format with uppercase AM or PM.
- am/pm: Uses a 12-hour format with lowercase am or pm.
- A/P: Uses a 12-hour format with uppercase A or P.
- a/p: Uses a 12-hour format with lowercase a or p.
- AMPM: 12-hour format using the morning or after designator specified in the Regional Settings in the Windows Control Panel.

You must enclose a comma or other separator or text in quotation marks as part of the format specifier.

Text and Memo field formats

When applied to text fields, format specifiers clarify the data contained within the fields. `tblContacts` uses several formats. The State text field has a > in the Format property to display the data entry in uppercase. The `OrigCustDate` field has an `mmm dd yyyy` format to display the date of birth as the short month name, a space, the day and a four-digit year (May 13 2007). The Active field has a format of `Yes/No` with lookup Display Control property set to Text Box.

Text and Memo fields are displayed as plain text by default. If a particular format is to be applied to Text or Memo field data, use the following symbols to construct the format specifier:

- `@` **(at sign):** A character or space is required.
- `&` **(ampersand):** A character is optional (not required).
- < **(less than symbol):** Force all characters to their lowercase equivalents.
- > **(greater than symbol):** Force all characters to their uppercase equivalents.

The custom format specifier may contain as many as three different sections, separated by semicolons:

- **First section:** Specifier for fields containing text
- **Second section:** Format for fields containing zero-length strings
- **Third section:** Format for fields containing Null values

If only two sections are given, the second section applies to both zero-length strings and null values. For example, the following specifier displays "None" when no string data is contained in the field, "Unknown" when a null value exists in the field. Otherwise, the simple text contained in the field is displayed:

```
@;"None";"Unknown"
```

Several examples of custom text formats are presented in Table 2-5.

TABLE 2-5

Format Examples

Format Specified	Data as Entered	Formatted Data as Displayed
>	Adam Smith	ADAM SMITH
#,##0;(#,##0);"-0-";"None"	15 -15 0 No Data	15 (15) -0- None
Currency	12345.67	$12,345.67
"Acct No." 0000	3271	Acct No. 3271
mmm yy	9/17/08	Sep 08
Long Date	9/17/08	Thursday, September 17, 2008

Yes/No field formats

A Yes/No field displays the words "Yes," "No," "True," "False," "On," or "Off," depending on the value stored in the field and the setting of the Format property for the field. Access predefines these rather obvious format specifications for the Yes/No field type:

- **Yes/No:** Displays "Yes" or "No"
- **True/False:** Displays "True" or "False"
- **On/Off:** Displays "On" or "Off"

Yes, True, and On all indicate the same "positive" value, while No, False, and Off indicate the opposite ("negative") value.

Access stores Yes/No data in a manner different from what you might expect. The Yes data is stored as –1, whereas No data is stored as 0. You'd expect it to be stored as 0 for No and 1 for Yes, but this isn't the case. Without a format setting, you must enter –1 or 0, and it will be stored and displayed that way.

You are also able to specify a custom format for Yes/No fields. For instance, assume you've got a table with a field that indicates whether the employee has attended an orientation meeting. Although a Yes or No answer is appropriate, maybe you want to get a little fancy with the field's display. By default, a check box is used to indicate the value of the Yes/No field (checked means Yes). To customize the appearance of the Yes/No field, set its Format property according to the following pattern:

```
;"Text for Yes values";"Text for No values"
```

Notice the placeholder semicolon at the front of this string. Also notice that each text element must be surrounded by quotes. In the case of the employee table, you might use the following Format property specifier:

```
;"Attendance OK";"Must attend orientation"
```

You must also set the Yes/No field's Display Control property to Text Box in order to change the default check box display to *text*.

CAUTION **There are two problems when changing the table-level format property of a logical, Yes/No field. First, if you enter a custom format like in the preceding example, you need to also change the default Lookup Display Control property from check box to text box to see the new format. Second, after the format is assigned and the text box is the display method, the user will only be able to enter a 0 for –1. The format property affects only how the value is displayed, not how it is entered into the table.**

Hyperlink data-type format

Access also displays and stores Hyperlink data in a manner different from what you would expect. The format of this type is composed of up to three parts:

- **Display Text:** The text that is displayed as a hyperlink in the field or control
- **Address:** The path to a file (UNC) or page (URL) on the Internet
- **Sub-Address:** A specific location within a file or page

The parts are separated by pound signs. The Display Text is visible in the field or control, while the address and sub-address are hidden. For example, `Microsoft Net Home Page#http://www.msn.com`.

Input Mask

The Input Mask property makes it easier for users to enter the data in the correct format. An input mask limits the way the user inputs data into the table or a form. For instance, you can confine the user to only entering digits into phone number, Social Security number, and employee ID fields. An input mask for a Social Security number might look like "000-00-0000." This mask requires input into every space, restricts entry to digits only, and does not permit characters or spaces.

An input mask specified as part of the field's properties is used anywhere the field appears (query, form, report).

The Input Mask property value is a string containing as many as three sections, each section separated by a semicolon.

- **First section:** Contains the mask itself, composed of the symbols shown below.
- **Second section:** Tells Access whether to store the literal characters included in the mask along with the rest of the data. For instance, the mask might include dashes to separate the parts of the Social Security number while a phone number may include parentheses and dashes. Using a 0 (zero) tells Access to store the literal characters as part of the data; a 1 tells Access to store only the data itself.
- **Third section:** Defines the "placeholder" character that tells the user how many characters are expected in the input area. Many input masks use pound signs (#) or asterisks (*) as placeholders.

The following characters are used to compose the input mask string:

- `0`: A digit is required, and plus (+) and (–) minus signs are not permitted.
- `9`: A digit is optional, and plus (+) and (–) minus signs are not permitted.
- `#`: Optional digit or space. Spaces are removed when the data is saved in the table. Plus and minus signs are allowed.
- `L`: A letter from A to Z is required.
- `?`: A letter from A to Z is optional.

- A: A character or digit is required.
- a: A character or digit is optional.
- &: Permits any character or space (required).
- C: Permits any character or space (optional).
- . **(period):** Decimal placeholder.
- , **(comma):** Thousands separator.
- : **(colon):** Date and time separator.
- ; **(semicolon):** Separator character.
- - **(dash):** Separator character.
- / **(forward slash):** Separator character.
- < **(less-than sign):** Convert all characters to lowercase.
- > **(greater-than sign):** Convert all characters to uppercase.
- ! **(exclamation mark):** Display the input mask from right to left. Characters fill the mask from right to left.
- \ **(back slash):** Display the next character as a literal.

The same specifiers are used on a field's property sheet in a query or form.

Input masks are ignored when importing data or adding data to a table with an action query.

An input mask is overridden by the Format property assigned to a field. In this case, the input mask is in effect only as data is entered and reformatted according to the format specifier when entry is complete.

The Input Mask Wizard

Although you can manually enter an input mask, you can easily create an input mask for Text or Date/Time type fields with the Input Mask Wizard. When you click the Input Mask property, the builder button (three periods) appears. Click the Build button to start the Wizard. Figure 2-18 shows the first screen of the Input Mask Wizard.

FIGURE 2-18

The Input Mask Wizard for creating input masks for Text and Date field types

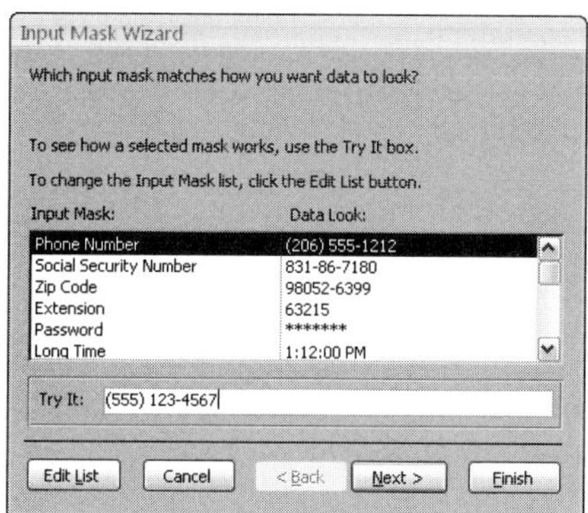

The Input Mask Wizard shows not only the name of each predefined input mask, but also an example for each name. You can choose from the list of predefined masks. Click in the Try It text box and enter a test value to see how data entry will look. After you choose an input mask, the next wizard screen enables you to refine the mask and specify the placeholder symbol (perhaps a pound sign [#] or "at" sign [@]). Another wizard screen enables you to decide whether to store special characters (such as the dashes in a Social Security number) with the data. When you complete the wizard, Access adds the input mask characters in the field's property sheet.

TIP **You can create your own input masks for Text and Date/Time fields by simply clicking the Edit List button and entering a descriptive name, input mask, a placeholder character, and a sample data content. Once created, the new mask will be available the next time you use the Input Mask Wizard.**

Enter as many custom masks as you need. You can also determine the international settings so that you can work with multiple country masks.

Caption

The Caption property determines what appears in the default label attached to a control created by dragging the field from the field list onto a form or report. The caption also appears as the column heading in Datasheet views (table or query) that include the field.

Be careful using the Caption property. Because the caption text appears as the column heading in Datasheet view, you may be misled by a column heading in a query's Datasheet view. When the field appears in a query, you do not have immediate access to the field's properties, so you must be aware that the column heading is actually determined by the Caption property. To be even more confusing, the caption assigned in the table's Design view and the caption assigned in a field's property sheet in the Query Design view are different properties and can contain different text.

Captions can be as long as 2,048 characters, more than adequate for all but the most verbose descriptions.

ValidationRule

The Validation Rule property establishes requirements for input into the field. Enforced by the Jet database engine, the validation rule ensures that data entered into the table conforms to the requirements of the application.

The Validation Rule property does not apply to check boxes, option buttons, or toggle buttons within an option group on a form. The option group itself has a Validation Rule property that applies to all of the controls within the group.

The value of the Validation Rule property is a string containing an expression that is used to test the user's input. The expression used as a field's Validation Rule property cannot contain user-defined functions or any of the Access domain or aggregate functions (DCount, DSum, and so on). A field's validation rule cannot reference forms, queries, or other tables in the application. (These restrictions do not apply to validation rules applied to controls on a form, however.) Field validation rules cannot reference other fields in the table, although a validation rule applied to a record in a table can reference fields in the same table (a record-level validation rule is set in the table's property sheet, rather than on an individual field).

In the "Understanding tblContacts Field Properties" section, later in this chapter, you'll see that a validation rule has been applied to the CreditLimit field. This validation rule (`< 250000`) causes an error message to appear (as shown in Figure 2-19) whenever a value greater than 250,000 is entered into the credit limit text box.

FIGURE 2-19

A data-validation warning box. This appears when the user enters a value in the field that does not match the rule specified in the design of the table.

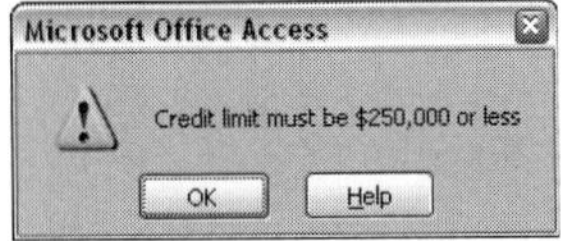

Validation rules are often used to ensure that certain dates fall after other dates (for instance, an employee's retirement date must fall after his starting date), to ensure nonnegative numbers are entered for values such as inventory quantities, and that entries are restricted to different ranges of numbers or text.

Dates are surrounded, or *delimited*, by pound signs (#) when used in Access expressions. If you want to limit the LastSalesDate data entry to dates between January 1, 2007, and December 31, 2008, enter **Between #1/1/07# and #12/31/08#**.

TIP **If you want to limit the upper end to the current date, you can enter a different set of dates, such as Between #1/1/00# and Date( ). Date( ) is a built-in VBA function that returns the current date, and is completely acceptable as part of a validation rule or other expression.**

When a field containing a validation rule is dragged onto a form, the new control's Validation Rule property is not set to the field's table-level validation rule value in the control's property sheet. Unless you enter a new validation rule value in the control's property sheet, the value in the property sheet is empty. Instead, the Access database engine enforces the field's validation rule behind the scenes, based on the value of the Validation Rule property for the field at the table level.

Field and control validation rules are enforced when the focus leaves the table field or form control. Record-level validation rules are enforced when moving to another record. Validation rules applied to both a table field and a form control bound to the field are enforced for both entities. The table-level rule is applied as data is edited on the bound control and as focus leaves the control.

You cannot create table-level validation rules for linked "foreign" tables, such as FoxPro, Paradox, or dBASE. Apply validation rules to controls bound to fields in linked foreign tables.

Validation Text

The `Validation Text` property contains a string that is displayed in a message box when the user's input does not satisfy the requirements of the `Validation Rule` property. The maximum length of the `Validation Text` property value is 255 characters.

When using the `Validation Rule` property, you should always specify a validation text value to avoid triggering the generic message box Access displays when the validation rule is violated. Use the `Validation Text` property to provide users with a helpful message that explains acceptable values for the field.

Required

The `Required` property directs Access to require input into the field. When set to Yes, input is required into the field within a table or into a control on a form bound to the field. The value of a required field cannot be Null.

The `Required` property is invalid for `AutoNumber` fields. By default, all `AutoNumber` fields are assigned a value as new records are created.

The Access database engine enforces the `Required` property. An error message is generated if the user tries to leave a text box control bound to a field with its `Required` property set to Yes.

The `Required` property can be used in conjunction with the`Allow Zero Length` property to determine when the value of a field is unknown or doesn't exist.

AllowZeroLength

The `Allow Zero Length` property specifies whether or not you want a zero-length string (`""`) to be a valid entry for a `Text` or `Memo` field. `Allow Zero Length` accepts the following values:

- **Yes:** A zero-length string is a valid entry.
- **No:** The table will not accept zero-length strings, and instead, inserts a Null value into the field when no valid text data is supplied.
- **Using Visual Basic:** `AllowZeroLength` (with no spaces!) can be set from Visual Basic for Applications (VBA). Use the `Allow Zero Length` property of the `TableDef` object to determine its setting or change its value.

Appropriate combination of the `Allow Zero Length` and `Required` properties enables you to differentiate between data that doesn't exist (which you'll probably want to represent as a zero-length string) and data that is unknown (which you'll want to store as a null value). VBA determines the difference between null and zero-length string values and takes appropriate action based on this information. In some cases you'll want to store the proper value in the `Text` or `Memo` field.

An example of data that doesn't exist is the case of a customer who doesn't have an e-mail address. The e-mail address field should be set to an empty (zero-length) string indicating that no address exists. Another customer who you are sure is an e-mail user but who hasn't supplied an e-mail address should have a null value in the e-mail address field, indicating that we don't know whether the person has an e-mail address.

An input mask can help your application's users distinguish when a field contains a null value. For instance, the input mask could be set to display "None" when the field contains a zero-length string.

The `Required` property determines whether a null value is accepted by the field, while the `Allow Zero Length` property permits zero-length strings in the field. Together, these independent properties provide the means to determine whether a value is unknown or absent for the field.

The interaction between `Required` and `Allow Zero Length` can be quite complicated. Table 2-6 summarizes how these two properties combine to force the user to input a value, or to insert either a Null or zero-length string into a field.

TABLE 2-6

Required and Allow Zero Length Property Combinations

Allow Zero Length	Required	Data Entered by User	Value Stored in Table
No	No	Null	Null
No	No	Space	Null
No	No	Zero-length string	Disallowed

Allow Zero Length	Required	Data Entered by User	Value Stored in Table
Yes	No	Null	Null
Yes	No	Space	Null
Yes	No	Zero-length string	Zero-length string
No	Yes	Null	Disallowed
No	Yes	Space	Disallowed
No	Yes	Zero-length string	Disallowed
Yes	Yes	Null	Disallowed
Yes	Yes	Space	Zero-length string
Yes	Yes	Zero-length string	Zero-length string

Indexed

The `Indexed` property tells Access you want to use a field as an index in the table. Indexed fields are internally organized to speed up queries, sorting, and grouping operations. If you intend to frequently include a certain field in queries (for instance, the employee ID or Social Security number), or if the field is frequently sorted or grouped on reports, you should set its `Indexed` property.

The valid settings for the Indexed property are as follows:

- **No:** The field is not indexed (default).
- **Yes (Duplicates OK):** The field is indexed and Access permits duplicate values in the column. This is the appropriate setting for values such as names, where it is likely that names like "Smith" will appear more than once in the table.
- **Yes (No Duplicates):** The field is indexed and no duplicates are permitted in the column. Use this setting for data that should be unique within the table, such as Social Security numbers, employee IDs, and customer numbers.

Indexes are discussed in more detail later in this chapter.

In addition to the primary key, you are able to index as many fields as necessary to provide optimum performance. Access accepts as many as 32 indexes per table. Keep in mind that each index extracts a small performance hit as new records are added to the table. Access dynamically updates the indexing information each time a new record is added. If a table includes an excessive number of indexes, a noticeable delay may occur as each new record is added.

The `Indexed` property is set in the field's property sheet or on the table's property sheet. Using the table index's property sheet is discussed in the earlier section on assigning primary keys. You must use the table's property sheet to set multi-field indexes.

AutoIndex Option

The Access Options dialog box (File ➪ Access Options ➪ Object Designers) contains an entry (AutoIndex on Import/Create) that directs Access to automatically index certain fields as they are added to a table's design. By default, fields that begin or end with `ID`, `key`, `code`, or `num` (for instance, `Employee ID` or `Task Code`) are automatically indexed as the field is created. Every time a new record is added to the table, the field's data is incorporated into the field's index. If there are other fields you'd like Access to automatically index as they are created, add new values to the `Auto Index on Import/Create` check box on the Object Designers tab in the Access Options dialog box (see Figure 2-20).

FIGURE 2-20

The Table Design area in the Options dialog box contains options for setting the AutoIndex on Import/Create specifier.

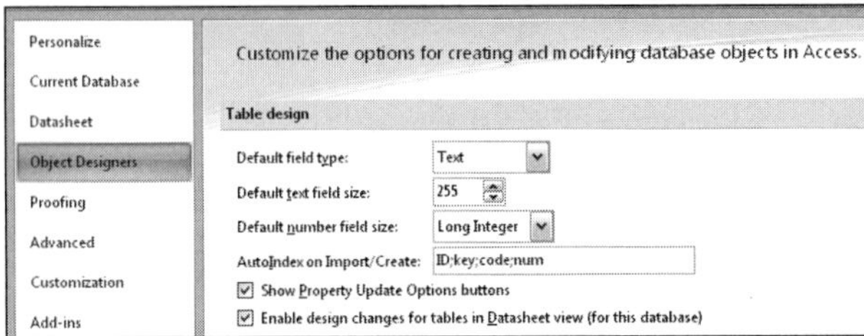

When to Index

Generally speaking, you should index fields that are frequently searched or sorted. Remember that indexes slow down certain operations such as inserting records and some action queries.

`Memo` and `OLE Object` fields cannot be indexed. It would be impossible for Access to maintain an index on these complete data types.

An index should not be used if a field contains very few unique values. For instance, you will not see a significant benefit from indexing a field containing a person's sex or state, or Yes/No fields. Because there is a limited domain of values in such fields, Access easily sorts the data in these fields.

Use a multiple-field index in situations where sorts are often simultaneously performed on multiple fields (for instance, first and last names). Access will have a much easier time sorting such a table.

Understanding tblContacts Field Properties

After you enter the field names, data types, and field descriptions, you may want to go back and further define each field. Every field has properties, and these are different for each data type. In `tblContacts`, you must enter properties for several data types. Figure 2-21 shows the property area for the field named `CreditLimit`; ten options are available in the General section of the property area. Notice that there are two tabs on the property box — `General` and `Lookup`. Lookup is discussed later in this chapter.

FIGURE 2-21

Property area for the Currency field named `CreditLimit`

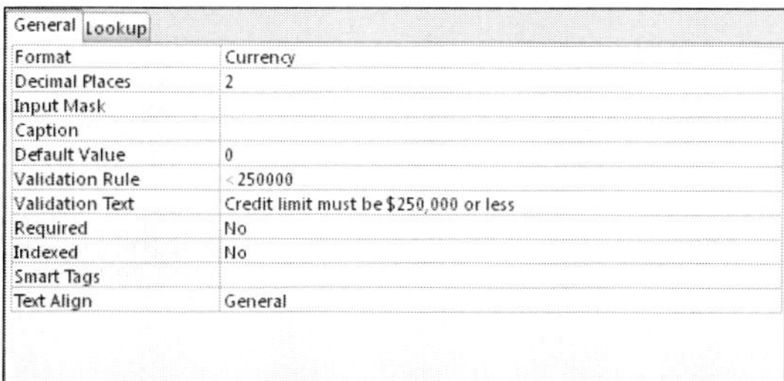

Figure 2-21 shows 11 properties available for the CreditLimit Currency field. Other types, such as `Number` and `Date/Time`, `Text`, or `Yes/No`, show more or fewer options.

Pressing F6 switches between the field entry pane and the property pane. You can also move between panes by clicking the desired pane. Some properties display a list of possible values, along with a downward-pointing arrow, when you move the pointer into the field. When you click the arrow, the values appear in a drop-down list.

Understanding the Lookup Property window

The Field Properties pane of the Table Design window has a second tab: the Lookup tab. After clicking this tab, you may see a single property, the Display Control property. This property is used for `Text`, `Number`, and Yes/No fields.

Figure 2-22 shows the Lookup Property window for the `Active Yes/No` field where Display Control is the only property. This property has three choices: `Check Box`, `Text Box`, and `Combo Box`. Choosing one of these determines which control type is used when a particular field is added to a form. Generally, all controls are created as text boxes except `Yes/No` fields, which are created as check boxes by default. For `Yes/No` data types, however, you may want to use the Text Box setting to display Yes/No, True/False, or another choice that you specifically put in the format property box.

If you are working with text fields instead of a `Yes/No` field and know a certain text field can only be one of a few combinations, select the combo box choice for the display control. When you select the Combo Box control type as a default, the properties change so that you can define a combo box.

CROSS-REF **You learn about combo boxes in Chapter 7 and again in Chapter 19.**

FIGURE 2-22

The Lookup property Display Control for a Yes/No field.

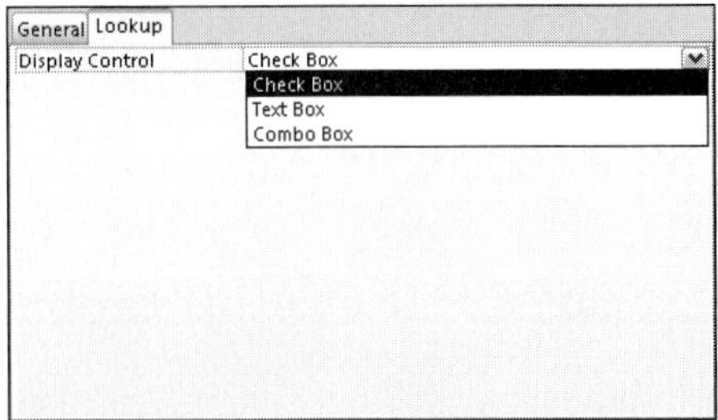

NOTE **The properties for a Lookup field are different for each data type. The Yes/No data type fields differ from text fields or numeric fields. Because a Lookup field is really a combo box (you learn more about these later), the standard properties for a combo box are displayed when you select a Lookup field data type.**

Setting the Primary Key

Every table should have a *primary key* — one or more fields with a unique value for each record. (This principle is called *entity integrity* in the world of database management.) In `tblContacts`, the `ContactID` field is the primary key. Each contact has a different `ContactID` value so that you can identify one from the other. `ContactID 17` refers to one and only one record in the Contacts table. If you don't specify a primary key (unique value field), Access can create one for you.

Understanding unique values

Without the ContactID field, you'd have to rely on another field or combination of fields for uniqueness. You couldn't use the LastName field because two customers could easily have the same last name. In fact, you couldn't even use the FirstName and LastName fields together (multi-field key), for the same reason — two people could be named James Smith. You need to come up with a field that makes every record unique. Looking at the table, you may think that you could use a combination of the LastName, FirstName, and Company fields, but theoretically, it's possible that two people working at the same company have the same name.

The easiest way to solve this problem is to add an AutoNumber field for the express purpose of using it as the table's primary key. This is exactly the situation with the Contacts table. The primary key of this table is ContactID, an AutoNumber field.

If you don't designate a field as a primary key, Access can add an AutoNumber field and designate it as the table's primary key. This field contains a unique number for each record in the table, and Access maintains it automatically.

Generally speaking, you may want to create and maintain your own primary key, even if you always use AutoNumber fields as primary keys:

- A primary key is always an index.
- An index maintains a presorted order of one or more fields that greatly speeds up queries, searches, and sort requests.
- When you add new records to your table, Access checks for duplicate data and doesn't allow any duplicates for the primary key field.
- By default, Access displays a table's data in the order of its primary key.

By designating a field such as ContactID as the unique primary key, you can see your data in a meaningful order. In our example, because the ContactID field is an AutoNumber, its value is assigned automatically by Access in the order that a record is put into the system.

Choosing a primary key

Although all of the tables in the Access Auto Auctions application use AutoNumber fields as their primary keys, you should be aware of the reasons why AutoNumbers make such excellent primary keys. The characteristics of primary keys include the following:

- The primary key must uniquely identify each record.
- The primary key cannot be null.
- The primary key must exist when the record is created.
- The primary key definition must remain stable — you should never change a primary key value once it is established.
- The primary key must be compact and contain as few attributes as possible.

The ideal primary key is, then, a single field that is immutable and guaranteed to be unique within the table. For these reasons, the Access Auto Auctions database uses the `AutoNumber` field exclusively as the primary key for all tables.

Creating the primary key

The primary key can be created in any of three ways. With a table open in Design View:

- Select the field to be used as the primary key and select the Primary Key button (the key icon) in the Tools group in the ribbon's Design tab.
- Right-click on the field to display the shortcut menu and select Primary Key.
- Save the table without creating a primary key, and allow Access to automatically create an `AutoNumber` field.

After you designate the primary key, a key icon appears in the gray selector area to the left of the field's name to indicate that the primary key has been created.

Creating composite primary keys

Although rarely done these days, it is possible to designate a combination of fields to be used as a table's primary key. Such keys are often referred to as *composite* primary keys. As indicated in Figure 2-23, select the fields that you want to include in the composite primary key, then click the key icon in the Tools ribbon tab. It helps, of course, if the fields lie right next to each other in the table's design.

FIGURE 2-23

Creating a composite primary key

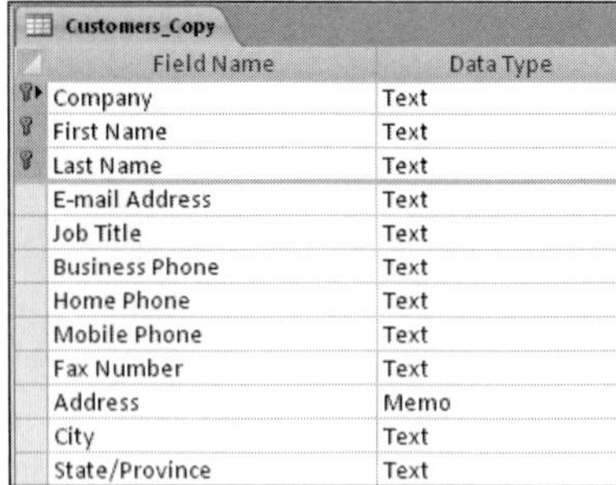

Customers_Copy

Field Name	Data Type
Company	Text
First Name	Text
Last Name	Text
E-mail Address	Text
Job Title	Text
Business Phone	Text
Home Phone	Text
Mobile Phone	Text
Fax Number	Text
Address	Memo
City	Text
State/Province	Text

Composite primary keys are primarily used when the developer strongly feels that a primary key should be comprised of data that occurs naturally in the database. There was a time when all developers were taught that every table should have a *natural* primary key.

The reason that composite primary keys are seldom used these days is because developers have come to realize that data is highly unpredictable. Even if your users promise that a combination of certain fields will never be duplicated in the table, things have a way of turning out differently than planned. Using a *surrogate* primary key, such as an AutoNumber, separates the table's design from the table's data. The problem with *natural primary keys* (meaning, data that occurs naturally in the table) is that, eventually, given a large enough data set, the values of fields chosen as the table's primary key are likely to be duplicated.

Furthermore, when using composite keys, maintaining relationships between tables becomes more complicated because the fields must be duplicated in all the tables containing related data. Using composite keys simply adds to the complexity of the database without adding stability, integrity, or other desirable features.

Indexing Access Tables

Data is rarely, if ever, entered into tables in a meaningful order. Usually records are added to tables in totally random order (with the exception of time-ordered data). For instance, a busy order entry system will gather information on a number of different customer orders in a single day. Most often this data will be used to report orders for a single customer for billing purposes or for extracting order quantities for inventory management. The records in the Orders table, however, are in chronological order, which is not necessarily helpful when preparing reports detailing customer orders. In that case, you'd rather have data entered in customer ID order.

To further illustrate this concept, consider the Rolodex card file many people use to store names, addresses, and phone numbers. Assume for a moment that the cards in the file were fixed in place. You could add new cards, but only to the end of the card file. This limitation would mean that "Jones" might follow "Smith," and in turn be followed by "Baker." In other words, there is no particular order to the data stored in this file.

An unsorted Rolodex like this would be very difficult to use. You'd have to search each and every card looking for a particular person, a painful and time-consuming process. Of course, this is not how we use address card files. When we add a card to the file, we insert it into the Rolodex at the location where it *logically* belongs. Most often, this means inserting the card in alphabetical order, by last name, into the Rolodex.

Records are added to Access tables as described in the "fixed" card file example earlier. New records are always added to the end of the table, rather than in the middle of the table where they may logically belong. However, in an order entry system you'd probably want new records inserted next to other records on the same customer. Unfortunately, this isn't how Access tables work. The *natural order* of a table is the order in which records were added to the table. This order is sometimes referred to as *entry order* or *physical order* to emphasize that the records in the table appear in the order in which they were added to the table.

Using tables in natural order is not necessarily a bad thing. Natural order makes perfect sense if the data is rarely searched or if the table is very small. Also, there are situations where the data being added to the table is highly ordered to start with. If the table is used to gather sequential data (like readings from an electric meter) and the data will be used in the same sequential order, there is no need to impose an index on the data.

But for situations where natural order does not suffice, Microsoft Access provides *indexing* to help you find and sort records faster. You specify the logical order for the records in a table by creating an *index* on that table. Access uses the index to maintain one or more internal sort orders for the data in the table. For instance, you may choose to index the `LastName` field that will frequently be included in queries and sorting routines.

Microsoft Access uses indexes in a table as you use an index in a book: To find data, Access looks up the location of the data in the index. Most often, your tables will include one or more *simple indexes*. A simple index is one that involves a single field in the table. Simple indexes may arrange the table's records in ascending or descending order. Simple indexes are created by setting the field's `Indexed` property to one of the following values:

- Yes (Duplicates OK)
- Yes (No Duplicates)

By default, Access fields are not indexed. However, it is hard to imagine a table that does not require some kind of index. The next section discusses why indexing is important to use in Access tables. Once you've read the following section, we're sure you'll agree that it's difficult to imagine an Access table that would not benefit from an index or two.

The importance of indexes

Microsoft's data indicates that more than half of all tables in Access databases contain *no* indexes. This number doesn't include the tables that are improperly indexed — it includes only those tables that have no indexes at all. It appears that a lot of people don't appreciate the importance of indexing the tables in an Access database.

As a demonstration of the power and value of indexes, the sample database for this chapter (`Chapter02.accdb`) contains two tables, each holding 46,796 records of identical data. `tblZipCodesIndexed` is indexed on the `City` field while `tblZipCodesNotIndexed` contains no indexes at all. The data in these tables is input in zip code order, not city order.

`Chapter02.accdb` also contains two queries and a form (`frmIndexTest`, shown in Figure 2-24) that provides a user interface to the two queries and underlying tables. The queries pull data from the indexed and non-indexed Zip Code tables. `qryFindCityIndexed` searches for a city in `tblZipCodesIndexed` while `qryFindCityNotIndexed` uses the unindexed tblZipCodesNotIndexed table. The results are displayed in the subform in the middle of frmIndexTest.

FIGURE 2-24

frmIndexTest provides a quick and easy way to verify the importance of indexes.

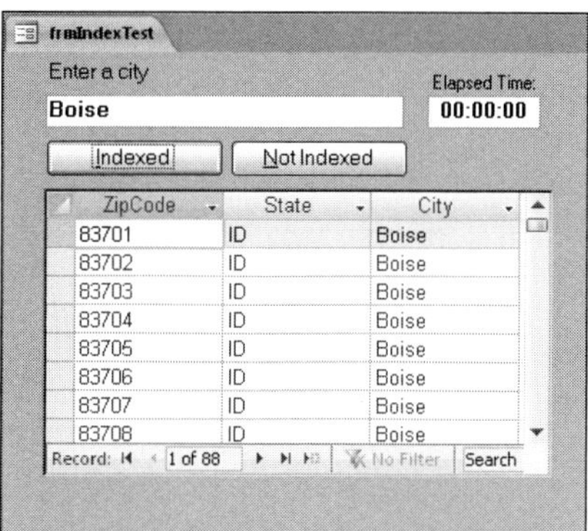

The query against the indexed table completes a search for "Boise" in less than 1 second while qryFindCityNotIndexed requires almost 5 seconds to perform the same search. It goes without saying that the actual time required to run a query depends very much on the computer's hardware, but performance enhancements of 500 percent and more are not at all uncommon when adding an index to a field.

Because an index means that Access maintains an internal sort order on the data contained in the indexed field, you can see why performance is enhanced by an index. You should index virtually every field that is frequently involved in queries or is frequently sorted on forms or reports.

Without an index, Access must search each and every record in the database looking for matches. This process is called a *table scan* and is analogous to searching through each and every card in Rolodex file to find all of the people who work for a certain company. Until you reach the end of the deck, you can't be sure you've found every relevant card in the file. Similarly Access much search every record in tblZipCodesNotIndexed to be sure it's found all of the cities matching "Boise."

It is interesting to note that the result set returned by a search for "Iowa City," which yields only 6 records takes just as long on the non-indexed table as the query for "Boise" (which returns 88 records) against the same table. This is because Access has to search the unindexed table from top to bottom, regardless of how many records are actually found during the search. Composing the view you see in Figure 2-24 takes almost no time at all and doesn't contribute to the overall time required to run the query.

As mentioned earlier in this chapter, a table's primary key field is always indexed. This is because the primary key is used to locate records in the table. Indexing the primary key makes it much easier for Access to find the required tables in either the current table or a foreign table related to the current table. Without an index, Access would have to search all of the records in the foreign table to make sure it has located all of the related records.

The performance losses due to unindexed tables can have a devastating effect on the overall performance of an Access application. Any time you hear a complaint about the performance of an application, consider indexing as a possible solution.

Multiple-field indexes

Multiple-field indexes (also called *composite indexes*) are easy to create. In Design view, click on the Indexes toolbar button or select the Indexes command on the View menu. The Indexes dialog box (see Figure 2-25) opens, allowing you to specify the fields to include in the index.

FIGURE 2-25

Multi-field (composite) indexes can enhance performance.

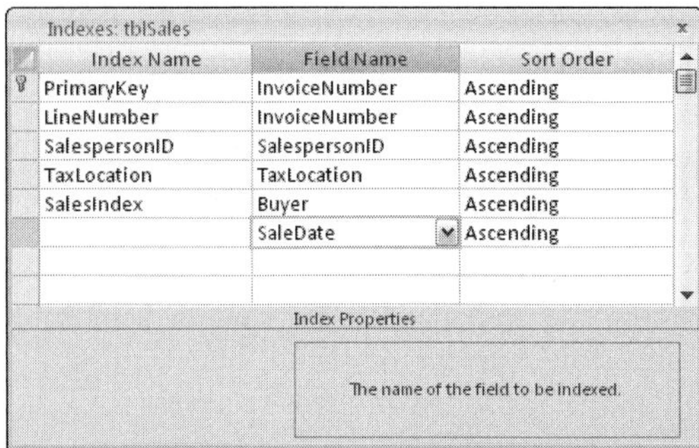

Enter a name for the index (`SalesIndex` in Figure 2-26) and tab to the Field Name column. Use the drop-down list to select the fields to include in the index. In this example `InvoiceNumber` and `OrderDate` are combined as a single index. Access considers both these fields when creating the sort order on this table, speeding queries and sorting operations that include both the `InvoiceNumber` and `OrderDate` fields.

As many as ten fields can be included in a composite index. As long as the composite index is not used as the table's primary key, any of the fields in the composite index can be empty.

Figure 2-26 shows how to set the properties of a composite index. The cursor is placed in the row in the Indexes dialog box containing the name of the index. Any row appearing immediately below this row that does not contain an index name is part of the composite index. Notice the three properties appearing below the index information in the top half of the Indexes dialog box.

FIGURE 2-26

It's easy to set the properties of a composite index.

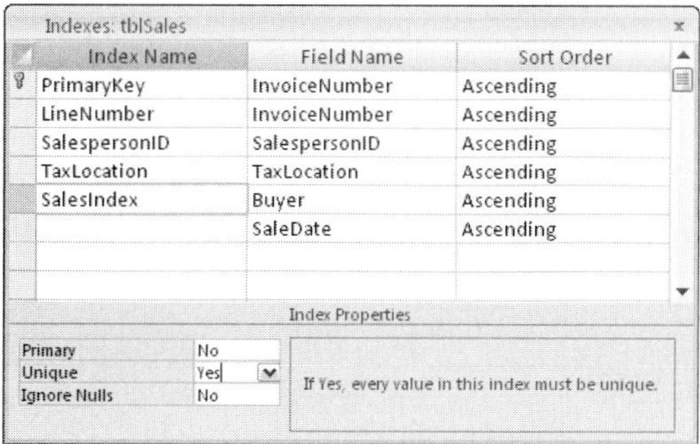

The index properties are quite easy to understand:

- `Primary`: When set to Yes, Access uses this index as the table's primary key. More than one field can be designated as the primary key, but keep the rules governing primary keys in mind, particularly those requiring each primary key value to be unique and that no field in a composite primary key can be empty. The default for the `Primary` property is `No`.
- `Unique`: When set to `Yes`, the index must be unique within a table. When applied to composite keys, the *combination* of field values must be unique — each field within the composite key can duplicate fields found within the table. A Social Security number field is a good candidate for a unique index, but a last name field should not be uniquely indexed.
- `Ignore Nulls`: If a record's index field contains a null value (which happens in a composite index only if all fields in the composite index are null) the record's index won't contribute anything to the overall indexing. In other words, unless a record's index contains some kind of value, Access doesn't know where to insert the record in the table's internal index sort lists. Therefore, you may want to instruct Access to ignore a record if the index value is null. By default, the `Ignore Nulls` property is set to `No`, which means Access inserts records with a null index values into the indexing scheme along with any other records containing null index values.

You should test the impact of the index properties on your Access tables and use the properties that best suit the data handled by your databases.

NOTE **A field can be both the primary key for a table and part of a composite index. You should index your tables as necessary to yield the highest possible performance without worrying about over-indexing or violating some arcane indexing rules.**

When to index tables

Depending on the number of records in a table, the extra overhead of maintaining an index may not justify creating an index beyond the table's primary key. Though data retrieval is somewhat faster than without an index, Access must update index information whenever you enter or change records in the table. In contrast, changes to nonindexed fields do not require extra file activity. You can retrieve data from nonindexed fields as easily (although not as *quickly*) as from indexed fields.

Generally speaking, it is best to add secondary indexes when tables are quite large, and indexing on fields other than the primary key speeds up searches. Even with large tables, however, indexing can slow performance if the records in tables will be changed often or new records will be added frequently. Each time a record is changed or added, Access must update all indexes in the table.

Given all the advantages of indexes, why not index everything in the table? What are the drawbacks of indexing too many fields? Is it possible to over-index tables?

First of all, indexes increase the size of the `.mdb` file somewhat. Unnecessarily indexing a table that doesn't really require an index eats up a bit of disk space for each record in the table. More important, indexes extract a performance hit for each index on the table every time a record is added to the table. Because Access automatically updates indexes each time a record is added (or removed), the internal indexing must be adjusted for each new record. If you have ten indexes on a table, Access makes ten adjustments to the indexes each time a new record is added or an existing record is deleted, causing a noticeable delay on large tables (particularly on slow computers).

Sometimes changes to the data in records causes adjustments to the indexing scheme. This is true if the change causes the record to change its position in sorting or query activities. Therefore, if you are working with large, constantly changing data sets that are rarely searched, you may choose *not* to index the fields in the table, or to minimally index by indexing only those few fields that are likely to be searched.

As you begin working with Access tables, it is likely you'll start with the simplest one-field indexes and migrate to more complex ones as your familiarity with the process grows. Do keep in mind, however, the tradeoffs between greater search efficiency and the overhead incurred by maintaining a large number of indexes on your tables.

It's also important to keep in mind that indexing does not modify the physical arrangement of records in the table. The natural order of the records (the order in which the records were added to the table) is maintained after the index is established.

Indexing tblContacts

You use the Indexes window to determine the specific characteristics of the indexes in a table. Notice that the Indexes window shown in Figure 2-27 contains four indexes. The first of these (on the `ContactID` field) is the table's Primary Key (you'll recall from the discussion above that Primary Keys are always uniquely indexed). The other indexes are built on single fields (`ZipCode`, `CustomerType`, and `TaxLocation`) and in ascending order.

FIGURE 2-27

The Indexes window that shows all the indexes built for `tblContacts`. You can add more indexes directly into this window.

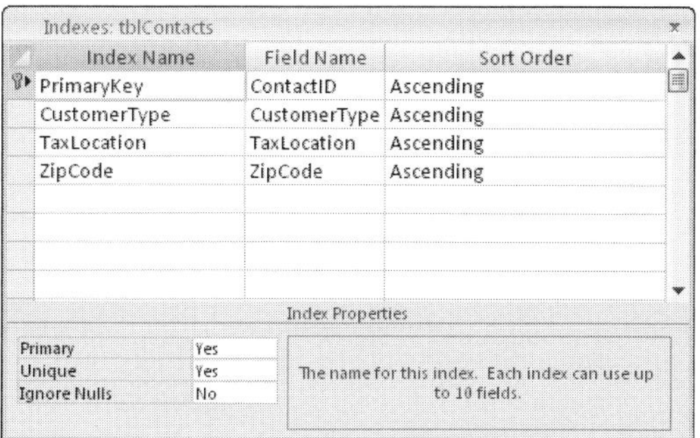

Printing a Table Design

You can print a table design by choosing the Analyze Table button in the Analyze group on the ribbon's Database Tools tab. The Analyze group contains a number of tools that makes it easy to document your database objects. When you select the Analyze Table button, Access shows you a dialog box that lets you select objects to print. In Figure 2-28, there is only one object (`tblContacts`) under the Tables tab. Select it by clicking the check box next to the table name.

You can also set various options for printing. When you click the Options button, a dialog box appears that enables you to select which information from the Table Design to print. You can print the various field names, all of their properties, the indexes, and even network permissions.

FIGURE 2-28

The Access Documenter dialog box

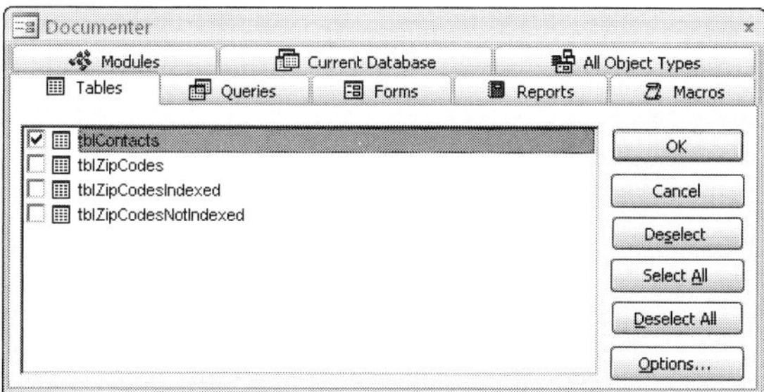

After you select which data you want to view, Access generates a report; you can view it in a Print Preview window or send the output to a printer.

TIP The Database Documenter creates a table of all the objects and object properties you specify. You can use this utility to document such database objects as forms, queries, reports, macros, and modules.

Saving the Completed Table

You can save the completed table design by choosing File ➪ Save or by clicking the Save button in the upper-left corner of the Access environment. If you are saving the table for the first time, Access asks for the name of the table. Table names can be up to 64 characters long and follow standard Access object-naming conventions.

If you have saved this table before and want to save it with a different name, choose File ➪ Save As and enter a different table name. This action creates a new table design and leaves the original table with its original name untouched. If you want to delete the old table, select it in the Navigation pane and press the `Delete` key. You can also save the table when you close it.

Manipulating Tables in a Database Window

As you create many tables in your database, you may want to use them in other databases or copy them for use as a history file. You may want to copy only the table structure. You can perform many operations on tables in the Navigation pane, including

- Renaming tables
- Deleting tables
- Copying tables in a database
- Copying a table from another database

You perform these tasks by direct manipulation or by using menu items.

Renaming tables

Rename a table with these steps:

1. **Select the table name in the Database window.**
2. **Click once on the table name, and press F2.**
3. **Type the new name of the table and press Enter.**

You can also rename the table by right-clicking on its name in the Navigation pane, and selecting Rename from the shortcut menu. After you change the table name, it appears in the Tables list, which re-sorts the tables in alphabetical order.

If you rename a table, you must change the table name in any objects where it was previously referenced, including queries, forms, and reports.

Deleting tables

Delete a table by selecting the table in the Navigation pane and pressing the Delete key. Another method is by right-clicking a table and selecting Delete from the shortcut menu. Like most delete operations, you have to confirm the delete by selecting Yes in a confirmation dialog box.

Copying tables in a database

The copy and paste options in the Clipboard group on the Home tab allow you to copy any table in the database. When you paste the table back into the database, you choose from three option buttons:

- Structure Only
- Structure and Data
- Append Data to Existing Table

Selecting the `Structure Only` button creates a new table, empty table with the same design as the copied table. This option is typically used to create a temporary table or an archive table to which you can copy old records.

When you select `Structure and Data`, a complete copy of the table design and all of its data is created.

Selecting the `Append Data to Existing Table` button adds the data of the selected table to the bottom of another. This option is useful for combining tables, such as when you want to add data from a monthly transaction table to a yearly history table.

Follow these steps to copy a table:

1. **Right-click the table name in the Navigation pane.**
2. **Choose Copy from the shortcut menu, or choose the Copy button in the Clipboard group on the Home tab.**
3. **Choose Paste from the shortcut menu, or choose the Paste button in the Clipboard group on the Home tab.**
4. **Provide the name of the new table.**
5. **Choose one of the Paste options (**`Structure Only`**,** `Structure and Data`**, or** `Append Data to Existing Table`**).**

6. **Click OK to complete the operation.**

Figure 2-29 shows the `Paste Table As` dialog box, where you make these decisions. To paste the data, you have to select the type of paste operation and type the name of the new table. When you are appending data to an existing table, you must type the name of an existing table.

FIGURE 2-29

Pasting a table activates this dialog box. You can paste only the structure, the data and structure, or the data to an existing table.

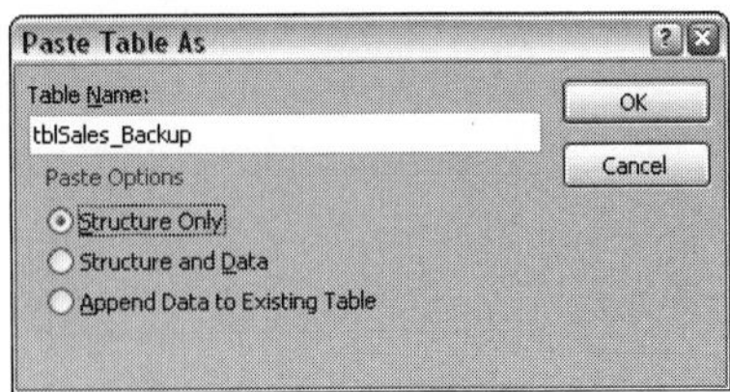

Copying a table to another database

Just as you can copy a table within a database, you can copy a table to another database. There are many reasons why you may want to do this. Possibly you share a common table among multiple systems, or you may need to create a backup copy of your important tables within the system.

When you copy tables to another database, the relationships between tables are not copied; Access copies only the table design and the data. The method for copying a table to another database is essentially the same as for copying a table within a database. To copy a table to another database, follow these steps:

1. **Right-click the table name in the Navigation pane.**
2. **Choose Copy from the shortcut menu, or choose the Copy button in the Clipboard group on the Home tab.**
3. **Open the other Access database.**
4. **Choose Edit Paste from the shortcut menu, or choose the Copy button in the Clipboard group on the Home tab.**
5. **Provide the name of the new table.**
6. **Choose one of the Paste options (`Structure Only`, `Structure and Data`, or `Append Data to Existing Table`).**
7. **Click OK to complete the operation.**

Adding Records to a Database Table

So far you have only created one table in the MyAccessAutoAuctions database: `tblContacts`.

Adding records is as simple as selecting the table name in the database container and clicking on its name to bring up the table in Datasheet view. Once opened, you can type in values for each field. Figure 2-30 shows adding records in datasheet mode to the table.

You can enter information into all fields except the Contact ID field (`ContactID`). `AutoNumber` fields automatically provide a number for you.

FIGURE 2-30

Adding records to a table using Datasheet view

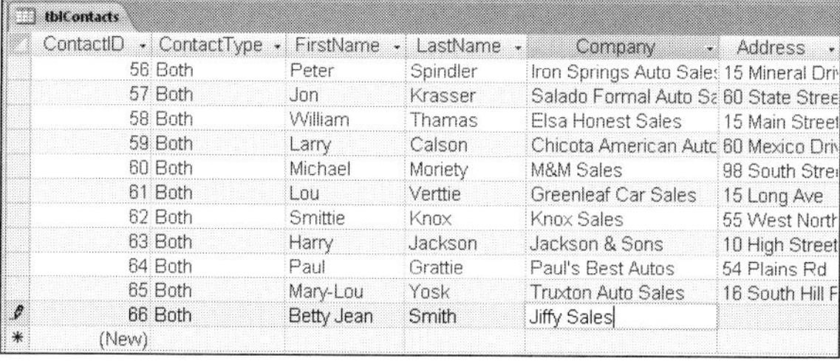

ContactID	ContactType	FirstName	LastName	Company	Address
56	Both	Peter	Spindler	Iron Springs Auto Sales	15 Mineral Dri
57	Both	Jon	Krasser	Salado Formal Auto Sa	60 State Stree
58	Both	William	Thamas	Elsa Honest Sales	15 Main Street
59	Both	Larry	Calson	Chicota American Autc	80 Mexico Driv
60	Both	Michael	Moriety	M&M Sales	98 South Stre
61	Both	Lou	Verttie	Greenleaf Car Sales	15 Long Ave
62	Both	Smittie	Knox	Knox Sales	55 West North
63	Both	Harry	Jackson	Jackson & Sons	10 High Street
64	Both	Paul	Grattie	Paul's Best Autos	54 Plains Rd
65	Both	Mary-Lou	Yosk	Truxton Auto Sales	16 South Hill F
66	Both	Betty Jean	Smith	Jiffy Sales	
(New)					

Although you can add records directly into the table through the Datasheet view, it is not the most efficient way. Adding records using forms is better.

Understanding the Attachment Data Type

Microsoft recognizes that database developers must deal with many different types of data. Although the traditional Access data types (Text, Currency, OLE Object, and so on) are able to handle many different types of data, until Access 2007 there was no way to accommodate *complete files* as Access data without performing some transformation on the file (such as conversion to OLE data).

Access 2007 adds the Attachment data type, enabling you to bring entire files into your Access database as "attachments" to a field in a table. When you click on an attachment field, Access opens a small dialog box (shown in Figure 2-31) enabling you to locate files to attach to the table. An attached file is actually incorporated into your Access database, but it's not transformed into one of the native Access data types.

FIGURE 2-31

Managing attachments in an Attachment field

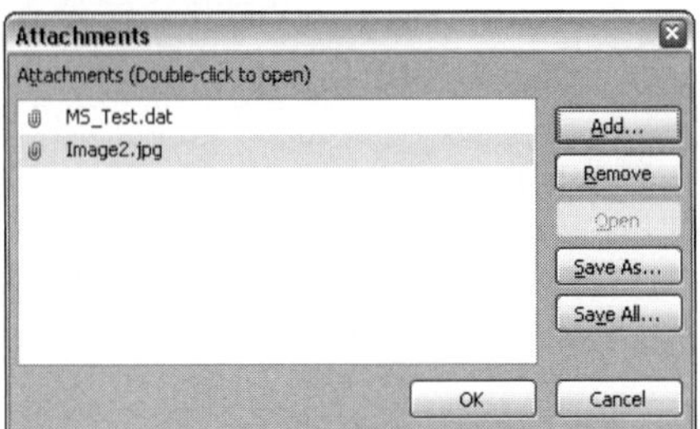

The Add button in Figure 2-31 opens the familiar Windows Choose File dialog box, enabling you to search for a file to attach to the field. The selected file is added to the list you see in Figure 2-21. Notice also that the Attachments dialog box includes buttons for removing attachments from the field and for saving attachments back to the computer's disk.

The significant thing to keep in mind about the Attachment data type is that a single attachment field in a table can contain multiple files. Obviously, because the attached data is incorporated into the database, the `.accdb` file will quickly grow if many attachments are added. You should use the Attachment data type only when its benefits outweigh the burden it places on an Access application.

Summary

This chapter has covered the important topics of creating new Access databases, and adding tables to Access databases. Although this chapter covered these topics from the perspective of creating brand-new databases and tables, the operations you performed in this chapter are identical to the maintenance procedures you perform on existing databases and tables.

The next chapter drills into the very important topics of data normalization, referential integrity, creating relationships, and other operations and procedures required to protect the integrity and reliability of data in your Access databases. Unless you have a very firm understanding of these important issues, you should take the time to review Chapter 3 and understand how Access supports professional database design.

Chapter 3

Designing Bulletproof Databases

We've already looked at one of the most basic assumptions about relational database systems — that is, that data are spread across a number of tables that are related through primary and foreign keys (see Chapter 1 for a review). Although this basic principle is easy to understand, it can be much more difficult to understand why and when data should be broken into separate tables.

Because the data managed by a relational database such as Access exist in a number of different tables, there must be some way to connect the data. The more efficiently the database performs these connections, the better and more flexible the database application as a whole will function.

Although databases are meant to model real-world situations or at least manage the data involved in real-world situations, even the most complex situation is reduced to a number of relationships between pairs of tables. As the data managed by the database become more complex, you may need to add more tables to the design. For instance, a database to manage employee affairs for a company will include tables for employee information (name, Social Security number, address, hire date, and so on), payroll information, benefits programs the employee belongs to, and so on.

When working with the actual data, however, you concentrate on the relationship between two tables at a time. You might create the employees and payroll tables first, connecting these tables with a relationship to make it easy to find all of the payroll information for an employee.

ON the CD-ROM **This chapter uses the database named `Chapter03.mdb`. If you haven't already copied it onto your machine from the CD, you'll need to do so now. If you're following the examples, you can use the tables in this database or create the tables yourself in another database.**

IN THIS CHAPTER

In Chapters 1 and 2 you saw examples of common relationships found in many Access databases. By far the most common type of table relationship is the one-to-many. The Access Auto Auction application has many such relationships: Each record in the Contacts table is related to one or more records in the Sales table (each contact may have purchased more than one item through Access Auto Auctions). (We cover one-to-many relationships in detail later in this chapter.) You can easily imagine an arrangement that would permit the data contained in the Contacts and Sales tables to be combined within a single table. All that's needed is a separate row for each order placed by each of the contacts. As new orders come in, new rows containing the contact and order information are added to the table.

The Access table shown in Figure 3-1 is an example of such an arrangement. In this figure, the `OrderID` column contains the order number placed by the contact (the data in this table have been sorted by `CustomerID` to show how many orders have been placed by each contact). The table in Figure 3-1 was created by combining data from the Contacts and Orders tables in the Northwind Traders sample database and is included in the `RelationshipsExamples.accdb` database file on this book's CD.

FIGURE 3-1

An Access table containing contact *and* orders data

tblCustomersAndOrders : Table

CustomerID	CompanyName	OrderID	ContactName	ContactTitle
ALFKI	Alfreds Futterkiste	10643	Maria Anders	Sales Represer
ALFKI	Alfreds Futterkiste	10692	Maria Anders	Sales Represer
ALFKI	Alfreds Futterkiste	10702	Maria Anders	Sales Represer
ALFKI	Alfreds Futterkiste	10835	Maria Anders	Sales Represer
ALFKI	Alfreds Futterkiste	10952	Maria Anders	Sales Represer
ALFKI	Alfreds Futterkiste	11011	Maria Anders	Sales Represer
ANATR	Ana Trujillo Emparedados y he	10308	Ana Trujillo	Owner
ANATR	Ana Trujillo Emparedados y he	10625	Ana Trujillo	Owner
ANATR	Ana Trujillo Emparedados y he	10759	Ana Trujillo	Owner
ANATR	Ana Trujillo Emparedados y he	10926	Ana Trujillo	Owner
ANTON	Antonio Moreno Taquería	10365	Antonio Moreno	Owner
ANTON	Antonio Moreno Taquería	10507	Antonio Moreno	Owner
ANTON	Antonio Moreno Taquería	10535	Antonio Moreno	Owner
ANTON	Antonio Moreno Taquería	10573	Antonio Moreno	Owner
ANTON	Antonio Moreno Taquería	10677	Antonio Moreno	Owner

Notice the `OrderID` column to the right of the `CompanyName` column. Each contact (like Alfreds Futterkiste) has placed a number of orders. Columns to the far right in this table (beyond the right edge of the figure) contain more information about each contact, including address and phone numbers, while columns beyond the company information contain the specific order information. In all, this table contains 24 different fields.

The design shown in Figure 3-1 is what happens when a spreadsheet application such as Excel is used for database purposes. Because Excel is entirely spreadsheet oriented, there is no provision for breaking up data into separate tables, encouraging users to keep everything in one massive spreadsheet.

Such an arrangement has a couple of problems:

- **The table quickly becomes unmanageably large.** The Northwind Traders Contacts table contains 11 different fields, while the Orders table contains 14 more. One field — `OrderID` — overlaps both tables. Each time an order is placed, all 24 data fields in the combined table would be added for each record added to the table.
- **Data are difficult to maintain and update.** Making simple changes to the data in the large table — for instance, changing a contact's phone or fax number — would involve searching through all records in the table, changing every occurrence of the phone number. It would be easy to make an erroneous entry or miss one or more instances. The fewer records needing changes, the better off the user will be.
- **A monolithic table design is wasteful of disk space and other resources.** Because the combined table would contain a huge amount of redundant data (for instance, a contact's address), a large amount of hard-drive space would be consumed by the redundant information. In addition to wasted disk space, network traffic, computer memory, and other resources would be poorly utilized.

A much better design — the relational design — moves the repeated data into a separate table, leaving a field in the first table to serve as a reference to the data in the second table. The additional field required by the relational model is a small price to pay for the efficiencies gained by moving redundant data out of the table.

Data Normalization

The process of splitting data across multiple tables is called normalizing the data. There are several stages of normalization; the first through the third stages are the easiest to understand and implement and are generally sufficient for the majority of applications. Although higher levels of normalization are possible, they're usually ignored by all but the most experienced and fastidious developers.

To illustrate the normalization process, we'll use a little database that a book wholesaler might use to track book orders placed by small bookstores in the local area. This database must handle the following information:

- Book title
- ISBN
- Author
- Publisher
- Publisher address
- Publisher city
- Publisher state

- Publisher zip code
- Publisher phone number
- Publisher fax
- Customer name
- Customer address
- Customer city
- Customer state
- Customer zip code
- Customer phone number

Although this data set is very simple, it's typical of the type of data you might manage with an Access database application, and it provides us with a valid demonstration of normalizing a set of data.

First normal form

The initial stage of normalization, called first normal form, requires that the table conform to the following rule:

> Each cell of a table must contain only a single value and the table must not contain repeating groups of data.

A table is meant to be a two-dimensional storage object, and storing multiple values within a field or permitting repeating groups within the table implies a third dimension to the data. Figure 3-2 shows the first attempt (`tblBookOrders1`) at building a table to manage bookstore orders. Notice that some bookstores have ordered more than one book. A value like `7 Cookie Magic` in the `BookTitles` field means that the contact has ordered seven copies of the cookbook titled *Cookie Magic*.

FIGURE 3-2

An unnormalized `tblBookOrders` table

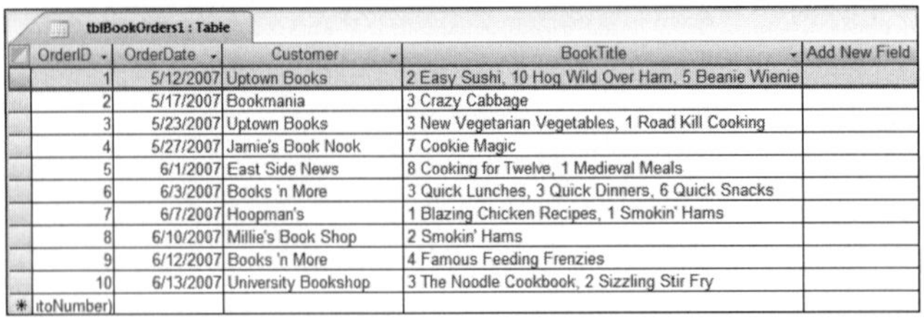

tblBookOrders1 : Table

OrderID	OrderDate	Customer	BookTitle	Add New Field
1	5/12/2007	Uptown Books	2 Easy Sushi, 10 Hog Wild Over Ham, 5 Beanie Wienie	
2	5/17/2007	Bookmania	3 Crazy Cabbage	
3	5/23/2007	Uptown Books	3 New Vegetarian Vegetables, 1 Road Kill Cooking	
4	5/27/2007	Jamie's Book Nook	7 Cookie Magic	
5	6/1/2007	East Side News	8 Cooking for Twelve, 1 Medieval Meals	
6	6/3/2007	Books 'n More	3 Quick Lunches, 3 Quick Dinners, 6 Quick Snacks	
7	6/7/2007	Hoopman's	1 Blazing Chicken Recipes, 1 Smokin' Hams	
8	6/10/2007	Millie's Book Shop	2 Smokin' Hams	
9	6/12/2007	Books 'n More	4 Famous Feeding Frenzies	
10	6/13/2007	University Bookshop	3 The Noodle Cookbook, 2 Sizzling Stir Fry	
* ıtoNumber)				

The table in Figure 3-2 is typical of a *flat-file* approach to building a database. Data in a flat-file database are stored in two dimensions (rows and columns) and neglects the third dimension (related tables) possible in a relational database system such as Microsoft Access.

Notice how the table in Figure 3-2 violates the first rule of normalization. Many of the records in this table contain multiple values in the `BookTitle` field. For instance, the book titled *Smokin' Hams* appears in records 7 and 8. There is no way for the database to handle this data easily. For instance, if you want to cross-reference the books ordered by the bookstores, you'd have to parse the data contained in the `BookTitle` field to determine which books have been ordered by which contacts.

A slightly better design is shown in Figure 3-3 (`tblBookOrders2`). The books' quantities and titles have been separated into individual columns. This arrangement makes it somewhat easier to retrieve quantity and title information, but the repeating groups for quantity and title continue to violate the first rule of normalization. (The row height in Figure 3-3 has been adjusted to make it easier for you to see the table's arrangement.)

FIGURE 3-3

Only a slight improvement over the previous design

tblBookOrders2 : Table

OrderID	OrderDate	Customer	Quant1	Title1	Quant2	Title2
1	5/12/2007	Uptown Books	2	Easy Sushi	10	Hog Wild Over Ham
2	5/17/2007	Bookmania	3	Crazy Cabbage		
3	5/23/2007	Uptown Books	3	New Vegetarian Vegetables	1	Road Kill Cooking
4	5/27/2007	Jamie's Book Nook	7	Cookie Magic		
5	6/1/2007	East Side News	8	Cooking for Twelve	1	Medieval Meals

The design in Figure 3-3 is still clumsy and difficult to work with. The columns to hold the book quantities and titles are permanent features of the table. The developer must add enough columns to accommodate the maximum number of books that could be purchased by a bookstore. For instance, let's assume the developer anticipates no bookstore will ever order more than 50 books at a time. This means that 100 columns would have to be added to the table (two columns—Quantity and Title—are required for each book title ordered). If a bookstore orders a single book, 98 columns would sit empty in the table, a very wasteful and inefficient situation.

Figure 3-4 shows `tblBookOrders`, a table in first normal form (abbreviated *1NF*). Instead of stacking multiple book orders within a single record, a second table is produced in which each record contains a single book ordered by a contact. More records are required, but the data are handled much more easily. First normal form is much more efficient because the table contains no unused fields. Every field is meaningful to the table's purpose.

FIGURE 3-4

First normal form at last!

tblBookOrders3 : Table

OrderID	OrderDate	Customer	Quantity	Title
1	5/12/2007	Uptown Books	10	Hog Wild Over Ham
1	5/12/2007	Uptown Books	5	Beanie Wienie Treats
1	5/12/2007	Uptown Books	7	Easy Sushi
2	5/17/2007	Bookmania	2	Crazy About Cabbage
3	5/23/2007	Uptown Books	1	Road Kill Cooking
3	5/23/2007	Uptown Books	3	New Vegetarian Vegetables
4	5/27/2007	Jamie's Book Nook	7	Cookie Magic
5	6/1/2007	East Side News	1	Medieval Meals
5	6/1/2007	East Side News	8	Cooking for Twelve
6	6/3/2007	Books 'n More	6	Quick Snacks

The table shown in Figure 3-4 contains the same data as shown in Figure 3-2 and Figure 3-3. The new arrangement, however, makes it much easier to work with the data. For instance, queries are easily constructed to return the total number of a particular book ordered by contacts, or to determine which titles have been ordered by a particular bookstore.

Your tables should *always* be in first normal form. Make sure each cell of the table contains a single value, and don't mix values within a cell.

The table design optimization is not complete at this point, however. Much remains to be done with the `BookOrders` data and the other tables in this application. In particular, the table shown in Figure 3-4 contains a lot of redundant information. The book titles are repeated each time customers order the same book, and the order number and order date are repeated for each row containing information about an order.

A more subtle error is the fact that the `OrderID` can no longer be used as the table's primary key. Because the Order ID is duplicated for each book title in an order, it cannot be used to identify each record in the table. Instead, the `OrderID` field is now just a key field for the table and can be used to locate all of the records relevant to a particular order. The next step of optimization corrects this situation.

Second normal form

A more efficient design results from splitting the data in `tblBookOrders` into two different tables to achieve second normal form (2NF). The first table contains the order information (for instance, the `OrderID`, `OrderDate` and `Customer`) while the second table contains the order details (`Quantity` and `Title`). This process is based on the second rule of normalization:

> Data not directly dependent on the table's primary key is moved into another table.

This rule means that a table should contain data that represents a single entity. The table in Figure 3-4 violates this rule of normalization because the individual book titles do not depend on the table's key field, the `OrderID`. Each record is a mix of book and order information. (For the meantime, we're ignoring the fact that this table does not contain a primary key. We'll be adding primary keys in a moment.)

At first glance, it may appear as though the book titles are indeed dependent on the Order ID. After all, the reason the book titles are in the table is because they're part of the order. However, a moment's thought will clarify the violation of second normal form. The title of a book is completely independent of the book order in which it is included. The same book title appears in multiple book orders; therefore, the Order ID has nothing to do with how a book is named. Given an arbitrary Order ID, you cannot tell anything about the books contained in the order other than looking at the Orders table.

The Order Date, however, is *completely* dependent on the Order ID. For each Order ID there is one and only one Order Date. Therefore, any Order Date is dependent on its associated Order ID. Order Dates may be duplicated in the table, of course, because multiple orders may be received on the same day. For each Order ID, however, there is one and only one valid Order Date value.

Second normal form often means breaking up a monolithic table into constituent tables, each of which contains fewer fields than the original table. In this example, second normal form is achieved by breaking the books and orders table into separate `Orders` and `OrderDetails` tables.

The order-specific information (such as the order date, customer, payment, and shipping information) goes into the Orders table, while the details of each order item (book, quantity, selling price, and so on) are contained by the OrderDetails table (not all of this data are shown in our example tables).

The new tables are shown in Figure 3-5. The `OrderID` is the primary key for the `tblBookOrders4` table. The `OrderID` field in the `tblBookOrderDetails` is a foreign key that references the `OrderID` primary key field in `tblBookOrders4`. Each field in `tblBookOrders4` (`OrderDate` and `Customer`) is said to be dependent on the table's primary key.

FIGURE 3-5

Second normal form: The OrderID field connects these tables together in a one-to-many relationship.

tblBookOrders4 : Table

OrderID	OrderDate	Customer
1	5/12/2007	Uptown Books
2	5/17/2007	Bookmania
3	5/23/2007	Uptown Books
4	5/27/2007	Jamie's Book Nook
5	6/1/2007	East Side News
6	6/3/2007	Books 'n More
7	6/7/2007	Hoopman's
8	6/10/2007	Millie's Book Shop
9	6/12/2007	Books 'n More
10	6/13/2007	Univeristy Bookshop

tblBookOrderDetails : Table

OrderID	Quantity	Title
1	10	Hog Wild Over Ham
1	5	Beanie Wienie Treats
1	7	Easy Sushi
2	2	Crazy About Cabbage
3	1	Road Kill Cooking
3	3	New Vegetarian Vegetables
4	7	Cookie Magic
5	1	Medieval Meals
5	8	Cooking for Twelve
6	6	Quick Snacks
6	3	Quick Dinners
6	3	Quick Lunches
7	1	Blazing Chickens
7	1	Smokin' Hams
8	2	Smokin' Hams
9	4	Famous Feeding Frenzies
10	2	Sizzling Stir Fry

The tblBookOrders4 and tblBookOrderDetails are joined in a one-to-many relationship. tblBookOrderDetails contains as many records for each order as are necessary to fulfill the requirements of the order. The OrderID field in tblBookOrders4 is now a true primary key. Each field in tblBookOrders4 is dependent on the OrderID field and appears only once for each order that is placed. The OrderID field in tblBookOrderDetails does not serve as the primary key for tblBookOrderDetails. In fact, tblBookOrderDetails does not even have a primary key, but one could be easily added.

The data in tblBookOrders4 and tblBookOrderDetails can be easily updated. If a bookstore cancels a particular book title in an order, the corresponding record is deleted from tblBookOrderDetails. If, on the other hand, a bookstore adds to an order, a new record can be added to tblBookOrderDetails to accommodate an additional title, or the Quantity field can be modified to increase or decrease the number of books ordered.

Breaking a table into individual tables that each describes some aspect of the data is called *decomposition,* a very important part of the normalization process. Even though the tables appear smaller than the original table (shown in Figure 3-2), the data contained within the tables are the same as before.

It's easy to carry decomposition too far — create only as many tables as are required to fully describe the dataset managed by the database. When decomposing tables, be careful not to lose data. For instance, if the tblBookOrders4 table contained a SellingPrice field, you'd want to make sure that field was moved into tblBookOrderDetails.

Later, you'll be able to use queries to recombine the data in tblBookOrders4 and tblBookOrderDetails in new and interesting ways. You'll be able to determine how many books of each type have been ordered by the different customers, or how many times a particular book has been ordered. When coupled with a table containing information such as book unit cost, book selling price, and so on, the important financial status of the book wholesaler becomes clear.

Notice also that the number of records in tblBookOrders4 has been reduced. This is one of several advantages to using a relational database. Each table contains only as much data as is necessary to represent the entity (in this case, a book order) described by the table. This is far more efficient than adding duplicate field values (refer to Figure 3-2) for each new record added to a table.

Further optimization: Adding tables to the scheme

The design shown in Figure 3-5 is actually pretty good. Yet, we could still do more to optimize this design. Consider the fact that the entire name of each customer is stored in tblBookOrders4. Therefore, a customer's name appears each time the customer has placed an order. Notice that Uptown Books has placed two orders during the period covered by tblBookOrders4. If the Uptown Books bookstore changed its name to Uptown Books and Periodicals, you'd have to go back to this table and update every instance of Uptown Books to reflect the new name.

Overlooking an instance of the customer's name during this process is called an *update anomaly* and results in records that are inconsistent with the other records in the database. From the database's perspective, *Uptown Books* and *Uptown Books and Periodicals* are two completely different organizations, even if we know that they're the same store. A query to retrieve all of the orders placed by Uptown Books and Periodicals will miss any records that still have Uptown Books in the `Customer` field because of the update anomaly.

Also, the table lacks specific information about the customers. No addresses, phone numbers, or other customer contact information are contained in `tblBookOrders4`. Although you could use a query to extract this information from a table named `tblBookStores` containing the addresses, phone numbers, and other information about the bookstore customers, using the customer name (a text field) as the search key is much slower than using a numeric key in the query.

Figure 3-6 shows the results of a refinement of the database design: `tblBookOrders5` contains a foreign key named `CustomerID` that relates to the `CustID` primary key field in the `tblBookStores` table. This arrangement uses `tblBookStores` as a lookup table to provide information to a form or report.

FIGURE 3-6

The numeric `CustomerID` field results in faster retrievals from `tblCustomers`.

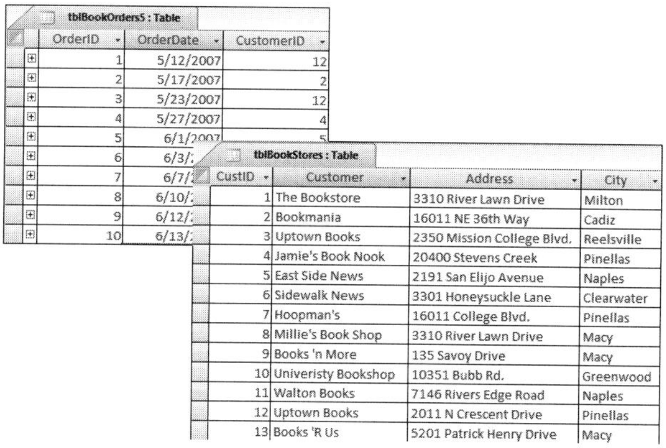

tblBookOrders5 : Table

OrderID	OrderDate	CustomerID
1	5/12/2007	12
2	5/17/2007	2
3	5/23/2007	12
4	5/27/2007	4
5	6/1/2007	5
6	6/3/	
7	6/7/	
8	6/10/	
9	6/12/	
10	6/13/	

tblBookStores : Table

CustID	Customer	Address	City
1	The Bookstore	3310 River Lawn Drive	Milton
2	Bookmania	16011 NE 36th Way	Cadiz
3	Uptown Books	2350 Mission College Blvd.	Reelsville
4	Jamie's Book Nook	20400 Stevens Creek	Pinellas
5	East Side News	2191 San Elijo Avenue	Naples
6	Sidewalk News	3301 Honeysuckle Lane	Clearwater
7	Hoopman's	16011 College Blvd.	Pinellas
8	Millie's Book Shop	3310 River Lawn Drive	Macy
9	Books 'n More	135 Savoy Drive	Macy
10	Univeristy Bookshop	10351 Bubb Rd.	Greenwood
11	Walton Books	7146 Rivers Edge Road	Naples
12	Uptown Books	2011 N Crescent Drive	Pinellas
13	Books 'R Us	5201 Patrick Henry Drive	Macy

Part of the speed improvement is due to the fact that the `CustomerID` field in `tblBookOrders5` is a long integer (4-byte) value instead of a text field. This means that Access has to manipulate only 4 bytes of memory when searching `tblBookOrders5`. The `Customer` field in `tblBookOrders4` was a text field with a width of 50 characters. This means that Access might have to manipulate as many as 50 bytes of memory when searching for matching records in `tblCustomers`.

A second advantage of removing the customer name from the orders table is that the name now exists in only one location in the database. If Uptown Books changes its name to Uptown Books and Periodicals, we now only have to change its entry in the `tblBookStores` table. This single change is reflected throughout the database, including all forms and reports that use the customer name information.

Breaking the rules

From time to time, you may find it necessary to break the rules. For instance, let's assume the bookstores are entitled to discounts based on the volume of purchases over the last year. Strictly following the rules of normalization, the discount percentage should be included in the `tblCustomers` table. After all, the discount is dependent on the customer, not on the order.

But maybe the discount applied to each order is somewhat arbitrary. Maybe the book wholesaler permits the salespeople to cut special deals for valued customers. In this case, you might want to include a `Discount` column in the book orders table, even if it contains duplicate information in many records. You could store the traditional discount as part of the customer's record in `tblCustomers`, and use it as the default value for the `Discount` column but permit the salesperson to override the discount value when a special arrangement has been made with the customer.

Third normal form

The last step of normalization, called third normal form (3NF), requires removing all fields that can be derived from data contained in other fields in the table or other tables in the database. For instance, assume the sales manager insists that you add a field to contain the total value of a book order in the orders table. This information, of course, would be calculated from the book quantity field in `tblOrderDetails` and the book unit price from the book information table.

There's no reason why you should add the new `OrderTotal` field to the `Orders` table. Access easily calculates this value from data that are immediately available in the database. The only advantage of storing order totals as part of the database is to save the few milliseconds required for Access to retrieve and calculate the information when the calculated data are needed by a form or report.

Removing calculated data has little to do with maintaining the database. The main benefit is saving disk space and memory, and reducing network traffic. Depending on the applications you build, you may find good reasons to store calculated data in tables, particularly if performing the calculations is a lengthy process, or if the stored value is necessary as an audit check on the calculated value printed on reports. It may be more efficient to perform the calculations during data entry (when data are being handled one record at a time) rather than when printing reports (when many thousands of records are manipulated to produce a single report).

Although higher levels of normalization are possible, you'll find that for most database applications, third normal form is more than adequate. At the very least, you should always strive for first normal form in your tables by moving redundant or repeating data to another table.

More on anomalies

This business about update anomalies is important to keep in mind. The whole purpose of normalizing the tables in your databases is to achieve maximum performance with minimum maintenance effort.

Three types of errors can occur from an unnormalized database design. Following the rules outlined in this chapter will help you avoid the following pitfalls:

- **Insertion anomaly:** An error occurs in a related table when a new record is added to another table. For instance, let's say you've added the `OrderTotal` field described in the previous section. After the order has been processed, the customer calls and changes the number of books ordered or adds a new book title to the same order. Unless you've carefully designed the database to automatically update the calculated `OrderTotal` field, the data in that field will be in error as the new data are inserted into the table.
- **Deletion anomaly:** A deletion anomaly causes the accidental loss of data when a record is deleted from a table. Let's assume that the `tblBookOrders` table contains the name, address, and other contact information for each bookstore. Deleting the last remaining record containing a particular customer's order causes the customer's contact information to be unintentionally lost. Keeping the customer contact information in a separate table preserves and protects that data from accidental loss. Avoiding deletion anomalies is one good reason not to use cascading deletes in your tables (see "Table Relationships," later in this chapter, for more on cascading deletes).
- **Update anomaly:** Storing data that are not dependent on the table's primary key causes you to have to update multiple rows anytime the independent information changes. Keeping the independent data (such as the bookstore information) in its own table means that only a single instance of the information needs to be updated. (For more on update anomalies, see "Further optimization: Adding tables to the scheme" earlier in this chapter.)

Denormalization

After hammering you with all the reasons why normalizing your databases is a good idea, let's consider when you might deliberately choose to denormalize tables or use unnormalized tables.

Generally speaking, you normalize data in an attempt to improve the performance of your database. For instance, in spite of all your efforts, some lookups will be time-consuming. Even when using carefully indexed and normalized tables, some lookups require quite a bit of time, especially when the data being looked up are complicated or there's a large amount of it.

Similarly, some calculated values may take a long time to evaluate. You may find it more expedient to simply store a calculated value than to evaluate the expression on the fly. This is particularly true when the user base is working on older, memory-constrained, or slow computers.

Be aware that most steps to denormalize a database schema result in additional programming time required to protect the data and user from the problems caused by an unnormalized design. For instance, in the case of the calculated Order Total field, you must insert code that calculates and updates this field whenever the data in the fields underlying this value change. This extra programming, of course, takes time to implement and time to process at runtime.

You must be careful, of course, to see that denormalizing the design does not cause other problems. If you know you've deliberately denormalized a database design and are having trouble making everything work (particularly if you begin to encounter any of the anomalies discussed in the previous section), look for workarounds that permit you to work with a fully normalized design.

Finally, always document whatever you've done to denormalize the design. It's entirely possible that you or someone else will be called in to provide maintenance or to add new features to the application. If you've left design elements that seem to violate the rules of normalization, your carefully considered work may be undone by another developer in an effort to "optimize" the design. The developer doing the maintenance, of course, has the best of intentions, but he may inadvertently reestablish a performance problem that was resolved through subtle denormalization.

Table Relationships

Many people start out using a spreadsheet application like Excel or Lotus 1-2-3 to build a database. Unfortunately, a spreadsheet stores data as a two-dimensional worksheet (rows and columns) with no easy way to connect individual worksheets together. You must manually connect each cell of the worksheet to the corresponding cells in other worksheets — a tedious process at best.

Two-dimensional storage objects like worksheets are called *flat-file databases* because they lack the three-dimensional quality of relational databases. Figure 3-7 shows an Excel worksheet used as a flat-file database.

FIGURE 3-7

An Excel worksheet used as a flat-file database

	A	B	C	D	E
1	CustomerID	CompanyName	OrderID	ContactName	ContactTitle
2	ALFKI	Alfreds Futterkiste	10643	Maria Anders	Sales Representative
3	ALFKI	Alfreds Futterkiste	10692	Maria Anders	Sales Representative
4	ALFKI	Alfreds Futterkiste	10702	Maria Anders	Sales Representative
5	ALFKI	Alfreds Futterkiste	10835	Maria Anders	Sales Representative
6	ALFKI	Alfreds Futterkiste	10952	Maria Anders	Sales Representative
7	ALFKI	Alfreds Futterkiste	11011	Maria Anders	Sales Representative
8	ANATR	Ana Trujillo Emparedados y helados	10308	Ana Trujillo	Owner
9	ANATR	Ana Trujillo Emparedados y helados	10625	Ana Trujillo	Owner
10	ANATR	Ana Trujillo Emparedados y helados	10759	Ana Trujillo	Owner
11	ANATR	Ana Trujillo Emparedados y helados	10926	Ana Trujillo	Owner
12	ANTON	Antonio Moreno Taquería	10365	Antonio Moreno	Owner
13	ANTON	Antonio Moreno Taquería	10507	Antonio Moreno	Owner

The problems with flat-file databases should be immediately apparent from viewing Figure 3-7. Notice that the customer information is duplicated in multiple rows of the worksheet. Each time a customer places an order, a new row is added to the worksheet. In this particular instance, only the order number is recorded as part of the worksheet, although the entire order could be included in the worksheet, including the order details. Obviously, this worksheet would rapidly become unmanageably large and unwieldy.

Consider the amount of work required to make relatively simple changes to the data in Figure 3-7. For instance, changing a customer's address would require searching through numerous records and editing the data contained within individual cells, creating many opportunities for errors.

Through clever programming in the Excel VBA language, it would be possible to link the data in the worksheet shown in Figure 3-7 with another worksheet containing the order detail information. It would also be possible to programmatically change data in individual rows. But such Herculean efforts are needless when you harness the power of a relational database system such as Microsoft Access.

Connecting the data

Recall that a table's primary key uniquely identifies the records in a table. Example primary keys for a table of employee data include the employee's Social Security number, a combination of first and last names, or an employee ID. Let's assume the employee ID is selected as the primary key for the employees table. When the relationship to the payroll table is formed, the `EmployeeID` field is used to connect the tables together. Figure 3-8 shows this sort of arrangement (see the "One-to-many" section, later in this chapter).

FIGURE 3-8

The relationship between the `tblEmployees` and `tblPayroll` tables is an example of a typical one-to-many relationship.

tblEmployees : Table

Employee ID	Last Name	First Name
1	Davolio	Nancy
2	Fuller	Andrew
3	Leverling	Janet
4	Peacock	Margaret
5	Buchanan	Steven
6	Suyama	Michael
7	King	Robert
8	Callahan	Laura
9	Dodsworth	Anne

tblPayroll : Table

EmployeeID	PayrollDate	CheckNumber	CheckAmount
1	4/15/2007	10344	1417.38
1	4/22/2007	10353	1417.38
2	4/15/2007	10345	3327.56
2	4/22/2007	10354	3327.56
3	4/15/2007	10346	1952.19
3	4/22/2007	10355	1952.19
4	4/15/2007	10347	1417.38
4	4/22/2007	10356	1417.38
5	4/15/2007	10348	2112.76
5	4/22/2007	10357	2112.76
6	4/15/2007	10349	1215.92
7	4/15/2007	10350	1215.92
8	4/15/2007	10351	978.55
9	4/15/2007	10352	1016.23

Although you can't see the relationship in Figure 3-8, Access knows it's there and is able to instantly retrieve all of the records from `tblPayroll` for any employee in `tblEmployees`.

The relationship example shown in Figure 3-8, in which each record of `tblEmployees` is related to several records in `tblPayroll`, is the most common type found in relational database systems but is by no means the only way that data in tables are related. This book, and most books on relational databases such as Access, discuss the three basic types of relationships between tables:

- One-to-one
- One-to-many
- Many-to-many

Figure 3-9 shows the relationships in the completed Access Auto Auctions database.

FIGURE 3-9

The Access Auto Auctions tables relationships

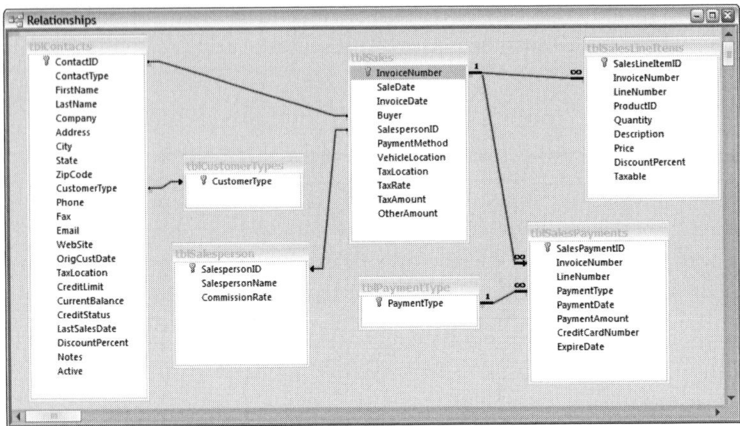

Notice that there are three one-to-many relationships between the primary tables (`tblSales-to-tblSalesPayments`, `tblSales-to-tblSalesLineItems`, and `tblContacts-to-tblContactsLog`), two one-to-many relationship between the primary tables (`tblSalesLineItems-to-tblProducts` and `tblSales-to-tblContacts`), and five one-to-many relations between the five lookup tables and the primary tables. The relationship that you specify between tables is important. It tells Access how to find and display information from fields in two or more tables. The program needs to know whether to look for only one record in a table or look for several records on the basis of the relationship. The `tblSales` table, for example, is related to the `tblContacts` table as a *many-to-one* relationship. This is because the focus of the Access Auto Auctions system is the sales. This means that there will *always* be only one contact (buyer) related to every sales record; that is, many sales can be associated with a single buyer (contact). In this case, the Access Auto Auctions system is actually using `tblContacts` as a lookup table.

NOTE **Relationships can be very confusing; it all depends upon the focus of the system. For instance, when working with the `tblContacts` and `tblSales` tables, you can always create a query that has a *one-to-many* relationship to the `tblSales` table, from the `tblContacts`. Although the system is concerned with sales (invoices), there are times that you will want to produce reports or views that are buyer-related instead of invoice-related. Because one buyer can have more than one sale, there will *always* be one record in the `tblContacts` table for *at least* one record in the `tblSales` table; there could be *many* related records in the `tblSales` table. So Access knows to find only one record in the `customer` table and to look for any records in the sales table (one or more) that have the same customer number.**

One-to-one

A one-to-one relationship between tables means that for every record in the first table, one and only one record exists in the second table. Figure 3-10 illustrates this concept.

FIGURE 3-10

A one-to-one relationship

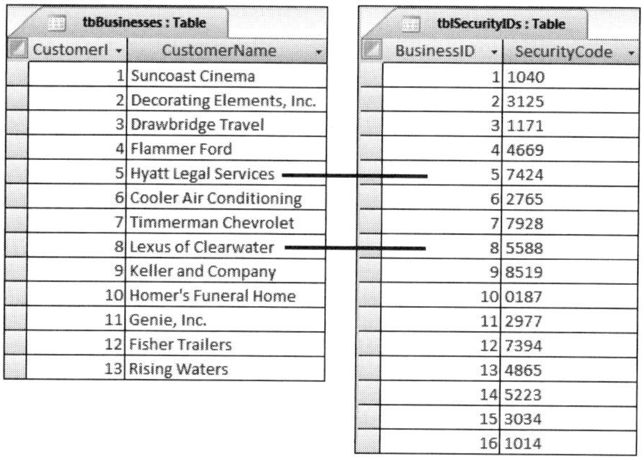

tbBusinesses : Table

Customerl	CustomerName
1	Suncoast Cinema
2	Decorating Elements, Inc.
3	Drawbridge Travel
4	Flammer Ford
5	Hyatt Legal Services
6	Cooler Air Conditioning
7	Timmerman Chevrolet
8	Lexus of Clearwater
9	Keller and Company
10	Homer's Funeral Home
11	Genie, Inc.
12	Fisher Trailers
13	Rising Waters

tblSecurityIDs : Table

BusinessID	SecurityCode
1	1040
2	3125
3	1171
4	4669
5	7424
6	2765
7	7928
8	5588
9	8519
10	0187
11	2977
12	7394
13	4865
14	5223
15	3034
16	1014

Pure one-to-one relationships are not common in relational databases. In most cases, the data contained in the second table are most often included in the first table. As a matter of fact, one-to-one relationships are generally avoided because they violate the rules of normalization. Following the rules of normalization, data should not be split into multiple tables if the data describe a single entity. Because a person has one and only one birth date, the birth date should be included in the table containing a person's other data.

There are times, however, when it's not advisable to store certain data along with other data in the table. For instance, consider the situation illustrated in Figure 3-10. The data contained in `tblSecurity` are confidential. Normally, you wouldn't want anyone with access to the public customer information (name, address, and so on) to have access to the confidential security code that the customer uses for purchasing or billing purposes. If necessary, the `tblSecurity` table could be located on a different disk somewhere on the network, or even maintained on removable media to protect it from unauthorized access.

Another instance of a one-to-one relationship is a situation where the data in a table exceed the 255-field limit imposed by Access. Although they're rare, there could be cases where you may have too many fields to be contained within a single table. The easiest solution is simply to split the data into multiple tables and connect the tables through the primary key (using the same key value, of course, in each table).

Yet another situation is where data are being transferred or shared between databases. Perhaps the shipping clerk in an organization doesn't need to see all of a customer's data. Instead of including irrelevant information such as job titles, birth dates, alternate phone numbers, and e-mail addresses, the shipping clerk's database contains only the customer's name, address, and other shipping information. A record in the customer table in the shipping clerk's database has a one-to-one relationship with the corresponding record in the master customer table located on the central computer somewhere within the organization. Although the data are contained within separate `.accdb` files, the links between the tables can be *live,* meaning that changes to the master record are immediately reflected in the shipping clerk's `.mdb` file.

Tables joined in a one-to-one relationship will almost always have the same primary key — for instance, `OrderID` or `EmployeeNumber`. There are very few reasons you would create a separate key field for the second table in a one-to-one relationship.

One-to-many

A far more common relationship between tables in a relational database is the one-to-many. In one-to-many relationships, each record in the first table (the *parent*) is related to one or more records in the second table (the *child*). Each record in the second table is related to one and only one record in the first table. Without a doubt, one-to-many relationships are the most common type encountered in relational database systems. Examples of one-to-many situations abound:

- **Customers and orders:** Each customer (the "one" side) has placed several orders (the "many" side), but each order is sent to a single customer.
- **Teacher and student:** Each teacher has many students, but each student has a single teacher (within a particular class, of course).
- **Employees and paychecks:** Each employee has received several paychecks, but each paycheck is given to one and only one employee.
- **Patients and treatments:** Each patient receives zero or more treatments for a disease.

As we discuss in the "Creating relationships and enforcing referential integrity" section, later in this chapter, Access makes it very easy to establish one-to-many relationships between tables. A one-to-many relationship is illustrated in Figure 3-11. This figure, using tables from the Northwind Traders database, clearly demonstrates how each record in the `Customers` table is related to several different records in the `Orders` table. An order can be sent to only a single customer, so all requirements of one-to-many relationships are fulfilled by this arrangement.

FIGURE 3-11

The Northwind Traders database contains many examples of one-to-many relationships.

Customers : Table

CustomerID	CompanyName
BLAUS	Blauer See Delikatessen
BLONP	Blondel père et fils
BOLID	Bólido Comidas preparadas
BONAP	Bon app'
BOTTM	Bottom-Dollar Markets
BSBEV	B's Beverages
CACTU	Cactus Comidas para llevar
CENTC	Centro comercial Moctezuma
CHOPS	Chop-suey Chinese
COMMI	Comércio Mineiro
CONSH	Consolidated Holdings
DRACD	Drachenblut Delikatessen
DUMON	Du monde entier
EASTC	Eastern Connection
ERNSH	Ernst Handel
FAMIA	Familia Arquibaldo
FISSA	FISSA Fabrica Inter. Salchichas S.A
FOLIG	Folies gourmandes

Record: 12 of 91 No Filter Search

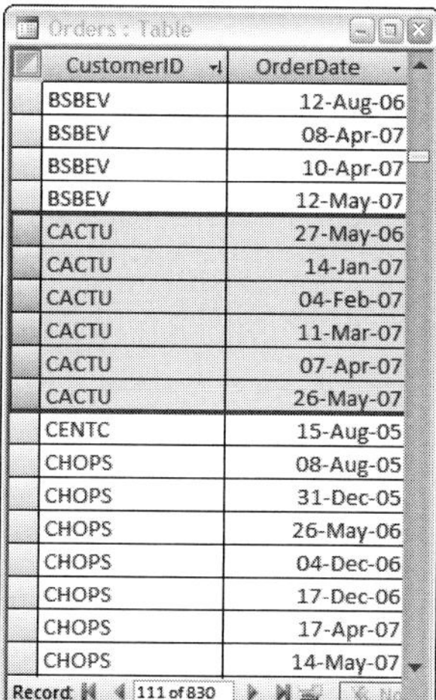

Orders : Table

CustomerID	OrderDate
BSBEV	12-Aug-06
BSBEV	08-Apr-07
BSBEV	10-Apr-07
BSBEV	12-May-07
CACTU	27-May-06
CACTU	14-Jan-07
CACTU	04-Feb-07
CACTU	11-Mar-07
CACTU	07-Apr-07
CACTU	26-May-07
CENTC	15-Aug-05
CHOPS	08-Aug-05
CHOPS	31-Dec-05
CHOPS	26-May-06
CHOPS	04-Dec-06
CHOPS	17-Dec-06
CHOPS	17-Apr-07
CHOPS	14-May-07

Record: 111 of 830

Although the records on the "many" side of the relationship illustrated in Figure 3-11 are sorted by the `CustomerID` field in alphabetical order, there is no requirement that the records in the many table be arranged in any particular order.

Although *parent-child* is the most common expression used to explain the relationship between tables related in a one-to-many relationship, you may hear other expressions used, such as *master-detail* applied to this design. The important thing to keep in mind is that the intent of referential integrity is to prevent lost records on the "many" side of the relationship. Referential integrity guarantees that there will never be an *orphan,* a child record without a matching parent record. As you'll soon see, it is important to keep in mind which table is on the "one" side and which is on the "many" side.

Notice how difficult it would be to record all of the orders for a customer if a separate table were not used to store the order's information. The flat-file alternative discussed in the "Table Relationships" section, earlier in this chapter, requires much more updating than the one-to-many arrangement shown in Figure 3-11. Each time a customer places an order with Northwind Traders a new record is added to the `Orders` table. Only the `CustomerID` (for instance, CACTU) is added to the `Orders` table as the foreign key back to the `Customers` table. Keeping the customer information is relatively trivial because each customer record appears only once in the `Customers` table.

Many-to-many

You'll come across many-to-many situations from time to time. In a many-to-many arrangement, each record in both tables can be related to zero, one, or many records in the other table. An example is shown in Figure 3-12. Each student in `tblStudents` can belong to more than one club, while each club in `tblClubs` has more than one member.

FIGURE 3-12

A database of students and the clubs they belong to is an example of a many-to-many relationship.

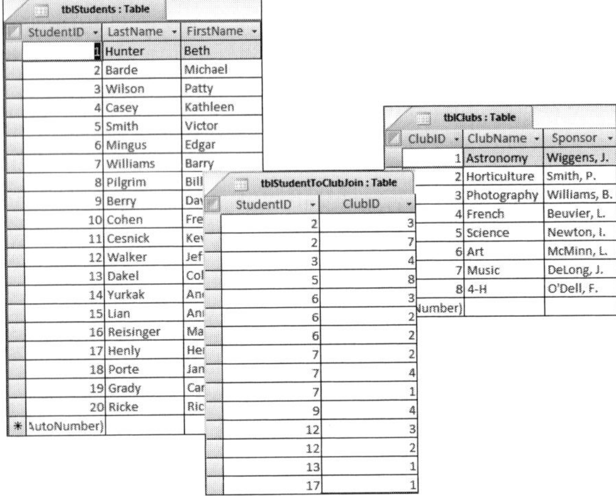

tblStudents : Table

StudentID	LastName	FirstName
1	Hunter	Beth
2	Barde	Michael
3	Wilson	Patty
4	Casey	Kathleen
5	Smith	Victor
6	Mingus	Edgar
7	Williams	Barry
8	Pilgrim	Bill
9	Berry	Da
10	Cohen	Fre
11	Cesnick	Ke
12	Walker	Jef
13	Dakel	Col
14	Yurkak	An
15	Lian	An
16	Reisinger	Ma
17	Henly	He
18	Porte	Jan
19	Grady	Car
20	Ricke	Ric
AutoNumber)		

tblStudentToClubJoin : Table

StudentID	ClubID
2	3
2	7
3	4
5	8
6	3
6	2
6	2
7	2
7	4
7	1
9	4
12	3
12	2
13	1
17	1

tblClubs : Table

ClubID	ClubName	Sponsor
1	Astronomy	Wiggens, J.
2	Horticulture	Smith, P.
3	Photography	Williams, B.
4	French	Beuvier, L.
5	Science	Newton, I.
6	Art	McMinn, L.
7	Music	DeLong, J.
8	4-H	O'Dell, F.
Number)		

As indicated in Figure 3-12, many-to-many relationships are somewhat more difficult to understand because they cannot be directly modeled in relational database systems like Access. Instead, the many-to-many relationship is broken into two separate one-to-many relationships, joined through a linking, or join, table. The join table has one-to-many relationships with both of the tables involved in the many-to-many relationship. This principle can be a bit confusing at first, but close examination of Figure 3-12 soon reveals the beauty of this arrangement.

In Figure 3-12, you can easily see that student ID 2 (Michael Barde) belongs to the music club, while student ID 12 (Jeffrey Wilson) is a member of the horticulture club. Both Michael Barde and Jeffrey Wilson belong to the photography club. Each student belongs to multiple clubs, and each club contains multiple members.

Because of the additional complication of the join table, many-to-many relationships are often considered more difficult to establish and maintain. Fortunately, Access makes such relationships quite easy to establish, once a few rules are followed. These rules are explained in various places in this book. For instance, in order to update either side of a many-to-many relationship (for example, to change club membership for a student), the join table must contain the primary keys of both tables joined by the relationship.

Many-to-many relationships are quite common in business environments:

- **Lawyers to clients (or doctors to patients):** Each lawyer may be involved in several cases, while each client may be represented by more than one lawyer on each case.
- **Patients and insurance coverage:** Many people are covered by more than one insurance policy. For instance, if you and your spouse are both provided medical insurance by your employers, you have multiple coverage.
- **Video rentals and customers:** Over a year's time, each video is rented by several people, while each customer rents several videos during the year.
- **Magazine subscriptions:** Most magazines have circulations measured in the thousands or millions. Most people subscribe to more than one magazine at a time.

The Access Auto Auctions database has a many-to-many relationship between `tblContacts` and `tblSalesPayments`, linked through `tblSales`. Each customer may have purchased more than one item, and each item may be paid for through multiple payments. In addition to joining contacts and sales payments, `tblSales` contains other information, such as the sale date and invoice number. The join table in a many-to-many relationship often contains information regarding the joined data.

Given how complicated many-to-many joins can be to construct, it is fortunate that many-to-many relationships are quite a bit less common than straightforward one-to-many situations.

Although Figure 3-12 shows a join table with just two fields (`StudentID` and `ClubID`), there is no reason that the join table cannot contain other information. For instance, the `tblStudentToClubJoin` table might include fields to indicate membership dues collected from the student for each club.

Pass-through

The last type of relationship we'll explore involves more than one table. Much as a many-to-many relationship involves an intermediate table, a pass-through relationship (which is sometimes called a `grandparent-grandchild relationship`) is necessary in some situations. In this type of relationship, the data in the grandparent table are related to records in a grandchild table through a third table. An example taken from Northwind Traders is diagrammed in Figure 3-13.

FIGURE 3-13

The order details information is related to the Customers table through the Orders table.

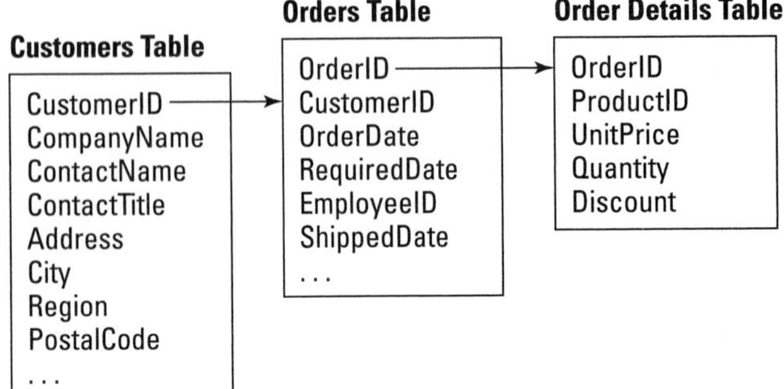

There is no direct connection between the Customers table (the grandparent) and the Order Details table (the grandchild). The Order Details table contains all of the information on the specific items included in a particular order. As indicated by Figure 3-13, you must use the Orders table (the parent table) to determine how many of a particular item have been purchased by a customer.

The only way to get information from the OrderDetails grandchild table is to first use the CustomerID field to reference all of the associated records in the Orders table. Then use the OrderID field to find all of its related items in the OrderDetails table.

From time to time, you'll find yourself building Access queries to extract just this kind of information. When you build these queries, you're actually constructing a pass-through relationship between the tables involved in the query.

The relationship between any two of the tables involved in the pass-through relationship (Customers to Orders or Orders to OrderDetails) is a one-to-many relationship.

Integrity Rules

Access permits you to apply referential integrity rules that protect data from loss or corruption. The relational model defines several rules meant to enforce the referential integrity requirements of relational databases. In addition, Access contains its own set of referential integrity rules that are enforced by the Jet database engine. Referential integrity means that the relationships between tables are preserved during updates, deletions, and other record operations.

Imagine a payroll application that contained no rules regulating how data in the database are used. It'd be possible to issue payroll checks that are not linked to an employee, or to have an employee who had never been issued a paycheck. From a business perspective, issuing paychecks to "phantom" employees is much more serious than having an employee who's never been paid! After all, the unpaid employee will soon complain about the situation, but paychecks issued to phantom employees raise no alarms. At least, that is, until the auditors step in and notify management of the discrepancy.

A database system must have rules that specify certain conditions between tables — rules to enforce the *integrity* of relationships between the tables. These rules are known as *referential integrity;* they keep the relationships between tables intact in a relational database management system. Referential integrity prohibits you from changing your data in ways that invalidate the relationships between tables.

Referential integrity operates strictly on the basis of the tables' key fields; it checks each time a key field, whether primary or foreign, is added, changed, or deleted. If a change to a value in a key field creates an invalid relationship, it is said to violate referential integrity. Tables can be set up so that referential integrity is enforced automatically.

Figure 3-14 illustrates one of several relationships in the Access Auto Auctions database. The Products table is related to the `SalesLinesItem` table through the `ProductID` field. The `ProductID` field in `tblProducts` is that table's primary key, while the `ProductID` field in `tblSalesLineItems` is a foreign key. The relationship connects each product with a line item on a sales invoice. In this relationship, `tblProducts` is the parent table, while `tblSalesLineItems` is the child table.

FIGURE 3-14

A typical database relationship

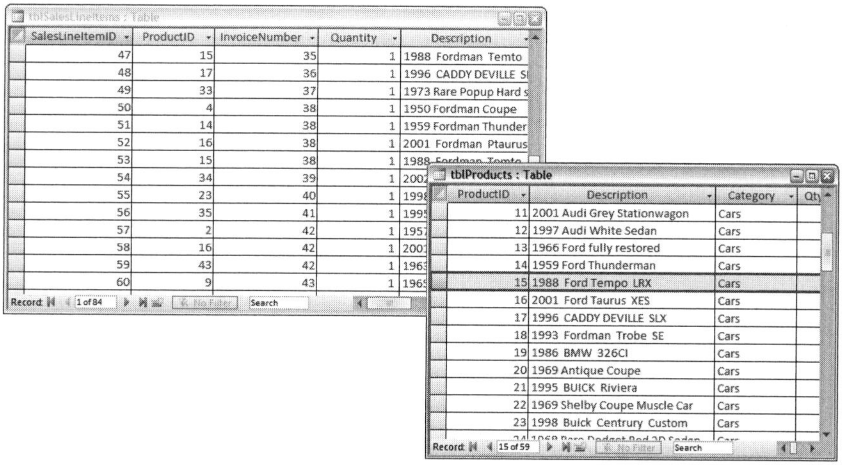

tblSalesLineItems : Table

SalesLineItemID	ProductID	InvoiceNumber	Quantity	Description
47	15	35	1	1988 Fordman Temto
48	17	36	1	1996 CADDY DEVILLE S
49	33	37	1	1973 Rare Popup Hard s
50	4	38	1	1950 Fordman Coupe
51	14	38	1	1959 Fordman Thunder
52	16	38	1	2001 Fordman Ptaurus
53	15	38	1	1988
54	34	39	1	200
55	23	40	1	199
56	35	41	1	199
57	2	42	1	195
58	16	42	1	200
59	43	42	1	196
60	9	43	1	196

Record: 1 of 84 No Filter Search

tblProducts : Table

ProductID	Description	Category	Qty
11	2001 Audi Grey Stationwagon	Cars	
12	1997 Audi White Sedan	Cars	
13	1966 Ford fully restored	Cars	
14	1959 Ford Thunderman	Cars	
15	1988 Ford Tempo LRX	Cars	
16	2001 Ford Taurus XES	Cars	
17	1996 CADDY DEVILLE SLX	Cars	
18	1993 Fordman Trobe SE	Cars	
19	1986 BMW 326CI	Cars	
20	1969 Antique Coupe	Cars	
21	1995 BUICK Riviera	Cars	
22	1969 Shelby Coupe Muscle Car	Cars	
23	1998 Buick Centrury Custom	Cars	

Record: 15 of 59 No Filter Search

Orphaned records are very bad in database applications. Because payroll information is almost always reported as which paychecks were issued to which employees, a paycheck that is not linked to an employee will not be discovered under most circumstances. It's easy to know which paychecks were issued to John Doe, but given an arbitrary paycheck record, it may not be easy to know that there is no legitimate employee matching the paycheck.

Because the referential integrity rules are enforced by the Access database engine, data integrity is ensured wherever the data appear in the database: in tables, queries, or forms. Once you've established the integrity requirements of your applications, you don't have to be afraid that data in related tables will become lost or disorganized.

We can't overemphasize the need for referential integrity in database applications. Many developers feel that they can use VBA code or user interface design to prevent orphaned records. The truth is that, in most databases, the data stored in a particular table may be used in many different places within the application. Also, given the fact that many database projects extend over many years, and among any number of developers, it's not always possible to recall how data should be protected. By far, the best approach to ensuring the integrity of data stored in any database system is by utilizing the power of the database engine to enforce referential integrity.

The general relational model referential integrity rules ensure that records contained in relational tables are not lost or confused. For obvious reasons, it is important that the primary keys connecting tables be protected and preserved. Also, changes in a table that affect other tables (for instance, deleting a record on the "one" side of a one-to-many relationship) should be rippled to the other tables connected to the first table. Otherwise, the data in the two tables will quickly become unsynchronized.

The first referential integrity rule states that no primary key can contain a null value. A *null value* is one that simply does not exist. The value of a field that has never been assigned a value (even a default value) is `null`. No row in a database table can have `null` in its primary key field because the primary purpose of the primary key is to guarantee uniqueness of the row. Obviously, `null` values cannot be unique and the relational model would not work if primary keys could be `null`.

Access automatically enforces the first referential integrity rule. As you add data to tables, you can't leave the primary key field empty without generating a warning (one reason the `AutoNumber` field works so well as a primary key). Once you've designated a field in an Access table as the primary key, Access will not let you delete the data in the field, nor will it allow you to change the value in the field so that it duplicates a value in another record.

When using a composite primary key made up of several fields, all of the fields in the composite key must contain values. None of the fields are allowed to be empty. The combination of values in the composite primary key must be unique.

The second referential integrity rule says that all foreign key values must be matched by corresponding primary keys. This means that every record in a table on the "many" side of a one-to-many relationship must have a corresponding record in the table on the "one" side of the relationship.

A record on the "many" side of a relationship without a corresponding record on the "one" side is said to be *orphaned* and is effectively removed from the database schema. Identifying orphaned records in a database can be very difficult, so you're better off avoiding the situation in the first place.

The second rule means that the following situations must be handled by the Jet engine:

- **Rows cannot be added to a "many" side table (the child) if a corresponding record does not exist on the "one" side (the parent).** If a child record contains a `ParentID` field, the `ParentID` value *must* match an existing record in the parent table.
- **The primary key value in a parent table cannot be changed if the change would create orphaned child records.**
- **Deleting a row on the "one" side must not orphan corresponding records on the "many" side.**

For instance, in our payroll example, the foreign key in each record in the `tblPayChecks` table (the "many" side) must match a primary key in `tblEmployees`. You cannot delete a record in `tblEmployees` (the "one" side) without deleting the corresponding records in `tblPayChecks`.

One of the curious results of the rules of referential integrity is that it is entirely possible to have a parent record that is not matched by any child records. Intuitively, this makes sense. A company may certainly have employees who haven't yet been issued paychecks. Or, the Access Auto Auctions company may recruit a new seller who doesn't have any cars for sale at the moment. Eventually, of course, most parent records are matched by one or more child records, but this condition is not a requirement of relational databases.

A somewhat less obvious outcome of these rules is that it is possible to have a child record that is not matched by a parent record, as long as the parent foreign key field does not contain a value. As you will recall, referential integrity requires that any value in a child table's foreign key field must be matched by the same value in the parent table. However, if the foreign key field in a child record is *completely* empty, there is no violation of referential integrity between the tables.

In practical terms, this situation is quite rare in Access applications. Virtually all database fields have some default value, such as zero, or an empty string (`""`). In the case of a numeric foreign key, by default, Access inserts zero into the field as new records are added to the table. Unless zero appears somewhere in the parent table, a referential integrity violation exists, and the new record will not be added. The only way around this situation is to delete the default value of zero for the foreign key field, or to ensure that the foreign key value is set to a valid `ParentID` value before adding the new record to the child table.

As you'll see in the next section, Access makes it easy to specify the integrity rules you want to employ in your applications. You should be aware, however, that not using the referential integrity rules means that you might end up with orphaned records and other data integrity problems.

Understanding Keys

When you create database tables, like those created in Chapter 2, you should assign each table a primary key. This key is a way to make sure that the table records contain only one unique value; for example, you may have several contacts named Michael Heinrich, and you may even have more than one Michael Heinrich (for instance, father and son) living at the same address. So in a case like this, you have to decide on how you can create a record in the `Customer` database that will let you identify each Michael Heinrich separately.

Uniquely identifying each record in a table is precisely what a primary key field does. For example, using the Access Auto Auction as an example, the `ContactID` field (a unique number that you assign to each customer or seller that comes into your office) is the primary key in the `tblContacts` table — each record in the table has a different `ContactID` number. (No two records have the same number.) This is important for several reasons:

- You do not want to have two records in your database for the same customer, because this can make updating the customer's record virtually impossible.
- You want assurance that each record in the table is accurate, thus the information extracted from the table is accurate.
- You do not want to make the table (and its records) any larger than necessary.

The ability to assign a single, unique value to each record makes the table clean and reliable. This is known as *entity integrity*. By having a different primary key value in each record (such as the `ContactID` in the `tblContacts` table), you can tell two records (in this case, customers) apart, even if all other fields in the records are the same. This is important because you can easily have two individual customers with a common name, such as Fred Smith, in your table.

Theoretically, you could use the customer name and the customer's address, but two people named Fred D. Smith could live in the same town and state, or a father and son (Fred David Smith and Fred Daniel Smith) could live at the same address. The goal of setting primary keys is to create individual records in a table that *guarantees* uniqueness.

If you don't specify a primary key when creating Access tables, Access asks whether you want one. If you say yes, Access uses the `AutoNumber` data type to create a primary key for the table. An `AutoNumber` field automatically updates each time a record is added to the table, and cannot be changed once its value has been established. Furthermore, once an `AutoNumber` value has appeared in a table, the value will never be reused, even if the record containing the value is deleted and the value no longer appears in the table.

Deciding on a primary key

As you learned previously, a table normally has a unique field (or combination of fields) — the primary key for that table — which makes each record unique. The primary key is an identifier that is often a text or `AutoNumber` data type. To determine the contents of this ID field, you specify a method for creating a unique value for the field. Your method can be as simple as letting Access automatically assign a value or using the first letter of the real value you are tracking along with a sequence number (such as A001, A002, A003, B001, B002, and so on). The method may rely on a random set of letters and numbers for the field content (as long as each field has a unique value) or a complicated calculation based on information from several fields in the table.

Table 3-1 lists the Access Auto Auctions tables and describes one possible plan for deriving the primary key values in each table. As this table shows, it doesn't take a great deal of work (or even much imagination) to derive a plan for key values. Any rudimentary scheme with a good sequence number always works. Access automatically tells you when you try to enter a duplicate key value. To avoid duplication, you can simply add the value of 1 to the sequence number.

TABLE 3-1

Deriving the Primary Key

Table	Possible Derivation of Primary Key Value
`tblContacts`	Individuals: `AutoNumber` field assigned by Access
`tblSales`	Invoice Number: `AutoNumber` field assigned by Access.
`tblSalesLineItems`	Invoice Number (from Sales) and an `AutoNumber` field set by Access
`tblProducts`	Product Number, entered by the person putting in a new product
`tblSalesPayments`	Invoice Number (from Sales) and an `AutoNumber` field set by Access
`tblContactLog`	Contact ID (from Contacts) and an `AutoNumber` field set by Access
`tblPaymentType`	Type of Payment: Visa, MasterCard, cash, and so on, used as lookup
`tblCustomerTypes`	Type of Customer: Dealer, Auctioneer, Parts, and so on, used as lookup
`tblSlaesperson`	Sales Person ID: `AutoNumber` field assigned by Access
`tblTaxRates`	Tax Location: Entered by the person putting in a new record
`tblCategories`	Category of Items: Entered by the person putting in a new record

Even though it is not difficult to use logic (implemented, perhaps, though VBA code) to generate unique values for a primary key field, by far the simplest and easiest approach is to use `AutoNumber` fields for the primary keys in your tables. The special characteristics of the `AutoNumber` field (automatic generation, uniqueness, the fact that it cannot be changed, and so on) make it the ideal candidate fore primary keys. Furthermore, an `AutoNumber` value is nothing more than a 4-byte integer value, making it very fast and easy for the database engine to manage. For all of these reasons, the Access Auto Auction exclusively uses `AutoNumber` fields as primary keys in its tables.

You may be thinking that all these sequence numbers make it hard to look up information in your tables. Just remember that, in most case, you never look up information by an ID field. Generally, you look up information according to the *purpose* of the table. In the `tblContacts` table, for example, you would look up information by customer name — last name, first name, or both. Even when the same name appears in multiple records, you can look at other fields in the table (zip code, phone number) to find the correct customer. Unless you just happen to know the contact ID number, you'll probably never use it in a search for information.

Recognizing the benefits of a primary key

Have you ever placed an order with a company for the first time and then decided the next day to increase your order? You call the people at the order desk. They may ask you for your customer number. You tell them that you don't know your customer number. Next, they ask you for some other information — generally, your zip code or telephone area code. Then, as they narrow down the list of customers, they ask your name. Once they've located you in their database, they can tell you your customer number. Some businesses use phone numbers or e-mail addresses as unique starting points.

Database systems usually have more than one table, and these tend to be related in some manner. For example, in the Access Auto Auctions database `tblContacts` and `tblSales` are related to each other via a link field named `Buyer` in `tblSales` and `ContactID` in `tblContacts`. The `tblContacts` table always has one record for each customer (buyer or seller), and the `tblSales` table has a record for the sales invoice that the customer makes (every time he purchases something). Because each customer is *one* physical person, you only need one record for the customer in the `tblContacts` table.

Each customer can make many purchases, however, which means you need to set up another table to hold information about each sale — thus, the `tblSales` table. Again, each invoice is *one* physical sale (on a specific day at a specific time). Each sale has one record in the `tblSales` table. Of course, you need to have some way to relate the buyer to the sales that the buyer makes in the `tblSales` table. This is accomplished by using a common field that is in both tables — in this case, the `Buyer` field in `tblSales` and `ContactID` in `tblContacts` (which has the identical type of information in both tables).

When linking tables, you link the primary key field from one table (the `ContactID` in the `tblContacts` table) to a foreign key field in the second table that has the same structure and type of data in it (the `Buyer` field in the `tblSales` table).

Besides being a common link field between tables, the primary key field in an Access database table has these advantages:

- **Primary key fields are always indexed, greatly speeding up queries, searches, and sorts that involve the primary key field.**
- **Access forces you to enter a value (or automatically provides a value, in the case of `AutoNumber` fields) every time you add a record to the table.** You're guaranteed that your database tables conform to the rules of referential integrity.
- **As you add new records to a table, Access checks for duplicate primary key values and prevents duplicates entries, thus maintaining data integrity.**
- **By default, Access displays your data in primary key order.**

TIP **An *index* is a special internal file that is created to put the records in a table in some specific order. For instance, the primary key field in the `tblContacts` table is an index that puts the records in order by `ContactID` field. Using an indexed table, Access uses the index to quickly find records within the table.**

Designating a primary key

From the preceding sections, you're probably very well aware that choosing a table's primary key is an important step towards bulletproofing a database's design. When properly implemented, primary keys help stabilize and protect the data stored in your Access databases. As you read the following sections, keep in mind that the cardinal rule governing primary keys is that the values assigned to the primary key field within a table must be unique. Furthermore, the ideal primary key is stable.

Single field versus composite primary keys

Sometimes, when an ideal primary key does not exist within a table as a single value, you may be able to combine fields to create a *composite* primary key. For instance, it is unlikely that a first name or last name alone is enough to serve as a primary key, but by combining first and last names with birth dates, you may be able to come up with a unique combination of values to serve as the primary key. As you'll see in the "Creating relationships and ensuring referential integrity" section, later in this chapter, Access makes it very easy to combine fields as composite primary keys.

The rules governing composite keys are quite simple:

- **None of the fields in a composite key can be null.**
- **Sometimes composing a composite key from data naturally occurring within the table can be difficult.** Sometimes records within a table differ by one or two fields, even when many other fields may be duplicated within the table.
- **Each of the fields can be duplicated within the table, but the combination of composite key fields cannot be duplicated.**

However, as with so many other issues in database design, composite keys carry a number of issues with them. First of all, composite keys tend to complicate a database's design. If you use three fields in a parent table to define the table's primary key, the same three fields must appear in every child table. Also, ensuring that a value exists for all of the fields within a composite key (so that none of the fields is null) can be quite challenging.

Most developers avoid composite keys unless absolutely necessary. In many cases, the problems associated with composite keys greatly outweigh the minimal advantage of using composite keys generated from data within the record.

Natural versus surrogate primary keys

Many developers maintain that you should only use natural primary keys. A *natural key* is derived from data already in the table, such as a Social Security number or employee number. If no single field is enough to uniquely identify records in the table, these developers suggest combining fields to form a composite primary key (we describe this process later in this section).

However, there are many situations where no "perfect" natural key exists in database tables. Although a field like `SocialSecurityNumber` may seem to be the ideal primary key, there are a number of problems with this type of data:

- **The value is not universal.** Not everyone has a Social Security number.
- **The value may not be known at the time the record is added to the database.** Because primary keys can never be null, provisions must be made to supply some kind of "temporary" primary key when the Social Security number is unknown, then other provisions must be made to fix up the data in the parent and child tables once the value becomes known.
- **Values such as Social Security number tend to be rather large.** A Social Security number is at least nine characters, even omitting the dashes between groups of numbers. Large primary keys unnecessarily complicate things and run more slowly than smaller primary key values.

By far the largest issue is that adding a record to a table is impossible unless the primary key value is known at the time the record is committed to the database. Even if temporary values are inserted until the permanent value is known, the amount of fix-up required in related tables can be considerable. After all, you can't change the value of a primary key if related child records exist in other tables.

A majority of experienced Access developers have come to consistently use `AutoNumber` fields as the primary keys in their tables. Although an `AutoNumber` value does not naturally occur in the table's data, because of the considerable advantages of using a simple numeric value that is automatically generated and cannot be deleted or changed, in most cases an `AutoNumber` is the ideal primary key candidate for most tables.

An artificially generated primary key is called a *surrogate key*. Historically, surrogate keys were only used as a last resort when no suitable natural key was available. Increasingly, however, surrogate keys are finding greater acceptance among database developers.

Creating primary keys

A primary key is created by opening a table in design view, selecting the field (or fields) that you want to use as a primary key, and clicking the Primary Key button on the toolbar (the button with the key on it). If you're specifying more than one field to create a composite key, hold down the Ctrl key while using the mouse to select the fields before clicking on the Primary Key toolbar button.

If you choose to use a surrogate primary key, such as an `AutoNumber` field, add the field to the table, select it, and click the Primary Key button on the toolbar.

The primary key is created when you save the table after designating the table's primary key. You'll see an error message if Access detects a problem (such as null or duplicate values) during the save process. Of course, there will be no problems with the selected primary key if the table contains no records.

Creating relationships and enforcing referential integrity

The Relationships window Database Ribbon icon lets you specify the relationships and referential integrity rules you want to apply to the tables involved in a relationship. Creating a permanent, managed relationship that ensures referential integrity between Access tables is easy:

1. **Choose Database Tools ➪ Relationships.**

   The Relationships window appears.

2. **Click on the Show Table button.**

   The Show Table dialog box (see Figure 3-15) appears.

FIGURE 3-15

Add the tables involved in a relationship in the Relationships window.

3. **Drag the primary key field in the one-side table and drop it on the foreign key in the many-side table.**

   In Figure 3-15, you would drag the `OrderID` field from `tblBookOrders5` and dropping it on `OrderID` in `tblBookOrdersDetails`. Access opens the Edit Relationships dialog box to enable you to specify the details about the relationship you intend to form between the tables. Notice that Access recognizes that the relationship between the `tblBookOrders5` and `tblOrderDetails` is a one-to-many.

4. **Specify the referential details you want Access to enforce in the database.**

   In Figure 3-16, Access ensures that deletions in the `tblBooksOrders5` table are rippled to the `tblOrderDetails` table, deleting the corresponding records there.

FIGURE 3-16

You enforce referential integrity in the Edit Relationships dialog box.

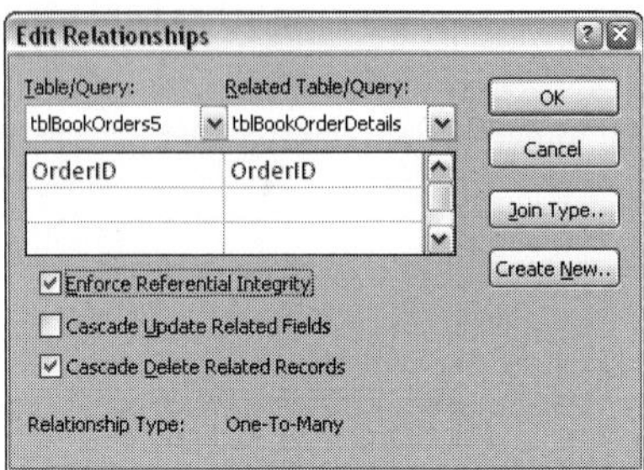

In Figure 3-16 if the Cascade Delete Related Records check box were left unchecked, Access would not permit you to delete records in `tblBookOrders5` until all of the corresponding records in `tblOrderDetails` were first manually deleted. With this box checked, deletions across the relationship are automatic.

5. **Click the Create button.**

   Access draws a line between the tables displayed in the Relationships window, indicating the type of relationship. In Figure 3-17, the 1 symbol indicates that `tblBookOrders` is the "one" side of the relationship while the infinity symbol designates `tblOrderDetails` as the "many" side.

FIGURE 3-17

A one-to-many relationship between `tblBookOrders5` and `tblBookOrderDetails`.

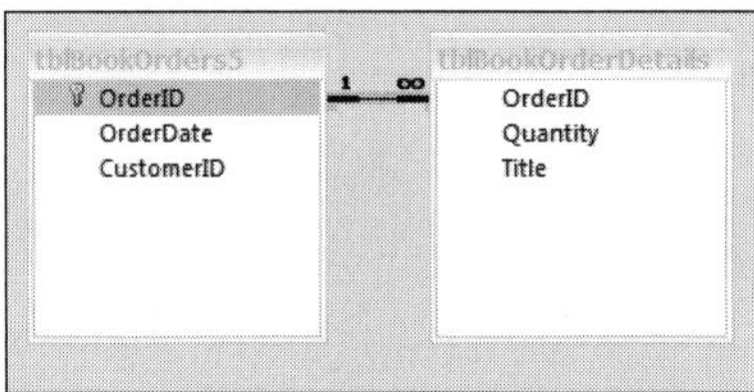

Specifying the Join Type between tables

The right side of the Edit Relations window has four buttons: Create, Cancel, Join Type, and Create New. Clicking the Create button returns you to the Relationships window with the changes specified. The Cancel button cancels the current changes and returns you to the Relationships window. The Create New button lets you specify an entirely new relation between the two tables and fields.

By default, when you process a query on related tables, Access only returns records that appear in both tables. Considering the payroll example from the "Integrity Rules" section, earlier in this chapter, this means that you would only see employees that have valid paycheck records in the paycheck table. You would not see any employees who have not yet received a paycheck. Such a relationship is sometimes called an *equi-join* because the only records that appear are those that exist on both sides of the relationship.

However, the equi-join is not the only type of join supported by Access. Click on the Join Type button to open the Join Properties dialog box. The alternative settings in the Join Properties dialog box allow you to specify that you prefer to see all of the records from either the parent table or child table, whether or not they are matched on the other side (it is possible to have an unmatched child record as long as the parent foreign key is null). Such a join (call an *outer join*) can be very useful because it accurately reflects the state of the data in the application.

In the case of the Access Auto Auction example, seeing all of the contacts, whether or not they have records in the Sales table, is what you're shooting for. To specify an outer join connecting contacts to sales, perform these steps:

1. **Click the Join Type button.**

   The Join Properties dialog box appears.

2. **Click the Include ALL Records from `'tblContacts'` and Only Those Records from `'tblSales'` Where the Joined Fields Are Equal check box.**

   The relationship between these tables should now look like what you see in Figure 3-18.

3. **Click OK.**

   You're returned to the Edit Relationships dialog box.

4. **Click OK.**

   You're returned to the Relationships window. The Relationships window should now show an arrow going from the `Contacts` table to the `Sales` table. At this point, you're ready to set referential integrity between the two tables.

FIGURE 3-18

The Join Properties dialog box, used to set up the join properties between the `Contacts` and `Sales` tables. Notice that it specifies all records from the `Contacts` table.

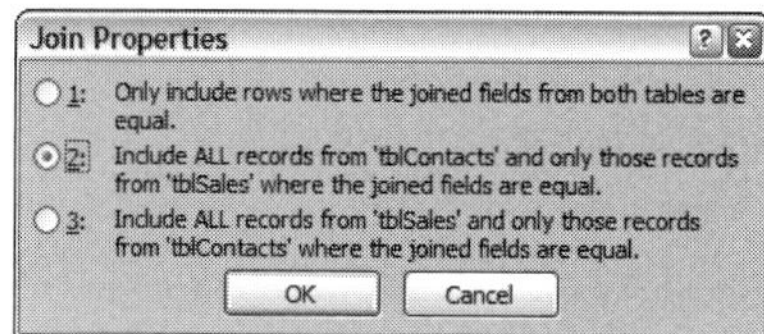

Establishing a join type for every relationship in your database is not absolutely necessary. In the following chapters, you'll see that you can specify outer joins for each query in your application. Many developers choose to use the default equi-join for all the relationships in their databases, and to adjust the join properties on each query to yield the desired results.

Enforcing referential integrity

After using the Edit Relationships dialog box to specify the relationship, verify the table and related fields, and specify the type of join between the tables, you should set referential integrity between the tables. Select the Enforce Referential Integrity check box in the lower portion of the Edit Relationships dialog box to indicate that you want Access to enforce the referential integrity rules on the relationship between the tables.

If you choose not to enforce referential integrity, you can add new records, change key fields, or delete related records without warnings about referential integrity violations — thus making it possible to change critical fields and damaging the application's data. With no integrity active, you can create tables that have orphans (Sales without a Contact). With normal operations (such as data entry or changing information), referential integrity rules should be enforced.

Enforcing referential integrity also enables two other options (cascading updates and cascading deletes) that you may find useful. These options can be checked in the Edit Relationships dialog box, as shown in Figure 3-19.

FIGURE 3-19

Referential Integrity set between the `tblSales` and `tblContacts` tables

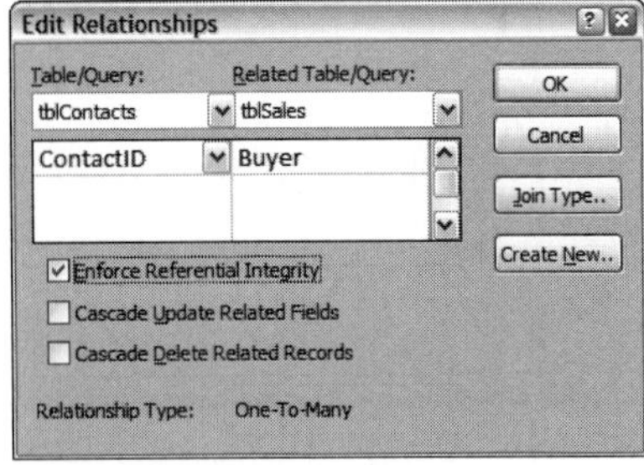

NOTE **You might find, when you specify Enforce Referential Integrity and click the Create button (or the OK button if you've reopened the Edit Relationships window to edit a relationship), that Access will not allow you to create a relationship and enforce referential integrity. The most likely reason for this behavior is that you're asking Access to create a relationship that violates referential integrity rules, such as a child table with orphans in it. In such a case, Access warns you by displaying a dialog box similar to that shown in Figure 3-20. The warning happens in this example because there are some records in the `Sales` table with no matching value in the `Salesperson`**

table. This means that Access cannot enforce referential integrity between these tables because the data within the tables already violate the rules.

FIGURE 3-20

A dialog box warning that referential integrity cannot be created between two tables due to integrity violations

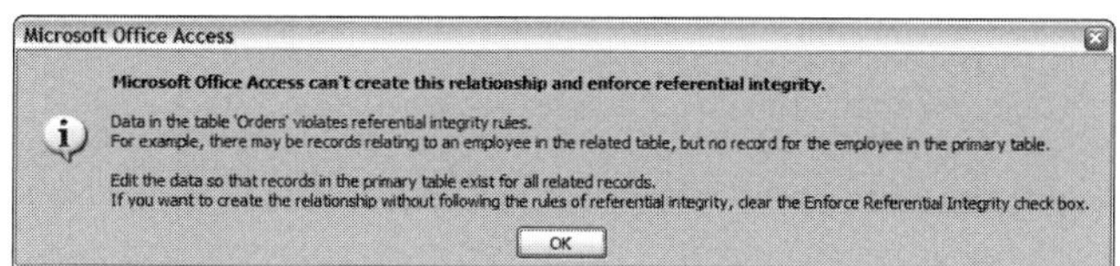

TIP **To solve any conflicts between existing tables, you can create a Find Unmatched query by using the Query Wizard to find the records in the many-side table that violate referential integrity. Then you can convert the Unmatched query to a Delete query to delete the offending records or add the appropriate value to the `SalespersonID` field.**

You could remove the offending records and return to the Relationships window and set referential integrity between the two tables. However, you should not do this, because `Salesperson` is not a critical field that requires referential integrity to be set between these tables.

Choosing the Cascade Update Related Fields option

If you specify Enforce Referential Integrity in the Edit Relationships dialog box, Access enables the Cascade Update Related Fields check box. This option tells Access that, as a user changes the contents of a related field (the primary key field in the primary table — `ContactID`, for example), the new `ContactID` is rippled through all related tables.

If this option is not selected, you cannot change the primary key value in the primary table that is used in a relationship with another table.

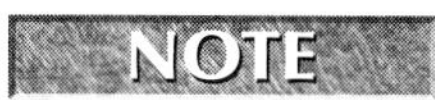
If the primary key field in the primary table is a related field between several tables, this option must be selected for all related tables or it won't work.

Generally speaking, however, there are very few reasons why the value of a primary key may change. The example we give in the "Connecting the Data" section, earlier in this chapter, of a missing Social Security number is one case where you may need to replace a temporary Social Security number with the permanent Social Security number after employee data have been added to the database. However, when using `AutoNumbers` or other surrogate key values, there is seldom any reason to have to change the primary key value once a record has been added to the database.

Choosing the Cascade Delete Related Records option

The Cascade Delete Related Records option instructs Access to delete all related child records when a parent record is deleted. Although there are instances where this option can be quite useful, as with so many other options, cascading deletes come with a number of warnings.

For example, if you have chosen Cascade Delete Related Records and you try to delete a particular customer (who moved away from the area), Access first deletes all the related records from the child tables — `Sales` and `SalesLineItems` — and then deletes the customer record. In other words, Access deletes all the records in the sales line items for each sale for each customer — the detail items of the sales, the associated sales records, and the customer record — with one step.

Perhaps you can already see the primary issue associated with cascading deletes. If all of a customer's sales records are deleted when the customer record is deleted, you have no way of properly reporting historic financial data. You could not, for instance, reliably report on the previous year's sales figures because all of the sales records for "retired" customers have been deleted from the database. Also, in this particular example, you would lose the opportunity to report on sales trends, product category sales, and a wide variety of other uses of the application's data.

TIP **To use this option, you must specify Cascade Delete Related Records for all of the table's relationships in the database. If you do not specify this option for all the tables in the chain of related tables, Access will not allow cascade deleting.**

Viewing all relationships

With the Relationships dialog box open, Choose View ➪ All Relationships to see all of the relationships in the database. If you want to simplify the view you see in the Relationships window, you can "hide" a relationship by deleting the tables you see in the Relationships window. Click on a table, press the Delete key, and Access removes the table from the Relationships window. Removing a table from the Relationships window does not delete any relationships between the table and other tables in the database.

Make sure that the Required property of the foreign key field in the related table (in the case of `tblBookOrders5` and `tblBookOrderDetails`, the foreign key is `OrderID` in `tblBookOrderDetails`) is set to Yes. This ensures that the user enters a value in the foreign key field, providing the relationship path between the tables.

The relationships formed in the Relationships window are permanent and are managed by Access. When you form permanent relationships, they appear in the Query Design window by default as you add the tables (queries are discussed in detail in Chapters 3 and 4). Even without permanent relationships between tables, you form temporary relationships any time you include multiple tables in the Query Design window.

CROSS-REF **If you connect to a SQL Server back-end database or use the Microsoft Database Engine and create an Access Data Project, the Relationships window is different. You can find more about this subject in Chapter 28.**

Deleting relationships

From time to time, you may find it necessary to delete relationships between tables. The Relationships window is simply a picture of the relationships between tables. If you open the Relationships window, click on each of the tables in the relationship and press the Delete key, you delete the picture of the tables in the relationship, but not the relationship itself. You must first click on the line connecting the tables and press Delete to delete the relationship, and then delete each of the table pictures to completely remove the relationship.

Application-specific integrity rules

In addition to the referential integrity rules enforced by the Access database engine, you can establish a number of business rules that are enforced by the applications you build in Access. In many cases, your clients or users will tell you the business rules that must be enforced by the application. It is up to you as the developer to compose the Visual Basic code, table design, field properties, and so on that implement the business rules expected by your users.

Typical business rules include items such as the following:

- The order entry clerk must enter his ID number on the entry form.
- Quantities can never be less than zero.
- The unit selling price can never be less than the unit cost.
- The order ship date must come after the order date.

Most often, these rules are added to a table at design time. Enforcing such rules goes a long way toward preserving the value of the data managed by the database. For instance, in Figure 3-21, the `ValidationRule` property of the `Quantity` field (`">=0"`) ensures that the quantity cannot be a negative number. If the inventory clerk tries to put a negative number into the `Quantity` field, an error message box pops up containing the validation text (`"Must not be a negative number"`).

You can also establish a tablewide validation rule that provides some protection for the data in the table. Unfortunately, only one rule can be created for the entire table, making it difficult to provide specific validation text for all possible violations.

Other approaches to enforcing business rules involve building VBA code that checks and verifies data entry at the form level, adding validation rules and validation text to controls on forms, and applying effective error trapping techniques to all the forms and user interface components of an application.

CROSS-REF **You can read examples of these techniques in Chapters 7, 8, and 10.**

FIGURE 3-21

A simple validation rule goes a long way toward preserving the database's integrity.

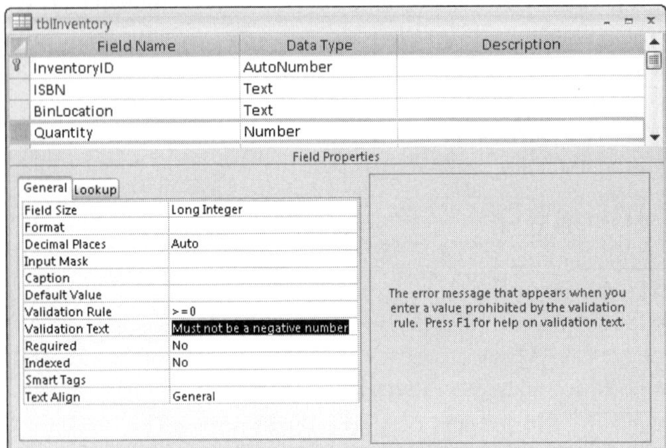

Default values are a valuable way to eliminate and enforce some business rules. For instance, in the case of an order entry form that requires the clerk's identification, you can use the `CurrentUser()` function (in a secured database) to return the user's login ID. Very often, a little clever programming is all you need to build an application that is secure, conforms to all business rules, yet is still easy and flexible for its users.

Summary

This chapter examines the relationships between tables in an Access database, and how you normalize the data for the best performance. We also studied the important topic of ensuring data security through the built-in integrity rules that are enforced by the Jet database engine. Most Access databases are built without adequate safeguards; make sure your database applications provide adequate protection for your user's data.

We're now ready to begin exploring using all that data. The next chapter takes on the challenging topic of constructing powerful, useful queries that return the data in a variety of ways. As you'll soon see, building queries in Microsoft Access 2007 is about much more than simply asking the database to return data to you. You'll learn how to control the sort order, combine data from multiple tables, and include expressions and other techniques that extend the flexibility of your queries.

Later, Chapter 5 explains the confusing topic of combining query operators such as `AND` and `OR` to achieve the desired results in a query. Access uses the same operators in a number of different places (such as VBA code and form and report design), so a firm understanding of this important topic extends well beyond query construction.

Chapter 4

Selecting Data with Queries

IN THIS CHAPTER

Understanding the different types of Access queries

Creating queries

Selecting tables and fields for queries

Displaying information in queries

Sorting information in queries

Selecting specific records in queries

Printing the results of queries

Adding more than one table to a query

Working around query limitations

Understanding types of joins

Changing the type of join

Creating an inner join and an outer join

Queries are an essential part of any database application. Queries are the tools that enable you and your users to extract data from multiple tables, combine it in useful ways, and present it to the user as a datasheet, on a form, or as a printed report.

You may have heard the old cliché, "Queries convert data to information." To a certain extent, this statement is true (that's why it's a cliché). The data contained within tables is not particularly useful because, for the most part, the data in tables appears in no particular order. Also, in a properly normalized database, important information is spread out among a number of different tables. Queries are what draw these various data sources together and present the combined information in such a way that users can actually work with the data.

In this chapter, you learn what a query is and how to create them. Using the Sales (`tblSales`), Contacts (`tblContacts`), Sales Line Items (`tblSalesLineItems`), and Products (`tblProducts`) tables, you create several types of queries for the Access Auto Auctions database.

On the CD-ROM This chapter will use the database named `Chapter04.accdb`. If you haven't already copied it onto your machine from the CD, you should do so now.

Understanding Queries

A database's primary purpose is to store and extract information. Information can be obtained from a database immediately after you enter the data or days, weeks, or even years later. Of course, retrieving information from database tables requires knowledge of how the database is set up.

For example, printed reports are often filed in a cabinet, arranged by date and by a sequence number that indicates when the report was produced. To obtain a specific report, you must know its year and sequence number. In a good filing system, you may have a cross-reference book to help you find a specific report. This book may have all reports categorized alphabetically by type of report and, perhaps, by date. Such a book can be helpful, but if you know only the report's topic and approximate date, you still have to search through all sections of the book to find out where to get the report.

Unlike manual databases, computer databases like Microsoft Access easily obtain information to meet virtually any criteria you specify.

This is the real power of a database — the capacity to examine the data in more ways than you can imagine. Queries, by definition, ask questions about the data stored in the database. Most queries are used to drive forms, reports, and graphical representations of the data contained in a database.

What is a query?

The word *query* comes from the Latin word *quærere*, which means "to ask or inquire." Over the years, the word *query* has become synonymous with *quiz, challenge, inquire,* or *question*. So, think of a query as a question or inquiry posed to the database about information contained in its tables.

A Microsoft Access query is a question that you ask about the information stored in your Access tables. You build queries with the Access query tools, and then save it as a new object in your Access database. Your query can be a simple question about data within a single table, or it can be a more complex question about information stored in several tables. After you submit the question, Microsoft Access returns only the information you requested.

Using queries this way, you ask the Access Auto Auctions database to show you only trucks that were sold in the year 2007. To see the *types* of trucks sold for the year 2007, you need information from three tables: `tblSales`, `tblSalesLineItems`, and `tblProducts`. Figure 4-1 is a typical Query Design window. Although it may look complex, it's actually very simple and easy to understand.

After you create and run a query, Microsoft Access retrieves and displays the requested records as a datasheet. This set of records is called a *recordset,* which is the set of records selected by a query. As you've seen, a datasheet looks just like a spreadsheet, with its rows of records and columns of fields. The datasheet (of the recordset) can display many records simultaneously.

You can easily filter information from a single table using the Search and Filter capabilities of a table's datasheet view (Filter by Selection and Filter by Form). Queries allow you to view information from a single table, or from multiple tables at the same time (as in Figure 4-1). Many database queries extract information from several tables.

FIGURE 4-1

A typical three-table select query. This query displays the sales date, number of trucks, and type of truck for all trucks sold in the year 2007.

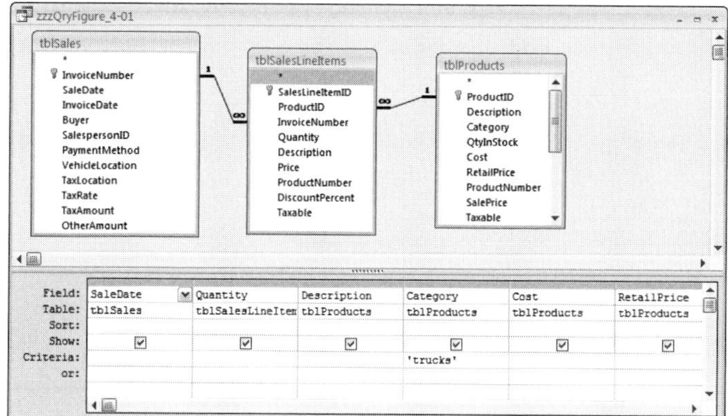

Clicking the Datasheet View button on the toolbar shows six records matching the query shown in Figure 4-1. This is a relatively easy-to-design query when you understand how to use the Access query designer. This simple query has many elements that demonstrate the power of the Access query engine: sorting a result set of records, specifying multiple criteria, and even using a complex `Or` condition in one of those fields.

You can build very complex queries using the same query designer. Suppose, for instance, that you want to send a notice to all previous buyers of more than one car in the past year that several new cars are available for auction. This type of query requires getting information from four tables: `tblContacts`, `tblSales`, `tblSalesLineItems`, and `tblProducts`. The majority of the information you need is in `tblContacts` and `tblProducts`.

In this case, you want Access to show you a datasheet of all Contact names and addresses where they have met your specified criteria (two or more cars purchased in 2007). In this case, Access retrieves customer names and cities from the `tblContacts` table and then obtains the number of cars from the `tblProducts` table, and the year of sale from the `tblSales` table. Figure 4-2 shows this relatively complex query. Access then takes the information that's common to your criteria, combines it, and displays all the information in a single datasheet. This datasheet is the result of a query that draws from the `tblContacts`, `tblSales`, `tblSalesLineItems`, and `tblProducts` tables. The database query performed the work of assembling all the information for you. Figure 4-3 shows the resulting datasheet.

FIGURE 4-2

A more complex query returning customers that purchased more than one car in 2007.

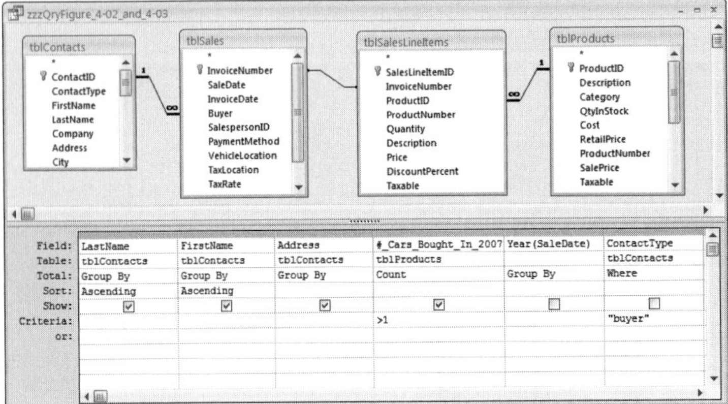

FIGURE 4-3

The resulting datasheet of the query shown in Figure 4-2.

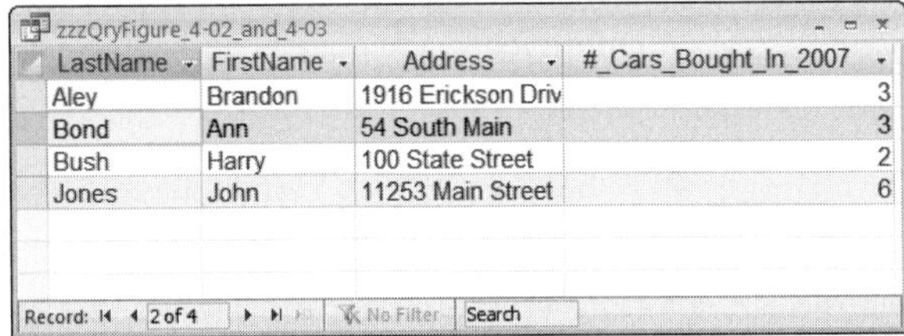
zzzQryFigure_4-02_and_4-03

LastName	FirstName	Address	#_Cars_Bought_In_2007
Aley	Brandon	1916 Erickson Driv	3
Bond	Ann	54 South Main	3
Bush	Harry	100 State Street	2
Jones	John	11253 Main Street	6

Record: 2 of 4 No Filter Search

Types of queries

Access supports many different types of queries, grouped into six basic categories:

- **Select:** These are the most common types of query. As its name implies, the select query selects information from one or more tables, creating a recordset. Generally speaking, the data returned by select query is updatable and is often used to populate forms and reports.
- **Total:** These are special type of select queries. Total queries provide sums or other calculations (such as count) from the records returned by a select query. Selecting this type of query adds a Total row in the QBE (Query by Example) grid.
- **Action:** These queries enable you to create new tables (Make Tables) or change data (delete, update, and append) in existing tables. Action queries affect many records as a single operation.

- **Crosstab:** These queries can display summary data in cross-tabular form like a spreadsheet, with row and column headings based on fields in the table. The individual cells of the recordset are computed or calculated from data in the underlying tables.
- **SQL:** There are three SQL (Structured Query Language) query types — Union, Pass-Through, and Data Definition. These queries are used for advanced database manipulation, such as working with client/server SQL databases like SQL Server or Oracle. You create these queries by writing specific SQL statements.
- **Top(n):** Top(n) queries enable you to specify a number or percentage of records you want returned from any type (select, total, and so on) of query.

Query capabilities

Queries are flexible. They provide the capability of looking at your data in virtually any way you can imagine. Most database systems are continually evolving and changing over time. Very often, the original purpose of a database is very different from its current use.

Here is a sampling of what you can do with Access queries:

- **Choose tables:** Obtain information from a single table or from many tables that are related by some common data. Suppose you're interested in seeing the customer name along with the items purchased by each type of customer. When using several tables, Access returns the data as a combined single datasheet.
- **Choose fields:** Specify which fields from each table you want to see in the recordset. For example, you can select the customer name, zip code, sales date, and invoice number from `tblContacts` and `tblSales`.
- **Choose records:** Select records based on selection criteria. For example, you may want to see records for only sellers in `tblContacts`.
- **Sort records:** You may want to sort records in a specific order. For example, you may need to see customers sorted by last name and first name.
- **Perform calculations:** Use queries to perform calculations on data. Perform calculations such as averaging, totaling, or counting fields and records.
- **Create tables:** Create a new table based on data returned by a query.
- **Base forms and reports on queries:** The recordset you create from a query may have just the right fields and data needed for a report or form. Basing a form or report on a query means that, every time you print the report or open the form, you will see the most current information in the tables.
- **Create graphs based on queries:** Create graphs from data returned by a query.
- **Use a query as a source of data for other queries (subquery):** Create additional queries based on records returned by another query. This is very useful for performing ad hoc queries, where you may repeatedly make small changes to the criteria. In this case, the second query is used to change the criteria while the first query and its data remain intact.

- **Make changes to tables:** Access queries can obtain information from a wide range of sources. You can retrieve data stored in dBASE, Paradox, Btrieve, and Microsoft SQL Server databases, as well as Excel spreadsheets, text files, and other data sources.

How recordsets work

Access takes the records that result from a query and displays them in a datasheet. The set of records is commonly called (oddly enough) a ***recordset***. Physically, a recordset looks much like a table. A recordset is, in fact, a ***dynamic*** set of records. The set of records returned by a query is not stored within the database, unless you have directed access to build a table from those records.

When you close a query, the query's recordset is gone; it no longer exists. Even though the recordset itself no longer exists, the data that formed the recordset remains stored in the underlying tables.

When you run a query, Access places the returned records into a recordset. When you save the query, only the structure of the query is saved, and not the returned records. Consider these benefits of *not* saving the recordset to a physical table:

- A smaller amount of space on a storage device (usually a hard drive) is needed.
- The query uses updated versions of records.

Every time the query is executed, it reads the underlying tables and re-creates the recordset. Because recordsets themselves are not stored, a query automatically reflects any changes to the underlying tables made since the last time the query was executed — even in a real-time, multiuser environment.

Creating a Query

After you create your tables and place data in them, you're ready to work with queries. To begin a query, choose the Create ribbon, and click on the Query Design button in the Other group. Access opens the query designer in response.

Figure 4-4 shows two windows. The underlying window is the Query Designer. Floating on top of the designer is the Show Table dialog box. The Show Table window is ***modal***, which means that you must do something in the dialog box before continuing with the query. Before you continue, you add the tables required for the query. In this case, `tblProducts` is highlighted to be added.

The Show Table dialog box shown in Figure 4-5 displays all tables and queries in your database. Double-click on `tblProducts` to add it to the query design. Close the Show Table dialog box after adding `tblProducts`. Figure 4-5 shows `tblProducts` added to the query.

FIGURE 4-4

The Show Table dialog box in the Query Design window.

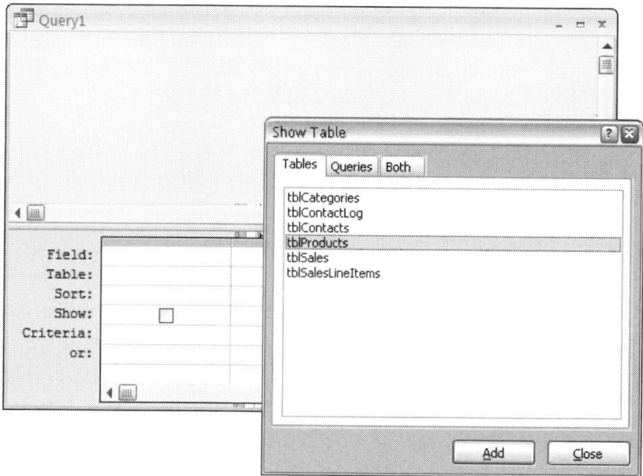

FIGURE 4-5

The Query Design window with `tblProducts` added to the Query Designer.

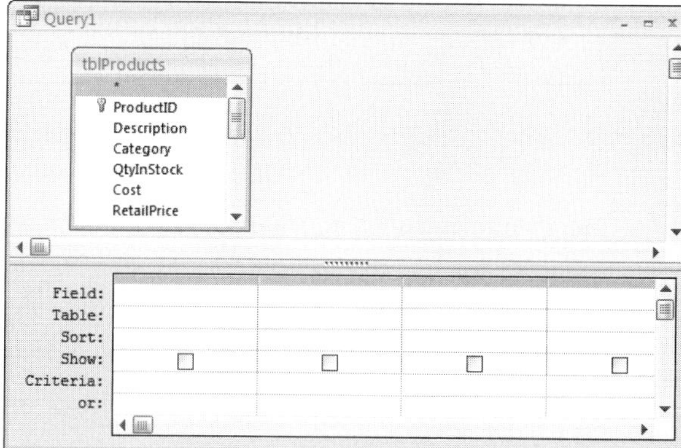

To add additional tables to the query, right-click on the query's design surface and select Show Table from the shortcut menu that appears. Alternatively, drag tables from the Navigation pane on to the Query Designer's surface.

Removing a table from the Query Designer is easy. Just right-click on the table in the Query Designer and select Remove Table from the shortcut menu.

Using the Query window

The Query window has two main views: Design view and Datasheet view. The difference between them is self-explanatory: The Design view is where you create the query, and the Datasheet view displays the records returned by the query.

The Query Design window should now look like Figure 4-5, with `tblProducts` displayed in the top half of the Query Design window.

The Query Design window consists of two sections:

- The table/query entry pane (top)
- The Query by Example (QBE) design grid (bottom)

The upper pane is where tables or queries and their fields are displayed. Tables and queries are displayed as small windows inside the top pane (the proper name of this window is Field List). The Field List window can be resized by clicking on the edges and dragging it to a different size.

The Query by Example (QBE) grid holds the field names involved in the query and any criteria used to select records. Each column in the QBE grid contains information about a single field from a table or query contained within the upper pane.

Navigating the Query Design window

The two window panes are separated horizontally by a pane-resizing bar (see Figure 4-5). Move the bar up or down to change the relative sizes of the upper and lower panes.

Switch between the upper and lower panes by clicking the desired pane or by pressing F6 to switch panes. Each pane has horizontal and vertical scrollbars to help you move around.

You actually build the query by dragging fields from the upper pane to the QBE grid.

Using the Query Design ribbon

The Query Design ribbon (shown in Figure 4-6) contains many different buttons specific to building and working with queries.

FIGURE 4-6

The Query Design ribbon

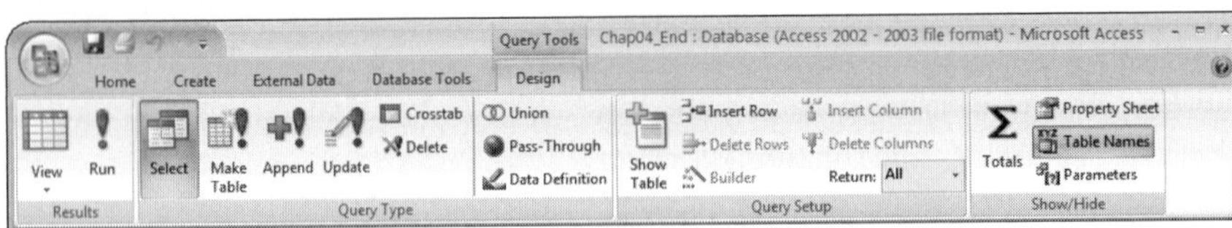

This ribbon has many buttons that can be helpful when designing your queries. Although each button is explained as it is used in the chapters of this book, here are the main buttons:

- **View:** Switches between the Datasheet view and Design view. The View drop-down control also enables you to display the underlying SQL statement behind the query (more on this later).
- **Save (in the Quick Access Toolbar):** Saves the query. It is a good idea to save your work often, especially when creating complex queries.
- **Make Table, Append, Update, and Crosstab:** Specify the type of query you are building.
- **Run:** Runs the query. Displays a select query's datasheet, serving the same function as the View button. However, when working with action queries, it actually performs the operations specified by the query.
- **Show Table:** Opens the Show Table dialog box.

The remaining buttons are used for more creating more advanced queries, printing the contents of the query, and displaying a query's property sheet.

Using the QBE grid of the Query Design window

As you saw earlier, Figure 4-5 displays an empty QBE grid, which has six labeled rows:

- **Field:** Where field names are entered or added.
- **Table:** Shows the table the field is from (useful in queries with multiple tables).
- **Sort:** Enables sorting instructions for the query.
- **Show:** Determines whether to display the field in the returned recordset.
- **Criteria:** Criteria that filter the returned records.
- **or:** This row is the first of a number of rows to which you can add multiple query criteria.

You learn more about these rows as you create queries in this chapter.

Selecting Fields

There are several ways to add fields to a query. You can add fields one at a time, select and add multiple fields, or select and add all fields. You use your keyboard or mouse to add fields.

Adding a single field

You add a single field in several ways. One method is to double-click the field name in the Field List (also called a Table window); the field name immediately appears in the first available column in the QEB pane. Alternatively, drag a field from a table in the top portion of the query designer, and drop it on a column in the QBE grid. Dropping a field between two other fields in the QBE grid pushes other fields to the right.

Another way to add fields to the QBE grid is to click an empty Field cell in the QBE grid, and select the field name from the drop-down list in the cell, or type the field's name into the cell. Figure 4-7 shows selecting the Cost field from the drop-down list. Once selected, simply move to the next field cell and select the next field you want to see in the query.

FIGURE 4-7

Adding fields in the QBE grid. Clicking the down arrow reveals a drop-down list from which you select a field.

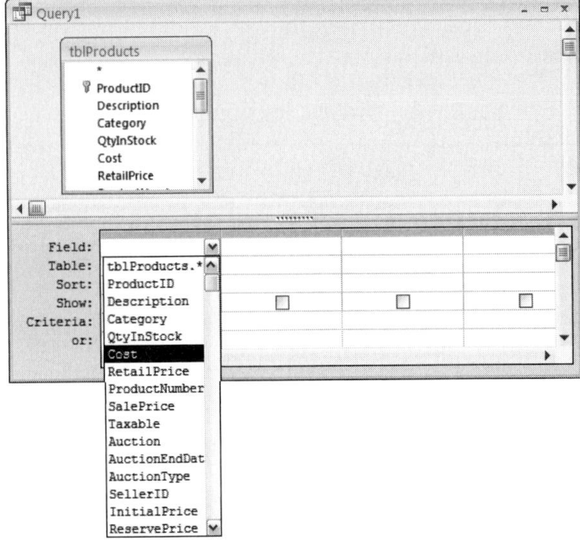

You'll find a similar list of all the tables in the query in a drop-down list in the Table row of the QBE grid.

After selecting the fields, run the query by clicking the Datasheet button or the Run button on the ribbon. Click the Design View button on the ribbon to return to the design window.

Adding multiple fields

You add multiple fields in a single action by selecting the fields from the Field List and dragging them to the QBE grid. The selected fields do not have to be contiguous (one after the other). Hold down the Shift key while selecting multiple fields. Figure 4-8 illustrates the process of adding multiple fields.

FIGURE 4-8

Selecting several fields to move to the QBE grid.

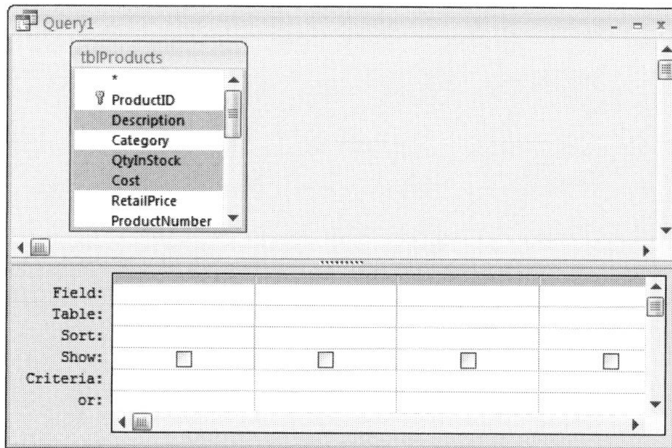

The fields are added to the QBE grid in the order in which they occur in the table.

You can also add all the fields in the table by clicking on the Field List's header (where it says `tblProducts` in Figure 4-9) to highlight all the fields in the table. Then drag the highlighted fields to the QBE grid.

Alternatively, click and drag the asterisk (*) from the Field List to the QBE grid. Although this action does not add all the fields to the QBE grid, the asterisk directs Access to include all fields in the table in the query.

FIGURE 4-9

Adding the asterisk to the QBE grid selects all fields in the table.

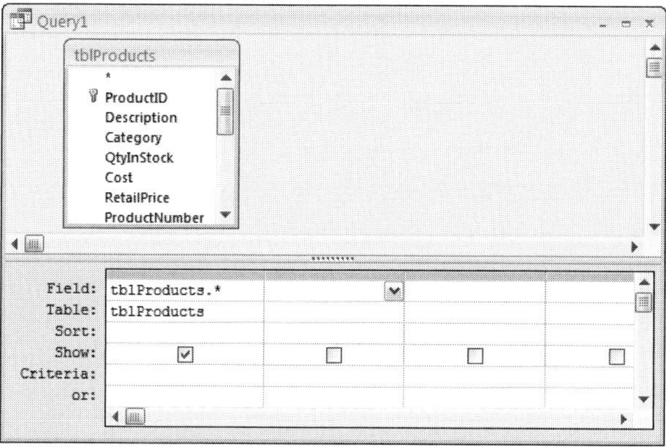

Unlike selecting all the fields, the asterisk places a reference to all the fields in a single column. When you drag multiple columns, as in the preceding example, you drag names to the QBE grid. If you later change the design of the table, you also have to change the design of the query. The advantage of using the asterisk for selecting all fields is that changes to the underlying tables don't require changes to the query. The asterisk means to select all fields in the table, regardless of the field names or changes in the number of fields in the table.

The downside of using the asterisk to specify all fields in a table is that the query, as instructed, returns all the fields in a table, whether or not every field is used on a form or report.

Displaying the Recordset

Click the Run button or the Datasheet button to view the query's results (see Figure 4-10).

FIGURE 4-10

The datasheet view of the query

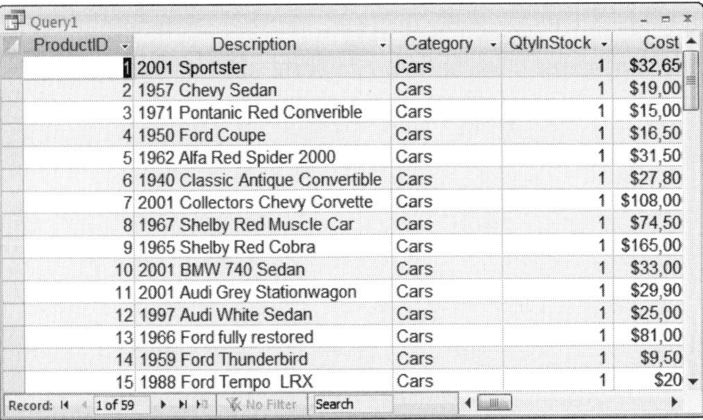

ProductID	Description	Category	QtyInStock	Cost
1	2001 Sportster	Cars	1	$32,65
2	1957 Chevy Sedan	Cars	1	$19,00
3	1971 Pontanic Red Converible	Cars	1	$15,00
4	1950 Ford Coupe	Cars	1	$16,50
5	1962 Alfa Red Spider 2000	Cars	1	$31,50
6	1940 Classic Antique Convertible	Cars	1	$27,80
7	2001 Collectors Chevy Corvette	Cars	1	$108,00
8	1967 Shelby Red Muscle Car	Cars	1	$74,50
9	1965 Shelby Red Cobra	Cars	1	$165,00
10	2001 BMW 740 Sedan	Cars	1	$33,00
11	2001 Audi Grey Stationwagon	Cars	1	$29,90
12	1997 Audi White Sedan	Cars	1	$25,00
13	1966 Ford fully restored	Cars	1	$81,00
14	1959 Ford Thunderbird	Cars	1	$9,50
15	1988 Ford Tempo LRX	Cars	1	$20

Working with records in Datasheet view is covered in detail in Chapter 6. As you can see in that chapter, filtering, sorting, rearranging, and searching within a datasheet is quite easy. Our simple select query did not transform the data in any way, so the data shown in Figure 4-10 is completely editable. We can modify existing data, delete rows, and even add new records to this data set, if we want.

When you're working with data in the datasheet, all the table and field properties defined at the table level are in effect. Therefore, validation rules, default values, and other properties assert themselves even though the datasheet is the result of a query.

Earlier versions of Access referred to an updatable datasheet as a *Dynaset*. This expression emphasized the fact that the datasheet was dynamically linked to its underlying data sources. However, this expression has fallen by the wayside because, very often the data in a query's datasheet is not updatable. For instance, transforming the data in any way, such as combining first and last names as a single field, makes the datasheet non-updatable. You'll see data transformations later in this chapter and in many other chapters in this book.

At any time, clicking the Design View button on the ribbon returns you to Query Design mode.

Working with Fields

There are times when you want to work with the fields you've already selected — rearranging their order, inserting a new field, or deleting an existing field. You may even want to add a field to the QBE grid without showing it in the datasheet. Adding a field without showing it enables you to sort on the hidden field, or to use the hidden field as criteria.

Selecting a field in the QBE grid

Before you can move a field's position, you must first select it. To select it, you will work with the field selector row.

The *field selector row* is the narrow gray area at the top of each column in the QBE grid at the bottom of the Query Designer. Recall that each column represents a field. To select the Category field, move the mouse pointer until a small selection arrow (in this case, a dark downward arrow) is visible in the selector row and then click the column. Figure 4-11 shows the selection arrow above the Category column just before it is selected.

FIGURE 4-11

Selecting a column in the QBE grid. The pointer changes to a downward-pointing arrow when you move over the selection row.

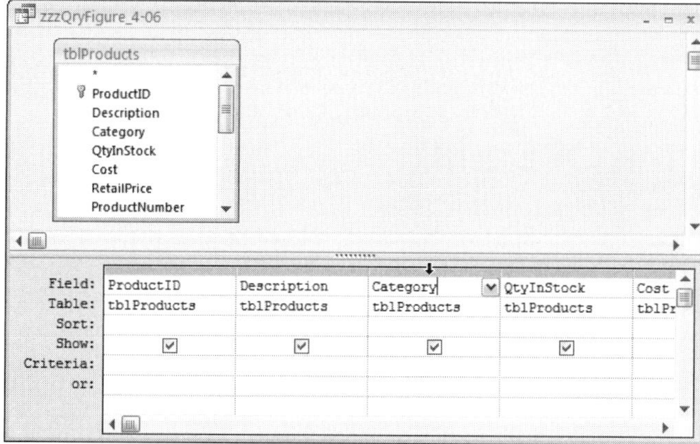

Select multiple contiguous fields by clicking the first field you wish to select and then dragging across the field selector bars of the other fields.

Changing field order

The left-to-right order in which fields appear in the QBE grid determines the order in which they appear in Datasheet view. You may want to move the fields in the QBE grid to achieve a new sequence of fields in the query's results. With the fields selected, you can move the fields on the QBE design by simply dragging them to a new position.

Left-click on a field's selector bar, and, while holding down the left mouse button, drag the field into a new position in the QBE grid.

Figure 4-12 shows the `Category` field highlighted. As you move the selector field to the left, the column separator between the fields `ProductID` and `Description` changes (gets wider) to show you where `Category` will go.

FIGURE 4-12

Moving the `Category` field to between `ProductID` and `Description`. Notice the QBE field icon below the arrow near the Description column.

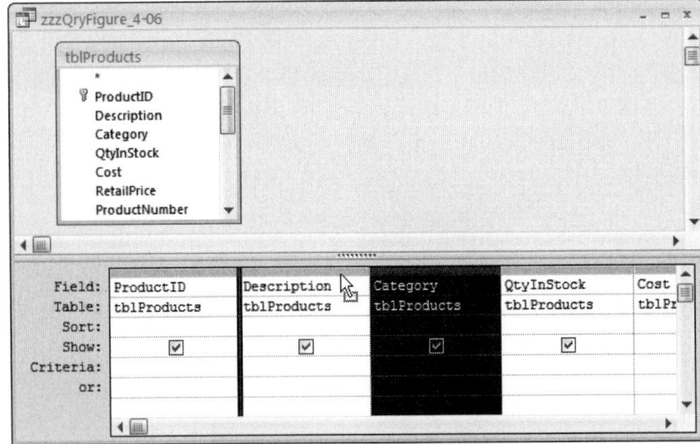

Resizing columns in the QBE grid

The QBE grid generally shows five or six fields in the viewable area of your screen. The remaining fields are viewed by moving the horizontal scroll bar at the bottom of the window.

There are times that you may want to shrink some fields to be able to see more columns in the QBE grid. You adjust the column width to make them smaller (or larger) by moving the mouse pointer to the margin between two fields, and dragging the column resizer left or right (see Figure 4-13). An easier way to resize columns in the QBE grid is to double-click on the line dividing two columns in the grid. Access "auto-sizes" the column to fit the data displayed in the column.

FIGURE 4-13

Resizing columns in the QBE grid

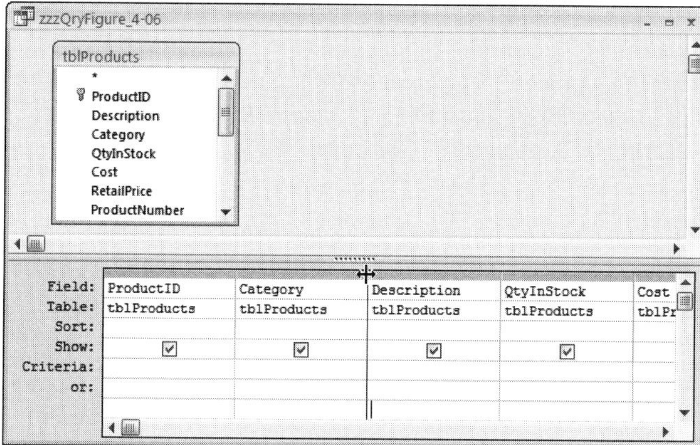

Removing a field

Remove a field from the QBE grid by selecting the field (or fields) and pressing the Delete key. You can also right-click on a field's selector and choose Cut from the shortcut menu.

Inserting a field

Insert new fields in the QBE grid by dragging a field from a Field List above the QBE grid and dropping it onto a column in the QBE grid. The new column is inserted to the left of the column you dropped the field on. Double-clicking a field in a Field List adds the new column at the far right position in the QBE grid.

Providing an alias for the field name

To make the query datasheet easier to read, you can provide aliases for the fields in your query. An alias becomes the field's heading in the query's datasheet, but does not affect the field's name or how the data is stored and used by Access. Aliases are sometimes useful to help users better understand the data returned by a query. As you will see in Chapter 18, data in queries are often transformed by performing simple operations such as combining a person's first and last name as a single field. In these situations, aliases are very useful because they provide an easily recognizable reference to the transformed data.

To follow along with this example, create a query using the fields from the `tblProducts` as shown in Figure 4-12. Follow these steps to establish an alias for the `ProductID` and `Description` fields:

1. **Click to the left of the *P* of the `ProductID` column in the top row of the QBE grid.**
2. **Type** Product-Number **followed by a colon (:) to the left of `ProductID`.**
3. **Click to the left of the *D* in the Description column and enter** Product Description: **to the left of the field name.**

   When you run the query, the aliases you created appear as the column headings. Figure 4-14 shows both the query in Design view and the query's datasheet. Notice that the `ProductID` and `Description` column sport their new aliases instead of their respective field names.

FIGURE 4-14

Aliases can be useful to help users understand data.

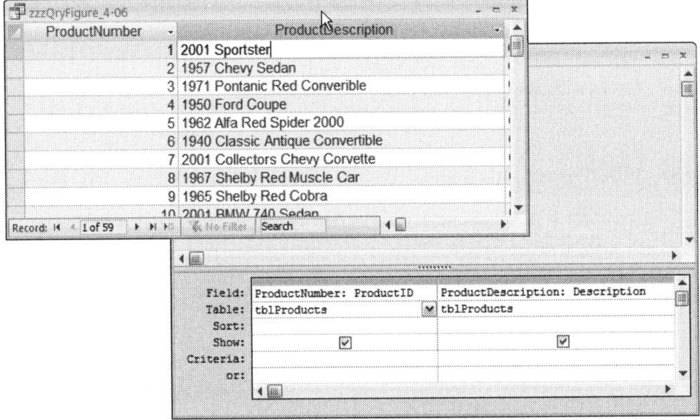

Aliases should be used with caution, however. Because an alias masks the name of the field underlying a datasheet, it's easy to become confused which column headings are aliases and which are field names. It is a complete waste of time looking for a field named `ProductDescription`, based on a datasheet column heading. It would be nice if Access somehow distinguished between aliases and field names in Datasheet view, but the only way to know for sure is to examine the query's design.

Showing a field

While performing queries, you may want to show only some of the fields in the QBE grid. Suppose, for example, you've chosen `ContactType`, `FirstName`, `LastName`, `Address`, `City`, and State. Then you decide that you want to temporarily look at the same data, without the ContactType and Address fields. You could start a new query adding all of the fields except Address and ContactType, or you can simply "turn off" the Address and ContactType fields by unchecking the check box in the Show row of each of these columns (see Figure 4-15).

FIGURE 4-15

The Show check box is unchecked for the Address and ContactType fields.

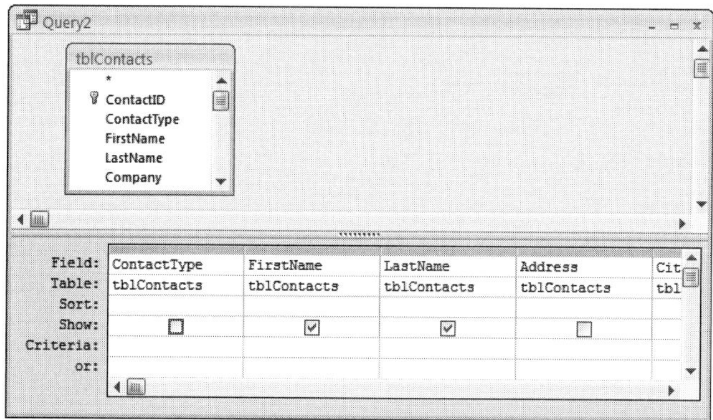

By default, every field you add to the QBE grid has its Show check box selected.

Another common reason to hide a field in the query is because the field is used for searching or sorting, but its value is not needed in the query. For instance, consider a query involving the invoices from the Access Auto Auctions database. For a number of reasons, the users may want to see the invoices sorted by the order date, even though the actual order date is irrelevant for this particular purpose. Simply include the OrderDate field in the QBE grid, set the sort order for the OrderDate field, and uncheck its Show box. Access sorts the data by the OrderDate field even though the field is not shown in the query's results.

CAUTION **If you save a query that has an unused field (its Show box is unchecked and no criteria or sort order is applied to the field), Access eliminates the field from the query. The next time you open the query, the field will not be included in the query's design.**

Changing the Sort Order

When viewing a recordset, you often want to display the data in a sorted order. You may want to sort the recordset to make it easier to analyze the data (for example, to look at all the tblProducts sorted by category).

Sorting places the records in alphabetical or numeric order. The sort order can be ascending (0 to 9 and A to Z) or descending (9 to 0 and Z to A). You can sort on a single field or multiple fields.

You input sorting directions in the Sort row in the QBE grid. To specify a sort order on a particular field (such as `LastName`), perform these steps:

1. **Position the cursor in the Sort cell in the `LastName` column.**
2. **Click the drop-down list that appears in the cell, and select the sort order (Ascending or Descending) you want to apply.**

   Figure 4-16 shows the QBE grid with ascending sorts specified for the `LastName` and `FirstName` fields. Notice that the `LastName` field is still showing the sort options available. Also notice that the word *Ascending* is being selected in the field's Sort: cell.

FIGURE 4-16

An ascending sort has been specified for the `LastName` and `FirstName` fields.

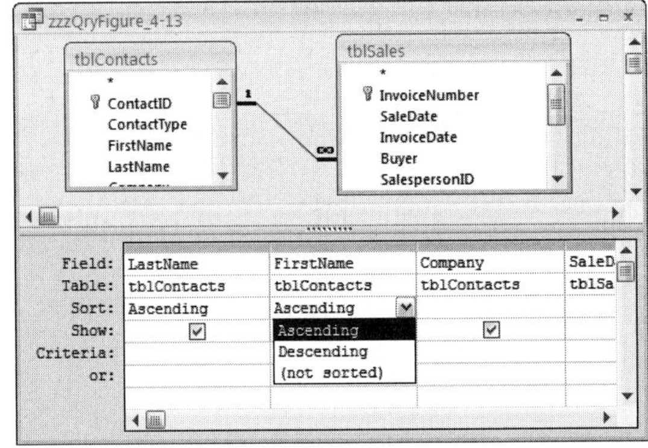

NOTE **You *cannot* sort on a Memo or an OLE object field.**

The left-to-right order in which fields appear in the QBE grid is important when sorting on more than one field. Not only to the fields appear in the datasheet in left-to-right order, they are sorted in the same order (this is known as *sort order precedence*). The leftmost field containing sort criteria is sorted first, the first field to the right containing sort criteria is sorted next, and so on. In the example shown in Figure 4-16, the `LastName` field is sorted first, and then the `FirstName` field.

Figure 4-17 shows the results of the query shown in Figure 4-16. Notice that the data is sorted by the values in the `LastName` column, and the values in the `FirstName` column are sorted within each name in the `LastName` column. This is why Ann Bond appears before John Bond in the query's data.

FIGURE 4-17

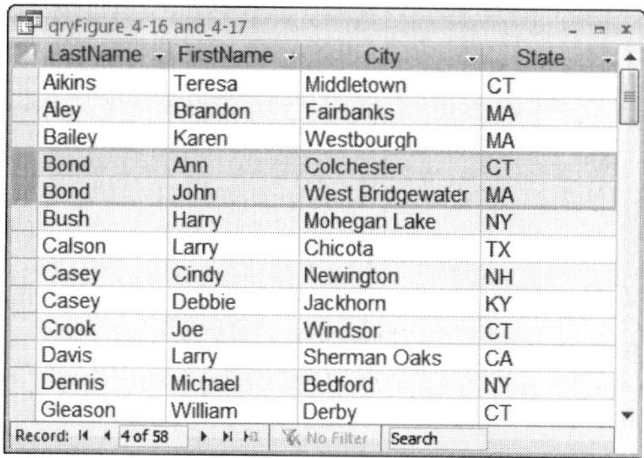

LastName	FirstName	City	State
Aikins	Teresa	Middletown	CT
Aley	Brandon	Fairbanks	MA
Bailey	Karen	Westbourgh	MA
Bond	Ann	Colchester	CT
Bond	John	West Bridgewater	MA
Bush	Harry	Mohegan Lake	NY
Calson	Larry	Chicota	TX
Casey	Cindy	Newington	NH
Casey	Debbie	Jackhorn	KY
Crook	Joe	Windsor	CT
Davis	Larry	Sherman Oaks	CA
Dennis	Michael	Bedford	NY
Gleason	William	Derby	CT

The order of the fields is critical when sorting on multiple fields.

Displaying Only Selected Records

So far, you've been working with all the records of the `tblContacts` and `tblProducts` tables. Most often users want to work only with records conforming to some criteria. Otherwise, too many records may be returned by a query, causing serious performance issues. For example, you may want to look only at contacts that are buyers and not sellers. Access makes it easy for you to specify a query's criteria.

Understanding selection criteria

Selection criteria are simply filtering rules applied to data as it is extracted from the database. Selection criteria instruct Access which records you want to look at in the recordset. A typical criterion might be "all sellers," or "only those vehicles that are not trucks," or "cars with retail prices greater than $45,000."

Selection criteria limit the records returned by a query. Selection criteria aid the user by selecting only the records a user wants to see, and ignoring all the others.

You specify criteria in the Criteria row of the QBE grid. You designate criteria as an expression. The expression can be as a simple example (like "Trucks" or "Not Trucks") or can take the form of complex expressions using built-in Access functions.

Entering simple string criteria

Character-type criteria are applied to Text-type fields. Most often, you will enter an example of the text you want to retrieve. Here is a small example that returns only product records where the product type is "Cars":

1. **Add `tblProducts` and choose the `Description`, `Category`, and `Cost` fields.**
2. **Type** CARS **into the Criteria cell under the Category column.**
3. **Run the query.**

   Only cars are displayed — in this case, 25 records (see Figure 4-18). Observe that you did not enter an equal sign or place quotes around the sample text, yet Access added double quotes around the value. Access, unlike many other database systems, automatically makes assumptions about what you want.

FIGURE 4-18

Specifying character criteria. In this case, because you want to see only cars, you enter "CARS" as the criteria.

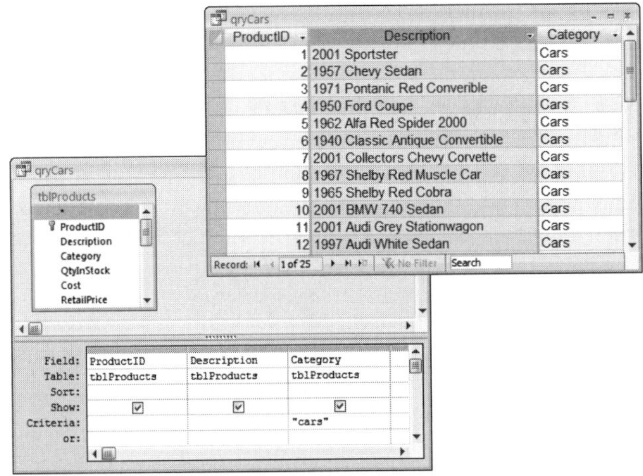

Figure 4-18 shows both the query design and the datasheet resulting from the query. This figure also illustrates one reason you may wish to hide a column in a query. There's no point in displaying "Cars" and every row in the third column. In fact, because this query only returns information about cars, the user can very well assume that every record references a car and there's no need to display a product category in the query. Unchecking the Category's Show box in the queries design would remove the Category column from the datasheet, making the data easier to understand.

You could enter the criteria expression in any of these other ways:

- CARS
- = CARS
- "CARS"
- = "Cars"

By default, Access is *not* case sensitive, so any form of the word *cars* works just as well as this query's criteria.

Figure 4-18 is an excellent example for demonstrating the options for various types of simple character criteria. You could just as well enter "Not Cars" in the criteria column, to return all products that are not cars (trucks, vans, and so on).

Generally, when dealing with character data, you enter equalities, inequalities, or a list of values that are acceptable.

This capability is a powerful tool. Consider that you have only to supply an example and Access not only interprets it but also uses it to create the query recordset. This is exactly what *Query by Example* means: You enter an example and let the database build a query based on the example.

To erase the criteria in the cell, select the contents and press Delete, or select the contents and Right Click Cut from the shortcut menu that appears. You can also right-click Paste to revert to the previous content (in this case, a blank cell).

Entering other simple criteria

You can also specify criteria for `Numeric`, `Date`, and `Yes/No` fields. Simply enter the example data in the criteria field.

It is also possible to add more than one criteria to a query. For example, suppose that you want to look only at contacts who are both sellers *and* buyers ("BOTH" type in the `ContactType` field), and those contacts have been customers since January 1, 2007 (where `OrigCustDate` is greater or equal to January 1, 2007). This query requires criteria in both the `ContactType` and `OrigCustDate` fields. To do this, it is critical that you place both examples on the same Criteria row. Follow these steps to create this query:

1. **Create a new query starting with `tblContacts`.**
2. **Add `ContactType`, `FirstName`, `LastName`, `State`, and `OrigCustDate` to the QBE grid.**
3. **Enter** BOTH **in the Criteria cell in the `ContactType` column.**
4. **Enter** >= 01/01/07 **in the Criteria cell in the `OrigCustDate` column.**
5. **Run the query.**

   Figure 4-19 shows how the query should look.

Access displays records of contacts that are both sellers and buyers that became customers after January 1, 2007 — in this example, two contact records.

CROSS-REF **Multi-criteria queries are covered in depth in Chapter 18.**

FIGURE 4-19

Specifying character and date criteria in the same query

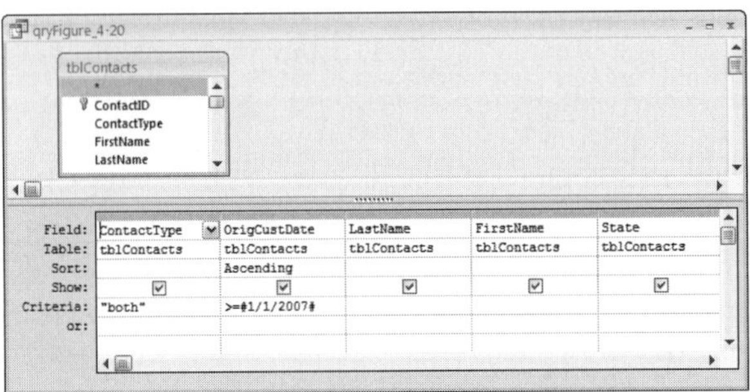

Access uses comparison operators to compare `Date` fields to a value. These operators include less than (<), greater than (>), equal to (=), or a combination of these operators. Notice that Access automatically adds pound sign (#) delimiters around the date value. Access uses these delimiters to distinguish between date and text data. The pound signs are just like the quote marks Access added to the "Cars" criteria. Because the `OrigCustDate` is a `DateTime` field, Access understands what you want and inserts the proper delimiters for you.

Operators and precedence are covered more in Chapter 5.

Printing a Query's Recordset

After you create your query, you can easily print all the records in the recordset. Although you can't specify a type of report, you can print a simple matrix-type report (rows and columns) of the recordset created by your query.

You do have some flexibility when printing a recordset. If you know that the datasheet is set up just as you want, you can specify some options as you follow these steps:

1. **Use the datasheet you just created for both sellers and buyers that have been customers since 01/01/2007.**
2. **If you are not in the Datasheet view, switch to the Query Datasheet mode by clicking the Datasheet button on the ribbon.**
3. **Choose File ➪ Print from the Query Datasheet window's ribbon**
4. **Specify the print options that you want in the Print dialog box and click OK.**

The printout reflects all layout options in effect when you print the dataset. Hidden columns do not print, and gridlines print only if the Gridlines option is on. The printout reflects the specified row height and column width.

Saving a Query

Click the Save button at the top of the Access screen to save your query. Access asks you for the name of the query if this is the first time the query has been saved.

After saving the query, Access returns you to the mode you were working in. Occasionally, you will want to save and exit the query in a single operation. To do this, click the Close Window button in the upper-right corner of the Query Designer. Access always asks you to confirm saving the changes before it actually saves the query.

Adding More Than One Table to a Query

Using a query to obtain information from a single table is common; often, however, you need information from several related tables. For example, you may want to obtain a buyer's name and vehicle type purchased by the contact. This query requires four tables: `tblContacts`, `tblSales`, `tblSalesLineItems`, and `tblProducts`.

In Chapter 2, you learned the importance of primary and foreign keys and how they link tables together. You learned how to use the Relationships window to create relationships between tables. Finally, you learned how referential integrity affects data in tables.

After you create the tables for your database and decide how the tables are related to one another, you are ready to build multiple-table queries to obtain information from several related tables. The query combines data from multiple tables and presents the data as if it existed in one large table.

The first step in creating a multiple-table query is to add the tables to the Query window:

1. **Create a new query by clicking the Query Design button in the Create ribbon tab.**
2. **Select** `tblContacts`, `tblSales`, `tblSalesLineItems`, **and** `tblProducts` **by double-clicking each table's name in the Show Table dialog box.**
3. **Click the Close button in the Show Table dialog box.**

NOTE **You can also add each table by highlighting the table in the list separately and clicking Add.**

Figure 4-20 shows the top pane of the Query Design window with the four tables you just added. Because the relationships were set at table level, the join lines are automatically added to the query.

NOTE **You can add more tables, at any time, by choosing Query ➪ Show Table from the Query Design Ribbon.**

FIGURE 4-20

The Query Design window with four tables added. Notice the join lines are already present.

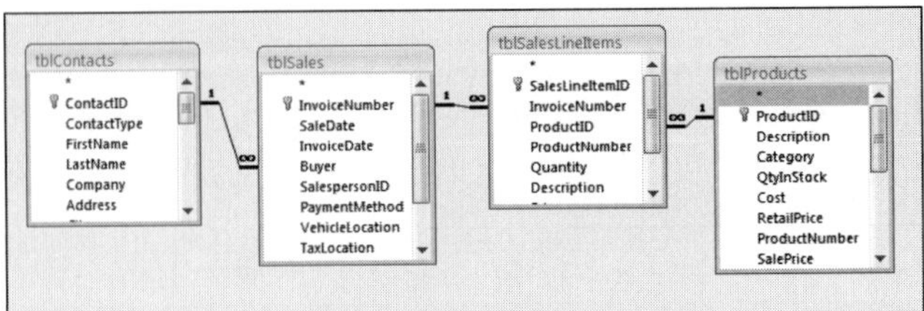

Working with the Table/Query Pane

As Figure 4-20 shows, a *join line* connects tables in the Query Designer. The join line connects the primary key in one table to the foreign key in another table.

CROSS-REF **These lines were predrawn because you already set the relationships between the tables earlier in Chapter 4.**

The join line

A *join line* represents the relationship between two tables in the Access database. In this example, a join line goes from `tblSales` to `tblContacts`, connecting `ContactID` in the `tblContacts` table to the `Buyer` field in `tblSales`. There are other join lines connecting the other tables in this query.

The join line is automatically created because relationships were set in the relationship builder. If Access already knows about the relationship, it adds the join line when the tables are added to a query.

If Referential Integrity is set on the relationship, Access displays a thicker line where the join line connects to the table in the Query Designer. This variation in line thickness tells you that Referential Integrity is set between the two tables. If a one-to-many relationship exists, the many-side table is indicated by an infinity symbol (∞).

Access will auto join to tables if the following conditions are met:

- Both tables have fields with the same name.
- The same-named fields are the same data type (text, numeric, and so on).
- One of the field is a *primary key* in its table.

Access 2007 automatically attempts to join the tables if a relationship exists. Access cannot set referential integrity on the join line.

Manipulating the Field List window

Each Field List window begins at a fixed size, which shows approximately four fields and perhaps 12 characters for each field. Each Field List is a resizable window and can be moved within the Query Designer. If there are more fields than will show in the Field List window, a scroll bar enables you to scroll through the fields in the Field List.

NOTE **After a relationship is created between tables, the join line remains between the two fields. As you move through a table selecting fields, the line moves relative to the linked fields. For example, if the scroll box moves down (toward the bottom of the window) in `tblContacts`, the join line moves up with the customer number, eventually stopping at the top of the table window.**

When you're working with many tables, these join lines can become confusing as they cross or overlap. As you scroll through the table, the line eventually becomes visible, and the field it is linked to becomes obvious.

Moving a table

Move the Field Lists by grabbing the title bar of a Field List (where the name of the table is) with the mouse and dragging the Field List to a new location. You may want to move the Field Lists for a better working view or to clean up a confusing query diagram.

You can move and resize the Field Lists anywhere in the top pane. Access saves the arrangement when you save and close the query. Generally speaking, the Field Lists will appear in the same configuration the next time you open the query.

Removing a table

There are times when you need to remove tables from a query. Any table can be removed from the Query window. Use the mouse to select the table you want to remove in the top pane of the Query window and press the Delete key. Or right-click on the Field List and choose Removed Table from the shortcut menu.

CAUTION **When you delete a table, join lines to that table are deleted as well. When you delete a table, there is no warning or confirmation dialog box. The table is simply removed from the screen, along with any of the table's fields added to the QBE grid.**

Adding more tables

You may decide to add more tables to a query or you may accidentally delete a table and need to add it back. You accomplish this task by clicking on the Show Table button on the Query Setup group in the Design ribbon. The Show Table dialog box appears in response to this action.

Adding Fields from More Than One Table

You add fields from more than one table to the query in exactly the same way as when you're working with a single table. You can add fields one at a time, multiple fields as a group, or all the fields from a table.

If you type a field name in an empty Field cell that has the same name in more than one table, Access enters the field name from the first table that it finds containing the field name.

If you select the field from the drop-down list in the Field cell, you see the name of the table first, followed by a period and the field name. For example, the `ProductID` in `tblSalesLineItems` is displayed as *tblSalesLineItems.ProductID*. This helps you select the right field name. Using this method, you can select a common field name from a specific table.

The easiest way to select fields is still to double-click the field names in the top half of the Query Designer. To do so, you may have to resize the Field Lists to see the fields that you want to select.

Viewing the table names

When you're working with two or more tables, the field names in the QBE grid can become confusing. You may find yourself asking, for example, just which table the field is from.

Access automatically maintains the table name that is associated with each field displayed in the QBE grid. Figure 4-21 shows the Query Designer with the name of each table displayed under the field name in the QBE grid.

FIGURE 4-21

The QBE grid with table names displayed. Notice that it shows all four table names.

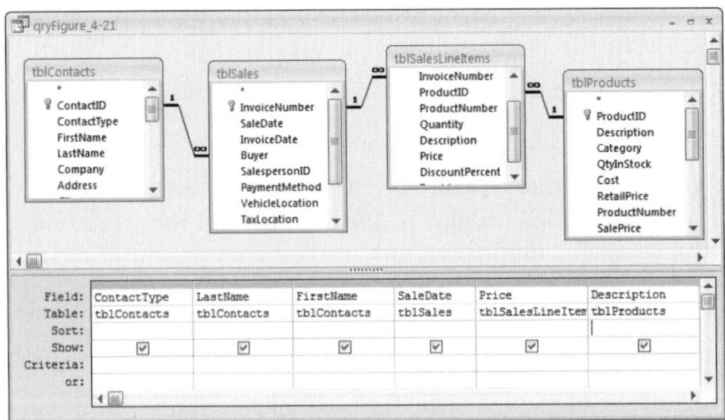

After you add fields to a query, you can view the returned records at any time. Figure 4-22 shows the data returned by the query in Figure 4-21.

FIGURE 4-22

Datasheet view of data from multiple tables. This resulting recordset, from the query, contains 84 records.

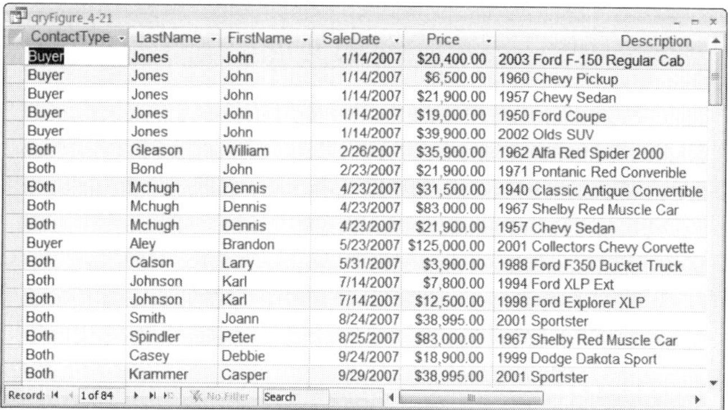

qryFigure_4-21

ContactType	LastName	FirstName	SaleDate	Price	Description
Buyer	Jones	John	1/14/2007	$20,400.00	2003 Ford F-150 Regular Cab
Buyer	Jones	John	1/14/2007	$6,500.00	1960 Chevy Pickup
Buyer	Jones	John	1/14/2007	$21,900.00	1957 Chevy Sedan
Buyer	Jones	John	1/14/2007	$19,000.00	1950 Ford Coupe
Buyer	Jones	John	1/14/2007	$39,900.00	2002 Olds SUV
Both	Gleason	William	2/26/2007	$35,900.00	1962 Alfa Red Spider 2000
Both	Bond	John	2/23/2007	$21,900.00	1971 Pontanic Red Converible
Both	Mchugh	Dennis	4/23/2007	$31,500.00	1940 Classic Antique Convertible
Both	Mchugh	Dennis	4/23/2007	$83,000.00	1967 Shelby Red Muscle Car
Both	Mchugh	Dennis	4/23/2007	$21,900.00	1957 Chevy Sedan
Buyer	Aley	Brandon	5/23/2007	$125,000.00	2001 Collectors Chevy Corvette
Both	Calson	Larry	5/31/2007	$3,900.00	1988 Ford F350 Bucket Truck
Both	Johnson	Karl	7/14/2007	$7,800.00	1994 Ford XLP Ext
Both	Johnson	Karl	7/14/2007	$12,500.00	1998 Ford Explorer XLP
Both	Smith	Joann	8/24/2007	$38,995.00	2001 Sportster
Both	Spindler	Peter	8/25/2007	$83,000.00	1967 Shelby Red Muscle Car
Both	Casey	Debbie	9/24/2007	$18,900.00	1999 Dodge Dakota Sport
Both	Krammer	Casper	9/29/2007	$38,995.00	2001 Sportster

Record: 1 of 84 No Filter Search

Adding multiple fields

The process of adding multiple fields in a multi-table query is identical to adding multiple fields in a single-table query. When you're adding multiple fields from several tables, you must add them from one table at a time. The easiest way to do this is to select multiple fields and drag them together down to the QBE grid.

You can select multiple contiguous fields by clicking the first field of the list and then clicking the last field while holding down the Shift key. You can also select noncontiguous fields in the list by holding down the Ctrl key while clicking individual fields with the mouse.

CAUTION **Selecting the * does have one drawback: You cannot specify criteria on the asterisk column itself. You have to add an individual field from the table and enter the criterion. If you add a field for a criterion (when using the *), the query displays the field twice — once for the * field and a second time for the criterion field. Therefore, you may want to deselect the Show cell of the criterion field.**

Understanding Multi-Table Query Limitations

When you create a query with multiple tables, there are limits to which fields can be edited. Generally, you can change data in a query's recordset, and your changes are saved in the underlying tables. The main exception is a table's primary key — a primary key value cannot be edited if referential integrity is in effect and if the field is part of a relationship.

To update a table from a query, a value in a specific record in the query must represent a single record in the underlying table. This means that you cannot update fields in a query that transforms data because most transformations group records and fields display aggregate information. Each field in a transformed recordset represents multiple fields in the underlying tables. There is no way to change the data in a transformed field and have it reflected in the underlying tables.

Updating limitations

In Access, the records in your tables may not always be updateable. Table 4-1 shows when a field in a table is updateable. As Table 4-1 shows, queries based on one-to-many relationships are updateable in both tables (depending on how the query was designed).

TABLE 4-1

Rules for Updating Queries

Type of Query or Field	Updateable	Comments
One table	Yes	
One-to-one relationship	Yes	
Results contains Memo field	Yes	Memo field updateable
Results contain Hyperlink	Yes	Hyperlink updateable
Results contain an OLE object	Yes	OLE object updateable
One-to-many relationship	Mostly	Restrictions based on design methodology (see text)
Many-to-one-to-many	No	Can update data in a form or data access page if RecordType = Recordset
Two or more tables with no join line	No	Must have a join to determine updateability
Crosstab	No	Creates a snapshot of the data
Totals Query (Sum, Avg, and so on)	No	Works with grouped data creating a snapshot
Unique Value property is Yes	No	Shows unique records only in a snapshot
SQL-specific queries	No	Union and pass-through work with ODBC data
Calculated field	No	Will recalculate automatically
Read-only fields	No	If opened read-only or on read-only drive (CD-ROM)
Permissions denied	No	Insert, replace, or delete are not granted
ODBC tables with no primary key	No	A primary key (unique index) must exist
Paradox table with no primary key	No	A primary key file must exist
Locked by another user	No	Cannot be updated while a field is locked by another

Overcoming query limitations

Table 4-1 shows that there are times when queries and fields in tables are not updateable. As a general rule, any query that performs aggregate operations or uses an ODBC (Open DataBase Connectivity) data source is not updateable. Most other queries can be updated. When your query has more than one table and some of the tables have a one-to-many relationship, there may be fields that are not updateable (depending on the design of the query).

Updating a unique index (primary key)

If a query uses two tables involved in a one-to-many relationship, the query must include the primary key from the one-side table. Access must have the primary key value so that they can find the related records in the two tables.

Replacing existing data in a query with a one-to-many relationship

Normally, all the fields in the many-side table (such as the `tblSales` table) are updateable in a one-to-many query. All the fields (*except* the primary key) in the one-side table (`tblCustomers`) can be updated. Normally, this is sufficient for most database application purposes. Also, the primary key field is rarely changed in the one-side table because it is the link to the records in the joined tables.

Design tips for updating fields in queries

If you want to add records to both tables of a one-to-many relationship, include the foreign key from the *many-side* table and show the field in the datasheet. After doing this, records can be added starting with either the one-side or many-side table. The *one* side's primary key field is automatically copied to the *many* side's join field.

If you want to add records to multiple tables in a form (covered in Chapters 7 and 8), remember to include all (or most) of the fields from both tables. Otherwise, you will not have a complete record of data in your form.

Creating and Working with Query Joins

By default, an Access query returns only records where data exists on both sides of a relationship. This means, for instance, that a query that extracts data from the Contacts table and the Sales table only returns records where contacts have actually placed sales, and will not show contacts who haven't yet placed a sale. If a contact record is not matched by at least one sales record, the contact data is not returned by the query. This means that, sometimes, the query does not return all of the records that you expect it to produce.

The situation described in the preceding paragraph is called an *inner join*, or an *equi-join*. Although this is the most common join type between tables in a query, there are instances where users want to see all of the data in a table (like the `tblContacts` table in the preceding example), whether or not those records are matched in another table. In fact, users often want to specifically see records that are *not* matched on the other side of the join. Consider a sales department that wants to know all the contacts who have *not* made a sale in the last year. You must modify the default query join characteristics in order to process this type of query.

You can create joins between tables in these three ways:

- By creating relationships between the tables when you design the database.
- By selecting two tables for the query that have a field in common that has the same name and data in both tables. The field is a primary key field in one of the tables.
- By creating joins in the query designer at the time you create the query.

The first two methods occur automatically in the Query Design window. Relationships between tables are displayed in the Query Designer when you add the related tables to a query. It also creates an automatic join between two tables that have a common field, provided that field is a primary key in one of the tables and the `Enable Auto Join` choice is selected (by default) in the Options dialog box.

If relationships are set in the relationship builder, you may add a table to a query and it will not automatically be related to another table, as in these examples:

- The two tables have a common field, but it is not the same name.
- A table is not related and cannot be logically related to the other table (for example, `tblContacts` cannot directly join the `tblSalesLineItems` table).

If you have two tables that are not automatically joined and you need to relate them, you join them in the Query Design window. Joining tables in the Query Design window does *not* create a permanent relationship between the tables. Rather, the join (relationship) applies only to the tables while the query operates.

Tables in a query have to be joined in some fashion or other. Including two tables with nothing in common (for instance, a query based on `tblContacts` and `tblProducts`, with nothing in between them) means that Access has no way to know which records in the `tblContacts` table match which records in the `tblProducts` table. Unless there is some way to relate the tables to one another, the query returns unusable data.

CAUTION **All tables in a query should be joined to at least one other table. If, for example, two tables in a query are not joined in some way, the query produces a *Cartesian product* (also known as the cross product) of the two tables. (This subject is discussed in the "Creating a Cartesian Product" section, later in this chapter). For now, note that a Cartesian product means that if you have five records in table 1 and six records in table 2, the resulting query will have 30 records (5 × 6) that will probably be useless.**

Joining tables

Figure 4-23 shows a simple query containing `tblSales`, `tblSalesLineItems`, `tblProducts`, and `tblCategories`. Notice that the join line between `tblProducts` and `tblCategories` is thinner than the other join lines and does not include the 1 and infinity symbols. This is an auto-join, formed when the Categories table was added to the query.

FIGURE 4-23

An auto-join between `tblProducts` and `tblCategories`

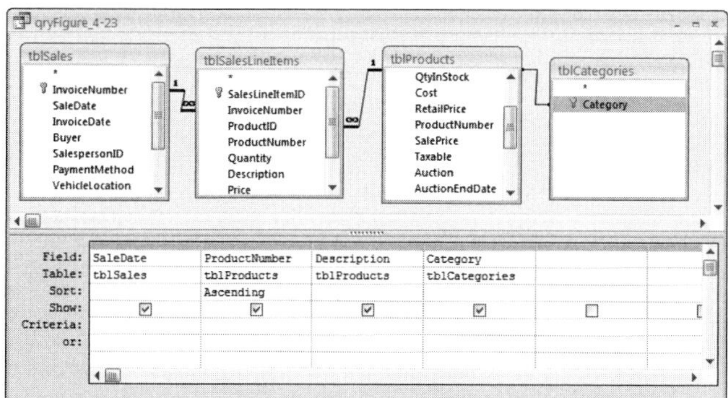

No formal relationship yet exists between `tblProducts` and `tblCategories`. However, Access found the `Category` field in both the tables, determined that the Category data type is the same in both tables, and that the `Category` field in `tblCategories` is the primary key. Therefore, Access added an auto-join between the tables.

NOTE **Tables are not joined automatically in a query if they are not already joined at the table level, if they do not have a common named field for a primary key, or if the AutoJoin option is off.**

If Access had not auto-joined `tblProducts` and `tblCategories` (perhaps because the `Category` field was named differently in the tables), you easily add a join by dragging the `Category` field from one table and dropping it on the corresponding field in the other table.

Specify the type of join

The problem with auto-joins is that, but default, they exhibit equi-join behavior as the query executes. In the case of the query in Figure 4-23, if a product record exists that does not have an assigned category (for instance, a car that was never assigned to a category) the query does not return any records where a product record is not matched by a category. Figure 4-24 shows the result of this query.

FIGURE 4-24

You can't tell that records are missing from this query.

SaleDate	ProductNumber	Description	Category
8/31/2007	CAR-002	1957 Chevy Sedan	Cars
1/14/2007	CAR-002	1957 Chevy Sedan	Cars
9/9/2008	CAR-002	1957 Chevy Sedan	Cars
6/12/2008	CAR-002	1957 Chevy Sedan	Cars
4/17/2008	CAR-002	1957 Chevy Sedan	Cars
4/23/2007	CAR-002	1957 Chevy Sedan	Cars
1/14/2008	CAR-002	1957 Chevy Sedan	Cars
2/23/2007	CAR-003	1971 Pontanic Red Converible	Cars
1/14/2007	CAR-004	1950 Ford Coupe	Cars
2/29/2008	CAR-004	1950 Ford Coupe	Cars
12/28/2007	CAR-004	1950 Ford Coupe	Cars
2/24/2008	CAR-005	1962 Alfa Red Spider 2000	Cars
2/26/2007	CAR-005	1962 Alfa Red Spider 2000	Cars
4/30/2008	CAR-036	1940 Classic Antique Convertible	Cars
9/5/2007	CAR-036	1940 Classic Antique Convertible	Cars
4/23/2007	CAR-036	1940 Classic Antique Convertible	Cars
2/24/2008	CAR-036	1940 Classic Antique Convertible	Cars

The problem in Figure 4-24 is that you can't even tell that records are missing. The only way you'd ever determine there should be more than 81 records is by carefully examining the sales records, or by composing another query that counts all sales, or performing some other audit operation.

You must modify the join characteristics between `tblProducts` and `tblCategories` to get an accurate picture of the Access Auto Auctions sales. Carefully right-click on the thin join line between `tblProducts` and `tblCategories`, and select the Join Properties command from the shortcut menu. This action opens the Join Properties dialog box (see Figure 4-25), enabling you to specify an alternate join between the tales.

FIGURE 4-25

Selecting an outer join for the query

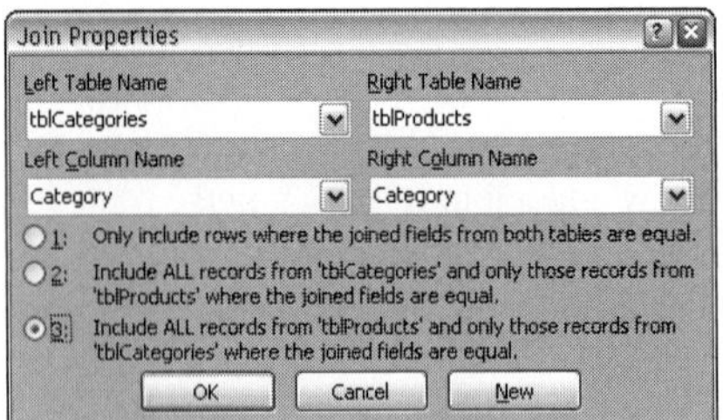

In Figure 4-25, the third option (Include All Records from 'tblProducts' . . .) has been selected (the first option is the default). Options 2 and 3 are called *outer joins* and direct Access to retrieve all records from the left (or right) table involved in the join, whether or not those records are matched on the other side of the join.

Figure 4-26 shows the result of the new join. In the lower-right corner of this figure you see how an outer join appears in the Access query design, while the rest of the figure shows the recordset returned by the query.

FIGURE 4-26

A right outer join corrects the problem in Figure 4-25.

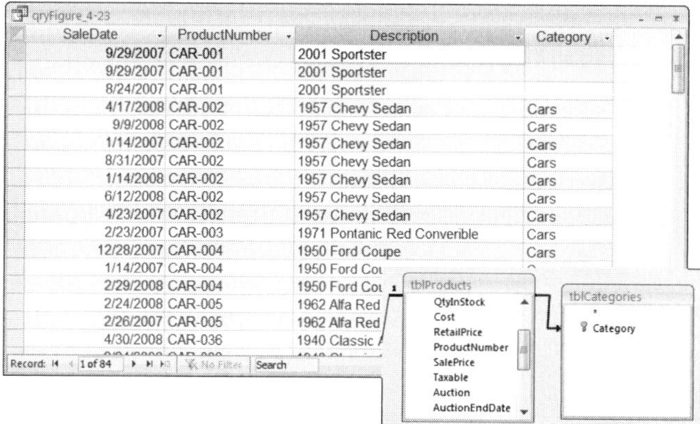

An outer join is represented by a join line with an arrow pointing at one of the tables involved in the join. In Figure 4-26, `tblProducts` is right-joined to `tblCategories`, which means all records from `tblProducts` are shown, whether or not there are matching records in `tblCategories`.

The larger portion of Figure 4-26 shows the recordset from the query. Notice that 84 records are now returned, and that the first three rows in the recordset have no `Category` value. The query now accurately reports the number of sales records.

Of course, you can easily create joins that make no sense, but when you view the data, you'll get less-than-desirable results. If two joined fields have no values in common, you'll have a datasheet in which no records are selected.

You can select either table first when you create a join.

You would never want to create a meaningless join. For example, you would not want to join the `City` field from the `tblContact` table to the `tblSalesDate` of `tblSales`. Although Access will enable you to create this join, the resulting recordset will have no records in it.

Deleting joins

To delete a join line between two tables, select the join line and press the Delete key. Select the join line by placing the mouse pointer on any part of the line and clicking once.

CAUTION **If you delete a join between two tables and the tables remain in the Query window unjoined to any other tables, the solution will have unexpected results because of the Cartesian product that Access creates from the two tables. The Cartesian product is effective for only this query. The underlying relationship remains intact.**

Access enables you to create multiple-field joins between tables (more than one line can be drawn). The two fields must have data in common; if not, the query will not find any records to display.

Understanding Table Join Types

In Chapter 3, you learned about table relationships and relating two tables by a common field. Access understands all types of table and query relations, including these:

- One-to-one
- One-to-many
- Many-to-one
- Many-to-many

When you specify a relationship between two tables, you establish rules for the type of relationship, not for viewing the data based on the relationship.

To view data in two tables, they must be joined through common fields in the two tables. Tables with established relationships are automatically joined through the relationship. Within a query, you can create ad-hoc joins or change existing joins, and as you've already seen, Access often auto-joins tables for you. Just as there are different types of relationships, there are different types of joins. In the following sections, you learn about a number of different types of joins:

- Equi-joins (inner joins)
- Outer joins
- Self-joins
- Cross-product joins (Cartesian joins)

Inner joins (equi-joins)

The default join in Access is known as an *inner join* or *equi-join*. It tells Access to select all records from both tables that have the same value in the fields that are joined.

NOTE **The Access manuals refer to the default join as both an equi-join and inner join (commonly referred to as an inner join in database relational theory). The Access Help system refers to it as an inner join. The terms *equi-join* and *inner join* are interchangeable; however, in the remainder of this chapter they are referred to as inner joins.**

If records are found in either table that do not have matching records in the other table, they are excluded from the returned recordset and are not shown in the datasheet. Thus, an inner join between tables is simply a join where records are selected when matching values exist in the joined field of both tables.

You can create an inner join between the `tblContacts` and `tblSales` tables by bringing these two tables into a new query and clicking on the join line to activate the Join Property dialog box and selecting the first choice: Only Include Rows Where the Joined Fields from Both Tables Are Equal.

Remember that you are looking for all records from these two tables with matching fields. The `ContactID` field and `Buyer` contain the common field values, so the inner join does not show any records for `contacts` that have no sales or any sales that do not relate to a valid `contactID` number. Referential integrity prevents sales records that are not tied to a contact number. Of course, it's possible to delete all sales from a contact or to create a new contact record with no sales records (possibly a seller instead of a buyer), but a sale should always be related to a valid contact (buyer). Referential integrity keeps a contact from being deleted or changed if there is a related sale.

It's possible to have a buyer in `tblContacts` who has no sales. With referential integrity controlling the relationship, it is impossible, to have a sale with no buyer. If you create a query to show contacts and their sales, any record of a contact without a sale is not shown in the returned recordset.

Changing join properties

You can change the default behavior of tables joined through formal relationships. Because default joins in Access queries are always inner joins, a query may under-report the returned data, as shown in Figure 4-24.

A join property is a rule that is enforced by Access. This rule tells Access how to interpret exceptions between two tables. For example, as you saw earlier, should the noncorresponding records be shown?

Access has several types of joins, each with its own characteristics or behaviors. Access enables you to change the type of join quickly by changing its properties. You change join properties by selecting the join line between tables and double-clicking the line or right-clicking and selecting Join Properties from the shortcut menu. When you do so, the Join Properties dialog box appears (Figure 4-27).

FIGURE 4-27

The Join Properties dialog box

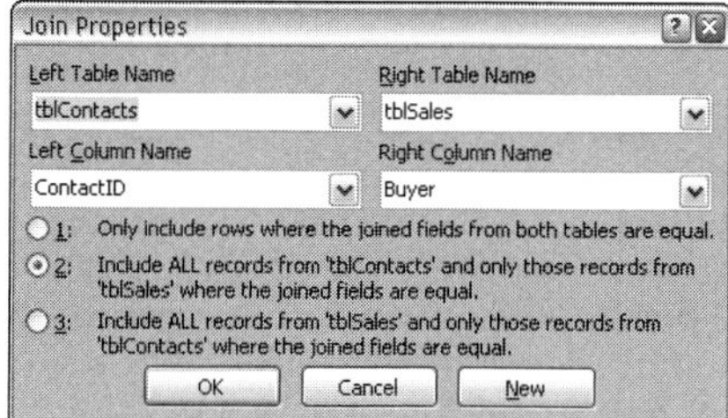

As Figure 4-27 shows, the Join Properties dialog box has two parts: the four combo boxes and three option buttons. For now, you focus on the three options buttons:

- Only include rows where the joined fields from both tables are equal. (This is the default.)
- Include ALL records from "tblContacts" and only those records from "tblSales" where the joined fields are equal.
- Include ALL records from "tblSales" and only those records from "tblContacts" where the joined fields are equal.

The first choice is commonly known as an *inner join*, and the other two are known as *outer joins*. These joins control the behavior of Access as it builds the recordset from the query.

Inner and outer joins

The Query Design window should now display two tables in the top pane of the Query window — `tblContacts` and `tblSales`, with four fields selected to display. If your query window does not have these two tables, create a new query and add them. The following sections use these tables as examples to explain how inner and outer joins operate.

Inner joins

You've already seen many examples of inner joins. The important thing to keep in mind about inner joins is that the records returned by an inner join will not include any records that are unmatched on either side of the join. A contact with no sales will not be shown; neither will a product without a specified category.

Creating a right outer join

Unlike inner joins (equi-joins), *outer joins* show all records in one table and any matching records in the other. The table or query that does not have a matching record simply displays an empty cell for the unmatched data when the recordset is displayed.

When you have created an outer join, the join line points to one of the tables (see Figure 4-26). The base of the arrow is attached to the "main" table — the one that returns all records. The arrow points to the right-joined (or left-joined) table — the one that may be missing a matching record.

So far the outer join examples you've seen have involved tables with no formal relationships. Figure 4-28 shows the results of an inner join between contacts and sales. Not all contacts have placed sales with Access Auto Auctions; perhaps they are sellers and not buyers.

The recordset contains 82 records and includes all contacts, whether or not they've placed sales.

FIGURE 4-28

A datasheet with a right outer join. It shows all contacts (buyers and sellers), including those with no sales.

qryOuterJoin

ContactType	LastName	FirstName	SaleDate
Buyer	Jones	John	1/14/2007
Buyer	Jones	John	12/11/2007
Buyer	Jones	John	2/25/2008
Seller	Masters	Hank	
Both	Minkler	Larry	4/14/2008
Both	Hammerman	Joe	
Buyer	James	Cary	8/2/2008
Buyer	Uno	Mark	
Buyer	Aley	Brandon	5/23/2007
Buyer	Aley	Brandon	8/31/2007
Buyer	Aley	Brandon	12/14/2007
Buyer	Aley	Brandon	9/9/2008
Both	Dennis	Michael	8/27/2008
Both	Martin	Mark	
Both	Johnson	Karl	7/14/2007
Both	Johnson	Karl	12/1/2007
Both	Johnson	Karl	1/14/2008
Both	Johnson	Karl	6/12/2008

Record: 1 of 82 No Filter Search

Creating a left outer join

Once in the query design, again double-click the join line between the `tblContacts` and `tblSales` tables. Select the third choice from the Join Properties dialog box (Include All Records from tblSales). Then click the OK button. The join line now has an arrow pointing to `tblContacts`. This is known as a *left outer join*. (If the arrow points to the right in the top pane, the join is known as a right outer join; if the arrow points to the left, it's a left outer join.)

If you create this left outer join query between the tables and select the Datasheet button to display the recordset, you will see that you again have 53 records. This simply means that there are no records in `tblSales` (sales without buyers). If there were one or more sales without buyers, this query would show them. The sales records, without buyers, would result from selecting the join property to include all records from `tblSales` (a *left outer join* in database terminology).

Any sales record without a buyer is known as an ***orphan*** record. Referential integrity can't be set in the Relationships window if there is an orphan record. If you attempt to set Referential Integrity between tables and you cannot, simply remove any orphan records and then return to the Relationships window to set up referential integrity between the tables.

Creating a Cartesian product

If you add both the `tblContacts` and `tblSales` tables to a query but don't specify a join between the tables, Access combines the first `tblContact` record with all the `tblSales` records; then it takes the second record and combines it with all the `tblSales` records and continues until all the `tblContacts` records have been combined with all of the `tblSales` records. Combining each record in one table with each record in the other table results in a Cartesian product (cross-product) of both tables. Because `tblContacts` has 58 records and `tblSales` has 53, the resulting recordset has 3,074 records.

Summary

This chapter has taken on the major topic of building select queries. Without a doubt, query creation is a daunting task, and one that takes a lot of practice. Even simple queries can return unexpected results, depending on the characteristics of the join between tables, and the criteria used to filter data in the underlying tables.

Queries are an integral and important part of any Access database application. Queries drive forms, reports, and many other aspects of Access applications.

Your best bet for mastering Access queries is to try increasingly difficult queries, and to always check your work. In the case of improperly joined tables, Access queries almost always under-report the data in the tables. You will discover the missing records only by carefully examining the data to ensure that your query is working properly.

Chapter 5

Using Operators and Expressions in Access

In previous chapters, you created queries using selected fields from one or more tables. You also sorted the data and set criteria to limit the results of a query. This chapter focuses on using operators and expressions to calculate information, compare values, and display data in a different format — using queries to build examples.

You aren't limited to using operators and expressions inside of queries. You'll also learn how to use them when creating calculated fields on forms and reports, and when programming in Visual Basic for Applications (VBA). This chapter only uses queries to demonstrate the use of operators and functions.

ON the CD-ROM This chapter will use the `Chapter05Start.accdb` database. If you haven't already copied it onto your machine from the CD, you'll need to do so now.

CROSS-REF For more on using operators and expressions on forms, reports, and in VBA, see Chapters 4, 9, and 13.

IN THIS CHAPTER

- Understanding operators, functions, and expressions and how they're used
- Reviewing types of operators
- Looking at types of functions
- Creating an expression
- Examining special identifier operators and expressions
- Creating and using text expressions as criteria
- Using the `Like` and `Not` operators and wildcards
- Creating and using date and numeric expressions as criteria
- Using the `And/Or` operators in single-field criteria
- Using the `In` and `Between...And` operators
- Searching for `Null` data
- Using the `And/Or` operators across several fields
- Using functions as expressions for criteria
- Creating and using a calculated field

What Are Operators?

Operators let you add numbers, compare values, put text strings together, format data, and perform a wide variety of tasks. You use operators to inform Access to perform a specific action against one or more items. The combination of operators and items is known as an *expression*.

You'll use operators every time you create an equation in Access. For example, operators specify data-validation rules in table properties, create calculated fields in forms and reports, and specify criteria in queries.

Operators indicate that an operation needs to be performed on one or more items. Some common examples of operators are:

```
=
&
And
Like
+
```

Types of operators

Here are the types of operators discussed in this chapter:

- Mathematical (arithmetic) operators
- Relational operators
- String operators
- Boolean (logical) operators
- Miscellaneous operators

Mathematical operators

There are seven basic mathematical operators. These are also known as arithmetic operators, because they're used for performing numeric calculations:

`*`	Multiply
`+`	Add
`-`	Subtract
`/`	Divide
`\`	Integer divide
`^`	Exponentiation
`Mod`	Modulo

By definition, you use mathematical operators to work with numbers. When you work with mathematical operators, numbers can be any numeric data type. The number can be an actual number (constant value), the value of a memory variable, or a field's contents.. Furthermore, you use these numbers individually or combine them to create complex expressions. Some of the examples in this section may seem complex, but trust us: You don't need a master's degree in mathematics to work through them.

The * (multiplication) operator

A simple example of when to use the multiplication operator is to calculate the total price of purchasing several items. You could design a query to display the number of items purchased and the price for each item. Then you could add a column — a *calculated field* — containing the value of the number of items purchased times the price per item. In this case, you could get that information from `tblSalesLineItems`, and the formula would be `[tblSalesLineItems].[Quantity] * [tblSalesLineItems].[Price]`.

NOTE **The standard Access notation for dealing with table names and field names in an expression is to enclose them in square brackets.**

TIP **Notice that you use the table name before the field name in the above example. Because your tables only have one field named `Price` and one field named `Quantity`, you could have skipped the table names; however, it's good practice to specify the name of the table where the field comes from, separating the table name from the field name by a single period.**

The + (addition) operator

If you want to create a calculated field in a query for adding the value of tax to the price, you would use an expression similar to this: `[TaxAmt]+[tblSalesLineItems].[Price]`. To use this expression, you would have to create another calculated field in the query named `[TaxAmt]` that you create using the multiplication operator — `TaxAmt: [tblSales].[TaxRate] * [tblSalesLineItems].[Price]`. You could also create a form for adding the values in fields, such as `GrossAmount` and `Tax`, in which case you would use the expression `[GrossAmount] + [Tax]`. This simple formula uses the addition operator to add the contents of both fields and display the result in the object containing the formula.

Besides adding two numbers, you can use the addition operator to concatenate two character strings — putting two text-based strings together to form a single text string. For example, you may want to combine the fields `FirstName` and `LastName` from `tblContacts` to display them as a single field. This expression is:

```
[tblContacts].[FirstName] + [tblContacts].[LastName]
```

NOTE **You use the table name before the field name. In this example, specifying the table name isn't necessary because your tables only have one field named `FirstName` and one field named `LastName`; however, it is good practice to specify the table name containing this field, separating the table name from the field name by a single period.**

CAUTION **Although you can *concatenate* (join) text strings by using the addition operator, you should use the ampersand (&) operator to avoid confusing Access. You can find more on this in the "String operators" section, later in this chapter.**

The – (subtraction) operator

An example of using the subtraction operator on the same form is to calculate the final invoice amount by subtracting a calculated discount from the price. The formula to determine the net invoice amount of an item would be as follows:

```
[tblSalesLineItems].[Price] - ([tblSalesLineItems].[Price] *
[tblSalesLineItems].[DiscountPercent])
```

NOTE **Although parentheses are not mathematical operators, they play an integral part in working with operators, as we discuss in the "Operator precedence" section, later in this chapter.**

The / (division) operator

You can use the division operator to divide two numbers and (as with the previous operators) display the result wherever you need it. Suppose, for example, that a pool of 212 people win the $1,000,000 lottery this week. The formula to determine each individual's payoff of $4,716.98 per person would be as follows:

```
1,000,000 / 212
```

The \ (integer division) operator

The integer division operator takes any two numbers (`number1` and `number2`), rounds them up or down to integers, divides the first by the second (`number1 / number2`), then drops the decimal portion of the result, leaving only the integer value. Here are some examples of how integer division differs from normal division:

Normal Division	Integer Conversion Division
100 / 6 = 16.667	100 \ 6 = 16
100.9 / 6.6 = 15.288	100.9 \ 6.6 = 14
102 / 7 = 14.571	102 \ 7 = 14

NOTE **Access rounds numbers based on the greater-than-0.5 rule: Any number with a decimal value of *x*.5 or less rounds down; greater than *x*.5 rounds up to the next whole number. This means that 6.49 and 6.5 become 6, but 6.51 and 6.6 become 7.**

CAUTION **The integer divide operator can be a confusing operator until you understand just what it does. Using it is equivalent to rounding both numbers in the division operation (101.9 = 102 and 6.6 = 7), then converting the answer to an integer (102 / 7 =14.571 = 14). *Remember:* It only rounds the numbers in the expression. It does not round the answer; it simply drops the remainder after the decimal point.**

The ^ (exponentiation) operator

The exponentiation operator (^) raises a number to the power of an exponent. Raising a number simply means indicating the number of times that you want to multiply a number by itself. For example, multiplying the value `4 x 4 x 4` (that is, 4^3) is the same as entering the formula `4^3`.

The Mod (Modulo) operator

The modulo operator (mod), or remainder operator, takes any two numbers (`number1` and `number2`), rounds them up or down to integers, divides the first by the second (`number1 / number2`), and then returns the remainder. Here are some examples of how modulo division compares to normal division:

Normal Division	Modulo Division	Explanation
10 / 5 = 2	10 Mod 5 = 0	10 is evenly divided by 5
10 / 4 = 2.5	10 Mod 4 = 2	10 / 4 = 2 with a remainder of 2
22.24 / 4 = 5.56	22.24 Mod 4 = 2	22 / 4 = 5 with a remainder of 2
22.52 / 4 = 5.63	22.52 Mod 4 = 3	23 / 4 = 5 with a remainder of 3

Relational operators

There are six basic relational operators (also known as *comparison operators*). They compare two values or expressions via an equation. The relational operators include the following:

=	Equal
<>	Not equal
<	Less than
<=	Less than or equal to
>	Greater than
>=	Greater than or equal to

The expressions built from relational operators always return either a logical value or `Null`; the value they return says Yes (True), No (not True; that is, False), or `Null` (unknown/no value).

Access actually returns a numeric value for relational operator equations. It returns a –1 (negative 1) for True and a 0 (zero) for False.

If either side of an equation is a `Null` value, the result will always be a `Null`.

The = (equal) operator

The equal operator returns a logical True if the two expressions being compared are the same. Here are two examples of the equal operator:

`[tblProducts].[Category] = "Car"`	Returns a `True` if the `Category` is a car; `False` is returned for any other `Category`.
`[tblSales].[SaleDate] = Date()`	Returns a `True` if the date in the `SaleDate` field is today.

The <> (not-equal) operator

The not-equal operator is exactly the opposite of the equal operator. In this example, the car example is changed to not-equal:

`[tblProducts].[Category] <> "Car"`	Returns a True if `Type of Category` is anything but a car.
`[tblProducts].[Category] != "SUV"`	Returns a True if `Type of Category` is anything but an SUV.

Notice that you have two different ways to express not equal to: The <> or `!=` symbols mean exactly the same thing.

The < (less-than) operator

The less-than operator returns a logical `True` if the left side of the equation is less than the right side, as in this example:

`[tblSalesLineItems].[Price] < 1000`	Returns a `True` if the `Price` field contains a value of less than 1000.

The <= (less-than-or-equal-to) operator

The less-than-or-equal-to operator returns a `True` if the left side of the equation is either less than or equal to the right side, as in this example:

`[tblSalesLineItems].[Price] <= 2500`	Returns a `True` if the value of `Price` equals 2500 or is less than 2500.
`[tblSalesLineItems].[Price] !> 1500`	Returns a `True` if the value of `Price` equals 1500 or is less than 1500.

Notice, in the second example, that you got the same results using the operator `!>` (not greater than). In other words, less than or equal to can be expressed using either operator, <= or `!>`.

Access 2007 is sensitive to the order of the operators. Access reports an error if you enter =<; the order is important. It must be less than or equal to (<=).

The > (greater-than) operator

The greater-than operator is the exact opposite of the less-than operator. This operator returns a `True` when the left side of the equation is greater than the right side, as in this example:

`[tblSales].[TaxRate] > 3.5`	Returns `True` if the value of `TaxRate` is greater than 3.5.

The >= (greater-than-or-equal-to) operator

The greater-than-or-equal-to operator returns a `True` if the left side of the equation is either greater than or equal to the right side. For example:

`[tblSales].[TaxRate] >= 5`	Returns a `True` if the value of `TaxRate` equals 5 or is greater than 5.
`[tblSales].[TaxRate] !< 5`	Returns a `True` if the value of `TaxRate` equals 5 or is greater than 5.

Notice, in the second example, that you got the same results using the operator `!<` (not less than). In other words, greater than or equal to can be expressed using either operator, >= or `!<`.

Access 2007 is sensitive to the order of the operators. Access reports an error if you enter =>; the order is important. It must be greater than or equal to (>=).

String operators

Access has three string operators, also know as *text operators*. Unlike the other operators, these work specifically with the Text data type:

`&`	Concatenation
`Like`	Similar to . . .
`NOT Like`	Not similar to . . .

The & (concatenation) operator

The concatenation operator concatenates or joins two or more values into a single string. This operator works similarly to the addition operator. Unlike the addition operator, however, the `&` operator always returns a string value. For instance, this example produces a single string:

```
[FirstName] & [LastName]
```

However, in the resultant string, no spaces are automatically added. If `[FirstName]` equals "Fred" and `[LastName]` equals "Smith", concatenating the field contents yields `FredSmith`. To add a space between the strings, you must add a string containing a space between the two fields:

```
[FirstName] & " " & [LastName]
```

This concatenation operator easily joins a string with a number- or date-type value. Using the `&` eliminates the need for special functions to convert numbers or dates to strings.

Suppose, for example, that you have a Number field, which is `HouseNumber`, and a Text field, which is `StreetName`, and that you want to build an expression that combines both fields. For this, enter the following:

```
[HouseNumber] & " " & [StreetName]
```

If `HouseNumber` has a value of `1600` and `StreetName` is `Pennsylvania Avenue N.W.`, the resulting string is:

```
"1600 Pennsylvania Avenue N.W."
```

Perhaps on a report you want to print the `OperatorName` field and the date and time the report was run at the bottom of the page. This can be accomplished by creating a calculated field using syntax similar to the following:

```
"This report was printed " & Now() & " by " & [OperatorName]
```

Notice the spaces after the word *printed* and before and after the word *by*. If the date is March 21, 2007, and the time is 4:45 p.m., the expression looks something like this:

```
This report was printed 3/21/07 4:45:40 PM by Jim Simpson
```

Knowing how the concatenation operator works makes maintaining your database expressions easier. If you always use the concatenation operator (&) — instead of the addition operator (+) — for creating concatenated text strings, you won't have to be concerned with the data types of the concatenated objects. Any formula that uses the `&` operator converts all the objects being concatenated to a string data type for you. Using the plus sign (+) to concatenate strings can sometimes lead to unpredictable results because Access must decide whether the operands are numbers or strings, and act accordingly. The concatenation operator forces Access to treat the operands as strings and always returns a string as a result.

If both operands are `Null`, the result is also a `Null`. If only one of the two objects is `Null`, Access ignores the `Null` object and builds the string from the other operand.

The Like (similar to) and Not Like operators

The `Like` operator, and its opposite, the `Not Like` operator, are used to compare two string expressions. These operators determine whether one expression matches, or doesn't match, the pattern of another expression. The resultant value of the comparison is a `True`, `False`, or `Null`.

The `Like` operator uses the following basic syntax:

```
expression Like pattern
```

Like looks for the *expression* in the *pattern;* if it is present, the operation returns a `True`. For example:

`[FirstName] Like "John"`	Returns a `True` if the first name is `John`.
[LastName] Like "SMITH"	Returns a `True` if the last name is `Smith`, `Smithson`, or any other name beginning with `"Smith"`, regardless of capitalization. (Wildcards like "*" are discussed in the next section.)
[State] Not Like "NY"	Returns a True for any state, except New York.

If either expression in the `Like` formula is a `Null`, the result is a `Null`.

This operator provides a powerful and flexible tool for string comparisons. Wildcard characters also increase the flexibility of the `Like` operator. (see the sidebar "Using Wildcards").

Using Wildcards

Access lets you use these five wildcards with the `Like` operator:

Character	Matches
?	A single character (A to Z, 0 to 9)
*	Any number of characters (0 to n)
#	Any single digit (0 to 9)
`[list]`	Any single character in the list
`[!list]`	Any single character not in the list

Both `[list]` and `[!list]` can use the hyphen between two characters to signify a range.

Here are some examples that use wildcards with the Like operator:

Expression	Result
`[tblContacts].[LastName] Like "Mc*"`	Returns a `True` for any last name that begins with "Mc" or "MC". "McDonald", "McJamison", "MCWilliams" all return `True`; "Jones" and "Mitchell" return `False`.
`[Answer] Like "[A-D]"`	Returns a `True` if the Answer is A, B, C, D, a, b, c, or d. Any other letter returns a `False`.
`"AB1989" Like "AB####"`	Returns a `True` because the string begins with the letters *AB* and is followed by any four numbers.
`[LastName] Not Like "[A,E,I,O,U]*"`	Returns a `True` for any last name that DOES NOT begin with a vowel. "Smith" and "Jones" return `True`; "Adams" and "O'Malley" return False.
`[City] Like "?????"`	Returns a `True` for any city that is five characters long.

If the pattern you're trying to match actually contains a wildcard character, you must enclose the wildcard character in brackets. In the example:

```
"AB*Co" Like "AB[*]C*"
```

the `[*]` in the third position of the pattern object will look for the asterisk as the third character of the string. Since the asterisk character is enclosed in brackets, it won't be mistaken for the asterisk wildcard character.

Boolean (logical) operators

Access uses six Boolean operators. Also referred to as *logical operators,* you use these for creating multiple conditions in expressions. Like relational operators, these always return either a logical `True` or `False` or a `Null`. Boolean operators include the following:

`And`	Logical and
`Or`	Logical inclusive or
`Eqv`	Logical equivalence
`Imp`	Logical implication
`Xor`	Logical exclusive or
`Not`	Logical not

The And operator

You use the *And operator* to perform a logical conjunction of two expressions; the operator returns the value `True` if both expressions return `True` values. The general syntax of an `And` operation is:

```
expression 1 And expression 2
```

Here is an example:

`[tblContacts].[State] = "MA" And [tblContacts].[ZipCode] = "02379-"`	Returns a True only if both expressions return True values.

If the expressions on both sides of the `And` operator are `True`, the result is a `True` value. Table 5-1 demonstrates the results.

TABLE 5-1

And Operator Resultants

Expression 1	Expression 2	Expression 1 And Expression 2
True	True	True
True	False	False
True	Null	Null

Expression 1	Expression 2	Expression 1 And Expression 2
False	True	False
False	False	False
False	Null	False
Null	True	Null
Null	False	False
Null	Null	Null

The Or operator

The `Or` operator is used to perform a logical disjunction of two expressions; the operator returns the value `True` if either condition returns a `True` value. The general syntax of an `Or` operation is

```
expression 1 Or expression 2
```

The following two examples show how the `Or` operator works:

`[LastName] = "Casey" Or [LastName] = "Gleason"`	Returns a True if LastName is either Casey or Gleason.
`[TaxLocation] = "TX" Or [TaxLocation] = "CT"`	Returns a True if the TaxLocation is either TX or CT.

If the condition of either side of the `Or` operator is true, the operator returns a `True` value. Table 5-2 demonstrates the results.

TABLE 5-2

Or Expression Resultants

Expression 1	Expression 2	Expression 1 Or Expression 2
True	True	True
True	False	True
True	Null	True
False	True	True
False	False	False
False	Null	Null
Null	True	True
Null	False	Null
Null	Null	Null

The Not operator

The *Not operator* is used for negating a numeric or boolean expression. The Not operator returns the value `True` if the expression is `False` and `False` if the expression is `True`. This operator reverses the logical result of an expression.

The general syntax of a `Not` operation is:

```
Not [numeric|boolean] expression
```

The following examples show how to use the *Not* operator:

`Not [Price] <= 100000`	Returns a `True` if `Price` is greater than 100000.
If Not (City = "Seattle") Then	Returns True for any city that is not Seattle

If the operand is `Null`, the Not operator returns `Null`. Table 5-3 demonstrates the results.

TABLE 5-3

Not Operator Resultants

Expression	Not Expression
True	False
False	True
Null	Null

Miscellaneous operators

Access has three very useful miscellaneous operators:

`Between...And`	Range
`In`	List comparison
`Is`	Reserved word

The Between...And operator

Use the `Between...And` operator to determine whether one expression's value is within a specific range of values. This is the general syntax:

```
expression Between value 1 And value 2
```

If the value of the expression is between `value 1` and `value 2`, or equal to *value 1* or *value* 2, the result is `True`; otherwise, it is `False`.

The following examples show how to use the `Between...And` operator:

`[TotalCost] Between 10000 And 19999`	Returns a `True` if the `TotalCost` is between 10,000 and 19,999, or equal to 10,000 or 19,999.
`[SaleDate] Between #1/1/2007# and #12/31/2007#`	Returns a True when the `SaleDate` is in the year 2007.

The In operator

The `In` operator is used to determine whether one expression's value is equal to any value in a specific list. This is the general syntax:

```
expression In (value1, value2, value3, ...)
```

If the value is found in the list, the result is `True`; otherwise, the result is `False`.

The following example uses the `In` operator as a field's criteria for a query:

```
In ('SUV','Minivans')
```

This displays only those vehicles that are SUVs or minivans.

The Is (reserved word) operator

The `Is` operator is used only with the keyword `Null` to determine whether an object has nothing in it. This is the general syntax:

```
expression Is Null
```

The following example uses the `Is` operator:

`[LastName] Is Null`	Returns `True` if no data was entered in the `LastName` field.

To eliminate records from a query where a particular field doesn't contain data, enter `Is Not Null` as the criteria for that field.

Operator precedence

When you work with complex expressions that have many operators, Access must determine which operator to evaluate first, and then which is next, and so forth. To do this, Access has a built-in predetermined order, known as *operator precedence*. Access always follows this order unless you use parentheses to specify otherwise.

Parentheses are used to group parts of an expression and override the default order of precedence. Operations within parentheses are performed before any operations outside of them. Inside the parentheses, Access follows the predetermined operator precedence.

Precedence is determined first according to category of the operator. The operator rank by order of precedence is:

1. Mathematical
2. Comparison
3. Boolean

Each category contains its own order of precedence, which we explain next.

The mathematical precedence

Within the general category of mathematical operators, this order of precedence is in effect:

1. Exponentiation
2. Negation
3. Multiplication and/or division (left to right)
4. Integer division
5. Modulo
6. Addition and/or subtraction (left to right)
7. String concatenation

The comparison precedence

Comparison operators observe this order of precedence:

1. Equal
2. Not equal
3. Less than
4. Greater than
5. Less than or equal to
6. Greater than or equal to
7. Like

The Boolean precedence

The Boolean operators follow this order of precedence:

1. Not
2. And
3. Or
4. Xor
5. Eqv
6. Imp

Precedence Order

Simple mathematics provides an example of order of precedence. Remember that Access performs operations within parentheses before operations that are not in parentheses. Also remember that multiplication and division operations are performed before addition or subtraction operations.

For example, what is the answer to this simple equation?

X=10+3*4

If your answer is 52, you need a better understanding of precedence in Access. If your answer is 22, you're right. If your answer is anything else, you need a calculator!

Multiplication is performed before addition by the rules of mathematical precedence. Therefore, the equation 10+3*4 is evaluated in this order: 3*4 is performed first, which yields an answer of 12. Twelve is then added to 10, which yields 22.

Look at what happens when you add parentheses to the equation. What is the answer to this simple equation?

X=(10+3)*4

Now the answer is 52. Within parentheses, the values 10 and 3 are added first; then the result (13) is multiplied by 4, which yields 52.

Moving beyond Simple Queries

Select queries are the most common type of query used; they select information (based on a specific criterion) from one or more related tables. With these queries, you can ask questions and receive answers about information that's stored in your database tables. In previous chapters, you work with queries that use simple criteria on a single field in a table with operators, such as equal (=) and greater than (>).

Knowing how to specify criteria is critical to designing and writing effective queries. Although queries can be used against a single table for a single criterion, many queries extract information from several tables using more complex criteria.

Because of this complexity, your queries are able to retrieve only the data you need, in the order that you need it. You may, for example, want to select and display data from the Access Auto Auctions database to get the following information:

- All buyers of Chevy cars or Ford trucks
- All buyers who have purchased something during the past 60 days
- All sales for items greater than $90,000
- The number of customers from each state
- Any customers that have made comments or complaints

As your database system evolves, you'll want to retrieve a subset of information like this. Select queries are the easiest way to obtain this information from one or more tables. Using operators and expressions, you create complex criteria to limit the number of records and calculated fields that display data differently than it's stored. This section uses select queries to demonstrate the use of these operators and expressions. Later, you'll apply this knowledge when working with forms, reports, and VBA code.

CROSS-REF **Chapter 4 gives an in-depth explanation of working with queries. For more on using operators and expressions on forms, reports, and in VBA, see Chapters 4, 9, and 13.**

Using query comparison operators

When working with select queries, you may need to specify one or more *criteria* to limit the scope of information shown. You specify criteria by using *comparison operators* in equations and calculations. The categories of operators are mathematical, relational, logical, and string. In select queries, operators are used in either the Field: or Criteria: cell of the QBE (Query by Example) pane.

Here's a good rule of thumb to observe:

> Use mathematical and string operators for creating calculated fields; use relational and logical operators for specifying criteria.

We discuss calculated fields in the "Creating a New Calculated Field in a Query" section, later in this chapter. You can find an in-depth explanation of operators in the "What Are Operators?" section, earlier in this chapter.

Table 5-4 shows most of the common operators that are used with select queries.

TABLE 5-4

Common Operators Used in Select Queries

Mathematical	Relational	Logical	String	Miscellaneous
* (multiply)	= (equal)	And	& (concatenate)	Between...And
/ (divide)	<> (not equal)	Or	Like	In
+ (add)	> (greater than)	Not	Not Like	Is Null
– (subtract)	< (less than)			Is Not Null

Using these operators, you can ferret out groups of records like these:

- Product records that include a picture
- A range of records, such as all sales between November and January

- Records that meet both And *and* Or criteria, such as all records that are cars and are not either a minivan or SUV
- All records that do *not* match a value, such as any category that is not a car

When you add a criterion to a query, you use the appropriate operator with an *example* of what you want. In Figure 5-1, the example is *Cars*. The operator is equal (=). Notice that the equal sign is *not* shown in the figure. The equal sign is the default operator for selection criteria.

FIGURE 5-1

The QBE pane shows a simple criterion asking for all vehicles where the Category is Cars.

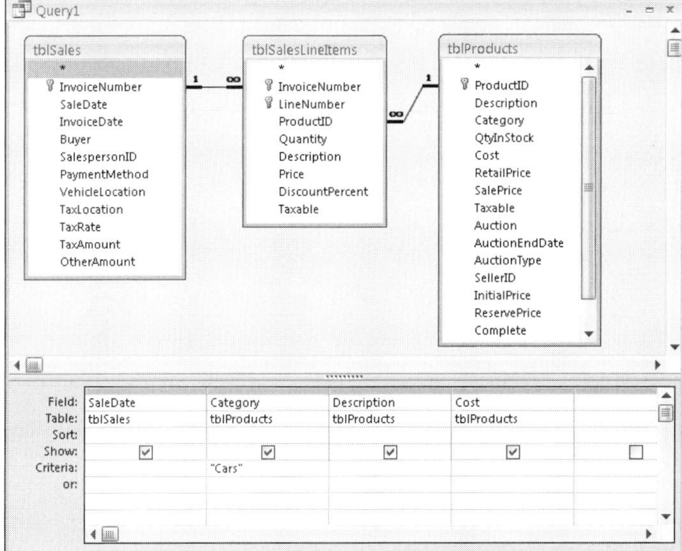

Understanding complex criteria selection

You build complex query criteria using any combination of the available operators shown in Table 5-4. For many queries, complex criteria consist of a series of Ands and Ors, as in these examples:

- State must be Connecticut *or* Texas
- City must be Sunnyville *and* state must be Georgia
- State must be MA *or* MO *and* city must be Springfield

These examples demonstrate the use of both logical operators: *And/Or*. Many times, you can create complex criteria by entering example data in different cells of the QBE pane. Figure 5-2 demonstrates how to create complex And/Or criteria without entering the operator keywords And/Or at all. This example displays all the buyers and their sales that satisfy the following criteria:

Live in either the state of Connecticut (CT) or the state of Massachusetts (MA) and whose product category is not a car.

You learn how to create this type of complex query in the "Entering Criteria in Multiple Fields" section, later in this chapter.

FIGURE 5-2

Creating complex And/Or criteria by example without using the And/Or operators. This Query uses both the Criteria row and the Or row of the QBE pane to combine the And/Or criteria through example.

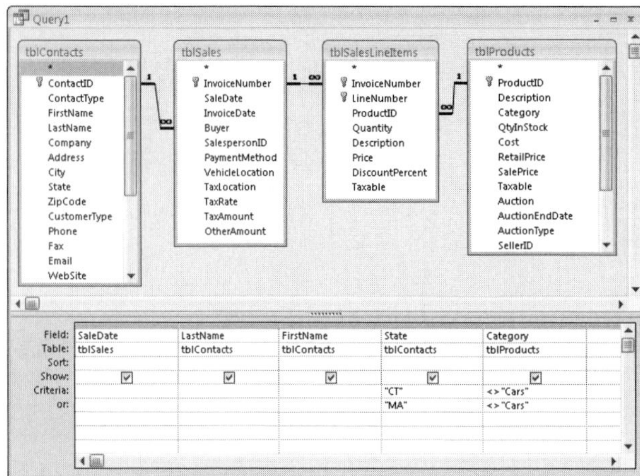

In the QBE pane, enter And criteria in the same row; enter Or criteria in different rows.

Access takes your graphical query and creates a single SQL `SELECT` statement to actually extract the information from your tables. Click the drop-down in the ribbon's View group and select SQL View to change the window's contents to display the SQL SELECT statement (shown in Figure 5-3), which Access creates from the fields and criteria placed in the QBE pane in Figure 5-2.

FIGURE 5-3

The SQL view for the query built in Figure 5-2. Notice that it contains a single `OR` statement and two `AND` statements (in the `WHERE` clause).

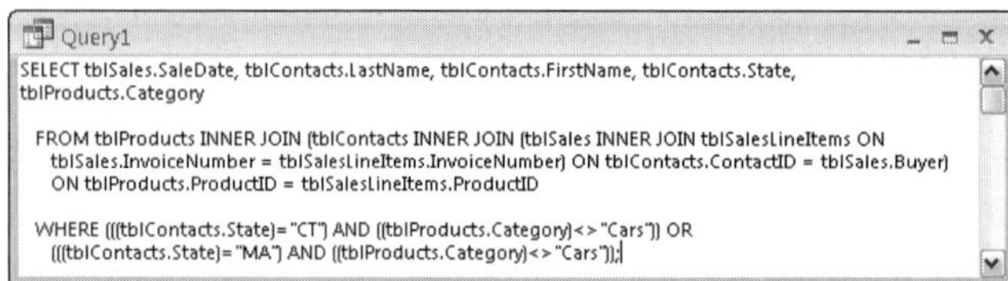

The SQL statement in Figure 5-3 has been separated by the author for clarification purposes. When you switch to SQL View in your database, you'll see one long multi-line statement with no breaks between sections.

NOTE Sometimes you see a field name referred to first by the table name and then by the field name, as shown in the SQL statement in Figure 5-3. When you see this kind of reference, it will have a dot (.) between the two names, such as `Customers.[Customer Name]`. This nomenclature tells you which table contains the field. This is especially critical when you're describing two fields that have the same name but are contained in different tables. In a multiple-table query, you see this format in the field list when you add a field to the QBE pane by clicking an empty column. You also see this format when you create a multiple-table form by using the field list. The general format is Table Name.Field Name. If the field name or table name contains spaces, you must surround the name with brackets [ ]; for example, `tblSales.[Date of Sale]` and `tblContacts.[Customer Last Name]`.

TIP We do not use spaces in table and field names; although many people do use spaces for better readability, it's a really good idea to not use spaces at all. This way, you don't have to use brackets around your field or object names. For example, name `tblContacts.[Customer Last Name]` without spaces between the words as `tblContacts.CustomerLastName`— eliminating the need for using brackets. Instead of using spaces, capitalize the first letter of each new word in the table and field name (e.g., tblSalesLineItems, FirstName, ZipCode, AuctionEndDate).

If you build an expression for this query (not the SQL statement), it looks similar to this example:

```
(tblContacts.State = "CT" AND tblProducts.Category <> "Cars") OR
(tblContacts.State = "MA" AND tblProducts.Category <> "Cars")
```

You must enter the category (<> `"Cars"`) for each state line in the QBE pane, as shown in Figure 5-2. In the "Entering Criteria in Multiple Fields" section, later in this chapter, you learn to use the `And/Or` operators in a Criteria: cell of the query, which eliminates the redundant entry of these fields.

TIP In this example, you looked for all vehicles that didn't contain cars in the `category` field. To find records that match a value, drop the use of the <> operator with the value. For example, enter the expression Cars to find all vehicles that have a category of cars. You don't have to use the equal (=) operator in the QBE pane when looking for matching values.

The `And/Or` operators are the most commonly used operators when working with complex criteria. The operators consider two different formulas (one on each side of the `And/Or` operators) and then determine individually whether they are `True` or `False`. Then the operators compare the results of the two formulas against each other for a logical `True/False` answer. For example, take the first `And` statement in the formula given in the preceding paragraph:

```
(tblContacts.State = "CT" AND tblProducts.Category <> "Cars")
```

The first half of the formula, `tblContacts.State = "CT"`, converts to a `True` if the state is `CT` (`False` if a different state; `Null` if no state was entered in the field).

Then the second half of the formula, tblProducts.Category <> "Cars", is converted to a True if the Category is anything except Cars (False if Cars; Null if no category was entered). The And compares the logical True/False from each side against the other side to return a True/False answer.

NOTE A field has a Null value when it has no value at all; it is the lack of entry of information in a field. Null is neither True nor False; nor is it equivalent to all spaces or zero — it simply has no value. If you never enter a city name in the City field and just skip it, Access leaves the field empty. This state of emptiness is known as Null.

When the result of an And/Or operation is True, the overall condition is True, and the query displays those records meeting the True condition. Table 5-5 reviews the True and False conditions for each operator.

TABLE 5-5

Results of Logical Operators And/Or

Left Side Is	Operator Is	Right Side Is	Resultant Answer Is
True	AND	True	True
True	AND	False	False
False	AND	True	False
False	AND	False	False
True	AND	Null	Null
Null	AND	True	Null
False	AND	Null	False
Null	AND	False	False
True	OR	True	True
True	OR	False	True
False	OR	True	True
True	OR	Null	True
Null	OR	True	True
False	OR	False	False
False	OR	Null	Null
Null	OR	False	Null

Notice that the result of an And operation is True only when both sides of the formula are True, whereas the result of an Or operation is True when either side of the formula is True. In fact, one side can be a Null value, and the result of the Or operation will still be True if the other side is True. This is the difference between And/Or operators.

Using functions in select queries

When you work with queries, you may want to use built-in Access functions to display information. For example, you may want to display items such as:

- The day of the week (Sunday, Monday, and so forth) for sales dates
- All customer names in uppercase
- The difference between two date fields

You can display all this information by creating calculated fields for the query. We discuss calculated fields in depth later in this chapter.

Referencing fields in select queries

When you work with a field name in queries, as you do with calculated fields or criteria values, you should enclose the field name in square brackets (`[]`). Access requires brackets around any field name that is in a criterion and around any field name that contains a space or punctuation. An example of a field name in brackets is the criterion `[tblSales].[SaleDate] + 30`.

If you omit the brackets (`[ ]`) around a field name in the criterion, Access may automatically place quotes around the field name and treat it as text instead of a field name.

Entering Single-Value Field Criteria

You'll encounter situations in which you want to limit the query records returned on the basis of a single field criterion, such as in these queries:

- Customer (buyer) information for customers living in the state of New York
- Sales of any motor homes
- Customers who bought anything in the month of January

Each of these queries requires a single-value criterion. Simply put, a *single-value criterion* is the entry of only one expression in a field. That expression can be example data, such as `NY`, or a function, such as `DatePart("m",[SaleDate]) = 1`. Criteria expressions can be specified for any data type: Text, Numeric, Date/Time, and so forth. Even OLE Object and Counter field types can have criteria specified.

NOTE

All the examples in this chapter rely on several tables: `tblContacts`, `tblSales`, `tblSalesLineItems`, and `tblProducts`. The `Chapter05Start.accdb` database contains the tables used in this chapter. The majority of these examples use only the `tblContacts` and `tblSales` tables.

Each series of steps in this chapter tells you which tables and fields make up the query. For most examples, you should clear all previous criteria. Each example focuses on the criteria line of the QBE pane. Examine each figure closely to make sure you understand the correct placement of the criteria in each example.

Entering character (Text or Memo) criteria

You use character criteria for Text or Memo data-type fields. These are either examples or patterns of the contents of the field. To create a text criterion to display customers who live in New York state, for example, follow these steps:

1. **Open a new query in Design View based on `tblContacts` and add the `FirstName`, `LastName`, and `State` fields to the QBE pane.**
2. **Click the Criteria: cell for `State` field.**
3. **Type** NY **in the cell.**

   Your query should look similar to the query shown in Figure 5-4. Notice that only one table is open and only three fields are selected. Click the Datasheet View command in the Home ribbon's Views group to see the results of this query.

FIGURE 5-4

The Datasheet window showing `tblContacts` open. You see the example data NY in the Criteria row under the `State` field.

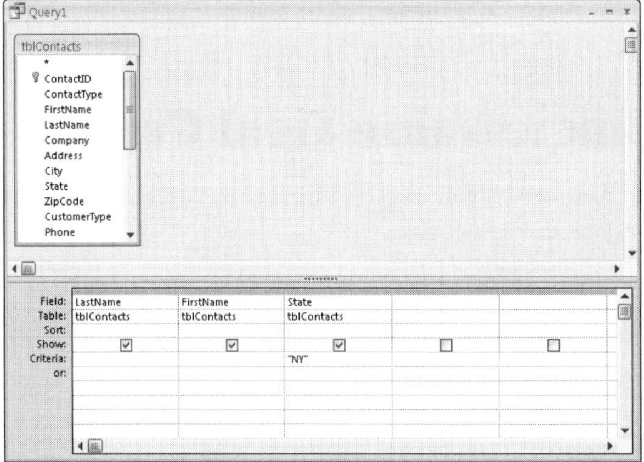

TIP **When specifying example-type criteria, it isn't necessary to match capitalization. Access defaults to case-insensitive when working with queries. Entering NY, ny, or nY provides the same results.**

You don't have to enter an equal sign before the literal word *NY* because Access uses the equal operator as the default operator. To see all states except Ny, you must enter either the <> (not equal) or the `Not` operator before the word *NY*.

You also don't have to type quotes around the word *NY*. Access assumes that you're using an example literal *NY* and adds the quotes for you automatically.

TIP If you type quotation marks, you should use the double quotation mark to surround literals. Access normally uses the single quotation mark as a remark character in its programming language. However, when you use the single quotation mark in the Criteria: cell, Access interprets it as a double quotation mark.

The Like operator and wildcards

In previous sections, you worked with *literal* criteria. You specified the exact field contents for Access to find, which was "NY" in the previous example. Access used the literal to retrieve the specific records. Sometimes, however, you know only a part of the field contents, or you may want to see a wider range of records on the basis of a pattern. For example, you may want to see all buyer information for those buyers who bought vehicles made in the 1950s (where descriptions begin with the characters *195*); so you need to check 1950, 1951, 1952, and so forth. Here's a more practical example: Suppose you have a buyer who has purchased a couple of red cars in the last year. You remember making a note of it in the `Comments` field about the color, but you don't remember which customer it was. To find these records, you're required to use a wildcard search against the *Comments* field in *tblProducts* to find any records that contain the word *Red*.

Access uses the string operator `Like` in the Criteria: cell of a field to perform wildcard searches against the field's contents. Access searches for a pattern in the field; you use the question mark (`?`) to represent a single character or the asterisk (`*`) for several characters. (This works just like filenames at the DOS level.) In addition to these two characters (`?` and `*`), Access uses three other characters for wildcard searches. Table 5-6 lists the wildcards that the `Like` operator can use.

The question mark (`?`) stands for any single character located in the same position as the question mark in the example expression. An asterisk (`*`) stands for any number of characters in the same position in which the asterisk is placed. Access can use the asterisk any number of times in an example expression. The pound sign (`#`) stands for any single digit (0-9) found in the same position as the pound sign. The brackets (`[]`) and the list they enclose stand for any single character that matches any one character in the list located within the brackets. Finally, the exclamation point (`!`) inside the brackets represents the `Not` word for the list — that is, any single character that does not match any character in the list within the brackets.

TABLE 5-6

Wildcards Used by the Like Operator

Wildcard	Purpose
`?`	A single character (0–9, Aa–Zz)
`*`	Any number of characters (0–*n*)
`#`	Any single digit (0–9)
`[list]`	Any single character in the list
`[!list]`	Any single character not in the list

These wildcards can be used alone or in conjunction with each other. They can even be used several times within the same expression. The examples in Table 5-6 demonstrate how you can use the wildcards.

To create an example using the `Like` operator, let's suppose that you want to find the record of a sports car with an exterior color of red. You know that the word *Red* is used in one of the records in the `Features` field of `tblProducts`. To create the query, follow these steps:

1. **Add the four tables:** `tblContacts`, `tblSales`, `tblSalesLineItems`, **and** `tblProducts`.
2. **Select** `LastName` **and** `FirstName` **from** `tblContacts`, **and select** `Description` **and** `Features` **from** `tblProducts`, **and add them to the QBE pane.**

   Although not necessary, you may want to set an Ascending sort order in the `LastName` and `FirstName` fields.
3. **Click the Criteria: cell of the** `Features` **field.**
4. **Type** * red * **in the cell.**

   Be sure to put a space between the first asterisk and the *r* and the last asterisk and the *d*—in other words, put spaces before and after the word *red.*

TIP **In the preceding steps, you put a space before and after the word *red.* If you did not, Access would find all words that have the word red in them, like *aired, bored, credo, fired, geared, restored,* and on and on. By placing a space before and after the word *red,* Access is being told to look for the word *red* only. Of course, it would not find *black/red* or *red/black* with spaces around the word. If you need to find these, you could put them as additional criteria in the or cells.**

When you click outside the Criteria: cell, Access automatically adds the `Like` operator and the quotation marks around the expression. Your query QBE pane should look similar to the one shown in Figure 5-5.

FIGURE 5-5

Using the `Like` operator with a select query in a `Memo` field. In this case, the query looks for the word *red* in the `Features` field.

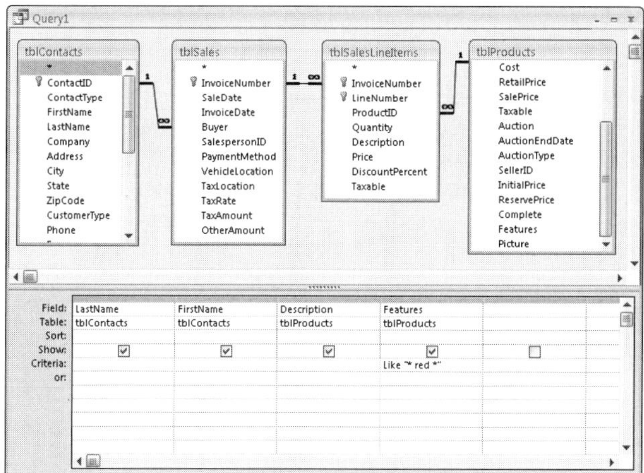

After creating this query, click on the Datasheet View command to view the query's results. It should look similar to the one shown in Figure 5-6.

FIGURE 5-6

The results of using the `Like` operator with a select query in a `Memo` field; the query looks for the word *red* in the `Features` field.

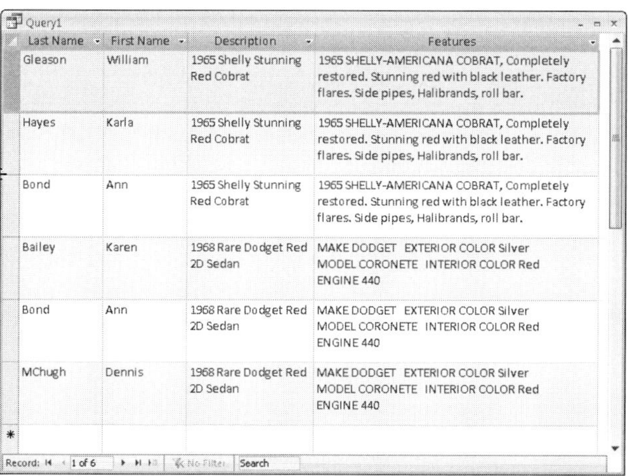

Last Name	First Name	Description	Features
Gleason	William	1965 Shelly Stunning Red Cobrat	1965 SHELLY-AMERICANA COBRAT, Completely restored. Stunning red with black leather. Factory flares. Side pipes, Halibrands, roll bar.
Hayes	Karla	1965 Shelly Stunning Red Cobrat	1965 SHELLY-AMERICANA COBRAT, Completely restored. Stunning red with black leather. Factory flares. Side pipes, Halibrands, roll bar.
Bond	Ann	1965 Shelly Stunning Red Cobrat	1965 SHELLY-AMERICANA COBRAT, Completely restored. Stunning red with black leather. Factory flares. Side pipes, Halibrands, roll bar.
Bailey	Karen	1968 Rare Dodget Red 2D Sedan	MAKE DODGET EXTERIOR COLOR Silver MODEL CORONETE INTERIOR COLOR Red ENGINE 440
Bond	Ann	1968 Rare Dodget Red 2D Sedan	MAKE DODGET EXTERIOR COLOR Silver MODEL CORONETE INTERIOR COLOR Red ENGINE 440
MChugh	Dennis	1968 Rare Dodget Red 2D Sedan	MAKE DODGET EXTERIOR COLOR Silver MODEL CORONETE INTERIOR COLOR Red ENGINE 440

Record: 1 of 6 No Filter Search

TIP To make your query look like the one shown in Figure 5-6, you need to widen the `Description` and `Features` fields to see more of the contents and expand the number of lines to show for each record. To make the height of each record more than one line, select the line between any two records in the record selector bar, as shown in Figure 5-6, between the first and second record. When the cursor becomes a small line with arrows pointing up and down, click and drag the field down to make each record show more lines.

Clicking on the Datasheet View command on the ribbon, you see that eight records match your query request — a red vehicle. Looking closer at the results, you see that although there are eight records that match your criteria of the word *red* in the `Features` field, they do not all show red exterior color cars. In this case, you will have to physically examine each record to see if the *exterior* color of the vehicle is red (versus the interior being red). If you need to see records where the `Features` may show black/red or red/black, you will need to refine your search. These records are only those that have the standalone word *red*.

Access automatically adds the `Like` operator and quotation marks if you meet these conditions:

- Your expression contains no spaces.
- You use only the wildcards `?`, `*`, and `#`.
- You use brackets (`[ ]`) inside quotation marks (`" "`).

If you use the brackets without quotation marks, you must supply the `Like` operator and the quotation marks.

Using the `Like` operator with wildcards is the best way to perform pattern searches through memo fields. It is just as useful in text and date fields as the examples in Table 5-7 demonstrate.

TABLE 5-7

Using Wildcards with the Like Operator

Expression	Field Used In	Results of Criteria
`Like "Ca*"`	`tblContacts.LastName`	Finds all records of contacts whose last name begin with *Ca*. Examples: Carson and Casey
`Like "* red *"`	`tblProducts.Features`	Finds all records of products with the word *red* anywhere within the `Features` field.
`Like "C*"`	`tblSales.TaxLocation`	Finds all records of sales in states that begin with the letter *C*.
`Like "9/*/2007"`	`tblSales.SaleDate`	Finds all records of sales for the month of September 2007.
`Like "## South Main"`	`tblContacts.Address`	Finds all records of contacts with houses containing house numbers between 10 and 99 inclusively. Examples: 10, 22, 33, 51 on South Main

Expression	Field Used In	Results of Criteria
`Like "[CDF]*"`	`tblContacts.City`	Finds all records of contacts for customers who live in any city with a name beginning with *C, D,* or *F.*
`Like "[!EFG]*"`	`tblContacts.City`	Finds all records of contacts who do not live in any city that begins with the letters *E, F,* or *G;* all other city records are displayed.

Table 5-7 shows several examples that can be used to search records in the tables of the Access Auto Auctions database.

Specifying non-matching values

To specify a non-matching value, you simply use either the `Not` or the <> operator in front of the expression that you don't want to match. For example, you may want to see all contacts who have purchased a vehicle , but you want to exclude buyers from New York state. Follow these steps to see how to specify this non-matching value:

1. **Open a new query in Design View, and add `tblContacts` and `tblSales`.**

TIP **If you only add the `tblContacts` table, you will see both sellers and buyers. When you add both tables, the query only displays buyers because `tblContacts.ContactID` is linked to `tblSales.Buyer`; the query only shows contacts who appear as a buyer in `tblSales` — thus eliminating the sellers.**

2. **Add LastName, FirstName, and State from tblContacts.**
3. **Click in the Criteria: cell of `State`.**
4. **Type** Not NY **in the cell.**

   Access automatically places quotation marks around NY if you don't do so before you leave the field. You can also use <> instead of the word `Not` as in Figure 5-7. The query should look similar to the one shown in Figure 5-7. The query selects all records *except* those for buyers who live in the State of New York.

NOTE **You can use the <> operator instead of `Not` in Step 4 of the previous instructions to exclude New York (NY). The result is the same with either operator. These two operators are interchangeable except with the use of the keyword `Is`. You cannot say `Is <> Null`. Rather, you must say `Not Is Null` or more accurately `Is Not Null`.**

FIGURE 5-7

Using the `Not` operator in criteria. Entering **Not NY** in the `State` field displays all records except those where the state is NY (New York).

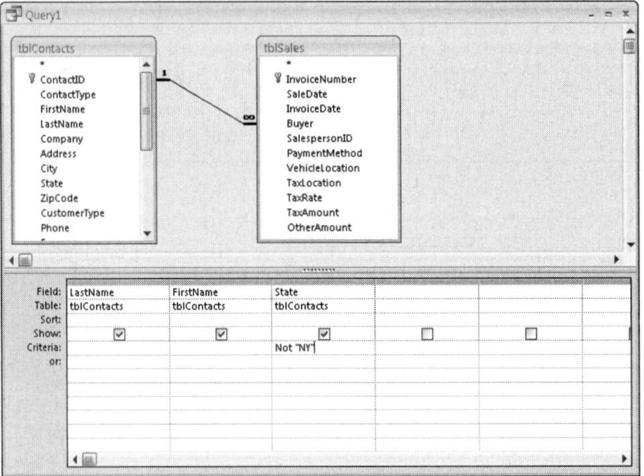

Entering numeric (Number, Currency, or Counter) criteria

You use numeric criteria with Number, Currency, or Counter data-type fields. You simply enter the numbers and the decimal symbol — if required — following the mathematical or comparison operator. For example, you may want to see all sales where the vehicle price was under $10,000. To create a query like this, follow these steps:

1. **Open a new query in Design View, and add `tblSalesLineItems` and `tblProducts`.**
2. **Add `Price` from `tblSalesLineItems`, and `Description` and `Category` from `tblProducts`.**
3. **Click in the Sort: cell for `Price`.**
4. **Select `Ascending` from the drop-down list.**
5. **Click in the Criteria: cell for `Price`.**
6. **Type <10000 in the cell.**

   When you follow these steps, your query looks similar to the query shown in Figure 5-8. When working with numeric data, Access doesn't enclose the expression with quotes, as it does with string criteria.

FIGURE 5-8

Criteria set for price of vehicles. Here the criteria is less than (<)10000.

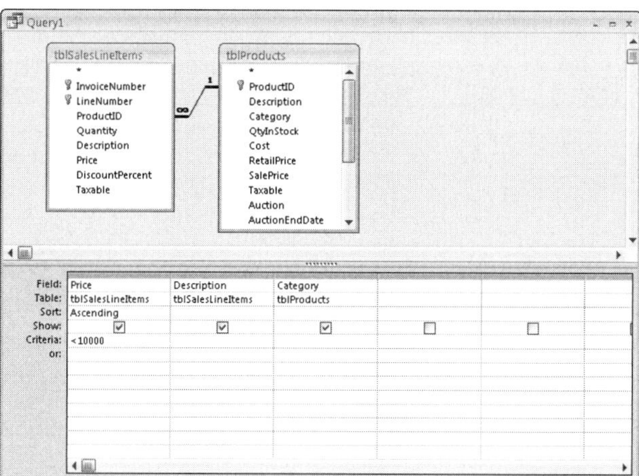

Running this query should show 24 records under $10,000 sorted by price from $700 to $7,800.

Numeric fields are generally compared to a value string that uses comparison operators, such as less than (<), greater than (>), or equal to (=). If you want to specify a comparison other than equal, you must enter the operator as well as the value. Remember that Access defaults to equal when an operator is not specified in criteria. That is why you needed to specify less than (<) 10000 in the previous example query for vehicles under $10,000.

Working with Currency and Counter data in a query is exactly the same as working with Numeric data; you simply specify an operator and a numeric value.

Entering Yes/No (logic) criteria

Yes/No criteria are used with Yes/No type fields. The example data that you supply in the criteria can be for only `Yes` or `No` states. You can also use the `Not` and the <> operators to signify the opposite, but the `Yes/No` data also has a `Null` state that you may want to check for. Access recognizes several forms of `Yes` and `No`. Table 5-8 lists all the available positive and negative values.

Thus, instead of typing **Yes**, you can type any of these in the Criteria: cell: **On**, **True**, **Not No**, **<> No**, **<No**, or **-1**.

NOTE **A `Yes/No` field can have three states: `Yes`, `No`, and `Null`. `Null` only occurs when no default value was set in a table and the value has not yet been entered. Checking for "Is Null" displays only records with no value, and checking for "Is Not Null" always displays all `Yes` or `No` records. After a `Yes/No` field check box is checked (or checked and then deselected), it can never be `Null`. It must be either `Yes` or `No` (–1 or 0).**

TABLE 5-8

Positive and Negative Values Used in Yes/No Fields

Yes	True	On	Not No	<> No	<No	-1
No	False	Off	Not Yes	<>Yes	>Yes	0

Entering a criterion for an OLE object

You can even specify a criterion for OLE objects: `Is Null` or `Is Not Null`. For example, suppose you don't have pictures for all the vehicles and you want to view only those records that have a picture of the vehicle — that is, those in which the picture is not null. You specify the `Is Not Null` criterion for the `Picture` field of `tblProducts`. After you do this, Access limits the records to those that have a picture in them.

Although `Is Not Null` is the correct syntax, you can also type `Not Null` and Access supplies the `Is` operator for you.

Entering Multiple Criteria in One Field

In previous sections of this chapter, you worked with single-condition criteria on a single field. As you learned in those sections, you can specify single-condition criteria for any field type. In this section, you work with multiple criteria based on a single field. For example, you may be interested in seeing all records in which the buyer comes from either New York, New Jersey, or Pennsylvania. Or perhaps you want to view the records of all the vehicles that were sold during the first quarter of the year 2007.

The QBE pane has the flexibility to solve these types of problems. You can specify criteria for several fields in a select query. Using multiple criteria, for example, you can determine which customers are from New York or New Jersey ("NY" or "NJ") or which vehicles were sold for the past 90 days (`Between Date() And Date() - 90`).

You use the `And` and `Or` operators to specify several criteria for one field.

Understanding an Or operation

You use an `Or` operation in queries when you want a field to meet either of two conditions. For example, you may want to see all the records where the customer lives in either NY or NJ. In other words, you want to see all records where a customer lives in New York, in New Jersey, or both. The general formula for this operation is:

```
[State] = "NY" Or [State] = "NJ"
```

If either side of this formula is `True`, the resulting answer is also `True`. To clarify this point, consider these conditions:

- Customer 1 lives in NY — the formula is `True`.
- Customer 2 lives in NJ — the formula is `True`.
- Customer 3 lives in NY and NJ — the formula is `True`.
- Customer 4 lives in CT — the formula is `False`.

Specifying multiple values for a field using the Or operator

The `Or` operator is used to specify multiple values for a field. For example, you use the `Or` operator if you want to see all records of buyers who live in CT or NJ or NY. To do this, follow these steps:

1. **Open a new query in Design View, and add `tblContacts` and `tblSales`.**
2. **Add `FirstName`, `LastName`, and `State` from `tblContacts` and `SalesDate` from `tblSales`.**
3. **Click in the Sort: cell of `State`.**
4. **Select Ascending from the drop-down list.**
5. **Click in the Criteria: cell of `State`.**
6. **Type** CT Or NJ Or NY **in the cell.**

   Your QBE pane should resemble the one shown in Figure 5-9. Access automatically places quotation marks around your example data — CT, NJ, and NY.

FIGURE 5-9

Using the `Or` operator. Notice the two `Or` operators under the `State` field — CT Or NJ Or NY.

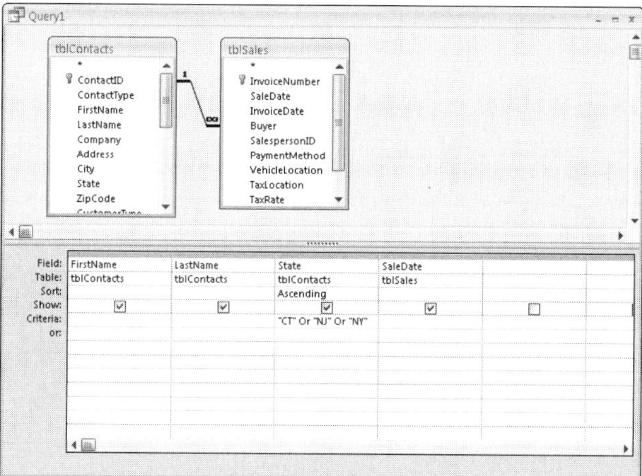

Using the Or: cell of the QBE pane

Besides using the literal `Or` operator in a single statement on the Criteria row under the `State` field, you can supply individual criteria for the field on separate rows of the QBE pane. To do this, enter the first criterion example in the Criteria: cell of the field. Then enter the second criterion example in the Or: cell of the same field. Enter the next criterion in the cell directly beneath the Or: example; and continue entering examples vertically down the column. This is equivalent to typing the `Or` operator between examples. Using the example in which you queried for NJ, NY, or CT, change your QBE pane to look like the one shown in Figure 5-10. Notice that each state abbreviation is on a separate row in the QBE pane.

FIGURE 5-10

Using the Or: cell of the QBE pane. You can place each bit of example data on its own row in the Or: cells.

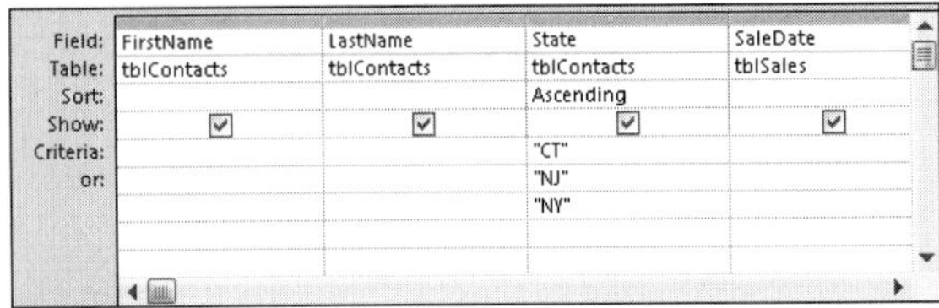

Access allows up to nine Or: cells for each field. If you need to specify more `Or` conditions, use the `Or` operator between conditions (for example: `CT Or NJ Or NY Or PA`).

Using a list of values with the In operator

Another method for specifying multiple values of a single field is using the In operator. The `In` operator finds a value that is one of a list of values. For example, type the expression **IN(CT, NJ, NY)** under the `State` field in the query used in Figure 5-10. The list of values in the parentheses becomes an example criterion. Your query should resemble the query shown in Figure 5-11.

In this example, quotation marks have been automatically added by Access around CT, NJ, and NY.

When you work with the `In` operator, each value (example data) must be separated from the others by a comma.

FIGURE 5-11

Using the `In` operator to find all records for buyer state being either CT, NJ, or NY.

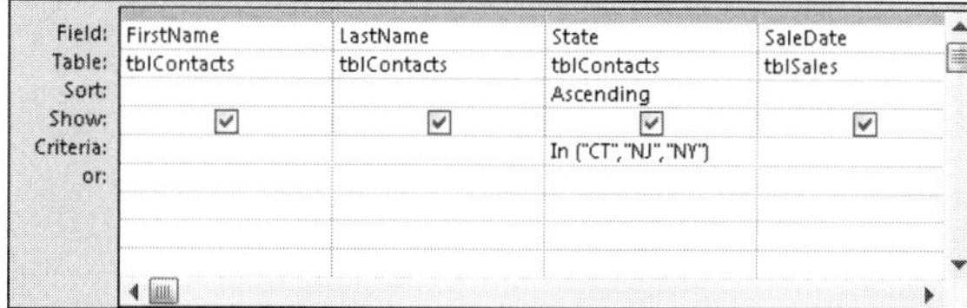

Understanding an And query

You use the `And` operator in queries when you want a field to meet two or more conditions that you specify. For example, you may want to see records of buyers that have purchased vehicles between October 1, 2007, and March 31, 2008. In other words, the sale had to have occurred during the last quarter of the year 2007 and first quarter of 2008. The general formula for this example is (parentheses are included in this example for clarity):

[SaleDate] >= 10/1/2007 And [SaleDate] <= 3/31/2008

Unlike the `Or` operation (which has several conditions under which it is `True`), the `And` operation is `True` only when both sides of the formula are `True`. To clarify use of the `And` operator, consider these conditions:

- `SaleDate` (9/22/2007) is not greater than 10/01/2007, but it is less than 3/31/2008 — the result is `False`.
- `SaleDate` (4/11/2008) is greater than 10/01/2007, but it is not less than 3/31/2008 — the result is `False`.
- `SaleDate` (11/22/2007) is greater than 10/01/2007, and it is less than 3/31/2008 — the result is `True`.

Both sides of the operation must be `True` for the `And` operation to be `True`.

Specifying a range using the And operator

The `And` operator is frequently used in fields that have Numeric or Date/Time data types. It is seldom used with Text data types, although it can be. For example, you may be interested in viewing all buyers whose names start with the letters *d*, *e*, or *f*. The `And` operator can be used here (> `"Cz"` `And` < `"G"`), although the `Like` operator is better (`Like "[DEF]*"`). Using an `And` operator with a single field sets a range of acceptable values in the field. Therefore, the key purpose of an `And` operator in a single field is to define a range of records to be viewed. For example, you can use the `And` operator to create a range criterion to display all buyers who have purchased vehicles between October 1, 2007, and March 31, 2008, inclusively. To create this query, follow these steps:

1. **Create a new query using** `tblContacts` **and** `tblSales`**.**
2. **Add** `FirstName` **and** `LastName` **from** `tblContacts` **and** `SaleDate` **from** `tblSales`**.**
3. **Click in the Criteria: cell of** `SaleDate`**.**
4. **Type** >= 10/1/2007 And <= 3/31/2008 **in the cell.**

   The query should resemble the one shown in Figure 5-12.

FIGURE 5-12

Using the `And` operator with numeric fields. Notice that this query shows all records for sales during the last quarter of 2007 and the first quarter of 2008.

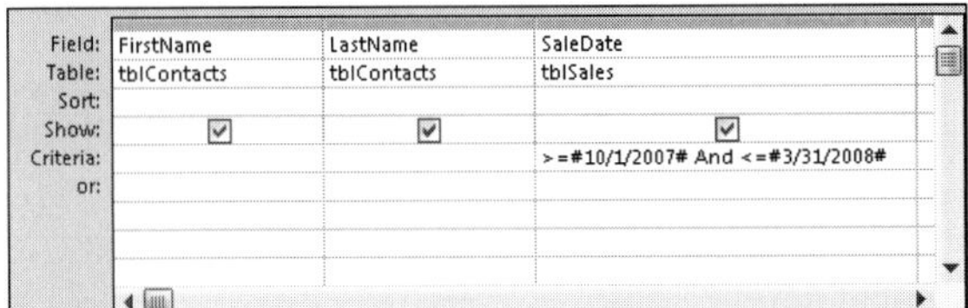

Using the Between...And operator

You can request a range of records based on criteria in a single field by using another method — the `Between...And` operator. With the `Between...And` operator, you can find records that meet a range of values — for example, all sales where the value of the vehicle was between $10,000 and $20,000. Using the example of sales between October 1, 2007, and March 31, 2008, create the query using the `Between...And` operator, as shown in Figure 5-13.

FIGURE 5-13

Using the `Between...And` operator. The results are the same as the query in Figure 5-12.

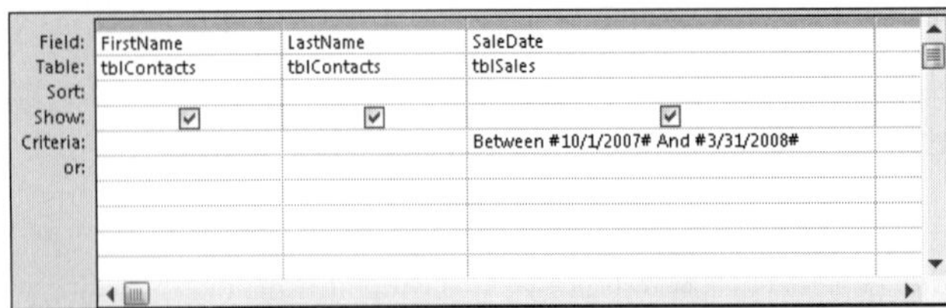

CAUTION **When you use the** `Between...And` **operator, the values entered in the** `Criteria` **field (in this example, 10/1/2007 and 3/31/2008) are (if they match) included in the results.**

Searching for Null data

A field may have no contents for several reasons: For example, perhaps the value wasn't known at the time of data entry, or the person who did the data entry simply forgot to enter the information, or the field's information was removed. Access does nothing with this field; it simply remains an empty field. (A field is said to be *null* when it's empty.)

Logically, a `Null` is neither `True` nor `False`. A `Null` field is not equivalent to all spaces or to zero. A `Null` field simply has no value.

Access lets you work with `Null` value fields by means of two special operators:

```
Is Null
Is Not Null
```

You use these operators to limit criteria based on `Null` values of a field. In the "Entering a criterion for an OLE object" section, earlier in this chapter, you learned that a `Null` value can be used to query for vehicles having a picture on file. In the next example, you look for buyers that don't have the `OrigCustDate` field filled in. To create this query, follow these steps:

1. **Create a new query using `tblContacts` and `tblSales`.**
2. **Add `OrigCustDate`, `FirstName`, and `LastName` from `tblContacts`, and `SaleDate` from `tblSales`.**
3. **Click in the Criteria: cell of `OrigCustDate`.**
4. **Type** Is Null **in the cell.**

   Your query should look like the query shown in Figure 5-14. Select the Datasheet View command to see the records that don't have a value in the `OrigCustDate` field. If you add a record to `tblContacts` and don't enter a value in this field, that record shows in this query's results since `OrigCustDate` contains a `Null` value.

FIGURE 5-14

If the table has records with the `OrigCustDate` field missing a value (the user clicked past the field), they'll be shown when you click Datasheet View command.

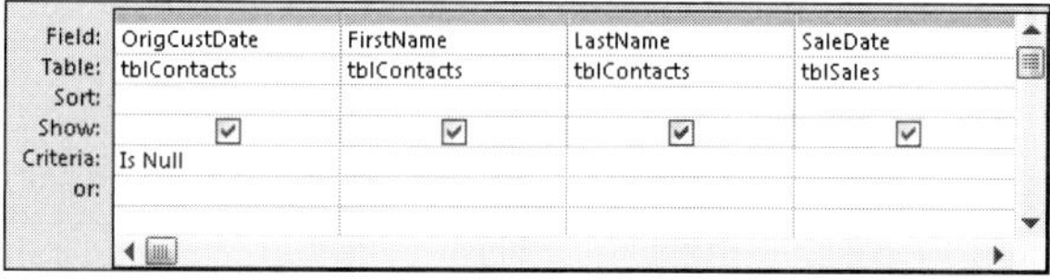

When using the `Is Null` and `Is Not Null` operators, you can enter `Null` or `Not Null` and Access automatically adds the `Is` to the Criteria field.

Entering Criteria in Multiple Fields

Previously in this chapter, you worked with single and multiple criteria specified in single fields. In this section, you work with criteria across several fields. When you want to limit the records based on several field conditions, you do so by setting criteria in each of the fields that will be used for the scope. Suppose you want to search for all sales of cars in Kansas (KS). Or, suppose you want to search for SUVs in Massachusetts or Connecticut. Or, suppose you want to search for all SUVs in Massachusetts or minivans in Connecticut. Each of these queries requires placing criteria in multiple fields and on multiple lines.

Using And and Or across fields in a query

To use the `And` operator and the `Or` operator across fields, place your example or pattern data in the Criteria: cells (for the `And` operator) and the Or: cells of one field relative to the placement in another field. When you want to use `And` between two fields, you place the example or pattern data across the same row in the QBE pane. When you want to use `Or` between two fields, you place the example or pattern data on different rows in the QBE pane. Figure 5-15 shows the QBE pane and a conceptual representation of this placement.

FIGURE 5-15

The QBE pane with `And/Or` criteria between fields using the Criteria: and or: rows

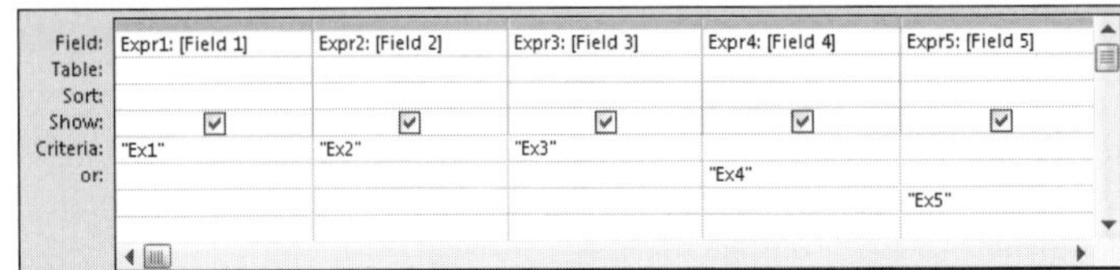

Figure 5-15 shows that if the only criteria fields present were `Ex1`, `Ex2`, and `Ex3` (with `Ex4` and `Ex5` removed), all three would be `And`-ing between the fields. If only the criteria fields `Ex4` and `Ex5` were present (with `Ex1`, `Ex2`, and `Ex3` removed), the two would be `Or`-ing between fields. As it is, the expression for this example is `(Ex1 And Ex2 And Ex3) Or Ex4 Or Ex5`. Therefore, this query displays a record if a value matches any of these criteria:

> `Ex1 And Ex2 And Ex3` (all must be `True`) or
>
> `Ex4` (this can be `True` and either/both of the other two lines can be `False`) or
>
> `Ex5` (this can be `True` and either/both of the other two lines can be `False`)

As long as one of these three criteria is `True`, the record appears in the query's results.

Specifying And criteria across fields of a query

The most common type of condition operator between fields is the `And` operator. You use the `And` operator to limit records on the basis of several field conditions. For example, you may want to view only the records of buyers who live in the state of Massachusetts and bought Chevys. To create this query, follow these steps:

1. **Create a new query using `tblContacts`, `tblSales`, `tblSalesLineItems`, and `tblProducts`.**
2. **Add `FirstName`, `LastName`, and `State` from `tblContacts` and `Description` from `tblProducts`.**
3. **Click the Criteria: cell of `State`.**
4. **Type** MA **in the cell.**
5. **Click the Criteria: cell for `Description`.**
6. **Type** Like *chevy* **in the cell.**

   Your query should look like the query shown in Figure 5-16. Notice that both example data are in the same row. If you look at the datasheet, you will see seven records that match the criteria one truck and six cars.

FIGURE 5-16

An `And` operator performing a Boolean operation based on two fields — `MA` in `State` and `Like *chevy*` in `Description`.

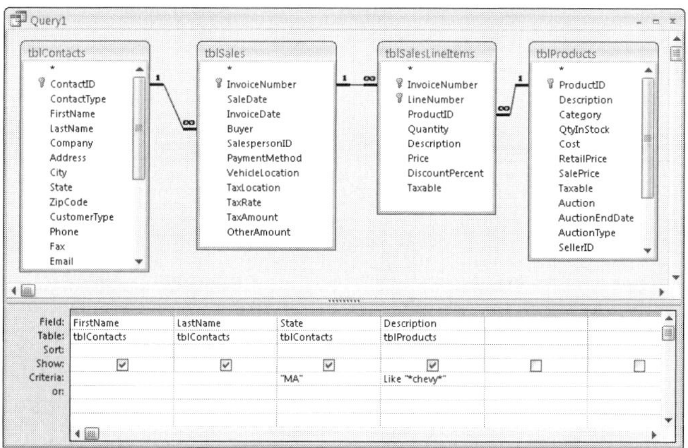

Because you placed data for both criteria on the same row, Access interprets this as an `And` operation — where both conditions must be `True`. If you click on the Datasheet View command, you see that you only have seven records in the query's results.

Specifying Or criteria across fields of a query

Although the `Or` operator isn't used across fields as commonly as the `And` operator, occasionally `Or` is very useful. For example, you may want to see records of any vehicles bought by contacts in Connecticut or you may want to see records on SUVs, regardless of the state they live in. To create this query, follow these steps:

1. **Use the query from the previous example, emptying the two criteria cells first.**
2. **Add** `Category` **from** `tblProducts`.
3. **Click the Criteria: cell of** `State`.
4. **Type** CT **in the cell.**
5. **Click in the Or: cell for** `Category` **(one line below the CT example).**
6. **Type** SUV **in the cell.**

   Your query should resemble the query shown in Figure 5-17. Notice that the criteria entered are not in the same row of the QBE pane for both fields. When you place the criterion for one field on a different line from the criterion for another field, Access interprets this as an `Or` between the fields. If you click on the Datasheet View command, you see that you now have 28 records in the query's results. You're seeing records where the `State` is "CT" or the `Category` is "SUV."

FIGURE 5-17

Using the `Or` operator between fields. Either condition must be `True`—either from the state of CT or the category of vehicle is SUV.

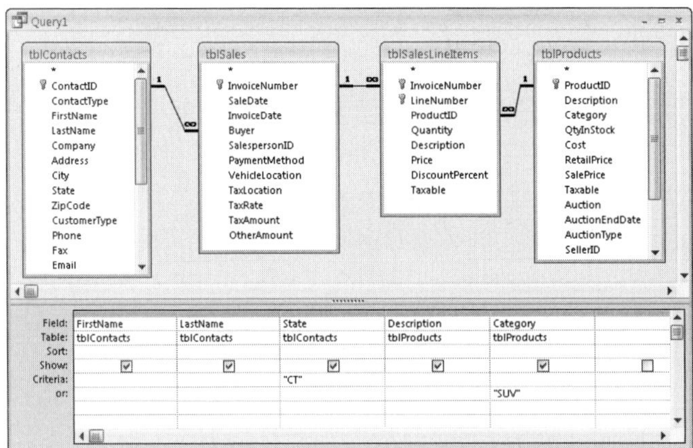

Using And and Or together in different fields

After you've worked with `And` and `Or` separately, you're ready to create a query using `And` and `Or` in different fields. In the next example, you want to display information for all buyers of SUVs in Connecticut and all buyers of trucks in New York. To create this query, follow these steps:

1. **Use the query from the previous example, emptying the two criteria cells first.**
2. **Click the Criteria: cell of `State`.**
3. **Type** CT **in the cell.**
4. **Click the Or: cell of `State`.**
5. **Type** NY **in the cell.**
6. **Click the Criteria: cell for `Category`.**
7. **Type** SUV **in the cell.**
8. **Click the Or: cell for `Category`.**
9. **Type** Trucks **in the cell.**

   Figure 5-18 shows how the query should look. Notice that `CT` and `SUV` are in the same row; `NY` and `Trucks` are in another row. This query represents two `And`s across fields, with an `Or` in each field.

FIGURE 5-18

Using `And`s and `Or`s across fields to select all SUVs for buyers that live in CT or all trucks whose buyers live in NY.

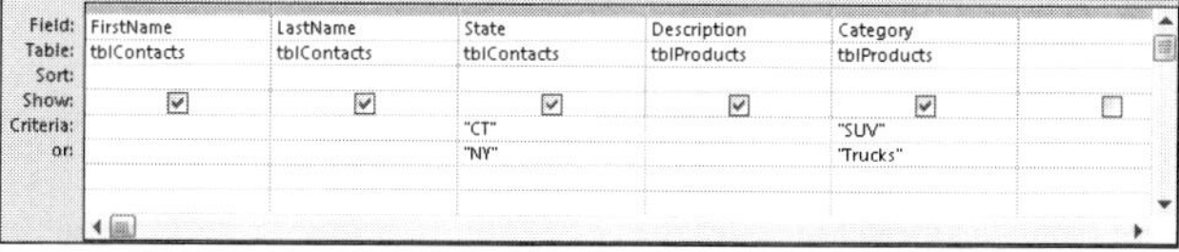

Clicking on the Datasheet View command displays eight records — four SUV records for CT and four truck records for NY.

A complex query on different lines

Suppose you want to view all records of Chevys that were bought in the first six months of 2007 where the buyer lives in Massachusetts, or any vehicle from buyers in California. In this example, you use three fields for setting criteria: `tblContacts.State`, `tblSales.SaleDate`, and `tblProducts.Description`. Here's the expression for setting these criteria:

```
((tblSales.SaleDate Between #1/1/2007# And #6/30/2007#) And
(tblProducts.Description = Like "*Chevy*" ) And
(tblContacts.State = "MA")) OR (tblContacts.State = "CA")
```

You can display this data by creating the query shown in Figure 5-19.

FIGURE 5-19

Using multiple Ands and Ors across fields. This is a rather complex Select query.

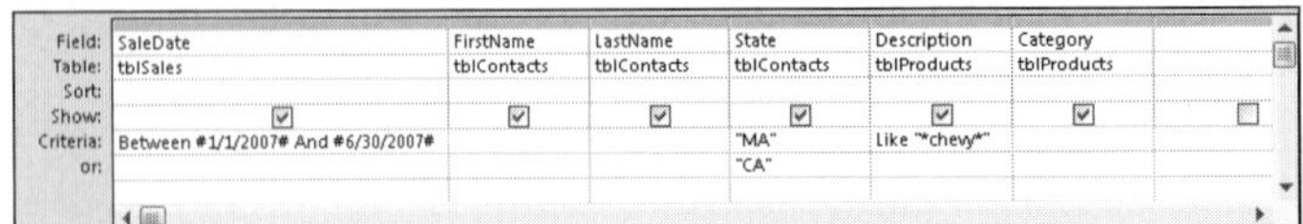

NOTE **You can enter the date 1/1/07 instead of 1/1/2007, and Access processes the query exactly the same. All Microsoft Office products process two-digit years from 00 to 30 as 2000 to 2030, while all two-digit years between 31 and 99 are processed as 1931 to 1999.**

Creating a New Calculated Field in a Query

Fields in a query are not limited to the fields from the tables in your database. You can also create *calculated fields* to use in a query. For example, you can create a calculated field named `Discount Amount` that displays the result of multiplying the value of the discount percent (`DiscountPercent`) times the price (`Price`) in the `tblSalesLineItem` table.

To create this calculated field, follow these steps:

1. **Create a new query using** `tblContacts`, `tblSales`, `tblSalesLineItems`, **and** `tblProducts`.
2. **Add** `FirstName` **and** `LastName` **from** `tblContacts`, **and** `Price` **and** `DiscountPercent` **from** `tblSalesLineItems`.
3. **Click the first empty Field: cell.**
4. **Type the following** DiscountAmt: tblSalesLineItems.Price * tblSalesLineItems .DiscountPercent **and click in another cell.**

   Your query should look like the one shown in Figure 5-20. The name of the calculated field is now `DiscountAmt`. If you didn't type the name in Step 4 above, Access automatically places Expr1: as the name before the calculation. Notice that the DiscountAmt expression does not completely show in Figure 5-20; however, it should match the expression entered in Step 4 above.

FIGURE 5-20

A calculated field, `Discount Amount`, was created by multiplying two fields from `tblSalesLineItems`.

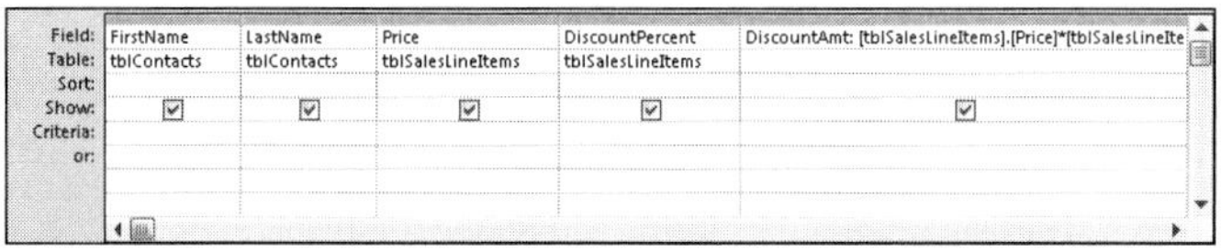

Field:	FirstName	LastName	Price	DiscountPercent	DiscountAmt: [tblSalesLineItems].[Price]*[tblSalesLineIte
Table:	tblContacts	tblContacts	tblSalesLineItems	tblSalesLineItems	
Sort:					
Show:	☑	☑	☑	☑	☑
Criteria:					
or:					

NOTE **A calculated field has to have a name (supplied either by the user or by Access). The name — which appears before the colon (:) — is needed as a heading for the datasheet column and as a reference to the field in a form, report, or another query. If you don't give a calculated field a name, Access will give it one for you (e.g., Expr1, Expr2, etc.).**

TIP **To see the entire contents of the field cell, drag the field until it is all visible or press the Shift+F2 keys to open the Zoom window.**

Notice that the general format for creating a calculated field is as follows:

```
CalculatedFieldName: Expression to build calculated field
```

Summary

In this chapter, you learned how to use various operators to create expressions in Access. You used mathematical operations to perform arithmetic calculations, relational operators to compare values, string operators to concatenate and match text patterns using wildcards, and Boolean operators to perform logical operations. You also used `Is`, `Not`, and `Between...And` operators.

You implemented these operators in queries to see them in action. You created simple and complex criteria, as well as calculated fields by creating expressions using the various types of operators. You learned the difference between using `And` and `Or` in your queries and how to set the QBE pane to get the desired results.

Chapter 6

Working with Datasheet View

In Chapter 2, you created a database named My Access Auto Auctions to hold the tables, queries, forms, reports, and macros you'll create as you learn Access. You also created a table named `tblContacts` using the Access 2007 table designer.

In this chapter, you'll use a datasheet to enter data into an Access table and display the data many different ways. Using Datasheet View allows you to see many records at once, in a the common spreadsheet-style format. In this chapter, you'll work with `tblContacts` and `tblProducts` to add, change, and delete data, as well as learn about different features available in Datasheet View.

ON the CD-ROM **This chapter uses the database named `Chapter06.accdb`. If you haven't already copied it onto your machine from the CD, you'll need to do so now.**

IN THIS CHAPTER

- **Displaying a datasheet**
- **Moving within a datasheet**
- **Opening a new datasheet**
- **Using special data-entry techniques**
- **Finding and replacing values**
- **Hiding, freezing, and rearranging datasheet columns**
- **Sorting or filtering records in a datasheet**
- **Saving and printing datasheets**

Understanding Datasheets

Using a datasheet is just one of the ways to view data in Access. A datasheet is similar to a spreadsheet because it displays data as a series of rows and columns. Figure 6-1 shows a typical Datasheet View of data. Each row represents a single record, and each column represents a single field in the table. Scroll up or down in the datasheet to see the rows (records) that don't fit on the screen; scroll left or right to see the columns (fields) that don't fit.

Datasheets are completely customizable, which allows you to view data in many ways. Changing the font size, column widths, and row heights makes more or less of the data fit on the screen. Rearranging the order of the rows and/or columns lets you organize the records and fields logically. Locking columns makes them stay in position as you scroll to other parts of the datasheet, and hiding columns makes them disappear. Filtering the data hides records that don't match a specific criteria.

FIGURE 6-1

A typical Datasheet View. Each row represents a single record in the table; each column represents a single field (like `Description` or `RetailPrice`) in the table.

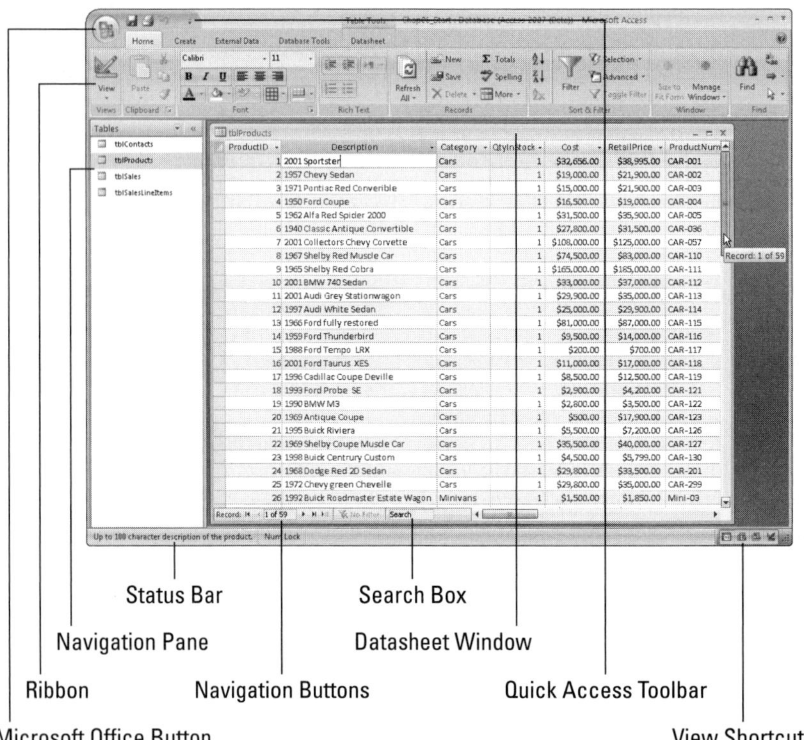

Quick Review of Records and Fields

A *table* is a container for storing related information — patient records, a card list (birthday, holiday), birthday reminders, payroll information, and so on. Each table has a formal structure comprised of fields, each with a unique name to identify and describe the stored information and a specific data type — text, numeric, date and time, and so on — to limit what users enter in these fields. When displayed in a *datasheet* (a two-dimensional sheet of information), Access displays these fields in columns.

The table is composed of records, which hold information about a single entity (like a single customer or a single product). One record is made up of information stored in all the fields of the table structure. For example, if a table has three fields — name, address, and phone number — then the first record only has one name, one address, and one phone number in it. The second record also has one name, one address, and one phone number in it. A datasheet is an ideal way of looking at all the table's contents at once. A single record appears as a row in the datasheet; each row contains information for that specific record. The fields appear as columns in the datasheet; each column contains an individual field's contents. This row-and-column format lets you see lots of data at once.

The Datasheet Window

The Datasheet window appears in the center of the Access window shown in Figure 6-1. This Datasheet window displays the data in rows and columns. Each record occupies one row, and each column — headed by a field name in the field title area — contains each field's values. The display arranges the records initially by primary key and the fields by the order in the table design.

At the top of the Access window, you see the title bar (displaying the database filename and Microsoft Access), the Quick Access toolbar, and the ribbon. At the bottom of the Access window, you see the status bar, which displays assorted information about the datasheet. For example, it may contain field description information (as in Figure 6-1, "Up to 100 character description of the product"), error messages, warnings, or a progress bar. If you gave the field a description when creating it, the field description that you enter for each field is displayed in the status bar. If a specific field doesn't have a field description, Access displays the words *Datasheet View.* Generally, error messages and warnings appear in dialog boxes in the center of the screen rather than in the status bar. If you need help understanding the meaning of a button in the toolbar, move the mouse over the button, hovering over it, and a ToolTip appears with a one- or two-word explanation.

The right side of the Datasheet window contains a scroll bar for moving quickly between records (up and down). As you scroll between records, a ScrollTip (shown in Figure 6-1) tells you precisely where the scroll bar takes you. In Access 2007, the size of the scroll bar thumb gives you a proportional look at how many of the total number of records are being displayed. In Figure 6-1, the scroll bar thumb takes up about 12 percent of the scroll area, and 28 of 60 records are shown onscreen. The bottom of the Datasheet window also contains a proportional scroll bar for moving among fields (left to right). The Navigation buttons — for moving between records — also appear in the bottom-left corner of the datasheet window.

Moving within a datasheet

You easily move within the Datasheet window using the mouse to indicate where you want to change or add to your data—just click a field and record location. In addition, the ribbons, scroll bars, and Navigation buttons make it easy to move among fields and records. Think of a datasheet as a spreadsheet without the row numbers and column letters. Instead, columns have field names, and rows are unique records that have identifiable values in each cell.

Table 6-1 lists the navigational keys that you can use for moving within a datasheet.

TABLE 6-1

Navigating in a Datasheet

Navigational Direction	Keystrokes
Next field	Tab
Previous field	Shift+Tab
First field of current record	Home
Last field of current record	End
Next record	Down arrow (↓)
Previous record	Up arrow (↑)
First field of first record	Ctrl+Home
Last field of last record	Ctrl+End
Scroll up one page	PgUp
Scroll down one page	PgDn

The Navigation buttons

The *Navigation buttons* (shown in Figure 6-2) are the six controls located at the bottom of the Datasheet window, which you click to move between records. The two leftmost controls move you to the first record or the previous record in the datasheet. The three rightmost controls position you on the next record, last record, or new record in the datasheet. If you know the record number (the row number of a specific record), you can click the record number box, enter a record number, and press Enter.

If you enter a record number greater than the number of records in the table, an error message appears stating that you can't go to the specified record.

FIGURE 6-2

The Navigation buttons of a datasheet

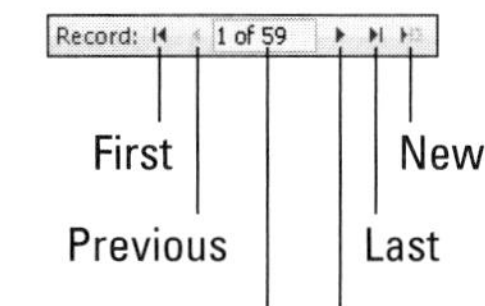

The Datasheet ribbon

The Datasheet ribbon (shown in Figure 6-3) provides a way to work with the datasheet. The Home ribbon has some familiar objects on it, as well as some new ones. This section provides an overview of the Home ribbon; the individual commands are described in more detail later in this chapter.

FIGURE 6-3

The Datasheet ribbon's Home tab

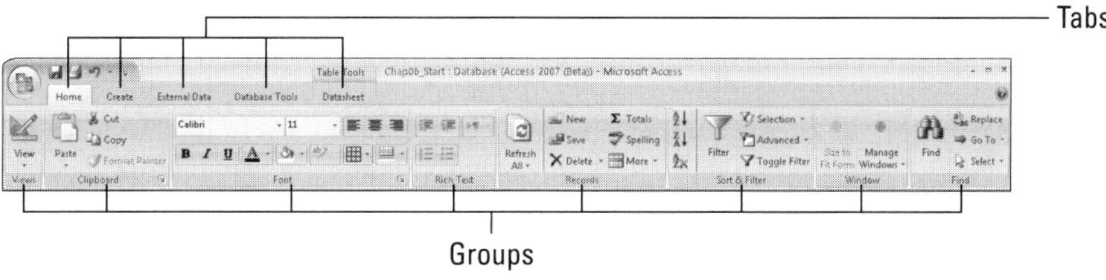

The Home ribbon is divided into the following groups:

- **Views:** The first group is the Views group, which allows you to switch between Datasheet View, PivotTable View, PivotChart View, and Design View. You can see all four choices by clicking the View command's down arrow (triangle pointing down). Clicking Design View permits you to make changes to the object's design (table, query, and so on). Clicking Datasheet View returns to the datasheet.
- **Clipboard:** The Clipboard group contains the Cut, Copy, and Paste commands. These commands work like the commands in other applications (Word, Excel, and so on). The Paste command's down arrow gives you three choices: Paste, Paste Special, and Paste Append. Paste Special gives you the option of pasting the contents of the clipboard in different formats (Text, CSV, Records, and so on). Paste Append pastes the contents of the Clipboard as a new record — provided a row with a similar structure was copied.

- **Font:** The Font group lets you change the look of the datasheet. Use these commands to change the font, size, bold, italic, color, and so on. Use the Align Left, Align Right, and Align Center commands to justify the data in the selected column. Click the Gridlines command to toggle gridlines on and off. Use the Alternate Fill/Back Color command to change the colors of alternating rows or to make them all the same.
- **Rich Text:** The Rich Text group lets you change a memo field's data if the field's Text Format property is set to Rich Text. Use these commands to add bullets or numbered lists and change the indentation levels. Highlighting text in a Rich Text field, and then selecting commands in the Font group, changes the highlighted text instead of the entire datasheet.
- **Records:** The Records group lets you save, delete, or add a new record to the datasheet. It also contains commands to show totals, check spelling, freeze and hide columns, and change the row height and cell width.
- **Sort & Filter:** The Sort & Filter group lets you change the order of the rows as well as limit the rows being displayed — based on criteria you want.
- **Find:** The Find group lets you find and replace data and go to specific records in the datasheet. Use the select command to select a record or all records.

Opening a Datasheet

Follow these steps to open a datasheet from the Database window:

1. **Using the `Chapter06.accdb` database from the CD, click Tables in the Navigation Pane.**
2. **Double-click the table name you want to open (in this example, `tblProducts`).**

An alternative method for opening the datasheet is to right-click on `tblProducts` and select Open from the pop-up menu.

If you are in any of the design windows, click on the Datasheet View command in the ribbon's View group to view your data in a datasheet.

Entering New Data

All the records in your table are visible when you first open it in Datasheet View. If you just created your table, the new datasheet doesn't contain any data. Figure 6-4 shows an empty datasheet. When the datasheet is empty, the first row contains an asterisk (*) in the record selector — indicating it's a new record.

FIGURE 6-4

An empty datasheet. Notice that the first record is blank and has an asterisk in the record selector.

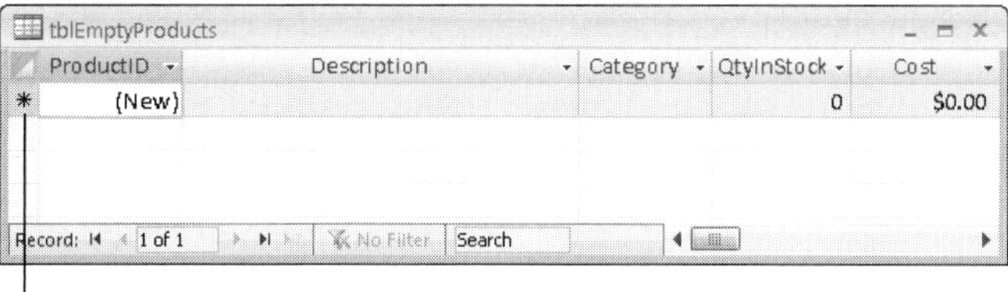

New Record Indicator

The new record appears at the bottom of the datasheet when the datasheet already contains records. Click the New Record command in the ribbon's Record group, or click the new record navigation button to move the cursor to the new row — or simply click on the last row, which contains the asterisk. The asterisk turns into a pencil when you begin entering data, indicating that the record is being edited. A new row — containing an asterisk — appears below the one you're entering data into. The new-record pointer always appears in the last row of the datasheet. Figure 6-5 shows adding a new record into `tblProducts`.

FIGURE 6-5

Entering a new record into the datasheet of `tblProducts`

New Row

Record Selectors

To add a new record to the open Datasheet View of the `tblProducts`, follow these steps:

1. **Click the New Record button.**
2. **Type in values for all fields of the table, moving between fields by pressing the Enter key or the Tab key.**

When adding or editing records, you may see three different record pointers:

- Record being edited
- Record is locked (multiuser systems)
- New record

CAUTION **If the record contains an `AutoNumber` field, Access shows the name (New) in the field. You cannot enter a value in this type of field; rather, simply press the Tab or Enter key to skip this field. Access automatically puts the number in when you begin entering data.**

Saving the record

Moving to a different record saves the record you're editing. Tabbing through all the fields, clicking on the Navigation buttons, clicking Save in the ribbon's Record group, and closing the table all write the edited record to the database. You'll know the record is saved when the pencil disappears from the record selector.

To save a record, you must enter valid values into each field. The fields are validated for data type, uniqueness (if indexed for unique values), and any validation rules that you have entered into the `Validation Rule` property. If your table has a primary key that's not an `AutoNumber` field, you'll have to make sure you enter a unique value in the primary key field to avoid the error message shown in Figure 6-6. Using an `AutoNumber` field as a table's primary key ensures you won't get this error message when entering data.

FIGURE 6-6

The error message Access displays when attempting to save a record with a duplicate primary key value entered into the new record. Use an `AutoNumber` field as your primary key to avoid this error.

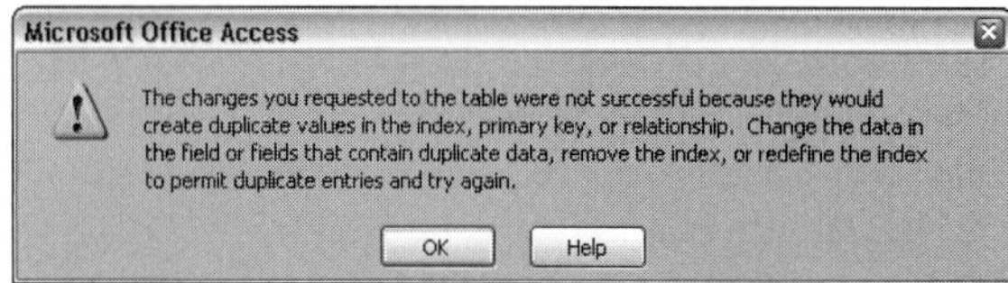

Microsoft Office Access
The changes you requested to the table were not successful because they would create duplicate values in the index, primary key, or relationship. Change the data in the field or fields that contain duplicate data, remove the index, or redefine the index to permit duplicate entries and try again.
OK
Help

TIP **The Undo button in the Quick Access toolbar reverses changes to the current record and to the last saved record. After you change a second record, you cannot undo the saved record.**

TIP **You can save the record to disk without leaving the record by pressing Shift+Enter.**

Now you know how to enter, edit, and save data in a new or existing record. Next you learn how Access validates your data as you make entries into the fields.

Understanding automatic data-type validation

Access validates certain types of data automatically. Therefore, you don't have to enter any data-validation rules for these data types when you specify table properties. The data types that Access validates automatically include

- Number/Currency
- Date/Time
- Yes/No

Access validates the data type when you move off the field. When you enter a letter into a Number or Currency field, you don't initially see a warning not to enter these characters. However, when you tab out of or click on a different field, you get a warning like the one shown in Figure 6-7. This particular warning lets you choose to enter a new value or change the column's data type to Text. You'll see this message if you enter other inappropriate characters (symbols, letters, and so on), enter more than one decimal point, or enter a number too large for a certain Number data type.

FIGURE 6-7

The warning Access displays when entering data that doesn't match the field's data type. Access gives you a few choices to correct the problem.

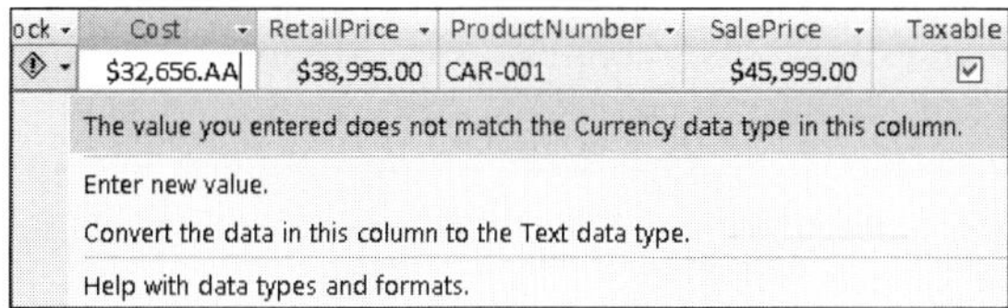

Access validates Date/Time fields for valid date or time values. You'll see a warning similar to the one shown in Figure 6-7 if you try to enter a date such as 14/45/05, a time such as 37:39:12, or an invalid character in a Date/Time field.

Yes/No fields require that you enter one of these defined values: Yes, True, -1, or a number other than 0 (it displays as a -1) for Yes; or No, False, Off, or 0 for No. Of course, you can define your own acceptable values in the Format property for the field, but generally these are the only acceptable values. If you enter an invalid value, the warning appears with the message to indicate an inappropriate value.

Display a check box in Yes/No fields to prevent users from entering invalid data.

Understanding how properties affect data entry

Because field types vary, you use different data-entry techniques for each type. Previously in this chapter, you learned that some data-type validation is automatic. Designing `tblContacts`, however, means entering certain user-defined format and data-validation rules. The following sections examine the types of data entry.

Standard text data entry

The first field — `ContactID` — in `tblContacts` is an AutoNumber field; the next 13 fields are Text fields. After skipping `ContactID`, you simply enter a value in each field and move on. The `ZipCode` field uses an input mask (`00000\-9999;0;`) for data entry. The `Phone` and `Fax` fields also use an input mask (`!\(999") "000\-0000;0;`). These are the only fields that use any special formatting via the input mask. Text fields accept any characters, unless you restrict them with an input mask.

To enter multiple lines in a Text or Memo field, press Ctrl+Enter to add a new line. This is useful, for example, in large text strings for formatting a multiple-line address field.

Date/Time data entry

The `OrigCustDate` and `LastSalesDate` fields in `tblContacts` are Date/Time data types, which both use a Short Date format (3/16/2007). However, you could have defined the format as Medium Date (16-Mar-07) or Long Date (Friday, March 16, 2007). Using either of these formats simply means that no matter how you type in the date — using month and year; day, month, and year; or month, day, and year — it always displays as the format specified (short date [3/16/07], medium date [16-Mar-07], or long date [Friday, March 16, 2007]). So if you type 4/8/08 or 8 Apr 08, Access displays the value in the defined format when you leave the field. The value 4/8/2008 is really stored in the table.

Formats only affect the display of the data. They do not change storage of data in the table.

Number/Currency data entry with data validation

The `CreditLimit` field in `tblContacts` has a validation rule assigned to it. It has a Validation Rule property to limit the amount of credit to $250,000. If the rule is violated, a dialog box appears with the validation text entered for the field. If you want to allow a contact to have more than $250,000 credit, change the validation rule in the table design.

OLE object data entry

You can enter OLE (Object Linking and Embedding) Object data into a datasheet, even though you don't see the object. An OLE Object field holds many different item types, including:

- Bitmap pictures
- Sound files

- Business graphs
- Word or Excel files

Any object that an OLE server supports can be stored in an Access OLE Object field. OLE objects are generally entered into a form so you can see, hear, or use the value. When OLE objects appear in datasheets, you see text that tells what the object is (for example, you may see Bitmap Image in the OLE Object field). You can enter OLE objects into a field in two ways:

- Pasting from the Clipboard
- Right-clicking on the OLE Object field and clicking on Insert Object from the pop-up menu

For thorough coverage of using and displaying OLE objects, see Chapter 24.

Memo field data entry

The second-to-last field in the table is `Notes`, which is a Memo data type. This type of field allows up to 65,536 characters of text for each field. Recall that you entered a long string (about 260 characters) into the Memo field. As you entered the string, however, you saw only a few characters at a time. The rest of the string scrolled out of sight. Pressing Shift+F2 displays a Zoom window with a scroll bar (see Figure 6-8) that lets you to see more characters at a time. Click the Font button at the bottom of the window to view all the text in a different font or size.

FIGURE 6-8

The Zoom window. Notice you can see a lot more of the field's data — not all 65,536 characters, but still quite a lot.

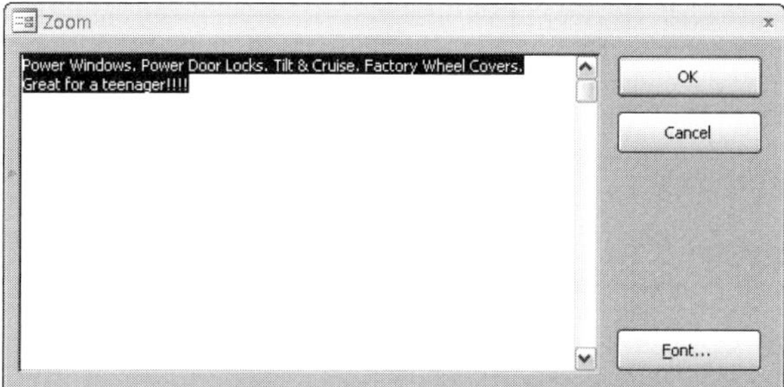

When you first display text in the Zoom window, all the text is selected and highlighted. You can deselect the text by clicking anywhere in the window. If you accidentally delete all the text or change something you didn't want to, click Cancel to exit back to the datasheet with the field's original data.

Use the Zoom window (Shift+F2) when designing Access objects (tables, forms, reports, queries) to see text that normally scrolls out of view.

Navigating Records in a Datasheet

Wanting to make changes to records after you've entered them is not unusual. You may want to change records for several reasons:

- You receive new information that changes existing values.
- You discover errors in existing values.
- You need to add new records.

When you decide to edit data in a table, the first step is to open the table — if it isn't already open. From the list of tables in the Navigation pane, double-click on `tblProducts` to open it in Datasheet View. If you're already in Design View for this table, click the Datasheet View button to switch views.

When you open a datasheet in Access that has related tables, a column with a plus sign (+) is added to access the related records, or subdatasheets.

Moving between records

You can move to any record by scrolling through the records and positioning your cursor on the desired one. With a large table, scrolling through all the records might take a while, so you'll want to use other methods to get to specific records quickly.

Use the vertical scroll bar to move between records. The scroll-bar arrows move one record at a time. To move through many records at a time, drag the scroll box or click the areas between the scroll box and the scroll-bar arrows.

TIP **Watch the ScrollTips when you use scroll bars to move to another area of the datasheet. Access does not update the record number box until you click a field.**

Use the five Navigation buttons (refer to Figure 6-2) to move between records. You simply click these buttons to move to the desired record. If you know the record number (row number of a specific record), click the record number box, enter a record number, and press Enter.

Also use the Go To command in the ribbon's Find group to navigate to the First, Previous, Next, Last, and New records.

Finding a specific value

Although you can move to a specific record (if you know the record number) or to a specific field in the current record, usually you'll want to find a certain value in a record. You can use one of these methods for locating a value in a field:

- Select the Find command (a pair of binoculars) from the ribbon's Find group
- Press Ctrl+F
- Use the Search box at the bottom of the datasheet window

The first two methods display the Find and Replace dialog box (shown in Figure 6-9). To limit the search to a specific field, place your cursor in the field you want to search before you open the dialog box. Change the Look In combo box to the table name to search the entire table for the value.

FIGURE 6-9

The Find and Replace dialog box. The fastest way to activate it is to simply press the Ctrl+F key combination.

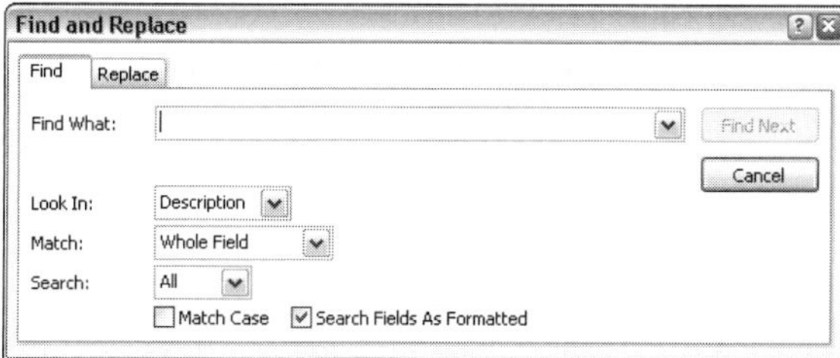

If you highlight the entire record by clicking the record selector (the small gray box next to the record), Access automatically searches through all fields.

The Find and Replace dialog box lets you control many aspects of the search. Enter the value you want to search for in the Find What combo box — which contains a list of recently used searches. You can enter a specific value or choose to use three types of wildcards:

* (any number of characters)

? (any one character)

\# (any one number)

To look at how these wildcards work, first suppose that you want to find any value in the `Description` field of `tblProducts` beginning with 2001; for this, you type **2001***. Then suppose that you want to search for values ending with Sedan, so you type ***Sedan**. If you want to search for any value that begins with 2001, ends with Sedan, and contains any number of characters in between, you type **2001*Sedan**.

CROSS-REF For more information on using wildcards, see Chapter 5.

The Match drop-down list contains three choices that eliminate the need for wildcards:

- Any Part of Field
- Whole Field
- Start of Field

The default is Whole Field, which finds only the whole value you enter. For example, the Whole Field option finds the value FORD only if the value in the field being searched is exactly FORD. If you select Any Part of Field, Access searches to see whether the value is contained anywhere in the field; this search finds the value FORD in the field values FORDMAN, 2001 FORD F-150, and FORD. A search for FORD using the Start of Field option searches from the beginning of the field, and returns no values because the `Description` field always begins with a year (1999, 2003, and so on).

In addition to these combo boxes, you can use two check boxes at the bottom of the Find and Replace dialog box:

- **Match Case:** Match Case determines whether the search is case-sensitive. The default is not case-sensitive (not checked). A search for SMITH finds smith, SMITH, or Smith. If you check the Match Case check box, you must then enter the search string in the exact case of the field value. (The data types Number, Currency, and Date/Time do not have any case attributes.)

  If you have checked Match Case, Access does not use the value Search Fields As Formatted (the second check box), which limits the search to the actual values displayed in the table. (If you format a field for display in the datasheet, you should check the box.)
- **Search Fields As Formatted:** The Search Fields As Formatted check box, the selected default, finds only text that has the same pattern of characters as the text specified in the Find What box. Clear this box to find text regardless of the formatting. For example, if you're searching the `Cost` field for a value of $16,500, you must enter the comma if Search Fields as Formatted is checked. Uncheck this box to search for an unformatted value (16500).

CAUTION **Checking Search Fields As Formatted may slow the search process.**

The search begins when you click the Find Next button. If Access finds the value, the cursor highlights it in the datasheet. To find the next occurrence of the value, click the Find Next button again. The dialog box remains open so that you can find multiple occurrences. Choose one of three search direction choices (Up, Down, All) in the Search drop-down list to change the search direction. When you find the value that you want, click Close to close the dialog box.

Use the search box at the bottom of the Datasheet window (refer to Figure 6-1) to quickly search for the first instance of a value. When using the search box, Access searches the entire datasheet for the value in any part of the field. If you type FORD in the search box, the datasheet moves as you type each letter. First, it finds an *F;* then it finds *FO* and so on. Once it finds the value, it stops searching. To find more than one instance, use the Find and Replace dialog box.

Changing Values in a Datasheet

If the field that you are in has no value, you can type a new value into the field. When you enter new values into a field, follow the same rules as for a new-record entry.

Replacing an existing value manually

Generally, you enter a field with either no characters selected or the entire value selected. If you use the keyboard (Tab or Arrow keys) to enter a field, you select the entire value. (You know that the entire value is selected when it is displayed in reverse video.) When you begin to type, the new content replaces the selected value automatically.

When you click in a field, the value is not selected. To select the entire value with the mouse, use any of these methods:

- Click just to the left of the value when the cursor is shown as a large plus sign.
- Double-click in the field. (This only works if the field doesn't contain spaces.)
- Click to the left of the value, hold down the left mouse button, and drag the mouse to select the whole value.
- Click in the field and press F2.

TIP **You may want to replace an existing value with the value from the field's Default Value property. To do so, select the value and press Ctrl+Alt+Spacebar. To replace an existing value with that of the same field from the preceding record, press Ctrl+' (single quote mark). Press Ctrl+; (semicolon) to place the current date in a field.**

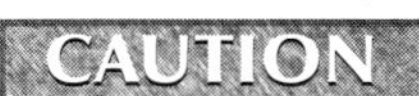

Pressing Ctrl+- (minus sign) deletes the current record.

Changing an existing value

If you want to change an existing value instead of replacing the entire value, use the mouse and click in front of any character in the field to activate Insert mode; the existing value moves to the right as you type the new value. If you press the Insert key, your entry changes to Overstrike mode; you replace one character at a time as you type. Use the arrow keys to move between characters without disturbing them. Erase characters to the left by pressing Backspace, or to the right of the cursor by pressing Delete.

Table 6-2 lists editing techniques.

TABLE 6-2

Editing Techniques

Editing Operation	Keystrokes
Move the insertion point within a field	Press the right-arrow (→) and left-arrow (←) keys
Insert a value within a field	Select the insertion point and type new data
Select the entire field	Press F2
Replace an existing value with a new value	Select the entire field and type a new value
Replace a value with the value of the previous field	Press Ctrl+' (single quote mark)
Replace the current value with the default value	Press Ctrl+Alt+Spacebar
Insert a line break in a Text or Memo field	Press Ctrl+Enter
Save the current record	Press Shift+Enter or move to another record
Insert the current date	Ctrl+; (semicolon)
Insert the current time	Ctrl+: (colon)
Add a new record	Ctrl++ (plus sign)
Delete the current record	Ctrl+- (minus sign)
Toggle values in a check box or option button	Spacebar
Undo a change to the current field	Press Esc or click the Undo button
Undo a change to the current record	Press Esc or click the Undo button a second time after you undo the current field

Fields that you can't edit

Some fields can't be edited, such as:

- **AutoNumber fields:** Access maintains AutoNumber fields automatically, calculating the values as you create each new record. AutoNumber fields can be used as the primary key.
- **Calculated fields:** Access uses calculated fields in forms or queries; these values are not actually stored in your table.
- **Locked or disabled fields:** You can set certain properties in a form to prevent editing for a specific field.
- **Fields in multiuser locked records:** If another user locks the record, you can't edit any fields in that record.

Using the Undo Feature

The Undo button on the Quick Access toolbar is often dimmed because there's nothing to undo. As soon as you begin editing a record, however, you can use this button to undo the typing in the current field. You can also undo a change with the Esc key; pressing Esc cancels either a changed value or the previously changed field. Pressing Esc twice undoes changes to the entire current record.

After you type a value into a field, click the Undo button to undo changes to that value. After you move to another field, you can undo the change to the preceding field's value by clicking the Undo button. You can also undo all the changes to an unsaved current record by clicking the Undo button after you undo a field. After you save a record, you can still undo the changes by clicking the Undo button. However, after the next record is edited, changes to the previous record are permanent.

CAUTION **Don't rely on the Undo command to save you after you edit multiple records. When working in a datasheet, changes are saved when you move from record to record and you can only undo changes to one record.**

Copying and Pasting Values

Copying or cutting data to the Clipboard is a Microsoft Windows task; it is not a specific function of Access. After you cut or copy a value, you can paste into another field or record by using the Paste command in the ribbon's Clipboard group. You can cut, copy, or paste data from any Windows application or from one task to another in Access. Using this technique, you can copy entire records between tables or databases, and you can copy datasheet values to and from Microsoft Word and Excel.

The Paste command's down arrow gives you three choices:

- **Paste:** Paste inserts the contents of the Clipboard into one field.
- **Paste Special:** Paste Special gives you the option of pasting the contents of the Clipboard in different formats (Text, CSV, Records, and so on).
- **Paste Append:** Paste Append pastes the contents of the Clipboard as a new record — provided a row with a similar structure was copied.

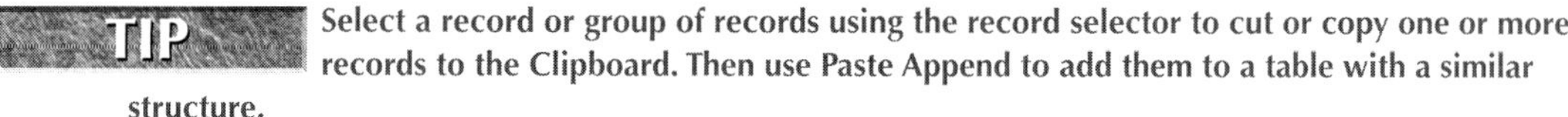

TIP **Select a record or group of records using the record selector to cut or copy one or more records to the Clipboard. Then use Paste Append to add them to a table with a similar structure.**

Replacing Values

To replace an existing value in a field, you can manually find the record to update or you can use the Find and Replace dialog box. Display the Find and Replace dialog box using these methods:

- Select the Replace command from the ribbon's Find group
- Press Ctrl+H

This dialog box allows you to replace a value in the current field or in the entire datasheet. Use it to find a certain value and replace it with a new value everywhere it appears in the field or table.

After the Find and Replace dialog box is active, you should first click the Replace tab and type in the value that you want to find in the Find What box. After you have selected all the remaining search options (turn off Search Fields As Formatted, for example), click the Find Next button to find to the first occurrence of the value. To change the value of the current found item (under the cursor), enter a value in the Replace With box and click the Replace button. For example, Figure 6-10 shows that you want to find the value *Motor Homes* in the `Category` field of `tblProducts` and change it to *Camper*.

FIGURE 6-10

Find and Replace dialog box with the Replace tab showing. In this case, you want to replace the value *Motor Homes* with *Camper.*

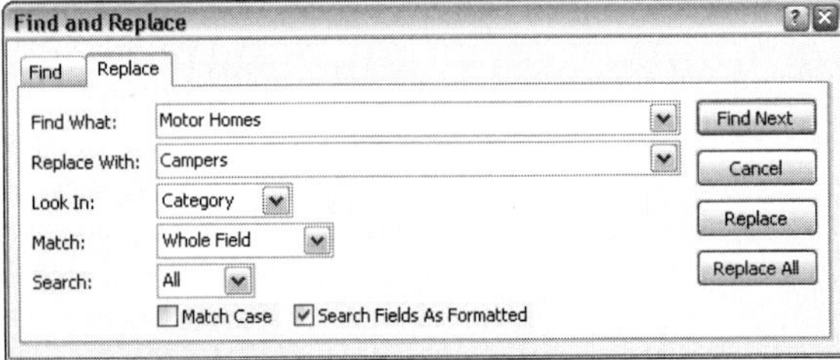

You can select your search options in the Find tab and then click the Replace tab to continue the process. However, it is far easier to simply do the entire process using the Replace tab. Enter the value you want to find and the value that you want to replace it with. After you have completed the dialog box with all the correct information, select one of the command buttons on the side:

- **Find Next:** Finds the next field that has the value in the Find What field.
- **Cancel:** Closes the form and performs no find and replace.
- **Replace:** Replaces the value in the current field only. (***Note:*** You must use the Find Next button first.)

- **Replace All:** Finds all the fields with the Find What value and replaces them with the Replace With value. Use this if you're sure that you want to replace all the values; double-check the Look In box to make sure you don't replace the values in the entire datasheet if you don't want to.

Adding New Records

There are a number of ways to add a record to the datasheet:

- Click on the datasheet's last line, where the record pointer is an asterisk.
- Click the new record Navigation button (the furthest button on the right).
- Click the New command from the ribbon's Records group.
- Click the Goto ➪ New command from the ribbon's Find group.
- Move to the last record and press the down-arrow (↓) key.
- Press Ctrl++ (plus sign).

Once you move to a new record, enter data into the desired fields and save the record.

Deleting Records

To delete records, select one or more records using the record selectors, then press the Delete key or click the Delete command in the ribbon's Records group. The Delete command's drop-down contains the Delete Record command, which deletes the current record, even if it's not selected. When you press Delete or choose the ribbon command, a dialog box asks you to confirm the deletion (see Figure 6-11). If you select Yes, the records are deleted. If you select Cancel, no changes are made.

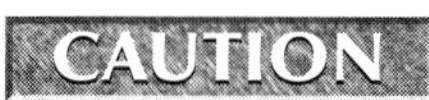

The Default value for this dialog box is Yes. Pressing the Enter key automatically deletes the records. If you accidentally erase records using this method, the action can't be reversed.

FIGURE 6-11

The Delete Record dialog box warns you that you are about to delete *x* number of records — the default response is YES (OK to delete) so be careful when deleting records.

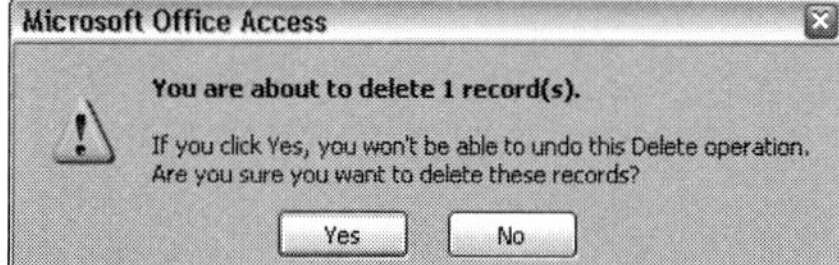

CAUTION If you have relations set between tables and checked Enforce Referential Integrity — for example, the `tblContacts` (Customer) table is related to `tblSales` — then you can't delete a parent record (`tblContacts`) that has related child records (in `tblSales`) unless the you also check the Cascade Delete check box. Otherwise, you receive an error message dialog box that reports `The record can't be deleted or changed because the table '<tablename>' includes related records.`

To select multiple contiguous records, click the record selector of the first record that you want to select and drag the mouse to the last record that you want to select. Or click to select the first record, then hold Shift and click on the last record you want in the selection.

Displaying Records

A number of techniques can increase your productivity when you add or change records. Change the field order, hide and freeze columns, change row height or column width, change display fonts, and change the display or remove gridlines to make data entry easier.

Changing the field order

By default, Access displays the fields in a datasheet in the same order that they appear in a table or query. Sometimes, you want to see certain fields next to each other in order to better analyze your data. To rearrange your fields, select a column by clicking the column heading, and then drag the column to its new location (as shown in Figure 6-12).

FIGURE 6-12

Selecting and dragging a column to change the field order

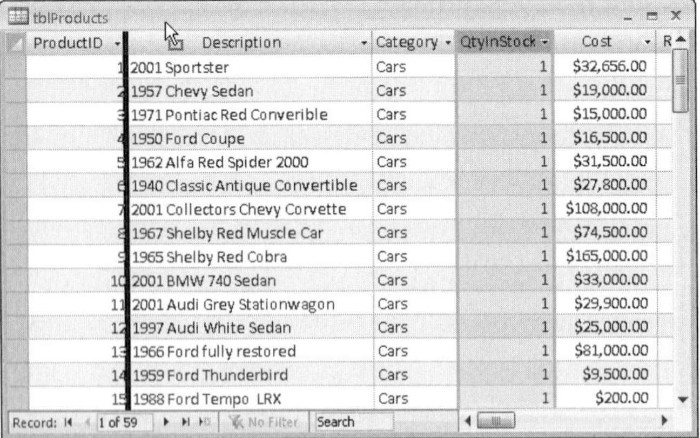
tblProducts

ProductID	Description	Category	QtyInStock	Cost
1	2001 Sportster	Cars	1	$32,656.00
2	1957 Chevy Sedan	Cars	1	$19,000.00
3	1971 Pontiac Red Converible	Cars	1	$15,000.00
4	1950 Ford Coupe	Cars	1	$16,500.00
5	1962 Alfa Red Spider 2000	Cars	1	$31,500.00
6	1940 Classic Antique Convertible	Cars	1	$27,800.00
7	2001 Collectors Chevy Corvette	Cars	1	$108,000.00
8	1967 Shelby Red Muscle Car	Cars	1	$74,500.00
9	1965 Shelby Red Cobra	Cars	1	$165,000.00
10	2001 BMW 740 Sedan	Cars	1	$33,000.00
11	2001 Audi Grey Stationwagon	Cars	1	$29,900.00
12	1997 Audi White Sedan	Cars	1	$25,000.00
13	1966 Ford fully restored	Cars	1	$81,000.00
14	1959 Ford Thunderbird	Cars	1	$9,500.00
15	1988 Ford Tempo LRX	Cars	1	$200.00

Record: 1 of 59 No Filter Search

You can select and drag columns one at a time, or select multiple columns to move at the same time. Suppose you want `QtyInStock` to appear before `Description` in the `tblProducts` datasheet. Follow these steps to make this change:

1. **Position the mouse pointer over the `QtyInStock` column heading.**

   The cursor changes to a down arrow.

2. **Click to select the column.**

   The entire `QtyInStock` column is now highlighted.

3. **Release the mouse button.**

4. **Click the mouse button on the column heading again.**

   The pointer changes to an arrow with a box under it.

5. **Drag the column to the left edge of the datasheet between the Product ID and Description field.**

   A thin black column appears between them (see Figure 6-12).

6. **Release the mouse button.**

   The column moves in front of the Description field of the datasheet.

With this method, you can move any individual field or contiguous field selection. To select multiple fields, click and drag the mouse across multiple column headings. Then you can move the fields left or right or past the right or left boundary of the window.

Moving fields in a datasheet does not affect the field order in the table design.

Changing the field display width

You can change the *field display width* (column width) either by specifying the width in a dialog box (in number of characters) or by dragging the column border. When you drag a column border, the cursor changes to the double-arrow symbol.

To widen a column or to make it narrower, follow these steps:

1. **Place the mouse pointer between two column names on the field separator line.**

   The mouse pointer turns into a small line with arrows pointing to the left and right — if you have it in the correct location.

2. **Drag the column border to the left to make the column smaller or to the right to make it larger.**

You can instantly resize a column to the best fit (based on the longest visible data value) by double-clicking the right column border after the cursor changes to the double arrow.

NOTE Resizing the column doesn't change the number of characters allowed in the table's field size. You are simply changing the amount of viewing space for the data contained in the column.

Alternatively, you can resize a column by right-clicking the column header and selecting Column Width from the pop-up menu to display the Column Width dialog box, as shown in Figure 6-13. Set the Column Width box to the number of characters you want to fit in the column or click the Standard Width check box to set the column to its default size. Click on Best Fit to size the column to the widest visible value.

FIGURE 6-13

The Column Width dialog box

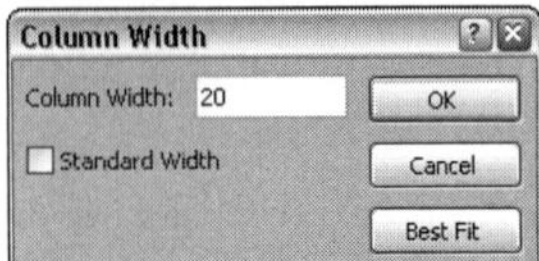

CAUTION You can hide a column by dragging the column gridline to the gridline of the next column to the left, or by setting the column width to 0 in the Column Width dialog box. If you do this, you must choose More ➪ Unhide Columns in the ribbon's Records group to redisplay the columns.

Changing the record display height

Sometimes you may need to increase the row height to accommodate larger fonts or text data displays of multiple lines. Change the record (row) height of all rows by dragging a row's border to make the row height larger or smaller, or you can choose More ➪ Row Height in the ribbon's Records group.

When you drag a record's border, the cursor changes to the vertical two-headed arrow you see at the left edge of Figure 6-14.

FIGURE 6-14

Changing a row's height. Simply put the mouse pointer between two rows. When the mouse pointer changes to arrows pointing up and down, drag to the desired height.

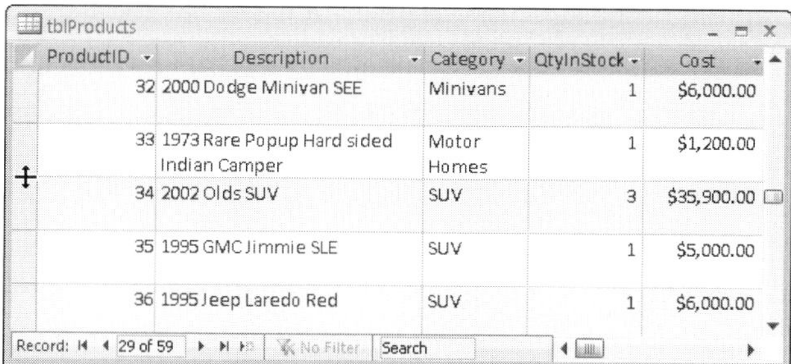

To increase or decrease a row's height, follow these steps:

1. **Place the mouse pointer between record selectors of two rows.**

   The cursor changes to the double pointing arrow (up and down).

2. **Drag the row border upward to shrink all row heights, or drag the border downward to increase all row heights.**

NOTE **The procedure for changing row height changes the row size for all rows in the datasheet. You can't have rows with different heights.**

You can also resize rows by choosing More ➪ Row Height in the ribbon's Records group. The Row Height dialog box appears; there you enter the row height in point size. Check the Standard Height check box to return the rows to their default size.

CAUTION **If you drag a record's gridline up to meet the gridline immediately above it in the previous record, all rows are hidden. This also occurs if you set the row height close to 0 (for example, a height of 0.1) in the Row Height dialog box. In that case, you must use the Row Height dialog box to set the row height to a larger number to redisplay the rows.**

Changing display fonts

By default, Access displays all data in the datasheet in the Calibri 11-point Regular font. Use the commands and drop-down lists in the ribbon's Font group (shown in Figure 6-15) to change the datasheet's text appearance.

FIGURE 6-15

Changing the datasheet's font directly from the ribbon. Choose font type style, size, and other font attributes for the entire datasheet.

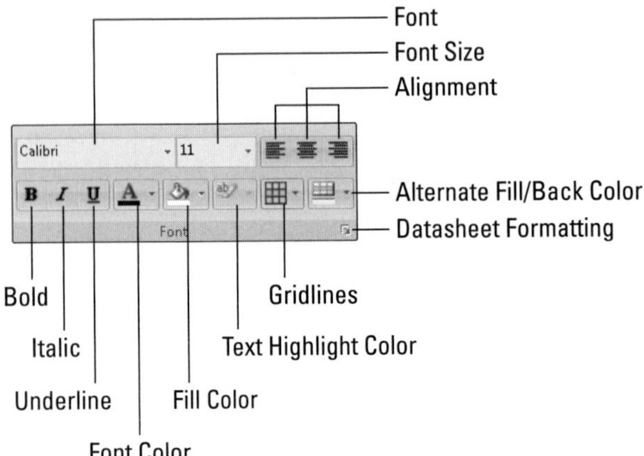

Setting the font display affects the entire datasheet. If you want to see more data on the screen, you can use a very small font. You can also switch to a higher-resolution display size if you have the necessary hardware. If you want to see larger characters, you can increase the font size or click the Bold button.

Displaying cell gridlines and alternate row colors

Normally gridlines appear between fields (columns) and between records (rows). You can set how you want the gridlines to appear using the Gridlines command in the ribbon's Font group (shown in Figure 6-15). Choose from the following options in the Gridlines drop-down list:

- Gridlines: Both
- Gridlines: Horizontal
- Gridlines: Vertical
- Gridlines: None

Use the Fill Color and Alternate Fill/Back Color drop-down lists to change the background colors of the datasheet. The Fill Color palette changes the color of the odd-numbered rows in the datasheet. The Alternate Fill/Back Color palette changes the color of the even-numbered rows. If you don't want alternating row colors, select No Color from the Alternate Fill/Back Color palette and the even-numbered rows will match the odd-numbered rows.

The Datasheet Formatting dialog box (shown in Figure 6-16) gives you complete control over the datasheet's look. Open this dialog box using the Datasheet Formatting command in the bottom-right corner of the ribbon's Font group. Use the Flat, Sunken, and Raised radio buttons under Cell Effect to change the grid to a 3D look. Click the Horizontal and Vertical check boxes under Gridlines Shown to toggle which gridlines you want to see. Change the Background Color, Alternate Background Color, and Gridline Color using the available color palettes. The sample in the middle of the dialog box shows you a preview of changes.

FIGURE 6-16

The Datasheet Formatting dialog box. Use this dialog box to customize the look of the datasheet.

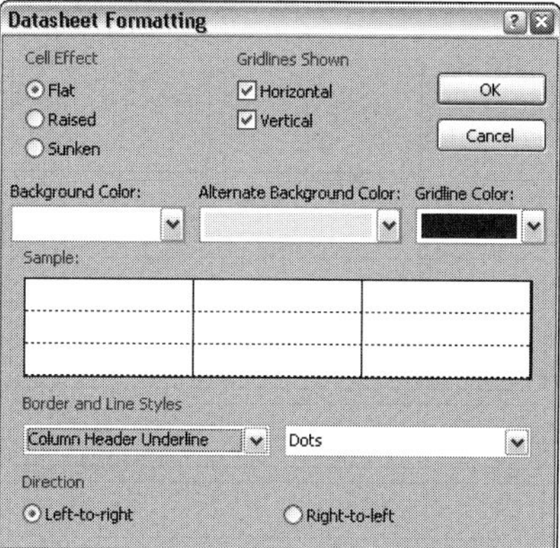

Use the Border and Line Styles drop-down lists to change the look of the gridlines. You can change the styles for the Datasheet Border and the Column Header Underline. Choose a different line style for each of the selections in the first drop-down list. The different line styles you can select from include

- Dash-Dot
- Dash-Dot-Dot
- Dashes
- Dots
- Double Solid
- Short Dashes
- Solid
- Sparse Dots
- Transparent Border

Figure 6-17 shows a datasheet with dots instead of solid lines and a higher contrast between alternating rows. You can use the various colors and styles to customize the datasheet's look to your liking.

FIGURE 6-17

Different line styles and row colors for the datasheet

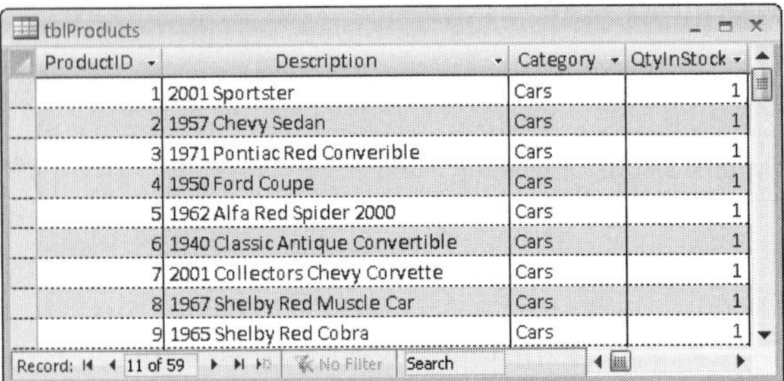

Aligning data in columns

Align the data to the left or right, or center it within a column using the alignment buttons. Choose alignments different from the default alignments Access chooses based on a field's data type (text aligns left, numbers/dates align right). To change the alignment of the data in a column, follow these steps:

1. **Position the cursor anywhere within the column that you want to change the alignment.**
2. **Click on the Align Left, Align Center, or Align Right commands in the ribbon's Font group (shown in Figure 6-15) to change the alignment of the column's data.**

Hiding and unhiding columns

Hide columns by dragging the column gridline to the preceding field or by setting the column width to 0. To hide a single column, follow these steps:

1. **Position the cursor anywhere within the column that you want to hide.**
2. **Choose More ➪ Hide Columns in the ribbon's Records group.**

   The column disappears. Actually, the column width is simply set to 0. You can hide multiple columns by first selecting them and then choosing More ➪ Hide Columns.

After you've hidden a column, you can redisplay it by choosing More ➪ Unhide Columns in the ribbon's Records group. This action displays a dialog box that lets you unhide columns selectively by checking next to each field. When you're finished, click Close; the datasheet appears, showing the desired fields. Also use this dialog box to hide one or more columns by unchecking the check box next to each field you want to hide.

Freezing columns

When you want to scroll left and right among many fields but want to keep certain fields from scrolling out of view, choose More ➪ Freeze in the ribbon's Records group. With this command, for example, you can keep the `ProductID` and `Description` fields visible while you scroll through the datasheet to find the product's features. The frozen columns are visible on the far-left side of the datasheet; other fields scroll out of sight horizontally. The fields must be contiguous if you want to freeze more than one at a time. (Of course, you can first move your fields to place them next to each other.) When you're ready to unfreeze the datasheet columns, simply choose More ➪ Unfreeze.

When you unfreeze columns, the column doesn't move back to its original position. You must move it manually.

Saving the changed layout

When you close the datasheet, you save all your data changes but you might lose all your layout changes. As you make all of these display changes to your datasheet, you probably won't want to make them again the next time you open the same datasheet. If you make any layout changes, Access prompts you to save the changes to the layout when you close the datasheet. Choose Yes to save the changes; choose No to preserve the layout when you opened the table. Save the layout changes manually by clicking Save on the Quick Access Toolbar.

If you're following the example, don't save the changes to `tblProducts`.

Saving a record

Access saves each record when you move off it. Pressing Shift+Enter or selecting Save from the ribbon's Records group saves a record without moving off it. Closing the datasheet also saves a record.

Sorting and Filtering Records in a Datasheet

The ribbon's Sort & Filter group (shown in Figure 6-18) lets you rearrange the order of the rows and narrow down the number of rows. Using the commands in this group, you'll display the records you want in the order you want them. The following sections demonstrate how to use these commands.

FIGURE 6-18

The Sort & Filter group. Change the record order and narrow the number of rows using commands in this group.

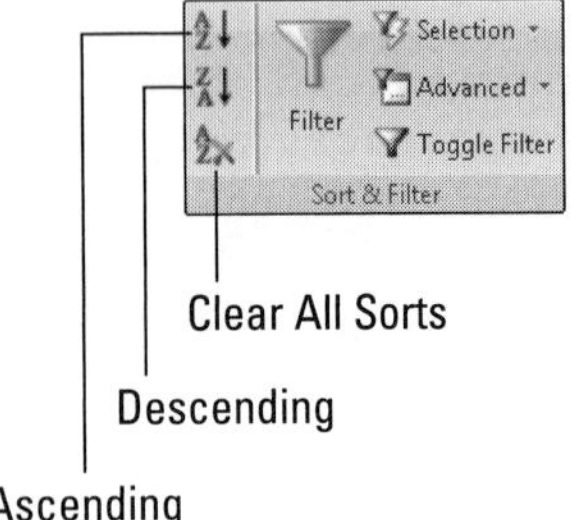

Clear All Sorts

Descending

Ascending

Using the QuickSort feature

Sometimes you may simply want to sort your records into a desired order. The QuickSort ribbon commands let you sort selected columns into either ascending or descending order. To use these commands, click in a field you want to sort by, then click Ascending (A–Z) or Descending (Z–A). The data redisplays instantly in the sorted order. Right-clicking on a column and selecting either Sort A to Z or Sort Z to A also sorts the data.

To sort your data on the basis of values in multiple fields, highlight more than one column: Highlight a column (as previously discussed), hold down the Shift key, and drag the cursor to the right. When you select one of the QuickSort commands, Access sorts the records into major order (by the first highlighted field) and then into orders within orders (based on subsequent fields). If you need to select multiple columns that aren't contiguous (next to each other), you can move them next to each other, as discussed earlier in this chapter.

To display the records in their original order, use the Clear All Sorts command.

Using Filter by Selection

Filter by Selection lets you select records on the basis of the current field value. For example, using `tblProducts`, move your cursor to the `Category` column and click the Ascending (A to Z) command. Access sorts the data by the vehicle's category. Now place your cursor in the `Category` column with the value Minivans. Press the Selection command in the ribbon's Sort & Filter group and choose Equals "Minivans"; Access displays the records where the `Category` is Minivans. Access gives you four choices when clicking the Selection command:

- Equals "Minivans"
- Does Not Equal "Minivans"

- Contains "Minivans"
- Does Not Contain "Minivans"

The area to the right of the Navigation buttons — at the bottom of the Datasheet window — tells you whether the datasheet is currently filtered; in addition, the Toggle Filter command on the ribbon is highlighted, indicating that a filter is in use. When you click this command, it removes the filter. The filter specification does not go away; it is simply turned off. Click the Toggle Filter command again to apply the same filter.

Filtering by selection is additive. You can continue to select values, each time pressing the Selection command.

Right-click the field content that you want to filter by and then select from the available menu choices.

If you want to further specify a selection and then see everything that doesn't match that selection (for example, where Description doesn't equal 2003 Mini Van), move the cursor to the field (the Description field where the value is 2003 Mini Van) that you want to say *doesn't match*, right-click on the datasheet, and then select Does Not Equal "2003 Mini Van". You are now left with six records — all minivans except the 2003 Mini Van.

When using the Selection command on numeric or date fields, select Between from the available command to enter a range of values. Enter the Smallest and Largest numbers or Oldest and Newest dates to limit the records to values that fall in the desired range.

Imagine using this technique to review sales by salespeople for specific time periods or products. Filtering by selection provides incredible opportunities to drill down into successive layers of data. Even when you click the Toggle Filter command to redisplay all the records, Access still stores the query specification in memory. Figure 6-19 shows the filtered datasheet.

FIGURE 6-19

Using Filter by Selection. In this case, you see all records for minivans except 2003 Mini Van records.

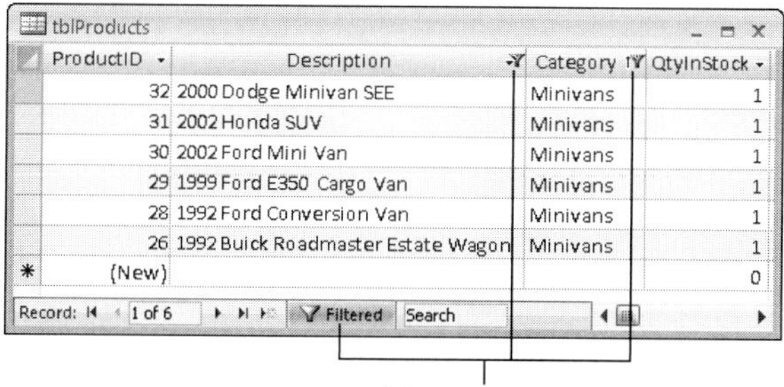

tblProducts

ProductID	Description	Category	QtyInStock
32	2000 Dodge Minivan SEE	Minivans	1
31	2002 Honda SUV	Minivans	1
30	2002 Ford Mini Van	Minivans	1
29	1999 Ford E350 Cargo Van	Minivans	1
28	1992 Ford Conversion Van	Minivans	1
26	1992 Buick Roadmaster Estate Wagon	Minivans	1
(New)			0

When a datasheet is filtered, each column has an indicator in the column heading letting you know if a filter is applied to that column. Hover the mouse over the indicator to see a ToolTip displaying the filter. Click on the indicator to specify additional criteria for the column using the pop-up menu shown in Figure 6-20. Click on the column heading's down-arrow for an unfiltered column to display a similar menu.

FIGURE 6-20

Filtering the Category field. Use the column filter menu to select criteria for a field.

The menu contains commands to sort the column ascending or descending, clear the filter from the field, select a specific filter, and check values you want to see in the datasheet. The available commands change based on the data type of the column. In this case, Text Filter lets you enter a criterion that filters the data based on data you type in.

The check boxes in this menu contain data that appears in the column. In this case, the choices are (Select All), (Blanks), Minivans, Cars, Motor Homes, SUV, and Trucks. Click (Select All) to see all the records regardless of this field's value. Click (Blanks) to see the records that don't contain data. Select any of the data values to limit the records where the field contains the selected values. Click on Minivans and Cars to display the records where `Category` is equal to Minivans or Cars.

If you want to filter data but you can't find the value that you want to use, but you know the value, click the Text Filters (or Number Filters, Date Filters, and so on) command and choose one of the available commands (Equals, Does Not Equal, Begins With, and so on) to display a dialog box where you type in the desired value.

Using Filter by Form

Filter by Form lets you to enter criteria into a single row on the datasheet. Each field becomes a combo box enabling you to select from a list of values in that field. An Or tab at the bottom of the window lets you specify *OR* conditions for each group. Choose Advanced ➪ Filter by Form in the ribbon's Sort & Filter group to enter Filter by Form mode, shown in Figure 6-21.

Select values from the combo boxes or type values you want to search for in the field. If you want to see records where the `Category` field is Minivans or Cars, select Minivans from the `Category` drop-down list, click the Or tab at the bottom of the window, and then select Cars from the `Category` drop-down list. To see records where `Category` is SUV and `QtyInStock` is 1, select SUV from the `Category` drop-down and type **1** in `QtyInStock`. Once you enter the desired criteria, click the Toggle Filter command to apply the filter.

FIGURE 6-21

Using Filter by Form lets you set multiple conditions for filtering at one time. Notice the Or tab at the bottom of the window.

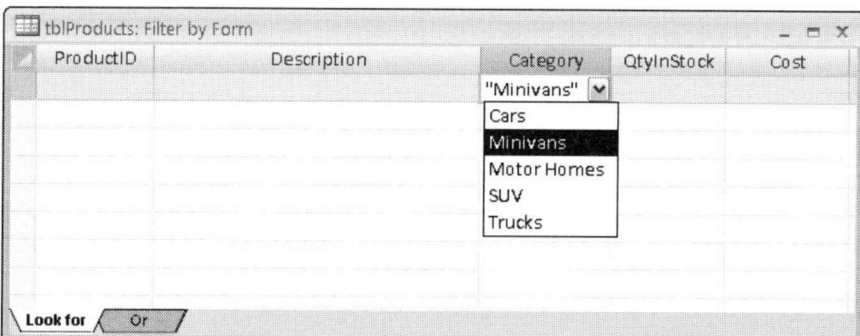

Enter as many conditions as you need using the Or tab. If you need even more advanced manipulation of your selections, you can choose Advanced ➪ Advanced Filter/Sort from the ribbon's Sort & Filter group to get an actual QBE (Query by Example) screen that you can use to enter more complex criteria.

Chapters 4 and 5 discuss queries and using operators and expression.

Printing Records

You can print all the records in your datasheet in a simple row-and-column layout. In Chapter 9, you learn to produce formatted reports. For now, the simplest way to print is to click the Print icon in the Quick Access toolbar. This prints the datasheet to the Windows default printer. Click on the Microsoft Office Button to view other print options, shown in Figure 6-22.

FIGURE 6-22

The Microsoft Office Print menu

The printout reflects all layout options that are in effect when the datasheet is printed. Hidden columns don't print. Gridlines print only if the cell gridline properties are on. The printout also reflects the specified row height and column width.

Only so many columns and rows can fit on a page; the printout takes up as many pages as required to print all the data. Access breaks up the printout as necessary to fit on each page. For example, the `tblProducts` printout may be six pages. Three pages across are needed to print all the fields in `tblProducts`; each record requires three pages in length. Each record of `tblContacts` may need four pages in length. The number of pages depends on your layout and your printer.

Printing the datasheet

You can also control printing from the Print dialog box, which you open by clicking the Microsoft Office Button, and then clicking on Print. From this dialog box, customize your printout by selecting from several options:

- **Print Range:** Prints the entire datasheet or only selected pages or records
- **Copies:** Determines the number of copies to be printed
- **Collate:** Determines whether multiple copies are collated

You can also click the Properties button and set options for the selected printer or select the printer itself to change the type of printer. The Setup button allows you to set margins and print headings.

Using the Print Preview window

Although you may have all the information in the datasheet ready to print, you may be unsure of whether to change the width or height of the columns or rows, or whether to adjust the fonts to improve your printed output. To preview your print job, either click the Print Preview command under the Print menu to display the Print Preview window. The default view is the first page in single-page preview. Use the ribbon commands to select different views and zoom in and out. Click Print to print the datasheet to the printer. Click the Close Print Preview command on the right side of the ribbon to return to Datasheet View.

Summary

In this chapter, you learned how to open and navigate around in a datasheet using the keyboard, ribbons, and navigation buttons. You learned to enter new records and edit data in existing records, as well as how to undo changes you made to the data. You saw what happens when Access validates each field based on its data type.

You also customized the fonts, colors, column widths, row heights, and other visual aspects of the datasheet. You froze and unfroze columns and hid them from view. Then, you limited the number of records using different types of filters and sorted the records using the QuickSort commands.

Chapter 7

Creating Basic Access Forms

Forms provide the most flexible way for viewing, adding, editing, and deleting your data. They are also used for *switchboards* (forms with buttons that provide navigation), dialog boxes that control the flow of the system, and the o displaying messages. Controls are the objects on forms such as labels, text boxes, buttons, and many others. In this chapter, you learn how to create different types of forms and get an understanding about the types of controls that are used on a form.

IN THIS CHAPTER

- Creating different types of forms
- Understanding controls
- Adding controls to a form
- Using the Field List
- Using the ribbon's Controls group
- Selecting controls
- Manipulating controls
- Understanding control properties
- Using the Property Sheet
- Control naming conventions

ON the CD-ROM In this chapter, you use `tblProducts` in the `Chapter07.accdb` database to provide the data necessary to create the examples used in this chapter.

Adding Forms Using the Ribbon

Use the Form group in the Create ribbon to add forms to your database. The commands in the Form group — shown in Figure 7-1 — let you create the following different types of forms:

- **Form:** Creates a new form that lets you enter information for one record at a time. You must have a table, query, form, or report open or selected to use this command.
- **Split Form:** Creates a split form that shows a datasheet in the upper section and a form in the lower section for entering information about the record selected in the datasheet.
- **Multiple Items:** Creates a form that shows multiple records in a datasheet, with one record per row.
- **PivotChart:** Instantly creates a PivotChart form.

- **Blank Form:** Instantly creates a blank form with no controls.
- **More Forms:** This drop-down list lets you start the Form Wizard or instantly create a Datasheet, Modal Dialog, or PivotTable.
- **Form Design:** Creates a new blank form and displays it in Design View.

FIGURE 7-1

The ribbon's Create tab. Use the Form group to add new forms to your database.

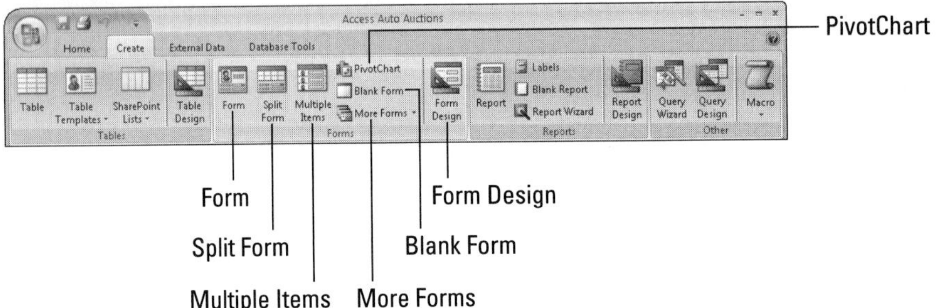

Creating a new form

Use the Form command in the ribbon's Form group to create a new form based on a table or query selected in the Navigation Pane. To create a form based on `tblProducts`, follow these steps:

1. **Select `tblProducts` in the Navigation Pane.**
2. **Click the Create tab on the ribbon, and then click on the Form command in the Form group.**

   Access creates a new form containing all the fields from `tblProducts` displayed in Layout View, shown in Figure 7-2. Layout View lets you see the forms data while changing the layout of controls on the form.

FIGURE 7-2

Creating a new form. Use the Form command to quickly create a new form with all the fields from a table or query.

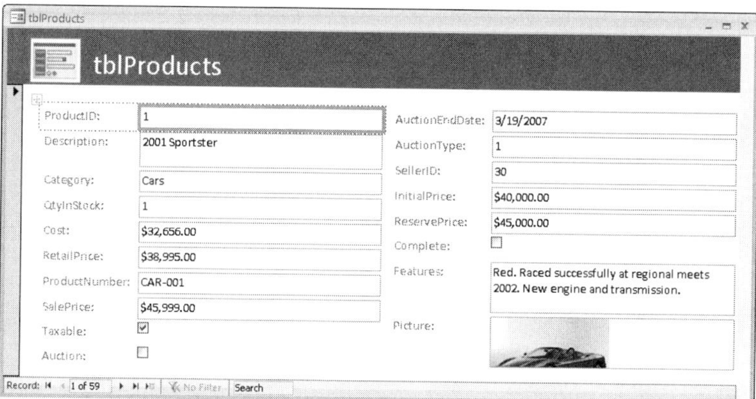

Creating a split form

Use the Split Form command in the ribbon's Form group to create a split form based on a table or query selected in the Navigation Pane. This new feature gives you two views of the data at the same time, letting you select a record from a datasheet in the upper section and edit the information in a form in the lower section. To create a split form based on `tblProducts`, follow these steps:

1. **Select `tblProducts` in the Navigation Pane.**
2. **Click the Create tab on the ribbon, and then click on the Split Form command in the Form group.**

   Access creates a new split form based on `tblProducts` displayed in Layout View, shown in Figure 7-3. Resize the form and use the splitter bar in the middle to make the lower section completely visible.

FIGURE 7-3

Create a split form when you want to select records from a list and edit them in a form. Use the splitter bar to resize the upper and lower sections of the form.

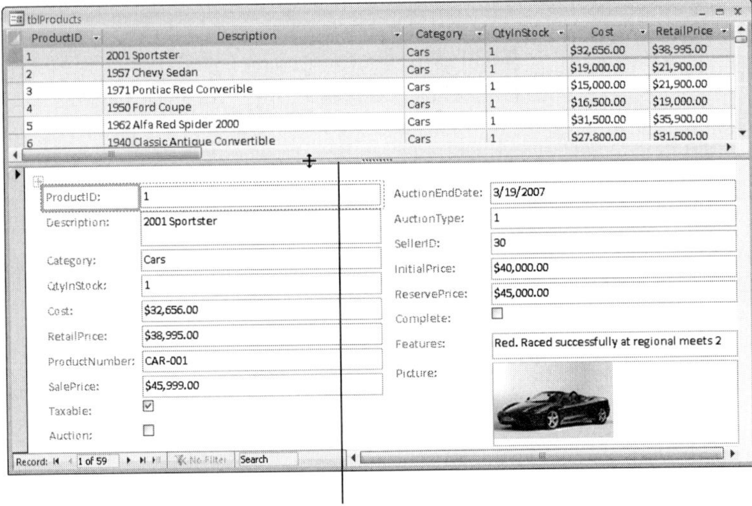

Creating a multiple-items form

Use the Multiple Items command in the ribbon's Form group to create a multiple-items form based on a table or query selected in the Navigation Pane. This new feature creates a form that looks like a datasheet, but it lets you add graphical elements, buttons, and other controls. To create a multiple-items form based on `tblProducts`, follow these steps:

1. **Select `tblProducts` in the Navigation Pane.**
2. **Click the Create tab on the ribbon, and then click on the Multiple Items command in the Form group.**

   Access creates a new multiple items form based on `tblProducts` displayed in Layout View, shown in Figure 7-4. Although the form looks similar to a datasheet, you can only resize the rows and columns in Design View and Layout View.

FIGURE 7-4

Create a multiple items form when you want to see data similar to Datasheet View but also want to add form controls such as buttons and graphical elements.

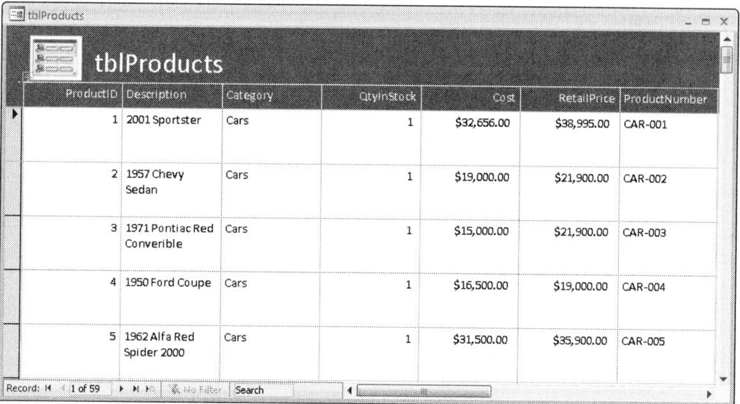

ProductID	Description	Category	QtyInStock	Cost	RetailPrice	ProductNumber
1	2001 Sportster	Cars	1	$32,656.00	$38,995.00	CAR-001
2	1957 Chevy Sedan	Cars	1	$19,000.00	$21,900.00	CAR-002
3	1971 Pontiac Red Converible	Cars	1	$15,000.00	$21,900.00	CAR-003
4	1950 Ford Coupe	Cars	1	$16,500.00	$19,000.00	CAR-004
5	1962 Alfa Red Spider 2000	Cars	1	$31,500.00	$35,900.00	CAR-005

Creating a form using the Form Wizard

Use the Form Wizard command in the Form group's More Forms drop-down list to create a form using a wizard. The Form Wizard visually walks you through a series of questions about the form that you want to create and then creates it for you automatically. The Form Wizard lets you select which fields you want on the form, the layout (Columnar, Tabular, Datasheet, Justified) of the form, the style (Access 2003, Access 2007, Apex, and so on), and the title on the form.

To start the Form Wizard based on `tblProducts`, follow these steps:

1. **Select `tblProducts` in the Navigation Pane.**
2. **Click the Create tab on the ribbon, and then click on the Form group's More Forms drop-down and select Form Wizard.**

   Access starts the Form Wizard shown in Figure 7-5. Choose which table or query you want the form based on using the Tables/Queries drop-down list. Use the buttons in the middle of the form to add and remove fields to the Available Fields and Selected Fields list boxes.

FIGURE 7-5

Use the Form Wizard to create a form with the fields you choose, as well as the layout and styles you want.

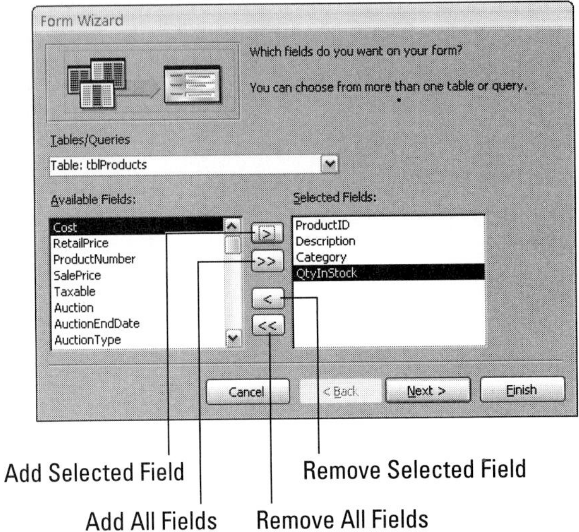

NOTE You can also double-click any field in the Available Fields list box to add it to the Selected Fields list box.

The series of buttons at the bottom of the form let you navigate through the other steps of the wizard. The types of buttons available here are common to most wizard dialog boxes:

- **Cancel:** Cancel the wizard without creating a form
- **Back:** Return to the preceding step of the wizard
- **Next:** Go to the next step of the wizard
- **Finish:** End the wizard using the current selections

CAUTION If you click Next or Finish without selecting any fields, Access tells you that you must select fields for the form before you can continue.

Creating a datasheet form

Use the Datasheet command in the Form group's More Forms drop-down list to create a form that looks like a table or query's datasheet. A datasheet form is useful when you want to see the data in a row and column format but want to limit which fields are displayed and editable. To create a datasheet form based on `tblProducts`, follow these steps:

1. Select `tblProducts` in the Navigation Pane.

2. Click the Create tab on the ribbon, and then click on the Form group's More Forms drop-down and select Datasheet.

You can view any form you create as a datasheet by selecting Datasheet View from the ribbon's View drop-down. A datasheet form appears in Datasheet View by default when you open it.

You can prevent users from viewing a form as a datasheet by setting the form's properties. You'll learn more about form properties later in this chapter.

Creating a blank form

Use the Blank Form command in the ribbon's Form group to create a form without any controls. To create a blank form based on `tblProducts`, follow these steps:

1. Select `tblProducts` in the Navigation Pane.

2. Click the Create tab on the ribbon, and then click on the Blank Form command in the Form group.

Access creates a new blank form based on `tblProducts` displayed in Layout View. In the next section, you'll learn how to add and customize controls on the form.

Use the Form Design command in the ribbon's Form group to create a blank form and display it in Design View.

Adding Controls

In this section, you'll learn how to change a form's design using Design View. You'll add, move, and resize different controls, as well as customize other aspects of a form.

Click on Design View from the View drop-down in the ribbon's View group to switch a form to Design View. The Design tab on the Form Tools ribbon — shown in Figure 7-6 — lets you add and customize controls on your form.

FIGURE 7-6

The Design tab lets you add and customize controls in a form's Design View.

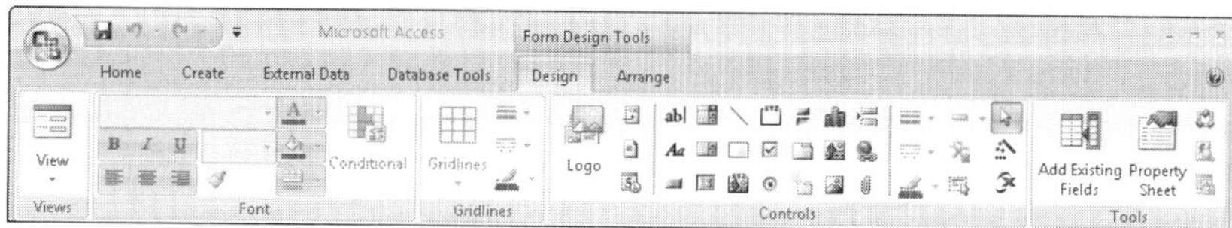

NEW FEATURE The Controls group on the ribbon's Design tab replaces the Toolbox from previous versions of Access.

Resizing the form area

The white area of the form is where you work. This is the size of the form when it is displayed. Resize the white area of the form by placing the cursor on any of the area borders and dragging the border of the area to make it larger or smaller. Figure 7-7 shows a blank form in Design View being resized.

FIGURE 7-7

Design View of a blank form. Resize the form area by dragging the bottom-right corner.

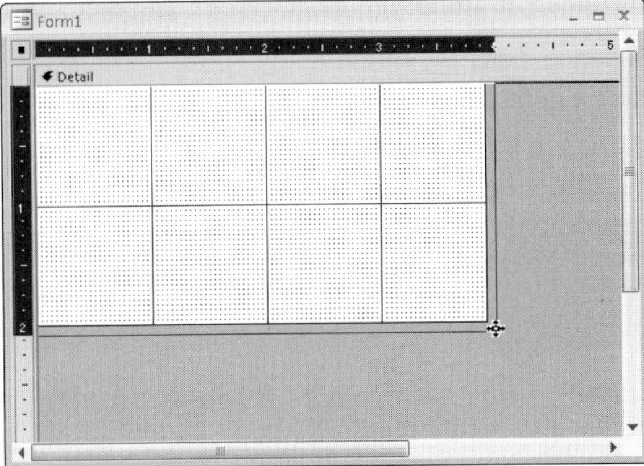

Saving the form

You can save the form at any time by clicking on Save in the Quick Access toolbar. When you're asked for a name for the form, give it a meaningful name (for example, `frmProducts`, `frmCustomers`, `frmProductList`). If you've already given the form a name, you won't be prompted for a name when you click Save.

When you close a form, Access asks you to save it. If you don't save a form, all changes since you opened the form (or the last time you pressed Save) are lost. You should frequently save the form while you work if you're satisfied with the results.

TIP **If you are going to make extensive changes to a form, you might want to make a copy of the form. If you want to work on the form `frmProducts`, you can copy and then paste the form in the database window, giving it a name like `frmProductsOriginal`. Later, when you have completed your changes and tested them, you can delete the original copy.**

Understanding controls

Controls and properties form the basis of forms and reports. It is critical to understand the fundamental concepts of controls and properties before you begin to apply them to custom forms and reports.

NOTE **Although this chapter is about forms, you will learn that forms and reports share many common characteristics including controls and what you can do with them. As you learn about controls in this chapter, you will be able to apply nearly everything you learn when you create reports.**

The term *control* has many definitions in Access. Generally, a control is any object on a form or report, such as a label or text box. These are the same controls that you use in any Windows application, such as Access, Excel, or Web-based HTML forms, or those that are used in any language, such as .Net, Visual Basic, C++, or even C#. Although each language or product has different file formats and different properties, a text box in Access is the same as a text box in any other Windows product.

You enter data into controls and display data using controls. A control can be bound to a field in a table (when the value is entered in the control it is also saved in some underlying table field), or it can be unbound and displayed in the form but not saved when the form is closed. A control can also be an object, such as a line or rectangle. Calculated fields are also controls, as are pictures, graphs, option buttons, check boxes, and objects. Some controls that aren't part of Access are developed separately — these are ActiveX controls. ActiveX controls extend the base feature set of Access 2007 and are available from a variety of vendors. Many ActiveX controls are shipped with Access 2007.

CROSS-REF **ActiveX controls are covered in Chapter 24.**

Whether you're working with forms or reports, essentially the same process is followed to create and use controls. In this chapter, we explain controls from the perspective of a form.

The different control types

Forms and reports contain many different control types. You can add these controls to forms using the Controls group shown in Figure 7-6. Hovering the mouse over the control displays a ToolTip telling you what the control is. Table 7-1 briefly describes each control.

TABLE 7-1

Controls in Access Forms and Reports

Control	What It Does
Text Box	Displays and allows users to edit data.
Label	Displays static text that typically doesn't change.
Button	Also called a command button. Calls macros or runs VBA code when clicked.
Combo Box	A drop-down list of values.
List Box	A list of values that is always displayed on the form or report.
Subform/Subreport	Displays another form or report within the main form or report.
Line	A graphical line of variable thickness and color, which is used for separation.
Rectangle	A rectangle can be any color or size or can be filled in or blank; the rectangle is used for emphasis.
Image	Displays a bitmap picture with very little overhead.
Option Group	Holds multiple option buttons, check boxes, or toggle buttons.
Check Box	A two-state control, shown as a square that contains a check mark if it's on and an empty square if it's off.
Option Button	Also called a radio button, this button is displayed as a circle with a dot when the option is on.
Toggle Button	This is a two-state button — up or down — which usually uses pictures or icons instead of text to display different states.
Tab Control	Displays multiple pages in a file folder type interface.
Page	Adds a "page" on the form or report. Additional controls are added to the page, and multiple pages may exist on the same form.
Chart	This chart displays data in a graphical format.
Unbound Object Frame	This frame holds an OLE object or embedded picture that is not tied to a table field and can include graphs, pictures, sound files, and video.
Bound Object Frame	This frame holds an OLE object or embedded picture that is tied to a table field.
Page Break	This is usually used for reports and indicates a physical page break.
Hyperlink	This control creates a link to Web page, a picture, an e-mail address, or a program.
Attachment	This control manages attachments for the Attachment data type.

The Use Control Wizards command, located on the right side of the Controls group, doesn't add a control to a form; instead, it determines whether a wizard is automatically activated when you add certain controls. The Option Group, Combo Box, List Box, Subform/Subreport, Bound and

Unbound Object Frame, and Command Button controls all have wizards that Access starts when you add a new control. You can also use the ActiveX Controls command (found in the bottom-right corner of the Controls group) to display a list of ActiveX controls, which you can add to Access 2007.

Understanding bound, unbound, and calculated controls

These are the three basic categories of controls:

- **Bound controls:** These are controls that are bound to a table field. When you enter a value into a bound control, Access automatically updates the table field in the current record. Most of the controls that let you enter information can be bound; these include OLE (Object Linking and Embedding) fields. Controls can be bound to most data types, including text, dates, numbers, Yes/No, pictures, and memo fields.
- **Unbound controls:** Unbound controls retain the entered value, but they don't update any table fields. You can use these controls for text label display, for controls such as lines and rectangles, or for holding unbound OLE objects (such as bitmap pictures or your logo) that aren't stored in a table but on the form itself. Unbound controls are also known as *variables* or *memory variables*.
- **Calculated controls:** Calculated controls are based on expressions, such as functions or calculations. Calculated controls are also unbound because they don't update table fields. An example of a calculated control is `=[SalePrice] - [Cost]`. This control calculates the total of two table fields for display on a form but is not bound to any table field.

The two ways to add a control

You add a control to a form in either of two ways:

- Click a button in the Design ribbon's Controls group and draw a new unbound control on the form.
- Drag a field from the Field List to add a bound control to the form.

A bound control is one that is linked to a table field, while an unbound control is one that is not bound to a table field. A control bound to a table places the data directly into the table by using the form.

Using the Controls group to add a control

By using the buttons in the Controls group to add a control, you decide which type of control to use for each field. The control you add is unbound (or not attached to the data in a table field) and has a default name such as Text21 or Combo11. After you create the control, you decide what table field to bind the control to, enter text for the label, and set any properties. You'll learn more about setting properties later in this chapter.

You can add one control at a time using the Controls group. To create three different unbound controls, perform these steps:

1. **Click the Create tab on the ribbon, and then click on the Form Design command in the Form group to create a new form in Design View.**
2. **Click the Design tab on the ribbon, and then click the Text Box button (ab|) in the Controls group.**

   The selected button appears with a colored background.
3. **Move the mouse pointer to the Form Design window.**

   The cursor changes to the Text Box icon.
4. **Click and hold down the mouse button where you want the control to begin, and drag the mouse to size the control.**
5. **Click the Option Button in the Controls group.**
6. **Move the mouse pointer in the Form Design window.**

   The cursor changes to the Option Button icon.
7. **Click and hold down the mouse button where you want the control to begin, and drag the mouse to size the control.**
8. **Click the Check Box button in the Controls group.**
9. **Move the mouse pointer in the Form Design window.**

   The cursor changes to the Check Box icon.
10. **Click and hold down the mouse button where you want the control to begin, and drag the mouse to size the control.**

    When you're done, your screen should resemble the one shown in Figure 7-8.

FIGURE 7-8

Unbound controls added from the Controls group

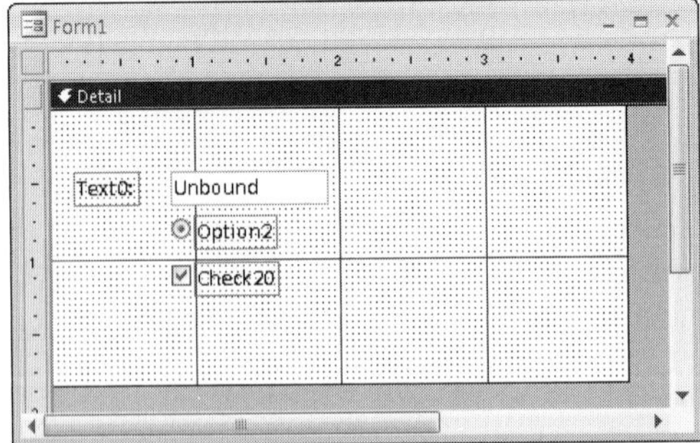

TIP Clicking the Form Design window with a control selected creates a default-sized control. If you want to add multiple controls of the same type, double-click on the icon in the Controls group, and then draw as many controls as you want on the form.

Using the Field List to add a control

The Field List displays a list of fields from the table or query the form is based on. You add bound controls to the form by dragging fields from the Field List onto the form. Select and drag them one at a time, or select multiple fields by using the Ctrl key or Shift key.

- Select multiple contiguous fields by holding down the Shift key and clicking the first and last fields that you want.
- Select multiple noncontiguous fields by holding down the Ctrl key and clicking each field that you want.

Click the Add Existing Fields command in the Design ribbon's Tools group to display the Field List. By default, the Field List appears docked on the right of the Access window, shown in Figure 7-9. This window is movable and resizable and displays a vertical scroll bar if it contains more fields than can fit in the window.

FIGURE 7-9

Click Add Existing Fields in the Tools group to show the Field List, docked on the right of the Access window.

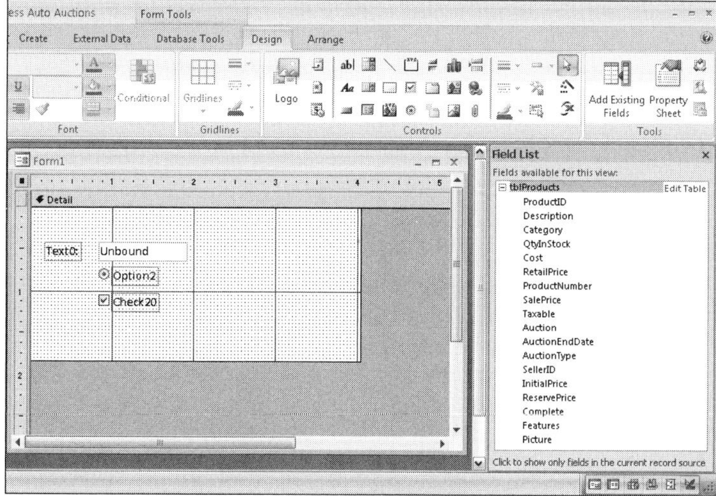

Generally, dragging a field from the Field List window adds a bound text box to the Form Design window. If you drag a Yes/No field from the Field List window, you add a check box. If you drag a field that has a Lookup property, you add a List Box control or Combo Box control. If you drag an

OLE field from the Field List window, you create a bound object frame. Optionally, you can select the type of control by selecting a control from the Controls group and dragging the field to the Form Design window.

CAUTION **When you drag fields from the Field List window, the first control is placed where you release the mouse button. Make sure that you have enough space to the left of the control for the labels. If you don't have sufficient space, the labels slide under the controls.**

You gain several distinct advantages by dragging a field from the Field List window:

- The control is bound automatically to the field that you dragged it from.
- Field properties inherit table-level formats, status-bar text, and data-validation rules and messages.
- The label control and label text are created with the field name as the caption.
- The label control is attached to the field control, so they move together.

Select and drag the `Description`, `Category`, `RetailPrice`, and `AuctionEndDate` fields from the Field List window to the form, as shown in Figure 7-10. Double-clicking a field also adds it to the form.

FIGURE 7-10

Drag fields from the Field List to add bound controls to the form.

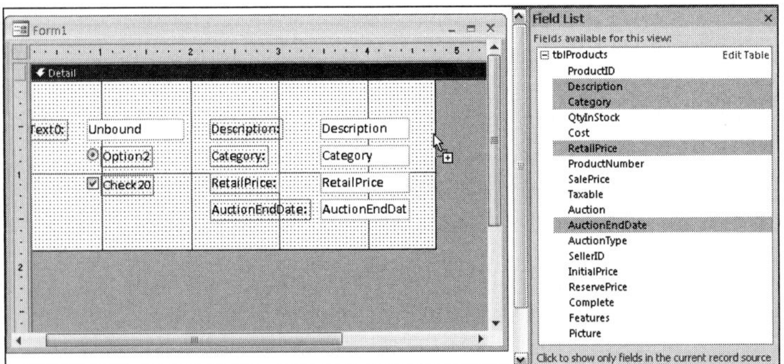

You can see four new controls in the form's Design View — each one consists of a Label control and a Text Box control (Access attaches the Label control to the text box automatically). You can work with these controls as a group or independently, and you can select, move, resize, or delete them. Notice that each control has a label with a caption matching the field name, and the Text Box control displays the bound field name used in the text box. If you want to resize just the control and not the label, you must work with the two controls separately.

Close the Field List by clicking the Add Existing Fields command in the ribbon's Tools group or the Close button on the Field List.

TIP **In Access, you can change the type of control after you create it; then you can set all the properties for the control. For example, suppose that you add a field as a Text Box control and you want to change it to a List Box. You can right-click the control and select Change To from the pop-up menu to change the control type. However, you can change only from some types of controls to others. You can change anything to a Text Box control; option buttons, toggle buttons, and check boxes are interchangeable, as are List Boxes and Combo Boxes.**

In Figure 7-10, notice the difference between the controls that were dragged from the Field List window and the controls that were created from the Controls group. The Field List window controls are bound to a field in `tblProducts` and are appropriately labeled and named. The controls created from the Controls group are unbound and have default names. The default names are automatically assigned a number according to the type of control.

Later, you learn how to change the control names, captions, and other properties. Using properties speeds the process of naming controls and binding them to specific fields. If you want to see the differences between bound and unbound controls, switch to Form View using the View command in the ribbon's View group. The `Description`, `Category`, `RetailPrice`, and `AuctionEndDate` controls display data since they're bound to `tblProducts`. The other three controls don't display data because they aren't bound to any data source.

If a form's Record Source property isn't set, you will not see a Field List window. You'll learn more about form properties in Chapter 8.

TIP **If you first select a control type in the Controls group and then drag a field from the Field List, a control is created (using the selected control type) that is automatically bound to the data field in the Field List.**

Which method to use

The deciding factor of whether to use the field list or the Controls group is this: Does the field exist in the table/query or do you want to create an unbound or calculated expression? By using the Field List window and the Controls group together, you can create bound controls of nearly any type. You will find, however, that some data types don't allow all the control types found in the Controls group. For example, if you select the Chart control type from the Controls group and drag a single field to the form, a text box control is added instead of a chart control.

The following properties always inherit their settings from the field's table definition:

- Format
- Decimal Places
- Status Bar Text (from the field Description)
- Input Mask
- Default Value
- Validation Rule
- Validation Text

Changes made to a control's properties don't affect the field properties in the source table.

Each type of control has a different set of properties, as do objects such as forms, reports, and sections within forms or reports. In the next few chapters, you learn about many of these properties as you use each of the control types to create more complex forms and reports.

Selecting Controls

After you add a control to the form, you can resize, move, or copy it. The first step is to select one or more controls. Depending on its size, a selected control may show from four to eight *handles* (small squares called *moving and sizing handles*) around the control — at the corners and midway along the sides. The Move handle in the upper-left corner is larger than the other handles and you use it to move the control. You use the other handles to size the control. Figure 7-11 displays some selected controls and their moving and sizing handles.

FIGURE 7-11

A conceptual view of selecting controls and their moving and sizing handles

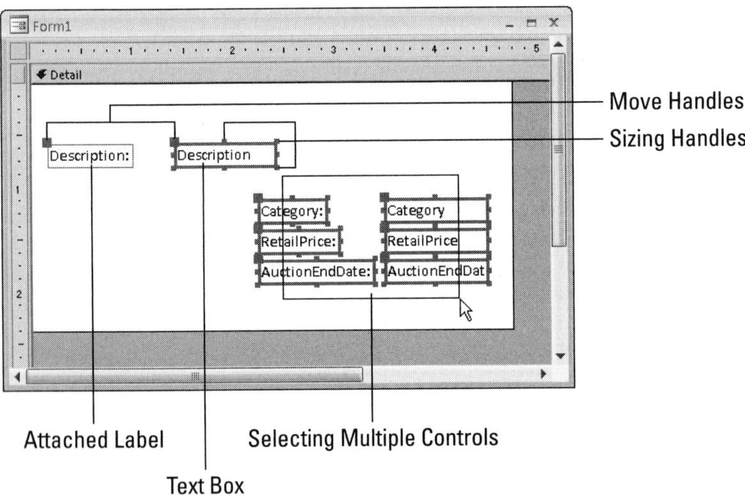

The Select command (top leftmost command) in the Controls group must be on for you to select a control. The pointer appears as an arrow pointing diagonally toward the upper-left corner. If you use the Controls group to create a single control, Access automatically reselects the pointer as the default.

Selecting a single control

Select any single control by clicking anywhere on the control. When you click a control, the handles appear. If the control has an attached label, the Move handle for the label also appears. If you select a label control that is part of an attached control, all the handles for the label control are displayed, and only the Move handle appears in the attached control.

Selecting multiple controls

You can select multiple controls in these ways:

- Click each desired control while holding down the Shift key.
- Drag the pointer through or around the controls that you want to select.
- Click and drag in the ruler to select a range of controls.

Figure 7-11 shows selecting the multiple bound controls graphically. When you select multiple controls by dragging the mouse, a rectangle appears as you drag the mouse. Be careful to only drag the rectangle through the controls you want to select. Any control you touch with the rectangle or enclose within it is selected. If you want to select labels only, make sure that the selection rectangle only encloses the labels.

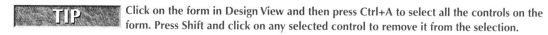

TIP **If you find that controls are not selected when the rectangle passes through the control, you may have the Selection behavior global property set to fully enclosed. This means that a control is selected only if the selection rectangle completely encloses the entire control. The normal default for this option is partially enclosed. Change this option by clicking the Microsoft Office Button and selecting Access Options. Then select Object Designers and set the Forms/Reports Selection behavior to Partially Enclosed.**

By holding down the Shift key, you can select several noncontiguous controls. This lets you select controls on totally different parts of the screen. Using Shift to select controls is different from using Shift to select files in Windows Explorer and fields in the Field List. You have to Shift+click on each control to add it to the selection.

Click on the form in Design View and then press Ctrl+A to select all the controls on the form. Press Shift and click on any selected control to remove it from the selection.

Deselecting controls

Deselect a control by clicking an unselected area of the form that doesn't contain a control. When you do so, the handles disappear from any selected control. Selecting another control also deselects a selected control.

Manipulating Controls

Creating a form is a multistep process. The next step is to make sure that your controls are properly sized and moved to their correct positions. The Arrange tab of the ribbon — shown in Figure 7-12 — contains commands used to assist you in manipulating controls.

FIGURE 7-12

The Arrange tab lets you work with moving and sizing control, as well as control the overall layout of the form.

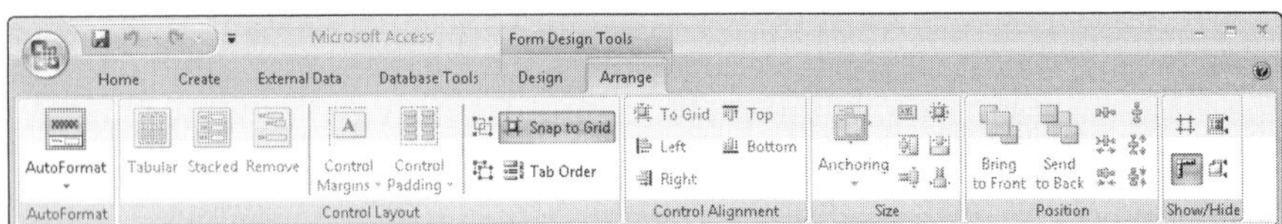

Resizing a control

You can *resize* controls by using any of the smaller handles on the control. The handles in the control corners let you make the field larger or smaller in both width and height — and at the same time. Use the handles in the middle of the control sides to size the control larger or smaller in one direction only. The top and bottom handles control the height of the control; the left and right handles change the control's width.

When the mouse pointer touches a corner handle of a selected control, the pointer becomes a diagonal double arrow. You can then drag the sizing handle until the control is the desired size. If the mouse pointer touches a side handle in a selected control, the pointer changes to a horizontal or vertical double-headed arrow. Figure 7-13 shows the Description control after being resized. Notice the double-headed arrow in the corner of the Description control.

FIGURE 7-13

Resizing a control

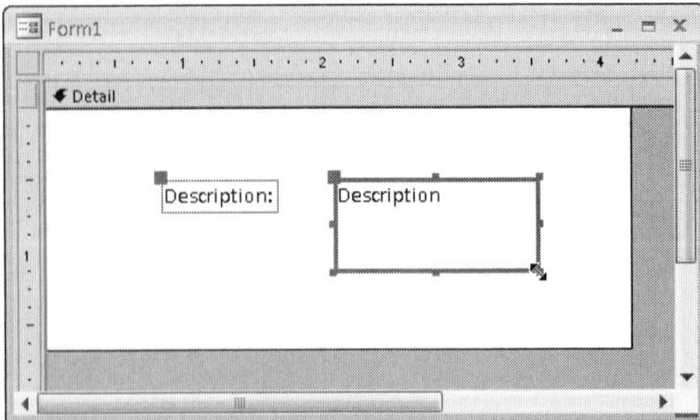

TIP You can resize a control in very small increments by holding the Shift key and pressing the arrow keys. This technique also works with multiple controls selected. Using this technique, a control changes by only 1 pixel at a time (or moves to the nearest grid line if Snap to Grid is selected in the Layout ribbon's Control Layout group).

When you double-click on any of the sizing handles, Access resizes a control to a best fit for the text in the control. This is especially handy if you increase the font size and then notice that the text is cut off either at the bottom or to the right. For label controls, note that this *best-fit sizing* adjusts the size vertically and horizontally, though text controls are resized only vertically. This is because when Access is in form-design mode, it can't predict how much of a field to display — the field name and field contents can be radically different. Sometimes, Access doesn't correctly resize the label.

Sizing controls automatically

The Size group on the Layout ribbon has several commands that help size controls based on the value of the data, the grid, or other controls. Here are the Size commands:

- **To Fit:** Adjusts control height and width for the font of the text they contain.
- **To Tallest:** Makes selected controls the height of the tallest selected control.
- **To Shortest:** Makes selected controls the height of the shortest selected control.
- **To Grid:** Moves all sides of selected controls in or out to meet the nearest points on the grid.
- **To Widest:** Makes selected controls the width of the widest selected control.
- **To Narrowest:** Makes selected controls the height of the narrowest selected control.

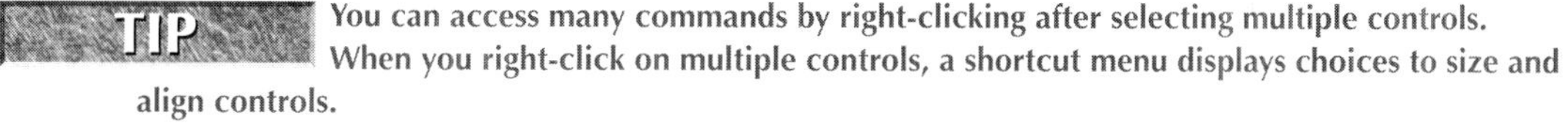

TIP You can access many commands by right-clicking after selecting multiple controls. When you right-click on multiple controls, a shortcut menu displays choices to size and align controls.

Moving a control

After you select a control, you can easily move it, using either one of these methods:

- Click on the control and hold the mouse button down; the cursor changes to a four-directional arrow. Drag the mouse to move the control to a new location.
- Click once to select the control and move the mouse over any of the highlighted edges; the cursor changes to a four-directional arrow. Drag the mouse to move the control to a new location.
- Select the control and use the arrow keys on the keyboard to move the control. Using this technique, a control changes by only 1 pixel at a time (or moves to the nearest grid line if Snap to Grid is selected in the Layout ribbon's Control Layout group).

When an attached label is created automatically with another control, it is called a *compound control*. If a control has an attached label, the label and control move together; it doesn't matter whether you click the control or the label.

You can move a control separately from an attached label by pointing to the Move handle of the control and then dragging it. Move the label control separately from the other control by pointing to the Move handle of the label control and dragging it separately.

Figure 7-14 shows a Label control that has been separately moved to the top of the Text Box control. The four-directional arrow cursor indicates that the controls are ready to be moved together. To see this cursor, the control(s) must already be selected.

FIGURE 7-14

Moving a control

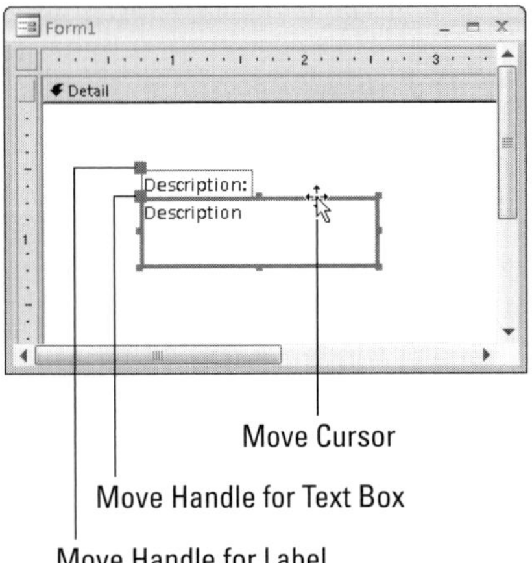

Press Esc before you release the mouse button to cancel a moving or a resizing operation. After a move or resizing operation is complete, click the Undo button on the Quick Access toolbar to undo the changes.

Aligning controls

You may want to move several controls so that they are all *aligned* (lined up). The Layout ribbon's Control Alignment group has several options described in the following list:

- **Left:** Aligns the left edge of the selected controls with that of the leftmost selected control.
- **Right:** Aligns the right edge of the selected controls with that of the rightmost selected control.
- **Top:** Aligns the top edge of the selected controls with that of the topmost selected control.

- **Bottom:** Aligns the bottom edge of the selected controls with that of the bottommost selected control.
- **To Grid:** Aligns the top-left corners of the selected controls to the nearest grid point.

You can align any number of selected controls by selecting a command from the Control Alignment group. When you choose one of the commands, Access uses the control that is the closest to the desired selection as the model for the alignment. For example, suppose that you have three controls and you want to left-align them. They are aligned on the basis of the control farthest to the left in the group of the three controls.

Figure 7-15 shows several sets of controls. The first set of controls is not aligned. The Label controls in the second set of controls have been left-aligned. The Text Box controls in the second set have been right-aligned. Each label, along with its attached text box, has been bottom-aligned.

FIGURE 7-15

An example of unaligned and aligned controls on the grid

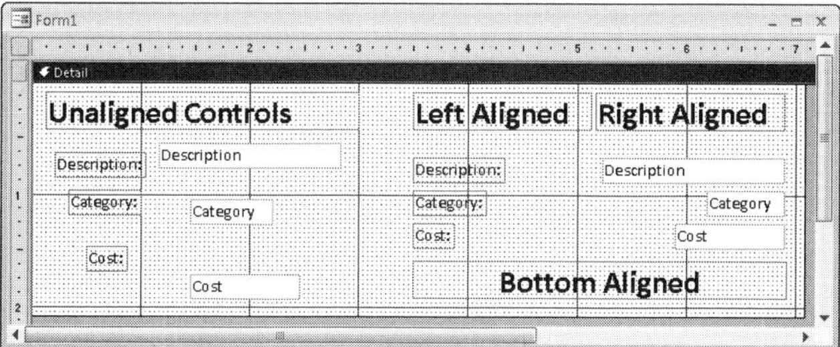

Each type of alignment must be done separately. In this example, you can left-align all the labels or right-align all the text boxes at once. However, you must bottom-align each label and its text control separately (three separate alignments).

The series of dots in the background of Figure 7-15 is the *grid*. The grid can assist you in aligning controls. Hide or display the grid by selecting the Show Grid command from the Layout ribbon's Show/Hide group. You can also hide or display the ruler using the Ruler command in the Show/Hide group.

Use the Snap to Grid command in the Layout ribbon's Control Layout group to align new controls to the grid as you draw or place them on a form. It also aligns existing controls to the grid when you move or resize them. Snap to Grid is on when it appears selected in the ribbon.

When Snap to Grid is on and you draw a new control by clicking on the form and dragging to size the control, Access aligns the four corners of the control to points on the grid. When you place a new control by clicking the control in the Field List and then dragging it to the form, only the upper-left corner is aligned.

As you move or resize existing controls, Access 2007 lets you move only from grid point to grid point. When Snap to Grid is off, Access 2007 ignores the grid and lets you place a control anywhere on the form or report.

TIP **You can temporarily turn Snap to Grid off by pressing the Ctrl key before you create a control (or while sizing or moving it). You can change the grid's *fineness* (number of dots) from form to form by using the Grid X and Grid Y Form properties. (Higher numbers indicate greater fineness.) You'll learn more about Form properties in Chapter 8.**

The Layout ribbon's Position group contains commands to adjust the space between multiple controls. These commands change the space between controls on the basis of the space between the first two selected controls. If the controls are across the screen, use horizontal spacing. If they are down the screen, use vertical spacing. These commands are as follows:

- **Equal Horizontal:** Makes the horizontal space between selected controls equal. You must select three or more controls for this command to work.
- **Increase Horizontal:** Increases the horizontal space between selected controls by one grid unit.
- **Decrease Horizontal:** Decreases the horizontal space between selected controls by one grid unit.
- **Equal Vertical:** Makes the vertical space between selected controls equal. You must select three or more controls for this command to work.
- **Increase Vertical:** Increases the vertical space between selected controls by one grid unit.
- **Decrease Vertical:** Decreases the vertical space between selected controls by one grid unit.

TIP **Aligning controls aligns the control boxes only. If you want to align the text within the controls (also known as *justifying the text*), you must use the Design ribbon's Font group and select the Left, Right, or Center commands.**

Modifying the appearance of a control

To modify the appearance of a control, select the control and click on commands that modify that control, such as commands in the Font group or Controls group. To change the text color and font of the `Description` label, follow these steps:

1. **Click `Description` label on the form.**
2. **In the Design ribbon's Font group, change the Font Size to 14, click the Bold command, and change the Font Color to blue.**
3. **Resize the `Description` label so the larger text fits (remember, you can double-click any of the sizing handles to autosize the label).**

Modifying the appearance of multiple controls

To modify the appearance of multiple controls at once, select the controls and click on commands to modify the controls, such as commands in the Font group or Controls group. To change the text color and font of the `Description`, `Category`, and `Cost` labels and text boxes, follow these steps:

1. **Select the three labels and three text boxes by dragging a selection box through them (refer to Figure 7-11).**
2. **In the Design ribbon's Font group, change the Font Size to 14, click the Bold command, and change the Font Color to blue.**
3. **Resize the labels and text boxes so the larger text fits (remember, you can double-click any of the sizing handles to autosize the controls).**

   As you click the commands, the controls' appearances change to reflect the new selections (shown in Figure 7-16). The fonts in each control increase in size, become bold, and turn blue. Any changes you make apply to all selected controls.

FIGURE 7-16

Changing the appearance of multiple controls at the same time

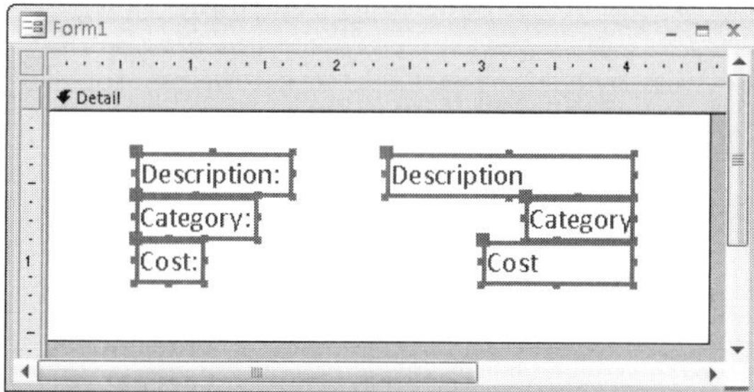

When multiple controls are selected, you can also move the selected controls together. When the cursor changes to the four-directional arrow, click and drag to move the selected controls. You can also change the size of all the controls at once by resizing one of the controls in the selection. All the selected controls increase or decrease by the same number of units.

Grouping controls

If you routinely change properties of multiple controls, you may want to group them together. To group controls together, select the controls by holding down the Shift key and clicking them or dragging the selection box through them. After the desired controls are selected, select the Group command from the Layout ribbon's Control Layout group. A box appears around the selected controls, as shown in Figure 7-17, indicating they're grouped together.

FIGURE 7-17

Grouping multiple controls together

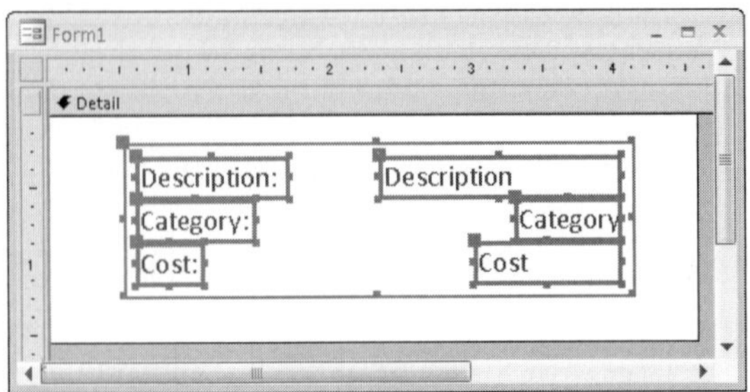

After you've grouped the controls together, whenever you click any of the controls inside the group, the entire group is selected. Double-click on a control to select just that one control. After a single control in the group is selected, you can click on any other control to select it.

To resize the entire group, put your mouse on the side you want to resize. After the double arrow appears, click and drag until you reach the desired size. Every control in the group changes in size. To move the entire group, click and drag the group to its new location. With grouped controls, you don't have to select all the controls every time you change something about them.

To remove a group, select the group by clicking any field inside the group, then select the Ungroup command from the Layout ribbon's Control Layout group.

Deleting a control

You can delete a control by simply selecting it in the form's Design View and pressing the Delete key on your keyboard. The control and any attached labels will disappear. You can bring them back by immediately selecting Undo from the Quick Access toolbar. You can also select Cut from the Home ribbon's Clipboard group or Delete from the Home ribbon's Records group.

You can delete more than one control at a time by selecting multiple controls and pressing Delete. You can delete an entire group of controls by selecting the group and pressing Delete. If you have a control with an attached label, you can delete only the label by clicking the label itself and then selecting one of the delete methods. If you select the control, both the control and the label are deleted. To delete only the label of the Description control, follow the next set of steps (this example assumes that you have the Description text box control in your Form Design window):

1. **Select the `Description` label control only.**
2. **Press Delete to remove the label from the form.**

Attaching a label to a control

If you accidentally delete a label from a control, you can reattach it. To create and then reattach a label to a control, follow these steps:

1. **Click the Label button on the Controls group.**
2. **Place the mouse pointer in the Form Design window.**

   The mouse pointer becomes the Text Box button.
3. **Click and hold down the mouse button where you want the control to begin; drag the mouse to size the control.**
4. **Type** Description: **and click outside the control.**
5. **Select the `Description` label control.**
6. **Select Cut from the Home ribbon's Clipboard group.**
7. **Select the `Description` text box control.**
8. **Select Paste from the Home ribbon's Clipboard group to attach the label control to the text box control.**

Another way to attach a label to a control is to click the informational icon next to the label, shown in Figure 7-18. This informational icon lets you know that this label is unassociated with a control. Click the Associate Label with a Control command from the menu, and then select the control you want to associate the label with.

FIGURE 7-18

Associating a label with a control

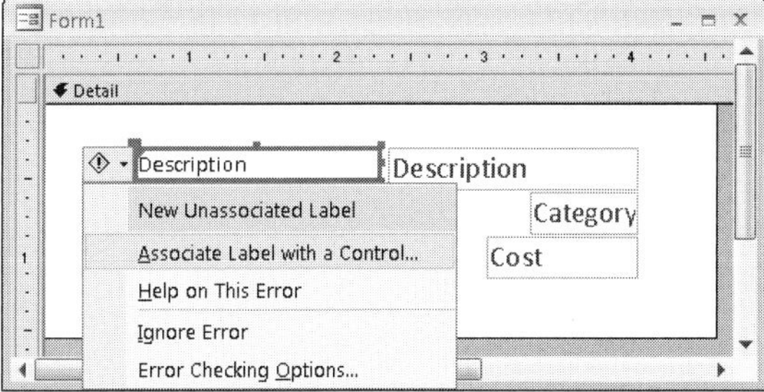

Copying a control

You can create copies of any control by copying it to the Clipboard and then pasting the copies where you want them. If you have a control for which you have entered many properties or specified a certain format, you can copy it and revise only the properties (such as the control name and bound field name) to make it a different control. This capability is useful with a multiple-page form when you want to display the same values on different pages and in different locations, or when copying a control from one form to another.

Changing the control type

In Figure 7-19, the Complete control is a check box. Although there are times you may want to use a check box to display a Boolean (Yes/No) data type, there are other ways to display the value, such as a toggle button. A toggle button is raised if it's true and depressed (or at least very unhappy) if it's false.

FIGURE 7-19

Become a magician and turn a check box into a toggle button.

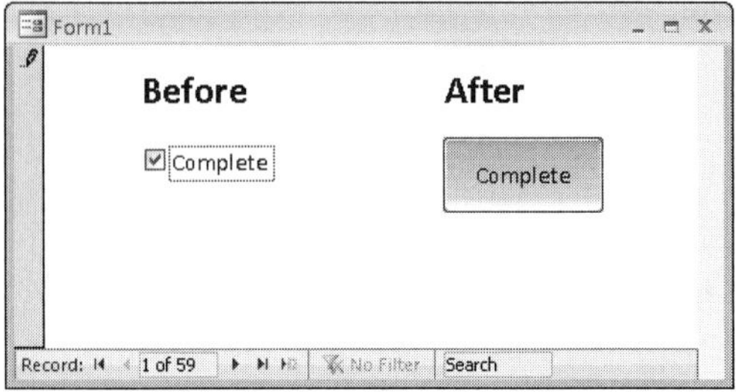

Use these steps to turn the check box into a toggle button:

1. **Select the Complete label control (just the label control, not the check box).**
2. **Press the Delete key to delete the label control because it is not needed.**
3. **Right-click the `Complete` check box, and choose Change To ➪ Toggle Button from the pop-up menu.**
4. **Resize the toggle button and click inside it to get the blinking cursor; then type** Complete **on the button as its caption (shown on the right of Figure 7-19).**

Understanding Properties

Properties are named attributes of controls, fields, or database objects that are used to modify the characteristics of a control, field, or object. Examples of these attributes are the size, color, appearance, or name of an object. A property can also modify the behavior of a control, determining, for example, whether the control is read-only or editable and visible or not visible.

Properties are used extensively in forms and reports to change the characteristics of controls. Each control on the form has properties. The form itself also has properties, as does each of its sections. The same is true for reports; the report itself has properties, as does each report section and individual control. The label control also has its own properties, even if it is attached to another control.

Everything from moving and resizing controls to changing fonts and colors that you do with the ribbon commands can be done by setting properties. In fact, all these commands do is change properties of the selected controls.

Displaying the Property Sheet

Properties are displayed in a Property Sheet (sometimes called a Property window). To display the Property Sheet for the Description text box, follow the steps below. You will be creating a new blank form.

1. **Drag the first five fields, `ProductID` through `Cost`, from the Field List window to the form's Design View.**
2. **Click the Description text box control to select it.**
3. **Click the Property Sheet command in the Design ribbon's Tools group to display the Property Sheet — which appears docked to the right side of the Access window, taking the place of the Field List.**

   The screen should look like the one shown in Figure 7-20.

FIGURE 7-20

Change an object's properties with the Property Sheet

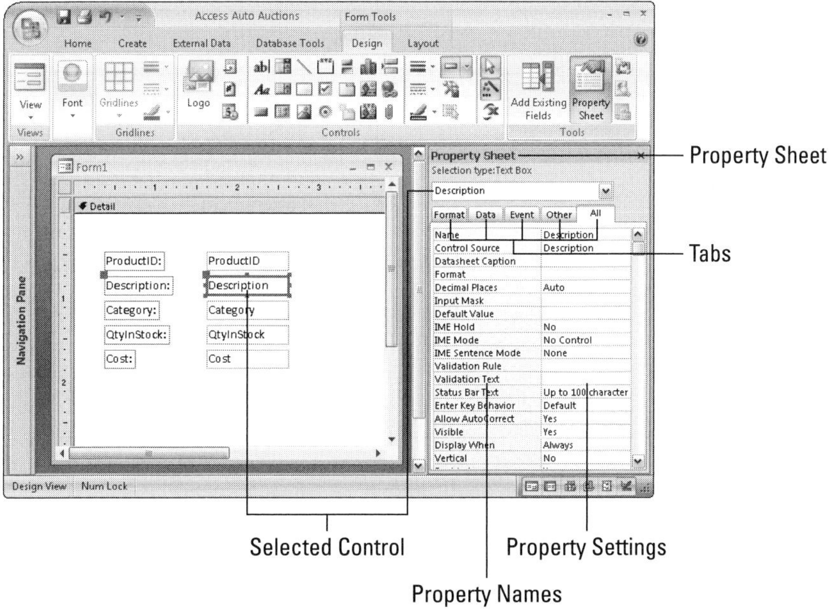

Because the Property Sheet is a window, it can be undocked, moved, and resized. It does not, however, have Maximize or Minimize buttons. There are several ways to display a control's Property Sheet if it's not visible:

- Select a control and click the Property Sheet command in the Design ribbon's Tools group.
- Double-click any control.
- Right-click any control and select Properties from the pop-up menu.

Understanding the Property Sheet

With the Property Sheet displayed, click on any control in Design View to display the properties for that control. Select multiple controls to display similar properties for the selected controls.

In Figure 7-20, the Property Sheet has been sized to fit the screen. By widening the Property Sheet, you can see more of its values; by increasing the length, you can see more controls at one time. The vertical scroll bar lets you move between various properties.

The Property Sheet has an All tab that lets you see all the properties for a control. Or you can choose another tab to limit the view to a specific group of properties. The specific tabs and groups of properties are as follows:

- **Format:** These properties determine how a label or value looks: font, size, color, special effects, borders, and scroll bars.
- **Data:** These properties affect how a value is displayed and the data source it is bound to: control source, input masks, validation, default value, and other data type properties.
- **Event:** Event properties are named events, such as clicking a mouse button, adding a record, pressing a key for which you can define a response (in the form of a call to a macro or a VBA procedure), and so on.
- **Other:** Other properties show additional characteristics of the control, such as the name of the control or the description that displays in the status bar.

CROSS-REF **The number of properties available in Access has increased greatly since early versions of Access. The most important properties are described in various chapters of this book. For a discussion of Event properties and Event procedures, see Part II of this book.**

Figure 7-20 shows the Property Sheet for the Description text box. The first column lists the property names; the second column is where you enter or select property settings or options.

Changing a control's property setting

There are many different methods for changing property settings, including the following:

- Entering or selecting the desired value in a Property window
- Changing a property directly by changing the control itself, such as changing its size

- Using inherited properties from the bound field or the control's default properties
- Entering color selections for the control by using the ribbon commands
- Changing label text style, size, color, and alignment by using the ribbon commands

You can change a control's properties by clicking a property and typing the desired value.

In Figure 7-21, you can see a down arrow and a button with three dots to the right of the `Control Source` property-entry area. Some properties display a drop-down arrow in the property-entry area when you click in the area. The drop-down arrow tells you that Access has a list of values from which you can choose. If you click the down arrow in the `Control Source` property, you find that the drop-down list displays a list of all fields in the data source — `tblProducts`. Setting the `Control Source` property to a field in a table creates a bound control.

FIGURE 7-21

The Property Sheet undocked

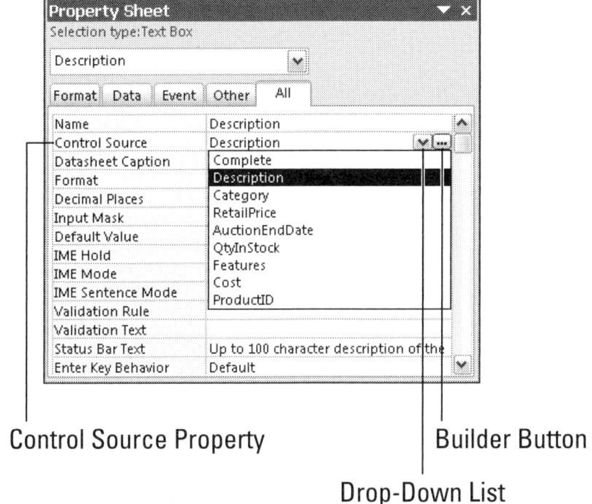

Some properties have a list of standard values such as Yes or No; others display varying lists of fields, forms, reports, or macros. The properties of each object are determined by the object itself and what the object is used for.

A nice feature in Access 2007 is the capability to cycle through property choices by repeatedly double-clicking on the choice. For example, double-clicking on the `Display When` property alternately selects Always, Print Only, and Screen Only.

The Builder button contains an ellipsis (three dots) and opens one of the many builders in Access — including the Macro Builder, the Expression Builder, and the Module Builder. When you open a builder and make some selections, the property is filled in for you. You will learn about builders later in this book.

Each type of object has its own property window and properties. These include the form itself, each of the form sections, and each of the form's controls. You display each of the property windows by clicking on the object first. The property window will instantly change to show the properties for the selected object.

Naming control labels and their captions

You might notice that each of the data fields has a Label control and a Text Box control. Normally, the label's `Caption` property is the same as the text box's `Name` property. The text box's `Name` property is usually the same as the table's field name — shown in the `Control Source` property. Sometimes, the label's `Caption` is different because a value was entered into the `Caption` property for each field in the table.

When creating controls on a form, it's a good idea to use standard naming conventions when setting the control's `Name` property. Name each control with a prefix followed by a meaningful name that you'll recognize later (for example, `txtTotalCost`, `cboState`, `lblTitle`). Table 7-2 shows the naming conventions for form and report controls. You can find a very complete, well-established naming convention online by searching for "Reddick Naming Convention."

TABLE 7-2

Form/Report Control Naming Conventions

Prefix	Object
`frb`	Bound Object frame
`cht`	Chart (Graph)
`chk`	Check Box
`cbo`	Combo Box
`cmd`	Command Button
`ocx`	ActiveX Custom Control
`det`	Detail (section)
`gft[n]`	Footer (group section)
`fft`	Form Footer section
`fhd`	Form Header section
`ghd[n]`	Header (group section)
`hlk`	Hyperlink
`img`	Image
`lbl`	Label
`lin`	Line

Prefix	Object
`lst`	List Box
`opt`	Option Button
`grp`	Option Group
`pge`	Page (tab)
`brk`	Page break
`pft`	Page Footer (section)
`phd`	Page Header (section)
`shp`	Rectangle
`rft`	Report Footer (section)
`rhd`	Report Header (section)
`sec`	Section
`sub`	Subform/Subreport
`tab`	Tab Control
`txt`	Text Box
`tgl`	Toggle Button
`fru`	Unbound Object Frame

The properties displayed in Figure 7-21 are the specific properties for the Description text box. The first two properties, `Name` and `Control Source`, are set to Description.

The `Name` is simply the name of the field itself. When a control is bound to a field, Access automatically assigns the `Name` property to the bound field's name. Unbound controls are given names such as Field11 or Button13. However, you can give the control any name you want.

With bound controls, the `Control Source` property is the name of the table field to which the control is bound. In this example, Description refers to the field with the same name in `tblProducts`. An unbound control has no control source, whereas the control source of a calculated control is the actual expression for the calculation, as in the example `=[SalePrice] - [Cost]`.

Summary

In this chapter, you learned how to add different types of forms to your database using the Create ribbon's Form group. You learned about the different types of controls and how to add them to the form. Then you learned how to move and resize these controls.

You also learned how properties are the building blocks of an object. The Property Sheet contains every attribute of the control, from where it's located on the form to what data it displays to what font it's displayed in. You learned how to display the Property Sheet and how to change a few properties, including the `Name` property using naming conventions.

Chapter 8

Working with Data on Access Forms

In Chapter 7, you learned about the tools necessary to create and display a form — Design View, bound and unbound controls, the Field List, and the ribbon's Controls group. In this chapter, you learn how to work with data on the form, view and change the form's properties, and use Access's new Layout View.

IN THIS CHAPTER

- Using Form View
- Navigating in a form
- Editing data in a form
- Entering pictures and data into OLE fields and Memo fields
- Using the date picker
- Switching views
- Printing a form
- Understanding form properties
- Changing the form's layout
- Setting the tab order
- Using the Field List
- Creating a calculated control

ON the CD-ROM In this chapter, you use `tblProducts` in the `Chapter08.accdb` database to provide the data necessary to create the examples used in this chapter.

Using Form View

Form View is where you actually view and modify data. Working with data in Form View is similar to working with data in a table or query's Datasheet View. Form View presents the data in a user-friendly format, which you create and design.

CROSS-REF For more information on working in Datasheet View, see Chapter 6.

To demonstrate the use of the Form View, follow these steps to create a new form based on `tblProducts`:

1. **Select `tblProducts` in the Navigation Pane.**
2. **Click the Create tab on the ribbon.**
3. **Click on the Form command in the Form group.**
4. **Click the Form View button on the Home tab's Views group to switch from Layout View to Form View.**

Figure 8-1 shows the Access window with the newly created form displayed in Form View. This view has many of the same elements as Datasheet View. At the top of the screen, you see the Access title bar, Quick Access toolbar, and the ribbon. The form in the center of the screen displays your data, one record at a time.

If the form contains more fields than can fit on-screen at one time, Access 2007 automatically displays a horizontal and/or vertical scroll bar that can be used to see the remainder of the data. You can also see the rest of the data by pressing the PgDn key. If you're at the bottom of a form, or the entire form fits on the screen, and press PgDn, you'll move to the next record.

The status bar at the bottom of the window displays the active field's Field Description that you defined when you created the table (or form). If no Field Description exists for a specific field, Access displays the words Form View. Generally, error messages and warnings appear in dialog boxes in the center of the screen (rather than in the status bar). The navigation buttons, search box, and view shortcuts are found at the bottom of the screen. These features lets you move quickly from record to record, find data quickly, or switch views.

FIGURE 8-1

A form in Form View

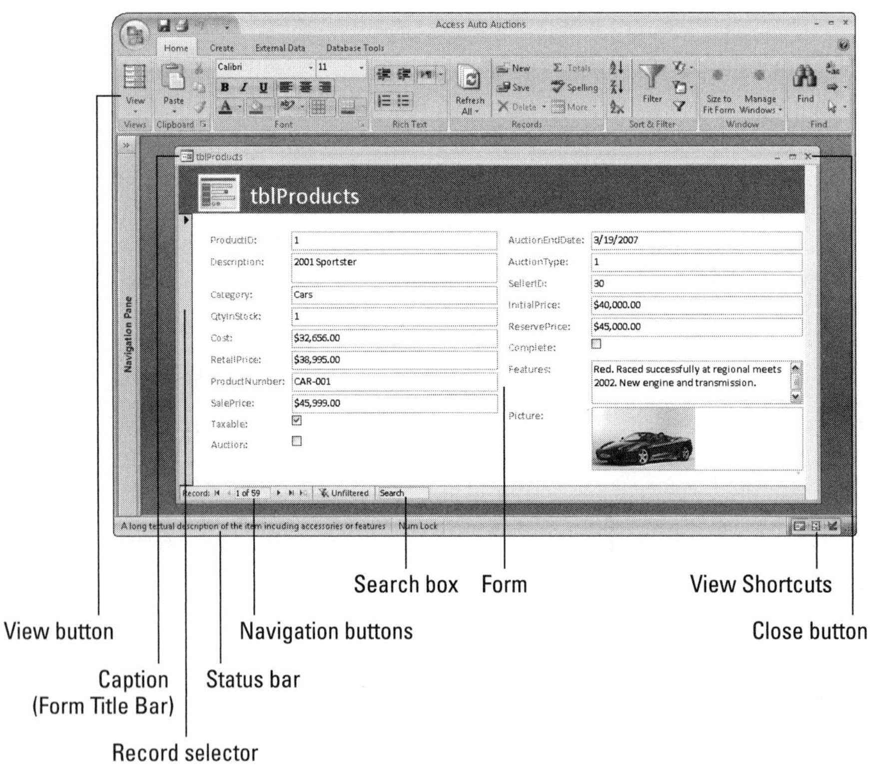

The Form ribbon

The Form ribbon (shown in Figure 8-2) provides a way to work with the data. The Home tab has some familiar objects on it, as well as some new ones. This section provides an overview of the form's Home tab; the individual commands will be described in more detail later in this chapter.

FIGURE 8-2

The Form ribbon's Home tab

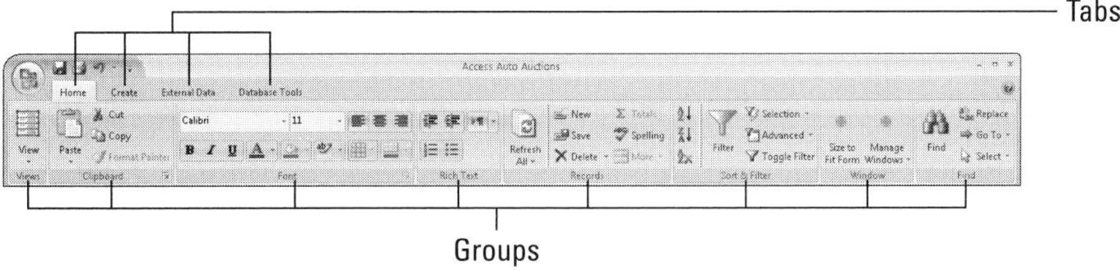

The first group is the View group, which allows you to switch between Form View, Datasheet View, PivotTable View, PivotChart View, Layout View, and Design View. You can see all six choices by clicking the command's down-arrow. Clicking Form View lets you manipulate data on the form. Datasheet View shows the data in a row-and-column format. Design View permits you to make changes to the form's design. Layout View lets you change the form's design while viewing data. PivotTable View and PivotChart View let you create PivotTables and PivotCharts based on the form's data. All these commands may not be available on all forms. By setting the form's properties, you can limit which views are available. You'll learn more about form properties later in this chapter.

The Clipboard group contains the Cut, Copy, and Paste commands. These commands work like the commands in other applications (Word, Excel, and so on). The Paste command's down arrow gives you three choices: Paste, Paste Special, and Paste Append. Paste Special gives you the option of pasting the contents of the Clipboard in different formats (Text, CSV, Records, etc.) Paste Append pastes the contents of the Clipboard as a new record — provided a record with a similar structure was copied.

The Font group lets you change the look of the datasheet in Datasheet View. Use these commands to change the font, size, bold, italic, color, and so on. Use the Align Left, Align Right, and Align Center commands to justify the data in the selected column. Click the Gridlines command to toggle gridlines on and off. Use the Alternate Fill/Back Color command to change the colors of alternating rows, or make them all the same. When modifying text in a memo field with the `Text Format` property set to `Rich Text`, you can use these commands to change the fonts, colors, and so on.

The Rich Text group lets you change a memo field's data if the field's `Text Format` property is set to `Rich Text`. Use these commands to add bullets or numbered lists and change the indentation levels.

The Records group lets you save, delete, or add a new record to the form. It also contains commands to show totals, check spelling, freeze and hide columns, and change the row height and cell width in Datasheet View.

The Sort & Filter group lets you change the order of the records, as well as limit the records being displayed — based on criteria you want.

The Find group lets you find and replace data and go to specific records in the datasheet. Use the select command to select a record or all records.

Navigating between fields

Navigating a form is nearly identical to navigating a datasheet. You can easily move around the form window by clicking the field that you want and making changes or additions to your data. Because the form window displays only as many fields as can fit on-screen, you need to use various navigational aids to move within your form or between records.

Table 8-1 displays the navigational keys used to move between fields within a form.

TABLE 8-1

Navigating in a Form

Navigational Direction	Keystrokes
Next field	Tab, right-arrow (→) or down-arrow (↓) key, or Enter
Previous field	Shift+Tab, left-arrow (←), or up arrow (↑)
First field of current record	Home or Ctrl+Home
Last field of current record	End or Ctrl+End
Next page	PgDn or Next Record
Previous page	PgUp or Previous Record

If you have a form with more than one page, a vertical scroll bar displays. You can use the scroll bar to move to different pages on the form. You can also use the PgUp and PgDn keys to move between form pages. You can move up or down one field at a time by clicking the scroll-bar arrows. With the scroll-bar button, you can move past many fields at once.

Moving between records in a form

Although you generally use a form to display one record at a time, you still need to move between records. The easiest way to do this is to use the Navigation buttons, as shown in Figure 8-3. The Navigation buttons let you move to the desired record.

The Navigation buttons (shown in Figure 8-3) are the six controls located at the bottom of the Form window, which you click to move between records. The two leftmost controls move you to the first record or the previous record in the form. The three rightmost controls position you on the next record, last record, or new record in the form. If you know the record number (the row number of a specific record), you can click the Record Number box, enter a record number, and press Enter.

FIGURE 8-3

The Navigation buttons of a form

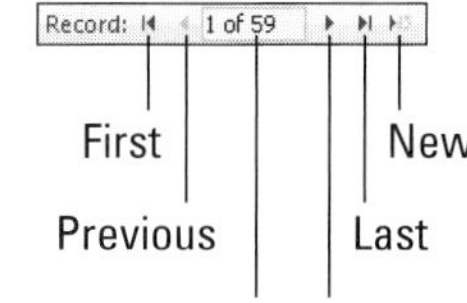

The record number between the Navigation buttons is a virtual record number. The number is not attached to any specific record — it's just an indicator as to the record number you're on given the current filter or sort. It will change with each time you filter or sort the records. The number to the right of the record number displays the number of records in the current view. The number of records displayed might not be the total number of records in the underlying table or query; this number changes when you filter the data on the form.

You can also press PgDn to move to the current field in the next record, or PgUp to move to the current field in the preceding record.

Changing Values in a Form

Earlier in the book, you learned techniques to add, change, and delete data within a table by using a datasheet. These techniques are the same ones you use within a form. Table 8-2 summarizes these techniques.

TABLE 8-2

Editing Techniques

Editing Technique	Keystrokes
Move insertion point within a control	Press the right-arrow (→) and left-arrow (←) keys
Insert a value within a control	Select the insertion point and type new data
Select the entire text in a control	Press F2
Replace an existing value with a new value	Select the entire field and type a new value
Replace value with value of preceding field	Press Ctrl+' (single quotation mark)
Replace current value with default value	Press Ctrl+Alt+Spacebar
Insert current date into a control	Press Ctrl+; (semicolon)
Insert current time into a control	Press Ctrl+: (colon)
Insert a line break in a Text or Memo control	Press Ctrl+Enter
Insert new record	Press Ctrl++ (plus sign)
Delete current record	Press Ctrl+- (minus sign)
Save current record	Press Shift+Enter or move to another record
Toggle values in a check box or option button	Spacebar
Undo a change to the current control	Press Esc or click the Undo button
Undo a change to the current record	Press Esc or click the Undo button a second time after you Undo the current control

Controls that you can't edit

Some controls can't be edited, such as:

- **Controls displaying AutoNumber fields:** Access maintains AutoNumber fields automatically, calculating the values as you create each new record.
- **Calculated controls:** Access uses calculated control in forms or queries; these values are not actually stored in your table.
- **Locked or disabled fields:** You can set certain properties to prevent editing for specific controls.
- **Controls in multiuser locked records:** If another user locks the record, you can't edit any controls in that record.

Working with pictures and OLE objects

OLE (Object Linking and Embedding) objects are objects not part of an Access database. These commonly include pictures but an OLE field can also contain links to objects such as Word documents, Excel spreadsheets, and audio files such as `.mp3`, `.wav`, or `.wmv` files. You can also include video files such as `.mpg` or `.avi` files.

In Datasheet View, you can't view a picture or any OLE object without accessing the OLE server (such as Word, Excel, or the Microsoft Media Player). In Form View, however, you can size the OLE control area to be large enough to display a picture, business graph, or any visual OLE object. You can also size text-box controls on forms so that you can see the data within the field — you don't have to zoom in on the value, as you do with a datasheet field.

Any object supported by an OLE server can be stored in an Access OLE field. OLE objects are entered into a form so that you can see, hear, or use the value. As with a datasheet, you have two ways to enter OLE fields into a form:

- Paste them in from the commands in the ribbon's Clipboard group.
- Right-click on the OLE field and click Insert Object from the pop-up menu to display the Insert Object dialog box, shown in Figure 8-4.

FIGURE 8-4

The Insert Object dialog box

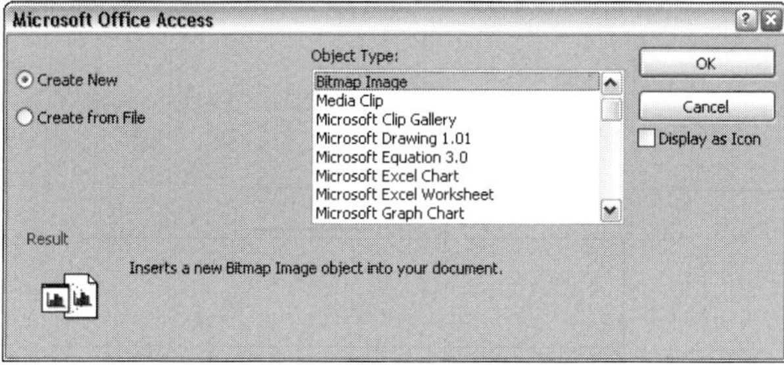

Use the Insert Object dialog box to add a new object to the OLE field, or add an object from an existing file. Choose the Create from File option button to add a picture or other OLE object from a file that already exists.

When displaying a picture in an OLE control, set the `Size Mode` property to control how the picture is displayed. The settings for this property are:

- **Clip:** Keeps the picture at its original size and truncates any portion of the picture that doesn't fit in the control.
- **Zoom:** Fits the picture in the control and keeps it in its original proportion, which may result in extra white space.
- **Stretch:** Sizes picture to fit exactly between the frame borders; this setting may distort the picture.

Memo field data entry

The `Features` field in the form shown in Figure 8-1 is a Memo data type. This type of field allows up to 65,535 bytes of text for each field. The first two sentences of data appear in the text box. When you click in this text box, a vertical scroll bar appears. Using this scrollbar, you can view the rest of the data in the control.

Better yet, you can resize the Memo control in the form's Design View if you want to make it larger to see more data. You can also press Shift+F2 and display a Zoom dialog box, as shown in Figure 8-5, which lets you see more data.

FIGURE 8-5

The Zoom dialog box

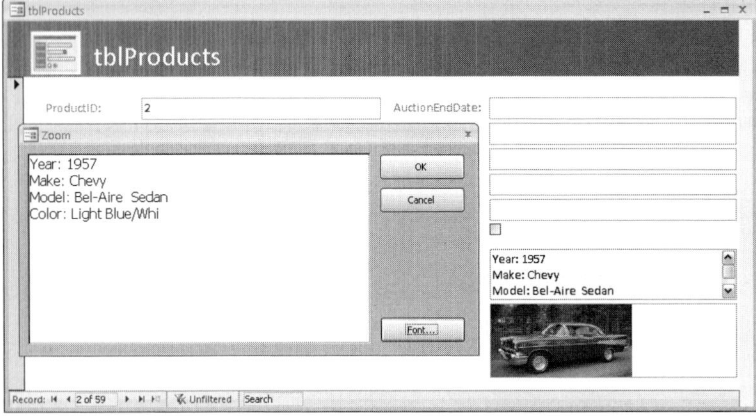

Date field data entry

The `AuctionEndDate` field in the form shown in Figure 8-5 is a Date/Time data type. This field is formatted to accept and show date values. When you click in this text box, a Date Picker icon appears next to it, as shown in Figure 8-6. Click the Date Picker to display a calendar from which you can choose a date.

If the Date Picker doesn't appear, switch to Design View and change the control's `Show Date Picker` property to `For dates`. Set the `Show Date Picker` property to `Never` if you don't want to use the Date Picker.

FIGURE 8-6

Using the Date Picker, new to Access 2007

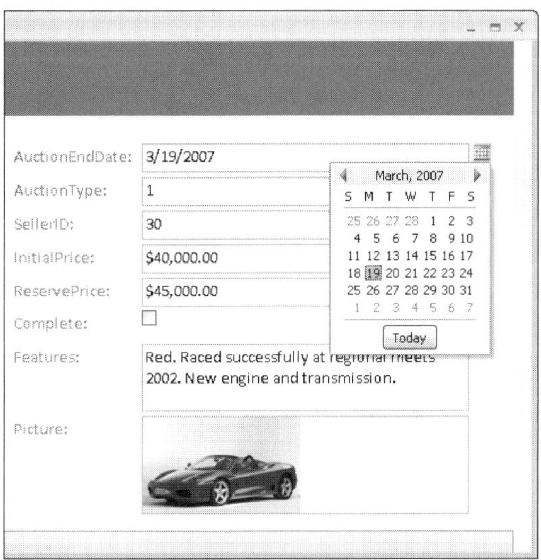

Using option groups

Option groups let you choose values from option buttons (sometimes called radio buttons). Option buttons let you select one value while deselecting the previous value. Option groups work best when you have a small number of choices to select from. Figure 8-7 shows an option group next to the `Auction` check box; both controls perform the same operation.

FIGURE 8-7

Using an option group to select a numeric value

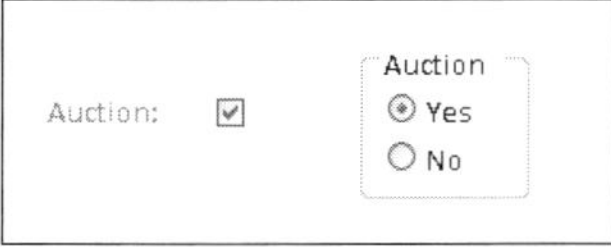

The easiest and most efficient way to create option groups is with the Option Group Wizard. You can use it to create option groups with multiple option buttons, toggle buttons, or check boxes. When you're through, all your control's property settings are correctly set. This wizard greatly simplifies the process and enables you to create an option group quickly. To create an option group, switch to Design View and select the Option Group command from the Design tab's Controls group. Make sure the Use Control Wizards command is selected.

Option groups can only be bound to numeric fields. When creating an option group for a Yes/No field (which is numeric), set the Yes value to –1 and the No value to 0.

Using combo boxes and list boxes

Access has two types of controls — *list boxes* and *combo boxes* — that enable you to show lists of data from which a user can select. The list box is always open and ready for selection, whereas the combo box has to be clicked to open the list for selection. Also the combo box enables you to enter a value that is not on the list and takes up less room on the form.

You may want to replace the Category text box with a combo box containing values from `tblCategories`, as shown in Figure 8-8. The easiest way to do this is with the Combo Box Wizard. This wizard walks you through the steps of creating a combo box that looks up values in another table. To create a combo box, switch to Design View and select the Combo Box command from the Design tab's Controls group. Make sure the Use Control Wizards command is selected.

FIGURE 8-8

Using a combo box to select value from a list

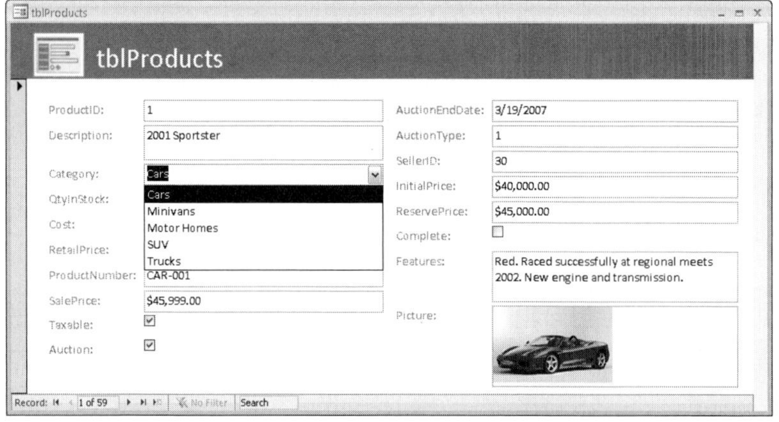

After you create the combo box, examine the `Row Source Type`, `Row Source`, `Column Count`, `Column Heads`, `Column Widths`, `Bound Column`, `List Rows`, and `List Width` properties. Once you become familiar with setting these properties, you can right-click a text box, select Change To ➪ Combo Box, and set the combo box's properties manually.

Switching to Datasheet View

While in the form, you can display a Datasheet View of your data by using one of the following methods:

- Click the Datasheet View command in the Home tab's Views group.
- Click the Datasheet View button in the View Shortcuts section at the bottom-right of the Access window.
- Right-click on the form's title bar — or any blank area of the form — and choose Datasheet View from the pop-up menu.

The datasheet is displayed with the cursor on the same field and record that it occupied in the form. If you move to another record and field and then redisplay the form, the form appears with the cursor on the field and with the record it last occupied in the datasheet.

To return to Form View — or any other view — select the desired view from the Views group, the View Shortcuts, or the pop-up menu.

Saving a record

Access saves each record when you move off it. Pressing Shift+Enter or selecting Save from the ribbon's Records group saves a record without moving off it. Closing the form also saves a record.

Printing a Form

You can print one or more records in your form exactly as they appear on-screen. (You learn how to produce formatted reports in Chapter 9.) The simplest way to print is to click the Print icon in the Quick Access toolbar. This prints the form to the Windows default printer. Click on the Microsoft Office Button to view other print options.

Printing a form is like printing anything else; you're in a WYSIWYG ("What You See Is What You Get") environment, so what you see on the form is essentially what you get in the printed hard copy. If you added page headers or page footers, they're printed at the top or bottom of the page. The printout contains any formatting that you specified in the form (including lines, boxes, and shading) and converts colors to grayscale if you're using a monochrome printer.

The printout includes as many pages as necessary to print all the data. If your form is wider than a single printer page, you need multiple pages to print your form. Access breaks up the printout as necessary to fit on each page.

You can also control printing from the Print dialog box, which you open by clicking the Microsoft Office Button, and then clicking on Print. From this dialog box, customize your printout by selecting from several options:

- **Print Range:** Prints the entire form or only selected pages or records
- **Copies:** Determines the number of copies to be printed
- **Collate:** Determines whether multiple copies are collated

You can also click the Properties button and set options for the selected printer or select the printer itself to change the type of printer. The Setup button allows you to set margins and print headings.

Using the Print Preview window

Although you may have all the information in the form ready to print, but you aren't sure whether that information will print on multiple pages or fit on one printed page. To preview your print job, click the Print Preview command under the Print menu to display the Print Preview window. The default view is the first page in single-page preview. Use the ribbon commands to select different views and zoom in and out. Click Print to print the form to the printer. Click the Close Print Preview command on the right side of the ribbon to return to Form View.

Working with Form Properties

You use form properties to change the way the entire form is displayed. This includes properties such as the form's background color or picture, the form's width, and so on. Tables 8-3 through 8-5 later in this chapter discuss some of the more important properties. Changing default properties is relatively easy: You select the property in the Property Sheet and set a new value. Following are some of the more important form properties that you may want to be aware of and may want to set.

The form selector is the area where the rulers meet; a small black square appears when the form is selected, as shown in Figure 8-9.

FIGURE 8-9

Using the form selector to display the form's Property Sheet

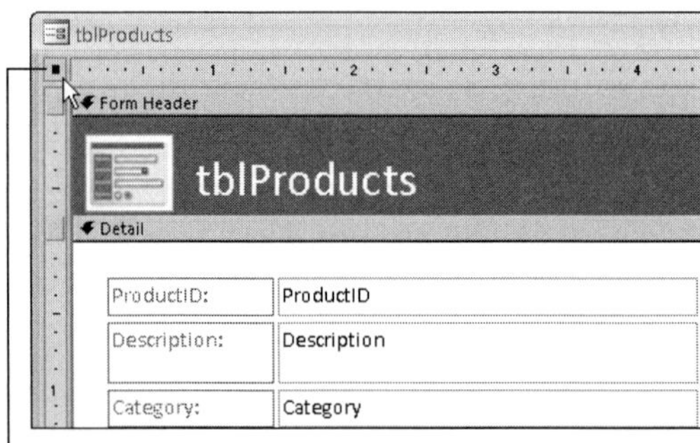

To set a form's properties, you have to show the Property Sheet for the form. Switch to Design View and use one of the following methods to display the form's Property Sheet:

- Click the form selector so a small black square appears, then click the Property Sheet command in the Design tab's Tools group.
- Click the Property Sheet command in the Design tab's Tools group, then select Form from the drop-down at the top of the Property Sheet.

- Double-click the form selector.
- Right-click the form selector and select Properties from the pop-up menu.

The form's Property Sheet appears docked to the right-side of the Access window. Because the Property Sheet is a window, it can be undocked, moved, and resized. It does not, however, have Maximize or Minimize buttons.

CROSS-REF For more information on working with the Property Sheet, see Chapter 7.

Changing the title bar text with the Caption property

Normally, the title bar displays the name of the form after it is saved. By changing the `Caption` property, you can display a different title on the title bar when the form is in Form View. To change the title bar text, follow these steps:

1. **Click the form selector to make sure the form itself is selected.**
2. **Click the Property Sheet command in the Design tab's Tools group.**
3. **Click the `Caption` property in the Property Sheet.**
4. **Type** Products, **as shown in Figure 8-10.**
5. **Click any other property or press Enter.**

FIGURE 8-10

Change the Caption property in the form's Property Sheet.

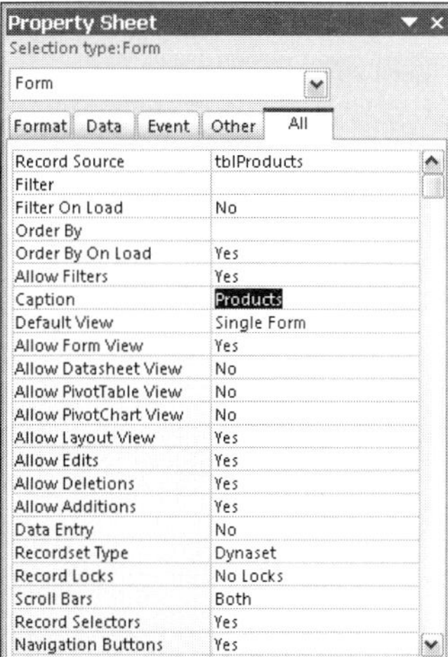

Switch to Form View to see the form's new title bar text. The caption you enter in the form's properties overrides the name of the saved form.

Creating a bound form

A bound form is one that places data into a table when the record is saved. Forms can be bound or unbound. To create a bound form, you must specify a data source in the form's `Record Source` property. In Figure 8-10, you can see the form's Property Sheet where the very first property is `Record Source`. If you want your form bound to a data source, this is where the name of the data source goes. Figure 8-10 shows the `Record Source` property set to `tblProducts`.

The data source can be on of three choices:

- **Table:** The name of a table from the current database file. The table can be a local table (stored in the database itself) or it can be linked to another Access database or an outside data source such as SQL Server.
- **Query:** The name of a query that references one or more tables from the current database file.
- **SQL Statement:** A SQL SELECT Statement that contains the name of a table or query.

If a form is unbound — the `Record Source` property is blank — you can't have any bound controls on the form (bound controls have their `Control Source` property set to a field in a table). If you add fields from the Field List and the `Record Source` property is blank, Access will set the `Record Source` property based on the fields you add.

CROSS-REF **For more information on adding bound controls with the Field List, see Chapter 7.**

Specifying how to view the form

Access 2007 uses several properties to determine how a form is viewed. The most common one is the `Default View`. The `Default View` property determines how the data is displayed when the form is first opened in Form View. There are six choices:

- **Single Form:** Displays one record at a time
- **Continuous Forms:** Shows more than one record at a time
- **Datasheet:** Row and column view like a spreadsheet or the standard query Datasheet View
- **PivotTable:** A datasheet with movable columns that can be swapped with rows
- **PivotChart:** A graph made from a PivotTable
- **Split Form:** A new feature in Access 2007 that gives you two views of the data at the same time, letting you select a record from a datasheet in the upper section and edit the information in a form in the lower section

Single Form is the default and displays one record per form page, regardless of the form's size. Continuous Forms tells Access to display as many detail records as will fit on-screen. Normally, you would use this setting to define the height of a very small form and to display many records at one time. Figure 8-11 shows such a continuous form with many records. The records have a small enough height that you can see a number of them at once.

FIGURE 8-11

The Continuous Forms setting of the Default View property shows multiple records at once. The Multiple Items form has its Default View set to Continuous Forms.

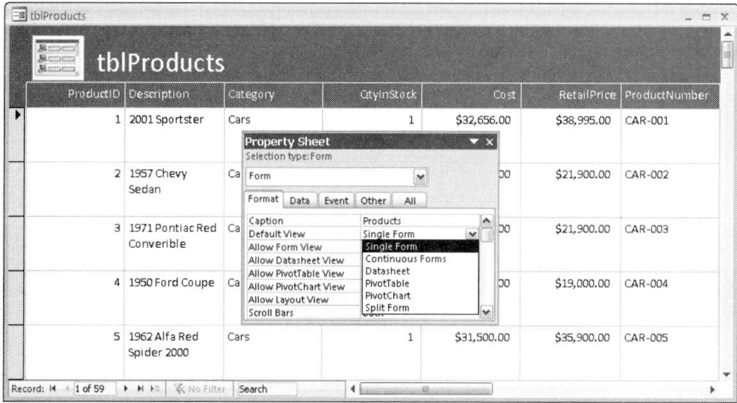

In Figure 8-11, you can see the form's Property Sheet with the choices for the `Default View` property.

A PivotTable form can display a field's values horizontally or vertically and then calculate the total of the row or column. Similar to this is the PivotChart, which displays a graphical analysis of data stored in a table, query, or form.

There are five separate properties to allow the developer to determine if the user can change the default view. These include `Allow Form View`, `Allow Datasheet View`, `Allow PivotTable View`, `Allow PivotChart View`, and `Allow Layout View`. The default settings are Yes to all of these properties, which lets you switch between Form View and Datasheet View, as well as PivotTable View and PivotChart View. If you set the `Allow Datasheet View` property to No, the Datasheet View commands (in the ribbon's Views group, the form's View Shortcuts, and right-click pop-up menu) won't be available; the data can be viewed only as a form. If you set the `Allow Form View` property to No, the Form View commands won't be available; the data can be viewed only as a datasheet.

Eliminating the Record Selector bar

The `Record Selectors` property determines whether the Record Selector bar (the vertical bar shown in Figure 8-1 on the left side of a form with a right-pointing arrow indicating the selected record) is displayed. The Record Selector bar is very important in multiple-record forms or datasheets because it's highlighted to indicate the current record and a pencil indicates that the record is being edited. Though the Record Selector bar is important for datasheets, you probably won't want it for a single record form. To eliminate it, simply change the form's `Record Selectors` property from Yes to No.

Set the Record Selectors property to No for your form.

Other form properties

Tables 8-3 through 8-5 list the most commonly used form properties and offers brief descriptions of each. You will learn more about many of these when they are used in examples throughout the chapters. Event properties are covered in Part II.

TABLE 8-3

Form Format Properties

Property	Description	Options
Caption	Displayed on the title bar of the displayed form.	N/A
Default View	Determines the type of view when the form is run.	Single Form: One record per page. Continuous Forms: (Default) As many records per page as will fit. Datasheet: Standard row and column Datasheet View. PivotTable: Displays a field's values horizontally or vertically; then calculates the total of the row or column. PivotChart: Graphical analysis of data. Split Form: Displays a datasheet in the upper portion and a form in the lower portion.
Allow Form View	Form View allowed (Yes/No).	N/A

Property	Description	Options
Allow Datasheet View	Datasheet View allowed (Yes/No).	N/A
Allow PivotTable View	PivotTable View allowed (Yes/No).	N/A
Allow PivotChart View	PivotChart View allowed (Yes/No).	N/A
Allow Layout View	Layout View allowed (Yes/No).	N/A
Scroll Bars	Determines whether any scroll bars are displayed.	Neither: No scroll bars are displayed. Horizontal Only: Displays only horizontal scroll bar. Vertical Only: Displays only vertical scroll bar. Both: Displays both horizontal and vertical scroll bars.
Record Selectors	Determines whether vertical Record Selector bar is displayed (Yes/No).	N/A
Navigation Buttons	Determines whether navigation buttons are visible (Yes/No).	N/A
Dividing Lines	Determines whether lines between form sections are visible (Yes/No).	N/A
Auto Resize	Form is opened to display a complete record (Yes/No).	N/A
Auto Center	Centers form on-screen when it's opened (Yes/No).	N/A
Border Style	Determines form's border style.	None: No border or border elements (scrollbars, navigation buttons). Thin: Thin border, not resizable. Sizable: Normal form settings. Dialog: Thick border, title bar only, cannot be sized; use for dialog boxes.
Control Box	Determines whether control menu (Restore, Move Size) is available (Yes/No).	N/A
Min Max Buttons	Specifies whether the "Min" and "Max" buttons appear in the form's title bar	None: No buttons displayed in upper-right corner of form. Min Enabled: Displays only Minimize button. Max Enabled: Displays only Maximize button. Both Enabled: Displays Minimize and Maximize buttons.

continued

TABLE 8-3 *(continued)*

Property	Description	Options
Close Button	Determines whether to display Close button in upper-right corner and a close menu item on the control menu (Yes/No).	N/A
Width	Displays the value of the width of the form; can be entered or Access fills it in as you adjust the width of the work area.	N/A
Picture	Enter the name of a bitmap file for the background of the entire form.	N/A
Picture Type	Determines whether picture is embedded or linked.	Embedded: Picture is embedded in the form and becomes a part of the database file. Linked: Picture is linked to the form. Access stores the location of the picture and retrieves it every time the form is opened.
Picture Size Mode	Determines how the picture is displayed.	Clip: Displays the picture at its actual size. Stretch: Fits picture to form size (non-proportional). Zoom: Fits picture to form size (proportional); this may result in the picture not fitting in one dimension (height or width).
Picture Alignment	Determines picture alignment.	Top Left: The picture is displayed in the top-left corner of the form, report window, or image control. Top Right: The picture is displayed in the top-right corner of the form, report window, or image control. Center: (Default) The picture is centered in the form, report window, or image control. Bottom Left: The picture is displayed in the bottom-left corner of the form, report window, or image control. Bottom Right: The picture is displayed in the bottom-right corner of the form, report window, or image control. Form Center: The form's picture is centered horizontally in relation to the width of the form and vertically in relation to the topmost and bottommost controls on the form.

Property	Description	Options
Picture Tiling	Used when you want to overlay multiple copies of a small bitmap; for example, a single brick can become a wall (Yes/No).	N/A
Grid X	Displays setting for number of points per inch when X grid is displayed.	N/A
Grid Y	Displays setting for number of points per inch when Y grid is displayed.	N/A
Layout for Print	Determines whether form uses screen fonts or printer fonts.	Yes: Printer Fonts. No: Screen Fonts.
Sub-datasheet Height	Determines the height of a sub-datasheet when expanded.	NA
Sub-datasheet Expanded	Determines the saved state of all subdatasheets in a table or query.	Yes: The saved state of subdatasheets is expanded. No: The saved state of subdatasheets is closed.
Palette Source	The palette for a form or report	(Default): Indicates the default Access color palette. You can also specify other Windows palette files (`.pal`), `.ico`, `.bmp`, `.db`, and `.wmf` files.
Orientation	Determines View Orientation.	Right-to-Left: Appearance and functionality move from right to left. Left-to-Right: Appearance and functionality move from left to right.
Moveable	Determines whether the form can be moved (Yes/No).	N/A
Split Form Orientation	Determines the look of a form in Split Form View.	Datasheet on Top: Datasheet appears at the top of the form. Datasheet on Bottom: Datasheet appears at the bottom of the form. Datasheet on Left: Datasheet appears to the left of the form. Datasheet on Right: Datasheet appears to the right of the form.
Split Form Datasheet	Determines whether data can be edited in the datasheet of a Split Form.	Allow Edits: Edits are allowed. Read Only: Data is read-only and cannot be changed.

continued

TABLE 8-3 *(continued)*

Property	Description	Options
Split Form Splitter Bar	Determines whether there's a splitter bar on a Split Form (Yes/No).	N/A
Save Splitter Bar Position	Determines whether the position of the Splitter Bar should be saved (Yes/No).	N/A
Split Form Size	Size of the form part of the Split Form.	N/A
Split Form Printing	Determines which section of a Split Form to print.	Form Only: Prints the form portion. Datasheet Only: Prints the datasheet section.
Navigation Caption	Overrides the word *Record* in the form's navigation buttons.	N/A

TABLE 8-4

Form Data Properties

Property	Description	Options
Record Source	Determines where the data to be displayed in the form is coming from, or where the data is going when you create a new record. Can be a table or a query.	N/A
Filter	Used to specify a subset of records to be displayed when a filter is applied to a form. Can be set in the form properties, a macro, or through VBA.	N/A
Filter on Load	Apply filter at form/report startup (Yes/No).	N/A
Order By	Specifies the field or fields used to order the data in the view.	N/A
Order By on Load	Apply sort at form/report startup (Yes/No).	N/A
Allow Filters	Determines whether a user will be able to display a filtered form (Yes/No).	N/A
Allow Edits	Determines whether a user will be able to edit data, making the form editable or read only (Yes/No).	N/A
Allow Deletions	Determines whether a user will be able to delete records (Yes/No).	N/A

Property	Description	Options
Allow Additions	Determines whether a user will be able to add records (Yes/No).	N/A
Data Entry	Determines whether form opens to a new blank record, not showing any saved records (Yes/No).	N/A
Recordset Type	Used to determine whether multi-table forms can be updated.	Dynaset: Only default table field controls can be edited. Dynaset (Inconsistent Updates): All tables and fields are editable. Snapshot: No fields are editable (Read Only in effect).
Record Locks	Used to determine default multiuser record locking on bound forms.	No Locks: Record is locked only as it is saved. All Records: Locks entire form's records while using the form. Edited Record: Locks only current record being edited.
Fetch Defaults	Determines whether default values should be retrieved (Yes/No).	N/A

TABLE 8-5

Form "Other" Properties

Property	Description	Option Definition
Pop Up	Form is a pop-up that floats above all other objects (Yes/No).	N/A
Modal	For use when you must close the form before doing anything else. Disables other windows. When Pop Up set to Yes, Modal disables menus and toolbar, creating a dialog box (Yes/No).	N/A
Cycle	Determines how Tab works in the last field of a record.	All Records: Tabbing from the last field of a record moves to the next record. Current Record: Tabbing from the last field of a record moves to the first field of that record. Current Page: Tabbing from the last field of a record moves to the first field of the current page.

continued

TABLE 8-5 *(continued)*

Property	Description	Option Definition
Menu Bar	Used to specify an alternate menu bar.	N/A
Toolbar	Use this property to specify the toolbar to use for the form. You can create a toolbar for your form by selecting the Customize option under the Toolbar command in the View menu.	N/A
Custom Ribbon ID	Name of loaded Ribbon customization to apply on open.	N/A
Shortcut Menu	Determines whether shortcut (right-click) menus are active (Yes/No).	N/A
Shortcut Menu Bar	Used to specify an alternate shortcut menu bar.	N/A
Fast Laser Printing	Prints rules instead of lines and rectangles (Yes/No).	N/A
Help File	Name of compiled Help file to assign custom help to the form.	N/A
Help Context Id	ID of context-sensitive entry point in the Help file to display.	N/A
Tag	Use this property to store extra information about your form.	N/A
Has Module	Use this property to show if your form has a class module. Setting this property to No can improve the performance and decrease the size of your database.	N/A
Use Default Paper Size	Use the default paper size when printing (Yes/No).	N/A
Display on SharePoint Site	Determines whether the form should be displayed on Microsoft Windows SharePoint Services?	Do Not Display: Don't display on SharePoint Services. Follow Table Setting: Use the form's underlying table setting.

Adding a Form Header or Footer

Although the form's Detail section usually contains the majority of the controls that display data, there are other optional sections in a form that you can add:

- **Form Header:** Displayed at the top of each page when viewed and at the top when the form is printed.
- **Page Header:** Displayed only when the form is printed; prints after the form header.
- **Page Footer:** Appears only when the form is printed; prints before the form footer.
- **Form Footer:** Displayed at the bottom of each page when viewed and at the bottom of the form when the form is printed.

A Form Header appears at the top of the form, while a Form Footer appears at the bottom. The Form Header and Footer remain on the screen, while any controls in the Detail section can scroll up and down.

Page Headers and Page Footers are displayed only if the form is printed. They do not appear when the form is displayed.

You can select the Form Header/Footer or Page Header/Footer commands from the Arrange tab's Show/Hide group in the form's Design View. These commands will place a Form Header/Footer or Page Header/Footer on the form.

Changing the Layout

In this section, you'll learn how to change a form's layout using Access's new Layout View. You'll add, move, and resize controls, as well as change a few other characteristics while viewing the form's data.

In the Home tab's Views group, click the Layout View command to switch to Layout View. Click on the ribbon's Arrange tab (shown in Figure 8-12) to show commands available to change the form while viewing data.

FIGURE 8-12

The Form ribbon's Arrange tab for Layout View

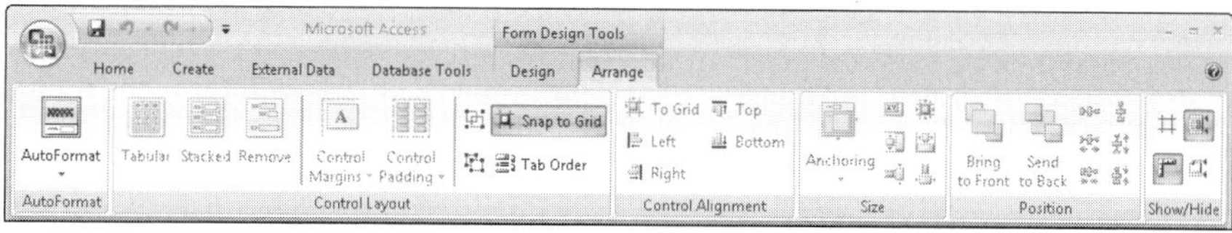

Changing a control's properties

In previous versions of Access, you had to make changes to the form in Design View. In Layout View, you can change these properties while looking at the data instead of the `Control Source`. Click the Property Sheet command in the Arrange tab's Tools group to display the Property Sheet for a selected Control.

CROSS-REF For more information on changing control properties with the Property Sheet, see Chapter 7.

Setting the Tab Order

If you move controls around or add a new control in between existing controls, you may notice that when you use Tab to move from control to control, the cursor jumps around the screen, skipping some control and moving fairly randomly around the screen. This route may seem strange, but that is the original order in which the controls were added to the form.

The *tab order* of the form is the order in which you move from control to control when you press Tab. The form's default tab order is always the order in which the controls were added to the form. If you move the controls around or even delete one control and re-add it for any reason, you'll probably need to change the tab order. Even though you may make heavy use of the mouse when designing your forms, the average data-entry person still uses the keyboard to move from control to control.

When you need to change the tab order of a form, select the Tab Order command from the Arrange tab's Control Layout group to display the Tab Order dialog box, shown in Figure 8-13. This dialog box shows the controls in the form that you can tab to; controls such as labels, lines, and other non-data controls don't appear.

FIGURE 8-13

The Tab Order dialog box

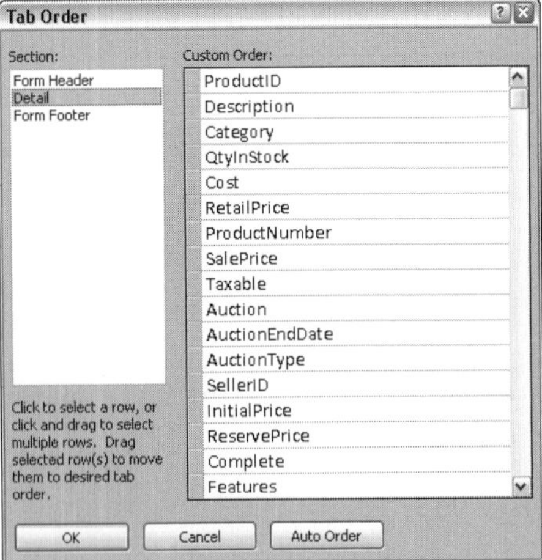

The Tab Order dialog box lets you select either one row or multiple rows at a time. Multiple contiguous rows are selected by clicking the first Selection bar and dragging down to select multiple rows. After the rows are highlighted, the selected rows can be dragged to their new positions.

The Tab Order dialog box has several buttons at the bottom of the window. The Auto Order button places the controls in order from left to right and from top to bottom, according to their position in the form. This button is a good place to start when you have significantly rearranged the controls. The OK button applies the changes to the form; the Cancel button closes the dialog box without changing the tab order.

Each control has two properties related to the Tab Order dialog box. The `Tab Stop` property determines whether pressing the Tab key lands you on the control. The default is Yes; changing the `Tab Stop` property to No removes the control from the tab order. When you set the tab order, you are setting the `Tab Index` property values. Moving the fields around in the Tab Order dialog box changes the `Tab Index` properties of those (and other) controls.

Aligning controls

You may want to move several controls so that they are all *aligned* (lined up). The Layout ribbon's Control Alignment group has several options for aligning controls: Left, Right, Top, and Bottom. These commands work the same as the Control Alignment commands described in Chapter 7, with the exception of aligning controls to the grid, which isn't available in Layout View.

Modifying the format of text in a control

To modify the formatting of text within a control, select the control by clicking it, then select a formatting style to apply to the control. The Layout View ribbon's Design tab—shown in Figure 8-14—contains additional commands for changing the format of a control.

FIGURE 8-14

The Form ribbon's Design tab for Layout View

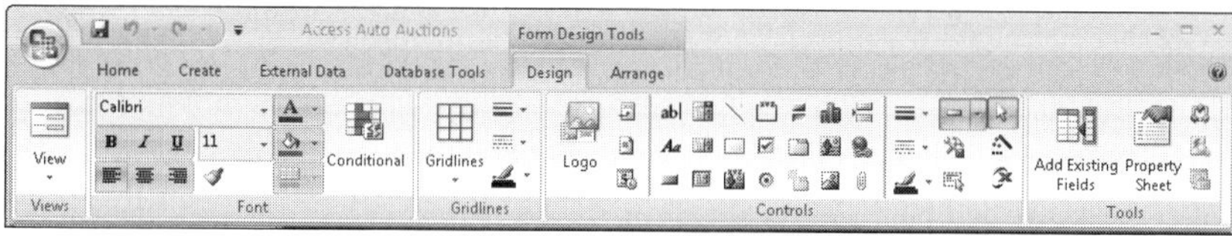

To change the fonts for the `Category` control, make sure you're in Layout View, then follow these steps:

1. **Select the `Category` control by clicking on it.**
2. **Change the Font Size to 14, and then click on the Bold button in the Design tab's Font group.**

   You probably can only see a portion of the label. The label control now needs to be resized to display all the text.

Using the Field List to add controls

The Field List displays a list of fields from table or query the form is based on. You add bound controls to the form by dragging fields from the Field List onto the form. Select and drag them one at a time, or select multiple fields by using the Ctrl key or Shift key. The Field List in Layout View works the same as the Field List in Design View, which is described in detail in Chapter 7.

Click the Add Existing Fields command in the Design tab's Controls group to display the Field List. By default, the Field List appears docked on the right of the Access window, shown in Figure 8-15. This window is movable and resizable and displays a vertical scrollbar if it contains more fields than can fit in the window.

To add fields from the Field List to a new form, follow these steps:

1. **Select `tblProducts` in the Navigation Pane.**
2. **Click the Create tab on the ribbon, and then click on the Blank Form command in the Form group to display a new form in Layout View.**
3. **If the Field List isn't displayed, click on the ribbon's Design tab, and then click the Add Existing Fields command from the Controls group.**
4. **Click the ProductID field in the Field List.**
5. **Hold the Shift key and click the Cost field in the Field List.**
6. **Drag the selected fields from the Field List to the Form, as shown in Figure 8-15.**

FIGURE 8-15

Adding fields from the Field List in a form's Layout View

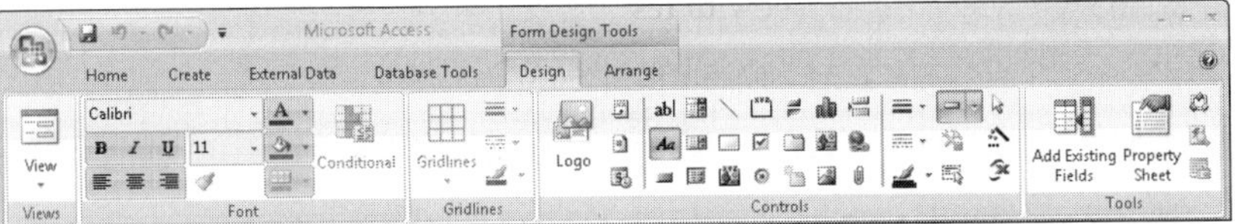

You can select noncontiguous fields in the list by clicking each field while holding down the Ctrl key. Each highlighted field can be dragged (as part of the group) to the form's Layout View.

Creating a Calculated Control

A calculated control displays a value that isn't stored in the form's underlying Record Source. To understand creation of a calculated control, you will now create one as follows:

1. **Select `tblProducts` in the Navigation Pane.**
2. **Click the Create tab on the ribbon, then click on the Blank Form command in the Form group to display a new form in Layout View.**
3. **Drag the `Cost` and `SalePrice` fields from the Field List onto the form.**
4. **Switch the form to Design View.**
5. **Click on the Text Box command in the Controls group and draw it on the form.**
6. **Set the `Name` property to `txtProfit`.**

   The `txt` prefix means the control is a text box.
7. **Set the `Control Source` property to `=[SalePrice]-[Cost]`.**
8. **Change the `Format` property to `Currency`.**
9. **Change the `Decimal Places` property to `2`.**
10. **Change the label's `Caption` property to `Profit:`.**
11. **Switch to Form View to test the calculation.**

    Your screen should look like one shown in Figure 8-16. The `txtProfit` control shows the difference between the `SalePrice` and `Cost`.

FIGURE 8-16

Creating a calculated control

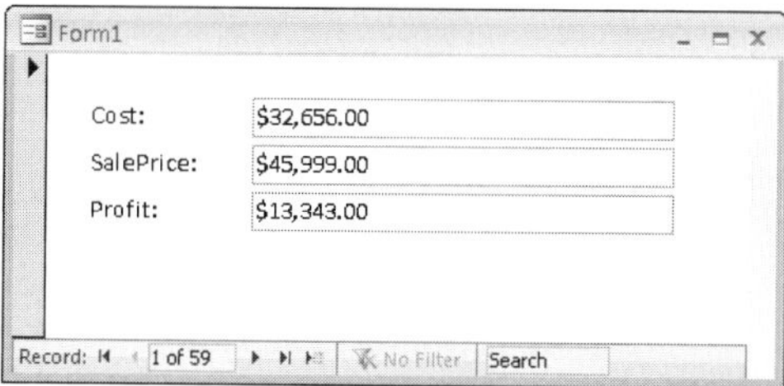

Converting a Form to a Report

By opening a form in Design View, clicking the Microsoft Office Button, and selecting Save As, you can save a form as a report. The entire form is placed in the report. If the form has form headers or footers, these are placed in the Report Header and Report Footer sections. If the form has page headers or page footers, these are placed in the Page Header and Page Footer sections in the report. After the design is in the Report Design window, it can be enhanced using the report design features. This allows you to add group sections and additional totaling in a report without having to re-create a great layout. You'll learn more about reports in later chapters.

Summary

In this chapter, you learned that working with data in Form View is similar to working with data in a table or query's Datasheet View. You learned how to navigate between fields and records and how to use controls such as option groups and combo boxes to facilitate data entry.

You also learned about a form's properties, including the different groupings and each property setting. You learned how setting some of these properties affects a form's appearance. You added a form header and footer and worked with the new Layout View, which lets you manipulate a form and its controls while viewing live data.

Chapter 9

Presenting Data with Access Reports

IN THIS CHAPTER

- Understanding the different types of Access reports
- Knowing the differences between reports and forms
- Understanding the process of building reports
- Creating reports with a Report Wizard
- Viewing reports on screen
- Printing reports
- Saving reports
- Understanding the 11 tasks necessary to create a great report
- Creating a report from a blank form
- Sorting and grouping data
- Adding label and text controls to your report
- Modifying the appearance of text and label controls
- Adding page breaks
- Copying an existing report

Reports provide the most flexible way of viewing and printing summarized information. Reports display information with the desired level of detail, while enabling you to view or print your information in almost any format. You can add multilevel totals, statistical comparisons, and pictures and graphics to a report. In this chapter, you learn to use Report Wizards as a starting point. You also learn how to create reports and what types of reports you can create with Access.

ON the CD-ROM **In this chapter, you create new reports using the report wizards and by creating a blank report without using a wizard. You use tables created in previous chapters. The `Chapter09.accdb` database file on the book's CD-ROM contains the completed reports described in this chapter.**

Understanding Reports

Reports present a customized view of your data. Report output is viewed onscreen or printed to provide a hard copy of the data. Reports provide summaries of the information contained in the database. Data can be grouped and sorted in any order and can create totals that add numbers, calculate averages or other statistics, and graphically display data. Reports can include pictures and other graphics as well as memo fields in a report. If you can think of a report you want, Access probably supports it.

Understanding report types

Four basic types of reports are used by businesses:

- **Tabular reports:** These print data in rows and columns with groupings and totals. Variations include summary and group/total reports.
- **Columnar reports:** These print data as a form and can include totals and graphs.
- **Mail-merge reports:** These create form letters.
- **Mailing labels:** These create multicolumn labels or snaked-column reports.
- **Graphs:** Visual representation of your data in a form such as a bar or a pie chart.

Tabular reports

Figure 9-1 is a typical tabular-type report (rptProductsSummary) displayed in print preview. *Tabular reports* (also known as *groups/totals reports*) are similar to a table that displays data in neat rows and columns. Tabular reports, unlike forms or datasheets, usually group data by one or more fields. Often, tabular reports calculate and display subtotals or statistical information for numeric fields in each group. Some reports include page totals and grand totals. You can even have multiple *snaked columns* so that you can create directories (such as telephone books). These types of reports often use page numbers, report dates, or lines and boxes to separate information. Reports may have color and shading and display pictures, business graphs, and memo fields. A special type of *summary* tabular report can have all the features of a *detail* tabular report but omit record details.

FIGURE 9-1

A tabular report (`rptProductsSummary`) displayed in Print Preview

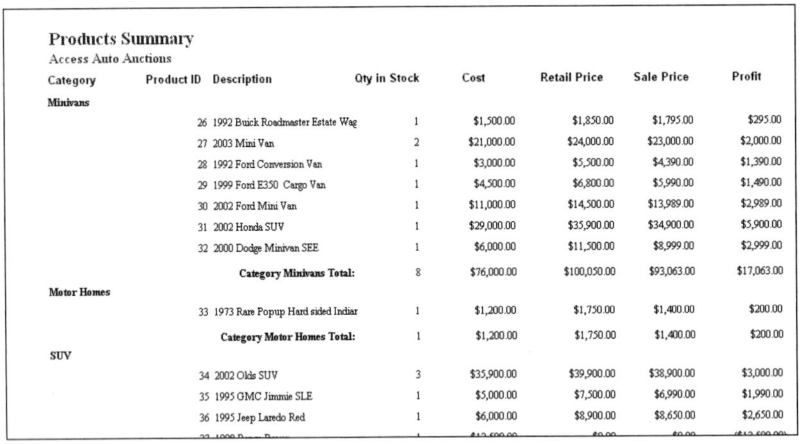

Products Summary

Access Auto Auctions

Category	Product ID	Description	Qty in Stock	Cost	Retail Price	Sale Price	Profit
Minivans							
	26	1992 Buick Roadmaster Estate Wag	1	$1,500.00	$1,850.00	$1,795.00	$295.00
	27	2003 Mini Van	2	$21,000.00	$24,000.00	$23,000.00	$2,000.00
	28	1992 Ford Conversion Van	1	$3,000.00	$5,500.00	$4,390.00	$1,390.00
	29	1999 Ford E350 Cargo Van	1	$4,500.00	$6,800.00	$5,990.00	$1,490.00
	30	2002 Ford Mini Van	1	$11,000.00	$14,500.00	$13,989.00	$2,989.00
	31	2002 Honda SUV	1	$29,000.00	$35,900.00	$34,900.00	$5,900.00
	32	2000 Dodge Minivan SEE	1	$6,000.00	$11,500.00	$8,999.00	$2,999.00
		Category Minivans Total:	8	$76,000.00	$100,050.00	$93,063.00	$17,063.00
Motor Homes							
	33	1973 Rare Popup Hard sided Indiar	1	$1,200.00	$1,750.00	$1,400.00	$200.00
		Category Motor Homes Total:	1	$1,200.00	$1,750.00	$1,400.00	$200.00
SUV							
	34	2002 Olds SUV	3	$35,900.00	$39,900.00	$38,900.00	$3,000.00
	35	1995 GMC Jimmie SLE	1	$5,000.00	$7,500.00	$6,990.00	$1,990.00
	36	1995 Jeep Laredo Red	1	$6,000.00	$8,900.00	$8,650.00	$2,650.00

Columnar reports

Columnar reports generally display one or more records per page, but do so vertically. Columnar reports display data very much as a data-entry form does but are used strictly for viewing data and not for entering data. Figure 9-2 shows part of a columnar report (rptProducts) in Print Preview.

FIGURE 9-2

A columnar report showing report controls distributed throughout the entire page

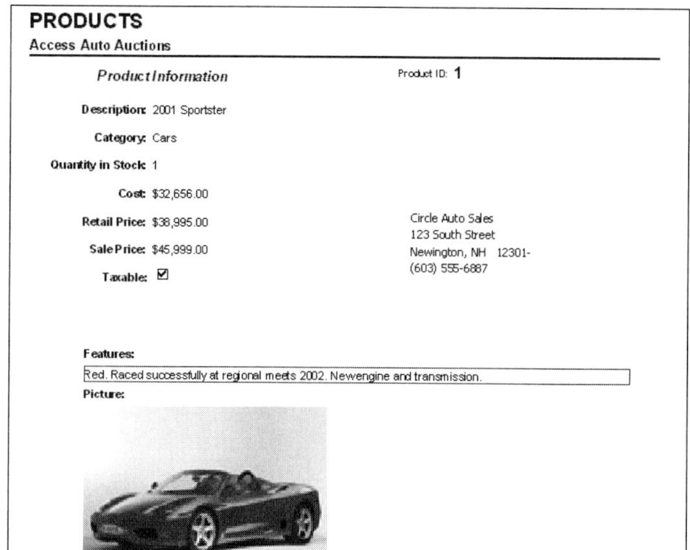

Another type of columnar report displays one main record per page (like a business form) but can show many records within embedded subforms. An invoice is a typical example. This type of report can have sections that display only one record and at the same time have sections that display multiple records from the *many* side of a one-to-many relationship — and even include totals.

Figure 9-3 shows an invoice report (rptInvoice) from the Access Auto Auctions database system in Report view.

In Figure 9-3, the information in the top portion of the report is on the "main" part of the report, whereas the product details near the bottom of the figure are contained in a subreport embedded within the main report.

Mailing labels

Mailing labels are also a type of report. You can easily create mailing labels, shown in Figure 9-4, using the Label Wizard to create a report in Access. The Label Wizard enables you to select from a long list of Avery label (and other vendors) paper styles, after which Access correctly creates a report design based on the data you specify to create your label. After the label is created, you can open the report in Design mode and customize it as needed.

FIGURE 9-3

An invoice report (rptInvoice)

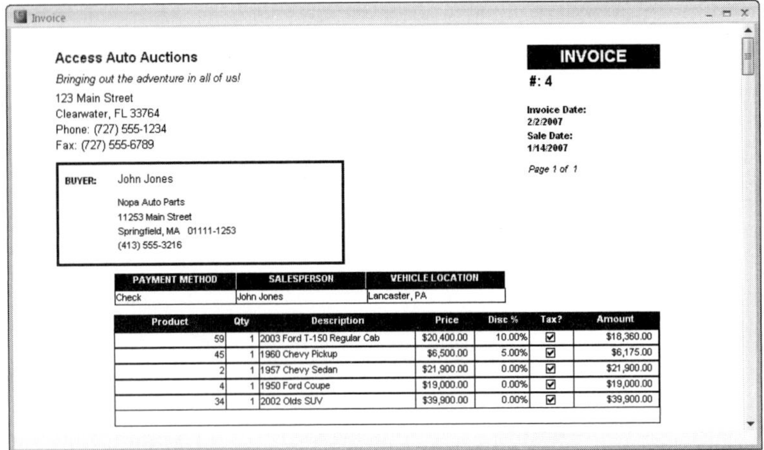

Invoice

Access Auto Auctions
Bringing out the adventure in all of us!
123 Main Street
Clearwater, FL 33764
Phone: (727) 555-1234
Fax: (727) 555-6789

INVOICE
#: 4
Invoice Date: 2/2/2007
Sale Date: 1/14/2007
Page 1 of 1

BUYER: John Jones
Nopa Auto Parts
11253 Main Street
Springfield, MA 01111-1253
(413) 555-3216

PAYMENT METHOD	SALESPERSON	VEHICLE LOCATION
Check	John Jones	Lancaster, PA

Product	Qty	Description	Price	Disc %	Tax?	Amount
59	1	2003 Ford T-150 Regular Cab	$20,400.00	10.00%	☑	$18,360.00
45	1	1960 Chevy Pickup	$6,500.00	5.00%	☑	$6,175.00
2	1	1957 Chevy Sedan	$21,900.00	0.00%	☑	$21,900.00
4	1	1950 Ford Coupe	$19,000.00	0.00%	☑	$19,000.00
34	1	2002 Olds SUV	$39,900.00	0.00%	☑	$39,900.00

FIGURE 9-4

`rptCustomerMailingLabels`, a typical mailing-label report

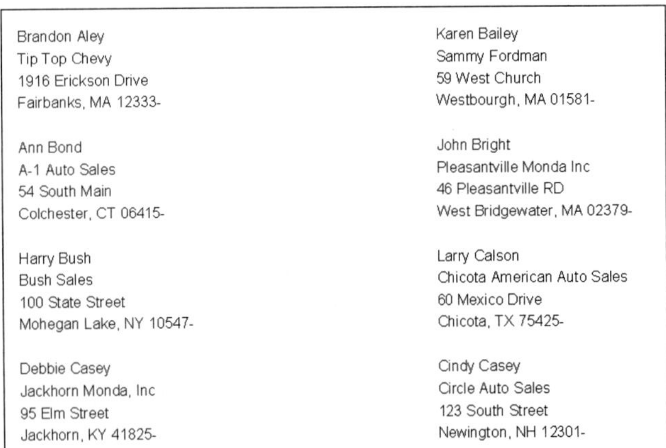

Brandon Aley
Tip Top Chevy
1916 Erickson Drive
Fairbanks, MA 12333-

Karen Bailey
Sammy Fordman
59 West Church
Westbourgh, MA 01581-

Ann Bond
A-1 Auto Sales
54 South Main
Colchester, CT 06415-

John Bright
Pleasantville Monda Inc
46 Pleasantville RD
West Bridgewater, MA 02379-

Harry Bush
Bush Sales
100 State Street
Mohegan Lake, NY 10547-

Larry Calson
Chicota American Auto Sales
60 Mexico Drive
Chicota, TX 75425-

Debbie Casey
Jackhorn Monda, Inc
95 Elm Street
Jackhorn, KY 41825-

Cindy Casey
Circle Auto Sales
123 South Street
Newington, NH 12301-

Distinguishing between reports and forms

The main difference between reports and forms is the purpose of the output. Whereas forms are primarily for data entry and interaction with the users, reports are for viewing data (either on-screen or in hard copy form). Calculated fields can be used with forms to display an amount based on other fields in the record. With reports, you typically perform calculations on a group of records, a page of records, or all the records processed during the report. Anything you can do with a form — except input data — can be duplicated by a report. In fact, you can save a form as a report and then customize the form controls in the Report Design window.

Understanding the process of creating a report

Planning a report begins long before you actually create the report design. The report process begins with your desire to view your data in a table, but in a way that differs from datasheet display. You begin with a design for this view; Access begins with raw data. The purpose of the report is to transform the raw data into a meaningful set of information. The process of creating a report involves several steps:

- Defining the report layout
- Assembling the data
- Creating the report design using the Access Report Design window
- Printing or viewing the report

Defining the report layout

You should begin by having a general idea of the layout of your report. You can define the layout in your mind, on paper, or interactively using the Access Report Designer. Good reports can first be laid out on paper, showing the controls needed and the placement of the controls. Very often, an Access report is expected to duplicate an existing paper report used by the application's consumers.

Assembling the data

After you have a general idea of the report layout, you should assemble the data needed for the report. Access reports use data from two primary sources: a single database table, or a recordset produced by the query. You can join many tables in a query and use the query's recordset as the record source for your report. A query's recordset appears to an Access report as if it were a single table.

As you learned earlier in this book, you specify the fields, records, and sort order of the records in a query. Access treats this recordset data as a single table (for processing purposes) in datasheets, forms, and reports. The recordset becomes the source of data for the report and Access processes each record to create the report. When the report is run, Access matches data from the recordset or table against the fields specified in the report and uses the data available at that moment to produce the report.

In this example, you use data from tblProducts to create a relatively simple tabular report.

Creating a Report with Report Wizards

Access enables you to create virtually any type of report. Some reports, however, are easier to create than others, especially when a Report Wizard is used as a starting point. Like Form Wizards, Report Wizards give you a basic layout for your report, which you can then customize.

Report Wizards simplify the layout process of your controls by visually stepping you through a series of questions about the type of report that you want to create and then automatically creating the report for you. In this chapter, you use Report Wizards to create tabular and columnar reports.

Creating a new report

The Access ribbon contains several commands for creating new reports for your applications. That Create tab of the ribbon includes a grouping called Reports containing several options such as Report, Labels, and Report Wizard. For this exercise, use the Report Wizard button to create a new report from tblProducts. Begin by clicking the Report Wizard button in the Reports group of the Create ribbon tab. The Report Wizard dialog opens, as shown in Figure 9-5.

FIGURE 9-5

The first screen of the Report Wizard after selecting a data source and fields

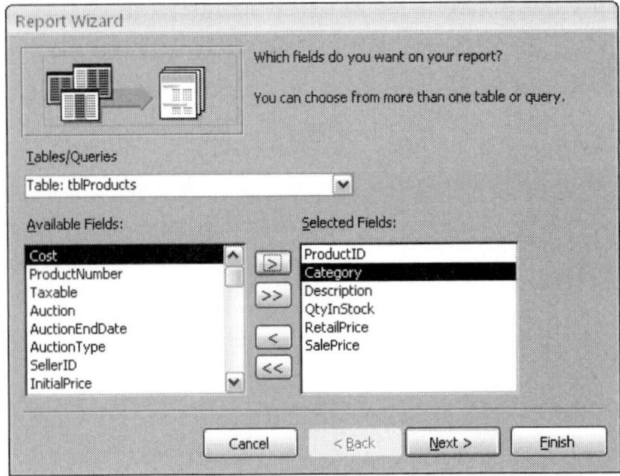

In Figure 9-5, tblProducts has been selected as the data source for the new report. Under the data source selection drop-down list is a list of available fields. Clicking on a field in this list and pressing the right pointing arrow moves the field from the Available Fields list to the Selected Field list, adding it to the report. For this exercise, select Product ID, Description, QtyInStock, RetailPrice, and SalePrice.

TIP **Double-click any field in the Available Fields list to add it to the Selected Fields list. You can also double-click any field in the Selected Fields list to remove it from the box. Access then moves the field back to the Available Fields list.**

You are limited to selecting fields from the original record source you started with. You can select fields from other tables or queries by using the Tables/Queries drop-down list in the Report Wizard. As long as you have specified valid relationships so that Access properly links the data, these fields are added to your original selection and you use them on the report. If you choose fields from unrelated tables, a dialog box asks you to edit the relationship and join the tables. Or, you can return to the Report Wizard and remove the fields.

After you have selected your data, click the Next button to go to the next wizard dialog box.

Selecting the grouping levels

The next dialog box enables you to choose which field(s) to use for grouping data. Figure 9-6 shows the Category field selected as the data grouping field for the report. The field selected for grouping determines how data appears on the report, and the grouping fields appear as group headers and footers in the report. Groups are most often used to combine data that are logically related. For instance, you may choose to group on CustomerID so that each customer's sales history appears as a group on the report. You use the report's group headers and footers to display the customer name and any other information specific to each customer.

The Report Wizard lets you specify as many as four group fields for your report. You use the Priority buttons to change the grouping order on the report. The order you select for the group fields is the order of the grouping hierarchy.

Select the Category field as the grouping field and click (>) to specify a grouping based on category values. Notice that the picture changes to show Category as a grouping field, as shown in Figure 9-6. Each of the other fields (ProductID, Description, QtyInStock, RetailPrice, and SalesPrice) selected for the report will appear within the Category groups.

FIGURE 9-6

Specifying the report's grouping

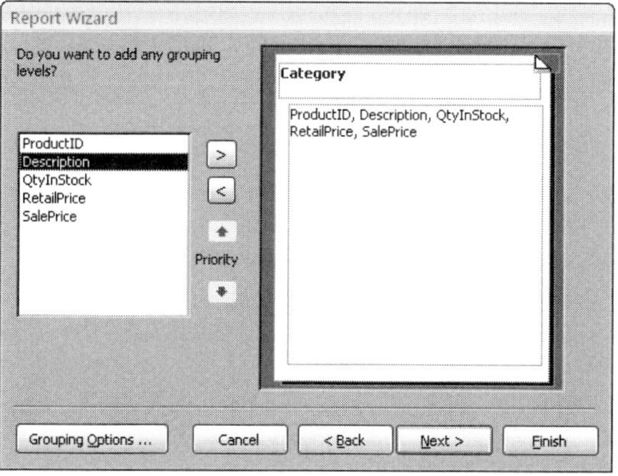

Defining the group data

After you select the group field(s), click the Grouping Options button at the bottom of the dialog box to display another dialog box, which enables you to further define how your report uses the group field.

For instance, you can choose to group by only the first character of a field chosen for grouping. This means that all records with the same first character in the grouping field are included as a single group. If you group a customers table by the CustomerName, and specify to group on the first character of the CustomerName field, a group header and footer appears for the set of all customers whose name begins with the same character. There would be a group for all records with a CustomerName beginning with the letter A, another group for all records with CustomerName beginning with the letter B, and so on.

The Grouping Options dialog box, which is displayed when you click the Grouping Options button in the lower-left corner of the Report Wizard screen, enables you to further define the grouping. This selection can vary in importance, depending on the data type.

The Grouping intervals list box displays different values for the various data types:

- **Text**: Normal, 1st Letter, 2 Initial Letters, 3 Initial Letters, 4 Initial Letters, 5 Initial letters
- **Numeric:** Normal, 10s, 50s, 100s, 500s, 1000s, 5000s, 10000s, 50000s, 100000s.
- **Date:** Normal, Year, Quarter, Month, Week, Day, Hour, Minute.

Normal means that the grouping is on the entire field. In this example, use the entire Customer Name field.

In this example, the default text-field grouping option of Normal is acceptable.

If you displayed the Grouping Options dialog box, click the OK button to return to the Grouping levels dialog box.

Click the Next button to move to the Sort order dialog box.

Selecting the sort order

By default, Access automatically sorts the grouped records in an order that helps the grouping make sense. For instance, after you have chosen the Customer Name field to group customer records, Access arranges the groups in alphabetical order by the CustomerName. However, for your purposes, it may be useful to specify a sort within each group. As an example, your users may want to see the customer records sorted by Order Date in descending order so that the newest orders appear near the top of for each customer group.

In our example, Access sorts data by the Category field. As Figure 9-7 shows, the data is also sorted by Description within each group.

The sort fields are selected by the same method you use for grouping fields in the report. You can select fields that you have not already chosen to group and use these as sorting fields. The fields chosen in this dialog box do not affect grouping. Instead, they affect only the sorting order in the Detail section fields. You select ascending or descending sort by clicking the button to the right of each sort field.

FIGURE 9-7

Selecting the field sorting order

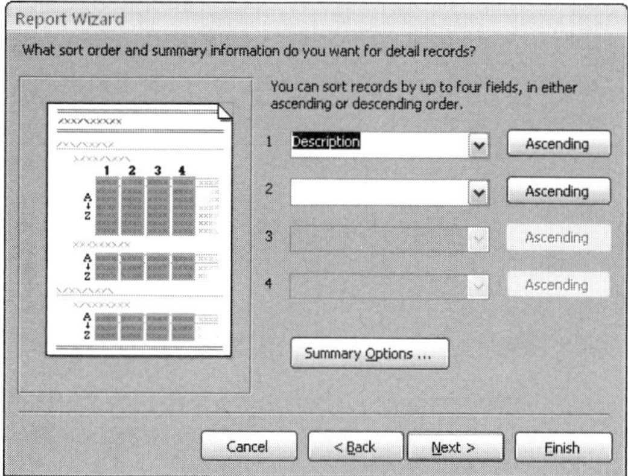

Selecting summary options

At the bottom of the sorting dialog box is a Summary Options button. Clicking this button displays the dialog box shown in Figure 9-8. This dialog box provides additional display options for numeric fields. As you can see in Figure 9-8, all of the numeric and currency fields are displayed and specified to be summed. Additionally, you can display averages, minimums, and maximums.

FIGURE 9-8

Selecting the summary options

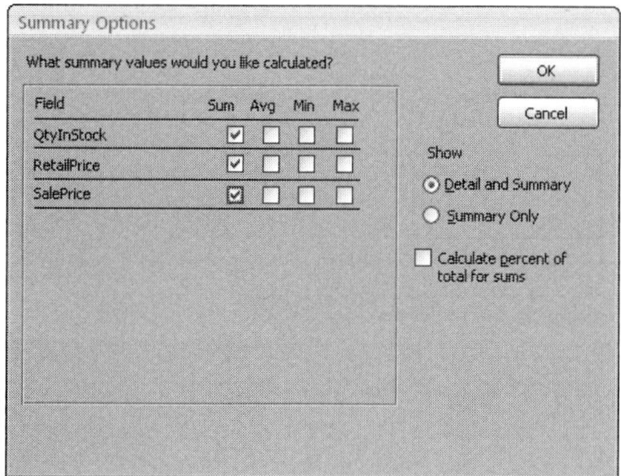

You can also decide whether to show or hide the data in the Detail section. If you select Detail and Summary, the report shows the detail data, whereas selecting Summary Only hides the Detail section and shows only totals in the report.

Finally, checking the Calculate percent of total for sums box adds the percentage of the entire report that the total represents below the total in the group footer. If, for example, you have three products and their totals are 15, 25, and 10, respectively, 30%, 50%, and 20% shows below their total (that is, 50)—indicating the percentage of the total sum (100%) represented by their sum.

Clicking the OK button in this dialog box returns you to the Sorting dialog box. There you can click the Next button to move to the next wizard dialog box.

Selecting the layout

Two more dialog boxes affect the look of your report. The first (shown in Figure 9-9) enables you to determine the basic layout of the data. The Layout area provides six layout choices that tell Access whether to repeat the column headers, indent each grouping, and add lines or boxes between the detail lines. As you select each option, the picture on the left changes to show how the choice affects the report's appearance.

You choose between Portrait (up-and-down) and Landscape (across-the-page) layout for the report in the Orientation area. Finally, the Adjust the field width so all fields fit on a page check box enables you to cram a lot of data into a little area. (A magnifying glass may be necessary!)

For this example, choose Stepped and Landscape, as shown in Figure 9-9. Then click the Next button to move to the next dialog box.

FIGURE 9-9

Selecting the page layout

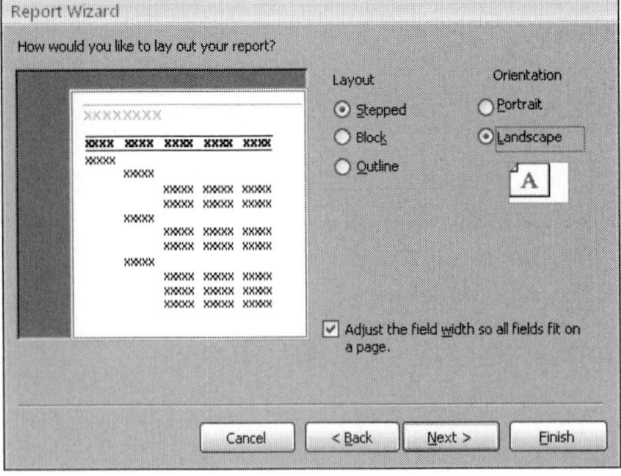

Choosing the style

After you choose the layout, select the style of your report from the dialog shown in Figure 9-10. Each style has different background shadings, font size, typeface, and other formatting. As each is selected, the picture on the left changes to show a preview. For this example, choose Opulent. Finally, click the Next button to move to the last dialog box.

FIGURE 9-10

Choosing the style of your report

You can customize the styles, or add your own with the AutoFormat option in the Arrange tab of the Access ribbon with a report open in Design view.

Opening the report design

The final Report Wizard dialog box contains a checkered flag, which lets you know that you're at the finish line. The first part of the dialog box enables you to enter a title for the report. This title appears only once, at the very beginning of the report, not at the top of each page. The report title also serves as the new report's name. The default titles is the name of the table or query you initially specified as the report's data source. The report just created in `Chapter09.accdb` is named `rptProducts_Wizard`.

Next, choose one of the option buttons at the bottom of the dialog box:

- Preview the report
- Modify the report's design

For this example, leave the default selection intact to preview the report. Clicking the Finish button displays the report in Report view. Click Finish to complete the Report Wizard and view the report (see Figure 9-11).

FIGURE 9-11

`rptProducts_Wizard` displayed in Report View

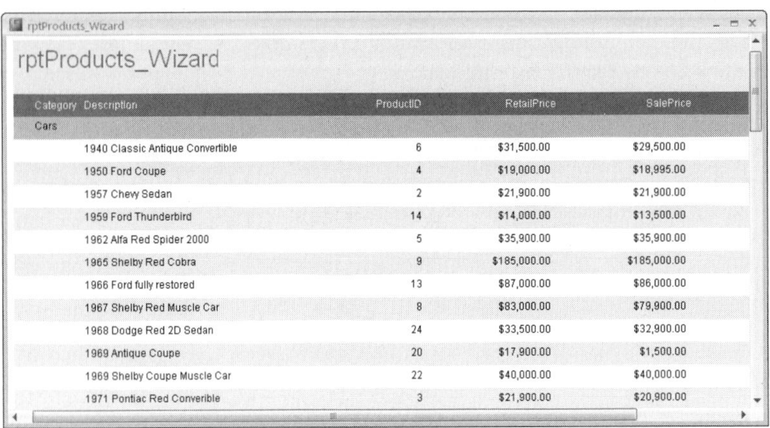

rptProducts_Wizard

Category	Description	ProductID	RetailPrice	SalePrice
Cars				
	1940 Classic Antique Convertible	6	$31,500.00	$29,500.00
	1950 Ford Coupe	4	$19,000.00	$18,995.00
	1957 Chevy Sedan	2	$21,900.00	$21,900.00
	1959 Ford Thunderbird	14	$14,000.00	$13,500.00
	1962 Alfa Red Spider 2000	5	$35,900.00	$35,900.00
	1965 Shelby Red Cobra	9	$185,000.00	$185,000.00
	1966 Ford fully restored	13	$87,000.00	$86,000.00
	1967 Shelby Red Muscle Car	8	$83,000.00	$79,900.00
	1968 Dodge Red 2D Sedan	24	$33,500.00	$32,900.00
	1969 Antique Coupe	20	$17,900.00	$1,500.00
	1969 Shelby Coupe Muscle Car	22	$40,000.00	$40,000.00
	1971 Pontiac Red Converible	3	$21,900.00	$20,900.00

Report view provides an overall view of the report, but it does not show the margins, page numbering, and how the report will look when printed on a piece of paper. To get a good idea of how a report will look when printed, right-click the report's title bar and select Print Preview from the shortcut menu that appears.

Using the Print Preview window

Figure 9-12 shows the Print Preview window in a zoomed view of rptProducts_Wizard. This view displays your report with the actual fonts, shading, lines, boxes, and data that will be on the printed report. Clicking the left mouse button changes the view to a *page preview* that shows the entire page.

The Access ribbon transforms to display controls relevant to viewing and printing the report. The Print Preview tab of the Access ribbon includes controls for adjusting the size, page orientation (Portrait or Landscape), and other viewing options. The Print Preview tab also includes a handy Print button for printing the report.

You can move around the page by using the horizontal and vertical scrollbars. Use the Page controls (at the bottom-left corner of the window) to move from page to page. These controls include VCR-like navigation buttons to move from page to page or to the first or last page of the report. You can also go to a specific page of the report by entering a value in the text box between the previous and next controls.

Right-clicking on the report and selecting the Multiple Pages option lets you view more than one page of the report in a single view. Figure 9-13 shows a view of the report in the Print Preview's multipage mode. Use the navigation buttons (in the lower-left section of the Print Preview window) to move between pages, just as you would to move between records in a datasheet. The Print Preview window has a toolbar with commonly used printing commands.

FIGURE 9-12

Displaying `rptReport_Wizard` in the zoomed preview mode

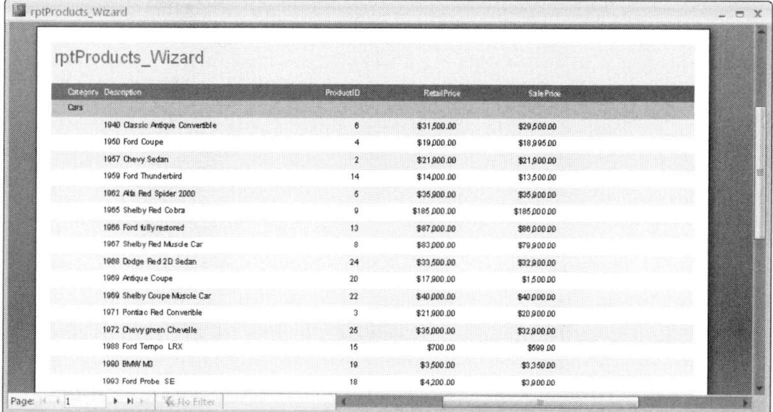

rptProducts_Wizard

Category	Description	ProductID	RetailPrice	SalePrice
Cars				
	1940 Classic Antique Convertible	6	$31,500.00	$29,500.00
	1950 Ford Coupe	4	$19,000.00	$18,995.00
	1957 Chevy Sedan	2	$21,900.00	$21,900.00
	1959 Ford Thunderbird	14	$14,000.00	$13,500.00
	1962 Alfa Red Spider 2000	5	$35,900.00	$35,900.00
	1965 Shelby Red Cobra	9	$185,000.00	$185,000.00
	1966 Ford fully restored	13	$87,000.00	$86,000.00
	1967 Shelby Red Muscle Car	8	$83,000.00	$79,900.00
	1968 Dodge Red 2D Sedan	24	$33,500.00	$32,900.00
	1969 Antique Coupe	20	$17,900.00	$1,500.00
	1969 Shelby Coupe Muscle Car	22	$40,000.00	$40,000.00
	1971 Pontiac Red Converible	3	$21,900.00	$20,900.00
	1972 Chevy green Chevelle	25	$35,000.00	$32,900.00
	1988 Ford Tempo LRX	15	$700.00	$699.00
	1990 BMW M3	19	$3,500.00	$3,350.00
	1993 Ford Probe SE	18	$4,200.00	$3,900.00

FIGURE 9-13

Displaying multiple pages of a report in Print Preview's page preview mode

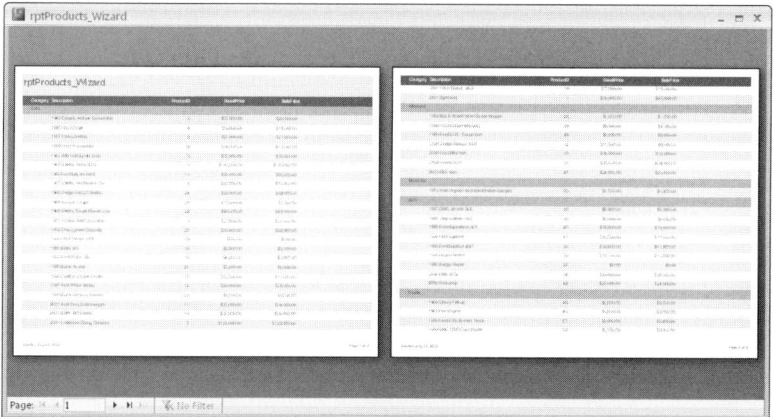

If, after examining the preview, you are satisfied with the report, click the Printer button on the toolbar to print the report. If you are dissatisfied, select the Close button to switch to the Report Design window and make further changes.

Viewing the Report Design window

Right-clicking the report's title bar and selecting Design View opens the Access Report Designer on the report. As shown in Figure 9-14, the report design reflects the choices you made using the Report Wizard.

FIGURE 9-14

The Report Design window

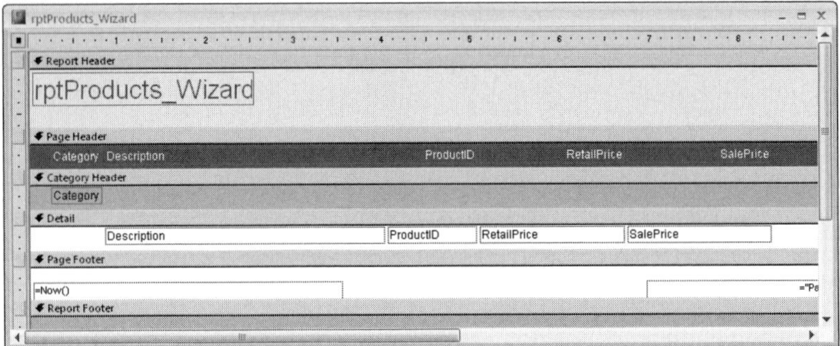

Return to the Print Preview mode by selecting the Print Preview button on the Report Design toolbar or by selecting the Print Preview option from the File menu. You can also select Print or Page Setup from the File menu. This menu also provides options for saving your report.

Printing a Report

There are several ways to print your report:

- Click the Print button in the Print Preview tab of the Access ribbon.
- Click File ➪ Print in the main Access window (with a report highlighted and the Navigation Pane).

Selecting File ➪ Print opens the standard Windows Print dialog box. You use this dialog to select the print range, number of copies, and print properties.

Clicking the Print button in the Access ribbon immediately sends the report to the default printer without displaying a Print dialog box.

Saving the Report

Save the report design at any time by selecting File ➪ Save, File ➪ Save As, or File ➪ Export from the Report Design window, or by clicking the Save button on the Quick Access Toolbar. The first time you save a report (or any time you select Save As or Export), a dialog box enables you to select or type a name.

Starting with a Blank Form

Previous chapters about forms introduced you to all the tools available in the Report Design window. When you create reports, you use some of these tools in a slightly different manner from the way you used them to create forms. Therefore, it is important to review some of the unique report menus and toolbar buttons.

You can view a report in four different views: Design, Report, Layout, and Print Preview. You can also print a report to the default Windows printer. You have already seen various preview windows in previous chapters. This chapter focuses on the Report Design window.

Layout view

The Report Design window is one place where you create and modify reports. You began working with a new report by selecting a table or query to serve as the new report's data source; then you click the Blank Report button in the Create tab of the main Access ribbon. The new report appears in Layout view as shown in Figure 9-15.

FIGURE 9-15

Layout view of a new report based on tblProducts

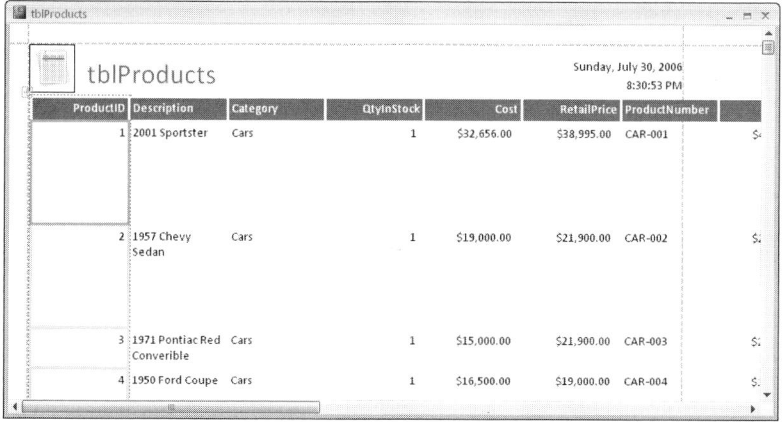

The ability to change a report's design in Layout view is a new feature of Access 2007. The main advantage of Layout view is that you can see the relative positions of the controls on the report's surface, as well as the margins, page headers and footers, and other report details.

The main constraint of Layout view is that you cannot make fine adjustments to a report's design unless you put the report in Design view. Layout view is primarily intended to allow you to adjust the relative positions of controls on the report. For instance, the icon that appears in the upper-left corner of the report shown in Figure 9-15 can be deleted by clicking on the icon and pressing the Delete button, or moved to another location by dragging it to a better location on the report's surface.

While in Layout view, you can also right-click any control and select Properties from the shortcut menu. The Property Sheet allows you to modify the default settings for the selected control.

Figure 9-16 shows the Access ribbon while a report is open in Layout view. Not surprisingly, the options on the ribbon are mostly involved with adjusting the appearance of the controls on the report.

FIGURE 9-16

The Access ribbon while a report is open in Layout view

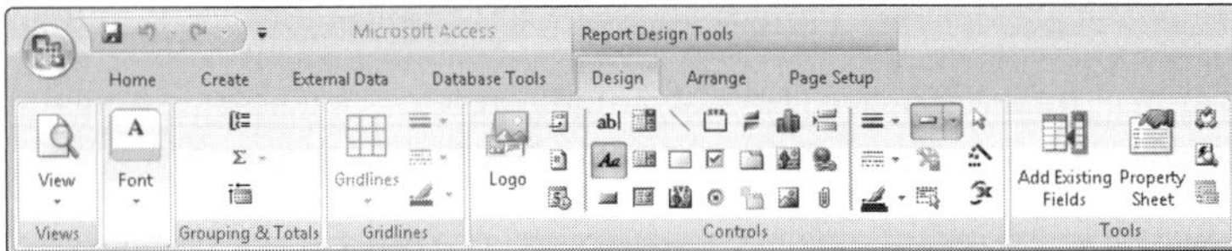

In Figure 9-16 notice that you cannot adjust the fine details of a control, such as its height or width, but you can adjust the font used for the control, the font size, the BackColor, and the ForeColor of a report control. To adjust a control's height and width, click on the control and drag its margins to the new height or width.

Report Design view

As an alternative to the Layout view, you may choose to use the more traditional Report Design view, which gives you a high level of control over the controls on a report, as well as the report itself. Right-click the report in Layout view, and select Design view from the shortcut menu to open the report in the traditional Access Report Designer (see Figure 9-17).

FIGURE 9-17

The new report open in Report Design view

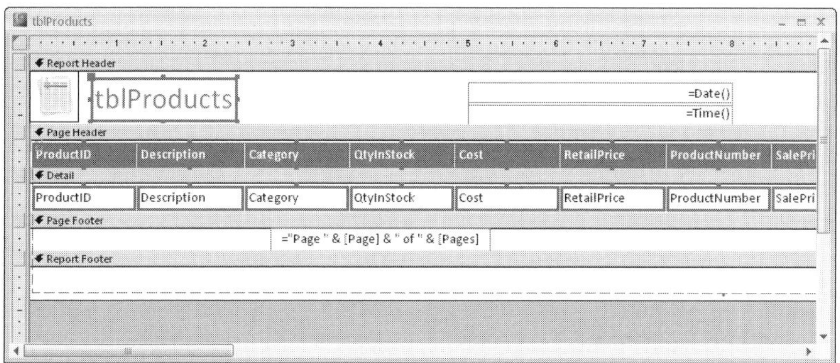

The Report Design ribbon is shown in Figure 9-18. Notice how much more complex the ribbon is when the report is in Design view than when it is open in Layout view. You have many more options for influencing how a report looks on the printed page in Design view than in Layout view.

FIGURE 9-18

The Report Design ribbon

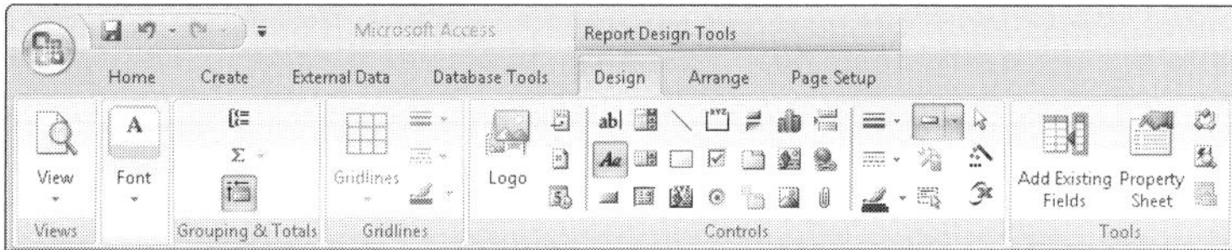

Banded Report Writer Concepts

In a report, your data is processed one record at a time. Depending on how you create your report design, each data item is processed differently. Reports are divided into *sections*, known as *bands* in most report-writing software packages. (In Access, these are simply called *sections*.) Access processes each record in the underlying data set, processing each section in order and deciding (for each record) whether to process fields or text in that section. For example, the report footer section is processed only after the last record is processed in the recordset.

In Figure 9-19 (`rptProductsSummary`) notice that the data on the report is grouped by ProductCategory (Minivans, Motor Homes, and so on). Each group has a *group header* containing the category name (The first category in this example is Minivans.) Each group also has a footer displaying summary information for the category. In Figure 9-19, the total profit is $17,063 on total sales of $93,063. The *page header* contains column descriptions (Product ID, Description, and so on), whereas the *report header* contains the report title (Products Summary). Finally, the *report footer* contains grand totals for the report, and the *page footer* shows the page number.

FIGURE 9-19

rptProductsSummary, a grouped report containing summary data

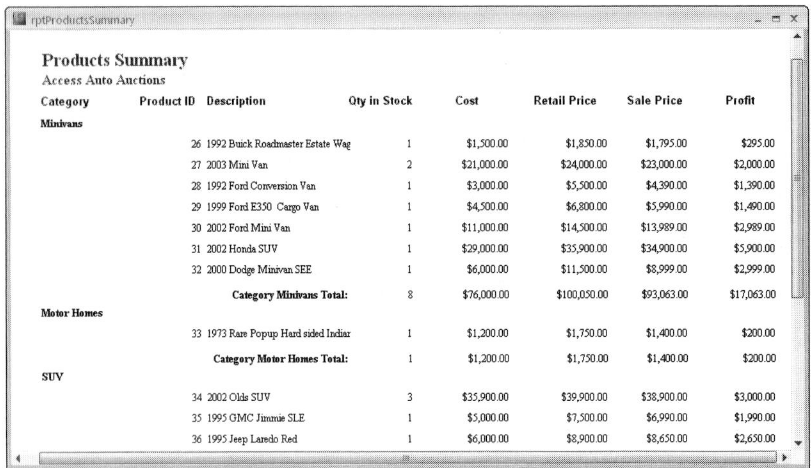

The following Access sections are available:

- **Report header:** Prints only at the beginning of the report; used for title page.
- **Page header:** Prints at the top of each page.
- **Group header:** Prints before the first record of a group is processed.
- **Detail:** Prints each record in the table or recordset.
- **Group footer:** Prints after the last record of a group is processed.
- **Page Footer:** Prints at the bottom of each page.
- **Report footer:** Prints only at the end of a report after all records are processed.

The Report Designer sections

Figure 9-20 shows rptProductSummary open in Design view. As you can see, the report is divided into seven sections. The group section displays data grouped by categories, so you see the sections Category Header and Category Footer. Each of the other sections is also named for the type of processing it performs.

You can place any type of text or text box controls in any section, but Access processes the data one record at a time. It also takes certain actions (based on the values of the group fields, the location of the page, or placement in the report) to make the bands or sections active. The example in Figure 9-20 is typical of a report with multiple sections. As you learned, each section in the report has a different purpose and different triggers.

FIGURE 9-20

The Report Design window

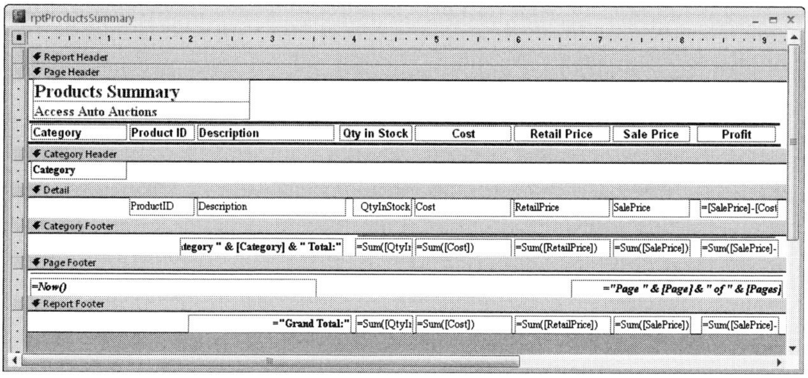

Page and report headers and footers are added as pairs. To add one without the other, resize the section you don't want to a height of zero or set its Visible property to No.

If you remove a header or footer section, you also lose the controls in those sections.

The Report Header section

Controls in the *Report Header section* are printed only once at the beginning of the report. A common use of a Report Header section is as a cover page or a cover letter or for information that needs to be communicated only once to the user of the report.

You can also have controls in the Report Header section print on a separate page, which enables you to create a title page and include a graphic or picture in the section. There is a Force New Page property in the Report Header section that can be set to After Section that will place the information in the report header into a separate page.

In Figure 9-20 the Report Header section is not used. Notice that the Report Header's height is zero.

Only data from the first record can be placed in a report header.

The Page Header section

Text or text box controls in the *Page Header section* normally print at the top of every page. If a report header on the first page is not on a page of its own, the information in the Page Header section prints just below the report header information on the first page. Typically, page headers serve as column headers in group/total reports; they can also contain a title for the report. In this example, placing the Products Summary report title in the Page Header section means that the title appears on every page.

The `page header` section shown in Figure 9-20 contains horizontal lines above and below the label controls. Each label control can be moved or sized individually. You can also change special effects (such as color, shading, borders, line thickness, font type, and font size) for each control.

Both the Page Header and Page Footer sections can be set to one of four settings (found in the Report's properties, not the section properties):

- **All Pages:** The page header and page footer print on every page.
- **Not with Report Header:** Neither the page header nor footer prints on a page with the report header.
- **Not with Report Footer:** The page header does not print with the report footer. The report footer prints on a new page.
- **Not with Report Header/Footer:** Neither the page header nor the footer prints on a page with the report header or footer.

The Group Header section

A *Group Header* section normally displays the name of the group, such as "Minivans" or "Motor Homes." Access knows when all the records in a group have been displayed in a Detail section when the group name changes. In this example, the detail records are all about individual products. The Category control in the Category Header tells you that the products within the group belong to the indicated category (Minivan or Motor Home). Group headers immediately precede Detail sections.

It is possible to have multiple levels of group headers and footers. In this report, for example, the data is only for categories. However, in some reports you might have groups of information with date values. You could group your sections by year or month and year, and within those sections by another group such as category.

NOTE **To set group-level properties such as Group On, Group Interval, Keep Together, or something other than the default, you must first set the Group Header and Group Footer property (or both) to Yes for the selected field or expression. You learn about these later in the chapter.**

The Detail section

The *Detail section* processes *every* record in the data and is where each value is printed. The Detail section frequently contains a calculated field such as profit that is the result of a mathematical expression. In this example, the Detail section simply displays information from the tblProduct table except for the last control. The profit is calculated by subtracting the cost from the SalePrice.

TIP **You can tell Access whether you want to display a section in the report by changing the section's Visible property in the Report Design window. Turning off the display of the Detail section (or by excluding selected group sections) displays a summary report with no detail or with only certain groups displayed.**

The Group Footer section

You use the *Group Footer section* to calculate summaries for all the detail records in a group. In the Products Summary report, the expression = `Sum([SalePrice] - [Cost])` adds a value calculated from all of the records within a category. In the Minivans group, this expression sums seven records. The value of this text box control is automatically reset to 0 every time the group changes. (You learn more about expressions and summary text boxes in later chapters.)

You can change the way summaries are calculated by changing the Running Sum property of the text box in the Report Design window.

The Page Footer section

The *Page Footer section* usually contains page numbers or control totals. In very large reports, such as when you have multiple pages of detail records with no summaries, you may want page totals as well as group totals. For the Products Summary Report, the page number is printed by combining the text page, and built-in page number controls. These controls show Page x of y where x is the current page number and y is the total number of pages in the report. A text box control with the following expression in the Control Source property can be used to display page number information that keeps track of the page number in the report:

```
="Page: " & [Page] & " of " & [Pages]
```

You can also print the date and the time printed. You can see the page number text box in the Page Footer section in Figure 9-20. The Page Footer in rptProductsSummary also contains the current date and time.

The Report Footer section

The *Report Footer section* is printed once at the end of the report after all the detail records and group footer sections are printed. Report footers typically display grand totals or other statistics (such as averages or percentages) for the entire report. The report footer for the Products Summary report uses the expression = `Sum` with each of the numeric fields to sum the amounts.

When there is a report footer, the Page Footer section is printed after the report footer.

The Report Writer in Access is a *two-pass report writer*, capable of preprocessing all records to calculate the totals (such as percentages) needed for statistical reporting. This capability enables you to create expressions that calculate percentages as Access processes those records that require foreknowledge of the grand total.

Creating a Report from Scratch

Fundamental to all reports is the concept that a report is another way to view the records in one or more tables. It is important to understand that a report is bound to either a single table or a query that brings together data from one or more tables. When you create a report, you must select which fields from the query or table you want to see in your report. Unless you want to view all the records from a single table, bind your report to a query. Even if you are accessing data from a single table, using a query lets you create your report on the basis of a particular search criterion and sorting order. If you want to access data from multiple tables, you have almost no choice but to bind your report to a query. In the examples in this chapter, all the reports are bound to a query (even though it is possible to bind a report to a table).

NOTE **Access lets you create a report without first binding it to a table or query, but you will have no controls on the report. This capability can be used to work out page templates with common text headers or footers such as page numbering or the date and time, which can serve as models for other reports. You can add controls later by changing the underlying control source of the report.**

Throughout the rest of this chapter, you learn the tasks necessary to create the Products Display Report (a part of the first page is shown in Figure 9-21). In these sections, you design the basic report, assemble the data, and place the data in the proper positions.

FIGURE 9-21

The Products Summary report

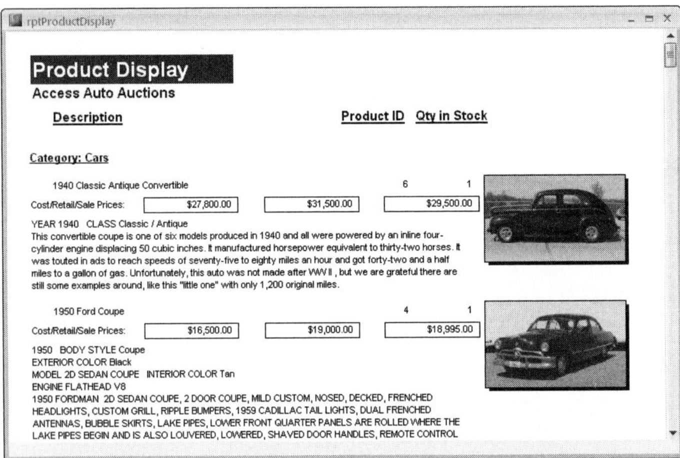

As with almost every task in Access, there are many ways to create a report without wizards. It is important, however, to follow some type of methodology, because creating a good report involves a fairly scientific approach. You should create a check list that is a set of tasks that will result in a good report every time. As you complete each task, check it off your list. When you are done, you will have a great-looking report. The following section outlines this approach.

Creating a new report and binding it to a query

The first step is to create a new, empty report and bind it to tblProducts. Creating a blank report is quite easy:

1. **Select the Create tab of the main Access ribbon.**
2. **Click the Blank Report button in the Reports ribbon group.**

   Access opens a blank report in Layout view, and positions a Field List dialog on top of the new report (see Figure 9-22).

FIGURE 9-22

A blank report in Layout view

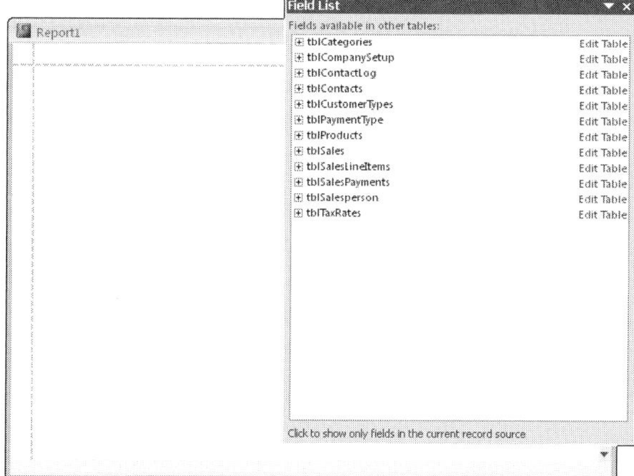

At this point, you have two different paths for adding controls to the report: continue working in Layout view, or switch to Design view. Each of these techniques has advantages over the other, but for the purposes of this exercise we'll use the Design view because it better demonstrates the process of building Access reports.

Right-click the report's title bar, and select Design view from the shortcut menu. The Report window transforms to the traditional Access banded Report Designer, as shown in Figure 9-23. This figure also shows the Field List open on tblProducts, allowing you to track fields from the list to the appropriate section on the new report.

FIGURE 9-23

Building the new report in Design view

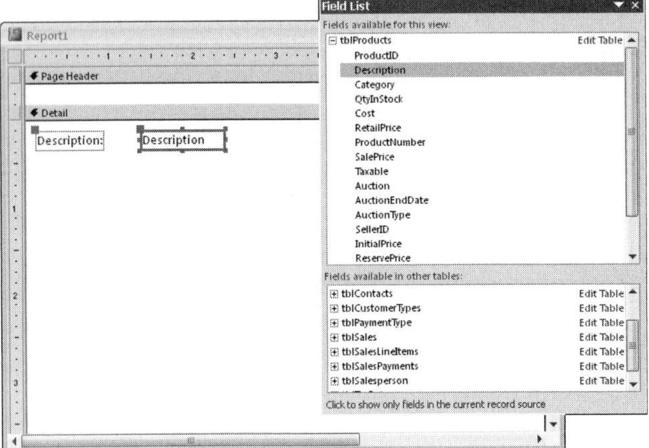

In Figure 9-23, the Description field has been dragged onto the Detail section of the report.

Defining the report page size and layout

As you plan your report, consider the page-layout characteristics as well as the kind of paper and printer you want to use for the output. As you make these decisions, you use several dialog boxes and properties to make adjustments. These specifications work together to create the desired output.

Click the Page Setup tab in the Access ribbon to select the report's margins, orientation, and other overall characteristics. Figure 9-24 shows a portion of the Access screen with the Page Setup tab selected, and the Margins option open.

FIGURE 9-24

The Page Setup dialog box showing the Page tab

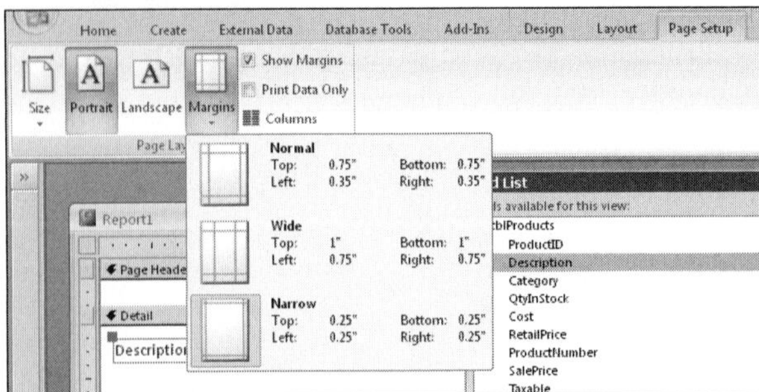

Notice that the Page Setup tab contains options for setting the paper size, the report's orientation (Portrait or Landscape), its margins, and other details. Dropping down either the Size or Margins option reveals a tab containing common settings for each of these options.

rptProductDisplay is to be a portrait report, which is taller than it is wide. You want to print on letter size paper (8½ x 11 inches), and you want the left, right, top, and bottom margins all set to 0.25 inches. In Figure 9-24 notice that the Narrow margins option is selected, which specifies exactly 0.25 inches for all four margin settings.

If the margins you need for your particular report are not shown in the margins tab, click the small button in the lower-right corner of the page layout group to open the common Windows Page Setup dialog. This dialog enables you to specify the margins, orientation, and other page layout specifications as you would in Microsoft Word or any other Windows application.

To set the right border for the Product Display report to 7 1/2 inches, follow these steps:

1. **Click the right edge of the report body (where the white page meets the gray background).**

   The mouse pointer changes to a double-headed arrow.

2. **Drag the edge to the 7½-inch mark.**

   If the ruler is not displayed in the Report Designer, select the Arrange tab, move to the Show/Hide group, and click the ruler icon.

NOTE **You can also change the Width property in the Property window for the report.**

TIP **If you run your report and every other page is blank, it is a sign that the width of your report exceeds the width of your page. To fix this problem, decrease your left and right margin size or reduce the report's width. Sometimes, when you move controls around, you accidentally make the report width larger than you originally intended. For example, in a portrait report, if your left margin + report width + right margin is greater than 8½ inches, you will see blank pages.**

Placing controls on the report

Access takes full advantage of drag-and-drop capabilities of Windows. The method for placing controls on a report is no exception:

1. **Click the Add Existing Fields button in the Tools group of the Design ribbon tab.**

   The Field List window appears.

2. **Click the desired Toolbox control to determine the type of control to create if they are to be different from the default control types for the fields.**

3. **Select each field that you want on your report and then drag them to the appropriate section of the Report Design window.**

Select multiple fields by holding down the Ctrl key as you click on fields in the Field List. Depending on whether you choose one or several fields, the mouse pointer changes shape to represent your selection as you drag fields on to the report.

The fields appear in the detail section of the report, as shown in Figure 9-25. Notice that for each field you dragged onto the report, there are two controls. When you use the drag-and-drop method of placing fields, Access automatically creates a label control with the field name attached to the Text control to which the field is bound.

FIGURE 9-25

The report with several fields added

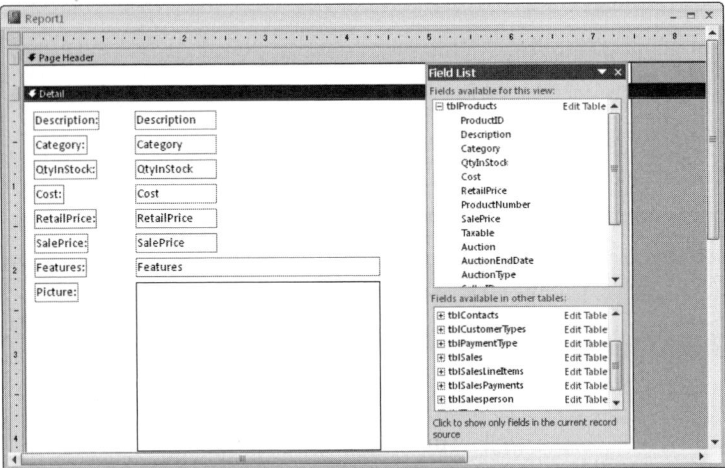

NOTE **Notice the Bound Object Frame control for the field named Picture. Access always creates a Bound Object Frame control for an OLE-type object found in a table. Also notice that the Detail section automatically resizes itself to fit all the controls. Above the Bound Object Frame control is the control for the memo field Features.**

Controls are needed for the customer information in the page header section. Before you do this, however, you must resize the page header to leave room for a title you will add later.

Resizing a section

To make room on the report for the title information in the page header, you must resize it. You resize by using the mouse to drag the bottom of the section you want to resize. The mouse pointer turns into a vertical double-headed arrow as it is positioned over the bottom of a report section. Simply drag the section border up or down to make the section smaller or larger.

Resize the Page Header section to make it about 3/4-inches high by dragging the bottom margin of the page header downwards. Use the Controls group on the Design ribbon tab to drag labels to the report. Add two labels to the Page Header, and enter **Product Display** as the Caption property of one label, and **Access Auto Auctions** to the other.

The labels you just added are unattached; they are not related to any other controls on the report. When you drag a field from the Field List Access adds not only a text box to contain the field's data, but also a label to provide an identifier for the text box. Labels that you drag from the Controls group on the Access ribbon are unattached and are not related to text boxes or any other control on the report.

You may notice the Page Header section expanding to accommodate the label controls that you dragged into the section. All the fields needed for the Product Display report are now placed in their appropriate sections.

To create a multiple-line label entry, press Ctrl+Enter to force a line break where you want it in the control.

TIP

If you enter a caption that is longer than the space in the Property window, the contents scroll as you type. Otherwise, open a Zoom box that gives you more space to type by pressing Shift+F2.

Modifying the appearance of text in a control

To modify the appearance of the text in a control, select the control by clicking its border (not in the control itself). You can then select a formatting style to apply to the label by clicking the appropriate button on the Formatting toolbar.

To make the titles stand out, follow these steps to modify the appearance of label text:

1. **Click the newly created report heading label Product Display.**
2. **Click the Bold button in Font group on the ribbon.**
3. **Click the arrow beside the FontSize drop-down box and select 18 from the drop-down list.**
4. **Repeat for the Access Auto Auctions label, using a 12 pt font and Bold.**

   The size of the labels may not fit their displayed text. To tighten the display or to display all the text when a label isn't big enough, double-click any of the sizing handles, and Access chooses an appropriate size for the label.

   Figure 9-26 shows these labels added, resized, and formatted in the report's Page Header section.

FIGURE 9-26

Adding unbound labels to the report

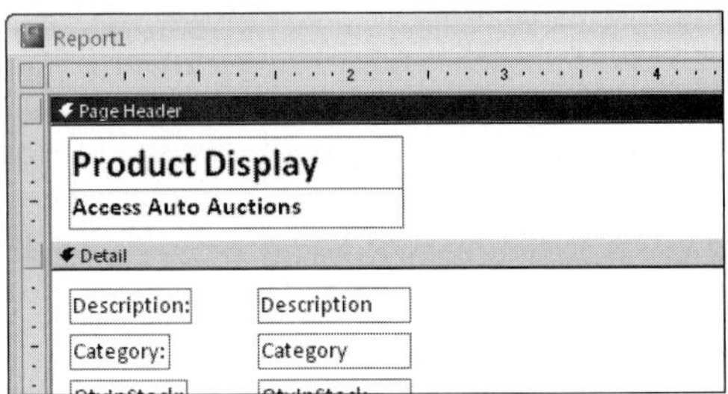

Working with text boxes and their attached label controls

So far, you added controls bound to fields in the tables and unbound label controls used to display titles in your report. There is another type of text box control that is typically added to a report: unbound text boxes that are used to hold expressions such as page numbers, dates, or a calculation.

Adding and using text box controls

In reports, text box controls serve two purposes. First, they enable you to display stored data from a particular field in a query or table. Second, they display the result of an expression. Expressions can be calculations that use other controls as their operands, calculations that use Access functions (either built-in or user-defined), or a combination of the two. You learned how to use a text box control to display data from a field and how to create that control.

Entering an expression in a text control

Expressions enable you to create a value that is not already in a table or query. They can range from simple functions (such as a page number) to complex mathematical computations.

CROSS-REF **Chapter 5 discusses expressions in greater detail.**

A *function* is a small program that, when run, returns a single value. The function can be one of many built-in Access functions or it can be user-defined. For example, earlier in this chapter you saw the `Now()` function used to return the current date and time for a text box located in a report's page footer. The following steps show you how to use an unbound text box to add a page number to your report:

1. **Click in the middle of the Page Footer section, resize the page footer so that it is a ½ inch in height**
2. **Drag a text box control from the Controls group on the Design ribbon tab and drop it into the Page Footer area. Make the text box about three-quarters of the height of the Page Footer section and about ½-inch wide.**

3. **Select the text box's attached label and change its contents to say** Page:.
4. **Select the text box control (it says "Unbound") and enter** = Page **directly into the text box.**

   Alternatively, you could open the Property sheet (press F4) and enter = **[Page]** as the text box's `ControlSource` property.
5. **Drag the new text box control until it is near the right edge of the report's page (see Figure 9-27).**

   You may want to also move the text box's label so that it is positioned close to the text box. The upper-left handle on the label moves the label independently of the text box.

FIGURE 9-27

Adding a page-number expression in a text box control

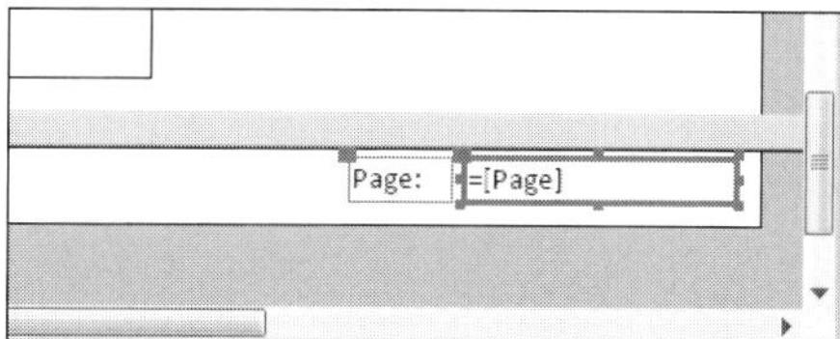

You can always check your result by clicking the Print Preview button on the toolbar and zooming in on the Page Footer section to check the page number.

Sizing a text box control or label control

You select a control by clicking it. Depending on the size of the control, from three to seven sizing handles appear — one on each corner except the upper-left corner and one on each side. Moving the mouse pointer over one of the sizing handles changes the mouse pointer to a double-headed arrow. When the pointer changes, click the control and drag it to the size you want. Notice that, as you drag, an outline appears indicating the size the label control will be when you release the mouse button.

If you double-click any of the sizing handles, Access resizes a control to best fit for text in the control. This feature is especially handy if you increase the font size and then notice that the text no longer fits the control.

Note that, for label controls, the *best-fit sizing* resizes both vertically and horizontally, although text controls resize only vertically. The reason for this difference is that in Report Design mode, Access doesn't know how much of a field's data you want to display. Later on, the field's name and contents might be radically different. Sometimes label controls are not resized correctly, however, and have to be adjusted manually.

You can also select Format ➪ Size ➪ To Fit to change the size of the label control text automatically.

Before continuing, you should check how the report is progressing. You should also save the report frequently as you make changes to it. You could send a single page to the printer, but is probably easier to view the report in Print Preview. Right-click the report's title bar, and select Print Preview from the shortcut menu. Figure 9-28 shows a zoomed print preview of the report's current appearance. The page header information is at the very top of the page, and the first product record appears below the header.

FIGURE 9-28

A print preview of the report

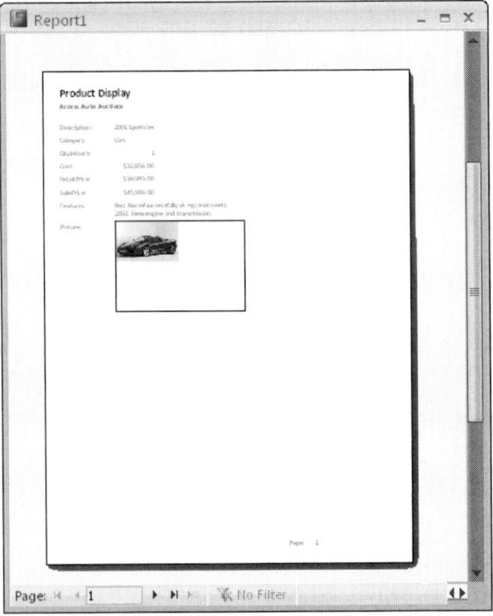

As you move the mouse over the print preview, the cursor changes to a magnifying glass. Click any portion of the view to zoom in so that can closely examine the report's layout. Only one record per page appears on the report because of the vertical layout. In the next section, you move the controls around and create a more horizontal layout.

Deleting and cutting attached labels from text controls

To create the report shown in Figure 9-19, you must move the text box labels from the Detail section to the Page Header section. Once moved, these controls appear as headings above each column of data and are repeated on each page of the report.

It's easy to delete one or more attached controls in a report. Simply select the desired controls and press Delete. However, if you want to *move* the label to the Page Header section (rather than simply deleting it), you can cut the label instead of deleting it. When removing attached controls, there are two choices:

- Delete only the label control.
- Cut the label control to the Clipboard.
- Delete or cut the label and the text box control.

Oddly enough, you cannot simply drag a label from the Detail section to the page header. Dragging an attached label from the Detail section drags its text box along with it. You must cut the label from the Detail section and paste it into the page header.

If you select the label control and cut it by pressing Ctrl+X or the Delete key, only the label control is removed. If you select the text box control and cut or delete it, the label and the text box controls are removed. To cut an attached label control (in this case, the Product ID controls and their attached label), follow these steps:

1. **Click the Close button on the toolbar to exit Print Preview mode.**
2. **Select the Product ID label control only in the Detail section.**
3. **Press Ctrl+X (Cut).**

   After you have cut the label, you may want to place it somewhere else. In this example, place it in the Page Header section.

Pasting labels into a report section

It is as easy to cut labels from controls placed in the Detail section and paste them into the page header as it is to delete the labels and create new ones in the page header. Regardless, you now paste the label you cut in the previous steps:

1. **Click anywhere in or on the Page Header section.**
2. **Press Ctrl+V (Paste).**

   The Product ID label appears in the page header.
3. **Repeat for the Description, Category, and Quantity in Stock labels.**
4. **Delete the remaining label controls in the Detail section, leaving all the text box controls.**

   If you accidentally selected the data text box control and both controls are cut or deleted, click the Undo toolbar button, or press Ctrl+Z, to undo the action.

TIP **If you want to delete only the text box control and keep the attached label control, right-click the label control and then select Copy from the shortcut menu. Next, to delete the text box control and the label control, press the Delete key. Finally, right-click anywhere on the form and select Paste from the shortcut menu to paste only the copied label control to the report.**

Moving label and text controls

Before discussing how to move label and text controls, it is important to review a few differences between attached and unattached controls. When an attached label is created automatically with a text control, it is called a *compound control*. In a compound control, whenever one control in the set is moved, the other control moves along with it. This means that, moving either the label or the text box also moves the related control.

To move both controls in a compound control, select either of the pair of controls with the mouse. As you move the mouse pointer over either of the objects the pointer turns into a hand. Click the controls and drag them to their new location. As you drag, an outline for the compound control moves with your pointer.

To move only one of the controls in a compound control, drag the desired control by its *move handle* (the large square in the upper-left corner of the control). When you click a compound control, it looks like both controls are selected, but if you look closely, you see that only one of the two controls is selected (as indicated by the presence of both moving and sizing handles). The unselected control displays only a moving handle. A pointing finger indicates that you have selected the move handles and can now move only one control. To move either control individually, select the control's move handle and drag it to its new location.

CROSS-REF **To move a label that is not attached, simply click any border (except where there is a handle) and drag it.**

To make a group selection, click with the mouse pointer anywhere outside a starting point and drag the pointer through (or around) the controls you want to select. A gray, outlined rectangle appears, showing the extent of the selection. When you release the mouse button, all controls the rectangle surrounds are selected. You can then drag the group of controls to a new location.

TIP **The global option File ➪ Access Options ➪ Object Designers ➪ Forms/Reports ➪ Selection Behavior is a property that controls the enclosure of selections. You can enclose them fully (the rectangle must completely surround the selection) or partially (the rectangle must touch only the control), which is the default.**

Make sure you also resize all the controls as shown in the figure. Change the size and shape of the Features memo field and the OLE picture field Picture. The OLE picture field displays as a rectangle with no field name in design view. It is to the right in Figure 9-29.

Place all the controls in their proper position to complete the report layout. You the controls arranged as shown in the example in Figure 9-29. You make a series of block moves by selecting several controls and positioning them close to where you want them. Then, if needed, you fine-tune their position. This is the way most reports are done.

Follow Figure 9-29 to begin placing the controls where they should be. Notice the Cost label in the Detail section has been renamed to Cost/Retail/Sale Prices.

FIGURE 9-29

Rearranging the controls on the report

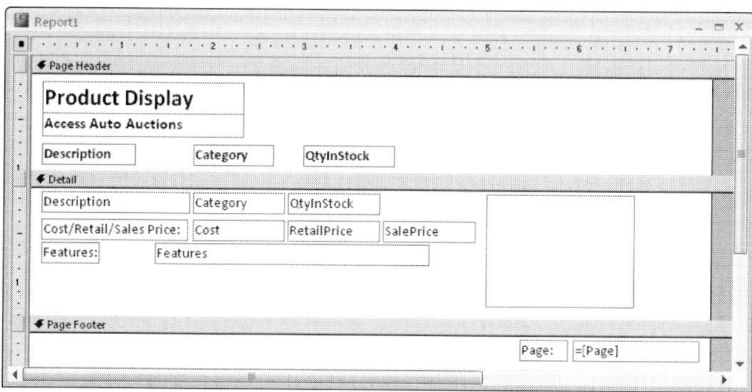

At this point, you're about halfway done. The screen should look like the one shown in Figure 9-29. (If it doesn't, adjust your controls until your screen matches the figure.) Remember that these screen pictures are taken with Windows set to 1024 x 768. If you are using a lower resolution, or have large fonts turned on the Windows Display Properties (in Control Panel), you have to scroll the screen to see the entire report.

These steps complete the rough design for this report. There are still properties, fonts, and sizes to change. When you make these changes, you have to move controls around again. Use the designs in Figure 9-29 only as a guideline. How it looks to *you*, as you refine the look of the report in the Report window, determines the final design.

Modifying the appearance of multiple controls

The next step is to apply bold formatting to all the label controls in the Page Header section directly above the section separator. The following steps guide you through modifying the appearance of text in multiple label controls:

1. **Select all label controls in the bottom of the Page Header section by individually clicking them while holding down the Shift key.**

   Alternatively, click in the vertical ruler immediately to the left of the labels in the Page Header. There are four label controls to select, as shown in Figure 9-29.

   Alternatively, you can drag a bounding box around the label controls in the page header.

2. **Click the Bold button on the toolbar.**

   After you make the final modifications, you are finished, except for fixing the picture control. To do this, you need to change properties, which you do in the next section.

NOTE This may seem to be an enormous number of steps because the procedures were designed to show you how laying out a report design can be a slow process. Remember, however, that when you click away with the mouse, you don't realize how many steps you are doing as you design the report layout visually. With a WYSIWYG (What You See Is What You Get) layout like an Access report, you may need to perform many tasks, but it's still easier and faster than programming. Figure 9-29 shows the final version of the design layout as seen in this chapter. In the next chapter, you continue to improve this report layout.

Changing label and text box control properties

To change the properties of a text or label control, you need to display the control's Property Sheet. If it is not already displayed, perform one of these actions to display it:

- Double-click the border of the control (anywhere except a sizing handle or move handle).
- Press F4.
- Right-click the mouse and select Properties.

The *Property Sheet* enables you to look at a control's property settings and provides an easy way to edit them. Using tools, such as the formatting windows and text-formatting buttons, on the Design ribbon also changes the property settings of a control. Clicking the Bold button, for example, sets the control's Font Weight property to Bold. It is usually easier and more intuitive to use the controls on the Design ribbon, but some properties are not accessible this way. In addition, sometimes objects have more options available through the Property Sheet.

The Size Mode property of an OLE object (bound object frame), with its options of Clip, Stretch, and Zoom, is a good example of a property that is available only through the Property Sheet.

The image control, which is a bound object frame, presently has its Size Mode property set to Clip, which is the default. With Clip, the picture is displayed in its original size and may be too large to fit in the frame. In this exercise, you change the setting to Stretch so that the picture is sized automatically to fit the picture frame.

CROSS-REF Chapter 24 covers the use of pictures, OLE objects, and graphs.

Follow these steps to change the property for the bound object frame control that contains the picture:

1. **Click the frame control of the picture bound object.**
2. **Click the Size Mode property and Click the arrow to display the drop-down list box.**
3. **Select Stretch.**

You might also consider changing the Border Style property to Transparent. When set to Transparent, no boxes drawn around the picture on the report.

These steps complete the changes so far to your report. A print preview of the first few records appears in Figure 9-30. If you look at the pictures, notice how the picture is properly displayed and the Features control now appears across the bottom of the Detail section.

FIGURE 9-30

The report displayed in print preview

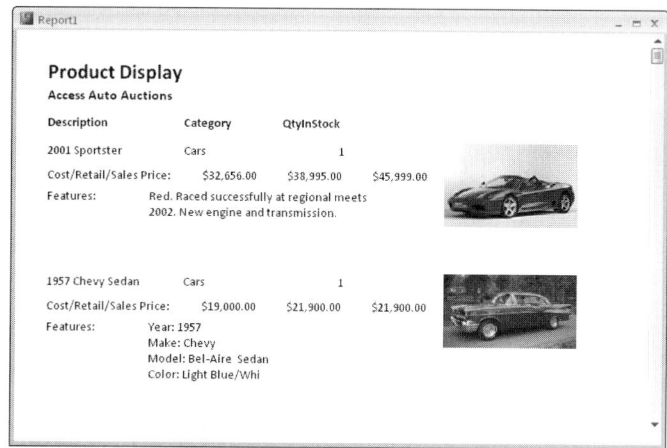

Growing and shrinking text box controls

When you print or print-preview controls that can have variable text lengths, Access provides options for enabling a control to grow or shrink vertically, depending on the exact contents of a record. The Can Grow and Can Shrink properties determine whether a text control resizes its vertical dimension to accommodate the amount of text contained in its bound field. Although these properties are usable for any text control, they are especially helpful for text box controls.

Table 9-1 explains the acceptable values for these two properties.

TABLE 9-1

Text Control Values for Can Grow and Can Shrink

Property	Value	Description
Can Grow	Yes	If the data in a record uses more lines than the control is defined to display, the control resizes to accommodate additional lines.
Can Grow	No	If the data in a record uses more lines than the control is defined to display, the control does not resize; it truncates the data display.
Can Shrink	Yes	If the data in a record uses fewer lines than the control is defined to display, the control resizes to eliminate blank lines.
Can Shrink	No	If the data in a record uses fewer lines than the control is defined to display, the control does not resize to eliminate blank lines.

To change the Can Grow settings for a text control, follow these steps:

1. **Select the Features text box control.**
2. **Display the Property window.**
3. **Click the Can Grow property; then click the arrow and select Yes.**

NOTE **The Can Grow and Can Shrink properties are also available for report sections. Use a section's Property Sheet to modify these values. Setting a report section's Can Grow and Can Shrink properties affects only the section, not the controls contained within the section.**

The report is starting to look good, but you may want to see groups of like data together and determine specific orders of data. To do this, you use sorting and grouping.

Sorting and grouping data

You can often make the data on the report more useful to users by grouping the data in informative ways. Suppose that you want to list your products first by category and then by description within each category. To do this, you use the Category and Description fields to group and sort the data.

Creating a group header or footer

Grouping on a field in the report's data adds two new sections (*Group Header* and *Group Footer*) to the report. In the following steps, you use the group header to display the name of the product category above each group of records. You won't use the Category group footer in this example because there are no totals by category or other reasons to use a group footer.

Follow these steps to create a Category group header:

1. **Click the Grouping button in the Grouping and Totals group of the Design ribbon tab.**

   You should see that the report's data already sorted by Description and Category.
2. **Click the Add a group button in the Group, Sort, and Total area.**
3. **Select Category from the field list, and Access adds Group on Category with A on top of the Group, Sort, and Total area.**

   Access adds Category Header and Category Footer sections to the report's design as soon as you select the Category field for grouping. The Category Header section appears between the Page Header and Detail sections. If you define a group footer, it appears below the Detail section. If a report has multiple groupings, each subsequent group becomes the one closest to the Detail section. The groups defined first are farthest from the Detail section.

The Group Properties pane (displayed at the bottom of the Sorting and Grouping box) contains these properties:

- **Group Header:** Yes creates a group header. No removes the group header.

- **Group Footer:** Yes creates a group footer. No removes the group footer.
- **Group On:** Specifies how you want the values grouped. The options you see in the drop-down list box depend on the data type of the field on which you're grouping. If you group on an expression, you see all grouping options as listed below.

For Text data types, there are two choices:

- **Each Value:** The same value in the field or expression
- **Prefix Characters:** The same first *n* number of characters in the field

For Date/Time data types, there are additional options:

- **Each Value:** The same value within the field or expression
- **Year:** Dates within the same calendar year.
- **Qtr:** Dates within the same calendar quarter
- **Month:** Dates within the same month
- **Week:** Dates within the same week
- **Day:** Dates on the same date
- **Hour:** Times within the same hour
- **Minute:** Times within the same minute

Currency, or Number data types provide three options:

- **Each Value:** Includes the same value in the field or expression
- **Interval:** Includes values falling within the interval you specify
- **Group Interval:** Specifies any interval that is valid for the values in the field or expression you're grouping on. The Group Interval has its own options:
  - **Keep Together:** Controls widows and orphans so that you don't have a header at the bottom of a page without detail until the next page
  - **Whole Group:** Prints header detail and group footer on one page
  - **With First Detail:** Prevents the contents of the group header from printing without any following data or records on a page
  - **No:** Does not keep data together

Sorting data within groups

Sorting enables you to determine the order in which the records are viewed on the report, based on the values in one or more controls. This order is important when you want to view the data in your tables in a sequence other than that of your input. For example, new products are added to tblProducts as they are needed on an invoice. The physical order of the database reflects the date and time a product is added. Yet, when you think of the product list, you probably expect it to be in alphabetical order by Product ID, and you want to sort it by Description of the cost of the product. By sorting in the report itself, you don't have to worry about the order of the data. Although you can sort the data in the table by the primary key or in a query by any field you want, there are good reasons to do it in the report. This way, if you change the query or table, the report is still in the correct order.

In the case of the products report, you want to display the records in each category group sorted by description. Follow these steps to define a sort order based on the Description field within the Category grouping:

1. **Click the Grouping button in the Design ribbon tab to display the Group, Sort and Total area, if it is not already open.**

   You should see that the Category group already exists in the report.
2. **Click the Add a Sort button in the Group, Sort and Total area.**
3. **Select Description in the field list. Notice that Sort Order defaults to Ascending.**
4. **Close the Group, Sort and Total area by clicking the X in the upper-right corner.**

   The Group, Sort and Total section should now look like Figure 9-31.

FIGURE 9-31

The Group, Sort and Total area completed

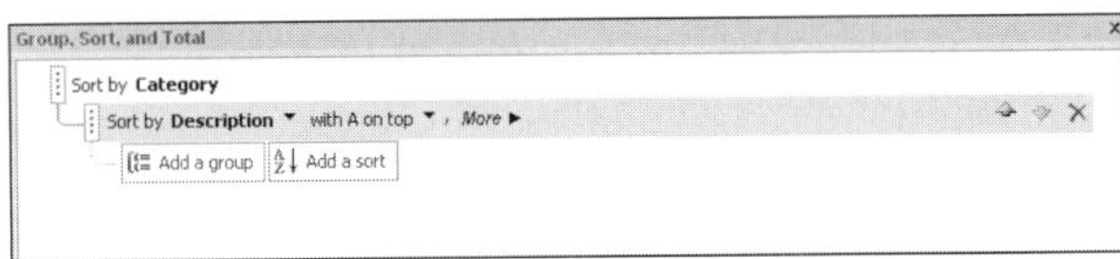

Although in this example you used a field, you can alternatively sort (and group) with an expression. To enter an expression, click the Add a sort or Add a group button in the Group, Sort and Total area and click the Expression button at the bottom of the field list. The Expression Builder dialog opens, enabling you to enter any valid Access expression, such as in `= [RetailPrice]-[Cost]`.

To change the sort order for fields in the Field/Expression column, simply click the drop-down arrow to the right of the button with the A on top to display the Sort Order list. Select Descending from the sort options that appear.

Removing a group header or footer

To remove a Page or Report Header/Footer section, display the Group, Sort and Total area, select the group or sort specifier to delete, and press the Delete key.

Hiding a section

Access also enables you to hide headers and footers so that you can break data into groups without having to view information about the group itself. You can also hide the Detail section so that you see only a summary report. To hide a section, follow these steps:

1. **Click the section you want to hide.**
2. **Display the section's Property Sheet.**
3. **Click the Visible property's text box.**
4. **Click the drop-down list arrow on the right side of the text box.**
5. **Select No from the drop-down list box.**

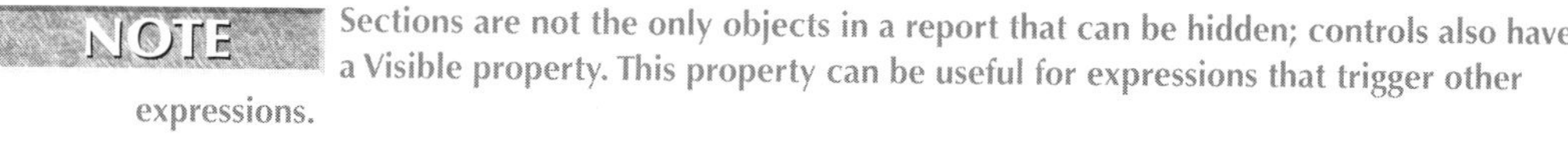

NOTE Sections are not the only objects in a report that can be hidden; controls also have a Visible property. This property can be useful for expressions that trigger other expressions.

Sizing a section

Now that you have created the group header, you might want to put some controls in the section, move some controls around, or even move controls between sections. Before you start manipulating controls within a section, you should make sure the section is the proper height.

To modify the height of a section, drag the top border of the section below it. If, for example, you have a report with a page header, Detail section, and page footer, change the height of the Detail section by dragging the top of the Page Footer section's border. You can make a section larger or smaller by dragging the bottom border of the section. For this example, change the height of the group header section to 3/8 inch with these steps:

1. **Move your mouse pointer to the bottom of the Category section.**

   The pointer changes to a horizontal line split by two vertical arrows.
2. **Select the top of the detail section (which is also the bottom of the Category Header section).**
3. **Drag the selected band lower until three dots appear in the vertical ruler (3/8").**

   The gray line indicates where the top of the border will be when you release the mouse button.
4. **Release the mouse button.**

Moving controls between sections

You now want to move the Category control from the Detail section to the Category Header section. You can move one or more controls between sections by simply dragging the control with your mouse from one section to another or by cutting it from one section and pasting it to another section. Follow these instructions to move the Category control from the Detail section to the Category section:

1. **Select the Category control in the Detail section.**
2. **Drag the Category control up to the Category Header section and drop it close to the vertical ruler, as shown in Figure 9-32.**

   You should now perform the following steps to complete the report design.
3. **Delete the Category label from the page header.**
4. **Move the ProductID control and its associated label after the Description control and its associated label, as shown in Figure 9-30.**
5. **Move the Description control and its associated label to the left so that it starts just to the right of the start of the Category control in the Category Header control.**

   By offsetting the first control in the Detail section slightly to the right of the start of the control in the Group Header section, you show the hierarchy of the data presented in the report. It now shows that each group of products is for the category listed in the group header.
6. **Lengthen the Description control so that it approaches the Product ID control.**

   Figure 9-32 shows this Property window and the completed report design. The Property sheet is opened in this figure so that you can see how the Force New Page property is set for the Category Header section.

FIGURE 9-32

Completing the Group Header section and forcing a page break before the Category Header section

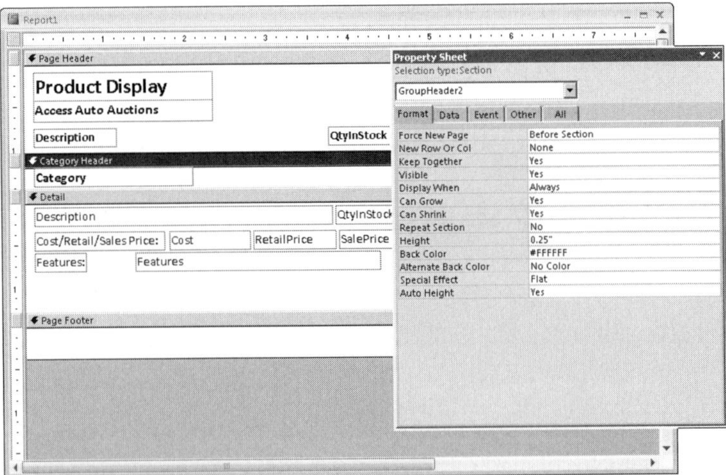

Adding page breaks

Access enables you to force page breaks based on groups. You can also insert forced breaks within sections, except in Page Header and Footer sections.

In some report designs, it's best to have each new group begin on a different page. You can achieve this effect easily by using the Force New Page property of a group section, which enables you to force a page break every time the group value changes.

The four Force New Page property settings are listed here:

- **None:** No forced page break (the default)
- **Before Section:** Starts printing the current section at the top of a new page every time there is a new group
- **After Section:** Starts printing the next section at the top of a new page every time there is a new group
- **Before & After:** Combines the effects of Before Section and After Section

To create the report you want, force a page break before the Category group with the Force New Page property in the Category header:

1. **Click anywhere in the Category header, or click the Category Header bar above the section.**
2. **Display the Property Sheet.**
3. **Select the Force New Page property, and select Before Section from the drop-down list in the property's box.**

Alternatively, you can set Force New Page property to After Section in the Category Footer section.

Sometimes, you don't want to force a page break on the basis of a grouping, but you still want to force a page break. For example, you may want to split a report title across several pages. The solution is to use the Page Break tool from the Controls group on the ribbon. Just drag the control and drop it on the report where you want a page break to occur every time the page prints.

Be careful not to split the data in a control. Place page breaks above or below controls; do not overlap them.

Making the Report Presentation Quality

As you near completion of testing your report design, you should also test the printing of your report. Figure 9-33 shows the first page of the Product Display report. There are a number of things still to do to complete the report.

The report is very boring, plain, and not something you want to give to anyone else. If your goal is to just look at the data, this report is done. However, you need to do more before you are really done.

Although the report has good, well organized data, it is not of professional quality. To make a report more visually appealing, you generally add some lines and rectangles, possibly some special effects such as shadows or sunken areas if you have a background on the report. You want to make sure sections have distinct areas separate from each other using lines or color. Make sure controls aren't touching each other (because text may eventually touch if a value is long enough). Make sure text is aligned with other text above or below and to the right or left.

In Figure 9-33, you can see some opportunities for professionalism.

FIGURE 9-33

The report is pretty plain and uninteresting at this point.

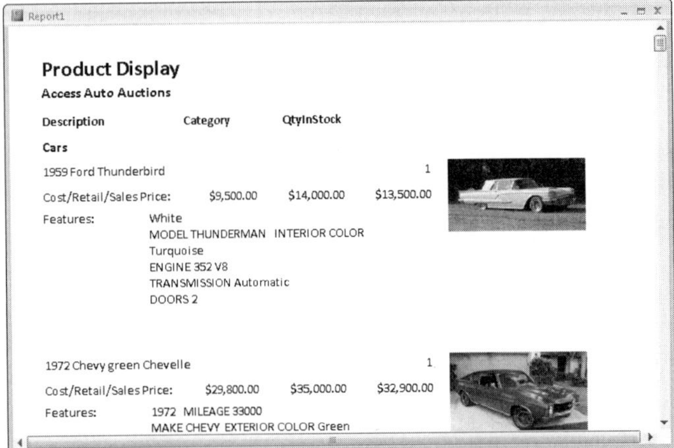

Adjusting the Page Header

The page header contains several large labels positioned far apart from each other. The column headers are too small and are just hanging there. They could be made one font size larger. The entire page header should be separated from the Detail section by a horizontal line.

If you wanted to add some color to your report, you could make the report name a different color. Be careful not to use too many colors unless you have a specific theme in mind. Most serious business reports use one or two colors, and rarely more than three with the exception of graphs and charts. Furthermore, colors are not much use when printed on most laser printers. Color laser printers are still not widely available, so adding a lot of color to your Access reports may not be something others will recognize or appreciate.

Figure 9-34 shows these changes. The Product Display label has been changed to a blue background color with white foreground text. This is done by first selecting the control and then selecting Blue for the background. They have also been placed under each other and left aligned. The rectangle around each of the controls was also properly sized by double-clicking each control's sizing handles.

The next step is to add a nice thick line separating the Page Header section from the Category Group Header section:

1. **Select the Line tool in the Controls ribbon group.**
2. **Place the mouse cursor near the far left side of the Page Header, just to the right and above of the 1 inch mark on the vertical toolbar, as shown in Figure 9-34.**

FIGURE 9-34

Adjusting controls in the page header

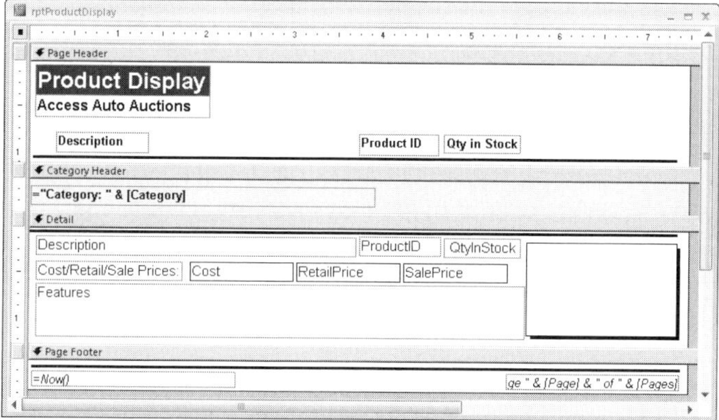

3. **Hold down the Shift key and then hold down the left mouse button and drag the mouse across the page header, releasing it just to the left of the 7½-inch mark.**

   Holding down the Shift key forces a nice, straight, horizontal line.

4. **Select the line and select the 2 pt line thickness from the Line Thickness icon on the toolbar, or select the 2 pt Border Width property from the line's Property window.**

   The Line Thickness icon should be next to the Border icon on the formatting toolbar.

Creating an expression in the group header

Figure 9-34 also shows that the Category field has been replaced by an expression. If you place the value of the category in the Group Header section, it looks out of place and may not be readily identifiable. Most data values should have some type of label to identify what they are.

The expression `="Category: " & [Category]` displays Category: followed by a space and the value of the Category field (such as Category: Cars) in the text box. The & symbol (the concatenation operator) joins strings. Make sure you leave a space after the colon or the value will not be separated from the label. The text control has been bolded, underlined, and the font point size increased as well.

You may find that Access complains about a circular reference on the Category text box after you change the control's ControlSource. This happens because the name of the control is Category, and the text box is bound to a field named Category. Access doesn't understand that `[Category]` in the expression you entered as the ControlSource actually refers to the field, not the text box. (A text box's value cannot be based on the text box's contents—that's the definition of *circular reference*.)

The solution is to rename the text box to distinguish it from its bound field. The logical name for this text box is `txtCategory`.

CAUTION **When you create a bound control, it uses the name of the data field as the default control name. Using the control in an expression without changing the name of your control, causes circular references. You must rename the control to something other than the original field name. This is another reason why a simple naming convention, such as prefixing text boxes with `txt` is such a good idea. You'll avoid a lot of nagging problems by adopting a naming convention for the controls on your Access reports.**

Follow these steps to complete the expression and rename the control:

1. **Select the Category control in the Category Group Header section.**
2. **Display the Property window for the control.**
3. **Change the Control Source property to** ="Category: " & [Category].
4. **Change the Name property to** txtCategoryDisplay.

Changing the picture properties and the Detail section

The Detail section is in fairly good shape. Make sure the Description control is slightly indented from the Category expression in the Group Header. A label should be created, as shown in Figure 9-34, identifying the values in the Cost, Retail Price, and Sale Price controls.

A line is also good to add to this Detail section to separate one record from another. This is often done when records occupy varying space within a group. Some records are shorter than others, and the separation between records may not be obvious to users.

Because you don't want two lines at the bottom of each page (you add a line to the Page Footer next), you put this line at the top of the Detail section:

1. **Select the Line tool in the Controls ribbon group.**
2. **Place the cursor near the far left side of the Detail section, just to the right and above the ⅛-inch mark on the vertical toolbar, as shown in Figure 9-35.**

FIGURE 9-35

Put the cursor near the far left of the Detail section.

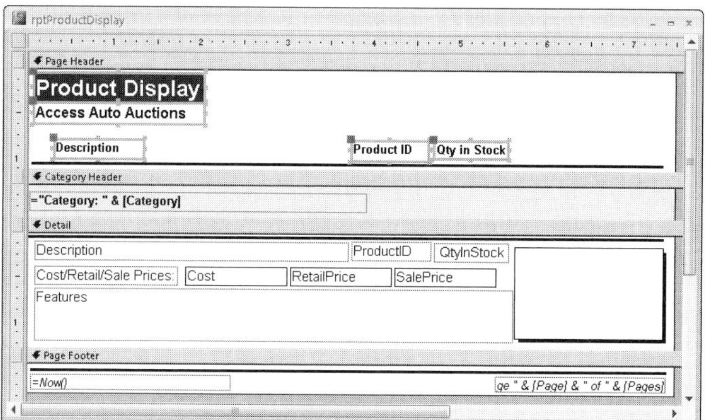

You may have to reposition controls in the Detail section to make room for the horizontal line.

3. **Hold down the Shift key and drag the line across the page header, releasing the mouse button just to the left of the 7½-inch mark.**
4. **Select the line and select 1 or 2 pt line thickness from the Line Thickness icon in the Controls ribbon group, or select the 1 or 2 pt BorderWidth property from the line's Property Sheet.**

Numeric data controls are right aligned by default. Because they are next to each other horizontally and not above each other vertically, they can be left or center aligned. Although the repeating groups of records are above each other, they are separated by a wide space and left alignment is okay.

One task to complete is to change the picture control to make the picture fit within the control and to add a shadow to dress up the picture and give it some depth. Follow these steps to complete these tasks:

1. **Select the Picture control in the Detail section.**
2. **Change the control's Size Mode property to Stretch.**
3. **Select Shadowed as the Special Effect property.**

Creating a standard page footer

The page footer currently contains a page number control that you added earlier in this chapter. Although *Page n of m* is at the bottom of the report, a date and time control would be nice as well. Many times, you print a copy of a report and then discover some bad data. You correct the values, print another copy, and discover you can't tell them apart. Having a print date and time solves this problem.

Follow these steps to create a date/time control:

1. **Select the Text Box control in the Controls group.**
2. **Select the Page Footer section and add a text box near the left edge.**
3. **Delete the label attached to the text box.**
4. **Enter** =Now() **as the text box's Control Source property.**

   This displays the current date and time when the report is run. If you use the `Date()` keyword, you only get the current date and not the current time.
5. **Select General Date from the control's Format property.**
6. **Select Align Left from the Font ribbon group.**

   The print date control should be left aligned, but make sure the page number control is right-aligned.

The last step is to move the controls down a little from the Page Footer section and add a line between the Page Header section and these controls:

1. **Select the date and page number controls and move them down 1/8 inch.**
2. **While they are selected, click the Italic icon on the Formatting toolbar.**
3. **Select the Line tool in the toolbox.**
4. **Draw a horizontal line above the print date and page number controls in the Page Footer section, and adjust its width.**

   Your screen should look like the one shown in Figure 9-36.

FIGURE 9-36

Adjusting controls in the Detail and Page Footer sections

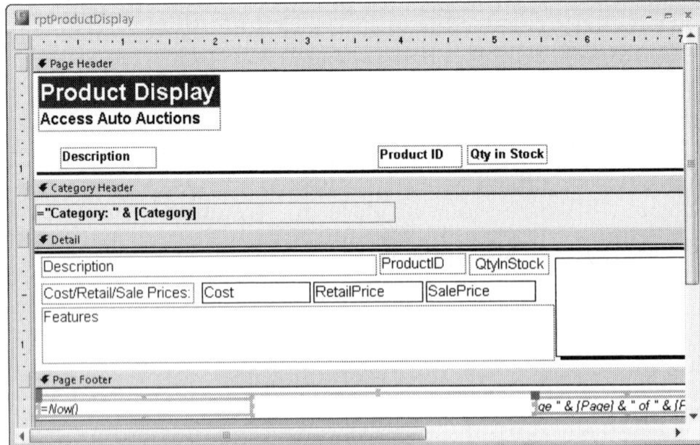

CAUTION If every even-numbered page is blank, you accidentally widened the report past the 8-inch mark. If you move a control to brush up against the right page-margin border or exceed it, the right page margin increases automatically. When it is past the 8-inch mark, it can't display the entire page on one piece of paper. The blank page you get is actually the right side of the preceding page. To correct this, make sure that all your controls are within the 8-inch right margin; then drag the right page margin back to 8 inches.

Saving your report

After all the time you spent creating your report, you'll want to save it. It is good practice to save your reports frequently, starting as soon as you create them. This prevents the frustration that occurs when you lose work because of a power failure. Save the report as follows:

1. **Select File ➪ Save, or click the Save button in the Quick Access toolbar in the upper -left area of the main Access window.**

   If this is the first time you have saved the report, the Save As dialog box appears.
2. **Type a valid Access object name. For this example, type** rptProductDisplayFinal.
3. **Click OK.**

   If you already saved your report, Access immediately saves your report.

Summary

Reports are an important and integral part of most Access applications. Very often reports are the most important aspect of Access applications, and are seen by people who never see the Access application running on a computer.

Access is endowed with an outstanding Report Designer. This long chapter has surveyed the wealth of report creation tools available to the Access developer. As long as this chapter is, it has only scratched the surface and presented the fundamental capabilities of the Access Report Designer.

In this chapter, you read about the different types of Access reports, learned how to use the Access Report Wizard to build reports, and then created reports from scratch. You also read about the many different ways to provide a report with data and to display data on the report. This chapter also discussed a number of techniques for summarizing data on Access reports.

Part II

Programming Microsoft Access

This part explains the art and science of Visual Basic for Applications (VBA) programming. Very few professional-quality Access applications have been written without liberal use of the VBA programming language and its capabilities. VBA provides you with powerful tools for adding capabilities and flexibility to your applications.

VBA is a fully qualified programming language and is used in many other Microsoft products, including all the main members of the Microsoft Office suite (Word, Excel, and PowerPoint), in addition to Microsoft Access.

Many user requirements simply cannot be implemented without using VBA code. VBA code provides functionality that goes far beyond simply opening forms and reports and controlling the user interface. You'll use VBA code to validate data, as well as transform and combine data in new and interesting ways. VBA code is used to import and export data, respond to user input, and handle the mistakes inevitably made by users.

VBA code enables you to seamlessly integrate with the other applications in Microsoft Office. For instance, using a surprisingly small amount of code, you can implement a very powerful mail-merge system by combining Access data with Word document templates. (We discuss application integration in Part III of this book, but we wanted to give you a preview of what's coming up next!)

IN THIS PART

As you'll see in this part, VBA is a large and somewhat complex programming language. If you aren't already using VBA, you'll want to carefully read the chapters in this part and work the examples until you're comfortable creating VBA modules and composing programming statements.

These chapters provide you with the essential skills necessary to become comfortable writing VBA code. You'll learn where VBA code lives within an Access application, how to compose VBA statements, and how to hook up VBA code to your forms and reports.

We can't overemphasize how important VBA programming skills are to professional database developers. Because VBA is used in so many different platforms (Access, Word, Excel, and so on), your programming skills are transferable to many situations beyond database development. Also, the VBA programming language is very similar to the languages used in Microsoft Visual Studio. Quite frankly, there is no limit to what you can accomplish with the skills you develop in learning Access VBA.

Chapter 10

VBA Programming Fundamentals

If you have created or worked with a simple Access application, you most likely created the application's operations by using macros. Although macros provide a quick and easy way to automate an application, writing Visual Basic for applications (VBA) modules is the best way to create applications. Using data access, repetitive looping, and branching, and adding features that macros simply cannot provide gives you more control over application development. In this chapter, you learn how to build an application framework and how to extend the power of an application using VBA.

IN THIS CHAPTER

- Converting macros to VBA
- Using the Command Button Wizard to create VBA code
- Understanding the basics of VBA
- Understanding modules
- Creating a new module
- Using the Module window

ON the CD-ROM Use the database file Chapter10.accdb in this chapter.

Understanding the Limitations of Macros

For a number of reasons, this book does not extensively cover Access macro creation. To begin with, there are enough important topics so that we have to choose which topics are covered in detail. Also, macros are pretty easy to learn on your own, and they are quite well documented in the Access online help.

But, by far, the biggest reason not to document macros is that, for the most part, macros do not belong in professionally built applications. At the very least, macros occupy a relatively minor position in most applications because of their rather serious limitations. Perhaps the greatest issue with macros is that they are guaranteed to be non-portable to other applications. You cannot use an Access macro anywhere other than Access. VBA code, on the other hand, is very portable to Word, Excel, Outlook, Visio, and even Visual Studio.NET (with changes). Learning to build great macros is not a career-booster the way that mastering VBA programming is.

NOTE **This is not meant to imply that macros have no place in Access 2007 applications. Microsoft has issues related to previous versions of Access macros. In particular, macros now include simple error handling (mostly jumping to a named location when an error occurs) and also include variables. These are significant updates to the Access macro engine but, in the opinion of many, are not enough to justify using macros in professional applications.**

Introducing Visual Basic for Applications

Although it is undoubtedly true that many readers of this book are experienced Access developers and are comfortable working with VBA, this chapter and the other chapters in this part of *Access 2007 Bible* assume the reader has no experience with VBA.

These chapters are included to provide a firm foundation for many of the techniques discussed in the latter chapters of this book. As you'll see in the chapters following Part II, many advanced Access techniques simply cannot be implemented without the use of VBA code.

Visual Basic for Applications (VBA), of course, is the programming language built into Access. VBA is shared among all of the Microsoft Office applications, including Word, Excel, Outlook, PowerPoint, and even Visio. If you are not already a VBA programmer, learning the VBA syntax and how to hook VBA into the Access event model is a definite career builder.

If you're new to programming, it is important not to become frustrated or overwhelmed by the seeming complexity of the VBA language. As with any new skill, you're much better off approaching VBA programming by taking it one step at a time. It is important to learn exactly what VBA can do for you and your applications, along with the general syntax, statement structure, and how to compose procedures using the VBA language.

This book is chock-full of examples for Access developers of how to use the VBA language to accomplish useful tasks. Each of the procedures you see in this book has been carefully tested and verified to work correctly. If you find that a bit of code in this book does not work properly for you, please take the time to ensure that you have used the example code exactly as presented in this book. Very often, the most difficult problems implementing any programming technique stem from simple errors such as misspelling or forgetting to include a comma or parentheses mark where required.

NOTE What's in a name? The expression "Visual Basic" is a source of endless confusion for people working with the Microsoft products. Microsoft has applied the name "Visual Basic" to a number of different products and technologies. For more than 10 years Microsoft marketed a stand-alone product named "Visual Basic" that was, in many ways, comparable and competitive with Microsoft Access. In 1995, Microsoft added the Visual Basic for Applications (VBA) programming language to Access, Word, and Excel in the Microsoft Office product. This name was chosen because the words used to write programs in the Visual Basic product are identical to those used when programming with the VBA language used in Access, Word, and Excel.

Although the VBA language used in the Visual Basic product is very similar to VBA as used in Access, they are not exactly the same. There are some things that can be done with the Visual Basic (product) language that cannot be done with Access VBA, and vice-versa. In this book, the expressions "VBA" and "Visual Basic" refer to the programming language built into Access, and should not be confused with the Microsoft product named Visual Basic or the newer products named Visual Basic.NET.

We actually begin our discussion of VBA programming by showing you how to migrate Access macros to the VBA language. There are a number of reasons why we have taken this approach to describing VBA. It is very likely that you understand how the macros in an Access application work. If your applications already include a several macros, it is very likely that you have seen these macros in action. Converting those macros to VBA code is a great way to learn basic VBA syntax. Also, after a macro is converted to VBA code, you may find simple and effective ways to extend the tasks supported by that code. Because the VBA programming language is very flexible, there are many things you can do using VBA that you can't do with Access macros. A few of these operations are discussed in the following section.

Understanding VBA Terminology

Before plunging into our discussion on VBA, let's review some basic VBA terminology:

Keyword: A word that has special meaning in VBA. For instance, in normal English language, the word *now* simply indicates a point in time. In VBA, `Now` is the name of a built-in VBA function that returns the current date and time.

Statement: A single VBA word or combination of words that constitute an instruction to be performed by the VBA engine.

Procedure: A collection of VBA statements that are grouped together to perform a certain task. You might, for instance, write a procedure that extracts data from a table, combines the data in a particular way, and displays the data on a form. Or, you might write three smaller procedures, each of which performs a single step of the overall process.

Function: There are two types of procedures: *subs* (subroutines) and functions. Subroutines are actually easier to understand — they perform a single task and then just go away. Functions, on the other hand, perform a task and then return a value. The procedure example described previously is actually a subroutine. It performs a specific task; then when it ends, it just goes away. The example where the operation is split into three smaller procedures includes a function. In this case, the first procedure that opens the database and extracts data most likely returns the data as a recordset, and the recordset is passed to the other procedures that perform the data combination and data display.

Module: Procedures live in modules. If statements are like sentences and procedures are like paragraphs, modules are the chapters or documents of the VBA language. A module consists of a number of procedures and other elements combined as a single entity within the application.

Variable: Variables are sometimes tricky to understand. Because Access is a database development tool, it makes sense that VBA code has to have some way of managing the data involved in the application. A variable is nothing more than a name applied to represent a data value. In virtually all VBA programs, you create and use variables to hold values such as customer names, dates, and numeric values manipulated by the VBA code.

VBA is appropriately defined as a *language*. And, just as with any human language, VBA consists of a number of words, sentences, and paragraphs, all arranged in a specific fashion. Each VBA sentence is a *statement*. Statements are aggregated as *procedures*, and procedures live within *modules*. A *function* is a specific type of procedure; one that returns a value when it's run. For instance, `Now()` is a built-in VBA function that returns the current date and time, down to the second. You use the `Now()` function in your application whenever it is necessary to capture the current date and time, such as when assigning a timestamp value to a record.

Each VBA statement is an instruction that is processed and executed by the VBA language engine built into Microsoft Access. Here is an example of a typical VBA statement that opens a form:

```
DoCmd.OpenForm "frmMyForm", acNormal
```

`DoCmd` is a built-in Access object that performs numerous tasks for you. Think of `DoCmd` as a little robot that can perform many different tasks. The `OpenForm` that follows DoCmd is the task we want `DoCmd` to run, and `frmMyForm` is (obviously) the name of the form to open. Finally, `acNormal` is a specifier that tells `DoCmd` we want the form opened in its "normal" view. The implication here, of course, is that there are other view modes that may be applied to opening a form. These modes include Design (acDesign) or Datasheet (acFormDS) view, and Print Preview (acPreview, when applied to reports).

In a nutshell, that's all there is to learning and using VBA.

Migrating from Macros to VBA

Should you now convert all the macros in your applications to VBA? The answer depends on what you are trying to accomplish. The fact that Access 2007 includes VBA does not mean that Access macros are no longer useful; it simply means that Access developers should learn VBA and add it to their arsenal of tools for creating Access applications.

VBA is not always the answer. Some tasks, such as creating global key assignments, can be accomplished only via macros. You can perform some actions more easily and effectively by using a macro than by writing VBA code.

When to use macros and when to use VBA

In Access, macros often offer an ideal way to take care of many details, such as opening reports and forms. You can build applications faster using macros because the arguments for each macro action are displayed in the macro editor (in the bottom portion of the Macro editor window). You don't have to remember complex or difficult syntax.

NOTE **Here's another naming issue: An Access macro is a stepwise list of actions that you compose using the Access macro editor. Microsoft Word and Excel use the word *macro* to refer to procedures written in the VBA programming language. When working with in the Access environment, a macro always refers to the stepwise set of instructions composed using the Access macro editor. Most Access developers refer to VBA code as either procedures or modules and virtually never refer to these objects as macros.**

Certain actions are easier to accomplish with macros than with VBA code. Actions such as opening and closing forms or opening reports are somewhat easier to accomplish with a simple macro than by writing VBA code.

Most often, VBA is much better choice. There are many things that can be accomplished with the VBA code and with macros:

- **Create and use your custom functions:** In addition to using built-in Access functions, you can use VBA to create and work with your own functions.
- **Trap and handle errors:** You can create error routines that detect an error and decide what action to take. These routines bypass the cryptic Access error messages.
- **Use Automation to communicate with other Windows applications:** You can write code to see whether a file exists before you take some action, or you can communicate with another Windows application (such as a spreadsheet), passing data back and forth.
- **Use the Windows API:** As you'll see in Chapter 30, you can use VBA code to hook into many resources provided by Windows, such as determining the user's Windows login name, or the name of the computer the user is working on.

- **Loop through records:** Very often, you need to open a set of records and perform some operation on those records one at a time. The only effective way to perform this type of operation is through VBA code.
- **Maintain the application:** Unlike macros, code can be built into a form or report, making maintaining the form or report more efficient. Additionally, if you move a form or report from one database to another, the event procedures built into the form or report travel with it.
- **Create or manipulate objects:** In most cases, you'll find that it necessary to work with an object in Design View. In some situations, however, you may want to manipulate the definition of an object in code. Using VBA, you can manipulate all the objects in a database, including the database itself.

TIP **If you create a form or report that will be copied to other databases, create your event procedures for that form or report in VBA instead of with macros. Because most macros are stored as separate objects in the database, you have to remember which ones are associated with the form or report you are copying. On the other hand, because VBA code can be attached to the form or report, copying the form automatically copies the VBA event procedures associated with it.**

Access 2007 supports embedded macros in forms, reports, and controls. An embedded macro lives within its host object (form, report, or control) and travels with the object if it is copied to another. Even then, however, embedded macros suffer from the performance issues associated with external macros and are not portable to any other systems like Word or Excel.

Converting existing macros to VBA

As you become comfortable with writing VBA code, you may want to rewrite existing macros as VBA procedures. As you begin this process, you quickly realize how mentally challenging the effort can be as you review every macro action in your macro libraries. You cannot cut and paste a macro into a VBA code module. You must analyze the task accomplished by each macro action and then add the equivalent VBA statements to your code.

Fortunately, Access provides a feature to convert macros to VBA code automatically. One of the options in the Save As dialog box is Save As Module. You can use this option when a macro file is highlighted in the Macros object window of the Database window. This option enables you to convert an entire macro group to a module in seconds.

To try the conversion process, convert the `mcrOpenContacts` macro in the Chapter10.accdb database and follow these steps to run the conversion process:

1. **Click the Macros object button of the Database window.**
2. **Select the `mcrOpenCustomers` macro.**
3. **Choose File ➪ Save As.**

   The Save As dialog box appears, as shown in Figure 10-1.

FIGURE 10-1

Saving a macro as a module

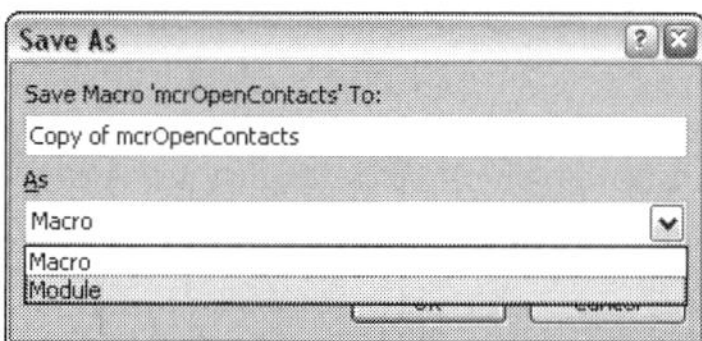

Access assigns a default name for the new module as "Copy of" followed by the macro name.

4. **Enter a more descriptive name for the new module and select module for the option and click OK.**

   The Convert Macro dialog box appears, as shown in Figure 10-2.

FIGURE 10-2

The Convert Macro dialog box

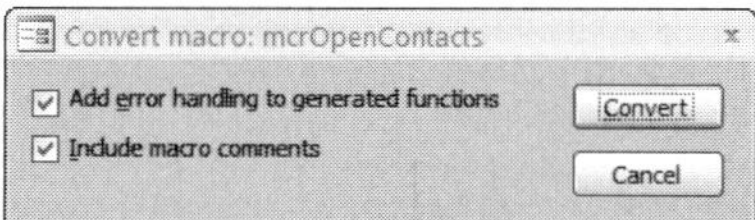

5. **Select the options that include error handling and comments, and click Convert.**

   Access briefly displays each new procedure as it is converted. When the conversion process completes, the `Conversion Finished!` message box appears.

Figure 10-3 shows the newly created VBA module (Converted Macro mcrOpenContacts). Notice that the module is named after the macro that was converted.

FIGURE 10-3

The newly converted module

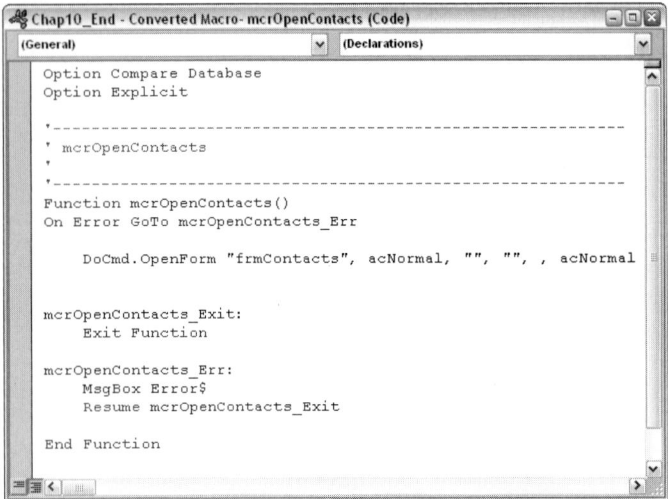

When you specify that you want Access to include error processing for the conversion, Access automatically inserts the `On Error` statement as the first statement in the procedure, telling Access to branch to other statements that display an appropriate message and then exit the function.

CROSS-REF **Handling errors is covered in Chapter 25.**

The statement beginning with `DoCmd` is the actual code that Access created from the macro. `DoCmd` methods mimic macro actions and perform important tasks such as opening forms and reports, and setting the value of controls.

Using the Command Button Wizard to create VBA code

One way to learn event procedures is to use the Command Button Wizard. When Access creates a command button with a wizard, it adds an event procedure attached to the button. You can open the event procedure to see how it works and then modify it to fit your needs.

Access supports more than 30 types of command buttons through the Command Button Wizard. These buttons include finding or printing records, or applying a filter to a form's data. Run this wizard by adding a command button to a form with the Use Control Wizards item selected in the Design tab of the Access ribbon. Figure 10-4 shows a Delete Record command button being created.

FIGURE 10-4

The Command Button Wizard

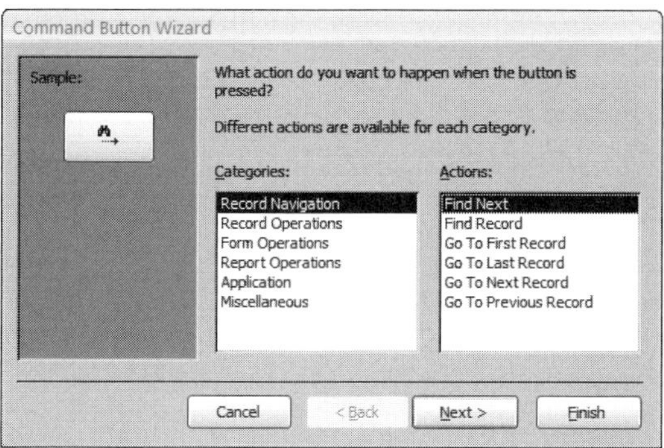

The `Chapter10.accdb` example database includes a form named frmButtonWizardSamples. This form, shown in Figure 10-5 in Design mode, contains a dozen command buttons created with the Command Button Wizard. Review the procedures for the buttons on this form to see how powerful VBA code can be.

FIGURE 10-5

Examples of Command Button Wizard buttons

Figure 10-6 shows the code for the Go To First Record command button.

FIGURE 10-6

The Go To First Record button's On Click procedure

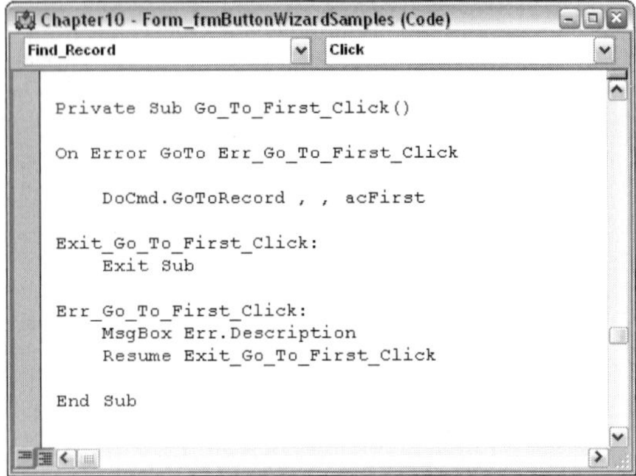
Chapter10 - Form_frmButtonWizardSamples (Code)
Find_Record
Click
Private Sub Go_To_First_Click()
On Error GoTo Err_Go_To_First_Click
DoCmd.GoToRecord , , acFirst
Exit_Go_To_First_Click:
Exit Sub
Err_Go_To_First_Click:
MsgBox Err.Description
Resume Exit_Go_To_First_Click
End Sub

The code produced by the Command Button Wizard is very simple, but effective.

Creating VBA Programs

Access has a wide variety of tools that enable you to work with tables, queries, forms, and reports without ever having to write a single line of code. At some point, you may begin building more sophisticated applications. You may want to "bulletproof" your applications by providing more intensive data-entry validation or implementing better error handling.

Some operations cannot be accomplished through the user interface, even with macros. You may find yourself saying, "I wish I had a way to..." or "There just has to be a function that will let me...." At other times, you find that you are continually putting the same formula or expression in a query or filter. You may find yourself saying, "I'm tired of typing this formula into...." or "Doggone it, I typed the wrong formula in this...."

For situations such as these, you need the horsepower of a high-level programming language such as VBA. VBA has become the common language for many Microsoft applications. VBA is a modern, structured programming language offering many of the programming structures available in most programming languages: If...Then...Else, Select Case, and so on. VBA is extensible (capable of calling Windows API routines) and can interact through ADO (ActiveX Data Objects), DAO (Data Access Objects), and with any Access or VBA data type.

Getting started with VBA programming in Access requires an understanding of its event-driven environment.

Understanding events and event procedures

In Access, unlike old-fashioned programming environments, the user controls the actions and flow of the application. The user determines what to do and when to do it, such as changing information in a field or clicking a command button. Users determine the flow of action and, through *events*, the application determines what action to take or ignore. In contrast, procedural-oriented programming languages require that the programmer determine the flow of actions the user must follow. In fact, the programmer must program for all possibilities of user intervention — for example, keystrokes a user may enter in error — and must determine what actions to take in response to the user.

Using macros and event procedures, you implement the responses to these actions. Access provides *event properties* for each control you place on a form. By attaching a VBA procedure to a control's event property, you do not have to worry about the order of actions a user may take on a particular form.

In an event-driven environment such as Access, the objects (forms, reports, and controls) respond to events. Basically, an event procedure is VBA code that executes when an event occurs. The code is directly attached to the form or report containing the event being processed. An Exit command button, for example, closes the form when the user clicks the button. Clicking the command button triggers its `Click` event. The event procedure is the VBA code attached to the `Click` event. The event procedure automatically runs every time the user clicks the command button.

There are two types of procedures:

- Sub
- Function

Sub and function procedures are grouped and stored in modules. The Modules object button in the Navigation Pane stores the common procedures that any of your forms can access. You *could* store all your procedures in a single module, but that wouldn't be a good idea. You'll probably want to group related procedures into separate modules, categorizing them by the nature of the operations they perform. For example, an `Update` module might include procedures for adding and deleting records from a table.

Subprocedures

Subprocedures do not return a value, and therefore, you cannot use subs in expressions or call them by assigning them to variables. All event procedures are subs.

These VBA statements within a sub are the code you want to run every time the procedure is executed. The following example shows an Exit command button's subprocedure:

```
Sub cmdExit_Click()
  DoCmd.Close
End Sub
```

The first line of this procedure notifies the VBA engine that the procedure is a Sub, and that its name is `cmdExit_Click`. If parameters (data passed to the procedure) are associated with this sub, they appear within the parentheses.

There is only one VBA statement within this Sub (`DoCmd.Close`). The `End Sub` statement at the bottom ends this procedure. The `cmdExit_Click ( )` subprocedure is attached to the Exit button's `Click` event. The event procedure closes the form when the user clicks the Exit command button.

Functions

A function returns a value. Use functions in expressions or assign a function to a variable. Like subprocedures, functions are often called by other functions or by subs.

Within the body of a function, you assign a return value to the function's name. You then can use the value that is returned as part of a larger expression. The following function calculates the square footage of a room:

```
Function nSquareFeet(dblHeight As Double, _
    dblWidth As Double) As Double

  'Assign this function's value:
  nSquareFeet = dblHeight * dblWidth

End Function
```

This function receives two parameters (`dblHeight` and `dblWidth`). Notice that the function's name (`nSquareFeet`) is assigned a value within the body of the function. The function is declared as a Double data type, so the return value is recognized by the VBA interpreter as a Double.

Use code like this to call this function:

```
dblAnswer = nSquareFeet(xHeight, xWidth)
```

One last point: notice the underscore character in the function's first line. An underscore at the end of a VBA statement (called a *continuation character*) instructs the VBA engine to include the next line as part of the same statement.

Understanding modules

Modules and their procedures are the principal objects of the VBA programming language. The code that you write is added to procedures that are contained in a module. VBA code modules can be independent, stand-alone objects (called *standard modules*) that are unrelated to specific forms or reports, or they can be integrated into forms and reports (usually referred to as *form modules* and *report modules*).

As you create VBA procedures for your Access applications, you use both types of modules.

Form and report modules

All forms and reports support events. The procedures associated with form and report events can be macros or VBA code. Every form or report you add to your database contains a VBA code module (unless its `Has Module` property is set to No). This form or report module is an integral part of the form or report, and is used as a container for the event procedures you create for the form or report. This method is a convenient way to place all of a form's event procedures in a single location.

Adding VBA event procedures to a form module is very powerful and efficient. Event procedures contained in a form's module become part of the form. When you export the form to another Access database, all of the form's event procedures go with it.

Modifying a control's event procedure is easy: simply click the ellipsis button (...) in the Property Sheet next to the event property, opening the form's code module. Figure 10-7 illustrates accessing the `Click` event procedure of the Delete button on the Contacts form.

FIGURE 10-7

Accessing a control's event procedure from the Property Sheet

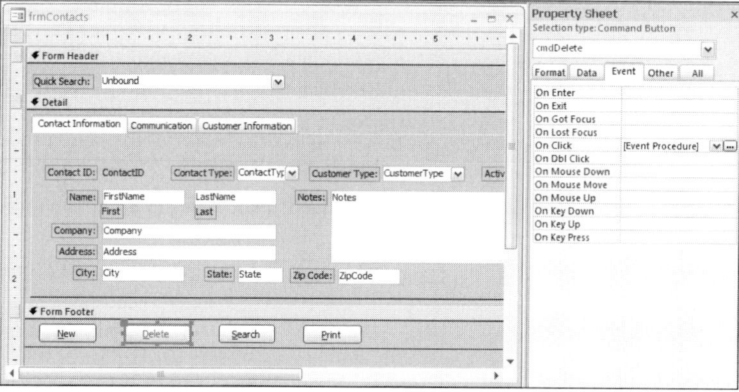

Notice the `[Event Procedure]` in the control's `On Click` property. It tells you that there is code attached to the control's event procedure. Clicking on the button with the ellipsis (three dots) opens the VBA code editor, displaying the event procedure.

Event procedures that work directly with a form or report belong in the module of the form or report. A form's module should contain only the declarations and event procedures needed for that form and its controls (buttons, check boxes, labels, text boxes, combo boxes, and so on). Placing procedures shared with other forms in a form's module doesn't make sense.

Standard modules

Standard modules are independent from forms and reports. Standard modules store code that is used from anywhere within your application. These procedures are often called *global* or *public* because they are accessible to all elements of your Access application.

Use public procedures throughout your application in expressions, macros, event procedures, and other VBA code. To use a public procedure, you simply reference it from VBA code in event procedures or any other procedure in your application.

TIP **Procedures *run*; modules *contain*. Procedures are executed and perform actions. Modules, on the other hand, are simple containers, grouping procedures and declarations together. A module cannot be run; rather, you run the procedures contained within the module.**

Standard modules are stored in the Module section of the Navigation Pane. As you read earlier, form and report modules are attached to their hosts and are accessed through the form or reports Property Sheets.

Generally speaking, you should group your procedures into categories. Most modules contain procedures that are related in some way.

Creating a new module

Using the Modules section of the Navigation Pane you create and edit VBA code contained in standard modules. You could, for example, create a Beep procedure that makes the computer beep as a warning or notification that something has happened in your program. Each procedure is a series of code statements that performs an operation or calculation.

Think of a module as a library or collection of procedures. Your Access databases can contain thousands of modules, although most Access applications include only a few dozen standard modules.

CROSS-REF **You will see many examples of creating functions and procedures in Chapters 11 through 14.**

For this example, you can use the Chapter10.accdb database, or open a new blank database. Add a new module by selecting the Create tab of the Access ribbon, dropping down the list under the Macro item, and selecting Module from the list (see Figure 10-8).

FIGURE 10-8

Adding a new module to an Access database

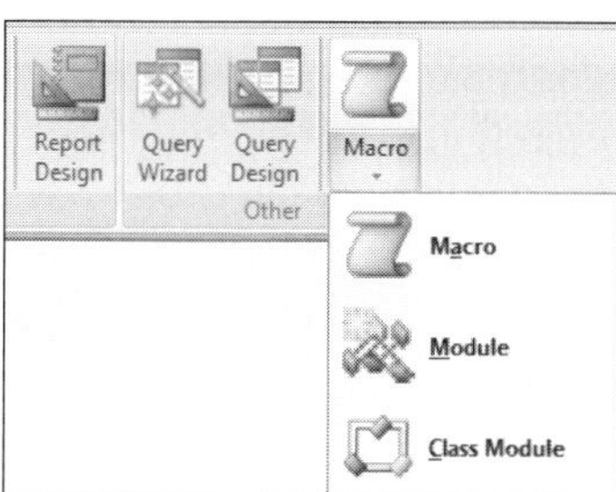

Access opens the VBA editor and adds a new module named `Module1` (see Figure 10-9).

FIGURE 10-9

The newly opened code in the VBA editor

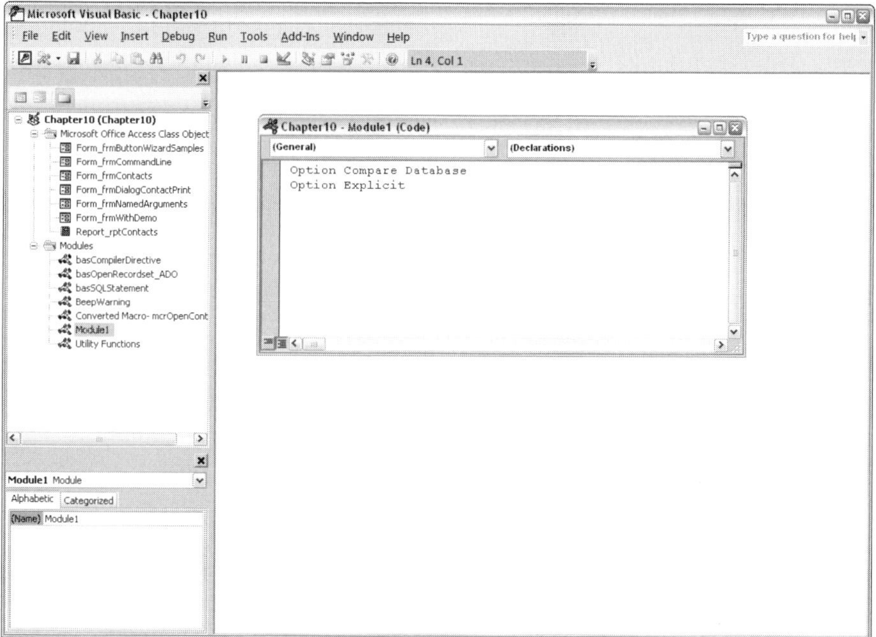

Working in the Code window

Whenever you create VBA procedures for your Access applications, you edit code in a code window. Although the Code window is confusing at first, it is easy to understand and use after you learn how each part is used.

NOTE **Notice that the Access 2007 Code window does not use the ribbon. Instead, the Code window appears much as it has in every version of Access since Access 2000. Therefore, in this book you'll see references to the Code window's toolbar and menu whenever we describe working with Access VBA modules.**

When you enter Design mode of a module — whether it is via a form or report module or the modules group on the Navigation Pane — the VBA editor and its menu and toolbar open to enable you to create or edit your procedures.

When you display VBA code within a form (or report) module, the Object and Procedure drop-down lists at the top of the Code window contain the form's controls and events. You select these objects and events to create or edit event procedures for the form. Form and report modules can also include procedures that are not related to a control's events.

The Object drop-down list for a standard module offers only one choice: General. The Procedure drop-down list contains only the names of existing procedures within the standard module.

The Code window's toolbar (shown in Figure 10-9) helps you create new modules and their procedures quickly. The toolbar contains buttons for the most common actions you use to create, modify, and debug modules.

The Code window — the most important area of the VBA editor — is where you create and modify the VBA code for your procedures. The Code window has the standard Windows features to resize, minimize, maximize, and move the window. You also can split the window into two areas by dragging the splitter bar downwards (the splitter bar is the little horizontal bar at the very top of the vertical scroll bar at the right edge of the Code window). Splitting the window enables simultaneous editing of two procedures. Each section of a split VBA Code window scrolls independently, and changes you make in one pane of a split window show in the other pane.

The Immediate window enables you to try a procedure while you are still in the module. See the "Checking your results in the Immediate window" section later in this chapter for an example.

Each VBA code module includes two or more sections:

- A Declarations section at the top of the module
- A section for each procedure

The Declarations section

You can use the Declarations section to declare (define) variables used in the module's procedures. A variable is a named storage location for a value. Examples of variables include:

- `intCounter` (an integer)
- `curMySalary` (a currency)
- `dtmDate` (a date/time)

CAUTION You may have noticed the `Option Explicit` line at the top of the VBA modules in this chapter's figures and example database. `Option Explicit` instructs the VBA compiler to require every variable to be "explicitly" declared. This means that every variable must be declared as a specific data type (integer, string, and so on). Explicit variable declaration is always a good idea because it prevents stray variables from creeping into an application and causing bugs. Without the `Option Explicit` directive at the top of the module, every time you type in an identifier that the VBA compiler does not recognize, it creates a new variable by that name. This means that, when using "implicit" variable declarations, if you have been using a variable named `strLastName` and type it in incorrectly (`strLstName`), the VBA compiler creates a new variable named `strLstName` and begins using it. Bugs caused by simple misspellings can be very difficult to detect, because the application doesn't raise any errors, and the only way to detect the cause of the bug is to go through the code one line at a time until you find the misspelling.

You are not required to declare all of a module's variables in the Declarations section, because variables are also declared within procedures.

Creating a new procedure

After you complete any declarations for the module, you are ready to create a procedure. Follow these steps to create a procedure called `BeepWarning`:

1. Open the Module1 module you previously created, as shown in Figure 10-9.
2. Go to any empty line in the Code window.
3. Type the code in exactly as shown in Figure 10-10.

FIGURE 10-10

Entering a new procedure in the Code window

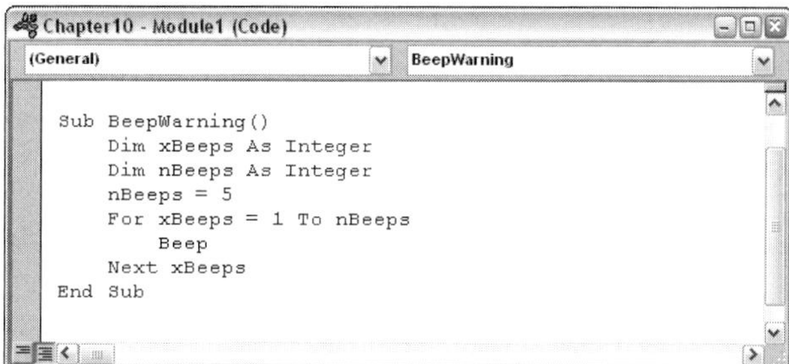

Notice that, as you enter the first line of the procedure, Access automatically added the `End Sub` statement to the procedure.

In this example, you are running the program five times. Don't worry about what the procedure does — you learn more about how to program specific tasks in Chapter 19.

Your completed function should look like the one shown in Figure 10-10.

When BeepWarning runs, it beeps for the number of times specified.

If you enter the name of a function you previously created in this module (or in another module within the database), Access informs you that the function already exists. Access does not enable you to create another procedure with the same name.

Using IntelliSense

Suppose that you know you want to use a specific command but can't remember the exact syntax. Access 2007 features two types of IntelliSense, called Auto List Members and Auto Quick Info, to help you create each line of code.

Auto List Members is a drop-down list that is automatically displayed when you type the beginning of a keyword that has associated objects, properties, or methods. For example, if you enter `DoCmd`, a list of the possible options displays, as shown in Figure 10-11. Scroll through the list box and press Enter to select the option you want.

FIGURE 10-11

Access 2007 Auto List Members help in a module

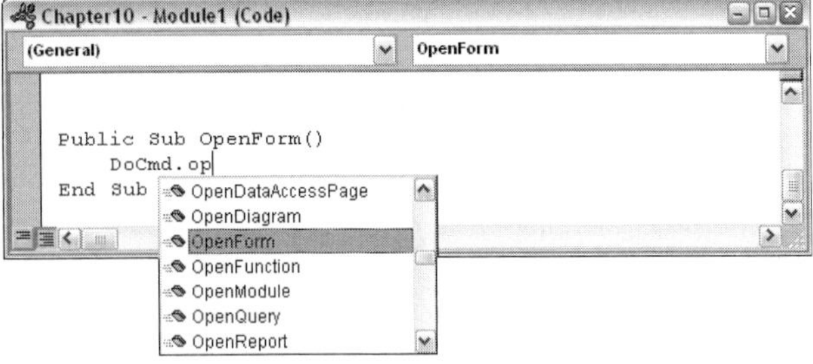

In this example, the `OpenForm` method is selected (actions associated with an object are called *methods*). After choosing an item in the list, more Auto List Members help is displayed. Or, if parameters are associated with the keyword, the other type of module help, Auto Quick Info is displayed, as shown in Figure 10-12. (In Figure 10-12, the AutoListMembers is cut off at the right edge. In fact, the Auto List Members help for the OpenForm method extends quite a ways beyond the edge of this figure.)

FIGURE 10-12

Access 2007 Auto Quick Info help in a module

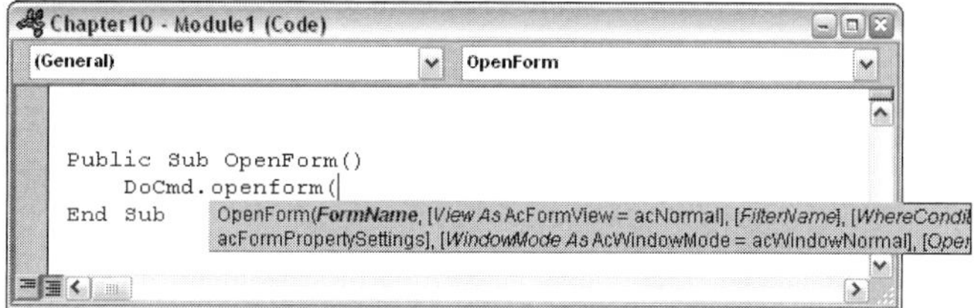

Auto Quick Info guides you through all the options (called *parameters*) for the specific item. The bold word (`FormName`) is the next parameter available for the `DoCmd` object. Figure 10-12 shows that there are many parameters available for the `OpenForm` command. The parameters are separated by commas, as each parameter is entered the next parameter is highlighted in bold. The position of parameters is significant; they cannot be rearranged without causing problems. Press the Esc key to hide Auto List Members help.

Compiling procedures

When you complete a procedure, you should compile it by choosing Debug ➪ Compile from the Code window menu. The compiler checks your code for errors (a process known as syntax checking), and the compiler converts the VBA code to a binary format your computer understands. An error window appears if the compilation is not successful.

Access compiles all procedures in the module, and all modules in the Access database, not just the current procedure and module.

Saving a module

When you finish creating a procedure, you save it by saving the module. Save the module by choosing File ➪ Save, or simply close the code editor to save the module automatically. Access prompts you for a name to apply to the module if no name has yet been assigned.

Creating procedures in the Form or Report Design window

All forms, reports, and their controls may have event procedures associated with their events. While you are in a form or report's Design View, you can add an event procedure in any of three ways:

- Choose `Build Event` from the shortcut menu (see Figure 10-13).

FIGURE 10-13

Shortcut menu for a control in the Form Design window

- Choose `Code Builder` in the Choose Builder dialog box when you click the ellipsis button to the right of an event in the Property dialog box.
- Type `[Event Procedure]` into the event property, or select it from the top of the event drop-down list (see Figure 10-14).

FIGURE 10-14

The properties sheet in the Form Design window

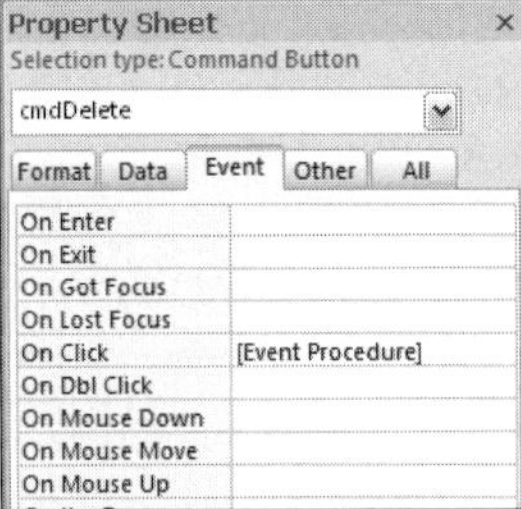

Whether you choose `Build Event` from the shortcut menu or click the ellipsis button in the Property dialog box, the Choose Builder dialog box appears. Choosing the `Code Builder` item opens the VBA code editor, as shown in Figure 10-15. Clicking the View Microsoft Access button in the Code window's toolbar toggles between the form designer and the VBA Code window.

FIGURE 10-15

A form module open in Design View

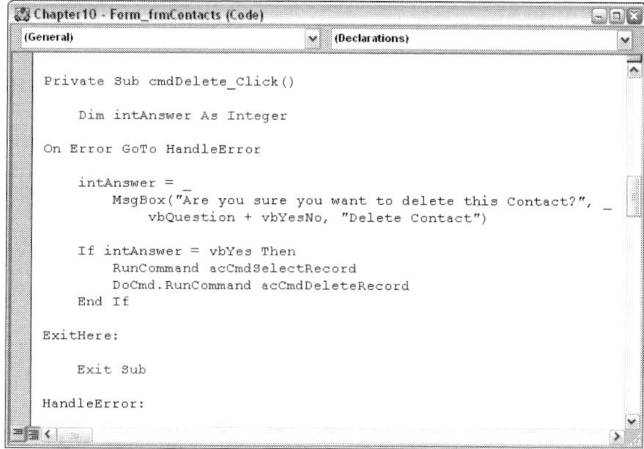

Editing an existing procedure

There a number of ways to access existing code behind a form or report. These are by far the most common:

- Use the `View Code` button in the Tools group in the Access ribbon (with the form or report open in Design View, of course).
- Select an event procedure from a control's event property, as demonstrated in Figure 10-7.

Opening a standard module is even easier. Simply select `Modules` in the Navigation Pane; then right-click on a module and select Design View from the shortcut menu (see Figure 10-16).

FIGURE 10-16

Selecting a module to edit

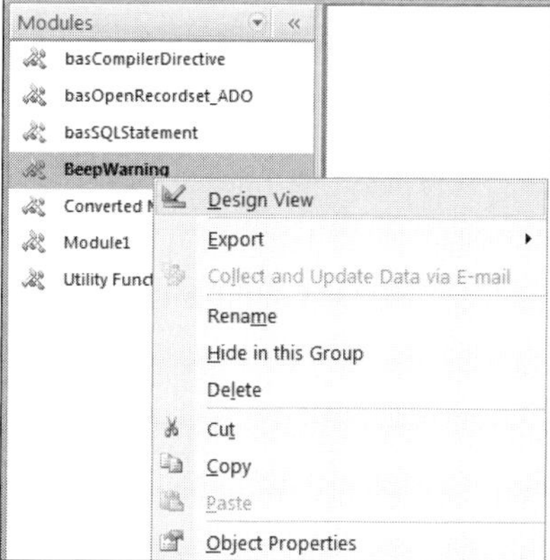

Checking your results in the Immediate window

When you write code for a procedure, you may want to try the procedure while you are in the module, or you may need to check the results of an expression. The Immediate window enables you to try your procedures without leaving the module. You can run the module and check variables. You could, for example, type ? and the name of the variable.

Use Ctrl+G to view the Immediate window, or select View ➪ Immediate Window in the VBA code editor. Figure 10-17 shows the Immediate window.

FIGURE 10-17

The Immediate window

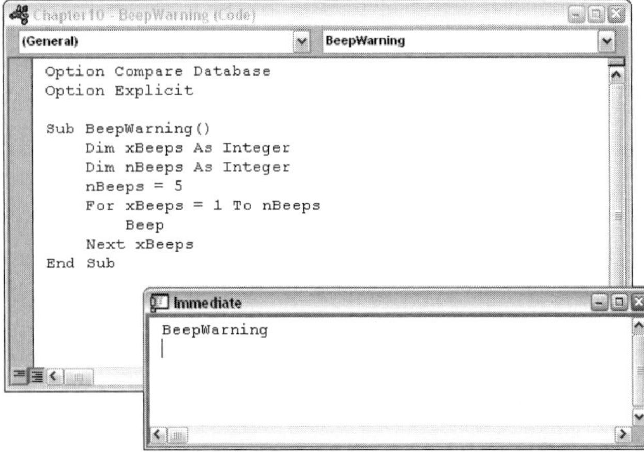

Running the `BeepWarning` procedure is easy. Simply type **BeepWarning** into the immediate window and press Enter. You may hear five beeps or only a continuous beep because the interval between beeps is short.

Figure 10-10, earlier in this section, shows the VBA code for this subprocedure.

You'll see many more examples of using the Immediate window in Chapter 15.

Understanding VBA Branching Constructs

The real power of any programming language is its capability to make a decision based on some condition. VBA provides two ways for a procedure to execute code conditionally: *branching* and *looping*.

Conditional execution

Often, a program in VBA performs different tasks based on some value. If the condition is `True`, the code performs one action. If the condition is `False`, the code performs a different action. An application's capability to look at a value and, based on that value, decide which code to run is known as conditional processing or *branching*.

The procedure is similar to walking down a path and coming to a fork in the path; you can go to the left or to the right. If a sign at the fork points left for home and right for work, you can decide which way to go. If you need to go to work, you go to the right; if you need to go home, you go to the left. In the same way, a program looks at the value of some variable and decides which set of code should be processed.

VBA offers two sets of conditional processing statements:

- `If...Then...Else...End If`
- `Select Case`

The If...Then...Else...End If construct

The `If...Then` and `If...Then...Else` construct checks a condition and, based on the evaluation, perform a single action. The condition must evaluate to a Boolean value (`True` or `False`). If the condition is `True`, the program moves to the next statement in the procedure. If the condition is `False`, the program skips to the statement following the `Else` statement, if present, or the `End If` statement if there is no `Else` clause.

In Figure 10-18, the code examines the value of the `ContactType`, and if the value is either `"Buyer"` or `"Both"`, the Customer page is made visible, otherwise the Customer page is made invisible.

FIGURE 10-18

The VBA code decides whether to display the Customers page of a tab control.

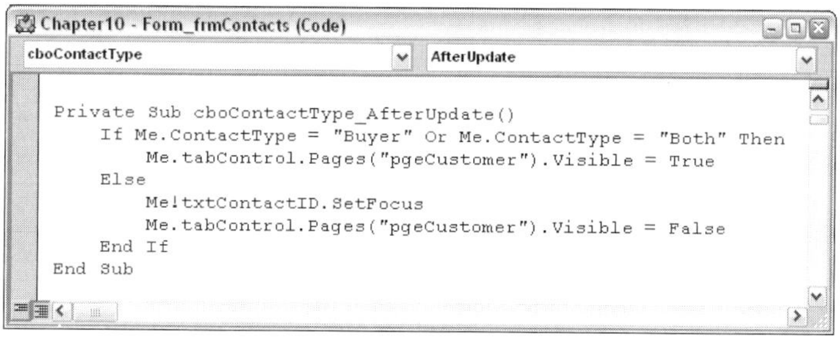

Chapter10 - Form_frmContacts (Code)

cboContactType | AfterUpdate

```
Private Sub cboContactType_AfterUpdate()
    If Me.ContactType = "Buyer" Or Me.ContactType = "Both" Then
        Me.tabControl.Pages("pgeCustomer").Visible = True
    Else
        Me!txtContactID.SetFocus
        Me.tabControl.Pages("pgeCustomer").Visible = False
    End If
End Sub
```

The Else statement is optional. Use Else to perform an alternative set of actions when the If condition is False:

```
If Condition Then
    [Action to perform when Condition is True]
Else
    [Action to perform when Condition is False]
End If
```

The Else clause can contain virtually any valid VBA statements, including another If... Then... Else...End If:

```
If Condition1 Then
    [Action to perform when Condition1 is True]
Else
    If Condition2 Then
        [Action to perform when Condition2 is True]
    Else
        [Action to perform when Condition2 is False]
    End If
End If
```

Needless to say, nested If... Then... Else...End If constructs can become quite complicated and confusing. The ElseIf clause sometimes helps reduce this confusion:

```
If Condition1 Then
    [Action to perform when Condition1 is True]
ElseIf Condition2 Then
    [Action to perform when Condition2 is True]
Else
    [Action to perform when Condition2 is False]
End If
```

In this example, notice that there is only one End If statement at the bottom of the construct.

When you have many conditions to test, the If...Then...ElseIf...Else conditions can get rather unwieldy. A better approach is to use the Select Case construct.

NOTE **In Figure 10-18 you may have noticed that the If statement actually contains two different conditions (Me.ContactType = "Buyer" and Me.ContactType = "Both"). In this case, if *either* condition is true, the "True" portion of the If...Then...Else...End If is executed. The Or clause means that the combined expression is true if the ContactType is *either* "Buyer" *or* "Both." If, on the other hand, an And clause was used between the conditions (such as Month = January And Day = 28), then *both* conditions must be true for the entire expression to evaluate to True.**

The Select Case...End Select statement

VBA offers the `Select Case` statement to check for multiple conditions. Following is the general syntax of the statement:

```
Select Case Expression

    Case Value1
        [Action to take when Expression = Value1]

    Case Value2
        [Action to take when Expression = Value2]

    Case ...

    Case Else
       [Default action when no value matches Expression]

End Select
```

Notice that the syntax is similar to that of the `If...Then` statement. Instead of a Boolean condition, the `Select Case` statement uses an expression at the very top. Then, each `Case` clause tests its value against the expression's value. When a `Case` value matches the expression, the program executes the next line or lines of code until it reaches another `Case` statement or the `End Select` statement. VBA executes the code for only one matching `Case` statement.

NOTE **If more than one `Case` statement matches the value of the test expression, only the code for the first match executes. If other matching `Case` statements appear after the first match, VBA ignores them.**

Figure 12-19 shows `Select...Case` used by `frmDialogContactPrint` to decide which of several reports to open.

FIGURE 10-19

Using the Select Case statement

Chapter10 - Form_frmDialogContactPrint (Code)

cmdPrint | Click

```
Select Case Me![grpTypeOfPrint]

    Case 1
        DoCmd.OpenReport "rptContacts", ReportDest, , _
          "[ContactID]=[Forms]![frmContacts]![txtContactID]"

    Case 2
        DoCmd.OpenReport "rptContacts", ReportDest

    Case 3
        DoCmd.OpenReport "rptContactListing", ReportDest

End Select
```

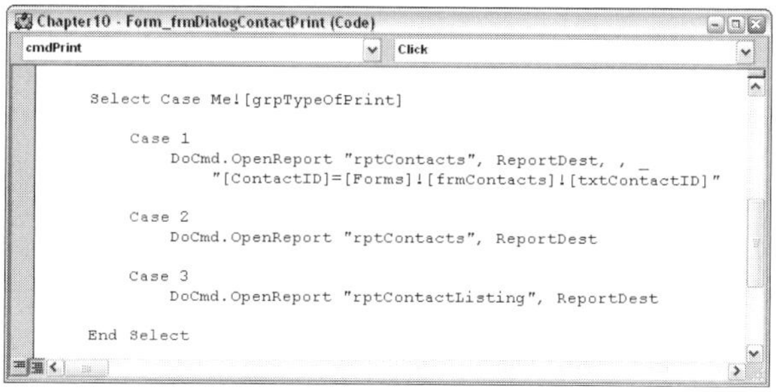

The `Case Else` statement is optional but is always a good idea. The `Case Else` clause is always the last `Case` statement of `Select Case` and is executed when none of the `Case` values match the expression at the top of the `Select Case` statement.

In some procedures, you may want to execute a group of statements more than one time. VBA provides some constructs for repeating a group of statements.

Repetitive Looping

Another very powerful process that VBA offers is repetitive looping — the capability to execute a single statement or a group of statements over and over. The statement or group of statements is repeated until some condition is met.

VBA offers two types of looping constructs:

- `Do...Loop`
- `For...Next`

Loops are commonly used to process records within a recordset, change the appearance of controls on forms, and a number of other processes that require repeating the same VBA statements multiple times.

The Do...Loop statement

`Do...Loop` is used to repeat a group of statements *while* a condition is `True` or *until* a condition is `True`. This statement is one of the most commonly used VBA looping constructs:

```
Do [While | Until Condition]
    [VBA statements]
    [Exit Do]
    [VBA statements]
Loop
```

Alternatively, the `While` (or `Until`) is placed at the bottom of the construct:

```
Do
    [VBA statements]
    [Exit Do]
    [VBA statements]
Loop [While | Until Condition]
```

Notice that `Do...Loop` has several options. The `While` clause causes the VBA statements within the `Do...Loop` to execute as long as the condition is `True`. Execution drops out of the `Do..Loop` as soon as the condition evaluates to `False`.

The `Until` clause works in just the opposite way. The code within the `Do...Loop` executes only as long as the condition is `False`.

Placing the `While` or `Until` clause at the top of the `Do...Loop` means that the loop never executes if the condition is not met. Placing the `While` or `Until` at the bottom of the loop means that the loop executes at least once because the condition is not evaluated until after the statements within the loop have executed the first time.

`Exit Do` immediately terminates the `Do...Loop`. Use `Exit Do` as part of a test within the loop:

```
Do While Condition1
    [VBA statements]
    If Condition2 Then
        Exit Do
    End If
    [VBA statements]
Loop
```

`Exit Do` is often used to prevent endless loops. An endless loop occurs when the condition's state (`True` or `False`) never changes within the loop.

In case you're wondering, `Condition1` and `Condition2` in this example may be the same. There is no requirement that the second condition be different from the condition used at the top of the `Do...Loop`.

Figure 10-20 illustrates how a `Do` loop may be used. In this particular example a recordset has been opened and each record is processed within the `Do` loop. In this example, the company's name is printed in the immediate window, but the data is not modified or used in any way.

FIGURE 10-20

Using the `Do...Loop` statement

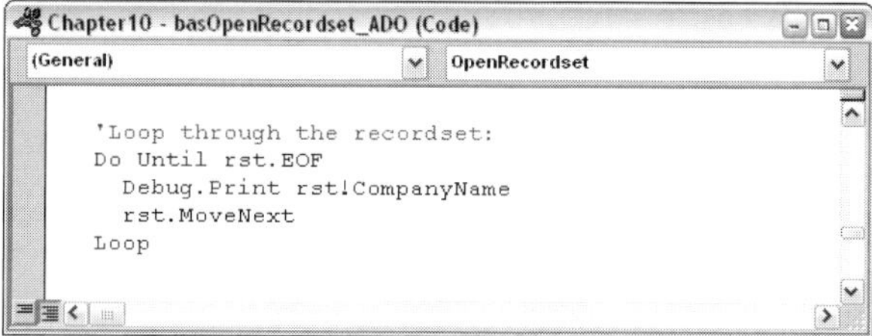

The `While` and `Until` clauses provide powerful flexibility for processing a `Do...Loop` in your code.

The For...Next statement

Use `For...Next` to repeat a statement block a set number of times. The general format of `For...Next` is:

```
For CounterVariable = Start To End
    [Statement block]
Next CounterVariable
```

We already saw an example of the `For...Next` loop. Earlier in this chapter, you saw a procedure named `BeepWarning` that looks like this:

```
Sub BeepWarning()
    Dim xBeeps As Integer
    Dim nBeeps As Integer

    nBeeps = 5

    For xBeeps = 1 To nBeeps
        Beep
    Next xBeeps

End Sub
```

In this procedure, `xBeeps` is the counter variable, `1` is the start, and `nBeeps` is the end. In this example, `xBeeps` starts at `1` and is incremented at the bottom of the `For...Next` loop at the Next `xBeeps` statement.

An alternate form of `For...Next` is:

```
For CounterVariable = Start To End Step StepValue
    [Statement block]
Next CounterVariable
```

The only difference here is the `StepValue` added to the first statement. The `Step` keyword followed by an increment causes the counter variable to the incremented by the step value each time the loop executes. For example, if *Start* is 10 and *End* is 100 and *StepValue* is 10, the counter variable starts 10 and increments by 10 each time the loop executes.

Working with Objects and Collections

Very often in Access applications is necessary to work with objects such as the controls on a form or a recordset object containing data extracted from the database. VBA provides several constructs specifically designed to work with objects and collections of objects.

The With statement

The `With` statement enables you to loop through all the members of a collection of objects, setting or changing the properties of each member. Any number of statements can appear between the `With` and `End With` statements. `With` statements can be nested.

As an example, consider the code using the following `For...Next` looping construct. This code loops through all members of a form's Controls collection, examining each control. If the control is a command button, the button's font is set to 10 point, Bold, Times New Roman:

```
Private Sub cmdOld_Click()
  Dim i As Integer
  Dim c As Control

  For i = 0 To Me.Controls.Count - 1
    Set c = Me.Controls(i)
    If TypeOf c Is CommandButton Then
      c.FontName = "Times New Roman"
      c.FontBold = True
      c.FontSize = 12
    End If
  Next
End Sub
```

Don't be confused by the different expressions you see in this example. The heart of this procedure is the `For...Next` loop. The loop begins at zero (the start value) and executes until the `i` variable reaches the number of controls on the form minus 1. (The controls on an Access form are numbered beginning with zero. The Count property tells you how many controls are on the form.) Within the loop, a variable named `c` is pointed at the control indicated by the `i` variable. The `If TypeOf...` statement evaluates the type of control referenced by the `c` variable.

Within the body of the `If...Then` branch, the control variable's properties (`FontName`, `FontBold`, and `FontSize`) are adjusted. Notice that the control variable is referenced in each of the assignment statements. Referencing control properties one at a time is a fairly slow process. If the form contains many controls, this code executes relatively slowly.

An improvement on this code uses the `With` statement to isolate one member of the controls collection and apply a number of statements to that control. The following listing uses the `With` statement to apply a number of font settings to a single control.

```
Private Sub cmdWith_Click()
  Dim i As Integer
  Dim c As Control

  For i = 0 To Me.Controls.Count - 1
    Set c = Me(i)
    If TypeOf c Is CommandButton Then
      With c
```

```
            .FontName = "Arial"
            .FontBold = True
            .FontSize = 8
          End With
        End If
      Next
    End Sub
```

The code in this example (`cmdWith_Click`) executes much faster than the previous example (`cmdOld_Click`). Once Access has a handle on the control (`With c...`), it is able to apply all the statements in the body of the `With` without having to fetch the control from the controls on the form as in `cmdOld_Click`.

Think of the `With` statement as if you are handing Access a particular item and saying "Here, apply all of these properties to *this* item." The previous example said "Go get the item named x and apply this property to it" over and over again. The speed difference in these commands is considerable.

The For Each statement

The code in `cmdWith_Click` is further improved by using the `For Each` statement to traverse the `Controls` collection. `For Each` walks through each member of a collection, making it available for examination or manipulation. The following code shows how `For Each` simplifies our example.

```
Private Sub cmdForEach_Click()
  Dim c As Control

  For Each c In Me.Controls
    If TypeOf c Is CommandButton Then
      With c
        .FontName = "MS Sans Serif"
        .FontBold = False
        .FontSize = 8
      End With
    End If
  Next
End Sub
```

The improvement goes beyond using fewer lines to get the same amount of work done. Notice we no longer need an integer variable to count through the `Controls` collection. We also don't have to call on the `Controls` collection's `Count` property to determine when to end the `For` loop. All of this overhead is handled silently and automatically for us by the VBA programming language engine.

The code in this listing is easier to understand than in either of the previous procedures. The purpose of each level of nesting is obvious and clear. You don't have to keep track of the index to see what's happening, and you don't have to worry about whether to start the `For` loop at 0 or 1. The code in the `For...Each` example is marginally faster than `With...End With` example because no time is spent incrementing the integer value used to count through the loop and Access doesn't have to evaluate which control in the collection to work on.

ON the CD-ROM **The Chapter10.accdb example database includes `frmWithDemo` (see Figure 10-21) containing all of the code discussed in this section. Each of the three command buttons along the bottom of this form uses different code to loop through the controls collections on this form, changing the font characteristics of the controls.**

FIGURE 10-21

`frmWithDemo` is included in Chapter10.accdb.

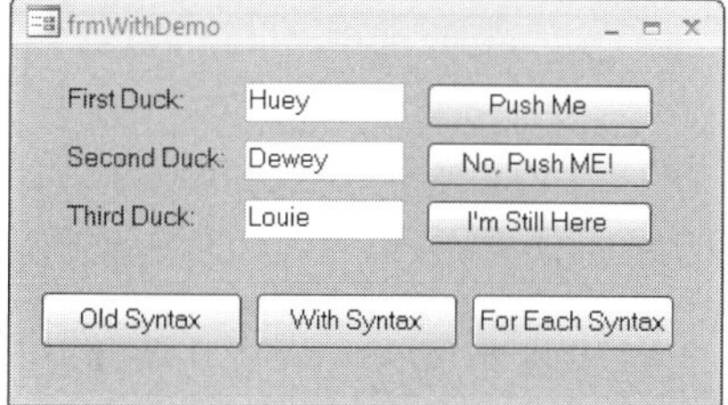

Using Compiler Directives

Conditional compilation directives are another feature of the Access VB language. In a conditional compilation directive, you declare the value of a constant that tells Access whether you want certain sections of code compiled and run. An example of using compiler directives is shown in Figure 10-22. In this example because the constant "`DEBUG1`" has been defined at the top of the local module, Access executes the `Debug.Print` statement. Otherwise, Access ignores the statements between the `#If` and `#End If` directives.

FIGURE 10-22

VBA compiler directives at work

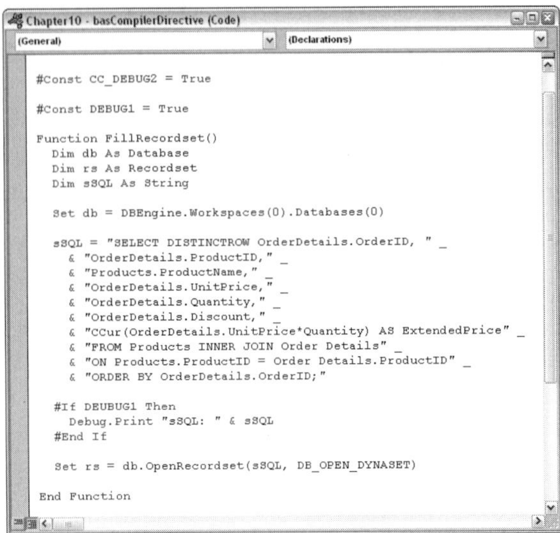

Chapter10 - basCompilerDirective (Code)
(General)
(Declarations)
#Const CC_DEBUG2 = True
#Const DEBUG1 = True
Function FillRecordset()
Dim db As Database
Dim rs As Recordset
Dim sSQL As String
Set db = DBEngine.Workspaces(0).Databases(0)
sSQL = "SELECT DISTINCTROW OrderDetails.OrderID, " _
& "OrderDetails.ProductID," _
& "Products.ProductName," _
& "OrderDetails.UnitPrice," _
& "OrderDetails.Quantity," _
& "OrderDetails.Discount," _
& "CCur(OrderDetails.UnitPrice*Quantity) AS ExtendedPrice" _
& "FROM Products INNER JOIN Order Details" _
& "ON Products.ProductID = Order Details.ProductID" _
& "ORDER BY OrderDetails.OrderID;"
#If DEUBUG1 Then
Debug.Print "sSQL: " & sSQL
#End If
Set rs = db.OpenRecordset(sSQL, DB_OPEN_DYNASET)
End Function

The following compiler directives are recognized by Access 2007:

- `#Const`: The `#Const` directive specifies a constant value that can be tested with the `#If` directive. The constant value specified by `#Const` is private to the module in which it appears and can be any data type (numeric, string, Boolean, and so on) recognized by Access. The syntax of `#Const` is:

  ```
  #Const Identifier = Value
  ```

  The Identifier name cannot conflict with the name of a variable or constant declared elsewhere in the module and cannot be the same as an Access 2007 keyword. For these reasons you may want to adopt a naming convention that avoids these conflicts, such as prefixing conditional constants with "CC_", your initials, or some other text. Using a naming convention will also make the conditional constants easier to find in your code. Many developers always use full upper case for all constants to make them easy to see in code.

- `#If...#Then...#Else...#End If`: The `#If` directive evaluates an expression which returns True or `False`. Place the statements you want processed when the expression is `True` between the `#If...Then` and the `#Else`; otherwise place them between the `#Else` and `#End If`. The syntax of these directives are:

  ```
  #If Expression Then
  ...Perform these statements
  #Else
  ...Perform these alternate statements
  #End If
  ```

  The `#Else` portion, of course, is optional.

The constant value established with `#Const` is seen only by the `#If` compiler directive and is ignored by your VBA code. Similarly, the `#If` directive cannot use a constant set up with the `Const` VBA keyword.

The compiler directives are a handy way to include debugging statements and optional code to an application. For instance, you may use compiler directives to exclude large portions of code during development because the code is not needed as you prepare and debug certain features.

Keep in mind that the `#Const` directive is a module-level constant declaration. This means it won't be seen outside of the module in which it appears, even if the module itself is global. In most cases the `#Const` directive appears in the module's Declarations section. Normally you want this directive to appear where it is easy to find and change, which means you want it in the same location from module to module. Also, if you are using compiler directives in more than one module, you should probably use the same constant value in all modules to help make your code easier to understand.

One important consideration is that the compiler directives affect the VBA code behind your application only as the code is compiled. Once you've compiled the code, you cannot change the directive at runtime. During compilation the Access VBA compiler detects the directives and either includes or excludes the code segments as specified by the directives. After the compiled code has been prepared by the compiler, you cannot change its contents.

Access 2007 Options for Developers

Many of the most important features in Access 2007 affect only developers. These features are hidden from end users and benefit only the person building the application. Spend some time exploring these features so that you fully understand their benefits. You'll soon settle on option settings that suit the way you work and the kind of assistance you want as you write your VBA code.

Editor tab in Options dialog box

The Options dialog box contains several important settings that greatly influence how you interact with Access as you add code to your applications. These options are accessed by opening a module in the VBA code editor, and selecting `Tools ➪ Options`.

- **AutoIndent:** AutoIndent causes code to be indented to the current depth in all successive lines of code. For instance, if you inserted four spaces (or tabs) in front of the current line of code, each line of code following the current line will be automatically indented four spaces.
- **Auto Syntax Check:** When the Auto Syntax Check option is selected, Access checks each line of code for syntax errors as you enter it in the code editor. Many experienced developers find this behavior intrusive and prefer to keep this option disabled, instead letting the compiler point out syntax errors. Most of the syntax errors caught by Auto Syntax Check are the most obvious spelling errors, missing commas, and so on.

- **Break on all Errors:** Break on All Errors causes Access to behave as if On Error GoTo 0 is always set, regardless of any error trapping you may set up in code. When this option is selected, Access stops on every error, making it easier to debug the code.
- **Require Variable Declaration:** This setting automatically inserts `the Option Explicit` directive into all VBA modules in your Access application. This option is *not* selected by default in Access 2007.
- **Compile on Demand:** Compile on Demand instructs Access to compile modules only when their functions are required somewhere else in the database. When this option is unchecked, all modules are compiled anytime any function is called.
- **Auto List Members:** This option pops up a list box containing the members of an object's object hierarchy in the Code window. In Figure 10-11 the list of Application objects appeared as soon as I typed as the period following `Application` in the VBA statement. You select an item from the list by continuing to type it in or scrolling the list and pressing the spacebar.
- **Auto Quick Info:** When Auto Quick Info has been selected Access pops up syntax help (refer to Figure 10-12) when you enter the name of a procedure (function, subroutine, or method) followed by a period, space, or opening parenthesis. The procedure can be a built-in function or subroutine or one that you've written yourself in Access VBA.
- **Auto Data Tips:** The Auto Data Tips option displays the value of variables when you hold the mouse cursor over a variable with the module in break mode. Auto Data Tips is an alternative to setting a watch on the variable and flipping to the Debug window when Access reaches the break point.

CROSS-REF **Debugging Access VBA is described in Chapter 15.**

Because they are so handy you'll almost certainly use one or more of the auto-help options in Access 2007. Of the other options available to you be sure not to overlook the ability to require variable declaration. Once you get used to having `Option Explicit` set on every module (including global and class modules) the instances of rogue and unexplained variables (which, in reality, are simple misspellings of declared variables) disappear. With Option Explicit set in every module, your code is more self-explanatory and easier to debug and maintain.

The Project Properties dialog box

All of the code components in an Access application, including all the modules, procedures, variables, and other elements are aggregated as the application's VBA *project*. The VBA language engine accesses modules and procedures as members of the project. Access manages the code in your application by keeping track of all of the code objects that are included in the project, which is different than and separate from the code added into the application as a runtime library or wizard.

Each Access project includes a number of important options. The Project Properties dialog (Figure 10-23) contains a number of settings that are important for developers. Open the Project Properties dialog by opening a module in the Code window, clicking the Tools menu, and selecting the project properties menu item. The project properties menu item is named after your database's project. For instance, in the Chapter10.accdb example database, the Code editor's Tools menu contains a `Chapter10 Properties` menu item.

FIGURE 10-23

The Project Properties dialog contains a number of interesting options.

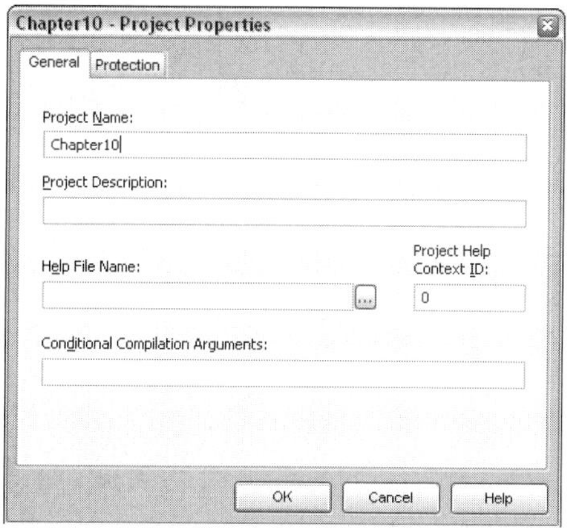

Project name

Certain changes in an application's structure require Access to recompile the code in the application. For instance, changing the code in a global module affects all statements in other modules using that code, so Access must recompile all the code in the application. Until the code is recompiled Access "decompiles" the application by reverting to the plain-text version of the code stored in the `.accdb` file and ignoring the compiled code in the `.accdb`. This means that each line of the code must be interpreted at runtime, dramatically slowing the application.

Sometimes insignificant modifications, such as changing the name of the project itself, are sufficient to cause decompilation. This happens because of the hierarchical nature of Access VBA. Because all objects are 'owned' by some other object, changing the name of a high-level object may change the dependencies and ownerships of all objects below it in the object hierarchy.

Access 2007 maintains a separate, independent project name for the code and executable objects in the application. Simply changing the name of the `.accdb` file is not enough to decompile the code in an Access 2007 application. By default, the project name is the same as the name of the `.accdb` but is not dependent on it. You can assign a unique name to the project with the Project Name text box in the General tab of the Project Properties dialog.

Project description

The Project Description is, as its name implies, a description for the project. Because this area is so small, it is not possible to add anything of significance that might be helpful to another developer.

Conditional compilation arguments

Earlier in this chapter (in the section titled "Using Compiler Directives") you learned about the new Access 2007 compiler directives. These directives instruct the Access VBA compiler to include or exclude portions of code, depending on the value of a constant established in the module's Declarations section.

One of the limitations of using compiler directives is that the constant declaration is local to the module. This means you have to use the `#Const` compiler directive to set up the constant in every module that includes the `#If` directive. This limitation can make it difficult to remove all of the `#Const` compiler directives to modify the code at the conclusion of development.

For instance, consider the situation where you want to use conditional compilation to include certain debugging statements and functions during the development cycle. Just before shipping the application to its users, of course, you want to remove the compiler directives from the code so that your users won't see the message boxes, status bar messages, and other debugging information. If your application consists of dozens of forms and modules, you have to make sure you find every single instance of the `#Const` directive to make sure you successfully deactivated the debugging code. (This is why it's such a good idea to apply a naming convention to the identifiers you use with the #Const directive.)

Fortunately, Access 2007 provides a way for you to set up "global" conditional compilation arguments. The General tab of the Project Properties dialog contains a text box where you can enter arguments to be evaluated by the conditional compilation directives in your code.

As an example, assume you've set up the following sort of statements in all the modules in your application:

```
#If CC_DEBUG2 Then
  MsgBox "Now in ProcessRecords()"
#End If
```

Rather than adding the constant directive (`#Const CC_DEBUG2 = True`) to every module in the application, you might enter the following text into the Conditional Compilation Arguments text box in the Advanced tab of the Options dialog:

```
CC_DEBUG2 = -1
```

This directive sets the value of `CC_DEBUG2` to -1 (`True`) for all modules (global and form and report class modules) in the application. You need only to change this one entry to `CC_DEBUG2=0` to disable the debugging statements in all modules in the application. Please note that you do not use the words `True` or `False` when setting compiler constants in the Project Properties dialog, even though you use these values within a VBA code module.

The syntax of the conditional compilation arguments in the Project Properties dialog is tricky. It does not recognize keywords such as `True` and `False`, and seems to accept only numeric arguments. You cannot, therefore, use text strings, variables, or intrinsic constants as arguments. Separate multiple arguments with colons.

Command-line arguments

The options dialog you open from the File menu (click on the large round Office button in the upper left corner of the main Access window, and select the `Access Options` button in the File menu) provides a number of interesting options. Click the `Advanced` tab and scroll down to the Advanced section near the bottom of the dialog. Notice the `Command-line arguments` text box at the very bottom of the Advanced section.

Many applications use command-line arguments to influence how the application behaves at runtime. You could, for instance, add a command-line argument to an Access database application that indicates whether the user was an experienced or novice user. The application might display help and other assistance that is appropriate for the user's experience level. (Use the `Command` function to return the arguments portion of the command line used to start Access or the Access runtime environment.)

It's always been difficult to pass a Windows application command-line arguments during development. Windows requires command-line arguments to be passed as text in the Target text box of a program icon's property sheet. Figure 10-24 shows such a property sheet. The text `/User Novice` in the Target text box is the command-line argument passed to the Access application as it starts up.

FIGURE 10-24

Adding a command-line argument to a shortcut pointing to a Windows application.

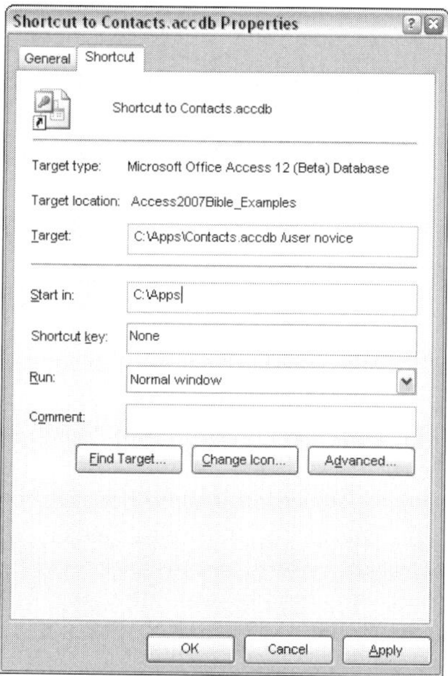

Before the `Command-Line Arguments` option was available there was no easy way to test the effect of command-line arguments in your application. Use this option to test and debug the command-line argument code you build into your applications.

Do not forget to remove the text from this option before distributing your application to end users. The text you enter in this option setting is persistent and will remain there until it is removed or changed.

ON the CD-ROM **Use the Command function to return the arguments portion of the command line used to start Access or the Access runtime environment. The `Chapter10.accdb` example database includes `frmCommandLine` (see Figure 10-25), a demonstration of the `Command` function. Use the Options dialog to set some command-line arguments for `Chapter10.accdb`; then click on the button on `frmCommandLine` to see the how `Command` retrieves the arguments.**

FIGURE 10-25

`Chapter10.accdb` includes `frmCommandLine` to demonstrate using command-line arguments in your applications.

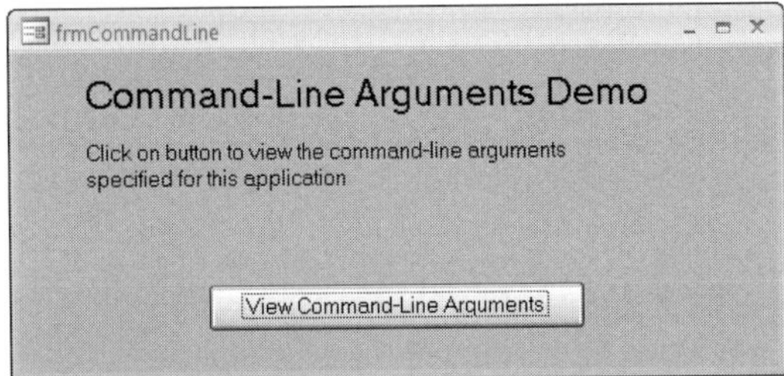

Summary

This chapter reviewed some of the important topics as you work with Access 2007 VBA. We took a look at the fundamental concepts of creating VBA modules and procedures and touched on the important topic of event-driven programming in Access 2007.

You also read that Access provides a large number of options and settings that influence how you work with your modules and procedures. The good news is that you have a lot of options controlling the appearance and behavior of the code editor in Access 2007. There is *no* bad news about writing code in Access 2007!

The `With..End`, `With`, and `For Each` constructs make it easy and efficient to traverse the members of object collections. Named arguments give you a lot more flexibility in passing parameters to functions and subroutines.

You continue your exploration of the VBA programming language in the next several chapters. In Chapters 11 through 15 you learn virtually every fundamental skill necessary to succeed as a VBA programmer. One important aspect of VBA programming is that it is a skill with no barriers. Your abilities as an Access VBA programmer are completely transferable to any of the other Microsoft Office products such as Word and Excel.

Chapter 11

Mastering VBA Data Types and Procedures

IN THIS CHAPTER

- Using variables
- Understanding the VBA data types
- Understanding subs and functions
- Creating VBA procedures
- Creating functions
- Calling procedures and functions
- Passing parameters to procedures and functions
- Handling values returned from a function

All VBA applications require *variables* to hold data while the program executes. Variables are like a white board where important information can be temporarily written and read later on by the program. For instance, when a user inputs a value on a form, you'll most often use a variable to temporarily hold the value until it can be permanently stored in the database or printed on a report. Simply put, a variable is the name you've assigned to a particular bit of data in your application. In more technical terms, a variable is a named area in memory used to store values during program execution.

Variables are transient and do not persist after an application stops running. And, as you'll read in the "Understanding variable scope and lifetime" section, later in this chapter, a variable may last a very short time as the program executes or may exist as long as the application is running.

In most cases, you assign a specific data type to each of the variables in your applications. For instance, you may create a string variable to hold text data such as names or descriptions. A currency variable, on the other hand, is meant to contain values representing monetary amounts. You should not try to assign a text value to a currency variable because a runtime error may occur as a result.

The variables you use have a dramatic effect on your applications. You have a lot options when it comes to establishing and using variables in your Access programs. Inappropriately using a variable can slow an application's execution or potentially cause data loss.

This chapter contains everything you need to know about creating and using VBA variables. The information in this chapter helps you use the most efficient and effective data types in your variables while avoiding the most common problems related to VBA variables.

In addition to variables, we'll take a look at a few more code editor options, working with VBA procedures, and passing parameters to procedures.

The Access VBA Editor

We'll be writing quite a bit of code in this chapter, and in the chapters that follow, and this seems as good a place as any to discuss a few options when using the VBA code editor and writing VBA code.

The Access 2007 Code editor (see Figure 11-1) supports a number of important features to help you write and manage VBA code. For instance, any line of code ending in an underscore character preceded by a space is recognized as a statement that is continued on the next line, making it easy to see all of the constituents of very long VBA statements. Notice the statement that starts out `If SysCmd` in Figure 11-1. This statement actually occupies two lines of code: the one containing the `If` statement and the line immediately under it.

FIGURE 11-1

The continuation character is a welcome feature in the Access 2007 VBA editor.

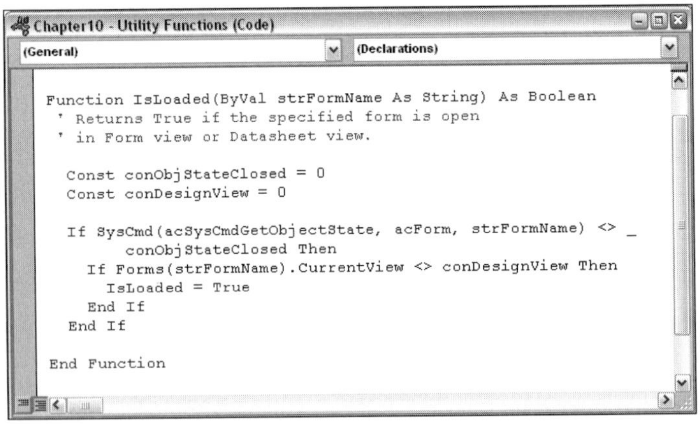

Chapter10 - Utility Functions (Code)

(General) (Declarations)

```
Function IsLoaded(ByVal strFormName As String) As Boolean
 ' Returns True if the specified form is open
 ' in Form view or Datasheet view.

  Const conObjStateClosed = 0
  Const conDesignView = 0

  If SysCmd(acSysCmdGetObjectState, acForm, strFormName) <> _
       conObjStateClosed Then
    If Forms(strFormName).CurrentView <> conDesignView Then
      IsLoaded = True
    End If
  End If

End Function
```

If you use continuation characters (and you will, we're sure!), be sure to indent the continued lines of code. Being able to recognize continued lines of code without having to keep track of the continuation characters is important.

The line continuation in Access 2007 is quite powerful. You can split long declaration lines such as Windows API declares (the Windows API is discussed in Chapter 30), and you can even split long strings into multiple lines. One particularly powerful use of the continuation character is illustrated later in this chapter (in Figure 11-14). In Figure 11-14, a long SQL statement is split across a number of lines of code. All that's needed on each subsequent line is the concatenation character (&) and as much of the string as you want to add on the line. Splitting long SQL statements this way makes it easy to see what's in the statement and, therefore, what fields end up in the resulting recordset.

Most often, however, continuation characters are used to break long, complex statements across multiple lines. Figure 11-2 shows an example of this use of the continuation character. In this figure, a long VBA statement that opens a new recordset is split into five lines of code. The continuation characters are placed after the commas separating the elements contained in the complex statement, making the statement easier to read and understand.

FIGURE 11-2

Use the continuation character to split long strings into multiple lines.

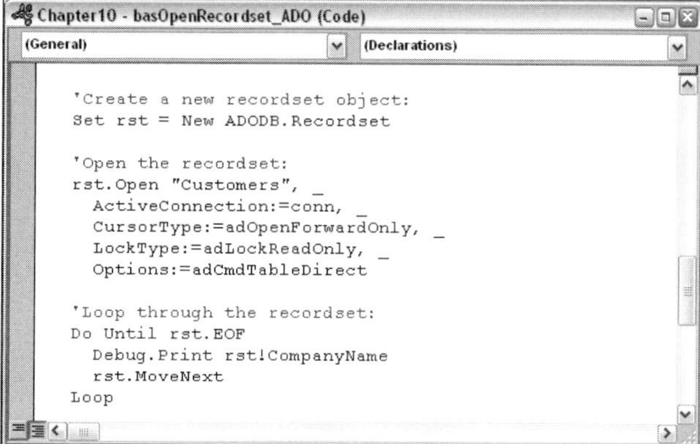

Another powerful feature of the Access code editor that is probably not evident in Figures 11-1 and 11-2 is the text colors used to set aside comments, keywords, and identifiers. Although it's not obvious in this book's figures, the comments in Figures 11-1 and 11-2 appear in a green font while the VBA keywords like `Function`, `Const`, and `If` are blue. Identifiers like `conObjStateClosed` and `conDesignView`, as well as the procedure name (`IsLoaded`) in Figure 11-1, are black.

You can adjust the editor font and text colors to suit your particular style. The Editor Format tab of the code Options dialog box (Tools ➪ Options from the code editor) contains all of the options necessary to select the font, font size, and colors for any number of different parts of the VBA syntax (see Figure 11-3).

FIGURE 11-3

The Options dialog box contains plenty of settings that affect the VBA code window.

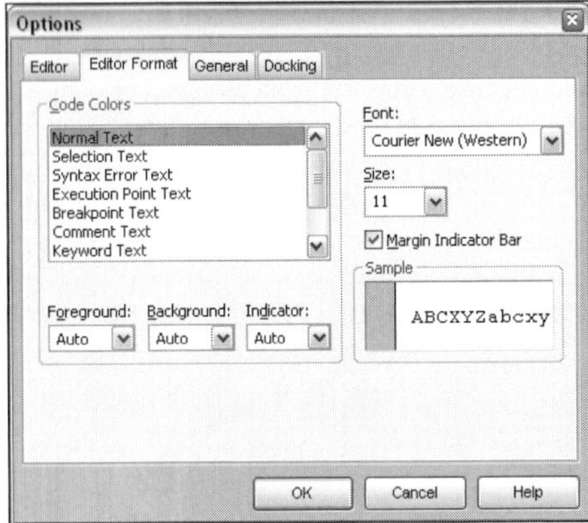

Another terrific feature of the Access 2007 code window is that the object drop-down list (shown in Figure 11-4) is alphabetically sorted. If you use a naming convention in Access 2007, all of the controls will be grouped by the control type. For instance, by using `cmd` as the prefix for command buttons, all of the command buttons are sorted together in the object list.

FIGURE 11-4

The object list in the Access 2007 code window is sorted alphabetically.

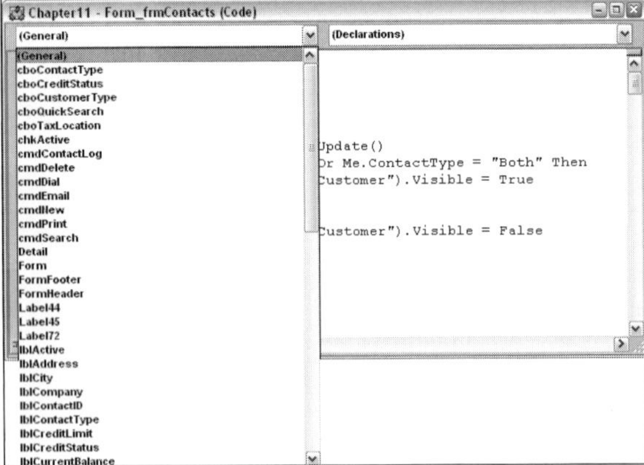

Using Variables

One of the most powerful concepts in programming is the *variable*. A variable is a temporary storage location for some value and is given a name. You can use a variable to store the result of a calculation, or you can create a variable to make the control's value available to another procedure.

To refer to the result of an expression, you use a variable's name to store the result. To assign an expression's result to a variable, you use the = operator. Following are some examples of expressions that assign values to variables:

```
counter = 1
counter = counter + 1
today = Date()
```

Figure 11-5 shows a simple procedure using several different variables.

FIGURE 11-5

Variable declarations are quite simple.

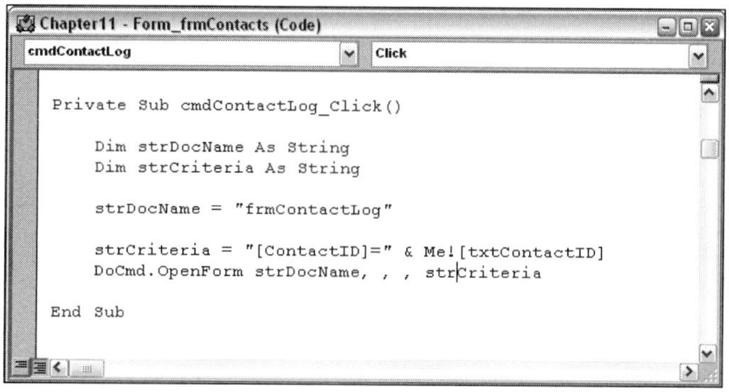

Chapter11 - Form_frmContacts (Code)

cmdContactLog | Click

```
Private Sub cmdContactLog_Click()

    Dim strDocName As String
    Dim strCriteria As String

    strDocName = "frmContactLog"

    strCriteria = "[ContactID]=" & Me![txtContactID]
    DoCmd.OpenForm strDocName, , , strCriteria

End Sub
```

Although this is a very simple example of using variable, it effectively demonstrates just about everything you need to know about using VBA variables:

- The `Dim` keyword establishes the new variables (`strDocName` and `strCriteria`) within a procedure.
- A variety of techniques can be used to assign a value to a variable. Figure 11-5 uses the = operator to assign a literal value (`frmContactLog`) to `strDocName`. Notice that `frmContactLog` is surrounded by quotation marks, making it a "literal" value. A value pulled from the `txtContactID` text box on the form's surface is combined with a literal string ("[ContactID]=") and assigned to the `strCriteria` variable. The data assigned to variables should always be appropriate for the variable's data type.

- The Dim statement includes the data type of the new variable. In Figure 11-5, both variables are declared as the String data type.
- A variety of techniques can be used to assign a value to a variable. Figure 11-5 uses the = operator to assign a literal value (frmContactLog) to strDocName. strCriteria is assigned a value that is derived from a literal string and a value pulled from the ContactID text box on the form's surface. The data assigned to variables should always be appropriate for the variable's data type.
- Variables are manipulated with a variety of operators. Figure 11-5 uses the concatenation operator (&) to combine = [ContactID] and the value in txtContactID.

There are a variety of ways to perform each of the tasks you see in Figure 11-5. For instance, as you'll read in the "Declaring variables" section later in this chapter, the Dim statement is not the only way to establish a variable. The = operator is not the only way to assign a value to a variable as you'll see in many of the chapters in this book. Also, it isn't necessary to use a variable like strCriteria to temporarily hold the value generated by combining two values. The two values could just as easily be combined on the fly within the DoCmd.OpenForm statement:

```
DoCmd.OpenForm "frmContactLog", _
    "[ContactID] = " & Me![txtContactID]
```

There are very few rules governing how you declare and use your variables. You should always strive for readability in your VBA code. In the small example shown in Figure 11-5, it's easy to see that strDocName holds the name of a form, especially because it is used as part of the DoCmd.OpenForm statement.

Naming variables

Every programming language has its own rules for naming variables. In VBA, a variable name must meet the following conditions:

- Must begin with an alphabetical character
- Must not contain an embedded period or type-declaration character
- Must have a unique name; the name cannot be used elsewhere in the procedure or in modules that use the variables
- Cannot contain spaces or punctuation characters
- Cannot be a reserved word, such as Sub, Module, or Form
- Must be no longer than 64 characters

Although you can make up almost any name for a variable, most programmers adopt a standard convention for naming variables. Some common practices include the following:

- Using a mix of uppercase and lowercase characters, as in TotalCost
- Using all lowercase characters, as in counter

- Preceding the name with the data type of the value; a variable that stores a number might be called `nCounter` while a variable holding a string might be named `strLastName`

One source of endless confusion to Access developers is the fact that Access object names (tables, queries, forms, and so on) may contain spaces, while variable names never include spaces. One reason not to use spaces in Access object names is to eliminate the confusion that is possible when mixing different naming conventions within a single applications. You really are better off being consistent in how you apply names to your Access objects, variables, procedures, and other application entities.

TIP **When creating variables, you can use uppercase, lowercase, or mixed-case characters to specify the variable or call it later. VBA variables are not case-sensitive. This fact means that you can use the `TodayIs` variable later without having to worry about the case that you used for the name when you created it; `TODAYIS`, `todayis`, and `tOdAyIs` all refer to the same variable. VBA automatically changes any explicitly declared variables to the case that was used in the declaration statement (`Dim` statement).**

When you need to see or use the contents of a variable, you simply reference its name. When you specify the variable's name, the computer program goes into memory, finds the variable, and gets its contents for you. This process means, of course, that you need to be able to remember and correctly reference the name of the variable.

VBA, like many other programming languages, allows you to create variables on the fly. In the `Counter = 1` example, at the beginning of this section, the Counter variable was not declared before the value `1` was assigned to it.

Declaring variables

There are two principle ways to add variables to your applications. The first method — called *implicit declaration* — is to let VBA automatically create the variables for you. As with most things that are not carefully controlled, you'll find that letting VBA prepare your variables for you is not necessarily a good idea and does not lead to the best performance or efficiency in your programs. (See the "Comparing implicit and explicit variables" section, later in this chapter, for a comparison of implicit declaration with the alternatives.)

Implicit declaration means that VBA automatically creates a variant data type variable for each identifier it recognizes as a variable in an application. (Variants are discussed in the "Working with Data Types" section, later in this chapter.) In the following listing, there are two implicitly declared variables (`strFirstName` and `strLastName`).

```
Private Sub Combine_Implicit()
  strFirstName = txtFirstName
  strLastName = txtLastName
  txtFullName = strFirstName & " " & strLastName
End Sub
```

The second approach to declaring variables is to explicitly declare them with one of the following keywords: `Dim`, `Static`, `Private`, or `Public`. The choice of keyword has a profound effect on the variable's scope within the application and determines where the variable can be used in the program. (Variable scope is discussed in the "Understanding variable scope and lifetime" section later in this chapter.)

The syntax for explicitly declaring a variable is quite simple:

```
Dim VariableName As DataType
Static VariableName As DataType
Private VariableName As DataType
Public VariableName As DataType
```

In each case, the name of the variable and its data type are provided as part of the declaration. VBA reserves the amount of memory required to hold the variable as soon as the declaration statement is executed. Once a variable is declared, it is not possible to change its data type, although it is quite easy to convert the value of a variable and assign the converted value to another variable.

The following example shows the `Combine_Implicit` sub rewritten to use explicitly declared variables.

```
Private Sub Combine_Explicit()
  Dim strFirstName As String
  Dim strLastName As String
  strFirstName = txtFirstName.Text
  strLastName = txtLastName.Text
  txtFullName = strFirstName & " " & strLastName
End Sub
```

So, if there's often very little difference between using implicit and explicit variables, why bother declaring variables at all? The following code demonstrates the importance of using explicitly declared variables in your applications.

```
Private Sub Form_Load()
  Department = "Manufacturing"
  Supervisor = "Joe Jones"
  Title = "Senior Engineer"

  'Dozens of lines of code go here

  txtDepartment = Department
  txtSupervisor = Superviser
  txtTitle = Title
End Sub
```

In this example code, the `txtSupervisor` text box on the form is always empty and is never assigned a value. A line near the bottom of this procedure assigns the value of a variable to a text box named `txtSupervisor`. Notice that the name of the variable (`Superviser`) is a misspelling of the intended variable (`Supervisor`). Because the source of the assignment appears to be a variable, VBA simply creates a new variant named `Superviser` and assigns it to the `txtSupervisor` text box to it. And, because the new `Superviser` variable has never been assigned a value, the text box always ends up empty. Misspellings such as this are very common and easy to overlook in long or complex procedures.

Furthermore, the code shown in this example runs fine, and causes no problem. Because this procedure uses implicit variable declaration, Access raises no error because of the misspelling, and the problem isn't detected until someone notices the text box is always empty. Imagine the problems you'd encounter in a payroll or billing application if variables go missing because of simple spelling errors!

When you declare a variable, Access sets up a location in the computer's memory for storing a value for the variable ahead of time. The amount of storage allocated for the variable depends on the data type you assign to the variable. More space is allocated for a variable that will hold a currency amount (such as $1,000,000) than for a variable that will never hold a value greater than, say, 255. This is because a variable declared with the Currency data type requires more storage than another variable declared as a Byte. Data types are discussed later in this chapter in the section titled "Working with Data Types."

Even though VBA does not require you to declare your variables before using them, it does provide various declaration commands. Getting into the habit of declaring variables is good practice. A variable's declaration assures that you can assign only a certain type of data to it — always a numeric value or only characters, for example. In addition, you attain real performance gains by pre-declaring variables. A programming best practice is to declare variables at the top of the procedure. This practice makes the program easier for other programmers to work with later on.

The Dim keyword

To declare a variable, you use the `Dim` statement (*Dim* is an abbreviation of the archaic *Dimension* programming term — because you are specifying the dimension of the variable). When you use the `Dim` statement, you must supply the variable name that you assign to the variable. The format for the `Dim` keyword is:

```
Dim [VariableName] [As DataType]
```

The following statement declares the variable `xBeeps` as an Integer data type:

```
Dim xBeeps As Integer
```

Notice that the variable name follows the `Dim` statement. In addition to naming the variable, use `As DataType` to specify a data type for the variable. The data type is the kind of information that will be stored in the variable: String, Integer, Currency, and so on. The default data type is known as *variant;* it can hold any type of data.

When you use the `Dim` statement to declare a variable in a procedure, you can refer to that variable only within that procedure. Other procedures, even if they are stored in the same module, do not know anything about the variable declared within a procedure. Such a variable is often described as *local* because it is declared *locally* within a procedure and is known only by the procedure that owns it (you'll read more about variable scope later in this chapter).

Variables can also be declared in the declarations section of a module. Then all the procedures in the module can access the variable. Procedures outside the module in which you declared the variable, however, cannot read or use the variable.

The Public keyword

To make a variable available to all modules in the application, use the Public keyword when you declare the variable. Figure 11-6 illustrates declaring a public variable.

FIGURE 11-6

Declaring a public variable

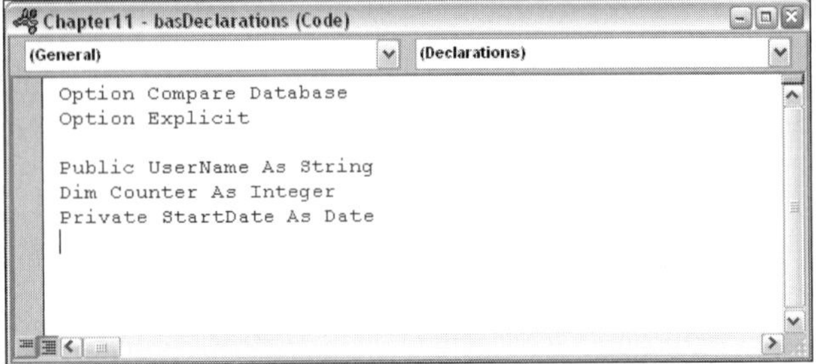

Notice that the statement is in the declarations section of the module. Public variables must be declared in the declarations section of the module, and not within a procedure.

CAUTION **You cannot declare a variable public within a procedure. It must be declared in the declarations section of a module. If you attempt to declare a variable public within a procedure, you receive an error message.**

Although you can declare a public variable in any module, it seems logical to declare public variables only within the module that will use them the most. The exceptions to this rule are true global variables that you want to make available to all procedures across modules and that are not specifically related to a single module. You should declare global variables in a single standard module so that you can find them easily.

TIP **It is possible to declare public variables in the code module attached to a form or report. Referencing these public variables from another module is a little bit different than referencing public variables declared in standard modules. To reference the value of a public variable declared behind a form or report from another module, you must qualify the variable reference, using the name of the form or report object. `frmMainForm.MyVariable`, for example, accesses a form named `frmMainForm` and obtains the value of the variable `MyVariable`.**

The Private keyword

The declarations section in Figure 11-6 shows the use of the `Dim` and `Private` statements to declare variables. Technically, there is no difference between `Private` and `Dim`, but using `Private` at the module level to declare variables that are available to only that module's procedures is a good idea. Declaring private variables does the following:

- Contrasts with `Dim`, which must be used at the procedure level, distinguishing where the variable is declared and its scope (`Module` versus `Procedure`)
- Contrasts with `Public`, the other method of declaring variables in modules, making understanding your code easier

TIP **You can quickly go to the declarations section of a module while you are working on code in a form's module by selecting `(Declarations)` from the Procedure drop-down list in the upper right corner of the Code editor. Another way to move to the declarations section is to select `(General)` in the Object drop-down list in the upper left corner of the Code editor. Refer to the Module window combo boxes in Figure 11-6.**

When you declare a variable, you use the `AS` clause to assign a data type to the variable. Because Access is a database development system, it's not surprising that variable data types are similar to field data types in an Access database table.

Working with Data Types

When you declare a variable, you also specify the data type for the variable. All variables have a data type. The type of variable determines what kind of information can be stored in the variable.

A string variable — a variable with a data type of string — can hold any character values ranging from A to Z, a to z, and 0 to 1, as well as formatting characters (`#`, `-`, `!`, and so on). Once created, a string variable can be used in many ways: comparing its contents with another string, pulling parts of information out of the string, and so on. If you have a variable defined as a string, however, you cannot use it to do mathematical calculations. Conversely, you cannot assign a number to a variable declared as a string.

Table 11-1 describes the 12 fundamental data types supported by VBA.

TABLE 11-1

VBA Data Types

Data Type	Range	Description
Boolean	True or false	2 bytes
Byte	0 to 255	1-byte binary data
Currency	–922,337,203,685,477,5808 to 922,337,203,685,477,5807	8-byte number with fixed decimal point
Decimal	+/-79,228,162,514,264,337,593,543,950,335 with no decimal point +/-7.9228162514264337593543950335 with 28 places to the right of the decimal; smallest non-zero number is +/0.0000000000000000000000000001	14 bytes
Date	01 Jan 100 to 31 Dec 9999	8-byte date/time value
Double	–1.79769313486231E308 to –4.94065645841247E–324 for negative values and 4.94065645841246544E-324 through 1.79769313486231570E+308 for positive values	8-byte floating-point number
Integer	–32,768 to 32,767	2-byte integer
Long	–2,147,483,648 to 2,147,483,647	4-byte integer
Object	Any object reference	4 bytes
Single	negative values: –3.402823E38 to –1.401298E –45 positive values: 1.401298E –45 to 3.402823E38	4-byte floating-point number
String (variable-length) 10 bytes plus length of string	0 to approximately 2,000,000,000	Varies by size of data
String (fixed-length)	1 to approximately 65,400	Length of string
Variant (with numbers)	Any numeric value up to the range of Double	16 bytes
Variant (with characters) 22 bytes plus length of string	0 to approximately 2,000,000,000	Varies by size of data

Most of the time, you use the String, Date, Integer, and Currency or Double data types. If a variable always contains whole numbers between –32,768 and 32,767, you can save bytes of memory and gain speed in arithmetic operations if you declare the variable an integer type.

When you want to assign the value of an Access field to a variable, you need to make sure that the type of the variable can hold the data type of the field. Table 11-2 shows the corresponding VBA data types for Access field types.

TABLE 11-2

Comparative Access and VBA Data Types

Access Field Data Type	VBA Data Type
AutoNumber (Long Integer)	Long
AutoNumber (Replication ID)	—
Currency	Currency
Computed	—
Date/Time	Date
Memo	String
Number (Byte)	Byte
Number (Integer)	Integer
Number (Long Integer)	Long
Number (Single)	Single
Number (Double)	Double
Number (Replication ID)	—
OLE object	String
Text	String
Hyperlink	String
Yes/No	Boolean

Now that you understand variables and their data types, you're ready to learn how to use them in writing procedures.

Comparing implicit and explicit variables

The default data type for VBA variables is the variant. This means that, unless you specify otherwise, every variable in your application will be a variant. As you read earlier in this chapter, the variant data type is not very efficient. Its data storage requirements are greater than the equivalent simple data type (a string, for instance) and the computer spends more time keeping track of the data type contained in a variant than for other data types.

Here's an example of how you might test for the speed difference when using implicitly declared variant variables and explicitly declared variables. This code is found behind `frmImplicitTest` in `Chapte11.accdb`:

```
'Use a Windows API call to get the exact time:
Private Declare Function GetTickCount _
    Lib "kernel32" () As Long

Private Sub cmdGo_Click()
  Dim i As Integer
  Dim j As Integer
  Dim sExplicit As Single

  txtImplicitStart = timeGetTime()

  For o = 1 To 10000
    For p = 1 To 10000
      q = i / 0.33333
    Next p
  Next o

  txtImplicitEnd = timeGetTime()

  txtImplicitElapsed = txtImplicitEnd - txtImplicitStart

  DoEvents

  txtExplicitStart = timeGetTime()

  For i = 1 To 10000
    For j = 1 To 10000
      sExplicit = i / 0.33333
    Next j
  Next i

  txtExplicitEnd = timeGetTime()
  txtExplicitElapsed = txtExplicitEnd - txtExplicitStart

End Sub
```

In this small test, the loop using implicitly declared variables required approximately 7.2 seconds to run while the loop with the explicitly declared variables required only 5.6 seconds. This is a performance enhancement of approximately 20 percent just by using explicitly declared variables.

Forcing explicit declaration

Access provides a simple *compiler directive* that forces you to always declare the variables in your applications. The `Option Explicit` statement, when inserted at the top of a module, instructs VBA to require explicit declaration of all variables in the module. If, for instance, you're working with an application containing a number of implicitly declared variables, inserting `Option Explicit` at the top of each module results in a check of all variable declarations the next time the application is compiled.

Since explicit declaration is such a good idea, it may not come as a surprise that Access provides a way to automatically ensure that every module in your application uses explicit declaration. The Editor tab of the Options dialog box shown in Figure 11-7 includes a Require Variable Declaration check box. This option automatically inserts the `Option Explicit` directive at the top of very module created after from this point in time onward.

FIGURE 11-7

Requiring variable declaration is a good idea in most Access applications.

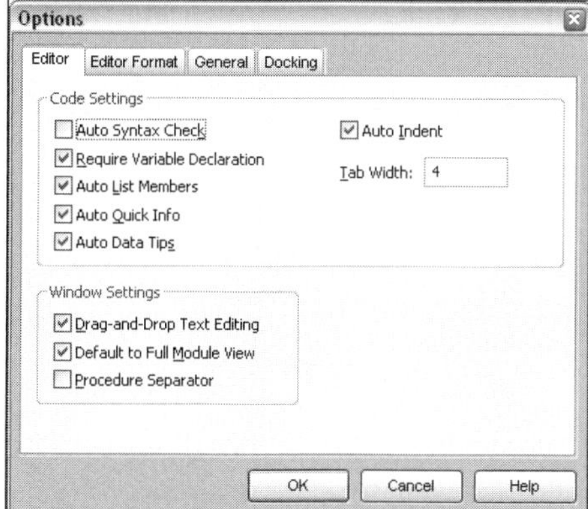

The Require Variable Declaration option does not affect modules already written. This option applies only to modules created after this option is selected, so you'll have to insert the Option Explicit directive in existing modules. As mentioned earlier in this chapter, `Require Variable Declaration` is not set by default in Access 2007. You must set this option yourself to take advantage of having Access add `Option Explicit` to all your modules.

Using a naming convention

Like most programming languages, applications written in VBA tend to be quite long and complex, often occupying thousand lines of code. Even simple VBA programs may require hundreds of different variables. VBA forms often have dozens of different controls on them, including text boxes, command buttons, option groups, and other controls. Keeping track of the variables, procedures, forms, and controls in even a moderately complicated VBA application is a daunting task.

One way to ease the burden of managing the code and objects in an application is through the use of a naming convention. A *naming convention* applies a standardized method of supplying names to the objects and variables in an application.

The most common naming convention used in Access applications uses a three- or four-character prefix (a *tag*) attached to the base name of the objects and variables in a VBA application. For instance, a text box containing a person's last name might be named `txtLastName`, while a command button that closes a form would be named `cmdClose`.

The names for variables follow a similar pattern. The string variable holding a customer name might be named `strCustomer` and a Boolean variable indicating whether the customer is currently active would be either `boolActive` or `fActive` (the `f` indicates a *flag* value).

Using a naming convention is not difficult. The code in this book uses one- and three-character prefixes exclusively. In most cases, when the use of the variable is obvious, a one-character prefix is used (for instance, `sLastName`) to keep code examples short and simple. In longer procedures, three-character prefixes are used on most variables. Most of the controls on the Access forms in the projects on this book's CD use three-character prefixes.

This simple naming convention even helps you select the most logical name to apply to the variables and objects in your applications. In virtually every case, you'll assign a name to a variable or object based on how that item is used in the application. In other words, using a naming convention encourages names based on the functionality provided by the variables and objects in your applications. After all, you should not be adding to an application variables and objects that do not have specific jobs to perform.

Understanding variable scope and lifetime

A variable is more than just a simple data repository. Every variable is a dynamic part of the application and may be used at different times during the program's execution. The declaration of a variable establishes more than just the name and data type of the variable. Depending on the keyword used to declare the variable and the placement of the variable's declaration in the program's code, the variable may be *visible* to large portions of the application's code. Alternatively, a different placement may severely limit where the variable can be referenced in the procedures within the application.

Examining scope

The visibility of a variable or procedure is called its *scope*. A variable that can be seen and used by any procedure in the application is said to have *public* scope. Another variable, one that is usable by a single procedure is said to have scope that is *private* to that procedure.

There are many analogies for public and private scope. For instance, a company is likely to have a phone number that is quite public (the main switchboard number) and is listed in the phone book. In addition to the main switchboard number, each office or room within the company may have its own extension number that is private within the company. A large office building will have a public street address that is known by anyone passing by the building. Each office or suite within the building will have a number that is private within that building.

Variables declared within a procedure are local to that procedure and cannot be used or referenced outside of that procedure. Most of the listings in this chapter have included a number of variables declared within the procedures in the listings. In each case, the `Dim` keyword was used to define the variable. *Dim* is shorthand for *dimension* and is a rather archaic expression that is an instruction to VBA to allocate enough memory to contain the variable that follows the `Dim` keyword. Therefore, `Dim intMyInt As Integer` allocates less memory (2 bytes) than `Dim dblMyDouble As Double` (8 bytes). There is no way to make a variable declared within a procedure visible outside of that procedure.

The `Public` keyword makes a variable visible throughout an application. `Public` can only be used at the module level and cannot be used within a procedure. Most often, the `Public` keyword is used only in standard (standalone) modules that are not part of a form. Figure 11-8 illustrates variables declared with three very different scopes.

Every variable declared in the general section of the standard module is public throughout the application unless the `Private` keyword is used. `Private` restricts the visibility of a variable to the module in which the variable is declared. In Figure 11-8, the X1 integer declared with `Public` scope at the top of the module will be seen everywhere in the application while the `Private` Y1 integer declared in the next statement is accessible only within the module.

A bit farther down in Figure 11-8, you see two procedures (A and B). Each procedure declares a variable that is usable only from within the procedure. In Procedure A, you see a variable named X2 declared as an integer and assigned the value 99. Just below this assignment is a reference to the Y1 variable defined at the top of the module. This is the variable that is accessible only from within the module. Procedure B defines an integer variable named Y2 and assigns it a value of 55. The X1 variable in Procedure B that is assigned the 19 value is the public X1 variable declared at the top of the module.

FIGURE 11-8

Variable scope is determined by the variable's declaration.

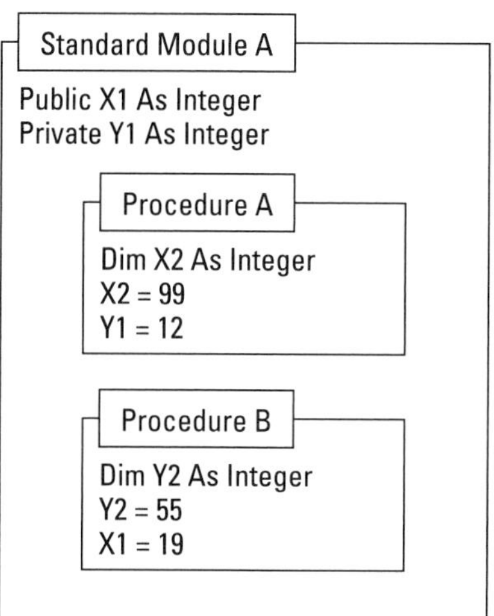

Determining a variable's lifetime

Variables are not necessarily permanent citizens of an application. Just as their visibility is determined by the location of their declaration, their *lifetime* is determined by their declaration as well. A variable's lifetime determines when it is accessible to the application.

By default, procedure-level variables exist only while the procedure is executing. As soon as the procedure ends, the variable is removed from memory and is no longer accessible. As already discussed, the scope of procedure-level variables is limited to the procedure and cannot be expanded beyond the procedure's boundaries.

A variable declared in the declarations section of a form's module exists as long as the form is open. All of the procedures within the form's module can use the module-level variables as often as they need, and they all share the value assigned to the variable. When the form is closed and removed from memory, all of its variables are removed as well.

The greatest variable lifetime is experienced by the variables declared in public (standard) modules. These variables are available as soon as the VBA application starts up, and they persist until the program is shut down and removed from memory. Therefore, public variables retain their values throughout the application and are accessible to any of the procedures within the program. Private variables (declared with the `Private` keyword) declared at the top of standard modules endure throughout the application, but following the rules of variable scope, are accessible only from within the module.

There is one major exception to the general rule that procedure-level variables persist only as long as the procedure is running. The `Static` keyword makes a variable persist between calls to the procedure. Once a value has been assigned to a static variable, that variable retains that value until it is changed in another call to the procedure.

An alternative to using static variables is to declare a global or module-level variable and use it each time a particular procedure is called. The problem with this approach is that a global or module-level variable is accessible to other procedures that are also able to modify its value. You can experience undesirable *side-effect bugs* by unwittingly changing the value of a widely scoped variable without realizing what has happened. Because of their procedure-limited scope, static variables are one way to avoid side-effect bugs.

Incidentally, declaring a procedure with the `Static` keyword makes all variables in the procedure static as well. In the following listing, both variables (`intStatic` and `intLocal`) in the `StaticTest2` sub are static, in spite of their local declarations within the procedure. The `Static` keyword used in the procedure's heading makes them both static.

```
Private Static Sub StaticTest2()
  Dim intStatic As Integer
  Dim intLocal As Integer

  intStatic = intStatic + 1
```

```
    intLocal = intLocal + 1

    txtStatic = intStatic
    txtLocal = intLocal
End Sub
```

Understanding Subs and Functions

The code in a VBA application lives in containers called *modules*. As you learned in Chapter 10, modules exist behind the forms in an Access application as well as in standalone modules. The modules themselves contain many procedures, variable and constant declarations, and other directives to the VBA engine.

The code within the modules is composed of procedures. There are two main types of procedures in VBA: *subroutines* or *subprocedures* (often called *subs*) and *functions*.

The general rules for procedures include the following:

- You must give the procedure a unique name within its *scope* (see "Understanding variable scope and lifetime," earlier in this chapter). Although it is not a good idea because of the chance of confusing the VBA engine or another person working with your code, it is possible to have more than one procedure with the same name, as long as the name is unique within each procedure's scope.
- The name you assign to a procedure cannot be the same as a VBA keyword or the name of a built-in VBA procedure.
- A procedure can't contain other procedures within it. A procedure can, however, call another procedure and execute the code in the other procedure at any time.

Because of the rules governing procedure scope, you cannot have two public procedures both named `MyProcedure`, although you could have two private procedures, both named `MyProcedure`, or one public procedure named `MyProcedure` and one private procedure named `MyProcedure`. The reason why it's a bad idea to use the same procedure name for multiple procedures, even when the procedures have different scopes, should be obvious.

The following sections cover some of the specifics regarding VBA procedures. Planning and composing the procedures in your modules is the most time-consuming part of working with VBA; therefore, it's important to understand how procedures fit into the overall scheme of application development.

Subroutines and functions both contain lines of code that you can run. When you run a subroutine or function, you call it. *Calling*, *running*, and *invoking* are all terms meaning *to execute* (or run) the statements (or lines of code) within the procedure or function. All of these terms can be used interchangeably (and they will be, by different developers). No matter how you invoke a VBA procedure — using the `Call` keyword, referencing the procedure by its name, or running it from the

Immediate window, they all do the same thing — which is to cause lines of code to be processed, run, executed, or whatever you want to call it.

The only real difference between a procedure and a function is that a function returns a value when called. *Returning a value* means that the function generates a value when it runs, and makes the value available to the code that called it. You can use a Boolean function to return a True or False value indicating, for example, where the operation it performed was successful. You could see if a file exists, if a value was greater than another value, or anything you choose. Function return dates, numbers, or strings. Functions can even return complex data types such as recordsets. In one of the examples in Chapter11.accdb, a function named `CalcTax` calculates the tax amount for an invoice and returns the value so that it can be placed into the tax control.

A subprocedure does not return a value. However, although a function directly returns a value to a variable created as part of the function call, there are other ways for functions and subprocedures to communicate values to form controls or declared variables in memory.

Understanding where to create a procedure

You create procedures in one of two places:

- In a standard VBA module
- Behind a form or report

You create a subprocedure or function in a standard module when the procedure will be shared by events in more than one form or report or by an object other than a form or report (queries can use functions to handle very complex criteria).

If the code you are creating will only be called by a single procedure or form, the subprocedure or function should be created in the form or report's module.

A module is a container for multiple subprocedures and functions.

Calling VBA procedures

VBA procedures are called in a variety of ways and from a variety of places. They can be called from events behind forms and reports or they can be placed in module objects and called by simply using their name or by using the `Call` statement. Here are some examples:

```
SomeSubRoutineName

Call SomeSubRoutineName

Somevalue = SomeFunctioName
```

Only functions return values that may be assigned to variables. Subprocedures are simply called, do their work, and end. Although functions return a single value, both subprocedures and functions can place values in tables, in form controls, or even in public variables available to any part of your program. You will see several examples of different ways to use subprocedures and functions in this chapter.

Creating subs

Conceptually, subroutines are easy to understand. A *subroutine* (usually called a *sub*, and sometimes called a *subprocedure*) is a set of programming statements that is executed as a unit by the VBA engine. VBA procedures can become complex, so this elementary description of subroutines is quickly overwhelmed by the actual subroutines you'll compose in the Visual Basic Code window.

Figure 11-9 shows a typical subroutine. Notice the `Sub` keyword that begins the routine, followed by the name of the subroutine. The declaration of this particular subroutine includes the `Private` keyword, which restricts the availability of this subroutine to the module containing the subroutine.

FIGURE 11-9

A typical subroutine in an Access application

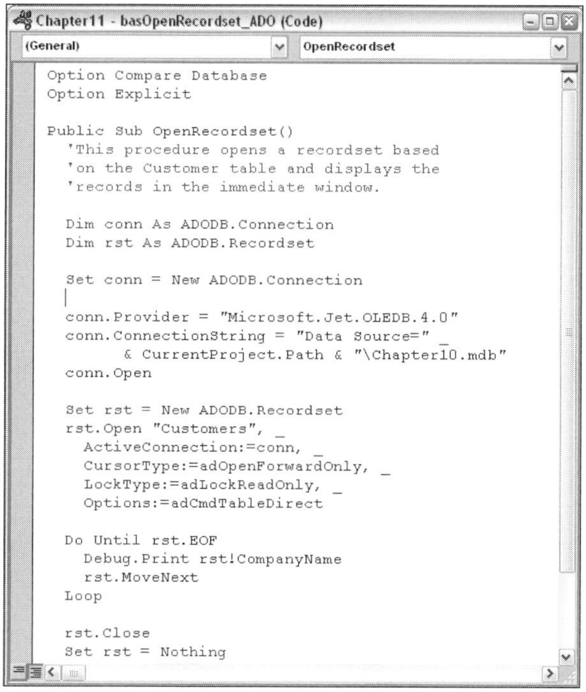

Chapter11 - basOpenRecordset_ADO (Code)

(General) | OpenRecordset

```
Option Compare Database
Option Explicit

Public Sub OpenRecordset()
  'This procedure opens a recordset based
  'on the Customer table and displays the
  'records in the immediate window.

  Dim conn As ADODB.Connection
  Dim rst As ADODB.Recordset

  Set conn = New ADODB.Connection

  conn.Provider = "Microsoft.Jet.OLEDB.4.0"
  conn.ConnectionString = "Data Source=" _
        & CurrentProject.Path & "\Chapter10.mdb"
  conn.Open

  Set rst = New ADODB.Recordset
  rst.Open "Customers", _
    ActiveConnection:=conn, _
    CursorType:=adOpenForwardOnly, _
    LockType:=adLockReadOnly, _
    Options:=adCmdTableDirect

  Do Until rst.EOF
    Debug.Print rst!CompanyName
    rst.MoveNext
  Loop

  rst.Close
  Set rst = Nothing
```

The subroutine you see in Figure 11-9 contains most of the components you'll see in almost every VBA sub or function:

- **Declaration:** All procedures must be *declared* so that VBA knows where to find them. The name assigned to the procedure must be unique within the VBA project. The *Sub* keyword identifies this procedure as a subroutine.
- **Terminator:** All procedures must be terminated with the `End` keyword followed by the type of procedure that is ending. In Figure 11-9, the terminator is `End Sub`.
- **Declarations area:** Although variables and constants can be declared within the body of the procedure, good programming conventions require variables to be declared near the top of the procedure where they'll be easy to find.
- **Statements:** A VBA procedure can contain many statements. Usually, however, you'll want to keep your VBA procedures small to make debugging as painless as possible. Very large subroutines can be difficult to work with, and you'll avoid problems if you keep them small. Instead of adding too many features and operations in a single procedure, place operations in separate procedures and call those procedures when those operations are needed.

At the conclusion of the subroutine in Figure 11-9, program flow returns to the code or action that originally called the sub. In this particular case, this subroutine runs in response to the form's `Load` event.

The first procedure you create in this chapter retrieves several values from the `cboBuyerID` combo box columns and uses them in the form. The `RowSource` of the `cboBuyerID` combo box contains six active columns, which are as follows:

VBA Column Number	Value
0	Name: `tblContacts.LastName & ", " & : tblContacts.FirstName`
1	`Company` (from `tblContacts`)
2	`DiscountPercent` (from `tblTaxRates`)
3	`TaxRate` (from `tblTaxRates`)
4	`TaxLocation` (from `tblContacts`)
5	`ContactID` (from `tblContacts`). This is the bound column of this combo box.

Combo-box row sources start with column 0, so column 2 is the third column in the row source.

The objective of this exercise is to learn about procedures, but it also serves to teach you some additional VBA commands. The code should be entered into the `cboBuyerID AfterUpdate` event.

To create an Event Procedure in a form, follow these steps:

1. **Select `cboBuyerID` in `frmSales` Design view.**
2. **Press F4 to display the Property window for the control.**
3. **Click in the `After Update` event in the Event tab of the property sheet and select `[Event Procedure]` from the `After_Update` event's drop-down list.**
4. **Press the builder button (...) to open the VBA Code editor.**
5. **Enter the following code into the VBA window, as shown in Figure 11-10.**

```
Me.Recalc
If Not IsNull(Me!cboBuyerID) Then
    'Verify that the DiscountPercent is valid:
    If Not IsNull(Me!cboBuyerID.Column(2)) Then
      'Get the DiscountPercent from Column 2:
      Me!txtDiscountRate = _
          Format(Me!cboBuyerID.Column(2),"Percent")
      'Get the Tax Location from Column 4:
      Me!txtTaxLocation = nz(Me!cboBuyerID.Column(4))
      'Get the Tax Rate from Column 3:
      Me!txtTaxRate = nz(Me!cboBuyerID.Column(3),0)
    End If
  Else
    'Invalid data found in the combo box,
    'so set all the text boxes to Null:
    Me!txtDiscountRate = Null
    Me!txtTaxLocation = Null
    Me!txtTaxRate = Null
End If
```

6. **Select `Compile Chapter11` from the Debug menu in the Code editor to check your syntax.**
7. **Close the VBA window and return to the `frmSales` form.**

The code first performs a `Recalc` on the form to update any values that may be in an incomplete state, like a buyer ID in the process of being selected or a line item that was in the process of being selected when the combo box was used. Any time you are doing data entry and need code to run to perform some process, it is a good idea to first run the form's `Recalc` command. The `Me.` refers to the current form and substitutes in this example for `Forms!frmSales!`.

The first `IF` statement checks to make sure a buyer ID was selected by making sure the current value of the combo box's bound column (`ContactID`) is not null. If it is not (a valid value was selected in the combo box), a second `IF` statement checks to make sure that not only the value of `cboBuyerID` is valid but also that the value of the third column (`DiscountPercent`) is not null.

If the `DiscountPercent` column (column 2) is valid, the values from that and other combo-box columns are used to fill controls on the form.

Notice the `nz` function on front of the statements that retrieve the value from column 3 and column 4 of the combo box. The `nz` function ("null to zero") prevents null or zero length string errors. For example, the following statement may cause an error if the value of `Me!cboBuyerID.Column(4)` is null:

```
Me!txtTaxLocation = nz(Me!cboBuyerID.Column(4))
```

The `nz` function around the right side of the equation sets it to a blank if the value is null.

The following line uses an alternative value to the default blank:

```
Me!txtTaxRate = nz(Me!cboBuyerID.Column(3),0)
```

This line of code sets the value of the equality to 0 if the third column in null.

Figure 11-10 shows the procedure created in the code editor after entering the procedure described earlier. After you complete entering these statements, press the Save button on the toolbar to save your code before closing the VBA window.

FIGURE 11-10

The `frmSales cboBuyerID AfterUpdate` event procedure in the VBA code window

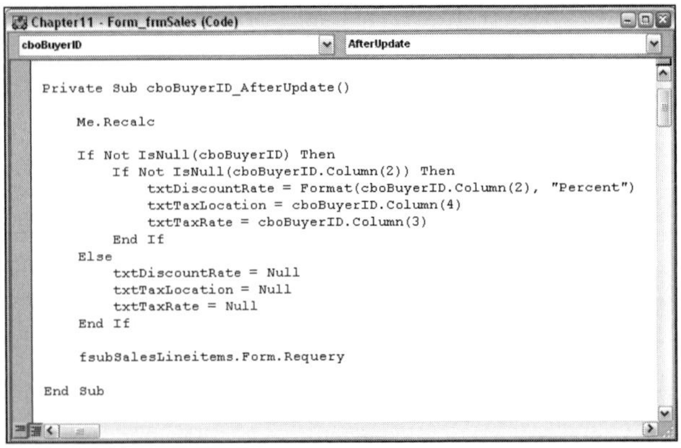

Chapter11 - Form_frmSales (Code)

cboBuyerID | AfterUpdate

```
Private Sub cboBuyerID_AfterUpdate()

    Me.Recalc

    If Not IsNull(cboBuyerID) Then
        If Not IsNull(cboBuyerID.Column(2)) Then
            txtDiscountRate = Format(cboBuyerID.Column(2), "Percent")
            txtTaxLocation = cboBuyerID.Column(4)
            txtTaxRate = cboBuyerID.Column(3)
        End If
    Else
        txtDiscountRate = Null
        txtTaxLocation = Null
        txtTaxRate = Null
    End If

    fsubSalesLineitems.Form.Requery

End Sub
```

The procedure behind this form runs each time the value of the `cboBuyerID` combo box changes. When the user changes the value of the buyer ID combo box, this code updates the value of the tax location and tax rate. However, you must then change the value of the tax amount. This code can now be added to this procedure. Later, you make a separate procedure from this new code.

Creating Functions

Functions differ from subprocedures in that functions return a single value. In these examples, you'll create functions to calculate the extension for a single line item, create a function to calculate the total of all the taxable line items, and then apply the current tax rate to that value.

Although functions can be created behind individual forms or reports, usually they are created in modules. This first function will be created in a new module that you will name `basSalesFunctions`. To do this, follow these steps:

1. **Select the Modules tab in the Navigation Pane.**
2. **Right-click the `basSalesFunctions` module and select Design view from the context menu.**

   The VBA window is displayed with the title basSalesFunctions (Code) in the title bar.
3. **Move to the bottom of the module, and enter the following code:**

```
Private CalcExtension( _
    Quantity As Integer, _
    Price As Currency, _
    DiscountPercent As Double _
    ) As Currency

    Dim Extension As Currency

    Extension = Quantity * Price

    CalcExtension = Extension - (Extension * DiscountPercent)

End Function
```

The first statement declares the variable `Extension` as the `Currency` data type. The `Extension` variable is used in an intermediate step. The next line of code creates a calculation assigning the product of two variables, `Quantity` and `Price`, to the previously declared variable, `Extension`. You might notice that the two variables on the right side of the equation are not declared.

Finally, the last line of code performs one more calculation to take the extension and apply any discount to it. The function's name is treated as if it is a variable and is assigned the value of the calculation. This is how a function gets the value that is returned to the calling program.

Handling parameters

Now, the question you should be asking is: Where are these variables coming from and how are they declared? The answer is simple. They are the passed parameters from the original function call.

The next step is to modify the `Function` statement at the top to handle the passed parameters and the returned data type.

Before you can create variables for the passed parameters, you must know what parameters are being passed. In this example, three parameters are passed.

Parameter Name	Data Type
`Quantity`	Integer
`Price`	Currency
`DiscountPercent`	Double

These parameter names can be anything you want them to be. Think of them as variables you would normally declare. All that is missing is the `Dim` statement. They do not have to be the same name as the variables used in the call to the function. Very often, you'll pass the names of fields in a table or controls on a form or variables created in the calling procedure as parameters to a procedure.

These variables are passed and their data types declared by placing them in parentheses after the function name with the syntax variable name as data type.

For example:

```
Public Function SomeProcedureName(var1 as datatype1, _
    var2 as datatype2)
```

For this example, you will change the first line as described in the following steps:

1. **Replace the original** `Public Function CalcExtension` **statement with:**

   ```
   Public Function CalcExtension( _
       Quantity As Integer, _
       Price As Currency, _
       DiscountPercent As Double _
       ) As Currency
   ```

2. **Select** `Compile Chapter11` **from the Debug menu to check your code.**
3. **Correct any errors you might find and then close the VBA window.**
4. **Save the module as** `basSalesFunctions`.

   Each parameter is listed in the form *var1 as datatype1* separated by commas. In this example, there are three parameters (`Quantity`, `Price`, and `DiscountPercent`). Each one corresponds to the table previously shown. After the parentheses, the data type declaration of the value is passed back to the calling program. `CalcExtension` is the name of the function and the variable, and its data type will be `Currency`.

   Your screen should look like the one shown in Figure 11-11.

FIGURE 11-11

The completed `CalcExtension` function

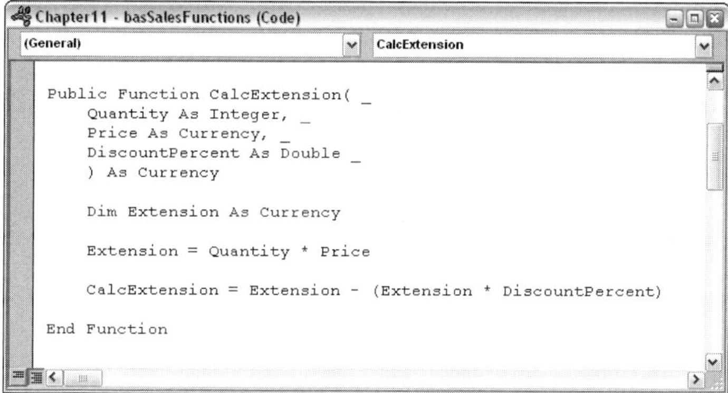
```
Public Function CalcExtension( _
    Quantity As Integer, _
    Price As Currency, _
    DiscountPercent As Double _
    ) As Currency

    Dim Extension As Currency

    Extension = Quantity * Price

    CalcExtension = Extension - (Extension * DiscountPercent)

End Function
```

Calling a function and passing parameters

Now that you have completed the function, it's time to test it.

Normally, a function call comes from a form or report event or from another procedure, and the call passes variables or the value of a control on a form or report. However, the function call may not even use variables. For example, you can test this function by going to the immediate window and using hard-coded numbers or characters known as literals.

Follow these steps to test the function:

1. **Press Ctrl+G to display the Immediate window.**
2. **Enter** ?CalcExtension(5, 3.50, .05).

   This statement passes the values as 5, 3.50, and .05 (5%) to the `Quantity`, `Price`, and `DiscountPercent` parameters, respectively. `CalcExtension` returns 16.625 using those values, as shown in Figure 11-12.
3. **Close the Immediate window and the VBA window and return to the Database window.**

FIGURE 11-12

Testing the `CalcExtension` function in the Immediate window

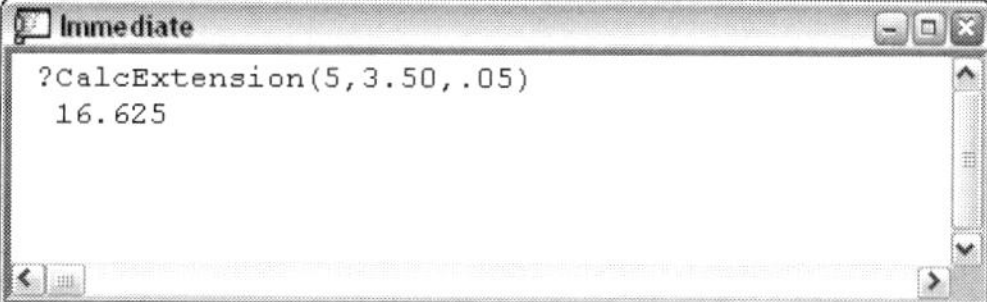

The next task is to use the function to calculate the extension. You can add a call to the function from the `frmSales` form's line item subform's `Amount` field. You can display the `frmSales` form in Design view, and then click into the `fsubSalesLineitems` subform, and finally click into the `txtAmount` control in the subform. Display the Property window and enter the following into the Control Source property, as shown in Figure 11-13.

```
=CalcExtension(Nz(txtQuantity,0),Nz(txtPrice,0),Nz(txtDiscountPercent,0))
```

This expression passes the values from three controls (`txtQuantity`, `txtPrice`, and `txtDiscountPercent`) in the subform to the `CalcExtension` function in the module and returns the value back to the control source of the `txtAmount` control each time the line is recalculated or any of the parameters change.

FIGURE 11-13

Adding a function call to the Control Source of a control

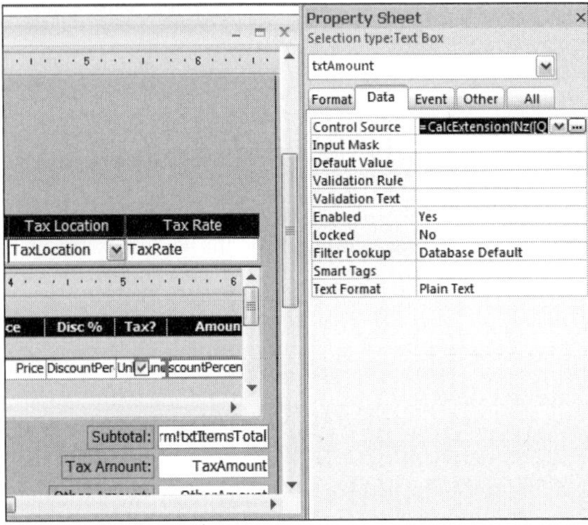

Of course, entering a function call or any expression into the control source of a control makes the control read-only. In this example, it is also an unbound control. There is no field in the `tblSalesLineItems` table that the `txtAmount` control is bound to. This is by design. Because the quantity, price, or discount can be changed, all three places would need to trigger a change to the amount.

Our business rule is that this value should always be calculated, and the user can enter the quantity and item number, override the price retrieved from the inventory table, and override the discount retrieved from the contacts table, but the calculation of extended amount (quantity * price * discount) is always used.

The `CalcExtension` function can be used in a variety of ways by other events within this form and by any form or report, because it *lives* in a module. If it were created behind the `frmSales` form, it would be accessible from only that form.

Creating a Function to Calculate Taxes

When you create a line item, you determine whether it is taxable. You can then add up all the extensions for all the taxable line items to determine the taxable total. This total can then be multiplied by the tax rate to determine the tax.

The Access Auto Auctions sales form (`frmSales`) includes a text box control for the tax amount. You could simply create an expression for the control's value such as:

```
=fSubSalesLineitems.Form!txtTaxableTotal * txtTaxRate
```

This expression references (`txtTaxableTotal`) in the subform (`fSubSalesLineitems`) and multiplies it by the tax rate (`txtTaxRate`) from the main form (`frmSales`).

However, although this expression displays the value of the tax, the expression entered into the `txtTaxAmount` control would make the `txtTaxAmount` control read-only because it contains an expression. You would not be able to override the calculated amount if you wanted to. The tax applied to a sale is one of the fields that needs to be changed once in a while for specific business purposes.

A better way than using a hard-coded expression is to create a function to calculate a value and then place the value of the calculation in the control. This way, you can simply type over the calculated value if needed.

You could enter the following line of code at the end of the `cboBuyerID AfterUpdate` event code you created previously. This way, each time you choose a new contact on the sales form, the tax is recalculated after the contact's tax rate is retrieved on the `frmSales` form.

```
Me.txtTaxAmount = _
  Me.fSubSalesLineitems.Form!txtTaxableTotal * Me.txtTaxRate
```

You could also enter this line of code in the `AfterUpdate` events behind the `Quantity`, `Price`, `DiscountPercent`, and `chkTaxable` controls. Each time the value in any of these controls changes, the value of the tax is updated. Actually, better would be to place this statement in the `AfterUpdate` event of `fsubSalesLineitems`. This way, the tax is recalculated each time a value is updated in any record of this form. Because `fsubSalesLineitems` is displayed as a datasheet, the `AfterUpdate` event fires as soon as the user moves to another line in `fsubSalesLineitems`.

Although you can use a simple expression that references controls on forms and subforms, this only works behind the form containing the code. Suppose you also need to calculate tax in other forms or in reports. There is a better way than relying on a form.

This is an old developer's expression: "Forms and reports lie; tables never lie." This means that the controls of a form or report often contain expressions, formats, and VBA code that may make a value seem to be one thing when the table actually contains a completely different value. The table containing the data is where the real values are stored and from where calculations and reports should retrieve data.

Figure 11-14 shows the `CalcTax` function. You can go to the `basSalesFunctions` module in `Chapter11.accdb` and enter this code into the `basSalesFunctions` module.

FIGURE 11-14

The `CalcTax` function

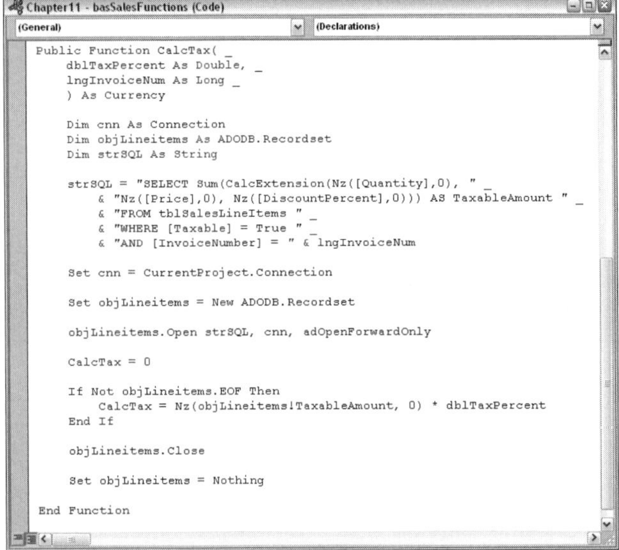


```
Public Function CalcTax( _
    dblTaxPercent As Double, _
    lngInvoiceNum As Long _
    ) As Currency

    Dim cnn As Connection
    Dim objLineitems As ADODB.Recordset
    Dim strSQL As String

    strSQL = "SELECT Sum(CalcExtension(Nz([Quantity],0), " _
        & "Nz([Price],0), Nz([DiscountPercent],0))) AS TaxableAmount " _
        & "FROM tblSalesLineItems " _
        & "WHERE [Taxable] = True " _
        & "AND [InvoiceNumber] = " & lngInvoiceNum

    Set cnn = CurrentProject.Connection

    Set objLineitems = New ADODB.Recordset

    objLineitems.Open strSQL, cnn, adOpenForwardOnly

    CalcTax = 0

    If Not objLineitems.EOF Then
        CalcTax = Nz(objLineitems!TaxableAmount, 0) * dblTaxPercent
    End If

    objLineitems.Close

    Set objLineitems = Nothing

End Function
```

The function is called from the `AfterUpdate` events behind the `txtQuantity`, `txtPrice`, or `txtDiscountPercent` controls in the subform. The `CalcExtension` function calculates the sum of the taxable line items from the `tblSalesItems` table. The `SQLstatement` combined with a bit of ADO code to determine the total. The calculated total amount is then multiplied by the `dblTaxPercent` parameter to calculate the tax. The tax is set to the variable `CalcTax` (the name of the expression).

TIP **Functions and subprocedures are important to the concepts of reusable code within an application. You should try to use functions and subprocedures and pass them parameters every time you can. A good rule is this: The first time you find yourself copying a group of code, it's time to create a procedure or function.**

Named arguments

Another significant feature of Access VBA is the use of *named arguments* for procedures. Without named arguments, the arguments passed to procedures must appear in the correct left-to-right order. With named arguments, you provide a name of each parameter passed to a subroutine or function. The subroutine or function uses the argument based on its name rather than on its position in the argument list. The following example illustrates this principle.

Assume your application includes the function shown here:

```
Function PrepareOutput(sStr1 As String, sStr2 As String, _
    sStr3 As String) As String

  PrepareOutput = sStr1 & " " & sStr2 & " " & sStr3

End Function
```

This function, of course, does nothing more than concatenate `sStr1`, `sStr2`, and `sStr3` and return it to the calling routine. The next example shows how this function might be called from another procedure.

```
Private Sub cmdForward_Click()
 txtOutput = PrepareOutput(txtFirstName, _
      txtLastName, txtHireDate)
End Sub
```

The arguments required by `PrepareOutput()` must be passed in left-to-right order. The results of this function are shown in Figure 11-15. The text in the Function output text box in the upper-right corner of this form shows the arguments in the order in which they appear in the text boxes on the left side of this form.

FIGURE 11-15

`frmNamedArguments` demonstrates the value of using named arguments in VBA procedures.

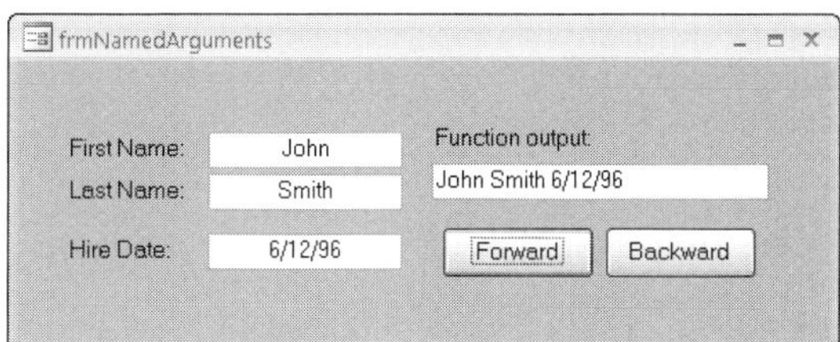

In Access 2007, arguments can be specified by name as we pass them to functions. Naming arguments makes them position-independent. Examine the code in the following list to see how named arguments work.

```
Private Sub cmdBackward_Click()
    txtOutput = PrepareOutput(sStr2:=txtLastName, _
        sStr3:=txtFirstName, sStr1:=txtHireDate)
End Sub
```

The thing to notice in `cmdBackward_Click` is that the arguments are not passed to `PrepareOutput()` in a specific order. As long as the names assigned to the arguments in this procedure match the names of the arguments expected by `PrepareOutput()`, Access VBA correctly uses the arguments in `PrepareOutput()`.

ON the CD-ROM **The `Chapter11.accdb` example database includes the `frmNamedArguments` you see in Figure 11-15 and Figure 11-16. The two buttons below the Function output text box pass the text from the First Name, Last Name, and Hire Date text boxes to the `PrepareOutput()` function using positional and named arguments.**

FIGURE 11-16

`PrepareOutput()` is able to use arguments submitted in any order as long as they're named.

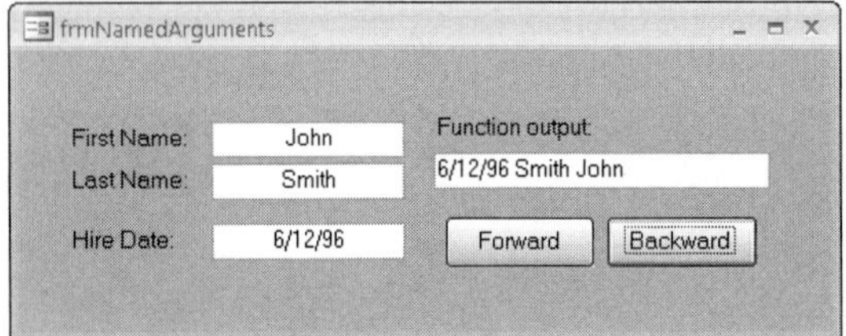

Summary

Building on the fundamentals presented in Chapter 10, this chapter took a closer — and longer — look at using VBA to build subprocedure and functions. You also saw many more ways to use VBA variables and data types in your Access applications.

We looked at some of the differences between subprocedures (or subroutines, if you prefer) and functions, passing parameter to procedures, and returning values from functions. Mastering the skills necessary to create strong VBA procedures, and correctly using the many different VBA variable types is an essential step towards building bulletproof Access applications.

Chapter 12

Understanding the Access Event Model

IN THIS CHAPTER

Understanding how events work

Learning how events are triggered

Understanding how event procedures work

Responding to events in forms and reports

Creating event procedures for forms

Creating event procedures for reports

Working with message boxes

Using variables and data types

Working with Visual Basic logical constructs

When working with a database system, the same tasks may be performed repeatedly. Instead of doing the same steps each time, you can automate the process with VBA.

Database management systems continually grow as you add records in a form, build new queries, and create new reports. As the system grows, many of the objects are saved for later use — for a weekly report or monthly update query, for example. You tend to create and perform many tasks repetitively. Every time you add contact records, for example, you open the same form. Likewise, you print the same form letter for contacts that have purchased a vehicle in the past month.

You can create VBA code throughout your application to perform these tasks. The VBA language offers a full array of powerful commands for manipulating records in a table, controls on a form, or just about anything else. This chapter continues the previous chapters' discussions of working with procedures in forms, reports, and standard modules.

ON the CD-ROM In this chapter, you will use the database file `Chapter12.accdb`. Please copy this database file from the book's CD if you wish to follow along with the examples presented in this chapter.

Programming Events

An Access event is the result or consequence of some user action. An Access event occurs when a user moves from one record to another in a form, closes a report, or clicks on a command button on a form. Even moving the mouse generates a continuous stream of events.

Access applications are event-driven. Access objects respond to many types of events. Access events are hooked into specific object properties. For example, checking or unchecking a check box triggers a `MouseDown` and a `MouseUp` event. These events are hooked into the check box through the `OnMouseDown` and `OnMouseUp` properties, respectively. You use VBA to compose event procedures that run whenever the user clicks on the check box.

Access events can be categorized into seven groups:

- **Windows (Form, Report) events:** Opening, closing, and resizing
- **Keyboard events:** Pressing or releasing a key
- **Mouse events:** Clicking or pressing a mouse button down
- **Focus events:** Activating, entering, and exiting
- **Data events:** Making current, deleting, or updating
- **Print events:** Formatting and printing
- **Error and timing events:** Happening after an error has occurred or some time has passed

In all, Access supports more than 50 different events that can be harnessed through VBA event procedures.

Of these types of events, by far the most common are the keyboard and mouse events. As you'll see in the following sections, forms and most controls recognize keyboard and mouse events. In fact, exactly the same keyboard and mouse events are recognized by forms and controls. The code you write for a mouse-click event on a command button is exactly the same sort of code that you might write for the mouse-click on a form.

In addition, most Access object types have their own unique events. The following sections discuss the majority of these events, but Microsoft has a habit of introducing new event capabilities with each new version of Access. Also, many ActiveX controls you might use in your Access applications may have their own unique and special events. When using an unfamiliar control or a new type of object in your Access applications, be sure to check out what events and properties are supported by the control or object.

How do events trigger VBA code?

You can create an event procedure that runs when a user performs any one of the many different events that Access recognizes. Access responds to events through special form and control properties. Reports have a similar set of events, tailored to the special needs and requirements of reports.

Figure 12-1 shows the property sheet for `frmProducts`. This form has many event properties. Forms aren't the only objects to have events. Each form section (page header, form header, detail, page footer, form footer) and every control on the form (labels, text boxes, check boxes, and option buttons, for example) has its own event.

FIGURE 12-1

The property sheet for `frmProducts`. Event procedures have been written for the `Current`, `BeforeDelConfirm`, and `Close` events.

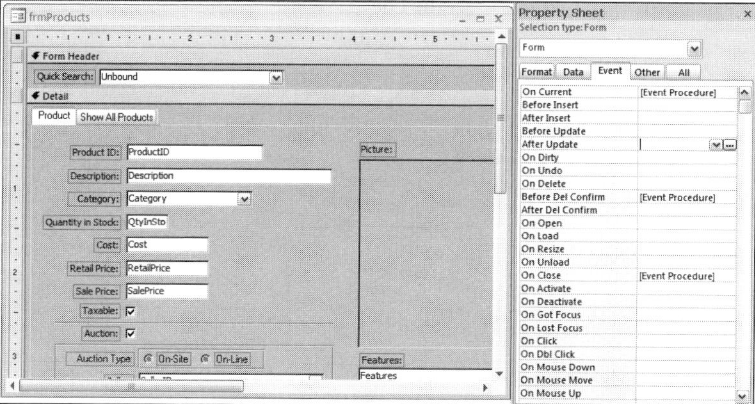

In Figure 12-1 notice that the property sheet is open on the Event tab. Access forms include more than 50 events, and each form section includes a number of events, as well as each control on the form. As you select a form section or a control on the form, the Event tab in the property sheet changes to show you the offense for that object.

In Figure 12-1, all of the events with existing event procedures contain `[Event Procedure]`, which indicates that the property has associated VBA code that executes whenever this event is triggered.

Where to trigger event procedures

In Access, you run event procedures through an object's event properties. There are no event properties for tables or queries.

Simply put, an event is how Access responds to a user's action. Events are triggered by actions such as opening a form or report, changing data in a record, clicking on a button, or closing a form or report. Access recognizes more than 60 events in controls, forms, and reports. Access provides event properties you use to tie VBA code to an object's events. For example, the `On Open` property is associated with a form or report opening on the screen.

You add an event procedure to a form or report by selecting the event property (`After Update`, for this example) in the object's property sheet. If no event procedure currently exists for the property, a drop-down arrow and builder button appear in the property's box, as shown in the `AfterUpdate` event property in Figure 12-1. The drop-down button exposes a short list containing `[Event Property]`. Selecting this option and then clicking on the builder button, takes you to the VBA code editor with an event procedure template already in place (see Figure 12-2).

FIGURE 12-2

An empty event procedure template for the form's `AfterUpdate` event

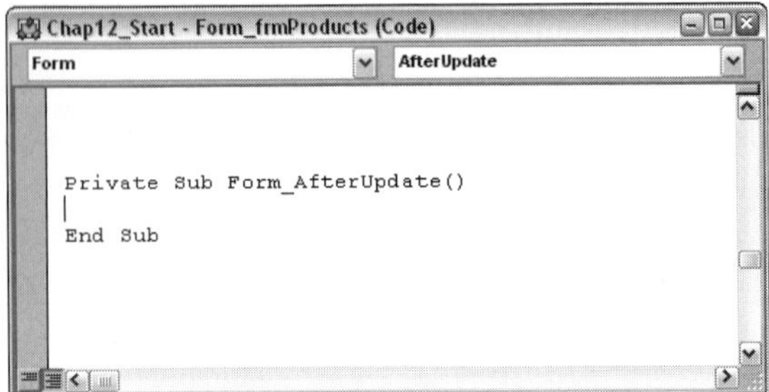

Notice the general format of the event procedure's declaration:

```
Private Sub Object_Event()
```

The `Object` portion of the procedure's name is, of course, the object raising the event, while the `Event` portion is the specific event raised by the object. In Figure 12-2 the object is `Form` and the event is `AfterUpdate`. Some events support arguments, which appear within the parentheses at the end of the declaration.

Common Events

Certain events are raised by many different Access objects. Microsoft has taken great care that these events behave exactly the same way, regardless of the object raising them. These events are also among the most commonly used by Access developers. Table 12-1 lists several of the most commonly used events.

TABLE 12-1

Events Common to Multiple Object Types

Event	Event Type	When the Event Is Triggered
`Click`	Mouse event	When you press and release (click) the left mouse button on a control in a form
`DblClick`	Mouse event	When you press and release (click) the left mouse button twice on a control/label in a form
`MouseDown`	Mouse event	When you press the mouse button while the pointer is on a form
`MouseMove`	Mouse event	When you move the mouse pointer over an area of a form

Event	Event Type	When the Event Is Triggered
`MouseUp`	Mouse event	When you release a pressed mouse button while the pointer is on a form
`MouseWheel`	Mouse event	When you spin the mouse wheel
`KeyDown`	Keyboard event	When you press any key on the keyboard when a form has focus or when you use a SendKeys macro action
`KeyUp`	Keyboard event	When you release a pressed key or immediately after the SendKeys macro
`KeyPress`	Keyboard event	When you press and release a key on a form that has the focus or when you use the SendKeys macro action

Not surprisingly, these events are all associated with the mouse and the keyboard because these are the user's primary means of inputting information and giving directions to an application. Not every object responds to every one of these events, but when an object responds to any of these events, the event exhibits exactly the same behavior.

Form Event Procedures

When you work with forms, you can create event procedures based on events at the form level, the section level, or the control level. If you attach an event procedure to a form-level event, whenever the event occurs, the action takes effect against the form as a whole (such as when you move to another record or leave the form).

To have your form respond to an event, you write an event procedure and attach it to the event property in the form that recognizes the event. Many properties can be used to trigger event procedures at the form level. Table 12-1 shows each property, the event it recognizes, and how the property works.

When referring to form events, we are talking about events that happen to the form as a whole — not about an event that can be triggered by a specific control on a form. Form events execute when moving from one record to another or when a form is being opened or closed. We cover responding to control events later in this chapter.

Primary form events

Access forms respond to many, many events. You'll never write code for most of these events because of their specialized nature. There are, however, some events that you'll program over and over again in your Access applications. Table 12-2 lists some of the most fundamental and important Access form events. Not coincidentally, these are also the most commonly programmed Access form events.

TABLE 12-2

Primary Form Events

Event	When the Event Is Triggered
`Current`	When you move to a different record and make it the current record
`BeforeInsert`	After data is first entered into a new record but before the record is actually created
`AfterInsert`	After the new record is added to the table
`BeforeUpdate`	Before changed data is updated in a record
`AfterUpdate`	After changed data is updated in a record
`Dirty`	When a record is modified
`Undo`	When a user has returned a form to clean state — record set back to unmodified state — opposite of On Dirty
`Delete`	When a record is deleted but before the deletion takes place
`BeforeDelConfirm`	Just before Access displays the Delete Confirm dialog box
`AfterDelConfirm`	After the Delete Confirm dialog box closes and confirmation has happened
`Open`	When a form is opened, but the first record is not displayed yet
`Load`	When a form is loaded into memory but not yet opened
`Resize`	When the size of a form changes
`Unload`	When a form is closed and the records unload, and before the form is removed from the screen
`Close`	When a form is closed and removed from the screen
`Activate`	When an open form receives the focus, becoming the active window
`Deactivate`	When a different window becomes the active window but before it loses focus
`GotFocus`	When a form with no active or enabled controls receives the focus
`LostFocus`	When a form loses the focus
`Timer`	When a specified time interval passes
`TimerInterval`	Specify the Interval in milliseconds
`BeforeScreenTip`	When the screen tip is activated

Form mouse and keyboard events

Access forms also respond to a number of mouse and keyboard events, as shown in Table 12-3.

TABLE 12-3

Form Mouse and Keyboard Events

Event	When the Event Is Triggered
`Click`	When you press and release (click) the left mouse button on a control in a form
`DblClick`	When you press and release (click) the left mouse button twice on a control/label in a form
`MouseDown`	When you press the mouse button while the pointer is on a form
`MouseMove`	When you move the mouse pointer over an area of a form
`MouseUp`	When you release a pressed mouse button while the pointer is on a form
`MouseWheel`	When you spin the mouse wheel
`KeyDown`	When you press any key on the keyboard when a form has focus; when you use a `SendKeys` macro action
`KeyUp`	When you release a pressed key or immediately after the `SendKeys` macro action
`KeyPress`	When you press and release a key on a form that has the focus; when you use the `SendKeys` macro
`KeyPreview` (Property)	Enables the form to respond to events before the controls on the form

Notice the `KeyPreview` property. This property, which is found only in forms, instructs Access to allow the form to see keyboard events before the controls on the form. By default, the controls on an Access form receive events before the form. This means that a form's controls mask key events from the form, and the form can never respond to those events. You must set the `KeyPreview` property to `Yes` (True) before the form responds to any of the key events (`KeyDown`, `KeyUp`, and so on).

Form data events

The primary purpose of Access forms is to display data. Not surprisingly then, Access forms have a number of events that are directly related to a form's data management (see Table 12-4). You will see these events programmed over and over again in this book, and will encounter event procedures written for these events virtually every time you work on an Access application.

TABLE 12-4

Form Data Events

Event	When the Event Is Triggered
`OnCurrent`	When you move to a different record and make it the current record
`BeforeInsert`	After data is first entered into a new record but before the record is actually created
`AfterInsert`	After the new record is added to the table
`BeforeUpdate`	Before changed data is updated in a record
`AfterUpdate`	After changed data is updated in a record
`OnDirty`	When a record is modified
`OnUndo`	When a user has returned a form to clean state — record set back to unmodified state — opposite of `OnDirty`
`OnDelete`	When a record is deleted but before the deletion takes place
`BeforeDelConfirm`	Just before Access displays the Delete Confirm dialog box
`AfterDelConfirm`	After the Delete Confirm dialog box closes and confirmation has happened
`Error`	When a runtime error is produced
`Filter`	When a filter has been specified but before it is applied
`ApplyFilter`	After a filter is applied to a form

Form PivotTable events

The more recent versions of Access include the ability to create PivotTables that display data in interesting ways. Although this book does not discuss PivotTables in detail, you may encounter PivotTables as you work with Microsoft Access. Because of the special requirements imposed by PivotTables, Access forms include a number of events, as shown in Table 12-5.

In Access 2007, a PivotTable is actually a special view of a table, created by selecting PivotTable View from the View group in the Home tab while a table is open in Datasheet View. A PivotChart is created from a table open in Datasheet view by clicking on the PivotChart button in the Forms group on the Create tab of the Access ribbon.

TABLE 12-5

Form PivotTable Events

Event	When the Event Is Triggered
`Timer`	When a specified time interval passes
`TimerInterval`	Specify the Interval in milliseconds
`BeforeScreenTip`	When the ScreenTip is activated
`CmdEnabled`	When a command has become enabled in a PivotChart or PivotTable
`CmdChecked`	When a PivotChart or PivotTable command has been selected
`CmdBeforeExecute`	When a PivotChart or PivotTable command has been selected from the ribbon, but not yet executed
`CmdExecute`	Immediately after a PivotTable or PivotChart command has been executed
`DataChange`	When PivotTable or PivotChart's data is changed or refreshed
`DataSetChange`	When a new data set for the chart changes (for example when filtered)
`PivotTableChange`	Whenever the list field, field set, or total is added or deleted in a PivotTable
`SelectionChange`	When a user makes a new selection; cannot be cancelled
`ViewChange`	When a different PivotTable view of the current data is opened
`Connect`	When a PivotTable connects to the underlying recordset
`Disconnect`	When a PivotTable disconnects from the underlying recordset
`BeforeQuery`	When a PivotTable is about to get a new data object
`Query`	When the PivotTable receives a new data object
`AfterLayout`	When the PivotChart has already been laid out but before any rendering is done
`BeforeRender`	When the PivotChart is about to paint itself on the screen (before drawing begins)
`AfterRender`	When the object has been rendered in the PivotChart
`AfterFinalRender`	When all the chart objects have been rendered

Form Access Data Project events

A fairly recent addition to Microsoft Access is the ability to create Access Data Projects (ADPs), a special type of database that is specifically designed to connect to SQL Server databases.

CROSS-REF **We discuss ADPs in Chapter 40, where you learn how to create ADPs, connect an ADP to a SQL Server database, and work with database objects managed by SQL Server.**

Access supports several events that are specifically designed to work with ADP databases (see Table 12-6). These events enable Access ADP databases to understand what is happening within SQL Server.

TABLE 12-6

Form ADP Events

Event	When the Event Is Triggered
`BeginBatchEdit`	Fires when a user begins editing a batch in ADPs (form in batch edit mode)
`UndoBatchEdit`	Fires when a user undoes edits in a batch in ADPs (form in batch edit mode)
`BeforeBeginTransaction`	Before a batch transaction begins in ADPs (form in batch edit mode)
`AfterBeginTransaction`	After a batch transaction begins in ADPs (form in batch edit mode)
`BeforeCommitTransaction`	After you request a commit, but before the commit actually takes place in ADPs (form in batch edit mode)
`AfterCommitTransaction`	After a commit has been completed in ADPs (form in batch edit mode)
`RollbackTransaction`	Fires a batch transaction rollback in ADPs (form in batch edit mode)

Control Event Procedures

Controls also raise events. A control's `BeforeUpdate` event fires as soon as focus leaves the control (more precisely, `BeforeUpdate` fires just before the focus leaves the control, allowing you to cancel the event if data validation fails), whereas a form's `BeforeUpdate` does not fire until you move the form to another record.

This means that a control's `BeforeUpdate` is good for validating a single control while the form's `BeforeUpdate` is good for validating multiple controls on the form. The form's `BeforeUpdate` would be a good place to validate that values in two different controls are in agreement with each other (such as a zip code in one text box, and the city in another text box), instead of relying on the `BeforeUpdate` in each of the controls.

Creating event procedures for control events is done exactly the same way you create procedures for form events. You select `[Event Procedure]` in the property sheet for the event; then add VBA code to the event procedure attached to the event. Table 12-7 shows each control event property, the event it recognizes, and how it works. As you review the information in Table 12-7, keep in mind that not every control supports every one of these events.

TABLE 12-7

Control Events

Event	When the Event Is Triggered
`BeforeUpdate`	Before changed data in the control is updated to the table
`AfterUpdate`	After changed data is updated in the control to the data
`Dirty`	When the contents of a form or text of combo box or tab control changes
`Undo`	When the form is returned to a clean state
`Change`	When the contents of a text box or combo box's text changes
`Updated`	When an ActiveX object's data has been modified
`NotInList`	When a value that isn't in the list is entered into a combo box
`Enter`	Before a control receives the focus from another control
`Exit`	Just before the control loses focus to another control
`GotFocus`	When a nonactive or enabled control receives the focus
`LostFocus`	When a control loses the focus
`Click`	When the left mouse button is pressed and released (clicked) on a control
`DblClick`	When the left mouse button is pressed and released (clicked) twice on a control or label
`MouseDown`	When a mouse button is pressed while the pointer is on a control
`MouseMove`	When the mouse pointer is moved over a control
`MouseUp`	When a pressed mouse button is released while the pointer is on a control
`KeyDown`	When any key on the keyboard is pressed when a control has the focus or when the `SendKeys` macro action is used
`KeyPress`	When a key is pressed and released on a control that has the focus or when the `SendKeys` macro action is used
`KeyUp`	When a pressed key is released or immediately after the `SendKeys` macro is used

TIP **When all is said and done, Access supports a very, very rich event model. Not many Access developers master every Access event, nor is there need to. Virtually every Access developer learns and uses the events that are important for the applications they are building, and learns the others as they go. There is no need to worry about memorizing all of these events — instead, just be aware that Access supports many different types of events and that they are there are if you need them.**

Event Order

Sometimes even a fairly simple action on the part of the user raises multiple events in rapid succession. As an example, every time the user presses a key on the keyboard, the following events are raised: `KeyDown`, `KeyPress`, and `KeyUp`. Similarly, pressing the left mouse button fires the `MouseDown` and `MouseUp` events, as well as a `Click` event. It is your prerogative as a VBA developer to decide which events you program in your Access applications.

Events do not occur randomly. Events actually fire in a predictable fashion, depending on which control is raising the event. Sometimes the trickiest aspect of working with events is keeping track of the order in which events occur. It may not be intuitive, for example, that the `Enter` event occurs before the `GotFocus` event (see Table 12-2) or that the `KeyDown` event occurs before the `KeyPress` event (see Table 12-3). In the following sections are the sequence of events for the most frequently encountered form scenarios.

Opening and closing of forms

When a form opens:

> `Open` (form) → `Load` (form) → `Resize` (form) → `Activate` (form) → `Current` (form) → `Enter` (control) → `GotFocus` (control)

When a form closes:

> `Exit` (control) → `LostFocus` (control) → `Unload` (form) → `Deactivate` (form) → `Close` (form)

Changes in focus

When the focus moves from one form to another:

> `Deactivate` (form1) → `Activate` (form2)

When the focus moves to a control on a form:

> `Enter` → `GotFocus`

When the focus leaves a form control:

> `Exit` → `LostFocus`

When the focus moves from one control to another control:

> `Exit` (control1) → `LostFocus` (control1) → `Enter` (control2) → `GotFocus` (control2)

When the focus leaves the record in which data has changed, but before entering the next record:

> `BeforeUpdate` (form) → `AfterUpdate` (form) → `Exit` (control) → `LostFocus` (control) → `Current` (form)

When the focus moves to an existing record in Form view:

`Current` (form) → `BeforeUpdate` (form) → `AfterUpdate` (form) → `Current` (form)

Changes to data

When data is entered or changed in a form control and the focus is moved to another control:

`BeforeUpdate` → `AfterUpdate` → `Exit` → `LostFocus`

When the user presses and releases a key while a form control has the focus:

`KeyDown` → `KeyPress` → `KeyUp`

When text changes in a text box or in the text-box portion of a combo box:

`KeyDown` → `KeyPress` → `Change` → `KeyUp`

After a value is entered in a combo box that isn't in the combo box list and the user attempts to move the focus to another control or record:

`KeyDown` → `KeyPress` → `Change` → `KeyUp` → `NotInList` → `Error`

When data in a control is changed and the user presses Tab to move to the next control:

Control1:

`KeyDown` → `BeforeUpdate` → `AfterUpdate` → `Exit` → `LostFocus`

Control2:

`Enter` → `GotFocus` → `KeyPress` → `KeyUp`

When a form opens and data in a control changes:

`Current` (form) → `Enter` (control) → `GotFocus` (control) → `BeforeUpdate` (control) → `AfterUpdate` (control)

When a record is deleted:

`Delete` → `BeforeDelConfirm` → `AfterDelConfirm`

When the focus moves to a new blank record on a form and a new record is created when the user types in a control:

`Current` (form) → `Enter` (control) → `GotFocus` (control) → `BeforeInsert` (form) → `AfterInsert` (form)

Mouse events

When the user presses and releases (clicks) a mouse button while the mouse pointer is on a form control.

`MouseDown → MouseUp → Click`

When the user moves the focus from one control to another by clicking the second control:

Control1:

`Exit → LostFocus`

Control2:

`Enter → GotFocus → MouseDown → MouseUp → Click`

When the user double-clicks a control other than a command button:

`MouseDown → MouseUp → Click → DblClick → MouseUp`

When the user double-clicks a command button:

`MouseDown → MouseUp → Click → MouseUp → Click`

Writing simple procedures to verify event sequence is quite easy.

Use the preceding information to determine which event should be harnessed in your application. Very often unexpected behavior can be traced to an event procedure attached to an event that occurs too late (or too early!) to capture the information that is needed by the application.

The `Chapter12.accdb` example database includes a form named `frmEventLogger` that prints every event for a command button, a text box, and a toggle button in the Debug window. This form is provided to demonstrate just how many Access events are triggered by minor actions. For instance, clicking the command button one time, then tabbing to the text box and pressing one key on the keyboard fires the following events:

```
cmdButton_MouseDown
cmdButton_MouseUp
cmdButton_Click
cmdButton_KeyDown
cmdButton_Exit
cmdButton_LostFocus
txtText1_Enter
txtText1_GotFocus
```

```
txtText1_KeyPress
txtText1_KeyPress
txtText1_KeyUp
txtText1_KeyDown
txtText1_KeyPress
txtText1_Change
txtText1_KeyUp
```

You'll have to open the Code editor and display the Immediate window to see these events displayed. From anywhere in the Access 2007 environment, press Ctrl+G and the Code editor instantly opens with the Immediate window displayed. Then, Alt+Tab back to the main Access screen, open the form, and click on the various controls and type something into the text box. You'll see a long list of event messages when you use Ctrl+G to return to the Immediate window.

Obviously, this is far more events than you'll ever want to program. Notice that, on the command button, both the `MouseDown` and `MouseUp` events fire before the `Click` event. Also, a `KeyDown` event occurs as the Tab key is pushed, and then the command button's `Exit` event fires before its `LostFocus` event. (The focus, of course, moves off of the command button to the text box as the Tab key is pressed.)

Also notice that the text box raises *two* `KeyPress` events. The first is the `KeyPress` from the Tab button, and the second is the `KeyPress` that occurs as a character on the keyboard is pressed. Although it may seem strange that the Tab key's `KeyPress` event has caught by a text box, it makes sense when you consider what is happening under the surface. The Tab key is a directive to move the focus to the next control in the tab sequence. Access actually moves the focus before passing the `KeyPress` event to the controls on the form. This means that the focus moves to the text box, and the text box receives the `KeyPress` raised by the Tab key.

Clearly, the event Access event model is very rich with events. It is very difficult sometimes to predict exactly which event fires before which other event. Sometimes the only way to understand the event sequence on an Access form is to write simple code that displays each event in the debug window.

Opening a form with an event procedure

Most applications require multiple forms and reports to accomplish the application's business functions. Instead of requiring the users of the application to browse the database container to determine which forms and reports accomplish which tasks, an application generally provides a *switchboard form* to assist users in navigating throughout the application. The switchboard provides a set of command buttons labeled appropriately to suggest the purpose of the form or report it opens. Figure 12-3 shows the switchboard for the Access Auto Auctions application.

FIGURE 12-3

Using a switchboard to navigate throughout the forms and reports of an application.

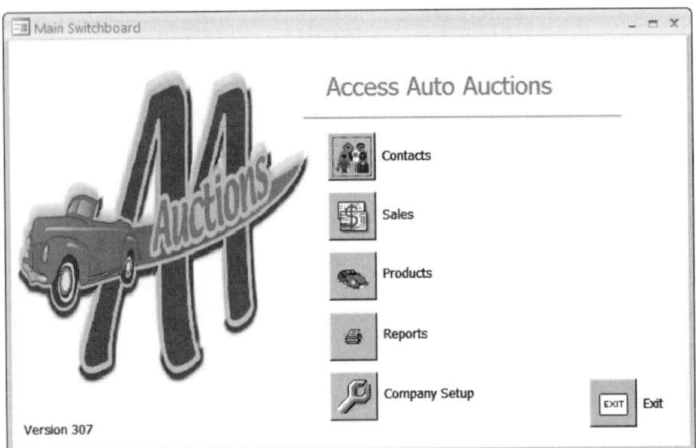

The Access Auto Auctions switchboard includes five command buttons. Each command button runs an event procedure when the command button is clicked. The Products command button, for example, runs the event procedure to open `frmProducts`. Figure 12-4 shows the Properties window for the Product command button, called `cmdProducts`. Figure 12-5 shows the VBA code for the `Click` event of the `cmdProducts` command button.

FIGURE 12-4

Specifying an event procedure for a control event

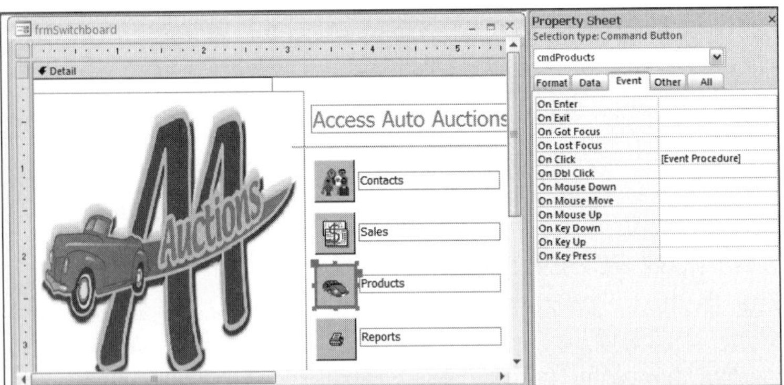

FIGURE 12-5

Using an event procedure to open a form

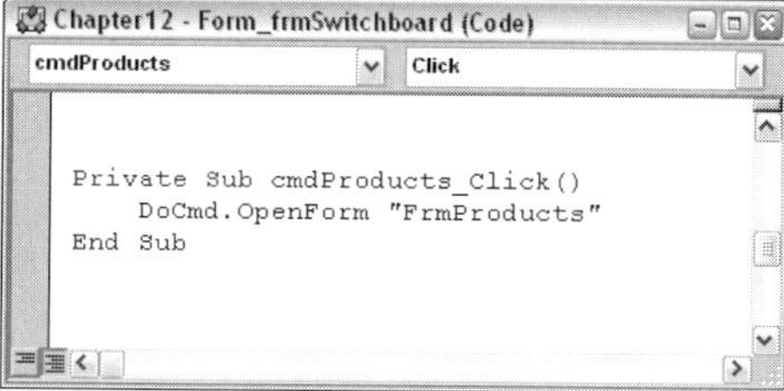
Chapter12 - Form_frmSwitchboard (Code)
cmdProducts
Click
Private Sub cmdProducts_Click()
DoCmd.OpenForm "FrmProducts"
End Sub

Running an event procedure when closing a form

At times, you'll want to perform some action when you close or leave a form. For example, you may want Access to keep an automatic log of the names of everyone using the form, or you may want to close the form's print dialog box automatically every time a user closes the main form.

To automatically close `frmDialogProductPrint` every time `frmProducts` is closed, create an event procedure for `frmProducts Close` event. Figure 12-6 shows the VBA code for `frmProducts Close` event.

FIGURE 12-6

Running an event procedure when a form closes

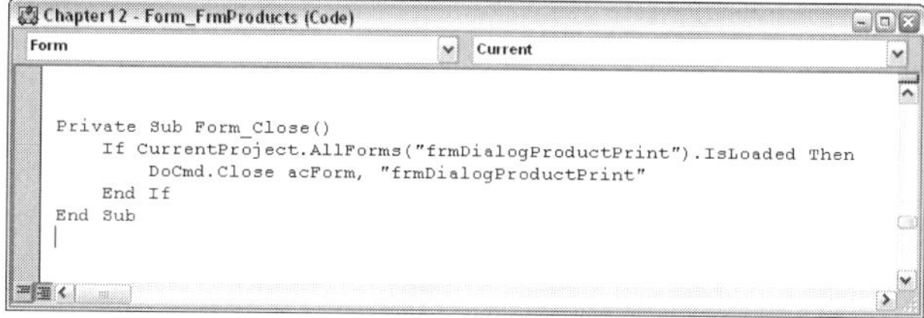
Chapter12 - Form_FrmProducts (Code)
Form
Current
Private Sub Form_Close()
If CurrentProject.AllForms("frmDialogProductPrint").IsLoaded Then
DoCmd.Close acForm, "frmDialogProductPrint"
End If
End Sub

The `Form_Close` event illustrated in Figure 12-6 first checks to see if the form `frmDialogProductPrint` is open. If it is open, the statement to close it executes. Although attempting to close a form that is not currently open does not cause an error, always check to see if an object is available before performing an operation on it (doing so is just good form).

Using an event procedure to confirm record deletion

Although you can use the Access Form View ribbon to delete a record in a form, a better practice is to provide a Delete command button on the form. A Delete button is a more user-friendly method because it provides a more obvious visual cue to the user as to how to delete a record. Additionally, the command button affords more control over the delete process because you can include code to verify the deletion before it is actually processed. Or you may need to perform a referential integrity check to ensure that deleting the record does not cause a connection to the record from some other table in the database to be lost.

Use the `MsgBox()` function to confirm a deletion. `cmdDelete`'s event procedure uses `MsgBox()` to confirm the deletion, as shown in Figure 12-7. For more information on using `MsgBox()`, see the section "Using the `MsgBox()` function," later in this chapter.

FIGURE 12-7

Using the `MsgBox( )` function to confirm a deletion

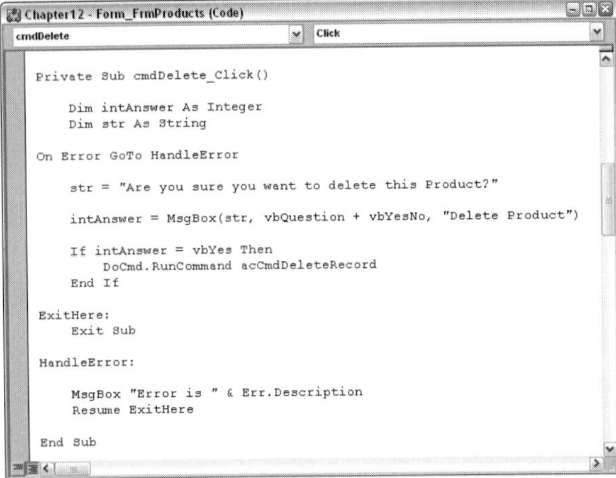

Chapter12 - Form_FrmProducts (Code)
cmdDelete
Click
Private Sub cmdDelete_Click()
Dim intAnswer As Integer
Dim str As String
On Error GoTo HandleError
str = "Are you sure you want to delete this Product?"
intAnswer = MsgBox(str, vbQuestion + vbYesNo, "Delete Product")
If intAnswer = vbYes Then
DoCmd.RunCommand acCmdDeleteRecord
End If
ExitHere:
Exit Sub
HandleError:
MsgBox "Error is " & Err.Description
Resume ExitHere
End Sub

When the `cmdDelete_Click( )` event procedure executes, Access displays a message box prompt, as shown in Figure 12-8. Notice that the message box includes two command buttons: Yes and No. Access displays the prompt and waits for the user to make a selection. The record is deleted only when the user confirms the deletion by clicking the Yes button.

FIGURE 12-8

A confirmation dialog box before deleting a record

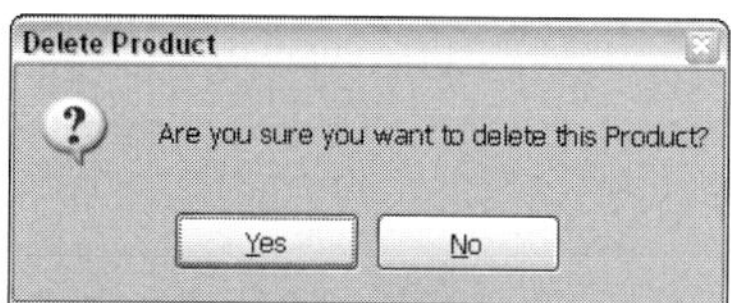
Delete Product
Are you sure you want to delete this Product?
Yes
No

CAUTION Before the `RunCommand acCmdDeleteRecord` statement executes, it first checks to see if deleting the record violates referential integrity rules that you have set up in the Relationships diagram. If a violation occurs, an Access error message displays and the deletion is cancelled.

CROSS-REF See Chapter 3 for more information on setting up referential integrity in a database.

Using the MsgBox() function

`MsgBox()` is a very powerful function that displays a message in a dialog box, waits for a response by the user, and then returns a value based on the user's selection. `MsgBox` has five arguments:

```
MsgBox(prompt[, buttons] [, title] [, helpfile, context])
```

- `prompt`: The text displayed as a question in the prompt.
- `buttons`: Numeric expression controlling the buttons and icons displayed in the message box.
- `title`: The text displayed in the title bar of the prompt.
- `helpfile` and `context`: Displays helpful information when you also include a Help button in the message box.

Only the prompt argument is required. If you don't specify the buttons or title arguments, Access displays only an OK button, no icon, and "Microsoft Access" as the title.

Access offers a wide range of button arguments. The buttons argument is composed of as many as four arguments added together:

- Number and type of buttons
- Icon style
- Default button
- Modality of the message box (that is, if all applications or just Microsoft Access must suspend while waiting for user selection)

The value that you specify for each section of the argument is actually an integer value. But Access provides built-in values, called *intrinsic constants,* so that you don't have to remember the numeric values. Table 12-8 lists the `MessageBox` intrinsic constants, the corresponding integer values, and the buttons each displays.

TABLE 12-8

Message Box Constants

Intrinsic Constant	Value	Description
`vbOKOnly`	0	Display OK button only.
`vbOKCancel`	1	Display OK and Cancel buttons.
`vbAbortRetryIgnore`	2	Display Abort, Retry, and Ignore buttons.
`vbYesNoCancel`	3	Display Yes, No, and Cancel buttons.
`vbYesNo`	4	Display Yes and No buttons.
`vbRetryCancel`	5	Display Retry and Cancel buttons.
`vbCritical`	16	Display Critical Message icon.
`vbQuestion`	32	Display Warning Query icon.
`vbExclamation`	48	Display Warning Message icon.
`vbInformation`	64	Display Information Message icon.
`vbDefaultButton1`	0	First button is default.
`vbDefaultButton2`	256	Second button is default.
`vbDefaultButton3`	512	Third button is default.
`vbDefaultButton4`	768	Fourth button is default.
`vbApplicationModal`	0	Application modal; the user must respond to the message box before continuing work in the current application.
`vbSystemModal`	4096	System modal; all applications are suspended until the user responds to the message box.
`vbMsgBoxHelpButton`	16384	Adds Help button to the message box.
`vbMsgBoxSetForeground`	65536	Specifies the message box window as the foreground window.
`vbMsgBoxRight`	524288	Text is right-aligned.
`vbMsgBoxRtlReading`	1048576	Specifies that text should appear as right-to-left reading on Hebrew and Arabic systems.

Using Table 12-8, specify the buttons argument of the MsgBox() function by specifying one or more of the constants, separating each constant with a + sign. For example, to display the Yes and No buttons, with Yes as the default button, the MsgBox statement looks like this:

```
intAnswer = MsgBox("Are you sure?", vbYesNo + vbDefaultButton1)
```

Adding a question mark icon changes the statement a bit:

```
intAnswer = MsgBox("Are you sure?", _
    vbYesNo + vbDefaultButton1 + vbQuestion)
```

You could use just the summed numeric value, but the statement is much harder to understand:

```
intAnswer = MsgBox("Are you sure?", 36)
```

The whole purpose of intrinsic constants is to make code easier to understand and write.

In addition to displaying the message box with the options you specify, the MsgBox() function also returns a value that indicates which button the user selected. Each button in the message box returns a unique value when selected. Table 12-9 shows each button and the value that MsgBox() returns.

TABLE 12-9

Message Box Return Values

Constant	Value	Description
vbOK	1	OK
vbCancel	2	Cancel
vbAbort	3	Abort
vbRetry	4	Retry
vbIgnore	5	Ignore
vbYes	6	Yes
vbNo	7	No

If the dialog box displays a Cancel button, pressing the Esc key is the same as selecting the Cancel button.

Report Event Procedures

Just as with forms, reports also use event procedures to respond to specific events. Reports respond to events for the overall report itself and at the section level. Individual controls on Access reports do not raise events.

Attaching an event procedure to the report runs code whenever the report opens, closes, or prints. Each section in a report (header, footer, etc.) also includes events that run as the report is formatted or printed.

Several overall report event properties are available. Table 12-10 shows the Access report events. As you can see, the list of report events is very similar to, but much shorter than, the form event list.

TABLE 12-10

Report Events

Event Property	When the Event Is Triggered
`Open`	When the report opens but before printing
`Close`	When the report closes and is removed from the screen
`Activate`	When the report receives the focus and becomes the active window
`Deactivate`	When a different window becomes active
`NoData`	When no data is passed to the report as it opens
`Page`	When the report changes pages
`Error`	When a runtime error is produced in Access

Running an event procedure as a report opens

Opening a report containing no data generally yields erroneous results. The report may display a title and no detail information. Or, it may display `#error` values for missing information. This situation can be a little scary for the user. Use the `NoData` event to avoid confusing the user. `NoData` fires as a report opens and there is no data available in the report's `RecordSource`. Use the `NoData` event procedure to display a message box describing the situation to the user and then cancel the report's opening. Figure 12-9 shows a typical `NoData` event procedure.

FIGURE 12-9

Running a NoData event procedure when there is no data for a report

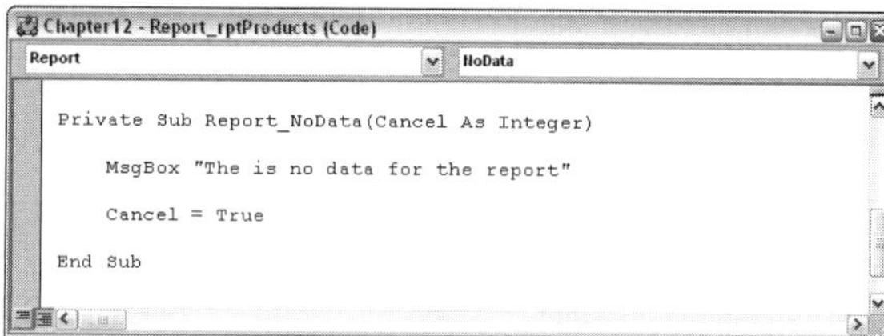

The Report_No Data event illustrated in Figure 12-9 first displays a message box to advise the user that the report contains no data. Then the event procedure cancels the report's opening by setting the Cancel parameter to True. Because the Cancel parameter is set to True, the report never appears on the screen and is never sent to the printer if no data exists for the report.

Many Access events are accompanied by parameters, such as the Cancel parameter you see in Figure 12-9. In this case, setting Cancel to True instructs Access to simply ignore the process that triggered the event. Because NoData was triggered as part of the report's opening process, setting Cancel to True prevents the report from being sent to the printer or being displayed on the screen. You'll see many examples of event property procedure parameters throughout this book.

Report Section Event Procedures

In addition to the event properties for the form itself, Access offers three event properties that you can use for report sections. Table 12-11 shows each property, the event it recognizes, and how it works.

TABLE 12-11

Report Section Events

Event	When the Event Is Triggered
Format	When the section is pre-formatted in memory before being sent to the printer. This is your opportunity to apply special formatting to controls within the section.
Print	As the section is sent to the printer. It is too late to format controls in a report section when the Print event fires.
Retreat	After the Format event but before the Print event; occurs when Access has to back up past other sections on a page to perform multiple formatting passes. Retreat is included in all sections except headers and footers.

Using the Format event

Use the `Format` event to apply special formatting to controls within a section before the section is printed. `Format` is useful, for instance, to hide controls you don't want to print because of some condition in the report's data. The event procedure runs as Access lays out the section in memory, but before the report is sent to the printer.

You can set the `OnFormat` and `OnPrint` event properties for any section of the report. However, `OnRetreat` is not available for the page header or page footer sections.

For example, you may want to hide some data on the form, based on certain conditions. If the condition is met, the event procedure uses the control's `Visible` property to show or hide the control. Figure 12-10 shows the Properties window for the `OnFormat` property of the detail section of the `rptProducts` report. Notice that the bar separating the Detail section from the `ProductID` header is selected so that the `OnFormat` property can be set for the Detail section.

FIGURE 12-10

Specifying an event procedure for a report's Detail section

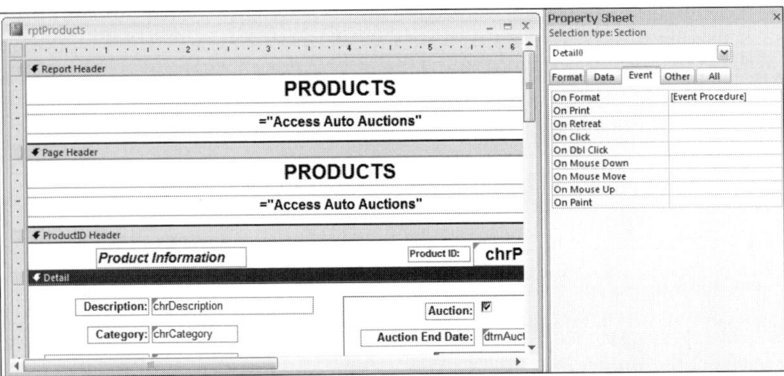

Figure 12-11 shows the VBA code for the Detail section's `Format` event.

FIGURE 12-11

Running an event procedure to display or hide a control on a report

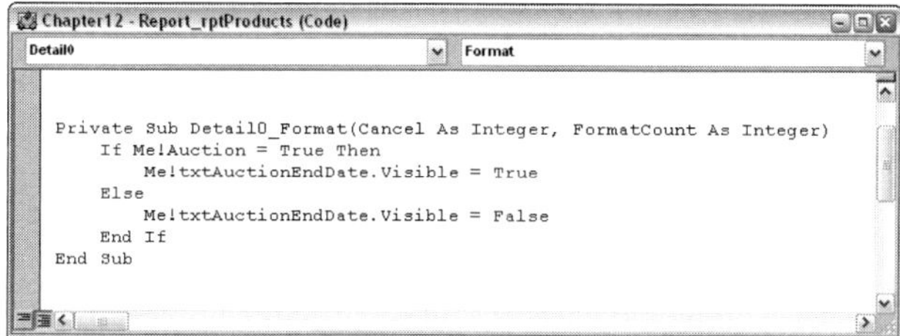
```
Private Sub Detail0_Format(Cancel As Integer, FormatCount As Integer)
    If Me!Auction = True Then
        Me!txtAuctionEndDate.Visible = True
    Else
        Me!txtAuctionEndDate.Visible = False
    End If
End Sub
```

The `Detail0_Format` event illustrated in Figure 12-11 first checks the value of the `Auction` control. If the value of `Auction` is `True`, `txtAuctionEndDate` is displayed; otherwise, `txtAuctionEndDate` is hidden.

You'll see many examples of using events and event procedures to manipulate forms, reports, and controls throughout this book.

Summary

A thorough understanding of the Access event model is an essential skill for serious Access developers. Access is unusually well equipped with events that enable developers to respond to virtually every move made by users. In addition, the data-driven events provide unique and total control over how Access works with and manages data.

The next chapter continues exploring the many uses of the VBA programming language in Access applications. There you'll learn many more details of adding powerful VBA procedures to Access forms and reports.

Chapter 13

Using Expressions in Queries and VBA Code

In this chapter, you gain a more complete understanding of expressions and functions. You have already seen and used expressions and functions in queries and forms in earlier chapters. This chapter focuses on more advanced expressions, and also discusses some of the most common built-in functions of Access. Built-in functions are very powerful in queries, forms, reports, and the VBA editor's Immediate window.

IN THIS CHAPTER

- Building expressions
- Using built-in VBA functions
- Referencing Access objects within expressions
- Using DLookup to look up data quickly

ON the CD-ROM This chapter uses the database named `Chapter13.accdb`. If you have not already copied it onto your machine from the CD, you need to do so now.

Understanding Expressions

Generally speaking, an *expression* is the means used to explain or model something to someone or something. An expression has a value — the expression 2 + 2 has a value of 4. Most expressions you use in Access have a value that is used by an Access application in place of a literal or simple numeric value.

In computer terms, an expression is generally composed of a combination of symbols, operators, numbers, strings, or identifiers that represent a numeric or string value. The expression is a representative object that Access uses to interpret something and, based on that interpretation, to obtain specific information. Simply put, an expression is a term or series of terms controlled by operators. Expressions are a fundamental part of Access operations. They are used to perform a calculation, manipulate characters, or test data.

You use expressions in Access to accomplish a variety of tasks. The same expression may serve as a WHERE clause in a SQL statement, as a filter for a form or report, or in VBA procedure. Expressions establish criteria for a query, or filter, control macros, and perform as arguments in user-defined functions.

Access evaluates an expression each time it is used. An expression used in a form or report is re-evaluated every time the form refreshes (as when changing records) to ensure accuracy of the results. If an expression is used as a criterion in a query, Access evaluates the expression every time the query is executed, thereby ensuring that the criterion reflects changes, additions, or deletions to records since the last execution of the query. If an expression is used in the table design as a validation rule, Access evaluates the expression each time the field's value is modified to determine whether the value is allowed in the field. Expressions used as table validation rules may include references to multiple fields within the table, whereas expressions used as field-level validation rules reference only that field's value.

To give you a better understanding of expressions, consider these examples:

```
= RTrim(LastName) & " " & RTrim(LastName)

= (Price-(Price * tblSalesLineItems.DiscountPercent)) < 25000

Taxable = True

ContactType = "Buyer" And State = "MA"

Sales.SalesDate Between 6/1/2007 And 4/30/2008
```

Each is a valid expression. Access can use them as validation rules, query criteria, calculated controls, control sources, and control-source properties. Some expressions use built-in functions like `RTrim()` in the first example. `RTrim` removes all spaces from the right side of the string passed as an argument (in this example, `LastName` and `FirstName`).

Figure 13-1 shows a query (qrySimpleExpression) that uses a simple expression in the first field of the returned data. Notice that it has concatenated (joined) the `FirstName` and `LastName` fields as a single value named `BuyerFullName`.

Figure 13-1 illustrates a special feature of Access queries. That is, the ability to create columns in the query's returned data that is derived from data in the data sources underlying the query. In this case, the query involves only two tables, and the derived field (BuyerFullName) is generated from two columns in the Contacts table.

FIGURE 13-1

A simple query using an expression. Notice that the expression has a name attached to it: 'Buyer Full Name'.

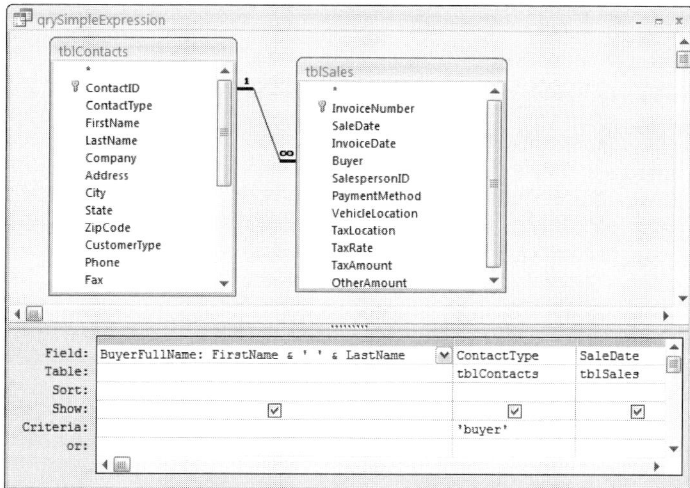

The parts of an expression

As the examples in the preceding section demonstrate, expressions can be simple or complex. Expressions can include a combination of operators, object names, functions, literal values, and constants.

Remembering that expressions don't need to contain all these parts, you should understand each of the following uniquely identifiable portions of an expression:

Operators: `>`, `=`, `*`, `And`, `Or`, `Not`, `Like`, and so on.

Operators indicate what type of action (operation) will be performed on one or more elements of an expression. Generally speaking, operators are either mathematical or Boolean (true/false) in nature.

Object names: `Forms![frmContacts]`, `LastName`, `Price`, `tblProducts.Description`

Object names, also known as *identifiers*, are the actual objects: tables, forms, reports, controls, or fields.

Functions: `Date()`, `DLookUp()`, `DateDiff()`

Functions always return a value. The resulting value can be created by a calculation, a data conversion result, or an evaluation. You can use a built-in Access function or a user-defined function that you create.

> **Literal values:** `100`, `Jan. 1, 2007`, `"Seller"`, `"[A-D]*"`

These are actual values that you supply to the expression. Literal values can be numbers, strings, or dates. Access uses the values exactly as they are entered.

> **Constants:** `Yes`, `No`, `Null`, `True`, `False`

Constants represent values that do not change.

The following example illustrates the parts of an expression:

> `[FollowUpDate] = Date() + 30` where:
>
> `[FollowUpDate]` is an object name or identifier, perhaps the name of a control on a form or a field in a recordset.
>
> = is an operator.
>
> `Date()` is a built-in VBA function.
>
> + is an operator.
>
> `30` is a literal.

Figure 13-2 shows a simple form (frmSimpleExpression) bound to a query named qryContactsAndContactLog. Notice the two data entry controls — Contacted On and Follow-up date. These controls are automatically populated with today's date (Contacted On) and 30 days from now (Follow-up Date). If the user leaves these controls empty when adding a new record, the form automatically adds the default values (today's date, and 30 days from now, respectively).

FIGURE 13-2

Using code that uses expressions to add field values to a record

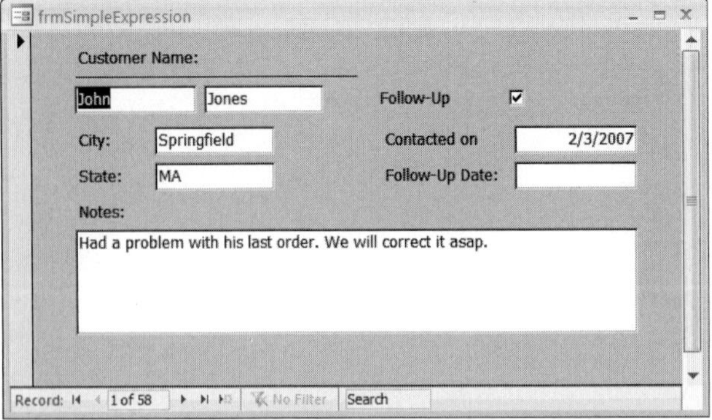

Figure 13-3 shows the code that contains the expressions to check values automatically in the fields in Figure 13-3.

FIGURE 13-3

The code used for updating the fields in Figure 13-2

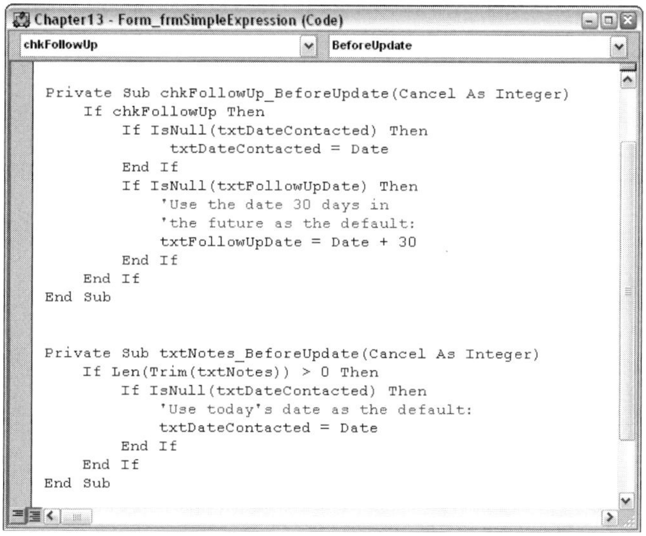

```
Chapter13 - Form_frmSimpleExpression (Code)
chkFollowUp                    BeforeUpdate

Private Sub chkFollowUp_BeforeUpdate(Cancel As Integer)
    If chkFollowUp Then
        If IsNull(txtDateContacted) Then
             txtDateContacted = Date
        End If
        If IsNull(txtFollowUpDate) Then
            'Use the date 30 days in
            'the future as the default:
            txtFollowUpDate = Date + 30
        End If
    End If
End Sub


Private Sub txtNotes_BeforeUpdate(Cancel As Integer)
    If Len(Trim(txtNotes)) > 0 Then
        If IsNull(txtDateContacted) Then
            'Use today's date as the default:
            txtDateContacted = Date
        End If
    End If
End Sub
```

Examining the code in Figure 13-3, you can see many expressions. A couple of them are `chkFollowUp`, `IsNull(txtDateContacted)`, and `IsNDateContacted = Date`. Notice that all three of these use the word `Me` with the field name. `Me` is a keyword that references the current parent object (form, report, or class module). It is only used in Visual Basic for Applications code.

NOTE **This chapter talks a lot about *identifiers* and *names*. Perhaps a little clarification is in order before we go too far in our discussion of expressions. An identifier is a *reference* to an object or to a value. For instance, I may point to a particular car in the parking lot and say, "That is my car." "My car" is an identifier and refers to one and only one car in the parking lot. If I've actually given a name to my car, I may say something like "The name of my car is Pokey." Once I've provided a name for the car, I can refer to it as either "my car" or "Pokey," and you'll know what I mean.**

In Access, you might refer to a form as Forms!frmContacts (the exclamation operator (!) is explained later in this chapter). Forms!frmContacts is an *identifier* that points to a particular form in the application. If instead, you wrote a VBA statement to open the same form, you might write the statement like this:

```
DoCmd.OpenForm "frmContacts"
```

In this case, `frmContacts` is the *name* of the form. It's confusing because you use the same word as an expression and as a name, but the context in which the word is used is important. The general rule is that names are surrounded by quotation marks (") and identifiers may or may not be surrounded by square brackets ([]), as explained later in this chapter.

Creating an expression

Expressions are commonly entered in Property windows, macro action arguments, and query criteria grids. Expressions are often used within VBA statements as well. As you enter an expression into a property box or grid cell, the text in the area shifts to the left so that you can continue to enter the expression. Although it is easy to enter an expression in this manner, it is often desirable to see the entire expression as you enter it. This is especially true when you are working with long, complex expressions. Access has a Zoom box (opened with Shift+F2) that shows even the longest expressions (see Figure 13-4).

FIGURE 13-4

The Zoom box makes it easy to see long expressions.

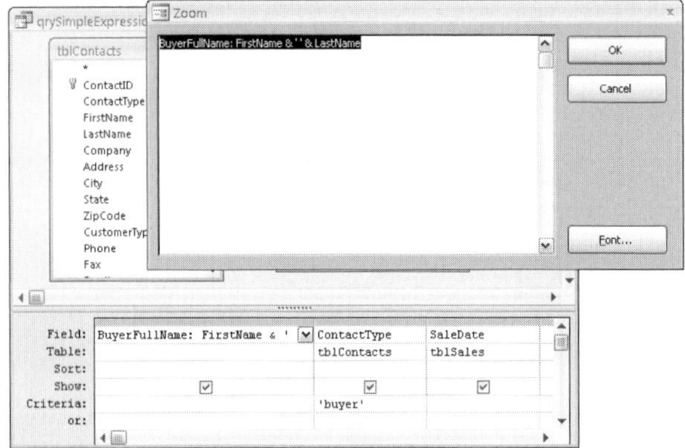

As you enter expressions, Access may insert certain characters for you when you change focus. Access checks your syntax and automatically inserts these characters:

- Brackets ([ ]) around identifiers that have no spaces or punctuation in the name. Brackets are much like quote marks (") and help Access understand the beginning and end of an identifier's name.
- Pound signs (#) around date values.
- Quotation marks (" ") around text that contains no spaces or punctuation in the body.

NOTE **The term *changing focus* refers to the movement of the insertion point out of the location where you are entering the expression, which is accomplished by pressing Tab or by moving the mouse and clicking another area of the screen.**

CAUTION **Access reports an error when it changes focus when Access doesn't understand the date you entered, when the name of the control contains spaces, when a control is not placed in brackets, when an end parenthesis is missing in a function, and on and on.**

Very often you have to manually enter the square brackets, quotation marks, or pound sign delimiters around identifiers to make sure Access understands what you mean.

Entering object names

Object names are identified by placing brackets ([ ]) around the element. Although the brackets are usually optional, Access requires the use of brackets when the object contains a space or punctuation in its name (like a dash). If these conditions are not present, you can ignore the brackets — Access inserts them automatically. The following expressions are syntactically identical:

```
Buyer & [Sales Person ID]
[Buyer] & [Sales Person ID]
```

CAUTION **The field name `SalespersonID` was changed in the previous example to `Sales Person ID`; placing spaces between the names demonstrates how to use brackets around the field name when it contains spaces. The example databases on this book's CD do not use spaces in object names.**

Notice that in both cases the brackets are placed around `Sales Person ID` because this object name contains spaces.

Many Access developers routinely include square brackets around identifier names. Brackets almost never cause problems and may help explain an identifier. Although it isn't necessary to enter brackets around objects such as `Buyer` in the second example, it is good programming practice to always surround object names with brackets for consistency in entry.

Entering text

Quotation marks around an element in an expression identify literal text. Access automatically places the quotation marks for you if you forget to add them (that is, as long as Access can figure out what you mean).

As an example, you can enter `Buyer` and `Both` into separate criteria cells of a query, and Access automatically adds the quotation marks around each of these entries. Access recognizes these as object names and helps you out by adding the quotation marks. Figure 13-5 illustrates how this works. Access automatically added the quotation marks around `Buyer` in the Criteria cell in the ContactType column.

FIGURE 13-5

Access adds the quotation marks around the query's criterion if it can tell what you mean.

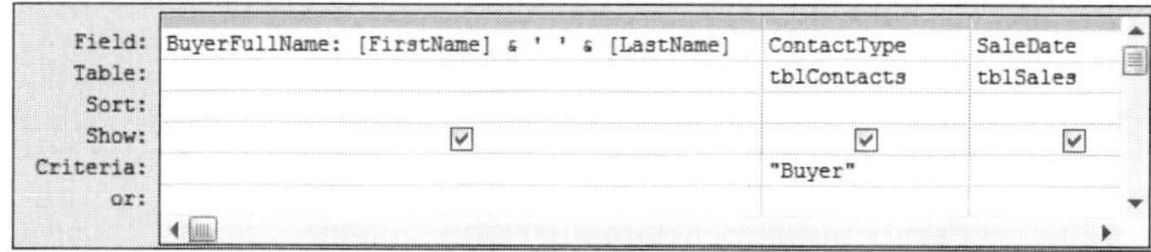

Entering date/time values

Pound signs (#) around a date/time element identify date/time data. Access evaluates valid date/time formats and places the pound signs around the element for you.

All the following expressions are recognized as date/time values by Access, and all mean May 13, 2009 when Windows is set to English (United States) local in Control Panel:

- `#May 13, 2009#`
- `#05/13/2009#`
- `#5-13-09#`
- `#13 May 2009#`
- `#13.May.2009#`

The pound signs are just like quotation marks around literal text or square brackets surrounding simple identifiers. In fact, pound signs are provided to help Access distinguish between mathematical operations (5/13/2009 means 5 divided by 13 divided by 2009) and dates (#5/13/2009# means May 13, 2009).

NOTE **Access's behavior (adding quotation marks, square brackets, and pound signs) can help you verify that you've written expressions correctly. If, for instance, you entered Buyer into the Criteria cell in the ContactType column, and Access did not immediately surround it with quotation marks, you'd know there was a problem. Perhaps the ContactType column isn't really a text data type, or you've entered the value into the wrong column. It's a good idea to let Access do what it does best, and take advantage of the help Access provides.**

Expression Builder

Access has an *Expression Builder* tool to help you build complex expressions. You can use the Expression Builder almost anywhere you can input an expression (such as when creating a calculated field on a form or report). You can activate the builder tool in two ways:

- Press the Build button on the toolbar (the button with the ellipsis on it)
- Click the right mouse button and select Build from the shortcut menu

Figure 13-6 shows the Expression Builder open on the field containing the buyer's first and last names expression. The Expression Builder lets you choose fields from tables, mathematical and string operators, and even Boolean operators like `And` and `Or`. After building an expression, simply click the OK button to place the new expression into the query or other container.

FIGURE 13-6

The Expression Builder provides a simple interface for creating expressions.

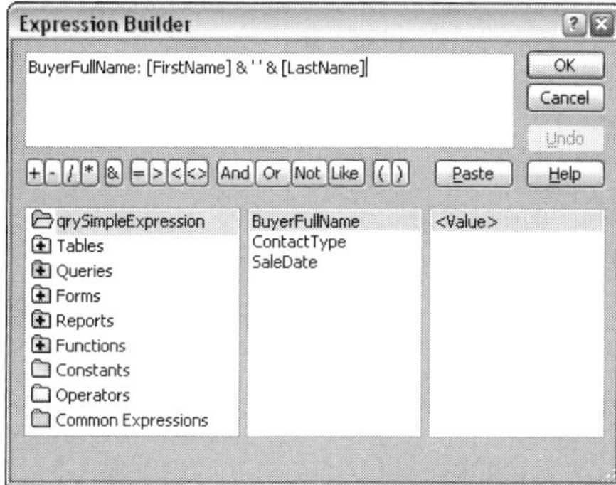

Special identifier operators and expressions

Access has two special *identifier operators*: the period (.) and the exclamation point (!). You'll frequently see these operators used in VBA code, a query's QBE grid, and object's property box, and other places in Access.

The exclamation point (often referred to as *bang*) and period (usually referred to as *dot*) are provided to help Access distinguish between objects, collections of objects, and properties and other attributes. Together, these operators are often referred to as *bang-dot* notation. We'll use tables and fields within tables as our first example of bang-dot notation.

Access tables provide many ways to store and present data. You can use fields and their contents, and field objects can be reused repeatedly. A field is often used in numerous forms and reports, using the same reference (the field name) in each instance.

For example, the SaleDate field in the `tblSales` is used in several different forms. When you want to use the SaleDate field in an expression for a comparison, how do you tell Access exactly which instance of the SaleDate field to use in the expression? It is possible to have several different forms open at the same time in an application. And, of course, there is always the field itself in `tblSales`. Which of these instances of SaleDate should be used in an expression?

With all this repetition, there must be a way to tell Access which SaleDate field object you want the expression to use. That is the purpose of the dot and exclamation point as operator identifiers. These symbols clarify which field to use.

A Few Words about Controls and Properties

When you create a form or report, you place many different objects on the form — fields bound to text boxes, labels, buttons, check boxes, combo boxes, lines, rectangles, and so on.

As you select and place these objects on a form, each object is assigned a control name. Access supplies a default control name according to predefined rules. For example, the name applied to a bound control (like a text box) defaults to the name of the field underlying the control. The field name appears in the text box on the form. The label for the text box is assigned the control name Text, with a sequence number attached to it (for example, Text11 or Text12). The sequence number is added to make each control name unique.

After all objects are placed on the form, you identify each object on the form (line, button, text box, and so on) by its control name. This control name is how you refer to a specific table field (or field on a form).

In most cases you change the default name that Access assigned to the object. The only requirement for the new control name is that it must be unique within the form or report that contains it.

Every object on the form (including the form itself) has associated properties. These are the individual characteristics of each object; as such, they are accessible by a control name. Properties control the appearance of the object (color, size, sunken, alignment, and so forth). They also affect the structure, specifying format, default value, validation rules, and control name. In addition, properties designate the behavior of a control — for instance, whether the field can grow or shrink and whether you can edit it. Behaviors also affect actions specified for the event properties, such as `On Enter` and `On Push`.

The ! (exclamation) operator

The exclamation mark (`!`) is used in conjunction with several reserved words. One such reserved word is `Forms`, which is a reference to the collection of *open* forms in an Access application. You cannot use `Forms` to refer to a form that is not currently open.

When `Forms` is followed by `!` Access is being told that the next object name is the form object that you want to refer to.

Additional keywords can be found in the next section, titled "Special Keywords and Properties."

As an example, say that you have a Description field (Description) that is in two different forms — frmProducts and frmSales, both of which are open on the screen at the same time. You want to refer to the Description field in frmProducts. The way to specify this form is by use of the ! and the `Forms` reserved word:

```
Forms![frmProducts]
```

or, more simply:

```
Forms!frmProducts
```

Now that the form is specified, further refine the expression to reference the `Description` field.

NOTE **Although earlier chapters cover controls and properties, by this point you should have a partial understanding of what properties and controls are (for a refresher, see the preceding sidebar).**

Actually, what you are specifying is a control on the form. That control uses the field you need, which is `Description`. In this case, the control has the same name as the field. Therefore, you refer to this specific control with the following expression:

```
Forms![frmProducts]![Description]
```

The second exclamation mark specifies a control on a form — one identified by the reserved word `Forms`.

NOTE **Strictly speaking, the exclamation mark separates a *collection* (collections are nothing more than aggregates of objects) from an *item* within the collection. In the preceding example, `Forms` is the collection, and `frmProducts` is a single item within the Forms collection.**

By following the properties of each object, starting with the Forms collection, you can trace the control source object back to a field in the original table.

In summary, the exclamation-point separator is always followed by an object name. This object name may be the name of a form, report, field, or other control.

The dot (.) identifier operator

The dot (`.`) is an operator used in expressions. Unlike the `!`, the dot (`.`) usually identifies a property or other attribute of an object. The following expression refers to the `Visible` property of the Description control in the previous example:

```
Forms![frmProducts]![Description].Visible
```

This expression refers to the value of the `Visible` property of the Description control on frmProducts. (You'll recall that the Forms collection refers only to forms that are currently open in the application.)

NOTE **Normally, the dot (`.`) identifier is used to obtain a value that corresponds to a property of an object (`frmProducts.Visible`). It is also used between a table's name and a field within the table: `tblSales.Buyer` and to refer to object methods: `DoCmd.OpenForm`. A method, as you'll recall from earlier chapters, is an action supported by an object.**

A thorough analysis of the two special identifier operators is beyond the scope of this book. Even so, you'll find that these identifiers enable you to create expressions that refer to any object in your Access application, and the values associated with its properties. Whenever you see bangs and dots you'll know that they are nothing more than operators that separate objects, properties, and methods.

NOTE **The word `Forms` has special meaning to Access. It actually refers to a *collection* of form objects. Each time you open a form in an Access application it is added to the Forms collection. There are several ways to refer to an individual form (such as "frmSales") within the Forms collection:**

```
Forms!frmSales.Caption
Forms("frmSales").Caption
Forms.Item("frmSales").Caption
Forms.Item(0).Caption
```

This assumes `frmSales` was the first form opened. Of these different ways (and, there are even more!), most developers choose the first (bang-dot notation: `Forms!frmSales.Caption`) or second (`Forms("frmSales").Caption`) syntax to refer to a form and its properties.

Special keywords and properties

Access uses many special keywords and properties to reference *active* objects. Two have already been referenced earlier in this chapter — the property `Me` used in VBA to reference forms or reports (as in `Me!txtLastName`) and `Forms` used to reference the current active form. Although there are many keywords and properties, the following list includes the most common keywords and properties you will use as references in your events and code for forms and reports:

- `Forms`: The complete collection of open forms in an application — used to specify a specific form. The Syntax is:

  `Forms!frmContacts`

- `Form`: The current active form — used to access an object on a sub form within a specific form. The syntax is:

  `Forms!frmMyForm.mySubFormObject.Form!theControlName`

- `Reports`: The complete collection of open reports in a database — used to specify a specific report. The syntax is:

  `Reports!rptContacts`

- `Screen`: The Screen object is used for the particular form, report, or control that has focus. The Screen object provides many properties to reference objects that currently have the focus. The syntax is:
  - `Screen.ActiveForm`: Used for active form
  - `Screen.ActiveReport`: Used for active report
  - `Screen.ActiveDatasheet`: Used for active datasheet
  - `Screen.ActiveControl`: Used for active control

  Be aware that a reference to a `Screen` property may be invalid if the referenced object (such as `ActiveDatasheet`) is not open on the screen, and does not have focus.

A Quick Review of Events and Properties

Simply put, an *event* is an indication that some action has occurred, or is occurring at this very moment. An event may indicate an action such as opening a form or report, changing data in a record, selecting a button, or closing a form or report. Access recognizes approximately 60 different events in forms, reports, and controls.

Access uses special *event properties* to hook events to objects. Each event has an associated event property. For example, the `OnOpen` event property is associated with a form or report's `Open` event.

To perform some action when the event is triggered, you create a macro or VBA code and associate it with the property (in the previous case, the `OnOpen` event property) through the event property on the object's property sheet. The event procedure runs when the event is raised by the object.

- `Me`: `Me` is a special property that is used to reference the active form, report, or class module. It can only be used in VBA code. The syntax is:
  - `Me!txtLastName`: The same as `Forms!frmContacts.txtLastName`)
  - `Me!txtLastName`: The same as `Screen.ActiveForm.txtLastName`)

As you work with your forms, report, and Visual Basic code, these special keywords and properties will be useful for writing efficient events.

Understanding Functions

Functions are procedures that, by definition, return a value. The value returned can be string, logic, or numeric, depending on the type of function. Access provides hundreds of built-in functions (such as `Date()`) that can be used in tables, queries, forms, and reports. You can also create your own user-defined functions (UDFs) using the Visual Basic for Applications language.

Using functions in Access

Functions perform specialized operations that enhance the utility of Access. Many times, you find yourself using functions as an integral part of Access. The following are examples of the types of tasks that functions can accomplish:

- Provide a default value for a field in a table
- Place the current date and time in a control on a report
- Convert data from one type to another
- Perform financial operations

- Format data in a table's field
- Look up and return a value based on some other value
- Perform an action upon the triggering of an event

Access functions perform financial, mathematical, comparative, and other operations. Functions are used just about everywhere in Access applications — in queries, forms, reports, validation rules, and so forth.

Many Access functions evaluate or convert data from one type to another; others perform an action. Some Access functions require the use of parameters; others operate without them.

NOTE **A *parameter* is a value that you supply to a function. The value can be an object name, a constant, or a quantity. Not all functions require parameters, and not all parameters are required.**

Access functions can be quickly identified because they always end with parentheses. If a function uses parameters, the parameters are placed inside the parentheses immediately after the function name.

Examples of Access functions are as follows:

- `Now()`: Returns the current date and time
- `Rnd()` : Returns a random number
- `DateAdd()`: Returns a date based on an interval added or subtracted from a date
- `Ucase()`: Returns the uppercase representation of a string
- `Format()`: Returns a formatted expression

Types of functions

Access offers several types of functions. They can be placed in the following general categories:

- **Conversion**: Convert one value to another.
- **Date/Time**: Return date and/or time values.
- **Financial**: Perform financial operations (such as NPV) on numeric values.
- **Mathematical**: Perform mathematical operations (SQRT) on numeric values.
- **String manipulation**: Transform, combine, or otherwise manipulate strings.

Immediate window

Microsoft Visual Basic has an *Immediate window* that you can use to test your code or functions. Figure 13-7 shows the Immediate window containing two lines of text — the `UCase()` function and its return value.

FIGURE 13-7

The Immediate window demonstrating the UCase() function.

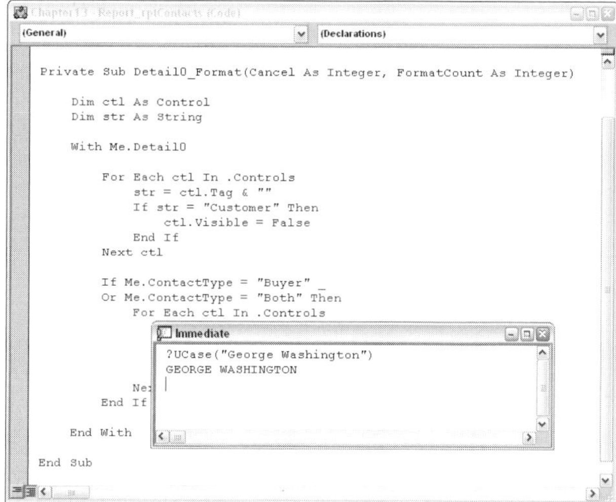

The Immediate window is a nice tool for checking on how a function works.

Activate the VBA editor by pressing Ctrl+G or by right-clicking a module in the Navigation Pane and selecting Design View from the shortcut menu. When you are in the VBA editor, select View ➪ Immediate Window or press `Ctrl+G`. When you are active, use the print command (a question mark: ?) to display the results of a function.

Conversion functions

Conversion functions change the data type from one type to another. A few common functions are listed here:

- `Str()`: Returns a string, converted from a numeric. It always reserves (adds) a leading space for the plus sign:
  - `Str(921.23)` returns `" 921.23"`. A leading space is added as a placeholder for a plus or minus sign.
  - `Str(-123)` returns `"-123"`. No leading space is added and the sign is displayed.
- `LCase()`: Returns a string that is converted to lowercase:
  - `LCase("Woodrow Wilson")` returns `"woodrow wilson"`.
- `UCase()`: Returns a string that is converted to uppercase:
  - `UCase("Abraham Lincoln")` returns `"ABRAHAM LINCOLN"`.

- `Val()`: Returns a numeric value found in a string up to the first non-numeric character in the string:
  - `Val("1234.56")` returns `1234.56`.
  - `Val("10 Farmview 2 Ct")` returns `10`. The 2 is after the first non-numeric character, `F`.
- `CDate()`: Converts a string to a date:
  - `CDate("04 Feb 07")` returns `02/04/2007`.
  - `CDate("February 4, 2007")` returns `02/04/2007`.
- `CSTR()`: Converts a numeric or Date to a string:
  - `CSTR(#Feb 04, 07#)` is converted to `"02/04/2007"`.
  - `CSTR(12345)` is converted to `"12345"`.
- `Format()`: Returns an expression according to the user-specified format:
  - `Format("Next",">")` returns `NEXT`.
  - `Format("123456789","@@@-@@-@@@@")` returns `113-45-6789`.
  - `Format(#12/25/07#,"d-mmmm-yyyy")` returns `25-December-2007`.
  - `Format(Date(), "Long Date")` returns the current date, such as `Wednesday, April 16, 2007`.
  - `Format(Now(), "Long Time")` returns the current time, down to the second: `2:37:58 PM`.

The `Format` function is one of the most powerful ways to display data in a specific format. You provide a format specifier by using keywords or a mask of symbols telling the `Format()` function how to display the data. Figure 13-8 shows a query using two `Format()` functions, both using a keyword — `Long Date` for the date and `Percent` for the discount percent.

FIGURE 13-8

The Format() function used in a query to display data in specific formats

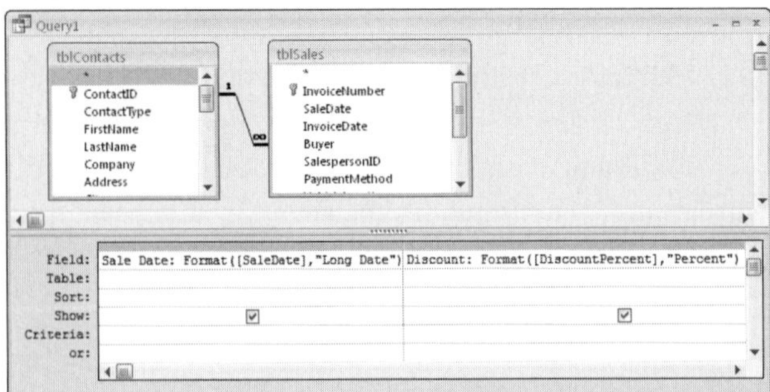

Figure 13-9 shows the resulting datasheet using the `Format()` function for the two fields. Notice that it shows the fields alongside each formatted field.

FIGURE 13-9

The datasheet from the Format() function used in Figure 13-8.

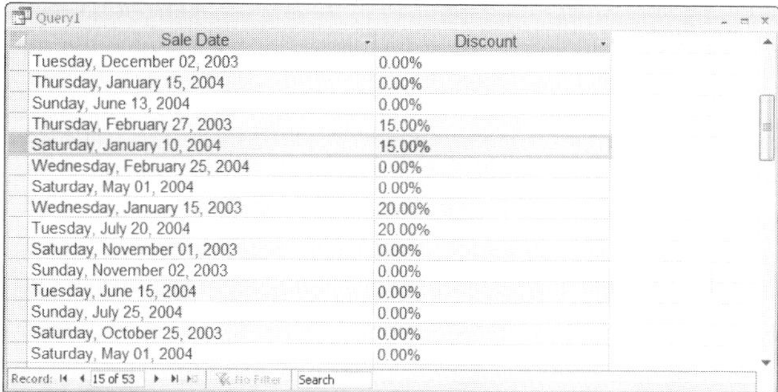

Sale Date	Discount
Tuesday, December 02, 2003	0.00%
Thursday, January 15, 2004	0.00%
Sunday, June 13, 2004	0.00%
Thursday, February 27, 2003	15.00%
Saturday, January 10, 2004	15.00%
Wednesday, February 25, 2004	0.00%
Saturday, May 01, 2004	0.00%
Wednesday, January 15, 2003	20.00%
Tuesday, July 20, 2004	20.00%
Saturday, November 01, 2003	0.00%
Sunday, November 02, 2003	0.00%
Tuesday, June 15, 2004	0.00%
Sunday, July 25, 2004	0.00%
Saturday, October 25, 2003	0.00%
Saturday, May 01, 2004	0.00%

Date/Time functions

Date/Time functions work with date and time expressions. The following are some common Date/Time functions:

- `Now()`: Returns the current date and time: `04/16/2007 12:22:34 PM`.
- `Time()`: Returns the current time in 12-hour format: `12:22:34 PM`.
- `Date()`: Returns the current date (versus `Now()`, which returns date and time): `04/16/2007`.
- `Month()`: Returns a whole number that represents the month portion of a date.
  - `Month(Now())` returns `04` (or today's month number).
- `Day()`: Returns a whole number that represents the day portion of a date.
  - `Day(Date())` returns `16` (or today's day number of the month)
- `Weekday()`: Returns a whole number that represents the day of week for a specific date.
  - `Weekday(Date())` returns `4` (for Wednesday or today's day of week number).
- `Year()`: Returns a whole number that represents the year portion of a date.
  - `Year(Date())` returns `2007` (or today's year).
- `DateDiff()`: Returns a number based on a specific time interval between two different dates. The time interval can be `d` (day), `ww` (weeks), `m` (months), `q` (quarters), `yyyy` (years). The syntax is:
  - `DateDiff("d", Date(), #02/04/92#)` returns `5550` (the number of days) if the current date is April 16, 2007.

  - `DateDiff("yyyy", Date(), #02/04/92#)` returns `15` (the number of years) if
  - `DateDiff("q", Date(), #02/04/92#)` returns `61` (the number of quarters) if the current date is April 16, 2007.
- `DateAdd()`: Returns a new date based on a specific time interval. The time interval can be `d` (day), `ww` (weeks), `m` (months), `q` (quarters), `yyyy` (years). The syntax is:
  - `DateAdd("d",22, Date())` returns `5/8/2007` if the current date is April 16, 2007.
  - `DateAdd("ww", 10, #01/01/2007#)` returns `3/11/2007`.
- `DatePart()`: Returns a number based on a specific time interval for a date. The time interval can be `d` (day), `y` (day of year), `w` (weekday), `ww` (weeks), `m` (months), `q` (quarters), `yyyy` (years). The syntax is:
  - `DatePart("y", Date())` returns `106` if the current date is April 16, 2007.
  - `DatePart("ww", Date())` returns `16` if the current date is April 16, 2007.
  - `DatePart("q", Date())` returns `2` if the current date is April 16, 2007.

Notice that all date manipulations are relative to the regional settings specified in Control Panel. The examples here use the English (United States) regional setting.

Financial (SQL) functions

Financial (SQL) functions perform aggregate financial operations on a set of values. The set of values is contained in a field. The field can be in a form, report, or query. Two common SQL functions are listed below:

- `Avg()`: An example is `Avg([Scores])`.
- `Sum()`: An example is `Sum([Gross Amount] + [Tax] + [Shipping])`.

Financial (monetary) functions

Financial (monetary) functions perform financial operations. Several monetary functions are listed below:

- `DDB()`: Returns the double-declining balance method of depreciation return. The syntax is:

  `DDB(`*`InitialCost, SalvageValue, LifeOfProduct, DepreciationPeriod`*`)`

  where:
  - `InitialCost` is a Double specifying the initial cost of the asset.
  - `SalvageValue` is the value of the asset at the end of its useful life (also a Double).
  - `LifeOfProduct` is an Integer that specifies the length of the useful life of the product (usually months or years).
  - `DepreciationPeriod` is a Double that specifies the period for which the depreciation is calculated.

- `NPV()`: Returns a Double floating-point value representing the net present value of an investment. The syntax of NPV is:

  `NPV(`*`DiscountRate, CashFlowArray()`*`)`

  where:

  - `DiscountRate` is the discount rate (expressed as a Double floating-point number) applied over the length of the period.
  - `CashFlowArray()` is an array of Double floating point numbers representing the cash flow values.

- `FV()`: Returns the future value of an annuity based on periodic, fixed payment and fixed interest rate. The syntax is:

  `FV(`*`Rate, PaymentPeriods, Payment`*` [, `*`PresentValue`*`] [, `*`Type`*`])`

  where:

  - `Rate` is a Double specifying the interest rate paid per period. If the interest rate is specified on an annual basis, but payments are made every month, divide the interest rate by 12 to get the interest rate per month.
  - `PaymentPeriods` is an Integer specifying the total number of payments in the annuity.
  - `Payment` is a Double indicating the payment made each period.
  - `PresentValue` (optional) is a Variant indicating the present value (usually expressed as a lump sum) of the series of payments.
  - `Type` (optional) indicates when the payment is made. A 1 indicates the payment is made at the beginning of each period, while 0 (zero) indicates the payment is made at the end of each period.

- `PV()`: Returns the present value of an annuity based on periodic, fixed payments to be paid in future and fixed interest rate. The syntax is:

  `PV(`*`Rate, PaymentPeriods, Payment`*` [, `*`FutureValue`*`] [, `*`Type`*`])`

  where:

  - `Rate` is a Double specifying the interest rate paid per period. If the interest rate is specified on an annual basis, but payments are made every month, divide the interest rate by 12 to get the interest rate per month.
  - `PaymentPeriods` is an Integer specifying the total number of payments in the annuity.
  - `Payment` is a Double indicating the payment made each period.
  - `FutureValue` (optional) is a Variant indicating the future value after making the last payment.
  - `Type` (optional) indicates when the payment is made. 1 indicates the payment is made at the beginning of each period, while 0 (zero) indicates the payment is made at the end of each period.

- `SYD()`: Returns the sum-of-years depreciation of an asset for a specific period. The syntax is:

  `SYD(CostOfAsset, SalvageValue, LengthOfUsefulLife, Period)`

  where
  - `CostOfAsset` is a Double representing the initial cost of the asset.
  - `SalvageValue` is a Double indicating the value of the asset at the end of its useful life.
  - `LengthOfUsefulLife` is a Double specifying the useful life of the asset (usually months).
  - `Period` is a Double indicating the period for which depreciation is calculated.
- `PMT()`: Returns the payment for an annuity based on periodic, fixed payment and fixed interest rate. The syntax is:

  `PMT(Rate, NumberOfPayments, PresentValue)`

  where:
  - `Rate` is a Double specifying the interest rate per period.
  - `NumberOfPayments` is an Integer indicating how many payments are made over the life of the annuity.
  - `PresentValue` is a Double indicating the present value (as a lump sum) that the series of payments is worth.

  `PMT(.005, 360, -110000)` returns payment amount of 659.51 for a 6 percent loan of 360 months for $110,000 USD.

Mathematical functions

Mathematical functions perform specific calculations. The following are some mathematical functions, with examples of how to use them.

- `Abs()`: Returns the absolute value of a number (the number without a sign):
  - `Abs(-14)` returns `14`.
  - `Abs(14)` results in `14`.
- `Fix()`: Determines the correct integer for a negative number:
  - `Fix(-1234.55)` results in `-1234`.
- `Int()`: Returns the integer of a specific value:
  - `Int(1234.55)` results in `1234`.
  - `Int(-55.1)` results in `-56`.
- `Round()`: Returns a number rounded to the specified number of decimals:
  - `Round(14.245, 2)` results in `14.24`; rounding occurs over `5`.
  - `Round(17.1351, 2)` results in `17.14`, rounding up to `.14`.

- `Rnd()`: Returns a random number:
  - `Rnd()` (with no argument) returns a random number — the next in the sequence of random numbers.
  - `Rnd(-1)` or any negative number returns the same random number every time, using the number as the seed (`-1` in this case).
  - `Rnd(1)` or any positive number returns a random number — the next in the sequence.
- `Sgn()`: Determines the correct sign of a number:
  - `Sgn(-14)` results in `-1` as will any negative number.
  - `Sgn(12)` results in `1` as will any positive number.
  - `Sgn(0)` results in `0`.
- `Sqr()`: Determines the square root of a number:
  - `Sqr(9)` returns `3`.
  - `Sqr(14)` returns `3.742`.

There is another mathematical operator, `MOD` (modulus division), which returns the remainder when one number is divided by another. For example:

- `10 MOD 2` results in an answer of `0` (10 is evenly divisible by 2 with no remainder).
- `10 MOD 3` results in an answer of `1` (10 is divisible by 3, 3 times with a remainder of 1).
- `10 MOD 4` results in an answer of `2` (10 is divisible by 4, 2 times with a remainder of 2).

String manipulation functions

String functions manipulate text-based expressions. Here are some common uses of these functions:

- `InStr()`: Returns a number that represents the first position of one string in another string:
  - `Instr("abcd123efg234", "23")` returns `6`, the start position of 23.
  - `Instr(7, "abcd123efg234", "23")` returns `11` — the 7 in the beginning tells `InStr()` to start after position 7 of the string.
- `Left()`: Returns the leftmost characters of a string:
  - `Left("abcdefg",4)` returns `"abcd"`.
- `Len()`: Returns the length of a string:
  - `Len("abcdefgh")` results in `8`.
- `Lcase()`: Returns the lowercase of the string:
  - `Lcase("Angus Young")` returns `angus young`.

- `LTrim()`: Removes leading spaces from a string:
  - `LTrim(" abcd")` returns `"abcd"`.
- `Mid()`: Returns characters from the middle of a string:
  - `Mid("abcdefgh",3,4)` returns `"cdef"`, starting at position 3 and reading 4 characters.
- `Right()`: Returns the rightmost characters of a string:
  - `Right("abcdefg",4)` returns `"defg"`.
- `RTrim()`: Removes trailing spaces from a string:
  - `RTrim("abcd ")` returns `"abcd"`.
- `Space()`: Inserts the specific number of spaces:
  - `Space(6)` returns six blank spaces.
- `Trim()`: Removes leading and trailing spaces from a string:
  - `Trim(" abcd ")` returns `"abcd"`.

Programming functions

Programming functions are those that don't fit in a specific category, yet are very useful in programming. The following are some programming functions, with examples of how to use them.

- `Choose()`: Returns a value based on an index parameter from a list.
  - `Choose(2, "Slow", "Average", "Fast")` returns `"Average"`.
  - `Choose(3, "A", "B", "C", "D")` returns `"C"`.
- `IsDate()`: Determines whether an expression is a valid date.
  - `IsDate("Feb 29, 2000")` returns `TRUE` because the year 2000 was a leap year.
  - `IsDate("Jup 4, 2007")` returns `FALSE`.
- `IIF()`: Immediate IF (IIF) is used to return either of two parts, based on an evaluation within the function:

```
Function TestIt(TestNum as Integer)
  'If TestNum is larger than 250, returns the word "Greater"
  'If TestNum is less than 250, returns the word "Smaller"
  TestIt = IIF(TestNum > 250, "Greater", "Smaller")
End Function
```

- `IsMissing()`: Determines whether a parameter has been passed to a function:

```
Dim ReturnVal As Integer
ReturnVal = ReturnCheck()

ReturnVal = ReturnCheck(4)

Function ReturnCheck(Optional ABC As Integer)
    If IsMissing(ABC) Then
```

```
        ReturnCheck = NULL
    Else
        ReturnCheck = ABC * 2
    End If
End Function
```

IsMissing is only valid when a parameter has been declared with the Optional keyword.

- IsNull(): Determines whether an expression has no value (no data — Null), returning True or False:
  - IsNull([LastName]) returns False if there is a value in the field or True if no value is present.
- NZ(): Use this function to return a zero, a zero-length string, or another value when a variant is null. The default is a zero-length string.
  - xName = "Mark"
  - ? Nz(xName) results in "Mark".
  - ? Nz(yName) results in "".
  - ? Nz(yName, 0) results in 0.

Domain functions

A *domain* is a set of records contained in a table, a query, or an SQL expression. A query's recordset is an example of a domain. Domain aggregate functions return statistics about a domain. Domain aggregate functions are often used to perform statistical calculations in VBA code. Domain aggregate functions are also used to specify criteria, update values, or even create calculated fields in a query expression.

Several examples of domain functions are listed here:

- DAvg(): Returns the arithmetic mean (average) of a set of values.
  - DAvg("Cost","tblProducts") determines the average cost of vehicles sold. Figure 13-10 shows an example (qryDAvg) using DAvg() to show only vehicles where the cost is greater than or equal to the average of all cars in tblProducts.
- DCount(): Returns the number of records specified.
  - DCount("ProductID","tblProducts", "Category = 'cars'") counts all records in tblProducts whose Category value is 'cars'. The answer should be 25 for the table.
- DFirst(): Returns a random record from a field in a table or query, when you need any value.
  - DFirst("LastName", "tblContacts") returns a random name from the LastName field. DLast() works the same.

- `DLookup()`: Returns the value of a specific field from the specified records.
  - `DLookUp("[Short Name]", "[tblPayType]", "[tblPayType].[PaymentType] = '"&[tblSales].[PaymentMethod]&"'")` finds the short name for all payment types in the query. Figure 13-11 (`qryDLookup`) shows how the query's field will look.
- `DMax()`: Returns the highest value in a range of values.
  - `DMax("Cost","tblProducts")` returns the highest cost ($165,000.00 USD) in `tblProducts`.
- `DMin()`: Returns the lowest value in a range of values.
  - `DMin("Cost","tblProducts")` returns the lowest price cost ($200.00 USD) in `tblProducts`.
- `DSum()`: Returns the sum for a set of records specified.
  - `DSum("Cost","tblProducts", "Category = 'cars'")` sums the `Cost` field in all records where the `Category` is `'cars'`. The answer is $779,356.00 USD.

FIGURE 13-10

Here the `DAvg()` function is used to show only records that are valued greater than or equal to the average of all vehicles.

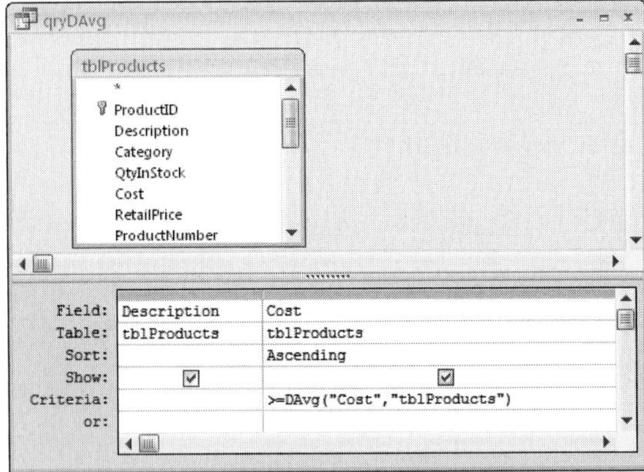

FIGURE 13-11

The DLookUp() function is being used in a query to show values found in a table not included in the query.

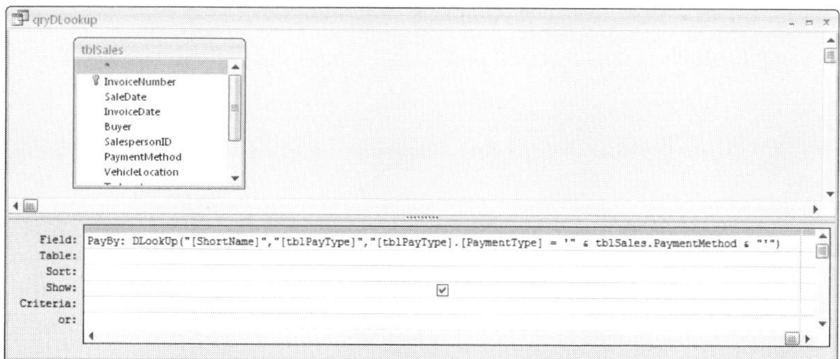

Although VBA code and fancy queries can produce the same results as the domain aggregate functions, using these functions is much easier and much faster than the equivalent code or queries.

Using the DLookUp() function for lookup tables

The DLookUp() function is difficult for people to understand. It is a way to find a specific field value by looking up information based on a condition. As its name implies, DLookUp() looks up information in a table (the domain) that is not currently open.

Although it can be easy to program and works well with small amounts of records, if your tables contain more than 5,000 records, you should probably perform the lookup with VBA code.

DLookUp has the following general syntax:

```
DLookUp("[Field]", "[Table]", "<Criteria>")
```

"[Field]" is the field in the table you want to search. "[Table]" is the table containing the field you want to display. "<Criteria>" specifies criteria used by the lookup function. The Criteria parameter is optional, but if you want to use different criteria for each record, it is essential.

The following simple example returns the address ("108 Thomas Road") from tblContacts where the ContactID is 27:

```
DLookup("Address", "tblContacts", "ContactID = 27")
```

When using DLookUp(), the format of your criteria is critical. Specifying the criteria is no problem when the lookup value is numeric, as in the preceding example. Formulating the criteria becomes much more difficult when working with string values.

The `Criteria` parameter has the following general syntax:

```
"[Field in Table] = '<Example>' "
```

You can replace the equal operator (=) with any Access operator such as > or <>.

`'<Example Data>'` in single quotes is usually a literal, such as 'Cars' or 'AMEX'. An example is:

```
DLookup("Address", "tblContacts", _
  "Company = 'Circle Auto Sales'")
```

In this example, because the name of the company (Circle Auto Sales) is a string, it must be surrounded by single-quotes.

`DLookup` becomes more complex when the `Criteria` value references a text field in a table. In this case, you must reference the table and the field, and let Access extract values from the field during the lookup. An example of a field reference is:

```
tblContacts.Company
```

You have to keep in mind that the field contains a string, so it must be surrounded by quote marks:

```
" & tblContacts.Company & "
```

The ampersands surround the value in the field with quotation marks.

Here comes the really confusing part. You'll recall that the `Criteria` parameter is a string:

```
"Company = 'Some String Value'"
```

In this case, the `Criteria` is a string that contains another string (the value in the field). Because you are using a string contained within a field in another table, you must be sure that the field's value is surrounded by the single quote marks. You saw such an example in Figure 13-11. This query was created by following these steps:

1. **Select `tblSales` in the Query Design window.**
2. **Double-click the SaleDate field in the table, and any other fields you want to look at.**
3. **In an empty field in the QBE pane, type the following:**

```
How Pay: DLookUp("ShortName", "tblPayType", _
  "tblPayType.PaymentType = '" _
  & tblSales.PaymentMethod & "'").
```

"ShortName" is the name of a field in tblPayType.

tblPayType is the domain for the DLookup function. This means you will extract data from tblPayType where the PaymentType field matches the PaymentMethod value in tblSales. In other words, you want to see the ShortName (such as "CHCK") from tblPayType where the PaymentType field value is the same as the PaymentMethod field in tblSales. The Criteria parameter for this example is:

```
"tblPayType.PaymentType = '" & tblSales.PaymentMethod & "'"
```

Notice that the tblSales.PaymentMethod field reference is surrounded by single quotes that are added through concatenation operators (the ampersands). On the left side, the single quote is enclosed within the double quotes containing the first part of the parameter, and the single quote to the right of the field reference is enclosed in two double quotes. The field reference itself is not enclosed in quotes ("tblSales.PaymentMethod") because Access would interpret this reference as a string literal.

The results for qryDLookup are shown in Figure 13-12. Notice that several records have no Payment method name, because these records have not yet been paid.

FIGURE 13-12

The datasheet using the DLookUp() function is used here in a query to show values found in another table.

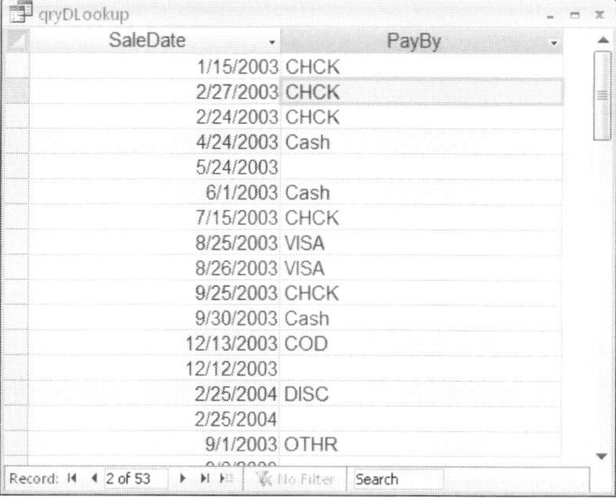

SaleDate	PayBy
1/15/2003	CHCK
2/27/2003	CHCK
2/24/2003	CHCK
4/24/2003	Cash
5/24/2003	
6/1/2003	Cash
7/15/2003	CHCK
8/25/2003	VISA
8/26/2003	VISA
9/25/2003	CHCK
9/30/2003	Cash
12/13/2003	COD
12/12/2003	
2/25/2004	DISC
2/25/2004	
9/1/2003	OTHR

Summary

Expressions are powerful tools you use in many places in Access applications. You use expressions as validation rules, to create fields within queries, as control properties, and embedded within your VBA code.

Access provides many functions that can be combined with identifiers, operators, and other information to build complex expressions. Very often a relatively simple expression replaces numerous lines of VBA code or substitutes for a fairly complex query.

Chapter 14 explains the heart of VBA programming in Access applications. Although many Access database applications are built entirely of bound forms, VBA procedures provide incredibly flexibility when dealing with data. As you'll see in Chapter 14, there is no substitute for manipulating individual records and fields using the ADO (ActiveX Data Objects) and DAO (Data Access Objects) syntaxes.

Chapter 14

Accessing Data with VBA Code

IN THIS CHAPTER

- Viewing and using SQL Statements
- Using ADO
- Updating tables
- Updating a calculated field
- Adding new records
- Deleting records
- Creating code that finds a record by using a form field
- Creating code that uses a bookmark to find a record
- Using a form's filter options
- Using a form to filter records
- Creating a parameter query
- Interfacing a parameter query to a form dialog

Data access and data management are at the core of any database application. Although you can do a fine job building applications with bound forms, using VBA code to access and manipulate data directly provides far greater flexibility than a bound application can. Anything that can be done with bound forms and controls can be done with a bit of VBA code using ADO (ActiveX Data Objects) to retrieve and work with data.

The Visual Basic for Applications (VBA) language offers a full array of powerful commands for manipulating records in a table, providing data for controls on a form, or just about anything else. This chapter provides some in-depth examples of working with procedures that use SQL and ADO to manipulate database data.

ON the CD-ROM In the `Chapter14.accdb` database, you will find a number of forms to use as a starting point and other completed forms to compare to the forms you change in this example. All of the examples in this chapter use modified versions of the `frmProducts` form and `tblProducts`.

Understanding SQL

Many of the VBA procedures that you write for working with Access data utilize Structured Query Language (SQL, usually pronounced "sequel" or "ess-que-ell") statements to retrieve data from a database, add new data to a database, or update records in a database. When you use the Access Query Designer to create a query, Access converts the query's design into a SQL statement. The SQL statement is what Access actually executes when the query runs.

SQL is a standardized language for querying and updating database tables, and it is used by many relational databases. Although Access SQL does not comply with ANSI SQL-92 (the generally-accepted specification for SQL language implementations), Access SQL shares many similarities with all SQL implementations. Your Access SQL statements run with very few changes in SQL Server or many other database systems.

Although forms and reports do have the ability to work with queries that are stored in an Access database, many times you'll find that creating a query on the fly in your code is quicker and easier than working with Access queries. SQL is relatively easy to understand and work with. This is a quick overview of SQL statements and how to create them in Access 2007.

Viewing SQL statements in queries

To view the SQL statement that Access creates while building a query, select View ➪ SQL View from the Access ribbon. Figure 14-1 shows a typical SQL statement that returns the product description, company name, and state for products purchased by contacts in Connecticut or New York.

FIGURE 14-1

A SQL statement in the SQL view window for an Access query

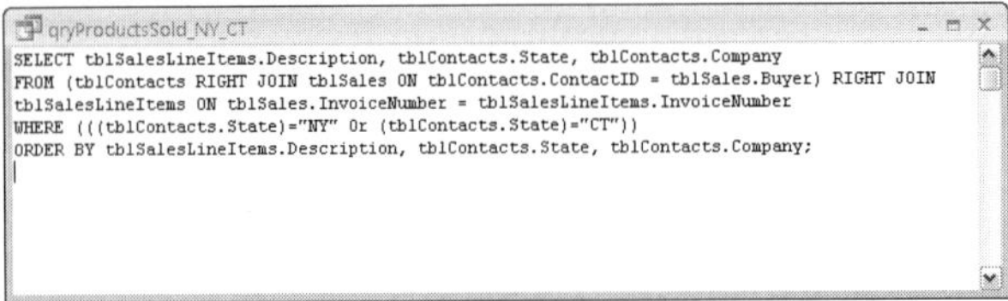

qryProductsSold_NY_CT
SELECT tblSalesLineItems.Description, tblContacts.State, tblContacts.Company
FROM (tblContacts RIGHT JOIN tblSales ON tblContacts.ContactID = tblSales.Buyer) RIGHT JOIN
tblSalesLineItems ON tblSales.InvoiceNumber = tblSalesLineItems.InvoiceNumber
WHERE (((tblContacts.State)="NY" Or (tblContacts.State)="CT"))
ORDER BY tblSalesLineItems.Description, tblContacts.State, tblContacts.Company;

Don't be put off by the apparent complexity of the SQL statement in Figure 14-1. The same query in Design view is shown in Figure 14-2. As you can easily see, the Access Query Designer hides much of the complexity of the underlying SQL statement.

Behind the scenes, as you add tables and choose fields in the Access Query Designer, Access composes a SQL statement that is stored within the database file. Anything you can do in the Query Designer can be expressed using the Access SQL syntax. Opening a query actually instructs Access to retrieve the SQL statement and compose the query view you see in the Query Designer.

You can make changes to the query using either the Design window or the SQL window. As you work with the query, you can alternate between view modes using the View drop-down in the Access ribbon. The changes you make in either view are immediately reflected in the alternative view.

FIGURE 14-2

The same query in Design view

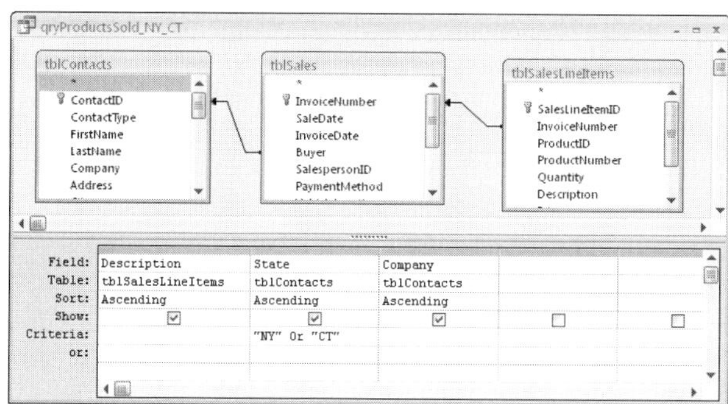

TIP **If you are proficient in creating SQL queries on your own, you can even create a new query directly in the SQL window. To add new lines to the SQL statement, simply press Enter, or add additional SQL text to the existing statement, while working in the SQL View window.**

An SQL primer

As you can see, one way to learn SQL syntax is to build a query in Design view; then view the corresponding SQL statement in the SQL view window. The example in Figure 14-1 utilizes the four most common SQL commands. Table 14-1 shows each command and explains its purpose.

TABLE 14-1

Four Common SQL Keywords

Keyword	Purpose in SQL Statement
`SELECT`	This keyword starts an SQL statement. It is followed by the names of the fields that are selected from the table or tables (if more than one is specified in the `FROM` clause). `SELECT` is a required keyword.
`FROM`	`FROM` is followed by the name(s) of the table(s) containing the fields specified in the `SELECT` command. `FROM` is a required keyword for `SELECT` queries. If more than one table is used you must also specify a `JOIN` type so that Access knows how the data in the tables are related.
`WHERE`	The `WHERE` keyword specifies conditions used to filter (limit) the records that are returned by the `SELECT`. The `WHERE` keyword is optional and is used only when you want to limit the records to a specific group on the basis of the condition.
`ORDER BY`	`ORDER BY` specifies the order in which you want the selected records to be sorted. The `ORDER BY` clause is optional and used when you want records returned in a specific sequence. Without an `ORDER BY` clause, Access returns records in an unpredictable order determined by the database engine (Jet).

Using these four basic keywords, you can build very powerful SQL statements to use in your Access forms and reports. By convention, SQL keywords are entered in all uppercase. This is not a requirement because Jet, the database engine built into Microsoft Access, is case-insensitive by default.

SQL statements may span many, many lines. The Jet database engine doesn't care how long a SQL statement is, or whether it spans multiple lines, as long as the SQL syntax (spaces, commas, and so on) is correct.

The SELECT keyword

The `SELECT` keyword is the first keyword used in two query types: in a select query or a make-table query. `SELECT` specifies the field(s) you want displayed in the result data.

After specifying the keyword `SELECT`, specify the fields you want included and displayed by the query. The general syntax is:

```
SELECT Field_one, Field_two, Field_three [,...]
```

where `Field_one`, `Field_two`, and so on, are replaced with the names of the table fields. Virtually any number of fields may be included in the SELECT statement.

Notice that commas separate each field in the list from the others. For instance use the following `SELECT` clause to specify Company Name and City fields in the `Contacts` table:

```
SELECT [Company Name], City
```

The last field name in the list is not followed by a comma.

The field name Company Name needs square brackets around it because it has a space in the name (see sidebar).

If you need to view fields from more than one table, specify the name of the tables in which to find the fields. The `SELECT` statement would, for example, look like this to select fields from both the `Contacts` and `Sales` tables:

```
SELECT tblContacts.Company, tblContacts.City,
tblSales.SaleDate, tblSales.InvoiceNumber
```

You'll recall that the "dot" between `tblContacts` and `Company` is an operator that indicates that `Company` is contained within `tblContacts`. In this context, the dot does not mean that `Company` is a property or method of `tblContacts`. This is an example of how context determines how Access interprets operators.

When you build a query using the Query Designer, Access automatically includes the table's name before the field name. Actually, the table name is optional. You only specify the table name if more than one table in the SQL statement has fields with exactly the same name. For instance, a field named Invoice Number may appear in both the `Sales` table and `SalesLineItems` tables. If you want to `SELECT` an invoice number field in your SQL statement, you must specify which of these to use — the one in `Sales` or the one in `SalesLineItems`.

Using the Brackets around Field Names

A field name that contains spaces requires the use of brackets. The brackets ([ ]) serve as delimiters to let the SQL parser know you are referring to a specific field. If the field name does not contain spaces, you do not need to use brackets. Access may insert brackets around field names, but they are generally unnecessary unless the field name contains spaces.

The square brackets surround just the field name (`tblMyTable.[My Field Name]`), not the table and field name (`[tblMyTable.My Field Name]`). Think of the square brackets as marking the beginning and end of an identifier.

The following SQL `SELECT` statement illustrates the syntax:

```
SELECT tblContacts.Company, tblContacts.City, _
tblSales.SaleDate, tblSales.InvoiceNumber
```

TIP **Although table names are not required for non-duplicate fields in an SQL statement, it's a good idea to use them for clarity. Anyone viewing your SQL statements will immediately know where each field is found in the database.**

You can use the asterisk wildcard (*) to specify that all fields in a table should be selected. If you're going to select all fields from more than one table, specify the table, a period (.), and the asterisk for each table:

```
SELECT tblContacts.*, tblContacts.*,
tblSales.*, tblSales.*
```

TIP **Generally speaking, it is not a good idea to use the asterisk to select all fields within a table. Your queries are guaranteed to run more slowly than necessary if you routinely extract more data than needed in your queries. By all means, select all of the fields that are necessary to satisfy the user's requirements, but do not make a habit of selecting all columns from all tables. Keep in mind that your queries pull everything specified by the SQL statement, whether or not the data is displayed on the form or report using the query.**

Specifying SELECT predicates

When you create an SQL `SELECT` statement, several *predicates* are available for the `SELECT` clause:

- `ALL`
- `DISTINCT`
- `DISTINCTROW`
- `TOP`

A *predicate* restricts or modifies the number of records returned. A predicate works in conjunction with the `WHERE` clause (actually, in SQL terminology, the `WHERE` condition) of an SQL statement.

The ALL predicate selects all records that meet the WHERE condition specified in the SQL statement. The ALL predicate is included by default. If you do not specify the keyword ALL, all records indicated by the SQL statement are returned by the query.

Use the DISTINCT predicate when you want to omit records that contain duplicate data in the fields specified in the SELECT statement. For instance, if you create a query and want to look at both the company name and the products the customer purchased, without considering the number of products of a single category, the SELECT statement for the query (qryCompaniesCategoriesDistinct) would be as follows:

```
SELECT DISTINCT tblContacts.Company, tblProducts.Category
FROM (tblContacts
INNER JOIN tblSales
ON tblContacts.ContactID = tblSales.Buyer)
INNER JOIN (tblProducts
INNER JOIN tblSalesLineItems
ON tblProducts.ProductID = tblSalesLineItems.ProductID)
ON tblSales.InvoiceNumber = tblSalesLineItems.InvoiceNumber
ORDER BY tblContacts.Company;
```

We'll ignore everything past the first line of this query for the meantime. Notice the DISTINCT clause that follows the SELECT keyword. The addition of the DISTINCT keyword has a profound effect on the records returned by this query.

If a customer (Paul's Best Autos) purchased two minivans — that is, has two minivan records (one 2002 Ford Mini Van and one 1992 Ford Conversion Van) in tblSalesLineItems — only one record with "Minivan" as the category appears in the resultset. Without the DISTINCT keyword, two records with "Minivan" as the category appear in the result set for Paul's Best Autos (see qryCompaniesCategoriesNotDistinct in Chapter14.accdb).

The DISTINCT predicate tells Access to show only one record if the values in the *selected* fields are duplicates (that is, same company name and same product category) — other fields in the underlying records may be different. Even though two different records are in tblSalesLineItems for the customer, only one is shown. DISTINCT eliminates duplicates based on the fields selected by the query.

The DISTINCT predicate is added to an Access query's SQL statement by setting the query's Unique Values property. Right-click in the upper portion of the Access Query Designer, and select Properties. Then, set the Unique Values property to Yes. Access adds the DISTINCT predicate to the SQL statement underlying the query for you.

Records returned by a query that includes the DISTINCT predicate are not updateable. Each record in the result set represents one or more records in the underlying tables, and there is no way for Access to know which records to update. Therefore, the data returned by a DISTINCT query are read-only.

The DISTINCTROW predicate is unique to Access. It works much like DISTINCT, with one big difference: It looks for duplicates on the basis of *all* fields in the table(s) underlying the query, not just the fields selected by the query.

For instance, if a customer has purchased two different product records in tblSalesLineItems, use the predicate DISTINCTROW in this SQL statement:

```
SELECT DISTINCTROW tblContacts.Company, tblProducts.Category
FROM (tblContacts
INNER JOIN tblSales
ON tblContacts.ContactID = tblSales.Buyer)
INNER JOIN (tblProducts
INNER JOIN tblSalesLineItems
ON tblProducts.ProductID = tblSalesLineItems.ProductID)
ON tblSales.InvoiceNumber = tblSalesLineItems.InvoiceNumber
ORDER BY tblContacts.Company;
```

In this example, both product records are displayed. DISTINCTROW looks for duplicates across all of the fields in the tables underlying the query, even if the field is not selected by the query. If any field in the underlying tables is different (in this case, the description field in the products table is different for the Minivan category), both records are displayed in the result set.

Generally speaking, Access queries behave as if DISTINCTROW is always included in the SQL statement. The only time you'll see a query with DISTINCTROW returns different records than a query without DISTINCTROW is when all of the tables underlying the query contain exactly the same records. Because all of the tables in a normalized database includes a primary key that uniquely identifies each row, it is unlikely a DISTINCTROW query will find identical records in tables joined by a query.

The DISTINCTROW predicate is added to a query's SQL statement by setting the query's Unique Records property to Yes. Unique Values (DISTINCT) and Unique Records (DISTINCTROW) are mutually exclusive and both cannot be set to Yes at the same time.

The TOP predicate enables you to restrict the number of records returned to the TOP <number> of values. For instance, the following SELECT statement displays the first five contact records (see qryCustomersTop5Sales in Chapter14.accdb):

```
SELECT TOP 5
Sum(tblSalesLineItems.Quantity*tblSalesLineItems.Price)
AS SaleAmount, tblContacts.Company
FROM (tblContacts
RIGHT JOIN tblSales ON tblContacts.ContactID=tblSales.Buyer)
RIGHT JOIN tblSalesLineItems
ON tblSales.InvoiceNumber=tblSalesLineItems.InvoiceNumber
GROUP BY tblContacts.Company
ORDER BY
Sum(tblSalesLineItems.Quantity*tblSalesLineItems.Price) DESC;
```

You can use the TOP predicate in conjunction with the ORDER BY clause to answer some practical business questions. This example (qryCustomersMostRecentSales) uses the TOP predicate with the ORDER BY clause:

```
SELECT TOP 5 Company FROM tblContacts
ORDER BY LastSalesDate DESC
```

This example returns a list of companies with the five most recent sales dates. In other words, the query lists all the companies and orders them by their last sales date in descending order (so that the most recent sales are at the top of the list), and then picks the first five companies in the ordered list.

The TOP predicate has an optional keyword, PERCENT, that displays the top number of records on the basis of a percentage rather than a number. To see the top two percent of your contacts, you use a SELECT statement like this example ((qryCustomersTop10PercentSales) :

```
SELECT TOP 10 PERCENT Company FROM tblContacts
ORDER BY LastSalesDate DESC
```

The FROM clause of an SQL statement

As the name suggests, the FROM clause specifies the tables (or queries) that contain the fields named in the SELECT statement. The FROM clause is required for SELECT queries. The FROM clause tells SQL where to find the records. If you fail to include a FROM clause in a SELECT statement, you will receive an error. Due to the required use of the FROM clause, some people refer to the SELECT statement as the SELECT . . . FROM statement.

When you're working with one table, the FROM clause simply specifies the table name:

```
SELECT Company, City
FROM tblContacts
```

When you are working with more than one table, you can supply a table expression to the FROM clause to specify how to retrieve data from the multiple tables. The FROM clause is where you set the relationship between two or more tables for the SELECT statement. The table expression can be one of three types:

- INNER JOIN . . . ON
- RIGHT JOIN . . . ON
- LEFT JOIN . . . ON

Use INNER JOIN . . . ON to specify the Access default inner or *equijoin*. To join two tables, you link them using a field that both tables have in common. For instance, the Contacts and Sales tables have a common field that identifies the buyer. To join the sales and contacts tables, the table expression syntax is (see qryInvoicesAndBuyers in Chapter14.accdb):

```
SELECT tblSales.InvoiceDate, tblSales.InvoiceNumber,
tblContacts.Company
FROM tblContacts
INNER JOIN tblSales
ON tblContacts.ContactID = tblSales.Buyer;
```

Notice that the `FROM` clause specifies the tables to use (`tblContacts`). Then the `INNER JOIN` portion of the `FROM` clause specifies the second table to use (`tblSales`). Finally, the `ON` portion of the `FROM` clause specifies which fields (`ContactID` in `tblContacts` and `Buyer` in `tblSales`) are used to join the table.

In the case of an inner join, it really makes no difference which table is specified in the `FROM` clause. Because records are selected only when values exist in both sides of the join (for instance, when `ContactID` 13 in `tblContacts` is joined to `Buyer` 13 in `tblSales`), Access gets data from both tables, regardless of which table is specified in the `FROM` clause.

The `LEFT JOIN` and `RIGHT JOIN` work exactly the same, except that they specify an *outer* join instead of an *inner* join. You use outer joins when you want to return records from a parent table even if the dependent table does not contain any records with matching values specified in the `ON` clause. The following example (`qryContactsAndInoviceNumbers`) shows a query coded as an outer join:

```
SELECT tblContacts.Company, tblSales.InvoiceNumber
FROM tblContacts
LEFT JOIN tblSales
ON tblContacts.ContactID = tblSales.Buyer;
```

In this example, the query includes contacts and the invoice numbers associated with sales placed by the contact.. If the query does not find a match in the `Sales` table, the Company is still shown in the resultset even if the `Sales` table contains no records matching the `ContactID` in the `Contacts` table. The `InvoiceNumber` field is blank when the contact has not yet placed a sale.

If you'd like to see all contacts who haven't placed a sale, add a simple filter to the query's design. In this case (`qryContactsWithNoInoviceNumbers`), the query selects records where the InvoiceNumber is Null:

```
SELECT tblContacts.Company, tblSales.InvoiceNumber
FROM tblContacts
LEFT JOIN tblSales
ON tblContacts.ContactID = tblSales.Buyer
WHERE tblSales.InvoiceNumber IS NULL;
```

In this particular example, there is no reason to include the `InvoiceNumber` as part of the `SELECT` clause because it will be blank (Null) in every record returned by the query. However, `InvoiceNumber` is included to clarify the query's intent.

The WHERE clause of an SQL statement

Use the `WHERE` clause of the SQL statement only when you want to specify a condition. This clause is optional, unlike `SELECT` and `FROM`.

The SQL statement in Figure 14-1 specifies the following `WHERE` clause:

```
WHERE (tblContacts.State="NY") Or (tblContacts.State="CT")
```

The `WHERE` condition can be any valid Boolean (`True` or `False`) expression. It can be an evaluation on a single field, as in the previous example, or a complex expression based on several criteria.

If you use the `WHERE` condition, it must follow the `FROM` clause of the SQL statement.

The ORDER BY clause

Use the `ORDER BY` clause to specify a sort order. It sorts the displayed data by the field(s) you specify after the clause, in ascending or descending order. Using the example in Figure 14-1, the query was sorted by all three of the fields in the `SELECT` clause:

```
ORDER BY tblSalesLineItems.Description, tblContacts.State,
tblContacts.Company;
```

The fields specified in the `ORDER BY` clause do not have to be the same fields specified in the `SELECT` clause. You can sort by any of the fields included in the tables you specify in the `FROM` clause.

Specifying the end of an SQL statement

Because an SQL statement can be as long as 64,000 characters, a way is needed to tell the database language that you've finished creating the statement. End an SQL statement with a semicolon (;).

NOTE **Access is very forgiving about the ending semicolon. If you forget to place one at the end of an SQL statement, Access assumes that it should be there and runs the SQL statement. On the other hand, if you accidentally place a semicolon inside an SQL statement, Access reports an error and attempts to tell you where it occurred.**

When you become proficient at creating SQL statements, you can begin using them to create very powerful programs that retrieve and manipulate data in your applications.

Creating Programs to Update a Table

Updating data in a table by using a form is easy. You simply place controls on the form for the fields of the table that you want to update. For example, Figure 14-3 shows `frmSales`. The controls on the form update data in `tblSales`, `tblSalesLineitems`, and `tblSalesPayments`.

FIGURE 14-3

Using a form to update data in tables

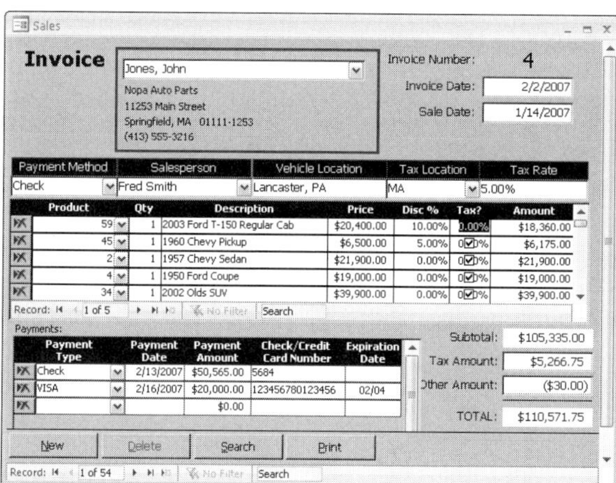

Sometimes, however, you want to update a field in a table that you do not want displayed on the form. When information is entered in the Sales form, for example, the field for the last sales date (`LastSalesDate`) in `tblContacts` should be updated to reflect the most recent date on which the contact purchased a product. When you enter a new sale, the value for the `LastSalesDate` field is the value of the `txtSaleDate` control on the Sales form.

Because the contact's last sales date refers to the control labeled Sale Date on the Sales form, you do not want the user to have to enter it in two places. Theoretically, you could place the `LastSalesDate` field as a calculated field that is updated after the user enters the Sale Date. Displaying this field, however, could be confusing and is irrelevant to the items for the current sale.

The best way to handle updating the `LastSalesDate` field is to use a VBA (Visual Basic for Applications) procedure. You can use VBA procedures to update individual fields in a record, add new records, or delete records.

Updating fields in a record using ADO

To update the `LastSalesDate` field in tblContacts by using a VBA procedure, you use the `After Update` event for the Sales form. The procedure is shown in Figure 14-4.

The `Form_AfterUpdate` procedure for the Sales form updates the LastSalesDate field in `tblContacts`. This procedure uses a special programming language to operate directly on a table in the Access Auto Auctions database.

FIGURE 14-4

Using ADO to update a table.

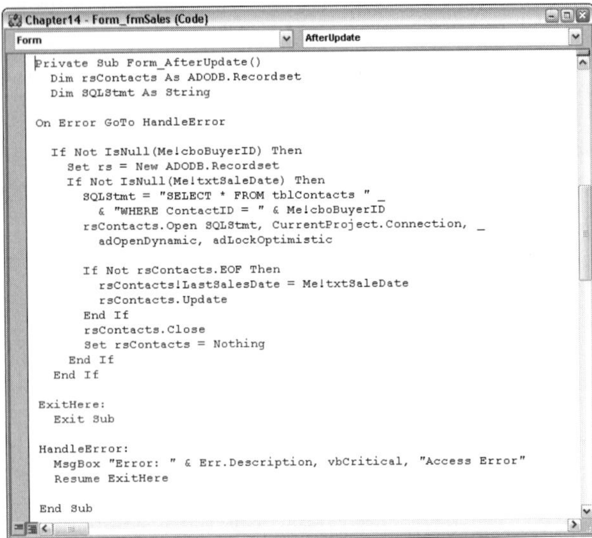

Chapter14 - Form_frmSales (Code)
Form
AfterUpdate
Private Sub Form_AfterUpdate()
Dim rsContacts As ADODB.Recordset
Dim SQLStmt As String
On Error GoTo HandleError
If Not IsNull(Me!cboBuyerID) Then
Set rs = New ADODB.Recordset
If Not IsNull(Me!txtSaleDate) Then
SQLStmt = "SELECT * FROM tblContacts " _
& "WHERE ContactID = " & Me!cboBuyerID
rsContacts.Open SQLStmt, CurrentProject.Connection, _
adOpenDynamic, adLockOptimistic
If Not rsContacts.EOF Then
rsContacts!LastSalesDate = Me!txtSaleDate
rsContacts.Update
End If
rsContacts.Close
Set rsContacts = Nothing
End If
End If
ExitHere:
Exit Sub
HandleError:
MsgBox "Error: " & Err.Description, vbCritical, "Access Error"
Resume ExitHere
End Sub

The programming syntax used to access and manipulate the data in an Access database is called ActiveX Data Objects, or ADO. ADO is a number of different objects, each with a set of properties and methods that enable you to perform a wide variety of data-oriented operations.

ADO is a versatile means of accessing data from various locations. The Access Auto Auctions examples you have seen so far show you how to use Access to update data in a local Access database. That is, all tables, queries, forms, and reports are stored in one Access database located either in a folder on your desktop or on a server. But Access, as a generic database development tool, can interact with all kinds of databases. You can develop forms and reports in one Access database that get their data from another Access database that may be on your local desktop or on a remote file server. You can even link to non-Access server databases like Oracle and SQL Server just as easily as linking to an Access database.

As a data access interface, ADO allows you to write programs to manipulate data in local or remote databases. Using ADO, you can perform database functions including querying, updating, data-type conversion, indexing, locking, validation, and transaction management.

Earlier versions of Access included the Data Access Objects (or DAO) data access interface. Improvements in data access technology have taken Access to new levels as a client-server development tool. ADO represents these improvements and provides a simpler, more powerful array of data access tools.

CAUTION VBA currently supports DAO. However, Microsoft does not plan to provide any future DAO enhancements. All new features will be incorporated only into ADO. You should use ADO for any new development projects. However, because DAO has been used for so long, you will frequently encounter DAO in existing Access applications. Therefore, this book includes examples of both the ADO and DAO syntaxes.

To use ADO properties and methods, you first declare an ADO object variable, instantiate it (create an instance of it), set its properties, and invoke its methods. When you are done with the variable, you should always set it to `Nothing` to remove it from memory. You'll see many examples of these steps throughout this book.

TIP DAO and ADO share some object names. Because both ADO and DAO have a Recordset type, you must precede the variable name with the appropriate class. When you are referring to a DAO recordset, you use the `DAO.Recordset` data type. ADO recordsets are referred to as type `ADODB.Recordset`.

Here is a fragment of a procedure showing how to use the ADO Recordset object to open a table:

```
Dim rs As ADODB.Recordset

Set rs = New ADODB.Recordset

rs.ActiveConnection = CurrentProject.Connection
rs.Source = "tblContacts"
rs.CursorType = adOpenDynamic
rs.LockType = adLockOptimistic

rs.Open
```

The ADO Recordset object provides the `Open` method to retrieve data from a table or query. A recordset is simply a set of records from a database table or the set of records that result from running a query.

The `Open` method has four parameters:

- `Source`: The data source to open. `Source` can be the name of a table (as in this example), the name of a query, or a SQL statement that retrieves records. When referencing a table, the table can be a local or linked table.
- `ActiveConnection`: Refers to a connection to a database. A connection is a communication line into the database. You use `CurrentProject.Connection` to refer to the current Access database.
- `CursorType`: ADO supports a number of different cursor types. A *cursor* is a pointer, or set of pointers, to records. Think of a cursor the way ADO keeps track of records. Depending on the property settings used to retrieve data, ADO cursors can move only *forward* through records (`adOpenForwardOnly`), or permit forward and backward movement (adOpenDynamic). A dynamic cursor (`adOpenDynamic`) allows movement in both directions, while `adOpenForwardOnly` permits only forward movement. The `CursorType` is explained in detail in Table 14-2.

- LockType: Determines how ADO locks records when updating. adLockOptimistic allows other users to work with a record that is locked by the ADO code, while adLockPessimistic completely locks other users out of the record while changes are made to the record's data.

This same ADO statement can be rewritten in a somewhat more condensed fashion:

```
Dim rs As ADODB.Recordset

Set rs = New ADODB.Recordset

rs.Open "tblContacts", CurrentProject.Connection, _
  adOpenDynamic, adLockOptimistic
```

In this example, the recordset properties are set as part of the Open statement. Either syntax is correct, and is completely the choice of the developer.

Here is another simple example extracting a single record, based on a ContactID:

```
Dim rs As ADODB.Recordset

Set rs = New ADODB.Recordset

rs.ActiveConnection = CurrentProject.Connection
rs.Source = _
  "SELECT * FROM tblContacts WHERE ContactID = 17"
rs.CursorType = adOpenDynamic
rs.LockType = adLockOptimistic

rs.Open
```

The SQL statement used to extract records returns a single record, based on the ContactID. In this case, because the LockType property is set to adLockOptimistic, the data in the record can be changed by the user.

Table 14-2 describes the permissible values for the CursorType property.

TABLE 14-2

ADO Cursor Values

ADO Cursor Type	Description
adOpenForwardOnly	You can only scroll forward through records. This improves performance in situations where you do not need to update, but are finding records and printing reports.
adOpenDynamic	Additions, changes, and deletions by other users are visible, and all types of movement through the recordset are allowed.

ADO Cursor Type	Description
adOpenStatic	A static copy of a set of records that you can use to find data or generate reports. Additions, changes, or deletions by other users are not visible.
adOpenKeySet	Returns a set of primary key values pointing to a snapshot of records in underlying tables. This cursor type is useful when data must be updated in the underlying tables, but viewing changes made by other users is not important to the user.

If you don't specify a CursorType or LockType, ADO creates the recordset as an adOpenForwardOnly/adLockReadOnly type recordset by default. This type of recordset is not updatable. If you need to make changes to the data in the recordset, you need an understanding of the various CursorType and LockType combinations and how they affect the capabilities of a recordset.

When you use ActiveX Data objects, you interact with data almost entirely through Recordset objects. Recordsets are composed of rows and columns, just like database tables. Once a recordset has been opened, you can begin working with the values in its rows and columns.

You've seen recordsets many times in this book. The records returned by a query are delivered as a recordset. Actually, when you open an Access table, Access arranges the table's records as a recordset, and presents it in Datasheet view. You never really "see" an Access table — you see only a representation of the table's data as a recordset displayed in Datasheet view.

Opening an updatable recordset — that is, by using the adOpenDynamic or adOpenKeySet cursor type, and specifying the adLockOptimistic lock type — the recordset opens in edit mode.

Before you change data in any of the recordset's fields, however, you need to make sure that you are in the record you want to edit. When a recordset opens, the current record is the first record. If the recordset contains no records, the recordset's EOF property is True.

A runtime error occurs if you attempt to manipulate data in a recordset that contains no records.

To update a field in the current record of the recordset, you simply assign a new value to the field. In Form_AfterUpdate procedure in Figure 14-4, you assign the value of txtSaleDate on the frmSales form to the recordset's LastSaleDate field.

After you change the record, use the recordset's Update method to commit the record to the database. The Update method copies the data from the memory buffer to the recordset, overwriting the original record. The entire record is replaced, not just the updated field(s).

Changes to an ADO recordset are automatically saved when you move to another record or close the recordset. In addition, the edited record is also saved if you close a recordset or end the procedure that declares the recordset or the parent database. However, you should use the Update method for better code readability and maintainability.

To cancel pending changes to a recordset in either ADO, use the record's `CancelUpdate` method. If it is important to undo changes to a record, you must issue the `CancelUpdate` method before moving to another record in an ADO recordset.

The `Close` statement at the end of the `Form_AfterUpdate` procedure closes the recordset. Closing recordsets when you finish using them is good practice. In Figure 14-4 notice also that the Recordset object is explicitly set to nothing (`Set rsContacts = Nothing`) to clear the recordset from memory. Omitting this important step can lead to "memory leaks" because ADO objects tend to persist in memory unless they are explicitly set to `Nothing` and discarded.

Updating a calculated field for a record

In the Sales form example, the `txtTaxAmount` control displays the tax that must be collected at the time of the sale. The tax amount's value is not a simple calculation. The tax amount is determined by the following items:

- The sum of the item amounts purchased that are taxable
- The customer's tax rate that is in effect on the sale date
- The value in `txtOtherAmount` and whether or not the `txtOtherAmount` is a taxable item

When the user changes information for the current sale, any one or all three of these factors can change the tax amount. The tax amount must be recalculated whenever any of the following events occur in the form:

- Adding or updating a line item
- Deleting a line item
- Changing the buyer to another customer
- Changing `txtTaxLocation`
- Changing txtOtherAmount

You use VBA procedures to recalculate the tax amount when any of these events occur.

Recalculating a field when updating or adding a record

Figure 14-5 shows the code for adding or updating a line item on the Sales form.

A single event can handle recalculating the tax amount when new line items are added or when a line item is changed—when an item's price is changed, for example. For both of these events, you can use the subform's `AfterUpdate` event. `AfterUpdate` occurs when a new record is entered or when any value is changed for an existing record.

The `Form_AfterUpdate` procedure for `fsubSalesLineItems` executes when a line item is added to the subform, or when any information is changed in a line item. The `Form_AfterUpdate` procedure recalculates the tax amount field on the Sales form. The dblTaxRate variable holds the customer's tax rate (the value of txtTaxRate on frmSales) and curTaxAmount stores the value returned by the CalcTax() function. CalcTax() calculates the actual tax amount. When the After_Update procedure calls CalcTax(), it passes two parameters: the value of dblTaxRate and the current line item's invoice number (Me.InvoiceNumber). Figure 14-6 shows the CalcTax() function.

FIGURE 14-5

Recalculating a field after a form is updated

Chapter14 - Form_fsubSalesLineitems (Code)

Form | AfterUpdate

```
Private Sub Form_AfterUpdate()

    Dim dblTaxRate As Double
    Dim curTaxAmount As Currency

    dblTaxRate = CDbl(Nz(Forms!frmSales!txtTaxRate, 0))

    curTaxAmount = CalcTax(dblTaxRate, Me.InvoiceNumber)

    If Forms!frmSales!chkOtherTaxable = True Then

        curTaxAmount = curTaxAmount _
          + (Nz(Forms!frmSales!txtOtherAmount, 0) * dblTaxRate)

    End If

    Forms!frmSales!txtTaxAmount = curTaxAmount

End Sub
```

FIGURE 14-6

Using ADO to recalculate a total field

Chapter14 - basSalesFunctions (Code)

(General) | CalcTax

```
Public Function CalcTax( _
    dblTaxPercent As Double, _
    lngInvoiceNum As Long) As Currency

    Dim cnn As Connection
    Dim objLineitems As ADODB.Recordset
    Dim strSQL As String

    strSQL = "SELECT Sum(CalcExtension(Nz([Quantity],0), " _
        & "Nz([Price],0), Nz([DiscountPercent],0))) AS TaxableAmount " _
        & "FROM tblSalesLineItems " _
        & "WHERE [Taxable] = True " _
        & "AND [InvoiceNumber] = " & lngInvoiceNum

    Set cnn = CurrentProject.Connection

    Set objLineitems = New ADODB.Recordset

    objLineitems.Open strSQL, cnn, adOpenForwardOnly

    CalcTax = 0

    If Not objLineitems.EOF Then
        CalcTax = Nz(objLineitems!TaxableAmount, 0) * dblTaxPercent
    End If

    objLineitems.Close

    Set objLineitems = Nothing

End Function
```

CalcTax uses ADO to create a recordset that sums the quantities and prices for the taxable items in tblSalesLineItems for the current sale. The function receives two parameters: the tax rate (dblTaxPercent) and the invoice number (lngInvoiceNum). The function's return value is initially set to 0 (zero) at the top of the function. The ADO code checks to see if the recordset returned a record. If the recordset is at the end of the field (EOF), the recordset did not find any line items for the current sale — and CalcTax remains set to 0. If the recordset does contain a record, the return value for CalcTax is set to the recordset's TaxableAmount field times the tax rate (dblTaxPercent).

When the Form_AfterUpdate procedure receives the result of the CalcTax() function, it continues to the next statement in the procedure. The next statement in Form_AfterUpdate checks to see if the Sales form's other taxable control (chkOtherTaxable) is True. If chkOtherTaxable is True, the procedure must also calculate tax on the Other Amount control. The calculation for the tax on Other Amount simply multiplies the value txtOtherAmount) by the tax rate (dblTaxRate) and adds this result to the curTaxAmount value returned by CalcTax().

At the end of the procedure, the txtTaxAmount is set to the curTaxAmount value.

When the Buyer, Tax Location, or Tax Rate controls are changed in the Sales form, you use the AfterUpdate event for the individual control to recalculate the tax amount. Figure 14-7 shows the code for the txtTaxRate_AfterUpdate event.

FIGURE 14-7

Recalculating a control after a control is updated

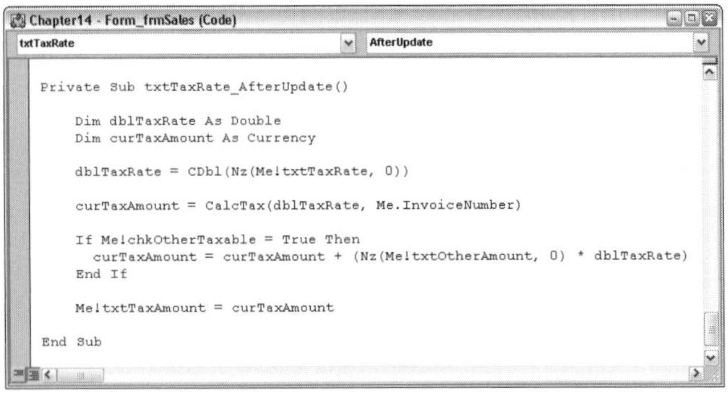

Chapter14 - Form_frmSales (Code)

txtTaxRate | AfterUpdate

```
Private Sub txtTaxRate_AfterUpdate()

    Dim dblTaxRate As Double
    Dim curTaxAmount As Currency

    dblTaxRate = CDbl(Nz(Me!txtTaxRate, 0))

    curTaxAmount = CalcTax(dblTaxRate, Me.InvoiceNumber)

    If Me!chkOtherTaxable = True Then
      curTaxAmount = curTaxAmount + (Nz(Me!txtOtherAmount, 0) * dblTaxRate)
    End If

    Me!txtTaxAmount = curTaxAmount

End Sub
```

The logic implemented in txtTaxRate_AfterUpdate is identical to the logic in fsubSalesLineItems_AfterUpdate. In fact, you can use the same code for the Buyer and Tax Location controls as well. The only difference between the code in Figures 14-5 and 14-7 is that the procedure in Figure 14-5 runs whenever a change occurs in the sales line items subform, while the code in Figure 14-7 runs whenever a change is made to txtTaxRate on the main form.

Checking the status of a record deletion

Use the form's `AfterDelConfirm` event to recalculate the txtTaxAmount control when deleting a line item. The form's `AfterDelConfirm` event (shown in Figure 14-8) is similar to the code for the subform's `AfterUpdate` event.

FIGURE 14-8

Recalculating a control after a record is deleted

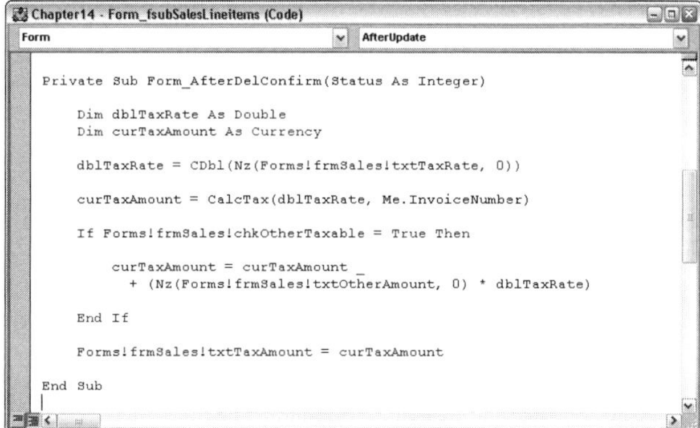


```
Private Sub Form_AfterDelConfirm(Status As Integer)

    Dim dblTaxRate As Double
    Dim curTaxAmount As Currency

    dblTaxRate = CDbl(Nz(Forms!frmSales!txtTaxRate, 0))

    curTaxAmount = CalcTax(dblTaxRate, Me.InvoiceNumber)

    If Forms!frmSales!chkOtherTaxable = True Then

        curTaxAmount = curTaxAmount _
          + (Nz(Forms!frmSales!txtOtherAmount, 0) * dblTaxRate)

    End If

    Forms!frmSales!txtTaxAmount = curTaxAmount

End Sub
```

Access always confirms deletions initiated by the user. Access displays a message box asking the user to confirm the deletion. If the user affirms the deletion, the current record is removed from the form's recordset and temporarily stored in memory so that the deletion can be undone if necessary. The `AfterDelConfirm` event occurs after the user confirms or cancels the deletion. If the `BeforeDelConfirm` event isn't canceled, the `AfterDelConfirm` event occurs after the delete confirmation dialog box is displayed. The `AfterDelConfirm` event occurs even if the `BeforeDelConfirm` event is canceled.

The `AfterDelConfirm` event procedure returns status information about the deletion. Table 14-3 describes the deletion status values.

TABLE 14-3

Deletion Status Values

Status value	Description
`acDeleteOK`	Deletion occurred normally
`acDeleteCancel`	Deletion canceled programmatically
`acDeleteUserCancel`	User canceled deletion

The Status argument for the `AfterDelConfirm` event procedure can be set to any of these values within the procedure. For instance, if the code in the `AfterDelConfirm` event procedure determines that deleting the record may cause problems elsewhere in the application, the Status argument should be set to `acDeleteCancel`:

```
If <Condition Indicates a Problem Elsewhere> Then
  Status = acDeleteCancel
  Exit Sub
Else
  Status = acDeleteOK
End If
```

The `Status` argument is provided to enable your VBA code to override the user's decision to delete a record if conditions warrant such an override. In the case that `Status` is set to `acDeleteCancel`, the copy of the record stored in the temporary buffer is restored to the recordset, and the delete process is aborted. If, on the other hand, `Status` is set to `acDeleteOK`, the deletion proceeds and the temporary buffer is cleared after the user moves to another record in the recordset.

Adding a new record

You can use ADO to add a record to a table just as easily as you can to update a record. Use the `AddNew` method to add a new record to a table. The following shows the ADO procedure for adding a new customer to the `Customer` table:

```
Private Sub New_Contact_Click()

  Dim rs As ADODB.Recordset

On Error GoTo HandleError

  Set rs = New ADODB.Recordset

  rs.Open "tblContacts", CurrentProject.Connection, _
    adOpenDynamic, adLockOptimistic

  With rs

    'Add new record to end of Recordset:
    .AddNew

    'Add data:
    ![LastName] = "Townshend"
    ![LastName] = "Charles"

    'Commit the changes:
    .Update
  End With
```

```
  rs.Close
  Set rs = Nothing

ExitHere:

  Exit Sub

HandleError:

  MsgBox Err.Description
  Resume ExitHere

End Sub
```

As you see in this example, using the `AddNew` method is similar to using ADO to edit recordset data. The `AddNew` method creates a buffer for a new record. After entering the `AddNew` command, you simply assign values to fields in the recordset. The recordset object's `Update` method adds the new record buffer to the end of the recordset, and to the underlying table.

Deleting a record

To remove a record from a table, you use the ADO method Delete. The following code shows the ADO procedure for deleting a record from `tblContacts`.

```
Private Sub Delete_Contact_Click()

  Dim rs As ADODB.Recordset
  Dim strSQL as string

On Error GoTo HandleError

  Set rs = New ADODB.Recordset

  strSQL = "SELECT * FROM tblContacts " _
    & "WHERE [ContactID] = " _
    & Me![txtContactID]

  rs.Open strSQL, CurrentProject.Connection, _
    adOpenDynamic, & adLockOptimistic

  With rs
    If not .EOF Then
      'Delete the record:
      .Delete
    End If
  End With

ExitHere:
```

```
    rs.Close
    Set rs = Nothing
    Exit Sub

  HandleError:

    MsgBox Err.Description
    Resume ExitHere

  End Sub
```

Notice that you do not follow the `Delete` method with `Update`. As soon as the `Delete` method executes, the record is removed from the recordset permanently.

Deleting records using ADO does not trigger the deletion confirmation dialog box. Generally speaking, changes made to data with ADO code are not confirmed because confirmation would interrupt the user's workflow.

Deleting related records in multiple tables

When you write ADO code to delete records, you need to be aware of the application's relationships. The table containing the record you are deleting may be participating in a one-to-many relationship with another table.

Take a look at the relationships diagram (see Figure 14-9) for the tables used in the Sales form example. `tblSales` has two dependent tables associated with it: `tblSalesLineItems` and `tblSalesPayments`.

FIGURE 14-9

Examining the tables of a one-to-many relationship

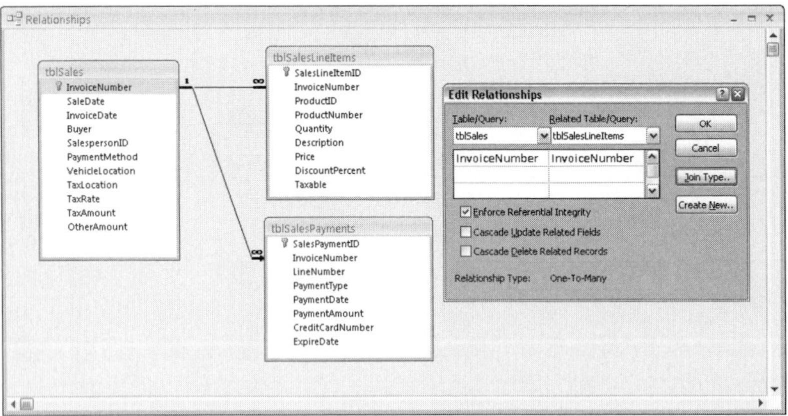

The Edit Relationships dialog box shows how the relationship is set up between the tables `tblSales` and `tblSalesLineItems`. The relationship type is a one-to-many (1:M) and referential integrity is enforced. A one-to-many relationship means that the parent table (`tblSales`), has a dependent table (`tblSalesLineItems`); whereas `tblSales` can contain only unique instances of the values in its primary key (`InvoiceNumber`), `tblSalesLineItems` may contain several records in the corresponding foreign key fields (`InvoiceNumber`) with the same value. This simply means that each `InvoiceNumber` may have many different sales line items associated with it.

When you enforce referential integrity on a one-to-many relationship, you are telling Access that a record in `tblSales` *cannot* be deleted if records with the same invoice number value exist in `tblSalesLineItems`. If Access encounters a delete request that violates referential integrity, Access displays an error message and the delete will be cancelled.

When you write ADO code to delete a record, you need to first check to see if there are any one-to-many relationships between the table containing the record to delete and any other tables in the database. If there are dependent tables, the records in the dependent tables need to be deleted before Access allows you to delete the record in the parent table.

Fortunately, you can write a single procedure using ADO code to delete records in both the dependent table or tables and the parent table. Figure 14-10 shows the code for the `cmdDelete` command button in the `frmSales` form.

FIGURE 14-10

Using ADO code to delete multiple records

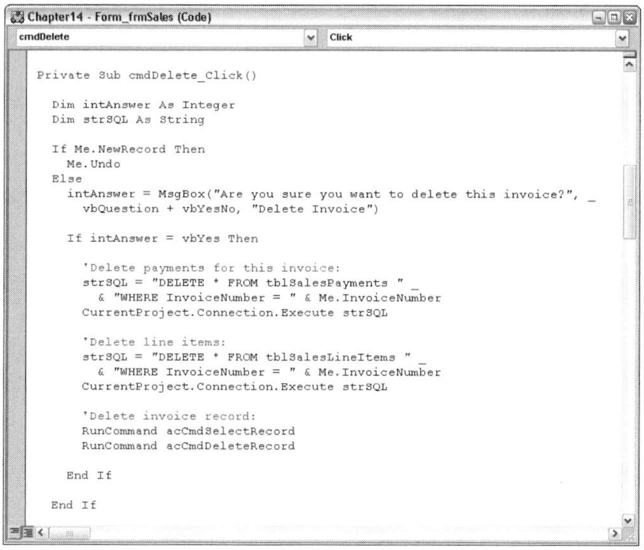

Chapter14 - Form_frmSales (Code)

cmdDelete | Click

```
Private Sub cmdDelete_Click()

  Dim intAnswer As Integer
  Dim strSQL As String

  If Me.NewRecord Then
    Me.Undo
  Else
    intAnswer = MsgBox("Are you sure you want to delete this invoice?", _
      vbQuestion + vbYesNo, "Delete Invoice")

    If intAnswer = vbYes Then

      'Delete payments for this invoice:
      strSQL = "DELETE * FROM tblSalesPayments " _
        & "WHERE InvoiceNumber = " & Me.InvoiceNumber
      CurrentProject.Connection.Execute strSQL

      'Delete line items:
      strSQL = "DELETE * FROM tblSalesLineItems " _
        & "WHERE InvoiceNumber = " & Me.InvoiceNumber
      CurrentProject.Connection.Execute strSQL

      'Delete invoice record:
      RunCommand acCmdSelectRecord
      RunCommand acCmdDeleteRecord

    End If

  End If
```

The cmdDelete_Click event procedure deletes records in tblSalesPayments, tblSalesLineItems, and tblSales that have an invoice number matching the current invoice number.

The first statement in cmdDelete_Click uses the NewRecord property to check to see if the current Sales form record is new. If the record is a new record, Me.Undo rolls back changes to the record. If the current record is not new, the procedure displays a message box to confirm that the user really wants to delete the record. If the user clicks the Yes button, the procedure deletes the records from the tables.

strSQL holds a SQL statement for locating and deleting records in tblSalesPayments with an invoice number that matches the invoice number on the Sales form. strSQL is passed as a parameter to the Execute method of the current project's (CurrentProject) connection. You can pass either the name of a query or an SQL statement as a parameter to the Execute method. The Execute method simply runs the specified query or SQL statement.

NOTE **If the query or SQL statement contains a WHERE clause and the Execute method does not find any records that meet the WHERE condition, no error occurs. If the query or SQL statement contains invalid syntax or an invalid field or table name, however, the Execute method fails and an error is raised.**

The same process is used to delete records in tblSalesLineItems.

After the tblSalesLineItems records are deleted, the tblSales record can then be deleted. The following listing shows the cmdDelete_Click procedure from frmSales in Chapter14.accdb:

```
Private Sub cmdDelete_Click()

  Dim intAnswer As Integer
  Dim strSQL As String

  If Me.NewRecord Then
    Me.Undo
    Exit Sub
  End If

  intAnswer = MsgBox("Are you sure you want to " _
    & " delete this invoice?", vbQuestion + vbYesNo, _
    "Delete Invoice")

  If intAnswer = vbNo Then
    Exit Sub
  End If

  'Delete payments for this invoice:
  strSQL = "DELETE * FROM tblSalesPayments " _
    & "WHERE InvoiceNumber = " & Me.InvoiceNumber
```

```
    CurrentProject.Connection.Execute strSQL

    'Delete line items:
    strSQL = "DELETE * FROM tblSalesLineItems " _
      & "WHERE InvoiceNumber = " & Me.InvoiceNumber
    CurrentProject.Connection.Execute strSQL

    'Delete invoice record:
    RunCommand acCmdSelectRecord
    RunCommand acCmdDeleteRecord

End Sub
```

Notice that this procedure includes two different `Exit Sub` statements. The first is executed if the current record happens to be a new record. Presumably, there is no reason to delete a new record, and, in fact, an attempt to delete a new record raises an error.

The second `Exit Sub` executes if the user chooses not to delete the record (the `MsgBox` function returns `vbNo`, in this case) after clicking the Delete button. If the user confirms the deletion (the value of `MsgBox`, in this case, is `vbYes`) , the code proceeds to delete the invoice records matching the current InvoiceNumber, then deletes the current record displayed on `frmSales`.

Summary

In the previous few chapters, you learned the basics of programming, reviewed some of the built-in functions, and experienced the various logical constructs. You learned about ADO and how to access data in tables and queries through SQL recordsets. You also learned a lot about forms and queries in previous chapters. In this chapter, you use all of this knowledge and learn how to display selected data in forms or reports using a combination of techniques involving forms, VBA code, and queries.

You'll see many other examples that use ADO (and DAO) to manipulate data in Access tables and recordsets throughout this book. A little bit of VBA code, coupled with either the ADO or DAO syntax, is able to perform complex operations without the use of queries or other database objects. Whenever possible the examples in this book are written in a generic fashion that is easily modified to fit other situations by replacing the names of fields, tables, and other objects. You should use VBA code whenever complex data management tasks are required by your applications, or in situations where users require more flexibility than provided by queries and forms alone.

Chapter 15

Using the VBA Debugging Tools

Access database applications prepared by even the very best developers have problems. By their very nature, database applications tend to be pretty complicated — especially by the time you consider table and query design, forms design and implementation, and all that VBA code that needs to be written for most databases. Something inevitably goes wrong and causes problems. If you're lucky, the problem and its cause are obvious and easily fixed. A somewhat worse condition exists when you know there's a problem but its source is not immediately apparent. The worst situation for all concerned are those bugs that silently and perniciously damage data or the representation of the data in an application without warning.

This chapter takes a look at the types of problems you'll encounter in Access applications and some of the steps you can take to uncover and repair these critters. This chapter largely ignores the errors caused by poor design: misrepresentation of data caused by ill-designed queries, update and insert anomalies causes by inappropriate application of referential integrity rules, and so on. For the most part, these problems occur because of failing to conform to proper design disciplines, misunderstanding Access query design, and so on. We can't do much to help you avoid these problems other than to encourage you to read — and reread — the chapters in Part I of this book.

What we can help you with, however, are the bugs that creep into your VBA code, particularly those bugs that cause noticeable problems with the data or user interface in your applications. Debugging Access VBA code is the focus of this chapter. This chapter assumes that you're comfortable designing and implementing the data structures in your applications and that the tables, queries, and other structural components of your databases are not a source of problems.

IN THIS CHAPTER

- Testing and debugging your applications
- Getting help with VBA
- Compiling procedures
- Handling runtime errors
- Using the Immediate window
- Using the Locals window
- Setting and working with breakpoints
- Viewing the Call Stack window

ON the CD-ROM This chapter is a departure from the other example files you've used in the book. The sample database file (`Chapter15.accdb`) contains the basic example code shown throughout this chapter. The code in `Chapter15.accdb` does not necessarily do anything useful. It's provided mostly as a "test bench" for practicing with the Access debugging tools, rather than as good examples of practical VBA code.

Many of the statements in the examples have been commented out because they contain syntax errors and other types of problems. You may have to remove the single quotes in front of some of the example statements to experience the error or view the assistance already built into Microsoft Access.

There are many more examples in `Chapter15.accdb` than are described in the text of this chapter. After you read the chapter, go back through all of the examples and try them. You'll learn more about debugging than you probably ever wanted to know, but the experience will serve you well as you develop and debug your programs.

It's no secret that testing and debugging VBA programming statements takes quite a bit of time. Good developers easily spend a third of their time designing a program, another third writing code, and another third testing and debugging. Very often, it's a good idea to have someone other than the developer test a program's operation. A person who is unfamiliar with an application will often do something the developer never expected, leading to new and surprising bugs.

Testing and Debugging Your Applications

Testing Access applications is an ongoing process. Each time you switch a form or report from design view to normal view, or leave the VBA Editor to run a bit of code, you're testing your application. Every time you write a line of code and move to another line, the VBA syntax parser checks the code you just wrote. Each time you change a property in a form or report and move your cursor to another property or another control, you're testing the form or report.

Testing is the time to see if your application runs the way you intend, or even if it runs at all. When you run an application and it doesn't work, you've found a *bug*. Fixing problems is most often referred to as *debugging*. This term dates back to the earliest electron tube computers. Legend has it that a moth shorted out an electrical circuit. The late Admiral Grace Hopper, an early pioneer in computing, coined the term *debugging* to describe the process of removing the moth.

You've already learned a lot about testing and debugging. When you run a report and no data appears, you've had to check the report's `RecordSource` property to ensure that the report is pulling the correct data. You may have viewed the data in a query or table to see if the data source is the problem. If you run a form and you see `#Name` or `#Error` in individual controls, you've learned to check the control's `ControlSource` property. Perhaps you have an incorrect reference to a table field or you spelled something wrong, and Access is unable to evaluate the reference.

Maybe you have too many parentheses in an expression, or you've used a control name in a formula that conflicts with an Access keyword. Each time you had this problem, you may have asked someone with more experience than you what the problem was, or perhaps you looked it up online or in a book, or you researched the syntax of the formula.

Most problems with query, form, and report design are pretty obvious. You know you have a problem when a query returns the wrong data, or a form or report fails to open or displays an error message as it opens. Behind the scenes, Access does a great deal to help you notice and rectify problems with your application's design. When you run forms and reports, Access often reports an error if it finds something seriously, and obviously, wrong.

It's much more difficult for Access to help you with incorrectly written code. Very often a problem in VBA code exists for months or even years before a user notices it. Even very poorly written code often runs without throwing errors or exhibiting obvious problems. However, determining exactly where a bug exists in VBA code, and figuring out what to do to repair the bug, can be very challenging. When you create VBA code, you're pretty much on your own when it comes to detecting and resolving problems. Fortunately, there are a wide variety of tools built into the editor to help you.

Understanding the Sources of Errors

Generally speaking, VBA errors fall into two broad categories. Syntactical errors are usually easily fixed by consulting the online language reference or a good book (such as this one!). Logical errors are another issue altogether. Logical errors occur when code does not do what is intended, yet does not cause overt problems like crashing or displaying error messages. Most of the time that you spend debugging Access applications involves uncovering the causes and resolving the logical errors that inevitably creep into VBA code. A third category of error (runtime errors) can often be avoided through proper end-user training, building defensive routines into your code, and so on.

Syntactical errors

Syntax errors are caused by using the VBA language incorrectly, much like mispronouncing a sentence in a foreign language. By far the most common bug in Access VBA code is the simple syntactical error caused by misspelling a keyword or a variable name; or misusing a procedure, property, or method. These errors are so easy to detect and correct that Access includes an option to automatically check for syntax errors. Figure 15-1 shows the Options dialog box (Tools ➪ Options while the VBA code editor window is open) open to the Editor tab. The Code Settings area in the upper-left quadrant of this dialog box contains a number of important options that help you write and debug the VBA code in your applications.

Notice the Auto Syntax Check check box in the Code Settings area. This option causes Access to check your code for syntax errors line by line as you type it into the code editor window. Figure 15-2 illustrates automatic syntax checking. In this figure, the `MsgBox` statement contains an error. Do you see it?

FIGURE 15-1

The Modules tab of the Options dialog box contains a number of important VBA coding options.

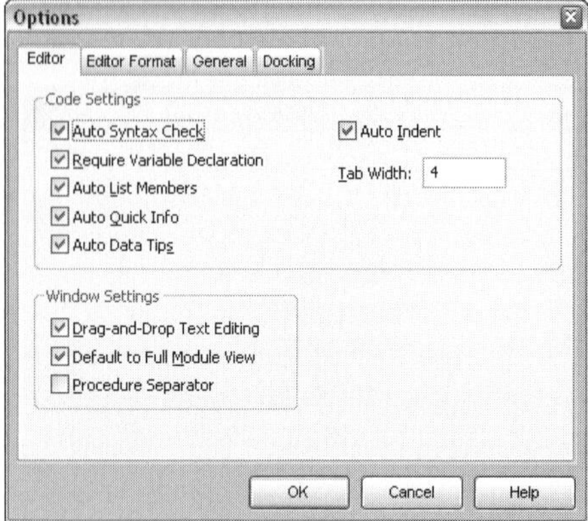

FIGURE 15-2

Automatic syntax checking can save you from simple bugs.

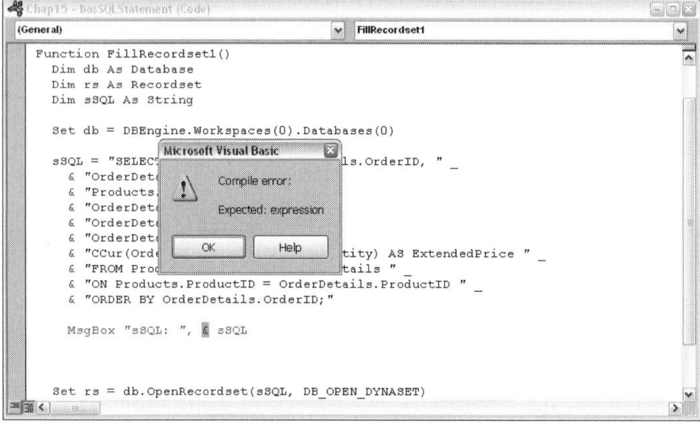

Notice the stray comma right after the `"sSQL: "` portion of the `MsgBox` line. No comma is needed here because the arguments to the `MsgBox` statement are not separated with commas. (The arguments to the `MsgBox` *function*, however, *are* separated with commas!) Access detects the stray comma and displays the statement in a red typeface to tell you there's a problem on that line. (If you don't like red, you can change the color of Syntax Error Text in the Code Colors area of the Editor Format tab of the Options dialog box).

Fixing syntax errors is straightforward: Simply examine the line for a misspelling, stray character, missing quotation marks, and so on. Very often, syntax errors are introduced by using parentheses where they aren't needed (or omitting them when they are necessary!), improperly placing square brackets, and so on.

TIP **Many syntax errors can be avoided by adhering to the naming conventions frequently mentioned in this book: avoid spaces in object names, use mixed-case names to make them easier to read, and so on. Anything you can do to make your code easier to understand goes a long way toward avoiding silly syntax errors.**

Logical errors

Logical errors can be somewhat more difficult to detect and remove. A logical bug occurs because of some mathematical error, misuse of the data in a record set, or other problem dealing with the data or program flow in the application.

Logical errors can be extremely dangerous and expensive if they go undetected for very long. Consider an application that calculates sales tax and adds the sales tax amount to invoices. Obviously, the sales tax must be calculated correctly or the customer will pay the wrong sales tax amount. The tax collector expects to collect the correct amount, even for customers who underpaid sales taxes on every sale during the fiscal year. Such an error can be very costly to a company in terms of extra expenses, fines, interest, and other penalties.

Here's another example of a logical error: Consider a situation in which a patient management program assumes that the user has entered both the first name and last name of the patient. After all, the patient data-entry form contains text boxes for both these values, so the user will certainly make sure both values are filled in, right? For perfectly valid reasons (for instance, an patient too young to know her own name or an elderly patient who can't recall his last name) either of these values may be missing from the data. A text box left empty contains a null value unless a default value has been provided. A logical error is generated when the application then tries to use the patient's first name in a find or sorting operation. If you're lucky, the logical error will be noticed by the user (perhaps through a pop-up dialog box or error message) and corrected before the data is committed to the database.

Other logical errors are created when an application incorrectly calculates the days between dates, uses the wrong value in a division or multiplication operation, and so on. Virtually any time data is mishandled or inappropriately used in your application, a logical error results.

Logical errors often require extensive debugging effort to correct. It goes without saying that debugging a complex application with many different forms and reports is more difficult than debugging a simple, straightforward desktop application.

Runtime errors

Runtime errors are usually traceable to some hardware failure. A hard-drive crash, of course, is an easily recognized runtime failure. Other runtime errors may be more subtle and difficult to deal with. For instance, a network glitch may cause data loss or make lookup data temporarily unavailable. Running out of swap disk space makes Windows run erratically or crash. Many computers are equipped with marginal memory, making it difficult or impossible to run large queries or use the built-in Access wizards.

CROSS-REF **Avoiding and dealing with runtime errors is difficult. There are many Windows application program interface (API) calls for performing system tests such as reporting free disk space, and checking the network. Chapter 30 discusses how to add Windows API function calls to your applications, including things like checking for available disk space. The examples in Chapter 30 are easily added to any Access application and may help you determine when the user's computer has run out of disk space or encountered other hardware failures.**

A second approach to avoiding runtime errors is to keep the database's `.data` file (`mdb` or `accdb`) well-maintained. Compact the data file frequently, particularly if data is frequently deleted or modified. The built-in repair utility is also useful for ensuring the physical integrity of the data file on the hard drive. Both the Compact and Repair commands are available by choosing the Manage tab on the Office menu (opened by clicking the large, round button in the upper-left corner of the main Access screen).

Avoiding errors

It shouldn't come as any surprise that your coding habits have a lot to do with the errors you encounter in your applications. Very often, the adoption of simple coding conventions eliminate all but the toughest syntax and logical errors in VBA code.

One coding suggestion is to put but a single variable declaration on a line of code. Consider the code you see in Figure 15-3. Although it's perfectly permissible to put all nine variable declarations together as a single `Dim` statement, you must scan the entire line to find the declaration of each of the variables.

FIGURE 15-3

Multiple declarations on a line make finding a variable's `Dim` statement difficult.

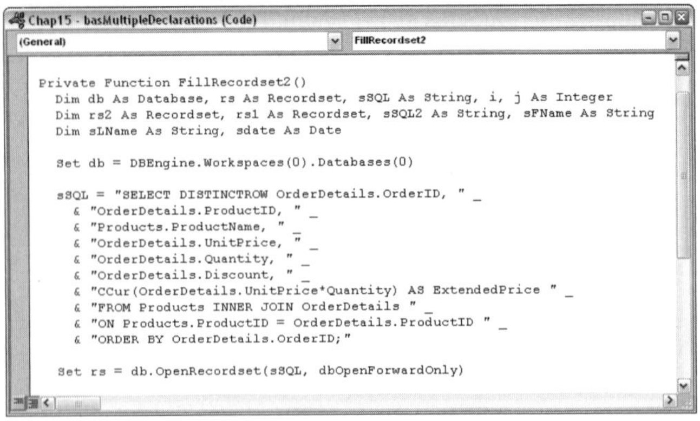

Chap15 - basMultipleDeclarations (Code)

(General) | FillRecordset2

```
Private Function FillRecordset2()
  Dim db As Database, rs As Recordset, sSQL As String, i, j As Integer
  Dim rs2 As Recordset, rs1 As Recordset, sSQL2 As String, sFName As String
  Dim sLName As String, sdate As Date

  Set db = DBEngine.Workspaces(0).Databases(0)

  sSQL = "SELECT DISTINCTROW OrderDetails.OrderID, " _
    & "OrderDetails.ProductID, " _
    & "Products.ProductName, " _
    & "OrderDetails.UnitPrice, " _
    & "OrderDetails.Quantity, " _
    & "OrderDetails.Discount, " _
    & "CCur(OrderDetails.UnitPrice*Quantity) AS ExtendedPrice " _
    & "FROM Products INNER JOIN OrderDetails " _
    & "ON Products.ProductID = OrderDetails.ProductID " _
    & "ORDER BY OrderDetails.OrderID;"

  Set rs = db.OpenRecordset(sSQL, dbOpenForwardOnly)
```

The problem in Figure 15-3 is that it's far too easy to overlook a variable or to misunderstand the data type assigned to a variable. It's quite easy to create a bug by assigning a variable an incorrect value. Other errors are caused by using a variable in an inappropriate context, such as using a string variable in a mathematical expression. In this particular case, VBA will use a numeric value stored in the string variable without throwing an error, but a runtime error is thrown if the string variable contains a text value (such as a person's name).

The long declaration in Figure 15-3 contains another, more subtle error. Notice that the declaration contains `i, j As Integer` at the end of the statement. Apparently the programmer intended that both `i` and j are declared as the Integer data type, but this is not what actually happens. VBA requires the `As <DataType>` clause for *each* variable declaration. If the `As <DataType>` is omitted, the variable is established as a Variant data type. Although the code you see in Figure 15-3 runs without errors, because the `i` variable is a variant, the code runs somewhat more slowly than it would if `i` were an Integer.

Figure 15-4 shows the same declarations reconfigured as multiple `Dim` statements. It's much easier to see the data type of the `rs1` variable in Figure 15-4. Let your eye run down the list of variable names until you reach `rs1` and see that it's a `Recordset` type variable. This is another reason why short, descriptive variable names are preferred over long descriptive names.

FIGURE 15-4

Single-variable `Dim` statements are easier to work with than declaring several variables as a single VBA statement.

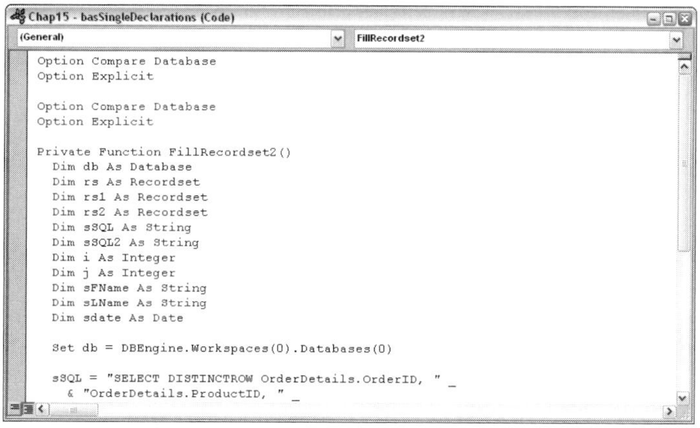

```
Chap15 - basSingleDeclarations (Code)
(General)                                FillRecordset2

Option Compare Database
Option Explicit

Option Compare Database
Option Explicit

Private Function FillRecordset2()
  Dim db As Database
  Dim rs As Recordset
  Dim rs1 As Recordset
  Dim rs2 As Recordset
  Dim sSQL As String
  Dim sSQL2 As String
  Dim i As Integer
  Dim j As Integer
  Dim sFName As String
  Dim sLName As String
  Dim sdate As Date

  Set db = DBEngine.Workspaces(0).Databases(0)

  sSQL = "SELECT DISTINCTROW OrderDetails.OrderID, " _
    & "OrderDetails.ProductID, " _
```

A second, less obvious change in Figure 15-4 is the fact that variables are grouped by data type. All of the `Recordset` variables are grouped together as are the `Integer` variables. You could carry this grouping one step farther by sorting the variables alphabetically by data type.

Spreading out your variable declarations does not appreciably affect compile times or runtimes. There is no difference in code module size once the code has been reduced to a binary format by the Access VBA compiler. In other words, there is nothing to be gained by condensing variable declarations into a few lines of code. Spreading out variable declarations makes them much easier to read without sacrificing execution or compilation speed.

Using the Module Options

The Editor tab in the Options dialog box (refer to Figure 15-1) contains a number of options that are important to the integrity of your VBA code. These options are summarized in the following sections.

TIP **The only drawback to the auto help built into Access 2007 is that the popup messages and help is sometimes obtrusive. But you can easily turn off these help features in the Modules tab. Also, on slow computers there can be a noticeable delay while Access retrieves the auto help. If you discover that the help you receive is not worth the wait, consider turning off the auto help features.**

Auto Syntax Check

When you select the Auto Syntax Check option, Access checks each line of code for syntax errors as you enter it in the code editor. Most of the syntax errors caught by Auto Syntax Check are the most obvious spelling errors, missing commas, and so on. It will not catch more subtle errors such as data type mismatch, and, of course, it won't catch logical errors.

Most Access developers leave Auto Syntax Check unselected. This option causes a message box to pop up over your code whenever Access detects a syntax error in your VBA statements. Access also turns the erroneous statement to red to indicate a problem whether or not Auto Syntax Check is selected. Most developers find that turning the statement to red is enough indication of a problem, and they don't want to be interrupted by the message box.

Break on All Errors

Break on All Errors forces Access stops at each and every error (regardless of the error handling you may have added to your application) to allow you to debug the statement generating the error. During the development process, you'll want to see errors as they occur instead of relying on the error handling you built into your code to make sure you understand what's generating the errors.

NOTE **Be sure to turn this option off before distributing the application to its end users.**

Require Variable Declaration

The Require Variable Declaration setting automatically inserts the Option Explicit directive into all VBA modules in your Access application. This means, of course, that all variables must be explicitly declared (with the Dim, Private, Public, or Static keyword) before they're used. This option is selected by default and is preferred by most experienced Access developers.

Compile on Demand

Compile on Demand instructs Access to compile modules only when their functions are required somewhere else in the database. When this option is unchecked, all modules are compiled any time any function is called. Unchecking this option makes sure that you see all errors that are detected by the compiler each time you make changes to the modules in your application. If you leave this option selected, the Access compiler will not recompile all of the code in the application, which means that some errors may slip through.

Auto List Members

This option pops up a list box containing the members of an object's object hierarchy in the code window. In Figure 15-5, you can see the list of Application objects that appeared as soon as I typed the period following `Application` in the VBA statement. It's your choice to locate an item in this list and select it or to continue typing in the object reference.

FIGURE 15-5

Auto List Members makes it easy to recall the members of an object's object hierarchy.

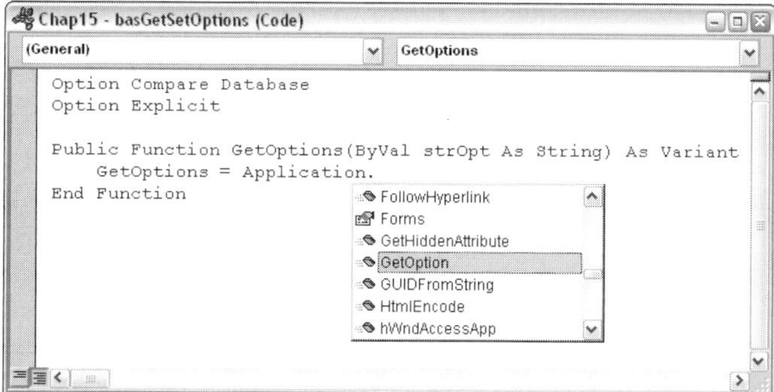

Auto Quick Info

When you select Auto Quick Info, Access pops up syntax help (see Figure 15-6) when you enter the name of a procedure (function, subroutine, or method) followed by a period, space, or opening parenthesis. The procedure can be a built-in function or subroutine or one that you've written yourself in Access VBA. This option helps you learn and understand the proper syntax of each command and method.

FIGURE 15-6

Auto Quick Info provides syntax reminders in the module window.

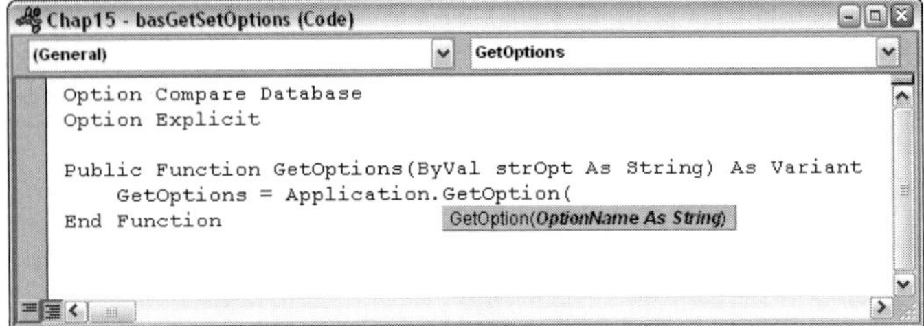

Auto Data Tips

Figure 15-7 shows Auto Data Tips in action. This option displays the value of variables when you hold the mouse cursor over a variable with the module in break mode. Auto Data Tips is an alternative to setting a watch on the variable and flipping to the Immediate window when Access reaches the break point. (You can find out more about watches in the "Setting watches" section, later in this chapter.)

FIGURE 15-7

Auto List Members makes it easy to recall the members of an object's object hierarchy.

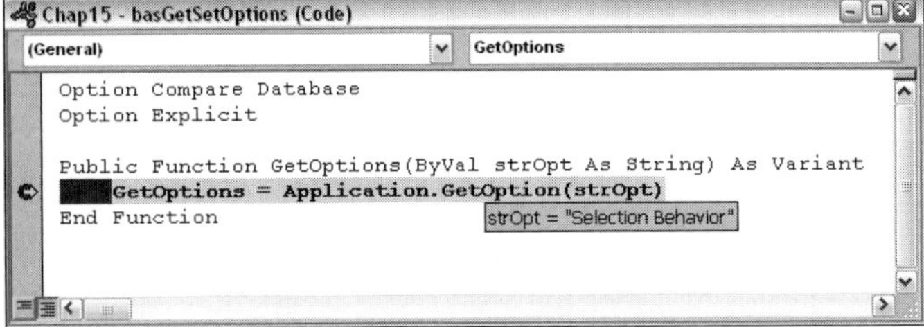

Compiling VBA Code

After you create a subprocedure or function and want to make sure that all of your syntax is correct, you should compile your procedures by choosing Debug ➪ Compile *<Project Name>* from the VBA code editor window menu (where *<Project Name>* is the name of the project set in the Tools ➪ Project dialog box). This action checks your code for errors and also converts the programs to a form that your computer can understand. If the compile operation is not successful, an error window appears, as shown in Figure 15-8.

This level of checking is more stringent than the single-line syntax checker. Variables are checked for proper references and type. Each statement is checked for all proper parameters. All text strings are checked for proper delimiters such as the quote marks surrounding `text string`. Figure 15-8 illustrates a typical compile-time error. In this case, the name of a method (`GetOption`) has been misspelled, and the compiler is unable to resolve the misspelled reference.

FIGURE 15-8

Viewing a compile error

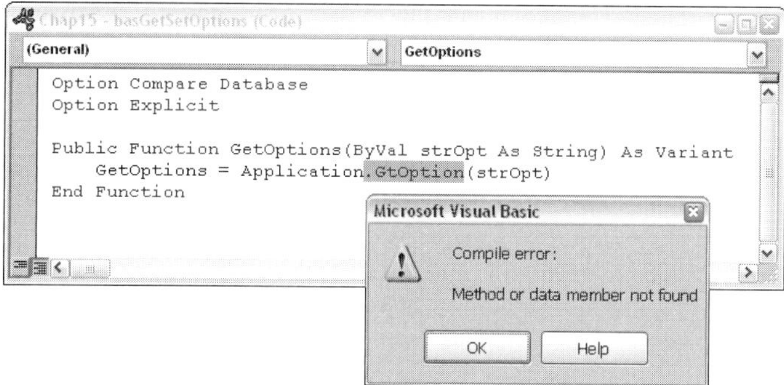

Access compiles all currently uncompiled procedures, not just the one you're currently viewing. If you receive a compilation error, you should immediately modify the code to rectify the problem. Then try to compile the procedure again. If there are further compile errors, you'll see the next error.

Unfortunately, the VBA compiler reports compilation errors one at a time. Most other compilers (such as the compilers in Visual Studio .NET) show you as many errors as they find during compilation.

TIP **When your application is compiled, you can't choose Debug ➪ Compile. Before implementing an application at the customer's site, you should make sure that your application is compiled.**

Your database is named with a standard Windows name, such as `Chapter15.accdb`, but there is an internal project name that Microsoft Access uses to reference the VBA code in your application. You'll see this name when you compile your database. When the database file is first created, the project name and the Windows filename will be the same. The project name is not changed when you change the Windows filename. You can change the project name by choosing Tools ➪ *<Project Name>* Properties (where *<Project Name>* is the current internal project name).

Compiling your database only makes sure that you have no syntax errors. The compiler can only check for language problems by first recognizing the VBA statement and then checking to see that you specify the right number of options and in the right order. The VBA compiler cannot detect logical errors in your code, and certainly cannot help with runtime problems.

After you compile your program, you should also compact your database. Every time you make a change to your program, Access stores both the changes and the original version. When you compile your program, it may double in size as the compiled and uncompiled versions of your code are stored. Compacting the database will reduce the size of the database by as much as 80 to 90 percent, because it eliminates all previous versions internally.

Traditional Debugging Techniques

There are two widely used debugging techniques that have been available since Access 1.0. The first is to insert `MsgBox` statements to display the value of variables, procedure names, and so on. The second common technique is to insert `Debug.Print` statements to output messages to the Immediate window.

Using MsgBox

Figure 15-9 shows an example of a `MsgBox` statement and the message box produced by the statement. In this example a long SQL statement is displayed in a message box to enable the developer to verify the statement was properly composed by the application.

FIGURE 15-9

The `MsgBox` statement makes a satisfactory debugging tool (with some limitations).

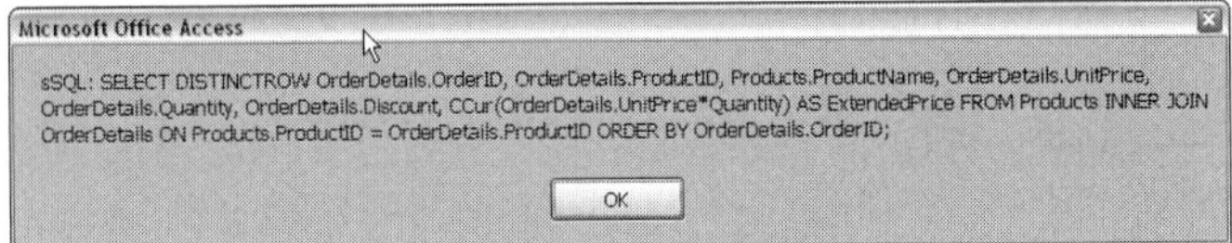

The advantages of using the `MsgBox` statement are obvious. `MsgBox` is easy to use and can be used to output virtually any type of data. The message box itself pops up right on the user interface, and you don't have to have the Immediate window open or flip to the Immediate window to view the message box. Also, the `MsgBox` statement is simple and easy to use and only occupies a single line of code.

There are also some problems associated with `MsgBox` statements. Never, ever forget to remove all `MsgBox` statements from your code before shipping to end users. There is nothing about the `MsgBox` statement to prevent it from popping up in front of an end user, causing all kinds of confusion and other problems. Also, message boxes are modal, which means you cannot flip to the code editor window or Immediate window to examine the value of variables or examine the code underlying the application. Using the `MsgBox` statement is an all-or-nothing proposition (with one exception described in the next section).

Using compiler directives

A refinement of the `MsgBox` technique is to use *compiler directives* to suppress the `MsgBox` statements unless a special type of constant has been set in the code or within the Access environment. Examine the code in Figure 15-10. Notice the `#Const` compiler directive above the `MsgBox` statement and the `#If` and `#End If` directives surrounding the `MsgBox` statement.

FIGURE 15-10

Compiler directives make it easy to include or exclude blocks of code from an application.

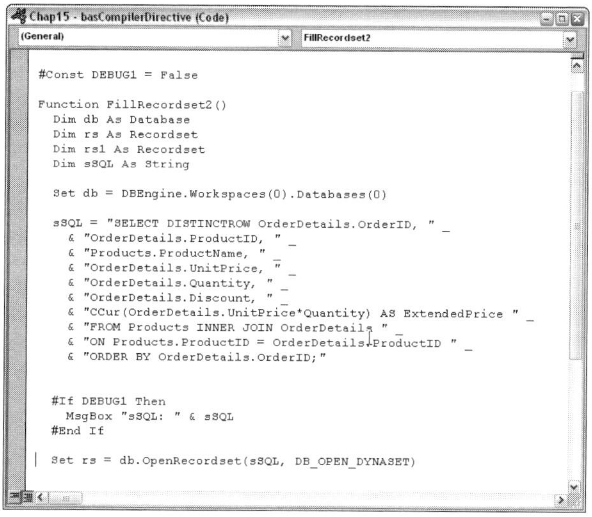

Chap15 - basCompilerDirective (Code)

(General) | FillRecordset2

```
#Const DEBUG1 = False

Function FillRecordset2()
  Dim db As Database
  Dim rs As Recordset
  Dim rs1 As Recordset
  Dim sSQL As String

  Set db = DBEngine.Workspaces(0).Databases(0)

  sSQL = "SELECT DISTINCTROW OrderDetails.OrderID, " _
    & "OrderDetails.ProductID, " _
    & "Products.ProductName, " _
    & "OrderDetails.UnitPrice, " _
    & "OrderDetails.Quantity, " _
    & "OrderDetails.Discount, " _
    & "CCur(OrderDetails.UnitPrice*Quantity) AS ExtendedPrice " _
    & "FROM Products INNER JOIN OrderDetails " _
    & "ON Products.ProductID = OrderDetails.ProductID " _
    & "ORDER BY OrderDetails.OrderID;"


  #If DEBUG1 Then
    MsgBox "sSQL: " & sSQL
  #End If

  Set rs = db.OpenRecordset(sSQL, DB_OPEN_DYNASET)
```

All of the keywords beginning with the pound sign (#) are seen only by the VBA compiler. These keywords (`#Const`, `#If`, `#Else`, and `#End If`) constitute directives to the VBA compiler to include (or exclude) certain statements in the compiled version of your project.

The `#Const` directive you see in Figure 15-10 can appear anywhere in the module as long as it is placed above the `#If` directive. The logical place for the `#Const` is in the module's declaration section, since `#Const` values are global to the module. In Figure 15-10, the compiler constant is set to `True`, which means the statements between `#If` and `#End If` will be compiled into the application's VBA project. In this case, the `MsgBox` statement is processed and appears in the user interface. Removing the `#Const` directive (perhaps by commenting it out) or setting its value to `False` suppresses the `MsgBox` statement.

Obviously, compiler directives are used for statements other than `MsgBox`. You could, for instance, use compiler directives to conditionally compile features, additional help, or other capabilities into an application. Compiler directives are particularly effective for suppressing `MsgBox` statements that are used for debugging purposes and must be squelched before giving the application to users.

Perhaps the biggest impediment to using compiler constants is that the `#Const` statement is module-level in scope. A compiler constant declared in one module is not seen by other modules in the application. This means that you must add the same compiler constants to every module you want to employ conditional compilation.

Access provides the Conditional Compilation Arguments option in the General tab of the application's Project Properties dialog box (Tools ➪ *<Application Name>* Properties) to get around this constraint. As shown in Figure 15-11, you use the Conditional Compilation Arguments section to specify any number of compiler constants that apply to the entire application. These settings make it very easy to toggle conditional compilation from a single location in the application, instead of changing the `#Const` statements in every module.

FIGURE 15-11

The Project Properties dialog provides a convenient way to set conditional compilation arguments for the entire application.

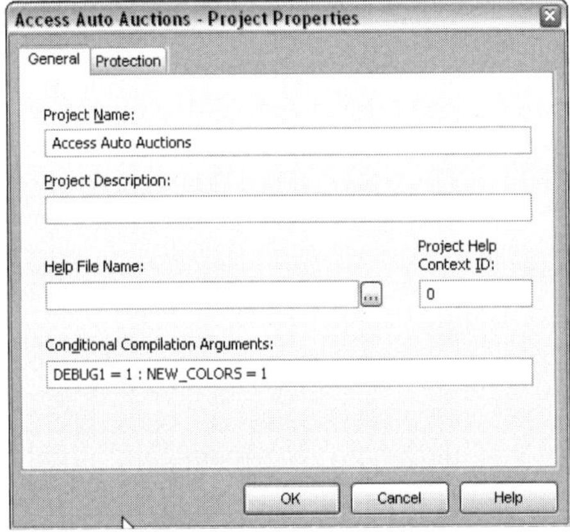

The Conditional Compilation Arguments and other settings set in the Project Properties dialog are relevant only to the current application. Unlike the options you set in the Tools ➪ Options dialog, the Project Properties settings are not shared among multiple Access applications.

TIP **In Figure 15-11, notice that the values assigned to the Conditional Compilation Arguments are all numeric. Assigning zero to a Conditional Compilation Argument sets the argument's *logical* value to False. Any nonzero value is interpreted as True. You cannot use the words "True" and "False" in the Conditional Compilation Arguments setting in the Project Properties dialog box.**

If you're confused about the conflicting terminologies applied to the VBA conditional compilation feature, you're not alone. In a VBA code module, you assign *conditional compilation constants* using the `#Const` keyword, yet in the Project Properties dialog box you set *Conditional Compilation*

Arguments. Also, you assign the `True` and `False` keywords to conditional compilation constants in a VBA module, but use 1 and 0 to assign True and False, respectively, to conditional compilation arguments. This is one place where the terminology and syntax used for the same purpose are quite different in different parts of an Access VBA project.

Using Debug.Print

The second commonly used debugging statement is using `Debug.Print` to output messages to the Immediate window. (`Print` is actually a method of the `Debug` object.) Figure 15-12 shows how the sSQL variable appears in the Immediate window.

FIGURE 15-12

Use `Debug.Print` to output messages to the Immediate window.

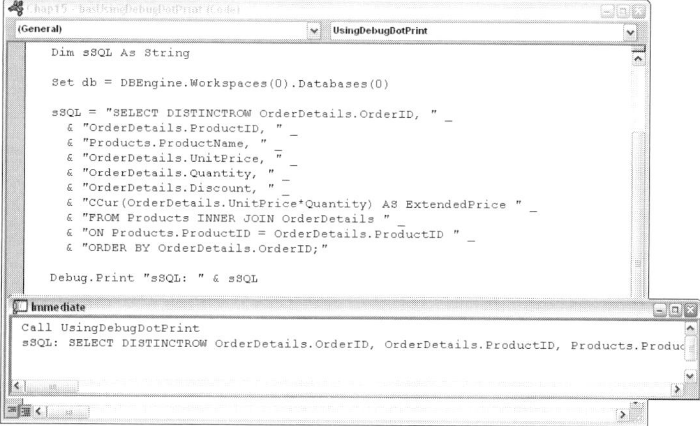

Unlike the `MsgBox` statement, you don't have to do anything special to suppress its output from the user interface. The output of `Debug.Print` only goes to the Immediate window, and because end users never see the Immediate window, you don't have to worry about a user encountering debug messages.

The problems with `Debug.Print` are obvious from Figure 15-12. Long strings do not wrap in the Immediate window. Also, the Immediate window must be brought to the top in order for you to view its output. But these limitations are relatively harmless and you'll frequently use `Debug.Print` in your applications.

NOTE **Some people have reported that excessive numbers of `Debug.Print` statements can slow an application. Even though the Immediate window is not visible, Access executes the `Debug.Print` statements it finds in its code. You might consider surrounding each `Debug.Print` statement with the compiler directives described in the preceding section to remove them from the end user's copy of the application.**

Using the Access Debugging Tools

Access 2007 features full debugging capabilities. Access 2007 includes a full complement of debugging tools and other capabilities.

Getting to know the Immediate window

Open the Immediate window (also called the Debug window) by choosing View ➪ Immediate or by pressing Ctrl+G. You can open the Immediate window any time. (For instance, you can open the Immediate window while you're working on a form's design.) You'll sometimes find it useful to test a line of code or run a procedure (both of which are supported by the Immediate window) while you're working on a form or report.

The Immediate window is shown in Figure 15-13. The Immediate window permits certain interactivity with the code and provides an output area for `Debug.Print` statements.

FIGURE 15-13

Get to know the Immediate window! You'll use it a lot in Access 2007.

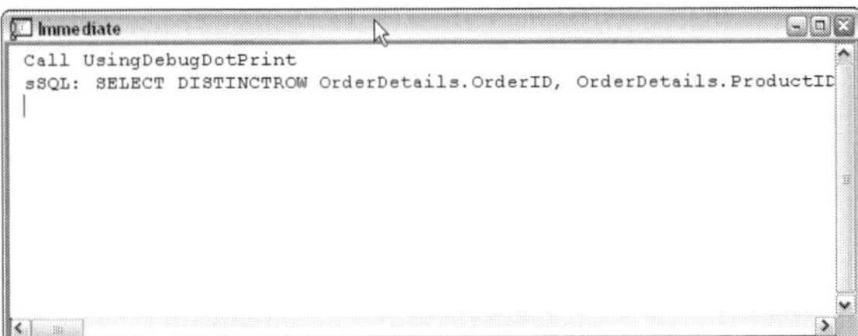

The basic debugging procedures include stopping execution so that you can examine code and variables, dynamically watching variable values, and stepping through code.

Running code with the Immediate window

One of the most basic uses of the Immediate window is to run code, such as built-in functions, or subroutines and functions that you've written. Figure 15-14 shows several examples of code that has been run in the Immediate window.

FIGURE 15-14

Running code from the Immediate window is a common operation.

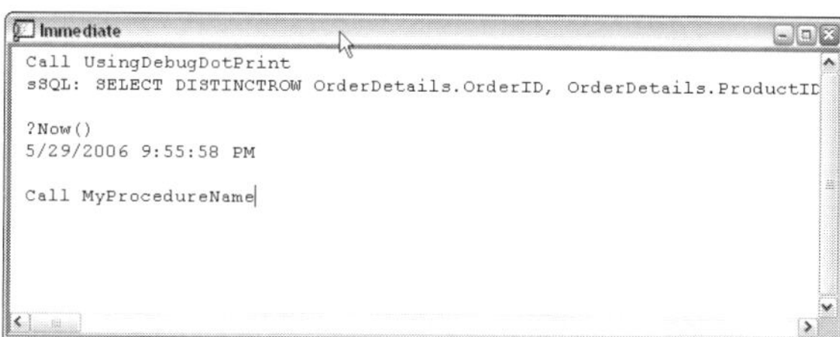

The `Now()` function has been run at the top of the Immediate window, returning the current date and time. The question mark (`?`) in front of the `Now()` function name is a directive to the Immediate window to display (or print) the value returned by `Now()`. The second example in Figure 15-14 shows the same convention used to run a function that's been added to the VBA project. You see the result of the function's execution, as long as the function is declared with the `Public` keyword, and any arguments required by the function are provided.

The third example in Figure 15-14 shows calling a subroutine from the Immediate window. Because subroutines do not return values, the question mark is not used. The `Call` keyword is optional when calling subroutines, but it's often included for clarity.

Suspending execution with breakpoints

You suspend execution by setting a *breakpoint* in the code. When Access encounters a breakpoint, execution immediately stops, allowing you to switch to the Immediate window to set or examine the value of variables.

Setting a breakpoint is easy. Open the code window and click on the gray Margin Indicator bar to the left of the statement on which you want execution to stop (see Figure 15-15). Alternatively, position the cursor on the line and click on the Breakpoint button. The breakpoint itself appears as a large brown dot in the gray bar along the left edge of the code window and as a brown highlight behind the code. The text of the breakpoint statement appears in a bold font. (All of these colors and font characteristics can be changed in the Modules tab of the Options dialog box.)

Removing a breakpoint involves nothing more than clicking on the breakpoint indicator in the Margin Indicator bar. Breakpoints are also automatically removed when you close the module.

FIGURE 15-15

Setting a breakpoint is easy.

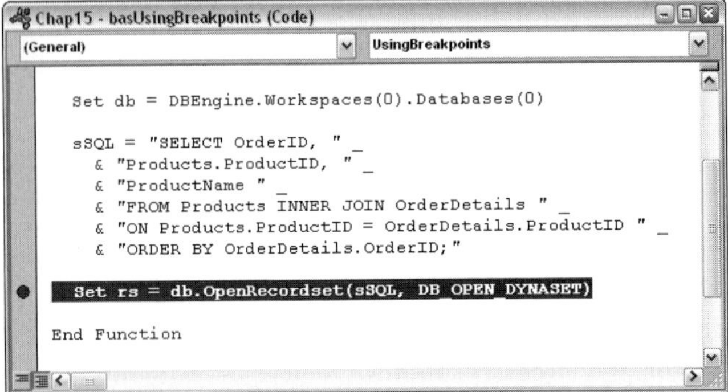

When execution reaches the breakpoint, Access halts execution and opens the module at the breakpoint (see Figure 15-16). You now use the Immediate window to examine the values of variables and perform other operations, or use any of the other debugging tools described in this section. Neither the code window nor the Immediate window are modal, so you still have full access to the development environment.

FIGURE 15-16

Execution stops on the breakpoint.

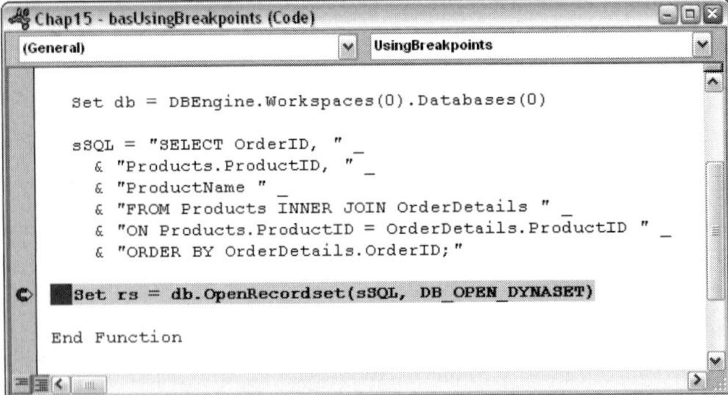

Figure 15-17 illustrates two techniques for viewing the values of variables while execution is stopped at a breakpoint. The Locals window contains the names and current values of all the variables in the current procedure. If you want to see the value of a variable in a slightly different format, use the Debug print command (?) to display the variable's value in the Immediate window. In Figure 15-17, the value of sSQL is displayed in the Immediate window.

FIGURE 15-17

The Immediate window contains a lot of valuable information.

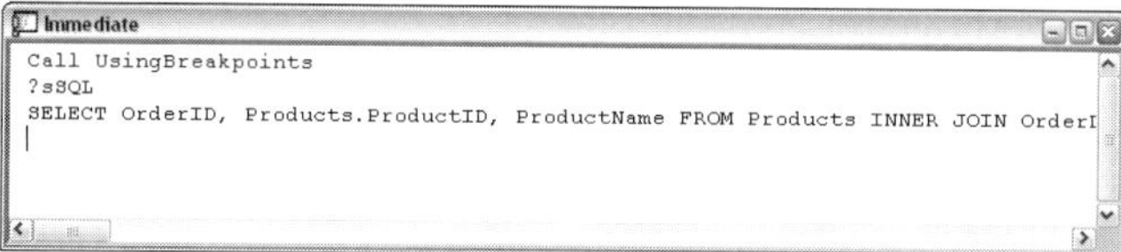

An alternative to setting breakpoints is to use `Stop` statements. The `Stop` statement halts execution but is more permanent than breakpoints. A `Stop` statement, like any other VBA statement, persists from session to session until explicitly removed. You can, however, surround the `Stop` statement with conditional compilation expressions and toggle their action by changing the value assigned to a conditional compilation constant. Figure 15-18 illustrates using the `Stop` statement.

FIGURE 15-18

`Stop` statements are a type of permanent breakpoint.

Chap15 - basUsingBreakpoints (Code)

(General) | UsingBreakpoints

```
    Set db = DBEngine.Workspaces(0).Databases(0)

    sSQL = "SELECT OrderID, " _
      & "Products.ProductID, " _
      & "ProductName " _
      & "FROM Products INNER JOIN OrderDetails " _
      & "ON Products.ProductID = OrderDetails.ProductID " _
      & "ORDER BY OrderDetails.OrderID;"

    Set rs = db.OpenRecordset(sSQL, DB_OPEN_DYNASET)
    Stop

End Function
```

Stepping through statements

The most fundamental operation at a breakpoint is to walk through the code, one statement at a time, to view what's happening to the application's logic and variables. Once you've reached a breakpoint, you use a few keystroke combinations to control the execution of the application. You're able to step through code one statement at a time, automatically walk through the local procedure, or step over the procedure and continue execution on the "other side" of the procedure.

In Figure 15-19, a breakpoint has been inserted near the top of the `FillRecordset1()` function. When execution reaches this point a break asserts itself, allowing us to take control of program execution.

FIGURE 15-19

Insert a breakpoint near the location of the code you want to step through.

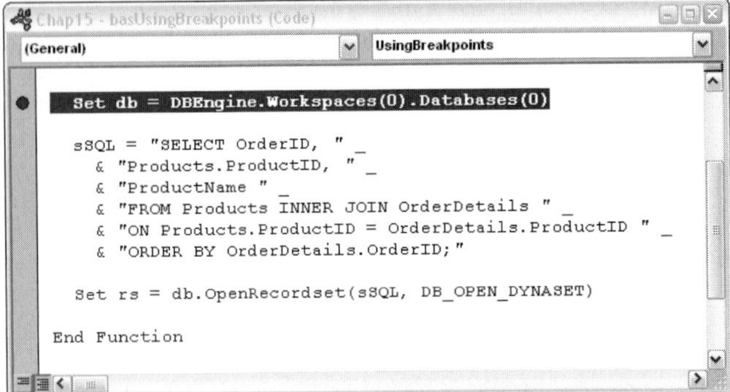

In Figure 15-20, the break has occurred and we've clicked on the Step Into button (or pressed F8). The Step Into button executes the next statement in the program's flow of execution. In this case, the SQL statement is composed and assigned to sSQL. If we wanted to view the value of sSQL at this point, we could flip to the Immediate window (Ctrl+G) and use `?sSQL` to print its value in the Immediate window. We could also have a watch set on sSQL and view its value in the Watch window (described in the section titled "Setting watches," later in this chapter).

FIGURE 15-20

Step Into executes one line at a time.

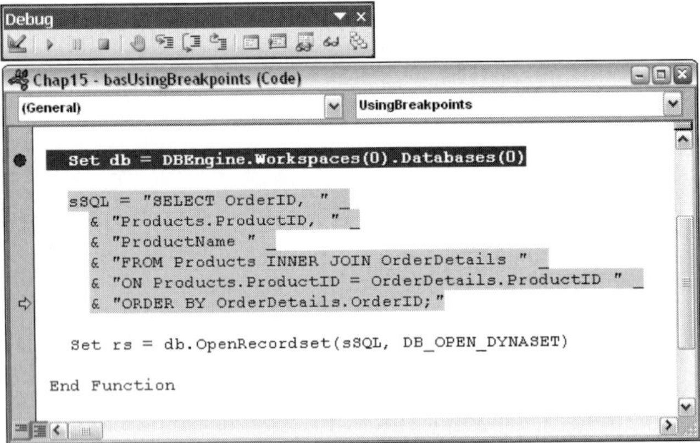

Notice the execution pointer (a yellow arrow) in the Margin Indicator bar pointing at the last line of the SQL statement. This arrow tells you where execution is actually stopped. The line pointed to by the arrow has not yet executed, so any action performed in the statement has not occurred.

Consecutive clicks on the Step Into button (or pressing F8) walks through the code one statement at a time. If a statement includes a call to another procedure, you'll be taken to that procedure and walked through it. If you want, you can use the Step Over button (or press Shift+F8) to step "through" the called routine. If you've previously debugged the called routine and you're sure it contains no errors, there is no reason to walk through its code. The code in the called routine is actually executed when you click on the Step Over button, changing any variables involved.

Once you're satisfied that you don't need to continue walking through the code, click on the Step Out button (or press Ctrl+F8) to complete the procedure. The Step Out button is handy if you've stepped into a called routine and you're sure there's nothing interesting going on in it.

One very nice feature in Access 2007 is the Auto Data Tips option in the Modules tab in the Options dialog box. With this option selected, you're able to view the value of any variable in a tooltip-like window by hovering the mouse pointer over the variable's name in the module window (see Figure 15-21).

FIGURE 15-21

Auto Data Tips are a powerful tool for debugging.

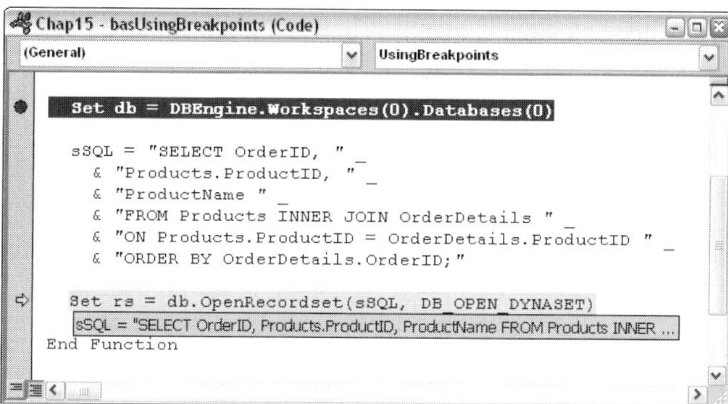

Keep in mind that the Auto Data Tips option must be selected in the Modules tab for the data tip you see in Figure 15-21 to appear.

Using the Locals window

The Locals window (View ➪ Locals Window) shows all variables that are currently in scope, saving you from having to examine each variable one at a time. The variable's name, its data type, and its current value are displayed.

Notice the items in the Locals window in Figure 15-22. Any line in the Locals window that begins with a plus sign icon will unfold to reveal more information. For instance, you can set a breakpoint on the `End Function` statement at the bottom of the function to halt execution so that you can examine the results of the `rs` assignment statement. Unfolding the `rs` entry in the Locals window reveals all the properties of the `rs` object and its contents (see Figure 15-22).

FIGURE 15-22

Use the Locals window to examine the values of complex objects.

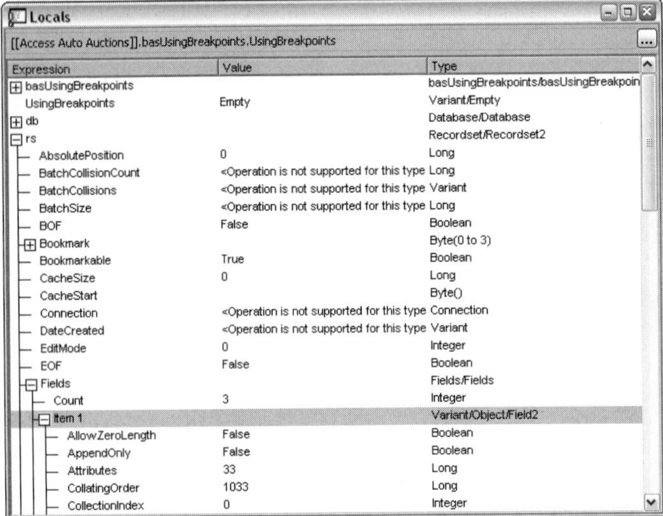

Setting watches

The Locals window can be overrun with variables in a large application, or in an application with many variables in scope. The Watch window enables you to specify just which variables you want to monitor as you single-step through your code. The value of a watched variable changes dynamically as the code runs (you need to be at some kind of breakpoint, of course, to actually see the values). The advantage of using the Watch window is that the variables displayed do not have to be from the local procedure. In fact, the variables in the Watch window can be from any part of the application.

Setting a watch is more complicated than using the Locals window or setting a breakpoint:

1. **Click on the Watch tab.**
2. **Right-click anywhere in the Watch window and select Add Watch from the shortcut menu.**
3. **Enter the name of the variable or any other expression in the Expression box of the Add Watch dialog box (see Figure 15-23).**

FIGURE 15-23

The Add Watch dialog box includes some powerful options.

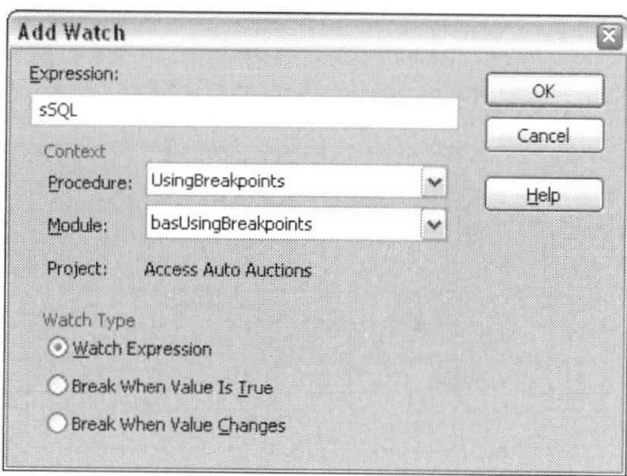

The Add Watch dialog box includes some important options. In addition to the name of a variable or expression (an expression might be something like `sSQL = ""`), there are options for specifying the module and procedure within the module to watch. In Figure 15-23, the Add Watch dialog box is set up to watch the `sSQL` variable in all procedures in all modules.

At the bottom of the Add Watch dialog box are the following options:

- **Watch Expression:** The variable's value will dynamically change in the Watch window. You must use an explicit breakpoint or `Stop` statement in order to observe the value of the watched variable.
- **Break When Value Is True:** This option asserts a break whenever the value of the watched variable or expression becomes `True`. If you set the expression to `sSQL = ""`, a breakpoint occurs whenever the value of the `sSQL` variable changes to an empty string.
- **Break When Value Changes:** This directive causes Access to halt execution whenever the value of the variable or expression changes. Obviously, this setting can generate a *lot* of breakpoints!

TIP **Use watches wisely. You don't want to be breaking into program execution too frequently or you'll never get through the code. On the other hand, you don't want to overlook some important change in the value of a variable because you didn't set a watch appropriately.**

Figure 15-24 shows the Watch window in action. The `sSQL` variable is displayed for all procedures in all modules.

FIGURE 15-24

The Watch window reveals all uses of a variable's details.

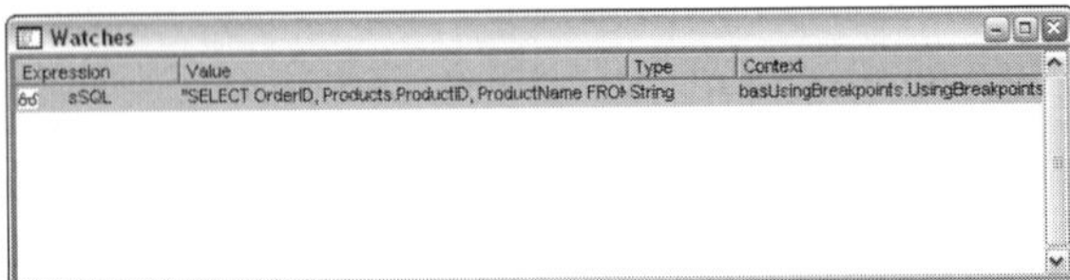

Using conditional watches

Although it can be quite entertaining to watch variables in the Locals or Watch windows, you may spend a great deal of unproductive time hoping to see something unexpected happen. You'll probably find it much more efficient to set a conditional watch on a variable, and instruct the VBA engine to break when the condition you've established is met.

The Add Watch dialog box (see Figure 15-25) accepts a Boolean (true or false) expression, such as `SalesTax < 0` in the text box near the top. You specify where in the application (which procedures and which modules) the expression is applied, and you tell Access what you want the VBA engine to do when the expression is evaluated. For our purposes, we want execution to break when the expression is `True`.

FIGURE 15-25

A conditional watch halts execution when the expression is true.

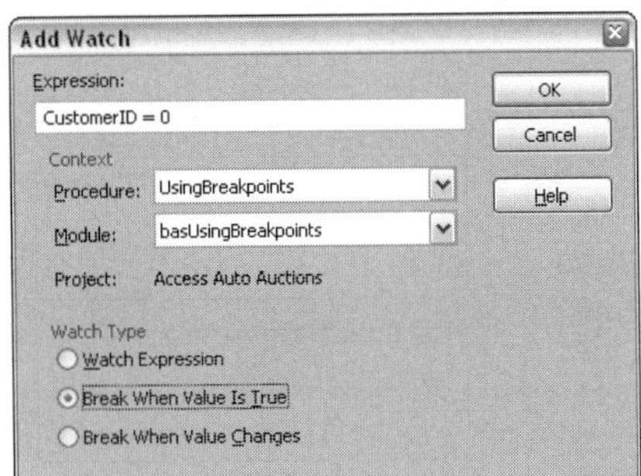

There are other ways to use conditional watches, such as using compound conditions (`X = True And Y = False`), and forcing a break whenever a value changes from the value set in the expression text box. The small example illustrated in Figure 15-25 only hints at the capabilities possible with conditional watches.

Using the Call Stack window

The last debugging tool we'll examine is a bit more difficult to understand because it involves multiple dimensions of execution. In many applications, you'll have procedures that call other procedures that call still other procedures. To our knowledge, there is no practical limit on the number of procedures that can be sequentially called in a VBA project. This means you may have a "tree" of procedures many levels deep, one level of which is causing problems in your application.

Imagine a function that performs a common operation (such as calculating sales tax) in an application. As a general rule, rather than include this function in every module in the application, you'll put the function into a single module, declare it with the `Public` keyword so that it's recognized and used by the entire application, and then call it from whichever procedure needs a sales tax calculation.

Furthermore, imagine that this application has many such functions and subroutines, each calling the other, depending on the application's logic at that moment. Finally, imagine that users report that the sales tax appears to be incorrectly calculated under some conditions, but not others.

It'd be possible to single-step through all of the code in the application, hoping to discover the cause of the erroneous sales tax. However, this would not be an efficient approach. It'd be much more efficient to set a conditional watch on an important variable within the sales tax function, forcing the code to break when the condition is `True`. Then, open the Call Stack window (see Figure 15-26) to view the path that the VBA engine has taken to reach this particular point in the code.

FIGURE 15-26

The Call Stack window shows you how the execution point reached its current position.

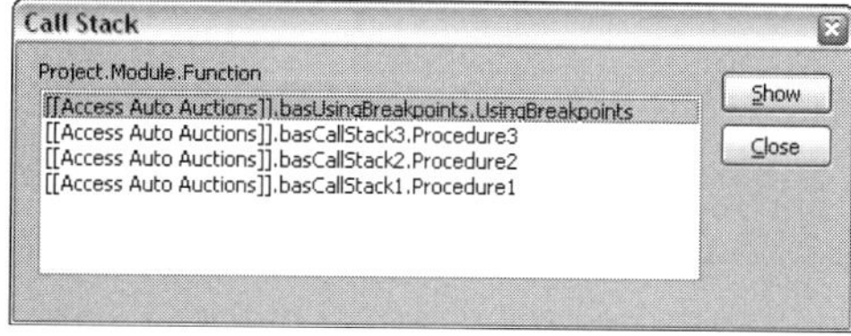

Double-click on any of the items listed in the Call Stack to be taken to the statement that sent execution to the next procedure. Using the Call Stack window in conjunction with conditional watches enables you to stop code wherever relevant, and to diagnose how code has executed up to the breakpoint.

Summary

This chapter takes a quick look at the important topic of debugging Access VBA code. The techniques you apply and the tools you use in debugging your code are highly individual choices. Not all developers feel comfortable using the Immediate window to watch variables. Not every developer uses breakpoints and the Step buttons to stop and control execution. At the same time, it's nice to know that these tools are available for your use when you're ready!

This chapter ends the section on VBA programming in Microsoft Access. You'll see many different ways of using VBA code to strengthen and enhance your Access applications in the following parts and chapters of this book.

The next part revisits the basic application building tasks you read about in the first part of this book. The next several chapters explain many of the most important aspects of application development, such as using external data in your Access applications, creating advanced queries, and building complex forms and reports. These chapters take the basic skills explained in the first two parts of this book and extend your understanding of Access application development.

Part III

More Advanced Access Techniques

Microsoft Access is a very sophisticated database-development system. Although the majority of casual Access developers never move beyond building simple forms and reports, you can do much more with Microsoft Access if you know how. The chapters in this part cover many, but not all, of the capabilities possible with Microsoft Access. The topics in these chapters range from creating advanced queries and integrating Access with other applications, to controlling the user interface and manipulating data with the VBA programming language.

This section of this book contains many examples that show how to use these techniques in Microsoft Access applications. You'll make good use of this book's CD as you work through the examples presented in these chapters.

This section also contains a chapter on multiuser database development. As you'll soon see, there are considerations in multiuser applications that never arise in single-user environments. You'll have to keep these principles and concerns in mind as you work on applications destined for multiuser environments to ensure that your applications don't confuse users or cause data loss as one user overwrites another user's work.

IN THIS PART

Chapter 16

Working with External Data

So far, you've worked with data in Access tables found within the current database. In this chapter, you explore the use of data from other types of files. You learn to work with data from database, spreadsheet, HTML, and text-based files. After we describe the general relationship between Access and external data, we explain the major methods of working with external data: linking and importing/exporting.

ON the CD-ROM This chapter uses the `Chapter16.accdb` database as well as several other files that you will use for linking. If you have not already copied these files onto your machine from the CD, you'll need to do so now.

The data linked or imported into Access applications comes in a bewildering variety of formats. There is no practical way to document every possible type of import or linking operation in a single chapter. Therefore, this chapter discusses the essential steps required to import or link to external data, and gives a few examples demonstrating how these processes are performed in Access 2007, instead of filling page after page with examples that may or may not be relevant to your work.

As you'll soon see, knowledge of the external data format is critical to a successful import or linking operation. You must have some notion of the external data format before you can successfully import data into your Access application or incorporate the data into your Access application through linking. This chapter points out many of the issues involved if you choose to import or link to external data; it's intended to be a guide as you perform these operations in your Access applications.

IN THIS CHAPTER

Access and External Data

Exchanging information between Access and another program is an essential capability in today's database world. Information is usually stored in a wide variety of application programs and data formats. Access, like many other products, has its own native file format, designed to support referential integrity and provide support for rich data types, such as OLE objects. Most of the time, this format is sufficient; occasionally, however, you need to move data from one Access database file to another, or even to or from a different software program's format.

Types of external data

Access has the capability to use and exchange data among a wide range of applications. For example, you may need to get data from other database files (such as FoxPro, dBASE, or Paradox files) or obtain information from a SQL Server, Oracle, or a text file. Access can move data among several categories of applications:

- Other Windows applications
- Macintosh applications (FoxBASE, FoxPro, Excel)
- Spreadsheets
- PC database-management systems
- Server-based database systems (SQL Server)
- Text and mainframe files

Methods of working with external data

Often, you need to move data from another application or file into your Access database, or vice versa. You may need to obtain information you already have in an external spreadsheet file. You can re-enter all the information by hand — or have it automatically imported into your database. Access has tools that enable you to move data from a database table to another table or file. It could be a table in Access, FoxPro, or Paradox; it could be an Excel spreadsheet file. In fact, Access can exchange data with more than 15 different file types:

- Access database objects (all types, all versions)
- dBASE
- Microsoft FoxPro
- Paradox
- Text files (ANSI and ASCII; DOS or OS/2; delimited and fixed-length)
- Lotus 1-2-3
- Microsoft Excel
- ODBC databases (Microsoft SQL Server, Sybase Server, Oracle Server, and other ODBC-compliant databases)

- HTML tables, lists, documents
- XML documents
- Microsoft Outlook and Outlook Express
- Microsoft Exchange documents
- Microsoft IIS
- Microsoft SharePoint
- Microsoft Active Server Pages
- Microsoft Word Merge documents
- Rich Text Format documents

Access works with these external data sources in several ways: linking, importing, and exporting. Table 16-1 describes these methods.

TABLE 16-1

Methods of Working with External Data

Method	Description
Link	Creates a link to a table in another Access database or links to the data from a different database format
Import	Copies data from a text file, another Access database, or another application's format into an Access table
Export	Copies data from an Access table to a text file, another Access database, or another application's format

As Table 16-1 shows, you can work with data from other sources in two ways: linking or importing. Both methods enable you to work with the external data. There is a distinct difference between the two methods:

- **Linking uses the data in its current file format (such as Excel or FoxPro).** The link to data remains in its original file. The file containing the link data should not be moved, deleted, or renamed. Otherwise, Access will not be able to locate the data the next time it's needed.
- **Importing makes a copy of the external data and brings the copy into the Access table.** The imported data is converted to the appropriate Access data type and is managed by Access from that point on.

Each method has clear advantages and disadvantages, covered in the following sections.

When to link to external data

Linking in Access enables you to work with the data in another application's format — thus, sharing the file with the existing application. If you leave data in another database format, Access actually changes the data while the original application is still using it. This capability is useful when you want to work with data in Access that other programs also need to work with. Another example is when you use Access as a front end for a SQL Server database — you can link to a SQL Server table and directly update the data, without having to batch-upload it to SQL Server.

If you plan to use a table from another Microsoft Access database, it's a good idea to simply link to it rather than import it. If another application continues to update and work with data, it's best to link to it.

You can link to the following types of data in Access: other Access tables (`.accdb`, `.accde`, `.mdb`, `.mda`, `.mde`), Excel spreadsheets, Exchange documents, Outlook documents, FoxPro, Paradox or dBASE, text files, HTML documents, SharePoint Team Services, and ODBC databases.

CAUTION **Access 2007 has the capability to link to HTML tables and text tables for read-only access. You can use and look at tables in HTML or text format; however, the tables cannot be updated and records cannot be added to them using Access. Also, if you are working with Paradox files and they don't have a primary key field defined, you will only be able to read the data — not change it.**

The biggest disadvantage of working with linked tables is that you lose the capability to enforce referential integrity between tables (unless you're linked to an Access database).

When to import external data

Importing data enables you to bring an external table or data source into a new Access table. By doing this, Access automatically converts data from the external format and copies it into Access. You can even import data objects into a different Access database or Access project than the one that is currently open. If you know that you'll use your data in Access only, you should import it. Generally, Access works faster with its own tables.

NOTE **Because importing makes another copy of the data, you may want to erase the old file after you import the copy into Access. Sometimes, however, you won't want to erase it. For example, the data may be sales figures from an Excel spreadsheet still in use. In cases such as this, simply maintain the duplicate data and accept that storing it will require more space.**

One of the principal reasons to import data is to customize it to meet your needs. After a table has been imported, you can work with the new table as if you'd built it in the current database.

With linked tables, on the other hand, you're greatly limited in the changes you can make. For example, you cannot specify a primary key or assign a data-entry rule, which means that you can't enforce integrity against the linked table.

TIP **Access opens only one database at a time. Therefore, you can't work directly with a table in a different database. If you need to work with tables or other Access objects (such as forms and queries) in another Access database, simply import the object from the other database into your current database.**

Data is frequently imported into an Access database from an obsolete system being replaced by a new Access application. When the import process is complete, the obsolete application can be removed from the user's computer. The data formerly managed by the obsolete system, such as an old FoxPro or dBASE application, is preserved in the Access database.

Data in unsupported programs

Although uncommon, there may be times when you need to work with data from a program that is not stored in the supported external database or file format. In cases such as this, the programs usually can export or convert their data in one of the formats recognized by Access. To use the data in these programs, export it into a format recognized by Access and then import it into Access. For example, many applications can export to the dBASE file format. If the dBASE format is not available, most programs, even those on different operating systems, can export data to delimited or fixed-width text files, which you can then import into Access.

Automating import operations

If you will be importing data from the same source frequently, you can automate the process with a macro or a VBA procedure. This can be very helpful for those times when you have to import data from an external source on a regular schedule or you have complex transformations that must be applied to the imported data.

Linking External Data

As the database market continues to grow, the need to work with information from many different sources will escalate. If you have information captured in a SQL Server database or an old Paradox table, you don't want to reenter the information from these sources into Access. Ideally, you want to open an Access table containing the data and use the information in its native format, without having to copy it or write a translation program to access it. For many companies today, this capability of accessing information from one database format while working in another is often an essential starting point for many business projects.

Copying or translating data from one application format to another is both time-consuming and costly. The time it takes can mean the difference between success and failure. Therefore, you want an intermediary between the different data sources in your environment.

Access can directly simultaneously link to multiple tables contained within other database systems. After an external file is linked, Access builds and stores a link to the table. Access easily links to other Access database tables as well as to non-Access database tables such as dBASE, FoxPro, and Paradox. A common practice is to split an Access database into separate databases, for easier use in a multiuser or client-server environment.

Linking to external database tables

In the "Methods of working with external data" section, earlier in this chapter, you saw a list of database tables and other types of files that Access links to. Access displays the names of link tables in the object list but uses a special icon to indicate that the table is linked and not contained within the current Access database. An arrow pointing to an icon indicates that the table name represents a link data source. Figure 16-1 shows several linked tables in the list, which are all external tables. Notice that all the linked tables have an icon containing is an arrow. (The icon clues you in to the type of file that is linked.)

FIGURE 16-1

Linked tables in an Access database. Notice that each linked table has an icon indicating its status as a linked table.

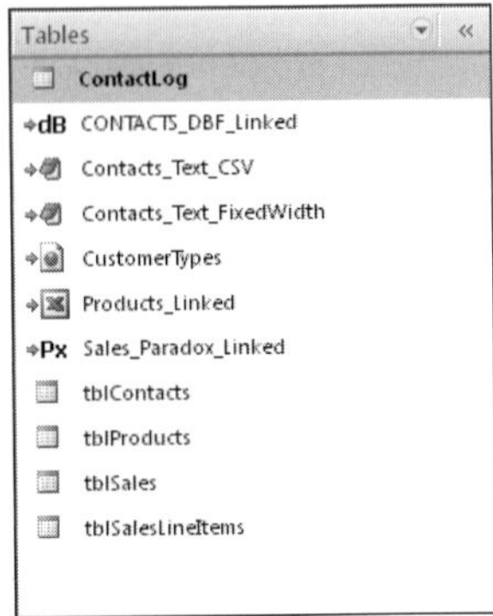

The icon indicates which type of file is linked to the current Access database. For instance, Excel has an *X* symbol in a box, Paradox has a *Px* symbol, and dBASE tables have a *dB* symbol.

After you link a table to your Access database, you use it as you would any other table. For example, Figure 16-2 shows a query using several linked tables: `Contacts` (from a dBase table), `Sales` (from a Paradox table), `SalesLineItems` (from a comma-delimited text file), and `Products` (from an Excel file).

This query shows the potential benefit of linking to a variety of data sources and seamlessly displays data from internal and linked tables. Figure 16-3 shows the datasheet returned by this query. Each column in this datasheet comes from a different linked data source.

FIGURE 16-2

A query designed using externally linked tables

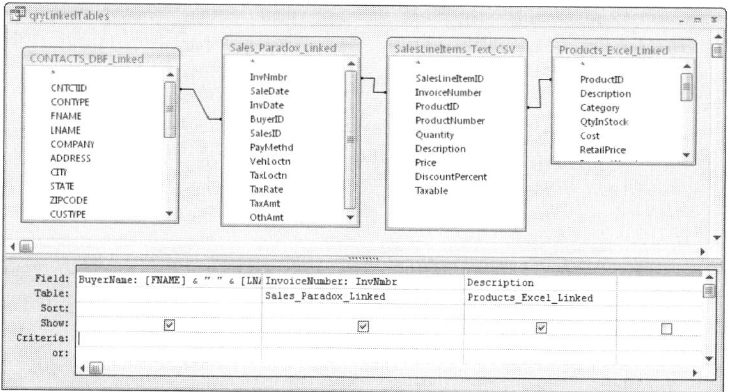

FIGURE 16-3

The datasheet view of externally linked data

BuyerName	InvoiceNumber	Description
John Jones	13	1999 Dodge Dakota Sport
John Jones	34	2001 Collectors Chevy Corvette
Larry Minkler	38	1950 Ford Coupe
Larry Minkler	38	1959 Ford Thunderbird
Larry Minkler	38	1988 Ford Tempo LRX
Larry Minkler	38	2001 Ford Taurus XES
Cary James	51	1965 Shelby Red Cobra
Brandon Aley	16	1996 Cadillac Coupe Deville
Brandon Aley	5	1962 Alfa Red Spider 2000
Brandon Aley	5	1965 Shelby Red Cobra
Brandon Aley	27	2001 Ford Taurus XES
Brandon Aley	53	1972 Chevy green Chevelle
Michael Dennis	52	1988 Ford Tempo LRX
Karl Johnson	43	1965 Shelby Red Cobra
Karl Johnson	30	2001 Collectors Chevy Corvette
Karl Johnson	43	1940 Classic Antique Convertible
Karl Johnson	7	1940 Classic Antique Convertible

In Figure 16-3, the column heading names come from the field names in the underlying external tables. For instance, the first column (BuyerName) is a combination of the `FNAME` and `LNAME` fields from the dBASE table, while the invoice number is from Paradox, and the `Description` field comes from Excel.

Figure 16-3 illustrates an important concept regarding using linked data in Access. Users will not know, nor will they care, where the data resides. All they want is to be able to see the data in a format they want and expect. Only you, the developer, understand the issues involved in bringing this data to the user interface. Other than the limitations of linked data (explained in the "Limitations of linked data" section), users will not be able to tell the difference between native and linked data.

NOTE **After you link an external table to an Access database, you should not move the table to another drive or directory. Access does not bring the external data file into the `.accdb` file; it maintains the link via the filename and the file's path. If you move the external table, you have to update the link using the Linked Table Manager, explained in the "Viewing or changing information for linked tables" section, later in this chapter.**

Limitations of linked data

Although this chapter describes using linked data as if it existed as native Access tables, certain operations cannot be performed on linked data. Furthermore, the prohibited operations depend, to a certain extent, on the type of data linked to Access.

These limitations are relatively easy to understand. Linked data is never "owned" by Access. External files that are linked to Access are managed by their respective applications. For instance, an Excel worksheet is managed by Microsoft Excel. It would be presumptive — and dangerous — for Access to freely modify data in an Excel worksheet. As an example, because many Excel operations depend on the relative positions of rows and columns in a worksheet, inserting a row into a worksheet may break calculations and other operations performed by Excel on the data. Deleting a row may distort a named range in the Excel worksheet, causing similar problems. Because there is no practical way for Access to understand all of the operations performed on an external data file by its respective owner, Microsoft has chosen to take a very conservative route and not allow Access to modify data that may cause problems for the data's owner.

The following list describes the limitations of linked data:

- **Excel data:** Existing data in an Excel worksheet cannot be changed, nor can rows be deleted or new rows added to a worksheet. For all intents and purposes, Excel data is treated in a read-only fashion by Access.
- **Text files:** For all practical purposes, data linked to text files is treated as read-only in Access. Although the data can be used in forms and reports, you can't simply and easily update rows in a link text file, nor can you delete existing rows in a text file. Oddly enough, you can add new rows to a text file. Presumably, this is because new rows will not typically break existing operations the way that deleting or changing the contents of a row may.

- **HTML:** HTML data is treated exactly as Excel data. You cannot modify, delete, or add rows to an HTML table.
- **Paradox and dBASE:** Because these are database files, you can pretty much perform the same data operations on Paradox and dBASE tables as you can on native access tables. This general statement applies only if a primary key is provided for each Paradox or dBASE table.
- **ODBC:** Briefly, ODBC is a data access technology that utilizes a driver between an Access database and an external database file, such as Microsoft SQL Server or Oracle. Again, generally speaking, because the linked data source is a database table, you can perform whatever database operations (modify, delete, add) as you would with a native Access table.

We discuss ODBC database tables in some detail in the "Linking to ODBC data sources" section, later in this chapter.

Linking to other Access database tables

Access easily incorporates data located in the other Access files by linking to those tables. This process makes it easy to share data among Access applications across the network or on the local computer. The information presented in this section applies to virtually any data file you linked to from an Access database. Rather than include examples of linking to every type of data file, this section explains the principles involved when linking to any type of data file. Later in this chapter, you'll see short sections explaining the differences between linking to an Access table and linking to each of the other types of data files recognized by Access.

NOTE **A very common practice among Access developers is splitting an Access database into two pieces. One piece contains the forms, reports, and other user interface components of an application, while the second piece contains the tables, queries, and other data elements of the application. There are many advantages to splitting Access databases, including certain performance benefits as well as easier maintenance. You can read about splitting Access databases in the "Splitting an Access database" section, later in this chapter. The process of linking to external Access tables described in this section is an essential part of a split database paradigm. The steps described in this section are frequently performed win managing split databases.**

After you link to another Access table, you use it just as you use another table in the open database. Follow these steps to link to `tblSalesPayments` in the Chapter16_Link.accdb database from the `Chapter16.accdb` database file:

1. **Open the `Chapter16.accdb` database.**
2. **Select the External Data ribbon, and then choose the type of data you want to access.**

   Access opens the Get External Data dialog box, shown in Figure 16-4.

FIGURE 16-4

Use the Get External Data dialog box to select the type of operation you want to perform on the external data sources.

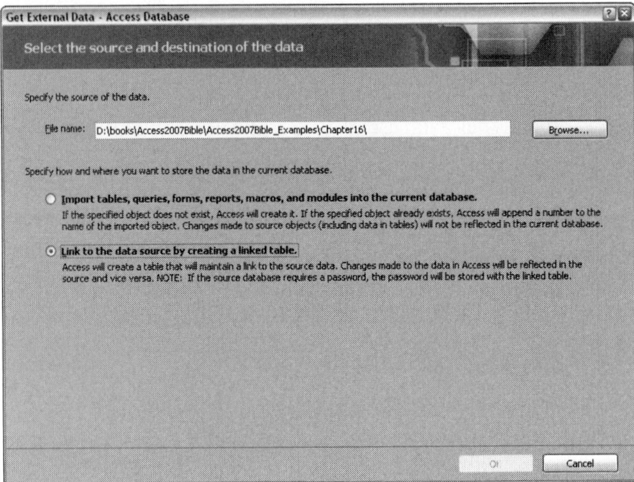

3. **Use the Browse button to open the Windows File Open dialog box, and locate the `.accdb` file you want to link to.**
4. **Find and select the `Chapter16_Link` file in the File Open dialog box and click the Open button.**

   The File Open dialog box closes and you're taken back to the Get External Data dialog box.
5. **Click the OK button in the Get External Data dialog box.**

   The Link Tables dialog box enables you to select one or more tables from the selected database (in this case, `Chapter16_Link`). Figure 16-5 shows the Link Tables dialog box open on Chapter16_Link.accdb.
6. **Select `tblSalesPayments` and click OK.**

   Double-clicking the table name will not select the table — you must highlight it and then click OK.

FIGURE 16-5

Use the Link Tables dialog box to select the Access table(s) for linking.

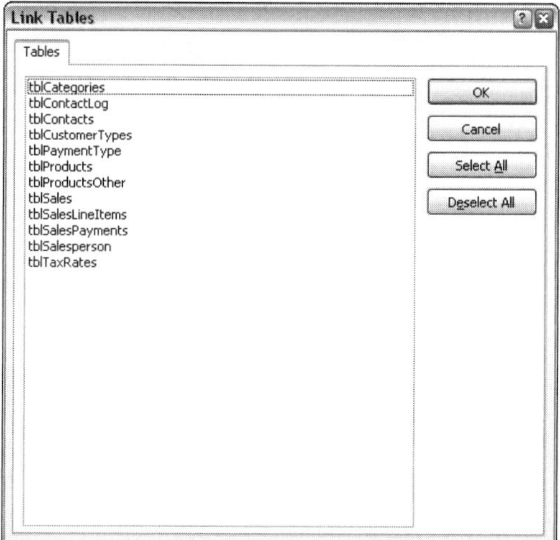

After you link `tblSalesPayments` from the `Chapter16_Link` database, Access returns to the object list and shows you the newly linked table. Figure 16-6 shows `tblSalesPayments` linked to the current database. Notice the special icon attached to `tblSalesPayments`. This icon indicates that this table is linked to an external data source. Hovering over the linked table with the mouse reveals the linked table's data source.

FIGURE 16-6

The Navigation Pane with `tblSalesPayments` added. Notice the icon indicating that this is a linked table.

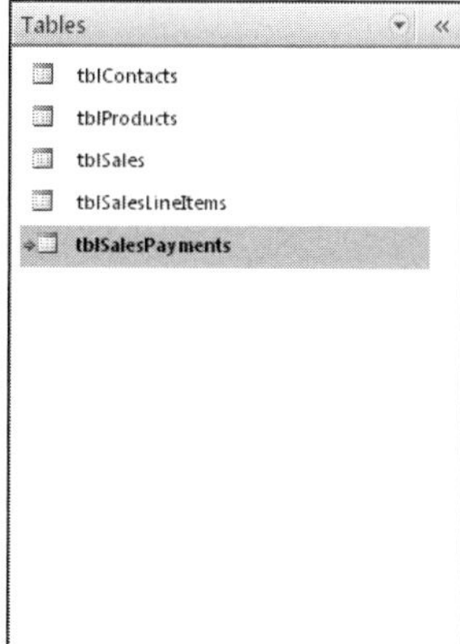

You can link more than one table at a time by selecting multiple tables before you click the OK button. Clicking the Select All button (naturally!) selects all the tables.

Linking to ODBC data sources

One significant advance with regard to data sharing has been the creation and support of Open Database Connectivity (ODBC) by Microsoft and other vendors. ODBC is a specification that software vendors use to create drivers for database products. This specification lets your Access application work with data in a standard fashion across platforms. If you write an application conforming to ODBC specifications, then your application will be able to use any other ODBC-compliant back end.

For example, say you create an Access application that uses a SQL Server database back end. The most common way to accomplish this requirement is to use the Microsoft SQL Server ODBC driver. After developing the application, you find that one of your branch offices would like to use the application as well, but they're using Oracle as a database host. If your application has conformed closely to ODBC syntax, then you should be able to use the same application with Oracle by purchasing an Oracle ODBC driver. Not only are vendors supplying drivers for their own products, but there are now software vendors who only create and supply ODBC drivers.

Linking to dBASE databases (tables)

Unlike Access, dBASE (and FoxPro and other xBase systems) store each table as a separate file with a `.dbf` extension. Each `.dbf` file may be accompanied by an `.ndx` or `.mdx` file containing the indexes associated with the dBASE table.

When you link to a dBASE table, Access may ask you if you want to link to the index file associated with the dBASE table. In almost every case, you'll want to include the index file in the linking operation. Otherwise, the dBASE data will be read-only and not updatable.

One other significant difference between Access and dBASE is that the links of table and field names are much shorter in dBASE than in Access, and are almost always expressed in all uppercase characters.

Linking to dBASE or other xBase data files is much like linking to an external Access table. The main difference is that you select dBASE (or FoxPro) from the Files of Type drop-down list in the File Open dialog box, and, because each xBase file is a table, you don't have to specify which table to link. Otherwise, the processes are virtually identical.

This book's CD includes a dBASE IV file named `CONTACTS.dbf` containing a copy of the `Contacts` table from the Access Auto Auctions application. You may want to use this file to practice linking the base tables.

Linking to Paradox tables

Linking to Paradox tables is much like linking to dBASE files. Each Paradox table is kept in a separate file with a `.db` extension. Each table's primary key and indexes is kept in a file with a `.px` or `.mb` extension. Otherwise, the Paradox linking operation parallels linking to dBASE files. Be sure to include the index file (if it exists) when linking to a Paradox `.db` file.

Linking to non-database data

You can also link to non-database data, such as Excel, HTML, and text files. When you select one of these types of data sources, Access runs a Link Wizard that prompts you through the process.

Linking to Excel

The main issues to keep in mind when linking to Excel data are:

- An Excel `.xls` workbook file may contain multiple worksheets. You must choose which worksheet within a workbook file to link.
- You may link to individual named ranges within an Excel worksheet.
- Excel columns may contain virtually any type of data.

The last bullet above is fairly important. Just because you have successfully linked to an Excel worksheet does not mean that your application will be able to use all of the data contained in the Excel worksheet. Because Excel does not limit the types of data contained in a worksheet, your application may encounter multiple types of data within a single column of a linked Excel worksheet. This means you may have to add code or provide other strategies for working around the varying types of data contained in an Excel worksheet.

This book's CD contains an Excel worksheet created by exporting the `Products` table from the Access Auto Auctions application. Use this file to practice importing Excel data, keeping in mind that, in practice, the data you're likely to encounter in Excel worksheets is far more complex and less orderly than the data contained in the `Products.xls` file.

By linking to an Excel table, you can update its records from within Access or any other application that updates Excel spreadsheets.

Follow these steps to link to the Excel `Products` spreadsheet:

1. **In the `Chapter16` database, select the Excel button on the External Data ribbon.**
2. **In the Get External Data dialog box, select Link to the Data Source by Creating a Linked Table, then click the Browse button.**

   The same Get External Data dialog box (see Figure 16-7) is used for both import and link operations. Therefore, be sure the correct operation is elected before continuing.

CROSS-REF **Importing data into Access is discussed in Chapter 17.**

FIGURE 16-7

The first screen of the Link Spreadsheet Wizard

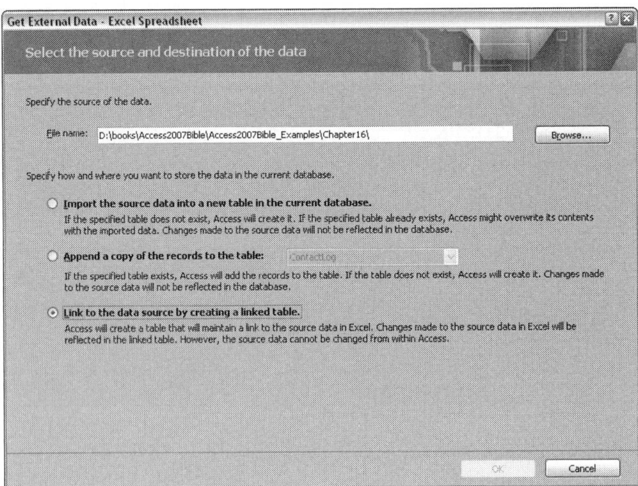

3. **Use the File Open dialog box to locate and open the Excel workbook file.**

   You'll be returned to the Link Spreadsheet Wizard (see Figure 16-8).

FIGURE 16-8

The main Link Spreadsheet Wizard screen

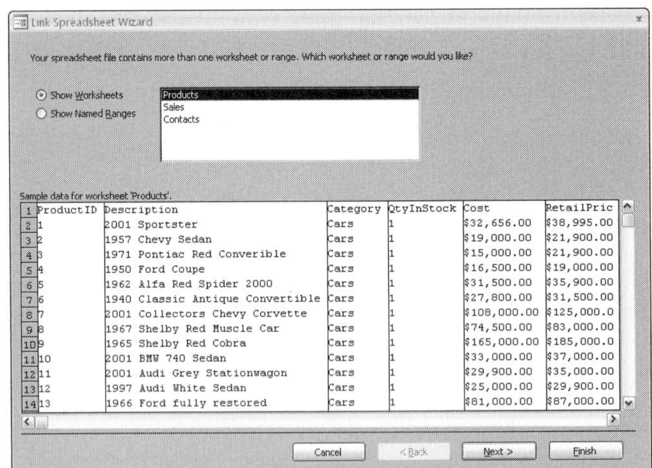

Notice that the Link Spreadsheet Wizard dialog contains options for selecting either worksheets or named ranges within the workbook file. In this example, there are three different worksheets (named `Products`, `Sales`, and `Contacts`) within the workbook file.

4. **Select the `Products` worksheet for this demonstration.**
5. **The Link Spreadsheet Wizard walks you through a number of different screens where you specify details such as First Row Contains Column Headings and the data type you want to apply to each column in the Excel worksheet.**
6. **The last screen of the Link Spreadsheet Wizard asks for the name of the newly linked table. The linked table is established as you click the Finish button and are returned to the Access environment.**

As with so many other things in database development, many decisions involved in linking to external data sources are based on how the data is to be used in the application. Also, the names you provide for fields and other details have a direct impact on your application.

Linking to HTML files

Linking to data contained in HTML documents is not covered in any detail in this book because of the rather severe limitations imposed by Access on this process. For instance, Access is unable to retrieve data from an arbitrary HTML file. The data must be presented as an HTML table, in a row and column format, and the data has to be relatively clean (absent any unusual data or mix of data, such as text, image, and numeric data combined within a single HTML table).

You're likely to encounter problems if more than one HTML table appears on the page, or if the data is presented in a hierarchical fashion (parent and child data).

All things considered, linking to arbitrary HTML documents is hit-or-miss at best. You're much better off linking to an HTML document specifically prepared as a data source for your Access application than to try working with arbitrary HTML files.

Furthermore, if someone is going to the trouble of creating specialized HTML documents to be used as Access data sources, it is probably more reliable for them to produce comma-separated values (CSV) or fixed-width text files. Comma-separated values, where the fields in each row are separated by commas, are a very common way to move data from one application to another. CSV and fixed-width file types are discussed in the next section.

Having said that, the process of linking HTML data is very similar to linking to Excel worksheets. Use the More drop-down list in the External Data tab and select HTML Document from the list. This action opens the same Get External Data dialog box you saw when linking to Excel worksheets. And, when you select the Link to the Data Source by Creating a Link Table option and click the Browse button, the File Open dialog box appears, enabling you to search for the HTML file you want to link. From this point on, the process of linking to HTML data is exactly parallel to linking to other types of data files, including providing field names and other details of the linked data (see Figure 16-9).

This book's CD includes a very simple HTML file named `CustomerTypes.html` in the `Chapter16` folder. The data in this file is, perhaps, overly simplistic, but it gives you the opportunity to practice linking to HTML documents. Because of the wide variety of ways that data is stored in HTML documents, it is not possible to generalize an approach to linking to HTML data. However, as you gain proficiency with the ability to link to external data sources, you may find linking to HTML a valuable addition to your Access skills.

FIGURE 16-9

The HTML Wizard screen that is used to name the column headings (field names) for the linked table

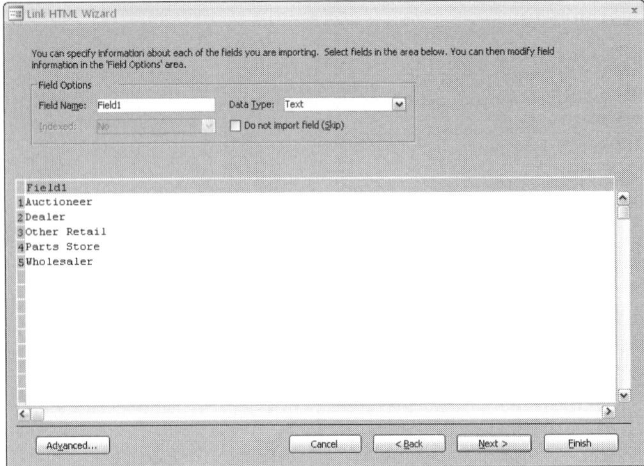

Linking to text files

A far more common situation is linking to data stored in plain text files. Most applications, including Microsoft Word and Excel, are able to publish data in a variety of text formats. The most common formats you're likely to encounter are *fixed-width* and *comma separated values* (CSV).

In a fixed-width text file, each line represents one row of a database table. Each field within a line occupies exactly the same number of characters as the corresponding field in the lines above and below the current line. For instance, a `Last Name` field in a fixed-width text file may occupy 20 characters, while a phone number field may only use 10 or 15 characters. Each data field is padded with spaces to the right to fill out the width allocated to the field. Figure 16-10 shows a typical fixed-width file open in Windows Notepad.

FIGURE 16-10

A typical fixed-width text file

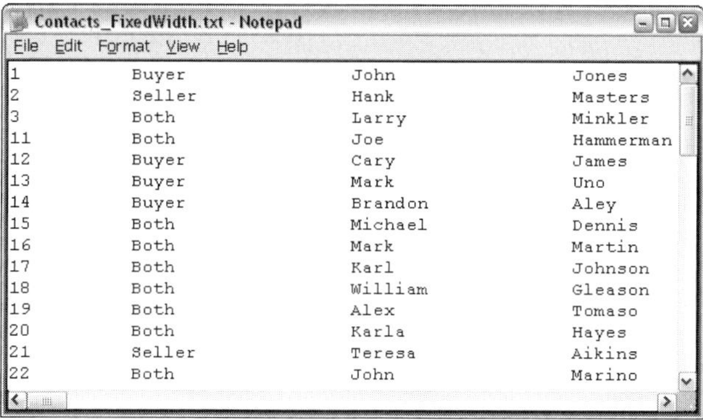
Contacts_FixedWidth.txt - Notepad

File Edit Format View Help

```
1           Buyer               John                Jones
2           Seller              Hank                Masters
3           Both                Larry               Minkler
11          Both                Joe                 Hammerman
12          Buyer               Cary                James
13          Buyer               Mark                Uno
14          Buyer               Brandon             Aley
15          Both                Michael             Dennis
16          Both                Mark                Martin
17          Both                Karl                Johnson
18          Both                William             Gleason
19          Both                Alex                Tomaso
20          Both                Karla               Hayes
21          Seller              Teresa              Aikins
22          Both                John                Marino
```

Comma-separated values are somewhat more difficult to understand. Each field is separated from the other fields by a comma character (`,`) and each field occupies as much space is necessary to contain the data. Generally speaking, there is little blank space between fields in a CSV file. The advantage of CSV files is that much more data can be contained in a CSV file because each field occupies only as much disk space as necessary to contain the data.

CSV files can be difficult to read when opened in Windows Notepad. Figure 16-11 shows a typical CSV text file.

FIGURE 16-11

CSV data is more compact than fixed-width text but is more difficult to read.

Contacts_CSV.txt - Notepad

File Edit Format View Help

```
1,"Buyer","John","Jones","Nopa Auto Parts","11253 Main Street
2,"Seller","Hank","Masters","Jiffy Auto Sales","623 Field Ro
3,"Both","Larry","Minkler","All Start Autos","971 E Main St",
11,"Both","Joe","Hammerman","Columbia Chevy","105 Main Street
12,"Buyer","Cary","James","James Auto Parts","59 South Street
13,"Buyer","Mark","Uno","Fillion Sales And Service","8908 No
14,"Buyer","Brandon","Aley","Tip Top Chevy","1916 Erickson D
15,"Both","Michael","Dennis","Newbury Auto","75 Main Street",
16,"Both","Mark","Martin","Peekskill Sales","51 Tolland Tnpk'
17,"Both","Karl","Johnson","KJ Auto Repair","350 Broadway St'
18,"Both","William","Gleason","R & G Monda Inc","196 East St
19,"Both","Alex","Tomaso","Tires National","46 School Street'
20,"Both","Karla","Hayes","Hayes Auctions","54 E Center Stre
21,"Seller","Teresa","Aikins","Middletown Auto Parts","100 N
22,"Both","John","Marino","Bill Thomas Sales, Inc","986 Buck
```

Text files are often used as intermediate data transfer vehicles between dissimilar applications. For instance, there may be an obsolete data-management system in your environment that is incompatible with any of the link or import data types in Access. If you're lucky, the obsolete system is able to output either fixed width or CSV files. Linking to or importing the fixed-width or CSV files may be the best option for sharing data with the obsolete system. At the very least, much less time is required linking or importing the data that would be involved in re-keying all of the information from the obsolete system into Access.

Finally, follow these steps to link to the `SalesLineItems` text file:

1. **Open the `Chapter16` database and select the External Data ribbon.**
2. **Click on the Text File button to open the Get External Data dialog box.**
3. **Be sure the Link to the Data Source by Creating a Link Table option is selected, and then click the Browse button.**

   The File Open dialog box appears.
4. **Locate the text file (either fixed-width, or CSV) and click the Open button.**
5. **Dismiss the other dialog boxes that appear.**

   You'll be taken to the Link Text Wizard dialog box.

   Generally speaking, Access makes pretty good guess at how the data in the file is delimited. Linking to text data involves nothing more than clicking on the Next button and verifying that Access has correctly identified the data in the file. Rather than show or describe each of the dialog boxes in the Link Text Wizard, you're encouraged to link to `Contacts_CSV.txt` and `Contacts_FixedWidth.txt`, both included on this book's CD.

   As you'll see when you link to these files, about the only input required from you is to provide a name for each of the fields Access finds in the text files. If you're lucky, the text file includes field names as the first row in the text file. Otherwise, linking to text files is a very simple operation.

Splitting an Access database

Very often, developers split an Access application into two databases. One (usually called the *back end*) contains only tables and (perhaps) queries, while the other (called the *front end*) contains the forms, queries, reports, macros, and modules included in the application. Splitting an Access database into multiple pieces is an extremely important operation when building applications for multiuser environments. The front-end database is installed on each user's machine, while the back-end database containing the tables is installed on the server. The split database arrangement has several major benefits:

- Everyone on the network shares one common set of data.
- Many people can simultaneously use and update data.

- Updating forms, reports, or other portions of the application generally means nothing more than providing a new front end to your users. The new front end can be put into service without affecting the data underlying the application, and, in fact, different users may work with different versions of the front-end database at the same time.

When creating an application for a multiuser environment, you should consider designing the objects that will be in your database, anticipating putting them into two Access databases. In general, putting all data elements (tables) in a separate database and all the visual objects (forms and reports) and code in another database usually proves more efficient. You will find it much easier to provide updates to your users by replacing the front-end database without having to worry about damaging the data underlying the application.

There are some things you just can't do with a linked table without doing a little extra work. These tasks include finding records and importing data. By using different techniques with linked tables, however, you can do anything you can do with a single database.

If you're starting from scratch, you first create a back-end database with just the tables for the application. You then create the front-end database and link the tables in the front end to the back end. This process is described in detail in Chapter 21. In the meantime, it is enough to understand that the primary consideration in a split database application is maintaining the linkage between the front-end and back-end databases.

Working with Linked Tables

After you link to an external table from another database, you use it just as you would any another Access table. You use linked tables with forms, reports, and queries just as you would native Access tables. When working with external tables, you can modify many of their features (for example, setting view properties and relationships, setting links between tables in queries, and renaming the tables).

One note on renaming linked tables: Providing a different name for the table inside of Access does not change the name of the file that is linked to the application. The name that Access refers to a link table is maintained within the Access application and does not influence the physical table that is linked.

Setting view properties

Although an external table is used like another Access table, you cannot change the structure (delete, add, or rearrange fields) of an external table. You can, however, set several table properties for the fields in a linked table:

- Format
- Decimal Places
- Caption
- Input Mask

- Unicode Compressions
- IME Sequence Mode
- Display Control

Setting relationships

TIP **Access enables you to set permanent relations at the table level between linked non-Access tables and native Access tables through the Relationships Builder. You cannot, however, set referential integrity between linked tables, or between linked tables and internal tables. Access enables you to create forms and reports based on relationships set up in the Relationships Builder, such as building a SQL statement used as the `RecordSource` property of a form or report.**

Linking to external Access tables maintains the relationships that may exist between the external tables. Therefore, when linking to a back-end database, the relationships you have established in the back end are recognized and honored by the front-end database.

Optimizing linked tables

When working with linked tables, Access has to retrieve records from another file. This process takes time, especially when the table resides on a network or in an SQL database. When working with external data, optimize performance by observing these basic rules:

- **Avoid using functions in query criteria.** This is especially true for aggregate functions, such as `DTotal` or `DCount`, which retrieve all records from the linked table before performing the query.
- **Limit the number of external records to view.** Create a query using criteria that limit the number of records from an external table. This query can then be used by other queries, forms, or reports.
- **Avoid excessive movement in datasheets.** View only the data you need to in a datasheet. Avoid paging up and down and jumping to the last or first record in very large tables. (The exception is when you're adding records to the external table.)
- **If you add records to external linked tables, create a form to add records and set the `DataEntry` property to `True`.** This makes the form an entry form that starts with a blank record every time it's executed.

Deleting a linked table reference

Deleting a linked table from the object list is a simple matter of performing three steps:

1. **In the object list, select the linked table you want to delete.**
2. **Press the Delete key, or right-click on the linked table and select Delete from the shortcut menu.**
3. **Click OK in the Access dialog box to delete the file.**

Deleting an external table deletes only its name from the database object list. The actual file is not deleted.

Viewing or changing information for linked tables

Use the Linked Table Manager Wizard to update the links when you move, rename, or modify tables or indexes associated with a linked table. Otherwise, Access will not be able to find the data file referenced by the link.

Select the Database Tools ribbon and click the Linked Table Manager button. Access displays the Linked Table Manager dialog box (shown in Figure 16-12), enabling you to locate the data files associated with the linked tables in the database. Click the check box next to a linked table and click OK. Access verifies that the file cannot be found and displays a Select New Location dialog box. Using this dialog box, find the missing file and reassign the linkage to Access. If all the files are already linked correctly, clicking OK makes Access verify all the linkages associated with all the selected tables.

If you know all of the linked data sources have been moved, click the `Always prompt for a new location` button. Access then prompts you for the new location, and links all of the tables as a batch process. You'll find this operation much faster than linking one or two tables at a time.

FIGURE 16-12

The Linked Table Manager enables you to relocate external tables that have been moved.

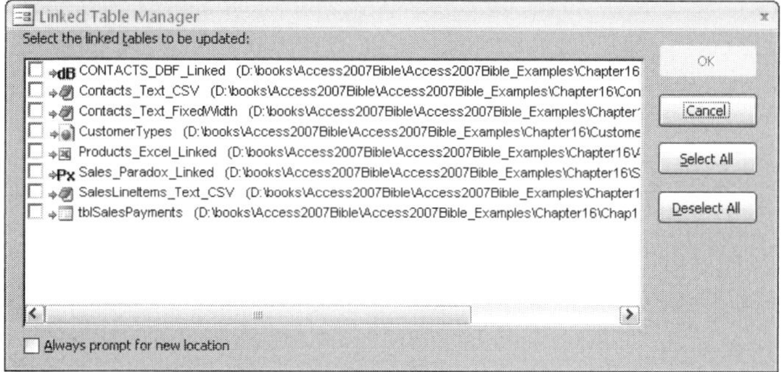

NOTE

If the Linked Table Manager Wizard is not present on your computer, Access automatically prompts you to provide the original Office CD so that Access can install the wizard. This may happen if you didn't instruct Office to install the Additional Wizards component during the initial installation process.

Using Code to Link Tables in Access

This section describes how to link tables to your Access application in code, instead of using the Access menus. It would be nice if you could just make the link once at development time and be done with the whole process. Occasionally, however, you may want to attach tables on the fly, to avoid losing a link. Testing your links whenever your application starts is a good practice — that way, you can keep users from getting any unplanned crashes or error messages. You'll find some examples of these routines in this section.

The following code examples use DAO instead of ADO. For purposes such as linking tables, DAO works just as fast (actually, considerably *faster*), and is simpler to implement, than ADO. The reason DAO is faster than ADO for simple operations such as linking tables is because DAO does not involve the overhead associated with declaring, instantiating, and discarding ActiveX controls. Because DAO is a much simpler object model, you'll find DAO is, arguably, a better fit for simple operations such as linking tables. ADO is definitely a better choice for complex data-management operations, but in some domains DAO still rules.

The Connect and SourceTableName properties

Open sample database for this chapter (`Chapter16.accdb`) and type the following in the Immediate pane of the Immediate window (use Ctrl+G to open the Immediate window):

```
? CurrentDB.TableDefs("ContactLog").Connect
```

you receive a `Null` value as the return. If, however, you type

```
? CurrentDB.TableDefs("Products").Connect
```

you receive a much different result. Access returns a long string that looks something like this (the path indicated at the end of this string may point to a different location):

```
Excel 8.0;HDR=NO;IMEX=2;DATABASE=C:\Data\AccessAutoAuctions.xls
```

In the first case, the `ContactLog` table is part of the current database, and Access finds it without any trouble. The `Products_Linked` table, on the other hand, is linked to an external Excel workbook file. The Connect property of the linked `Products` contains information that Access uses to physically locate the Excel workbook file and form a link to it.

The difference between the `Connect` property for the `Contacts` and `Products` tables is where the tables originate. The `Connect` property of an Access table found within the current database is null because the table originates in the database you're in. There's nothing to connect to, or more appropriately, by default, the connection always exists. However, your ODBC, Excel, and linked Access data sources will always have a `Connect` property that explicitly tells Access what type of data is contained in the linked data source, and where the data source file can be found.

The `Connect` property string is composed of a number of different parameters, some of which are required, depending on the type of external data you're using. If you're accessing one of the ISAM formats that Access directly supports (Excel, dBASE, FoxPro, Paradox, and so on), the connect string is much more abbreviated, taking this form:

```
Object.Connect="Type;DATABASE=Path"
```

where `Object` is the name of the object variable for your `TableDef`, and `Type` is the type of database you're connecting to, such as dBASE IV, Excel 8.0, Text, and so on.

The `Path` parameter can be the complete path to the file, not including the filename itself, or it might include the filename as well, depending on the type of data source. For instance, when connecting to another Access table, you include the entire path, like `C:\Access\Samples\Nwind.mdb`. The same is true of an Excel file.

To connect to a dBASE file, however, you only have to tell Access the path to the file, not the `.dbf` file itself. The difference is in whether or not the object you'll be connecting to exists within another object, or whether the table is the file that you're going after. That's where the `SourceTableName` property comes in.

The `SourceTableName` property tells Access which object to take data from. If you want to connect to a dBASE file, you want your table definition to come from the `.dbf` itself. If, however, you're connecting to an Excel file, you might want the table to be based on a range of cells or a single worksheet within the workbook in the `.xls` file, not the entire spreadsheet file. Connecting to another Access `.accdb` or `.mdb` is the same way. To link to the `Customers` table in `Northwind.accdb`, your connect string tells Access that the value of the `DATABASE` parameter is `C:\Access\Samples\Northwind.mdb` and that the `SourceTableName` property of your `TableDef` is `Customers`. If you want to connect to a dBASE file named `NewEmp.dbf` located in the root directory of `C:`, you tell Access that the `DATABASE` is `C:\` and the `SourceTableName` is `NewEmp.dbf`.

The AttachExcel function (listed below) shows you how to connect to a named range within an Excel spreadsheet. To connect to a spreadsheet, you have to specify what kind of spreadsheet it is, where the spreadsheet file exists, and the range you want to connect to. You can use either a named range or a range of cells (such as A1:B20). You can also tell Access that the spreadsheet you're connecting to contains field names in the first row. The default for this parameter is `Yes`.

To use the `AttachExcel()` function, the calling procedure must pass the spreadsheet name, the new name for the Access table, and a valid Excel range name.

ON the CD-ROM **The following function is located in the `basAttachExcel` module in `Chapter16.accdb` on the book's companion CD-ROM.**

The following statement invokes the AttachExcel function, linking a range named `Names` to a table named `ExcelDemo`:

```
AttachExcel(""Emplist.xls"", ""ExcelDemo"", "Names")
```

The AttachExcel function returns a Boolean value reporting whether the Excel file was successfully attached (True) or not (False):

```
Function AttachExcel( _
    ByVal sFileName As String, _
    ByVal sTableName As String, _
    ByVal sRangeName As String _
    ) As Boolean

  Const conCannotOpen = 3432
  Const conNotRange = 3011
  Const conTableExists = 3012

  Dim db As DAO.Database
  Dim td As DAO.TableDef

  Dim sConnect As String
  Dim sMsg As String
  Dim sFunction As String

On Error GoTo HandleError

  AttachExcel = False
  sFunction = "AttachExcel"

  ' Check for existence of worksheet:
  sFileName = CurDir() & "\" & sFileName

  ' If the file isn't found, notify
  ' the user and exit the procedure:
  If Len(Dir(sFileName)) = 0 Then
    MsgBox "The file " & sFileName _
        & " could not be found"
    MsgBox "Please move the file to " _
        & CurDir() & " to continue"
    Exit Function
  End If
  Set db = CurrentDb

  ' Create a new tabledef in the current database:
  Set td = db.CreateTableDef(sTableName)

  ' Build connect string:
  sConnect = "Excel 8.0;HDR=YES;DATABASE=" & sFileName
  td.Connect = sConnect

  ' Specify Range Name sRangeName:
  td.SourceTableName = sRangeName
```

```
    ' Append new linked table to TableDefs collection:
    db.TableDefs.Append td

    'Return True:
    AttachExcel = True

ExitHere:

    Exit Function

HandleError:

    Select Case Err
      Case conCannotOpen
          sMsg = "Cannot open " & sFileName

      Case conTableExists
          sMsg = "The table " & sTableName & _
               " already exists."

      Case conNotRange
          sMsg = "Can't find the " & sRangeName & " range."

      Case Else
          sMsg = "Error#" & Err & ": " & Error$

    End Select

    MsgBox sMsg, vbExclamation + vbOKOnly, _
         "Error in Procedure " & sFunction

    AttachExcel = False
    Resume ExitHere

End Function
```

Connect strings and source table names are more involved when you're using ODBC data sources. For instance, when you connect to a SQL Server ODBC data source, you have the option of specifying the type of source you'll be using (ODBC), the DSN (data source name), the application you're using, the table within the data source that contains the data you want, the workstation using the application, and a user ID and password. Not all of these parameters are available to every ODBC data source, so you need to consult your ODBC driver manual to find out what you can and can't use.

By the way, you might not want to hard-code a user ID and password in your connect string but instead use some combination of Access and a customized security setup that allows you to capture a user's ID and password when the user logs in to your application and then pass those values dynamically.

One final example we've included in this section is one that shows you how to connect to a text file. As we mention in the "Linking to text files" section, earlier in this chapter, you can link to delimited or fixed-width text files. Linking to a text file follows the same process as the previous examples; the biggest difference is the DSN parameter. Before you can link to a text file, you must create an import specification that tells Access what the file looks like.

In previous versions of Access, you created import/export specs only when you imported or exported fixed files; but Access 2007 lets you create a spec for delimited files as well. If you use the Import Wizard, Access creates an import specification for you. The connect string for a text file is the name of the import spec you've created. The `Database` parameter is the path to the file, and the `SourceTableName` property is the filename you want to link to, without the file extension.

The following function is located in the `basLinkText` module in `Chapter16.accdb` on this book's companion CD-ROM.

```
Function LinkText( _
    ByVal sFileName As String, _
    ByVal sDSN As String, _
    ByVal sFMT As String, _
    ByVal sHDR As String, _
    ByVal sIMEX As String, _
    ByVal sTableName As String _
    ) As Boolean

  Dim db As DAO.Database
  Dim td As DAO.TableDef
  Dim x As Integer
  Dim sType As String
  Dim sPath As String
  Dim sPathAndFileName As String
  Dim sDatabase As String
  Dim sConnect As String
  Dim sMsg As String
  Dim sFunction As String
  Const conTableExists = 3012

On Error GoTo HandleError

  LinkText = False
  sFunction = "LinkTxt"

  ' Check for existence of file:
  sPath = CurDir() & "\"
  sDatabase = sPath & sFileName

  If Len(Dir(sDatabase)) = 0 Then
    MsgBox "The File " & sFileName & _
           "could not be found"
```

```
    MsgBox "Copy the file to " & CurDir() _
           & " to continue"
    Exit Function
  End If

  ' Create Tabledef:
  Set db = CurrentDb
  Set td = db.CreateTableDef(sTableName)

  sType = "Text;"
  sDSN = "DSN=" & sDSN & ";"
  sFMT = "FMT=" & sFMT & ";"
  sHDR = "HDR=" & sHDR & ";"
  sIMEX = "IMEX=" & sIMEX & ";"

  sDatabase = "DATABASE=" & sPath
  sConnect = sType & sDSN & sFMT & sHDR & sIMEX & sDatabase

  td.Connect = sConnect
  td.SourceTableName = sFileName
  db.TableDefs.Append td

  LinkText = True

ExitHere:

  Exit Function

HandleError:

  Select Case Err

    Case conTableExists
        sMsg = "The table " & sTableName _
            & " already exists."

    Case Else
        sMsg = "Error#" & Err & ": " & Error$

  End Select

  MsgBox sMsg, vbExclamation + vbOKOnly, _
       "Error in Procedure " & sFunction

  LinkText = False
  Resume ExitHere

End Function
```

Assuming you have created an import link specification named EmployeeImport Link Specification, the following statement uses the LinkText() function to link data from the Empimp.txt text file to a new table named EmployeeLink.

The sample database, Chap16Start.accdb, already contains this import link specification and the LinkText() function.

The text file ImpFixed.txt, which contains fixed-length data, is also found in the Chapter16 folder on the companion CD. Use a statement like the following to link ImpFixed.txt to a table named EmployeeLink:

```
LinkText("ImpFixed.txt", _
    "EmployeeImport Link Specification", _
    "Fixed", "NO", "2", "EmployeeLink")
```

To import a comma-delimited text file named ImpDelim.txt (also found on the companion CD-ROM) for which you have created a corresponding import link specification, you can use the following statement:

```
LinkText("ImpDelim.txt", _
    "EmployeeImport Link Specification Delimited", _
    "Delimited", "NO", "2", "EmployeeLink2")
```

As you can see, there are dozens of combinations you can use when linking to external data sources. The connect strings for each can get a little confusing, but there is a way to make connecting easy. If you pretend you're an end user and use the wizards, the process can be a lot easier. Once you step through the process of linking the table you want using the Link Wizard, open the Debug window and query the Connect and SourceTableName properties of the table you've linked. Once you do, you'll have all you need to build the VBA code for doing the same thing programmatically. Just copy the connect string from the Debug window and paste it into your procedure.

Checking links

You (or, more accurately, your users) will at some point encounter a situation where a linked table in one of your applications becomes unavailable. For example, suppose your application links to a SQL Server database and the network goes down. One of your users, who does not know the network is down, sits down at his workstation and tries to pull up your application. As soon as the attempt is made to access data from the attached table, an error occurs and your uninformed user panics. Here's another common scenario: Suppose your application is linking to an Excel spreadsheet, but someone decides to clean up a directory and moves, renames, or deletes the spreadsheet. Again, an error occurs when someone tries to access data from the linked table. You may not be able to prevent these situations, but you can plan for them ahead of time.

The following function, CheckLinks, should probably be run as a startup routine for your application, or in addition to any procedures you run when your application is accessed. You can pass the function the name of an attached table, and test to see if the link is still valid. All the procedure does is try to open the table as a recordset. If the OpenRecordset method fails, either the table doesn't exist in the database or the link has been lost. All this function has to do is flash a descriptive message to the user and a return value to announce that the application should proceed no further.

The following function is located in the `basTestLinks` module in `Chapter16.accdb` on the book's companion CD-ROM.

```
Function TestLink(sTablename As String) As Boolean
  Dim db As DAO.Database
  Dim rs As DAO.Recordset
  Dim iStartODBC As Integer
  Dim iEndODBC As Integer
  Dim sDataSrc As String
  Dim iODBCLen As Integer
  Dim sMessage As String
  Dim iReturn As Integer

On Error GoTo HandleError

  Set db = CurrentDb

  'Open a recordset to force an error:
  Set rs = db.OpenRecordset(sTablename)

  'If the link is valid, exit the function:
  TestLink = True

ExitHere:

  If Not rs Is Nothing Then
    rs.Close
    Set rs = Nothing
  End If

  Exit Function

HandleError:
  'If the link is bad, determine what the problem
  'is, let the user know, and exit the function:
  Select Case Err

      Case 3078    'Table doesn't exist:

          sMessage = "Table '" & sTablename _
               & "' does not exist in this database"

      Case 3151    'Bad link
          'Extract the name of the odbc DSN
          'to use in your custom error message:
```

```
            iStartODBC = InStr(Error, "to '") + 4

            iEndODBC = InStr(Error, "' failed")
            iODBCLen = iEndODBC - iStartODBC

            sDataSrc = Mid$(Error, iStartODBC, iODBCLen)

            sMessage = "Table '" & sTablename _
                 & "' is linked to ODBC datasource '" _
                 & sDataSrc _
                 & "' which is not available at this time"

        Case Else
            sMessage = Err.Description

    End Select

    iReturn = MsgBox(sMessage, vbOKOnly)

    'Return failure:
    TestLink = False

    Resume ExitHere

End Function
```

Summary

Linking to external data sources is an essential requirement for many access applications. Microsoft Access is equipped to deal with virtually any type of external data, including obsolete database types such as dBASE and Paradox as well is more modern data types such as HTML and XML.

With few exceptions, linking to virtually any external data source requires very few steps on the part of a developer. The Access linking wizards are very similar, regardless of the data type involved in the link operation. The code required to automatically link to external data sources is not extensive and is easily incorporated into Access applications. Access also provides tools such as the Linked Table Wizard to help you manage linked tables in your applications.

Chapter 17 deals with the important topic of importing data into Access applications. Although the process is very similar to linking to external data sources, importing moves the data into an Access database permanently. As you'll see in Chapter 17, virtually the same steps are required to import data as were required to link to external data.

Chapter 17

Importing and Exporting Data

In Chapter 16, you discovered how Access 2007 can be used to link to external data sources and files. A link allows you to view data in Access, where the data is stored in something like an Oracle database, or an XML document. So, in the case of linking, Access is being used as an interface into data, which is stored outside of Access. In this chapter, you'll discover that importing and exporting are quite different from linking. An import into Access allows the creation of data inside an Access database, from some external source such as an XML document. An export from Access means you create something. For example, export to an XML document from data stored in an Access database.

IN THIS CHAPTER

Importing and exporting external data

Creating import/export specifications

Exporting to external tables and files

ON the CD-ROM This chapter uses various files for importing, plus two Access 2007 databases: `Chapter17_1.accdb` and `Chapter17_2.accdb`. Both databases will be used for importing and exporting. If you haven't already copied these files onto your machine from the CD, you'll need to do so now.

Types of Imports and Exports

Before examining the processes of importing and exporting, let's take a brief look at the various options for importing into Access and exporting from Access.

Access can use and exchange data among a wide range of applications. For example, you may need to get data from other databases, such as FoxPro, dBASE, or Paradox databases. Or you might need to obtain information from a SQL Server, an Oracle database, a text file, or even an XML document. Access can move data among several categories of applications, database engines, and even different platforms (mainframes and Macintosh computers).

CROSS-REF **We cover all these items in Chapter 16.**

Open up the `Chapter17.accdb` database in Access 2007, and you can see for yourself. Click the External Data ribbon tab at the top of the screen in Access 2007. You'll see options for Import, Export, Collect Data, and SharePoint Lists. At this point, what all these things are is not too important. The point is, you're now looking at all the numerous options for importing and exporting with Access 2007.

Both the Import and Export options include the following:

- Another Access database (virtually any Access version)
- Excel spreadsheet
- SharePoint List
- Text file
- XML document

NOTE **At the bottom-right corner of both the Import and the Export options, you'll see a drop-down button. That's the thing with the little down arrow on the right. Click the More drop-down list and you'll see additional import or export options.**

The additional Import options include the following:

- ODBC connected database (SQL Server, Oracle, another Access database)
- HTML document
- Outlook folder
- dBase and Paradox file
- Lotus 1-2-3 file

The Export option includes the following in addition to those listed earlier:

- ODBC connected database (SQL Server, Oracle, another Access database)
- HTML file
- dBase and Paradox databases
- Lotus 1-2-3 file
- Merge with a Word document

Importing External Data

An import copies externally stored data into an Access database, resulting in the imported data utilizing the format of an Access database. When you import a file (unlike when you link tables), you copy the contents from an external file into an Access table. You can import external file information from several different sources, as we discussed in the previous section.

You can import information to new tables or existing tables, depending on the type of data being imported. All data types can be imported to new tables. However, some types of imports — such as spreadsheets and text files — may have to be imported into existing tables, because text files and spreadsheets don't necessarily have table structure. So, it has to already exist.

When Access imports data from an external file, it does not erase or destroy the external file or external data source, because Access merely reads the data. Therefore, you'll have two copies of the data: the original file (in its original format) and the new Access table.

Importing from another Access database

You can import objects from a source database into the current database. The objects you import can be tables, queries, forms, reports, macros, or modules. Import an object into the current Access database by following these generic steps:

1. **Open the target database you want to import into.**

   In this case open the `Chapter17_1.accdb` database.

2. **Click the External Data tab.**
3. **Click the Access option in the Import section and select the filename of the source Access database as `Chapter17_2.accdb`.**
4. **The next screen will give you options as to what you can import, as shown in Figure 17-1, where all sorts of things can be imported.**
5. **Select one of the tables and click OK.**

   If an object already exists in the target database, then a sequential number will be added to the imported object, distinguishing it from the original already present in the open target database. If `tblDepartments` already exists, the new imported table will be `tblDepartments1`.

6. **The next screen you get is a very useful feature in that it allows you to store the import process in a VBA macro coded procedure; that procedure can be executed again at a later date by opening the Saved Imports option on the Import section of the External Data tab in Access 2007.**

   You simply click on the task and the import will be executed again. It couldn't be easier.

FIGURE 17-1

Many types of Access database objects can be imported from one Access database into another.

7. **You can also import the VBA export macro process as a regularly scheduled Outlook Task (which executes periodically in the calendar scheduling system of your Outlook e-mail software).**

   Now, isn't that just neat!

Importing spreadsheet data

You can import data from Excel or Lotus 1-2-3 spreadsheets to a new or existing table. The key to importing spreadsheet data is that it must be arranged in tabular (columnar) format. Each cell of data in a spreadsheet column must contain the same type of data. Figure 17-2 demonstrates correct and incorrect columnar-format data.

NOTE **You can import or link all the data from a spreadsheet, or just the data from a named range of cells. Naming a range of cells in your spreadsheet can make importing into Access easier. Often a spreadsheet is formatted into groups of cells. One group of cells may contain a listing of sales by customer, for example. The section below the sales listing may include total sales for all customers, totals by product type, or totals by month purchased. By naming the range for each group of cells, you can limit the import to just one section of the spreadsheet.**

FIGURE 17-2

Access can import data from a spreadsheet, but there are some restrictions.

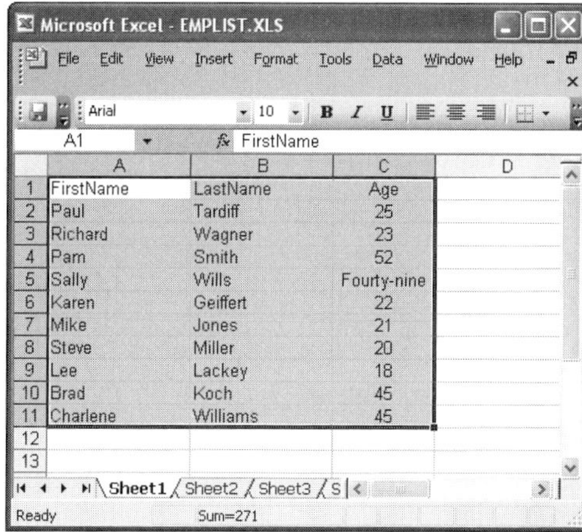

	A	B	C	D
1	FirstName	LastName	Age	
2	Paul	Tardiff	25	
3	Richard	Wagner	23	
4	Pam	Smith	52	
5	Sally	Wills	Fourty-nine	
6	Karen	Geiffert	22	
7	Mike	Jones	21	
8	Steve	Miller	20	
9	Lee	Lackey	18	
10	Brad	Koch	45	
11	Charlene	Williams	45	
12				
13				

Figure 17-2 represents cells in a spreadsheet to be imported. There is a problem with Column C in the spreadsheet in Figure 17-2. The Age column should contain all numbers, but it contains a single text description of the age of 49. This is likely to cause an error so it has to be changed to that shown in Figure 17-3.

FIGURE 17-3

Data types between a spreadsheet and Access should be the same for each column

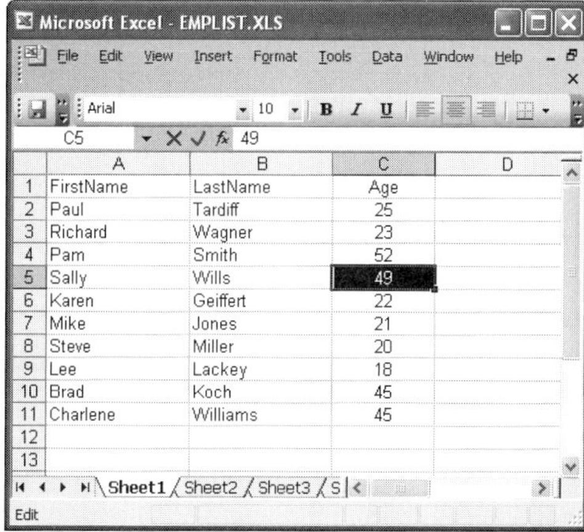

	A	B	C	D
1	FirstName	LastName	Age	
2	Paul	Tardiff	25	
3	Richard	Wagner	23	
4	Pam	Smith	52	
5	Sally	Wills	49	
6	Karen	Geiffert	22	
7	Mike	Jones	21	
8	Steve	Miller	20	
9	Lee	Lackey	18	
10	Brad	Koch	45	
11	Charlene	Williams	45	
12				
13				

To import the Excel spreadsheet named `emplist.xls`, follow these steps:

1. **Click the Excel button under the External Data tab.**
2. **Select the filename for the Excel spreadsheet file and click OK.**

   The next screen displays the first step in the Import Spreadsheet Wizard, resembling that shown in Figure 17-4.

FIGURE 17-4

The first Import Spreadsheet Wizard screen

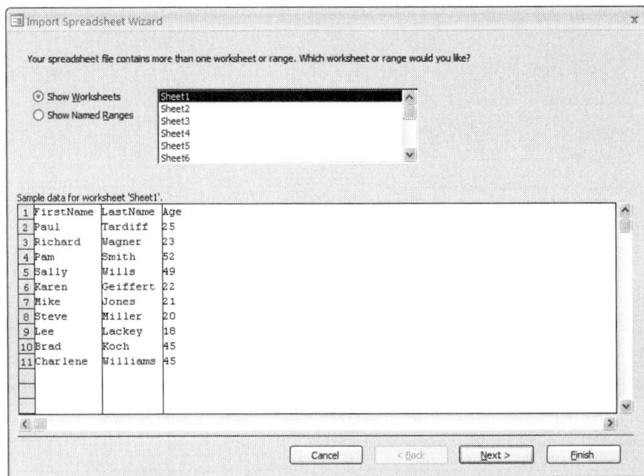

3. **Click Next to move to the second screen and select the First Row contains Column Heading check box.**

   You don't want the column headings FirstName, LastName, and Age being stored as fields. Apart from that, the Age header will change the field Age to a text datatype, and a number is best stored as a number.

4. **Click Next.**
5. **On the next screen, you can remove fields from the import. You can also specify a new name for the field, set its data type, and even create an index on a field. When you're done, click Next.**
6. **You can now set a primary key. Assuming you didn't change the name of the `FirstName` field, select the radio button to select your own primary key, and select the `FirstName` field as the primary key.**

A primary key uniquely identifies each row in a table, in this case prohibiting more than one employee with the same name.

7. **Click Next, specify the new table name, and click the Finish button.**
8. **Again, you can save the import process as a macro for later re-execution.**

The new table will now appear in your target Access database window. A standard Access table has been created from the original spreadsheet file.

CAUTION **Importing an Excel file with the same name as a linked Excel file could cause problems. It might be best to give the newly imported table a new name and avoid issues, unless you actually intend to replace an existing table.**

Importing a SharePoint list

A SharePoint list is essentially a data source, which is available from a SharePoint site, running a SharePoint server. It's a way of sharing data over the Internet. We examine SharePoint Services in Chapter 23 and Chapter 38.

Importing text file data

There are many reasons for text file output such as B2B (Business to Business data transfers and mainframes). Mainframe data, is ordinarily output from the mainframe computer using text files, when used in desktop applications. You can import from two different types of text files: delimited and fixed-width. Access uses a single wizard for both types of text files. The Import Text Wizard assists you in identifying the fields for the import/export specification. You may recognize this wizard structure and its screens if you've ever imported text data into something like Excel or Word.

Delimited text files

Delimited text files are sometimes known as *comma-delimited* or *tab-delimited files;* each record is on a separate line in the text file. The fields on the line contain no trailing spaces, normally use commas or tab characters as field separators, and might have certain fields be enclosed in *delimiters* (such as single or double quotation marks). Sometimes text fields are enclosed in quotation marks or some other delimiter. This is an example comma delimited text file:

```
1,Davolio,Nancy,5/1/92 0:00:00,4000
2,Fuller,Andrew,8/14/92 0:00:00,6520
3,Leverling,Janet,4/1/92 0:00:00,1056
4,Peacock,Margaret,5/3/93 0:00:00,4000
5,Buchanan,Steven,10/17/93 0:00:00,5000
6,Suyama,Michael,10/17/93 0:00:00,1000
7,King,Robert,1/2/94 0:00:00,1056
8,Callahan,Laura,3/5/94 0:00:00,1056
9,Dodsworth,Joe,11/15/94 0:00:00,1056
```

Notice that the file has nine records (rows of text) and six fields. A comma separates each field. Text fields are not delimited with double quotation marks, as this behavior is a little dated. The starting position of each field, after the first one, is different. Each record has a different length because the field lengths are different.

To import a delimited text file named `impdelim.txt`, follow these steps:

1. **Open the `Chapter17_1.accdb` database.**
2. **Select the External Data tab.**
3. **Click Text File in the Import section.**
4. **Find the text file using the Browse button, select it, and click OK.**

   The next screen you get is the Import Text Wizard, as shown in Figure 17-5.

FIGURE 17-5

The first Import Text Wizard screen

Import Text Wizard

Your data seems to be in a 'Delimited' format. If it isn't, choose the format that more correctly describes your data.

- Delimited - Characters such as comma or tab separate each field
- Fixed Width - Fields are aligned in columns with spaces between each field

Sample data from file: C:\MANUSCRIPTS\WILEY\ACCESS2007\17\IMPDELIM.TXT.

```
1 1,Davolio,Nancy,5/1/92 0:00:00,4000
2 2,Fuller,Andrew,8/14/92 0:00:00,6520
3 3,Leverling,Janet,4/1/92 0:00:00,1056
4 4,Peacock,Margaret,5/3/93 0:00:00,4000
5 5,Buchanan,Steven,10/17/93 0:00:00,5000
6 6,Suyama,Michael,10/17/93 0:00:00,1000
7 7,King,Robert,1/2/94 0:00:00,1056
8 8,Callahan,Laura,3/5/94 0:00:00,1056
9 9,Dodsworth,Joe,11/15/94 0:00:00,1056
```

Advanced... Cancel < Back Next > Finish

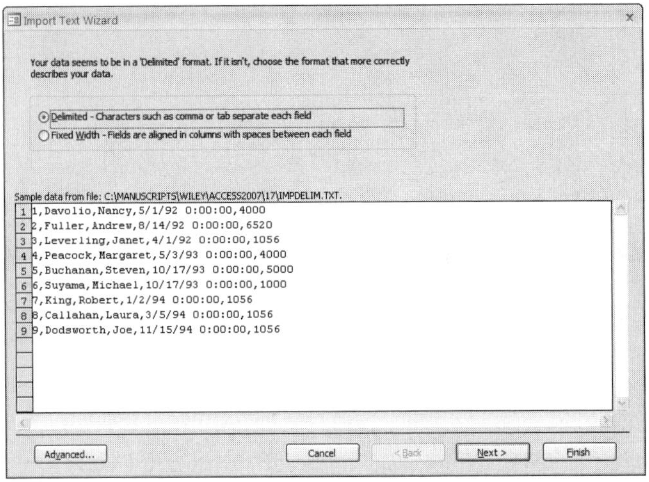

This screen in Figure 17-5 displays the data in the text file and lets you choose between delimited or fixed-width. The default for the wizard is delimited.

NOTE **Notice, at the bottom of the screen, the button marked Advanced. Click it to further define the import specifications. You'll learn more about this option in the "Fixed-width text files" section; generally, it's not needed for delimited files. Click the Cancel button to return to the Import Text Wizard.**

5. **Click Next to display the next Import Text Wizard screen.**

   As you can see in Figure 17-6, this screen enables you to determine which type of separator to use in the delimited text file. Generally, this separator is a comma, but you could use a tab, semicolon, space, or other character (such as an asterisk), which you enter in the box next to the Other option button. You can also decide whether to use text from the first row as field names for the imported table. It has correctly assigned the comma as the separator type and the text qualifier as quotation marks (").

NOTE A *separator* is the specific character that was placed between the fields in a delimited text file — often it is a comma or semicolon, although it can be any specific character. There can be a problem with the separator used — for example, in this case, the separator is a comma — if any of the fields have a comma in them. It could cause a problem when trying to import the data. (With the last name of JONES, Peter versus the next name of SMITH, Johnathan, Sr., Smith's record has what appears to be an extra field in the last name — Sr.) This can cause all sorts of problems when importing the data. The *Text Qualifier*, for delimited text files refers to the marks that are often placed around text fields versus numeric and date fields. Often they are single quotation marks or double quotation marks.

FIGURE 17-6

The second Import Text Wizard screen

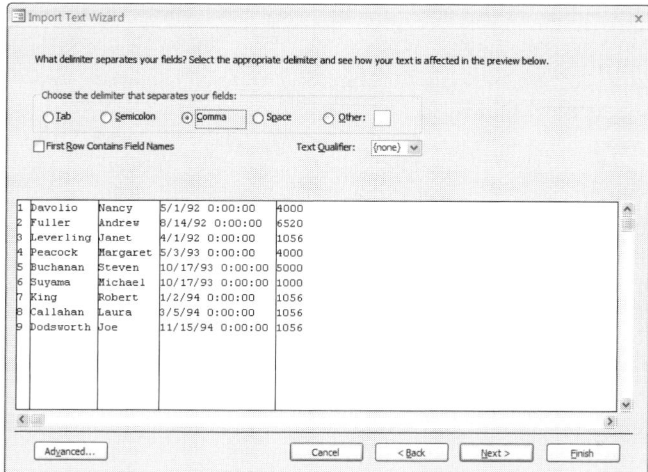

6. **The next few screens allow you to change field names, do things with primary keys, set an import table name, save the import steps as a VBA macro — all the same stuff as before. The detailed specifications of importing and exporting are fairly consistent for many types of importing and exporting.**

   Access creates a new table, using the same name as the text file's name; then it displays an information box informing you that it created the table successfully. Clicking the OK button returns you to the database. The filename appears in the Access Database window, where Access has added the table Names.

NOTE You can import records from a delimited text file that has fields with no values. To specify a field with no value, simply leave no characters between the commas (not even a space character). An empty field at the end of a row is indicated by the line ending with a comma. Obviously, a field containing a comma will cause a problem and the entire field should be enclosed in double quotes. This prevents the contained comma from being interpreted as a field delimiter.

Fixed-width text files

Fixed-width text files also place each record on a separate line. However, the fields in each record are of a fixed length. If the field contents are not long enough, trailing spaces are added to the field, as shown in the following example (the same as the previous example, except without the commas):

```
1          Davolio      Nancy     5/1/92 0:00:00      4000
2          Fuller       Andrew    8/14/92 0:00:00     6520
3          Leverling    Janet     4/1/92 0:00:00      1056
4          Peacock      Margaret  5/3/93 0:00:00      4000
5          Buchanan     Steven    10/17/93 0:00:00    5000
6          Suyama       Michael   10/17/93 0:00:00    1000
7          King         Robert    1/2/94 0:00:00      1056
8          Callahan     Laura     3/5/94 0:00:00      1056
9          Dodsworth    Joe       11/15/94 0:00:00    1056
```

Notice that the fields are not separated by delimiters. Rather, they start at exactly the same position in each record. Each record has exactly the same length. If the data in a field is not long enough, trailing spaces are added to fill the field.

Notice that text values, such as first and last names, are not surrounded by quotation marks. There is no need for delimiting text values because each field is a specific width. Anything within a field's position is considered data and does not require delimiters such as quotation marks.

You can import either a delimited or a fixed-width text file to a new table or existing Access table. If you decide to append the imported file to an existing table, the file's structure must match that of the Access table you're appending to.

NOTE **If the Access table being imported has a primary key field, the text file cannot have any duplicate primary key values or the import will report an error and fail to import rows with duplicate primary key values.**

In fixed-width text files, each field in the file has a specific width and position. Files downloaded from mainframes are the most common fixed-width text files. As you import or export this type of file, you must specify an import/export setup specification. You create this setup file by using the Advanced options of the Import Table Wizard.

To import a fixed-width text file, follow these steps:

1. **Open the `Ch17_1.accdb` database in Access 2007.**
2. **Click the External Data tab and select Text File import.**
3. **When browsing (by clicking the Browse button), find a file called `impfixed.txt`, select it to import, and click OK.**
4. **You get the same screen as shown in Figure 17-5, except with the Fixed Width radio button option selected (Access guesses for you). Click Next.**

   Your next screen looks like the one shown in Figure 17-7.

FIGURE 17-7

An Import Text Wizard screen for fixed-width text files

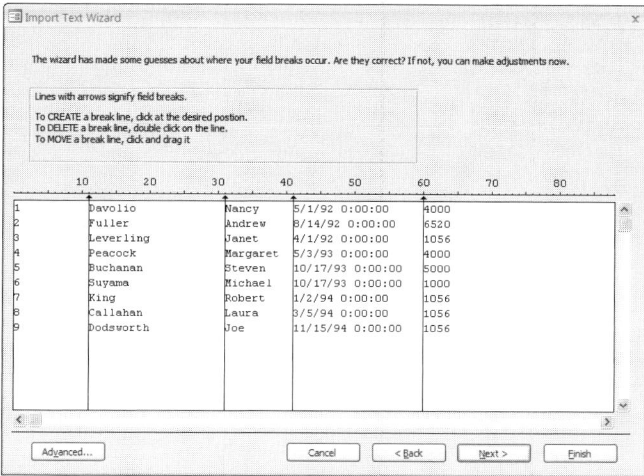

5. **Read the text at the top of the window.**

   You can actually create more break lines (to break data into fields), move the break lines around, and delete existing ones. Access guesses at the best split of data into columns, based on the most consistent breakup of data across the different rows. In this case, the data columnar splitting is very consistent.

6. **Click Next to display the next Import Text Wizard screen.**

   This screen makes intelligent guesses as to where columns begin and end in the file, basing the guess on the spaces in the file.

7. **Click the Advanced button to activate the Import Specification screen (see Figure 17-8) for the table to be imported.**

   Figure 17-8 shows the Import Specification screen active. This window is atop the Import Text Wizard window. This Import Specifications window is activated by clicking the Advanced button in the Import Text Wizard.

FIGURE 17-8

The Import Specification screen for importing a fixed-width text file

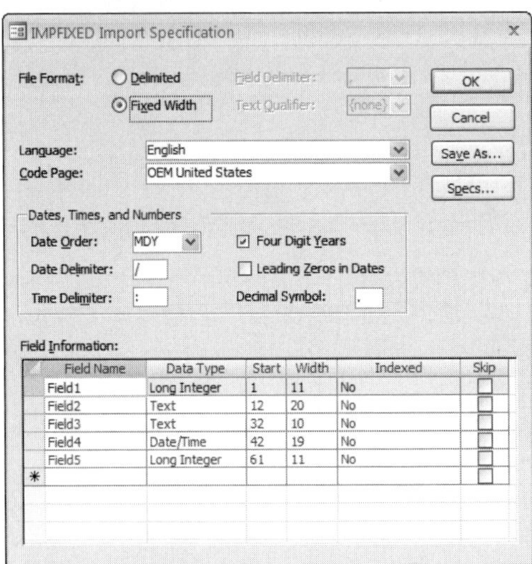

The section labeled Dates, Times, and Numbers describes how date, time, and numeric information is formatted in the import file.

8. **Make sure that the Four Digit Years check box is selected.**
9. **Click the Leading Zeros in Dates check box.**

   The month and day in the data being imported includes a leading zero for numbers less than 10.

10. **Click in the Date Order combo box and make sure it's set to MDY (month day year).**

    The bottom half of the Import Specifications dialog box has a section named Field Information. This section lists the name, data type, and position of each field in the import table. Although you can manually type the specifications for each field in this file, in this example you can accept the field information that Access has created for you and return to the Import Text Wizard.

11. **Click a sequence of OK buttons and Next buttons. You get to specify a primary key and other import details, and eventually reach the Finish button, which you click to execute the import process.**

CAUTION **If you made a mistake and Access could not import the records correctly, perhaps you failed to specify the correct type of date conversion to get this type of error. Access will report a message like this: "Finished importing file XXX to table XXX. Not all your data was successfully imported. Error descriptions with associated row numbers of bad records can be found in Microsoft Access table YYYErrors." Note that XXX and YYY will be actual names. You can read about troubleshooting import errors in the "Troubleshooting import errors" section, later in this chapter.**

Using the Import Specification window

In earlier versions of Access, you had to specify the import/export specifications manually, specifying field lengths, delimited or fixed text, type of delimiter, how to export date fields, and so on. You can still specify this information by using the Import Specification window, as shown in the previous step-by-step example. Using the graphical tools (built into the Import Wizard) of Access is easier, though.

Although the Import Text Wizard generally does a good job of importing your data correctly, at times you may need to specify field lengths and data types manually. If you use the Import Specification dialog box (shown in Figure 17-8), you can change or set all the options on one screen, which can be helpful.

One advantage of using this screen is the capability to specify the type of file to be imported from or exported to. The Language and Code Page fields determine the type of format. The default language is English. The Code Page combo box displays the code page types that are available for the language you select. Specifically, these choices are available for the English language:

- OEM United States
- Unicode
- Unicode (Big-Endian)
- Unicode (UTF-7)
- Unicode (UTF-8)
- Western European (DOS)
- Western European (ISO)
- Western European (Windows)

The default value is the Western European (Windows). Notice that in Figure 17-8 it has been changed to OEM United States. You may need to set this value if you're running a language that does not use the Roman character set used in English, French, German, and so on. You can also specify the Field Delimiter option for delimited text files; the delimiter is used to separate the fields. You do this by using a special character such as a comma or semicolon. Four field-separator choices are available in this combo box:

;	Semicolon
{tab}	Tabulation mark
{space}	Single space
,	Comma

When working with delimited files, you can also specify your own field separator directly in this combo box.

Also, when working with delimited files, you can specify the Text Qualifier. It specifies the type of delimiter to be used when you're working with Text-type fields. Normally, the text fields in a delimited file are enclosed by specified delimiters (such as quotation marks). This is useful for specifying Number-type data (such as Social Security numbers) as Text type rather than Number type (it won't be used in a calculation). You have three list box choices:

{none}	No delimiter
"	Double quotation mark
'	Single quotation mark

The default value is a double quotation mark. This list box is actually a combo box; you can enter your own delimiter. If the one you want is not among these three choices, you can specify a different text delimiter by entering a new one directly in the combo box—for example, the caret symbol (^).

NOTE **If you use comma-delimited files, created by other PC-based databases, you should set the text qualifier to the double quotation mark (") and the field delimiter to a comma (,) if that is what they are in the text file being imported or linked. You can always open the incoming data file in Notepad or Word to examine how the data is delimited.**

When Access 2007 imports or exports data, it converts dates to a specific format (such as MMDDYY). In the example MMDDYY, Access converts all dates to two digits for each portion of the date (month, day, and year), separating each by a specified delimiter. Thus, January 19, 2006, would be converted to 1/19/06. You can specify how date fields are to be converted, using one of six choices in the Date Order combo box:

- DMY
- DYM
- MDY
- MYD
- YDM
- YMD

These choices specify the order for each portion of a date. The D is the day of the month (1–31), M is the calendar month (1–12), and Y is the year. The default date order is set to the U.S. format of month, day, and year. When you work with European dates, the order must be changed to day, month, and year.

You use the Date Delimiter option to specify the date delimiter. This option tells Access which type of delimiter to use between the parts of date fields. The default is a forward slash (/), but this can be changed to any user-specified delimiter. In Europe, for example, date parts are separated by periods, as in 22.10.06.

NOTE **When you import text files with Date-type data, you must have a separator between the month, day, and year or else Access reports an error if the field is specified as a Date/Time type. When you're exporting date fields, the separator is not needed.**

With the Time Delimiter option, you can specify a separator between the segments of time values in a text file. The default value is the colon (:). In the example 12:55, the colon separates the hours from the minutes. To change the separator, simply enter another in the Time Delimiter box.

You select the Four Digit Years check box when you want to specify that the year value in date fields will be formatted with four digits. By checking this box, you can export dates that include the century (such as in 1881 or 2001). The default is to include the century.

The Leading Zeros in Dates option is a check box where you specify that date values include leading zeros. You can specify, for example, that date formats include leading zeros (as in 02/04/03). To specify leading zeros, check this box. The default is without leading zeros (as in 2/4/03).

Importing an XML document

Importing XML documents is easy with Access 2007. This type of processing can be used to transfer information between disparate platforms, databases, operating systems, applications, companies, planets, universes — you name it! That's the intention of XML. XML creates standards for data, metadata, and even the processing of that data. Those standards are more than adequately provided for in Access 2007.

Presenting XML in Access 2007 needs to be done in an odd way. You could easily import a simple XML document in your Access database. However, the best way to find out how well Access 2007 caters to XML is to begin by exporting something into XML.

Follow these steps to export data from Access 2007 into an XML document:

1. **Open the** `Chapter17_1.accdb` **database in Access 2007.**
2. **Under the External Data tab, in the Export section, click the More drop-down button, and click XML File.**
3. **Browse to and select an XML file to export to, and click the OK button.**
4. **The next screen is like the one shown in Figure 17-9.**

FIGURE 17-9

The first export window for exporting to an XML document

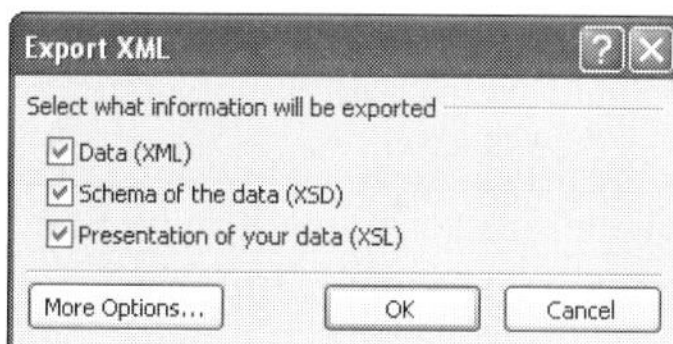

The screen in Figure 17-9 shows that multiple layers and levels of XML data, metadata, and processing capability can all be exported. It gets even better. Click the More Options button. XML is the basic XML document. A basic XML document includes both data in its textual values, plus metadata in its elements, attributes, and relationships between the elements across the entire document. XML Schema Definition (XSD), gives the capability to essentially map relational tables to XML documents — directly! In other words, the Access 2007 database will *understand* everything in the XML document, without any extra processing. That's what XSD is used for.

Also eXtensible Style Sheets (XSL) provides for transformation processing. A direct display of an XML document in a browser is very technical and quite ugly. XSL allows for transformation to beautify, personalize, and functionally empower the presentation of XML data in a browser.

5. **The next screen on from Figure 17-9 will give you further capabilities to exercise Access 2007 taking, what appears to be, full advantage of the power of XML.**

   We're very impressed with the way that Access 2007 deals with XML. The only thing that is missing is an internally stored database and fully XML functionally XML datatype. The most sophisticated relational databases have only just introduced XML datatypes.

To import that same XML document just created, select the External Data tab, go to XML file in the Import section, find the XML file by browsing to it, and click OK. Importing is the same process as exporting, implementing the same process as in Steps 1 to 5 above — in reverse.

Importing an HTML document

Access 2007 enables you to import HTML tables as easily as any other database, Excel spreadsheet, or text file. You simply select the HTML file you want to import and use the HTML Import Wizard. It works exactly like the link HTML Wizard described in detail earlier in this chapter.

And just like demonstrating XML in the previous section, let's do this one in reverse as well. First, you export a table to get HTML data. Then import from the HTML document created, to create a new table in Access.

Follow these steps to export data from Access 2007 into an HTML document:

1. **Open the `Chapter17_1.accdb` database in Access 2007.**
2. **Under the External Data tab, in the Export section, click the More drop-down button, and click HTML File.**
3. **Browse to and select an HTML file to export to. Check the top two check boxes under the header "Specify export options." The first of the two options preserves relational table information, which you need for later importing.**
4. **The next screens will present you with HTML output options, and VBA macro export processing save options. Keep clicking until you finish.**

As for XML import and export, the result is similar for HTML. The fundamental difference between importing XML and HMTL documents, is based on the basic difference between HTML and XML. The HTML import process imports data in much the same way as would a text file import, using similar wizard options. XML, on the contrary, is metadata and functionally empowered in itself. Access 2007 takes advantage of the power of XML.

Importing Access objects other than tables

You can import other Access database tables or any other object in another database. You can, therefore, import an existing table, query, form, report, macro, or module from another Access database. You can also import custom toolbars and menus.

As a simple demonstration, follow these steps:

1. **Open the** `Chapter17_1.accdb` **database in Access 2007.**
2. **Under the External Data tab, in the Import section, click the Access option to import from another Access database.**
3. **Browse to the** `Chapter17_2.accdb` **database and click OK.**

   Figure 17-10 shows that you can import tables, queries, forms, reports, macros, and modules. This encompasses anything and everything.

FIGURE 17-10

Importing Access object other than tables

When including tables, queries, forms, reports, macros, or modules—all in the same import—you can select objects from each and then import them all at once.

Importing an Outlook folder

Importing Outlook folders means you can pick folders in your e-mail tools (Outlook Express and Outlook). And you can import them into a database. For example, you can import your Contacts folder in your Outlook e-mail installation, into a table in your database. Figure 17-11 demonstrates this very clearly to anyone ever having used Outlook or Outlook Express — and that's something that anyone with Microsoft Windows on his computer is likely to have indulged in.

FIGURE 17-11

Importing Outlook folders from your e-mail tool

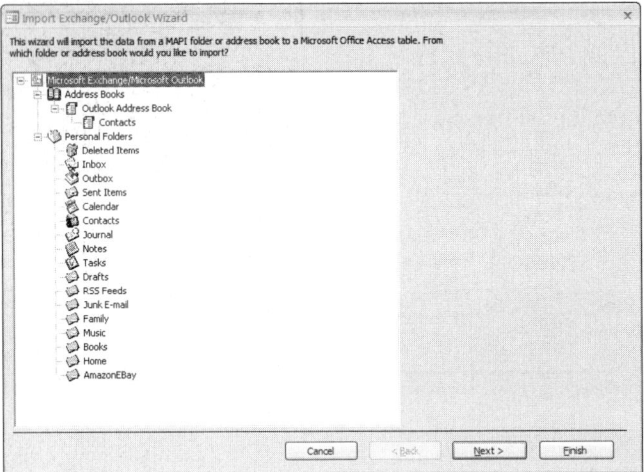

In fact, importing an Outlook folder such as your list of contacts in Outlook even allows you to create a table with a primary key, adjust the import to include specific fields and set datatypes. You can even save the import process as a VBA macro for later execution.

Importing through ODBC drivers

In this situation, you need to connect to an external relational database, which can be connected to using an Object Database Connectivity (ODBC) driver. ODBC drivers are one of the industry standards for establishing some of heterogeneous communication between database engines and application software development kits, quite often from multiple vendors.

Follow these steps in Access 2007 just to show you how easy this is:

1. **Open the** `Chapter17_1.accdb` **database in Access 2007.**
2. **Under the External Data tab, in the Import section, click the More drop-down button, and select the ODBC option.**

3. You will be asked to select a table name to export to. Leave as is and click OK.
4. You will get a window with title Select Data Source. Click on the Machine Data Source tab and you get the window as shown in Figure 17-12.

FIGURE 17-12

Importing Outlook folders from your e-mail tool

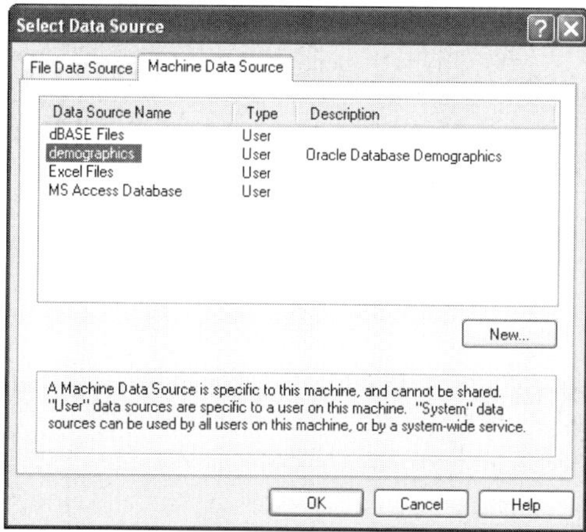

5. **So, Figure 17-12 shows you that you have to create a data source.**

   A File Data Source stores it connection data in a file and is easily shared among a number of different computers. A Machine Data Source is stored in the Windows registry and is much more difficult to use on multiple machines. In our situation, we used Oracle Database. We create a Machine Data Source called demographics.
6. **You will be prompted to log in to our Oracle Database using the user name specified in the Machine Data Source we have created in Step 5 above, as shown in Figure 17-13.**

FIGURE 17-13

Connecting to an Oracle database using an ODBC driver

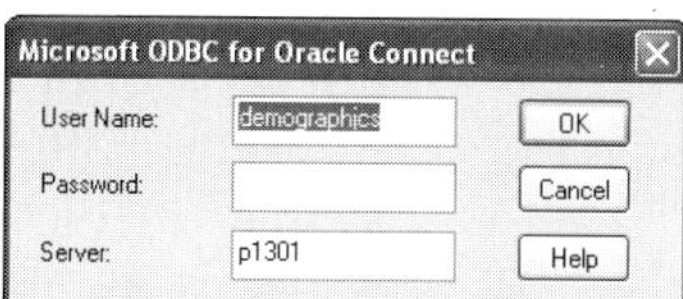

CROSS-REF An ODBC driver allows connecting to specific database objects in a database. Chapter 16 discussed links. Using a link, the data is stored in the Oracle database. Using an import such as this, data is copied into the Access database, and changes are not replicated between either database.

The result of the import looks like what you see in Figure 17-14.

FIGURE 17-14

An import from an ODBC database makes a snapshot copy of data

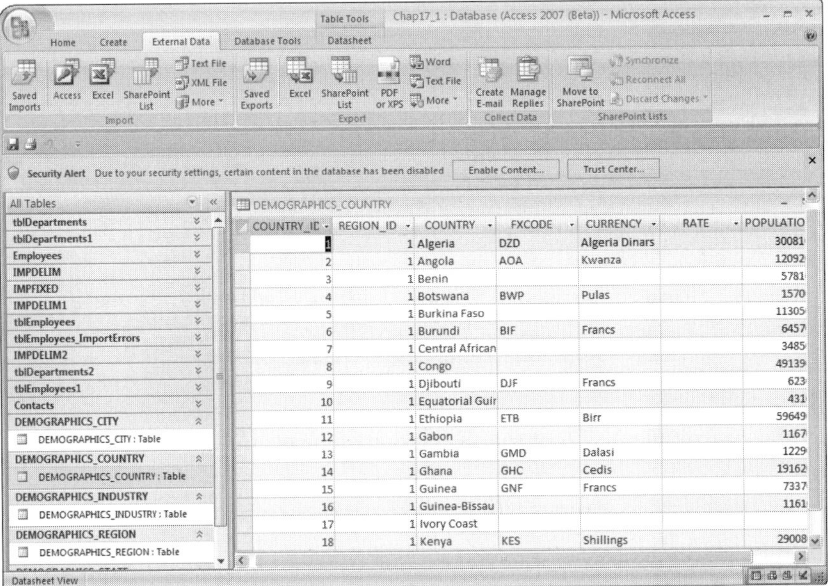

Importing non-Access, PC-based database tables

When importing data from PC-based databases, you can import two basic categories of database file types:

- dBASE
- Paradox

Each type of database can be imported directly into an Access table. The native data types are converted to Access data types during the conversion.

You can import any Paradox (3.0 through 8), dBASE III, dBASE IV, or dBASE 5 database table into Access. To import one of these, simply select the correct database type in the Files of Type box during the import process.

After selecting the type of PC-based database, select which file you want to import; Access imports the file for you automatically.

If you try to import a Paradox table that is encrypted, Access prompts you for the password after you select the table in the Select File dialog box. Enter the password and click OK to import an encrypted Paradox table.

When Access imports dBASE fields, it converts them from their current data type into an Access data type. Table 7-1 lists how the data types are converted.

TABLE 7-1

Conversion of Data Types from dBASE to Access

xBASE Data Type	Access Data Type
Character	Text
Numeric	Number (property of Double)
Float	Number (property of Double)
Logical	Yes/No
Date	Date/Time
Memo	Memo

When importing any dBASE database file in a multiuser environment, you must have exclusive use of the file. If other people are using it, you will not be able to import it.

As with dBASE tables, when Access imports Paradox fields, the Paradox fields are converted from their current data type into an Access data type. Table 7-2 lists how the data types are converted.

TABLE 7-2

Conversion of Data Types from Paradox to Access

Paradox Data Type	Access Data Type
Alphanumeric	Text
Number	Number (property of Double)
Short Number	Number (property of Integer)
Currency	Number (property of Double)
Date	Date/Time
Memo	Memo
Blob (Binary)	OLE

Modifying imported table elements

After you import a file, you can refine the table in Design View. The following list itemizes and discusses some of the primary changes you may want to make to improve your table:

- **Add field names or descriptions.** You may want to change the names of the fields you specified when you imported the file. For example, xBASE databases enable no more than 10 characters in their names and no spaces.
- **Change data types.** Access may have guessed the wrong data type when it imported several of the fields. You can change these fields to reflect a more descriptive data type (such as Currency rather than Number, or Text rather than Number).
- **Set field properties.** You can set field properties to enhance the way your tables work. For example, you may want to specify a format or default value for the table.
- **Set the field size to something more realistic than the 255 bytes (characters) Access allocates for each imported text field.** Make the names descriptive enough without the need to make them too long — for example, "Last Name" versus "Last Name of the Car Buyer or Seller." "Last Name" is sufficient to clarify what the contents of the field are.
- **Define a primary key.** Access works best with tables that have a primary key. You may want to set a primary key for the imported table.

Troubleshooting import errors

When you import an external file, Access may not be able to import one or more records, in which case it reports an error when it tries to import them. When Access encounters errors, it creates an Access table named Import Errors (with the user's name linked to the table name). The Import Errors table contains one record for each record that causes an error.

After errors have occurred and Access has created the Import Errors table, you can open the table to view the error descriptions.

Import errors for new tables

Access may not be able to import records into a new table for the following reasons:

- A row in a text file or spreadsheet may contain more fields than are present in the first row.
- Data in the field cannot be stored in the data type Access chose for the field. (This could be text in a numeric field — best case will import as zeros — or numeric trying to store in a date field.)
- On the basis of the first row's contents, Access automatically chose the incorrect data type for a field. The first row is correct, but the remaining rows are blank.
- The date order may be incorrect. The dates are in YMD order, but the specification calls for MDY order. (When Access tries to import 991201 [YYMMDD], it will report an error because it should be in the format of 120199 [MMDDYY].)

Import errors for existing tables

Access may not be able to append records into an existing table for the following reasons:

- The data is not consistent between the text file and the existing Access table.
- Numeric data being entered is too large for the field size of the Access table.
- A row in a text file or spreadsheet may contain more fields than the Access table.
- The records being imported have duplicate primary key values.

The Import Errors table

When errors occur, Access creates an Import Errors table you can use to determine which data caused the errors.

Open the Import Errors table and try to determine why Access couldn't import all the records. If the problem is with the external data, edit it. If you're appending records to an existing table, the problem may be with the existing table; it may need modifications (such as changing the data types and rearranging the field locations). After you solve the problem, erase the Import Errors file and import the data again.

NOTE **Access attempts to import all records that do not cause an error. If you re-import the data, you may need to clean up the external table or the Access table before re-importing. If you don't, you may have duplicate data in your table.**

If importing a text file seems to take an unexpectedly long time, it may be because of too many errors. You can cancel importing by pressing Ctrl+Break.

Exporting to External Formats

An export copies data from an Access table to some other software tool or data source, such as an XML document. The exported result uses the format of the other data source and not the format of an Access database. You can copy data from an Access table or query into a new external file. This process of copying Access tables to an external file is called exporting. You can export tables to several different sources.

In general, anything imported can also be exported, unless otherwise stated in this chapter.

Exporting objects to other Access databases

You can export objects from the current database to another Access database. The objects you export can be tables, queries, forms, reports, macros, or modules. To export an object to another Access database, follow these generic steps:

1. **Open the source database that has the objects you want to export.**
2. **Select the More drop-down button under the Export section of the External Data tab.**

3. **The next option is a destination option Access database. You have to browse to, or type in, an existing target unopened Access database.**

   The target database cannot be open; otherwise, there will be a locking conflict.

4. **You will then be prompted to export objects from the source database.**

   Tables can be exported as data only or data and metadata.

5. **If an object already exists in the target database, you will be prompted with an option to replace the object in the target database. Otherwise, choose to create a new object in the target database.**

   What we did in this situation was to export data and metadata for one of the tables in the database for this chapter.

6. **The last step enables you to save the export configuration for future use. This option can be quite handy if you frequently perform the same export process.**

NOTE If you attempt to export an object to another Access database that has an object of the same type and name, Access warns you before copying. You then have the option to cancel or overwrite.

Exporting through ODBC drivers

Exporting using an ODBC driver connection to a relational database other than Access, is as simple as the importing process. You connect to the external database (in our case, an Oracle database). You then select a table to export, which is then copied back into the Oracle database from the Access 2007 import copy of the table, as shown in Figure 17-15.

FIGURE 17-15

Exporting Access tables to an ODBC data source relational database

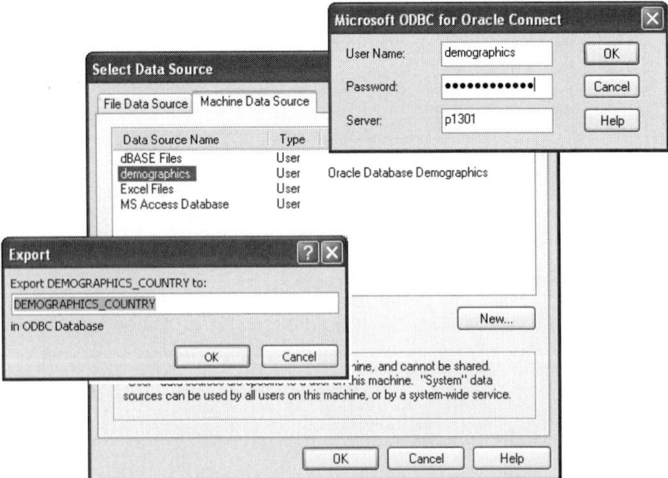

Functionality exclusive to exports

These export types are exclusively export-capable because their outputs are essentially read only as far as Access 2007 is concerned. This functionality is over and above that of previously introduced import functionality. You can export Access database table data into the following read-only formats:

- **Microsoft Word:** Word documents can be produced as direct Access 2007 database exports. The result is shown in Figure 17-16.

FIGURE 17-16

An Access to Microsoft Word document export

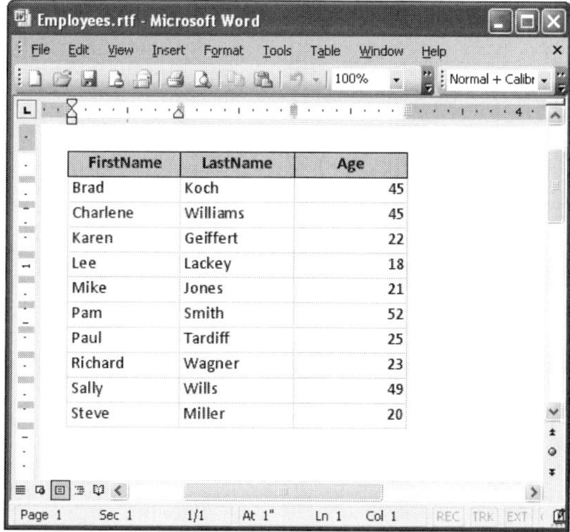

FirstName	LastName	Age
Brad	Koch	45
Charlene	Williams	45
Karen	Geiffert	22
Lee	Lackey	18
Mike	Jones	21
Pam	Smith	52
Paul	Tardiff	25
Richard	Wagner	23
Sally	Wills	49
Steve	Miller	20

NOTE **You can import from Word into Access by converting the Word document into a text file first. You could even use Word in combination with Excel to produce a delimited text file.**

- **Microsoft Word Mail Merge:** A specialized Word document export function is that of Mail Merge using Word. In this case, you can create Word documents, for subsequent printing, of letters, labels and envelopes. You can even do sending of e-mail messages.
- **Snapshot Viewer:** The Snapshot Viewer allows for a database snapshot report. In database parlance, a snapshot is a consistent picture of an entire database at a specific point in time. In other words, if any data changes during the process of taking the snapshot, the snapshot contains data states before those changes. So, if you start a snapshot, and add a record to a table, the snapshot will not contain the new record.

Summary

The ability to generate files externally to a database like Access increases general functionality enormously. For example, simple text files can be exported from Access and then imported into other software tools at a later stage. XML documents and HTML pages can be executed directly in a browser, and copying data to an ODBC data source provides data to other database engines, such as SQL Server and Oracle Database. It follows that the ability to import from various sources, including the aforementioned, provides the same functionality as exporting, but in the opposite direction.

The next chapter covers working with reading from an Access database. It deals with more complex queries, and in greater detail, than in earlier chapters.

Chapter 18

Advanced Access Query Techniques

In this chapter, you work with more complex queries in greater detail than you did in earlier chapters. So far, you have worked with types of select queries and parameters. Earlier parts of this book explained relatively simple select queries, in which you select specific records from one or more tables based on some criteria. You also learn about action queries, which enable you to change the field values in your records automatically and add or delete records.

ON the CD-ROM This chapter uses the database named `Chapter18.accdb`. If you have not already copied it onto your machine from the CD, you need to do so now. This database is a direct ODBC import from an Oracle database. All the field names from the Oracle database are expressed in uppercase characters. See Chapter 17 for details about importing data into Access applications.

IN THIS CHAPTER

Using Calculated Fields

Queries are not limited to fields from tables; you can also use *calculated fields* (created by performing some calculation). A calculated field can be created in many different ways, including the following:

- Concatenating two Text type fields using the ampersand character (&)
- Performing a mathematical calculation on two Number type fields
- Using an Access function to create a field based on the function

In this first example, you create a simple calculated field, DiscountPrice, from the ListPrice and a discount percentage value, in the `BOOKS_EDITION` table. Follow these steps:

1. **Start up Access and open the database for this chapter, Ch18.accdb.**
2. **Create a simple query by opening the Query Wizard in the Other group on the Access ribbon.**
3. **Select the ISBN and LIST_PRICE fields from the BOOKS_EDITION table. Click Next.**
4. **Follow the options, selecting to create a detail query and click Next.**
5. **Modify the design of the query on exiting the Query Wizard.**
6. **Right click a new field and enter the expression** DiscountPrice: LIST_PRICE * 0.75.

   This discounts the list price of all books by 25%.

NOTE **You did not have to type in the name of the table before each field name because you are only using one table. However, it is good practice to do so. You could have entered** **`DiscountPrice: BOOKS_EDITION.LIST_PRICE * 0.75`.**

7. Click the great big Run button at the left side of the Access 2007 ribbon. (It has a huge red exclamation mark in it.)

   The result is shown in Figure 18-1.

FIGURE 18-1

Using calculated fields

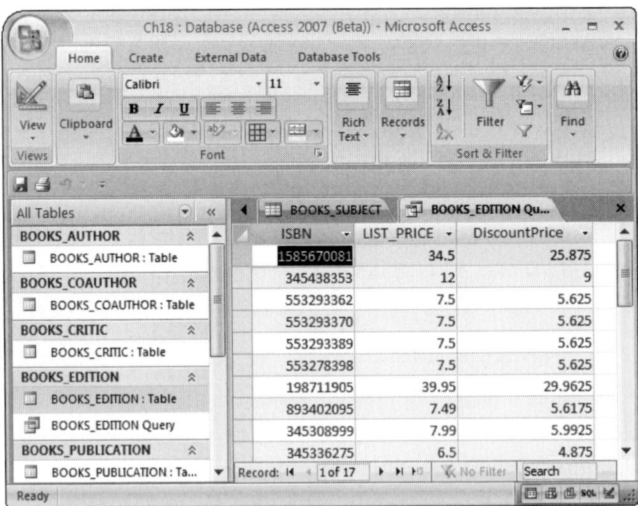

Access has an *Expression Builder* that helps you create any expression, such as a complex calculated field for a query. To create a calculated field using the Expression Builder interface, follow these steps:

1. **From the previous example, click the View button at the top left of the screen, and then select Design View.**

   This gets you back to the Query Wizard editor.

2. **To execute the Expression Builder right-click any field, in the empty column to the right of the discounted price.**
3. **Select Build from the menu and click.**

   You now have an expression builder on your screen. This screen has a box at the top and three boxes underneath it filled with all sorts of things.

4. **Now click Functions in the left column below, and then click Built-In Functions.**
5. **Scroll down the right-most of the lower selection windows, find the `IIf` function, and select it.**

NOTE **An IIF function is called an immediate IF function. In programming terms an `IIF` function can be included inline within a mathematical expression. The syntax for an `IIF` expression is `IIF(expression,dotruething,dofalsething)`. If the result is true then one expression is executed. Otherwise the false expression is executed. The result is an expression passed back to the calling expression.**

6. **To cut a long story short, use both the `IIf` and `IsNull` functions to create the expression as shown in Figure 18-2.**

FIGURE 18-2

Using the Expression Builder to create calculated fields

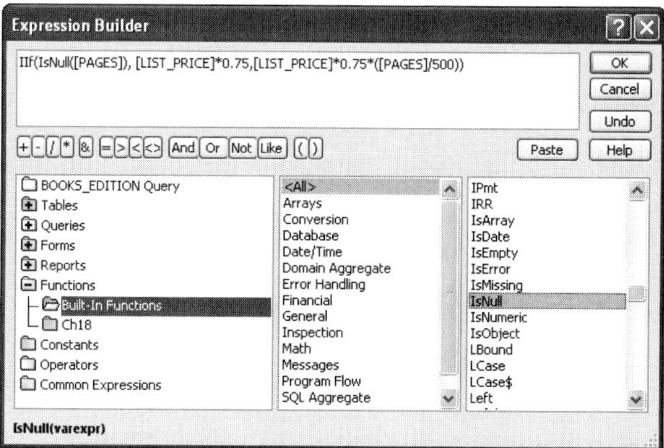

NOTE The `IsNull` function allows selection of two expressions based on the null content of a field (or expression). Why is this needed in a database? A null value in an expression produces a null result regardless of all the other contents in an expression.

7. **At the top left of the screen, click the View button again, followed by the SQL View option.**

   You should see a SQL Statement that looks something like this:

   ```
   SELECT BOOKS_EDITION.ISBN, BOOKS_EDITION.LIST_PRICE,
   [LIST_PRICE]*0.75 AS DiscountPrice,
   IIf(IsNull([PAGES]),[LIST_PRICE]*0.75,[LIST_PRICE]*0.75*([PAGES
   ]/500)) AS Expr1
   FROM BOOKS_EDITION;
   ```

   In the case of the PAGES field in the preceding expression, there is no point performing a calculation including a null value. It makes sense to add the PAGES field, from the `BOOKS_EDITION` table, while you are still in Design View.

8. **Click the View button again, and select the Datasheet View option.**

   The result should look something like the screen shown in Figure 18-3.

FIGURE 18-3

Executing a query as a Design View execution

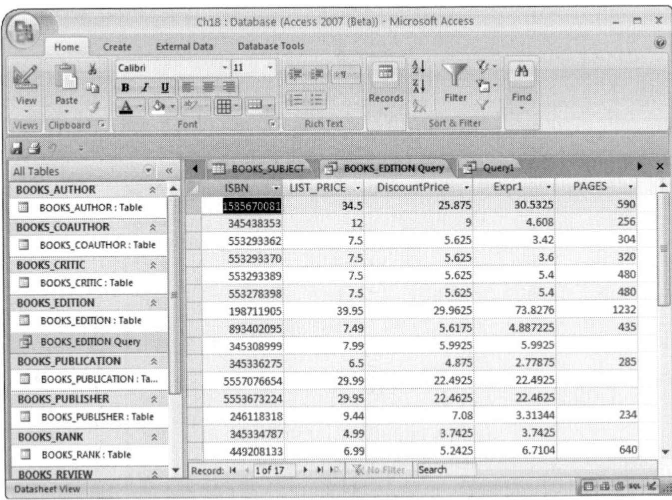

ISBN	LIST_PRICE	DiscountPrice	Expr1	PAGES
1585670081	34.5	25.875	30.5325	590
345438353	12	9	4.608	256
553293362	7.5	5.625	3.42	304
553293370	7.5	5.625	3.6	320
553293389	7.5	5.625	5.4	480
553278398	7.5	5.625	5.4	480
198711905	39.95	29.9625	73.8276	1232
893402095	7.49	5.6175	4.887225	435
345308999	7.99	5.9925	5.9925	
345336275	6.5	4.875	2.77875	285
5557076654	29.99	22.4925	22.4925	
5553673224	29.95	22.4625	22.4625	
246118318	9.44	7.08	3.31344	234
345334787	4.99	3.7425	3.7425	
449208133	6.99	5.2425	6.7104	640

In addition to creating calculated fields from fields in a single table, you can also create them using fields from multiple tables. When using linked tables, you can even create calculated fields based on values stored in other Access databases.

Finding the Number of Records in a Table or Query

To quickly determine the total number of records in an existing table or query, use the `Count(*)` function. This is a special parameter of the `Count( )` function. For example, to determine the total number of records in the `BOOKS_EDITION` table, follow these steps:

1. **Start a new query using the `BOOKS_EDITION` table.**
2. **Click the first empty Field cell in the Query Design View.**
3. **Type** Count(*) **in the cell.**

   You should get 17 records, unless you have changed your database for this chapter.

The `Count(*)` function can also be used to determine the total number of records that match a specific criterion. For example, you may want to know how many contacts you have in the `tblContacts` table that are not sellers (buyers or both) and that live in Connecticut. Follow these steps to ascertain the number in the table:

1. **Start a new query and select the `BOOKS_EDITION` table.**
2. **Click the first empty Field: cell in the Design View pane.**
3. **Type** Count(*) **in the cell.**
4. **Double-click the `PAGES` field in the table to add it to the query.**
5. **Deselect the Show cell for the `PAGES` field.**

   Only the field containing the summary `Count(*)` function can be shown in the datasheet because you are displaying the total, and not each individual edition of each book. You're adding them all together. If you try to display any additional fields, Access reports an error.
6. **Type** >300 **into the Criteria cell for `PAGES`.**
7. **Replace Expr1 in the first field containing the `COUNT(*)` function to** Total over 300 Pages.
8. **Click the big View again, and select Datasheet View.**

   You should get a result of 10.

Finding the Top (n) Records in a Query

Access not only enables you to find the number of records in an existing table or query, but it also provides the capability of finding the query's first (n) records (that is, a set number or percentage of its records).

So, let's find the first 10 editions of all books, out of all 17 books, as returned by a query. This time let's add in the title of the book. Follow these steps:

1. **Create a new query using the `BOOKS_EDITION` and `BOOKS_PUBLICATION` tables.**

   The two are related based on the publication of each edition so they should be joined based on the PUBLICATION_ID field, which is present in both tables.

2. **Create the join by selecting the PUBLICATION_ID field in one table, holding the left mouse button down, and rolling the mouse over to the same field in the other table.**

3. **Verify the relationship created in Step 2 by right-clicking the line between the two tables.**

4. **Select Join Properties on the menu that pops up.**

   The result should look like Figure 18-4.

FIGURE 18-4

Verifying a join between two tables

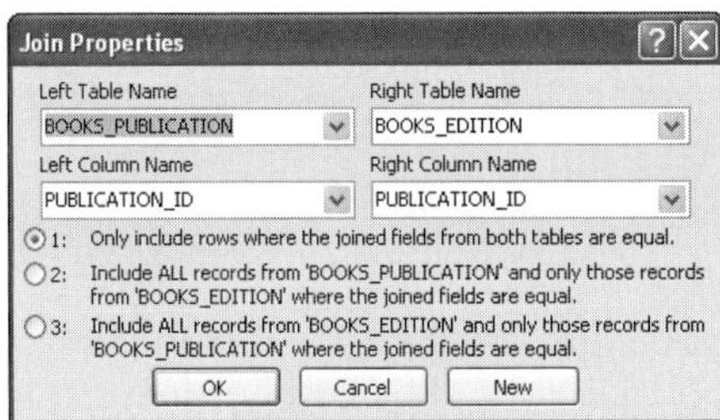

Figure 18-4 shows that the two tables are joined based on the common field PUBLICATION_ID, which is correct. Find the SQL code for this query by selecting the SQL View option from the View icon (the big button on at the left end of the Access ribbon). This is the SQL code for the query, clearly showing the JOIN:

```
SELECT TOP 10 BOOKS_PUBLICATION.TITLE, BOOKS_EDITION.ISBN,
   BOOKS_EDITION.PRINT_DATE, BOOKS_EDITION.FORMAT
FROM BOOKS_PUBLICATION INNER JOIN BOOKS_EDITION
   ON BOOKS_PUBLICATION.PUBLICATION_ID =
BOOKS_EDITION.PUBLICATION_ID
ORDER BY BOOKS_PUBLICATION.TITLE;
```

5. **Now you can go to the field specifications and add fields to the query. Add the TITLE, ISBN, PRINT_DATE, and FORMAT fields. Additionally, specify an ascending sort order on book titles.**

6. At this point, you can click the View button to see that there are 17 records in the resulting dynaset.
7. Click the View button to return to Design View.
8. Select the Design button on the top-most tab menu. Under the Query Setup section, you should see a drop-down button labeled Return. Let the mouse hover over the box and you should get a ToolTip on the screen. Select a value of 10 (you can manually enter a value as well). You should get 10 records returned when executing the query.
9. If you click the selection arrow of the Top Values combo box, a series of default values will appear. These default values are 5, 25, 100, 5%, and All.

When executing this particular query I got 10 records when requesting 5. This is because the Return selection box returns the first 5 unique records, plus any duplicates.

How Queries Save Field Selections

When you open a query design, you may notice that the design has changed since you last saved the query. When you save a query, Access rearranges (even eliminates) fields on the basis of several rules:

- If a field does not have the Show box checked but has criteria specified, Access moves it to the rightmost columns in the QBE pane.
- If a field does not have the Show box checked, Access eliminates it from the QBE pane column unless it has sorting directives or criteria.
- If you create a totaling expression with the Sum operator in a total query, Access changes it to an expression using the Sum function.

Because of these rules, your query may look very different after you save and reopen it. In this section, you learn how this happens (and some ways to prevent it).

Hiding (not showing) fields

Sometimes you won't want certain fields in the Design pane to show in the actual dynaset of the datasheet. You may remember from a query executed previously in this chapter, you specified to return only books with more than 300 pages. The query returned a total count of all books, not each book. It was imperative to display only the total count of books and exclude the display of the number of pages in each book.

To *hide*, or exclude, a field from the dynaset, you simply click off the Show box under the field you want to hide. Figure 18-5 shows Design View of the previous query, where the Show check box is set to blank for the PAGES field.

FIGURE 18-5

The easiest way to hide a field is to uncheck the Show check box for the field

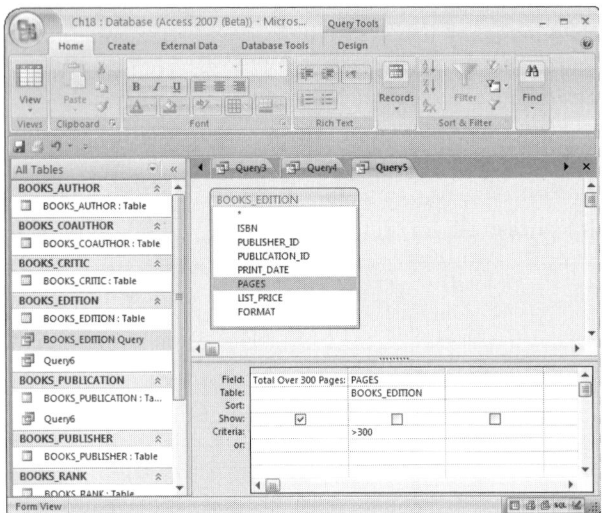

If you hide any fields in Design View that are not used for sorting or filtering criteria, Access automatically eliminates them from the query when you save it. If you want to use these fields and need to show them later, you have to add them back in from Design View.

If you're creating a query to be used by a form or report, you must show any fields it will use, including any field to which you want to bind a control.

Renaming fields in queries

When working with queries, you can rename a field to describe the field's contents more clearly or accurately. This new name is the one that would be shown in the datasheet of the query. You have already seen renaming of expression in queries. Renaming fields is very similar. You are essentially renaming the field in the resulting query and not in the table.

So, again you can use a previous query: this time the Top (n) query example. In Design View of the join query change the PRINT_DATE column header (field name), from PRINT_DATE to **Published**. Here is the SQL query code for that altered query:

```
SELECT TOP 10 BOOKS_PUBLICATION.TITLE, BOOKS_EDITION.ISBN,
   BOOKS_EDITION.PRINT_DATE AS Published, BOOKS_EDITION.FORMAT
FROM BOOKS_PUBLICATION INNER JOIN BOOKS_EDITION
   ON BOOKS_PUBLICATION.PUBLICATION_ID = BOOKS_EDITION.PUBLICATION_ID
ORDER BY BOOKS_PUBLICATION.TITLE;
```

In SQL code a field is renamed using the `AS` clause, as shown in the previous script. In Access Design View, change the header for the column to *name*: *field*, as for any other expression. So, in Design View simply change PRINT_DATE to **Published: PRINT_DATE**.

NOTE **If you specified a caption name for the field in the table designer, this name will be used in the query.**

If you rename a field, Access uses only the new name for the heading of the query datasheet; it does the same with the control source in any form or report that uses the query. Any new forms or reports you create on the basis of the query use the new field name.

NOTE **Access does not change the actual field name in the underlying table. However, any subsequent process used in the query can utilize the altered field name.**

When working with renamed fields, you can use an *expression name* (the new name you specified) in another expression within the same query. For example, you may have a calculated field called FullName that uses an Access function to join the first and last names fields of a person's name. You can refer later on in the query to the `FullName` expression.

NOTE **When you work with referenced expression names, you cannot have any criteria specified against the field you're referring to.**

Hiding and unhiding columns in Design View

Sometimes you may want to hide specific fields returned by a query. You can do this, as already seen, by unchecking the Show check box in Design View. You can also reduce the width a column to nothing, by dragging the width of the column with your mouse, in the Datasheet View, until the column is no longer visible.

Setting Query Properties

While creating a query, you can set query properties several ways: click the Properties button on the toolbar; right-click Properties and choose it from the shortcut menu. Access displays a Query Properties dialog box. Your options depend on the query type and on the table or field with which you're working.

You can use the *query-level properties* just as you would the properties in forms, reports, and tables. Query-level properties depend on the type of query being created and on the table or field with which you're working. Table 18-1 shows the query-level properties you can set.

TABLE 18-1

Query-Level Properties

Property	Description	Query	Select	Crosstab	Update	Delete	Make-Table	Append
Description	Text describing table or query	X	X	X	X	X	X	X
Default View	Values Datasheet, Pivot Table, or Pivot Chart	X	X	X				
Output All Fields	Show all fields from the underlying tables in the query	X					X	X
Top Values	Number of highest or lowest values to be returned	X					X	X
Unique Values	Return only unique field values in the dynaset	X					X	X
Unique Records	Return only unique records for the dynaset	X	X		X	X	X	X
Run Permissions	Establish permissions for specified user	X	X	X	X	X	X	X
Source Database	External database name for all tables/queries in the query	X	X	X	X	X	X	X
Source Connect Str	Name of application used to connect to external database	X	X	X	X	X	X	X
Record Locks	Records locked while query runs (usually action queries)	X	X	X	X	X	X	X
Recordset Type	Which records can be edited: Dynaset, Dynaset (inconsistent updates), or Snapshot	X	X	X				
ODBC Time-out	Number of seconds before reporting error for opening DB	X	X	X	X	X	X	X

Property	Description	Query	Select	Crosstab	Update	Delete	Make-Table	Append
Filter	Filter name loaded automatically with query	X	X					
Order By	Sort loaded automatically with query	X	X					
Max Records	Max number of records returned by ODBC database	X	X					
Orientation	Set view order for fields from left-to-right or right-to-left	X	X	X	X	X	X	X
SubDatasheet Name	Identify subquery	X	X	X	X		X	X
Link Child Fields	Field name(s) in subquery	X	X	X	X		X	X
Link Master Fields	Field name(s) in main table	X	X	X	X		X	X
Subdatasheet Height	Maximum height of subdatasheet	X	X	X	X		X	X
Subdatasheet Expanded	Records initially in their expanded state?	X	X	X			X	X
Column Headings	Fixed-column headings			X				
Use Transaction	Run action query in transaction?				X	X	X	X
Fail on Error	Fail operation if errors occur				X	X		
Destination Table	Table name of destination						X	X
Destination DB	Name of database						X	X
Dest Connect Str	Database connection string						X	X

As you can see, working with queries offers many options for how the fields can be displayed and properties for each specific type of query.

Creating Queries That Calculate Totals

Many times, you want to find information in your tables based on data related to the total of a particular field or fields. For example, you may want to find the total number of contacts who are both buyers and sellers or the total amount of money each buyer has spent on vehicles last year. Access supplies the tools to accomplish these queries without the need for programming.

Access performs calculation totals by using numerous aggregate functions, which let you determine a specific value based on the contents of a field. For example, you can determine the average price for vehicles by type, the maximum and minimum price paid for a vehicle, or the total count of all records in which the type of contact is a buyer or both. Performing each of these examples as a query results in a dynaset of answer fields based on the mathematical calculations you requested.

CROSS-REF **You have already worked with counts using the `Count (*)` function in the previous section. The `Count(*)` function is an aggregate function.**

To create a total query, you can use the Summary Query editor in the Query Wizard tool. You can also elect to create totals in Design View by clicking the Totals button with the sigma character on it (Σ).

Query Wizard summaries

When using the Query Wizard to create a query, one of the screens presents an option to create a detail query, or a summary query. A detail query shows every field in every record. A summary query gives you options to aggregate. Follow these steps: Create a new query. Click the Summary Options button and find the screen mentioned previously. You ultimately get a screen that looks as shown in Figure 18-6.

FIGURE 18-6

Creating summary options for aggregate queries

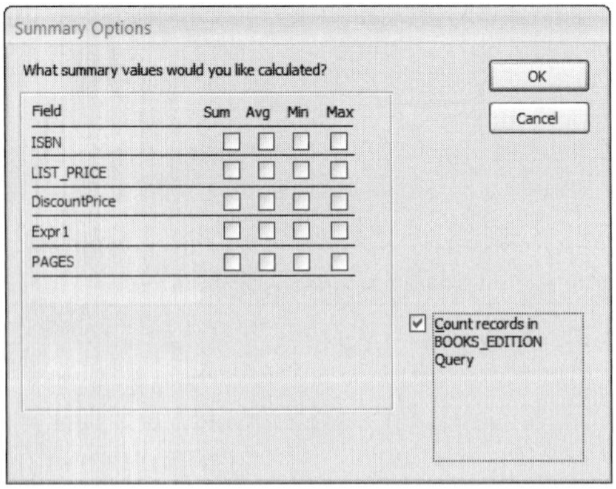

Summary Options

What summary values would you like calculated?

Field	Sum	Avg	Min	Max
ISBN	☐	☐	☐	☐
LIST_PRICE	☐	☐	☐	☐
DiscountPrice	☐	☐	☐	☐
Expr1	☐	☐	☐	☐
PAGES	☐	☐	☐	☐

OK

Cancel

☑ Count records in BOOKS_EDITION Query

What Is an Aggregate Function?

The word *aggregate* implies gathering a mass (a group or series) of things, on which the function acts as though the collection is a single entity. Therefore, an aggregate function is a function that takes a group of records and performs some mathematical function against the entire group. The function can be a simple count or a complex expression you specify, based on a series of mathematical functions.

Aggregate queries in Design View

To create a query that performs a total calculation, create a select query and then activate the Total by clicking the Totals button (with the Σ character), at the top right of the Design window.

If not already present a new row appears in the query design, containing either a summary function or the words Group By. You have created an aggregate query. All that remains is to select fields to aggregate on and to remove those fields from the summary record output if the aggregation removes them from the query.

The result of aggregation using either the Query Wizard or Design View will be a query that looks something like this:

```
SELECT DISTINCTROW [BOOKS_EDITION Query].ISBN,
   Sum([BOOKS_EDITION Query].LIST_PRICE) AS SumOfLIST_PRICE
FROM [BOOKS_EDITION Query]
GROUP BY [BOOKS_EDITION Query].ISBN;
```

Although only eight options are shown in Table 18-2, you can choose from 12. You can view the remaining options by using the scroll bar on the right side of the box. The 12 options can be divided into four distinct categories: group by, aggregate, expression, and total field record limit. Table 18-2 lists each category, its number of Total options, and its purpose.

TABLE 18-2

Four Categories of Total Options

Category	Number of Options	Purpose of Operator
Group By	1	Groups common records. Access performs aggregate calculations against the groups.
Aggregate	9	Specifies a mathematical or selection operation to perform against a field.
Expression	1	Groups several total operators and performs the group totals.
Where	1	Filters records before record limit, performing a total calculation against a field.

The Group By, Expression, and Where categories have one option each. The Aggregate category has nine options, all of which are used by the other three categories. The following sections provide details about the options available in each category.

Group By category

This category has one option, the Group By option. You use this option to specify that a specific field in Design View is used as a grouping field. For example, if you select the field LIST_PRICE, the Group By option tells Access to group all books together. This option is the default for all Total: cells.

Expression category

Like the Group By category, the Expression category has only one option: Expression. This is the second-from-last choice in the drop-down list. You use this option to tell Access to create a calculated field by using one or more aggregate calculations in the field box of Design View.

Where category

The Where category is the third category that has a single option: the Where option. This option is the last choice in the drop-down list. When you select this option, you tell Access that you want to specify limiting criteria against an aggregate type field, as opposed to a Group By or an Expression field. The limiting criteria are performed *before* the aggregate options are executed. By specifying the Where option, you are telling Access to use this field only as a limiting criteria field, before it performs the aggregate calculation.

Aggregate category

The Aggregate category, unlike the others, has multiple options that you can choose from (a total of nine options): Sum, Avg, Min, Max, Count, StDev, Var, First, and Last. These options appear as the second through tenth options in the drop-down list. Each option performs an operation on your data (check out Table 18-3 for how you can use each option) and supplies the new data to a cell in the resulting dynaset. Aggregate options are what database designers think of when they hear the words *total query.* Each of the options performs a calculation against a field in the Design View pane of the query, returning a *single answer* in the dynaset.

For example, you may want to determine the maximum (Max), minimum (Min), and average (Avg) value of each format of books. You can also use it to find a single value in the table, without creating an aggregate grouping.

The Group By, Expression, and Where categories of options can be used against any type of Access field. For example, Text, Memo, or Yes/No datatypes. Some of the aggregate options can be performed against certain field types only. For example, you cannot perform a Sum option against Text type data. And you can't you use a Max option against an OLE object.

Table 18-3 lists each option, what it does, and which field types you can use with the option.

TABLE 18-3

Aggregate Options for Total: Where

Option	Returns	Field Type Support
Count	Number of non-Null values in a field	AutoNumber, Number, Currency, Date/ Time, Yes/No, Text, Memo, OLE object
Sum	Total of values in a field	AutoNumber, Number, Currency, Date/ Time, Yes/No
Avg	Average of values in a field	AutoNumber, Number, Currency, Date/ Time, Yes/No
Max	Highest value in a field	AutoNumber, Number, Currency, Date/ Time, Yes/No, Text
Min	Lowest value in a field	AutoNumber, Number, Currency, Date/ Time, Yes/No, Text
StDev	Standard deviation of values in a field	AutoNumber, Number, Currency, Date/ Time, Yes/No
Var	Population variance of values in a field	AutoNumber, Number, Currency, Date/ Time, Yes/No
First	Field value from the first record in a number, table, or query	AutoNumber, Currency, Date/Time, Yes/No, Text, Memo, OLE object
Last	Field value from the last record in a number, table, or query	AutoNumber, Currency, Date/Time, Yes/No, Text, Memo, OLE object

So, aggregate queries can be built in various ways. What are these different types of aggregate queries?

Grand totals in aggregates

A grand total aggregation is essentially a query summarizing multiple records into a single return record. The totals `Count(*)` function previously demonstrated in this chapter is a perfect example.

Subtotals in aggregates

A subtotal is sometimes know as a control break total and is essentially the creation of subtotals within a larger grand total for the entire query, or a total for a parent subtotal. Let's say you have a query joining three tables, as shown in Figure 18-7.

FIGURE 18-7

A multiple table join query

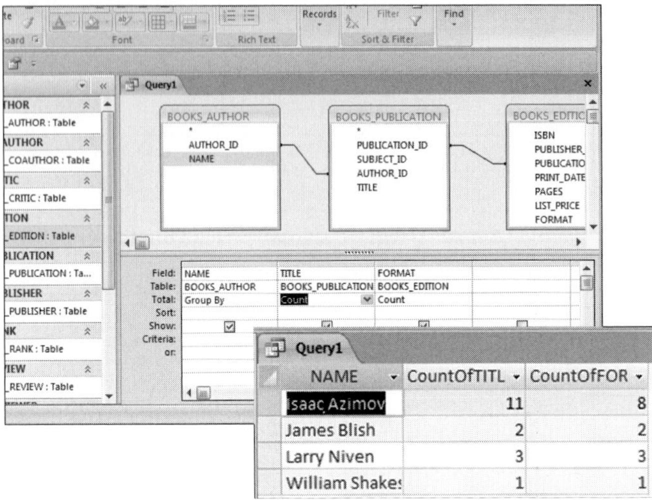

This query returns a total for book formats, within each author and title:

```
SELECT BOOKS_AUTHOR.NAME, BOOKS_PUBLICATION.TITLE,
Count(BOOKS_EDITION.FORMAT) AS CountOfFORMAT
FROM (BOOKS_AUTHOR INNER JOIN BOOKS_PUBLICATION
ON BOOKS_AUTHOR.AUTHOR_ID = BOOKS_PUBLICATION.AUTHOR_ID)
INNER JOIN BOOKS_EDITION
ON BOOKS_PUBLICATION.PUBLICATION_ID =
BOOKS_EDITION.PUBLICATION_ID
GROUP BY BOOKS_AUTHOR.NAME, BOOKS_PUBLICATION.TITLE;
```

You can also get multiple layers of subtotals by aggregating more fields, in this case the title and the format. The query looks like this:

```
SELECT BOOKS_AUTHOR.NAME,
Count(BOOKS_PUBLICATION.TITLE) AS CountOfTITLE,
Count(BOOKS_EDITION.FORMAT) AS CountOfFORMAT
FROM (BOOKS_AUTHOR INNER JOIN BOOKS_PUBLICATION
ON BOOKS_AUTHOR.AUTHOR_ID = BOOKS_PUBLICATION.AUTHOR_ID)
INNER JOIN BOOKS_EDITION
ON BOOKS_PUBLICATION.PUBLICATION_ID =
BOOKS_EDITION.PUBLICATION_ID
GROUP BY BOOKS_AUTHOR.NAME;
```

Note in the preceding query that the `group by` clause is only a single field. The Design View and query results look as shown in Figure 18-8.

FIGURE 18-8

Aggregating to produce subtotals on multiple layers

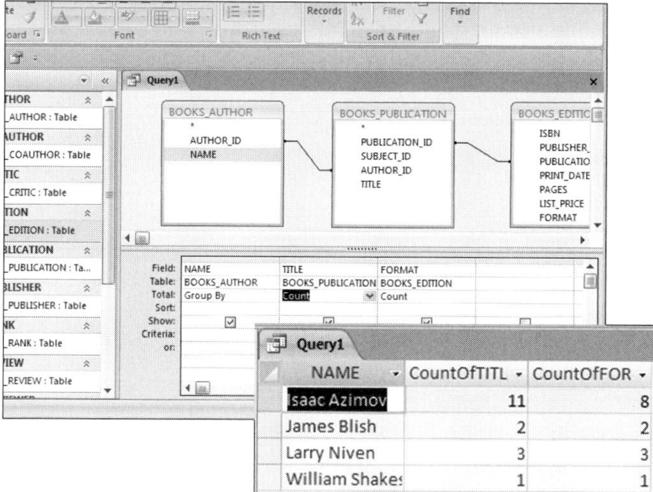

Filtering aggregates with criteria

In addition to grouping records for total queries, you can specify criteria to limit the records that will be processed or displayed in a total calculation. When you're specifying record criteria in total queries, several options are available. A criterion against any of these three fields can be created:

- Group By
- Aggregate Total
- Non-Aggregate Total

Using any one, any two, or all three of these criteria types, you can easily limit the scope of your total query to finite criteria. So, Design View of a query is shown in Figure 18-9.

FIGURE 18-9

Filtering aggregate queries

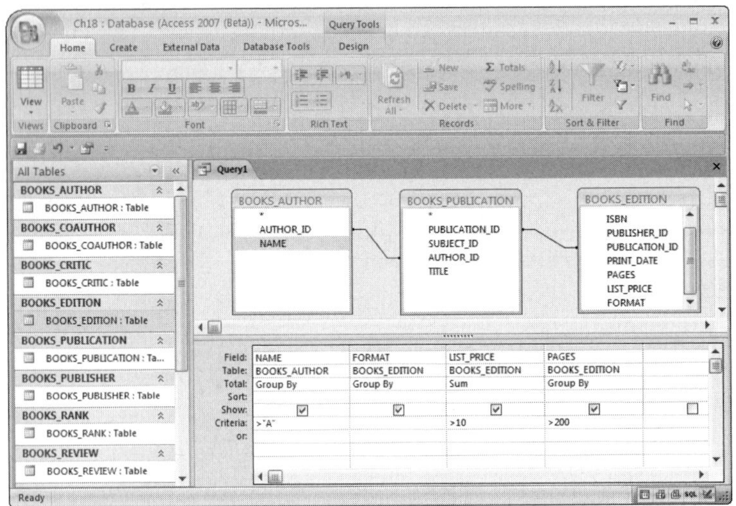

In Figure 18-9 there are filtering criteria for three fields: NAME, LIST_PRICE, and PAGES. This is the query for Design View shown in Figure 18-9:

```
SELECT BOOKS_AUTHOR.NAME, BOOKS_EDITION.FORMAT,
Sum(BOOKS_EDITION.LIST_PRICE) AS SumOfLIST_PRICE,
BOOKS_EDITION.PAGES
FROM (BOOKS_AUTHOR INNER JOIN BOOKS_PUBLICATION
ON BOOKS_AUTHOR.AUTHOR_ID = BOOKS_PUBLICATION.AUTHOR_ID)
INNER JOIN BOOKS_EDITION
ON BOOKS_PUBLICATION.PUBLICATION_ID =
BOOKS_EDITION.PUBLICATION_ID
GROUP BY BOOKS_AUTHOR.NAME, BOOKS_EDITION.FORMAT,
BOOKS_EDITION.PAGES
HAVING (((BOOKS_AUTHOR.NAME)>"A*")
AND ((Sum(BOOKS_EDITION.LIST_PRICE))>10)
AND ((BOOKS_EDITION.PAGES)>200));
```

There is actually something very wrong with the previous query. It is not that the query will not actually function, because it will. The issue is that all filtering is placed into a `HAVING` clause, which appears after the `GROUP BY` clause. Filters not applicable to groups created by a `GROUP BY` clause should be placed into a `WHERE` clause. The `WHERE` clause is executed before the `ORDER BY` and `GROUP BY` clauses. Why summarize what is not returned by a query? For a query with 10 rows this is no problem. For a query reading 1 million rows, and expected to filter down to 1000 rows, before applying grouping functionality, this becomes a fairly serious performance problem.

Crosstab Queries

This type of query is an excellent analytical tool. It enables you to create queries and reports where classifications of data (fields) are mixed, matched, and compared against data values (values in fields).Crosstab queries are useful for summarizing information, a little like a spreadsheet. In its simplest form, a crosstab enables you to compare data values with each other. Those comparisons can even be in one table.

For example, you may want to create a query that displays summaries by comparing different factors about books. Figure 18-10 shows a crosstab report, where totals for books by all authors are shown, broken down by the format of the book. The format can be paperback, hardcover, or even a book on tape (audio).

FIGURE 18-10

A simple crosstab report

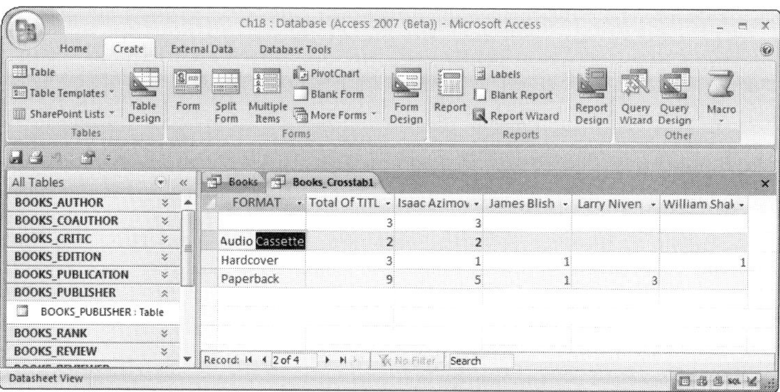

You cannot use simple relational database SQL commands to create analytical reports such as crosstabs. Years ago, you would have created intermediary tables. With current technology, you can make use of specialized SQL commands, such as `CUBE`, `ROLLUP`, and `GROUPING SETS` clauses.

Details of `CUBE`, `ROLLUP`, and `GROUPING SETS` clauses can be found as part of SQL standards at `ansi.org`.

Access handles these types of queries such as crosstabs slightly differently, and also more easily than regular ANSI standards. The following is the SQL coding behind the query shown in Figure 18-10, where Access 2007 uses something called the `TRANSFORM` and `PIVOT` commands:

```
TRANSFORM Count(Books.[TITLE]) AS CountOfTITLE
SELECT Books.[FORMAT], Count(Books.[TITLE]) AS [Total Of TITLE]
FROM Books
GROUP BY Books.[FORMAT]
PIVOT Books.[Author];
```

In the previous script the author name is used as a pivot, meaning it is used as a pivot or comparison against the aggregation in the query, or the summary result in the query. The summary result in the query is the count of all books for each format. The TRANSFORM command sends book counts to the PIVOT command, which creates the crosstab summary.

Another point to note is that the Books object selected from in the previous query is not a table, but actually a query of three tables that looks like this (to get enough data and provide enough groupings with small enough number of values):

```
SELECT BOOKS_AUTHOR.NAME AS Author, BOOKS_PUBLICATION.TITLE,
BOOKS_EDITION.FORMAT
FROM
(BOOKS_AUTHOR INNER JOIN BOOKS_PUBLICATION
ON BOOKS_AUTHOR.AUTHOR_ID = BOOKS_PUBLICATION.AUTHOR_ID)
INNER JOIN BOOKS_EDITION
ON BOOKS_PUBLICATION.PUBLICATION_ID =
BOOKS EDITION.PUBLICATION ID;
```

This query is named "Books" such that it can be called by the crosstab query.

The previous crosstab query was created using the Crosstab Query Wizard, in the following sequence of steps:

1. **Use the Query Design screen to create a join query of the BOOKS_AUTHOR, BOOKS_EDITION, and BOOKS_PUBLICATION tables.**

NOTE **Yes, it could all be manually coded. However, when first using Access 2007 it makes sense to use the wizards first, if only to discover the unique flavor of SQL coding used in Access 2007. For example, SQL Server and Oracle SQL coding are not the same as Access.**

The result in the Query editor should look something like that shown in Figure 18-11.

In Figure 18-11 three tables are selected. They are appropriately joined. One field is selected from the two parent tables (BOOKS_AUTHOR and BOOKS_EDITION), and two fields from the child table lowest in the hierarchy (BOOKS_PUBLICATION).

3. **Right-click the tab at the top-left of the Query Design editor, change the name of this query to Books, and save the query.**
4. **Now execute the Query Wizard tool and select a crosstab query. When prompted you also need to select the Books query, which was created in the preceding steps.**
5. **The next prompt asks for row headings. Examine Figure 18-10 and you will see that row headers are different formats for books.**
6. **The next choice is for column headings, which in Figure 18-10 are shown as being the names of authors. The title of the book is left over to perform the count function summary on.**

The result of the query will be the same as Figure 18-10.

FIGURE 18-11

Creating a join query for a crosstab report

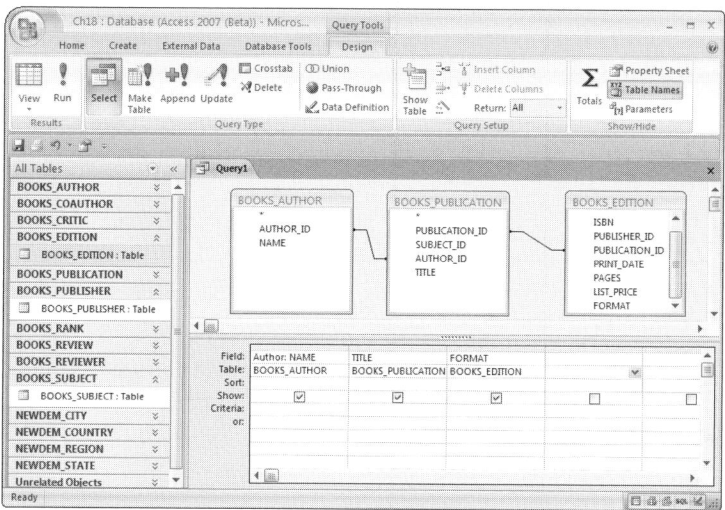

Crosstab queries and their underlying join queries can get a lot more complex than this. It all depends on how many layers are used. The problem with too many layers, both vertically and horizontally, is that you end up with a really huge report. For example, a spreadsheet with hundreds of rows and columns is not much use as a summary. The same applies to crosstab reports.

Duplicate and Unmatched Queries

The Query wizard can also create two other types of queries:

- **Find Duplicates Query Wizard:** Shows duplicate records in a single table on the basis of a field in the table.
- **Find Unmatched Query Wizard:** Shows all records that do not have a corresponding record in another table (for example, a sale with an invalid contact). This is the same thing as an outer join between two tables.

Find Duplicates Query Wizard

This wizard helps you create a query that reports which records in a table are duplicated using a field, or fields, in the table as a basis. Access asks which fields you want to use for checking duplication and then prompts you to enter some other fields that you may want to see in the query. Finally, Access asks for a title and then it creates and displays the query.

This type of wizard query can help you find duplicate key violations, a valuable trick when you want to take an existing table and make a unique key field with existing data. If you try to create a unique key field and Access reports an error, you know that you have Nulls in the field or you have duplicate records. The query helps find the duplicates.

So, let's say I join three tables again like this:

```
SELECT BOOKS_AUTHOR.NAME, BOOKS_PUBLICATION.TITLE,
BOOKS_EDITION.FORMAT, BOOKS_EDITION.LIST_PRICE
FROM (BOOKS_AUTHOR INNER JOIN
BOOKS_PUBLICATION
ON BOOKS_AUTHOR.AUTHOR_ID = BOOKS_PUBLICATION.AUTHOR_ID)
INNER JOIN BOOKS_EDITION
ON BOOKS_PUBLICATION.PUBLICATION_ID =
BOOKS_EDITION.PUBLICATION_ID;
```

I store it as a query and execute a query against the query, but this time retrieving only the NAME field. And I store the new query as Duplicate Authors. The result is as shown in Figure 18-12, with numerous duplicate author names.

FIGURE 18-12

A query that returns duplicated values

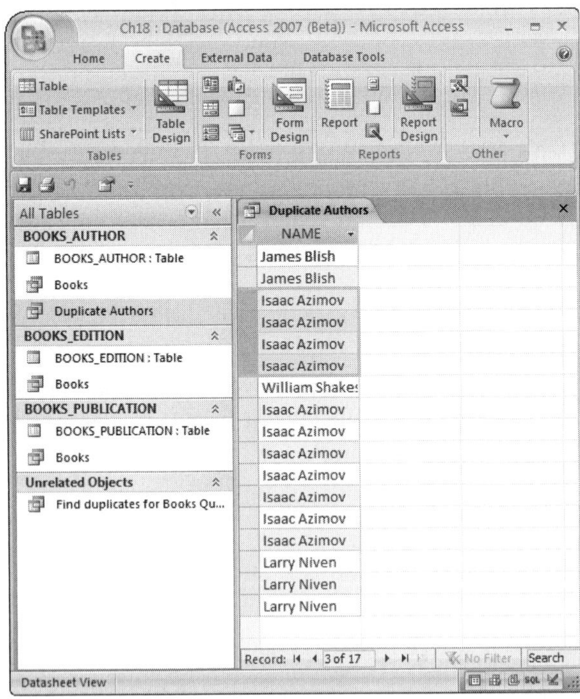

Now you can create a Find Duplicates query to find the duplicate values:

1. **Open up the Query Wizard and select Find Duplicates query.**
2. **Select the Duplicate Authors query, select the Name field, and execute.**

   The result is shown in Figure 18-13, where each author is shown once, with the number of duplications in the next column.

FIGURE 18-13

A find duplicates query

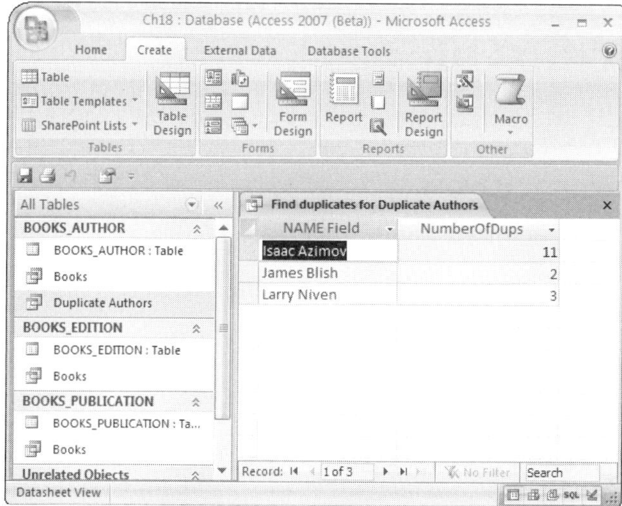

Find Unmatched Query Wizard

This wizard helps you create a query that reports any orphan or widow records between two tables.

An *orphan* is a record in a *many*-side table that has no corresponding record in the one-side table. A *widow* is a record in the *one* side of a one-to-many or one-to-one table that does not have a corresponding record in the other table.

Access asks for the names of the two tables to compare; it also asks for the link field name between the tables. Access prompts you for the fields that you want to see in the first table and for a title. Then it creates the query.

This type of query can help find records that have no corresponding records in other tables. If you create a relationship between tables and try to set referential integrity but Access reports that it cannot activate the feature, some records are violating integrity. This type of query helps find them quickly.

You can go ahead and execute the Query Wizard, and create a Find Unmatched query between any two tables. The result will be something like that shown here:

```
SELECT BOOKS_EDITION.ISBN
FROM BOOKS_EDITION LEFT JOIN BOOKS_PUBLICATION
ON BOOKS_EDITION.[PUBLICATION_ID] =
BOOKS_PUBLICATION.[PUBLICATION_ID]
WHERE (((BOOKS_PUBLICATION.PUBLICATION_ID) Is Null));
```

As you can see, a Find Unmatched query is essentially just another term for an outer join. Outer joins are covered in Chapter 4.

SQL-Specific Queries

Access has three query types that cannot be created by using the QBE pane; instead, you type the appropriate SQL (Structured Query Language) statement directly in the SQL View window. These *SQL-specific* queries are as follows:

- **Union query**: Combines fields from more than one table or query into one recordset
- **Pass-through query**: Enables you to send SQL commands directly to ODBC (Open Database Connectivity) databases using the ODBC database's SQL syntax
- **Data definition query**: Enables you to create or alter database tables or create indexes in a database, such as Access databases, directly

NOTE **To create any of these queries, right-click in Design View, select SQL Specific, and then select from the menu that appears. You can also select these queries from the menu at the top left of the window.**

- **Subqueries**: In addition to these three special SQL-specific queries, you can use SQL in a subquery (inside a standard Access query) to define a field or define criteria for a field.

Creating union queries

A union query merges the results of two other queries, so you can go into Design View and create a query. Follow these steps:

1. **Create a query design and add the** BOOKS_AUTHOR **table to Design View.**
2. **Put both the fields in the table into the query.**
3. **Now select a Union query by clicking the button at the top of the window or right-clicking and selecting Union inside SQL Specific.**

NOTE **A text editor pops up in place of the design on the screen. This is because you have to select two tables for a union. They could even be the same tables. Selecting the same table twice also reverts to the editor.**

This is what union query looks like, and this is what you can type into the editor:

```
SELECT * FROM BOOKS_AUTHOR
UNION
SELECT * FROM BOOKS_AUTHOR;
```

The result is as shown in Figure 18-14.

FIGURE 18-14

A union query retrieving rows from the same table twice

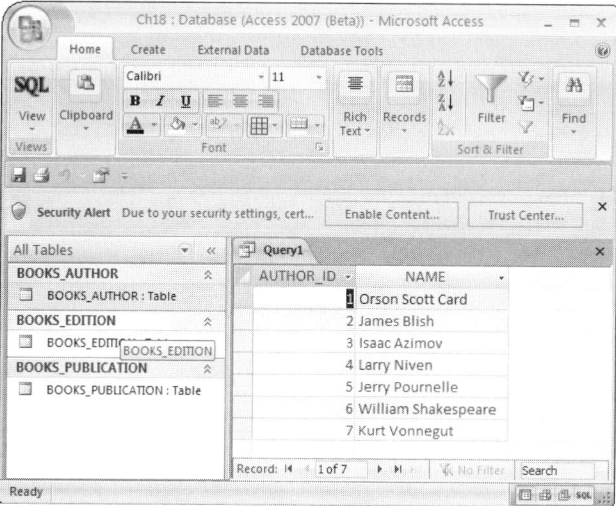

General restrictions on union queries are that the number of fields retrieved by both queries is the same:

- Datatypes for all fields in both queries must match, field for field, and in the correct sequence.
- Fields not in the select list in either query can be replaced with a NULL as in the following example:

```
SELECT AUTHOR_ID, NAME, NULL FROM BOOKS_AUTHOR
UNION
SELECT PUBLICATION_ID, FORMAT, ISBN FROM BOOKS_EDITION;
```

The result is as shown in Figure 18-15.

FIGURE 18-15

A union query on two different tables

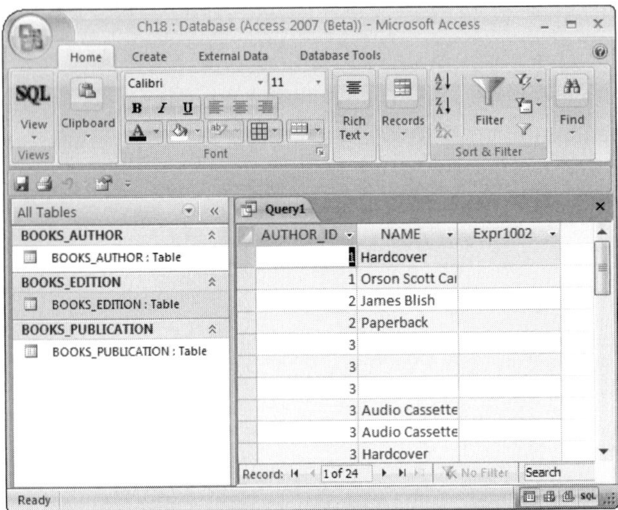

There's a problem with the previous two queries, most obviously with the first one. The BOOKS_AUTHOR table is selected from twice, and there is only one copy of the records. This happens because duplicate records have been removed.

When you use the Union command in the SQL SELECT statement, it copies only those records that are not duplicates when it joins the tables. The contents of all the fields being selected in the SQL Union query determine whether duplication exists. If two records have the same contents in all the fields selected, they are considered duplicates and only one record is displayed. If there are other fields not used in the Union query that have different values, they are not used to determine duplicity. If you want to see all records from the Union of two tables, simply use the keyword ALL after the UNION command: UNION ALL SELECT.

So the query can be changed as follows:

```
SELECT * FROM BOOKS_AUTHOR
UNION ALL
SELECT * FROM BOOKS_AUTHOR
ORDER BY AUTHOR_ID;
```

And the result is as shown in Figure 18-16.

FIGURE 18-16

A union all query returns all records, including duplicated records

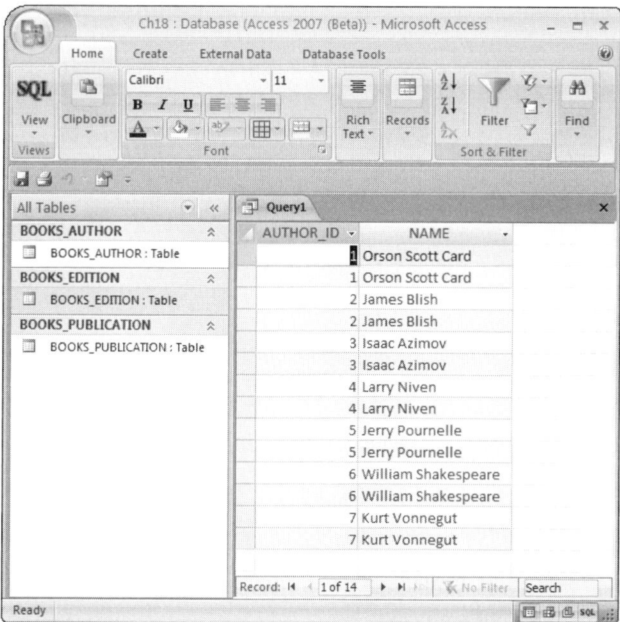

Additionally, the query was enhanced with an `ORDER BY` sorting clause, showing very clearly in Figure 18-16 that each author is repeated.

The `ORDER BY` sorting command is applied to the results of the union, not the first or second queries alone. In other words, the sort is executed after the union has finished executing.

Creating pass-through queries

A *pass-through query* sends SQL commands directly to an SQL database server (such as Microsoft SQL Server, Oracle, and so on). Often these database servers are known as the back end of the system, with Access being the client tool or front end. You send the command by using the syntax required by the particular server. Be sure to consult the documentation for the appropriate SQL database server.

You can use pass-through queries to retrieve records, or change data, or to run a server-side stored procedure or trigger. They can even be used to create new tables at the SQL server database level (versus local tables).

After you create a pass-through query, you need to specify information about the database you want to connect to. You can type a connection string in the `ODBCConnectStr` property of the query property sheet directly or click Build and enter the information about the server you want to connect to. If you do not specify a connection string, you are prompted for the connection information when you run the query.

Creating data definition queries

Of the three SQL-specific queries, the *data definition query* is the least useful against local tables. Everything that can be done with it also can be done by using the design tools in Access. The data definition query is, however, an efficient way to create or change database objects. With a data definition query, any of these SQL statements can be used:

- `CREATE TABLE`
- `ALTER TABLE`
- `DROP TABLE`
- `CREATE INDEX`
- `DROP INDEX`

For example, you could type the following code into the SQL query window (Data Definition Query) to create a local Access table named `TelephoneList`:

```
CREATE TABLE TelephoneList
( [TeleID] integer, [FullName] text,
[Address1] text, [Address2] text,
[Address3] text, [Country] text,
[Phone 1] text, [Phone 2] text,
[FaxPhn 1] text, [Notes] memo,
CONSTRAINT [Index1] PRIMARY KEY ([TeleID]) );
```

After it is created, this query could be run to create a new table named `Telephone List`. You could create a second data-definition query to create an index for the table. For instance, you could create an index that would be in order by country and full name:

```
CREATE INDEX CountryName
ON TelephoneList ([Country], [FullName]);
```

You can have only one SQL statement in each data-definition query.

Creating SQL subqueries in an Access query

Access 2007 enables you to create an SQL `SELECT` statement inside another select query or action query. You can use these SQL statements in the Field row to define a new field or in the Criteria row to define criteria for a field. Using subqueries, you can do the following:

- Find values in the primary query that are equal to, greater than, or less than values returned by the subquery using the `ANY`, `IN`, or `ALL` reserved words.
- Test for the existence of a result from a subquery using the `EXISTS` or `NOT EXISTS` reserved words.
- Using the `ANY`, `IN`, or `ALL` reserve words in a subquery, you can compare values in the main query to the results of the subquery (not equal, equal, greater than, or less than).
- Create nested subqueries (subqueries within subqueries).

You can place an SQL statement in the Field cell or in the Criteria cell of the design grid. You would place it in the Field cell to create a new field for the query. In contrast, you can use an SQL statement in the Criteria cell of a field to define the criteria used for limiting the records of the cell.

Action Queries

An action query defines a query that does something more than simply select a specific group of records and then present it to you in a dynaset. The word "action" suggests performing some operation, influencing, or affecting something. The word is synonymous with operation, performance, and work. An action query can be considered a select query that is given a *duty* to perform against a specified group of records in the dynaset.

Types of action queries

When you create any query, Access creates it as a select query automatically. You can specify a different type (such as action) from within the query design tool.

Action queries can not be created using the Query Wizard tool. Open the Query Design screen and create an action query by right-clicking on the background, and selecting Make Table, Update Query, Append Query, or Delete Query from the menu. The four different types of action queries perform the following functions:

- **Make Table Query**: Makes a selection of records from a database, saving those records into a new table (it makes a new table). For example, you want to create history tables and then copy all inactive records to them. You consider a record inactive if a customer hasn't bought anything in more than two years. You decide to remove the inactive records from your active database tables. Use a make-table query to create the history tables and a delete query to remove the unwanted records.
- **Update Query**: Updates data in a table that already exists.
- **Append Query**: Adds new records to a table that already exists. For example, one of your former customers, whom you haven't heard from for more than four years, wants to make a purchase; you need to bring the old information back into the active file from the backup files. Use an append query to add records from your back-up tables to your active tables.

- **Delete Query**: Deletes data in a specified table that matches a set of criteria (a filter).

TIP **You can quickly identify action queries in the Database window by the special exclamation point icons that sit beside their names (to the right side).**

CAUTION **Unlike select queries, which display data in a specific manner, action queries perform actions against the data stored in the underlying tables. This action may be copying the information (data) to another table, modifying the contents of records within the current table, or even deleting records in the current table.**

CAUTION **Because of the destructive nature of action queries, it is a good idea to observe the following rules: Always back up your table *before* performing the action query, and always create and view the action query (use the Datasheet button on the toolbar) before *performing it.***

Viewing the results of an action query

Action queries perform a specific task many times, which can be destructive. Be very careful when using them. It's important to view the changes that they will make (by selecting Datasheet View) before you run the action query and to verify afterward that they made the changes that you anticipated. Before you learn how to create and run an action query, it's also important to review the process for seeing what your changes will look like *before* you change a table permanently.

Viewing a query before using update and delete queries

Before actually performing an action query, you select Datasheet View to see which set of data the action query will work with. Meanwhile, when you're updating or deleting records with an action query, the actions take place on the underlying tables that the query is currently using. To view the results of an update or a delete query, click the Datasheet button to see whether the records will be updated or deleted before committing the action.

NOTE **If your update query makes changes to the fields you used for selecting the records, you may have to look at the underlying table or change to a select query to see the changes. For example, if you delete a set of records with an action button, the resulting select dynaset of the same record criteria will show that no records exist and that the condition specified has been performed. By removing the delete criteria, you can view the remaining table and verify that all specified records have been deleted.**

Switching to the result table of a make-table or append query

Unlike the update or delete queries, make-table and append queries copy resultant records to another table. After specifying the fields and the criteria in the Design window, the make-table and the append queries copy the specified fields and records to another table. When you run the queries, the results take place in another table, not in the current table.

Scoping Criteria

Action queries can use any expression composed of fields, functions, and operators to specify any limiting condition that you need to place on the query. Scoping criteria are one form of record criteria. Normally, the record criteria serve as a filter to tell Access which records to find and/or leave out of the dynaset. Because action queries do not create a dynaset, you use scoping criteria to specify a set of records for Access to operate on.

Selecting a Datasheet View shows you a dynaset of only the criteria and fields that were specified, not the actual table that contains the new or added records. To view the results of a make-table or append query, open the new table and view the contents to verify that the query worked correctly. If you won't be using the action query again, do not save it. Delete it.

Action queries cannot be reversed

Action queries copy or change data in underlying tables. After an action query is executed, it cannot be reversed. Therefore, when you're working with action queries, create a select query first to make sure that the record criteria and selection are correct for the action query.

CAUTION **Action queries are destructive; before performing one, always make a backup of the underlying tables. You may also consider removing the action query from your database after the action has been performed if the query will not be used again.**

Creating Action Queries

Creating an action query is similar to creating a select query. You specify the fields for the query and any *scoping criteria*. In addition to specifying the fields and criteria, you must tell Access to make this query an action-specific query of Append To, Table, Update To, or Delete.

Creating an update action query to change values

In this section, you learn to handle an event that requires changing many records. The type of query used is called an *update* action query.

It's possible to update each record in a table individually by using a form or even creating a select query dynaset to make these changes in the datasheet; however, this process can take a very long time if there are many records to change. The method is not only time-consuming but also inefficient. In addition, this method lends itself to typing errors as you enter new text into fields.

The best way to handle this type of event is to use an *update* action query to make many changes in just one operation. You save time and eliminate many of those typos that crop up in manually edited records.

Let's create an update action query:

1. **Create a very simple query that selects all records and fields from the** `BOOKS_AUTHOR` **table.**
2. **Right-click the background, go to Query Type, and select Update Query.**

   This option is also on the Query Type menu at the top-left of the page. This is what you get in the SQL View:

   ```
   UPDATE BOOKS_AUTHOR SET BOOKS_AUTHOR.[NAME] = "Unknown";
   ```

Essentially, you can now execute that this update query from elsewhere, and the names of authors in the `BOOKS_AUTHOR` table will be set to `Unknown`.

An update action query is the SQL equivalent of an `UPDATE` statement, which updates one or more records in a table.

Creating a new table using a make-table query

You can use an action query to create new tables based on scoping criteria. To make a new table, you create a make-table query. Consider the following situation as an example that might give rise to this particular task and for which you would create a make-table query.

Let's create a make-table query:

1. **Create a very simple query that selects all records and fields from the** `BOOKS_AUTHOR` **table.**
2. **Right-click the background, go to Query Type, and select Make-Table Query.**

   This option is also on the Query Type menu at the top-left of the page. This is what you get in the SQL View:

   ```
   SELECT BOOKS_AUTHOR.AUTHOR_ID,
   BOOKS_AUTHOR.NAME INTO [New Authors]
   FROM BOOKS_AUTHOR;
   ```

NOTE **All a make-table query does is select rows with a query and insert them into another table. This is the ANSI standard SQL equivalent of an `INSERT INTO ... SELECT ...` statement.**

When you're creating numerous make-table queries, you need to select Make-Table Query from the Query Type button on the toolbar or select Query Type followed by Make-Table from the menu; either method renames the make-table query each time. Access assumes that you want to overwrite the existing table if you don't reselect the make-table option. Access warns you about overwriting before performing the new make-table query; as an alternative, you could change the destination table name on the Property Sheet.

Creating queries to append records

As the word *append* suggests, an append query attaches or adds records to a specified table. An append query adds records *from* the table you're using to another table. The table you want to add records to must already exist. You can append records to a table in the same database or in another Access database.

Append queries are useful for adding information to another table on the basis of some scoping criteria. Even so, append queries are not always the fastest way of adding records to another database. For example, if you need to append all fields and all records from one table to a new table, the append query is not the best way to do it. Instead, use the Copy and Paste options on the Edit menu when you're working with the table in a datasheet or form.

NOTE **You can add records to an open table. You don't have to close the table before adding records. However, Access does not automatically refresh the view of the table that has records added to it. To refresh the table, press Shift+F9. This action requires the table so that you can see the appended records.**

When you're working with append queries, be aware of these rules:

- If the table you're appending records to has a primary key field, the records you add cannot have Null values or duplicate primary key values. If they do, Access will not append the records and you will get no warning.
- If you add records to another database table, you must know the location and name of the database.
- If you use the asterisk (*) field in a field's row in Design View, you cannot also use individual fields from the same table. Access assumes that you're trying to add field contents twice to the same record and will not append the records.
- If you append records with an AutoNumber field (an Access-specified primary key), do not include the AutoNumber field if the table you're appending to also has the field and record contents (this causes the problem specified in the first rule). Also, if you're adding to an empty table and you want the new table to have a new AutoNumber number (that is, order number) based on the criteria, do not use the AutoNumber field.

By following these simple rules, your append query will perform as expected and become a very useful tool. Let's create a append query:

1. **Create a very simple query that selects all records and fields from the** `BOOKS_AUTHOR` **table.**
2. **In the Design View for the query, right-click the background, go to Query Type, and select Append Query.**

   This option is also on the Query Type menu at the top-left of the page. This is what you get in the SQL View:

   ```
   INSERT INTO authors
   SELECT
   FROM BOOKS_AUTHOR;
   ```

NOTE All an append query is doing is executing an insert into one table, from a query. This is another ANSI standard SQL equivalent of an `INSERT INTO ... SELECT ...` statement.

NOTE When you're using the append query, only fields with names that match in the two tables are copied. For example, you may have a small table with six fields and another with nine fields. The table with nine fields has only five of the six field names that match fields in the smaller table. If you append records from the smaller table to the larger table, only the five matching fields are appended; the other four fields remain blank.

CAUTION If you create an append query by using the asterisk (*) field and you also use a field from the same table as the All asterisk field to specify a criterion, you must take the criteria field name out of the Append To row. If you don't, Access reports an error. Remember that the field for the criterion is already included in the asterisk field.

Creating a query to delete records

Of all the action queries, the *delete query* is the most dangerous. Unlike the other types of queries you've worked with, delete queries remove records from tables permanently and *irreversibly*.

Like other action queries, delete queries act on a group of records on the basis of scoping criteria.

A delete action query can work with multiple tables to delete records. If you intend to delete related records from multiple tables, however, you must do the following:

- Define relationships between the tables in the Relationships Builder.
- Check the Enforce Referential Integrity option for the join between tables.
- Check the Cascade Delete Related Records option for the join between tables (for one-to-one or one-to-many relationships).

When working with one-to-many relationships without defining relationships and turning Cascade Delete on, Access deletes records from only one table at a time. Specifically, Access deletes the *many* side of the relationship first. Then you must remove the many table from the query and delete the records from the *one* side of the query.

This method is time-consuming and awkward. Therefore, when you're deleting related records from one-to-many relationship tables, make sure that you define relationships between the tables and check the Cascade Delete box in the Edit Relationships dialog box. By doing this, you can delete from all related tables by creating a single Delete query.

CAUTION Because of the permanently destructive action of a delete query, always make back-up copies of your tables before working with them.

Let's create a delete query:

1. **Create a very simple query that selects all records and fields from the `BOOKS_AUTHOR` table.**

2. **Right-click the background, go to Query Type, and select Delete Query.**

   This option is also on the Query Type menu at the top-left of the page. This is what you get in the SQL View:

   ```
   DELETE BOOKS_AUTHOR.AUTHOR_ID, BOOKS_AUTHOR.NAME
   FROM BOOKS_AUTHOR;
   ```

All a delete query is doing is executing a `delete` command on multiple records.

Remember that a delete query permanently and irreversibly removes the records from the table(s). Therefore, it is important to back up the records to be deleted *before* you delete them.

Saving an action query

Saving an action query is just like saving any other query. From Design mode, you can save the query and continue working by clicking the Save button on the toolbar (or by selecting File followed by Save from the Query menu). If this is the first time you're saving the query, Access prompts you for a name in the Save As dialog box.

You can also save the query by exiting the tool.

Running an action query

After you save an action query, you can run it by double-clicking its name in the Query container (window). Access warns you that an action query is about to be executed and asks for confirmation before it continues with the query.

Troubleshooting action queries

When you're working with action queries, you need to be aware of several potential problems. While you're running the query, any of several messages may appear, including messages that several records were lost because of *key violations* or that records were *locked* during the execution of the query. This section discusses some of these problems and how to avoid them.

Data-type errors in appending and updating

If you attempt to enter a value that is not appropriate for the specified field, Access doesn't enter the value; it simply ignores the incorrect values and converts the fields to Null values. When you're working with append queries, Access appends the records, but the fields may be blank!

Key violations in action queries

When you attempt to append records to another database that has a primary key, Access will not append records that contain the same primary key value.

Access does not enable you to update a record and change a primary key value to an existing value. You can change a primary key value to another value under these conditions:

- The new primary key value does not already exist.
- The field value you're attempting to change is not related to fields in other tables.

Access does not enable you to delete a field on the *one* side of a one-to-many relationship without first deleting the records from the *many* side.

Access does not enable you to append or update a field value that duplicates a value in a *unique index field*. A unique index field is a field that has the Index property set to Yes (No Duplicates).

Record-locked fields in multiuser environments

Access will not perform an action query on records locked by another user. When you're performing an update or append query, you can choose to continue and change all other values. But remember this: If you enable Access to continue with an action query, you won't be able to determine which records were left unchanged!

Text fields

When appending or updating to a text field that is smaller than the current field, Access truncates any text data that doesn't fit in the new field. Access does not warn you that it has truncated the information.

Summary

Queries are the heart of every database applications. Queries are responsible for converting diffuse data contained in tables into information that users can actually use. Without queries, you'd have to write VBA code for every data extraction and transformation, rather than relying on a powerful database object that performs these tasks for you.

It is unlikely you will ever use all of the techniques described in this chapter. The Access implementation of the SQL language is quite extensive and supports many highly advanced query and SQL language constructs. Combining these capabilities with your other hard-earned Access development skills adds considerably to the sophistication of your Access applications.

Chapter 19

Advanced Access Form Techniques

User interface is a term you hear frequently in discussions about personal computer software. In virtually all applications built with Microsoft Access, the user interface consists of a series of Access forms. If you intend to develop successful Access applications, you need to understand Access forms inside out.

This chapter helps you improve your understanding of forms. You first take a look at how to programmatically manipulate the many controls that constitute the building blocks out of which forms are constructed. You examine, also, some powerful ways to take advantage of subforms. A section of the chapter is then devoted to presenting a grab-bag of forms-related programming techniques that will help you create forms that wring the best performance from Access and your computer. Then, we discuss the Query By Form feature that enables you to build an intuitive form-based interface between users and Access queries.

IN THIS CHAPTER

Setting Control Properties

The building blocks of Access forms are known as *controls*. The form design toolbox contains 16 types of controls from which you can build forms: labels, text boxes, option groups, toggle buttons, option buttons, check boxes, combo boxes, list boxes, command buttons, images, unbound (OLE) object frames, bound (OLE) object frames, page breaks, subforms, lines, and rectangles.

Each control on an Access form has a set of properties that determines how it looks and acts. In Design View, you can determine property settings for any object by selecting the object and displaying its property sheet. To display the property sheet, right-click the object and click Properties in the pop-up menu or select the object and click the Properties button on the ribbon. Once the property sheet is open, just click any other control in the form to display the control's property settings. Figure 19-1 shows the property sheet for the Next command button on the Contacts form in the `Chapter19.accdb` application. As you are designing a form, you set control properties by changing the values stored in each control's property sheet.

FIGURE 19-1

The property sheet for the New command button

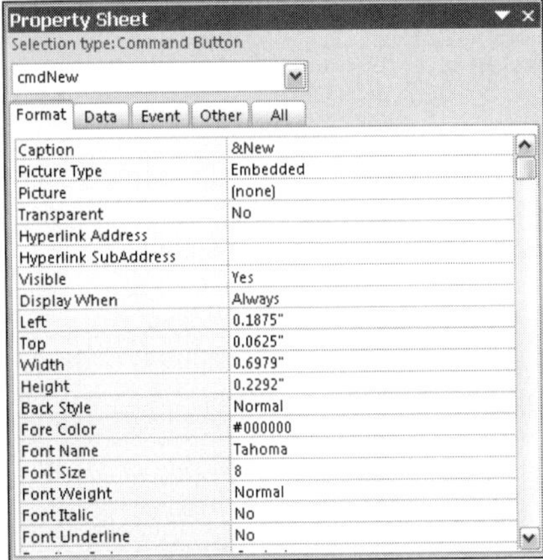

The form itself also has its own set of properties. If you display the property sheet in Design View before selecting a specific control, Access lists the form's properties in the property sheet, as indicated by the caption "Form" in the property sheet's title bar (see Figure 19-2). To display the form's properties in the property sheet after first displaying a control's properties, click a completely blank area in the form design window (outside the form's defined border).

FIGURE 19-2

The property sheet for the Contacts form

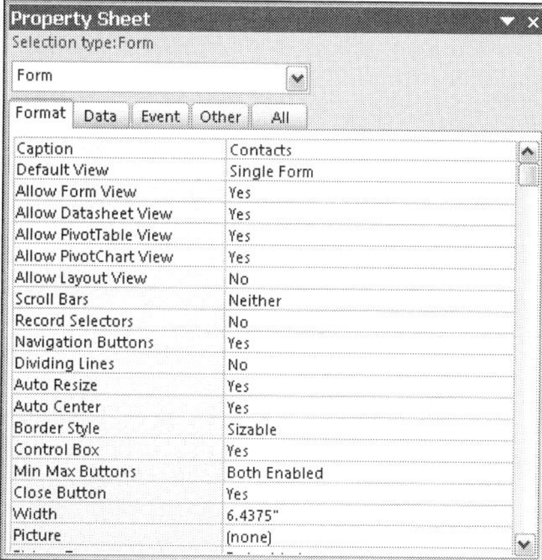

Customizing default properties

Whenever you use a tool in the form Design View toolbox to create a control, the control is created with a *default* set of property values. While this may seem obvious, what you may not know is that you can set these default values yourself. For example, if you want all list boxes in your form to be flat rather than sunken, it is more time-efficient to change the default SpecialEffect property to Flat before you design the form, rather than changing the SpecialEffect property of every list box individually.

In addition to saving you time while designing a form, customizing default properties can speed the saving and loading of forms. When you save the form design, Access saves the default control properties as well as those property values that differ from the default property settings for that type of control. If most controls on the form use the default property settings, the saved form takes less space, saves faster, and subsequently loads faster when your application uses it (but doesn't save memory).

To set control defaults, select a tool in the toolbox and then set properties in the property sheet. Notice that the title in the property sheet is Selection type: Default <ControlType>. As you set the control's properties, you are actually setting the default properties for this type of control. Rather than adding the control to the form, select another control (such as the Select control in the upper-right corner of the Controls group) to "lock down" the default settings. Then, when you reselect the control, the control's default properties have been set the way you want.

Manipulating controls at runtime

The form design capabilities of Access are so robust that you can sometimes get so engrossed in designing beautiful forms that you lose site of the fact that all Access form controls are programmatically accessible at runtime. It can sometimes turn out to be very convenient to change the design of a form on the fly, based on input from the user. For example, a list box that contains information that is relevant only some of the time doesn't have to be displayed all the time. A well-designed form hides irrelevant choices whenever possible. You can achieve this and similar functionality by assigning values to control and form properties at runtime.

Following are a few properties that are often good candidates for dynamic assignment at runtime:

- `Enabled` **property:** If you want a control to be visible but grayed-out, set the `Enabled` property to `False`. Clicking the grayed-out control has no effect. This technique enables you to maintain a consistent form design, and helps the user get familiar with the location of the various controls on the form but prevents the user from selecting a control that is irrelevant to the current operation.
- `Visible` **property**: You can easily toggle the display of any control by assigning `Yes` or `No` to the control's `Visible` property. While the control is invisible, it is also inactive and cannot receive the focus. An invisible control cannot respond to events as well. Making a control invisible is sometimes more appropriate than simply disabling the control, especially in the case of irrelevant text, combo, or list boxes.
- `Caption` **property**: By dynamically assigning values to a control's `Caption` property, you can get the control to serve double- or triple-duty. This technique is especially useful when two command buttons serve mutually exclusive functions and don't need to appear on the form at the same time. For example, you might place a command button with the caption `&New Patient Data` on your application's main switchboard form. This button opens a form for adding a new record to your Patient database. After the new patient data has been entered, but before the full transaction has been committed to the database, you could change the command button's caption to `&Edit Patient Data` using the button's `Caption` property.

  You can also use the active form's `Caption` property creatively to display information about the current record. Each time the current event occurs, assign a new value to the `Caption` property that contains pertinent information from the current record.
- `RowSource` **property**: Use the `RowSource` property of a combo or list box control to synchronize the list contents with values in other controls in the active form. For example, if the `txtDepartment` control contains the value `Sales` you can use the `cboPhoneList` combo box's `RowSource` property to cause only members of the sales department to be listed in the combo box.
- `BackColor` **and** `ForeColor` **properties:** Judicious use of color can be very effective in accenting important information. Access enables you to dynamically change the color of controls as they receive/lose the focus or to reflect a characteristic of the data by assigning values to the `ForeColor` and/or `BackColor` properties.

- `Left`, `Top`, `Width`, **and** `Height` **properties:** Using these properties, you can control the position and dimensions of a control on the form.
- `MenuBar`, `ShortcutMenu`, `ShortcutMenuBar`: If you have defined custom menu bars, shortcut menus, and/or shortcut menu bars, you can use these form properties to change the menu bar, shortcut menu, and/or shortcut menu bar that the form displays.
- **Custom Ribbon ID:** If the current application includes custom ribbons, the ribbon IDs appear in this property's drop-down list. Access shows and hides the assigned ribbon as the form is opened and closed.

The `SetProperty` function included in the following procedure can be used to set the value of any property of any open form or any property of any control in an open form:

```
Function SetProperty( _
     ByVal strFormName As String, _
     ByVal strCtrlName As String, _
     ByVal strPropName As String, _
     ByVal strNewValue As Variant) As Boolean

  Dim frmName As Form
  Dim strMsg As String
  Dim strFunction As String
  Dim strObjName As String

On Error GoTo HandleError

  SetProperty = False
  strFunction = "SetProperty"

  'If no control name is passed, must be a form:
  If strCtrlName = "" Then
    GoTo SetFormProperty
  End IF

SetControlProperty:
  'Assign new control property value:
  strObjName = strCtrlName
  Set frmName = Forms(strFormName)
  frmName(strCtrlName).Properties( _
    strPropName) = strNewValue
  SetProperty = True
  GoTo ExitHere

SetFormProperty:
  'Assign new form property value:
  strObjName = strFormName
  Set frmName = Forms(strFormName)
  frmName.Properties(strPropName) = strNewValue
```

```
    SetProperty = True
    GoTo ExitHere

ExitHere:

    Exit Function

HandleError:
    Select Case Err

      Case 2450
        strMsg = "'" & strFormName & "' is not an open form"

      Case conNotControl
        strMsg = "'" & strCtrlName _
          & "' is not a control on '" & strFormName & "'"

      Case 2465
        strMsg = "'" & strPropName _
          & "' is not a property of '" & strObjName & "'"

      Case Else
        strMsg = "Error#" & Err & ": " & Err.Description

      End Select

      MsgBox strMsg, vbExclamation + vbOKOnly, _
        "Error in Procedure " & strFunction

    SetProperty = False
    Resume ExitHere

End Function
```

This function takes four arguments, the name of the form, the name of the control (if any), the name of the property, and the new value of the property. It returns a value of `True` if the operation is successful and `False` if it is not. For example, to disable the `GoToNew` button in the Employees form, you could use the following statement:

```
intRetVal = SetProperty("Employees", "GoToNew", "Enabled", 0)
```

To set the value of a form property, pass a blank string (`""`) as the control name. For example, to set the `frmEmployees` form's caption (in the `Chapter19.accdb` database) to `Sales Department`, you can use the following statement:

```
intRetVal = SetProperty("frmEmployees", "", _
  "Caption", "Sales Department")
```

Hiding and shown controls is easily done by adjusting the control's `Visible` property. You may want to hide certain controls (such as command buttons or text boxes) when they are irrelevant to the user's current task. You may also want to hide controls if the user is not permitted to perform the operation (such as deleting an existing record). Rather than simply disabling the control (by setting its `Enabled` property to `False`), hiding the control makes it invisible on the form's surface. Invisible controls are less likely to confuse users than controls that are visible, but cannot be accessed or used. The following statement hides a command button named `cmdDeleteRecord` on the employees form:

```
intRetVal = SetProperty("frmEmployees", "cmdDeleteRecord", _
  "Visible", "False")
```

Reading control properties

If your application manipulates the control properties, at various times you will need to read the value of a control's property. The following `GetProperty` function returns the value of any property of any open form or any property of any control in an open form. If the function encounters an error, it returns the value `ERROR`.

```
Function GetProperty( _
    ByVal strFormName As String, _
    ByVal strCtrlName As String, _
    ByVal strPropName As String) As Variant

  Dim frmName As Form
  Dim strMsg As String
  Dim strFunction As String
  Dim strObjName As String

On Error GoTo HandleError

  GetProperty = "ERROR"
  strFunction = "SetProperty"

  'If no control name is passed, must be a form:
  If strCtrlName = "" Then
    GoTo GetFormProperty
  End If

GetControlProperty:
  'Get control property value:
  strObjName = strCtrlName
  Set frmName = Forms(strFormName)
  GetProperty = _
      frmName(strCtrlName).Properties(strPropName)
  GoTo ExitHere

GetFormProperty:
```

```
    'Get form property value:
    strObjName = strFormName
    Set frmName = Forms(strFormName)
    GetProperty = frmName.Properties(strPropName)
    GoTo ExitHere

ExitHere:

    Exit Function

HandleError:
    Select Case Err

      Case 2450
        strMsg = "'" & strFormName & "' is not an open form"

      Case 2465
        strMsg = "'" & strCtrlName _
            & "' is not a control on '" & strFormName & "'"

      Case 2455
        strMsg = "'" & strPropName _
          & "' is not a property of '" & strObjName & "'"

      Case Else
        strMsg = "Error# " & Err & ": " & Err.Description

    End Select

    MsgBox strMsg, vbExclamation + vbOKOnly, _
      "Error in Procedure " & strFunction
    Resume ExitHere

End Function
```

Notice that the GetProperty function returns a variant data type value. A variant is returned because the function may return a property object, or — in the event of a problem accessing the property — a string containing the word "ERROR". If a runtime error is triggered by the GetProperty function, a string containing the error number and message is returned.

Working with Subforms

Subforms are an indispensable tool for displaying information from two different tables or queries on the screen together. Typically, subforms are used where the main form's record source has a one-to-many relationship with the subform's record source. Many records in the subform are associated with one record in the main form.

Access uses the `LinkMasterFields` and `LinkChildFields` properties of the subform control to choose the records in the subform that are related to each record in the main form. Whenever a value in the main form's link field changes, Access automatically re-queries the subform.

When creating a subform, you may want to display subform aggregate information in the master form. For example, you may want to display the count of the records in the subform somewhere on your main form. For an example of this technique, see the `txtItemCount` control in `frmCustomerSales` in `Chapter19.accdb`. In this case the `ControlSource` expression in the `txtItemCount` control is:

```
="(" & [subfPurchases].[Form]![txtItemCount] & " items)"
```

The result of this expression is shown in Figure 19-3.

FIGURE 19-3

Aggregate data from a subform can be displayed on the main form.

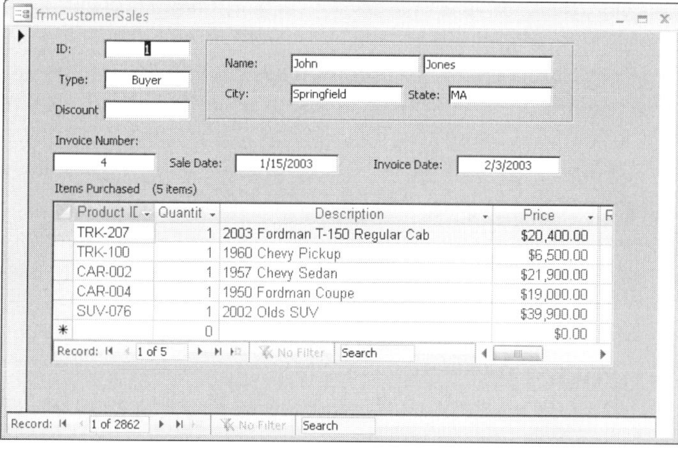

Before you can put aggregate data in the master form, its value must be found in the subform. Place a text box wherever you want in the subform, and set its `Visible` property to `No` (False) so that it is hidden. Put an aggregate expression, such as `= Count([ProductID])`, into its `ControlSource` property.

In the main form, insert a new text box with `ControlSource` set to the following value:

```
=[Subform1].Form![Aggregate Control]
```

where `Subform1` is the name of the control on the main form that contains the embedded subform and `Aggregate Control` is the name of the control on the subform that contains the aggregate data.

The control on the main form updates every time you change its value in the subform.

Access treats a subform control in the same manner as other controls on the main form. You can set a subform control's properties, and refer to it with a `GoToControl` command, and use code to set and read the values of controls on the subform. Use the following syntax versions to refer to subform properties, subform controls, and subform control properties, respectively:

```
Forms![FormName]![SubformName].Form.SubFormProperty
Forms![FormName]![SubformName].Form![ControlName]
Forms![FormName]![SubformName].Form![ControlName] _
      .ControlProperty
```

where `SubformName` refers to the name you've given the subform control, which is not necessarily the same as the name of the form as it appears in the Navigation pane.

When using subforms within subforms, use the following syntax:

```
Forms![FormName]![SubformName].Form![SubSubformName] _
      .Form.SubSubFormProperty
Forms![FormName]![SubformName].Form![SubSubformName] _
      .Form.[ControlName]
Forms![FormName]![SubformName].Form![SubSubformName] _
      .Form.[ControlName].ControlProperty
```

Form Design Techniques

Following is a grab bag of form design tips that you may find handy; they have been gathered from numerous sources. Hopefully they will inspire you to come up with many more on your own.

Using the Tab Stop property

From time to time you may place a control on a form that is intended to trigger a fairly drastic result, such as deleting a record, or printing a long report. If you want to reduce the risk that the user might activate this control by accident, you may want to make use of the `Tab Stop` property.

For example, suppose you have placed a command button named `cmdDelete` on a form that deletes the current record. You don't want the user to click this button by mistake. Modify the `Tab Stop` property of the `cmdDelete` button to `No` to remove the button from the form's tab order (the default is `Yes`). A user will have to explicitly click on the button to activate it and will not be able to accidentally choose it while entering data.

Tallying check boxes

If you ever need to count the number of `True` values in a check box field, consider using the following expression:

```
Sum(Abs([CheckBoxField]))
```

Abs converts all the -1's to 1's and the Sum function adds them up. To count False values, use the following expression:

```
Sum([CheckBoxField] + 1)
```

True values (-1's) are converted to 0 and False values (0's) are converted to 1 before being summed.

Adding animation

Using the Timer event, it is pretty simple to add animation to Access forms. You can move a control on the form at quick intervals or rapidly change the appearance of the control. To create the appearance of animation:

1. **Embed a picture on the form.**
2. **Set the TimerInterval property of the form to around 100 (milliseconds).**
3. **Assign the following event procedure to the Timer event:**

```
Private Sub Form_Timer()
  'Move the image down and to the right.
  ctlImage.Left = ctlImage.Left + 200
  ctlImage.Top  = ctlImage.Top  + 100
End Sub
```

Screen positions in VBA are given in twips — 1/1440 of an inch. This event procedure moves the image in the ctlImage control down and to the right on the form every 1/10th of a second.

The frmAnimation form in Chapter19.accdb uses the technique described here to move an airplane bitmap across the form. A couple of other techniques are used to create a bit of animation. The following event procedure, associated with the Timer event, causes a bitmap of a pencil eraser to move back and forth by manipulating the Image control's PictureAlignment property. The procedure also causes a globe to spin by using the Visible property of three different bitmaps that are positioned one on top of the other:

```
Private Sub Form_Timer()

On Error GoTo HandleError

  'Wiggle the eraser:
  If Eraser.PictureAlignment = 2 Then
    Eraser.PictureAlignment = 3
  ElseIf Eraser.PictureAlignment = 3 Then
    Eraser.PictureAlignment = 4
  ElseIf Eraser.PictureAlignment = 4 Then
    Eraser.PictureAlignment = 3
  End If

  '"Spin" the globe:
  If World1.Visible = -1 Then
```

```
      World1.Visible = 0
      World2.Visible = -1
    ElseIf World2.Visible = -1 Then
      World2.Visible = 0
      World3.Visible = -1
    ElseIf World3.Visible = -1 Then
      World3.Visible = 0
      World1.Visible = -1
    End If

    'Now, move the plane:
    Plane.Left = Plane.Left + 200
    Plane.Top = Plane.Top + 100

  ExitHere:

    Exit Sub

  HandleError:
    Plane.Left = 0
    Plane.Top = 800
    Resume ExitHere

  End Sub
```

The `TimerInterval` property is set to `200`. Set it to a longer interval to slow down the animation.

Notice that the `Error` event is used to start the plane over again. Otherwise the plane "crashes" off the edge of the form.

Using SQL for a faster refresh

You can generate faster combo box refreshes on a form by making the control's row source a SQL statement instead of a query name. Complete the following steps:

1. **Generate the query using the standard procedure.**
2. **Make the query the control's `RowSource` property and make sure the combo box is correctly populated.**
3. **When everything works correctly, display the query in Design View and select SQL from the View menu.**
4. **Cut and paste the SQL statement into the combo box's `RowSource` property.**

Selecting data for overtyping

When users edit existing data in a form, they usually prefer to type over existing data without having to first select the existing data. The following function when triggered by each control's `GoFocus` event has this effect:

```
Function SelectAll()
  SendKeys "{Home}" 'Moves the cursor to first position
  SendKeys "+{End}" 'Selects all positions up to the last
                    'and as a reversed image easy to see
                    'and overtype.
End Function
```

Toggling properties with Not

A handy way to toggle properties that take Boolean values, such as the `Visible` property, is to use the `Not` operator. For example, the following VB statement toggles the object's `Visible` property, regardless of the actual value of the property:

```
Object.Visible = Not Object.Visible
```

For example, if `Visible` is `True`, its value is set to `False`, hiding the object. By using the `Not` operator, you don't have to test for the current value of the property.

`Chapter19.accdb` contains a simple form demonstrating this capability. `frmFlashingLabel` contains two label controls (`lblRed` and `lblBlue`) placed on top of one another. `lblRed's` `Visible` property is initially set to `No`, making it invisible. Then the following code runs every time the form's Timer event fires:

```
Private Sub Form_Timer()
  lblRed.Visible = Not lblRed.Visible
  lblBlue.Visible = Not lblBlue.Visible
End Sub
```

This code simply alternates the `Visible` property of each of the label controls. Since `lblRed` was initially invisible, it is made visible in the first pass, and so on. Although there are many other ways to implement this form trick, this example adequately demonstrates the value of the `Not` operator when dealing with property values.

Creating an auto-closing form

If you want a form to close automatically as soon as the user moves to another form, do the following:

1. **Create an event procedure for the `Deactivate` event that includes the following statement:**

   `Me.TimerInterval = 1`

2. **Create an event procedure for the `Timer` event that includes the following statement:**

   `DoCmd.Close`

Your form automatically closes as soon as you go to any other form.

Combo box techniques

Combo boxes and list boxes are powerful tools in your form-building toolbox, but they can be complicated to set up. When you build combo boxes and list boxes it is important to keep in mind the distinction between `ControlSource`, which is the table or query field to and from which the control saves and loads data, and `RowSource`, which is the source of the data displayed in the list. Because combo and list boxes support multiple columns, they allow you to easily related data from another table without basing your form on a query that joins the tables. This technique, which involves a bound combo or list box control that stores an ID number but displays names in a list, is used in the Organization combo box in the Contacts_Northwind form in `Chapter19.accdb` as well as in several of the forms found in the Northwind sample database.

For example, suppose you're creating a form to display information about your clients and customers (your "contacts"), and you want to identify the organization with which these contacts are associated. In a well-designed database, you store only an organization ID number with each contact record, while you store the organization's name and other information in a separate table. You want your form to include a combo box that displays organization names and addresses in the list but stores organization ID numbers in the field. (For an example of this technique, see `frmContacts_Northwind` in `Chapter19.accdb`.)

To accomplish your design goal, create a multiple-column combo box. Set the `ControlSource` to the `OrgID` field (the field in the `Contacts` table that contains the organization ID number for each contact person). Set the `RowSourceType` property of the combo box to `Table/Query`. You could base the list on a table, but you want the list of names to be sorted; instead, set the `RowSource` property to a query that includes `OrgID` numbers in the first field, and organization names sorted ascending in the second field. The best way to do this is using the Query Builder for the `RowSource` property to create a SQL statement; alternatively, you can create and save a query to provide the list. In `frmContacts_Northwind` example (the Organization combo box), the `RowSource` query is as follows:

```
SELECT Organizations.OrgID, Organizations.Name,
Organizations.AddressLine1, Organizations.AddressLine2,
Organizations.City, Organizations.State,
Organizations.ZipCode, Organizations.Country
FROM Organizations ORDER BY Organizations.Name
```

Because you are interested in seeing all this data listed in the combo box, set the `ColumnCount` property to `8`. You hide the `OrgID` column in a minute, but you need it in the combo box `RowSource` because it contains the data that is saved by the control when a row is selected by the user. This column is identified by the combo box's `BoundColumn` property (set to `1` by default). The bound column containing ID numbers doesn't have to be visible to the user. The `ColumnWidths` property contains a semicolon-separated list of visible column widths for the columns in the drop-down menu. Access uses default algorithms to determine the widths of any columns for which you do not explicitly choose a width. If you choose a width of 0 for any column, that column is effectively hidden from the user on the screen, but it is not hidden from the rest of your forms, VBA code, or macros. In this case you set the property to the following:

```
0";1.4";1.2";0.7";0.7";0.3;0.5";0.3"
```

This indicates to Access that you want the first column to be invisible and sets explicit column widths for the other columns.

The second column, in this case the organization name, is the one the user's text input is matched against. The first visible column in the combo box is always used for this purpose. Figure 19-4 shows the resulting drop-down list. Although this is a rather extreme example of loading a combo box with data, it effectively illustrates the power of the Access combo box control.

FIGURE 19-4

The drop-down list for the Organizations combo box

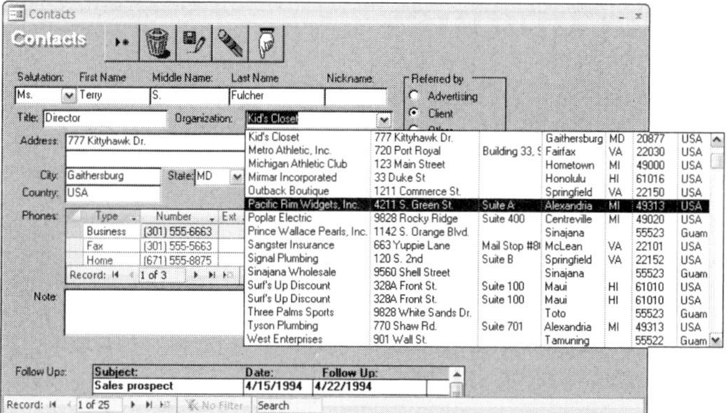

When working with combo boxes, if you set the `Limit to List` property to `Yes`, the user is required to choose only from the entries in the drop-down list. You can then construct an event procedure for the control's `NotOnList` event to handle what should happen if a user enters a value not in the list. You may want to open a form into which the user can enter new information; or perhaps you want to display a message box that instructs the user what procedure to follow to add data.

Determining whether a form is open

The following code shows a function that reports whether the form passed in as `strFName` is currently open. It simply enumerates all members of the `Forms` collection, looking to see if `strFName` matches the name of any open form.

```
Function IsFormOpen(strFName As String) As Integer

  'This function returns true if a form is open:

  Dim i As Integer

  'Assume False:
```

```
        IsFormOpen = False

        For i = 0 To Forms.Count - 1
          If Forms(i).Name = strFName Then
            IsFormOpen = True
            Exit Function
          End If
        Next

      End Function
```

Advanced Forms Techniques

Access 2007 contains many powerful and exciting features in its forms design and user interface capabilities. As you well know, the forms in your applications are the main component of the user interface. To a large extent a user's perception of an application's ease of use and strength is determined by the attractiveness and effectiveness of its user interface. You'll be pleased to know that Microsoft has provided Access 2007 forms with significant capabilities to control the user interface. Many of these features have been in Access for a very long time, but haven't been discovered by many developers.

Page Number and Date/Time controls

Most Access reports and many forms contain more than one page, and very often forms and reports include the current date and time. Many developers add this information to a form or report with an unbound text box, and use the `Page` property or `Date( )` function to return this information to the unbound text box. Access simplifies this process with the Page Numbers and Date and Time commands on the Insert menu (see Figure 19-5).

FIGURE 19-5

These commands simplify adding the page number or date to forms and reports.

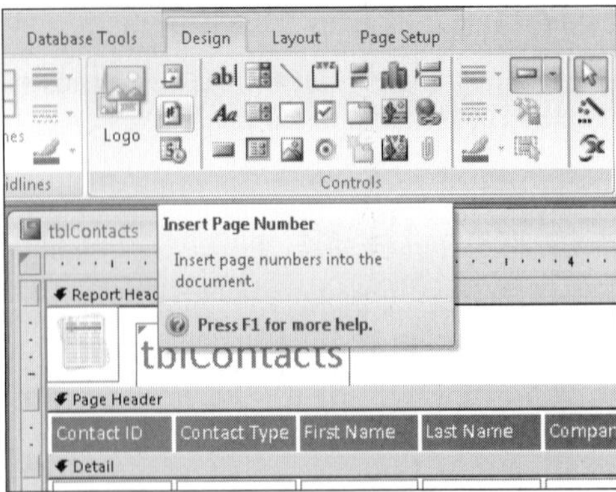

When these commands are selected Access first asks you how you want the data displayed (see Figure 19-6). Then it inserts an unbound text box onto the form or report.

FIGURE 19-6

Tell Access how you want the page numbers or date to appear.

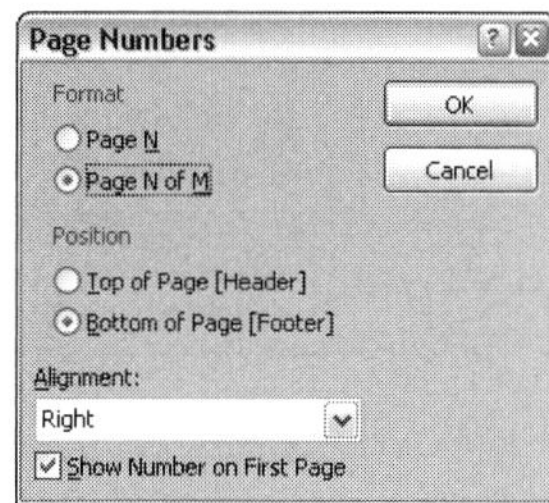

If you've asked for the page number to appear in the header or footer area, Access automatically adds these objects to your form and pops the unbound page number text box where you've indicated (see Figure 19-7). You are free to reposition the unbound text boxes anywhere you wish, of course. Adding page numbers and dates to forms and reports takes only a few seconds and is completely foolproof in Access 2007.

FIGURE 19-7

Access intelligently places the unbound controls on the form for you.

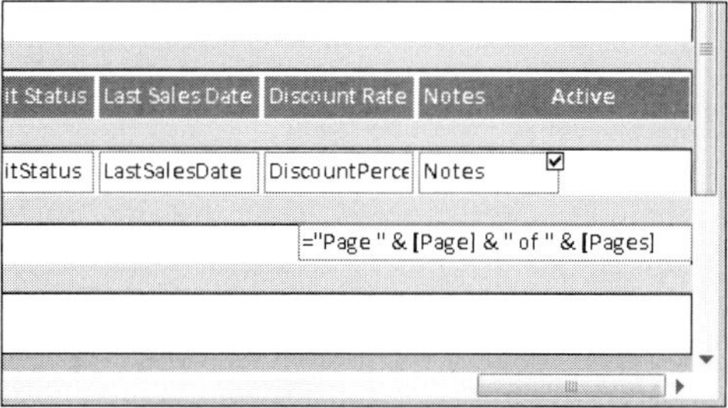

Image control

A subtle and often overlooked performance issue in Access applications occurs when static images are added to forms. Images are often added to Access forms as OLE objects, which means that a certain amount of memory and disk space is required to maintain the image's connection to its parent application. This overhead is used even when the image is a company logo or other graphic that will not be changed or edited at runtime.

Access 2007 simplifies this process and provides a great deal more flexibility with the Image control. The Image control places an image frame onto a form or report, but does not burden the image object with the overhead associated with OLE objects. The Image control accepts virtually any type of image data type recognized by Windows (`.bmp`, `.pcx`, .ico, `.dib`, `.gif`, `.wmf`, and so on), and enables you to specify the path to the image file at runtime in its `Picture` property. The Image control also accepts image data stored in an Access table, although it does not provide the flexibility of in-place editing.

Control "morphing"

Surely one of the most frustrating problems when building Access forms is the need to specify the control type as a control is added to a form. For instance, consider the issues involved when you add a list box to an Access form, specify the `ControlSource`, `RowSourceType`, `RowSource`, and other properties and then discover there's not enough room on the form for the list box. In this case, it seems the only solution is to remove the list box, add a combo box and reset all of the properties, even though the properties for the combo box are identical for the list box you just removed.

In Access 2007 you are able to change a control to any other compatible type (a process sometimes called *morphing* the control). For instance, a text box can be changed to a label, list box, or combo box. Simply right-click the control and select the Change To command from the shortcut menu to see the options. Figure 19-8 shows the options for changing a text box control.

FIGURE 19-8

Access 2007 lets you change the type of a control without losing the properties you've already set.

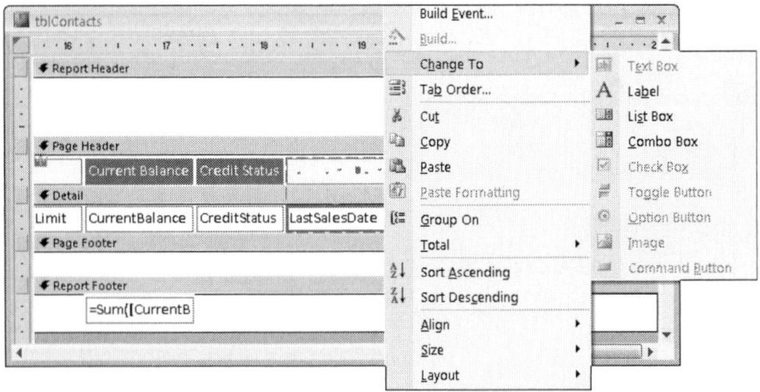

The choices you see in the shortcut menu make sense for the type of control you're changing. For instance, an option button can be changed to a check box or toggle button, but not to a text box.

Format Painter

Access 2007 includes a format painter that functions much like the same feature in Word. When creating a form, you set the appearance of a control (its border, font, special effects like sunken or raised) then click the Format Painter button from the Font group on the ribbon's Design tab to copy the properties to a special internal buffer. When you click another control of the same type, the appearance characteristics of the selected control are transferred to the second control. In Figure 19-9 the format properties of the First Name text box are about to be "painted" onto the Last Name text box (notice the little paintbrush adjacent to the mouse pointer to tell you you're in "paint" mode).

FIGURE 19-9

The Format Painter makes it easy to "paint" the appearance of a control onto other controls on a form.

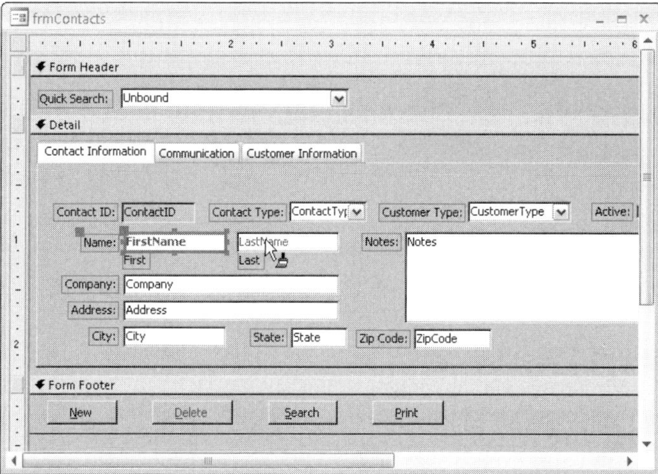

The Format Painter can be locked by double-clicking its button on the Access ribbon. It is important to note that not all properties are painted onto the second control. The size, position, and data properties of the control are not affected by the Format Painter. Only the most basic text properties are influenced by the Format Painter.

Offering more end-user help

Beginning with Office 4.x all Microsoft products have featured ToolTip help — those little yellow "post-it notes" that appear when you hold the mouse cursor over a control or button. (Microsoft calls these prompts "control tip help.")

You add ToolTips to Access 2007 forms by adding the help text to the control's `ControlTip Text` property (see Figure 19-10). By default the text in a ToolTip does not wrap, but you can add a new line character by pressing Ctrl+Enter in the ControlTip text wherever you want the break to appear.

FIGURE 19-10

ToolTip help makes your applications easier to use.

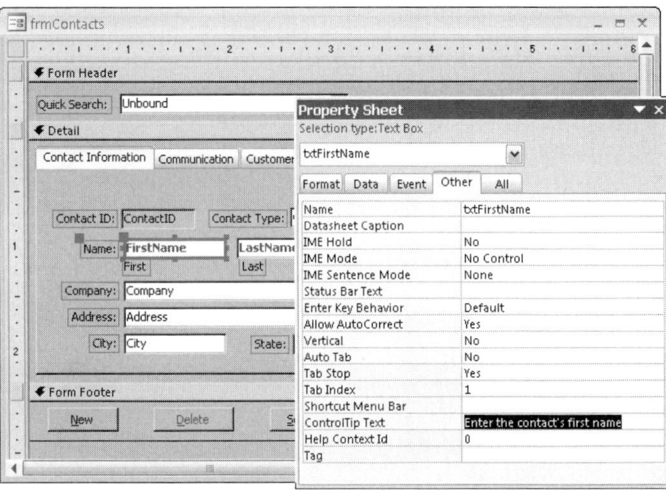

In general, you should consistently use ToolTips throughout an application. After your users become accustomed to ToolTips they expect them on all but the most obvious controls.

Adding background pictures

Attractive forms are always a valuable addition to Access applications. It's difficult to add color or graphics to forms without obscuring the data contained on the form. Access 2007 makes it easy to add a graphic to the background of a form much as a "watermark" may appear on expensive bond paper. The picture can contain a company logo, text, or any other graphic element. The picture is specified by the form's `Picture` property and can be embedded in the form or linked to an external file. If the picture is linked, the graphic displayed on the form changes any time the external file is edited.

The picture can also be positioned at any of the form's four corners or centered in the middle of the form. Although the picture can be clipped, stretched, or zoomed to fit the dimensions of the form, you cannot modify the picture to make it smaller (other than editing the image file, of course). Figure 19-11 shows a small background picture positioned in the upper-right corner of `frmContacts`.

FIGURE 19-11

A small `.bmp` file has been added to `frmContacts` as the Picture property.

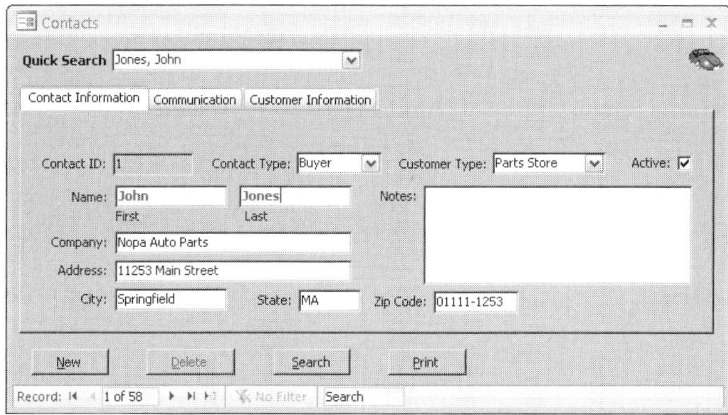

You can even make controls on a form transparent so that the form's background picture shows through the controls (see Figure 19-12). In this case (`frmEmployees_Background`), the background of each label control is set to `Transparent`, letting the form's background picture show through.

FIGURE 19-12

Transparent controls allow the background picture to show through.

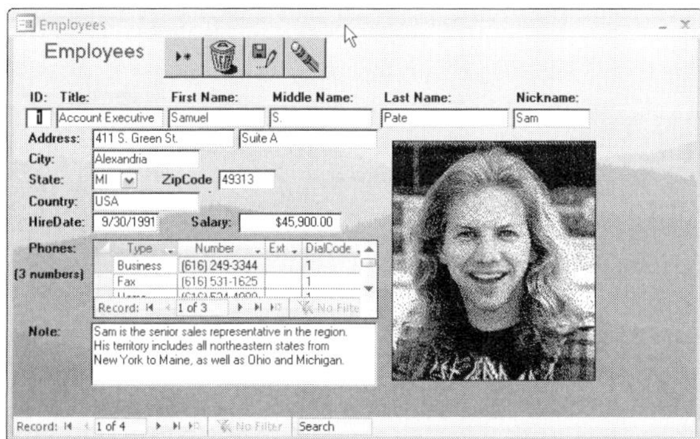

Obviously, it's easy to overdo the background picture added to Access forms, but, when carefully used, background pictures can make forms easier for users to understand.

Be forewarned, however, that background pictures added to a form noticeably slow down the form's appearance on the screen. Generally speaking, you should use a background picture when the benefit provided by the picture outweighs the unavoidable performance degradation caused by the picture's presence.

Form events

The Access 2007 form events allow you to fine-tune your form's behavior when filters are applied or removed from the form's underlying data source.

ApplyFilter

The `ApplyFilter` event fires whenever the user applies a filter by clicking one of the filter buttons (Ascending, Filter, Selection, and so on) in the Sort & Filter ribbon group. You can use the `ApplyFilter` event to test the user's filtering criteria to make sure the filter makes sense. Use the form's `Filter` property to determine whether the filter being applied contains valid criteria, or to modify the `Filter` property in code.

You can also use the `ApplyFilter` event to hide certain fields that should not be viewed by all users, or to pop up a dialog requesting additional identification information such as an "extra" password or username.

Finally, because `ApplyFilter` is triggered when you click Remove Filter button in the Sort & Filter group, you can use this event to reveal hidden fields, reset the `Filter` property to its former value, and so on.

Filter event

The `Filter` event is similar to the `ApplyFilter` in that it is triggered whenever the user invokes one of the built-in forms filtering options. The `Filter` event triggers before the `ApplyFilter` event and is useful for displaying your own filtering form, removing controls that should not be used in a filter by form session, and so on. Together the `Filter` and `ApplyFilter` events give you a great deal of control over user access to the built-in filtering capabilities in Access 2007.

Using the Tab Control

A tab control, of course, provides a several pages, each accessed through a tab at the top, bottom, or side of the dialog. Figure 19-13 shows `frmContacts`, a perfect example of a tabbed Access form. `frmContacts` contains three tabs, allowing the form to contain many more controls than possible without the tab control. Each of the tabs along the top of the form reveals a different page of the form's data. Each page contains many controls. Figure 19-13 shows buttons, labels, and text boxes. Each control on the page behaves independently of all other controls on the form and can be accessed through Access VBA code as an independent unit.

As you might guess, the tab control is fairly complex. The tab control includes its own properties, events, methods, and object collections. You have to know and understand these items before effectively using the tab control in your applications.

FIGURE 19-13

The tab control allows a form to host a large amount of data.

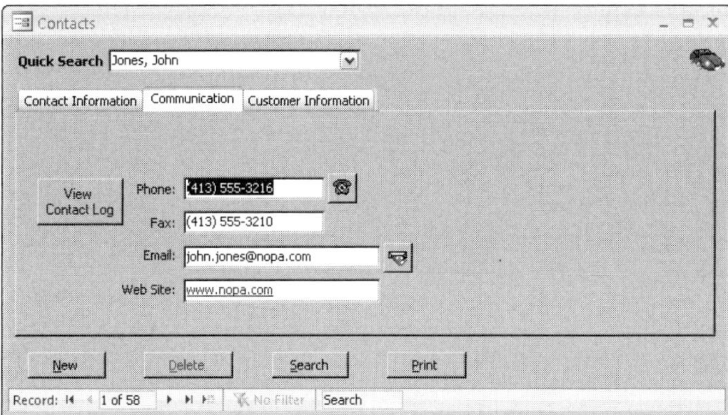

A tab control consists of a number of `Page` objects, each a member of the control's `Pages` collection. Developers often use the expression tab when referring to the pages of a tabbed dialog box. In this chapter the expressions Page and tab are used interchangeably. Each page includes a `Controls` collection consisting of the controls that have been added to that page. A page is added to the `Pages` collection with the `Add` method of the `Pages` object; whereas a page is removed from the dialog with the `Pages` object's `Remove` method. From the user interface, the quickest and easiest way to add or delete a page is to right-click the control and select the appropriate command from the shortcut menu (see Figure 19-14).

FIGURE 19-14

The tab control's shortcut menu contains relevant commands.

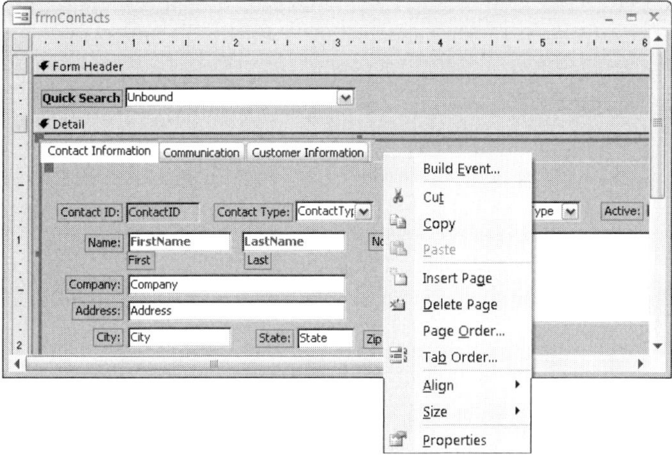

Using the Add and Remove methods to add new pages or delete existing pages from a tab control is not very practical for a number of reasons. First of all, both methods require the form to be in Design View before they are able to modify the tab control. The Add method does not return a handle to the new tab. Therefore, it is difficult if not impossible to manipulate the properties of the new tab. Furthermore, the Delete method acts on the tab with the highest index and does not accept an index or page name as an argument. Therefore, you have to be very careful to make sure you are actually removing the tab you think you are.

In addition to these methods, the tab control contains the relevant properties shown in Table 19-1. Use these properties to tailor the tab controls in your applications to suit the needs of your users.

TABLE 19-1

Important Tab Control Properties

Property	Description
Caption	Applies to each page in the tab control. Provides the text that appears on the tab.
MultiRow	Applies to the tab control. Determines whether the tabs appear as a single row or as multiple rows. You cannot specify how many tabs appear in each row. Instead, Access adds as many rows as necessary to display all tabs, given their respective widths.
Style	By default tabs appear as tabs. The alternative (Buttons) forces the tabs to appear as command buttons.
TabFixedHeight	This value determines the height (in inches or centimeters, depending on the units of measurement settings in the Windows Control Panel) of the tabs on the control. When the TabFixedHeight set to 0, the tab height is determined by the size of the font specified for the tab control.
TabFixedWidth	This value determines the width (in inches or centimeters) of the tabs on the control. Text that is too wide to fit on the tab when the TabFixedWidth value is set is truncated. When the TabFixedWidth is set to 0, the width of the tab is determined by the font size selected for the tab control and the text specified in the tab's Caption property.
Picture	Applies to each page on the tab control. The Picture property specifies an image (.bmp, .ico, or built-in picture) to display on the tab.

The tab control itself has a Value property that tells you which tab is selected. Value changes each time a tab is selected. Figure 19-15 shows frmTabControl2, a form included in Chapter19.accdb on this book's companion CD-ROM. This form demonstrates some of the properties of the tab control and its pages.

FIGURE 19-15

frmTabControl2 in the Chapter19.accdb example database demonstrates important tab control properties.

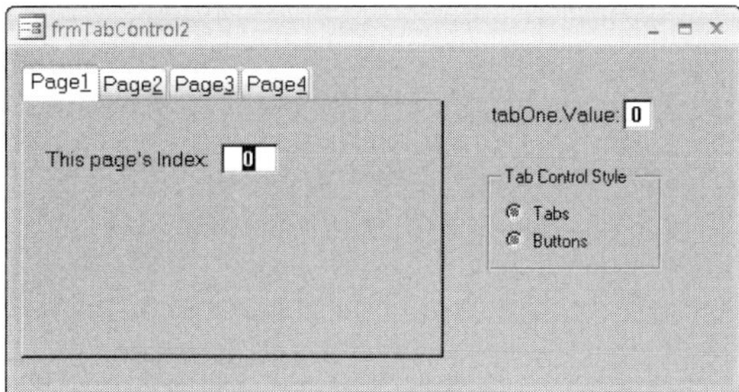

The `Value` property of a tab control indicates which page is currently selected. It returns an integer that indicates the position of the selected page in the Pages collection. For example, if the first page in a tab control is selected, the `Value` property returns 0, the index number of the first page in the `Pages` collection. If the second page is selected, the `Value` property returns `1`, and so on. The page's position within the collection corresponds to the value of the `PageIndex` property for that page.

A tab control can contain virtually any type of control, including text boxes, combo and list boxes, option buttons and check boxes, and OLE objects. A tab control can even include other tab controls! Although a form can contain multiple tab controls, it is probably not a good idea to overload the user by putting more than one tab control on a form. After all, the reason you use tab controls in an application is to simplify the form by fitting multiple pages of controls within a single control. In most cases, there is no point in challenging the user with more than one tab control on a form.

Using Dialog Boxes to Collect Information

The dialog box is one of the most valuable user interface components in Windows applications. When properly implemented, dialog boxes provide a way to extend the available screen space on the computer. Rather than having to place every text box, option button, and other user input control on the main form, dialog boxes provide a handy way to move some of these controls to a convenient pop-up device that is on the screen only when needed.

Dialog boxes usually collect a certain type of information, such as font attributes or hard-copy parameters. Dialog boxes are a valuable way to prefilter or qualify user input without cluttering the main form. Or use a dialog box to allow the user to enter query criteria before running a query that populates a form or report, or to gather information that is added to a report's header or footer area.

Although they are forms, dialog boxes should not look like or behave as other forms in the application do. Dialog boxes often pop up over the user's work. When properly implemented, dialog boxes also provide a means to simply cancel the query without breaking anything on the user's workspace.

A typical query form implemented as a dialog box is shown in Figure 19-16. This simple form gathers information that is used to query the database for order information.

FIGURE 19-16

A dialog box used to collect data for an ad-hoc query.

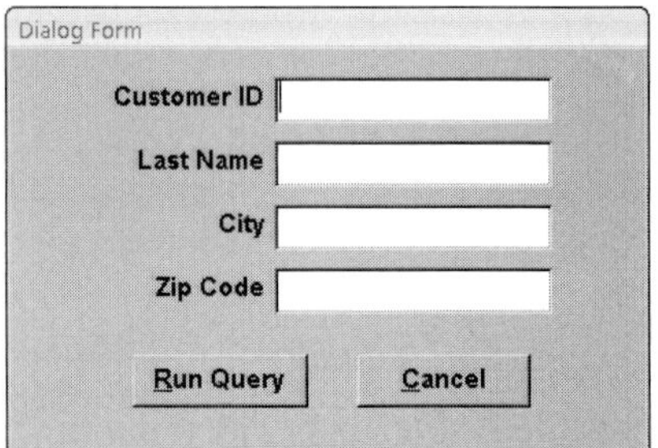

The relevant properties of this dialog box include those listed in Table 19-2.

TABLE 19-2

Property Settings for Dialog Forms

Property	Setting	Purpose
`ScrollBars`	Neither	Scroll bars aren't needed on a dialog.
`NavigationButtons`	No	Navigation buttons aren't needed.
`PopUp`	Yes	Keeps form on top.
`Modal`	Yes	Prevents the user from working with another part of the application until the dialog box is removed.
`RecordSelectors`	No	Not needed.
`BorderStyle`	Dialog	Specifies wide borders that can't be resized. Also removes Minimize and Maximize buttons.
`ShortcutMenu`	No	Not needed.

After these changes have been made, you have a form that is always on top of the user's work and won't leave the screen until the user clicks the Run Query or Cancel button.

There are a couple of rules you should follow when constructing dialog boxes. These rules ensure that your dialog boxes conform to the generally accepted behavior for Windows dialog boxes.

Composing the SQL statement

A temporary `querydef` object is created when the user clicks the Run Query button. Although you are simply opening the query on the screen, the temporary query could just as easily serve as the `RecordSource` of a form or report.

```
Private Sub cmdRunQuery_Click()
  Dim db As DAO.Database
  Dim QD As DAO.QueryDef
  Dim where As Variant

  Set db = CurrentDb

  'Delete existing dynamic query, trap error if it does not
exist.
  On Error Resume Next
  db.QueryDefs.Delete ("MyQuery")
  On Error GoTo 0

  'Note Single quotes surrounding text fields [Ship Country]
  'and [Customer ID]
  'Note NO Single quotes surrounding Numeric field [Employee ID]
  where = Null

  If Not IsNull(txtContactID.Value) Then
   where = where _
    & (" [ContactID]= " & Me![txtContactID] & " ")
  End If

  If Not IsNull(txtLastName.Value) Then
    If Len(where) > 0 Then
        where = where _
          & (" AND [LastName]= '" & Me![txtLastName] & "' ")
    Else
        where = where _
          & (" [LastName]= '" & Me![txtLastName] & "' ")
    End If
  End If

  If Not IsNull(txtCity.Value) Then
    If Len(where) > 0 Then
        where = where _
```

```
            & (" AND [City]= '" & Me![txtCity] & "' ")
      Else
          where = where _
            & (" [City]= '" & Me![txtCity] & "' ")
      End If
    End If

    If Not IsNull(txtZipCode.Value) Then
      If Len(where) > 0 Then
          where = where _
            & (" AND [ZipCode]= '" & Me![txtZipCode] & "' ")
      Else
          where = where _
            & (" [ZipCode]= '" & Me![txtZipCode] & "' ")
      End If
    End If

    Set QD = db.CreateQueryDef("MyQuery", _
       "SELECT * FROM Contacts WHERE " & where & ";")

    DoCmd.OpenQuery "MyQuery"

    'Me.Visible = False
    DoCmd.Close acForm, Me.Name

  End Sub
```

Notice that the SQL statement is built up with the contents of the text boxes on the form. Each text box's value is added only when the text box is not null. Also, the length of the query string is evaluated before adding to the `SELECT` clause. The AND is added only when the `SELECT` clause already contains a value so that the resulting SQL string looks something like this:

```
SELECT * FROM Contacts
WHERE ContactID = 17 AND City = 'New York';
```

Adding a default button

There should be a button on the form that is automatically selected if the user presses the Enter key while the dialog is open. The default button does not have to be selected by the user to be triggered; Access does this automatically as the user presses the Enter key.

For instance, the user enters 17 in the Customer ID text box and presses the Enter key. Unless a default button is specified, the input cursor simply drops down to the Ship City text box. If you've designated the Run Query button as the dialog's default, Access interprets the Enter key press as a `Click` event for the Run Query button.

Set the Run Query's `Default` property to `Yes` to make it the default for this dialog. Only one button on a form can have its `Default` property set to `Yes` — if you move to the Cancel button and set its `Default` property to `Yes`, Access silently changes the Run Query's `Default` property to `No`.

Normally, the designated default button is on the left of the form. If you've arranged the command buttons vertically on a form, the top button should be the default.

You should select a button that won't cause trouble if accidentally triggered as the default for a form. For instance, to avoid the risk of losing data, it's probably not a good idea to set a button that performs a delete action query as the default. In this case, you may decide to make the Cancel button the default.

Setting a Cancel button

The Cancel button on a form is automatically selected if the user presses the Esc key while the form is open. In most cases, you simply want the dialog box to disappear if the user hits the Esc key while the dialog is open.

Set a button's `Cancel` property to designate it as the form's Cancel button. In our example, `cmdCancel` has been designated the dialog's Cancel button. As with the default button, only one button on a form can be the Cancel button. Access triggers the Cancel button's `On Click` event whenever the user presses the Esc key.

Removing the control menu

After you've designated default and Cancel buttons, you have no need for the control menu button in the upper-left corner of the form. Set the form's `Control Box` property to `No` to hide the control menu button. Once the control menu box is removed, the user will have to use the Cancel or Run Query buttons to remove the form from the screen.

Closing the form

The dialog form remains on the screen on top of the query results. The following line was added to the `Click` event of the Run Query button to remove the form from the Access desktop:

```
DoCmd Close acForm, Me.Name
```

In some cases, however, you'll want to continue to reference information in the dialog box after the user is "done" with it. In these cases you should hide the dialog form, rather than close it. Use the following statement at the bottom of the `Click` event to hide the dialog form as the query opens:

```
Me.Visible = False
```

As with any user interface component, always completely test any dialog box. Because it "takes over" the user's desktop, you want to make sure the dialog behaves as expected and does not impede or annoy the user in any way.

Summary

This chapter has assisted you in understanding Access 2007 forms. You now have a better grasp on the workings of the Access event model, and you know how to programmatically manipulate the many controls that constitute the building blocks out of which forms are constructed. You also have a larger bag of tricks from which to draw when you are building Access forms.

The advanced forms features in Access 2007 boggle the mind. It is unlikely you will use all of the new forms design tricks in your first Access 2007 application, but it's nice to know what you can do with this truly remarkable development platform.

Chapter 20

Advanced Access Report Techniques

IN THIS CHAPTER

- Learning techniques to add to your Access reports
- Adding alphabetically and numerically sorted lists to reports
- Using report events and VBA code to enhance reports
- Hiding headers and other report sections at runtime
- Adding extra white space between detail sections
- Applying special formatting to even and odd pages

Back in the bad old days, most computer-generated reports were printed on pulpy, greenbar paper in strict row-and-column (called *tabular*) format. The user was expected to further process the data to suit his particular needs — often, a time-consuming process that involved manually summarizing or graphing the data.

Things have changed. Visually oriented business people want useful, informative reports produced directly from their databases. No one wants to spend time graphing data printed in simple tabular format nowadays. Users want the software to do much of the work for them. This means that reporting tools such as Microsoft Access must be able to produce the high-quality, highly readable reports users demand.

Because Access is a Windows application, you have all the super-duper Windows facilities at your disposal: TrueType fonts, graphics, and a graphical interface for report design and preview. In addition, Access reports feature properties and an event model (although with fewer events than you saw on forms) for customizing report behavior. You use the Visual Basic language to add refinement and automation to the reports you build in Access.

In this chapter, we provide some general principles and design techniques to keep in mind as you build Access reports. These principles will help make your reports more readable and informative.

ON the CD-ROM All of the examples presented in this chapter can be found in the sample database named `Chapter20.accdb` on this book's CD-ROM. Please note that many of the figures in this chapter appear with the report Design view grid turned off to make the report design details easier to see.

Hide Repeating Information

An easy improvement to tabular reports is to reduce the amount of repeated information on the report. Figure 20-1 shows a typical tabular report produced by Access (`rptTabularBad`), based on a simple query of the Northwind Traders data.

FIGURE 20-1

Simple tabular reports can be confusing and boring.

rptTabularBad

Northwind Sales: January 2008

Name	Order ID	Order Date	Company Name
Andrew Fuller	10407	01-Jan-08	Ottilies Käseladen
Andrew Fuller	10414	08-Jan-08	Familia Arquibaldo
Andrew Fuller	10422	16-Jan-08	Franchi S.p.A.
Anne Dodsworth	10411	04-Jan-08	Bottom-Dollar Markets
Janet Leverling	10409	03-Jan-08	Océano Atlántico Ltda.
Janet Leverling	10410	04-Jan-08	Bottom-Dollar Markets
Janet Leverling	10413	08-Jan-08	La maison d'Asie
Janet Leverling	10415	09-Jan-08	Hungry Coyote Import Store
Janet Leverling	10420	15-Jan-08	Wellington Importadora
Janet Leverling	10429	23-Jan-08	Hungry Owl All-Night Grocers
Janet Leverling	10432	25-Jan-08	Split Rail Beer & Ale
Janet Leverling	10433	28-Jan-08	Princesa Isabel Vinhos
Janet Leverling	10434	28-Jan-08	Folk och fä HB

The report in Figure 20-1 was produced with the Access Report Wizard, selecting the tabular report format and all defaults. The query underlying this report selects data from the Customers, Orders, and Employees tables in `Northwind.accdb` and is shown in Figure 20-2. Notice that the data returned by this query is restricted to the month of January 2008. Also, the first and last names of employees are concatenated as the `Name` field.

FIGURE 20-2

The simple query underlying `rptTabularBad`

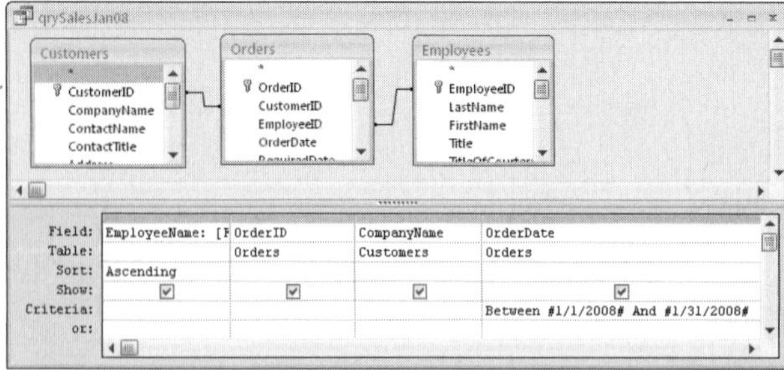

You can significantly improve the report in Figure 20-1 simply by hiding repeated information in the Detail section. As soon as Andrew Fuller's name is given, there's no need to repeat it for every sale that Andrew made in January 2008. The way the data is arranged on `rptTabularBad`, you have to search for where one employee's sales data ends and another employee's data begins.

Making the change to hide the repeated values is very easy:

1. **Open the report in Design view.**
2. **In the Detail section, select the `Name` field containing the employee's first name and last name.**
3. **Open the Property Sheet for the `Name` field (see Figure 20-3).**

FIGURE 20-3

The default property values sometimes lead to unsatisfactory results.

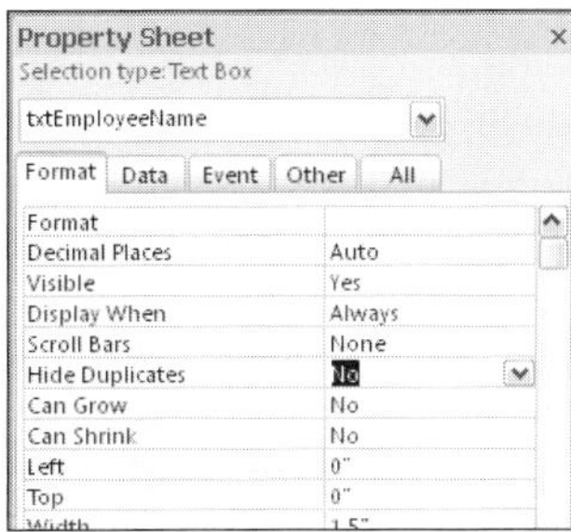

4. **Change the Hide Duplicates property to Yes.**

   The default is No, which directs Access to display every instance of every field.
5. **Put the report back to Print Preview mode and enjoy the new report layout (shown in Figure 20-4).**

   The report shown in Figure 20-4 is `rptTabularGood`.

FIGURE 20-4

Much better! Hide that repeating information.

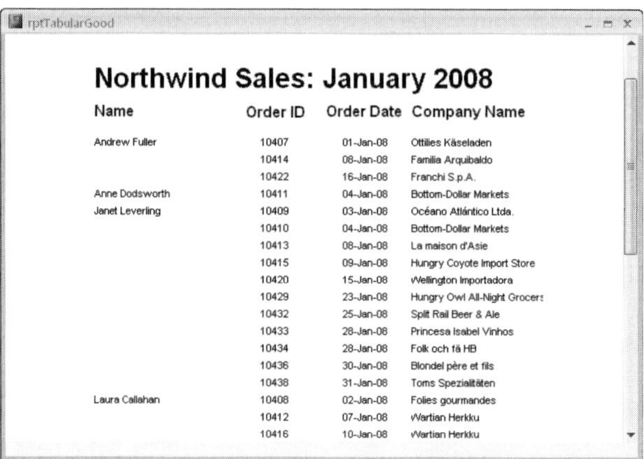

Distinguishing the sales figures for individual employees in Figure 20-4 is much easier than when the repeating information is printed on the report. Notice that no fancy programming or report design was required. A simple property-value change resulted in a much more readable and useful report. (Mainframe report designers working with high-speed line printers, and traditional report writers would *kill* for a report as good looking as the one shown in Figure 20-4!)

The `Hide Duplicates` property only applies to records that appear sequentially on the report. As soon as Access has placed a particular `Name` value on the report, the name won't be repeated in records immediately following the current record. In Figure 20-4, the records are sorted by the `EmployeeName` field, so all records for an employee appear sequentially as a group. If the report were sorted by another field (for instance, `OrderID` or `OrderDate`) the `HideDuplicates` property set on the `Name` field would apply only to those instances where the employee's name coincidentally appeared sequentially in multiple records on the report.

Alphabetically Group Data

Data is often displayed with too much granularity to be useful. As you saw in Figure 20-1, a report displaying every sale made by every employee arranged in a tabular format can be difficult to read. And, as you saw in the revised example, anything you do to reduce the overload of tabular reports can make the data more meaningful.

Sometimes even grouping data doesn't help much. Have you ever seen a book index where every major topic appeared in bold with minor topics within the major topic indented below the bold heading? Some book indexes use boldface for virtually *everything* (including topics with no subordinate subtopics below them), creating a confusing, hard-to-read page. A much better arrangement is to group data into alphabetically sorted groups. Dictionaries and encyclopedias use alphabetical groupings for their data. Imagine how difficult it would be to find a person's phone number if the data weren't carefully grouped by the letters of the alphabet and then arranged into alphabetical order within the group!

The Sorting and Grouping dialog box (which you can get to by choosing the Group and Sort button in the Grouping & Totals group in the Design tab) controls how data is grouped on Access reports. Sorting alphabetically simply arranges the records in alphabetical order based on the first character of the company name, while grouping by company name will create a separate group for each company.

Typically, data is grouped on the entire contents of a field or combination of fields. Simple grouping on the `CompanyName` field means that all records for Bottom Dollar Markets appear together as a group. You can, however, override the default and group based on *prefix characters* by changing the `Group On` property in the Sorting and Grouping dialog box (see Figure 20-5).

FIGURE 20-5

Alphabetical grouping is easy!

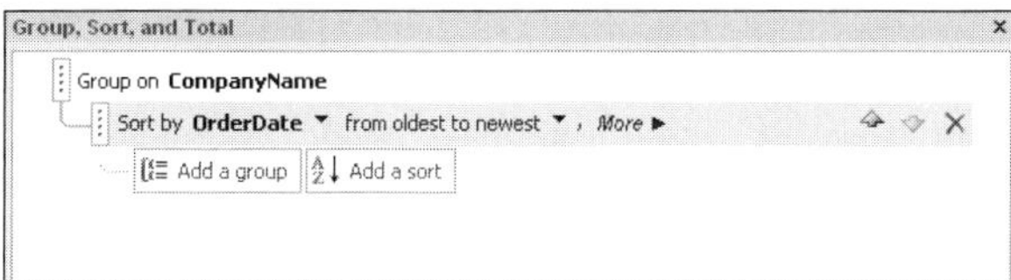

When you select Prefix Characters, the `GroupInterval` property tells Access how many characters to consider when grouping on prefix characters. In our case, Group Interval is set to 1, meaning, "Consider only the *first* character when grouping." Notice also that the `CompanyName` field is set to Ascending Sort, which causes alphabetic grouping starting at names beginning with *A* and progressing to names beginning with *Z*. With this combination of properties, all companies starting with *A* will be grouped together, those beginning with *B* will be in another group, and so on.

For this example, a slightly different report is used to illustrate prefix character grouping. This report (`rptSalesJan08Alpha1`, shown in Figure 20-6) shows purchases during the month of January 2008, sorted by customer name. The order date, order ID, and the employee filling the order are shown across the page. The result of the sorting and grouping specification in Figure 20-5 is shown in Figure 20-6. (Hide Duplicates has been set to Yes for the `CompanyName` field so that each customer appears only once in the list.)

It's important to note that the data shown in Figure 20-6 is identical to the data in Figure 20-4. In fact, the same record source (`qrySalesJan08`, shown in Figure 20-2) is used for both of these reports. Often, a data rearrangement yields useful information. For instance, you can easily see that Around the Horn placed two orders in January with the same sales agent, Janet Leverling.

FIGURE 20-6

A rearrangement of the data shown in Figure 20-4, earlier in this chapter

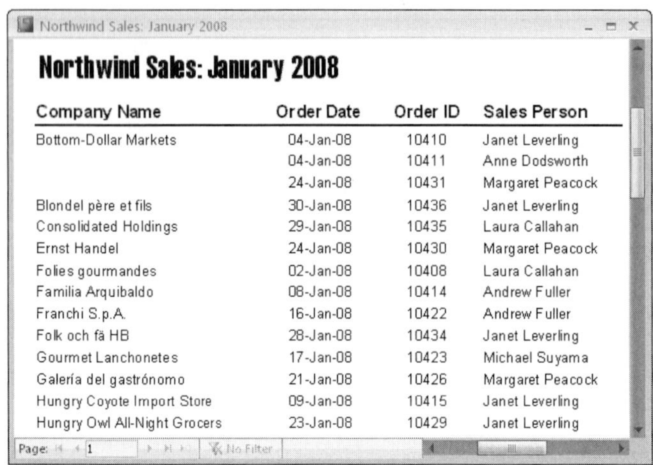

Northwind Sales: January 2008

Company Name	Order Date	Order ID	Sales Person
Bottom-Dollar Markets	04-Jan-08	10410	Janet Leverling
	04-Jan-08	10411	Anne Dodsworth
	24-Jan-08	10431	Margaret Peacock
Blondel père et fils	30-Jan-08	10436	Janet Leverling
Consolidated Holdings	29-Jan-08	10435	Laura Callahan
Ernst Handel	24-Jan-08	10430	Margaret Peacock
Folies gourmandes	02-Jan-08	10408	Laura Callahan
Familia Arquibaldo	08-Jan-08	10414	Andrew Fuller
Franchi S.p.A.	16-Jan-08	10422	Andrew Fuller
Folk och fä HB	28-Jan-08	10434	Janet Leverling
Gourmet Lanchonetes	17-Jan-08	10423	Michael Suyama
Galería del gastrónomo	21-Jan-08	10426	Margaret Peacock
Hungry Coyote Import Store	09-Jan-08	10415	Janet Leverling
Hungry Owl All-Night Grocers	23-Jan-08	10429	Janet Leverling

Let's assume we want to refine the `rptSalesJan08Alpha1` report by labeling the groups with the letters of the alphabet. That is, all customers beginning with *B* (B's Beverages, Berglunds snabbköp, Blondel père et fils, and so on) are in one group, all the *C* customers (Comércio Mineiro, Consolidated Holdings, and so on) in another group, and so on. Within each group the company names are sorted in alphabetical order. The sales to each customer are further sorted by order ID.

To emphasize the alphabetical grouping, a text box containing the first character for each group has been added to the report (see rptSalesJan08Alpha2 in Figure 20-7). Although our data set in this example is rather small, in large reports such headings can be useful.

FIGURE 20-7

An alphabetic heading for each customer group makes the rptSalesJan08Alpha2 report easier to read.

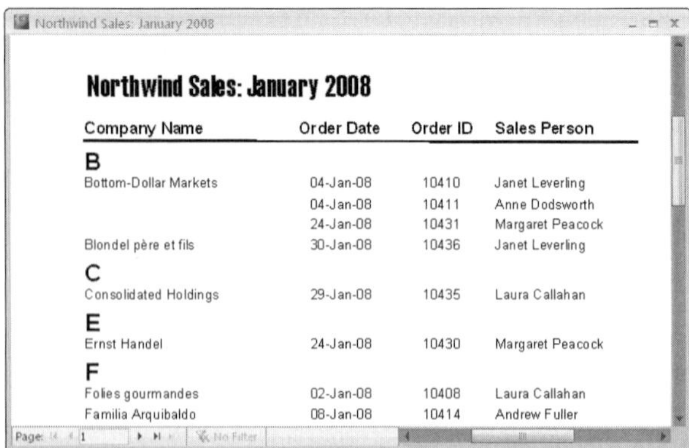

Northwind Sales: January 2008

Company Name	Order Date	Order ID	Sales Person
B			
Bottom-Dollar Markets	04-Jan-08	10410	Janet Leverling
	04-Jan-08	10411	Anne Dodsworth
	24-Jan-08	10431	Margaret Peacock
Blondel père et fils	30-Jan-08	10436	Janet Leverling
C			
Consolidated Holdings	29-Jan-08	10435	Laura Callahan
E			
Ernst Handel	24-Jan-08	10430	Margaret Peacock
F			
Folies gourmandes	02-Jan-08	10408	Laura Callahan
Familia Arquibaldo	08-Jan-08	10414	Andrew Fuller

Adding the text box containing the alphabetic character is easy:

1. **Choose View ➪ Design.**
2. **Choose View ➪ Sorting and Grouping.**

   The Sorting and Grouping dialog box appears.
3. **Set the `Group Header` property for `CompanyName` to Yes.**

   This will add a band for a group based on the `CompanyName` information.
4. **Open the `CompanyName` group header and add an unbound text box to the `CompanyName` group header.**
5. **Set the text box's `Control Source` property to the following expression:**

   ```
   =Left$([CompanyName],1)
   ```
6. **Set the other text box properties (Font, Font Size, and so on) appropriately.**

   When you're done, the report in Design view should appear as shown in Figure 20-8.

FIGURE 20-8

`rptSalesJan08Alpha2` in Design view

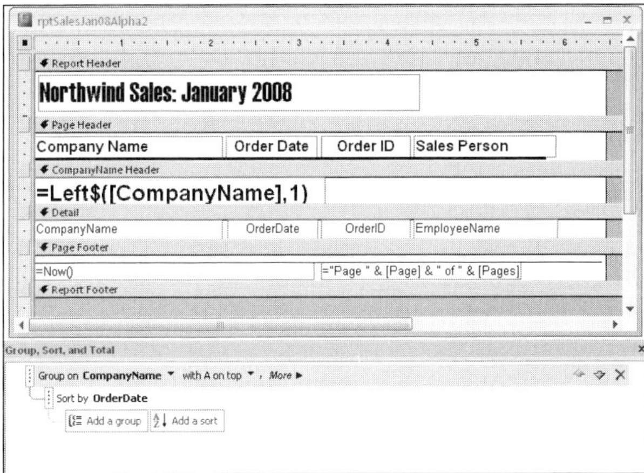

Notice the `CompanyName` group header that was added by the Group Header setting in the Sorting and Grouping dialog box. The Property Sheet for the unbound text box is shown so you can see the expression used to fill the text box.

This little trick works because all of the rows within a `CompanyName` group have the first character in common. Using the `Left$()` function to peel off the first character and use it as the text in the text box in the group header provides an attractive, useful heading for the `CompanyName` groups.

Group on Date Intervals

Many reports require grouping on dates or date intervals (day, week, or month). For instance, Northwind Traders may want a report of January 2008 sales grouped on a weekly basis so that week-to-week patterns emerge.

Fortunately, the Access report engine includes just such a feature. An option in the Sorting and Grouping dialog box enables you to quickly and easily group report data based on dates or date intervals. Just as we grouped data based on prefix characters in an earlier example, we can group on dates using the group's `GroupOn` property. Figure 20-9 shows the January 2008 sales report grouped by each week during the month. This report is named `rptSalesJan08ByWeek`.

FIGURE 20-9

The January 2008 sales data grouped by each week during the month

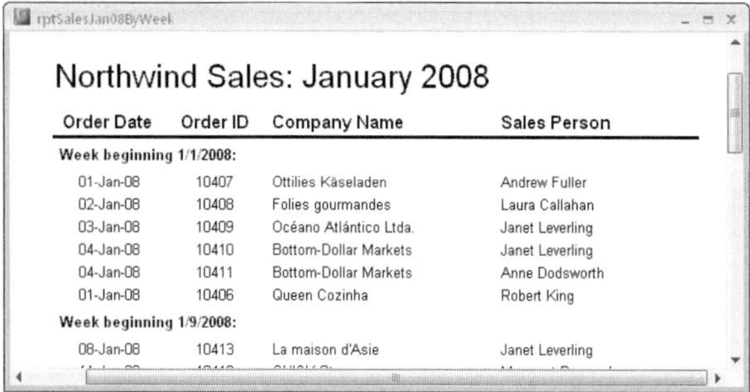

This report is easy to set up. Open the Sorting and Grouping dialog again and establish a group for the `OrderDate` field. Set the `OrderDate GroupHeader` option to Yes and drop-down the Group On list (see Figure 20-10). Notice that Access is smart enough to present Group On options (Year, Qtr, Month, Week, and so on) that make sense for date/time fields like `OrderDate`. Selecting Week from this list instructs Access to sort the data on the `OrderDate`, grouped on a week-by-week basis.

FIGURE 20-10

`OrderDate` is a date/time field, so the grouping options are relevant for date and time data.

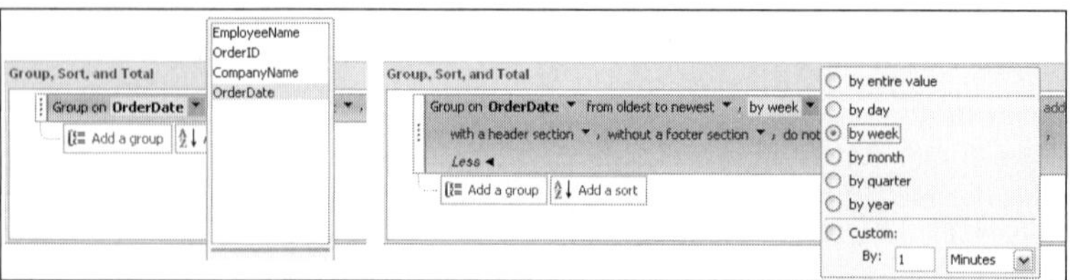

The label at the top of the group identifying the week (the first one reads `Week beginning 1/1/08:`) is the product of the following expression in an unbound text box in the `OrderDate` group header:

```
="Week beginning " & [OrderDate] & ":"
```

See the Design view of `rptSalesJan08ByWeek` in Figure 20-11. Notice the unbound text box in the `OrderDate` group header. This text box contains the value of the order date that Access used to group the data in the `OrderDate` grouping.

FIGURE 20-11

The Design view of `rptSalesJan08ByWeek`. Notice the expression in the `OrderDate` group header.

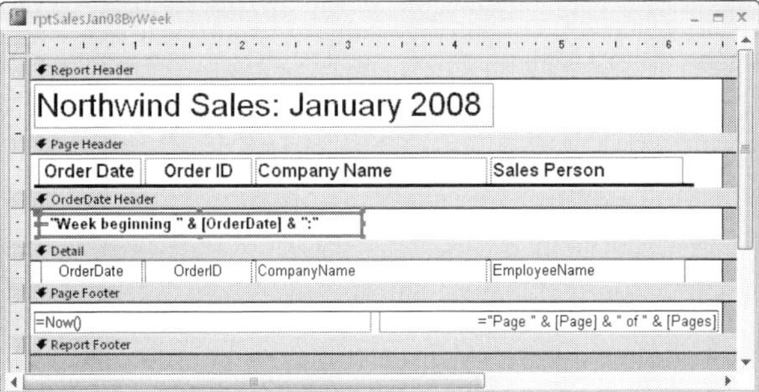

Create Numbered Lists

By default, the items contained on an Access report are not numbered. They simply appear in the order determined by the query or table underlying the report, or the order dictated by the settings in the Sorting and Grouping dialog box.

Sometimes it would be useful to have a number assigned to each entry on a report or within a group on a report. You might need a number to count the items in a list or uniquely identify items in the list. For instance, an order details report might contain an item number for each item ordered, plus a field for items ordered, showing how many things were ordered.

The Access Running Sum feature provides a way to assign a number to each item in a list on an Access report. For instance, the Northwind Traders sales management has asked for a report showing the sum of all purchases by each customer during the month of January, sorted in descending order so that the top purchaser appears at the top. Oh, yes — and they want a number assigned to each line in the report to provide a ranking for the Northwind customers.

What an assignment! The query to implement this request is shown in Figure 20-12 (`qrySalesJan08`). This query sums the purchases by each customer for the month beginning

1/1/08 and ending 1/31/08. Because the Purchases column is sorted in descending order, the customers buying the most product will appear at the top of the query results set. The `OrderDate` field is not included in the query results and is used only as the query's selection criterion (notice the *Where* in the Total row).

FIGURE 20-12

An interesting query that sums data and sorts the query results in descending order

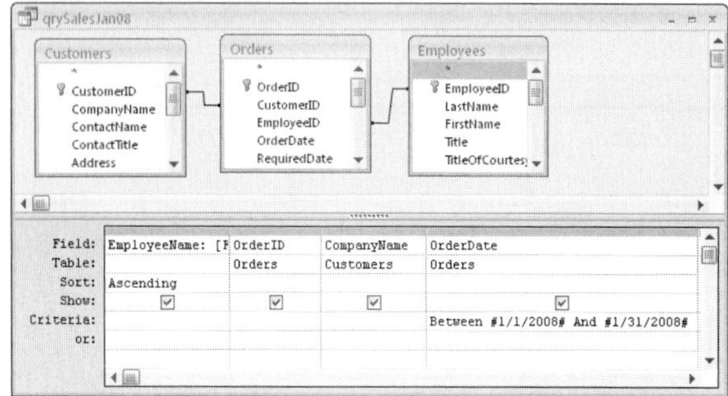

Although you could do much of this work at runtime using VBA to programmatically sum the values returned by the query or a SQL statement in the report's `RecordSource` property, you should always let the Access query engine perform aggregate functions. All Access queries are optimized when you save the query. You're guaranteed that the query will run as fast as possible — much faster than a filter based on a SQL statement in a report's `RecordSource` property.

Also, the Access query builder's aggregate functions perform flawlessly. Furthermore, Jet will perform the aggregate function exactly the same way every time the query is run. There is no reason you should be tempted to manually sum data when the query will do it for you.

The basic report (`rptUnNumberedList`) prepared from the data provided by `qrySalesJan08` is shown in Figure 20-13. All sorting options have been removed from the Sorting and Grouping dialog box to permit the records to arrange themselves as determined by the query.

Adding a Ranking column to the simple report you see in Figure 20-13 is not difficult. Although the information that's shown in Figure 20-13 is useful, it's not what the user asked for.

To add a Ranking column to the report, use the `RunningSum` property of an unbound text box to sum its own value over each item in the report. When the `RunningSum` property is set to Over Group, Access adds 1 to the value in this text box for each record displayed in the Detail section of the report (`RunningSum` can also be used within a group header or footer). The alternate setting (Over All) instructs Access to add 1 each time the text box appears in the entire report (see Figure 20-14). Add an unbound text box to the left of the `CompanyName` text box on the report, with an appropriate header in the Page Header area. Set the `RecordSource` property for the text box to =1 and the `RunningSum` property to Over All.

FIGURE 20-13

A straightforward report (`rptListUnNumbered`) produced with data from `qrySalesJan08`

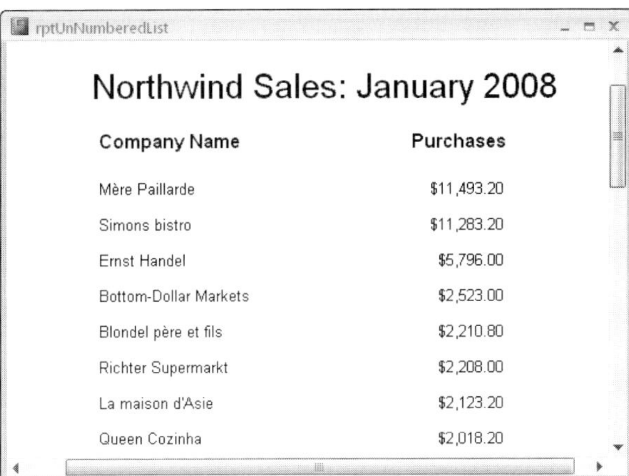

FIGURE 20-14

The value in the unbound text box named `txtRank` will be incremented by 1 for each record in the report.

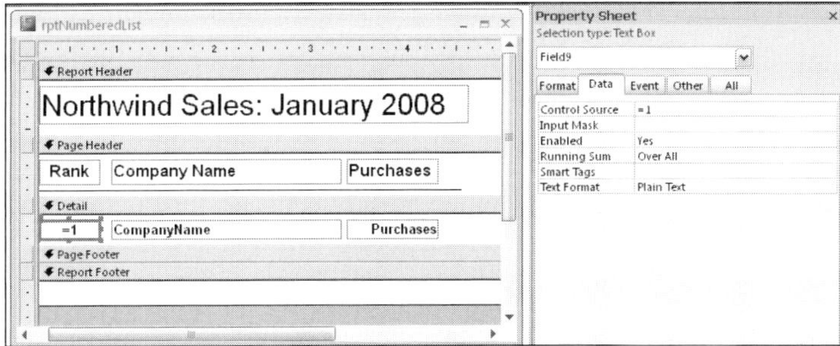

When this report (`rptNumberedList`) is run, the Rank column is filled with the running sum calculated by Access (see Figure 20-15). Once again, the data in this report is the same as in other report examples. The main difference is the amount of manipulation done by the query before the data arrives at the report and the additional information provided by the running sum.

FIGURE 20-15

The Running Sum column provides a ranking for each customer in order of purchases during January.

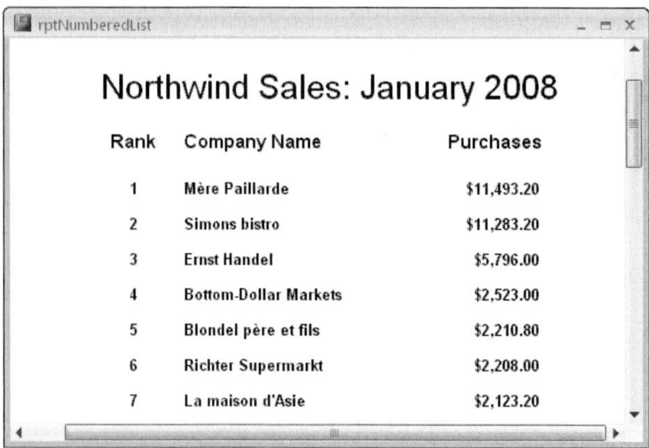

Reports can contain multiple running sum fields. You could, for instance, keep a running sum to show the number of items packed in each box of a multiple-box order while another running sum counts the number of boxes. The running sum starts at 0 (zero), hence the need to initialize it to 1 in the `Control Source` property on the Property Sheet.

You can also assign a running sum within each group by setting the `RunningSum` property of the unbound text box to `Over Group` instead of `Over All`. In this case, the running sum will start at zero for each group. Therefore, be sure to set the `ControlSource` property of a group's running sum to 1.

Add Bullet Characters

You can add bullet characters to a list instead of numbers, if desired. Rather than use a separate field for containing the bullet, however, it's easier to simply concatenate the bullet character to the control's `RecordSource` property. Access will "glue" the bullet character to the data as it is displayed on the report, eliminating alignment problems that might occur with a separate unbound text box.

The design of `rptBullets` is shown in Figure 20-16. Notice the bullet character in the `txtCompanyName` text box as well as in the Property Sheet for this text box.

FIGURE 20-16

The bullet character is added to the `ControlSource` property of the `txtCompanyName` text box.

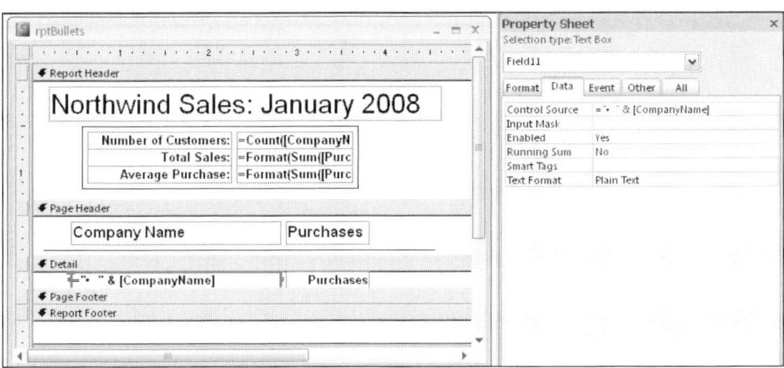

The bullet is added by exploiting a Windows feature. Position the text insertion character in the `RecordSource` property for the `CompanyName` field and type in **0149** while holding down the Alt key. Windows inserts the standard Windows bullet character, which you see in the Property Sheet. Looking at Figure 20-16, you can see that the bullet character is inserted correctly into the text box on the report. The expression you use in the `ControlSource` property is the following:

```
= "∞ " & [CompanyName]
```

where the bullet is inserted by the Alt+0149 trick.

You can produce the same effect by using the following expression in the text box:

```
= Chr(149) & " " & [CompanyName]
```

This expression concatenates the bullet character (returned by `Chr(149)`) with the data in the `CompanyName` field.

The report now appears as shown in Figure 20-17. You may want to add a few extra spaces after the bullet to pad the white space between the bullet and the text. Because the bullet character and `CompanyName` field have been concatenated together in the text box, they will be displayed in the same typeface. Also, adding the bullet character to the text box containing the company name guarantees the spacing between the bullet and first character of the company name will be consistent in every record. When using proportionally spaced fonts such as Arial, it can sometimes be difficult to get precise alignment between report elements. Concatenating data in a text box eliminates spacing problems introduced by proportionally spaced characters.

FIGURE 20-17

Use a Windows feature to insert the bullet in front of the CompanyName field.

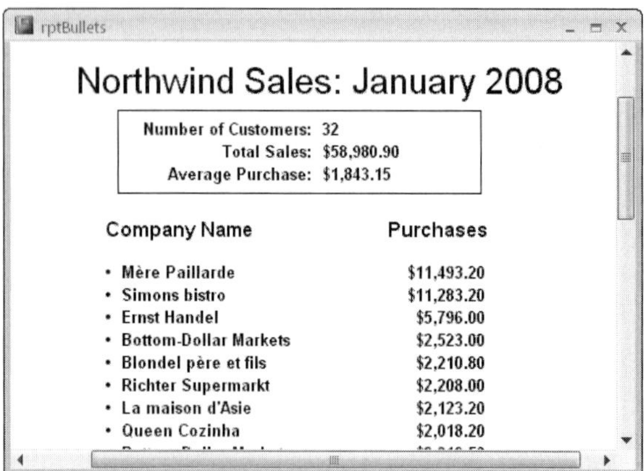

You may want to add other special characters to the control. For a complete display of the characters available in the font you've chosen for the text box control, run `Charmap.exe`, the Windows Character Map application. Be sure to select the font you've chosen for the text box control. The only constraint on the characters you use on an Access report is that the font used in the text boxes on the report must contain the specified characters. Not all Windows TrueType character sets include all of the special characters, like bullets.

Add Emphasis at Runtime

You might add a number of hidden controls to your reports to reduce the amount of clutter and unnecessary information. You can hide and show controls based on the value of another control. You hide a control, of course, by setting its `Visible` property to False (or No) at design time. Only when the information contained in the control is needed do you reset the `Visible` property to True.

An example might be a message to the Northwind Traders customers that a certain item has been discontinued and inventory is shrinking. It's silly to show this message for every item in the Northwind catalog; and including the number of units in stock, in conjunction with a message that a particular item has been discounted, might encourage buyers to stock up on the item.

Figure 20-18 shows `rptPriceList` in Print Preview mode. Notice that the Guarana Fantastica beverage product appears in italics, the price is bold italics, and the `Only 20 in stock!` message appears to the right of the product information.

FIGURE 20-18

Can you tell Guarana Fantastica is on sale?

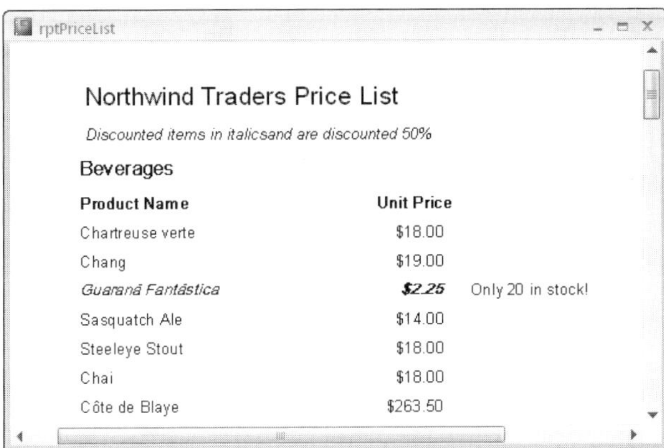

Figure 20-19 reveals part of the secret behind this technique. The text box under the unit price is actually unbound. The text box bound to the `UnitPrice` field appears to the far right of the Detail section but is hidden from the user's view by setting its `Visible` property to No. Just to the left of the hidden `UnitPrice` field is a hidden check box representing the `Discontinued` field. `txtMessage`, which contains the `Only x units in stock!` message is also hidden.

FIGURE 20-19

`rptPriceList` in Design view reveals how this effect is implemented.

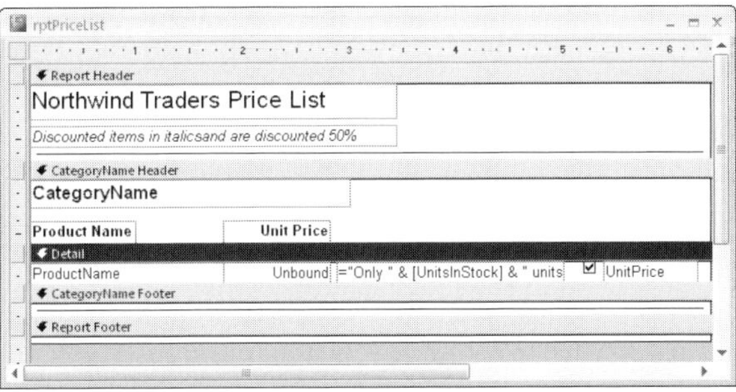

Use the Detail section's `Format` event to switch the `Visible` property of `txtMessage` to True whenever `txtDiscontinued` contains a True value. The code is quite simple:

```
Private Sub Detail1_Format(Cancel As Integer,
    FormatCount As Integer)
```

```
    If Me![Discontinued] Then
      txtProductName.FontItalic = True
      txtPrice.FontItalic = True
      txtPrice.FontBold = True
      txtPrice = Me![UnitPrice] * 0.5
      txtMessage.Visible = True
    Else
      txtProductName.FontItalic = False
      txtPrice.FontItalic = False
      txtPrice.FontBold = False
      txtPrice = Me![UnitPrice]
      txtMessage.Visible = False
    End If
  End Sub
```

In this code fragment, "Me" is a shortcut reference to the report. You must explicitly turn the italics, bold typeface, and other font characteristics off when the product is not discontinued. Otherwise, once a discontinued product has been printed, all products following the discontinued product will print with the special font characteristics. The font characteristics you set in a control's Property Sheet are just the initial settings for the control; if you change any of those properties at runtime, they stay changed until modified again. Similarly, `txtMessage` must be hidden once it's been displayed by setting its `Visible` property to False.

Hide a Page Header

Sometimes you need to display a page header or footer on just the first page of a report. An example is a terms and conditions clause in the header of the first page of an invoice. You want the terms and conditions to appear on the first page of the invoice but not on subsequent pages.

Add an unbound text box control to the report with its `ControlSource` property set to the expression `=HideHeader()`. Delete the text box's label and set the text box's text color to White and its border to Transparent to make it invisible on the report. You can't actually set the control's `Visible` property to No; if you did, the control wouldn't be able to respond to events.

The `HideHeader()` function is as follows:

```
Function HideHeader()
  Reports![rptInvoice].Section(3).Visible = False
  'Section(3) is a reference to the
  'report page header reference
  HideHeader = True
End Function
```

The invisible text box can be placed virtually anywhere on the first page but is most logically located in the page footer. The assumption is that, because the page header is the first item printed on the page, you'll always get the first page header. Once the page footer containing the invisible text box has been processed, the page header's `Visible` property will be set to False, and the page header will not be seen on any other pages in the report.

Avoid Empty Reports

If Access fails to find valid records to insert into the Detail section of a report, all you'll see is `#Error` in the Detail section when the report is printed. To avoid this error, attach code to the report's `Open` event that checks for valid records and sets a flag to cancel the print event if no records are found.

The `NoData` event is triggered when Access tries to build a report and finds no data in the report's underlying recordset. Using `NoData` is easy:

```
Private Sub Report_NoData(Cancel As Integer)
  MsgBox "The report has no data. Printing is canceled"
  Cancel = True
End Sub
```

The `Cancel = True` statement instructs Access to stop trying to open the report. The user will see the dialog box shown in Figure 20-20 and will avoid getting a report that can't be printed. (Open `rptEmpty` in `Chapter20.accdb` for this example.)

FIGURE 20-20

Better than `#Error` in all the text boxes in the report!

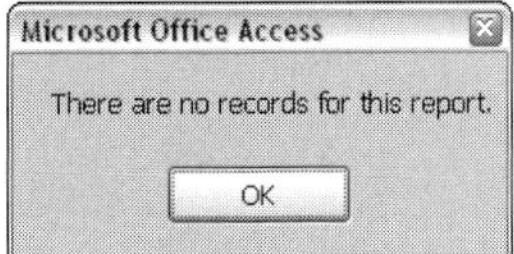

Because the `NoData` event is tied to the report itself, don't look for it in any of the report's sections. Simply add this code as the report's `NoData` event procedure and your users will never encounter a report full of `#Error` messages.

An older technique applicable to older versions of Access is to use the `Dcount()` function to check the number of records in the report's `RecordSource`. If `DCount` returns 0, set the flag and continue.

```
If DCount("*", Me.RecordSource) = 0 Then
  Cancel = True
  MsgBox "There are no records for this report."
EndIf
```

Start a New Page Number for Each Group

Sometimes a report will contain a number of pages for each group of data. You may want to reset page numbering to 1 as each group prints, so that each group's printout will have its own page-numbering sequence. For example, assume you're preparing a report with sales data grouped by region. Each region's sales may require many pages to print, and you're using the `ForceNewPage` property to ensure that grouped data doesn't overlap on any page. But how do you get the page numbering within each group to start at 1?

The report's `Page` property, which you use to print the page number on each page of a report, is a settable property. This means that you can reset `Page` at any time as the report prints. Use the group's `Format` event to reset the report's `Page` property to 1. Every time a group is formatted, `Page` will be reset to 1 by the following code:

```
Sub GroupHeader2_Format ()
  Page = 1
End Sub
```

Use the `Page` property to display the current page number in the page header or footer as usual. For instance, include the following expression in an unbound text box in the page footer:

```
= "Page " & [Page]
```

There does not appear to be a way to count the pages within a group so that you could put a "Page *x* of *y*" in the page footer, where *y* is the number of pages within the group.

Avoid Null Values in a Tabular Report

Null values in reports can cause errors, particularly when the field containing the null value is part of an expression in another control on the report. Instead of simply ignoring the null value and the resulting errors, you may decide that forcing a zero into the field is preferable.

The following expression in a numeric field's `ControlSource` property will solve this problem. In this expression, the field is contained in a text box named `txtField`:

```
=IIf([Field] Is Null,0,[Field]).
```

This immediate `If` statement sets the value of `txtField` to 0 if the value of `Field` (the data) is null; otherwise, `txtField` is set to the value of Field.

Alternatively, you could create the following function, which performs the same actions:

```
Function NullToZero(ByVal varValue as Variant)
  NullToZero = IIf(IsNull(varValue), 0, varValue)
End Function
```

This function accepts a value (like Field) as the `varValue` parameter and tests it with the `IIf`; then the function assumes the value of `varValue` or zero, depending on the result of the `IIf`.

Add More Information to Report

You probably know that the following expression in an unbound text box will print the current page and number of pages contained in the report:

```
="Page " & [Page] & " of " & [Pages]
```

Both `Page` and `Pages` are report properties that are available at runtime and can be included on the report.

But consider the value of adding other report properties on the report. Most of the report properties can be added to unbound text boxes as long as the property is enclosed in square brackets. For the most part, these properties are only of value to you as the developer, but they may also be useful to your users.

For instance, the report's `Name`, `RecordSource`, and other properties are easily added the same way. Figure 20-21 demonstrates how unbound text boxes can deliver this information to a report footer or some other place on the report.

FIGURE 20-21

`rptMoreInfo` demonstrates how to add more information to your reports.

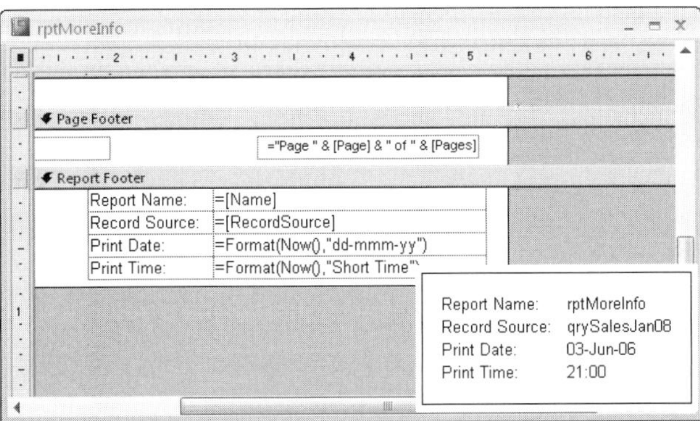

The inset in the lower-right part of Figure 20-21 shows the information provided by adding the four text boxes to this report. Very often, the user is not even aware of the name of a report — the only text the user sees associated with the reports he prints are whatever appears in the title bar (in other words, the report's `Caption` property). If a user is having problems with a report, it might be helpful to display the information you see in Figure 20-21 in the report footer.

Add the User's Name to a Bound Report

An unbound text box with its `ControlSource` set to an unresolved reference will cause Access to pop up a dialog box requesting the information necessary to complete the text box. For instance, an unbound text box with its `RecordSource` set to the following pops up the dialog box you see in the middle of Figure 20-22 when the report is run:

```
=[What is your name?]
```

The text entered into the text box is then displayed on the report. (`rptUserName` in `Chapter20.accdb` on this book's companion CD demonstrates this technique.)

FIGURE 20-22

Use an unbound text box to capture useful information.

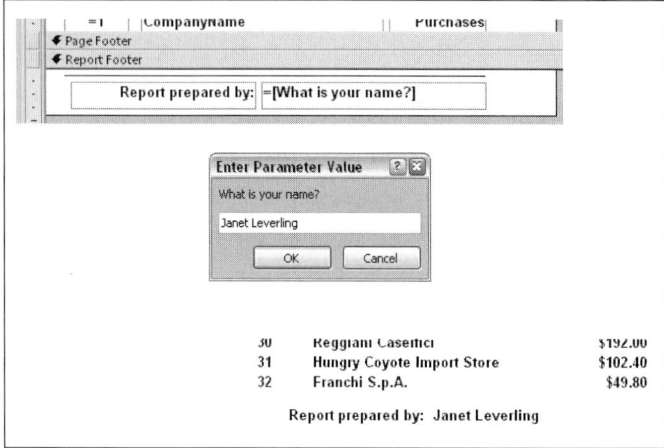

The unbound text box on the report can be referenced by other controls on the report. The Parameter dialog appears before the report is prepared for printing, which means that the data you enter into the dialog box can be used in expressions, calculations, or the Access Basic code behind the report.

Add Vertical Lines between Columns

You can easily add a vertical line to a report section whose height is fixed (like a group header or footer). Adding a vertical line to a section that can grow in height (like a Detail section on a grouped report) is more difficult. It's really difficult to get a vertical line between columns of a report (see `rptVerticalLines` in Figure 20-23). If you simply add a vertical line to the right side of a section of a snaking columns report, the line will appear to the right of the rightmost column on the page. You have to be able to specify where vertical lines will appear on the printed page.

FIGURE 20-23

Vertical lines in `rptVerticalLines` help segregate data.

rptVerticalLines

Northwind Sales: January 2008

Name	Order Date	Order ID	Company Name
Andrew Fuller	10407	01-Jan-08	Ottilies Käseladen
Andrew Fuller	10414	08-Jan-08	Familia Arquibaldo
Andrew Fuller	10422	16-Jan-08	Franchi S.p.A.
Anne Dodsworth	10411	04-Jan-08	Bottom-Dollar Markets
Janet Leverling	10409	03-Jan-08	Océano Atlántico Ltda.
Janet Leverling	10410	04-Jan-08	Bottom-Dollar Markets
Janet Leverling	10413	08-Jan-08	La maison d'Asie
Janet Leverling	10415	09-Jan-08	Hungry Coyote Import Store
Janet Leverling	10420	15-Jan-08	Wellington Importadora
Janet Leverling	10429	23-Jan-08	Hungry Owl All-Night Grocers
Janet Leverling	10432	25-Jan-08	Split Rail Beer & Ale
Janet Leverling	10433	28-Jan-08	Princesa Isabel Vinhos
Janet Leverling	10434	28-Jan-08	Folk och fä HB
Janet Leverling	10436	30-Jan-08	Blondel père et fils

Page: 1 No Filter

Although you add most controls at design time, sometimes it's necessary to explicitly draw a control as the report is prepared for printing. The easiest approach in this case is to use the report's `Line` method to add the vertical line at runtime. The following subroutine, triggered by the Detail section's `Format` event, draws a vertical line 3.5 inches from the left printable margin of the report:

```
Sub Detail1_Format ()
  Dim X1 as Single
  X1 = 3.5 * 1440
  Me.Line (X1, 0)-(X1, 10000)
End Sub
```

The syntax of the `Line` method is as follows:

```
object.Line (X1, Y1) - (X2, Y2)
```

The `Line` method requires four arguments. These arguments (`X1`, `X2`, `Y1`, and `Y2`) specify the top and bottom (or left and right, depending on your perspective) coordinates of the line. Notice that all calculated measurements on a report must be specified in twips (there are 1,440 twips per inch). In our case, `X1` and `X2` are the same value and we're forcing the line to start at the very top of the Detail section (0) and to extend downward for 10,000 twips.

You might wonder why I'm using 10,000 as the `Y2` coordinate for the end of the line. Access will automatically "clip" the line to the height of the Detail section. Because the line control does not contain data, Access will not expand the Detail section to accommodate the line you've drawn in code. Instead, Access draws as much of the 10,000-twip line as needed to fill the detail section, then it stops. The maximum value for `Y2` is 32,767.

The same procedure could be used to draw vertical lines for each section on the report. In the report example (`rptVerticalLines`) in the database accompanying this chapter (`Chapter20.accdb`), we've chosen to add line controls to the report instead. Using the Line control when the height of the report section is fixed (for instance, in the group header and footer) is simply faster than drawing the line for each of these sections.

TIP **The double horizontal lines you see in Figure 20-23 were created by putting two line controls across the page and setting their Top properties 0.0174 inches different. For instance, in the group footer section the "top" line's Top property is set at 0.0799 inches, while the "bottom" line's Top property is set to 0.0625 inches. The exact spacing is relatively unimportant — in fact, Access will force the space increments between the lines to conform to the spacing allowed by the computer's default printer. In this particular case, the minimum space acceptable by the computer's printer was 0.0174 inches. Your computer's printer may accept a different spacing, so you should experiment to see what works best for you.**

Add a Blank Line Every *n* Records

Detail sections chock-full of dozens or hundreds of records can be difficult to read. It's just too easy to lose your place when reading across columns of figures and when the rows are crowded together on the page. Wouldn't it be nice to insert a blank row every fourth or fifth record in a Detail section? It's much easier to read a single row of data in a report (`rptGapsEvery5th` in `Chapter20.accdb`) where the records have been separated by white space every fifth record (see Figure 20-24).

FIGURE 20-24

Using white space to break up tabular data can make it easier to read.

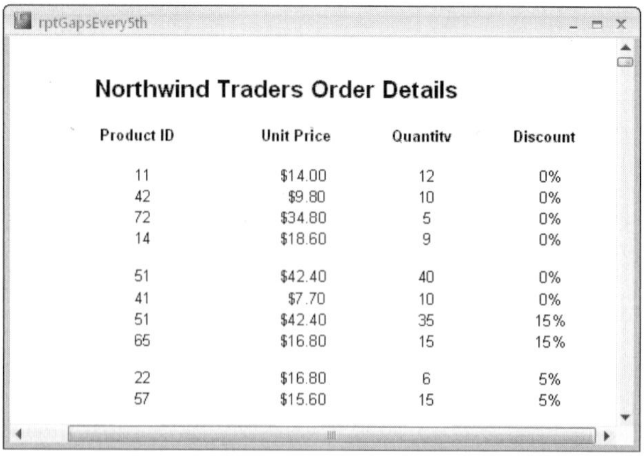

rptGapsEvery5th

Northwind Traders Order Details

Product ID	Unit Price	Quantity	Discount
11	$14.00	12	0%
42	$9.80	10	0%
72	$34.80	5	0%
14	$18.60	9	0%
51	$42.40	40	0%
41	$7.70	10	0%
51	$42.40	35	15%
65	$16.80	15	15%
22	$16.80	6	5%
57	$15.60	15	5%

Access provides no way to insert a blank row in the middle of a Detail section. You can, however, trick Access into inserting white space in the Detail section now and then with a little bit of programming and a couple of hidden controls.

Figure 20-25 reveals the trick behind the arrangement you see in Figure 20-24. An empty, unbound text box named `txtSpacer` is placed below the fields containing data in the Detail section. To the left of `txtSpacer` is another unbound text box named `txtCounter`.

FIGURE 20-25

This report trick uses hidden unbound text boxes in the Detail section.

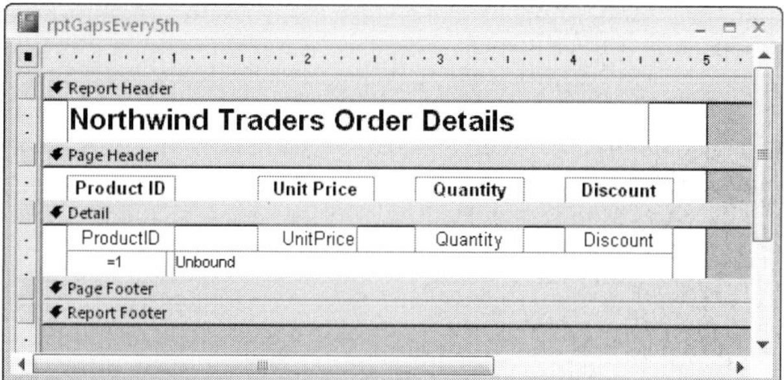

Set the following properties for `txtSpacer`, `txtCounter`, and the Detail section.

TABLE 20-1

Properties for the "Blank Line" Example

Control	Property	Value
`txtSpacer`	`Visible`	Yes
	`CanShrink`	Yes
`txtCounter`	`Visible`	No
	`RunningSum`	OverAll
	`ControlSource`	=1
	`CanShrink`	Yes
`Detail1`	`CanShrink`	Yes

These properties effectively hide the unbound `txtSpacer` and `txtCounter` controls and permit these controls and the Detail section to shrink as necessary when the `txtSpacer` text box control is empty. Even though txtSpacer is visible to the user, Access shrinks it to 0 height if it contains no data. The txtCounter control never needs any space because its Visible property is set to No, hiding it from the user.

The last step is to enter the following code as the Detail section's procedure for the Format event:

```
Sub Detail1_Format ()
  If (txtCounter Mod 4) = 0 Then
    txtSpacer = " "
  Else
    txtSpacer = Null
  End If
End Sub
```

The Format event occurs as Access begins to format the controls within the Detail section. The value in txtCounter is incremented each time a record is added to the Detail section. The Mod operator returns whatever number is left over when the value in txtCounter is divided by 4. When txtCounter is evenly divisible by 4, the result of the txtCounter Mod 4 expression is zero, which causes a space character to be assigned to txtSpacer. In this situation, because txtSpacer is no longer empty, Access increases the height of the Detail section to accommodate txtSpacer, causing the "empty" space in every fourth record printed in the Detail section. You never actually see txtSpacer because all it contains is an empty space character.

txtCounter can be placed anywhere within the Detail section of the report. Make txtSpacer as tall as you want the blank space to be when it is revealed on the printout.

Even-Odd Page Printing

If you've ever prepared a report for two-sided printing, you may have encountered the need for knowing whether the data is being printed on the even side of the page or the odd side of the page. Most users prefer the page number to be located near the outermost edge of the paper. On the odd-numbered page, the page number should appear on the right edge of the page, while on the even-numbered side, the page number must appear on the left side of the page. How, then, do you move the page number from side to side?

The easiest way to determine whether the current page is even or odd is with the Mod operator. The Mod operator performs modulus division on two numbers and returns the remainder of the division expressed as a whole integer. For instance, 5 Mod 2 is 1 (5 divided by 2 leaves a remainder of 1). Any even number is evenly divided by 2, leaving no remainder. Therefore, 2 Mod 2 is 0 (zero), 4 Mod 2 is 0, and so on. We can easily exploit the Mod function to tell us when the current page is even or odd with the following small function:

```
Function IsEven(iTest As Integer) As Integer
  If iTest Mod 2 = 0 Then
    IsEven = True
  Else
    IsEven = False
```

```
  End If
End Function
```

Assuming the page number appears in the Page Footer section of the report, we can use the page footer's `Format` event to determine whether the current page is even or odd, and move the text box containing the page number to the left or right side of the page accordingly.

The basic design of `rptEvenOdd` is shown in Figure 20-26. Notice that the `txtPageNumber` is right-aligned to ensure that the page number appears as close to the right margin as possible.

FIGURE 20-26

`txtPageNumber` moves from the right to the left edge of the paper.

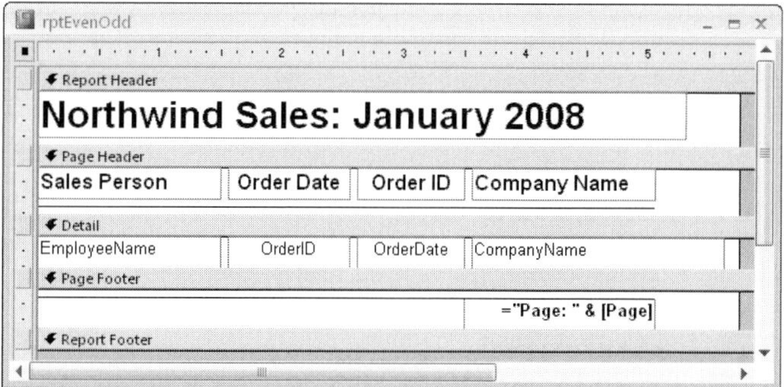

The `Page Footer Format` event procedure is a bit more involved than the `IsEven` function shown earlier. Because the Page Number text box is rather wide (we don't know how many pages are in the report, so the extra width ensures that there's adequate space in the box to accommodate almost any number), simply moving the text box to the left margin leaves the text in the text box too far to the right. We have to adjust the `TextAlign` property of `txtPageNumber` to shift the page number all the way to the left side of the text box. `ALIGN_LEFT` and `ALIGN_RIGHT` are integer constants set at 1 and 3, respectively, in the Declarations section of the report's code module.

```
Sub PageFooter1_Format ()
  If (Me.Page Mod 2) = 0 Then
    txtPageNumber.Left = 0
    txtPageNumber.TextAlign = ALIGN_LEFT
  Else
    txtPageNumber.Left = 3.5 * 1440
    txtPageNumber.TextAlign = ALIGN_RIGHT
  End If
End Sub
```

In this event procedure, any time the expression `Me.Page Mod 2` is zero (meaning, the page number is even) the `Left` property of `txtPageNumber` is set to 0 and its `TextAlign` property is set to `ALIGN_LEFT (1)`. On odd-numbered pages, `TextAlign` is set to `ALIGN_RIGHT (3)`.

Notice how the `Left` property of `txtPageNumber` is set on odd-numbered pages. The expression `3.5 * 1440` is used to determine the `Left` property's setting. You may recall that, by default, all positioning information in Access Basic is done using twips as the unit of measure. There are 1,440 twips in an inch, so this expression moves `txtPageNumber` to a position 3.5 inches from the left print margin on the page.

Like magic, this event procedure causes the Page Number text box to move from the right side on odd-numbered pages to the left side on even-numbered pages (see Figure 20-27).

FIGURE 20-27

`txtPageNumber` jumps from right to left.

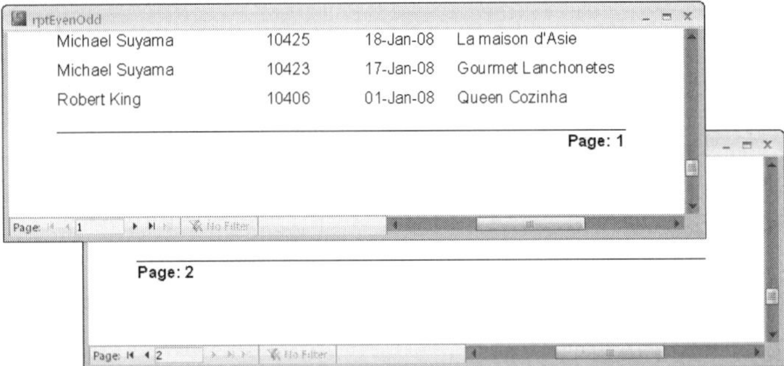

Display All Reports in a Combo Box

The names of all the top-level database objects are stored in the `MSysObjects` system table. You can run queries against `MSysObjects` just as you can run queries against any other table in the database. It's easy to fill a combo box or list box with a list of the report objects in an Access database.

Choose Table/Query as the RowSource Type for the list box and put this SQL statement in the `RowSource` of your list box to fill the box with a list of all reports in the database:

```
SELECT DISTINCTROW [Name] FROM MSysObjects
WHERE [Type] = -32764
ORDER BY [Name];
```

The `-32764` identifies report objects in `MSysObjects`, one of the system tables used by Microsoft Access. The results are shown in Figure 20-28. Notice that reports do not have to be open for this technique to work. `MSysObjects` knows all of the objects in the database, so no reports will escape detection using this technique.

FIGURE 20-28

`frmReports` displays the reports in `Chapter20.accdb`.

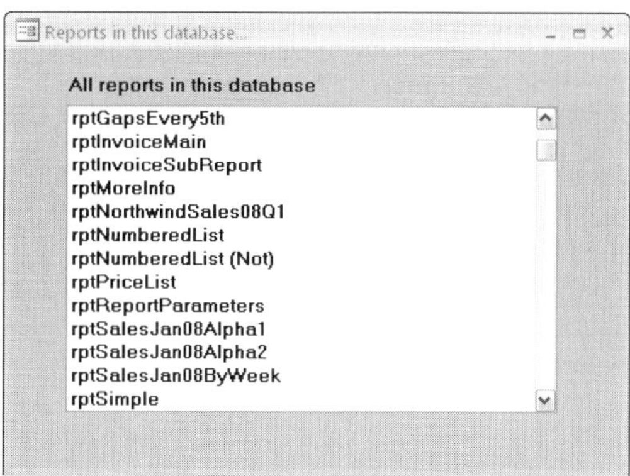

If you're using a naming convention for your database objects, use a prefix to show only the reports you want. The following code returns only those reports that begin with *tmp:*

```
SELECT DISTINCTROW [Name] FROM MSysObjects
WHERE [Type] = -32764 AND Left([Name], 3) = "tmp"
ORDER BY [Name];
```

Because `MSysObjects` stores the names of all database objects, you can return the names of the other top-level database objects as well. Just substitute the `-32764` as the type value in the preceding SQL statement with the Table 20-2 values to return different database object types.

To view the `MSysObjects` table, set the Show System Objects setting to Yes in the System Objects dialog box (which you can get to by right-clicking on the Navigation Pane's title bar, and selecting `Navigation Options` from the shortcut menu). `MSysObjects` does *not* have to be visible for this trick to work.

TABLE 20-2

Microsoft Access Object Types and Values

Object	Type Value
Tables	6
System tables	1
Forms	-32768
Modules	-32761
Macros	-32766
Queries	5

Use Different Formats in the Same Text Box

On some reports, you may want the format of certain fields in a record to change according to the values in other fields on the report. A good example is a journal voucher report in a multicurrency financial system in which the voucher detail debit or credit amount format varies according to the number of decimal places used to display the currency value.

Unfortunately, a control in a Detail section of a report can have but a single format specified in its Property Sheet. Use the following trick to flexibly set the format property at runtime. The `FlexFormat()` function uses the built in `Format()` function to provide dynamic formatting to controls on a form or report:

```
Function FlexFormat (iFmt As Integer) As String
  Select Case iFmt
     Case 1 : FlexFormat = "##0.0;(##0.0)"
     Case 2 : FlexFormat = "##0.00;(##0.00)"
     Case 3 : FlexFormat = "##0.000;(##0.000)"
     Case 4 : FlexFormat = "##0.0000;(##0.0000)"
  End Select
End Function
```

`FlexFormat()` returns a string containing the new format of the field. The returned string depends on the `iFmt` parameter passed to `FlexFormat()`.

Assume that the field to be dynamically formatted has its `ControlSource` set to [Amount]. The format of the Amount text box should vary depending on the value of the `CurrDecPlaces` field in the same record. `CurrDecPlaces` is an Integer data type. To use `FlexFormat`, change the `ControlSource` property of the Amount text box to the following:

```
=Format([Amount],FlexFormat([CurrDecPlaces]))
```

The Amount text box will be dynamically formatted according to the value contained in the `CurrDecPlaces` text box. This trick may be generalized to format fields other than currency fields. By increasing the number of parameters of the user-defined formatting function, the formatting can be dependent on more than one field, if necessary.

Fast Printing from Queried Data

A report that is based on a query can take a long time to print. Because reports and forms cannot share the same recordset, once a user has found the correct record on a form it's a shame to have to run the query over again to print the record on a query. A way to "cache" the information on the form is to create a table (we'll call it `tblCache`) containing all of the fields that will eventually be printed on the report. Then, when the user has found the correct record on the form, copy the data from the form to `tblCache`, and open the report. The report, of course, is based on `tblCache`.

The query is run only once to populate the form. Copying the data from the form to `tblCache` is a very fast operation, and multiple records can be added to `tblCache` as needed. Because the report is now based on a table, it opens quickly and is ready to print as soon as the report opens.

Hide Forms during Print Preview

Very often, a report opened in Print Preview will be obscured by forms that are open on the screen. The easiest way to prevent forms from getting in the way during Print Preview is to simply hide them as the report opens, and then reveal them when the report is closed.

The `RunReport()` function opens a report for previewing and hides all open forms during print preview. To restore the forms after previewing the report, set the report's `OnClose` property to `=MakeFormsVisible(-1)`.

```
Function RunReport(RepName as string)
  Dim intErrorCode as Integer

  DoCmd.OpenReport RepName, acPreview
  intErrorCode = MakeFormsVisible(0)
End Function

Function MakeFormsVisible (YesNo)
  Dim intCounter As Integer

  On Error GoTo MakeFormsVisible_Error

  For intCounter = 0 To Forms.Count - 1
    'If you want to make sure a hidden form is not
    'displayed use the forms(intCounter).formname
    'statement to get the form name.
    Forms(intCounter).Visible = YesNo
  Next

MakeFormsVisible_Exit:
    Exit Function
MakeFormsVisible_Error:
    Msgbox "Error " & Err.Number & ": " & Err.Description
    'Make sure all forms are restored if an error occurs.
    For intCounter = 0 To forms.count - 1
       forms(intCounter).visible = -1
    Next
    Resume MakeFormsVisible_Exit
End Function
```

A Few Quick Report Tips

In addition to the more verbose report tips discussed earlier in this chapter, you might be interested in the following very short report tips.

Center the title

Centering a report title directly in the middle of the page is often difficult. The easiest way to guarantee that the title is centered is to stretch the title from left margin to right margin, and then click the Center Align button.

Easily align control labels

Keeping text boxes and their labels properly aligned on reports is sometimes difficult. Because a text box and its label can be independently moved on the report, all too often the label's position must be adjusted to bring it into alignment with the text box.

You can eliminate text-box labels completely by including the label text as part of the text box's record source. Use the concatenation character to add the label text to the text box's control source:

```
= "Product: " & [ProductName]
```

Now, whenever you move the text box, both the label and the bound record source move as a unit. The only drawback to this technique is that you must use the same format for the text box and its label.

Micro-adjust controls

The easiest way to adjust the size of text boxes on a form in tiny increments is to hold down the Shift key and press the arrow key corresponding to Table 20-3.

TABLE 20-3

Micro-Adjustment Keystroke Combinations

Shift Combination	Adjustment
Shift+Left Arrow	Reduce width
Shift+Right Arrow	Increase width
Shift+Up Arrow	Reduce height
Shift+Down Arrow	Increase height

Another resizing technique is to position the cursor over any of the sizing handles on a selected control and double-click with the left mouse button. The control will automatically "size to fit" the text contained within the control. This quick method can also be used to align not only labels but also text boxes to the grid.

To micro-adjust a control's position, hold down the Ctrl key as you press the arrows keys. The selected control will move in tiny increments in the direction indicated by the arrow keys you press.

Always assign unique names to controls

If you use the Report Wizard or drag fields from the Field List when designing your reports, Access assigns the new text boxes the same names as the fields in the recordset underlying the report. For instance, if you drag a field named `Discount` from the field list, both the `Name` and `ControlSource` properties of the text box are set to Discount.

If another control on the report references the text box, or if you change the `ControlSource` of the text box to a calculated field, such as

```
=IIf([Discount]=0,"N/A",[Discount])
```

you'll see `#Error` when you view the report. This happens because Access can't distinguish between the control named `Discount` and the field in the underlying recordset named `Discount`.

You must change the `Name` property of the control to something like `txtDiscount` so that Access can tell the difference between the control's name and the underlying field.

Use Snaking Columns in a Report

When the data displayed on a report doesn't require the full width of the page, you may be able to conserve the number of pages by printing the data as snaking columns, as in a dictionary or phone book. Less space is wasted and fewer pages need to be printed, speeding the overall response of the report. More information is available at a glance and many people find snaking columns more aesthetically pleasing than simple blocks of data.

For the examples in this section, we need a query that returns more data than we've been using up to this point. Figure 20-29 shows the query we'll be using to prepare the sample reports in this section.

FIGURE 20-29

This query returns more detailed information than we've been using.

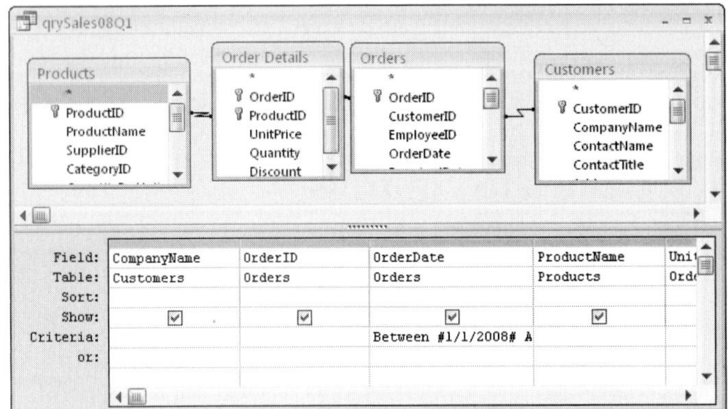

This query returns the following information: company name, order date, order ID, product name, unit price, and quantity for the period from January 1, 2008, to March 31, 2008.

The initial report design to contain this data is shown in Design view in Figure 20-30. This rather complex report includes a group based on the order ID for each order placed by the company, as well as a group based on the company itself. This design enables us to summarize data for each order during the quarter, as well as for the company for the entire quarter.

FIGURE 20-30

Notice how narrow the records in this report are.

The same report in Print Preview is shown in Figure 20-31. Notice that the report really doesn't make good use of the page width available to it. In fact, each record of this report is only 3.25 inches wide.

FIGURE 20-31

The report makes poor use of the available page width.

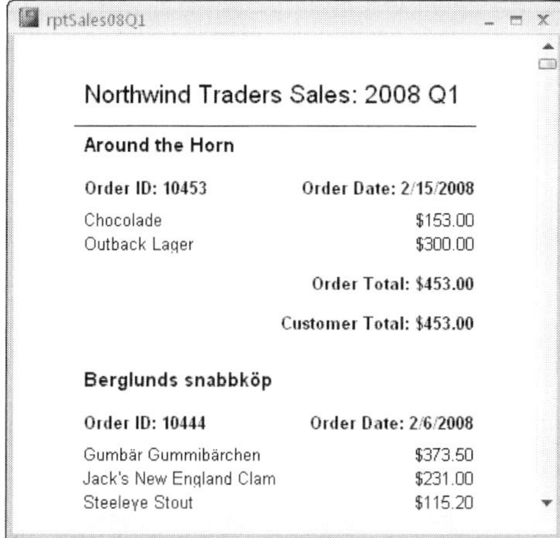

Setting a report to print as snaking columns is actually part of the print setup for the report, not an attribute of the report itself. Choose File ➪ Page Setup to open the Page Setup dialog box, and then select the Arrange tab. Change the Number of Columns value to 2. As you change Number of Columns from 1 to 2, the Column Layout area near the bottom of the Arrange tab becomes active, showing you that Access has selected the Across, Then Down option to print items across the page first, and then down the page. Although this printing direction is appropriate for mailing labels, it's not what we want for our report. Select the Down, Then Across option to direct Access to print the report as snaking columns (Figure 20-32).

When working with snaking columns, make sure the proper Column Layout option is selected. If you neglect to set the Column Layout to Down, Then Across, the snaking columns will be laid out horizontally across the page. This common error can cause a lot of confusion because the report won't look as expected (see Figure 20-33). The reports shown in Figures 20-32 and 20-33 are the same with the exception of the Column Layout setting.

FIGURE 20-32

Only a few changes are needed to produce snaking columns.

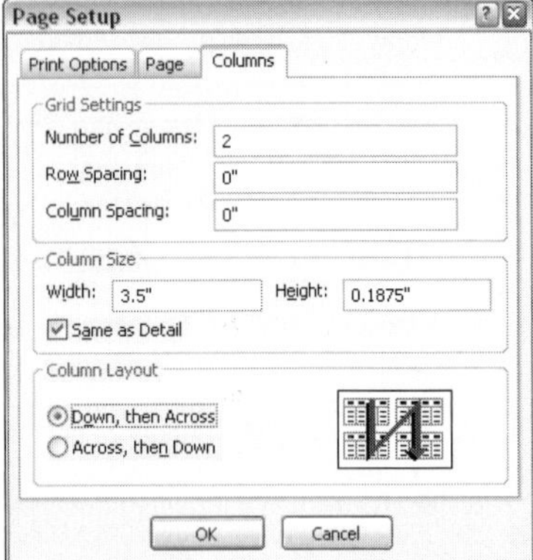

FIGURE 20-33

The wrong Column Layout setting can be very confusing!.

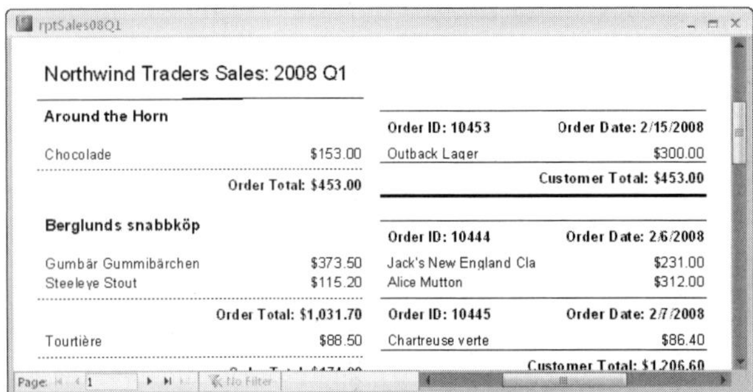

As long as the Same as Detail check box is *not* checked, Access intelligently adjusts the Column Spacing and other options to accommodate the number of items across that you've specified for the report. With Same as Detail checked, Access will force the columns to whatever width is specified for the columns in Design view, which might mean that the number of columns specified in the Number of Columns parameter won't fit on the page.

Figure 20-34 clearly demonstrates the effect of changing the report to a snaking two-column layout. Before the change, this report required 11 pages to print all the data. After this change, only seven pages are required.

FIGURE 20-34

Snaking multiple columns conserve page space and provide more information at a glance.

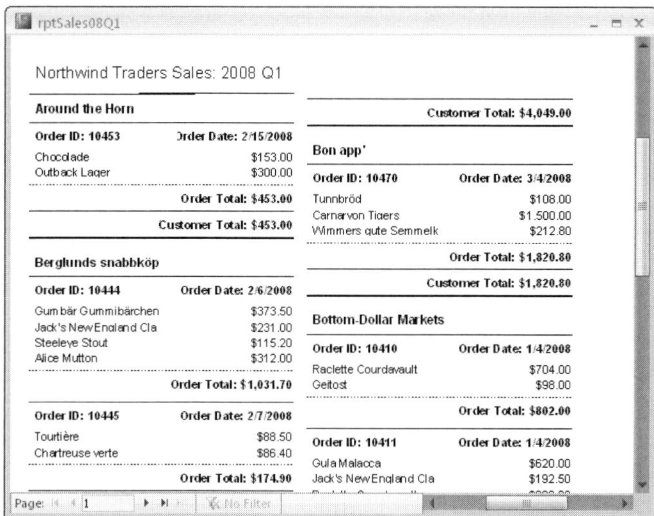

You may be wondering about the other print options in the Page Setup dialog box (refer to Figure 20-32). Here is a short description of each of the relevant settings in the Arrange tab of the Page Setup dialog box:

- **Number of Columns:** Specifies the number of columns in the report. You should be aware that Number of Columns affects only the Detail section, Group Header section, and Group Footer section of the report. The Page Header section and Page Footer section are not duplicated for each column.
- **Row Spacing:** Additional vertical space allowed for each detail item. Use this setting if you need to force more space between detail items than the report's design allows.
- **Column Spacing:** Additional horizontal space allowed per column. Use this setting if you need to force more space between columns in the report than the design allows.
- **Item Size - Same as Detail:** The column width and detail height will be the same as on the report in Design view. This property is useful when you need to fine-tune the column placement on a report (for instance, when printing the data onto preprinted forms). Making adjustments to the report's design will directly influence how the columns print on paper.
- **Column Size - Width and Height:** The width and height of a column. These options are handy when printing onto preprinted forms to ensure that the data falls where you want it to.
- **Column Layout:** How the items are to be printed: either Across, Then Down or Down, Then Across.

Keep in mind that the measurement units you see in the Page Setup dialog box are determined by the Windows internationalization settings. For instance, in Germany or Japan where the metric system is used, the units of measure will be centimeters instead of inches. Also, you must allow for the margin widths set in the Margins tab of the Page Setup dialog box (see Figure 20-35).

FIGURE 20-35

All report page settings must consider the margin widths.

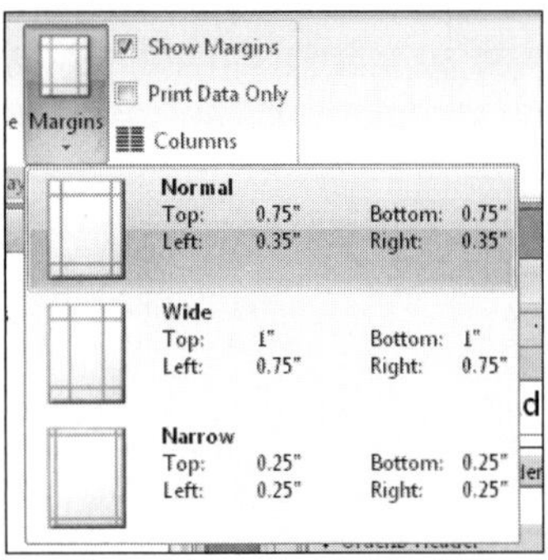

For instance, if you specify a Column Size Width of 3.5" and the left margin is set to 1", this means the right edge of the column will actually fall 4.5 inches from the left physical edge of the paper, or more than halfway across an 8.5-x-11-inch sheet of paper. These settings will not allow two columns, each 3.5 inches wide, to print on a standard letter-size sheet of paper. In this case, you might consider reducing the left and right margins until the 3.5-inch columns fit properly. (Don't worry about setting the margins too small to work with your printer. Unless you're working with a nonstandard printer, Windows is pretty smart about knowing the printable area available with your printer and won't allow you to set margins too small.)

Exploiting Two-Pass Report Processing

In Chapter 19, we mention that Access uses a two-pass approach when formatting and printing reports. We'll now explore what this capability means to you and how you can exploit both passes in your applications.

The main advantage of two-pass reporting is that your reports can include expressions that rely on information available anywhere in the report. For example, placing a control with the `Sum()` function in a header or footer means that Access will use the first pass to accumulate the data required by the function, and then use the second pass to process the values in that section before printing them.

Another obvious example is putting an unbound text box in the footer of a report containing the following expression:

```
="Page " & [Page] & " of " & [Pages]
```

The built-in `Pages` variable (which contains the total number of pages in the report) isn't determined until Access has completed the first pass through the report. On the second pass, Access has a valid number to use in place of the `Pages` variable.

The biggest advantage of two-pass reporting is that you're free to use aggregate functions that depend on the report's underlying record source. Group headers and footers can include information that can't be known until the entire record source is processed.

There are many situations where aggregate information provides valuable insight into data analysis. Consider a report that must contain each salesperson's performance over the last year measured against the total sales for the sales organization, or a region's sales figures against sales for the entire sales area. A bookstore might want to know what portion of its inventory is devoted to each book category.

Figure 20-36 shows such a report. The Number of Customers, Total Sales, and Average Purchase information at the top of this report (`rptSummary`) are all part of the report header. In a one-pass report writer, the data needed to perform these calculations would not be available until the bottom of the page, after all of the records have been processed and laid out.

FIGURE 20-36

The summary information is part of the report's header.

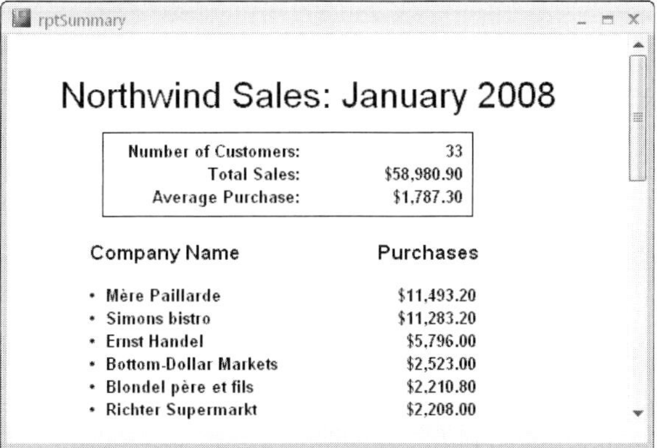

A glance at `rptSummary` in Design view (Figure 20-37) reveals the text boxes in the report header containing the summary information. The expressions used in the unbound text boxes are as follows:

```
Number of Customers: =Count([CompanyName])
Total Sales: =Format(Sum([Purchases]),"Currency")
Average Purchase: =Format(Sum([Purchases])/ _
     Count([CompanyName]), "Currency")
```

The `Count()` and `Sum()` functions both require information that isn't available until the entire report has been processed. As long as Access can find the arguments provided to these functions (`CompanyName` and `Purchases`) in the underlying recordset, the calculations proceed without any action by the user.

FIGURE 20-37

`rptSummary` in Design view

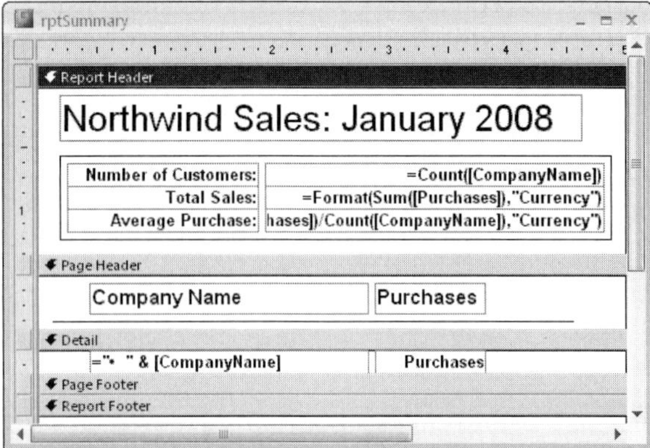

Summary

This chapter examines a number of advanced report design concepts and techniques. Most of the "tricks" described in this chapter simply exploit the built-in properties and features of Access reports to yield more information or to make the reports easier to read. Anything you can do to help your users understand the data contained in their Access databases will be greatly appreciated, we're sure!

The next several chapters explorer some of the more interesting and challenging aspects of working with Microsoft Access. Chapter 21 takes on the issue of creating applications that will be simultaneously used by more than one person. Although multiuser applications may seem easy to produce, there's much more than meets the eye.

Chapters 22 explorers *automation*, the process of controlling one application (such as Microsoft Word) from another application (Microsoft Access, of course!). There you'll see how easy (or difficult!) it can be to share data between Windows applications and control printing and other operations with automation.

Chapter 21

Building Multiuser Applications

IN THIS CHAPTER

- Understanding the issues in multiuser applications
- Splitting Access databases
- Configuring Access for multiuser access
- Considering your locking options
- Looking at record-locking errors
- Handling locking errors
- Using unbound forms in multiuser environments

You've created a really nifty application. After you finished your masterpiece, you tested, poked, and prodded it every which way imaginable. Finally, you gave it to your users, who tried it out and thought it was pretty nifty, too. Everything worked the way it was supposed to: The application's form navigation was smooth and quick, queries ran fast, and there were no errors during data entry.

So who is this guy on the other end of the phone line complaining about record locks? You didn't have any record-locking problems during testing. But then again, you didn't test your application in a multiuser environment. After all, Access is supposed to handle all those issues for you, right? Almost, but not quite. There's still a lot you need to know about using Access applications in multiuser environments before you can be confident that users will not encounter unwarranted record locks, frustration, and possible data loss.

This chapter shows you how to avoid some of the pitfalls of failing to plan for multiuser issues when developing applications in Microsoft Access. The key phrase here is *failing to plan*. In order to create a successful multiuser application, you must anticipate the environment in which the application will be run (single-user, multiuser, desktop, network, and so on), and you must take into consideration what kind of database application you are developing (data entry, client-server, and so on). This chapter covers some of the planning issues you should keep in mind and ways to handle problems you might encounter.

Much of what we discuss in this chapter is related to the security issues we discuss in Chapter 29. The Access record-locking mechanism is designed to prevent accidental data loss or corruption by controlling which of several users is able to make updates to records in a database. Access security, on the other hand, prevents unauthorized users from viewing or changing not only the data but the database objects such as forms and reports. Hand in hand, record locking and security combine to ensure the integrity of the application and its data.

NOTE **Some of the examples in this chapter are given using both ADO and DAO syntax. Although ADO is far superior to DAO for most purposes, many Access developers spend time maintaining applications written with DAO code. Because proper handling of multiuser issues is so important in many environments, we felt it was necessary to show both the proper ADO and DAO code involved with record locking and handling lock contention.**

Network Issues

In order to have a multiuser application, you have to have a network of some kind. Generally, the type of network you use doesn't matter. The multiuser issues are basically the same regardless of the underlying networking technology. The speed of your network, the type of data source that you're accessing, and the location of your application's files are all important considerations when planning your network installation. Although we've listed these as three separate items, they're all related to the primary issue of database performance. No matter how well it's written, if your application performs poorly due to network bottlenecks, the application will get the blame, not the network.

Network performance

When you develop applications in Access, a good rule of thumb is to always plan for the lowest common denominator — that is, write your database applications as if they were going to be used on the most minimally equipped computer possible. Preparing databases that will be used in networked environments is no different. There are a lot of different network topologies and speeds out there — everything from remote-access dialup lines running on slow modems to megabit networks and dedicated T1 lines.

TIP **Plan ahead: If you're writing an application that will be used in a high-speed, low-traffic network environment; then you can afford to be a little extravagant and less stringent in your control of record-locking issues. If, however, your application will be used by salesmen on the road dialing in to retrieve customer and order information using modems of 56 K baud, then your focus should be very conservative, and you should design to accommodate the frequent updates likely in this scenario.**

File location

File location can change the performance of your application more than you may think. Where you locate your files depends on the environment. For instance, if your network contains diskless workstations, then you have no choice but to run the entire application from the server (an unfortunate, but unavoidable, choice). However, if each workstation has a hard drive with plenty of free space available, you may want to locate some files on the server and some on each workstation. You may want to put all of the files on each workstation except the data files that will be shared by all users.

The following scenarios assume that you're splitting your database into a *back-end Access data file* (`.accdb` or `.mdb`, containing data tables only) and a *front-end database* (an Access data file containing code modules and form, report, and query objects). (We discuss splitting Access databases in detail later in this chapter.)

This method of maintaining your applications has advantages in any environment, but it offers you even more advantages in a networked multiuser environment. Here are some of the advantages and disadvantages of different file-location scenarios:

- **All files on server:** The primary advantage of locating all your application files on a server is that updating your application is easy because everything is in a single location. You can easily post a new `.accdb` or `.mdb` file on a file server or shared folder in a Windows network. The disadvantages, however, far outweigh the advantage. Performance is poor due to the fact that every read, write, or execute request must first pass around the network to the server, and then a response must be sent back around the network to the client. This approach greatly increases network traffic, especially in an environment with many users. Try to avoid this scenario, if possible.
- **Distributed installation:** A distributed installation is a good choice for most environments. In this design, you install a copy of Access and the front-end database on the user's local machine, leaving the back-end database application and linked data files on the server. Less network traffic is generated and less time is spent waiting for requests to be sent back and forth around the network. This installation allows for moderately simple upgrades because the majority of the most volatile files are in one central location. One problem you may experience is decreased performance from several users accessing your application databases at the same time.
- **All files on client:** In this scenario, you would have all executables — `.exe` files, `.dll` files, and application files — located on each client, and only data files on the server. Your data files would be attached to your application database. You would gain performance because network traffic and requests would be kept to a minimum and because you wouldn't have several users hitting your application at the same time — only the data. This scenario is not conducive to easy upgrades, however. Most of the time, your application's front end will be the one that changes the most. If the application is located on a client workstation, you'll have to go to each workstation and upgrade it individually (unless you're using some kind of distribution software, like Microsoft System Center Configuration Server).

NOTE **Microsoft's System Center Configuration Server (SCCS) is an add-on for network systems running Windows 2003 Server as the file server and either Windows 2000, Windows XP, or Windows Vista on the user's desktop. SMS enables the system administrator to install and manage software from a central location, making it much easier to upgrade operating system and application software on large networks.**

Data sources

Access is a versatile development environment because of its ability to read many kinds of external data sources. This ability, however, can cause problems for your applications. Even if you're just reading a plain ol' Access `.accdb` or `.mdb` located on your sever, there are still issues you need to consider. Access is a client-centric application. In many instances, when you execute a query against a table located in an Access database located on your network, Access goes out to the server, brings back all the records needed to perform the query, and then processes the request on the client. The next time you get a chance, run a really big query on your workstation while watching the number of packets being sent to that address. It's fun to see your network utilization go from 35 percent to 90 percent just because of one query. All this traffic and the huge amount of data you can potentially transfer over a network can kill performance.

This client-centric nature can be seen especially when using ODBC data sources. Access still acts the same way, but because ODBC is another layer that Jet has to go through, performance can be even worse, especially when querying large recordsets. But ODBC and client-server applications are in high demand right now, so you have to find an acceptable solution to these performance problems. You can do a couple of things to speed performance when using data sources other than native Access tables:

- **Use SQL pass-through.** SQL pass-through allows you to send a SQL statement (or stored procedure name) to a host database to let it execute the request, returning only the result set (instead of the entire recordset) for local processing. This ability takes advantage of the host platform's capabilities, and it keeps network traffic down. The disadvantage to SQL pass-through is that you must use the host database's SQL syntax instead of letting Access generate the SQL request for you. This makes your application less portable to other database platforms and doesn't let you take advantage of Access's QBE facility.
- **Use transactions.** Transactions (the `BeginTrans` and `CommitTrans` methods of an ADO `Connection` object or DAO `Workspace` object) allow you to cache reads, edits, and updates in local memory instead of reading from or writing to disk or your external data source. If you know that you'll be doing several updates or reads within a VBA procedure, enclose the updates in transaction statements. Better performance is achieved because you don't have to wait on your request to be sent back around the network to your data source, and because all writes are done at one time (when the `CommitTrans` method is executed) instead of each time the `Update` method is executed. Listing 21-1 shows the use of transactions within a VBA procedure. (Be sure that the `Microsoft DAO Object Library` library is selected in the Tools ➪ References dialog in the Code Editor window.)

LISTING 21-1

Demonstrating DAO Transactions

```
Function UpdateRecords()
    Dim db As DAO.Database
    Dim ws As DAO.Workspace
```

```
    Dim rs As DAO.Recordset
    Set db = CurrentDb
    Set ws = DBEngine.OpenDatabase("C:\Data\MyDB.accdb")
    Set rs = db.OpenRecordset("Employees", dbOpenTable)

    'Begin transaction:
    ws.BeginTrans

    rs.MoveFirst
    Do While Not rs.EOF
        rs.Edit
        rs.Fields("CompanyName") _
            = UCase(rs.Fields("CompanyName"))
        rs.Update
        rs.MoveNext
    Loop

    'Commit transaction:
    ws.CommitTrans

ExitHere:
    rs.Close
    Set rs = Nothing
    Exit Function

HandleError:
    'Rollback transaction:
    ws.Rollback
    GoTo ExitHere

End Function
```

Special network situations

Before ending this section, some mention of remote users needs to be made. With portable computing power increasing and becoming less expensive, more of your applications will have to be developed with remote or home users in mind. Although broadband Internet access is widely available, many users may still be using dialup to access your company's network. In these situations, you can do a few things to make performance more acceptable:

- **Place files on the client.** Put as much of your application on the remote computer as possible. Executables across a dialup line are unacceptable. The more you can put on the client, the fewer complaints you'll receive.
- **Use database replication.** One of the best features of Microsoft Access is the ability to replicate databases. This facility has more potential and probably solves more problems than any new feature. In the past, you had to create some kind of scheme whereby you kept up with changes to a host and remote database independently and, upon dialing in,

passed those changes to the server and remote using a MAPI message or a VBA procedure. The potential for error was extremely high and the process was difficult to plan. Now you can place local copies of your database on each remote client and, upon dialing in, replicate all changes, deletions, and additions to the server database, then pass a copy of the master's updates back to the client. Not only does this solve many remote problems, but it can also work in wide area network (WAN) settings where line speed is still an issue and data doesn't have to be real-time. For specifics on Access replication, see Chapter 31.

Database Open Options

By default, each time a user opens an Access database, other users are able to open and make changes to the same database. The "shared" mode of opening Access databases is great for most users because everyone is able to work with the data as if no one else was using the same tables and records. However, Shared mode also leads to update conflicts when more than one user wants to simultaneously change the same record.

It's easy to change the open mode of an Access database. The Open dialog box (see Figure 21-1) contains an option that directs Access to open the database exclusively (for single-user access). When you don't select the Exclusive option, the database is opened for shared access, permitting simultaneous multiuser access to the data.

FIGURE 21-1

By default, Access 2007 databases are opened in Shared mode.

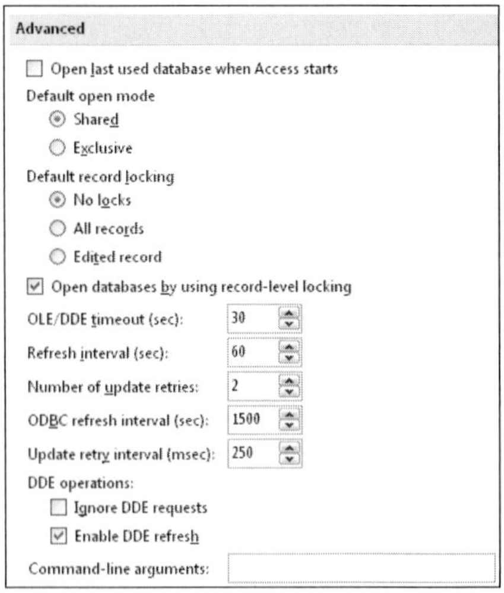

The essential step to multiuser databases, therefore, is to make sure that the database in question has been opened for shared access. You can easily change the default Exclusive open mode for Access databases, as shown later in this chapter.

Listing 21-2 shows the ADO and DAO code necessary to open an Access database exclusively. The options passed to the Connection object as it is opened are not particularly well documented.

LISTING 21-2

Using ADO to Open a Database Exclusively

```
Public Sub OpenDatabaseTestADO()

    Dim cnn As ADODB.Connection
    Dim str As String

    str = "Provider=Microsoft.Jet.OLEDB.4.0;" _
        & "Data Source=C:\Data\MyDB.accdb"
    Set cnn = New ADODB.Connection
    cnn.Mode = adModeShareExclusive
    cnn.ConnectionString = str
    cnn.Open

    '... Your code goes here ...

    cnn.Close
    Set cnn = Nothing
End Sub


Public Sub OpenDatabaseTestDAO()
  Dim db As Database
  Set db = DBEngine.OpenDatabase("C:\Data\MyDB.accdb")

  '... Your code goes here ...

  db.Close
  Set db = Nothing
End Sub
```

When opening a database with DAO code, you pass a parameter to the `OpenDatabase` method of the `Workspace` object to instruct Jet which open mode to use. Notice the False value passed as the second argument to the `OpenDatabase` method in Listing 21-2.

The syntax of the DAO `OpenDatabase` method is:

```
Set Database = Workspace.OpenDatabase (dbName _
    [, Exclusive] [, Read-only] [, Connect])
```

where:

- `dbName` is the name of the database to open
- `Exclusive` is the flag instructing whether to open `dbName` in Exclusive or Shared mode. True means open the database exclusively; False means open in Shared mode.
- `Read-only` is a flag telling Jet to open the database in read-only mode.
- `Connect` is the connect string required by the ODBC database.

By default, a database opened with the `OpenDatabase` method is opened in Shared mode (`Exclusive` is False). You should, of course, specify either True or False as the `Exclusive` value. Better yet is to use constants such as `OPEN_EXCLUSIVE` or `OPEN_SHARED` (which you have set to True and False, respectively) to make your code more self-documenting.

Splitting Databases for Network Access

One common technique employed by most experienced Access developers working in multiuser environments is splitting the database into front-end and back-end components. This relatively simple operation can yield big benefits in terms of networked application performance and future maintenance on the application.

There is at least one extremely good reason why we should explore splitting Access databases. Although you can place a single copy of an `.accdb` or `.mdb` file onto a shared computer on the network, the performance degradation from such a design is considerable. Although Jet is able to service many, many simultaneous data requests, the overhead associated with moving large volumes of data into and out of an Access database is considerable.

Using an Access database stored on a remote computer involves much more than simply moving data from the remote computer to the local machine. All of the form, menu, and ribbon definitions must be transported to the local computer so that Windows can "construct" the user interface on the local computer's monitor. The Windows installation on the local computer must intercept and transmit any keyboard and mouse events to the remote computer so that the proper code will run in response to these events. Finally, the single copy of Jet on the remote computer must fulfill all data requests, no matter how trivial or demanding. The impact of all of these actions is compounded by increasing the number of users working with the same remotely installed copy of the database.

Fortunately, most of these issues disappear when the database application is split into front-end and back-end components. The local Windows installation handles the user interface from information stored in the front-end database. All code is run on the user's desktop computer, rather than on the remote machine. Also, the locally installed copy of Jet is able to handle all local data requirements, while only those requests for remote data are passed on to the back-end database.

Before getting into the details of splitting a database, let's consider some of the problems associated with single-file databases. To begin with, unlike some other development systems, all of the objects in an Access database application are stored in a single file, the familiar `.accdb` or `.mdb` you work with every day. Other database systems like FoxPro for Windows maintain a number of different files for each application, usually one file per object (form, table, and so on). Although having to deal with multiple files complicates database development and maintenance somewhat, updating a single form or query involves nothing more than replacing the related file with the updated form or query file.

Updating an Access database object is somewhat more complicated. As you've probably discovered, replacing a form or query in an Access database used by a large number of users can be quite a problem. Replacing a form or other database object often requires hours of work importing the object into each user's copy of the database.

A second consideration is the network traffic inherent in single-file Access databases. Figure 21-2 shows an example of the problem. This figure illustrates a common method of sharing an Access database. The computer in the upper-left corner of the figure is the file server and holds the Access database file. Assume for a moment that the entire database is contained within a single `.accdb` on the file server, and the database has been enabled for shared data access. Each workstation in Figure 21-2 has a full copy of Access (or the Access runtime) installed.

FIGURE 21-2

A database kept on a file server can generate a large amount of traffic on the network.

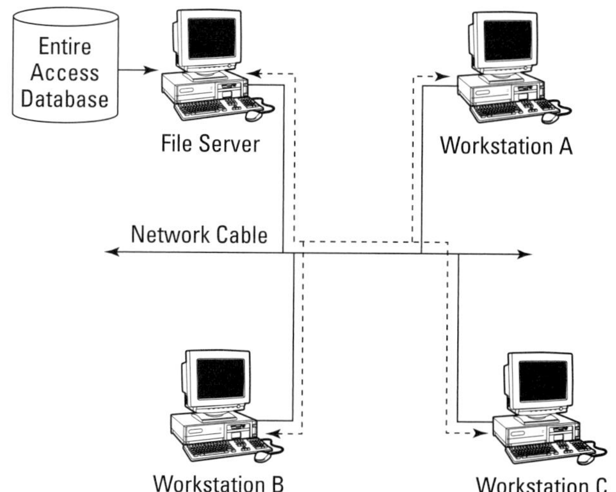

Now, what happens when the user on Workstation C opens the database? The Access installation on that machine must locate the `.accdb` on the file server, open that file, and start up the application. This means that any splash forms, queries, and other startup activities must take place across the network before the user is able to work with the database. Any time a form is opened or a query is run, the information necessary to fulfill the query must travel across the network, slowing the operation. In Figure 21-2 the network load is indicated by a thick, dashed line.

The situation shown in Figure 21-2 is made even worse when more than one user is using the same database. In this case, the network traffic is increased by the queries, forms opening, and other operations performed by each additional user's copy of Access. Imagine the dashed line getting thicker with each operation across the network.

The split database model is illustrated in Figure 21-3. Notice that the back-end database resides on the server while individual copies of the front-end database are placed on each workstation. Each front-end database contains links to the tables stored in the back-end `.accdb` file. For performance reasons, the front-end databases may also contain certain tables that are more efficiently used from the local machine than when they are stored on the file server. The front-end databases also contain the forms, reports, queries, and other user interface components of the application.

FIGURE 21-3

A database kept on a file server can generate a large amount of traffic on the network.

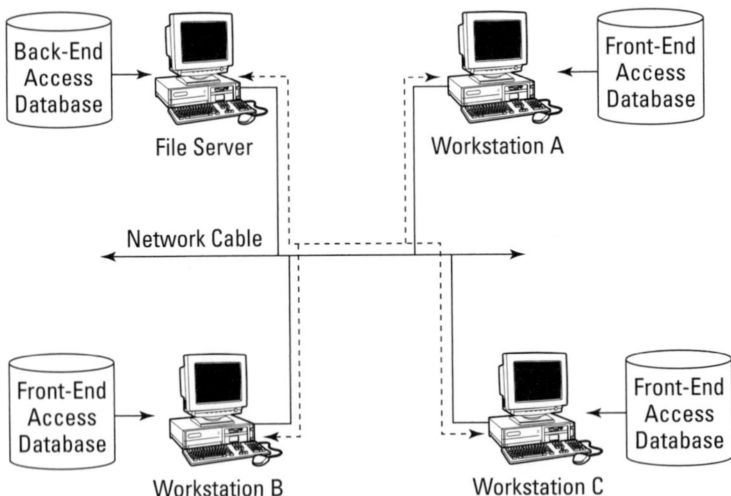

The network traffic is reduced in Figure 21-3 because only linking information and data returned by queries is moved across the network. A user working with the database application uses the forms, queries, reports, macros, and code stored in the local front-end `.accdb` file. Because the front end is accessed by a single user, response time is much improved because the local copy of

Access is able to instantly open the database and begin the startup operations. Only when actually running queries does the network traffic increase.

The second major benefit of the design in Figure 21-3 is that updating the forms, reports, and other application components requires nothing more than replacing the front-end database on each user's computer and reestablishing the links to the table in the back-end database. In fact, the design in Figure 21-3 supports the notion of customized front ends, depending on the requirements of the user sitting at each workstation. For instance, a manager sitting at Workstation A might need access to personnel information that is not available to the people sitting at workstations B and C. In this case the front-end database on Workstation A includes the forms, queries, and other database objects necessary to view the personnel information.

Figure 21-4 illustrates an elegant solution to the need to keep the front-end databases up to date. Instead of manually copying an updated front-end database to each user's workstation, the users in Figure 21-4 replicate their locally installed database with the front-end replica master located on the file server. As you'll see in Chapter 31, Access replicates database objects like forms and reports, as well as the data contained in tables.

FIGURE 21-4

Access replication can ease the task of updating local copies of database objects.

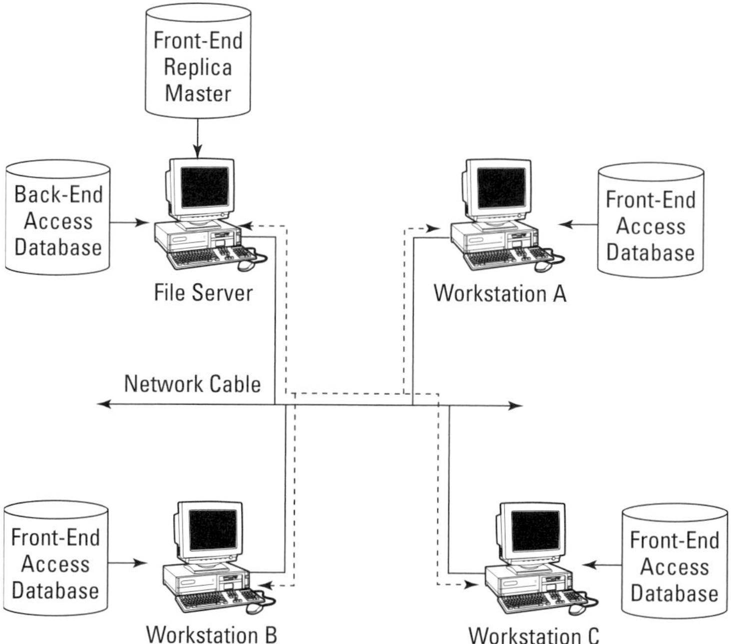

Where to put which objects

Not all tables need to be put into the back-end database. Generally speaking, any object that rarely changes should be kept in the front-end database, while those objects that change frequently are kept in the back-end `.accdb` file. Keeping tables in the local `.accdb` reduces network traffic — there's no reason to move static data such as state abbreviations, city names, and zip codes across the network. The local tables require updating only when the data changes.

The local `.accdb` also contains all of the user interface objects, including forms, reports, queries, macros, and modules. Keeping the user interface components on the local machine dramatically improves performance. There is no need to move forms, queries, or reports across the network. These objects are much more easily manipulated on the local machine than when accessed across the network.

All shared tables and tables that are changed at regular intervals really should be placed in the back-end database kept on the server. The server database is opened in shared mode, making all of its objects accessible to multiple users. The tables in the server database are linked to the front-end `.accdb` on each user's desktop. (There is no problem with simultaneously linking the same table to multiple databases.)

Obviously, with more than one person using the data within a table, the possibility exists that the same record will be edited by multiple users. Jet handles this problem by locking a record as it is edited by a user. A lock contention occurs when more than one user tries to update the same record. Only one user will have "live" access to the record — all other users will either be locked or have their changes held up until the record holder is done making changes.

We explain the Jet locking mechanism in detail later in this chapter.

Using the Database Splitter add-in

The Database Splitter helps you split an application into front-end and back-end databases. This wizard enables you to build and test your database to your heart's content, and then lightens the burden of preparing the application for multiuser access.

As an experiment, let's take a look at splitting the Northwind Traders database into front-end and back-end `.accdb` files. You start the Database Splitter by choosing the Tools tab of the Add-ins ribbon, then clicking on the Database Splitterin the Database Utilities group. The opening wizard screen (see Figure 21-5) explains the actions of the Database Splitter and suggests that you make a backup of the database before proceeding.

FIGURE 21-5

The Database Splitter is a very simple wizard.

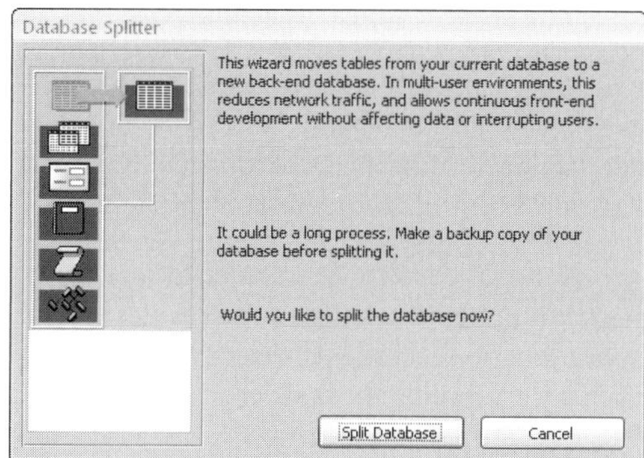

The only other information that the Database Splitter requires is where you want to put the back-end database. Figure 21-6 shows the familiar Explorer-style file dialog box that lets you specify the location of the back-end `.accdb` file. By default, the back-end database has the same name as the original database with a `_be` suffix added to the name (for example, `MyDB_be.accdb`). You should plan to put the back end exactly where it will reside in the production environment. Because the front-end database will contain links to the back-end database, and because links are path-specific, the links would have to be refreshed if the back end were moved after being built by the Database Splitter.

FIGURE 21-6

Specify the permanent location of the back-end database in the Create Back-end Database dialog box.

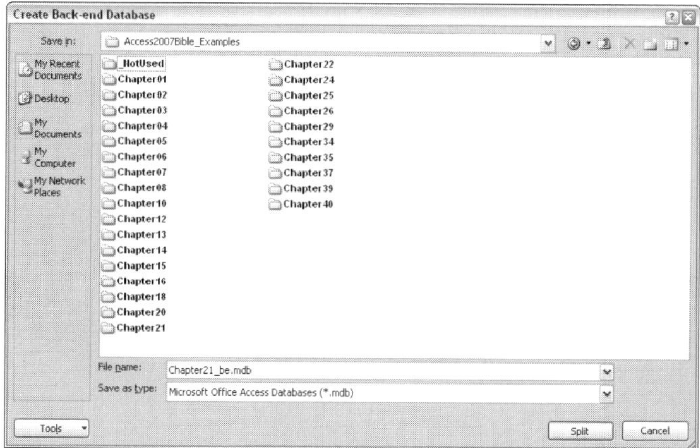

When you click on the Split button shown in Figure 21-6, the Database Splitter database creates the back-end database, exports all tables to it, deletes the tables in the local database, and creates links to the back-end tables. In other words, the Database Splitter performs precisely the same steps you'd have to perform manually if the Database Splitter weren't available.

You should be prepared for this process to take a little while, especially on large databases. Because Access has to create the new database, transfer tables to it, and create the links back to the original database, the splitting process can easily require more than a few minutes. Don't worry if the process appears to be taking longer than you expect — you'll be well rewarded for your efforts!

Figure 21-7 shows the Access Database Explorer after splitting the Northwind Traders database. The back-end database only contains the tables exported from `Northwind.accdb`. Notice that all of the tables in `Northwind.accdb` have been moved to the back-end database. You'll have to import any local tables from the back-end database before distributing the front end to the users.

FIGURE 21-7

The Database Splitter creates links for all tables in the database.

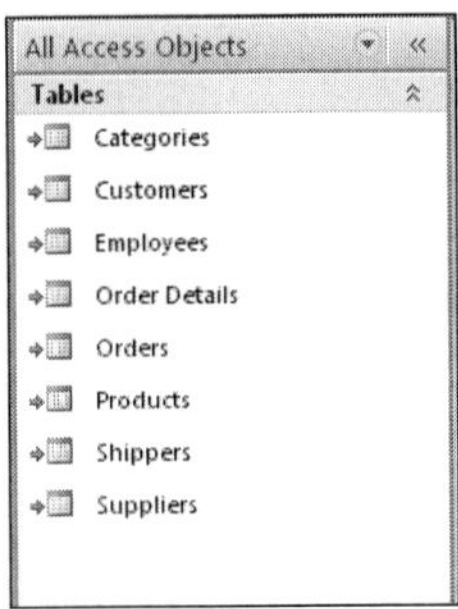

Keep in mind that in spite of the Database Splitter's simple interface, there is a lot going on behind the scenes. Splitting a large database can take several to many minutes to complete. The Database Splitter is rather naive about system considerations such as available disk space. Make sure adequate disk space exists on the target machine to accommodate the back-end database.

Locking Issues

In multiuser situations, one of the most nagging problems involves a situation where two or more users try to access the same record at the same time. Although Access lets you alter the way it locks records using built-in options, the best cure for record-locking problems is a combination of Access's record-lock settings, careful planning, and VBA error-handling procedures.

Access has long been criticized for its handling of record locks. Some of the older ISAM databases, and even some high-end server products, give you the ability to lock an individual row within a table or recordset. The advantage of this individual record-lock ability is its certainty: You know that only one person can access one record at a time. You can easily code procedures to handle single-record locks. In systems using record-locking schemes, it's easy to know which individual record is locked and handle lock contentions against that one record.

Access uses either row-level (record) locks or page locks. A page is a 2K-sized section of your table that Access pulls into memory when you want to change a record within a table. When using page locking (which is a good option if performance is an issue), Access locks the entire 2K page containing the record. If the record is greater than 2K, Access locks as many 2K pages as necessary to lock all of the record's data.

Page locking makes more efficient use of system resources by caching data locally, allowing you to have more responsive applications. The page-locking scheme in Access also corresponds to the locking behavior of high-end client-server database engines like SQL Server. After you've mastered the page locking mechanisms in Access, you have a much better understanding of how locking works in client-server environments.

When using record-level locking, Access locks only the record currently being edited. Record-level locking is a good option when many users are simultaneously editing and updating records. The only lock contention that occurs in such a situation happens when two users happen to change the same record at the same time.

Record-level locking is the default in Access 2007. If you choose to use page-level locking, open the Access Options dialog box (File ➪ Access Options ➪ Advanced) and deselect the Open Databases by Using Record-Level Locking check box. In most environments, however, you'll find that record-level locking works just fine.

When you design your applications, the type of database application that you're creating should drive the locking strategy that you apply to your applications. Decision support or EIS-type applications usually do not need any locks (No Locks or Read-Only access), because most users only view data and do not change or add new records to the underlying tables. However, if the records in your application are constantly changing as people add new records or edit existing data, then your locking strategy will be much more complex.

Access's built-in record-locking features

Access has several settings available at runtime and design time that you can change to control the locking behavior of your applications. The Access Options dialog box contains an Advanced page that contains record-lock settings for your databases (see Figure 21-8). Once set, these become the default behavior for your database and its objects. You can, however, change these defaults in code and in each individual form you create.

FIGURE 21-8

The Advanced tab in the Access Options dialog box

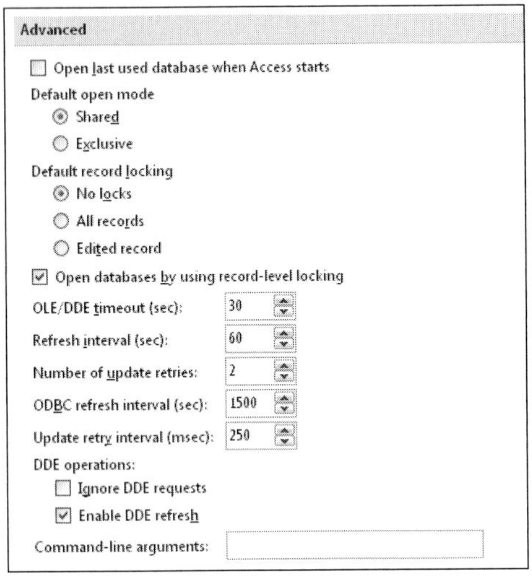

Advanced

☐ Open last used database when Access starts

Default open mode

◉ Shared

○ Exclusive

Default record locking

◉ No locks

○ All records

○ Edited record

☑ Open databases by using record-level locking

OLE/DDE timeout (sec): 30

Refresh interval (sec): 60

Number of update retries: 2

ODBC refresh interval (sec): 1500

Update retry interval (msec): 250

DDE operations:

☐ Ignore DDE requests

☑ Enable DDE refresh

Command-line arguments:

Default record locking controls whether or how Access handles locking when your users add, edit, or change records within a recordset. Once set, these settings apply globally to the objects you create within your database. The same settings exist within the Design view of forms, which will override the default settings of the Advanced tab.

- **No Locks:** Also called *optimistic locking,* this setting allows you or your users to add or edit a record without locking the page in which it exists. The only locking occurs during the split second when the update is actually written to the Access table. Thus, when No Locks is set, someone may be able to start an edit but may not be able to finish it. The No Locks setting is most appropriate in environments where users will be adding many records simultaneously. This will allow all adds to be started and almost all updates to be committed (unless two people save the record at the same time). Your error-handling routines must anticipate the errors that occur when the record is committed. The No Locks setting is called *optimistic locking* because you have every expectation that the record commit will proceed without error.
- **All Records:** The All Records setting locks an entire recordset as long as the user has the table, form, or query open for viewing. This setting really has no practical use in a dynamic multiuser environment. The only time it should be used is when you're doing some kind of administrative updates to a table and don't want anyone else editing records during the time you are updating.
- **Edited Record:** Also called *pessimistic locking*, this setting locks a record when a user tries to obtain a record for editing. Access locks the record (or page) at the moment a user begins editing a record, as opposed to No Locks, which locks the page only at the instant

the record is updated. Pessimistic locking is appropriate in applications where data will be changed frequently but not added. Pessimistic locking is a good choice in situations where data changes frequently. In these environments, you don't want two users trying to edit the same record at the same time. If they do, one user has the potential to overwrite the changes of the other. With Edited Record locking on, your application can capture an error when the second user tries to obtain the lock for editing. The application then notifies the user to wait until the other user is finished.

Default Open Mode

The Default Open Mode setting in the Advanced tab of the Access Options dialog box should always be set to Shared in multiuser applications (Shared is the default in Access 2007). After all, if everyone tried to open the application in Exclusive mode, no two users could use the database at the same time. You may use the Exclusive mode as the administrator to update files and tables, add forms, and so on.

Number of Update Retries

When two users try to update the same record at the same time, Access captures the error and tries to recover using the Number of Update Retries setting. The Number of Update Retries option tells Access how many times to attempt to update the record (where *x* is the number you have set) before it raises an error condition. In situations where you anticipate a high number of locking conflicts, set this option to a high number (10 is the maximum number of retries you can set, 2 is the default).

Update Retry Interval

This option controls the period of time Access waits to retry a lock. The maximum number is 1,000 (one second); the default is 250 (one-quarter second). Adjust this setting to accommodate the latency imposed by the network, slow computers, and other hardware constraints. An unnecessarily long Retry Interval and a high Number of Update Retries can result in an uncomfortably long interval before the user sees a locking error message. In most cases, using the No Locks option (optimistic locking) in conjunction with a brief Update Retry Interval, and a minimum number of update retries is adequate.

Refresh Interval

In multiuser environments, data is extremely volatile because it can be changed by many different people during the course of a day or even an hour. You want users to see the most current data displayed on forms and datasheets, so that they don't make decisions based on information that is no longer valid. Refresh Interval tells Access how long to wait before refreshing the data displayed in a form or datasheet with current data. This does not requery the data; it only refreshes it. Requerying reissues the query behind the recordset displayed. To illustrate the difference, imagine that two users are editing data and one deletes a record from a table that the other is viewing. When Access refreshes the underlying table for User 2, the record viewed will display `#Deleted` in all the columns of the record. If the form or datasheet is queried once again, the new recordset does not display the record at all because it no longer resides in the underlying table.

In situations where data will be added or edited frequently, set this number fairly low, say, 3 seconds. The default is 30, the minimum 0, and the maximum 32,766.

ODBC Refresh Interval

This setting is much like the previous one, except that special considerations must be made when using external data sources. ODBC links can be slow, and queries executed against these back-end databases can consume a lot of time and increase network traffic. When using ODBC data sources, the ODBC Refresh Interval should be set higher than you would set the Refresh Interval of an Access database. You'll notice that the default is 1,500 seconds (25 minutes!), much higher than the previous Refresh Interval. Its maximum number is also much smaller: 3,600. Before setting this option, experiment with the speed of your queries and tables, and monitor network resources when you issue reads from your back end. Setting the ODBC Refresh Interval too low will really bog down the system as Access hits the ODBC data source looking for data changes.

Record-Lock Error Handling

Even though you plan ahead and set Access's default settings to a number you think will handle record-locking problems in your application, you're bound to encounter conflicts sometime. The more users you have hitting your application, the better the chance that you'll encounter a locking conflict. You can capture the errors that Access throws up, however, and use VBA to communicate conflict solutions to your users.

In an effort to correct some performance problems and locking conflicts in earlier versions of Access, Microsoft has developed Access 2007 so that it caches more data in memory and writes data to disk only after the cache has been filled (unless specified in the engine's Registry keys). Although these enhancements do increase performance, they can make it harder to trap lock errors on specific records.

Here's an example: Mike is changing data on Machine A. Elizabeth is editing data on Machine B. Mike and Elizabeth both change the same record, but the record changed is cached in memory on Machine A along with several other records. Finally, Machine A runs out of cache space and flushes the cache to disk. Because a locking violation has occurred (even though time and records have long since passed the violation), Access flags an error. But because the record is being written along with several others, figuring out exactly which record lock caused the error is difficult.

Another problem with Access's caching behavior is latency. Because data is being stored in cache on each machine, changes that may have occurred to data on each machine will not be reflected to other users until the cache is flushed to disk. In order to solve both of these problems, you must use explicit transactions in your procedures. Explicit transactions enclose each transaction with `workspace.BeginTrans` and `workspace.CommitTrans` (ADO transactions are managed by the Connection object). Be aware, however, that you can encounter locking problems within your transactions, so be sure to provide adequate error handling.

By this time, you've gotten a taste of what can happen in your multiuser applications: Performance can suffer, and users can change each other's data and encounter errors when a locking conflict occurs. The good news is that you can plan for the errors, specifically by trapping for errors 3260, 3186, 3188, and 3197. The next sections explain what each of these errors means, and give you some routines to help you use them (instead of becoming their victim). In the following sections, we cover Error 3188 along with Error 3186.

A function to handle lock errors

Many of the routines in the following code listings call an error-handling function named `ErrorRoutine()`. Instead of each procedure having to trap and interpret every possible error, many developers condense error handling as a single public function (such as `ErrorRoutine`), and have the function interpret and handle errors as they occur. Each procedure in the application is responsible for trapping errors, but the errors are passed to `ErrorRoutine` for handling. `ErrorRoutine` may notify the user, log the error, or simply ignore the error, depending on the details of the error incident.

The `ErrorRoutine` function (shown in Listing 21-3) uses the `Err` object's `Number` property to determine which locking error has occurred, and takes action based on the error number and the `Flag` parameter to appropriately handle Jet locking problems. Most likely, you'll want to modify each error number to suit your users and their environment.

As you'll see in Chapter 25, there is but a single `Err` object in any VBA project, such as a Microsoft Access application. The `Error` object contains all of the details of an error incident, and because there is only one `Err` object in the entire project, any routine (such as `ErrorRoutine`) can use the information provided by the `Err` object.

`ErrorRoutine` accepts a single argument (`Flag`) that instructs `ErrorRoutine` to take specific actions depending on the value of `Flag`. You'll see this parameter passed to `ErrorRoutine` in the following sections. At this point, don't be too concerned with the details of how `ErrorRoutine` operates. You'll see the explanation for each of the branches in the `Select Case` statement in the following sections.

LISTING 21-3

A Function to Handle Locking Errors

```
Public Function ErrorRoutine(Flag As Integer) As Integer
    Dim lngCounter As Long
    Dim lngReturn As Long
    Dim strMessage As String

    Select Case Err.Number

        Case 3021
            'Let the error pass

        Case 3186
            '3186-Couldn't Save; currently
            'locked by user x on machine y.
            If Flag < 10 Then
              For lngCounter = 0 To 15000
                  'Empty loop for short delay...
              Next lngCounter
              ErrorRoutine = 3
            Else
              ParseError Err, Error
              ErrorRoutine = 4
            End If

        Case 3188
            'Record is locked by another
            'session on the same machine:
            MsgBox "The Record Could Not Be Locked " _
                & "Because It Is Locked On Your Machine"

        Case 3197
            '3197-Data has changed; Operation stopped.
            'Offer the user a chance to cancel
            'the edit or save the changes
            strMessage = "The record you are trying " _
                & "to save has been changed " _
                & "since your edit began." _
                & vbCrLf & vbCrLf _
                & "Do you want to save it anyway?"
            lngReturn = MsgBox(strMessage, vbYesNo)
            Select Case lngReturn
                Case vbYes
                    'Return 3:
                    ErrorRoutine = 3
                Case vbNo
                    'Return 4:
```

```
                ErrorRoutine = 4
            End Select

        Case 3260
            '3260—Couldn't Update; currently
            'locked by user x on machine y.
            'Record is locked on another machine:
            If Flag < 10 Then
                For lngCounter = 0 To 15000
                    'Empty loop for short delay...
                Next lngCounter
                ErrorRoutine = 3
            Else
                ParseError Err, Error
                ErrorRoutine = 4
            End If

        Case 3421
            strMessage = _
                "The Add was cancelled due to a " _
              & "type conversion error"
            lngReturn = MsgBox(strMessage, vbOKOnly)

        Case Else
            strMessage = _
                "The Error Number Was " & Err & " " & Error
            lngReturn = MsgBox(strMessage, vbInformation)
    End Select

End Function
```

Notice that `ErrorRoutine()` contains the error-handling segments for each of the errors discussed in the following sections. `ErrorRoutine()` could be extended, of course, to include the `ParseError()` subroutine, error logging and more extensive messaging, among other features.

Error 3260: Couldn't update; currently locked by user . . .

Remember pessimistic locking (see the "Access's built-in record-locking features" section, earlier in this chapter)? Error 3260 most often occurs when pessimistic locking is enabled in an application. It occurs when a user tries to lock a record for editing but another user already has the record locked (because that person is editing it). You can choose to try again within your code, but one of the problems inherent in pessimistic locking is that a user can hold a record for editing for an indefinite period of time. This means that you have to provide a failure mechanism within your code just in case you can't obtain the lock after trying several times.

Before you waste time on edit procedures, make sure you can obtain a lock on the record you want to edit. You can check to see if the record is locked by forcing the error (if there is one). All you have to do is enable pessimistic locking and try to edit the desired record. In an ADO application, pessimistic locking is implemented by setting the LockType parameter of the Recordset object's Open method:

```
rst.Open "Customers", _
  ActiveConnection:=conn, _
  CursorType:=adOpenForwardOnly, _
  LockType:=adLockReadOnly, _
  Options:=adCmdTableDirect
```

The enumerated values for LockType are shown in Table 21-1.

TABLE 21-1

Enumerated Values for LockType

Enumerated Constant	Numeric Value	Description
adLockBatchOptimistic	4	Specifies optimistic batch updates. This value is required for Batch Update mode.
adLockOptimistic	3	Optimistic locking on a record-by-record basis. The lock is applied only when the Update method is called.
adLockPessimistic	2	Pessimistic locking on a record-by-record basis. The lock is applied right after the user begins editing the record.
adLockReadOnly	1	The data is read-only.
adLockUnspecified	–1	No lock type specified.

In a DAO environment, use the LockEdits property (a Boolean) of a Recordset object to specify the default record-locking behavior of a recordset. Set LockEdits to True to specify pessimistic locking:

```
Recordset.LockEdits = True
```

Set LockEdits to False for optimistic locking:

```
Recordset.LockEdits = False
```

Listing 21-4 creates a recordset based on the Employees table and an EmployeeID passed to the function as an argument. It then sets record locking to pessimistic locking and tries to lock the record for editing. If the edit fails, the error handler (see the "A function to handle lock errors" section earlier in this chapter) uses an empty loop to wait a few seconds before trying the edit again. After four tries, the edit fails and the user is notified of the failure.

LISTING 21-4

Testing a Record Lock Using Pessimistic Locking

```
Function PessimisticLockRecordADO(ID As Long)
    Dim cnn As ADODB.Connection
    Dim rs As ADODB.Recordset
    Dim str As String
    Dim lngTryCount As Long

On Error GoTo LockRecord_Error

    str = "Provider=Microsoft.Jet.OLEDB.4.0;" _
        & "Data Source=C:\Data\MyDB.accdb"
    Set cnn = New ADODB.Connection

    str = "SELECT * FROM Employees WHERE " _
        & "Employees.Fields('EmployeeID') = " & ID

    'Open the recordset:
    rs.Open "Customers", _
      ActiveConnection:=cnn, _
      CursorType:=adOpenForwardOnly, _
      LockType:=adLockPessimistic, _
      Options:=adCmdTableDirect
    'Try to update a field:
    rs.Fields("LastName") = UCase(rs.Fields("LastName"))

LockRecord_Exit:
    rs.Close
    Set rs = Nothing
    cnn.Close
    Set cnn = Nothing
    Exit Function

LockRecord_Error:
    'Update Retry Count:
    lngTryCount = lngTryCount + 1
    'Call Error Routine, passing
    'in the number of retries:
    Select Case ErrorRoutine(lngTryCount)
        Case 3
            'Try again at the same statement
            'that caused the error:
            Resume
        Case 4
            MsgBox "Edit Cancelled"
            GoTo LockRecord_Exit
```

continued

LISTING 21-4 *(continued)*

```
    End Select
End Function



Function PessimisticLockRecordDAO(ID As Long)
    Dim db As DAO.Database
    Dim rs As DAO.Recordset
    Dim strSQL As String
    Dim lngTryCount As Long
    Dim lngCounter As Long

On Error GoTo LockRecord_Error

    Set db = CurrentDb
    sSQL = "SELECT * FROM Employees WHERE " _
         "Employees.Fields("EmployeeID") = "  & ID
    Set rs = db.OpenRecordset(sSQL)
    'Set record locking to Pessimistic Locking:
    rs.LockEdits = True
    rs.Edit
    rs.Fields("LastName") = UCase(rs.Fields("LastName"))

LockRecord_Exit:
    rs.Close
    Exit Function

LockRecord_Error:
    'Update Retry Count:
    lngTryCount = lngTryCount + 1
    'Call Error Routine, passing
    'in the number of retries:
    Select Case ErrorRoutine(lngTryCount)
        Case 3
            'Try again at the same statement
            'that caused the error:
            Resume
        Case 4
            MsgBox "Edit Cancelled"
            GoTo LockRecord_Exit
    End Select
End Function
```

The portion of code from `ErrorRoutine()` that handles this error is shown in the following listing. This code fragment contains an empty loop that provides a little bit of time for the lock to be released. As long as the value of `Flag` is less than 10, the loop will be executed and the value of `ErrorRoutine()` is set to 3. If `ErrorRoutine()` has been called 10 or more times, `ErrorRoutine()` is set to 4, which ends the attempt to rectify the situation.

```
    Case 3260
        ' Record is locked on another machine
        If Flag < 10 Then
          For lngCounter = 0 To 15000
              'Empty loop for short delay...
          Next lngCounter
          ErrorRoutine = 3
        Else
          ParseError Err, Error
          ErrorRoutine = 4
        End If
```

Error 3186: Couldn't save; currently locked by user x on machine y

Sound familiar? This error is much like Error 3260, except for one difference: 3260 states that the record couldn't be updated; 3186 states that the record couldn't be saved. You can't update a record that you can't get a lock on for editing (pessimistic locking). But if you can get a lock on a record but not save it, it must be an optimistic record-locking error.

As an example, let's say two users are trying to edit the same record, but one is using pessimistic locking and the other is using optimistic locking. Both can pull the record into memory for updating because one of the two users is set to optimistic locking. If the user with optimistic locking tries to save while the pessimist is still editing, the optimist one is likely to get Error 3186. The same could happen if two optimistic updates were committed at the same time (a less likely situation).

Listing 21-5 shows how to test for locking status on a record that's been obtained using optimistic locking. Actually, there's not much difference except that an edit takes place (`rs.Fields("Lastname") = "Smith"`) using optimistic locking (`LockType: =adLockOptimistic`). Contrary to Listing 21-4, the error occurs as the record is updated instead of as it is edited. Again, when the error occurs, the global error handler is called to deal with the error.

LISTING 21-5

Testing a Record Lock Using Optimistic Locking

```
Function OptimisticLockRecordADO(ID As Long)
    Dim cnn As ADODB.Connection
    Dim rs As ADODB.Recordset
```

continued

LISTING 21-5 *(continued)*

```
    Dim str As String
    Dim lngTryCount As Long

On Error GoTo LockRecord_Error

    str = "Provider=Microsoft.Jet.OLEDB.4.0;" _
        & "Data Source=C:\Data\MyDB.accdb"
    Set cnn = New ADODB.Connection

    str = "SELECT * FROM Employees WHERE " _
        & "Employees.Fields('EmployeeID') = " & ID

    'Open the recordset:
    rs.Open "Customers", _
      ActiveConnection:=cnn, _
      CursorType:=adOpenForwardOnly, _
      LockType:=adLockOptimistic, _
      Options:=adCmdTableDirect
    'Try to update a field:
    rs.Fields("LastName") = UCase(rs.Fields("LastName"))

LockRecord_Exit:
    rs.Close
    Set rs = Nothing
    cnn.Close
    Set cnn = Nothing
    Exit Function

LockRecord_Error:
    'Update Retry Count:
    lngTryCount = lngTryCount + 1
    'Call Error Routine, passing
    'in the number of retries:
    Select Case ErrorRoutine(lngTryCount)
        Case 3
            'Try again at the same statement
            'that caused the error:
            Resume
        Case 4
            MsgBox "Edit Cancelled"
            GoTo LockRecord_Exit
    End Select
End Function
```

Again, a `Select Case` construct is used to handle the value returned by `ErrorRoutine()`. The function is stopped only when the value of ErrorRoutine() is 4. The portion of `ErrorRoutine()` for handling Error 3186 is shown in the following listing:

```
Case 3186
    ' Record is locked on another machine
    If Flag < 10 Then
      For lngCounter = 0 To 15000
          'Empty loop for short delay...
      Next lngCounter
      ErrorRoutine = 3
    Else
      ParseError Err, Error
      ErrorRoutine = 4
    End If
```

The code in this listing is identical to Listing 21-4. Because of the similarities between errors 3260 and 3186, they may be handled with the same logic. In fact, you can combine the `Case` routines for errors 3260 and 3186 into a single statement:

```
Case 3260, 3186:
```

What about Error 3188?

Error 3188 occurs when someone has more than one instance of a database open on the same machine and tries to lock the same record in both sessions. Error handling is simple for this error; it is included in the global error handler (`ErrorRoutine()`) in the Chapter21.accdb example database.

To keep this error from occurring altogether, try to keep users from starting more than one instance of your application. You can do this using the `FindWindow` API in your startup routine. Check for a running instance of Access at startup, and close the second instance if another is present.

The error handler called by both of these examples is really very simple. It merely reads the current error and uses a `Select` statement to decide what to do. The only errors we've included in this module (`modErrorHandlers`) relate to this chapter. You'll notice that the `ErrorRoutine` function has entries for error numbers 3186 and 3260. Each of these calls another subroutine, `ParseError`. `ParseError` (in module `modParseError`) accepts the error number and error message as arguments, and parses the user name and the machine name from errors 3260 and 3186. It doesn't matter which error has occurred because the parsing routine looks only for the `"user"` and `"on machine"` string values within the error message, so it's pretty generic. In fact, this same subroutine is called from both errors. You can make the default Access error message more descriptive, and you can also make use of the user ID and machine number within your error log (if you keep one). The code follows:

```
Public Sub ParseError(lngErr As Long, strError As String)
  Dim strUser As String
  Dim strMachine As String
  Dim lngUserStart As Long
  Dim lngMachineStart As Long
  Dim lngMachineEnd As Long

  lngUserStart = InStr(1, strError, "user") + 5
  lngMachineStart = _
```

```
        InStr(lngUserStart, strError, " on machine")
    lngMachineEnd = InStr(lngMachineStart, strError, ".")
    strUser = Mid$(strError, lngUserStart, _
        lngMachineStart - lngUserStart)
    strMachine = Mid$(strError, lngMachineStart + 12, _
        lngMachineEnd - (lngMachineStart + 12))
    MsgBox "The Record Could Not Be Locked " _
        & "Because It Is Locked On " _
        & strMachine & " By " & strUser
End Sub
```

Error: 3197: Data has changed; operation stopped

Error 3197 can be one of the most confusing errors to an end user if it isn't captured through a VBA error handler. It usually occurs when optimistic locking is enabled in an application, but it may also occur in an environment containing mixed record-lock settings as well. Mike starts an edit on his machine. During the course of the edit (Mike is a slow typist), Elizabeth starts and finishes an edit on the same record. This means that the underlying data that Mike is editing is no longer valid, so an error is flagged when he tries to issue the `Update` method. The resulting Access message box is shown in Figure 21-9.

FIGURE 21-9

The Access error message for Error 3197

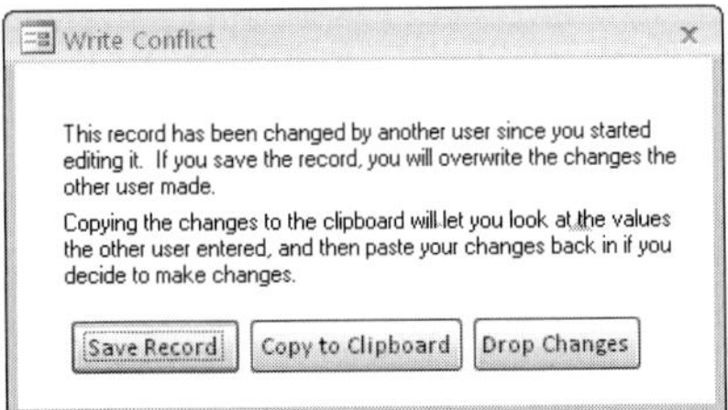

By default, Access gives your users three choices: Save the record with the changes they have made, copy the changes to the clipboard, or abort the changes altogether. Options 1 and 3 make sense, but Option 2 (Copy to Clipboard) has never seemed practical to me. Anyway, there are too many choices for the average person to make, especially when the options aren't self-explanatory. The best option is to offer the user the option of saving his changes or aborting the edit, and then deliver the message in a format that's easy to understand. Besides a meaningful error message, you might want to offer to show your users the changes that have been made by refreshing the current form or opening a form based on the record that has been changed.

The actual error handling is straightforward. A record update throws up an error the first time it is executed. It is at this point that your code captures the error. Then all you have to do is give the user the options you think best. If the user chooses to save the record, the update does cause an error the next time you issue it (unless another locking conflict occurs). Listing 21-6 shows an example of this type of procedure. Like the previous examples, an edit is attempted; but if it fails, control is transferred to the error handler. However, in the previous examples the edit either failed or didn't fail after 10 retries. `SaveChanges()` just gives the user a chance to overwrite or cancel.

LISTING 21-6

Handling "Data has changed" errors

```
Function SaveChanges(ID As Long)
    Dim cnn As ADODB.Connection
    Dim rs As ADODB.Recordset
    Dim str As String
    Dim lngTryCount As Long

On Error GoTo LockRecord_Error

    str = "Provider=Microsoft.Jet.OLEDB.4.0;" _
        & "Data Source=C:\Data\MyDB.accdb"
    Set cnn = New ADODB.Connection

    str = "SELECT * FROM Employees WHERE " _
        & "Employees.Fields('EmployeeID') = " & ID

    'Open the recordset:
    rs.Open "Customers", _
      ActiveConnection:=cnn, _
      CursorType:=adOpenForwardOnly, _
      LockType:=adLockOptimistic, _
      Options:=adCmdTableDirect

    'Try to update a field:
    rs.Fields("LastName") = UCase(rs.Fields("LastName"))

LockRecord_Exit:
  ' Exit The Procedure
  rs.Close
  Exit Function

LockRecord_Error:
    Select Case ErrorRoutine(0)
        Case 3
            rs.Update
            MsgBox "Record Was Updated!"
        Case 4
            MsgBox "Edit Was Cancelled!"
    End Select
    GoTo LockRecord_Exit

End Function
```

The portion of `ErrorRoutine()` for handling this error is shown here. Notice how the user is prompted for the action to be taken. The messaging in this routine is easier to understand than what you see in Figure 21-9, and the user's wishes are carried out in a more sophisticated manner than the default Access actions. Notice also that the option to copy the data to the clipboard is not provided because this routine assumes that the user wants either to save the record or to abandon changes.

```
Case 3197
     ' Offer the user a chance to cancel
     ' the edit or save the changes
     strMessage = "The record you are trying " _
        & "to save has been changed " _
        & "since your edit began" _
        & vbCrLf & vbCrLf _
        & "Do you want to save it anyway?"
     lngReturn = MsgBox(strMessage, vbYesNo)
     Select Case lngReturn
         Case vbYes
             ErrorRoutine = 3
         Case vbNo
             ErrorRoutine = 4
     End Select
```

Using Unbound Forms in Multiuser Environments

Everything in the previous discussion is relevant to any multiuser Access environment. However, when you use a *bound form* (a form with an attached recordset), you're more likely to encounter some of the negative situations mentioned. Yet another way to decrease the likelihood of encountering multiuser errors is to create and use unbound forms. Unbound forms have advantages and disadvantages, but they may be worth exploring if you want more control over your applications.

Unbound forms give you complete control over your user interface. All the updating, movement, editing, adding, and saving is executed by code, rather than by Access's default behavior. Record-locking errors are less frequent because the user has direct control over edits and updates, instead of relying on Access to do the dirty work.

Consider this scenario: Two users are sharing an application across a network. The application uses a pessimistic locking strategy and forms directly bound to the underlying recordsets. Both users try to edit a particular record at the same time and — *bam!* — a locking error occurs. Why? Because when both users try to edit the record, only the first user gets to lock the record. The lock stays in effect until the record is updated in the recordset by the user who got there first. Meanwhile, the other user has to wait.

However, when using unbound forms, editing a record on a form probably won't trigger record locks. There's nothing behind the form, so no recordset locks are established. When the user clicks on the Save button, the application probably does a quick add or update to the recordset, only holding the lock for a split second. You're much less likely to hit a lock error with unbound forms.

You may, however, immediately see the disadvantages of this situation: Access does a lot for you when you bind forms to underlying recordsets. The less you let Access do, the more code you'll have to write. The more code you write, the more you have to maintain and update. The more you maintain, the less predictable your applications will become. It's a vicious cycle but one that may be necessary for complex applications. You also can't take advantage of all the valuable actions that Access performs on your behalf. Access is pretty smart and doesn't screw up too often. Also, you can't use continuous forms when no recordset is attached to the form, which can be a very useful view of your data.

ON the CD-ROM **We've put together a sample unbound form in the example database for this chapter (`Chapter28.accdb`) located on the companion CD. The form, named `frmEmployees`, works much like a typical form: you can go to the first record, next record, last record, and previous record, and add, edit, and save records in the `Employees` table. But there is no data behind this form. All the work takes place in a collection of routines in the `modUnboundMethods` module. We'll take you through each method and discuss how it works and how you can apply it to your own forms. The form is shown in Figure 21-10.**

FIGURE 21-10

The unbound `Employees` form

Creating an unbound form

Creating an unbound form doesn't take a lot of special skill, just some planning ahead of time and a few shortcuts. We try to make the process as easy as possible by first creating a bound form that looks and behaves as close to the finished product as we can. The reason we do this is because all our fields get named correctly, they keep the formatting we've set for them in my tables, we don't have to set label captions, and so forth. The naming part is important, for reusability reasons that you'll discover as we populate controls with data. After we've finished creating the look of the form, we move to the `RecordSource` property of the form and delete it. Ta da! You now have an unbound form. Of course, it doesn't do anything, but it looks good.

Making it work

There are several events your form has to respond to, such as advancing to a record, adding, editing, updating, and so forth. To do this, I've created a separate routine that responds to each event. Each procedure accepts at least the name of the calling form and the recordset it's based on. You tell the form what recordset you want to use by placing its name in the form's `Tag` property.

The Tag property

The routines in the following section make extensive use of the `Tag` property of forms and controls. The `Tag` property is unique in that it doesn't do anything. That's what makes it so useful. You can use it as a place to store information for later retrieval or to keep track of where you are in a process. Here's a good example of what you can do with the `Tag` property: Suppose you want your application to have the ability to fill in each new record with data from the previous record. Using the `Tag` property, you can store the current record's values in each control's `Tag` property, and, upon moving to the next new record, fill in the form's controls with the values stored in the `Tag`. It's a whole lot easier than doing a lookup using a hidden field on a form and the `Seek` method on a clone of the form's recordset, which is an alternative we've seen some people use.

The `Tag` property was introduced way back in Access Version 2, but many developers don't know it exists or aren't sure what it's for. We encourage you to use this property often.

The form Open event

The first event you must respond to is the `Open` event of the form. When this event fires, there are a few things that need to be done to populate the unbound form. The first is to open the recordset that will be filled with the data displayed on the form. You don't have to do this — you could just open a new recordset instance in each routine behind the form — but it's faster to just have a recordset open and waiting as the form opens. The second thing you need to do is update the form with some data. Again, you don't have to, but many times a user expects to see something on a form when it opens. The Declarations section of the form contains two public variables, `db` (database) and `rs` (recordset). The form's `Open` event runs a very short procedure that sets the database and recordset variables to their proper values and calls the `Unbound Display` routine that loads the first record of the recordset into the form's fields:

```
Private cnn As ADODB.Connection
Private rs As ADODB.Recordset

Private Sub Form_Open(Cancel As Integer)
    Dim intReturn As Integer
    Dim str As String
    str = "Provider=Microsoft.Jet.OLEDB.4.0;" _
        & "Data Source=C:\Data\MyDB.accdb "
```

```
    Set cnn = New ADODB.Connection
    cnn.Open (str)

    Set rs = New ADODB.Recordset
    rs.Open "tblCustomers", _
        ActiveConnection:=cnn, _
        CursorType:=adOpenForwardOnly, _
        LockType:= adLockOptimistic, _
        Options:=adCmdTableDirect

    intReturn = UnboundDisplay(Me, rs)
End Sub
```

The real work begins in the `UnboundDisplay` procedure. Like most of the unbound methods, this routine accepts the name of the form and the name of the open recordset. The key to making this practical is making your routines as reusable as possible. It's good practice anytime but especially in situations where you'll be doing the same type of routine several times. For instance, you shouldn't create routines that require a recordset named `Employees`, because the database may have unbound forms based on other tables that act the same way as the `Employees` form. `UnboundDisplay` is a reusable function. Because we created the form as a bound form first, the control names on the form should be the same as the field names in the recordset. Because you have the recordset open, the names of the controls on your form are readily available. `UnboundDisplay` cycles through the recordset, setting the value of each form control equal to the value of its corresponding recordset field value. The following listing shows the code for `UnboundDisplay`:

```
Function UnboundDisplay( _
    frm As Form, _
    frmRS As Recordset) As Integer

    Dim ctlName As String
    Dim lngReturn As Long
    Dim x As Integer

On Error GoTo Display_Err

    frmRS.MoveFirst  'Move to the first record

    'Cycle through the recordset, setting the
    'value of each control on the form.
    For x = 0 To frmRS.Fields.Count - 1
        ctlName = frmRS.Fields(x).Name
        frm.Controls(ctlName).Value = frmRS.Fields(x).Value
    Next x

Display_End:
    Exit Function

Display_Err:
    'If there's an error, switch to
```

```
    'the error handling procedure:
    lngReturn = ErrorRoutine(0)
    GoTo Display_End

End Function
```

Moving through records

A user can move through records on the Employee form in either of two ways: by using one of the navigation buttons we've created (you can't use Access's navigation buttons on an unbound form) or by searching for a record using a combo box. The navigation buttons we've created are based on four routines, each of which work similarly. The UnboundMoveFirst and UnboundMoveLast routines accept the name of the form you're using and the open recordset as arguments. All they do is issue a MoveFirst or MoveLast method on the recordset variable to move to the desired location.

```
Function UnboundMoveFirst( _
    frm As Form, _
    frmRS As Recordset) As Integer

    Dim ctlName As String
    Dim x As Integer
    Dim lngReturn As Long

On Error GoTo MoveFirst_Err

    frmRS.MoveFirst

    For x = 0 To frmRS.Fields.Count - 1
      ctlName = frmRS.Fields(x).Name
      frm.Controls(ctlName).Value = frmRS.Fields(x).Value
    Next x

MoveFirst_End:
    Exit Function

MoveFirst_Err:
    lngReturn = ErrorRoutine(0)
    GoTo MoveFirst_End
End Function
```

NOTE **The code for UnboundMoveLast is not given here because it is nearly identical to UnboundMoveFirst. Simply use MoveLast instead of MoveFirst, and make a few other minor changes, and you've got UnboundMoveLast.**

The UnboundMoveNext and UnboundMovePrevious procedures accept the name of the form and recordset, but they also include the employee ID of the currently displayed employee record. When you call the MoveNext or MovePrevious procedure, the function that was called sets the index of the recordset to the primary key and does a seek to place the cursor at the name of the employee whose record is displayed. If the record is found (`If Not frmRS.NoMatch`), which should always be the case unless the record displayed is the last or first record in the recordset, you issue a `MoveNext` or `MovePrevious` method on the recordset to move to the desired record. The last step in the procedure is to update the controls on your form with data from the recordset.

NOTE The code for `UnboundMovePrevious` is not given here because it is nearly identical to `UnboundMoveFirst`. Simply use `MovePrevious` instead of `MoveNext`, and make a few other minor changes and you've got `UnboundMoveFirst`.

```
Function UnboundMoveNext( _
    frm As Form, _
    frmRS As DAO.Recordset, _
    lValue As Long) As Integer

    Dim ctlName As String
    Dim x As Integer
    Dim lngReturn As Long

On Error GoTo MoveNext_Err

    'Move to the next employee record:
    frmRS.INDEX = "PrimaryKey"
    frmRS.Seek "=", lValue  'Search for displayed employee

    If Not frmRS.NoMatch Then
        ' Move to the next employee record
        frmRS.MoveNext
        For x = 0 To frmRS.Fields.Count - 1
            ctlName = frmRS.Fields(x).Name
            frm.Controls(ctlName).Value = _
            frmRS.Fields(x).Value
        Next x
    End If

MoveNext_End:
    Exit Function

MoveNext_Err:
    lngReturn = ErrorRoutine(0)
    GoTo MoveNext_End
End Function
```

The second method for changing position within the form's recordset is by using a combo box. The combo box `cboEmployee` uses the employee's ID number which is the bound column of the combo box. It is passed to the `UnboundSearch` function (shown here) as the variable `lValue`, which is called when the `AfterUpdate` event is triggered. `UnboundSearch` sets the recordset's index property to `EmployeeID` then uses the `Seek` method to locate the employee chosen. If a match is found after using the `Seek` method, the now familiar looping routine is used to extract field values from the recordset and fill in the corresponding controls on the `Employees` form. The code is shown here:

```
Function UnboundSearch( _
    frm As Form, _
    frmRS As DAO.Recordset, _
    lValue As Long) As Integer

    Dim ctlName As String
    Dim x As Integer
    frmRS.Index = "PrimaryKey"
    frmRS.Seek "=", lValue

    If Not frmRS.NoMatch Then
        For x = 0 To frmRS.Fields.Count - 1
            ctlName = frmRS.Fields(x).Name
            frm.Controls(ctlName).Value = _
                frmRS.Fields(x).Value
        Next x
    End If
End Function
```

Editing data

The last action you need to provide for in your unbound form is editing. You must be able to add, remove, edit, and save data. The `Employees` form does all of these (except deletions, but that can be accomplished using the `Delete` method and the examples shown here). Although it's really not that involved, these routines are the reason you created an unbound form in the first place. Because they don't take any action on the recordset until update time, your users shouldn't have trouble with locks.

When someone clicks on the Add button, a couple of things happen:

- **The controls on the form are selectively enabled or disabled.** By default, this form is set to browse data, as evidenced by the disabled data entry fields and disabled Save command button. When an add takes place, the data entry fields and Save button are enabled, but everything else is disabled (to keep users from wandering until the add is successfully completed). When the users type information into form controls, they're really just typing the data into placeholders. No action has occurred in the recordset.
- **We need to set some value to let us know what kind of action we have in progress.** To do this, the Save button's `Tag` property is set to `Add`. Later, this value will be retrieved and sent to the update routine.

When the Save command button is hit, its `OnClick` event runs the `UnboundSave` procedure, passing the procedure the value of the button's `Tag` property. Listing 21-7 shows the procedure. Notice that every effort has been made to assure a successful update: Locking is set to optimistic locking (`LockEdits = False`), and transactions are used on the current workspace. The procedure uses a `Select` statement and the value passed from the `Tag` property to decide what action should be taken. The update is essentially the reverse of the `UpdateDisplay` procedure, with a few exceptions. An `AddNew` (or `Edit`) method is invoked, and again we step through each field in the recordset's Fields collection, this time updating values in the recordset instead of updating controls on the form.

Another difference is the use of the EmployeeID's Tag property. If you open the form and check the Tag property of the control EmployeeID, you'll see the string value Key. This lets the procedure know that this value should not be updated. Why? It's a counter (AutoNumber), and you can't update a counter. If you try, the routine will flag an error. After all the fields have been set, the update method is invoked. This is the only time a record-lock error can occur — this split second. If it does fail, which is unlikely, the procedure can roll back the transaction.

LISTING 21-7

UnboundSave

```
Function UnboundSave( _
    frm As Form, _
    frmRS As DAO.Recordset, _
    ID As Long, _
    sAction As Variant) As Integer

    Dim ws As Workspace
    Dim ctlName As String
    Dim ctl As Control
    Dim x As Integer

On Error GoTo Save_Err

    frmRS.LockEdits = False   ' Pessimistic Locking
    Set ws = DBEngine.Workspaces(0)

    Select Case sAction
        Case "Add"
            ws.BeginTrans
            frmRS.AddNew
            For x = 0 To frmRS.Fields.Count - 1
                ctlName = frmRS(x).Name
                Set ctl = frm.Controls(ctlName)
                If ctl.Tag = "Key" Then
                    'Do nothing...
                Else
                    frmRS.Fields(ctlName).Value = ctl.Value
                End If
            Next x

        Case "Edit"
            frmRS.Index = "PrimaryKey"
            frmRS.Seek "=", Flag
            ws.BeginTrans
            frmRS.Edit
            For x = 0 To frmRS.Fields.Count - 1
                ctlName = frmRS(x).Name
```

continued

LISTING 21-7 *(continued)*

```
                Set ctl = frm.Controls(ctlName)
                If ctl.Tag = "Key" Then
                Else
                    frmRS.Fields(ctlName).Value = ctl.Value
                End If
            Next x

        Case Else
            GoTo Save_End

    End Select
    frmRS.UPDATE
    ws.CommitTrans

Save_End:
    Exit Function

Save_Err:
    ws.Rollback
    GoTo Save_End
End Function
```

The process for editing a record is the same, except that the `Tag` property of the `cmdSave` command button is set to `Edit`, and the `Seek` method is used in the `UnboundSave` procedure to search for the record that has been edited. Once the match is found, the `Edit` method is invoked and the fields in the recordset are updated.

After the update is complete, the private form procedure `EnableButtons` is called (from the `cmdSave` button's `OnClick` event), and the appropriate fields are enabled/disabled.

Summary

Access is perfect for single-user database application development. It's also excellent in a multiuser environment, but there are more opportunities for things to go wrong. You have to do some careful planning before creating multiuser applications, in order to ensure their success. You have to take into consideration network speed, number of users, type of application (data-entry, EIS), and update volume (high number of additions, high number of edits, high number of data selection) when planning and implementing a multiuser Access application. Only after extensive planning can you decide on the best approach for handling Access's record-locking behavior. You should decide which of the wide variety of options (retries and refresh rate, trapping errors, using bound or unbound forms, and so on) make the most sense for your users, and carefully apply those techniques to your applications.

Chapter 22

Integrating Access with Other Applications

IN THIS CHAPTER

- Using Automation to integrate with other applications
- Adding Automation references
- Creating an instance of an Automation object
- Getting an existing object instance
- Closing an instance of an Automation object
- Using Microsoft Word to create an Automation example
- Using Word's Macro Recorder
- Collecting data with Outlook 2007

As companies standardize their computer practices and software selections, it is becoming more and more important to develop *total* solutions: in other words, solutions that integrate the many procedures of an organization. Usually, various procedures are accomplished by using different software packages, such as Word for letter writing, Exchange and Outlook for mailing and faxing, PowerPoint for presentations, and Excel for financial functions. If the organization for which you are developing has standardized on the Microsoft Office suite, you can leverage your knowledge of Visual Basic for Applications to program for all of these products.

NOTE *Automation,* formerly called *OLE Automation,* is a means by which an application can expose objects, each with its own methods and properties that other applications can create instances of and control through code. Not all commercial applications support Automation, but more and more applications are adopting Automation to replace the outdated DDE interface. Consult with a specific application's vendor to find out whether it supports or plans to support Automation in the program.

ON the CD-ROM This chapter uses a database named `Chapter22.accdb`. A Word template file, named `Thanks.dotx`, is also included for use in this chapter. If you have not already copied these files onto your computer from the CD, you need to do so now. Because this chapter relies on the use of VBA code, it and the forms that are driven by it have already been created for you.

Using Automation to Integrate with Office

The Microsoft Office applications mentioned in the previous section all support Automation. Using Automation, you can create objects in your code that represent other applications. By manipulating these objects (setting properties and calling methods), you can control the referenced applications as though you were programming directly in them, thus allowing you to create seamless integrated applications by using Automation.

Creating Automation references

Applications supporting Automation provide information about their objects in an *object library*. The object library contains information about an application's properties, methods, and *classes*. An application's class is its internal structure for objects; each class creates a specific type of object — a form, a report, and so on. To reference an application's objects, VBA must determine which specific type of object is being referenced by an object's variable in your code. The process of determining the type of an object variable is called *binding*. You can use two methods for binding an object — *early binding* and *late binding*.

Early binding an object

Using the References dialog box in the Access VBA editor window, you can explicitly reference an object library. When you explicitly reference an object library, you are performing early binding. Automation code executes more quickly when you use early binding than when you use late binding.

To access the References dialog box of VBA, you need to activate the VBA editor window by either creating a new module or displaying the design of an existing module.

To create a reference, first create a new module or open an existing module in the VBA editor window. After you open a module in the VBA editor the References menu command is available in the Tools menu. Figure 22-1 shows the References selection on the Tools menu. Select Tools ➪ References to access the References dialog box. Figure 22-2 shows the References dialog.

FIGURE 22-1

The References option is available on the Tools menu only after you have a module in Design or New view in Access.

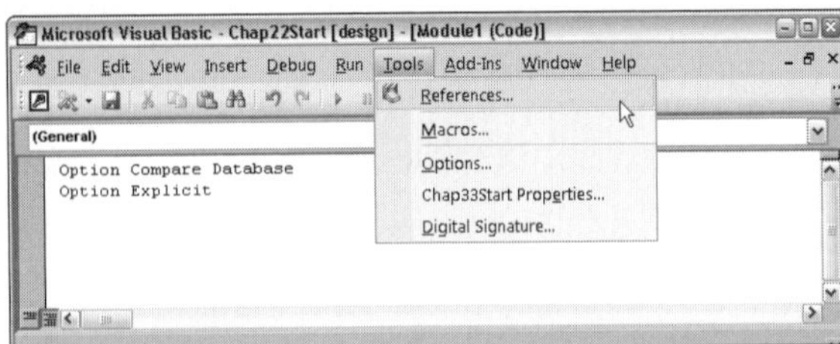

FIGURE 22-2

Early binding by setting references is the most efficient way to perform Automation.

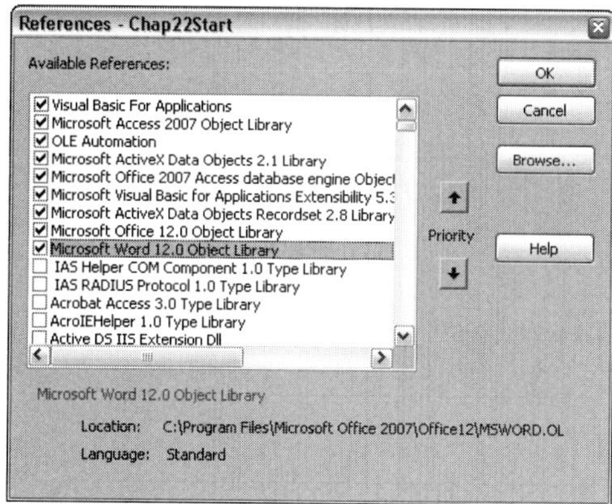

In the References dialog box, you specify all the references that your application needs for using Automation or for using other Access databases as library databases. To select or deselect a reference, click its check box.

For this chapter, you need to make sure that several reference libraries are active. You may not initially have the following four references available (checked):

```
Microsoft DAO 3.6 Object Library
Microsoft ActiveX Data Objects Recordset 2.8 Library
Microsoft Word 12.0 Object Library
Microsoft Office 12.0 Object Library
```

If these libraries aren't active (or, visible at the top of the list), find them in the selection list box by scrolling to them, and then check them.

After you reference an Automation object library, you can explicitly declare object variables from the referenced library. The VBA IntelliSense help feature displays the objects contained within the library as you type, as shown in Figure 22-3. In addition, after you select an object and enter a period (.), IntelliSense shows you the available classes within the object (see Figure 22-4).

Late binding an object

If you don't explicitly reference an object library by using the References dialog box, you can set an object's reference in code by first declaring a variable as an object and then using the Set command to create the object reference. This process is known as *late binding*.

To create an object to reference Microsoft Word, for example, you can use the following code:

```
Dim WordObj As Object
Set WordObj = New Word.Application
```

The `Set` command is discussed in the next section.

If you create an object for an application that is not referenced, an IntelliSense drop-down, such as the ones shown in Figures 22-3 and 22-4, won't display.

FIGURE 22-3

When an Automation Server is referenced, its objects are immediately known by VBA.

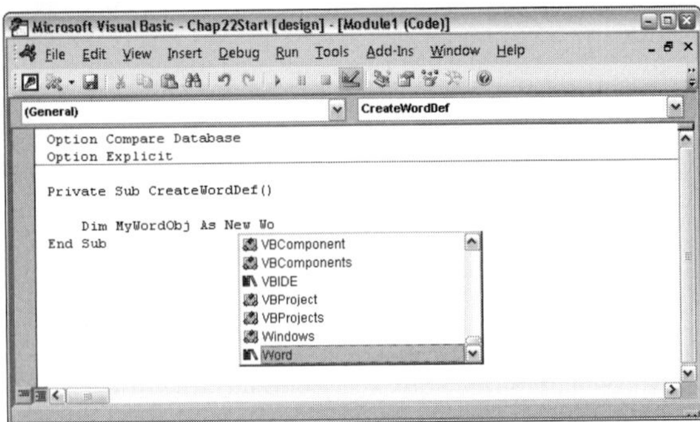

Figure 22-3 shows the IntelliSense drop-down that appears immediately after you type the word new in the `Dim` statement. At this point, you can select one of the application object name types displayed (such as *Word*) or enter a new application object name type that you define.

In Figure 22-3, IntelliSense shows *Word*, which is a library, as indicated by the books icon. This icon distinguishes a library object from a simpler class object in the list, such as VBProject. Libraries contain one or more classes, whereas classes contain properties, methods, and events. The class objects you see in Figure 22-3 (`VBComponent`, `VBComponents`, `VBProject`, and so on) are included within other libraries referenced by the `Chapter22.accdb` application.

FIGURE 22-4

The VBA IntelliSense feature makes it easy to use Automation Servers.

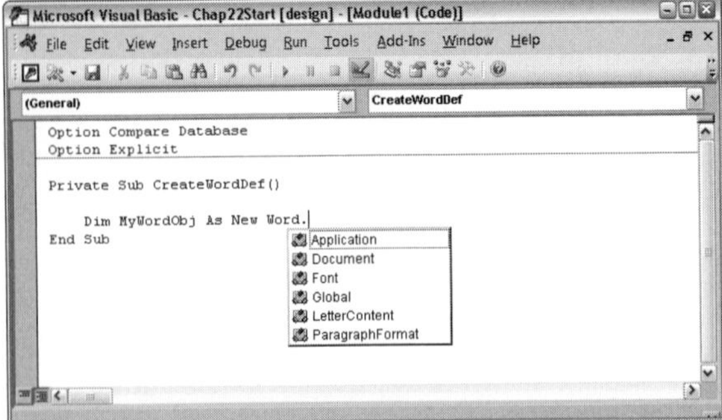

Figure 22-4 shows the IntelliSense drop-down list that appears when you type a period (.) after the object type *Word*. This drop-down list helps you by displaying all known object types that can be associated with the particular primary object name. In this case, clicking the Application object type adds this to the *Word.* portion of the object, thus *Word.application*.

Creating an instance of an Automation object

To perform an Automation operation, the operating system needs to start the application — if it isn't already started — and obtain a reference, or *handle*, to it. This reference will be used to access the application. Most applications that support Automation, called *Automation Servers,* expose an Application object. The Application object exists at the top of the object application's hierarchy and often contains many objects, as well.

Using the New keyword to create a new instance

The simplest (and most efficient) method to create any Automation object is to *early bind* the specific Automation Server reference library to the module by activating it, using the Tools ➪ References menu. After you bind it, you then create a new instance of the object with the `New` keyword. In the examples shown in Figure 22-3 and Figure 22-4, the variable `MyWordObj` is set to a new instance of Word's `Application` object. If you have not bound the Microsoft Word Object Library, you need to do so or you will receive an error.

If you don't create a reference to the Automation Server with the References dialog box, VBA doesn't recognize the variable's object type and generates an error on compile.

Early binding simply means that a reference is made to an Automation Server before the code is run. As you'll see in the next section, you could *late bind* an Automation Server by referencing the server from within a VBA statement. Late binding means that the reference to the server is made only after the code has started running.

Every time you create an instance of an Automation Server with the `New` keyword, a new instance of the application is started. If you don't want to start a new instance of the application, use the `GetObject` function, which is discussed later in this chapter. Not all Automation Servers support the `New` keyword. Consult the specific Automation server's documentation to determine whether it supports the `New` keyword. If the `New` keyword is not supported, you must use the `CreateObject` function, which is discussed in the following section, to create an instance of the Automation Server.

Using the CreateObject function to create a new instance

In addition to creating an instance of an object library by using the `New` keyword, you can create an instance of an object library by using the `CreateObject` function. You use the `CreateObject` function to create instances of object libraries that do not support the `New` keyword. To use the `CreateObject` function, first declare a variable of the type equal to the type of object that you want to create. Then use the `Set` statement in conjunction with the `CreateObject` function to set the variable to a new instance of the object library.

For example, Microsoft Binder doesn't support the `New` keyword, but it does provide an object library, so you can reference it by using the References dialog box. To early bind the object library of Binder, use the `CreateObject` function, as shown in the following code:

```
Dim BinderObj As OfficeBinder.Binder
Set BinderObj = CreateObject("Office.Binder")
```

NOTE **In the preceding example, the object library name for Binder is `OfficeBinder.Binder`, and the class instance is `"Office.Binder."` You can view the names of object libraries and their available classes by using the Object Browser.**

You create a *late bound* object instance with the `CreateObject` function. In this case the object variable is declared as a generic Object data type. For example, the following code uses late binding to create an instance of the Office Binder object:

```
Dim BinderObj As Object
Set BinderObj = CreateObject("Office.Binder")
```

If you have different versions of the same Automation Server on your computer, you can specify the version to use by adding it to the end of the class information. For example, the following code specifies Office 12 as the Automation Server:

```
Dim WordObj As Object
Set WordObj = CreateObject("Word.Application.12")
```

Word 2007 doesn't require you to specify a version when creating instances of Word object libraries. The version of Word installed on the user's computer is used when a reference is made to `Word.Application`. In fact, you get an error if you try to specify a version number. Therefore, the following syntax may be more reliable in environments where different versions of Word are used by different users:

```
Set WordObj = CreateObject("Word.Application")
```

Getting an existing object instance

As stated previously in this chapter, using the `New` keyword or the `CreateObject` function creates a new instance of the Automation Server. If you don't want a new instance of the server created each time you create an object, use the `GetObject` function. The format of the `GetObject` function is as follows:

```
Set objectvariable = GetObject([pathname][, class])
```

The `pathname` parameter is optional. To use this parameter, you specify a full path and filename to an existing file for use with the Automation Server.

The specified document is then opened in the server application. Even if you omit the parameter, you must still include the comma (`,`).

The `class` parameter is the same parameter that's used with the `CreateObject` function. See Table 22-1 for a list of some class arguments used in Microsoft Office.

TABLE 22-1

Class Arguments for Common Office Components

Component	Class Argument	Object Returned
Access	`Access.Application`	Microsoft Access Application object
Excel	`Excel.Application`	Microsoft Excel Application object
Excel	`Excel.Sheet`	Microsoft Excel Workbook object
Excel	`Excel.Chart`	Microsoft Excel Chart object
Word	`Word.Application`	Microsoft Word Application object
Word	`Word.Document`	Microsoft Word Document object

For example, to work with an existing instance of Microsoft Word, but not a specific Word document, you can use the following code:

```
Dim WordObj as Word.Application
Set WordObj = GetObject(, "Word.Application")
```

To get an instance of an existing Word document called `MyDoc.Docx`, on your C: drive, you can use the following code:

```
Dim WordObj as Word.Application
Set WordObj = GetObject("C:\MyDoc.Docx", "Word.Application")
```

Of course, this code is always placed in a new function or sub that you declare in your module.

Working with Automation objects

After you have a valid instance of an Automation Server, you manipulate the object as though you were writing code within the application itself, using the exposed objects and their properties and methods.

For example, when developing directly in Word, you can use the following code to change the directory that Word uses when opening an existing file:

```
ChangeFileOpenDirectory "C:\My Documents\"
```

Consult the development help for the Automation Server (Word, Excel, and so on) for specific information on the objects, properties, and methods available.

Just as in Access, Word is implicitly using its `Application` object; the command `ChangeFileOpenDirectory` is really a method of the `Application` object. Using the following code, you create an instance of Word's `Application` object and call the method of the object:

```
Dim WordObj As New Word.Application
WordObj.ChangeFileOpenDirectory "C:\My Documents\"
```

TIP **When using Automation, you should avoid setting properties or calling methods that cause the Automation Server to ask for input from the user via a dialog box. When a dialog box is displayed, the Automation code stops executing until the dialog box is closed. If the server application is minimized or behind other windows, the user may not even be aware that he or she needs to provide input and therefore may assume that the application is locked up.**

Closing an instance of an Automation object

Automation objects are closed when the Automation object variable goes out of scope. Such a closing, however, doesn't necessarily free up all resources that are used by the object, so you should explicitly close the instance of the Automation object. You can close an Automation object by doing either of the following:

- Using the `Close` or `Quit` method of the object (consult the specific Automation Server's documentation for information on which method it supports)
- Setting the object variable to nothing, as follows:

  `Set WordObj = Nothing`

The best way to close an instance of an Automation object is to combine the two techniques, like this:

```
WordObj.Quit
Set WordObj = Nothing
```

An Automation Example Using Word

Perhaps the most common Office application that is used for Automation from a database application like Access is Word. Using Automation with Word, you can create letters that are tailored with information from databases. The following section demonstrates an example of merging information from an Access database to a letter in Word by using Automation and Word's bookmarks. Ordinarily, you create a merge document in Word and bring field contents in from the records of an Access database. This method relies on using Word's MergeField, which is replaced by the contents of the Database field. It normally requires that you perform this action in Word — thus limiting the scope and capability of the function. For example, you merge all records from the table that is being used rather than a single record.

The following example uses the Orders form, which calls a module named `WordIntegration`. The `WordIntegration` module contains a function named `MergetoWord()` that uses the Word `Thanks.dotx` template file.

NOTE When you attempt to run this example, you must make sure that the path for the template in the VBA code is the actual path in which the `Thanks.dotx` template file resides. This path may vary from computer to computer.

The items that are discussed in this Word Automation example include the following:

- Creating an instance of a Word object
- Making the instance of Word visible
- Creating a new document based on an existing template
- Using bookmarks to insert data
- Activating the instance of Word
- Moving the cursor in Word
- Closing the instance of the Word object without closing Word

This example prints a thank-you letter for an order based on bookmarks in the thank-you letter template (`Thanks.dotx`). Figure 22-5 shows the data for customers; Figure 22-6 shows the data entry form for orders; Figure 22-7 shows the `Thanks.dotx` template; and Figure 22-8 shows a completed merge letter.

FIGURE 22-5

Customer data used in the following Automation example is entered on the Customers form.

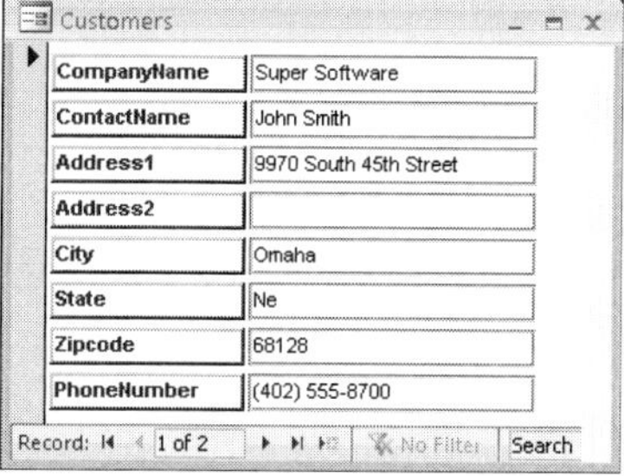

FIGURE 22-6

Each customer can have an unlimited number of orders. Thank-you letters are printed from the Orders form.

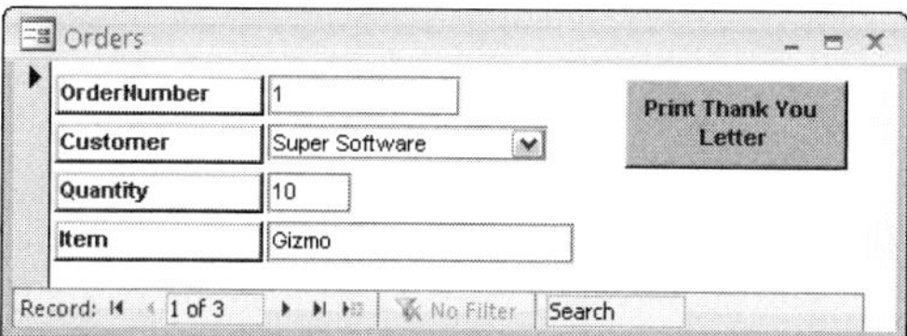

The bookmarks in Figure 22-7 are shown as grayed large I-beams (text insert). The bookmarks are normally not visible, but you can make them visible by selecting the Show Bookmarks check box in the Show Document Content section on the Advanced Tab of the Word Options screen. The names won't be visible — only the bookmark holders (locations) will be visible, as shown in Figure 22-7.

FIGURE 22-7

The `Thanks.dotx` template contains bookmarks where the merged data is to be inserted.

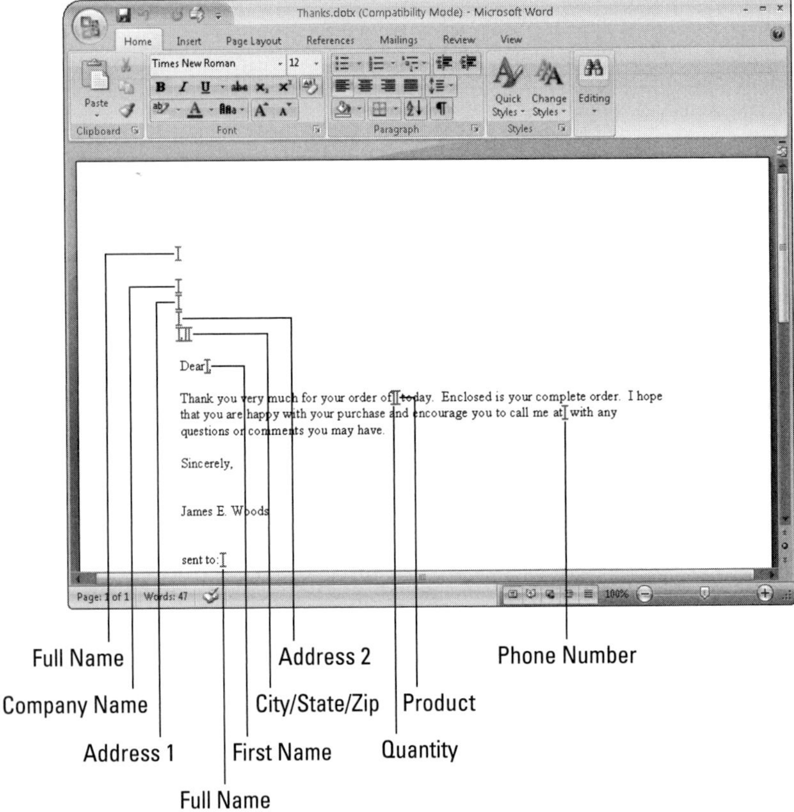

CAUTION If you click the Print Thank You Letter button in Access while Word is open with an existing document that lacks the bookmark names specified in the code, the fields will simply be added to the text inside Word at the point where the cursor is currently sitting.

FIGURE 22-8

After a successful merge, all the bookmarks have been replaced with their respective data.

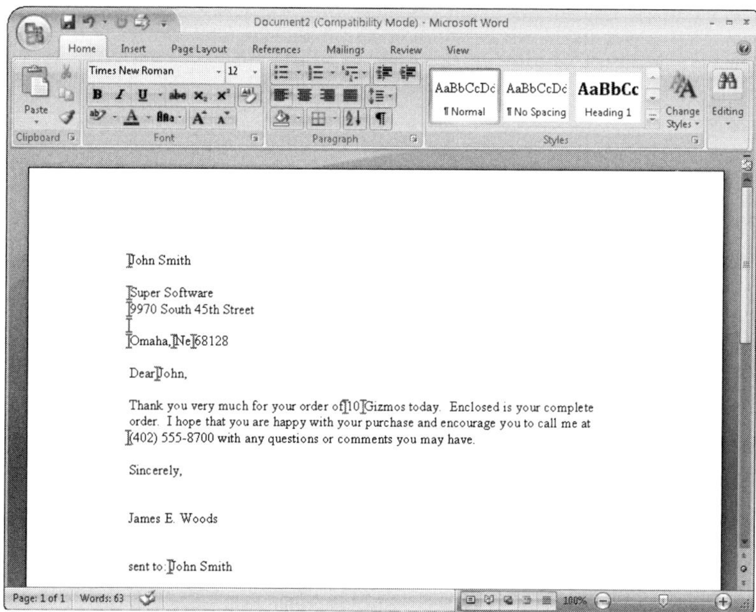

When the user clicks the Print Thank You Letter button on the Orders form, Word generates a thank-you letter with all the pertinent information. The following code shows the `MergetoWord` function in its entirety so you can see in-depth how it works.

```
Public Sub MergetoWord()
' This method creates a new document in
' MS Word using Automation
On Error Resume Next
  Dim rsCust As New ADODB.Recordset
  Dim sSQL As String
  Dim WordObj As Word.Application
  Dim iTemp As Integer
  sSQL = "SELECT * FROM Customers " _
    & "WHERE CustomerNumber = " _
    & Forms!Orders![CustomerNumber]
  rsCust.Open sSQL, CurrentProject.Connection
  If rsCust.EOF Then
    MsgBox "Invalid customer", vbOKOnly
    Exit Function
```

```
End If

DoCmd.Hourglass True

'Try to get a running instance of Word:
Set WordObj = GetObject(, "Word.Application")
If Err.Number <> 0 Then
  'An error is thrown if Word is not running,
  'so use CreateObject to start up Word:
  Set WordObj = CreateObject("Word.Application")
End If

'Make sure the user can see Word:
WordObj.Visible = True

'Warning:
'Specify the correct drive and path to the
'file named Thanks.dotx in the line below.

WordObj.Documents.Add _
Template:="C:\Thanks.dotx", NewTemplate:=False

With WordObj.Selection
  .GoTo what:=wdGoToBookmark, Name:="FullName"
  .TypeText rsCust![ContactName]

  .GoTo what:=wdGoToBookmark, Name:="CompanyName"
  .TypeText rsCust![CompanyName]

  .GoTo what:=wdGoToBookmark, Name:="Address1"
  .TypeText rsCust![Address1]

  .GoTo what:=wdGoToBookmark, Name:="Address2"
  If IsNull(rsCust![Address2]) Then
    .TypeText ""
  Else
    .TypeText rsCust![Address2]
  End If

  .GoTo what:=wdGoToBookmark, Name:="City"
  .TypeText rsCust![City]

  .GoTo what:=wdGoToBookmark, Name:="State"
  .TypeText rsCust![State]

  .GoTo what:=wdGoToBookmark, Name:="Zipcode"
  .TypeText rsCust![Zipcode]

  .GoTo what:=wdGoToBookmark, Name:="PhoneNumber"
```

```
      .TypeText rsCust![PhoneNumber]

      .GoTo what:=wdGoToBookmark, Name:="NumOrdered"
      .TypeText Forms!Orders![Quantity]

      .GoTo what:=wdGoToBookmark, Name:="ProductOrdered"
      If Forms!Orders![Quantity] > 1 Then
        WordObj.Selection.TypeText Forms!Orders![Item] & "s"
      Else
        WordObj.Selection.TypeText Forms!Orders![Item]
      End If

      .GoTo what:=wdGoToBookmark, Name:="FName"

      iTemp = InStr(rsCust![ContactName], " ")

      If iTemp > 0 Then
        .TypeText Left$(rsCust![ContactName], iTemp - 1)
      End If
      .GoTo what:=wdGoToBookmark, Name:="LetterName"
      .TypeText rsCust![ContactName]

      DoEvents
      WordObj.Activate
      .MoveUp wdLine, 6
    End With

    'Set the Word Object to Nothing to free resources:
    Set WordObj = Nothing
    DoCmd.Hourglass False

End Sub
```

The `MergeToWord` function uses the `With` construct to reduce the amount of code used to reference the object variable. All of the property and method references within the body of the `With..End With` construct refer to the `WordObj.Selection object`. The `WordObj` object is set to `Nothing` at the end of the subroutine to remove the Word automation server from memory.

Creating an instance of a Word object

The first step in using Automation is to create an instance of an object. The sample creates an object instance with the following code:

```
On Error Resume Next
...
Set WordObj = GetObject(, "Word.Application")
If Err.Number <> 0 Then
  Set WordObj = CreateObject("Word.Application")
End If
```

Obviously, you don't want a new instance of Word created every time a thank-you letter is generated, so some special coding is required. This code snippet first attempts to create an instance by using an active instance (a running copy) of Word. If Word is not a running application, an error is generated. Because this function has `On Error Resume Next` for error trapping, the code doesn't fail, but instead proceeds to the next statement. If an error is detected (the `Err.Number` is not equal to `0`), an instance is created by using `CreateObject`.

Making the instance of Word visible

When you first create a new instance of Word, it runs invisibly. This approach enables your application to exploit features of Word without the user even realizing that Word is running. In this case, however, it is desirable to let the user edit the merged letter, so Word needs to be made visible by setting the object's `Visible` property to `True` by using this line of code:

```
WordObj.Visible = True
```

CAUTION **If you don't set the object instance's `Visible` property to `True`, you may create hidden copies of Word that use system resources and never shut down. A hidden copy of Word doesn't show up in the Task tray or in the Task Switcher.**

Creating a new document based on an existing template

After Word is running, a blank document needs to be created. The following code creates a new document by using the `Thanks.dotx` template:

```
WordObj.Documents.Add _
Template:="C:\Thanks.dotx", NewTemplate:=False
```

The path must be corrected in order to point to the `Thanks.dotx` template on your computer.

The `Thanks.dotx` template contains bookmarks (as shown in Figure 22-7) that tell this function where to insert data. You create bookmarks in Word by highlighting the text that you want to make a bookmark, selecting the Bookmark command from the Link group on Word 2007's Insert ribbon, and then entering the bookmark name and clicking Add.

Using Bookmarks to insert data

Using Automation, you can locate bookmarks in a Word document and replace them with the text of your choosing. To locate a bookmark, use the `Goto` method of the `Selection` object. After you have located the bookmark, the text comprising the bookmark is selected. By inserting text (which you can do by using Automation or simply by typing directly into the document), you replace the bookmark text. To insert text, use the `TypeText` method of the `Selection` object, as shown here:

```
WordObj.Selection.Goto what:=wdGoToBookmark, Name:="FullName"
WordObj.Selection.TypeText rsCust![ContactName]
```

NOTE You can't pass `Null` to the `TypeText` method. If the value may possibly be `Null`, you need to check ahead and make allowances. The preceding sample code checks the `Address2` field for a `Null` value and acts accordingly. If you don't pass text to replace the bookmark — even just a zero length string (`" "`) — the bookmark text remains in the document.

Activating the instance of Word

To enable the user to enter data in the new document, you must make Word the active application. If you don't make Word the active application, the user has to switch to Word from Access. You make Word the active application by using the `Activate` method of the `Word` object, as follows:

```
WordObj.Activate
```

TIP Depending on the processing that is occurring at the time, Access may take the focus back from Word. You can help to eliminate this annoyance by preceding the `Activate` method with a `DoEvents` statement. Note, however, that this doesn't always work.

Moving the cursor in Word

You can move the cursor in Word by using the `MoveUp` method of the `Selection` object. The following example moves the cursor up six lines in the document. The cursor is at the location of the last bookmark when this code is executed:

```
WordObj.Selection.MoveUp wdLine, 6
```

Closing the instance of the Word object

To release resources that are taken by an instance of an Automation object, you should always close the instance. In this example, the following code is used to close the object instance:

```
Set WordObj = Nothing
```

This code closes the object instance, but not the instance of Word as a running application. In this example, the user needs access to the new document, so closing Word would defeat the purpose of this function. You can, however, automatically print the document and then close Word. If you do this, you may even choose not to make Word visible during this process. To close Word, use the `Quit` method of the Application object, as follows:

```
WordObj.Quit
```

Inserting pictures by using bookmarks

It is possible to perform other unique operations by using bookmarks. Basically, anything that you can do within Word, you can do by using Automation. The following code locates a bookmark that marks where a picture is to be placed and then inserts a .bmp file from disk. You can use the following code to insert scanned signatures into letters:

```
WordObj.Selection.Goto what:=wdGoToBookmark, Name:="Picture"
WordObj.ChangeFileOpenDirectory "D:\GRAPHICS\"
WordObj.ActiveDocument.Shapes.AddPicture _
  Anchor:=Selection.Range, _
  FileName:="D:\GRAPHICS\PICTURE.BMP", LinkToFile:=False,
  SaveWithDocument:=True
```

Using Office's Macro Recorder

Using Automation is not a difficult process when you understand the fundamentals. Often, the toughest part of using Automation is knowing the proper objects, properties, and methods to use. Although the development help system of the Automation Server is a requirement for fully understanding the language, the easiest way to quickly create Automation for Office applications like Word is with the Macro Recorder.

Most versions of Office applications have a Macro Recorder located on the Word 2007's Developer ribbon (see Figure 22-9). When activated, the Macro Recorder records all events, such as menu selections and button clicks, and creates VBA code from them.

FIGURE 22-9

The Macro Recorder in Word is a powerful tool to help you create Automation code.

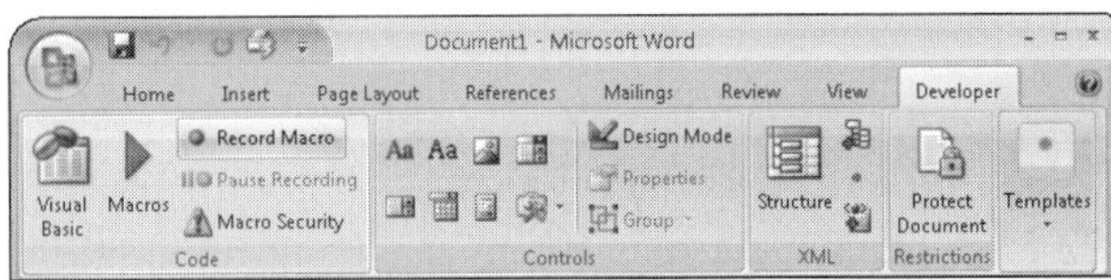

TIP **If you don't see the Developer tab in Word 2007, open the Word Options from the Microsoft Office Button, click Personalize and select the Show Developer tab in the Ribbon check box.**

After selecting Record Macro from the Developer ribbon's Code group, you must give your new macro a name (see Figure 22-10). In addition to a name, you can assign the macro to a button or keyboard combination and select the template (`.dotm` file) in which to store the macro. If you are creating the macro simply to create the VBA code, the only thing that you need to be concerned with is the macro name.

After you enter a macro name and click OK, the Macro Recorder begins recording events and the arrow changes to an open pointer attached to a cassette, as shown in Figure 22-11. You can stop recording events by clicking the Stop Recording button (the button with a square next to it). To pause recording events, click the Pause Recording button.

FIGURE 22-10

Enter a macro name and click OK to begin recording the macro. In this example, the macro is named MyMacro.

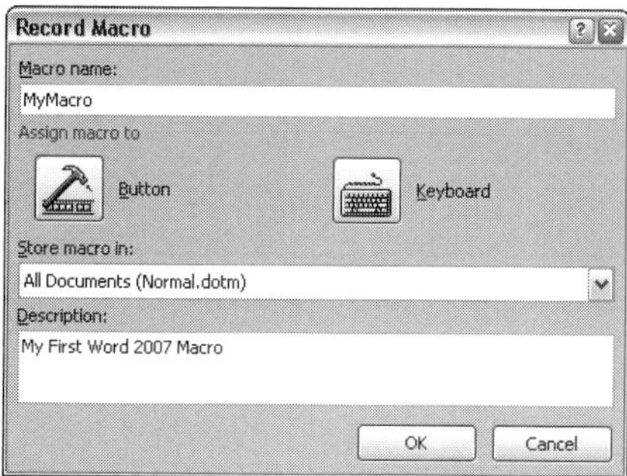

FIGURE 22-11

The Macro Recorder records all events until you click the Stop Recording button.

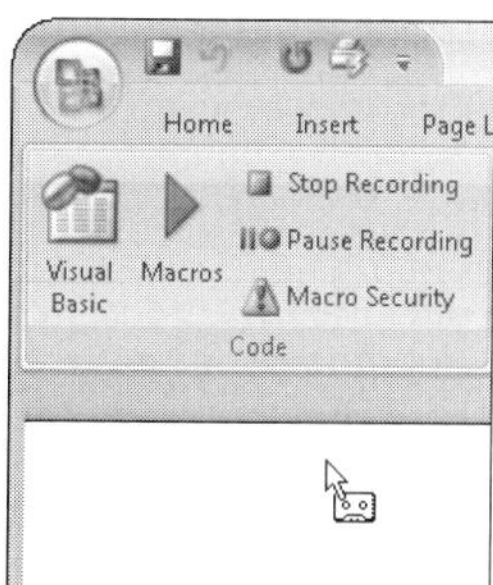

After you finish recording a macro, you can view the VBA code created from your events. To view the macro code, click the Macros button on the ribbon to display a list of all saved macros. Then select the macro that you recorded and click the Edit button to display the VBA editor with the macro's code. Figure 22-12 shows the VBA editor with a macro that recorded the creation of a new document using the Normal template and the insertion of a picture using the Picture From File command from the Insert ribbon's Illustrations group.

In the application for which a macro is created, the Application object is used explicitly. When you use the code for Automation, you must create an Application object accordingly. For example, the preceding macro uses the following code to create a new document:

```
Documents.Add Template:="Normal", _
  NewTemplate:= False, DocumentType:=0
```

This code implicitly uses the Application object. To use this code for Automation, copy the code from the VBA editor, paste it into your Access procedure, and create an object that you use explicitly, as follows:

```
Dim WordObj as New Word.Application
WordObj.Documents.Add Template:="Normal", _
  NewTemplate:= False, DocumentType:=0
```

FIGURE 22-12

The VBA code recorded by Word's Macro Recorder

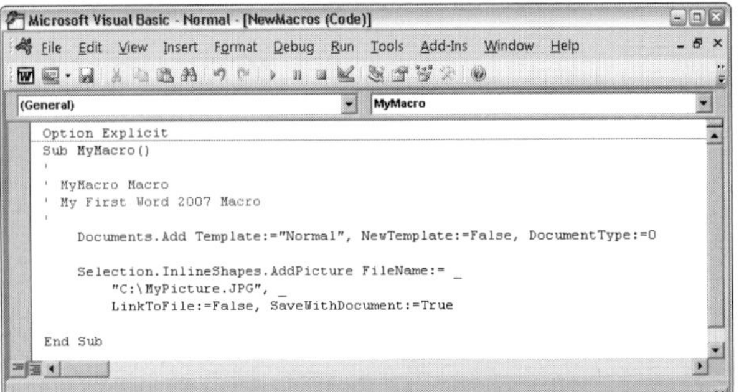

The Macro Recorder enables you to effortlessly create long and complete Automation code without ever needing to read the Automation Server's documentation. Try using the Macro Recorder to generate VBA code instead of typing it from scratch.

Collecting Data with Outlook 2007

Access 2007 includes a new feature that lets you use Outlook 2007 to collect data from one or more users. This feature automatically creates a data-entry form in an Outlook e-mail message, gives you several options for sending, and then adds or modifies data in the database. This saves you lots of time when sending out surveys or updating contact information by letting users without access to your application do data entry.

Creating an e-mail

Creating an e-mail consists of a number of steps, which Access presents in a wizard when you click the Create E-mail button in the Collect Data group of the External Data ribbon (shown in Figure 22-13). You must select a table or query in the Navigation Pane before creating an e-mail. You can't collect data if there's nowhere to store it.

FIGURE 22-13

Use the Collect Data group on the External Data ribbon to use Outlook 2007 to get information from users.

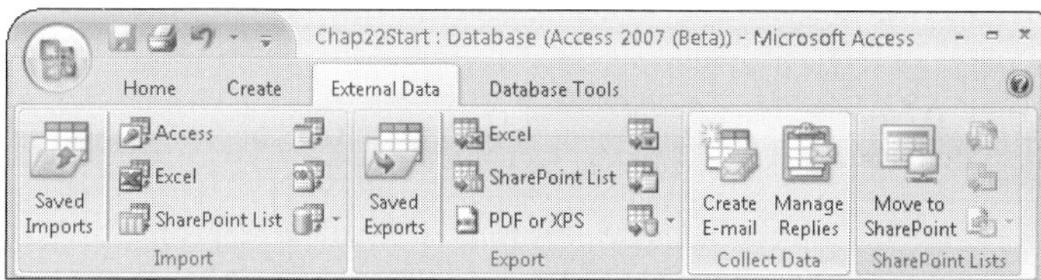

Click the `Customers` table, and then click the Create E-mail button to start the Collect Data wizard. The opening page of the wizard explains the new feature and the steps required to create an e-mail message. Click Next to begin setting up the e-mail.

Choose the type of data-entry form you want to use to collect data. Choose either HTML or an InfoPath form. The HTML form option creates an HTML e-mail message and the only requirement for the recipient is that their e-mail program supports HTML. The Microsoft Office InfoPath form option creates an InfoPath form and requires the recipients to have both Outlook 2007 and InfoPath 2007 installed on their computers. For this example, click HTML form; then click Next.

Choose whether you're collecting new data or updating existing data. Choose the Collect new information only option to send the recipient(s) a blank form. Any data collected is appended to the database. Choose the Update existing information option to send the recipient information to review and update. Any data collected overwrites the older information in your table. You can update existing information only if the recipients' e-mail addresses are stored in the table. For this example, click Update existing information, and then click Next.

Select which fields you want to include in your form. You can also set the text of the label that appears next to each field and whether the field is read-only. For this example, add all the fields from the `Customers` table (shown in Figure 22-14); then add spaces to each of the labels by clicking the field on the right, and changing the label to display in the field properties section of the form; then click Next.

Decide how you want to process the replies. Select the Automatically process replies and add data to Customers check box to let Outlook and Access do all the work from the Access Data Collection Replies folder in Outlook 2007. If you want to prevent records from being added, check the Only allow updates to existing data check box. For this example, check both check boxes and click Next.

Specify the field in the database that contains the recipient's e-mail address. If the e-mail address is in the table or query the e-mail form is based on, select The current table or query option and select the field — in this example, the EMailAddress field. If the e-mail address is in an associated table, you have to select the An associated table option; then select the field in the current table that identifies who receives the e-mail, the associated table, and the field in the associated table that contains the e-mail address. For this example, select the current table; then click Next.

FIGURE 22-14

Select the fields to add to the e-mail form; then set the caption and read-only check box for each field.

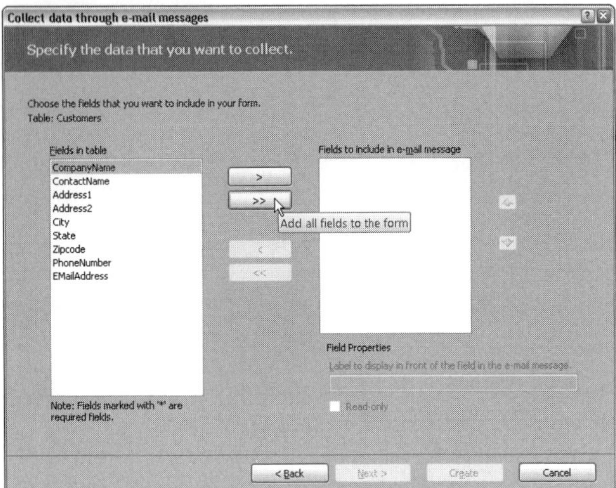

Customize the e-mail message by typing a subject, introduction, and choosing whether you want the e-mail addresses in the To, Cc, or Bcc fields (shown in Figure 22-15).

FIGURE 22-15

Customize the e-mail message you're sending.

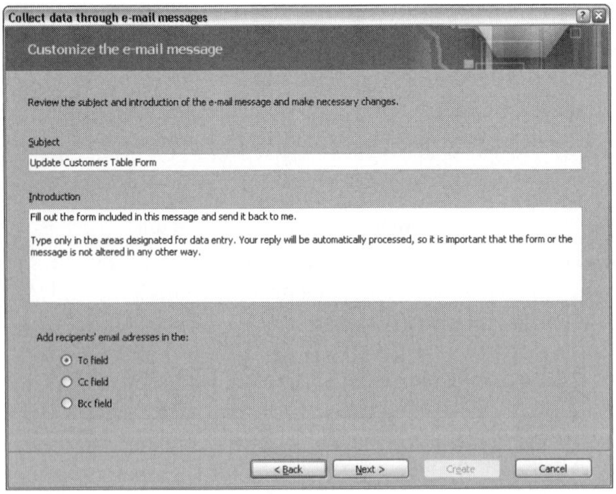

Collect data through e-mail messages

Customize the e-mail message

Review the subject and introduction of the e-mail message and make necessary changes.

Subject

Update Customers Table Form

Introduction

Fill out the form included in this message and send it back to me.

Type only in the areas designated for data entry. Your reply will be automatically processed, so it is important that the form or the message is not altered in any other way.

Add recipients' email adresses in the:

To field

Cc field

Bcc field

< Back Next > Create Cancel

Accept the default settings; then click Next to review the instructions for managing the e-mails. Click Next again, verify the recipients, and create the e-mail. Check all the recipients and click Send to create the e-mail messages (shown in Figure 22-16).

FIGURE 22-16

The resulting data-entry form sent to each recipient.

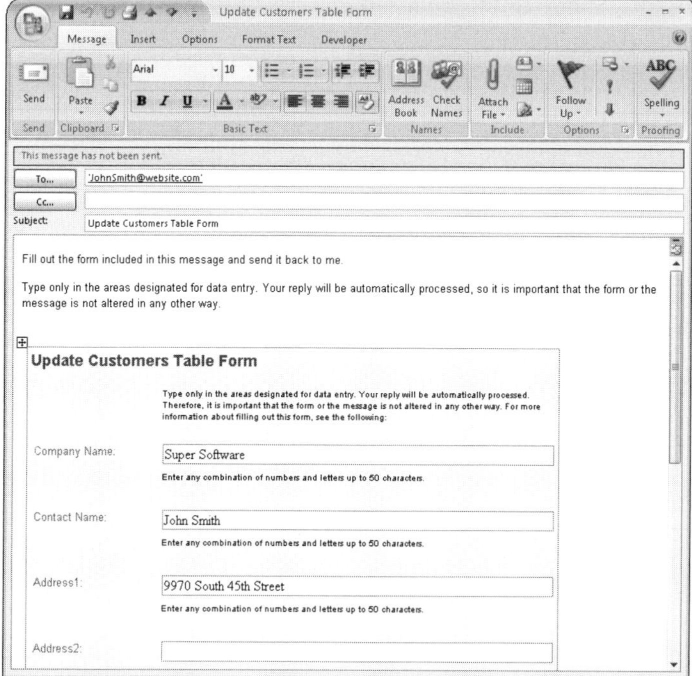

These steps vary depending on the choices you make. Using InfoPath gives you a different look and functionality. Adding new data creates a blank form. After creating the e-mails, you need to manage the replies, which the next section covers.

Managing replies

After sending an e-mail to collect data, click the Manage Replies button in the Collect Data group of the External Data ribbon (shown in Figure 22-13) to manage the e-mail messages you sent. The Manage Data Collection Messages dialog (shown in Figure 22-17) lets you see which e-mails you sent and when you sent them, resend the messages, and delete the messages.

FIGURE 22-17

Use the Manage Data Collection Messages dialog to manage replies to the e-mail forms you sent.

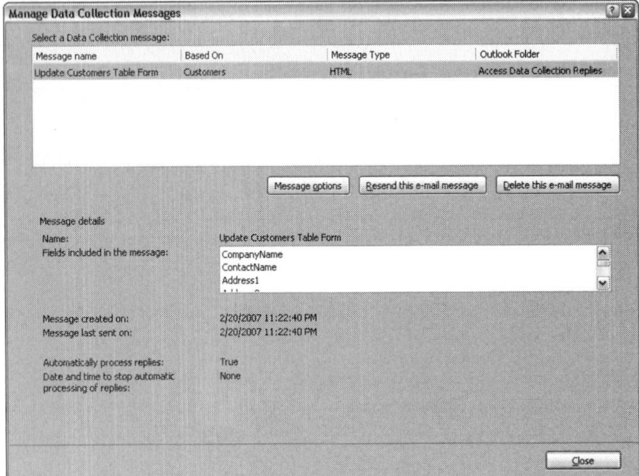

The list at the top of the dialog shows the message details: the message name, the table or query the e-mail is updating, the message type, and the Outlook folder where the replies are stored. The message details section at the bottom of the form displays information about the selected message: the fields included in the message, the date/time the message was created and last sent, whether to process replies automatically, and the date/time to stop processing the replies.

Click the Resend this e-mail message button to send the highlighted message again. This walks you through a few steps of the Create E-mail wizard, letting you choose the same recipients, or a different list of recipients. Follow the steps of the wizard to resend the message.

Click on the Delete this e-mail message button to stop processing replies to the message. If Outlook receives any replies to the message after you delete the message, it treats those messages as regular e-mail replies.

Import settings

The Message options button lets you customize the highlighted message. Click this button to display the Collect Data Using E-mail Options dialog (shown in Figure 22-18), which lets you specify the import settings and automatic processing settings. Changes you make to these settings do not affect the replies already in your Outlook mailbox.

FIGURE 22-18

Display the message options to customize the settings for importing and automatic processing of replies.

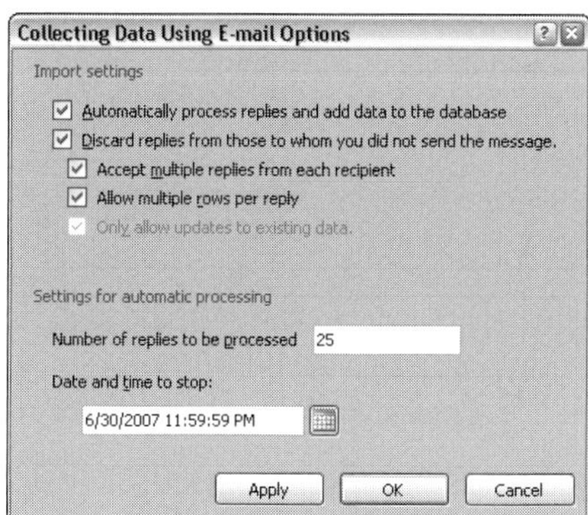

Select the Automatically process replies and add data to the database check box to let Access and Outlook do all the work. This option lets Access process the replies as soon as they reach the Outlook 2007 Inbox. If you don't select this option, you must manually process the replies, which is covered later in this chapter.

The Discard replies from those to whom you did not send the message check box lets you process the replies from the original recipients of the e-mail. If this option is selected, replies from other recipients are stored in Outlook's destination folder, but they won't be automatically processed. You can, however, manually process the replies. Uncheck this option to automatically process all replies, regardless of who they're from.

If you choose to discard replies from non-original recipients, select the Allow multiple replies from each recipient check box to process all replies from each recipient. Deselect this check box to process only the first reply from each recipient; you can manually process — or delete — any subsequent replies. If you're using InfoPath 2007, this option controls only the number of replies, not the number of records in a single reply. InfoPath lets users update multiple records in a single reply. With the check box deselected, Access only processes the first InfoPath reply and ignores any subsequent replies.

Select the Allow multiple rows per reply check box if you're using InfoPath 2007 and you want to allow the recipients to add more records by clicking Insert a row at the bottom of the e-mail message. Deselect this check box if you want to process only one record per reply.

Also, when using InfoPath 2007, select the Only allow updates to existing data check box to ignore any new records the recipients add to the reply and process just the updates to existing records. If you want to allow recipients to add new records, clear this check box.

Settings for automatic processing

The settings for automatic processing let you choose when to stop automatically processing replies. These settings apply only to the automatic processing of replies.

The Number of replies to be processed text box lets you set the number of replies from all recipients that you want to automatically process. If you want to process all the replies, enter a large value in the text box. Replies received after you reach the specified value will be stored in the destination folder, but won't be processed automatically. You can, however, manually process the replies.

The Date and Time to stop option lets you pick a date and time to quit automatically processing the replies. Replies received after the specified date and time are stored in the destination folder, but aren't processed automatically. You can, however, manually process the replies. Leave this blank to process replies forever.

Manually processing replies

If you want to control which replies to process and when to process them, deselect the Automatically process replies and add data to the database check box in the Collect Data Using E-mail Options dialog (shown in Figure 22-18). You also need to manually process replies that aren't processed automatically, due to the import settings and settings for automatic processing, described in the previous sections.

To manually process each reply, you have to use Outlook 2007. The replies reach your Outlook destination folder, but they aren't processed automatically. To process a reply manually, right-click the reply; then click Export data to Microsoft Office Access from the pop-up menu (shown in Figure 22-19). The resulting dialog lets you verify the information being updated; click OK to process the data.

The Collect Data feature in Access 2007 is a powerful tool letting you separate some users from your applications. If you want to add or update data to your database application, create a data-entry form, send it to the users you want data from, and then process the replies automatically or manually.

FIGURE 22-19

Process replies manually from Outlook 2007.

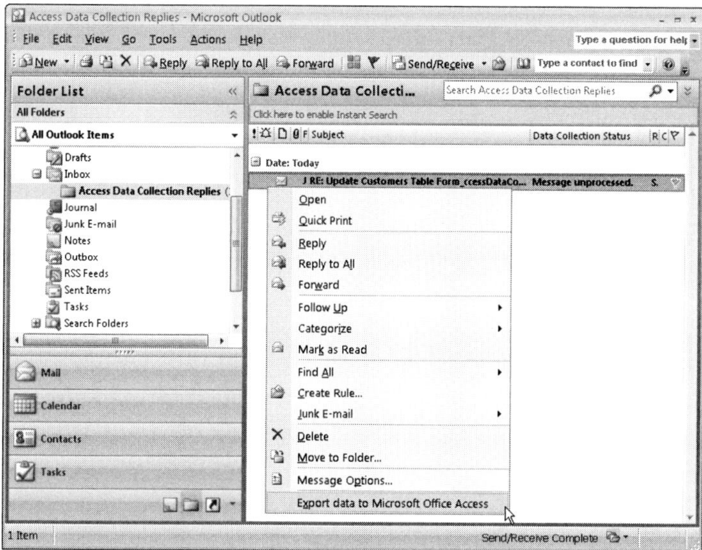

Summary

In this chapter, you learned how to use Automation to interact with other applications. You learned about the Automation references and how to create Automation objects. Then you used Automation to take control of the Word object to insert data from Access into a Word document using Word's bookmarks. Then you used Word's Macro Recorder to generate VBA code, so you don't have to learn Word's object model.

You also learned how to collect data using Outlook 2007. You walked through the steps to create an e-mail to update the data in the `Customers` table, sent the e-mail, and monitored the replies. Using Outlook 2007 and Access 2007 together lets you gather information from users without doing data entry or giving them access to your application.

Chapter 23

Integrating Access with SharePoint

Access and SharePoint can be transparently integrated, seamlessly sharing data across the Internet. Access data can very simply be linked to, or copied from, a data source located on a SharePoint Web site. The result is data stored on a SharePoint Web site somewhere, appearing to be stored in a table in Access. The connection between SharePoint Services and an Access installation can be executed over a TCP/IP connection. This means that the connection can run over the Internet. So, in technical terms, the overall result is that SharePoint can provide an external source of data to Access, similar to how an external database such as SQL Server can provide data to Access, over an ODBC connection.

the CD-ROM **This chapter uses the `Chapter23.accdb` database. If you haven't already copied it onto your machine from the CD, you'll need to do so now.**

IN THIS CHAPTER

- Getting familiar with SharePoint
- Knowing what a SharePoint Service is
- Understanding SharePoint Portal Server
- Looking at SharePoint applications
- Seeing the integration of a SharePoint Service with Access 2007
- Looking at how operating systems work with SharePoint
- Working with SharePoint Lists

What Is SharePoint?

SharePoint is essentially a storage framework (at a specific location), where information can be shared across a network. Current implementations of SharePoint are typically local area network (LAN) implementations within a company, sometimes shared with client or partners. SharePoint is primarily used for intranet installations, helping to share information across a company network.

SharePoint helps companies implement collaborative sharing of information within the company and even with the company's customers. The result is what could be termed *collaborative* Web sites that can even be allowed to go across firewalls if necessary. The real issue with the scalability of SharePoint implementations is network bandwidth. Simply put, sharing large amounts of information takes very large bandwidth capacity. A large portion of Internet users still use slow-speed modem connections to access the Internet, so SharePoint is somewhat impractical for general Internet use. Of course, the information being shared by SharePoint software could be kept simple, but that might defeat the purpose of using SharePoint in the first place. Simplicity can probably be more effectively catered to with a tool that's simpler than SharePoint.

Various pieces of software are involved in a SharePoint implementation. Some software pieces are only available with Windows Server 2003. In general, SharePoint consists of two primary pieces of software: SharePoint Services and a SharePoint Portal Server.

What is SharePoint Services technology?

SharePoint Services technology supplies the basic structure allowing for sharing of information across an intranet. This allows for companies to share data across their internal networks. Also, companies often share their intranets with their clients — typically, in partnerships. So, an intranet does not specially apply to only a single company. The types of data that intranet users will want to share is varied, but it's also very likely to include large and complex structures such as word-processing documents, spreadsheets, and perhaps even large reports and charts.

Essentially, SharePoint Services technology is a process that provides a service to users.

What is a SharePoint Portal Server?

A server process, or server computer, is a provider of information. A server serves information up to user computers across a network. In the case of Web services — Intranet or internet — a Web service perform tasks such as generating Web pages from data in a database, or based on requests by specific users, providing user- or group-specific Web page content. One of the most important functions of server computers is as application servers and Web servers. These types of servers manage sharing of connections to a high-intensity computer such as a database server. The Internet can host millions of users at one time. It is impossible to expect a single database server to service data requests for even more than a thousand users all at once. So a server process serves up information from one computer to another. A database computer is a database server. Web servers and application servers serve up information from a lower tier (such as a database server computer) to the Internet community.

A SharePoint Portal Server provides a portal between a SharePoint data source and an application using that data, such as Access. The SharePoint Portal Server essentially manages connections between the data and requests for access to that data. A SharePoint Portal Server is a process (a computer program), running on a Windows Server computer, which performs a similar role to that of a Web server or an application server.

SharePoint Portal Server is only available on Windows Server 2003 operating system and not Windows XP. Not even Windows XP Professional is a suitable server for SharePoint Portal Server.

The implication is that SharePoint Portal Server is only available with a server-level operating system such as Windows Server 2003. What this really means is actually very simple: A computer known as a server is used to serve information to users. The intention of a database server is to serve up data. Web servers and application servers are even more specialized, in that they help to manage the large number of users who want to talk to a database, and all at the same time.

So, a server process simply serves information. Therefore, SharePoint Portal Server and SharePoint Services serve up data to users. That is what a SharePoint Portal Server is. And that is why SharePoint Portal Server is constructed to execute on top of SharePoint Services.

In truth, SharePoint Portal Server provides extra functionality in addition to that of simple SharePoint Services functionality. That extra functionality includes capabilities such as indexing, fast searching (using that indexing), specialized targeting modifications depending on the user population (or even individual users), and security in the form of username and password verification. In other words, not anyone can use SharePoint Services — you need a username and password. Confidential information will remain confidential.

SharePoint Applications: Types of Web Sites

There are all sorts of possibilities for sharing of information using SharePoint Web sites. Figure 23-1 and Figure 23-2 show an example SharePoint Web site allowing all sorts of information sharing of numerous types and flavors.

FIGURE 23-1

Example applications for SharePoint Services, part 1

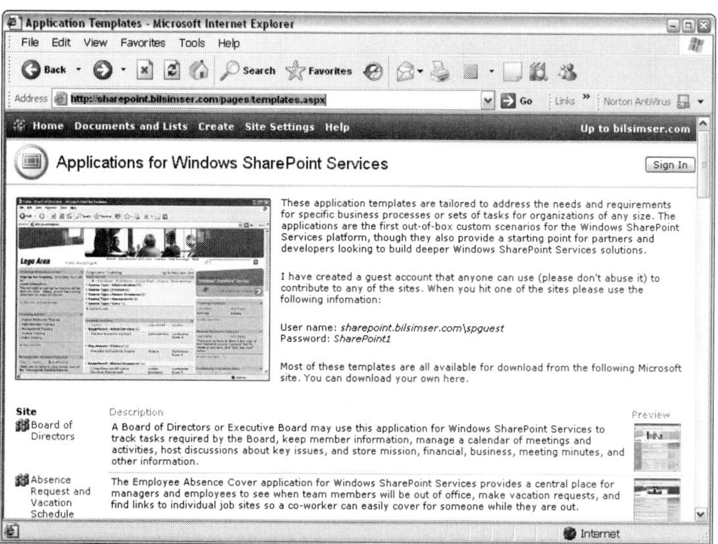

FIGURE 23-2

Example applications for SharePoint Services, part 2

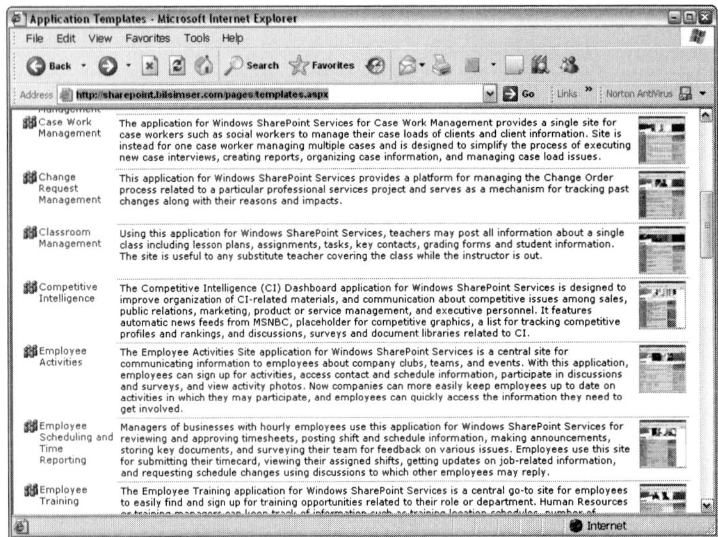

Figure 23-1 and Figure 23-2 are snapshots of a Web site at `http://sharepoint.bilsimser.com/pages/templates.aspx`. A similar version of this URL is currently (at the time of writing this book) available at `www.microsoft.com/technet/prodtechnol/sppt/wssapps/default.mspx`.

The Microsoft SharePoint site contains more application templates in addition to those shown in Figure 23-1 and Figure 23-2, including:

- Discussion database
- Document library
- Event coordination
- Expense reimbursement request
- Help desk
- Human resources programs and forms
- Information technology (IT) developer
- Legal document review management
- Loan initiation
- Meeting management
- New product development

- Performance review
- Professional services contractual services
- Professional services resourcing
- Project team site
- Public official activity and issue management
- Public relations
- Publication review center
- Recruiting resource center
- Request for proposal
- Room and equipment reservation
- Team room
- Travel request

The scale and scope of the number of different types of topics should give you an idea of the flexibility of SharePoint software.

Some of the most common implementations of SharePoint Services are storing of version-controlled documents, holding records and minutes of meetings, and listing contacts. Traditionally, e-mail is used for passing documents back and forth within a company. The potential for mixing up different versions of the same document is immense. Also, storing all those potentially uncontrollable copies of the same document takes up a lot of disk space. File shares are commonly used where the possibility of mixing up document versions, or even of accidental deletion of documents, can cause serious problems. Many of these issues can be alleviated by using something like SharePoint Services.

Figure 23-3 shows another site, similar to the one shown in Figure 23-1 and Figure 23-2.

FIGURE 23-3

A Microsoft-based application for a SharePoint Services Web site

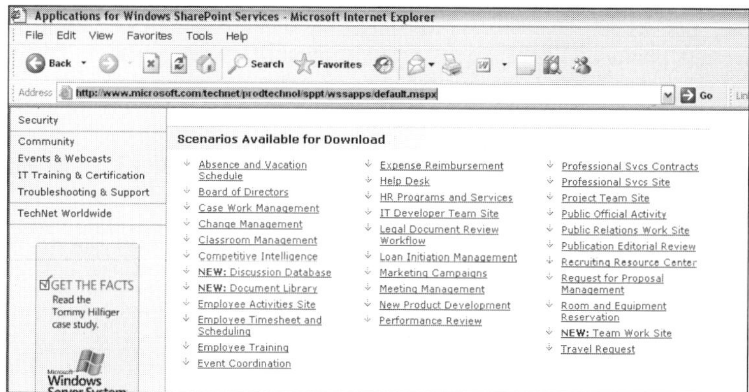

The Web site shown in Figure 23-3 is similar to the one shown in Figure 23-1 and Figure 23-2. It contains some of the same applications. The URL for the Microsoft Web site shown in Figure 23-3 is `www.microsoft.com/technet/prodtechnol/sppt/wssapps/default.mspx`.

One further and final point to make is specific capabilities of an application-specific SharePoint application. For example, a document sharing Web site can implement, track, and correct versioning of documents. On the contrary, something like a SharePoint meetings application can be used to contain functionality provided in Microsoft Outlook, such as when meetings are, how often meetings recur, who is supposed to attend, who did attend, and so on. It's all Microsoft Office compatible, so it has all the capabilities of other Office applications such as Excel and Outlook.

What Is a SharePoint List?

SharePoint Lists are an important part of SharePoint Services technology in general. They provide a basis of static information (for example, contact lists, task list, lists of links to Web sites, among others). These are all lists that can be stored as a SharePoint List object, even in an Access 2007 database.

Typically, a SharePoint List is known as a SharePoint List type, or even a SharePoint List data type. In relational database terminology a *data type* is essentially a definition for storing data. A table is a data type. In the case of Access (which is a relational database), Access 2007 can only link to a SharePoint List on a SharePoint Web site. Access cannot copy or store the data that is located on a SharePoint Web site.

Access 2007 allows specific types, of what can only be assumed to be the most commonly used types of SharePoint List data types. These are contacts, tasks, issues, and events. Access 2007 does allow creation of a custom-designed SharePoint List and can also use an already existing SharePoint List.

NOTE **SharePoint List types are also referred to as multivalued fields or multivalued lists. Relational database modeling terminology often refers to comma delimited string lists of string values, as *multivalued lists* or *multivalued fields.***

You now have a general idea of SharePoint technology, including SharePoint Services, the SharePoint Portal Server, types of SharePoint applications, and SharePoint List data types.

Introducing a SharePoint Services Web Site

Before going into the detail of describing how Access 2007 integrates with SharePoint technology, you need to get a picture in your mind of what a SharePoint Web site is.

So, what is a SharePoint Web site? And what is its function and purpose? The first question will be answered by example in this section. The second question is easy to answer. The function and purpose of a SharePoint Services Web site is provision, servicing, and management of information — and optionally to a specified group of users. Now back to the first question. What is a SharePoint Web site? We'll just demonstrate.

The following URL is a fictional SharePoint Web site for demonstrating and testing of the beta version of Microsoft SharePoint Services: `www.somesharepointsite.net`. This URL is meant to simply demonstrate how easily Access 2007 links to SharePoint resources, rather than as a bona fide SharePoint Services location. The fictional URL contains multiple SharePoint Services portals for different users. Each user has his own username and password to access the site.

Some items of information have been added to the SharePoint Services above, including lists, documents, calendar events, tasks, and so on. A full list of site content specific to this book (and its principal author) is shown in Figure 23-4.

FIGURE 23-4

Data content can be altered from a SharePoint Services Web site.

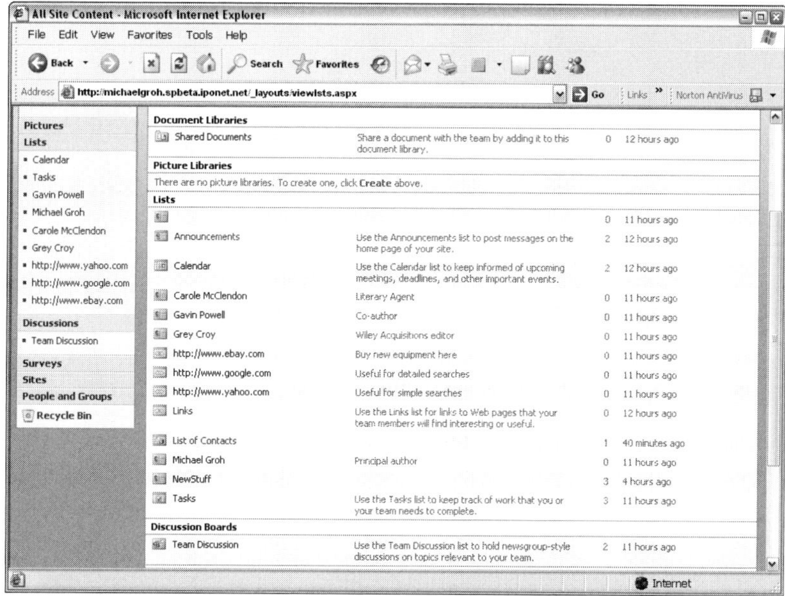

Figure 23-5 shows a calendar with multiple entries, which were added just to make things a little interesting.

Figure 23-6 shows recent and prospective tasks and team discussions.

FIGURE 23-5

A calendar SharePoint Services Web site

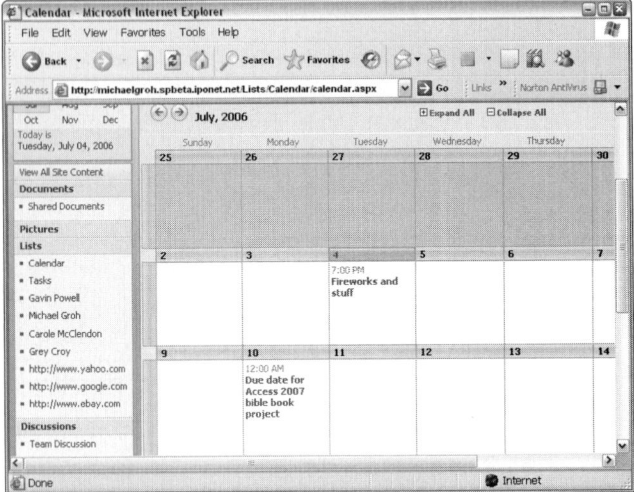

FIGURE 23-6

Task and discussion SharePoint Services

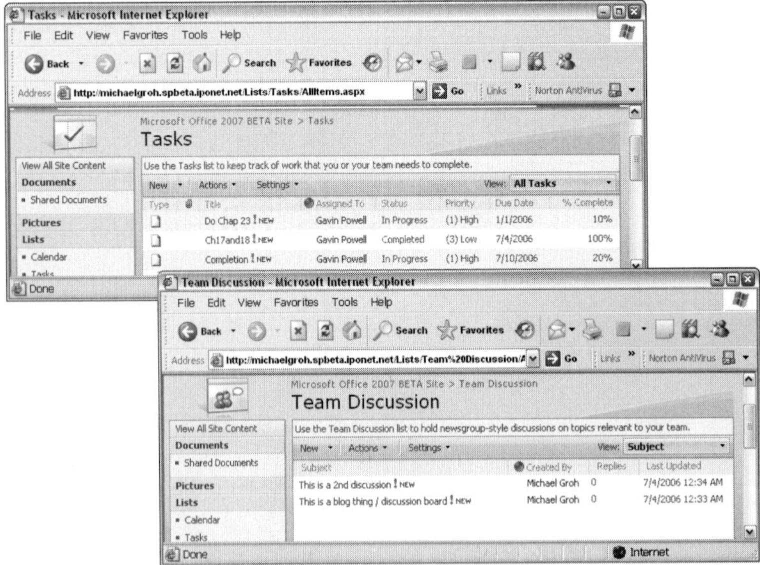

And all this information can be altered in detail from the SharePoint Services Web site, as shown in Figure 23-7 and Figure 23-8.

FIGURE 23-7

Adding, changing, or deleting a calendar item in a SharePoint Services Web site

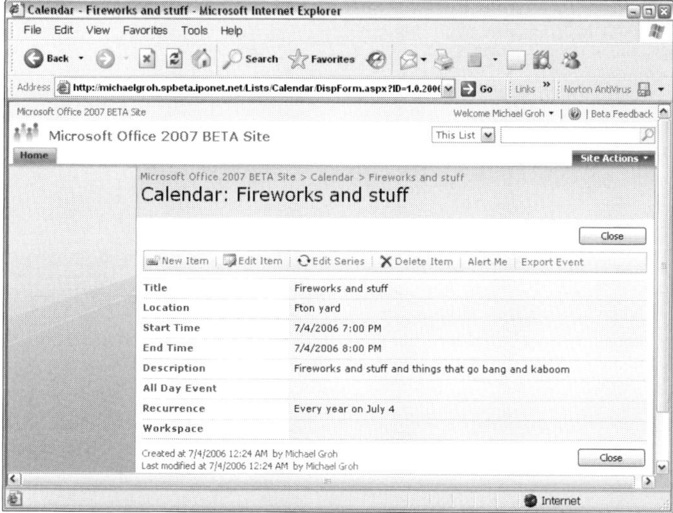

The screens shown in Figure 23-8 are displayed when clicking the link, shown as Fireworks and Stuff in Figure 23-5.

SharePoint is able to manage virtually any type of data you want to share with other people. Although this example concerns a specific project, SharePoint is suitable for many other purposes. For instance, a Boy Scout troop could use SharePoint for keeping track of its members and their merit badges. A bowling club could maintain tournament schedules and player rankings as SharePoint Lists.

FIGURE 23-8

Changing a calendar item in a SharePoint Services Web site

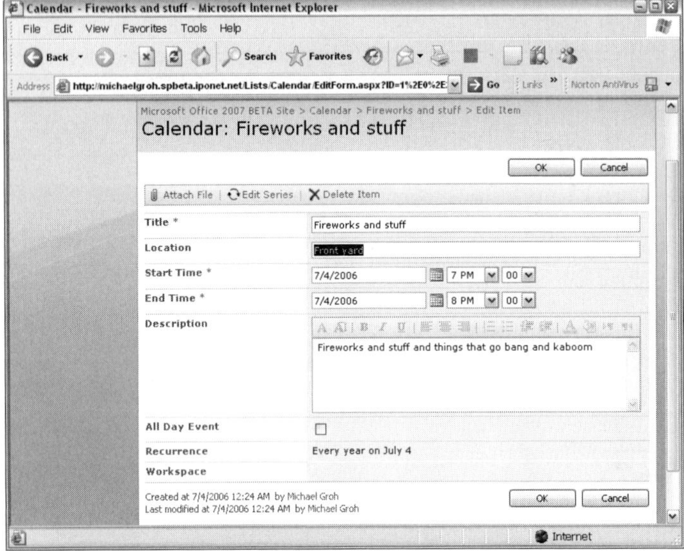

Integrating Access 2007 and SharePoint

Integrating Access 2007 and SharePoint Services consists of the following elements:

- The data content of Access tables can be stored on the Internet. This can be done by copying tables from Access to SharePoint Lists (on a SharePoint Services Web site).
- You can even create a SharePoint Services Web site using the Access interface.
- You can build rich content entry forms in Access, based on data content in SharePoint Services data sets.

In other words, you pass information back and forth across the Internet, between an Access database and SharePoint Services. You can also do this data transfer processing in both directions. Figure 23-9 demonstrates how Access can be used as a rich content interface, and a SharePoint Services Web site is used to store data.

As shown in Figure 23-9, Access becomes solely a user interface, and the SharePoint Services Web site becomes the database. This database effectively allows multiple Access interfaces to share the same data.

FIGURE 23-9

Access can provide a rich content interface to a SharePoint Services Web site "database"

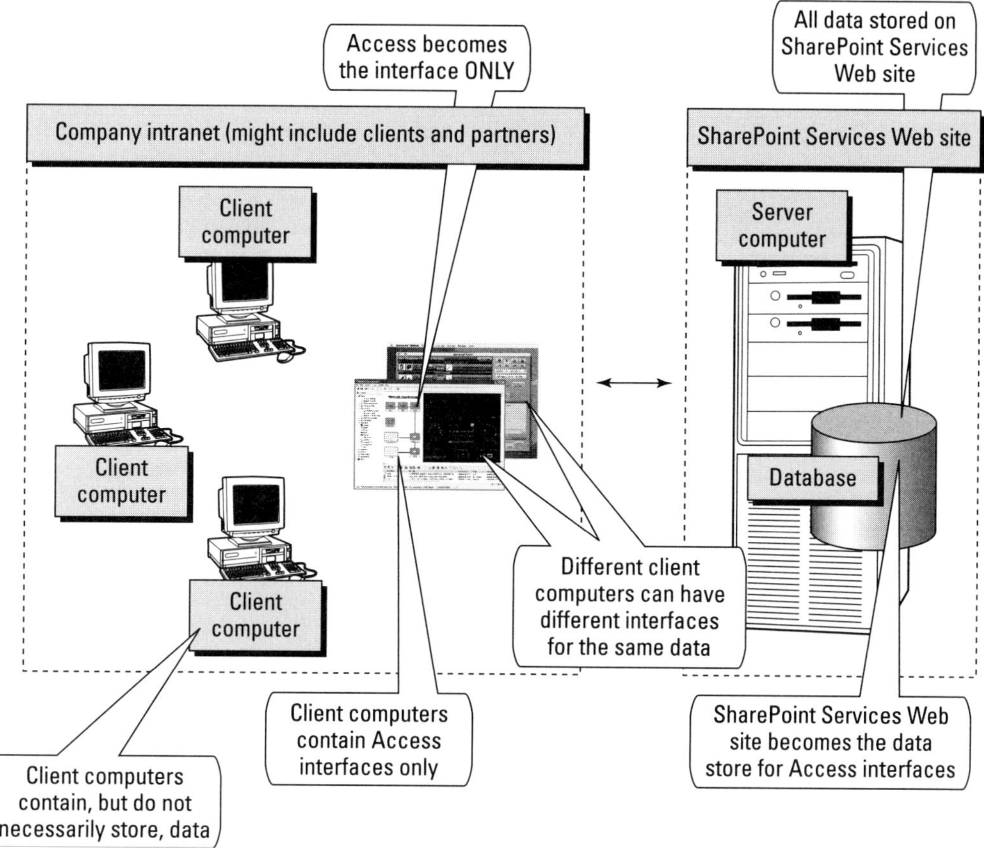

Sourcing data from a SharePoint Services Web site

You can execute an Access database from the SharePoint Services Web site, and push data from the Web site into an Access database — automatically. This is not necessarily a sequence of steps you can follow, because you would have to substitute the SharePoint Services Web site we're using for another, and one you can use. So, if you can't follow these steps, then just read them, and look at the pretty pictures:

1. **Execute a SharePoint Services Web site in your browser.**
2. **Isolate one of the SharePoint Lists on the page, and choose Actions ➪ Access, as shown in Figure 23-10.**

FIGURE 23-10

Executing an Access database from a SharePoint Service Web site

The result of selecting Access as in Figure 23-10 is what you see in Figure 23-11.

FIGURE 23-11

Linking between an Access database and a SharePoint Services Web site

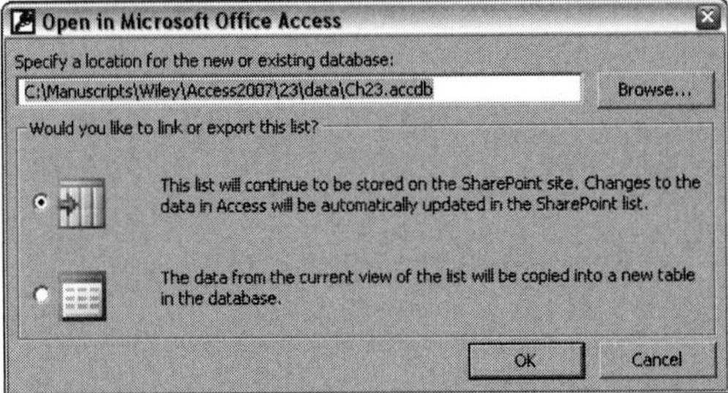

As shown in Figure 23-11, you can either make a copy of SharePoint Services Web site data — into an Access database — or you can create a link between Access and the Web site, allowing changes in Access to automatically propagate to the Web site.

3. **Select the Access database, leave the link option selected, and click OK.**

   You selected the calendar SharePoint List on the SharePoint Services Web site. The result is the calendar data in the Access database you executed, as shown in Figure 23-12.

   After a brief pause in the Access database, and a quick refresh of the SharePoint Services Web site display in the browser, the changes are clearly shown in Figure 23-13. And it's all automatic. Now that's integration!

FIGURE 23-12

Passing data into Access from a SharePoint Services Web site

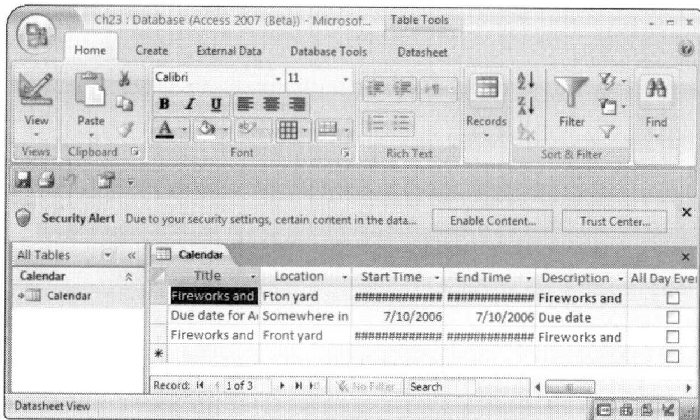

FIGURE 23-13

Changes propagate automatically from Access to SharePoint Services

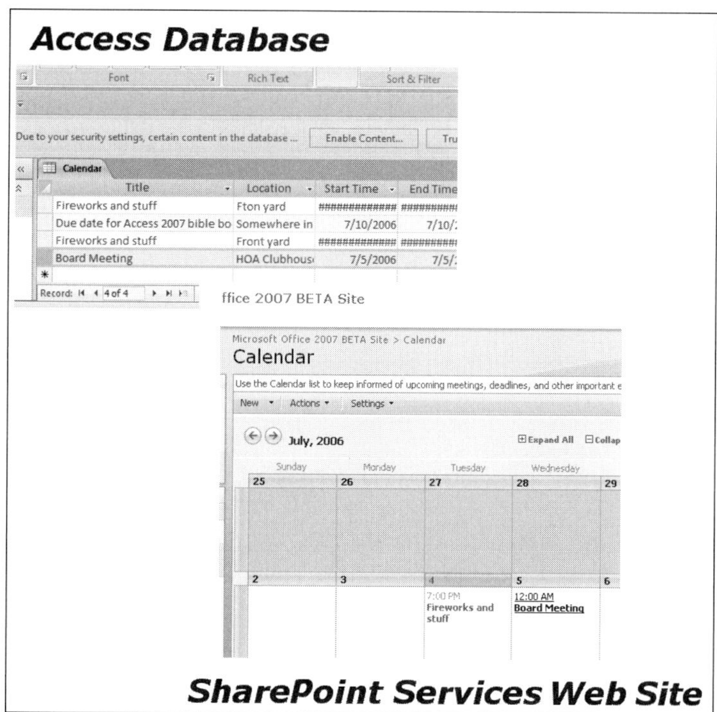

4. **Now you can get something else from the SharePoint Services Web site (for example, tasks, as shown in Figure 23-14).**

FIGURE 23-14

Getting another SharePoint List from the SharePoint Services

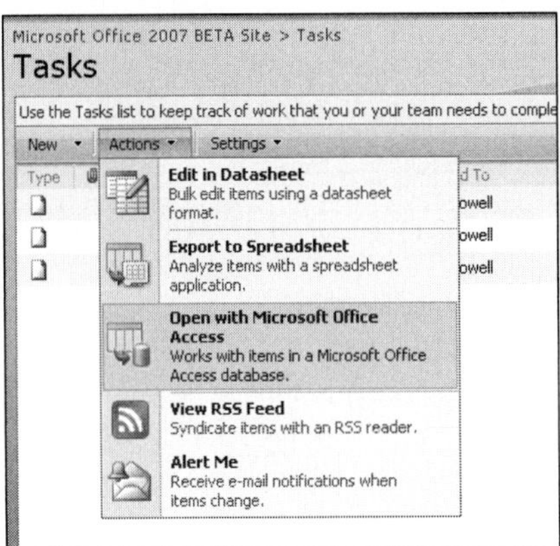

5. **The tasks are added to the same database as before, as shown in Figure 23-15.**

   In the case of the data transfer shown in Figure 23-15, both tasks and a list of people (people allocated to tasks) are passed back to the Access database.

FIGURE 23-15

More data is passed from SharePoint Services to Access database.

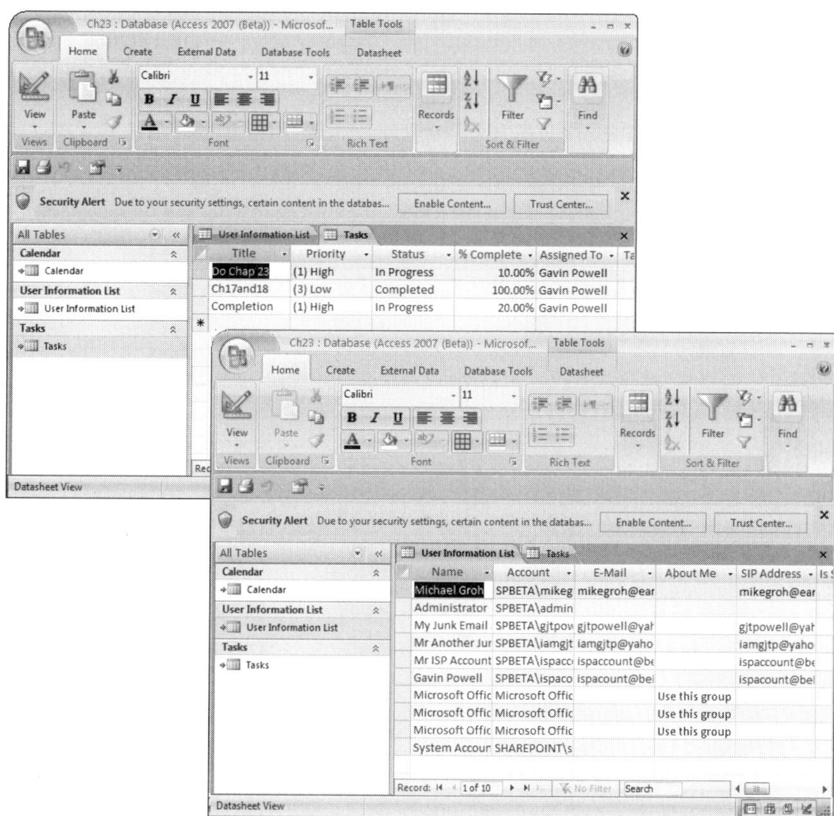

Sourcing data from an Access database

In the previous section, you began with the SharePoint Services Web site. This time, you begin with the Access database, and no SharePoint Services started in a browser. In other words, you work only with the Access database. So follow these steps, using a similar SharePoint Services Web site if possible; otherwise, just read the steps:

1. **Open up an Access database.**

   In this case, open the same database as before, which is `Chapter23.accdb`.

   Assuming that nothing has changed with your database from the previous section, your Access database screen should look something like the one shown in Figure 23-16.

FIGURE 23-16

Connecting from Access to a SharePoint Services Web site

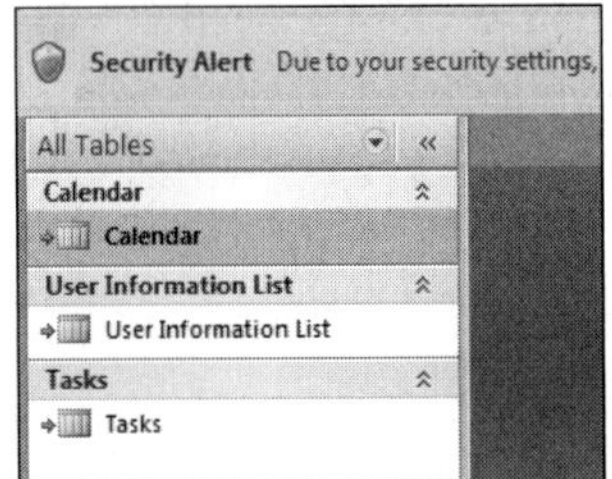

   Figure 23-16 should show the data already added in the previous section.

2. **Click the Create tab at the trop of the Access window, select SharePoint List from the SharePoint List option, and select Contacts.**

   The next screen you see is the one shown in Figure 23-17.

   Figure 23-17 allows you to select a Web site to connect to. This Web site is a SharePoint Services technology that you will get data from. You have to type in a name for the Web site, as shown by the circle highlighting the typed-in name *Here's a list of contacts.* Otherwise, you won't be able to click the OK button to continue. This is because the Access database needs to know what to call whatever it is you're linking to from Access to the SharePoint Services Web site.

3. **You should be prompted to log in with a username and password as shown in Figure 23-18.**

   And as you see, the list of contacts is now accessible from Access, as shown in Figure 23-19. There was nothing to copy from the SharePoint Services. So a single contact was added in Access, which propagated to the SharePoint Services automatically.

FIGURE 23-17

Select a SharePoint Services Web site to connect to.

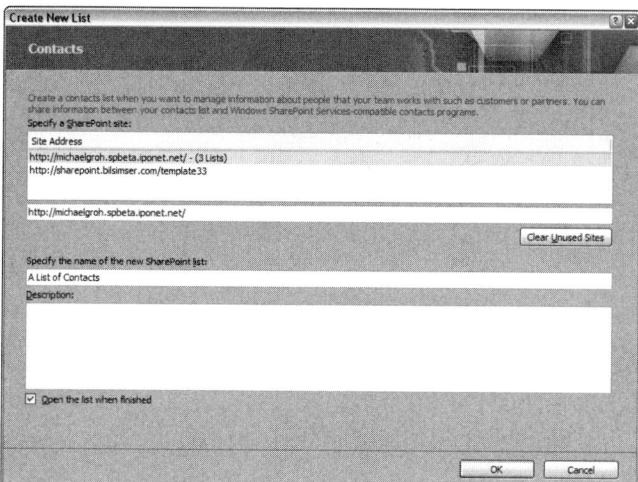

FIGURE 23-18

SharePoint Services Web sites require security.

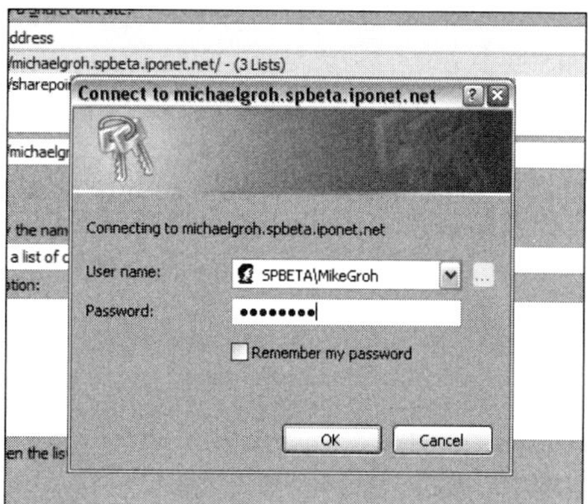

FIGURE 23-19

SharePoint Services Web site link into an Access database

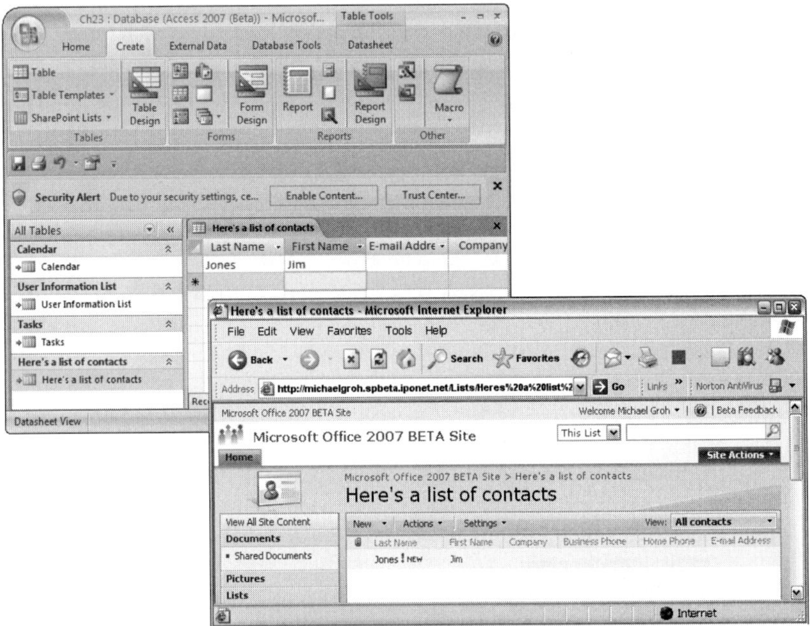

SharePoint and Different Operating Systems

Different Microsoft Windows operating systems, or different variants of Windows, has varying capabilities with respect to SharePoint Services. Windows Server 2003 will provide the most flexible and scalable options, if that is what you need:

- **Windows 2K:** Very basic integration with SharePoint Services only. SharePoint Portal Server is exclusive to Windows Server 2003. Data stored with SharePoint Services can be edited from Access 2000 and beyond.
- **Windows XP:** A little better than Windows 2K, allowing access to more Office products (Office 2002 and beyond).
- **Windows Server 2003:** Best integration plus provision of SharePoint Services as a portal server process as well, allowing for typical server capabilities such as much better scalability and processing capacity.

SharePoint Lists as External Data

A SharePoint List is maintained from a SharePoint Services Web site, or from something like an Access database. Making changes to the data at the service Web site prompts an immediate update. Much like the updating from changes in an Access database, changing data on a SharePoint Services Web site is performed automatically. Access 2007 can be used to maintain the integration between Access and a SharePoint Service Web site in other ways. Figure 23-20 shows various options that can be used to manage that integration process.

FIGURE 23-20

Access 2007 to SharePoint Services Web site integration options

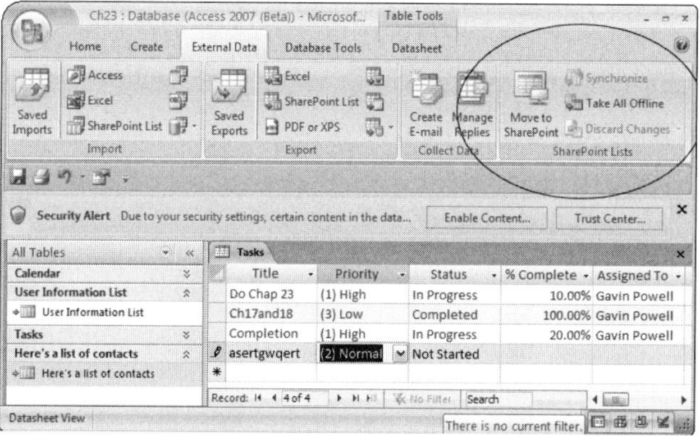

As you can see in Figure 23-20 the following points are useful to remember:

- **Move to SharePoint:** Parts of an Access database, such as a table not part of a SharePoint Services Web site, can be copied to the SharePoint Services Web site.
- **Synchronize and Discard Changes:** Normally, the integration process of propagation of changes between SharePoint Services and an Access database is executed automatically. When this is not the case, the two disparate data sets can be synchronized, or changes not yet implemented from Access to SharePoint Services can be abandoned.
- **Take All Offline:** Access objects, which are linked to objects on a SharePoint Services Web site, can be taken offline altogether, such that changes are no longer propagated in either direction.

Importing a SharePoint List into Access and exporting a SharePoint List from Access use the same process as that shown in Figure 23-17 and Figure 23-18. Figure 23-21 shows that the importing and exporting processes for SharePoint Lists objects are simple processes of connecting Access and the SharePoint List Web site and performing the external data import or export.

FIGURE 23-21

Access 2007 to SharePoint Services Web site importing and exporting is simple.

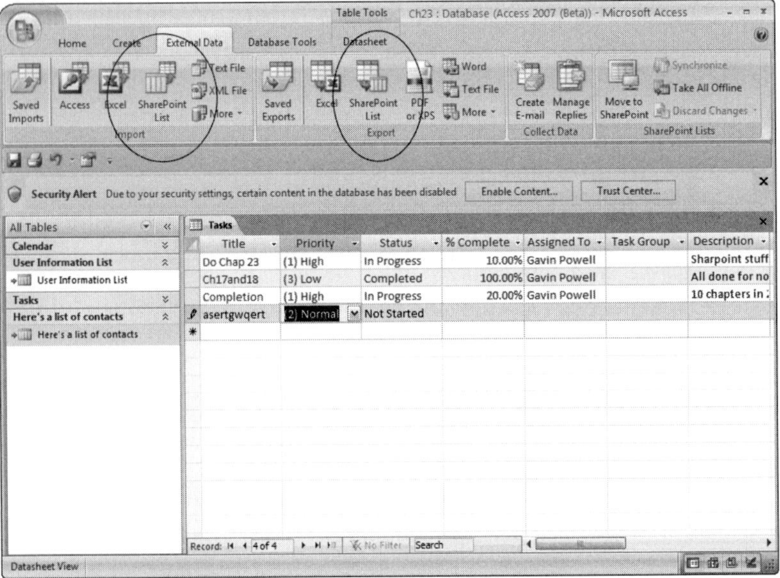

Summary

SharePoint Services are a major advance for Access developers. Microsoft is very clearly committed to SharePoint, and the ability to link Access to SharePoint data sources will only increase over time. SharePoint provides a flexible, secure, efficient data repository that is Web-accessible. Anyone with access to the Internet is able to access a SharePoint Web site and (assuming they present the appropriate credentials to SharePoint's security system) is able to not only access, but to modify and add data to the SharePoint site through Access 2007.

SharePoint integration is just one more example of Microsoft's commitment to enhancing Access's ability to integrate with diverse data sources. Although the other Microsoft Office 2007 applications also integrate with SharePoint, it is a sure bet that Access 2007 will take a dominant role when working with SharePoint. With its ability to provide the users with powerful forms and informative reports, Access is a natural tool to use when building SharePoint client-side interfaces.

Chapter 24

Using ActiveX Controls

Access provides many powerful tools for enhancing your forms and reports. These tools let you add pictures, graphs, sound, and even video to your database application. Chart wizards make it easy to build business graphs and add them to your forms and reports. ActiveX controls extend the power of Access 2007; new features borrowed from Microsoft Office 2007 make using Access forms more productive than ever.

In this chapter, you learn about the different types of graphical and ActiveX objects you can add to your system. You learn how to manipulate them to create professional, productive screen displays and reports. You also learn how to use some of the new Office 2007 tools that work with Access 2007 forms.

the CD-ROM **This chapter uses the `Chapter24.accdb` database. If you haven't already copied it onto your machine from the CD, you'll need to do so now.**

IN THIS CHAPTER

- Understanding the differences between bound and unbound objects
- Reviewing the differences between linking and embedding
- Learning the different ways of storing these objects
- Modifying an existing OLE object from your form design
- Creating a graph and linking it to a form
- Customizing graphs
- Using Office integration in Access 2007
- Creating an Excel PivotTable
- Creating an Excel PivotChart

Understanding Objects

Access gives you the capability of embedding pictures, video clips, sound files, business graphs, Excel spreadsheets, and Word documents. You can also link to any OLE (Object Linking and Embedding) object within forms and reports. Therefore, Access lets you not only use objects in your forms but also edit them directly from within your forms.

Looking at the types of objects

As a general rule, Access can add any type of picture or graphic object to a form or report. You can interact with OLE objects with great flexibility. For example, you can link to an entire spreadsheet, a range of cells, or even an individual cell.

Access can embed and store any binary file within an object frame control, including even sound and full-motion video. As long as you have the software driver for the embedded object, you can play or view the contents of the frame.

These objects can be bound to a field in each record *(bound)* or to the form or report itself *(unbound)*. Depending on how you want to process the OLE object, you may either place *(embed)* the copy directly in the Access database or tell Access where to find the object *(link)* and place it in the bound or unbound object frame in your form or report. The following sections describe the different ways to process and store both bound and unbound objects by using embedding and linking.

Using bound and unbound objects

A *bound object* is an object displayed (and potentially stored) within a field of a record in a table. Access can display the object on a form or print it on a report.

A bound object is bound to an OLE object data type field in the table. If you use a bound object in a form, you can add and edit pictures or documents, record by record, the same way you can edit other data. To display a bound OLE object, you use a *bound object frame control*. In Figure 24-1, the picture of the Porsche is a bound object. Each record stores a photograph of the car in the `Picture` field in the `tblProducts` table. You can enter a different picture for each record.

An *unbound object* is not stored in a table; it is placed on the form or report. An unbound object control is the graphic equivalent of a label control. These are generally used for OLE objects in the form or report itself. They don't belong to any of the record's fields. Unbound objects don't change from record to record.

An *image control* that displays a picture is another example of an unbound object. Although an unbound OLE object frame allows you to edit an object by double-clicking on it and launching the source application (Paint, Word, Excel, a sound or video editor or recorder, and so on), an image control only displays a bitmap picture (usually in `.bmp`, `.jpg`, or `.gif` format) that cannot be edited.

TIP **Always use an image control for unbound pictures; it uses far fewer computer resources than an OLE control and significantly increases performance.**

In Figure 24-1 the image of the car is a bound OLE object; the expected profit value is an unbound object because it is not directly stored in the table. However, the expected profit value is calculated for each record in the form. So, there is a dependency between the expected profit and whatever record is currently displayed on the form. This means the graph is updated each time data in the record changes.

FIGURE 24-1

Bound and unbound objects

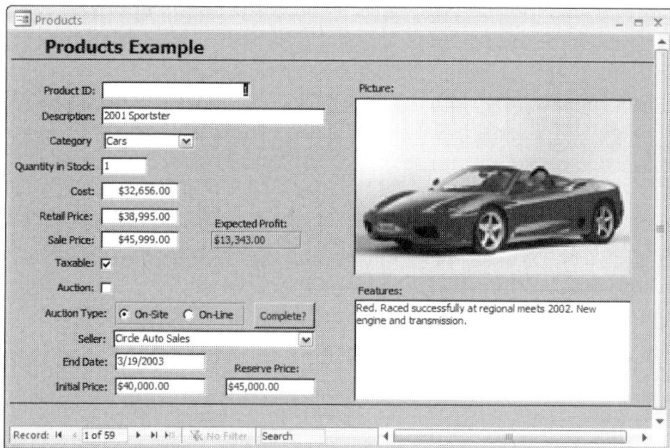

Linking and embedding

The basic difference between linking and embedding objects within a form or report is that *embedding* the object stores a copy of it within your database. *Linking* an object from another application does not store the object in your database; instead, the external location of the object is stored. Linking an object gives you two benefits:

- You can make changes to the object using the source application, without opening Access.
- The Access database only uses space for the file path and filename to the external reference.

CAUTION **If the external file is moved to another directory (or if the file is renamed), the link to Access is broken. Therefore, opening the Access form that is linked to the object will result in an error message.**

One benefit of embedding is that you don't have to worry about someone changing the location or name of a linked file. It is embedded. So, the file is part of the Access `.accdb` database file. Embedding does have its costs, however. The first is that it takes up space in your database — sometimes a great deal of space. Some pictures can take several megabytes. In fact, if you embed an `.avi` video clip of just 30 seconds in your database for one record, it can use 10MB or more of space. Imagine the space that 100 records with video could use.

After the object is embedded or linked, you can use the source application (such as Excel or Paintbrush) to modify the object directly from the form. To make changes to these objects, you only have to display the object in Access and double-click on it. This automatically launches the source application and lets you modify the object.

When you save the object, it is saved within Access.

Suppose that you've written a document management system in Access and have embedded a Word file in an Access form. When you double-click on the image of the Word document, Word is launched automatically and you can edit the document.

NOTE **When you use a linked object, the external application is started, and when you modify the object the changes are made to the external file, not within your database as they are with an embedded file.**

NOTE **To edit an OLE object, you must have the associated OLE application installed in Windows. If you have embedded an Excel `.xls` file but don't own Excel, you can view the spreadsheet (or use its values), but you won't be able to edit or change it.**

Embedding Objects

You can embed objects in both unbound and bound object frames, as well as in image frames. Embedding places the object in the Access database, where it is stored in the form, the report, or a record of a table.

ON the CD-ROM **In this section, you use the form shown in Figure 24-2. You can find the form in the Access Auto Auctions database file, named `frmProductExampleStart`.**

FIGURE 24-2

The frmProductExampleStart form

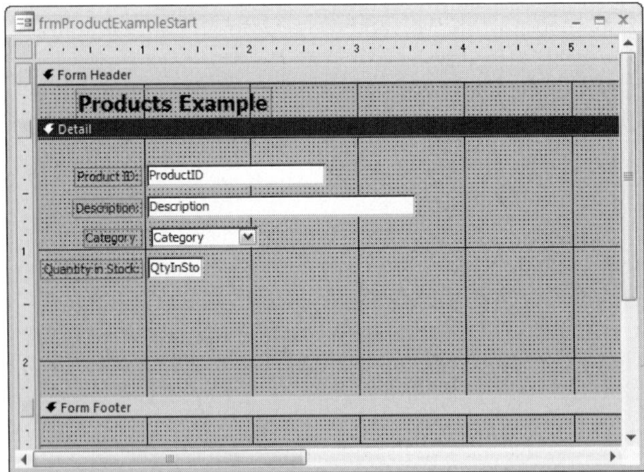

Embedding an unbound object

Access provides two methods you can use to embed an unbound object in a form or report:

- You can simply paste an object on the form or report. Access adds an image or unbound object frame that contains the object.
- You can add an unbound object frame or image frame and then insert the object or picture into the frame.

Pasting an unbound object

If the object you want to insert is not an OLE object, you *must* first copy in the source application and then paste the object on the form. Generally today most applications include OLE technology and can be recognized by the Insert menu option. Sometimes, you may just want to select an image using Windows Explorer and copy and paste the object to an Access form. As an example, to cut or copy an object and then paste it into an image or unbound object frame, follow these steps:

1. **Create or display any object by using any source application like Word, Excel, or Paint.**
2. **Select the object and copy into the buffer by pressing Ctrl+C.**
3. **Display the Access form or report in Design View and paste from the buffer by pressing Ctrl+V.**

This process automatically adds an unbound object frame for an OLE object (such as Word or Excel) or an Image control for a Paint picture and then embeds the pasted object in it.

If the object you paste into a form is an OLE object and you have the OLE application loaded, you can still double-click on the object to edit it. For example, you can highlight a range of cells in an Excel worksheet and paste the highlighted selection into an Access form or report. You can use the same highlight-and-paste approach with a paragraph of text in Word and paste it on the Access form or report. You can paste both OLE and non-OLE objects on a form or report with this method, but you'll see that there are other ways to add an OLE object.

Inserting an image-type object

You can also use the second method to embed OLE objects or pictures into an unbound object frame or image frame. Suppose that you want to embed a file containing a Paint picture. In Figure 24-1, the picture of the Access Auto Auctions logo appears on the form in the form header in an *image control*. You can embed the picture by either pasting it into the image control or by inserting the object into the *image frame* (the rectangle that contains and displays the picture). Follow these steps to add an image control:

1. **Open the form `frmProductExampleStart` in Design View.**
2. **Select the Image frame tool on the Toolbox (see Figure 24-3).**

   The icon is under the Design tab (at the top of the Access window), in the Controls section, and looks like a little mountain with the sun rising over it).

FIGURE 24-3

Creating an image frame

3. **Draw a rectangle in the Form Header (refer to Figure 24-3), to add the image frame.**

   When you add an image frame, the Insert Picture dialog box appears. This dialog box, shown in Figure 24-4, displays the filenames of the image objects you have on your system.

4. **To embed an existing graphic, select the file called `porsche.bmp` in the Navigation window (shown in Figure 24-4), and click the OK button.**

Access embeds and displays the picture in the unbound object frame, as you can see in Figure 24-5. Notice that, in this figure, the picture may not appear to be displayed correctly. In this case, the image is too small for the image frame. You can correct this by simply resizing the image frame until it looks right. Otherwise, you can also use the Size Mode property. To get the Properties window up on the screen, right-click the image and select the Properties option from the menu.

FIGURE 24-4

The Insert Picture dialog box

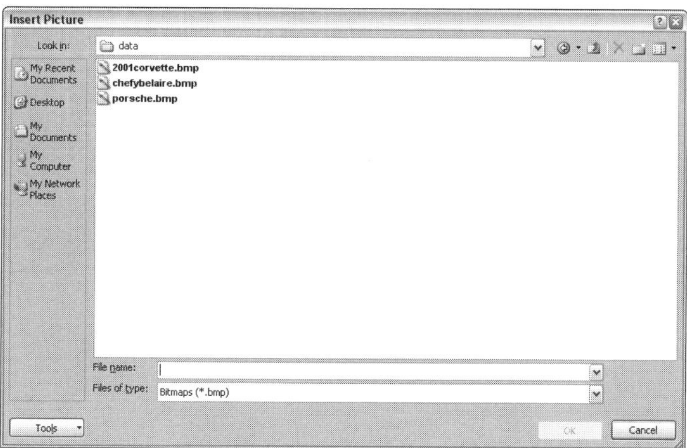

Figure 24-5 also shows some of the other properties of the Image control. The Picture property is set to the path and filename of the image you selected. The Picture Type property below has two choices. The default is Embedded and saves a copy of the bitmap picture in the database container in a compressed form. The other Picture Type option is Linked and stores the image externally to the Access database. This setting will maintain a link to the original picture. However, if you move the bitmap, the picture will no longer be displayed and the link will be broken.

FIGURE 24-5

The image frame property sheet

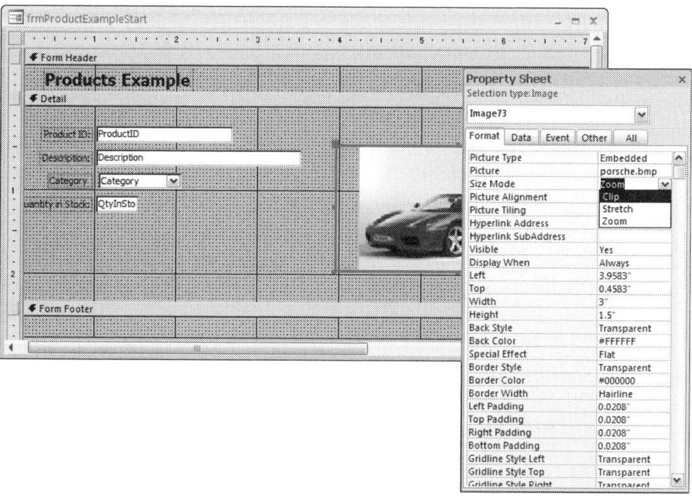

Changing the display of an image

After you add an image to a form or a report, you may want to change the size of the object or the object frame. If you embed a small picture, you may want to adjust the size of the object frame to fit the picture. Similarly, you might want to reduce the size of the picture to fit a specific area on your form or report.

To change the appearance and proportions of the object you embedded, you must change the size of the image frame and set the Size Mode property. In Figure 24-6, you see the result of the three choices for the Size Mode property, as well as the correct view of the picture:

- **Clip:** Shows the picture at its actual size, truncating both the right and bottom
- **Stretch:** Fits the picture within the frame, distorting the picture's proportions
- **Zoom:** Fits the picture proportionally within the frame, possibly resulting in extra white space

FIGURE 24-6

Results of using the various scaling options

You should use the Clip option only when the frame is the exact size of the picture or when you want to crop the picture. Stretch is useful when you can accept a slight amount of distortion in the picture. Although using Zoom fits the picture to the frame and maintains the original proportions, it may leave empty space in the frame. To change the Size Mode setting for the `porsche.bmp` file on the `frmProductExampleStart` form, follow these steps:

1. **Select the image frame in Design View.**
2. **Display the Property Sheet.**
3. **Change the Size Mode setting to Stretch.**

When you have added a picture with a frame (border) that is much larger than the picture itself and you have selected a Size Mode of Clip, the picture normally is centered within the frame. You can control this by using one of the Picture Alignment options, which are Center, Top Left, Top Right, Bottom Left, and Bottom Right.

Embedding bound objects

You can store pictures, spreadsheets, word-processing documents, or other objects as data in a table. For example, you can store a Paintbrush picture, an Excel worksheet, or an object created in any other OLE application, such as a sound clip, an HTML document, or even a video clip from a movie.

You store objects in a table by creating a field in your table that uses the OLE Object data type. After you create a blank bound object frame, you can bind its Control Source to the OLE Object field in the table. You can also drag the field to the form from the Field List window and it will be automatically bound.

You can then use the bound object frame to embed an object into each record of the table.

NOTE **You can also insert objects into a table from the Datasheet View of a form, table, or query, but the objects cannot be displayed in a view other than Form. When you switch to Datasheet View, you'll see text describing the OLE class of the embedded object. For example, if you insert a `.bmp` picture into an OLE object field in a table, the text Picture appears in Datasheet View.**

Adding a bound OLE object

The image added in the previous section was not bound, in that it was not bounded, linked, connected in any way, to the database. To add an embedded OLE object in a new bound object frame, follow these steps:

1. **Remove the unbound image from the previous section.**
2. **Select the Bound Object Frame button from the Toolbox (t).**
3. **Drag and size the frame, as shown in Figure 24-7.**
4. **Display the properties sheet.**
5. **Type** Picture **in the Control Source property of the Data tab.**

   This is the name of the OLE field in the `tblProducts` table that contains pictures of the cars.
6. **Set the Size Mode property to Zoom, on the Format tab, so that the picture will be zoomed proportionally within the area you define.**
7. **Select and delete only the bound object frame label (OLEBoundxx:).**
8. **Close and save the changes to this form.**

FIGURE 24-7

Creating a bound object frame

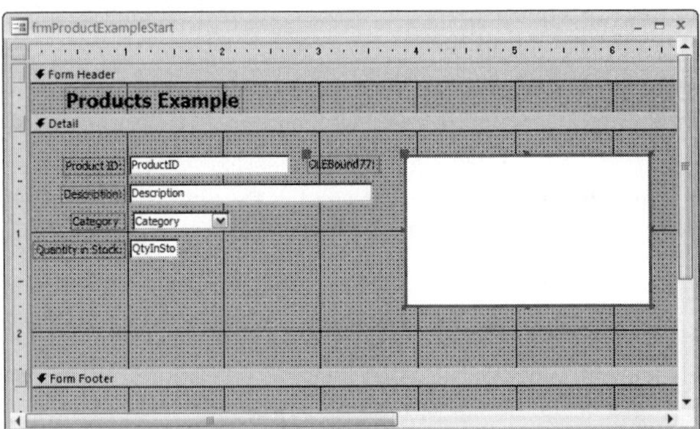

Adding a picture to a bound object frame

After you define the bound object frame control and place it on a form, you can add pictures to it in several ways. You can paste a picture into a record or insert a file object into the frame. You insert the file object for a bound frame in nearly the same way you would insert an unbound object or image frame. The only difference is that, where an unbound image frame has a picture inserted in the design screen, a bound object frame contains a picture that is stored in a table, so the picture is inserted in Form View like any other data.

To insert a picture or other object into a bound object frame, display the form in Form View, move to the correct record (each record can have a different picture or object), select the bound object frame, and then right-click on the object, and select the Insert Object option from the pop-up menu. The dialog box is a little different. Because you can insert any OLE object (in this example, a picture), you first have to choose Create from File, and then choose the first option, Bitmap Image. You can then select the actual picture. When you're through, the picture or object appears in the bound object frame in the form.

NOTE **If you create the object (instead of embedding an existing file), some applications display a dialog box asking whether you want to close the connection and update the open object. If you choose Yes, Access embeds the object in the bound object frame or embeds the object in the datasheet field along with text describing the type object, such as Excel or Word.**

After you embed an object, you can start its source application and edit it from your form or report. Simply select the object in Form View and double-click it.

Editing an embedded object

After you have an embedded object, you may want to modify the object itself. You can edit an OLE object in several ways. Normally, you can just double-click on it and launch the source application; then you can edit the embedded OLE object. As an example, you could follow these steps to edit the picture of the car in Windows Paint or whatever your default application is for editing bitmaps:

1. **Display the form `frmProductExampleStart` in Form View.**
2. **Move to record 2 (or whichever record contains blue car) and select the picture bound object frame of the car.**
3. **Double-click the picture.**

   The screen changes to an image-editing environment with Windows Paint, Microsoft Photo Editor, or your default bitmap editor's menus and functions available. You may see the icon on the taskbar for the product (Microsoft Photo Editor) in Figure 24-8. Choose Maximize on the icon to edit the picture if in-place editing is not allowed in Access.

CAUTION If you get the message `The OLE object was changed to a picture or the link was broken`, it just means that our pictures may not be compatible with your system. Insert your own picture and try again.

CAUTION Another error message might be `OLE server isn't registered`. If you get this error message, you need to register some DLL files in Windows. Go to `www.microsoft.com` and search for OLE server.

NOTE Windows supports full in-place editing of OLE objects. Instead of launching a different program, it changes the look of the menus and screen to match Windows Paint, temporarily adding that functionality to Access.

4. **Make any changes you want to the picture.**
5. **Click on any other control in the form to close Paint or Microsoft Photo Editor.**

If you make any changes, you'll be prompted to update the embedded object before continuing.

CAUTION In most cases, you modify an OLE object by double-clicking on it. When you attempt to modify either a sound or video object, however, double-clicking on the object causes it to use the player instead of letting you modify it. For these objects, you must use the Edit menu; select the last option, which changes (according to the OLE object type) to let you edit or play the object. You can also convert some embedded OLE objects to static images, which breaks all OLE links and simply displays a picture of the object.

FIGURE 24-8

Editing the embedded object

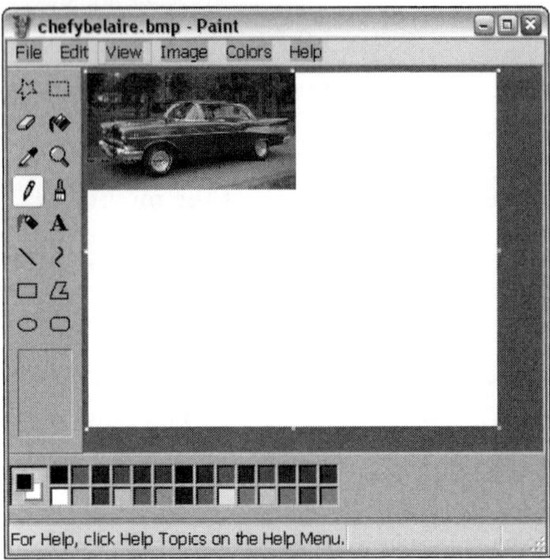

Linking Objects

Besides embedding objects, you can link them to external application files in much the same way as you would embed them. As you learned earlier, the difference is that the object itself is not stored in the form, the report, or the database table. Instead, Access stores the filename and path to the object, saving valuable space in the `.accdb` file. This feature also allows you to edit the object in its source application without having to go through Access.

When you create a link from a file in another application (for example, Microsoft Excel) to a field in a table, the information is still stored in its original file.

Suppose that you decide to use the OLE Object field to store an Excel file containing additional information about the car's sales. If the Excel file contains history about the sales, you might want to link the information from the `tblProducts` record to this file.

Before linking information in a file to a field, however, you must first create and save the file in the source application.

ON the CD-ROM **On the CD-ROM is a file named `Car2.xls`, which is an Excel worksheet. However, you can use any spreadsheet or word-processing file in this example.**

To link information to a bound object, use the following steps showing you how to use the Picture bound object frame to link a `tblProducts` table record to an Excel worksheet:

1. Open Microsoft Excel or the source application, and load the document that contains the information you want to link to.
2. Select the information you want to link, as shown in Figure 24-9.
3. Press Ctrl+C to copy into the buffer.

FIGURE 24-9

Copying a range from Microsoft Excel

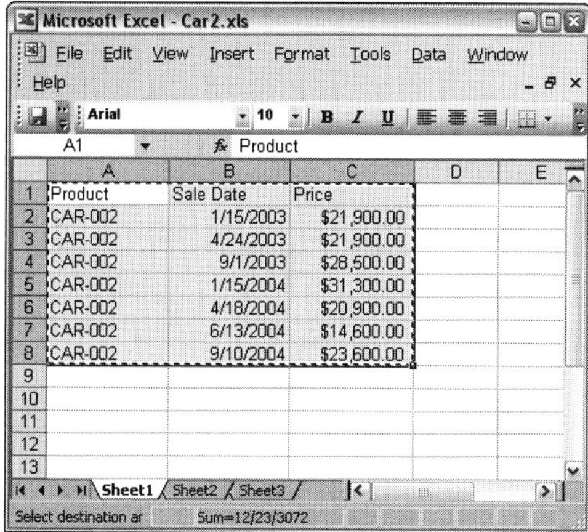

After you copy the range to the Clipboard, paste it into the bound object frame in the Access form by using the Paste Special option of the Edit menu.

The Clipboard is also known as *the buffer.*

4. Switch to Access and open the form `frmProductExampleStart` in Form View.
5. Go to record number 2 in the Access form or the record that contains blue car.
6. Select the bound object frame.
7. Right-click and select Paste.

   This will copy the data content into the bound object, not the Excel spreadsheet object.
8. Add the spreadsheet object by right-clicking the mouse and selecting Insert Object.
9. Follow the prompts to select an Excel Worksheet object, browse for, and select the file to add.

   This will allow you to edit the spreadsheet object from within the Access form, when it is running.

The linked Excel worksheet appears in the bound object frame, as shown in Figure 24-10. Access creates the link and displays the object in the bound object frame or it links the object to the datasheet field, displaying text (such as Microsoft Excel) that describes the object. When you double-click on the picture of the worksheet, Excel is launched and you can edit the data.

FIGURE 24-10

The linked worksheet

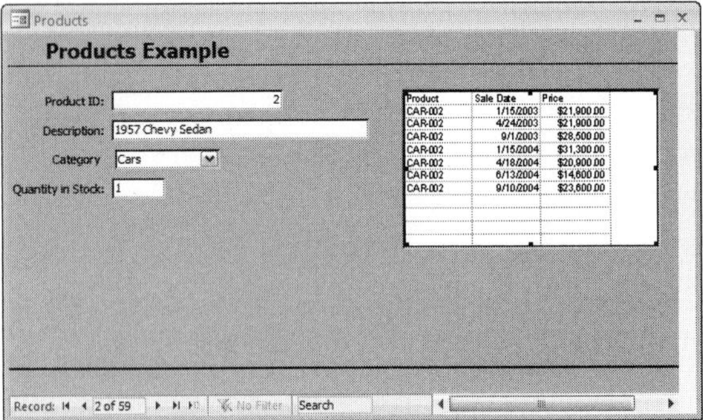

Creating a Graph or Chart

You use Microsoft Graph to chart data from any of your database tables or data stored within other applications (such as Microsoft Excel). Microsoft Graph creates graphs in a wide variety of styles, such as bar graphs, pie charts, line charts, and others. Because Graph is an embedded OLE application, it does not work by itself; you have to run it from within Access. It is dependent on Access.

NOTE **The terms *graph* and *chart* are used interchangeably in this chapter. Technically, you use Microsoft Graph to create a chart. There are many chart types that Microsoft Access cannot create. These have little to do with data, and include organization charts and flow charts.**

After you embed a graph, it behaves as any other OLE object. You can modify it from the Design View of your form or report by double-clicking on the graph itself, or edit it from the Form or Datasheet View of a form. The following sections describe how to build and process graphs that use data from within an Access table, as well as from tables of other OLE applications.

The different ways to create a graph

Access provides several ways to create a graph and place it on a form or a report. Using the Graph form or Report Wizard, you can create a graph as a new form or report, add it to an existing form or report, or add it to an existing form and link it to a table data source. (To use this third method, in form Design View, click on the Unbound Object frame tool on the Toolbox and then choose Microsoft Graph Chart.) Unless you're already an experienced Graph user, familiar with it from previous versions of Access or Excel, you'll find it easier to create a new graph from the Toolbox. If you examine the Toolbox, however, you won't see a Chart Wizard icon. You must first customize the Toolbox so that you can add a graph to an existing form by using the Chart Wizard.

As a general rule (for both types of graph creation), before you enter a graph into a form or report that will be based on data from one or more of your tables, you must specify which table or query will supply the data for the graph. You should keep in mind several rules when setting up your query:

- Make sure that you've selected the fields containing the data to be graphed.
- Be sure to include the fields containing the labels that identify the data.
- Include any linking fields if you want the data to change from record to record.

Creating graphs using the Toolbox

Figure 24-11 shows the Design tab, under the Design View when editing a form. The graph object selected is highlighted in Figure 24-11 with a circle drawn around it.

FIGURE 24-11

Adding a graph to a form

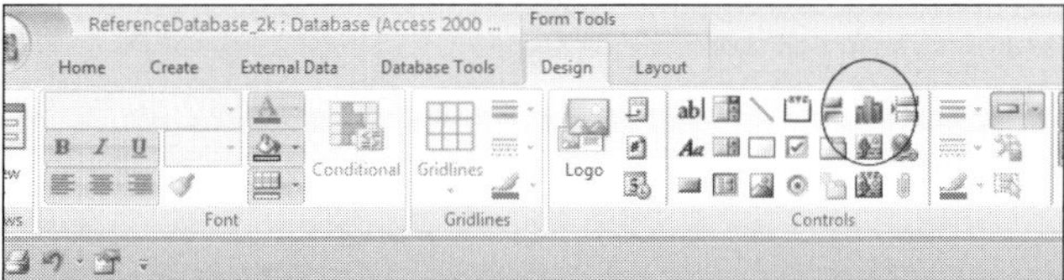

Embedding a Graph in a Form

As you learned earlier in this chapter, you can both link and embed objects in Access tables, and display objects on Access forms. Next you create and display a graph based on the Access Auto Auction data and display it in a form.

This graph will show the dates a car was sold and the dollars received each time. When you move through the records in the `tblProducts` table, the form will display the data in graph format for each car's prices. You'll use the same form that you've used so far throughout this chapter.

Assembling the data

As a first step in embedding a graph, make sure that the query associated with the form provides the information you need for the graph. In this example, you need both the `dtmSalesDate` and the `curPrice` fields from the `tblSalesLineItems` table as the basis of the graph. You also need the idsInvoiceNumber field from the tblSales table to use as a link to the data on the form. This link allows the data in the graph to change from record to record.

Sometimes, you'll need to create a query when you need data items from more than one table. In this example, you select all the data you need right from the wizard. Access builds the query (actually a SQL statement) for you automatically.

Build the query like this:

1. **In the leftmost, main drop-down menu, select Queries.**
2. **Click the Create tab (at the top), and the Query Design tool in the Other section.**
3. **Select the tblSales, and tblsSalesLineItems from the menu.**
4. **Click the Add button and close the Show Tables window.**

   The two tables should be linked with the invoice number (InvoiceNumber).
5. **Select ProductID from the line items table, and drag it onto the first Field box entry in the design specifications on the lower half of the Design View screen.**
6. **Place the SaleDate field from the sales table into the second column.**
7. **Place the Price field from the line items table into the third column.**
8. **Set the Sort option for the first two columns to an ascending sort.**
9. **Right-click the top of the window for the query designed, select Save from the menu, and store the query as qryChartExample.**
10. **Test the query by clicking the Datasheet View option from the View menu, just to make sure it's doing something useful.**

Adding the graph to the form

The following steps detail how to create and place the new graph on the existing form. You should be in the Design View of the form named frmProductExampleStart. The following steps take you through the wizard to create the desired graph and link it to your form:

1. **Select the Insert Chart tool you added to the Toolbox and draw a chart onto the form Design View.**
2. **Click the mouse button and hold it down while dragging the box to the desired size for the graph.**

   Access displays the Chart Wizard dialog box you use to embed a graph in the form. As shown in Figure 24-12, the first Chart Wizard screen lets you select the table or query with the data for the chart. By using the row of option buttons under the list of tables, you view all the tables, all the queries, or both.

FIGURE 24-12

Selecting the query for the source of data for the graph

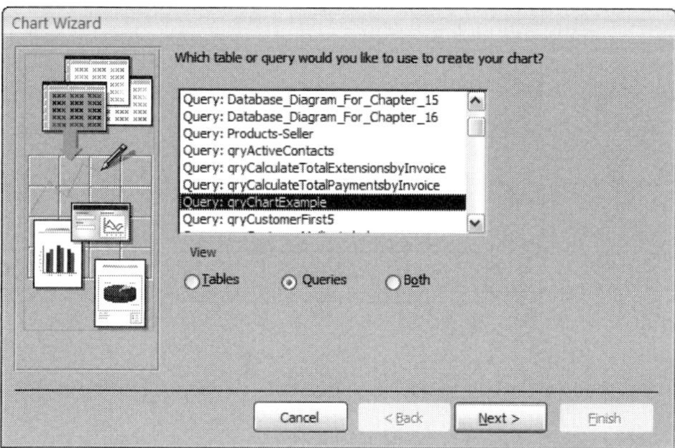

3. **Choose Query: qryChartExample as the data source for the graph and click Next.**

   The second screen of the Chart Wizard lets you select fields to include in your graph. You could select all the fields listed by double-clicking on them to move them to the Fields for Chart box or by clicking on the >> button to move the fields all at once. However, you want to add them in a specific order.

4. **Select the fields by double-clicking on them in the following specific order:** `SaleDate`, `ProductID`, `Price`.

5. **Click Next.**

   The third Chart Wizard screen (Figure 24-13) lets you choose the type of graph you want to create and determine whether the data series are in rows or columns.

6. **In this example, select a column chart.**

   You'll customize it later using the graph options. As you click on each of the graph types, an explanation appears in the box in the lower-right corner of the screen.

7. **Select the Column Chart, as shown in Figure 24-13, and click Next.**

   Column charts are easy to work with.

   Access 2007 may do something weird at this stage. The `SaleDate` field must be used for the *x*-axis. The `Price` must be used for *y*-axis; this determines the height of the bars on the histogram. If you want to change the assumptions, drag the field buttons on the right side of the screen to the simulated graph area. You drag the buttons to the little boxes, and delete anything that should not be in the little boxes. You should eventually have what is shown in Figure 24-12.

FIGURE 24-13

Selecting the type of chart

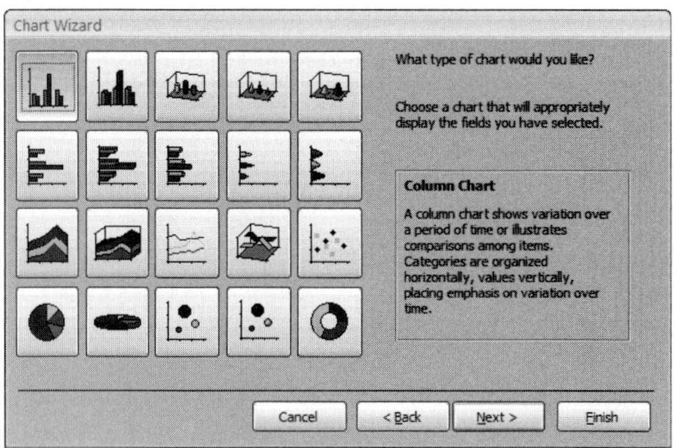

NOTE **It is important to only choose the fields that you'll use for the graph if you want the wizard to figure out for you what to graph.**

You may notice in Figure 24-14, that each of the fields on the left side of the screen is a button. By double-clicking on a field-button you further define how the data is used in the graph.

NOTE **There is a button on the top-left corner of the Chart Wizard that lets you preview that chart at any time. This way, you can see the results of your selections.**

Generally, the *x*-axis variable is either a date or a text field. The *y*-axis field is almost always a number. That number can be an aggregation, as in the case shown in Figure 24-12. Only numeric and date fields, such as the *y*-axis variable Price, can be further defined.

8. **Double-click on the `SumOfPrice` field on the left side of the screen.**

   The dialog box shown in Figure 24-15 appears. You can define options for summarizing the field. Remember that there may be many records for a given summary; in this example, many cars may have been sold in the same month.

TIP **If you had several numeric fields, you could drag them (or any multiple fields), to the left side for a multiple series; these would appear in a legend and display more than one bar or lines in the graph. You can also drag the same field to both the *x*-axis and the Series indicator, as long as you're grouping differently. For example, you could group the `SalesDate` by month and use it again in the Series grouped by year. Without using the `SalesDate` field a second time as the series variable, you would have one bar for each month in sequential order. For example, Jan01, Feb01, Mar01 . . . Dec01, Jan02, Feb02, and so on. By adding the `SalesDate` as a series variable and grouping it by year, you could get pairs of bars. Multiple bars can be created for each month, each a different color and representing a different year and a legend for each year.**

FIGURE 24-14

Laying out the chart's data elements

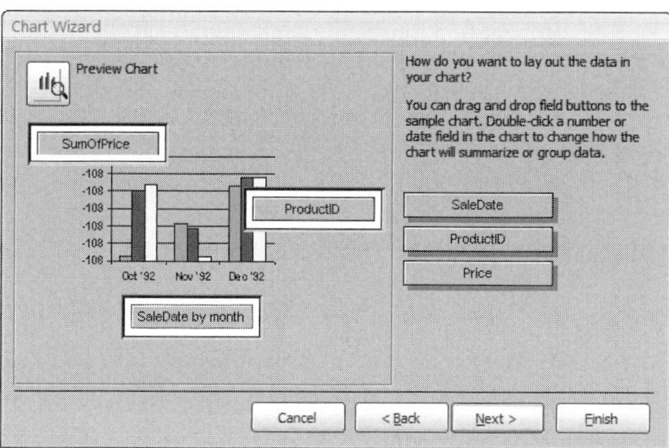

FIGURE 24-15

Selecting options to summarize the *y*-axis numeric field

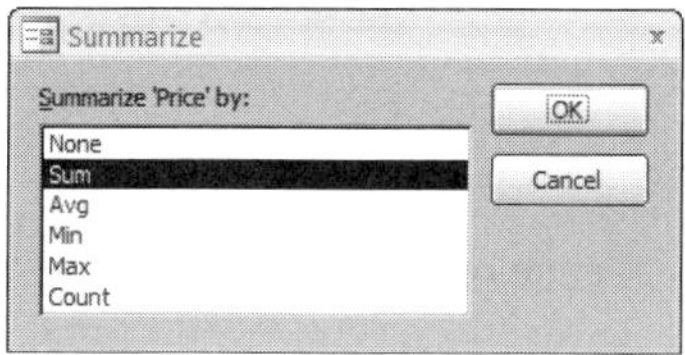

9. **As shown in Figure 24-15, Sum is selected as the summarizing type.**

   You could change it to Avg to get a graphical representation of an average amount of prices — instead of summing all the price amounts. Click Cancel to accept Sum.

You must supply a numeric variable for all the selections except Count, which can be any data type.

10. **Double-click SaleDate by month, and the dialog box shown in Figure 24-16 appears to let you choose the date hierarchy from larger to smaller rollups.**

    The choices include Year, Quarter, Month, Week, Day, Hour, and Minute. If you have data for many dates within a month and want to roll it up by month, choose Month. In this example, you want to see all the detail data. Because the data is in Sales by date (mm/dd/yy), you would select Day to view all the detail records.

11. **For this example, change the default selection from Month to Day and click OK.**

FIGURE 24-16

Choosing group options for a date field

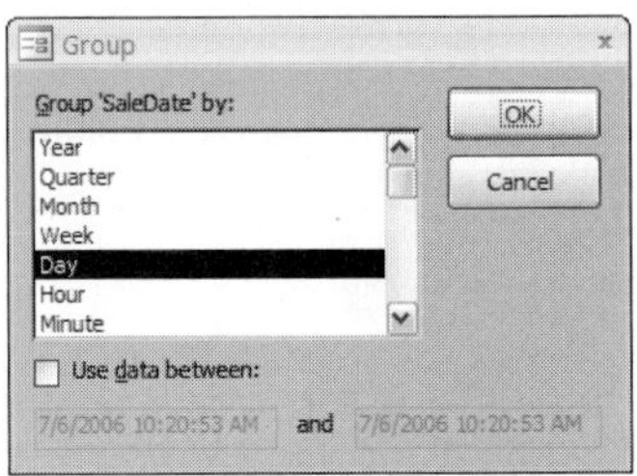

12. **After you change the group options from Month to Day for the `SaleDate` field, click on Next to go to the next wizard screen.**

    Figure 24-17 shows the field linking box. If you run the Chart Wizard from inside an existing form, you have the option to link a field in the form to a field in the chart. Even if you don't specify the field when you select the chart fields, you can make the link as long as the field exists in the selected table.

    In this example, Access has correctly selected the `ProductID` field, from both the `frmProductsExampleStart` form and the `qryChartExample` query. This way, as you move from record to record, which is keyed by Product ID, in the `frmProductExampleStart` form, the graph changes to display the data for that product.

13. **Click Next to move to the last wizard screen.**

FIGURE 24-17

Linking fields between the form and the graph

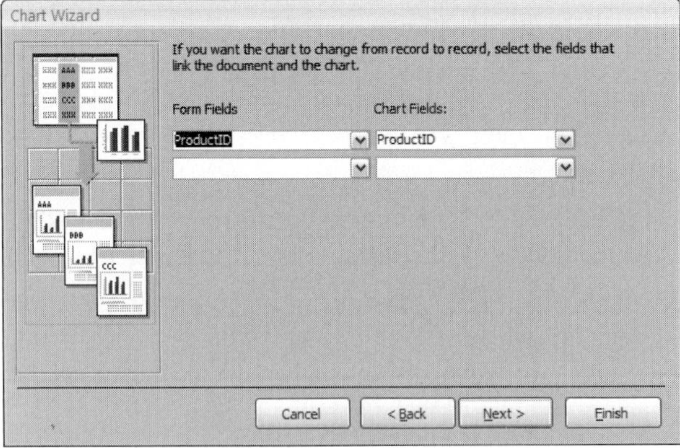

14. **The last Chart Wizard screen, shown in Figure 24-18, lets you enter a title and determine whether a legend is needed.**

    You won't need one for this example because you have only one data series.

FIGURE 24-18

Specifying a chart title and legend

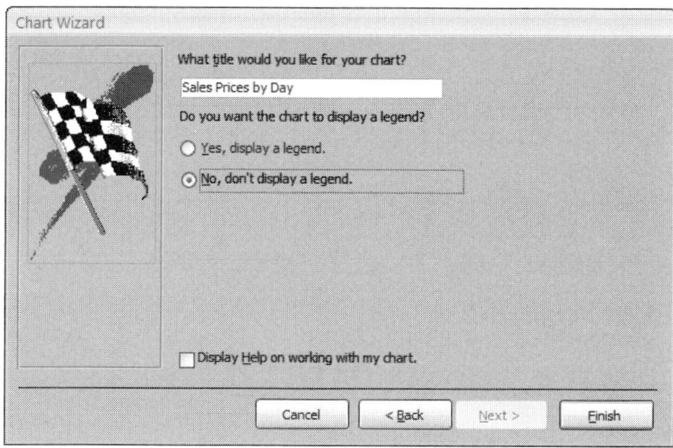

15. **Enter Sale Prices by Day for the graph title.**
16. **Select the button next to the text `No, don't display a legend` and click Finish to complete the wizard.**

    The sample chart appears in the graph object frame on the design screen. This is shown in Figure 24-19. Until you display the form in Form View, the link to the individual product is not established, and the graph is not recalculated to show the sale dates for a specific car's record.

    In fact, the graph shown is a sample preview. So, it doesn't use any of your data. If you were worried about where that strange-looking graph came from, don't be.

17. **Click the Form View button on the ribbon to display the `ProductExampleStart` form and recalculate the graph.**

    Figure 24-20 shows the final graph in Form View.

FIGURE 24-19

The graph in the Form Design window

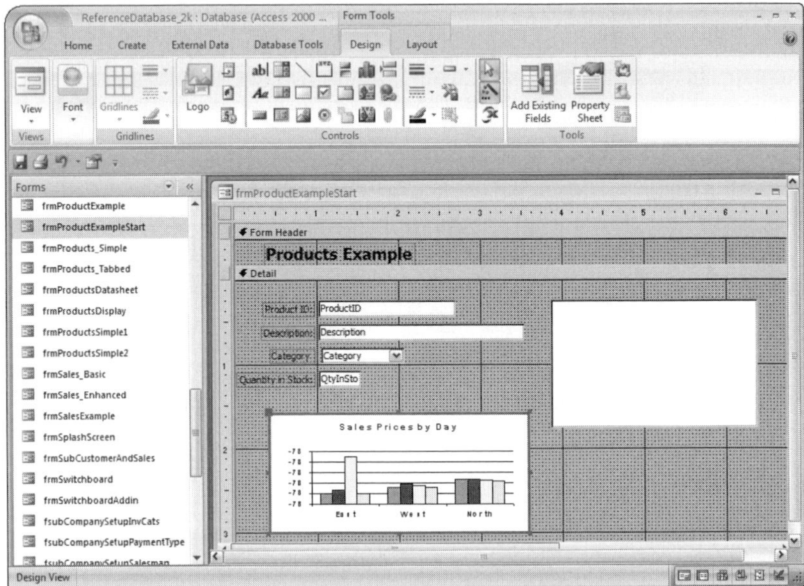

FIGURE 24-20

Recalculating the graph in Form View

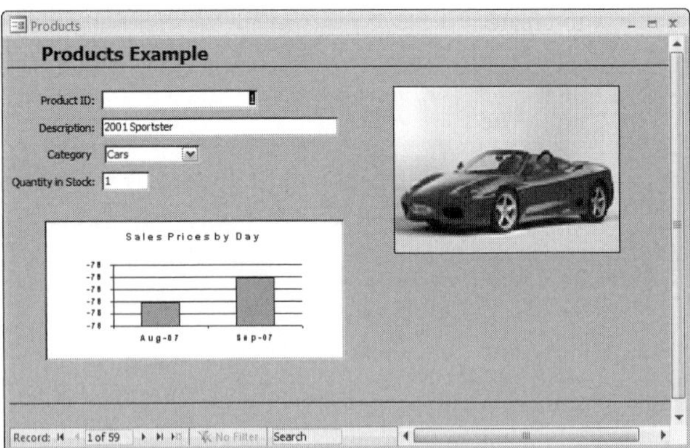

In Figure 24-19, you saw the graph and the property sheet. You display a graph by using a *graph frame,* which shows its data in either Form View or Design View. Now take a look at some properties in the property sheet. The Size Mode property is initially set to Stretch. You can change this to Zoom or Clip, although the graph should always be displayed proportionally. You can also size and move the graph to fit on your form. When you work with the graph in the Graph window, the size of the graph is the same size it will be in the Design window.

The Row Source property setting comes from the table or query you used with the graph, but it appears as a SQL statement that is passed to the Graph. The SQL statement (more on this later) created for this graph is as follows:

```
TRANSFORM Sum([Price]) AS [SumOfPrice]
SELECT (Format([SaleDate],"DDDDD"))
FROM [qryChartExample]
GROUP BY (Int([SaleDate])),(Format([SaleDate],"DDDDD"))
PIVOT [ProductID];
```

The next two properties — Link Child Fields and Link Master Fields — control data linking to the form's data. Using the link properties, you link the graph's data to each record in the form. In this example, the ProductID from the current Product record is linked to Sales records with the same ProductID value.

To change the appearance of the graph, double-click on the graph in Design View to open Microsoft Graph. After you make the changes you want, select File and Exit to return to Microsoft Access and go back to Design View.

Customizing a graph

After you create a graph within Access, you enhance it by using the tools within Microsoft Graph. As demonstrated in the preceding section, just a few mouse clicks will create a basic graph. In many cases, the basic chart that you create presents the idea you want to get across. In other cases, however, it may be necessary to create a more illustrative presentation. You accomplish this by adding any of these enhancements:

- Entering free-form text to the graph to highlight specific areas of the graph
- Changing attached text for a better display of the data being presented
- Annotating the graph with lines and arrows
- Changing certain graphic objects with colors and patterns
- Moving and modifying the legend
- Adding gridlines to reflect the data better
- Manipulating the 3-D view to show your presentation more accurately
- Adding a bitmap to the graph for a more professional presentation
- Changing the graph type to show the data in a different graphic format, such as Bar, Line, or Pie
- Adding or modifying the data in the graph

Integration with Microsoft Office

Access is not only integrated with Windows, it now shares many major components with all Microsoft Office tools. If you're an Excel or Word user, you'll be especially thrilled. Access has an integrated Spell Checker that is used to make sure that the data stored in Access tables and database objects is spelled correctly. The dictionary is shared across all Office applications. There are also specific technical dictionaries for legal, medical, and foreign languages and also several custom dictionaries that store your own technical words.

Checking the spelling of one or more fields and records

You can check the spelling of your data in either Form View or Datasheet View. In Form View, you spell-check only a single record, or a single field within a record. To check the spelling of data in Datasheet View, select the field or text containing spelling you want to check, and then click on the Spelling button (the icon with the check mark and the small letters ABC above it) in the Records group on the Home ribbon tab.

When you click on the icon, Access checks the field (or selected text within the field) for spelling, as shown in Figure 24-21.

FIGURE 24-21

Spell-checking in Access

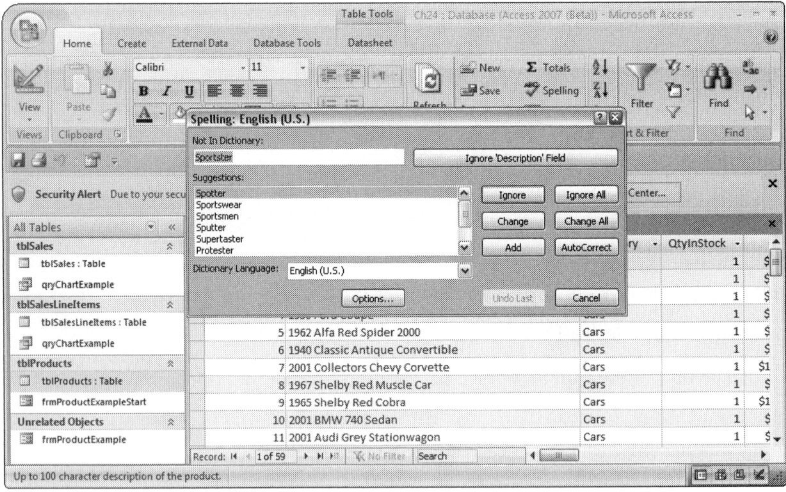

In the Spelling dialog box that appears, click on Add if you want to add the word in the Not In Dictionary box to the custom dictionary.

You can select only one field at a time in Form View. You'll probably want to use only Form View to spell-check selected memo data. You must switch to Datasheet View to select multiple fields or records. To check the spelling of data in Datasheet View, you would select the records, columns, fields, or text within a field containing spelling you want to check and then click on the Spelling icon.

You can also check the spelling in a table, query, or form in the Database window by clicking on the table, query, or form object containing spelling you want to check.

You only spell-check the data inside the objects. Access cannot spell-check control names.

Using OLE automation with Office

Access 2007 takes advantage of drag and drop. You do it from a Datasheet View across Excel and Word. You can instantly create a table in a Word document (or add a table to an Excel spreadsheet) by simply copying and pasting (or dragging and dropping) data from an Access datasheet to a Word document or an Excel spreadsheet. (Obviously, you must have Word or Excel installed on your computer to take advantage of these features.)

Creating an Excel-type PivotTable

Access contains a PivotTable Wizard to create Excel PivotTables based on Access tables or queries. A *PivotTable* is like a cross-tabulation of your data. You define the data values for rows, columns, pages, and summarizing.

A PivotTable is like a cross-tab query, except more powerful.

Before beginning a PivotTable, make sure to display a simple datasheet containing the data you want to analyze. Figure 24-22 shows a query using the `tblContacts`, `tblSales`, and `tblSalesLineItems` tables, in addition to the `qryCalculateTotalPaymentsbyInvoice` query. All this is used to create an analysis of sales.

FIGURE 24-22

This query combines various tables and a query for later PivotTable use.

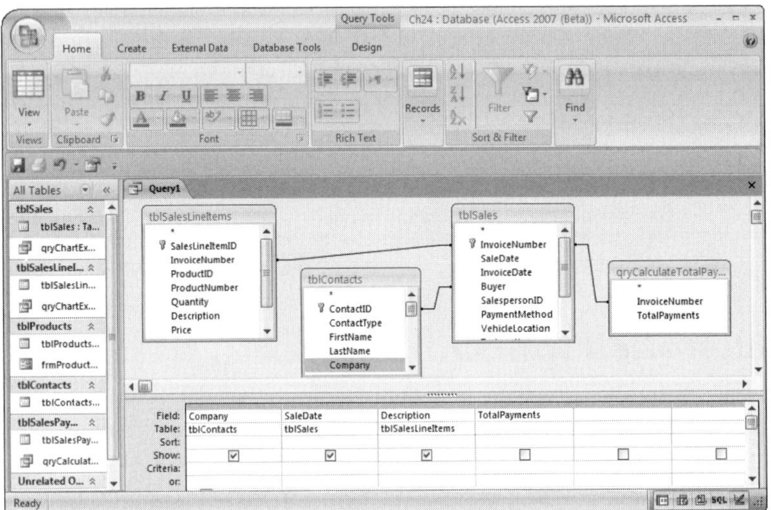

After you create a query, display the datasheet to make sure that the data you expect to see is displayed, and that the type of data lends itself to PivotTable analysis. There should be many different groupings of data because a PivotTable is intended to manipulate, or pivot about, different data categories.

A category is the equivalent of a type table in a relational database terminology.

As shown in Figure 24-23, this data is perfect for PivotTable analysis. There are many customers, each having several purchases, on several dates, plus a total payment for each sale.

After the data is reviewed, you can create a PivotTable. You start by selecting the View menu with the query in Figure 24-23 still open, and then the PivotTable View on the menu. After you begin the PivotTable Wizard process, you see an introductory screen describing exactly what to put where, as shown in Figure 24-24.

FIGURE 24-23

The datasheet version of the query shown in Figure 24-22

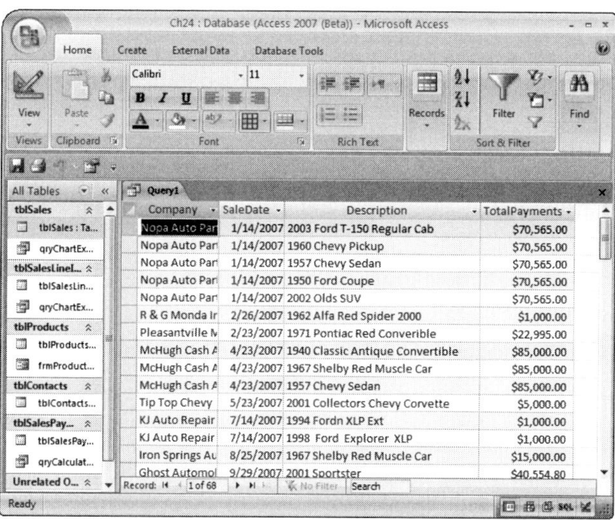

FIGURE 24-24

The PivotTable layout design wizard

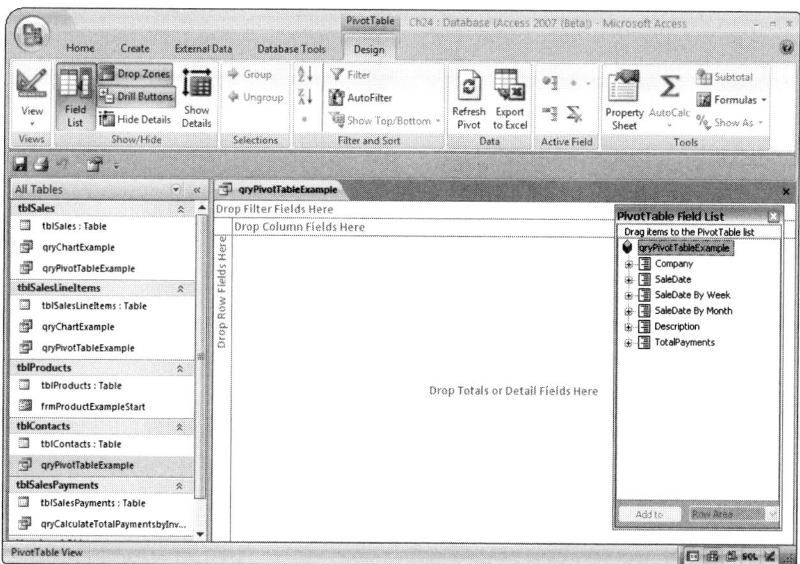

Figure 24-24 shows a number of sections plus a field list selection box. The `qryPivotTableExample` query is selected. You can create a PivotTable report by following through with these steps:

This is where it gets really easy and your PivotTable design screen starts to look like a spreadsheet.

1. **Select the Description field in the PivotTable field list window.**

   This is the name of the car.

2. **Drag the field from the field list window, and drop it onto the left-hand side row box that has `Drop Row Fields Here` written in it. Easy, right?**

3. **Now select the SaleDate by Month field, and drag and drop it onto the top box or column heading box (Drop Column Fields Here).**

   So far, you've created rows and columns, where the data will be matched up and summarized based on meeting points between cars and sale date months of those cars.

4. **Now drag the Company field onto the top box (Drop Filter Fields Here).**

   Underneath the word *Company* you will see the word *All*. That means you are retrieving data for all companies. You can select one or more companies if you so wish, as shown in Figure 24-25, by clicking the Company filter field as a spin control.

FIGURE 24-25

Selecting companies to filter with

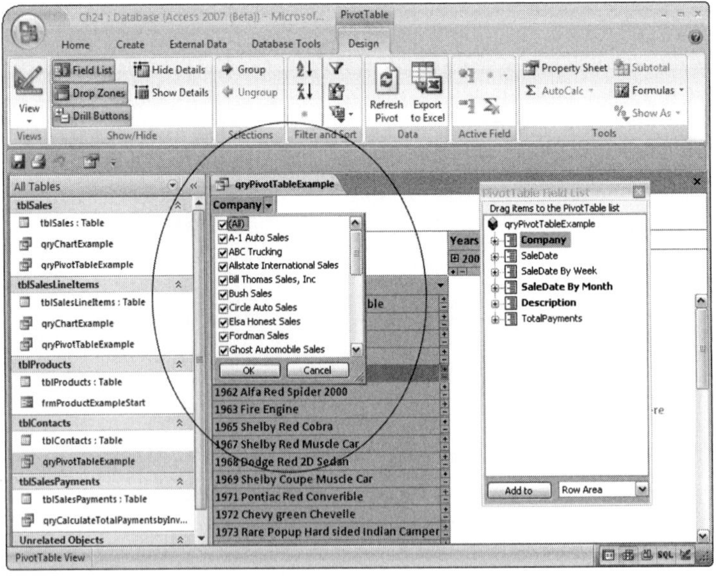

5. **Drag and drop the `TotalPayments` field, and drop it onto the central section (Drop Totals or Detail Fields Here).**

   The result is shown in Figure 24-26.

FIGURE 24-26

A PivotTable design with all sections selected

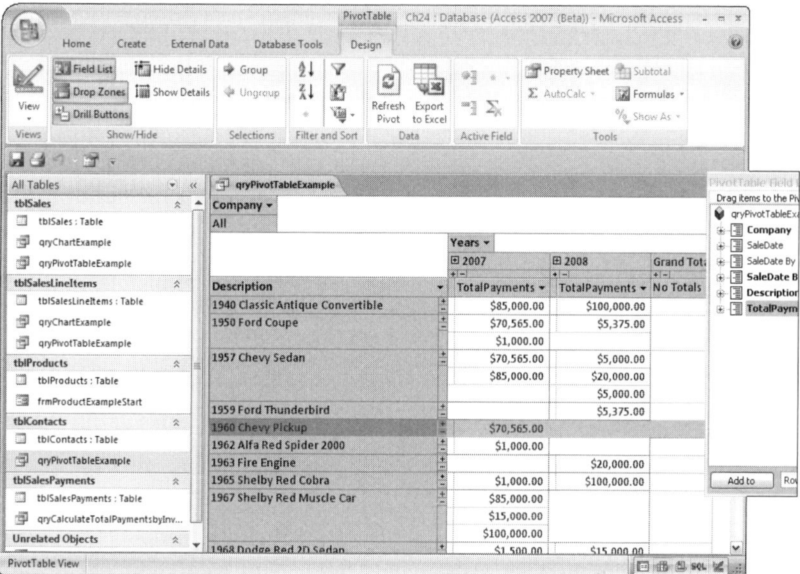

6. **You can now click the various plus signs (to add in totals), or minus signs (to remove totals). Click the plus sigh underneath Grand Totals. And also click the plus sign to the left of the 2008 column header.**

   You get the result shown in Figure 24-27.

FIGURE 24-27

A PivotTable can be drilled down into for more or less detail, using the plus and minus signs.

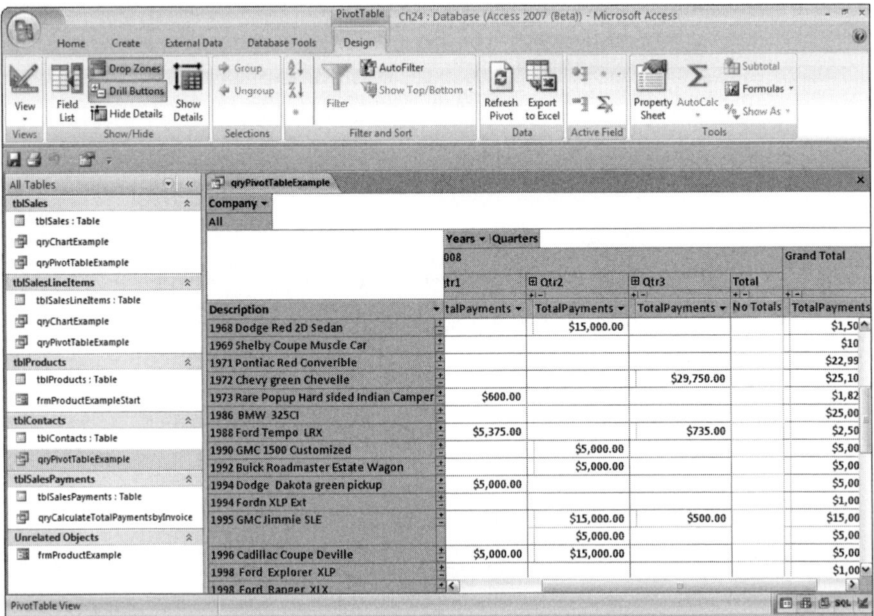

7. **Now go to the View button and select PivotChart View.**

   The screen changes to that shown in Figure 24-28.

   In Figure 24-28, the `SaleDate` field was dragged and dropped onto the Drop Data Fields Here box. The chart gives a slightly more entertaining, summarized picture of the data.

FIGURE 24-28

A PivotChart can also be selected.

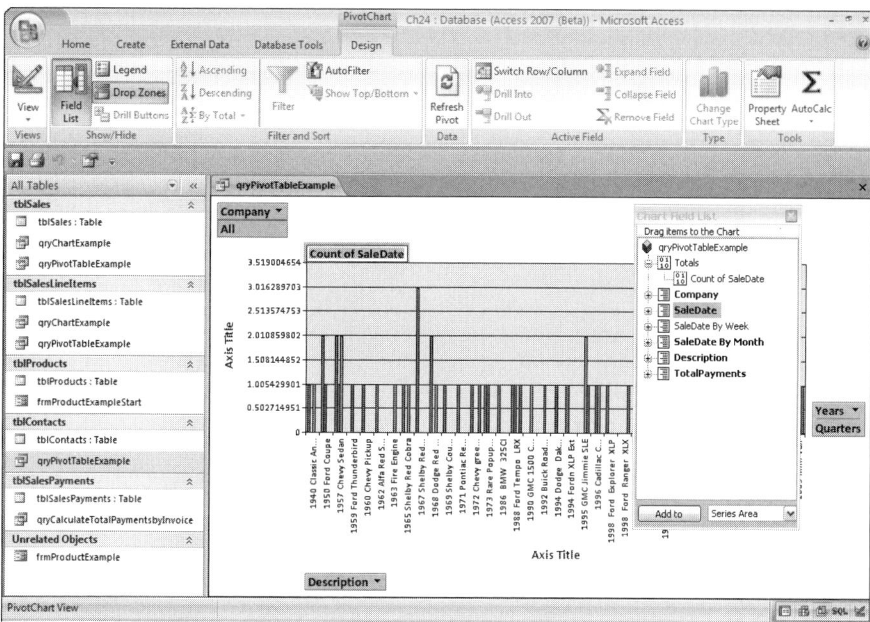

Summary

The ability to include only objects such as Microsoft Graph in Access applications is a very powerful feature. ActiveX controls provide utility that simply cannot be reproduced any other way. It would be virtually impossible to re-create the sophisticated graphs and charts possible with Microsoft Graph using Access or even a powerful graphical design tool.

Microsoft Graph is particularly attractive because its built-in wizards make creating even complex graphs and charts a simple task. As you saw in this chapter, Microsoft Graph provides numerous options for customizing the appearance of Access displayed in graphs and charts.

The next chapter concludes our discussion of advanced Access techniques. There, you'll learn the basics of trapping runtime errors and handling them in such a way that users are not bothered or interrupted by the errors. Proper error handling is one of the distinctions of professionally designed and built applications. Graceful error handling is one of the earmarks of professional database development, and you'll be happy to note that VBA provides all of the tools necessary to add powerful, efficient error handling to your Access applications.

Chapter 25

Handling Errors and Exceptions

Access database applications prepared by even the very best developers have problems. By their very nature, database applications tend to be fairly complicated when you consider table and query design, forms and reports, and implementation details. All the VBA code that needs to be written for most databases can inevitably result in coding errors. If you're lucky the problem and its cause are obvious and are easy to fix. The situation becomes difficult when you know there's a problem, but its source is not immediately apparent. The worst situation for all concerned are those bugs that silently and perniciously damage data, or the representation of data in an application, and without any warning.

This chapter takes a look at the types of errors you'll encounter in Access applications, and some of the steps you can take to uncover and repair these little critters. This chapter largely ignores the errors caused by poor design: those of misrepresentation of data caused by ill-designed queries, update and insert anomalies caused by inappropriate application of referential integrity rules, and so on. For the most part the causes of poor design errors are rooted in failure to conform to proper design disciplines, misunderstanding Access query design, among other causes. Careful attention to database design principles is required to produce truly robust Access applications.

IN THIS CHAPTER

NOTE There is no database for this chapter as the chapter contains only fairly simple VBA code examples.

Dealing with Errors

We all have to deal with the errors that occur in our applications. Even the best-written code fails now and then, very often because of problems with data entry or poorly trained users. Other times errors occur because we've written the code incorrectly, or we haven't adequately tested and debugged an application before distributing to users.

Logical errors

Logical errors can be sometimes be difficult to detect and remove. A logical error (a bug), often occurs because of some mathematical error: Perhaps a data was misused of in a recordset, or maybe there is some other problem dealing with the data or program flow of the application, or unexpected input from the user is not properly checked by the application.

For instance, consider the situation where a patient management program assumes the user has entered both the first name and last name for a patient. Let's also say that a patient data entry form contains text boxes for both these values. So, the user typing in the details will certainly fill in both values. Right?

Either of the first or last names might be missing from the data. There could be a perfectly valid reason. For instance, there could be a patient too young to know their own name or an Alzheimer's patient who can't recall his or her last name. A text value left as empty contains a null value, unless a default value has been provided. A logical error is generated if the application then tries to use the patient's first name in a lookup or sorting operation. If you're lucky, the user will notice the logical error. The user could be informed through the use of a pop-up dialog box or error message, and the error corrected before the data is committed to the database.

Other logical errors are created when, for instance, an application incorrectly calculates the days between dates, uses the wrong value in a division or multiplication operation, and so on. Virtually any time data is mishandled or inappropriately used in your application, a logical error is likely to be the result.

The obvious solution to the missing first name / last name situation described earlier is to add some VBA code to the form's `BeforeUpdate` event to verify that both a first and last name have been entered, and notify the user that one or both names are missing. Alternatively, the application may insert a default value such as "N/A" for the first and last names when either has been left blank.

Even so, a well-mannered application should detect errors when they occur, and handle them gracefully. Access, like most Windows applications, handles errors in a fairly unfriendly fashion, popping up a dialog box that may or may not adequately describe the error to the user. A carefully written application traps these errors before Access takes over, handling them without disturbing the user's workflow.

Runtime errors

Assuming you get past the syntax checking using the VBA editor and your code compiles, the errors that occur as the user works with an application are generally referred to as *runtime errors*. Runtime errors occur for a multitude of reasons. When they do occur, a runtime error causes one of following four things to happen:

- A fatal error and the application crashes
- An untrapped error and the default Access error dialog box appears
- The error is handled by the application and your code takes care of the problem
- An unanticipated application error that may or may not cause problems with your Access application

Fatal errors

A *fatal error* is a non-recoverable and crashes the application. These errors are generally a result of an operation outside the Access environment, and there is no way for Access to handle it. In most cases, your code won't be able to trap and respond to fatal errors. An example of this type of error is calling a poorly written Windows API function. As you'll see in Chapter 30, Windows API functions are extremely fussy about the type and number of parameters passed to them. Because Windows API functions execute outside of Access, there is no way for VBA code to trap an API error. In extreme cases, your users encounter the dreaded blue screen of death often seen when a computer is infected by a virus.

Because you cannot do much about these fatal errors other than fix them, you should concentrate on the types of errors you can control.

Simple runtime errors

Runtime errors often give no direct indication of an error condition, such as a pop-up message on a screen. More likely a runtime error is detected after the fact, when something with the data is discovered to be erroneous. For instance, a report may contain blank text boxes when the user expects to see names and other data. This situation could even occur a long time after the data entry error has occurred, and the error may occur many times before its discovery.

On rare occasions, runtime errors are traceable to a hardware failure such as a full disk or network problems, leading to the frequent "*&#^ computer's fault!" complaint. Modern desktop computers are much more reliable than they were a few years ago, making this a rare occurrence. Most application errors are caused by the people who program computers. Many hardware failures, such as a hard-drive crash, are easily recognized by the user.

Other runtime errors may be less obvious and more difficult to deal with. For instance, a network glitch may cause data loss or make lookup data temporarily unavailable. Running out of swap disk space makes Windows run erratically or crash. Many computers are equipped with marginal memory, making it difficult or impossible to run large queries or use the built-in Access wizards.

A second approach to avoiding runtime errors is to keep an Access database file well maintained by periodically running a compact and repair cycle:

1. **Click the round File icon at the very extreme top left of the Access 2007 window.**
2. **Select the Manage option from the menu.**
3. **Click the Compact and Repair database option from the menu, as shown in Figure 25-1.**

What used to be compact and repair functionality in Access 2003 is now under the Microsoft Office Diagnostics option, in the Windows menu for Microsoft Office.

FIGURE 25-1

Compacting and repairing a database

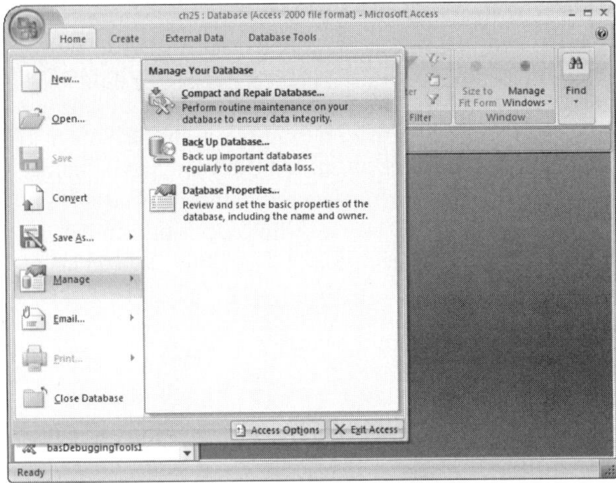

Prudence dictates frequent diagnostic attention to an Access 2007 `.accdb` file, particularly if data is often deleted or modified. A compact and repair cycle can also help to ensure physical integrity of the `.accdb` file on the hard drive.

Default error handling in Access

Access, Visual Basic, and the other VBA applications, such as Word and Excel, can handle errors for you. Unfortunately, the built-in error handling in most applications is not really intended for end users. Figure 25-2 shows a typical runtime error message produced by Access. Notice how unhelpful the message is. Most users have no idea how to respond to the error message shown in Figure 25-2. This error message includes technical expressions, such as "type mismatch." Unless appropriate training has been provided, it is unlikely the user will simply guess at the correct action to take in response.

The error in Figure 25-2 occurs because the procedure declares and creates a text string variable and a numeric variable and then tries to assign the numeric variable the value of the text string. The type mismatch occurs because you can't assign nonnumeric characters to a numeric variable.

FIGURE 25-2

Built-in error messages are usually not helpful.

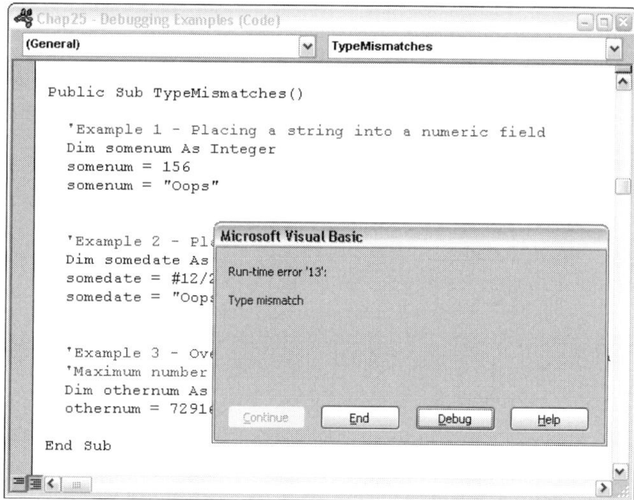

The error message in Figure 25-2 reports `Runtime error '13':` — which happens to be a type mismatch. Unless you know the problem, how does this message help you? Without a great deal of experience, how do you then fix this type of problem? In fact, how do you determine what the problem is? Clearly, this message box is not much help to a user who has entered character data into a text box that should be filled with a numeric value.

In the error dialog box in Figure 25-2, notice the Debug button. The Debug button stops the program, opens the VBA code editor, and places a breakpoint on the offending statement. The program is in a state of limbo. All the values of temporary variables are intact, and you can view them to help you solve the error. The End button causes the program to stop running, and you cannot use any tools to check the problem.

The Access Error dialog box shown in Figure 25-2 appears for *untrapped errors*. This can be good for development because problems can be traced to the specific line of code that caused the error. When you click the Debug button, the VBA window opens and highlights the guilty line of code. But this is not the kind of reaction you generally want with your applications and end users. For this reason, having an error handler and making it a *handled error* is much better. You can sometimes not just alert the user of a problem, but maybe prevent the user from even worrying about the problem by having the code take some action to work around the error or correct the problem.

Unanticipated errors

The last type of error is the unknown or unanticipated application error. This is most often a logical error in the code. Often no error is displayed because the program is working exactly the way it was coded. For example, an endless loop occurs if you forget to advance a record pointer as you traverse a recordset or the condition ending a `Do.Loop` never happens. The problem is that the code is doing the wrong thing, even though it is executing as programmed.

The unanticipated error is often the hardest type of problem to resolve. There are several different ways to handle these errors:

- Check the results programmatically by redundantly checking the results.
- Use the Watch window or breakpoints to watch the code run line by line.

A well-written application may prevent runaway, endless loops by counting how many times the loop has executed and forcing an end to the loop when the maximum value has been exceeded. Other sophisticated ways of handling unanticipated errors include keeping track of the number of times a particular function has been called, or monitoring how long it takes for a query to execute or a form or report to open. Such extreme measures are not necessary in the vast majority of Access applications, but you should be aware that there are solutions to virtually any unexpected application problem.

Which Errors Can Be Detected?

There are several hundred trappable errors that can occur in VBA applications. Only a minor portion of these hundreds of errors are likely to occur in your applications. The question is, then, which of the remaining fifty or one hundred relevant errors should you trap in your applications?

Most developers begin simply and write an error handler that catches one or two of the most obvious errors. In the case of the navigation buttons on an Access or Visual Basic form, you should trap the error that occurs when the user tries to move off either end of the recordset. Such an error is readily anticipated and is the result of normal navigation through a recordset.

However, say a problem makes it so the recordset itself cannot be created. The solution might not be as obvious. There are many reasons why the `OpenRecordset` method may fail. Perhaps the table cannot be found because it's been deleted or a link to the table is broken. Or, there could be an error in the SQL statement used to create the recordset and no records are returned. During development you may never see an error caused by an empty recordset because your test data is always available.

Experience will tell you which errors are expected as you write your VBA procedures. But, you should always prepare for the unexpected.

What is an error handle?

VBA provides extensive runtime error handling capabilities. You are able to add code to your applications to detect when an error occurs. Other code directs the program to handle anticipated errors in a predictable fashion. Still other code can catch unanticipated errors, automatically correcting the problem, preventing data loss, and reducing support costs.

Almost all error-handling routines in VBA programs require a three-step process:

1. **Trap the error.**
2. **Redirect program flow to error handler.**
3. **Direct program flow out of error handler back to main body of procedure.**

It is important to note that all VBA error handling is done locally. That is, each procedure contains its own error handling code. Although a procedure's error handler can call other functions and subroutines, the error handler exists entirely within the procedure causing the error. In fact, as discussed later in this chapter, after you start implementing error handling, it is important to include error handling code in almost every procedure. An error that occurs in a procedure without error handling is passed back to the routine that called the procedure, causing some confusion as to which procedure actually failed.

Setting a basic error trap

The VBA engine is constantly looking for problems and immediately notifies you when something unexpected happens. The default error message is generally technical in nature. A single line of VBA code is all that's necessary to intercept an error and redirect program flow to code that provides a more user-friendly approach to error resolution.

The following procedure shows how error handling is implemented in VBA procedures:

```
Sub RoutineA()
On Error GoTo HandleError
  MsgBox "Now in routine A"
ExitHere:
  MsgBox "Now leaving routine A"
  Exit Sub
HandleError:
  MsgBox "Error in routine A"
  Resume ExitHere
End Sub
```

The `On Error` statement near the top of the procedure sets the error trap for the routine. Code near the bottom of the routine implements the error-handling mechanism for this subroutine. The error-handling code in this procedure is the very least you can include in your procedures to handle runtime errors effectively. The error-handling statements in this procedure are the template you can consistently use in all your VBA programs.

The `On Error` clause informs VBA that you want to defeat the built-in VBA error-handling system by sending execution to the location identified by the `"HandleError"` label. The `GoTo Label` statement is an unconditional branch (in the event of an error) to a label somewhere within the procedure.

NOTE **A VBA *label* is nothing more than an identifier (such as `"HandleError"`) followed by a colon. A word by itself on a line in a VBA procedure is interpreted as the name of a procedure, variable, or VBA keyword, and VBA tries to evaluate it. When followed by a colon, the VBA interpreter understands that the word is actually a label and should not be executed or evaluated.**

The `On Error` statement is a switch that disables the default VBA error handling. This statement switches the VBA engine away from its built-in error handling and redirects error handling to your code. After you set the error trap with the `On Error` statement, you suppress the appearance of the default Access error dialog boxes.

After an error occurs the VBA engine's normal operation is suspended. Normal execution is directed to the error handler and further error trapping is inhibited. If an error occurs in your error handler VBA responds with its default behavior. Some resources available to you (discussed later in this chapter) determine which error occurred and exactly where the error occurred. You also have several options as to where you want program flow to commence after the error handler has done its job.

It is important to note that there is nothing special about the labels used in the error handling statements. `"HandleError"` and `"ExitHere"` are just words; they convey no special meaning to Access or the VBA language engine. Choose any label you wish — `HandleError` and `ExitHere` are used throughout this book simply because VBA developers understand these labels. In fact, you can use exactly the same labels and every VBA procedure. This fact makes it easier to copy and paste the error-handling template from one procedure to another in your Access application.

Trapping Errors with VBA

Several situations can cause a great of frustration for your application users: A program that has been operating without a hint of trouble suddenly crashes, popping up a dialog box containing a contradictory or confusing error message. Another problem is a program behaving inconsistently. In one situation the program operates in a predictable fashion, reliably churning out reports and displaying the results of calculations. Under other conditions the program, operating on seemingly identical data, behaves erratically, stopping execution or perhaps displaying the data in unexpected ways.

A third, much more dangerous situation, is a program that appears to be functioning properly but is in fact corrupting data. (*Corruption* in this context simply means unexpectedly changing the value of the data.) This program silently makes changes to the data or reports erroneous values without indicating an error exists. An example is a program that calculates currency exchange rates. The user of this program may believe the program is correctly calculating the monetary exchange values while in fact the program is actually reporting incorrect results.

CAUTION **The worst type of situation occurs when the values returned by the program appear to be correct, but are in fact wrong.**

Using VBA error-handling techniques, you can add code to your applications to prevent unexpected crashes or inconsistent behavior. Unfortunately, there is little you can do to correct a poorly programmed application. If calculations are being performed incorrectly, there is little that the VBA engine can do to correct these types of error. VBA code can be utilized to gracefully cater to unexpected behavior in Access.

Access 2007 provides several basic programming elements used for catering to errors, including the following:

- The `Error` event
- The `Errors` collection
- The `Err` object
- VBA Error statements

The following sections detail each of these program elements.

The Error event

Access provides a special `Error` event when running a bound form or report. The `Error` event provides a nice way to trap an error that occurs in the database engine supplying data to the form or report. You need to create an event procedure for the `Error` event to trap these errors. The procedure looks like one of the following, depending on whether it was a form or a report:

```
Sub Form_Error(DataErr As Integer, Response As Integer)
   'Insert error handler here
End Sub

Sub Report_Error(DataErr As Integer, Response As Integer)
   'Insert error handler here
End Sub
```

There are two arguments for these subroutines: `DataErr` and `Response`. `DataErr` is the error code returned by the Access database engine when an error occurs. Note that the `Err` object is superseded by `Error` event, and is not helpful when this event is triggered by a problem with the data underlying the form or report. You must use the `DataErr` argument to determine which error occurred. The second argument, `Response`, is set to either of the following constants by the procedure:

- `AcDataErrContinue`: Ignore the error and continue without displaying the default Access error message.
- `AcDataErrDisplay`: Display the default Access error message. (This is the default.)

When you use `AcDataErrContinue`, you can then supply a custom error message or handler in place of the default error message.

The following is a typical `Form_Error` event procedure:

```
Private Sub Form_Error(DataErr As Integer, _
      Response As Integer)
```

```
    Dim strMsg As String

    Select Case DataErr
      Case 7787  'OverwriteErr:
        strMsg = "You lose. Click on OK to see"_
          & "updates for other people."
        MsgBox strMsg, vbOKOnly + vbInformation


        Response = acDataErrContinue

      Case 7878 'DataChangedErr:
        strMsg = "Another user has changed this" _
          & "data while you were looking at it." _
          & vbCrLf & "Click OK to see " _
          & "the other user changes."
        MsgBox strMsg, vbOKOnly + vbInformation


        Response = acDataErrContinue

      Case Else
        'Default for any other errors:
        Response = acDataErrDisplay

    End Select
  End Sub
```

This particular error-handling routine traps the errors on a bound form that occur when multiple users make simultaneous changes to the same record. The Access database engine raises the error, allowing the form to intelligently notify the user that a problem has occurred.

Notice how `DataErr` is examined to see if its value is `7787` or `7878`, and an appropriate action (notifying the user of the problem) is taken to handle the problem. Response is set to `acDataErrContinue` to notify Access that the form's data error has been handled.

If any other error occurs, `Reponse` is set to `acDataErrDisplay`, allowing Access to present the user with the default error message. Hopefully the user can make some sense of the error message, or at least notify someone of the situation.

Keep in mind that the form and report `Error` event fires only in response to data errors detected by the database engine. The `Error` event is not related to problems caused by the user, other than inappropriate data entry, and a failure to add or update the wrong kind of data in the database.

The ADO Errors collection

When an error occurs in an ADO object, an error object is created in the `Errors` collection of the `Connection` object. These are referred to as *data access errors*. When an error occurs, the collection is cleared and the new set of objects is put into the collection. Although the collection exists only for the most recent error event, the event could generate several errors. Each of these errors is stored in the `Errors` collection. The `Errors` collection is an object of the `Connection` object, not ADO.

The `Errors` collection has one property, `Count`, which contains the number of errors or error objects. It has a value of zero if there are no errors. There are a few properties of the `Error` object. These include `Description`, `HelpContext`, `HelpFile`, `Number`, and `Source`. When there are multiple errors, the lowest-level error is the first object in the collection, and the highest-level error is the last object in the collection.

When an ADO error occurs, the VBA `Err` object contains the error number for the first object in the `Errors` collection. You need to check the `Errors` collection to see whether additional ADO errors have occurred.

In the following code, you find an error handler that can be used in a procedure that deals with an ADO connection. When an error occurs, the code following the label `ErrorHandler` runs and first checks to see if the `Error` object contains any items. If it does, it checks to see if the error is the same as the `Err` object. If it is the same, the error was an ADO error and the variable `strMessage` contains the descriptions of all the errors in the `Errors` collection. If it is not an ADO error, the error is from VBA and the single `Err.Description` value is displayed:

```
Sub ADOTest()
  Dim cnn As New ADODB.Connection
  Dim errX As ADODB.Error
  Dim strMessage As String

On Error GoTo HandleError

  'Insert your code here
ExitHere:

  Exit Sub

HandleError:

  If cnn.Errors.Count > 0 Then

    If Err.Number = cnn.Errors.Item(0).Number Then

      'Error is an ADO Connection Error:
      For Each errX In cnn.Errors
        strMessage = strMessage & Err.Description & vbCrLf
      Next
      MsgBox strMessage, , "ADO Error Handler"
    End If

    Resume ExitHere
```

```
    Else
       'The error is a VBA Error:
      MsgBox Err.Description, vbExclamation, _
        "VBA Error Handler"

      Resume ExitHere

    End If

End Sub
```

The Err object

The Err object is a part of the VBA language and is always present in every Access application. When an error occurs, information about the error is stored in the Err object, enabling you to examine the Err object and learn the details of the error.

The Err object contains information about only the most recent error and does not contain information about more than one error at a time. When a new error occurs, the Err object is cleared and updated to include information about that most recent error.

The Err object has several properties, including Number, Description, and Source. The Number is the VBA number of the ; Description gives you a little more information about the error. The Source property is not normally very useful in Access applications; it identifies the VBA project that generated the error, which, in Access applications, is the name of the Access application by default.

The Err object also has two methods: Clear, to clear information from the Err object; and Raise, to simulate an error.

The Description property returns the built-in description of the error that has occurred. Whether you choose to use this description is entirely up to you. Perhaps the most important property of the Err object is the Number associated with the error. The following listing shows how you might use the Err.Number property to determine which error has triggered the error handler.

The following procedure demonstrates the use of the Err object and its Number attribute:

```
Sub GenericProcedure()

On Error GoTo HandleError

    'Other VBA statements here

ExitHere:
    'Shut down statements here
   Exit Sub
```

```
HandleError:

  Select Case Err.Number
    Case X
       'Handle X case
      Resume ExitHere
    Case Y
       'Handle Y case
      Resume ExitHere
    Case Z
       'Handle Z case
      Resume ExitHere
    Case Else   'Unanticipated error
      MsgBox Err.Number & " " & Err.Description
      Resume ExitHere
  End Select

End Sub
```

The `Select Case` statement in the error handler, in the procedure called `GenericProcedure` uses the `Err.Number` property to execute any of a number of responses to the error. The beauty of `Select Case` is that the error-handling code can be extended as far as necessary. There is no practical limit on the number of `Case` statements that can be contained within the `Select Case` construct, and multiple `Err.Number` values can be handled by the same `Case`.

In each `Case` construct you choose whether to include the `Resume ExitHere` statement. For instance, perhaps `Case Y` fixes the problem, and you really want the code to return to the statement that caused the error so that it can be executed a second time. In this case, rather than `Resume ExitHere`, use a simple `Resume` statement with no target label. `Resume` instructs VBA to go back to the statement that caused the problem and execute it again.

Obviously, the `Select Case` construct is not the only way to handle multiple error conditions. You could, for instance, use nested `If..Then..Else` and `If..Then..ElseIf` statements. However, you'll find that the If statement is not easily extensible and the logical flow through nested If..Then..Else statements can be difficult to follow.

A bit later in this chapter you'll read about the special `Resume` statement you use to redirect program flow out of the error handler.

VBA Error statement variations

You've already seen several examples of the basic VBA statements for handling errors:

- `On Error`
- `Resume`

There are a number of forms of the `On Error` statement:

- `On Error Resume Next`
- `On Error GoTo <label>`
- `On Error GoTo 0`

An error trap is a section of code that is executed when some kind of an error occurs. That error can be specifically specified, or it can be general. Essentially, when an error is detected by an error trap, then whatever the error trap dictates (the code the trap contains) is what is executed.

There are obviously numerous ways to deal with errors within forms, reports, and code. Each form and report, as well as each function and subroutine, can and probably should have an error-handling routine. It is not unusual to see a good part of the development effort devoted to error handling. Probably the most common routine is the following one:

```
Function SampleCode
   'Dim statements here
On Error goto HandleError

   'Insert functional code here

ExitHere:
  Exit Function

ErrorHandler:
   'error handler code here
  Msgbox err.description
   'either enter a resume statement here
   'or nothing and let the function end
  Resume ExitHere

End Function
```

The `On Error` statement enables the error handler, and if an error occurs, execution branches to the first line after the label `ErrorHandler`. This label could be any valid VBA label. The error-handler code would deal with the error and then either resume execution back in the body of the procedure or just exit the function or subroutine. The inclusion of the `Msgbox` statement in the error handler is a typical way of informing the user what happened.

When an error occurs in a called function or subroutine that doesn't have an enabled error handler, VBA returns to the calling procedure looking for an enabled error handler. This process proceeds up the call stack until an error handler is found. If no error handler is found, execution stops with a default Access error message displayed.

On Error Resume Next

The `On Error Resume Next` statement ignores the line causing an error. Processing continues at the line immediately following the line causing that error. No error-handling routine is called. This statement is useful if you want to sometimes ignore errors. The following procedure shows that, for any error dealing with the error log table, the rest of the routine will simply be ignored and passed over:

```
Sub LogError(iNumber As Integer, sDesc As String)
  Dim db As Database
  Dim rs As Recordset
On Error Resume Next
  Set db = CurrentDb()
  Set rs = db.OpenRecordset("SELECT * FROM ErrorLog")
  If Err.Number <> 0 Then
     'Put code here to create The table ErrorLog
  End If
  rs.Close
End Sub
```

`On Error Resume Next` must be used appropriately. After `On Error Resume Next` is set, Access ignores all errors until the procedure ends or until another error directive is encountered, as in this example:

```
Sub LogError(iNumber As Integer, sDesc As String)
  Dim db As Database
  Dim rs As Recordset
On Error Resume Next
  Set db = CurrentDb()
  Set rs = db.OpenRecordset("SELECT * FROM ErrorLog")
  If Err.Number <> 0 Then
     'Put code here to create The table ErrorLog
  End If
On Error GoTo HandleError

  ... Other code here ...

End Sub
```

In this case, the `On Error Resume Next` causes Access to ignore the error that occurs if the ErrorLog table does not exist. Once past this section of code, the `On Error GoTo HandleError` statement you've seen in several places in this chapter establishes the usual error handler for the remainder of the procedure.

On Error GoTo <label>

The `On Error GoTo <label>` statement enables an error-handling routine. This is the standard error handling directive described earlier in this chapter. This statement enables error handling for the procedures. Here is another example of using `On Error GoTo <label>` as a simple error-handling operation:

```
Sub LogMoreErrors(iNumber As Integer, sDesc As String)
  Dim db As Database
```

```
    Dim rs As Recordset

  On Error GoTo HandleError

    Set db = CurrentDb()
    Set rs = db.OpenRecordset("SELECT * FROM ErrorLog")
    If Err.Number <> 0 Then
       'Put code here to create The table ErrorLog
    End If
    rs.Close

  ExitHere
    Exit Sub

  HandleError:
    MsgBox Err.Number & " " & Err.Description
    Resume ExitHere

  End Sub
```

Keep in mind that you are free to use any labels you wish as the targets of the `On Error` and `Resume` statements. The labels you see here were chosen simply because of the obvious purposes they serve.

On Error GoTo 0

The `On Error GoTo 0` statement disables error handling. This statement also resets the properties of the `Err` object. The following procedure shows an example of using `GoTo 0`. After processing has bypassed the `Delete` method, the `On Error GoTo 0` statement disables further error traps. This means any errors that occur after this statement will be handled by the default VBA error mechanism:

```
Sub DeleteTableDef()
  Dim db As Database
  Set db = CurrentDb()
On Error Resume Next
  db.TableDefs.Delete "tblTemp"
On Error GoTo 0
   'More code here
End Sub
```

Although in most cases it is not desirable to let VBA handle its own errors, one situation where you may choose to use `On Error GoTo 0` is during the development process. Assume you're working on a complex procedure that has a number of different failure modes. You're never really sure you're trapping for all possible errors, so you may want to disable error handling temporarily so that you'll be sure to see all errors that occur past the error trap you've prepared.

VBA Resume statements

As with the `On Error` statement, there are a number of forms of the `Resume` statement:

- `Resume`
- `Resume Next`
- `Resume <label>`

Using the `Resume` statement is all about gaining better and more effective program control over the occurrence of errors.

You shouldn't simply fall out of the error handlers in your procedure. You've probably noticed that the error handler usually appears near the very bottom of a procedure. It's tempting to just let the `End Sub` statement after the error handler terminate the procedure after the error has been managed. There are several problems with this approach:

- **The VBA error mechanism is left in an indeterminate state.** You'll recall that as soon as the error occurs VBA enters a special "error" mode. This mode persists until the VBA engine encounters a `Resume` statement (more on `Resume` later), or until another error occurs. Even though the end of the procedure resets VBA's error mode, you should not count on this happening, particularly in deeply nested procedure calls.
- **VBA procedures often open recordsets, establish object variables, and perform other tasks that may be left incomplete unless shut down in a predictable fashion.** For instance, assume a procedure has opened a disk file and an error occurs. Unless the disk file is explicitly closed you run the risk of damaging the disk's file structure. Using the `Resume` statement to redirect flow to the procedure's shut down code provides a single point at which to close resources that are no longer needed.

Every VBA error handler should include some form of the Resume statement. This special VBA command instructs the VBA engine to resume normal execution. Depending on how you write the `Resume` statement, you can redirect program execution to any of a number of different points within the procedure.

The `GoTo` statement will not work in place of `Resume`. `GoTo` is an unconditional branch to another location within the current procedure and does not reset the VBA engine error status.

Resume

The `Resume` statement (with no label) returns execution to the line at which the error occurred. This statement is typically used when the user must make a correction, or when the error handler has repaired the problem causing the error. This might occur if you prompt the user for the name of a file to open and the user enters a filename that doesn't exist. You can then force the execution of the code back to the point where the filename is requested.

In almost all cases, the `Resume` keyword assumes that the error handler repairs the error condition. Otherwise you'll find yourself in an endless loop. Unless the error condition is corrected, every time the line causing the error is executed the error occurs, triggering the `Resume` statement, causing the cycle to repeat itself an infinite number of times. The following procedure shows how the `Resume` statement fits into a robust error handler, where judicious use of `Resume` can simplify coding:

```
Public Sub ResumeDemo()

On Error GoTo HandleError

   'Statement causing error occurs here:
  Kill "C:\Temp.txt"

ExitHere:
  Exit Sub

HandleError:

  If MsgBox("Error! Try again?", vbYesNo) = vbYes Then
    Resume
  Else
    Resume Exit_ResumeDemo
  End If

End Sub
```

If the `Temp.txt` file cannot be found, processing jumps down to the error handler. A message box pops up with Yes and No buttons on it asking the user whether to try again to delete the file. If the user selects the Yes button (vbYes) processing moves back to the `Kill` statement. The cycle repeats itself until either the `Temp.txt` file becomes available and is deleted or until the user clicks the No button on the message box.

Resume Next

When your error handler corrects or works around the problem that caused the error, the `Resume Next` statement is used. `Resume Next` returns execution to the line immediately following the line at which the error occurred.

The assumption with `Resume Next` is that either the error handler corrected the error condition or that the error was relatively minor in nature and that it's appropriate for processing to simply continue at the statement following the error condition.

The following procedure shows how to use `On Error Resume Next`. This simple error-logging routine tries to create a recordset object by selecting all fields from a table named `ErrorLog`. The call to the `OpenRecordset` method fails if `ErrorLog` is unavailable. If `ErrorLog` cannot be opened an error occurs, but because of the `Resume Next` directive processing simply falls through to the `If` statement immediately following the `OpenRecordset`. The code to create `ErrorLog` is missing from this routine, but the logic should be clear.

```
Sub LogErrors(iNumber As Integer, sDesc As String)
  Dim db As Database
  Dim rs As Recordset
On Error Resume Next
  Set db = CurrentDb()
  Set rs = db.OpenRecordset("SELECT * FROM ErrorLog")
  If Err.Number <> 0 Then
     'Put code here to create tblErrorLog
  End If
  rs.AddNew
  rs![TimeStamp] = Now()
  rs![Number] = iNumber
  rs![Description] = sDesc
  rs.Update
  rs.Close
  Set rs = Nothing
End Sub
```

The `LogError` sub in the previous procedure does not capture the situation that occurs if `ErrorLog` cannot be created. In fact, if errors occur as the code tries to assign values to the fields in `LogError`, processing simply continues to fall through to the next statement until a successful statement is encountered. In most cases this means execution ends up in an unpredictable location. It also means subsequent errors are not properly trapped.

Resume <label>

`Resume <lable>` is the standard method for exiting an error handler. If you need to continue execution at some other place besides the line that caused the error or the line after the line that caused the error, the `Resume <label>` statement should be used. It returns execution to the line specified by the label argument.

The label must be a label appearing within the current procedure. You cannot resume execution at a point outside of the currently executing procedure. If you must use the code in another procedure as part of the error handler, simply call it at a point above the `Resume` statement.

NOTE **When using error traps, one option is to redirect processing to an error trap, and log the error to a log file. After that, you could always continue processing. The result is that processing is not halted, perhaps prudent for less critical error situations.**

One important aspect of `Resume <label>` is that program execution is typically directed to the procedures exit point. This gives you a handy place to put all of a procedure's clean-up code, so that it executes whether or not an error occurs:

```
Sub LogErrors(iNumber As Integer, sDesc As String)
  Dim db As Database
  Dim rs As Recordset
On Error GoTo HandleError
  Set db = CurrentDb()
```

```
    Set rs = db.OpenRecordset("SELECT * FROM ErrorLog")
    If Err.Number <> 0 Then
       'Put code here to create tblErrorLog
    End If
    rs.AddNew
    rs![TimeStamp] = Now()
    rs![Number] = iNumber
    rs![Description] = sDesc
    rs.Update

ExitHere:
     'These steps are followed whether or not an error
     'has occurred. This means there is a single place
     'in this procedure for "clean up" code:
    rs.Close
    Set rs = Nothing
    Exit Sub

HandleError:
    'Handle the error here
    Resume ExitHere

End Sub
```

In this short example, the statements following the `ExitHere` label are executed whether or not an error has occurred. You should always close recordset objects and set them to `Nothing` to conserve memory. These "clean up" statements normally appear near the bottom of procedures, but in this example are located midway through the subroutine. Execution of this procedure actually ends when the `Exit Sub` statement executes.

Summary

This chapter surveys the important topic of adding error handling in Access applications. All VBA hosts (Access, Word, Excel, and so on) use identical error-handling paradigms. This means that all the code you saw in this chapter is applicable to any VBA host application.

Error handling is enabled with the `On Error` keywords. The typical error-handling process is to trap the error, redirect program execution to the code segment handling the error, and then resume out of the error handler. Most procedures use the `Resume` statement to redirect program flow to a common exit point in the procedure. The code following the exit label performs any clean up (closing and discarding object variables, closing files that are open, and so on) and is executed whether or not an error occurs in the procedure.

Part IV

Professional Database Development

The chapters in this part cover issues that concern professional database developers, including securing databases from unauthorized access, enhancing the user interface with toolbars and menus, and *replicating* (exchanging) data from one Access database to another.

This part builds on the information provided in earlier chapters. In this part, you'll find answers to many questions and problems facing Access developers, such as identifying a user as the user logs on to an application, exploiting object-oriented programming with the VBA language, and using advanced data management techniques with ActiveX Data Objects (ADOs).

It is entirely possible that some developers will never use many of the capabilities described in the chapters in this part. However, far too often, even advanced developers overlook the capabilities provided by a system like Microsoft Access simply because they're too busy or too involved in other work to truly learn what Access is capable of. This part takes you on a tour of some of the high-end features provided by Microsoft Access so that you'll know they're there, and you'll have a blueprint for using these capabilities in your own applications.

IN THIS PART

Chapter 26

Optimizing Access Applications

When Microsoft introduced 32-bit Access, a number of new performance concerns came part and parcel with the new features and functions. Microsoft continues to make a conscious effort to enhance the performance of Access 2007 with improvements in Jet as well as compilation techniques and features such as the formerly undocumented decompile command. The end result is that Microsoft has helped to ease your burden, but in no way has it completely taken it from you.

TIP **The published minimum RAM requirement for a computer to run Access 2007 on Windows XP (SP2 or later), Windows Server 2003 (or higher), or Windows Vista is 256MB — with an emphasis on *minimum*. If you're going to do serious development with Access 2007, you should have at least 512MB of RAM or, preferably, 1GB or more. With today's computers and memory prices, this amount of memory is a valuable investment. In fact, simply adding more memory (512MB to 1GB) will increase speed much more than changing your processor or speed, due to the fact that Access 2007 must use the hard drive as a virtual memory area if it doesn't have enough memory. Hard drives are slow, and big hard drives are even slower — regardless of the processor speed.**

IN THIS CHAPTER

Understanding Module Load on Demand

One of the great features of Visual Basic for Applications (the core language of Microsoft Access) is the *load on demand* functionality of VBA. Using load on demand, Access loads code modules only as they are needed or referenced. In early versions of Access, on-demand loading of modules wasn't fully realized because loading a module loaded the entire module's potential call tree. With Access 2007, the load on demand feature truly does help reduce the amount of RAM needed and helps your program run faster.

TIP **Because Access doesn't unload code after it has been loaded into memory, you should periodically close your application while you develop. When developing, you have a tendency to open and work with many different procedures in many different modules. These modules stay in memory until you close Access.**

Organizing your modules

When any procedure or variable is referenced in your application, the entire module that contains the procedure or variable is loaded into memory. To minimize the number of modules loaded into memory, you need to organize your procedures and variables into logical modules. For example, it's a good idea to place all Global variables in the same module. If only one Global variable is declared in a module, the entire module is loaded into memory. By the same token, you should put only procedures that are always used by your application (such as start-up procedures) into the module containing the Global variables.

Access 2007 prunes the call tree

The *call tree* for a procedure contains any additional functions or procedures that the current procedure (or function) has referenced within it, as well as those referenced by the newly loaded functions and procedures, and so forth. Because a procedure may reference numerous additional functions/procedures (stored in different modules) based on the action taken by the procedure, this loading of all potentially called functions/procedures takes a lot of time and memory.

Remember that when a procedure or function is called, the entire module in which that function is stored is placed in memory.

Therefore, a potential call tree consists of all the procedures that *could* be called by the current procedure that you are calling. In addition, all the procedures that could be called from *those* procedures and so forth are also part of the potential call tree. For example:

1. **If you call Procedure A, the entire module containing Procedure A is loaded.**
2. **Modules containing variable declarations used by Procedure A are loaded.**
3. **Procedure A has lines of code that call Procedures B and C — the modules containing Procedure B and Procedure C are loaded. (Even if the call statements are in conditional loops and are never executed, they are still loaded because *potentially* they could be called.)**
4. **Any procedures that could be called by Procedure B and Procedure C are loaded, as well as the entire modules containing those potential procedures.**
5. **And so on and so on. . .**

Fortunately for all Access developers, this complete loading of a potential call tree has been addressed in Access 2007. Access 2007 automatically compiles modules on demand, instead of loading the entire potential call tree. However, you can turn this feature off, thus making Access 2007 compile all modules at one time. Do this in the Visual Basic for Applications program rather than in Access. Access 2007 links directly to VBA's development environment for working with Visual Basic code. To check the status of the Compile on Demand option, follow these steps:

1. **Select the Modules object type from the Navigation Pane.**
2. **From the ribbon's Create tab, select Module from the Macro drop-down in the Other group to activate the Visual Basic Development Environment.**
3. **Select Tools ➪ Options. The Options dialog box appears.**
4. **Select the General tab.**
5. **Verify that the Compile on Demand check box, located on the bottom right of the dialog box, is checked. If it's not, check it. Figure 26-1 shows the dialog box with the option selected.**

FIGURE 26-1

For maximum performance, leave the Compile on Demand check box selected.

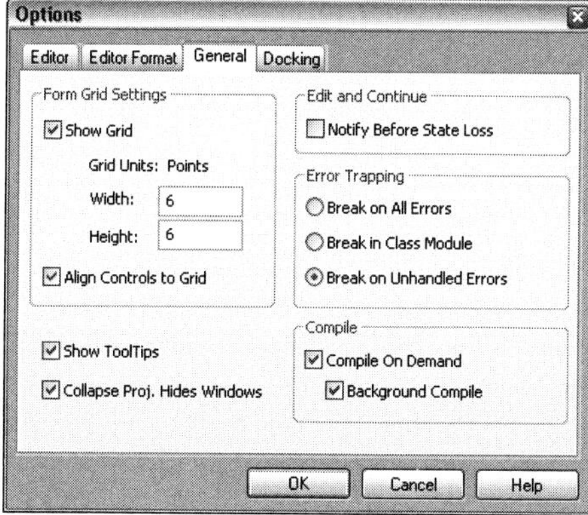

6. Click OK.
7. **Select File ➪ Close and Return to Microsoft Access (Alt + Q) or click the Access button (first button on toolbar) if you want to return to Access and leave the VBA window open.**

TIP **Unless you have a specific reason to do so, never deselect the Compile on Demand option. When you deselect this option, you can conceivably cause *all* of the modules in a database to load and compile, simply by calling just one procedure.**

With the Compile on Demand option selected, Access 2007 won't load the entire call tree of a module, but it will load a portion of the call tree of the executed procedure. For example, if you call procedure A in module A, any modules that contain procedures referenced in procedure A are loaded and compiled. However, Access 2007 doesn't take into consideration procedures that may be called from other procedures in module A, and it doesn't look at the potential call tree of the modules loaded because one of their procedures is referenced in procedure A. Because Access 2007 loads modules one-deep from the executed procedure's immediate call tree only—and *not* the module's call tree—your applications should load and execute many times faster than they did in previous versions.

Even though Access 2007 has made a significant improvement in the way modules are loaded and compiled, you can still do a number of things to reduce the number of modules loaded and compiled. For example, you should never place infrequently called procedures in a module with procedures that are called often. At times, this may make your modules less logical and harder to conceptualize. For example, you might have a dozen functions that perform various manipulations to contact information in your application. Ordinarily, you might make one module called "`modContacts`" and place all the contact-related procedures and variables into this one module. Because Access loads the entire module when one procedure or variable in it is called, you might want to separate the contact-related procedures into separate modules (one for procedures that are commonly used and one for procedures that are rarely used and not referenced in commonly used procedures).

TIP **You need to be aware at all times that all modules having procedures referenced in a procedure of a different module are loaded when that procedure is called. In your application, if any of your common procedures reference a procedure that isn't commonly used, place the uncommon procedure in the same module with the common procedures to prevent a different module (containing the uncommon procedures) from being loaded and compiled. You may even decide to use more than two modules if you have very large amounts of code in multiple procedures that are rarely called. Although breaking related procedures into separate modules may make your code a little harder to understand, it can greatly improve the performance of your application.**

To fully take advantage of Compile on Demand, you have to carefully plan your procedure placement. Third-party tools can be invaluable for visualizing where all of the potential calls for various procedures are located.

Using the Access 2007 Database File Format

Access 2007 supports several file formats, including Access 2002-2003, Access 2000, and Access 97. The Access 2007 format (`.accdb`) supports several new features, such as multivalued fields and attachments, not available in previous versions (`.mdb`). The new file format cannot be opened or linked to earlier versions of Access (although you can link tables in earlier versions to an accdb file), does not support replication, and does not support user-level security. If you need to use the database with earlier versions of Access or use replication or user-level security, you must use an earlier version file format.

You can open and even run Access 97 database files, but you can't make any design changes. You can open Access 2002-2003 and Access 2000 database files and make any desired changes to them. However, you'll only be able to use features specific to those versions. Some of the new features in Access 2007 won't be available.

The default database file format in Access 2007 is `.accdb`. You can convert database saved in a previous format by opening the database in Access 2007, clicking the Microsoft Office button in the upper-left corner of the main Access screen, and selecting Convert. From the Convert Database Into dialog box, give the file a new name with the `.accdb` extension and click Save.

TIP **Change the default file format for new files by clicking the Microsoft Office button, selecting Access Options, and clicking the Personalize tab. Under the Creating Databases section, change the Default file format to Access 2007, Access 2002-2003, or Access 2000, as shown in Figure 26-2.**

FIGURE 26-2

For maximum performance, change the default file format to Access 2007.

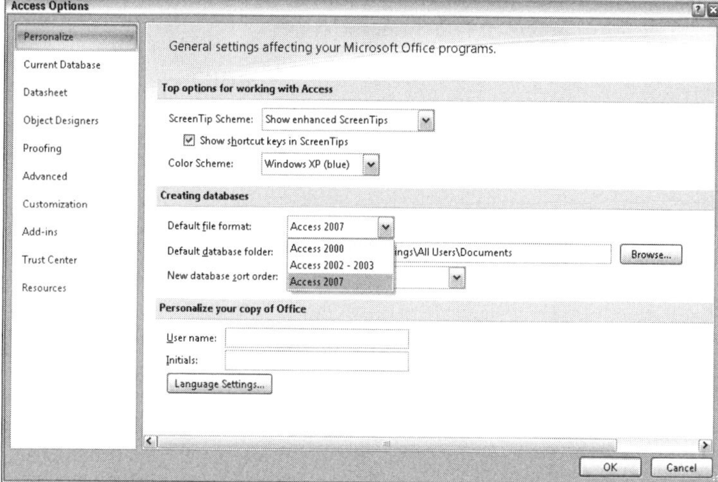

The Access 2007 file format should only be used in an Access 2007 environment where all users are using Access 2007. In addition to complete compatibility with all Access 2007 features, you may experience some performance advantages when using the Access 2007 file format with larger databases. However, in a mixed environment of Access 2000, 2002-2003 and Access 2007 users, you should stay with the Access 2002-2003 file format for compatibility with Access 2002-2003 users. The same holds true for Access 2000 compatibility; stay with the Access 2000 file format. An Access 2003 program can attach to Access 97 data files, but if you are trying to accommodate Access 97 users, you should not upgrade the Access 97 data files.

Distributing .accde Files

One way to ensure that your application's code is always compiled is to distribute your database as an `.accde` file. When you save your database as an `.accde` file, Access compiles all code modules (including form modules), removes all editable source code, and compacts the database. The new `.accde` file contains no source code, but continues to work because it does contain a compiled copy of all of your code. Not only is this a great way to secure your source code, but it also allows you to distribute databases that are smaller (because they contain no source code) and always keep their modules in a compiled state. Because the code is always in a compiled state, less memory is used by the application, and you suffer no performance penalty for code being compiled at runtime.

In addition to not being able to view existing code because it is all compiled, the following restrictions apply:

- You can't view, modify, or create forms, reports, or modules in Design View.
- You can't add, delete, or change references to object libraries or databases.
- You can't change your database's VBA project name by using the Options dialog box.
- You can't import or export forms, reports, or modules. Note, however, that tables, queries, and macros can be imported from or exported to non-`accde` databases.

TIP **If you want to create a demo of your application — and if you don't want the users to be able to see your code or form and report designs — you should create an `.accde` file. Because the designs of your forms, reports, and all code modules are simply not present (they are stored in a compiled version only), you don't have to worry about someone stealing or even modifying your designs and code. An `.accde` file is also good for distributing your work in environments where you don't want the user to change your designs.**

Because of these restrictions, it may not be possible to distribute your application as an `.accde` file. For example, if your application creates forms at runtime, you would not be able to distribute the database as an `.accde` file.

CAUTION **You have no way to convert an `.accde` file back into a normal database file. Therefore, always save and keep a copy of the original database! When you need to make changes to the application, you must open the normal database and then create a new `.accde` file before distribution. If you delete your original database, you will be unable to access any of your objects in Design View.**

To create an `.accde` file, follow these steps:

1. **Save and close all the database objects.**

   If you don't close these objects, Access attempts to close them for you, prompting you to save changes where applicable. When working with a shared database, all users must close the database; Access needs exclusive rights to work with the database.

2. **Select the Make ACCDE command from the Database Tools group of the Database Tools ribbon (see Figure 26-3).**

   The Save As dialog box appears.

FIGURE 26-3

Use the Make ACCDE command on the Database Tools ribbon to create an .accde file.

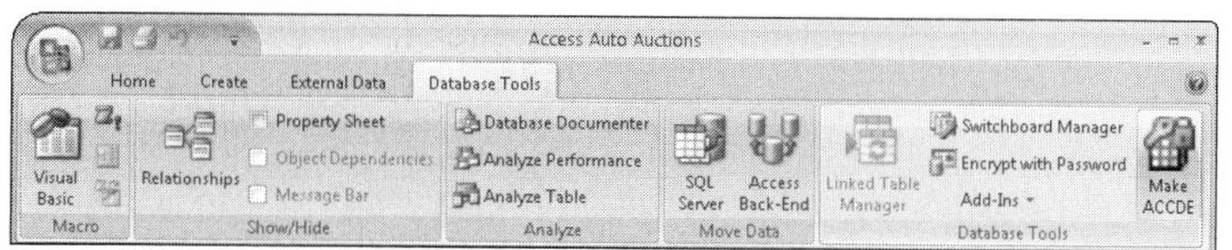

3. **In the Save As dialog box, specify a name, drive, and folder for the database.**

   Don't attempt to save the `.accde` file with the same filename (including the filename extension) as the original database.

CAUTION **Don't delete or overwrite your original database! As stated previously, you have no way to convert an `.accde` file to a normal database, and you can't edit any objects in an `.accde` file. If you delete or otherwise lose your original database, you will never again be able to access any of the objects in the design environment.**

NOTE **You can create an `.accde` file only if you first convert the database into the Access 2007 format. If the file is in an Access 2002-2003 format, you can create an `.mde` file — the Access 2002-2003 equivalent.**

Understanding the Compiled State

Understanding how Access performs Compile on Demand is critical to achieving maximum performance from your Access application. However, it is also paramount that you understand what compilation is and what it means for an application to be in a compiled state.

Access has two types of code — code that you write and code that Access can understand and execute. Before VBA procedure that you have written can be executed, the code must be run through a compiler to generate code in a form that Access understands — compiled code.

Access lacks a true compiler and instead uses partially compiled code and an interpreter. A true compiler converts source code to machine-level instructions, which are executed by your computer's CPU. Access converts your source code to an intermediate state that it can rapidly interpret and execute. The code in the converted form is known as *compiled code*, or as being in a *compiled state*.

If a procedure is called that isn't in a compiled state, the procedure must be compiled and the compiled code passed to the interpreter for execution. In reality, as previously stated, this doesn't happen at the procedure level, but at the module level. When you call a procedure, the module containing the procedure and all modules that have procedures referenced in the called procedure are loaded and compiled. You can manually compile your code, or you can let Access compile it for you on the fly. It takes time to compile the code, however, so the performance of your application suffers if you let Access compile it on the fly.

In addition to the time required for Access to compile your code at runtime, uncompiled programs use considerably more memory than compiled code does. When your application is completely compiled, only the compiled code is loaded into memory when a procedure is called. If you run an application that is in a decompiled state, Access loads the decompiled code and generates the compiled code as needed (explained previously). Access does not unload the decompiled code as it compiles, so you are left with two versions of the same code in memory.

Even on computers with large amounts of installed memory, loading both the compiled and uncompiled versions of modules takes more time than loading compiled modules alone.

There is one drawback to compiled applications: They use more hard drive space than their decompiled versions. This is because both the compiled and decompiled versions of the code are stored on the hard drive.

Hard drive space shouldn't often become a problem, but if you have an application with an enormous amount of code, you can save hard drive space by keeping it in a decompiled state. Remember that a trade-off is made between hard drive space used and the performance of your database. Most often, when given the choice, a user would rather give up a few megabytes of hard drive space in exchange for faster applications.

TIP **You can use this space-saving technique to your advantage if you need to distribute a large application and your recipients have a full development version of Access. By distributing the uncompiled versions, you need much less hard drive space to distribute the application, and the end users can compile it again at their location. If you are going to do this, you should put the entire application into a decompiled state. The topic of fully decompiling an application is discussed later in this chapter.**

Putting your application's code into a compiled state

You have only one way to put your entire application into a compiled state: Use the Compile [*Database Name*] menu item from the Debug menu on the Modules toolbar in the VBA editor window (see Figure 26-4). You must have a module open to access the Debug menu. Generally, you should always use the Compile [*Database Name*] command to ensure that all of the code is saved in a compiled state. Complex applications may take a long time to compile, and in general, you may choose to compile your Access projects only before distributing to end users or before performing benchmark tests.

FIGURE 26-4

Compile [*Database Name*] (in this example, Chapter 38) is the only way to fully compile your application.

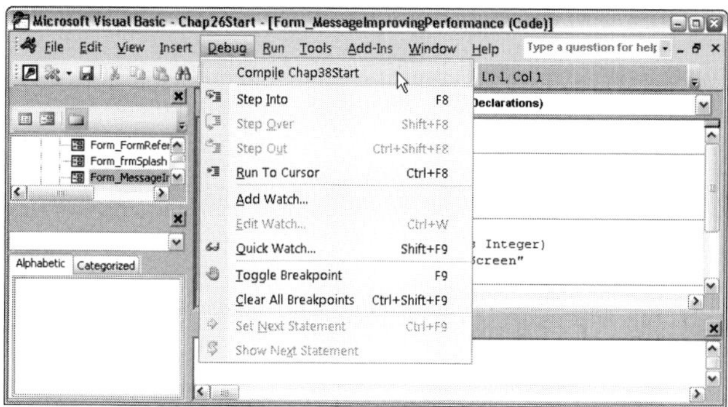

NOTE **When you use the Compile option in the Debug menu, you see the name of your project. This is the name that you used to save your database file the first time that it was created or saved. If you later rename the database file, the project name doesn't change. You can change it by opening the Tools menu in the module window and selecting the current project name with the word *Properties* beside it.**

Access 2007 has a Background Compile option. Figure 26-1 shows this option under Compile on Demand — the default value for this option is True (selected). This option tells Access to compile code in the background rather than to compile it all at one time.

TIP **It is especially important to close your application after performing a Compile [*Database Name*]. To compile all of your modules, Access needs to load every single one of them into memory. All this code stays in memory until you close Access.**

Losing the compiled state

One of the greatest roadblocks to increasing the performance of Access applications was the fact that an application could be uncompiled very easily. When the Access application was in an uncompiled state, Access had to constantly compile code as it was called. In fact, losing the compiled state was so easy to do in previous versions of Access that it would often happen without developers even realizing that they had done it.

In Access 2007, only portions of code affected by certain changes are put into an uncompiled state — not the entire application. By itself, this is a tremendous improvement over previous versions of Access.

The following actions cause portions of your code to be uncompiled:

- Modifying a form, report, control, or module. (If you don't save the modified object, your application is preserved in its previous state.)

- Adding a new form, report, control, or module (including adding new code behind a form).
- Deleting or renaming a form, report, control, or module.
- Adding or removing a reference to an object library or database by using the References command on the Tools menu.

Okay, so you think that you have a handle on code that loses its compiled state? Well, here are a couple of gotchas to consider:

- If you modify objects — such as reports or forms — at runtime through VBA code, portions of your application are put into an uncompiled state when the objects are modified. (Wizards often do this.)
- If your application creates objects like reports or forms on the fly, portions of your application are put into an uncompiled state when the objects are created. (Wizards often do this as well.)

CAUTION **When you change a project name (but not the filename), the entire application loses its compiled state. Because of this, you should change the project name only if absolutely necessary, and you should compile your database immediately after changing the project name.**

Distributing applications in a compiled or uncompiled state

When distributing your Access application, you need to take into consideration a couple of issues concerning compilation.

Distributing source code for your application

First and foremost, if you distribute source code and allow your users access to modify or add objects, you must make them completely aware of the compilation issues. If your users don't fully comprehend what is happening with your application's compiled state, you can be sure that you will receive phone calls about how your program seems to be getting slower the more that users make changes to objects.

Putting an application in an uncompiled state

If your application is the type that will be constantly changing its compiled state (due to creating forms and reports dynamically), or if end users will be making modifications to the application's objects often, or if distributed file size is an issue, you may want to consider distributing the database in a fully uncompiled state.

To put your entire application into an uncompiled state, follow these steps:

1. **Create a new database.**
2. **Import all of your application objects into the new database.**
3. **Compact the new database.**

CROSS-REF Later in this chapter, you also learn how to decompile the project manually. This has more benefits than simply letting the project become partially or completely uncompiled.

Organizing commonly used code that is never modified into a library

After your application is finished and ready for distribution, you may want to consider placing all commonly used code that will never be modified by an end user into a library database. A *library database* is an external database that your application database can reference and access. You will incur slight overhead by calling code from the library rather than by accessing it directly in the parent application, but the benefit is that the library code will never be put into a decompiled state — even if your application creates or modifies objects on the fly or if your users add new objects or modify existing objects. This technique can greatly increase an application's performance and keep the performance relatively consistent over time. Chapter 33 discusses the process of creating Access libraries.

The first step for referencing procedures in an external database is to create the external database with all its modules, just as you would do in an ordinary Access database.

CAUTION Any procedures that you declare as Private are not made available to the calling application, so plan carefully what you want to expose (declare as Public) and don't want to expose to other databases.

After you create the database and its modules, you must create a reference to that database in your application database (which is the database that your users will run). To create a reference, first open any module in your application in the VBA editor. With a module open in Design View, a new command — References — is available from the Tools menu (see Figure 26-5). Select Tools ➪ References to access the References dialog box (see Figure 26-6).

FIGURE 26-5

The References option appears on the Tools menu only when you have a module open and selected in Design View.

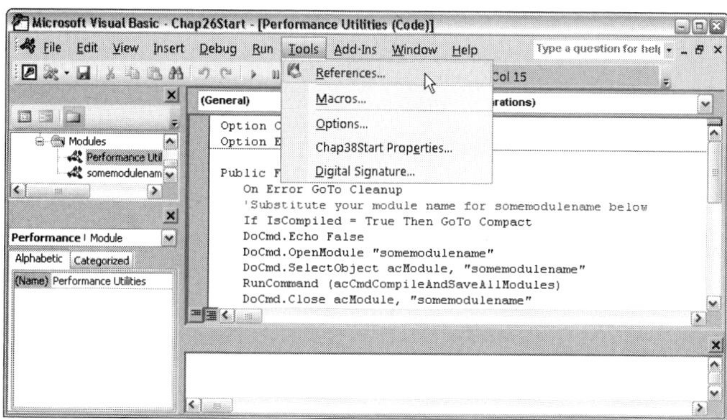
Microsoft Visual Basic - Chap26Start - [Performance Utilities (Code)]
File Edit View Insert Debug Run Tools Add-Ins Window Help
References...
Macros...
Options...
Chap38Start Properties...
Digital Signature...
Modules
Performance Util
somemodulenam
Performance Module
Alphabetic Categorized
(Name) Performance Utilities
(General)
Option C
Option E
Public F
On Error GoTo Cleanup
'Substitute your module name for somemodulename below
If IsCompiled = True Then GoTo Compact
DoCmd.Echo False
DoCmd.OpenModule "somemodulename"
DoCmd.SelectObject acModule, "somemodulename"
RunCommand (acCmdCompileAndSaveAllModules)
DoCmd.Close acModule, "somemodulename"

FIGURE 26-6

The References dialog box is where you resolve references to OLE automation servers and Access library databases.

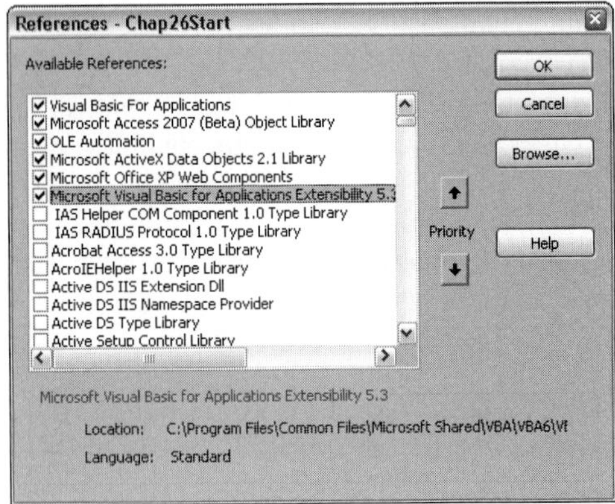

In the References dialog box, you specify all the references that your application needs for using OLE automation or for using other Access databases as library databases. When making a reference to another Access database, as opposed to an OLE server created with another development tool like Visual Basic, you probably need to browse for the database. Use the Browse dialog box as if you were going to open the external database. After you have selected the external Access database, it shows up in the References dialog box with a selected check box to indicate that it is referenced.

To remove a reference, access the References dialog box again and deselect the referenced item by clicking its check box. After you have made all the references that you need to make, click OK.

After a database is referenced, you can call the procedures in the referenced database as if they existed in your application database. No matter what happens in your application database to cause code to decompile, the referenced database always stays in a compiled state unless it is directly opened in Access and modified.

To reference an external Access database to call its procedures, follow these steps:

1. **Create the library database and its modules.**
2. **Open the database in which you want to use the external procedures.**
3. **Open any module in Design View.**
4. **Select Tools ⇨ References.**
5. **Select the OLE server that you want to register.**

   If it is an Access database, you probably need to use the Browse feature to locate it.

TIP If your application uses *add-in databases* (a special type of library database), you should open the add-in database for read-only access. Opening add-ins for read-only access increases performance because Jet doesn't have to maintain locking information for the add-in database in an `.laccdb` file.

Creating a library reference for distributed applications

If you are distributing your application, references stay in tact only if the calling database and the library database are in the same or relative path. For example, if the main database is in `C:\myapp` on your machine, and if the library database is in `C:\myapp\library`, the reference remains intact if the library database is located in the same relative path, such as in `C:\newdir` for the main database and `C:\newdir\library` for the library database. If the relative path won't remain consistent upon distribution, your application's users must manually add the reference or you must create the reference with VBA code.

The following procedure creates a reference to the file whose name is passed to it. For this function to work, the full filename with path must be passed:

```
bResult = CreateReference("C:\My Documents\MyLib.accdb").
```

The function is:

```
Public Function CreateReference(strFileName As String) _
    As Boolean
  Dim ref As Reference
On Error GoTo HandleError
  Set ref = References.AddFromFile(strFileName)
  CreateReference = True

ExitHere:
  Exit Function

HandleError:
  MsgBox Err & ": " & Err.Description
  CreateReference = False
  Resume ExitHere

End Function
```

You can verify that a reference is set by using the `ReferenceFromFile` function. To verify a reference, pass the function, the full path, and the filename like this:

```
bResult = _
  ReferenceFromFile("C:\Windows\System32\mscal.ocx")
```

The function returns `True` if the reference is valid and `False` if it isn't.

With the References collection, the primary concern of using and distributing libraries — losing references upon distribution — is now gone. However, library databases still have one major drawback: Access doesn't support circular references. This means that the code in your library databases can't reference variables or call procedures that exist in your parent database.

Whether you distribute your application as one database or as a primary database that uses library databases, if your applications are static (meaning that they don't allow modification of objects by end users or wizards, and don't perform object modifications on themselves) you should always distribute the databases in a fully compiled state so that your users experience the highest possible level of performance.

Improving Absolute Speed

When discussing an application's performance, the word *performance* is usually synonymous with speed. You will find two types of speed in software development — absolute and perceived. *Absolute speed* refers to the actual speed at which your application performs a function, such as how long it takes to run a certain query. *Perceived speed* is the phenomenon of an end user actually perceiving one application to be faster than another application, even though it may indeed be slower. This phenomenon of perceived speed is often a direct result of visual feedback provided to the user while the application is performing a task. Absolute speed items can be measured in units of time; perceived speed can't be measured in this manner.

Of course, some of the most important items for increasing actual speed are the following:

- Keeping your application in a compiled state
- Organizing your procedures into "smart" modules
- Opening databases exclusively
- Compacting your databases regularly

Opening a database exclusively

You should always open a database exclusively in a single-user environment. If your application is a standalone application (meaning that nothing is shared over a network), opening the database in exclusive mode can really boost performance. If your application is run on a network and shared by multiple users, you won't be able to open the database exclusively. (Actually, the first user can open it exclusively, but if he does, no other user can access the database until the first user closes it.) The preferred method for running an application in a network environment is to run Access and the main code `.accdb` file locally, and then link to a shared database containing the data on the server. If your application is used in this manner, you can open and run the code database exclusively, but you can't use exclusive links to the shared data.

To open a database exclusively in Access 2007, click the Open button down arrow and select Open Exclusive in the Open Database dialog box (see Figure 26-7).

FIGURE 26-7

Select the Open Exclusive button on the Open button pull-down to open a database in a single-user environment to increase the performance of the database.

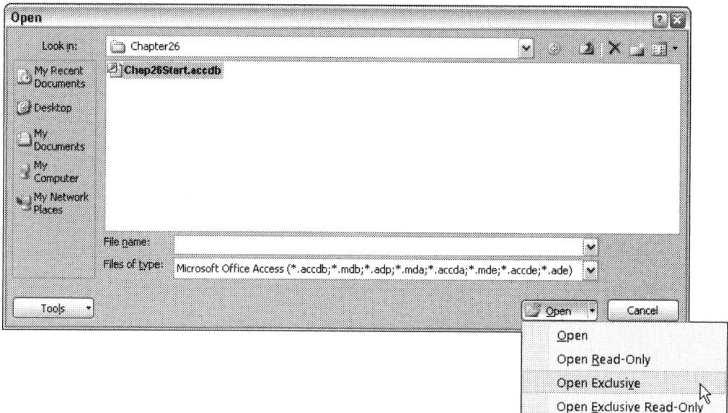

TIP **Click the Microsoft Office button and select Access Options; then click the Advanced tab. Under the Advanced section, change the Default open mode to Exclusive if you always want to open a database exclusively. The default open mode is Shared.**

Compacting a database

Another often-overlooked way of maximizing your database's performance is to compact your database regularly. When records are deleted from a database, the hard drive space that held the deleted data is not recovered until a compact is performed. In addition, a database becomes fragmented as data is modified in the database. Compacting a database defragments the database and recovers used hard drive space.

All the preceding methods are excellent (and necessary) ways to help keep your applications running at their optimum performance level, but these are not the only tasks that you can perform to increase the absolute speed of your application. Almost every area of development, from forms to modules, can be optimized to give your application maximum absolute speed.

If you use Jet as your data access engine, an Access application can run only so fast. With Jet, each time you open a table, run a query, or perform an operation on data, all the data referenced by the process or query must be moved from the data database (assuming that you have split your program and data database files) to the computer that's running the program. This means that you may be moving a lot of data across your network. This is simply not fast. An Access project that's using the Microsoft SQL Server Desktop Engine (MSDE 2000) or SQL Server 2005 Express Edition can use stored procedures to minimize network traffic and can drastically speed up applications with large data databases. If you are working with large amounts of data, consider writing the application using SQL Server as your back-end database file.

Tuning your system

One important aspect of performance has nothing to do with the actual application design — that is, the computer on which the application is running. Even though it's impossible to account for all the various configurations your clients may have, you can do some things for your computer and recommend that end users do them for theirs:

- Equip the computer with as much RAM as possible. This step often becomes an issue of dollars. However, RAM prices continue to decrease, and adding to a computer's RAM is one of the most effective methods that you can employ to increase the speed of Access.
- Don't use wallpaper. Removing a standard Windows wallpaper background can free up anywhere from 25K to 250K of RAM, and removing complicated bitmaps or high-color bitmaps can free up even more space.
- Close all applications that aren't being used. Windows makes it very handy to keep as many applications loaded as you want — on the odd chance that you may need to use one of them. Although Windows XP and Windows Vista are pretty good at handling memory for multiple open applications, each running application still uses RAM. On machines with little RAM, unnecessary open applications can significantly degrade performance.
- Make sure that your Windows swap file is on a fast drive with plenty of free space. If possible, you should also set the minimum hard drive space available for virtual memory to at least twice the physical RAM installed and make it a permanent swap file.
- Defragment your hard drive often. Defragmenting a hard drive allows data to be retrieved from the drive in larger sections, thus causing fewer direct reads and less repositioning of the read heads.

Getting the most from your tables

In addition to reviewing all the technical issues discussed in the preceding sections, it is advantageous to get back to the basics when designing your applications. Tools like Access enable novices to create relational databases quickly and easily, but they don't teach good database design techniques in the process. An exception to this statement is the Table Analyzer Wizard. However, even though the Table Analyzer Wizard offers suggestions that are often helpful in learning good design technique, its recommendations should *never* be taken as gospel. The Table Analyzer has proven to be wrong on many occasions. Click the ribbon's Database Tools tab, then click the Analyze Table command in the Analyze group to start the Table Analyzer Wizard.

Entire volumes of text have been devoted to the subject of database theory. Teaching database theory is certainly beyond the scope of this chapter (or even this book). However, you should be familiar with many basics of good database design.

Creating efficient indexes

Indexes help Access find and sort records faster and more efficiently. Think of these indexes as if they were book indexes. To find data, Access looks up the location of the data in the index and then retrieves the data from its location. You can create indexes based on a single field or on multiple fields. Multiple-field indexes enable you to distinguish between records in which the first field may have the same value. If they are defined properly, multiple-field indexes can be used by Microsoft's Rushmore query optimization, which is the technology that Jet uses to optimize the speed at which queries execute, based on the search and sort fields of the queries and indexes of the tables included in the queries.

Deciding which fields to index

People new to database development typically make two mistakes: First, not using indexes and, second, using too many indexes (usually putting them on every field in a table). Both of these mistakes are serious — sometimes a table with indexes on every field may give *slower* performance than a table with no indexes. Why? When a record is saved, Access must also save an index entry for each defined index. This can take time and use a considerable amount of hard drive space. The time used is rarely noticed in the case of a few indexes, but many indexes can require a huge amount of time for record saves and updates. In addition, indexes can slow some action queries (such as append queries) when the indexes for many fields need to be added or updated while performing the query's operations. Figure 26-8 shows the index property sheet for a sample `tblContacts` table.

FIGURE 26-8

Note that common search fields like ZipCode, CustomerType, and TaxLocation are indexed.

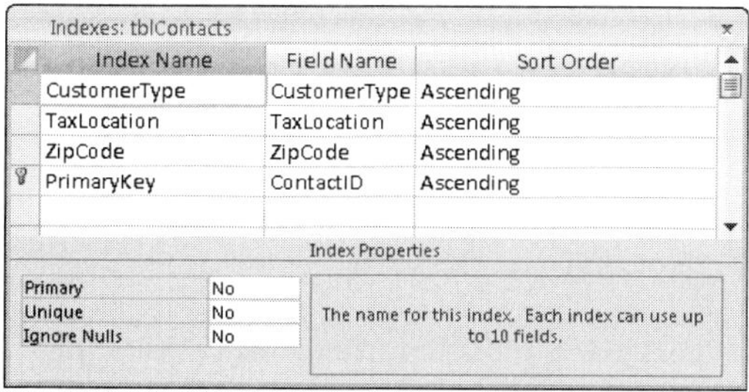

When you create a primary key for a table, the field (or fields) used to define the key is automatically indexed, and you can index any field unless the field's data type is Memo or OLE Object. You should consider indexing a field if all the following factors apply:

- The field's data type is Text, Number, Currency, or Date/Time.
- You anticipate searching for values stored in the field.
- You anticipate sorting records based on the values in the field.

- You will join the field to fields in other tables in queries.
- You anticipate storing many different values in the field. (If many of the values in the field are the same, the index may not significantly speed up searches or sorting.)

When defining an index, you have the option of creating an ascending (the default) or a descending index.

TIP **Jet can use a descending index when optimizing queries only when the equal sign (=) operator is used. If you use an operator other than the equal sign, such as <, >, <=, or >=, Jet can't use the descending index. If you plan on using operators other than an equal sign on an index, you should define the index as an ascending index.**

Using multiple-field indexes

When frequently searching or sorting by multiple fields at the same time, you can create an index on the combined fields. For example, if you often set criteria for `LastName` and `FirstName` fields in the same query, it makes sense to create a multiple-field index on both fields.

When sorting a table by a multiple-field index, Access first sorts by the first field defined for the index. If the first field contains records with duplicate values, Access then sorts by the second field defined for the index, and so on. This creates a drill-down effect. For a multiple-field index to work, a search criterion *must* be defined for the first field in the index, but not for additional fields in the index. In the preceding example, if you wanted to search for someone with the first name *Robert,* but you didn't specify a last name to use in the search, the second field in the index wouldn't be used. If you need to perform searches on the second field in a multiple-field index, but are not always specifying criteria for the first field in the index, you should create an index for the second field in addition to the multiple-field index.

Continuing with the `LastName, FirstName` index: To search for the first name *John*, the multiple-field index wouldn't be used because you would be attempting to search only on the second field in the index.

Getting the most from your queries

The performance problems of many Access applications result from query design. Database applications are all about looking at and working with data, and queries are the heart of determining what data to look at or work with. Queries are used to bind forms and reports, fill list boxes and combo boxes, make new tables, and many other functions within an Access application. Because they are so widely used, it is extremely important to optimize your queries. A query that is properly designed can provide results minutes to hours faster than a poorly designed query that returns the same result set. Consider the following:

- When designing queries and tables, you should create indexes for all fields that are used in sorts, joins, and criteria fields. Indexes enable Jet to quickly sort and search through your database.

TIP **Sorting and searching is much faster if the indexes are unique rather than nonunique. Also, if you are using conditions in your queries, queries can run faster if the index is based on ascending order (as opposed to reverse, z to a, or descending order).**

- When possible, use a primary key in place of a regular index when creating joins. Primary keys don't allow nulls and give the Rushmore query optimizer more ways to use the joins.
- Limit the columns of data returned in a select query to only those you need. If you don't need the information from a field, don't return it in the query. Queries run much faster when they return less information.

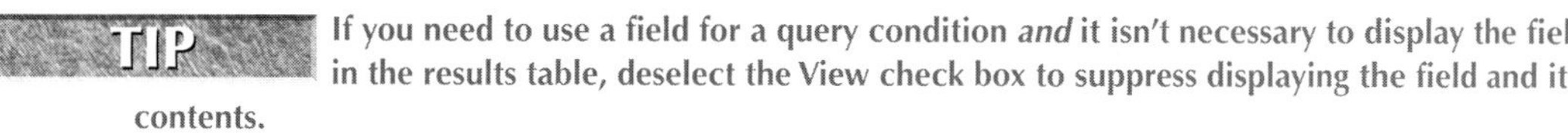

TIP **If you need to use a field for a query condition *and* it isn't necessary to display the field in the results table, deselect the View check box to suppress displaying the field and its contents.**

- When you need to return a count of the records returned by an SQL statement, use `Count(*)` instead of `Count([FieldName])` because `Count(*)` is considerably faster. `Count(*)` counts records that contain null fields; `Count([FieldName])` checks for nulls and disqualifies them from being counted. If you specify a field name instead of using the asterisk, `Count` doesn't count records that have a null in the specified field.

TIP **You may also replace `FieldName` with an expression, but this slows down the function even further.**

- Avoid using calculated fields in nested queries. A calculated field in a subordinate query considerably slows down the top-level query. You should use calculated fields only in top-level queries, and even then, only when necessary.
- When you need to group records by the values of a field used in a join, specify the `Group By` for the field that is in the same table that you are totaling. You can drag the joined field from either table, but using `Group By` on the field from the table that you are totaling yields faster results.
- Domain aggregate functions, such as `DLookup` or `DCount`, that are used as expressions in queries slow down the queries considerably. Instead, you should add the table to the query or use a subquery to return the information that you need.
- As with VBA code modules, queries are compiled. To compile a query, Jet's Rushmore query optimizer evaluates the query to determine the fastest way to execute the query. If a query is saved in a compiled state, it runs at its fastest speed the first time that you execute it. If it isn't compiled, it takes longer the first time that it executes because it must be compiled, but it then runs faster in succeeding executions. To compile a query, run the query by opening it in Datasheet View and then close the query without saving it. If you make changes to the query definition, run the query again after saving your changes and then close it without saving it.
- If you really want to squeeze the most out of your queries, experiment by creating your queries in different ways (such as specifying different types of joins). You will be surprised at the varying results.

Getting the most from your forms and reports

Forms and reports can slow an application by taking a long time to load or process information. You can perform a number of tasks to increase the performance of forms and reports.

Minimizing form and report complexity and size

One of the key elements to achieving better performance from your forms and reports is reducing their complexity and size. Try these methods to reduce a form's or report's complexity and size:

- Minimize the number of objects on a form or report. The fewer objects used, the fewer resources needed to display and process the form or report.
- Reduce the use of subforms. When a subform is loaded, two forms are in memory — the parent form and the subform. Use a list box or a combo box in place of a subform whenever possible.
- Use labels instead of text boxes for hidden fields because text boxes use more resources than labels do. Hidden fields are often used as an alternative to creating variables to store information.

You can't write a value directly to a label like you can to a text box, but you can write to the labels caption property using VBA like this: `Label1.Caption = "MyValue"`.

- Move some code from a form's module into a standard module. This enables the form to load faster because the code doesn't need to be loaded into memory. If the procedures that you move to a normal module are referenced by any procedures executed upon loading a form (such as in the form load event), moving the procedures won't help because they are loaded anyway as part of the potential call tree of the executed procedure.
- Don't overlap controls on a form or report.
- Place related groups of controls on form pages. If only one page is shown at a time, Access doesn't need to generate all of the controls at the same time.
- Use a query that returns a limited result set for a form's or report's `RecordSource` rather than use a table or underlying query that uses tables. The less data returned for the `RecordSource`, the faster the form or report loads. In addition, return only those fields actually used by the form or report. Don't use a query that gathers fields that won't be displayed on the form or report (except for a conditional check).

Using bitmaps on forms and reports

Bitmaps on forms and reports make an application look attractive and can also help convey the purpose of the form or report (as in a wizard). However, graphics are always resource-intensive, so you should use the fewest possible number of graphic objects on your forms and reports. This helps to minimize form and report load time, increase print speed, and reduce the resources used by your application.

Often you will display pictures that a user never changes and that are not bound to a database. Examples of such pictures include your company logo on a switchboard or static images in a wizard. When you want to display images like these, you have two choices:

- Use an Unbound Object Frame.
- Use an Image control.

If the image will never change and if you don't need to activate it in a form's Design View, use an Image control. Image controls use fewer resources and display faster. If you need the image to be a linked or embedded OLE object that you can edit, use an Unbound Object Frame. You can convert OLE images in Unbound Object Frames.

TIP **If you have an image in an Unbound Object Frame that you no longer need to edit, you can convert the Unbound Object Frame to an Image control by right-clicking the control and selecting Change To ➪ Image from the pop-up menu.**

TIP **When you have forms that contain unbound OLE objects, you should close the forms when they are not in use to free up resources. Also avoid using bitmaps with many colors — they take considerably more resources and are slower to paint than a bitmap of the same size with fewer colors.**

If you want to display an Unbound OLE object but don't want the user to be able to activate it, set its `Enabled` property to `False`.

Speeding up list boxes and combo boxes

It's important to pay attention to list boxes and combo boxes when optimizing your application. You can take a number of steps to make your combo boxes and list boxes run faster:

- When using multipage forms that have list boxes or combo boxes on more than one page, don't set the RowSource of the list boxes or combo boxes until the actual page containing the control is displayed.
- Index the first field displayed in a list box or combo box. This enables Access to find entries that match text entered by the user much faster.
- Although it's not always practical, try to refrain from hiding a combo box's bound column. Hiding the bound column causes the control's searching features to slow down considerably.
- If you don't need the search capabilities of AutoExpand, set the AutoExpand property of a combo box to No. Access is then relieved of the task of constantly searching the list for entries matching text entered in the text portion of the combo box.
- When possible, make the first nonhidden column in a combo or list box a text data type, and not a numeric one. To find a match in the list of a combo box or list box, Access must convert a numeric value to text to do the character-by-character match. If the data type is text, Access can skip the conversion step.

- Often overlooked is the performance gain achieved by using saved queries for RecordSource and RowSource properties of list boxes and combo boxes. A saved query gives much better performance than an SQL SELECT statement because an SQL query is optimized by Rushmore on the fly.

TIP **You will find one problem with combo boxes present in Access 2007, which poses a performance concern. Because Access 2007 supports hyperlinks, Access has to perform some additional work when first painting a combo box; it needs to determine the data type of the combo box.**

The result is that the combo box takes a little longer to paint — up to a couple of seconds on some computers. If your combo box is a bound combo box, this isn't a problem because Access gets the data type from the ControlSource's data type. In addition, if you save a RowSource for the combo box when you save the form, Access determines the data type from the RowSource and doesn't need to determine the data type at runtime. The only time that this paint delay is an issue is when you have an unbound combo box that has its RowSource set programmatically. When this is the case, the combo box takes slightly longer to paint the first time it is displayed.

Getting the most from your modules

Perhaps the area where you'll be able to use smart optimization techniques most frequently is in your modules. For example, in code behind forms, you should use the Me keyword when referencing controls. This approach takes advantage of the capabilities of Access 2007; using Me is faster than creating a form variable and referencing the form in the variable. Other optimization techniques are simply smart coding practices that have been around for many years. You should try to use the optimum coding technique at all times. When in doubt, try different methods to accomplish a task and see which one is fastest.

TIP **Consider reducing the number of modules and procedures in your application by consolidating them whenever possible. A small memory overhead is incurred for each module and procedure that you use, so consolidating them may free up some memory.**

Using appropriate data types

You should always explicitly declare variables using the Dim function rather than arbitrarily assign values to variables that haven't been dimmed. To make sure that all variables in your application are explicitly declared before they are used in a procedure, while in the VBA development environment, select Tools ➪ Options, choose the Editor tab, and then set the Require Variable Declarations option on the tab (second from the top in the Code settings section).

Use integers and long integers rather than singles and doubles when possible. Integers and long integers use less memory, and they take less time to process than singles and doubles do. Table 26-1 shows the relative speed of the different data types available in Access.

TABLE 26-1

Data Types and Their Mathematical Processing Speed

Data Type	Relative Processing Speed
Integer/Long	Fastest
Single/Double	Next to Fastest
Currency	Next to Slowest
Variant	Slowest

In addition to using integers and long integers whenever possible, you should also use integer math rather than precision math when applicable. For example, to divide one long integer by another long integer, you can use the following statement:

```
x = Long1 / Long2
```

This statement is a standard math function that uses floating-point math. You can perform the same function by using integer math (notice that the mathematical sign is the regular slash versus the backward slash) with the following statement:

```
x = Long1 \ Long2
```

Of course, integer math isn't always applicable. It is, however, commonly applied when returning a percentage. For example, you can return a percentage with the following precision math formula:

```
x = Total / Value
```

However, you can perform the same function using integer math by first multiplying the Total by 100 and then using integer math like this:

```
x = (Total * 100) \ Value
```

You should also use string functions ($) where applicable. When you are manipulating variables that are of type String, use the string functions (for example, `Str$()`) as opposed to their variant counterparts (`Str()`). If you are working with variants, use the non-$ functions. Using string functions when working with strings is faster because Access doesn't need to perform type conversions on the variables.

When you need to return a substring by using `Mid$()`, you can omit the third parameter to have the entire length of the string returned. For example, to return a substring that starts at the second character of a string and returns all remaining characters, use a statement like this:

```
strReturn = Mid$(strMyString, 2)
```

When using arrays, use dynamic arrays with the `Erase` and `ReDim` statements to reclaim memory. By dynamically adjusting the size of the arrays, you can ensure that only the amount of memory needed for the array is allocated.

TIP **In addition to using optimized variables, consider using constants when applicable. Constants can make your code much easier to read and won't slow your application if you compile your code before executing it.**

Writing faster routines

You can make your procedures faster by optimizing the routines that they contain in a number of ways. If you keep performance issues in mind as you develop, you will be able to find and take advantage of situations like the ones discussed here.

Some Access functions perform similar processes but vary greatly in the time that they take to execute. You probably use one or more of these regularly, and knowing the most efficient way to perform these routines can greatly affect your application's speed:

- `For/Next` statements are normally faster than `Select Case` statements are. They tend to process less logic.
- The `IIF()` function is much slower than a standard set of `If/Then/Else` statements is.
- The `With` and `For Each` functions accelerate manipulating multiple objects and/or their properties.
- Change a variable with `Not` instead of using an `If . . . Then` statement. (For example, use `x = Not(y)` instead of `If y = true then x= false`.)
- Instead of comparing a variable to the value `True`, use the value of the variable. (For example, instead of saying `If X = True` then . . ., say `If X` then . . .)
- Use the `Requery` method instead of the `Requery` action. The method is significantly faster than the action.
- When using OLE automation, resolve references when your application is compiled rather than at runtime by using the `GetObject` or `CreateObject` functions.

Using control variables

When referencing controls on a form in code, there are some very slow ways and some very fast ways to use references to form objects. The slowest possible way is to reference each control explicitly. This requires Access to search for the form name sequentially, starting with the first form name in the database and continuing until it finds the form name in the forms list (`msysObjects` table). If the form name starts with a `z`, this can take a long time if the database contains many forms. For example:

```
Forms![frmSales]![SaleDate] = something
Forms![frmSales]![InvoiceDate] = something
Forms![frmSales]![SalespersonID] = something
```

If the code is in a class module behind the `frmSales` form, you can use the `Me` reference. The `Me` reference refers to the open object (forms or reports) and substitutes for `Forms![formname]`. This is a much faster method because it can go right to the form name. For example:

```
Me![SaleDate] = something
Me![InvoiceDate] = something
Me![SalespersonID] = something
```

If your code is not stored behind the form but is in a module procedure, you can use a control variable like the following:

```
Dim frm as Form
set frm = Forms![frmSales]
frm![SaleDate] = something
frm![InvoiceDate] = something
frm![SalespersonID] = something
```

This way, the form name is looked up only once. An even faster way is to use the `With` construct. For example:

```
With Forms![frmSales]
  ![SaleDate] = something
  ![InvoiceDate] = something
  ![SalespersonID] = something
End With
```

You can then reference the variable rather than the actual control. Of course, if you don't need to set values in the control but rather use values from a control, you should simply create a variable to contain the value rather than the reference to the control.

Using field variables

The preceding technique also applies to manipulating field data when working with a recordset in VBA code. For example, you may ordinarily have a loop that does something like this:

```
...
Do Until tbl.EOF
  MyTotal = MyTotal + tbl![OrderTotal]
  tbl.MoveNext
Loop
```

If this routine loops through many records, you should use the following code snippet instead:

```
Dim MyField as Field
...
Set MyField = tbl![OrderTotal]
Do Until tbl.EOF
  MyTotal = MyTotal + MyField
  tbl.MoveNext
Loop
```

The preceding code executes much faster than code that explicitly references the field in every iteration of the loop.

Increasing the speed of finding data in code

Use the `FindRecord` and `FindNext` methods on indexed fields. These methods are much more efficient when used on a field that is indexed. Also, take advantage of bookmarks when you can. Returning to a bookmark is much faster than performing a `Find` method to locate the data.

The procedure shown in Listing 26-1 is an example of using a bookmark. Bookmark variables must always be dimmed as variants, and you can create multiple bookmarks by dimming multiple variant variables. The following code opens the `tblCustomers` table, moves to the first record in the database, sets the bookmark for the current (first) record, moves to the last record, and finally repositions back to the bookmarked record. For each step, the `debug.print` command is used to show the relative position in the database as evidence that the current record changes from record to record.

LISTING 26-1

Using a Bookmark to Mark a Record

```
Public Sub BookmarkExample()

  Dim rs As Recordset
  Dim bk As Variant

  Set rs = Workspaces(0).Databases(0).OpenRecordset( _
    "tblContacts", dbOpenTable)

  'Move to the first record in the database:
  rs.MoveFirst

  'Print the position in the database:
  Debug.Print rs.PercentPosition

  'Set the bookmark to the current record:
  bk = rs.Bookmark

  'Move to the last record in the database:
  rs.MoveLast

  'Print the position in the database:
  Debug.Print rs.PercentPosition

  'Move to the bookmarked record:
  rs.Bookmark = bk

  'Print the position in the database:
  Debug.Print rs.PercentPosition
```

```
    rs.Close
    Set rs = Nothing
End Sub
```

Eliminating dead code and unused variables

Before distributing your application, remove any *dead code* — code that is not used at all — from your application. You will often find entire procedures, or even modules, that once served a purpose but are no longer called. In addition, it isn't uncommon to leave variable declarations in code after all code that actually uses the variables has been removed. By eliminating dead code and unused variables, you reduce the amount of memory your application uses and the amount of time required to compile code at runtime.

Although it isn't easy and is often impractical, removing large numbers of comments from your code can decrease the amount of memory used by your application.

Other things that you can do to increase the speed of your modules include opening any add-ins that your application uses for read-only access and replacing procedure calls within loops with in-line code. Also, don't forget one of the most important items: Deliver your applications with the modules compiled.

Increasing Network performance

The single most important action that you can take to make sure that your networkable applications run at their peak performance is to run Access and the application database on the workstation and link to the shared network database. Running Access over the network is much slower than running it locally.

Improving Perceived Speed

Perceived speed is how fast your application appears to run to the end user. Many techniques can increase the perceived speed of your applications. Perceived speed usually involves supplying visual feedback to the user while the computer is busy performing some operation, such as constantly updating a percent meter when Access is busy processing data.

Using a splash screen

Most professional Windows programs employ a splash screen, as shown in Figure 26-9. Most people think that the splash screen is simply to show the product's name and copyright information and the registered user's information, but this isn't entirely correct. The splash screen greatly contributes to the perceived speed of an application. It shows the user that something is *happening*, and it gives users something to look at (and hence occupy their time) for a few seconds while the rest of the application loads.

NOTE In large applications, you may even display a series of splash screens with different information, such as helpful hints, instructions on how to use the product, or even advertisements. These are known as ***billboards***.

FIGURE 26-9

A splash screen to display product and version information

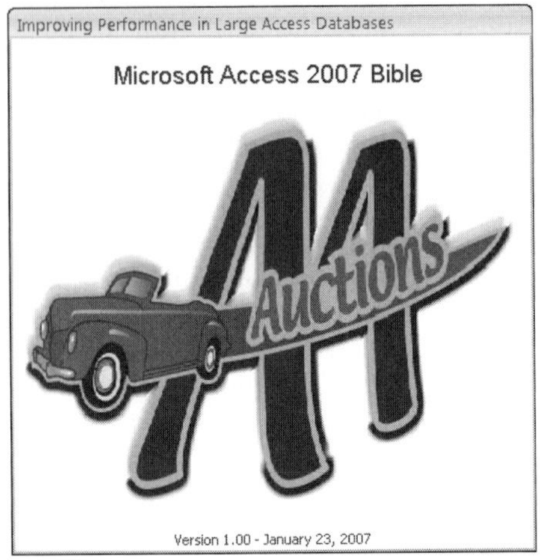

To create a splash screen, create a basic form with appropriate data, such as your application information, logo, and registration information. Then set this form as the Display Form in the Current Database options. Setting the form as the Display Form ensures that the splash screen is the first form to be loaded. You then want to call any initialization procedures from the `On Open` event of the splash form. A good splash screen should automatically disappear after a few seconds. To make this happen, use the timer event. `Chapter26.accdb` contains a simple splash screen named `frmSplashScreen` to help get you started and includes some simple code to initialize the timer and remove the form after a few seconds.

CROSS-REF For more information on splash screens and setting Current Database options (including the Display Form), see Chapter 35.

You need to remember a few issues when using splash screens:

- Never use custom controls in a start-up form. Custom controls take time to load and consume resources.
- Minimize code in start-up forms. Use only code that is absolutely necessary to display your start-up form and use a light form if possible.
- The start-up form should call only initialization procedures. Be careful about call trees; you don't want your start-up form to trigger the loading of many modules in your application.

Loading and keeping forms hidden

If you have forms that are displayed often, consider hiding them rather than closing them. To hide a form, set its `Visible` property to `False`. When you need to display the form again, set its `Visible` property back to `True`. Forms that remain loaded consume memory, but they display more quickly than forms that must be loaded each time they are viewed. In addition, if you are *morphing* a form or report (changing the way it looks by changing form and control properties), keep the form hidden until all changes are made so that the user doesn't have to watch the changes take place.

Using the hourglass

When your application needs to perform a task that may take a while, use the hourglass. The hourglass mouse pointer shows the user that the computer is not locked up but is merely busy. To turn on the hourglass cursor, use the `Hourglass` method like this:

```
DoCmd.Hourglass True
```

To turn the hourglass back to the default cursor, use the method like this:

```
DoCmd.Hourglass False
```

Using the built-in progress meter

In addition to using the hourglass, you should consider using the progress meter when performing looping routines in a procedure. The progress meter gives constant visual feedback that your application is busy, and it shows the user in no uncertain terms where it is in the current process.

ON the CD-ROM **`Chapter26.accdb` includes two types of progress meters. Using the standard Microsoft Access progress meter that is displayed in the status bar creates the first type that is discussed in this chapter. The other meter is a pop-up form that uses a colored rectangle to show the progress of an activity.**

The sample database file `Chapter26.accdb` contains a number of progress meter samples. Each uses the progress meter a little differently but all run the same example. The example creates 50,000 records in a table named *SampleData*. Each of the examples uses a simple form with several text box controls and a button to start the process. The basic progress meter form in Design View is shown in the following figure. Each of the examples contains code to display either the built-in Access progress meter or one within the pop-up form. Each contains a button to start the process, as well as two text boxes to display the start time and end time of the process.

The following code demonstrates how to use the built-in progress meter in a loop to show the meter starting at 0 percent and expanding to 100 percent, 1 percent at a time. The first example is named `ProgressMeterUsingBuiltInAccessMeter`. This example doesn't actually use the text box in the sample progress meter form, but rather uses the progress meter built into Microsoft Access that displays as a bar at the bottom-left corner of the screen in the status bar.

If you don't display the status bar, you won't see the built-in progress meter when it runs.

The code to initialize, update, and remove the meter is shown in Figure 26-10.

FIGURE 26-10

Code to run the built-in progress meter

Microsoft Visual Basic - Chap26Start - [Form_ProgressMeterUsingBuiltInAccessMeter (Code)]

```
Option Compare Database
Option Explicit
Dim ReturnValue As Integer

Private Sub Start_Click()
  Me.StartTime = Now
  Me.Repaint

  Dim rst As New ADODB.Recordset, i As Long, lngCounter As Long
  DoCmd.SetWarnings False
  DoCmd.RunSQL ("delete * from sampletable")
  DoCmd.SetWarnings True
  rst.Open "SELECT * FROM SampleTable", CurrentProject.Connection, _
      adOpenDynamic, adLockOptimistic

  lngCounter = 50000

  'Display message and initialize status bar.
  ReturnValue = SysCmd(SYSCMD_INITMETER, "Creating Records", lngCounter)
  For i = 1 To lngCounter
    ReturnValue = SysCmd(SYSCMD_UPDATEMETER, i)
    rst.AddNew
    rst!Name = "somename"
    rst!Address = "100 Anyplace Rd"
    rst!Salary = 25000 + 2 * i
    rst!dateoftxn = #3/15/1999# + i
    rst!complete = True
    rst.Update
  Next i

  rst.Close
  Me.EndTime = Now
  ReturnValue = SysCmd(SYSCMD_REMOVEMETER)

End Sub
```

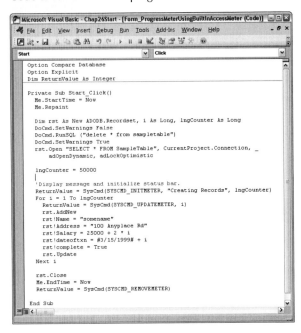

The first step for using the percent meter is initializing the meter. You initialize the meter by calling the `SysCmd` function like this:

```
ReturnValue = SysCmd(acSysCmdInitMeter, "Creating Records", lngCounter)
```

The `acSysCmdInitMeter` in this line is an Access constant that tells the function that you are initializing the meter. The second parameter is the text that you want to appear to the left of the meter. Finally, the last value is the maximum value of the meter (in this case, 100 percent). You can set this value to anything that you want. For example, if you were iterating through a loop of 50,000 records, you may set this value to 50,000. Then you can pass the record count at any given time to the `SysCmd` function; Access decides what percentage the meter shows as filled.

After the meter has been initialized, you can pass a value to it to update the meter. To update the meter, you call the `SysCmd` function again and pass it the `acSysCmdUpdateMeter` constant and the new update meter value. Remember, the value that you pass to the function is not necessarily the percent displayed by the meter. It can be the number of records processed or any number that when divided by the initial counter provides a percentage from 1 to 100. For example, if 50,000 records are being processed and the number 12,500 is passed to the meter, it will display 25 percent.

```
ReturnValue = SysCmd(acSysCmdUpdateMeter, i)
```

After all the records are processed, you want to remove the meter from the status bar. To do this, use the following command. (There are no parameters to pass when you remove the meter.)

```
ReturnValue = SysCmd(acSysCmdRemoveMeter)
```

The progress meter displayed in the status bar is shown in Figure 26-11.

FIGURE 26-11

The progress meter displayed in the status bar

Creating a progress meter with a pop-up form

To run the sample progress meter that uses the pop-up form, open the form `ProgressMeter CallingEveryRecord` and click the Search button. The progress meter form appears, and the bar grows from 0 to 100 percent. This may take 15 to 20 seconds on a high-end machine, but a little longer on a slower machine.

The Progress Meter form in progress is shown in Figure 26-12.

FIGURE 26-12

A graphical progress meter

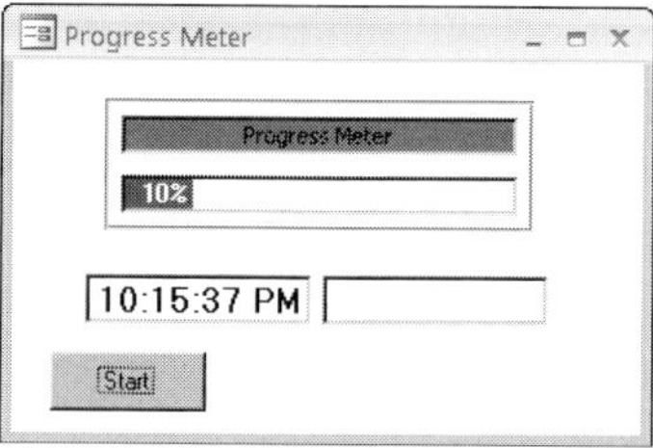

This progress meter has some advantages over the standard Microsoft Access progress meter. The progress meter that comes with Access uses the status bar to display the meter and isn't always as visible as you may want it to be. The pop-up progress meter pops up in the middle of the screen and is immediately visible to the user. The meter that comes with Access, however, usually displays faster because it requires less overhead to run, although with longer tasks the difference may not be noticeable. The speed of the pop-up meter can be controlled by updating the meter every *x* percent. Therefore, if the form meter is set for fast execution, it displays with speed comparable to that of the built-in meter.

The progress meter form is created from a few simple controls, as shown in Figure 26-12. It contains a rectangle control, two label controls, and option group controls. In Figure 26-12, you can see that the rectangle is shown 10 percent completed. In reality, the width of the rectangle is manipulated by the program that is used to display the meter's progress. The width is reset to 0 when the progress meter starts, and it is slowly built back to its original length.

The code for the progress meter is also simple and shown in its entirety, including the three-line function that is called in Figure 26-13.

FIGURE 26-13

The Progress Meter form call to the pop-up progress meter

Microsoft Visual Basic - Chap26Start - [Form_ProgressMeterCallingEveryRecord (Code)]

File Edit View Insert Debug Run Tools Add-Ins Window Help

(General) SetPMeter

```
Public Function SetPMeter(p As Single)
  'p is percent of total
  Me.PMeterBar.Width = p * Me.PMeter.Width
  Me.PMeterBar.Caption = Format(p, "##%")
  Me.Repaint
End Function

Private Sub Start_Click()
  Me.StartTime = Now
  Me.Repaint
  Dim rst As New ADODB.Recordset, i As Long, lngCounter As Long
  DoCmd.SetWarnings False
  DoCmd.RunSQL ("delete * from sampletable")
  DoCmd.SetWarnings True
  rst.Open "SELECT * FROM SampleTable", CurrentProject.Connection, _
      adOpenDynamic, adLockOptimistic

  lngCounter = 50000
  For i = 1 To lngCounter
    rst.AddNew
    rst!Name = "somename"
    rst!Address = "100 Anyplace Rd"
    rst!Salary = 25000 + 2 * i
    rst!dateoftxn = #3/15/1999# + i
    rst!complete = True
    SetPMeter i / lngCounter
    rst.Update
  Next i
  rst.Close
  Me.EndTime = Now
End Sub
```

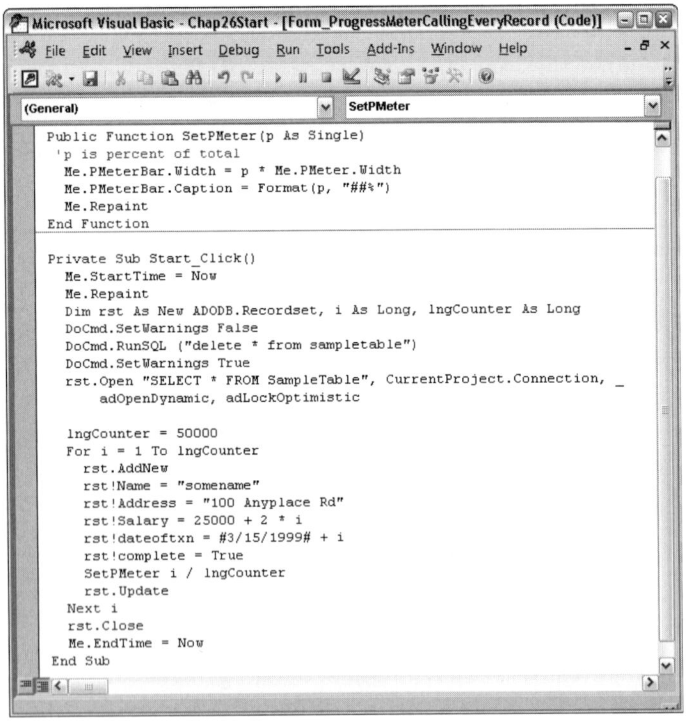

The code that calls the meter is one simple line buried in the middle of the iteration loop. It calls the display function by passing it the iteration number and total number of iterations expected. In this example, `i` is the record number being processed and `lngCounter` is the expected 50,000 records.

```
SetPMeter i / lngCounter
```

The function `SetPMeter` consists of only three lines: one to display the rectangle and manipulate its width, one to display the caption on the bar as it grows inside the rectangle in the form, and one to repaint the screen each time so that the bar is animated.

```
Public Function SetPMeter(p As Single)
 'p is percent of total
  Me.PMeterBar.Width = p * Me.PMeter.Width
  Me.PMeterBar.caption = Format(p, "##%")
  Me.Repaint
End Function
```

Speeding up the progress meter display

This routine is called whenever you want to update the progress meter. You can decide when to do this. Generally, you should call the progress meter only when it is likely to be updated. If you know that you have 1000 records, you may call the meter every 10 records; if you have 10,000 records, you may call the meter every 100 records.

Although this code is simple, it is not the best option. In fact, because this code calls the progress meter for every record, it is much slower than the built-in progress meter. A better approach is to call the progress meter only once in a while. The following code can replace the call in the code previously discussed:

```
If (i / lngCounter) * 100 = Int((i / lngCounter) * 100) Then
  SetPMeter i / lngCounter
End If
```

The `If` statement checks to see whether the calculation of the completion percentage is an integer (whole number). This calls the progress meter function (`SetPMeter`) that moves the progress meter rectangle and displays the percentage completed. It is called only 100 times to move the rectangle; even though the `If` statement is run 50,000 times, you may wonder why the `If` statement is faster. The reality is that the `If` statement takes very few resources to process, but a function that changes the width of a rectangle or control, writes to the screen, and then repaints the screen uses a lot of resources — as evidenced by the time to process falling by 90 percent.

Follow these steps to integrate the Progress Meter into your application:

1. **Import the Progress Meter form into your application.**
2. **Change the code behind the form to interact with your application.**

Working with Large Program Databases in Access 2007

When someone mentions large databases in Microsoft Access, they are generally thinking about a database with tables that contain hundreds of thousands of data records. Though this can be considered to be a large database, another definition is a database that contains hundreds of objects — tables, queries, forms, reports, and thousands of lines of VBA program code. Although you can sometimes solve data performance problems by changing the back end from Jet to SQL Server, you will probably have to deal with much more complex problems if you create applications with many queries, forms, reports, and lots of VBA module code.

If your database has hundreds of objects, especially forms and reports, you may have run into problems that cause your database to exhibit strange behavior. These include

- Not staying compiled or not compiling at all
- Growing and growing and growing in size, even after compiling and compacting
- Running slower and slower
- Displaying the wrong record in linked subforms
- Displaying compile errors when you know that the code is correct
- Corrupting constantly

Compacting your database doesn't always work as advertised. Compiling and saving all modules becomes a long wait with a seemingly perpetual hourglass. After you compact and open the database, it is uncompiled again. If you work with large databases, chances are good that you have had these experiences. This section shows you how to solve these problems and get you up and running fast again.

How databases grow in size

Many things can cause a database to grow. Each time that you add an object to an Access 2007 database (`.accdb`) file, it gets larger. And why shouldn't it? You are certainly using more space to define the properties and methods of the object. Reports and forms take the most space because the number of properties associated with each form or report and each control on a form or report uses space. Table attachments (links) and queries take up very little space, but VBA code grows proportionally to the number of lines in both modules and code behind forms and reports. If you store data in your program database, this also takes up space proportionally to the number of records in the table. Many other things cause a database to grow.

Each time you add another new form or report, more space is used. Each time you add a new control and define some properties, even more space is used. When you define any event in a form or report that contains even a single line of VBA code, more overhead is used, because the form or report is no longer a lightweight object but one that is VBA-aware. This requires more space and resources than a lightweight form or report containing no VBA code. If you embed images into your forms and reports, these also will use space. Embedding bound OLE aware data, such as pictures, sound, video, or Word or Excel documents, uses more space than unbound objects or images.

Each time that you make a change to any object — even a simple one — a duplicate copy of the object is created until you compact the database. Within even a few hours of work, Access 2002 databases can begin to grow larger and larger. If the database contains thousands of lines of VBA code, the database can grow to two or three times its original size very quickly, especially when compiled and before it is compacted.

Compiling and compacting may not be enough

As you add, delete, and modify objects, Access doesn't always clean up after itself. You have probably learned that after you make changes to your objects, especially VBA code, you should open any module and select Debug ➪ Compile [*Database Name*], save the module, and close the Visual Basic Development Environment. After you do this, click the Microsoft Office button and select Manage; then click Compact and Repair Database. This action compacts the database to the same name and reopens the database running any startup commands or autoexec macros that you may have. If you prefer to be less aggressive, close the database first and compact the database to a different name, effectively creating a compacted backup. You can then use the new database or delete the old one and rename the new database to the original name.

Compiling and compacting may not be enough to solve some of the problems mentioned at the beginning of the section. Databases have been known to grow in size after compiling and compacting — even without adding new objects, code, or data. Sometimes, strange things happen to databases without a good explanation. The database might not compile code properly if the database is too large, or you may see compile errors on perfectly written code. The database may run slowly even if there's nothing wrong. There are still a few techniques to use, even when you think you're out of options.

Rebooting gives you a clean memory map

We have always noticed that strange behavior in any program gets better when you reboot your system. Access is particularly bad at *memory leaks*, especially if you're going in and out of form, report, and module design. If you don't want to reboot, at least close your database and exit Access before beginning the examination of your problem.

Fixing a single corrupt form by removing the record source

Sometimes, you may have a single form that doesn't run properly. To fix this, try opening the form in Design View and removing any record source. Then, close and save the form. Reopen the form in Design View and reenter the original (or a new) record source. This may fix your problem. When the record source of an Access form or report is changed, it forces various pieces of internal code behind the form to be rebuilt. Sometimes, this simple process works.

Creating a new database and importing all objects

It's important to have your database as clean as possible. Although we're not sure if gremlins crawl into some obscure portion of the database file, we are sure that you can't import or export them. A technique that usually proves to be successful is to simply create a new database and then import all of the objects from the original database. Access 2007 makes it easy to import all of your objects by using the Select All button found in the Import Objects dialog box. You can get to this dialog box by first opening a new empty database; then click the External Data tab and click the Access command on the Import group, selecting the database you're having problems with, and then clicking the Import option button (not the Link option button). Click OK then import all of the database objects.

If you have any custom menus and toolbars, Import/Export specifications, or Navigation Pane groups, you should remember to use the Options button and check off those options as shown in Figure 26-14. The default for these options is False. If you have created any current database properties in the database, you have to create them again because they are not importable.

CAUTION **If you use externally referenced libraries or add-ins, you must manually reference these libraries in the new database. You can display a module and use the Tools ➪ References menu to do this.**

FIGURE 26-14

Importing database objects the Options button pressed

Using the decompile option in Access 2007

A little known start-up, command-line option is called `/decompile`. You may have seen many of the command-line options, such as `/nostartup`, `/cmd`, and `/compact`. This option starts

Access 2007 in a special way and, when a database is opened, saves all VBA modules as text. This works with module objects and all the code behind forms and reports.

To do this, go to the Windows Start menu Run command and type **msaccess /decompile** as shown in Figure 26-15. Hold down the Shift key before you launch Microsoft Access. This prevents any startup forms or autoexec macro processes from running. You don't want the database to run code that forces even a single module to be compiled. This prevents the decompile process from actually doing any good.

FIGURE 26-15

Starting Access 2007 with the decompile command-line option

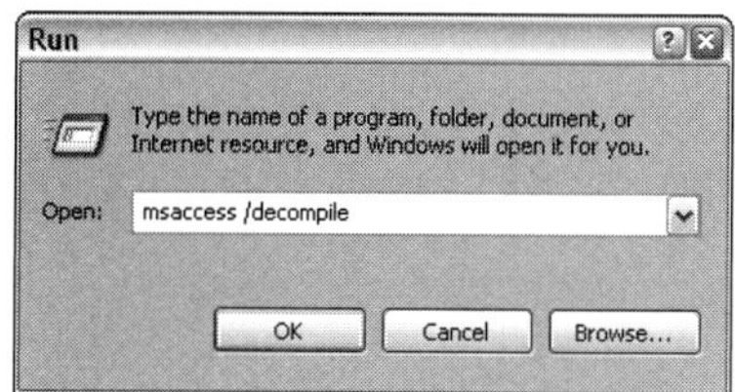

Access appears to start as usual. It takes about three minutes to open a database and decompile all of the objects in a 20MB database. At this point, the real question is whether the database gets sufficiently smaller, runs faster, and stays compiled after it was compiled and compacted.

After the database window is displayed, close Access. Don't just close the database window — actually exit Microsoft Access.

After you exit Access, you can restart Access normally. You can then open your database, open any module, and select Debug ➪ Compile *projectname* where *projectname* is simply the name of your project (original database filename). After the database compiles, you should close the module, return to the Access window, and compact and repair the database. You should find that Access runs these procedures much faster than usual.

Make sure that you immediately exit Access 2007 after it finishes decompiling and then start Access again before running Compile projectname or Compact and Repair Database.

Recapping the six steps to large database success

If you're ready to release your application for a real test by the users, you should follow the steps below to insure a clean-running system:

1. **Reboot your computer to clean up memory.**
2. **Create a new Access database and import all the objects. Then close Access.**
3. **Restart Access by using the `/decompile` option while holding down the Shift key. Close Access after the database window is displayed.**

4. **Restart Access normally while holding down the Shift key.**
5. **Compile the database.**
6. **Compact and Repair the database.**

By releasing a clean, fully compiled and compacted system your application runs faster and has fewer technical or maintenance problems.

Detecting an uncompiled database and automatically recompiling

It's very important that you make sure that a database is always in a compiled state. If you release your application as a modifiable `.accdb` file, your customers may make simple or even complex changes to your application and then complain because their system is running slowly. Although some of your customers may be serious developers, our experience is that many customers who make changes to Access databases don't know about compilation or compacting.

To see if your database is compiled, open the Visual Basic window for any module, display the Debug window at the bottom of the editor, and type **? IsCompiled()**, as shown in Figure 26-16. If the database is compiled, it displays `True`. If it is in a decompiled state, it displays `False`, as shown in Figure 26-16.

FIGURE 26-16

Checking to see if an Access 2007 program is compiled

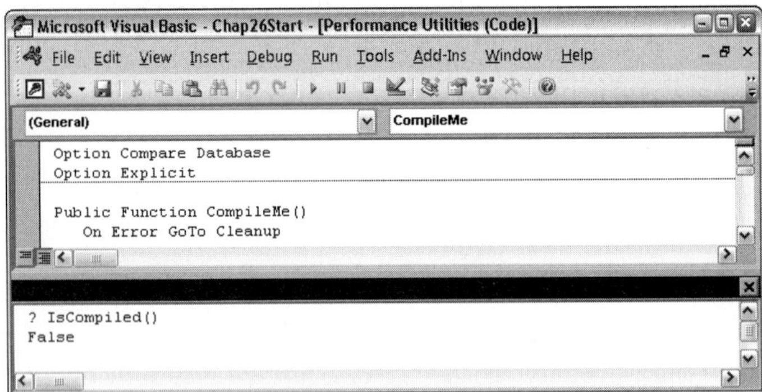

To solve this problem, you can create an interface that automatically detects whether the database is not in a compiled state and then gives the user the option of compiling the application. This automatic detection runs each time the database is opened. The user still has to compact the database, but the hard part is compiling. Figure 26-17 shows the message that is automatically displayed if the database is uncompiled. The code is shown in the following example.

FIGURE 26-17

A form to help the user compile your application

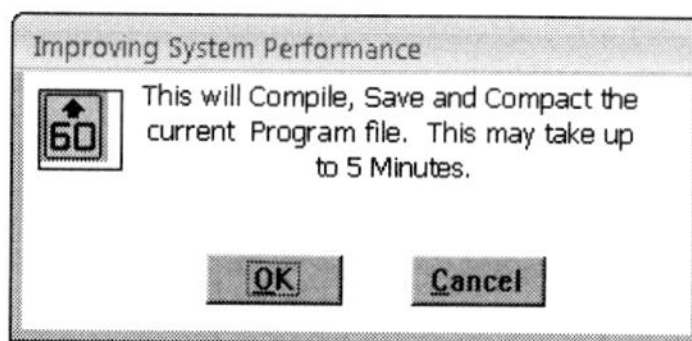

One line of code can be added anywhere in your program to detect an uncompiled application and start the process:

```
If IsCompiled() = False Then DoCmd.OpenForm "MessageImprovingPerformance"
```

The code uses the Access 2007 built-in function `IsCompiled` to determine the compiled state of the application. If the application isn't compiled, the form is displayed, as shown in Figure 26-17. Users have two choices. If they are still testing, they may not want to compile yet. If they want to compile, they simply have to click the Yes button.

The compile and compact code is shown in Figure 26-18. The application is compiled first and then compacted. If the database is already compiled, the compile function is skipped and the database is only compacted. You can simply insert this module and the message box into any application and call the form.

Making small changes to large databases — Export

One final tip for working with large databases: Always work with a copy of the program file and export the changed objects. When you are making lots of changes to a few objects to try a new technique or to get a stubborn algorithm to work, you are constantly opening and closing objects. This tends to negatively affect large databases. Work with a copy of the database, and then when you have the changes just the way you want, you can export the changed objects from the test database to the production database. Any object that you export with the same name as the production database is exported with a 1 at the end of the name. You can then open the production database, delete the original objects, and rename the changed objects that have a 1 on the end of their name. New objects are obviously exported with their name intact.

The fewer changes to a large database, the better off you are. By following the tips and techniques in this section, you will have fewer problems and you will be more productive.

FIGURE 26-18

A module to automatically compile and compact your database

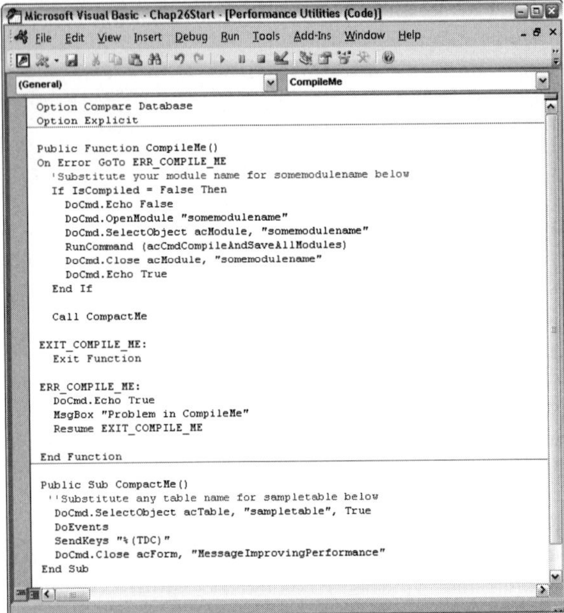

Microsoft Visual Basic - Chap26Start - [Performance Utilities (Code)]
File Edit View Insert Debug Run Tools Add-Ins Window Help
(General)
CompileMe
Option Compare Database
Option Explicit
Public Function CompileMe()
On Error GoTo ERR_COMPILE_ME
'Substitute your module name for somemodulename below
If IsCompiled = False Then
DoCmd.Echo False
DoCmd.OpenModule "somemodulename"
DoCmd.SelectObject acModule, "somemodulename"
RunCommand (acCmdCompileAndSaveAllModules)
DoCmd.Close acModule, "somemodulename"
DoCmd.Echo True
End If
Call CompactMe
EXIT_COMPILE_ME:
Exit Function
ERR_COMPILE_ME:
DoCmd.Echo True
MsgBox "Problem in CompileMe"
Resume EXIT_COMPILE_ME
End Function
Public Sub CompactMe()
''Substitute any table name for sampletable below
DoCmd.SelectObject acTable, "sampletable", True
DoEvents
SendKeys "%(TDC)"
DoCmd.Close acForm, "MessageImprovingPerformance"
End Sub

Summary

In this chapter, you learned techniques to improve the performance and operation of your database. You learned how to set up tables, queries, forms, and reports to optimize performance. You saw techniques to take a problem database and turn it into a working database. You even used methods to make the user think the application was running faster.

Through judicious use of the techniques discussed in this chapter, you can increase the performance of your Access application to the highest level possible.

Chapter 27

Advanced Data Access with VBA

IN THIS CHAPTER

- Creating code that finds a record by using a form control
- Creating code that uses a bookmark to find a record
- Using the form's filter options
- Using a form to filter records
- Creating a parameter query
- Interfacing a parameter query to a form dialog

In the previous few chapters, you learned the basics of programming, reviewed some built-in VBA functions, and experienced the various VBA logical constructs. You learned about ADO and how to access data in tables and queries through SQL recordsets. You also learned a lot about forms and queries in previous chapters. In this chapter, you use all this knowledge and learn how to display selected data in forms or reports using a combination of techniques involving forms, Visual Basic code, and queries.

ON the CD-ROM In the `Chapter27.accdb` database, you will find several forms to use as a starting point and other completed forms to compare to the forms you change in this example. All of the examples use a modified version of the frmProducts form and `tblProducts`.

Adding an Unbound Combo Box

When viewing a form, you often have to page through hundreds or even thousands of records to find the record or set of records you want to work with. You can teach your user how to use the Access "find" features and wildcards, what to do to see other records, and so on, but this defeats the purpose of a programmed application. If you build an application, you want to make it easier for your users to become productive with your system, not teach them Microsoft Access.

Figure 27-1 shows the frmProducts form with an additional control at the top — a combo box that is not bound to any control source in the form. The unbound combo box is used to look up a record in `tblProducts` and then display the record in the form using a bit of code. You see several ways to do this in the chapter.

FIGURE 27-1

The frmProductsExample1 form with an unbound combo box

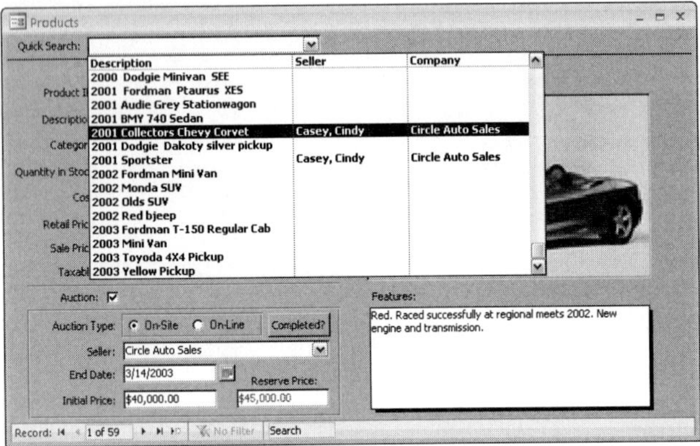

The design for the combo box is shown in Figure 27-2. Notice that the Control Source property is empty. This combo box is not bound to any field in a table. It is used only by the form. There are four columns that can be viewed in the query for the Row Source, as shown in Figure 27-3. The first is the Description from `tblProducts`. The second and third columns are taken from `tblContacts`. The second column is the seller from an auction's Last Name and First Name together. The third column is the seller's company. The last column is not displayed and is the ProductID field in `tblProducts`.

FIGURE 27-2

The Property window for the unbound combo box control

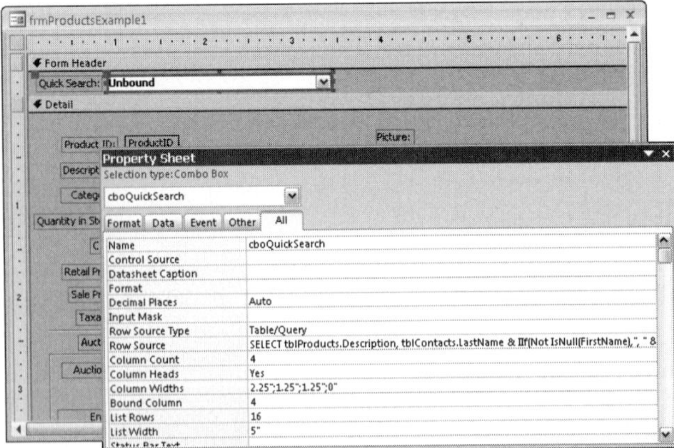

This column is also the bound column for the combo box and is the value the combo box will equal when a description record is selected in the combo box. Notice that the fourth column width is 0, which hides the displayed value when the combo box is pulled down.

The Column Heads property is set to Yes because whenever there are three or more displayed columns, you should display column heads as well.

FIGURE 27-3

The query behind the Row Source property of `cboQuickSearch`

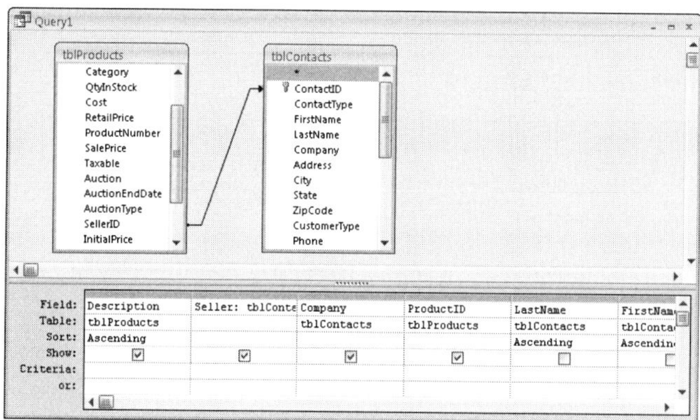

This combo box will be used for all the examples in this chapter. Next you see how to find records in a variety of ways using the combo box and the code behind it.

Using the FindRecord Method

The first form to look at is frmProductsExample1. You enhance the code behind the form and the combo box that selects a specific record.

When a user selects a record using a combo box, it triggers the `AfterUpdate` event. This example uses the `AfterUpdate` event procedure to find the record selected in the combo box.

The `FindRecord` method locates a record in any field by specifying a value passed to it as a parameter. This is equivalent to using the binoculars in the Access ribbon to find a record.

To create an event procedure behind the combo box, follow these steps:

1. **Display the frmProductsExample1 form in Design view, click cboQuickSearch, and display the Property window (press F4).**
2. **Select the Event tab and click the `AfterUpdate` event.**

3. **Click the combo box arrow in the `AfterUpdate` event property and select Event Procedure.**
4. **Click the Builder button that appears in the right side of the property.**

   The procedure appears in a separate VBA code window. The shell of the event procedure (`Private Sub cboQuickSearch_AfterUpdate()`...`End Sub`) is automatically created. As you have learned, whenever you create an event procedure, the name of the control and event are part of the subprocedure.
5. **Enter the four lines of code exactly as shown in Figure 27-4.**

FIGURE 27-4

Using the `FindRecord` method to find a record

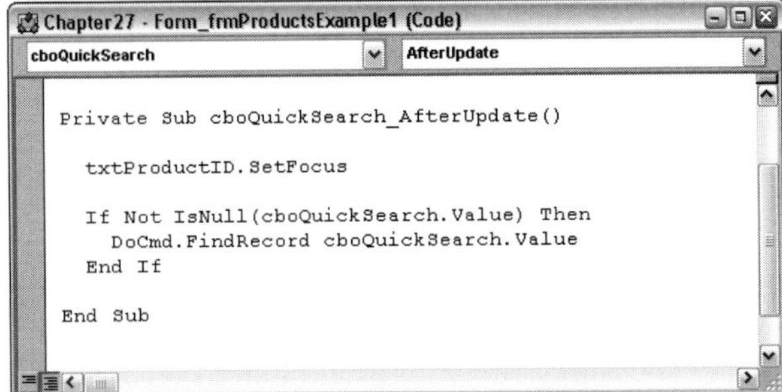

The first line is:

```
txtProductID.SetFocus
```

This statement moves the cursor to the txtProductID control. Just as you need to manually move the cursor to a control in order to use the Find icon in the Access ribbon, you must place the cursor in the control. In this case, you're moving the cursor to the control containing the ProductID value because the search will look for a particular ProductID.

The next block of code is:

```
If Not IsNull(cboQuickSearch.Value) Then
    DoCmd.FindRecord cboQuickSearch.Value
End If
```

This block of code first checks to make sure that cboQuickSearch contains a value (is not null) before using the `FindRecord` method. If a value is found in the combo box, the `FindRecord` method uses the combo box's value (which happens to be the selected item's ProductID) to search for the selected vehicle's record.

The first value found by the `FindRecord` method is determined by a series of parameters, including whether the case is matched and whether the search is forward, backward, or the first record found. Enter `DoCmd.FindRecord` in the code window and press the spacebar to see all available options. The `FindRecord` method finds only one record at a time while allowing all other records to be viewed.

Using the Bookmark to Locate a Record

The `FindRecord` method is a good way to search when the control you want to use to find a record is displayed on the form. It is also a good way if the value being searched for is a single value. However, many times multiple values are used as look-up criteria. A bookmark is another way of finding a record.

You can use the form named frmProductsExample2 to follow this example.

Figure 27-5 shows code to use a bookmark that is added behind the `AfterUpdate` event of the combo box.

FIGURE 27-5

Bookmark code used to find a record

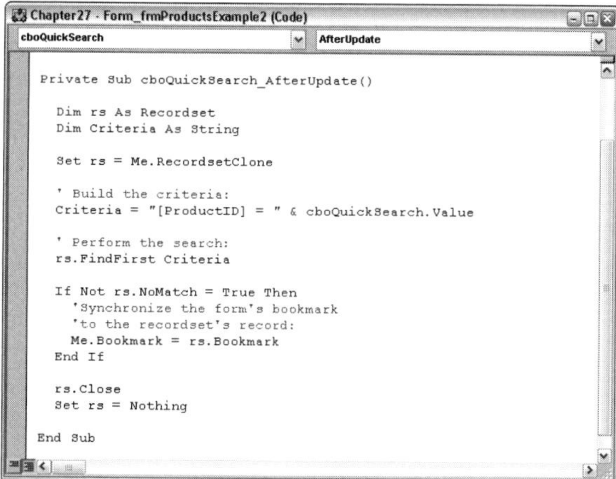

The first three lines are:

```
Dim rs As Recordset
Dim strCriteria As String
Set rs = Me.RecordsetClone
```

The first two lines declare a recordset named rs and a string named `Criteria`. These will be used later in the code. The next line sets the recordset to a copy of the form's bound recordset (the RecordsetClone).

The `Recordset` object's `FindFirst` method requires a search string containing criteria to look up in the recordset (yes, that is correct — you're actually asking the recordset to search itself for a particular record, based on some criteria).

The criteria string can be as complicated as needed. The following statement concatenates the field name `ProductID` with the value of cboQuickSearch:

```
strCriteria = "[ProductID] = " & cboQuickSearch.Value
```

Notice the parts of the criteria string that are concatenated.

The first part is a double quote, then the field name followed by an equal sign:

```
[ProductID] =
```

The value of `Me. cboQuickSearch` is then added to the string. Assuming the value of `cboQuickSearch` is `17`, the string is now:

```
[ProductID] = 17
```

TIP **Creating criteria in code is sometimes complicated. Remember that the objective is to build a string that could be copied into a query SQL window and run as is. Often, the best way to create a criteria string is to create a query design, switch to SQL view, and then copy the SQL to a code window. Then, break up the code's `WHERE` clause into field names and control values, inserting concatenation symbols and delimiters. In this example, there is no `WHERE` clause but the idea is the same.**

After the criteria string is completed, you use the recordset's `FindFirst` method to search for the record. The following line uses the `FindFirst` method of the recordset, passing the criteria string like the `WHERE` clause of a SQL statement:

```
rs.FindFirst strCriteria
```

The `FindFirst` method looks for a record matching the criteria property's value.

NOTE **You don't have to create a `Criteria` variable and then set the criteria string to it. You can simply place the criteria after the `rs,FindFirst` method, like this:**

```
rs.FindFirst  "ProductID = " & cboQuickSearch.Value
```

However, when you have complex criteria, it may be easier to create the criteria separately from the command that uses the criteria string so you can debug the string separately.

The next lines are used to determine whether the record pointer in the form should be moved. Notice the `Bookmark` property referenced in the following code block. A bookmark is nothing more than a pointer to a record in a recordset. The `FindFirst` method positions the recordset's bookmark on the found record.

```
If Not rs.NoMatch = True Then
  Me.Bookmark = rs.Bookmark
End If
```

If no record was found, the `NoMatch` property is `True`. Because you want to set the bookmark if a record *is* found, you need the computer equivalent of a double negative. Essentially, it says if there is "not no record found" then the bookmark is valid. Why Microsoft chose `NoMatch` instead of `Match` (which would reduce the logic to `If rs.Match Then...`) is a mystery to everyone.

An alternative way to write the logic for checking the NoMatch property is:

```
If rs.NoMatch = False Then
  Me.Bookmark = rs.Bookmark
End If
```

If a matching record is found, the form's bookmark (`Me.Bookmark`) is set to the found recordset's bookmark (`rs.Bookmark`) and the form repositions itself to the bookmarked record. This does not filter the records but merely positions the form's bookmark on the first record matching the criteria. All other records are still visible in the form.

The last lines of code simply close and discard the recordset.

NOTE **Criteria can be as complex as you need them to be, even involving multiple fields of different data types. Remember that strings must be delimited by single quotes (not double quotes, because double quotes surround the entire string), dates are delimited by pound signs (#), and numeric values are not delimited.**

The `FindFirst/bookmark` method is preferable to using `FindRecord` because it allows for more complex criteria and doesn't require the control being searched to be visible. You don't have to preposition the cursor on a control to use the recordset's `FindFirst` method.

Filtering a Form Using Code

Although using the `FindRecord` or `FindFirst` methods allow you to quickly locate a record meeting the criteria you want, it still shows all the other records in a table or query recordset and doesn't necessarily keep all the records together. Filtering a form lets you view only the record or set of records you want, hiding all non-matching records.

Filters are good when you have large recordsets and want to view only the subset of records matching your needs.

Figure 27-6 shows the two lines of code necessary to create and apply a filter to a form's recordset. Each form contains a `Filter` property that specifies how the bound records are filtered. Usually the `Filter` property is blank and means the form is unfiltered (all of the records are displayed).

FIGURE 27-6

Code for filtering and clearing a filter behind a form

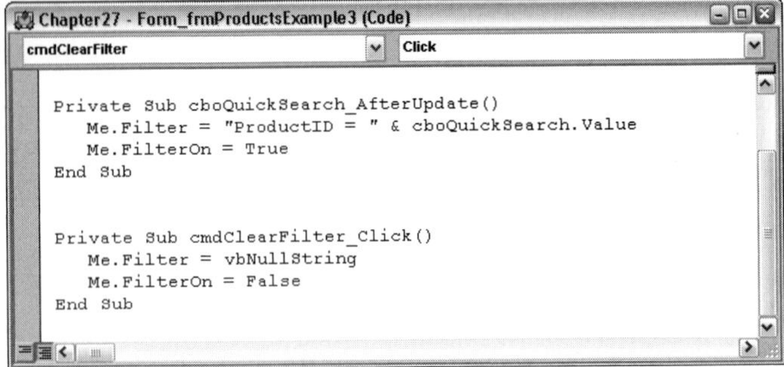

The first line of code sets form's `Filter` property:

```
Me.Filter = "ProductID = " & cboQuickSearch.Value
```

Notice that this is exactly the same string used as the criteria passed to the recordset's `FindFirst` property.

The second line of code (`Me.FilterOn = True`) turns on the filter. You can put all the criteria that you want in a filter property, but unless you explicitly set the `FilterOn` property to `True`, the filter is never applied to the form's recordset. The filter hides all the records that do not meet the criteria, showing only the records meeting the filter's value.

```
Me.FilterOn = True
```

CAUTION **If you create a form filter and then save the form design with the filter set, the filter is saved with the form. The next time the form is opened, the filter is active. Always clear the filter manually from the form's `Filter` property before saving the form.**

Whenever you turn on a filter, you must create a way to turn it off. If you look at the top of Figure 27-7, you can see a small button (cmdClearFilter) next to the combo box. This button turns off the filter and sets the form's `Filter` property to an empty string (`vbNullString`). The second procedure shown in Figure 27-6 is the button's `Click` event procedure:

```
Private Sub cmdClearFilter_Click()
  Me.Filter = vbNullString
  Me.FilterOn = False
End Sub
```

FIGURE 27-7

frmProductsExample3 uses the form's Filter and FilterOn properties.

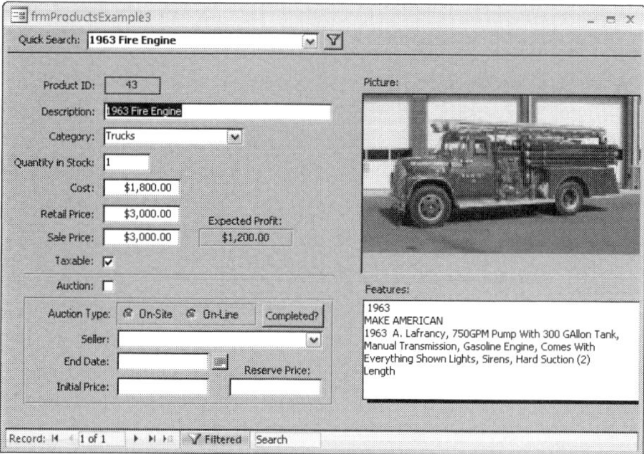

Using a Query to Filter a Form Interactively

At times you want to have one form control another. There may be times when you want a recordset to display selected data based on instant user decisions. For example, each time a report is run, a dialog box is displayed and the user enters a set of dates or selects a product or customer. One way to do this is to use a parameter query.

Creating a parameter query

A parameter query is any query that contains criteria based on a reference to a variable, a function, or a control on a form. Normally, you enter a value such as `"SMITH"`, `26`, or `6/15/04` in a criteria entry area. You can also enter a variable such as `[Enter the Last Name]` or a reference to a control on a form such as `Forms!frmProducts![cboQuickFind]`.

The `Chapter27.accdb` database contains a parameter query named qryProductParameterQuery.

The simplest way to create a parameter query is to create a select query, specify the query's criteria, and run the query to make sure it works. Then change the criteria to the following:

```
Like [<some prompt>] & "*"
```

where `some prompt` is the question you want to ask the user. Figure 27-8 shows a parameter query that prompts the user whenever the query is run to enter the Product Category.

FIGURE 27-8

Creating a simple parameter query

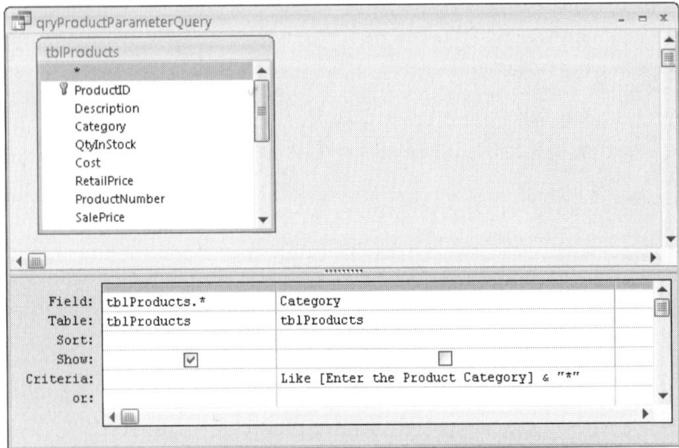

Any time the query is run, even if it is used as the record source for a form or report or the row source for a list or combo box, the parameter is displayed — and depending on what is entered, the query criteria filters the query results. Figure 27-9 shows the Parameter dialog box open, asking for the product category value required by the query.

FIGURE 27-9

Running the parameter query

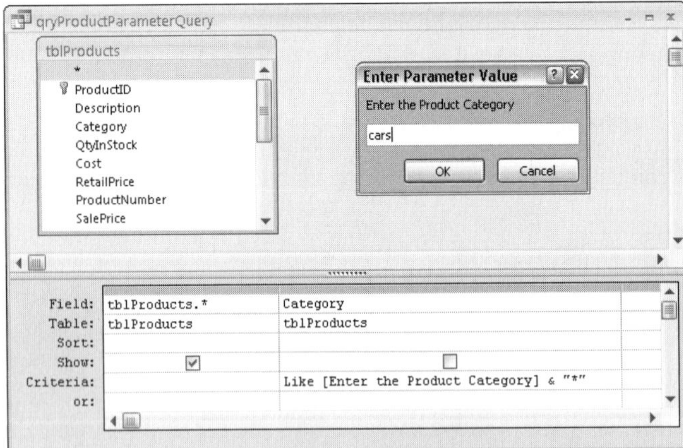

You may remember learning that the `Like` operator allows for wildcard searches. For example, if you want to filter the query records for any product category that starts with "car" (or "CAR"), you enter `CAR` when the parameter dialog box displays the question `Enter the Product Category`. Without the parameter, you would have to enter `Like "CAR*"` in the criteria area of the query. Also, because the wildcard "`*`) is included as part of the parameter, users don't have to include the wildcard when they respond to the parameter dialog.

TIP **The wildcards `*` (anything after this position) and `?` (one character in this position) can be used with a `Like` operator in any query or SQL string.**

Figure 27-10 shows the Query Parameters dialog (opened by right-clicking the query's upper area and selecting Parameters from the shortcut menu). You use the Query Parameters dialog to specify parameters that require special formatting, such as date/time entries or specially formatted numbers. One text entry has been entered in the Query Parameters dialog to show how it works. You enter the name of the parameter text and then choose the data type.

FIGURE 27-10

The Query Parameters dialog

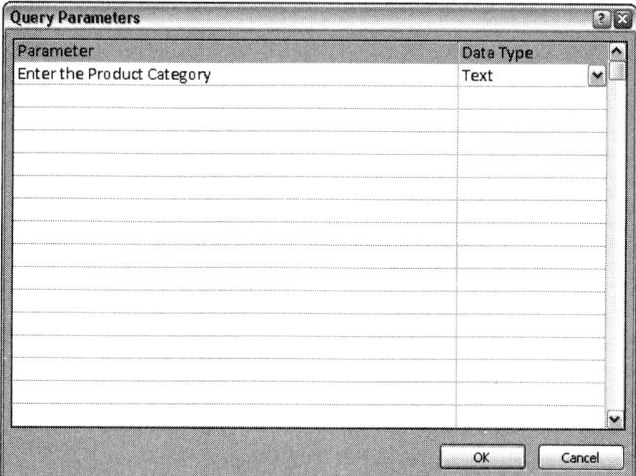

TIP **If you want to add more complex parameters, such as a range of dates, use an expression such as `Between [Enter the Start Date] and [Enter the End Date]` as a criteria in a date field. This would display two separate parameter dialog boxes and then filter the date value appropriately.**

Creating an interactive dialog box

The problem with parameter queries is that they are suitable for only simple parameters. It is fairly difficult to use parameter queries for entering complex criteria. A better technique is to create a simple form and place controls in the form that are used by a query as criteria.

Figure 27-11 shows frmFilterProducts, which contains a combo box for selecting a record. On the left side of Figure 27-11 the combo box is closed while the right side shows the combo box open.

FIGURE 27-11

Creating a dialog box for selecting records

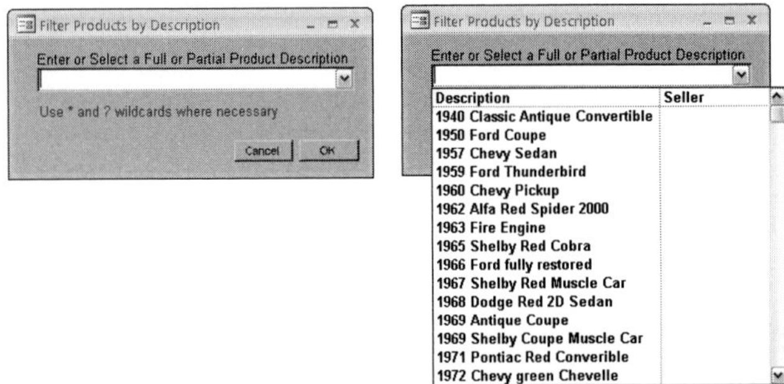

A combo box gives the user the choice of selecting a single record from a set of records or entering a wildcard (if the combo box's Limit to List property is False). The combo box (cboDescription) shown in Figure 27-11 contains two columns — Description and Seller. The Description is the bound column and makes the selected description available to a query that references the combo box, as shown in Figure 27-12.

Figure 27-12 shows qryProductFormReference. This query selects all the fields in `tblProducts` based on the description retrieved from the combo box on frmFilterProducts. Notice the expression in the query criteria area:

```
Like [Forms]![frmFilterProducts]![cboDescription] & "*"
```

This expression references `cboDescription` in `frmFilterProducts`. `cboDescription` returns the value of the selected description or a selection like 1992, which would show all of the vehicles with descriptions beginning with 1992.

FIGURE 27-12

Creating a query that references a form control

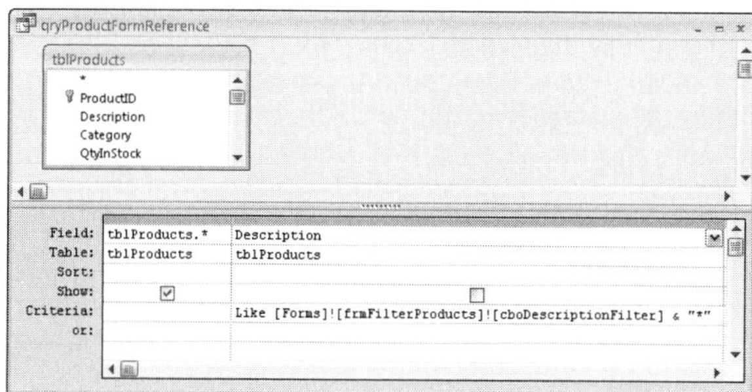

Linking the dialog box to another form

The frmFilterProducts dialog box (you saw this back in Figure 27-11) does more than just create a value that can be referenced from a query. It actually contains code to open frmProductsExample4. The `RecordSource` property of frmProductsExample4 is set to qryProductFormReference.

Figure 27-13 shows the `cmdCancel_Click` and `cmdOK_Click` event procedures behind the Cancel and OK buttons found on frmFilterProducts.

FIGURE 27-13

Creating a dialog box that opens a form

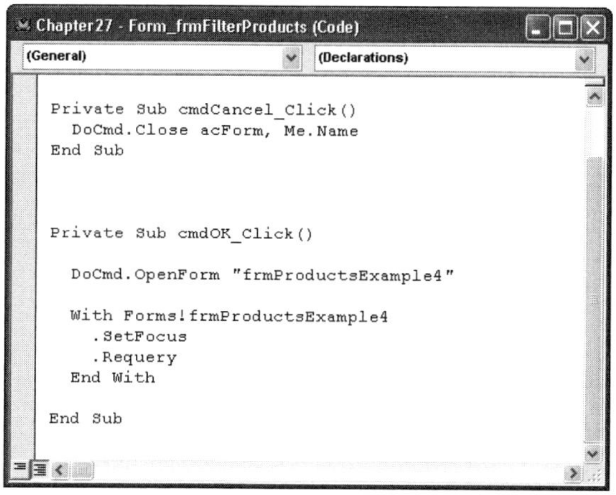

Chapter27 - Form_frmFilterProducts (Code)

(General) (Declarations)

```
Private Sub cmdCancel_Click()
  DoCmd.Close acForm, Me.Name
End Sub


Private Sub cmdOK_Click()

  DoCmd.OpenForm "frmProductsExample4"

  With Forms!frmProductsExample4
    .SetFocus
    .Requery
  End With

End Sub
```

Using the With Keyword

The `With` keyword is used to save time by not referencing the controls on the form explicitly (which means directly): for example, Forms!frmProductsExample4.SetFocus. This requires Access to search alphabetically through the list of forms in the database container. If there are 500 forms (and some large systems have this many or more) and the form name started with z, this would take a measurable amount of time. Because there is more than one reference to the form, this would have to take place multiple times. The `With` command sets up an internal pointer to the form so that all subsequent references to the form control or property or to use a form method (like `Requery` or `SetFocus`) are much faster.

When you use the `With` keyword and reference the form name, you simply use a dot (`.`) or a `!` to reference a control, property, or method just like the Forms!FormName was first. You can see this in Figure 27-13.

For each `With`, you must have an `End With`.

The cmdOK_Click event procedure code opens frmProductsExample4, sets the focus on it, and then requeries the form to make sure the latest selection is used on the form. The `SetFocus` method is necessary to move focus to the form that is opened. The `Requery` method isn't strictly required because a form automatically requeries its record source the first time it is opened. However, if the form is already opened — for example, if you use the dialog box a second time to search for another record — the `Requery` method ensures the form displays fresh data.

Summary

This chapter examines several fairly advanced techniques for working with data on Access forms. In each case, a few lines of VBA code are all you need to make a form more efficient and effective for users.

We looked at several different filtering and searching techniques for bound Access forms. Each bound Access form includes a `RecordsetClone` property that references the set of records bound to the form. You saw how a recordset's `FindFirst` method and `Bookmark` property work together to locate and display data selected by the user.

You also reviewed the process of building parameter queries that include the parameter as part of the query's design, and another example where the parameter references a control on a dialog form.

The techniques described in this chapter greatly extend the utility of Access forms and empower users to quickly look up data without having to learn the built-in filtering and searching features of Access forms.

Chapter 28

Bulletproofing Access Applications

IN THIS CHAPTER

Defining bulletproofing

Looking at the characteristics of bulletproof applications

Understanding that bulletproofing goes beyond code

Identifying the principles of bulletproofing

Developing to a specification

Securing the environment

Providing user feedback

Adding logging to applications

One of my favorite old movies is *Desk Set*, starring Spencer Tracy and Katharine Hepburn. In this movie (produced in 1957), Spencer Tracy plays a computer consultant responsible for installing a large computer system in Katharine Hepburn's office. Typical of computers in older movies, the massive wall-to-wall mainframe featured in *Desk Set* understands plain-English queries ("How many ounces of gold were mined in South Africa in the last ten years?") and is equipped with a galaxy of flashing lights that indicate when the machine is "thinking." And of course, the machine and its software work flawlessly, delivering the requested information in seconds (after much clicking, clacking, and spinning of the huge tape drives, of course).

As we all know, Hollywood's vision of computer systems has always been far from reality. Even now, in the 21st century, computers still can't "understand" plain-English commands, hardware still doesn't perform flawlessly, and users still have trouble getting their applications to do what they want and need them to do. Most important, software cannot be made to anticipate what the user wants. How many times have you heard people complain that they know the computer can do what they want but they just can't get it to happen?

TIP **In this chapter, the expressions *end user, user, client,* and *customer* all mean the same thing: the person or group of people using the application you've created. Although the terms *client* and *customer* are normally applied to the parties who pay to have the application produced, thinking of *all users* as clients should be your first step toward producing bulletproof applications. Always think of your users as the important people they are, and your work will reflect a conscientious attitude and a professional approach.**

What Is Bulletproofing?

Advanced database systems like Access bring valuable data and information directly to the user's desktop. Unlike traditional mainframe and midrange databases, very often the data contained in an Access database resides on the user's computer or is only slightly removed by being connected to a file server on a LAN. In either case, the valuable data contained in an Access database is exposed to potential loss or corruption by a well-meaning user.

For instance, unless you have added appropriate data validation to the applications you build, it's far too easy for a user to enter "bad" data into the database, causing errors later on. Or if you haven't applied adequate levels of security, an unauthorized user may accidentally (or intentionally) change sensitive data. At the very least, security prevents unauthorized users from viewing confidential information. When applied to their fullest, the Access security features will ensure that valuable data is not accessed by any but the most trusted and reliable users.

By one definition, *bulletproofing* an application means that you trap all errors, preventing crashes and unexpected behavior. This book assumes that you're already a good programmer who understands that properly handling errors is a required part of any database development project.

CROSS-REF **Chapters 15 and 25 explain how to "crash-proof" Access applications and how to remove errors that may silently and perniciously mangle the data entrusted to the databases you build.**

In this chapter, the term *bulletproofing* means applying safeguards to the data in an application through various techniques and methods. The objective of this chapter is to explain a development philosophy that leads to highly reliable and secure databases that protect the valuable data entrusted to them.

As you'll see, protecting the data very often means limiting the user's interaction with the Access environment. Data must be validated as it is input by the user to prevent inappropriate values from distorting the user's interpretation of the information contained in the database. Other techniques described in this chapter make Access applications easier to learn and use, reducing the possibility that a simple misunderstanding harms the data.

Characteristics of Bulletproof Applications

Although, as a developer, you want to provide users with maximum flexibility, you simply can't allow full access to the entire database environment. If users have unrestricted access to tables, queries, forms, and other database objects, chaos will inevitably ensue. Through mischief or ignorance, damaging changes to the database's structure and logic will occur. Only the most disinterested and unimaginative user will resist the temptation to "improve" the forms and reports you've carefully crafted.

Perhaps the most important step to bulletproofing applications is to provide end users with the Access runtime environment, described in Chapter 35. As you'll see in Chapter 35, the Access runtime provides full support (well, almost full support) of all the features you build into Access databases without giving end users the tools needed to change the underlying database structures. Chapter 35 also explains how to add context-sensitive help to Access databases, an important part of adding documentation to an application.

Unrestricted access to tables could mean deletion or modification of multiple records. Even though Access warns of most changes to data, an untrained user may ignore these warnings and proceed with the changes.

Applications that have been bulletproofed protect the data through a number of techniques:

- **Rock-solid construction:** No database exhibiting unexplained crashes, general protection faults (GPFs), or other instabilities can be considered bulletproof. First and foremost, an Access application must be reliable and free from programming bugs that lead to crashes or other undesirable behavior.

CROSS-REF **Chapter 15 explains how to use the built-in debugging tools and how to test a database to improve its reliability.**

- **Self-documenting behavior:** Built-in security features — helpful text on the screen, warning messages that caution the user when something dangerous is about to happen, and context-sensitive help to explain how the application should be used — guide the user.
- **Controlling the flow through the application:** Controlling an application's flow channels the user through the application in a logical sequence that's best suited to the application's purposes.
- **Error handling that stops otherwise damaging actions on the part of the user:** You shouldn't let a user destroy, delete, or modify data without understanding what's happening. Whenever possible, warn the user before he performs an irreversible action.
- **Providing feedback so that the user is never left in the dark about the database status:** Long operations are indicated by progress meters, an hourglass cursor, or other visual indicators.

Some of these concepts are covered in this chapter, while others are explained in chapters elsewhere in this book.

Bulletproofing Goes Beyond Code

Bulletproofing means much more than simply writing the right VBA code in your Access programs. You must adopt a certain attitude that leads to the careful, methodical approach necessary to succeed in bulletproofing applications. This means taking a professional approach to your development activities. Here are some guidelines. (If you're already employing these procedures in your applications, the following will serve as reminders.)

Document the code you write

Include comments, use naming conventions, and name your procedures and variables logically. Don't, for instance, accept the default names Access provides for database objects such as forms and controls. The default names are simply a convenience for simple applications and should not be used in professional-quality work. Figure 28-1 is an example of clear commenting and documenting. Imagine even this small section of code without comments and it's easy to see how important documentation is.

CROSS-REF **The chapters in Part II describe many valuable Access programming techniques.**

FIGURE 28-1

Well-documented code is easier to maintain and is less likely to lead to coding errors.

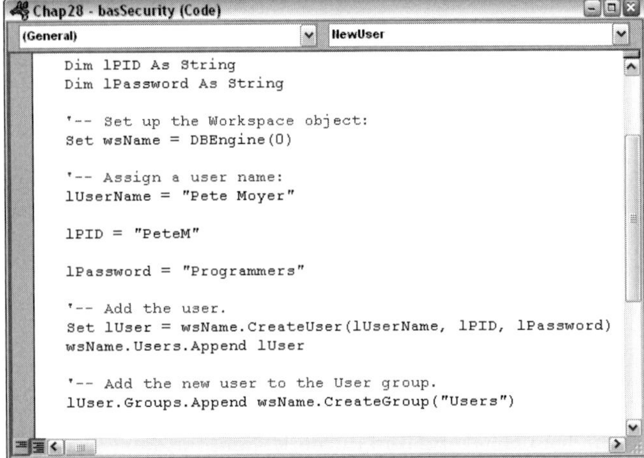

Build to a specification

All of your serious development work should be done to specification. A written specification is your best guarantee that you're creating what the users expect. (We discuss specifications in the "Develop to a Specification" section later in this chapter.)

Document the application

The applications you deliver to end users should be accompanied by printed documentation that explains how the applications are meant to be used. End-user documentation doesn't have to include descriptions of the internal structure or logic behind the user interface. It should, however, explain how the forms and reports work, describe things the users should be wary of (for instance, changing existing data), and include printouts of sample reports. Use screenshots to illustrate the documentation. Be sure the documentation includes the exact version number in the title or footer so that users can verify that the documentation is the right version for the software they're using.

The users of your applications will benefit from the online Help you build into the database. Online Help, of course, means everything from the ToolTips you attach to the controls on a form to status-bar text, to sophisticated context-sensitive and "What's This" Help you build with the Microsoft Office Developer Extension tools.

Use professional installation tools

The days of distributing an application as zipped files on a floppy disk are long gone. Microsoft Windows has become so popular that every possible type of user is working with applications running under this operating system. This means that many end users are people with virtually no computer experience, and you can't expect them to create directories, unzip files, and create program icons on their own.

In many cases, an Access application is simply copied across a network or copied to a CD-ROM or DVD. Other times, a more formal distribution package is needed by users. Chapter 35 explains the process of preparing Access applications for distribution to remote users. The Microsoft Office Developer Extensions include a very nice deployment wizard that walks you through all the steps necessary to build an effective distribution package. Figure 28-2 is an example of an application setup screen that will guide the user through the applications installation.

FIGURE 28-2

A professional-quality installation program adds a welcome touch to most applications.

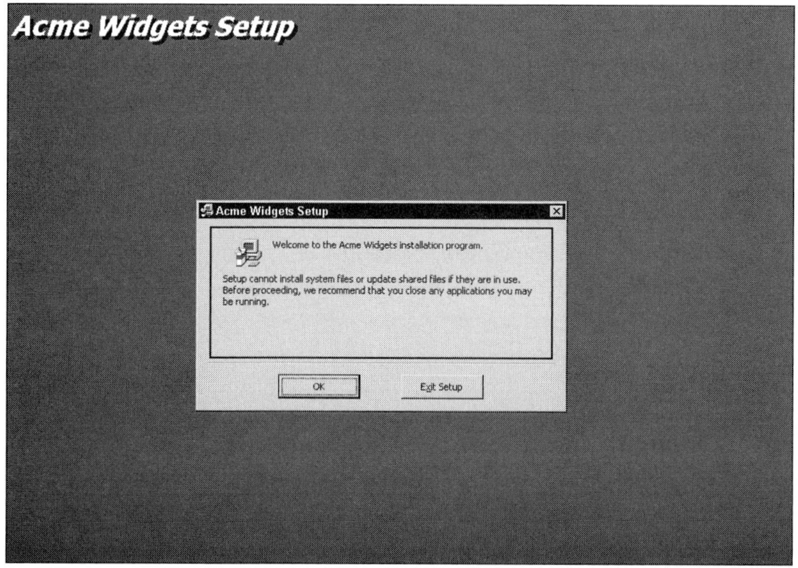

Remember that the user's first impression of your work is often based on how easily the application installs. If the user encounters problems or can't understand how to get the program installed on his computer, you're off to a bad start with the very people you've worked so hard to please.

Provide the Access runtime module to users

Although Access 2007 is included in the Microsoft Office Professional package, it's probably not a good idea to give the full development environment wide distribution in your organization. The most direct approach to preventing users from modifying the design of tables, forms, and other database objects is to only give them the Access runtime version. Although the runtime program requires the same memory and disk space as the full development environment, all of the menu options required to modify database objects have been removed and are not accessible to users. In the runtime environment, even the Database window is hidden.

As a registered owner of the Visual Studio Tools for the Microsoft Office System, you are permitted to distribute as many copies of the Access runtime and its support files as you want. The ActiveX custom controls, the Replication Manager (described in Chapter 31), and other utilities may also be distributed as necessary.

When you follow Microsoft's guidelines as you prepare a distributable application, your users may not even be aware that they're using Microsoft Access. You can modify or hide the runtime's title bar, menus, toolbars, dialog boxes, and other components to create a highly customized environment for your application.

Consider the user's skill and training requirements

If you know in advance that the majority of your users are relatively unskilled or untrained, or if they won't have a lot of on-site support, you should "overengineer" the messaging and Help file in the application. On the other hand, if the users are relatively experienced in computing, less handholding will be necessary.

One valuable technique used by many developers is to keep messages such as you see in Figure 28-3 in a table within the database. Figure 28-4 shows such a table and a message box displaying the first message in this table.

This table and the accompanying form (`frmMessageDemo`) are included in this chapter's example database (`Chapter28.accdb`) on this book's CD-ROM.

FIGURE 28-3

The messages you provide your users don't have to be extensive or sophisticated.

FIGURE 28-4

A simple message table and message box containing Help text

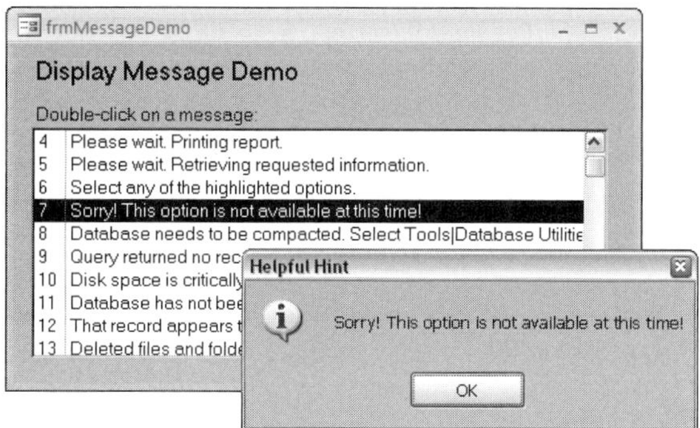

In practice, the `MessageID` is used to reference a particular message in this table. You could store the `MessageID` in the `Tag` field of a control or form and invoke the message when some error has occurred or when the user presses a button on a form. The message could also be displayed in the Access status bar or in a designated message area on a form. The code required to display a message stored in this table is quite simple:

```
Public Function DisplayMessage(iMsgNumber As Long)
  Dim sMsg As String
  Dim sSQL As String
  Dim db As DAO.Database
  Dim rs As DAO.Recordset

  Set db = CurrentDb()
  sSQL = "SELECT * FROM tblMessages WHERE " & _
         "MessageID = " & iMsgNumber & ";"
  Set rs = db.OpenRecordset(sSQL)

  MsgBox rs("Message"), vbInformation, "Helpful Hint"

End Function
```

The beauty of this little messaging system is that you could easily add a form to the application that permits users to add to the message list or change the existing text messages. Because the `MessageID` field is an AutoNumber, new messages are sequentially numbered without dealing with primary-key collisions. You'll also have to provide a form that sets a control or form's `Tag` property whenever a new message has been added to the database.

You could extend the messaging concept a bit and provide multiple levels of help. For instance, a novice user receives more extensive help than a more experienced user, while an expert should be able to turn off help completely.

Why Not Just Use Windows Help?

The messaging system described in this section is not intended to replace the Help files built with the Microsoft Office Developer Extension's Help authoring system (called the Microsoft Help Workshop). There are many things that can be done in a Windows Help file (such as displaying a graphic) that are difficult or impossible to do in an Access message box. But if your applications make frequent use of the Access status bar to display Help or error text, or if you want to provide your users with the flexibility of changing the messages themselves, a "home-grown" messaging system might be an appropriate solution.

Understand the user's motivations

The people using your applications have a number of basic needs that must be met. The applications you produce are expected to save time and/or money, produce new business, replace obsolete paper methods, reduce staffing requirements, or improve data reliability. Your applications may be expected to meet several or all of these objectives. Whatever the situation, you should have a firm understanding of what is needed. The better you understand the client's goals, the more you can concentrate on the most important aspects of the application.

Check for obvious hardware errors

Whenever possible, you should monitor how much disk space, memory, and other resources are available to the application. Many problems users encounter are avoided by simply testing to confirm that adequate disk space exists. As you'll read in Chapter 31, the databases in a replica set grow every time they are replicated, even if there are no data changes (replication events are logged in each database in the replica set). It is possible, therefore, for an Access data file to completely fill up a small hard drive over time, causing the application (and Windows itself) to fail. All of the error messages you see in Figure 28-5 were caused by running out of disk space on the computer.

FIGURE 28-5

Careful planning will help to avoid the unpleasant events that trigger these error messages.

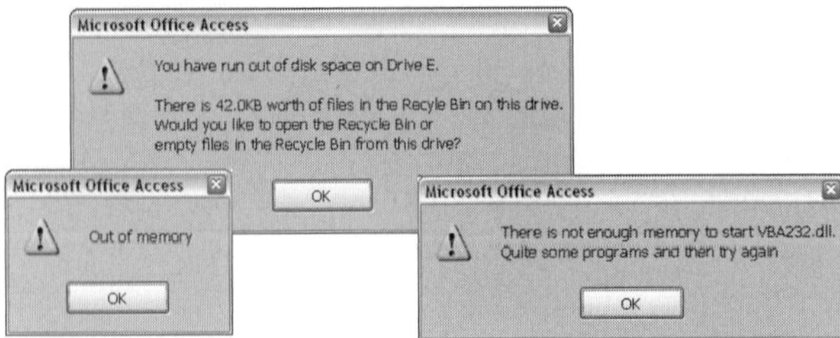

What Does Disk Space Have to do With Memory Errors?

You may be wondering why inadequate disk space leads to the memory errors you see in Figure 28-5. Windows uses disk space as *virtual memory* when all of the physical memory (RAM) on the machine has been used. Windows creates virtual memory by allocating disk space to use as a *swap file* to temporarily store things that otherwise must be stored in memory. Windows continues allocating available disk space until nothing is left, leading to the "memory" error messages in Figure 28-5. To the application there is no difference between running out of physical memory or swap space — a memory error is a memory error, regardless of the cause.

Unfortunately, the VBA language built into Access does not provide functions for checking free disk space or available memory. You must resort to Windows API calls to interrogate the system for this information. Chapter 15 explains how to call Windows API functions from your databases.

Continue to improve the product

A developer's work is never done. Surely you came up with new ideas as you built the basic application, or your clients pestered you with improvement requests as they beta-tested the interim builds. Although not allowing "off-spec" changes to interfere with the main development effort is important, you should record these ideas and use them as starting points for the next iteration of the product.

In many cases, improvements to the application consist of enhancements to the user interface. If you discover that users misunderstand how to enter data, perhaps you need to add more label text to the forms to serve as guidance. Or, if people complain that the application is hard to use, you might have to add more menu options or liberally use "plain English" throughout the program.

In the "Add Logging to your applications" section, later in this chapter, you'll read about building usage logs into your applications. A properly designed and maintained usage log provides invaluable information about how the database is being used. You may be surprised at how often errors occur, or how rarely a particular form or report is used. Any feedback you get from your users or the application itself will help you as you begin the next phase of what might turn out to be an endless project.

Principles of Bulletproofing

A few simple rules go a long way toward bulletproofing your applications. The following principles are easily applied to most any Access application, and once you've implemented them, the techniques and objects you've built are easily exported to future databases.

Make the application easy to start

You shouldn't expect users to locate the Access data file (`.accdb` or `.mdb`) or to use the File Open dialog box in Access to invoke the application. Adding items to the Windows Start menu or to a program group isn't difficult. When properly implemented, a program icon creates the impression that the application exists as an entity separate from Access and endows it with a status equivalent to Word, Excel, or other task-oriented programs.

Creating a program icon is not difficult. Many freeware and shareware versions of icon editors are available online. The `Chap28.accdb` example database comes with its own program icon (`Earth.ico`) for you to experiment with. You designate the program icon in the Access 2007 startup options (see the next section) or by setting a program icon in Windows Explorer.

Follow these steps to establish a program icon for an Access database:

1. **Hold down the Ctrl key as you drag the Access 2007 program icon to a new position in the Office 2007 program folder.**

   This copies the existing Access 2007 icon.
2. **Press F2 while the icon is highlighted and type in the new caption for the icon.**
3. **Press Alt+Enter. (Alternatively, right-click on the icon and select Properties from the shortcut menu.)**

   The Properties dialog box for the icon opens.
4. **Select the Shortcut tab in the Properties dialog box and add a complete path reference to the application's `.accdb` or `.mdb` file to the Target text box.**

   In Figure 28-6 the application database's path is `C:\Apps\Contacts.mdb`. Notice that the Target text box contains the path to the Access 2007 executable.
5. **The icon properties dialog lets you specify an icon to use in the application folder or Windows desktop (see Figure 28-7). Click on the Change Icon button and use the Browse button in the Change Icon dialog to locate the icon file (`.ico` extension) you want to use.**

Use startup options

When properly designed, users should not even be aware that they're working with Microsoft Access. Use the Access 2007 Application Options (see Figure 28-8) to hide the Navigation pane, and replace the default menus and ribbons with application-specific menus and ribbons. These options give the application control from the start, instead of having to wrest it away from the user once things are under way.

FIGURE 28-6

It's easy to get Access to automatically open a database from a program icon.

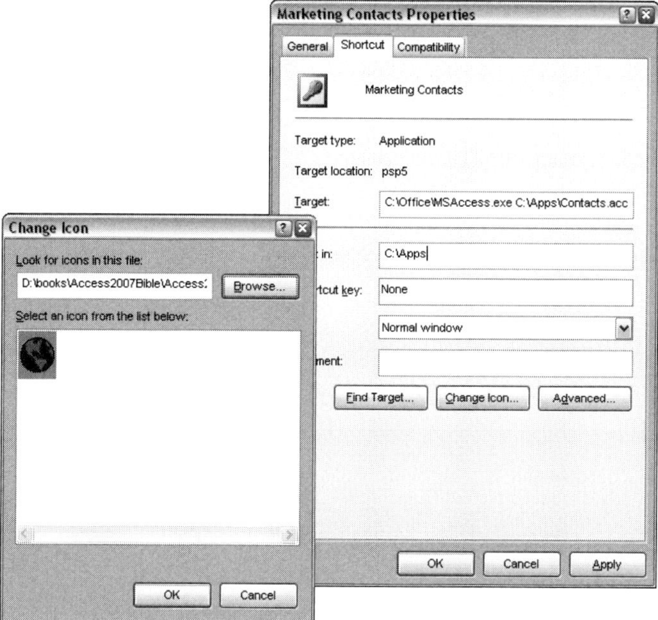

FIGURE 28-7

A colorful icon can make an application easy to find in a crowded folder or desktop.

FIGURE 28-8

The Access Application Options help you simplify the user interface.

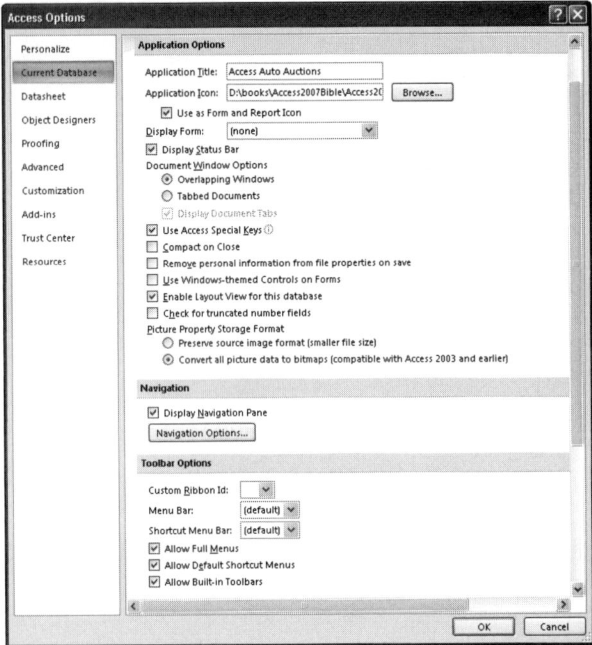

Figure 28-8 illustrates the first step to simplifying the user interface. The Current Database dialog box (File ➪ Access Options) includes options for hiding the Navigation pane, disabling the default ribbons, and trapping the built-in "special keys" (like Ctrl+F6) that may otherwise confuse users.

For example, notice the Application Icon option in the Application Options dialog box in Figure 28-8. The icon file (`.ico`) that you specify in this text box is used in the Access title bar, replacing the default form icon you see in Figure 28-9. The same icon appears at the top of reports displayed in Print Preview.

The icon you specify using the Windows properties (described in the "Make the application easy to start" section, later in this chapter) do not affect the Access application itself. For instance, the icon you assign to the application icon on the Windows desktop or in a program folder does not show up in the Access title bar and does not appear on the Windows taskbar. You must specify an icon in the .database's Startup dialog box to see the icon in the Access title bar.

FIGURE 28-9

The application icon you specify in the Startup dialog box replaces the default icons in form and report title bars.

TIP **The user can bypass all of the startup options by holding down the Shift key as the database opens. See the "Disable Startup Bypass" section, later in this chapter, to see how you can disable this Access feature. Once you've disabled the startup bypass, only the most sophisticated user will be able to reinstate the bypass feature.**

Use a login form

The user's name or ID can be valuable information, even if not part of a security scheme. In the "Maintain usage logs" section, later in this chapter, you'll read about logging activity during a database session to provide an audit trail that helps determine what went wrong and who was responsible when failures occur as people work with the database. The login information you see in Figure 28-10 can be an invaluable aid to deciphering the audit trail.

FIGURE 28-10

Capture useful information on the login form.

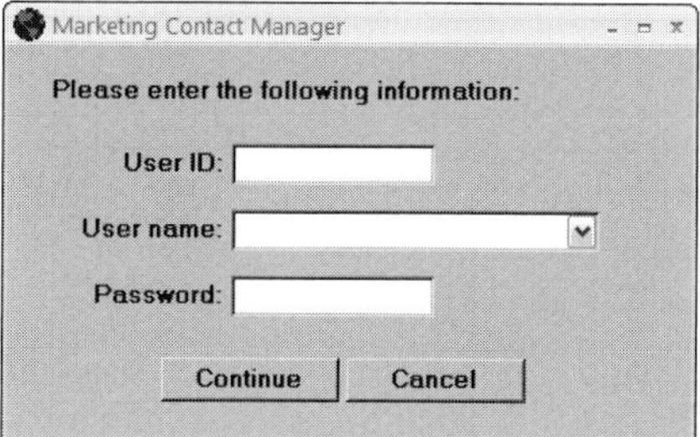

The login information should also include the date and time the user logged in to the application. You shouldn't make the user enter this information, however. The built-in `Now()` function returns the current system time and date and can be used in any logging features you build into the application.

Confirm the user ID and password from the login form with data stored in a hidden table. You could even include code to temporarily link to the password table in an "administration" database that resides in another location on the network. Store the user ID from the login form in a global variable to use in error logs, send e-mail messages, or stamp records with the user's identification.

In any case, set the `Modal` property of the login form to `Yes` (True) to prevent the user from accessing any other part of the application until the user ID, username, and password have been verified.

Use the predefined `Password` value for the Password text box's `InputMask` property to display an asterisk for each character entered into this box.

Although a simple login form such as you see in Figure 28-10 does not deter a determined hacker or sophisticated user, the average user will comply with the request for the user information on this form. When used in conjunction with the `BypassSetupKey` property (which prevents the user from using the Shift key to bypass the startup options) described later in this chapter, a startup form such as you see in Figure 28-10 provides a reliable login procedure for most applications.

Use a splash screen

Although a splash screen (also called a *startup form*) might not sound like a bulletproofing technique, one aspect of professional application development is providing high-quality information to the user in a timely fashion. An appropriately designed splash screen gives the user such valuable information as the version number of the database application, the user name (or login ID), the date the database was most recently replicated, and so on. A simple splash screen is shown in Figure 28-11.

CROSS-REF **Chapter 26 describes adding splash screens to Access applications and how to add valuable data to the splash screen.**

FIGURE 28-11

A splash screen confirms the application name and version number.

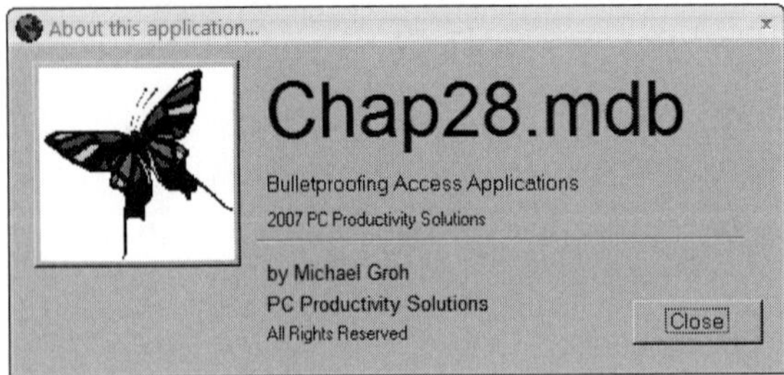

Add switchboards to the application

Switchboard forms are an invaluable way to keep users focused on using the database as intended. A switchboard form presents the user with a limited number of choices for working with the application and makes the application easier to use. You could use the user's login information to determine which of a number of switchboard forms to use. For instance, a manager with a higher level of privileges may be given a form with more options than a clerical worker would be given.

Figure 28-12 shows the switchboard form from the Access Auto Auctions database. Each button in this switchboard triggers some action within the database or leads to another switchboard form.

FIGURE 28-12

Switchboard forms control a user's access to the application.

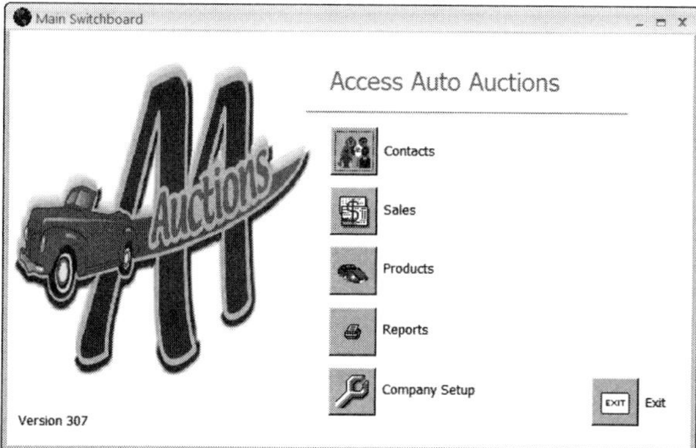

Control the ribbons

In most applications, you don't want the user to have access to dangerous ribbon commands. If, for instance, users are able to access the export or import commands in the External Data ribbon, they may be tempted to experiment with exporting and importing data. This could have serious repercussions on the security and integrity of the data stored in the database.

Removing default ribbon command options requires a bit of work, but is worth the trouble. Actually, you don't remove ribbon items as much as you replace the built-in ribbons with custom ribbons that become part of the database.

CROSS-REF **Chapter 34 explains how to create custom ribbons containing virtually any built-in or custom commands or functions.**

In addition, Access 2007 allows you to easily modify the Quick Access bar in the upper-left corner of the Access environment. Figure 28-13 shows the Quick Access toolbar customization dialog box. You open this dialog from the File menu.

FIGURE 28-13

Creating a custom Quick Access bar in Access 2007 isn't too difficult.

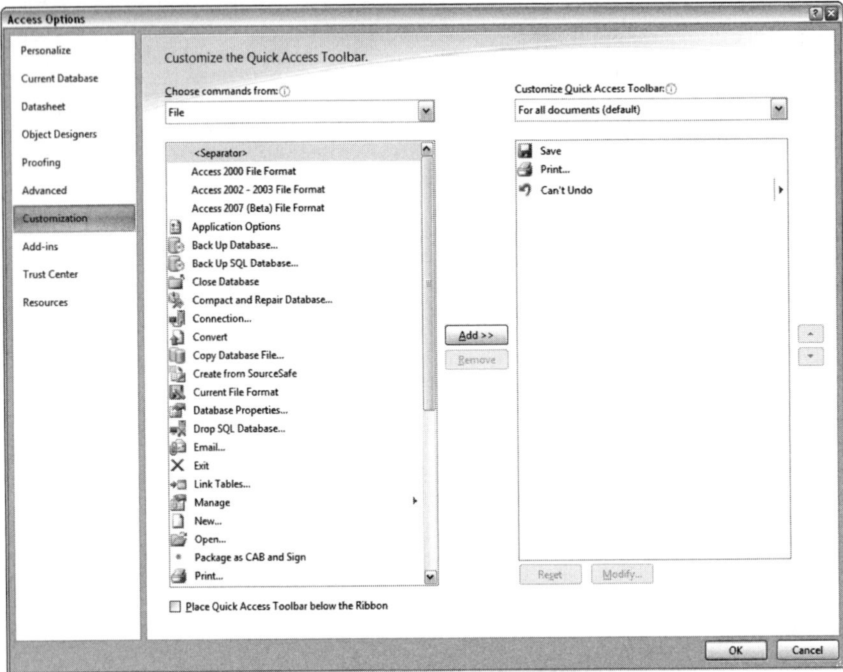

Figure 28-14 shows a Quick Access toolbar after adding several new commands. The two File menus you see in this figure are equivalent except that the one on the right has had certain commands removed with the Menu Builder.

FIGURE 28-14

The Quick Access toolbar is easy to customize.

Hide the Navigation Pane and remove menus

Notice the Display Navigation Pane check box, the Allow Full Menus check box, and the Allow Built-in Toolbars check box in the startup dialog box in Figure 28-8. When not selected, these check boxes hide the Navigation Pane and remove the built-in menus from the Access environment. This means, of course, that your application will be totally reliant on the switchboard forms and toolbars you create, but it is a good way to control the user's access to the environment.

Display one form at a time

If appropriate for the application, you'll probably want to restrict the user to a single form to avoid problems. Many inexperienced users are confused by the multiple document interface (MDI) paradigm used by Access. Having too many forms open on the screen can lead the user to jump from task to task in no particular order.

As an alternative to displaying a single form at a time, you can also use the `Modal` property to force a form to retain the focus during some operation. A good example is selecting from a number of reports to print. Once the user has decided to print a report, you might want to keep him focused on that task, instead of allowing him to jump back to the data-entry form. With access to both printing and data entry, the user might start a print job, jump back to data entry as the print job begins (to make changes to the data), and then wonder why the printout doesn't include the changes made after the printing has begun. Or Access may lock the records the user is trying to change during the print event.

Trap unwanted keystrokes

Many simple keystrokes (like pressing the Delete key) can lead to data loss. The easiest way to capture keystrokes is to create an AutoKeys macro that simply remaps dangerous keystrokes to harmless equivalents. The problem with AutoKeys, however, is that the remapped keystrokes are applied globally, rather than locally on a particular form. You can set up any number of keystroke macros, however, and enable or disable keys as the user enters and leaves forms.

Build bulletproof forms

You can take several steps to make each form in an application virtually bulletproof:

- **Remove the Control Box, Min, Max, and Close buttons from the form at design time.** Your users will be forced to use the navigation aids you've built into the application to close the form, ensuring that your application is able to test and verify the user's input.
- **Always put a Close or Return button on forms to return the user to a previous form in the application.** The buttons should appear in the same general location on every form and should be consistently labeled. Don't use "Close" on one form, "Return" on another, and "Exit" on a third.
- **Set the `ViewsAllowed` property of the form to `Form` at design time.** This will prevent the user from ever seeing a form as a datasheet.
- **Use modal forms where appropriate.** Keep in mind that modal forms force the user to respond to the controls on the form — the user can't access any other part of the application while a modal form is open.

- **Use your own navigation buttons that check for EOF (End of File) and BOF (Beginning of File) conditions.** Use the `OnCurrent` event to verify information or set up the form as the user moves from record to record.
- **Use the `StatusBarText` property on every control, to let the user know what's expected in each control.** The `Control TipText` property should also be set on all relevant controls.
- **Disable the Del key or trap the `OnDelete` event to confirm deletions.**

Validate user input

One of the most important bulletproofing techniques is to simply validate everything the user enters into the database. Capturing erroneous data input during data entry is one of the most import safeguards you can build into your applications. In many cases, you can use the table-level validation (determined by each field's `ValidationRule` and `ValidationText` properties) provided by Jet, but in many other cases you'll want more control over the message the user receives or the actions taken by the database in response to erroneous input.

One of the major problems with the `ValidationRule` property is that it isn't checked until the user actually tabs to the next control, making it impossible to capture erroneous null values. You're much better off in many cases validating entries in code. Very often you'll want to validate all controls on a form from the `BeforeUpdate` event instead of checking each and every control on the form.

Keep the user informed

An uninformed user is a dangerous user. Keep the user informed of the database status through the hourglass mouse cursor, message boxes, status-bar text, and progress meters. A simple progress meter (see the "Creating and using a progress meter" section, later in this chapter) can keep a user from frustration during long queries or printouts. The last thing you want a user doing is hitting keys in a panic, thinking the application has crashed or is hung up.

Also, always warn the user when something dangerous (like a delete query that removes data from the database) is about to happen. You don't have to inform users of trivial or expected actions, but make them aware when irreversible changes are being made.

Maintain usage logs

In the "Adding Logging to Applications" section, later in this chapter, you'll read about adding usage logs to your applications. These logs—which capture information such as the user's name or ID, the date, and the time—provide valuable information, especially in the event that an error occurs. Although you can easily record too much information, a properly designed usage log will permit you to pinpoint whether a certain type of error always seems to occur when a particular user is working with the system or when a certain query is run.

The logging information you add to a database might include updating a time stamp on records in a table when changes are made. Be aware, however, that the more logging you do, the slower the application becomes. The log information will cause the database to grow as well, unless the log information is stored in another location.

You can even tailor the level of logging to suit particular users or user groups. Using the information captured on a login form, the application can determine at startup what level of logging to impose during the session. To make reviewing the logs much easier, you can even log to a table located in an external database in a different location on the network.

Develop to a Specification

All databases are meant to solve some problem experienced by users. The problem might be some inefficiency in their current methods or an inability to view or retrieve data in a format they need. Or you may simply be converting an obsolete database to a more modern equivalent. The effectiveness of the solution you build will be judged by how well it resolves the problem the users are having. Your best guarantee of success is to carefully plan the application before building any table, query, or form. Only by working to a plan will you know how well the application will solve the user's problem.

Most Access development projects follow this general sequence of events:

1. **Define the problem.**

   Something is wrong or inadequate with the current methods — a better system is needed and Access appears to be a good candidate to produce the new system.

2. **Determine the requirements.**

   Interviews with the client yield a description of the basic features the program should provide. The product of these discussions is the *design specification,* a written document that outlines and details the application.

3. **Design the application.**

   The developer uses the initial design specification to design the basic structure of the database and its user interface.

4. **Develop the application.**

   This is where most developers spend most of their time. You spend a great deal of time building the tables, queries, forms, and other database objects needed to meet the specification produced in Step 2.

5. **Test.**

   The developer and client exercise the application to verify that it performs as expected. The application is tested against the requirements defined in the design specification, and discrepancies are noted and corrected for Step 6.

6. **Distribute and roll out.**

   After the application's performance has been verified, it is distributed to its users. If necessary, users are trained in the application's use and instructed on how to report problems or make suggestions for future versions.

Many inexperienced Access developers dive right into development without adequately defining the application's objectives or designing the database's structure. Unless the application is incredibly simple, a developer who does not work to a specification will surely end up with a buggy, unreliable, and trouble-prone database.

Another major error is allowing the database to stray too far from the initial design specification. Adding lots of bells and whistles to an otherwise simple and straight-forward database is all too tempting. If implementation digresses too far from the design specification, the project may fail because too much time is spent on features that do not directly address the user's problem.

Before any work begins, most professional application developers demand that the client submit a written document describing the intended application and specifying what the program is expected to do. A well-written design specification includes the following information:

- **Expected inputs:** What kind of data (text, numeric, binary) will the database have to handle? Will the data be shared with other applications like Excel or another database system? Does the data exist in a format that is easily imported into an Access database, or will the data have to be re-keyed at runtime?
- **User interface:** Will the users be comfortable with simple forms, or will they need custom menus, ribbons, and other user-interface components? Is context-sensitive online help required?
- **Expected outputs:** What kind of reports are needed by the user? Will simple select queries be adequate to produce the desired results, or are totals, crosstabs, and other advanced queries necessary as well?

The whole point of a design specification is to avoid adding unplanned features that decrease the database's reliability without contributing to its utility. Writing a design specification before beginning the actual implementation will consistently yield the following benefits:

- **A guide to development effort:** Without some kind of design specification, how can you possibly know whether you're building an application that truly meets the client's expectations? As you work through the development phase, you can avoid adding features that don't contribute to the application's objectives and concentrate on those items that the client has identified as having priority.
- **Verification that the application meets expectations:** All aspects of the application must be tested to verify its operation. The best way to conduct testing is to confirm that all design objectives have been met and that no unexpected behavior is observed during the testing phase.

- **Minimization of design changes during implementation:** Many problems can be avoided by sticking to the specification. One of the easiest ways to break an application is to add new features not included in the original design. If the application was properly planned, the specified features will have been designed to work together. Introducing new features once development has begun will most likely result in a less reliable system.

Overall, a well-written design specification provides the basis for creating tight, bulletproof applications that fulfill the user's requirements. At the conclusion of the project, the finished database can be compared to the design specification, and its effectiveness in addressing the original problem can be objectively evaluated. Without the design specification written at the beginning of a project, there is no valid measure of how well the application resolves the problem that inspired the project in the first place.

Securing the Environment

Obviously a serious Access application must be secured from unauthorized users. The built-in security system (enforced by the Jet database engine, not by Access) provides multiple levels of security. You can, for instance, secure a single database object (form, table, report) from individuals, groups, or individuals within groups. A user can even have multiple levels of security (provided the user has been assigned multiple login names). All of the Access security objects, their properties, and methods are accessible throughout Access Visual Basic code.

CROSS-REF **The Access security system is described in detail in Chapter 29. As you'll see in Chapter 29, it is possible to use code to add any level of security into an Access application required by the users.**

Setting Startup Options in Code

The options you set in the Current Database dialog box (refer to Figure 28-8) apply globally to every user who logs into the database. There are times when you want to control these options through startup code instead of allowing the global settings to control the application. For instance, a database administrator ought to have access to more of the database controls (menus, the Navigation Pane) than a data-entry clerk has.

Every option you see in the Options dialog box, except for options on the Module tab, can be set through code. You are able to use Access VBA to control the settings of the `Application` object properties listed in Table 28-1.

TABLE 28-1

Startup Option Properties of the Application Object

Startup Option	Property to Set	Data Type
Application title	AppTitle	dbText
Application icon	AppIcon	dbText
Display form	StartupForm	dbText
Display database window	StartupShowDBWindow	dbBoolean
Display status bar	StartupShowStatusBar	dbBoolean
Menu bar	StartupMenuBar	dbText
Shortcut menu bar	StartupShortcutMenuBar	dbText
Allow full menus	AllowFullMenus	dbBoolean
Allow default shortcut menus	AllowShortcutMenus	dbBoolean
Allow built-in toolbars	AllowBuiltInToolbars	dbBoolean
Allow toolbar changes	AllowToolbarChanges	dbBoolean
Allow viewing code after error	AllowBreakIntoCode	dbBoolean
Use Access special keys	AllowSpecialKeys	dbBoolean

Depending on the username (and password) provided on the login form, you can use VBA code in the splash screen or switchboard form to set or reset any of these properties. Clearly these properties have much to do with controlling the Access environment at startup.

Disable Startup Bypass

In old versions of Access, developers used the AutoExec macro to do things like hide the database container, open a startup form, and execute some startup code. The problem was that any user could easily bypass the AutoExec macro by holding down the Shift key while opening the database.

The Access startup properties provide some relief from reliance on startup macros and other routines. Unfortunately the user is still able to bypass your carefully designed startup options by holding down the Shift key as the application starts. This action, of course, will reveal the application's design and objects that you've hidden behind the user interface.

Fortunately, the Access designers anticipated the need for bulletproofing an application's startup by providing a database property named `AllowBypassKey`. This property, which accepts `True` or `False` values, disables (or enables) the Shift key bypass at application startup.

Because AllowBypassKey is a developer-only property, it is not built into Access databases. You must create, append, and set this property sometime during the development process. Once appended to the database's Properties collection, you can set and reset it as needed.

Here is the code you need to implement the AllowBypassKey property:

```
Function SetBypass(BypassFlag As Boolean) As Boolean
'Returns True if value of AllowBypassKey
'is successfully set to BypassFlag.

  On Error GoTo SetBypass_Error

  Dim db As DAO.Database
  Set db = CurrentDb
  db.Properties!AllowBypassKey = BypassFlag

SetBypass_Exit:
  Exit Function

SetBypass_Error:
  If Err = 3270 Then
    'AllowBypassKey property does not exist
    MsgBox "Appending AllowBypassKey property"
    db.Properties.Append _
         db.CreateProperty("AllowBypassKey", _
         dbBoolean, BypassFlag)
    SetBypass = True
    Resume Next
  Else
    'Some other error
    MsgBox "Unexpected error: " & Error$ _
         & " (" & Err & ")"
    SetBypass = False
    Resume SetBypass_Exit
  End If
End Function
```

This function first tries to set the AllowBypassKey property to whatever value is passed in as BypassFlag. If the attempt to set the property generates an error, indicating that the AllowBypassKey property doesn't exist, the error trap checks to see if the error value is 3270. If it is, the AllowBypassKey property is created and appended to the database's Properties collection after being set to the BypassFlag value.

If the error is anything other than 3270, the function simply exits and doesn't try to resolve the problem.

ON the CD-ROM The **`AllowBypassKeyDemo`** objects (**`frmAllowBypassKeyDemo`** and **`modAllowBypassKey`**) in the **`Chap26.mdb`** sample file on this book's companion CD-ROM demonstrate how to set and use the **`AllowBypassKey`** property. The **`frmAllowBypassKeyDemo`** form contains two toggle buttons that alternately enable or disable the bypass feature.

Setting property values

You use the Application object's `SetOption` method to set each of these properties, and the `GetOption` method to retrieve the current value. The syntax of the `SetOption` method is:

```
Application.SetOption OptionName, Setting
```

where `OptionName` is the name of an option in Table 28-1, and `Setting` is one of a number of different data types, depending on the option being manipulated with `SetOption`.

In most cases, unless the property has already been set in the Access Options dialog box, the property has not been appended to the `Application` object's properties collection. You must make sure the property exists before trying to set its value in code. The following function sets the value of a startup property, creating and appending the property to the `Application` object's Properties collection if the property does not exist:

```
Function AddStartupProperty(PropName As String, _
     PropType As Variant, PropValue As Variant) _
     As Integer
  'Consult the Access online help for the PropName
  'and PropType for each of the startup options.
  'Adding a property requires the appropriate
  'PropType variable or the property creation fails.
  Dim MyDB As DAO.Database
  Dim MyProperty As Property
  Const _PropNotFoundError = 3270
  Set MyDB = CurrentDB
  On Error GoTo AddStartupProp_Err

  'The following statement will fail if the
  ' property named PropName doesn't exist.
  MyDB.Properties(PropName) = PropValue
  AddStartupProperty = True

AddStartupProp_OK:
  Exit Function

AddStartupProp_Err:
  'Get here if property doesn't exist.
  If Err = _PropNotFoundError Then
    'Create the new property and set it to PropValue
    Set MyProperty = MyDB.CreateProperty(PropName, _
         PropType, PropValue)
```

```
      'You must append the new property
      'to the Properties collection.
      MyDB.Properties.Append MyProperty
      Resume
    Else
      'Can't add new property, so quit
      AddStartupProperty = False
      Resume AddStartupProp_OK
    End If
  End Function 'AddStartupProperty
```

Using AddStartupProperty() is quite easy. You must know the exact property name and data type of the property before invoking AddStartupProperty(). The following subroutine demonstrates how to set a startup property with AddStartupProperty():

```
Sub cmdAddProperty_Click()
  Dim iRetVal As Integer
  iRetVal = AddStartupProperty("AppTitle", dbText,
       "Marketing Contact Management")
  iRetVal = AddStartupProperty("AppIcon", dbText,
       "C:\My Documents\World.ico")
End Sub
```

Notice that both the AppTitle and AppIcon properties are string data types (dbText).

Use the RefreshTitleBar method to see the changes made by setting either the AppTitle or AppIcon property. The syntax of RefreshTitleBar is simple:

```
Application.RefreshTitleBar
```

Getting property values

Getting the value of a property is much easier than setting a property's value. The GetOption method returns the value of a property. The syntax of GetOption is as follows:

```
vRetVal = GetOption(PropertyName)
```

where vRetVal is a variant and PropertyName is the name of a property in Table 28-1. The following code fragment shows how to use the GetOption method to read an option property:

```
Dim vRetVal As Variant

' Get the current setting.
vRetVal = Application.GetOption("AppTitle")
```

A variant is used to capture the return value because of the different data types used for startup properties. Also, a property that has not yet been set may be null, and the variant is the only type of variable that can accept null values without error.

TIP **`GetOption` works for any of the options you see in the Options dialog box (Tools ➪ Options). For instance, the following statement returns the current setting of the Hidden Objects check box in the View tab of the Options dialog box:**

```
vRetVal = Application.GetOption("Hidden Objects").
```

Providing User Feedback

You can use any of numerous techniques to provide feedback to the user. One of the easiest ways to communicate (but sometimes the most annoying to the user) is with the `MsgBox` function. Although message boxes are easy to add to applications, they're always modal and require the user to acknowledge the message before it's dismissed. Message boxes can disrupt the workflow if the user is constantly required to dismiss multiple message boxes containing low-value information. In fact, flooding a user with silly message boxes containing unimportant information may cause a user to ignore truly important messages.

In many situations, message boxes are invaluable. A message box can be used to obtain confirmation before performing an irreversible action, or to deliver important information.

The `MsgBox` function accepts a number of parameters that specify the message text, which buttons to display on the message box, and the text to display in the message box title bar. The `MsgBox` function returns a value indicating which button displayed on the message box has been clicked by the user. The syntax of `MsgBox` is as follows:

```
MsgBox(Prompt[, Buttons][, Title][, HelpFile, Context])
```

where the function parameters are:

- `Prompt`: The message displayed in the message box. `Prompt` can be a maximum of approximately 1,024 characters. Separate lines in `Prompt` with a carriage return character (`Chr(13)`), a linefeed character (`Chr(10)`), or a carriage return-linefeed character combination (`Chr(13) & Chr(10)`) between the lines.
- `Buttons`: A numeric expression that defines the number and type of buttons to display in the message box, the icon style to use, which button to use as the default button, and the modality of the message box. The `Buttons` parameter completely defines the nature of the message box; therefore, there are many different values for this parameter. Table 28-2 contains all of the possible values. If omitted, the default value for `Buttons` is 0.
- `Title`: The text to display in the title bar of the message box. If you omit the title, the name of the application is used in the title bar.
- `HelpFile`: A string that is the name of the Help file to use to provide help for the dialog box. If the `HelpFile` parameter is provided, the `Context` parameter must also be provided.
- `Context`: The help context number assigned to the message-box Help topic. If the `Context` parameter is provided, `HelpFile` must also be provided.

Table 28-2 lists the valid values for the `Buttons` parameter. When more than one button or setting is required, sum the `Constant` values and pass the total to the `MsgBox()` function.

TABLE 28-2

MsgBox Button Constants

Button Constant	Value	Description
`vbOKOnly`	0	Display only the OK button.
`vbOKCancel`	1	Display the OK and Cancel buttons.
`vbAbortRetryIgnore`	2	Display Abort, Retry, and Ignore buttons.
`vbYesNoCancel`	3	Display Yes, No, and Cancel buttons.
`vbYesNo`	4	Display Yes and No buttons.
`vbRetryCancel`	5	Display Retry and Cancel buttons.
`vbCritical`	16	Display Critical Message icon.
`vbQuestion`	32	Display Warning Query icon.
`vbExclamation`	48	Display Warning Message icon.
`vbInformation`	64	Display Information Message icon.
`vbDefaultButton1`	0	First button in message box is default.
`vbDefaultButton2`	256	Second button in message box is default.
`vbDefaultButton3`	512	Third button in message box is default.
`vbDefaultButton4`	768	Fourth button in message box is default (new at Access 2007).
`vbApplicationModal`	0	Make the message box application modal — the user must respond to the message box before continuing work in the current application.
`vbSystemModal`	4096	Make the message box "System modal" — all applications are suspended until the user responds to the message box.

The `Button` value you provide `MsgBox` can be a combination of several options. For instance, the following command pops up a message box containing the famous `Are you sure?` message seen in many Windows applications. The message box contains Yes, No, and Cancel buttons:

```
iRetVal = MsgBox("Are you sure?", _
     vbQuestion + vbYesNoCancel, "Confirm, please")
```

Alternatively, a number can be used in place of the VBA intrinsic constants. The following statement is equivalent to the previous example:

```
iRetVal = MsgBox("Are you sure", 35, "Confirm, please")
```

The 35 is the sum of `vbQuestion (value = 32)` and `vbYesNoCancel (value = 3)`. You'll find using the VBA intrinsic constants is more self-explanatory. Figure 28-15 is an example of different message boxes.

FIGURE 28-15

Message boxes come in a variety of sizes and display a number of different icons.

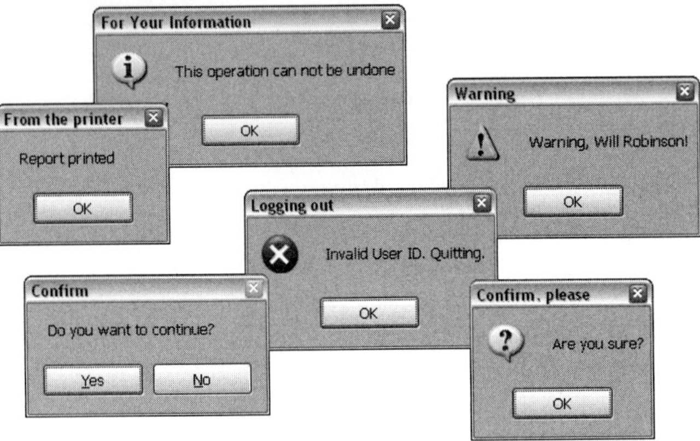

`MsgBox()`, like all VBA functions, returns a value. The value returned depends on which button displayed on the message box is clicked by the user. By default, a message box contains a single OK button, and the return value of the `MsgBox()` function is `1` when the OK button is clicked. The return values of the different message box buttons are shown in Table 28-3.

TABLE 28-3

MsgBox Return Values

Button Pressed	Constant Returned	Value Returned
OK	`vbOK`	1
Cancel	`vbCancel`	2
Abort	`vbAbort`	3
Retry	`vbRetry`	4
Ignore	`vbIgnore`	5
Yes	`vbYes`	6
No	`vbNo`	7

ON the CD-ROM The form named `frmMsgBoxDemo` in the `Chap28.mdb` example database contains a number of different varieties of message boxes and command buttons. You'll see how the different VBA constants influence the command buttons displayed in message boxes and how each command button returns a different value.

Creating and using a progress meter

Setting up and using a progress meter requires an initializing step, then incrementing the meter to its next value. As you increment, you don't just increment a counter that is managed by `SysCmd`. You must explicitly set the meter's value to a value between 0 and the maximum you set at initialization.

ON the CD-ROM The following code and demonstration is contained in a form named `frmSysCmdDemo` in the `Chapter28.accdb` database.

Use the `acSysCmdInitMeter` constant to initialize the meter. You must pass some text that is used to label the meter as well as the meter's maximum value:

```
Private Sub cmdInitMeter_Click()
  Dim vRetVal As Variant

  MeterMax = 100
  vRetVal = SysCmd(acSysCmdInitMeter, _
      "Reading Data", MeterMax)

End Sub
```

When this subroutine is run, the Access status bar appears, as shown in Figure 28-16.

FIGURE 28-16

The progress meter after initialization

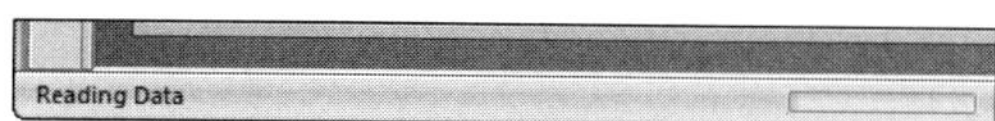

Incrementing the meter is a little tricky. In the following subroutine, the global variable `MeterInc` is incremented by 10 and the meter's position is set to the value of `MeterInc`.

```
Private Sub cmdIncrementMeter_Click()
  Dim vRetVal As Variant

  MeterInc = MeterInc + 10
  vRetVal = SysCmd(acSysCmdUpdateMeter, MeterInc)

End Sub
```

Figure 28-17 shows the progress meter after five increments. It's easy to see that the meter has moved a distance proportional to the value of `MeterInc` after being incremented five times.

FIGURE 28-17

The progress meter midway in its movement

A meter is a valuable way to keep the user informed of the progress of a lengthy process. Because you control its initial value and the rate at which it increments, you are able to fairly precisely report the application's progress to its users.

Adding Logging to Applications

Throughout this chapter you've seen multiple references to logging errors. An error log provides an excellent way to perform a postmortem on an application that does not operate properly. By adding error logging to each subroutine and function that might fail at runtime, you can see exactly what happened at the time an error occurred, instead of relying on the user's description of the error.

Error logging can produce undesirable results at times. For instance, an error that causes an endless loop can easily consume all available disk space on the user's computer if each iteration of the loop adds a message to an error log. Use error logging wisely. You may want to add error logging to *every* procedure in an application during the beta-test process, and reduce the number of calls to the logging procedure just before distributing the application to its users. You may even provide some way that users can turn on error logging if they encounter a reproducible problem in a database application.

You can easily activate or deactivate the calls to logging before distributing the application to users using the compiler directives described in Chapters 8 and 11. For instance, the following call to the `Logger()` function will be ignored if the `DEVELOPMENT` constant has not been defined in the application.

```
#If DEVELOPMENT Then
  Logger("Begin function TestuserInput()   ", Now())
#End If
```

During the development cycle, include the following statement in the Declarations section of the form module, and calls to `Logger()` will be enabled. Before compiling and distributing to the user, either comment out this statement or set the `DEVELOPMENT` constant to 0.

```
#Const DEVELOPMENT = 1
```

The function shown in the following listing provides an elementary form of error logging. `LogError()` writes the following information to a table named `tblErrorLog`:

- The current date and time
- The procedure name that produced the error
- The error number

- The error description
- The form that was active at the time the error occurred (may be null if no form is open)
- The name of the control that was active at the time the error occurred (may be null if no control is selected)

```
Function LogError (ProcName As String, _
     ErrNum As Integer, ErrDescription) As Integer

  Dim MyDB As DAO.Database
  Dim tblErr As Table
  Set MyDB = CurrentDB()
  Set tblErr = MyDB.OpenTable("tblErrorLog")
  tblErr.AddNew
  tblErr("TimeDateStamp") = Now
  tblErr("ErrorNumber") = ErrNum
  tblErr("ErrorDescription") = ErrDescription
  tblErr("ProcedureName") = ProcName
  ' The following may be null if no form
  ' or control is currently active.
  tblErr("FormName") = Screen.ActiveForm.FormName
  tblErr("ControlName") = Screen.ActiveControl.ControlName

  tblErr.Update
  tblErr.Close
End Function
```

This simple subroutine adds to an existing table named `tblErrorLog`. What you do with the data in this table is up to you. You may, for instance, trigger a hard copy of the error log's report at the end of a session, or e-mail the report to a database administrator. A sophisticated application would create `tblErrorLog` at the first instance of a logged error, and then check for the existence of `tblErrorLog` at the end of the session.

`tblErrorLog` contains the fields listed in Table 28-4.

TABLE 28-4

Structure of tblErrorLog

Field Name	Data Type
`TimeDateStamp`	Date/Time
`ErrorNumber`	Long Integer
`ErrorDescription`	String 255
`ProcedureName`	String 64
`FormName`	String 64
`ControlName`	String 64

The ProcedureName, FormName, and ControlName fields are 64 characters in length — long enough to accommodate the longest possible names for these Access database objects. Error descriptions are usually short, but you want to provide as much space as possible to hold them.

A prototype of using LogError() is shown in the following subroutine. Notice that the LogError() function is triggered by the subroutine's error handler. After the error is logged, you handle the error by other code that may be needed.

```
Sub MySubroutine
  On Error GoTo MyErrorHandler
  <Your code goes here>
  Exit Sub
MyErrorHandler:
  LogError("MySubroutine", Err.Number, Err.Description)
  <Handle error here>
  Resume
End Sub
```

The most critical items in the error log are the date and time, the error number, and the error description. The procedure name is useful, but it has to be hard-coded for each procedure (subroutine or function) you log with LogError().

Summary

This chapter has taken a quick look at the steps required to bulletproof Access applications. Although it's true that entire books could be written on this important subject, the concepts presented in this chapter will be adequate for most Access applications.

Obviously, bulletproofing a database application takes a lot of time. Validating all of the data entry on every form or adding status bar messages to every control in an application isn't easy. But the time you spend bulletproofing your databases will be paid back many times over in reduced support calls and happier users.

Chapter 29

Securing Access Applications

Although Access provides the interface to maintain security options, it is Jet that actually performs security functions. The Jet security model has changed little from Access 95 to Access 2003. Jet's security in those versions is a workgroup-based security model; all users in a workgroup are bound to the same security rules. The rules enforced for individual users may vary from user to user based on the permissions assigned to each user.

Microsoft removed the user-level security features from the new Access 2007 (`.accdb`) format but retained the functionality to manage user-level security for previous versions of Access databases (`.mdb` files). Microsoft retained the functionality in Access 2007 to manage user-level security for the older file formats; however, you can't set user-level security for an Access 2007 database. Other options, such as setting a database password, are available for all database versions.

ON the CD-ROM **In this chapter, you will use the database file `Chapter29.mdb`. This is in an Access 2000 format database file that demonstrates all the functionality, including user-level security, not available in an `.accdb` file.**

IN THIS CHAPTER

- Understanding Jet security
- Deciding on a security level to implement
- Creating a database password
- Using the /runtime option
- Using the Current Database options
- Manipulating users and groups
- Securing objects by using permissions
- Using the Access Security Wizard
- Protecting Visual Basic code
- Encrypting or encoding a database
- Using the Trust Center

Understanding Jet Security

Jet security is defined at the object level for individuals or groups of users. The Jet security model is rather complex, but it isn't too difficult to understand when broken down into its core components, which are as follows:

- Workgroups
- Groups
- Users

- Object owners
- Object permissions

The two main reasons for employing user-level security are

- To protect sensitive data in the database.
- To prevent users from accidentally breaking an application by changing the objects (tables, queries, and so on) of the application.

By using passwords and permissions, you can allow or restrict access of an individual or groups of individuals to the objects (forms, tables, and so on) in your database. This information, known as a *workgroup,* is stored in a workgroup information file.

Understanding workgroup files

Jet stores security information for databases in workgroup information files, usually the default file is named SYSTEM.MDW. This workgroup information file is a special Access database that contains a collection of usernames and passwords, user group definitions, object owner assignments, and object permissions. The `SYSTEM.MDW` file is often located, by default, in `C:\Documents and Settings\<user name>\Application Data\Microsoft\Access\`.

When Access opens a database, it reads the workgroup information file associated with the database. Access reads the file to determine who is allowed — and at what level — to access the objects in the database and what permissions they have to those objects.

You can use the same workgroup file for multiple databases. After you enable security for a database, however, users must use the workgroup information file containing the security information. If users use a workgroup other than the one used to define security, however, they are limited to logging into the database as the Admin user with any permissions the database administrator assigned to Admin user.

TIP **When securing a database, one of the first things to do is remove all permissions for the Admin user. Removing these permissions prevents other users from opening the database as the Admin user by using another Access workgroup file and obtaining the rights of the Admin user. Users can still open the database as the Admin user by using a different workgroup, but they won't have any object permissions. This measure is discussed later in this chapter in the section "Working with workgroups."**

Understanding permissions

The permissions in Jet security are defined at the object level. Each object, such as a form or report, has a specific set of permissions. The system administrator defines which permissions each user or group of users has for each object. Users may belong to multiple groups, and they always inherit the highest permission setting of any of the groups to which they belong.

For example, every table object has a set of permissions associated with it: Read Design, Modify Design, Read Data, Update Data, Insert Data, Delete Data, and Administrator. (See Table 29-1, later in this chapter, for a complete list of permissions and their meanings.) The database administrator has the ability to assign or remove any or all of these permissions for each user or group of users in the workgroup. Because the permissions are set at the object level, the administrator may give a user the ability to read data from Table A, as well as read data from and write data to Table B, but prevent the user from even looking at Table C. In addition, this complexity allows for unique security situations, such as having numerous users sharing data on a network, each with a different set of rights for the database objects. All security maintenance functions are performed from the Users and Permissions command in the Administrator group on the Database Tools ribbon (see Figure 29-1).

FIGURE 29-1

All user-level security functions are performed from the Database Tools ribbon.

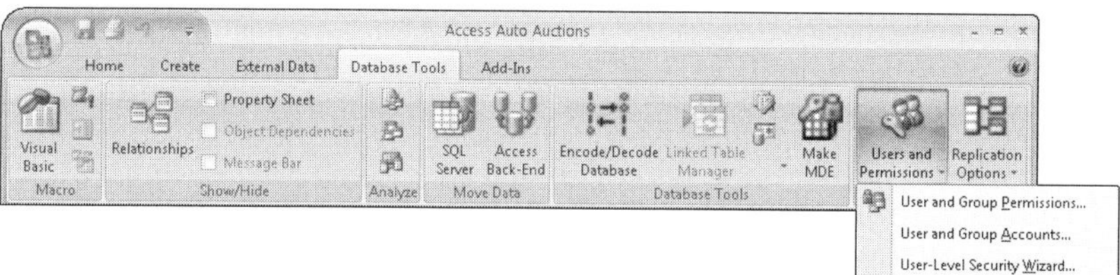

Understanding security limitations

You need to be aware of the fact that you can't depend on the Jet security model to be foolproof. For example, security holes have been discovered and exposed in previous versions of Access — in effect, unprotecting every database distributed under the assumption that the code and objects were protected. The amount of resources involved in developing an application is often huge, and protecting that investment is essential. The most that you can do for protection is to implement the Jet security model fully and properly and use legally binding licensing agreements for all your distributed applications. Unfortunately, the security of your databases is at the mercy of software hackers.

You should monitor the Microsoft Update service on the Web at `windowsupdate.com/` to keep your Windows operating system and Office programs up to date.

We recommend that you use Microsoft Access security to lock up your tables and prevent access to the design of your forms, reports, queries, and modules. However, if you want to control data at the form level — for example, suppose you want to hide controls or control access to specific form-level controls or data — you have to write your own security commands. You can also use the operating system (Windows) to prevent access to the folders.

Choosing a Security Level to Implement

As an Access developer, you must determine the level of security appropriate for your application; not every database needs user-level security. If your application contains non-sensitive data or is implemented in a fairly low-risk workgroup, you may not need the powerful permission protection of Jet's security. For applications that need to be secure, you need to answer the following questions:

- Which users are allowed to use the database?
- Can individual users be categorized into similar groups?
- Which objects need to be restricted for individual users or groups?

After you have made these determinations, you are ready to begin implementing security in your application. Access includes a tool to help you implement security — the User-Level Security Wizard (available from the Users and Permissions command's drop-down list in the Administrator group on the Database Tools ribbon). This chapter teaches you how you can implement security using Access's interface; each security element is discussed in detail. A thorough understanding of the workings of the security model is essential in developing well-secured applications. (The wizard is discussed later in this chapter.)

ON the CD-ROM **This chapter uses two example databases: `Chapter29.mdb` and `AAASecureWizard`. Later in this chapter, you see how the second database is created from the first database. You should copy the `Chapter29.mdb` database from the CD, included with this book, into a folder on your hard drive.**

Creating a Database Password

You can use Jet security at its most basic level simply by controlling who can open the database. You control database access by creating a password for the databases that you want to protect. When you set a database password for a database, users are prompted to enter the password each time they attempt to access the database. If they don't know the database password, they are not allowed to open the database. When using this form of security, you are not controlling specific permissions for specific users; you are merely controlling who can and can't access the secured database.

To create a database password, follow these steps:

1. **In Access, open the `Chapter29.mdb` database exclusively.**

NOTE **You *must* open the database exclusively to set the database password. To open the database exclusively, click Open Exclusive from the Open pull-down menu in the lower-right corner of the Open dialog box, as shown in Figure 29-2.**

2. **Select the Set Database Password command from the Database Tools group on the Database Tools ribbon.**

FIGURE 29-2

Opening a database in exclusive mode

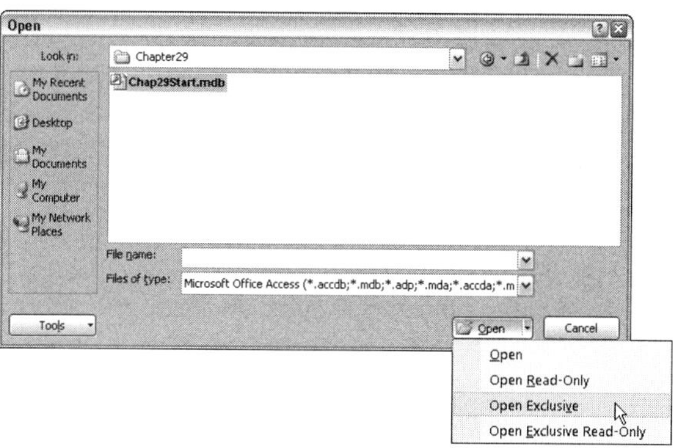

3. **In the Password field, type the password that you want to use to secure the database (see Figure 29-3). For this example, use the password** bible.

   Access does *not* display the password; rather, it shows an asterisk (*) for each letter.

FIGURE 29-3

Creating a database password is the simplest way to secure your database.

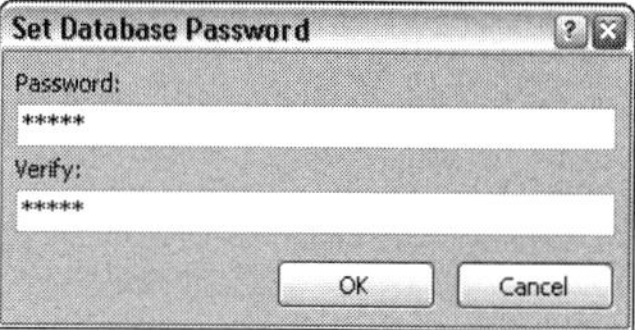

4. **In the Verify field, type the password again.**

   This security measure ensures that you don't mistype the password (because you can't see the characters that you type) and mistakenly prevent everyone, including you, from accessing the database.

TIP For maximum security, when entering a password you should follow standard password naming conventions. That is, you should make the password a combination of letters and numbers that won't represent any easily known or deduced combination. People often unwisely use a birthday, their name, their address number, or a loved one's name, which are all poor choices for passwords because another person could deduce them fairly easily. On the other hand, you shouldn't make the password so difficult to remember that you and others accessing the database will have to write it down to use it. A written password is a useless password.

5. **Click OK to save the password.**

CAUTION **You can't synchronize replicated databases that have database passwords. If you plan to use Jet's replication features and you need database security, you must use user-level security.**

After you save the database password, any user who attempts to open the database must enter the password. Although this method controls *who* can access the database, it doesn't control *what* users are allowed to do with the objects and data after they have opened the database. To control objects, you need to fully implement Jet's user-level security, which is discussed in the following section.

NOTE **After a database has been protected with a database-level password, you must supply the password when linking to any of its tables. This password is stored in the definition of the link to the table.**

To remove a database password, follow these steps:

1. **In Access, open the secure database exclusively.**

   You must open the database exclusively to be able to remove the database password.
2. **Select the Unset Database Password command from the Database Tools group on the Database Tools ribbon.**

   This command replaced the command labeled Set Database Password before the database password was set.
3. **In the Password field, type the password of the database (see Figure 29-4).**

FIGURE 29-4

You can remove a database password by entering the password in the Unset Database Password dialog box.

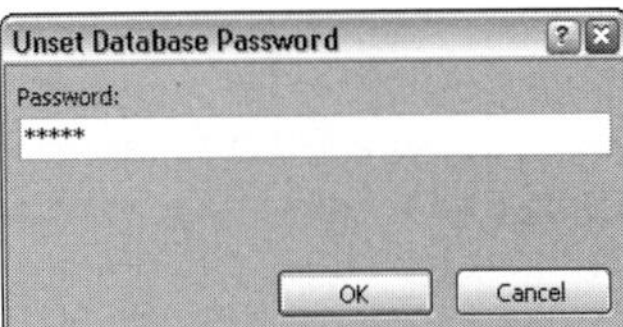

4. **Click OK to unset the password.**

If you remove a database password from an Access database, users are no longer required to enter a password to access the database unless you have enabled user-level security.

NOTE **Any user who knows the database password has the ability to change or remove the database password. You can prevent this situation by removing the Administer permissions from the database for all users except the database administrator. This is discussed in more detail later in this chapter.**

Using Visual Basic to Set a Password

You also can set a database password using Visual Basic code. The following code changes the database password of the currently opened database:

```
Public Sub ChangeDatabasePassword()
  On Error GoTo ChangeDatabasePasswordErr
  Dim strOldPassword As String, strNewPassword As String
  Dim db As DAO.Database
  Set db = CurrentDb
  strOldPassword = ""
  strNewPassword = "shazam"
  db.NewPassword strOldPassword, strNewPassword
  Exit Sub
  ChangeDatabasePasswordErr:
    MsgBox Err & ":  " & Err.Description
    Exit Sub
  End Sub
```

If no database password is set, you pass a zero-length string (`""`) as the old password parameter. If a database password is assigned and you want to remove the password, pass the database password as the old password parameter and pass a zero-length string (`""`) as the new password.

CAUTION **Microsoft Access stores the database password in an unencrypted form. If you have sensitive data, this can compromise the security of the password-protected database. When data security is critical, you should consider defining user-level security to control access to sensitive data. User-level security is covered in depth later in this chapter.**

For an Access 2007 database (`.accdb` file), the Encrypt with Password command in the Database Tools group adds a password to the database. You have to open the database exclusively to set and unset the password. When you encrypt an Access 2007 database with a password, the data is unreadable by other tools and forces any user opening the database to enter a password. This higher level of security is available only in the `.accdb` file format.

Using the /runtime Option

If you're not concerned with protecting your application but simply want to prevent users from mistakenly breaking your application by modifying or deleting objects, you can force your application to be run in Access's *runtime mode*. When a database is opened in Access's runtime mode, all the interface elements that allow changes to objects are hidden from the user. In fact, while in runtime mode, it is impossible for a user to access the Navigation Pane. When using the runtime option, you must ensure that your application has a startup form that gives users access to any objects you want them to access. Normally this is the main menu or main switchboard of your application.

TIP **To assign a form as a startup form, open the database that you want to use, click the Microsoft Office Button, select Access Options, and click Current Database on the left side of the window. Under Application Options, set the Display Form to the form you want to be the startup form for the application. Startup forms are covered more in depth in the following section.**

To create a shortcut to start your application in Access's runtime mode, follow these steps, using the `Chapter29.mdb` database:

1. **Go to the folder that contains Microsoft Access (`MSACCESS.exe`).**

NOTE **On most computers, the `MSAccess.exe` file is located in the `C:\Program Files\Microsoft Office\Office12\` folder.**

2. **Highlight the Microsoft Access program and select File ➪ Create Shortcut, or right-click the program file and select Create Shortcut from the pop-up menu.**

   Windows creates a shortcut in the same folder, naming it Shortcut to MSAccess.exe.

3. **Right-click the newly created shortcut, select Properties from the menu, and then click the Shortcut tab when the Properties dialog box opens.**

4. **In the Target: field, append the following parameters to the path of `MSAccess.exe` (program): A space, the full path name and filename of the database (in quotation marks) to open in runtime mode, another space, and then** /runtime.

   For example, the following command line starts Access and opens the `Chapter29.mdb` database in runtime mode on our computers:

   ```
   C:\Program Files\Microsoft Office\Office12\MSAccess.exe
   C:\Access 2007 Access Auto Auctions\Chapter29.mdb" /runtime
   ```

NOTE **The path to `MSAccess.exe` should have already been in the Target: field. Note that Windows automatically places the path and filename for `MSAccess.exe` in quotation marks. The `/runtime` switch should not be enclosed in quotes. If you enclose the `/runtime` switch in quotes, an error occurs when you attempt to execute the shortcut.**

5. **After you've specified the path and filename, placing the /runtime switch at the end of the Target field, you can optionally remove the path name in the Start In field.**

   Figure 29-5 shows how the Shortcut properties should look at this point.

6. **After the fields have been updated, click the Apply button to process the changes and save the shortcut.**

7. **You can rename the shortcut icon to any name that you want and move it from the current folder to another folder, or even to the desktop.**

   After you have created the shortcut, you can distribute or re-create the same shortcut for each user installation.

FIGURE 29-5

Modifying the Target and Start in fields of the shortcut by using the /runtime switch of Access 2007

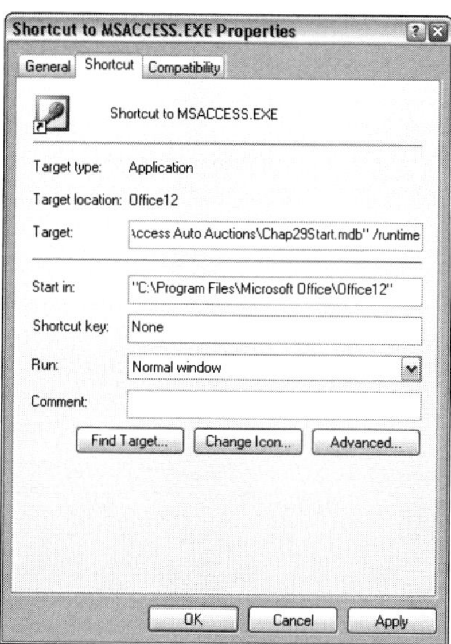

If your database has a password associated with it, the user will still be prompted to enter the password prior to opening the database.

NEW FEATURE

Access contains a new extension — `.accdr` — that automatically puts your Access 2007 database in the runtime environment when it's opened. Change your database file's extension from `.accdb` to `.accdr` to create a locked-down version of your Access 2007 database. Change the extension back to `.accdb` to restore full functionality.

Using the Current Database Options

A slightly less secure alternative to using the `/runtime` option or the `.accdr` extension is to set the Current Database options. This alternative is not a complete solution for situations where tight security is paramount. Figure 29-6 shows the Access Options window, accessible from the Microsoft Office Button. These options are available for both the `.accdb` and `.mdb` file formats.

FIGURE 29-6

The Current Database options provide another way to secure an application.

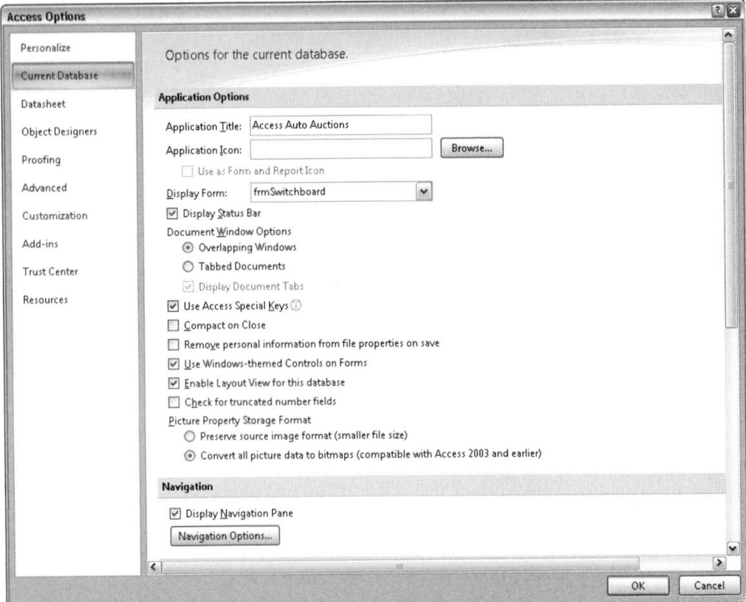

By making the appropriate specifications in the Access Options window, you can do the following:

- Assign a title to the application
- Assign an application icon to the application
- Assign a form or data access page to immediately run when the database is open
- Prevent the Navigation Pane from being displayed
- Prevent the status bar from being displayed
- Designate a menu bar to be used on startup of your application.
- Designate a shortcut menu to be used on startup of your application
- Prevent full menus from being displayed
- Prevent Access's built-in shortcut menus from being displayed
- Prevent users from modifying toolbars (toolbar/menu changes)
- Prevent users from using Access's special keys to display the Navigation Pane, Immediate window, or VB window, or pause execution

To designate `frmSwitchboard` as the default form to open whenever the `Chapter29.mdb` database opens, follow these steps:

1. **Open the `Chapter29.mdb` database and select Access Options from the Microsoft Office Button, and then click Current Database.**
2. **Click the Display Form field and select `frmSwitchboard` from the drop-down list (refer to Figure 29-6).**
3. **Click OK.**

CROSS-REF Chapter 35 covers the Current Database options in more detail.

After you have assigned a form to open automatically, you can also specify that the Navigation Pane or status bar not be displayed to give even greater security to your application. Using a database password and the Current Database options, you can assign minimum security to the database and your application.

CAUTION The user can bypass these options by simply holding down the Shift key while opening the database. However, if you assign a database password, users are required to enter the password to use the database.

Using the Jet User-Level Security Model

Most often when security is required, setting a database password and runtime option is simply not enough. Access 2003 and earlier allowed you to set user-level security. While this is no longer available in Access 2007 databases, you can still administer databases created in previous versions of Access.

When you need more security, you can use Access user profiles that are implemented by the user-level/object permissions security of Jet. The Jet Database Engine offers additional levels of customization and security for your application. When using Jet level security, you need to complete the following series of steps:

1. **Select or create a workgroup database.**
2. **Define the workgroup database's security groups.**
3. **Create the users of the workgroup database.**
4. **Define permissions for each user and security group.**
5. **Enable security by setting an Admin user password.**

What Is Jet and a User Profile?

When you create a Microsoft Access database (`.mdb` or `.mde`), Access uses an internal program to create and work with the database and its objects. Microsoft calls this internal program the *Jet Database Engine*. Its purpose is to retrieve and store data in user and system databases. Some people refer to the Jet engine as a *data manager* that the database system is built upon. Jet works only with Access databases; it doesn't work with other ODBC databases, such as SQL Server, Oracle, and others. When you installed Access, the installation program created several Registry settings for the Jet engine. You can use the Registry Editor to examine and even change these settings for Access. However, we highly recommend you not change the setting in the Microsoft Windows Registry.

Using Jet, you can build an Access user profile, comprised of a special set of Window's Registry keys, to override the standard Access and Jet database engine settings.

Enabling security

Jet database security is always on. Whenever a new workgroup database is created, an Admin user is automatically created within the workgroup. This Admin user has no password assigned to it. When the Admin password is blank, Access assumes that any user attempting to open the database is the Admin user, and that this user is automatically logged in to the database as the Admin user. To force Access (Jet) to ask for a valid username and password to log in to the database (see Figure 29-7), you simply create a password for the Admin user. (Creating passwords is discussed later in this section.) To disable security, clear the Admin user's password. The security permissions that you designed are still in effect, but Access doesn't ask for a username and password; it logs on all users as the Admin user and gives them any permissions assigned to the Admin user. Be careful about clearing the Admin user's password when you have modified other users' permissions.

FIGURE 29-7

When security is enabled, Jet forces all users to enter a valid username and password to use the secured database.

TIP **Any changes that you make to security won't take effect until you restart Access. If you have cleared the Admin password only to find that some or all of the Admin user's permissions have been revoked, open the database and create a password for the Admin user. Then exit Access and restart Access (not the database). When you restart Access, you are prompted to enter a username and password.**

Working with workgroups

A *workgroup* is a collection of users, user groups, and object permissions. You can use a single workgroup file for all of your databases, or you can use different workgroups for different databases. The method that you use depends on the level of security that you need. If you give Administrative rights to users of some databases but not to users of other databases, you need to distribute separate workgroup files with each database. Access always uses a workgroup file when you open it. By default, this workgroup file is the `System.mdw` workgroup file. This file comes with Access 2007.

Creating a new workgroup

If you've used the Workgroup Administrator in previous versions of Access to create and join workgroups, you'll be sad to see it's been removed from Access 2007. To create a new workgroup file, use the Workgroup Administrator in previous versions of Access or use the User-Level Security Wizard, covered later in this chapter.

Joining an existing workgroup

The Workgroup Administrator in previous versions of Access also let you switch between workgroup files. In Access 2007, you must use the `/wrkgrp` switch on the command line to use a specific workgroup.

To create a shortcut that opens an Access database using existing workgroup, follow these steps:

1. **Go to the folder that contains Microsoft Access (`MSAccess.exe`).**
2. **Highlight the Microsoft Access program and select File ➪ Create Shortcut, or right-click the program file and select Create Shortcut from the pop-up menu.**

   Windows creates a shortcut in the same folder, naming it Shortcut to `MSAccess.exe`.
3. **Right-click the newly created shortcut, select Properties from the menu, and then click the Shortcut tab when the Properties dialog box opens.**
4. **In the Target field, append the following parameters to the path of `MSAccess.exe` (program): A space, the full pathname and filename of the database to open in run-time mode, another space, and then `/wrkgrp`.**

   For example, the following command line starts Access and opens the `Chapter29.mdb` database with the AutoAuction workgroup file:

   ```
   "C:\Program Files\Microsoft Office\Office12\MSAccess.exe"
   "C:\Access 2007 Access Auto Auctions\Chapter29.mdb" /wrkgrp
   "C:\Access 2007 Access Auto Auctions\AutoAuction.mdw"
   ```

Working with users

Every time a user opens an Access (Jet) database, Jet must identify the user opening the database. In Access, security is always enabled, regardless of whether you explicitly created a workgroup for your database. If you did not define a workgroup, Jet assumes that any user who opens the database is the Admin user. When a new workgroup is created, Access automatically creates a default user named Admin. The Admin user automatically receives full permissions to all objects in the database. Obviously, when you secure a database, you don't want everyone to be able to open the database with full permissions on all objects, so you must create additional users for the workgroup.

Adding and deleting user accounts

To add, delete, and edit user information, you use the User and Group Accounts dialog box (see Figure 29-8). To open the User and Group Accounts dialog box, select User and Group Accounts from the Users and Permissions command's drop-down in the Administrator group on the Database Tools ribbon. The Users tab of the User and Group Accounts dialog box consists of two sections: User and Group Membership. You use the User section to create and maintain usernames and passwords. You use the Group Membership section to assign users to user groups. Assigning users to groups is discussed in detail later in this chapter.

FIGURE 29-8

Creating and maintaining users in the User and Group Accounts dialog box.

To fully secure your database with users and groups, you should generally follow these steps:

1. **Create a new user.**
2. **Add the new user to the Admins group.**
3. **Remove the Admin user from the Admins group.**
4. **Assign all object ownerships to the new user.**

When you create a user, you supply the username and a personal identifier. Jet then combines these two items and processes them in a special algorithm, producing a unique security ID (SID). It is this SID that Jet uses to recognize users. To re-create a user in the workgroup, you need to know the username and the personal ID (PID) that was used to create the user. Consequently, you should always write down and store all usernames and PIDs that you create in a safe place.

To create a new user in a workgroup, follow these steps:

1. **Open the database** `Chapter29.mdb`.
2. **Select User and Group Accounts from the Users and Permissions command's drop-down in the Administrator group on the Database Tools ribbon.**
3. **Select the New button in the User section to display the New User/Group dialog box (see Figure 29-9).**

FIGURE 29-9

Jet combines the username and Personal ID to create a unique SID for the user.

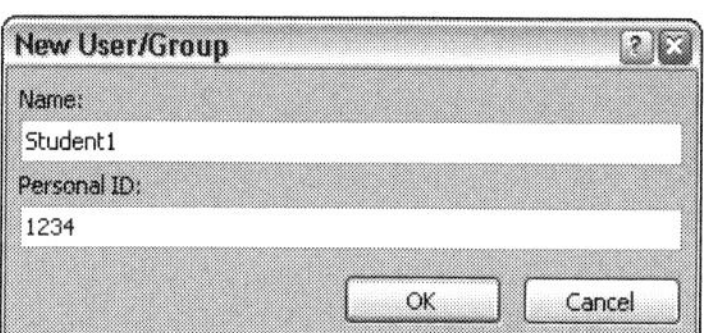

4. **Enter the name** Student1 **for the name, and enter a unique Personal ID of** 1234.

   You can enter any appropriate information into these two fields, if you don't want to use these example names. Write this information down and store it in a safe place; you will need it if you have to re-create the user in the workgroup.
5. **Click OK to save the new user.**

After you create the new user, Student1, you can assign group memberships and/or a password for the user. Notice that Student1 is automatically a member of the Users group. Any new member must at least belong to this group. You can make Student1 a member of the Admins group by simply clicking the Add button in the Group Membership section.

CAUTION **To secure your database fully, you must remove all permissions for the Admin user. (Defining Group Permissions is covered later in this chapter.) All Admin users share the same SID in all workgroups, on all machines. If you don't remove the permissions for the Admin user, an unauthorized user using a different workgroup can open the database as the Admin user with all permissions of the Admin user. The Admin user can't be deleted, so the Admin user account needs to be adjusted accordingly.**

If you want to delete the user Student1 that you just created, follow these steps:

1. **Display the User and Group Accounts dialog box.**
2. **From the User Name drop-down list, select Student1.**
3. **Click the Delete button to delete the selected user.**

Creating and changing user passwords

Any user who is a member of the Admins group can remove a password from any user account. A user who is a not a member of the Admins group can change his or her own password. However, a user who is not a member of the Admins group cannot change or create a password for any other user.

CAUTION **When Access opens and a password has been assigned to any user, the Logon dialog box displays (refer to Figure 29-7).**

If no passwords are assigned to any users, however, Access automatically opens, using the Admin user. This means that any additional users that you create in Security will *not* be able to set a password. To correct this, you need to create a password for the Admin user. Then exit from Access and restart Access, logging on as the user whose password you want to change.

To create or change the Admin password, follow these steps:

1. **Open the database** `Chapter29.mdb`.
2. **Display the User and Group Accounts dialog box.**

CAUTION **Make sure that the username selected is Admin (not Student1 that you created earlier).**

3. **Click the Change Logon Password tab (see Figure 29-10).**

FIGURE 29-10

The Change Logon Password tab of the User and Group Accounts dialog box. Notice that the name is "Admin" and can't be changed.

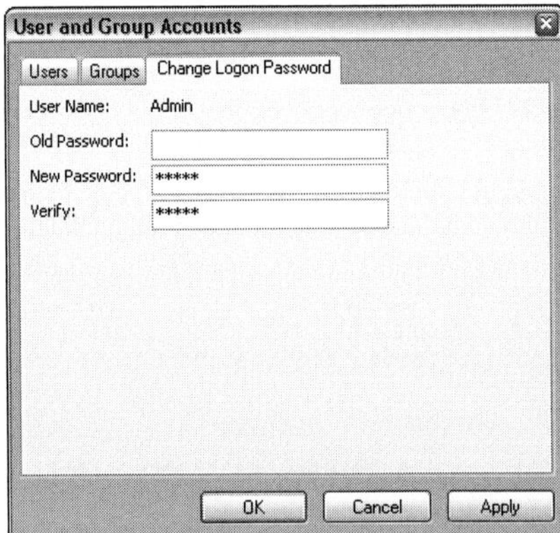

4. **Because no password has been assigned to Admin, leave the Old Password field blank.**

TIP If you are logging on as the Admin user after you have assigned a password, or if a password exists for the user that you logged on as, enter it in the Old Password field. If no password is assigned to the user, leave the Old Password field blank.

5. **Move to the New Password field and enter the new password** Admin **(or any other password that you want to assign — remember that Access's security is case-sensitive) in the New Password field.**

   Access *won't* show you the word that you are typing; rather, it shows an asterisk for each character that you type.

6. **Move to the Verify field and enter the new password** Admin **again.**

   Again, remember that Access's security is case-sensitive. Each character is represented with an asterisk.

7. **Click the Apply button to save the new password for the Admin user.**

8. **Click OK to close the User and Group Accounts dialog box.**

TIP After you have created a password for the user, you have to exit from Access and restart it for the changes to take effect. Simply closing the database and opening it again won't activate the security changes (such as assigning a password to Admin) that you made.

Any user who is a member of the Admins group can clear the password of another user, so that user can log on if he or she has forgotten his or her password.

To change another person's password, you have to restart Access and open the database by logging on as the user whose password you want to change.

Working with groups

Groups are collections of users. A user may belong to one or more groups. You use groups to group multiple users who have the same object permission privileges. You can then define object permissions to the group once, versus having to assign them individually for each user. When you create a new user, you simply add the user to the group that has the object permission privileges that the new user should have.

For example, you may have a number of users in a credit department and in a sales department. If you want to allow all these users to look at a customer's credit history but restrict the sales staff to viewing only basic customer information, you have the following options:

- Create an individual user account for each user in each department and assign object permissions for each user.
- Allow all users in the credit department to log on as one user, and allow all users in the sales department to log on as a different user. You can then restrict the object permissions for each of these two users.

- Create an individual user account for each user in each department and create a group account for each department. You can then make the permissions assignments for each of the two groups and place each user into his or her respective group to inherit the group's permissions.

Although creating a unique user account and assigning specific permissions to each user is a valid scenario, it is an administrator's nightmare. If policy dictates that one department needs permissions added or revoked, the change has to be made to each of the users' accounts in that department.

The second method is straightforward and simple but presents many problems. If a user transfers from one department to another, he knows the usernames and passwords for both departments and may be able to retrieve data that he is no longer authorized to view. In addition, if an employee leaves, the username and password need to be changed, and each user of the workgroup has to be made aware of the change. In a multiuser environment, creating a unique user account for each user and grouping them accordingly is a much better solution.

With the third option, the change can be made to the department group once, and all users inherit the new permission settings. It's recommended you set the permissions at the group level, rather than the individual user level.

Adding and deleting groups

Just as Access automatically creates an Admin user in all new workgroups, it also automatically creates two groups: Users and Admins. Every user account in the system belongs to the Users group; you can't remove a user from the Users group. The Admins group is the all-powerful, super-user group. Users in Admins can add and delete user and group accounts, as well as to assign and remove permissions for any object for any user or group in the workgroup. In addition, a member of the Admins group has the ability to remove other user accounts from the Admins group. For this reason, you need to carefully consider which users you allow to be a member of the Admins group. The Admins group and the Users group are permanent groups; they can never be deleted.

TIP **Access doesn't enable you to remove all users from the Admins group; one user must belong to the Admins group at all times (the default is the user named Admin). If you were allowed to remove all users from the Admins group, you could set security so tightly that you would never be able to bypass it yourself! In general, when securing a database, you should place only one user and one back-up user in the Admins group.**

NOTE **Unlike the Admin user's SID, which is identical in every Access workgroup, the Admins group's SIDs are not identical from workgroup to workgroup, so unauthorized users using a workgroup other than the one that you used to define security can't access your database as a member of the Admins group. The Users group's SIDs are the same throughout all workgroups, however, so you need to remove all permissions for the Users group. If you don't remove permissions from the Users group, any user in any workgroup can open your database with the Users group's permissions.**

To create a new group named Sales, follow these steps:

1. **Open Access and then open the `Chapter29.mdb` database and log in with the Admin username and password. Then display the User and Group Accounts dialog box.**
2. **Select the Groups tab.**
3. **Click the New button to display the New User/Group dialog box (see Figure 29-11).**

FIGURE 29-11

Jet uses the group name and personal identifier to create a unique SID for a group, just as it does for user accounts.

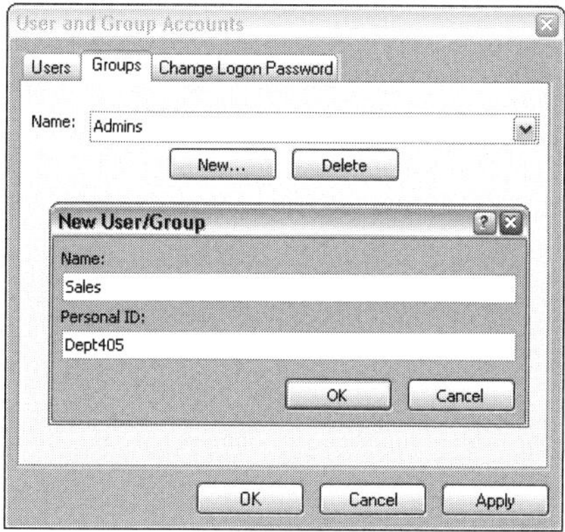

4. **Just as you do to create users, enter the group name** Sales **and a personal ID of** Dept405.

   If you aren't following along with this example, you can enter your own group name and personal ID. Also, just as before, write down this information and put it in a safe place because you will need it if you ever need to re-create the group.
5. **Click OK to save the new group.**
6. **After this is complete, click OK in the User and Group Accounts dialog box to save your work.**

If, at a later time, you want to delete the Sales group that you just created, follow these steps:

1. **Display the User and Group Accounts dialog box.**
2. **Select the Groups tab (refer to Figure 29-11).**
3. **From the drop-down list, select the Sales group.**
4. **Click the Delete button to delete the selected group.**

Assigning and removing group members

Assigning users to and removing users from groups is a simple process. You use the Users tab on the User and Group Accounts dialog box to add to and remove users from a group. You may place any user in any group, and a user may belong to more than one group. You cannot remove a user from the Users group nor can you remove all users from the Admins group; you must always have at least one user in the Admins group.

To add the user Student1 to the new group Sales, follow these steps:

1. **Open `Chapter29` and display the User and Group Accounts dialog box.**
2. **From the User Name drop-down list, select the user Student1 to modify the group assignments.**
3. **To assign the user Student1 to the group Sales, select the Sales group in the Available Groups list and click the Add button (see Figure 29-12).**

   The Sales group displays in the Member Of list.

FIGURE 29-12

Assigning users to groups makes controlling object permissions much easier for the system administrator.

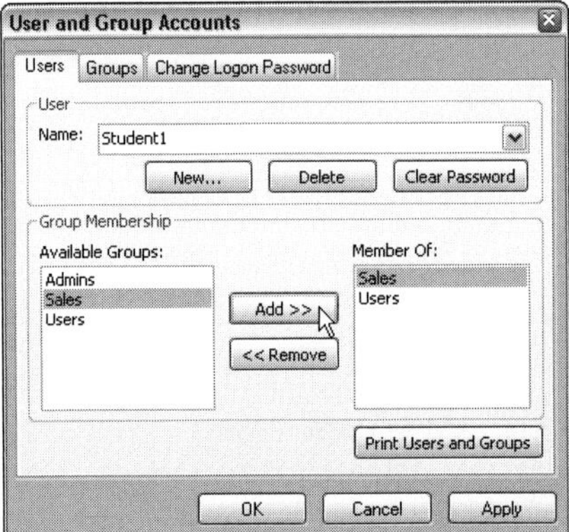

4. **Click OK to save the new group assignments.**

To remove the user Student1 from the group Sales, follow these steps:

1. **Display the User and Group Accounts dialog box.**

Make sure that the username selected is Student1 (not Admin).

2. **Select the group Sales in the Member Of list and click the Remove button.**

   The Sales group no longer displays in the Member Of list.

3. **Click OK to save the new group assignments.**

4. **Because Jet uses the same SIDs for all Admin user accounts throughout all workgroups, you always need to remove the Admin user from the Admins group when securing a database.**

   Figure 29-12 shows that the user Student1 has been added to the Sales group. Notice that Student1 is a member of two groups: Users and Sales. Before leaving this section, assign Student1 to the Admins group so that you can use this example later in this chapter.

The only remaining task is to set the appropriate object permissions for the Users and Sales groups.

Securing objects by using permissions

After you define your users and groups, you must determine the appropriate object permissions for each group. Permissions control who can view data, update data, add data, and work with objects in Design View. Permissions are the heart of the Jet security system and can be set only by a member of the Admins group, by the owner of the object (see the next section), or by any user who has Administrator permission for an object.

Setting an object's owner

Every object in the database has an owner. The *owner* is a user account in the workgroup that is designated to always have Administrator rights to the object. Administrator rights override the permissions defined for the logged-on user or defined for any of the user's groups. You can designate one user to be the owner of all the objects in a database, or you can assign an owner to individual objects.

Access queries require special consideration when assigning owners to objects. When creating a query, you can set the `Run Permissions` property of the query to either User's or Owner's (see Figure 29-13). When a password is defined for a workgroup, `Run Permissions` is automatically set to User's. Setting `Run Permissions` to User's limits the query users to viewing only the data that their security permissions permit. If you want to enable users to view or modify data for which they do not have permissions, you can set the `Run Permissions` property to Owner's. When the query is run with the Owner's permissions (`WITH OWNERACCESS OPTION` in an SQL statement), users inherit the permissions of the owner of the query. These permissions are applicable only to the query and not to the entire database.

TIP **When a query's `Run Permissions` property is set to Owner's, only the owner can make changes to the query. If this restriction poses a problem, you may want to set the owner of the query to a group rather than to a user account. Note that only the owner of an OwnerAccess query can change the query's owner.**

NOTE **If you haven't assigned passwords to Admin or other users, the user is automatically assumed to be Admin and the query's `Run Permissions` property is set to Owner's.**

FIGURE 29-13

Setting a query's Run Permissions determines which users can run or modify the query.

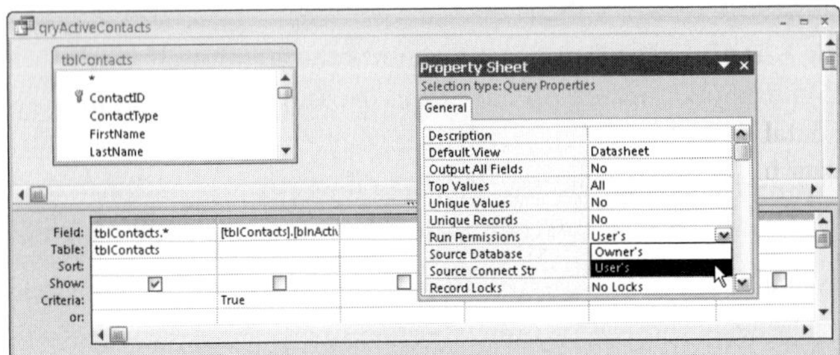

To change the owner of any object in the database, follow these steps:

1. **Select User and Group Permissions from the Users and Permissions command's drop-down list in the Administrator group on the Database Tools ribbon to display the User and Group Permissions dialog box.**
2. **Select the Change Owner tab (see Figure 29-14).**

FIGURE 29-14

Transferring ownership of one or more tables from the Admin user to the Sales group

3. **Select the object (or objects) whose ownership you want to transfer.**

   You can select the type of objects to display by changing the Object Type drop-down list.

4. Select the user or group that you want to make the owner of the selected object. To select a group name, first select the List: Groups radio button.
5. Click the Change Owner button to change the object's owner to the selected user or group.

NOTE Each object in a database has an owner. The database itself also has an owner. You can view the owner of the database by selecting Database from the Object Type drop-down list. You can't change an object's owner by using Access's interface. The only way to change a database's owner is to log on as the user that you want to make the owner of the database, create a new database, and then import the original database into the new database by using the External Data ribbon. When you import a database, the current user is assigned as the new owner of the database and all of its database objects. This is essentially what the Security Wizard (discussed later in this chapter) does for you.

Setting object permissions

Object permissions are the heart of Jet security. You can set one or more object permissions at a time for a user or group. When assigning permissions, you must keep in mind that some permissions automatically imply other permissions. For example, if you assign a user Read Data permission for a table, the Read Design permission is also granted because a table's design must be available to access the data. A more complex example is assigning permission for Insert Data—this automatically grants permission for Read Data and Read Design.

An object's permission assignments are persistent until one of the following conditions occurs:

- A member of the Admins group changes the object's permissions.
- The object is saved with a new name by using the Save As command from the File menu.
- The object is cut and pasted in the Database window.
- The object is imported or exported.

If any of the preceding actions occurs, all permissions for the manipulated object are lost and you need to reassign them. When you perform any of these actions, you are actually creating a new object. Access assigns default permissions for each object type.

There are two ways that permissions can be granted to a user:

- Explicit permissions are permissions granted directly to a user. When you manually assign permissions to a user, no other user's permissions are affected.
- Implicit permissions are permissions granted to a group. All users belonging to a group inherit the permissions of that group.

NOTE Because permissions can be assigned implicitly and because some permissions grant other permissions (Insert Data, Read Data, and Read Design permissions), users may be able to grant themselves permissions that they do not currently have. Because of this possibility, you must plan carefully when assigning permissions to groups of users and to individual users.

To assign or revoke a user's permissions for an object, follow these steps:

1. **Display the User and Group Permissions dialog box and select the Permissions tab.**
2. **In the Object Type drop-down list, select the type of object whose permissions you want to change.**
3. **In the User/Group Name list box, select the user or group account that you want to modify.**

   To see a list of all Groups, click the List Groups radio button under the User/Group Name list box.
4. **In the Object Name list box, select the object (or objects) that you want to modify.**
5. **In the Permissions grouping section, select or unselect the permissions check boxes for the object(s).**
6. **Click Apply to save the permission assignments.**

Remember that Admin user SIDs are identical throughout all workgroups. So after you assign Administer permissions to a specific user, you need to remove all permissions for the Admin user to secure your database. Figure 29-15 shows the Admin user's permissions being revoked for all tables in the database. Notice that all check boxes have been cleared for all tables. Clearing the check boxes prevents an Admin user from doing anything with table objects. You must repeat the process for each Object type until the Admin user has no permissions for any object.

FIGURE 29-15

Removing all permissions for the Admin user is critical to securing your database.

Setting default object permissions

You can create default permission assignments for each type of object in a database. These default permissions are assigned when you create new objects in the database. You set the default permissions just as you set them for any other object's permissions. You select the user or group to assign the default permissions, but you do not select a specific object name. Instead, select the first item in the Object Name list that is enclosed in <> and begins with New. When you select the Object Type Table, for example, you select <New Tables/Queries> in the Object Name list. When you assign permissions for users and groups to these <New> items, the permissions are used as defaults for all new objects of that type.

CAUTION **When removing default permissions for table objects, make sure that users have the necessary permissions to create new tables. Otherwise, users will not be able to execute make-table queries.**

Setting database permissions

Just as objects in a database have permissions, the database itself also has its own permissions. Selecting Database from the Object Type drop-down list displays the database permissions that can be modified (see Figure 29-16). The database permissions enable you to control who has administrative rights to the entire database, who can open the database exclusively (locking out other users), and who can open or run the database.

FIGURE 29-16

Assigning permissions for the entire database

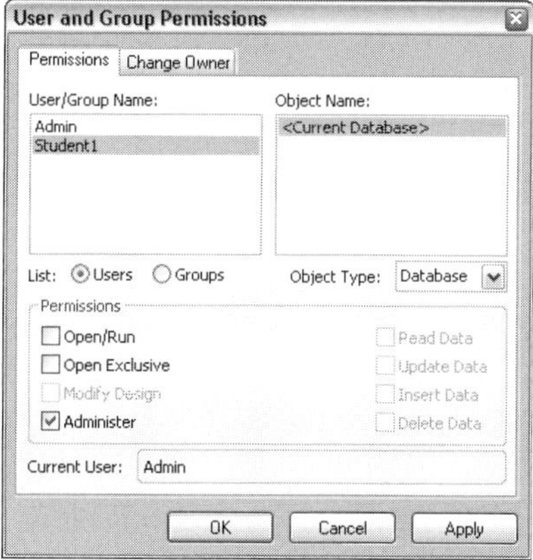

Securing your database for distribution: A basic approach

If you are securing a database for distribution, setting up detailed security for multiple users for all the objects in your database may not be important to you. Often, the only concern with shipping a secured database is protecting your development investment by securing the design of the application's objects and code. If you need this type of protection, you can distribute your application as an `.mde` or `.accde` file (see the section "Protecting Visual Basic Code"). Another method is to follow these steps:

1. **Create a workgroup to distribute with your database.**
2. **Remove the Admin user from the Admins group.**
3. **Remove all permissions for the Users group.**
4. **Remove all design permissions for the Admin user for all objects in the database.**
5. **Do not supply a password for the Admin user.**

Remember that if you do not specify a password for the Admin user, Access logs on all users as the Admin user. Because the Admin user has no rights to the design of any object, users cannot access objects or code in Design View.

Table 29-1 summarizes the permissions that you can assign.

TABLE 29-1

Summary of Assignable Permissions

Permission	Permits a User To	Applies To
Open/Run	Open a database, form, or report, or run a macro.	Databases, forms, reports, and macros
Open Exclusive	Open a database with exclusive access.	Databases only
Read Design	View objects in Design View.	Tables, queries, forms, and macros
Modify Design	View and change the design of objects, or delete them.	Tables, queries, forms, and macros
Administer	For databases, set database password, replicate a database, and change start-up properties. For database objects, have full access to objects and data, including the ability to assign permissions.	Databases, tables, queries, forms, reports, and macros
Read Data	View data.	Tables and queries
Update Data	View and modify but not insert or delete data.	Tables and queries
Insert Data	View and insert but not modify or delete data.	Tables and queries
Delete Data	View and delete but not modify or insert data.	Tables and queries

Using the Access Security Wizard

Access includes the Security Wizard tool to assist you in securing your database. The Security Wizard makes it easy for you to select the objects to secure. It then creates a new database containing secured versions of the selected objects. The Security Wizard assigns the currently logged-in user as the owner of the objects in the new database and removes all permissions from the Users group for those objects. The original database is not modified in any way. Only members of the Admins group and the user who ran the Security Wizard have access to the secured objects in the new database.

TIP

When you use the Security Wizard, make sure that you are logged in as the user that you want to become the new database's owner. You must already belong to the Admins group and you cannot log on as Admin. If you log on as Admin, Access reports an error when you attempt to run the Security Wizard. If you receive this error, simply log on as another Admins group user.

To start the Security Wizard, log onto the database as a user who is a member of the Admins group. Then select User-Level Security Wizard from the Users and Permissions command's drop-down in the Administrator group on the Database Tools ribbon.

Follow these steps to create and open the AAASecureWizard database.

These steps assume that you have created the user Student1 and assigned the user to the Admins group.

1. **Exit Access and open the folder that contains `Chapter29.mdb`. Copy this file and name the new copy `AAASecureWizard.mdb`.**
2. **Start Access and open the AAASecureWizard database.**

   When Access attempts to open the database, the Logon dialog box displays. The Logon dialog box displays automatically because the AAASecureWizard database inherited its permissions from the original database (`Chapter29`).
3. **Enter** Student1 **in the Name field and click OK.**

   The user Student1 has no assigned password. Access opens the AAASecureWizard database.
4. **Select User-Level Security Wizard from the Users and Permissions command's drop-down in the Administrator group on the Database Tools ribbon to start the wizard.**

   The wizard's first page displays a message advising you that you need to use the existing workgroup information file, or it can create a new one for the current open database (see Figure 29-17).
5. **Select Create a new workgroup information file and click the Next button.**

   When you select Create a new workgroup information file, the next screen, shown in Figure 29-18, asks you for the filename for the new file, a Workgroup ID number (WID) — which you should write down and save — and, optionally, your name and company.
6. **When the new workgroup information file screen appears, it automatically assigns a random 20-character string of numbers and letters to the WID (Workgroup ID) field. You can change this WID to any value.**

FIGURE 29-17

The Security Wizard helps jump-start your security implementation.

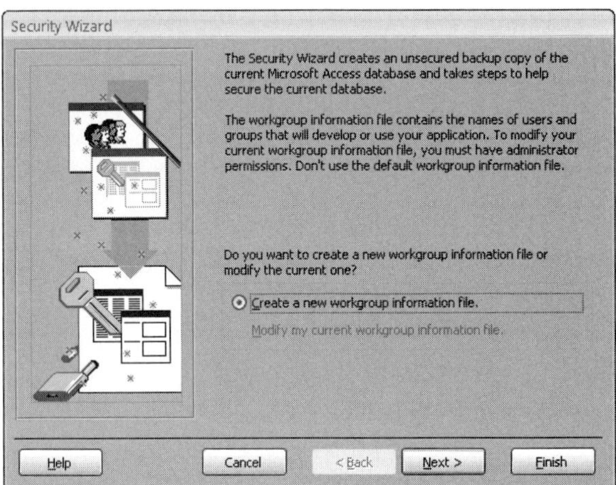

FIGURE 29-18

Assigning a unique WID and name to new workgroup information file

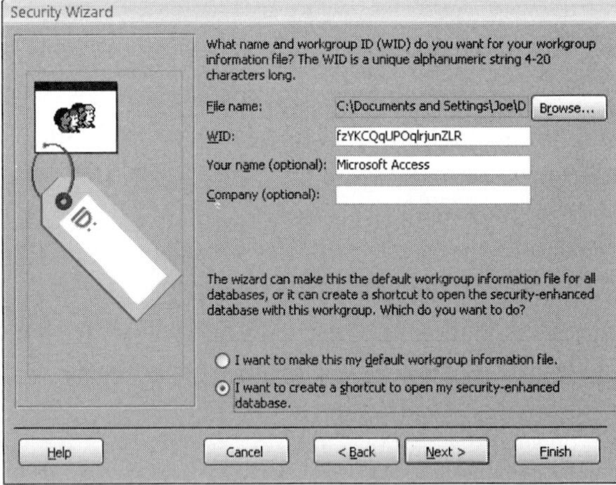

7. As Figure 29-18 shows, you can choose to make this the new default workgroup file for all databases (not recommended), or have Access create a shortcut to use this file only for this database (default). Selecting the option to create a shortcut associates this file with only one database. Click the Next button to display the next screen of the wizard.

8. The next screen of the wizard, shown in Figure 29-19, lets you select the objects to secure. By default, the wizard secures all objects in the database. If you deselect an object type (such as Tables or Forms), none of the objects of that type are exported to the secured database. If you do not want to restrict security permissions for a set of objects but still want those objects included in the new secured database, be sure to select the objects in the wizard. Later on, modify the user and group permissions for those objects in the new secured database. When you are satisfied with your object selections, click the Next button to continue.

FIGURE 29-19

Selecting the objects to secure

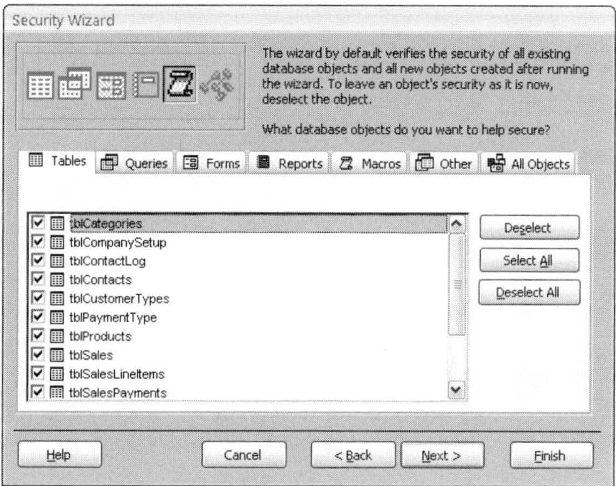

9. The next screen of the wizard, shown in Figure 29-20, asks you to create an optional security group account for a series of group actions.

   These include

   - **Backup Operators:** Can open the database exclusively for backing up and compacting
   - **Full Data Users:** Can edit data, but not alter design
   - **Full Permissions:** Has full permissions for all database objects, but can't assign permissions
   - **New Data Users:** Can read and insert data only (no edits or deletions)
   - **Project Designers:** Can edit data and objects, and alter tables or relationships
   - **Read-Only Users:** Can read data only
   - **Update Data Users:** Can read and update, but can't insert or delete data or alter design of objects

10. Check all the optional security groups displayed in the wizard screen. After you select all groups, click the Next button to continue.

FIGURE 29-20

Additional optional security groups for the database

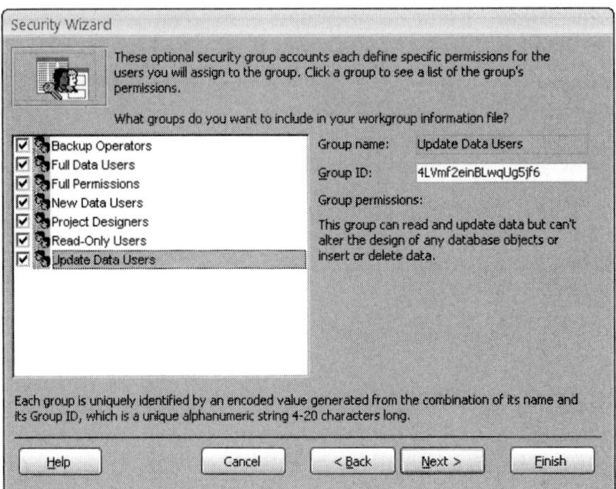

11. Notice that the next page of the wizard, shown in Figure 29-21, lets you choose to grant permissions to the Users group (the default is no permissions). By selecting Yes, you are able to assign rights to all object types in the database. Figure 29-21 shows this page with the Yes option selected. However, you should select the default choice: No — the Users group should not have any permissions. Click the Next button to continue to the next wizard screen.

FIGURE 29-21

Choosing whether to assign permissions to the Users group

Security Wizard
All users belong to the Users group in all workgroup information files. By default the wizard assigns no permissions to the Users group, but you may want to assign limited permissions to this group. Don't assign full permissions to the Users group, because this will remove all security.
Would you like to grant the Users group some permissions?
Yes, I would like to grant some permissions to the Users group.
No, the Users group should not have any permissions.
Database Tables Queries Forms Reports Macros
Open/Run
Open Exclusive
Modify Design
Administer
Read Data
Update Data
Insert Data
Delete Data
CAUTION: Anyone with a copy of Access will have the same permissions that you assign to the Users group!
Help
Cancel
< Back
Next >
Finish

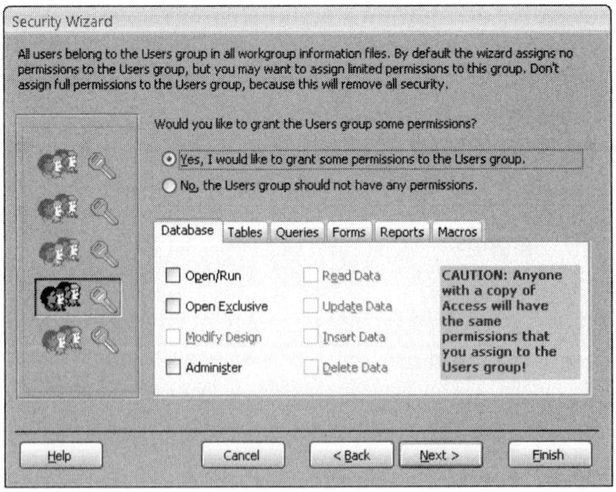

CAUTION If you decide to grant any permissions to the Users group, you should be aware that anyone with a copy of Access will have the same permissions that you assign to this group. Essentially, you are exposing the database to a security breach if you assign rights to this group.

12. The next page, shown in Figure 29-22, lets you add users to the workgroup information file. To add a user, enter the name and password information in the appropriate fields and click the Add a New User button.

FIGURE 29-22

Adding users and passwords to the workgroup information file

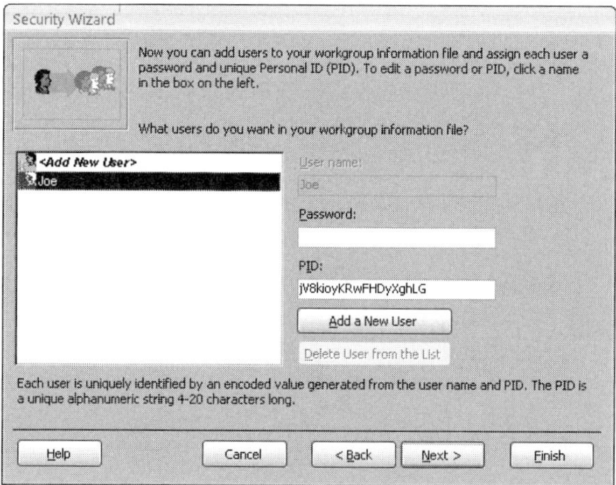

As Figure 29-22 shows, you can also remove users from the list by simply selecting their name from the list box on the left and selecting the Delete User from the List button. Click the Next button to continue.

13. The next wizard screen to display, shown in Figure 29-23, enables you to assign users to groups in your workgroup information file. If you added optional groups from the previous page (as shown in Figure 29-20), you can assign a user to any of these groups by checking the appropriate check box. To assign rights to a user, simply select the user from the drop-down list and then assign that user to groups using the check boxes. By default, all users, except the person creating the wizard, are assigned to new groups. Click the Next button to continue on to the next screen.

14. The last page of the wizard displays, as shown in Figure 29-24. In this screen, the Security Wizard asks you to provide a name for the old, and now unsecure, database. The default name is the same name as the current database with the extension `.bak`. Click the Finish button to finish creating the new secure database.

FIGURE 29-23

Adding users to groups for group rights

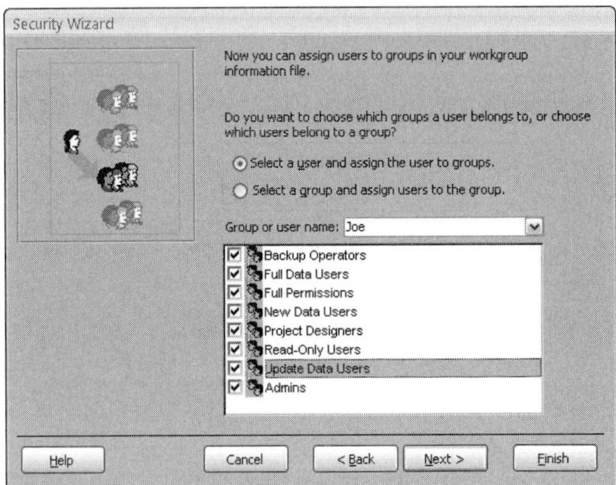

FIGURE 29-24

In the final wizard screen, the Security Wizard asks you to assign a name to the old database.

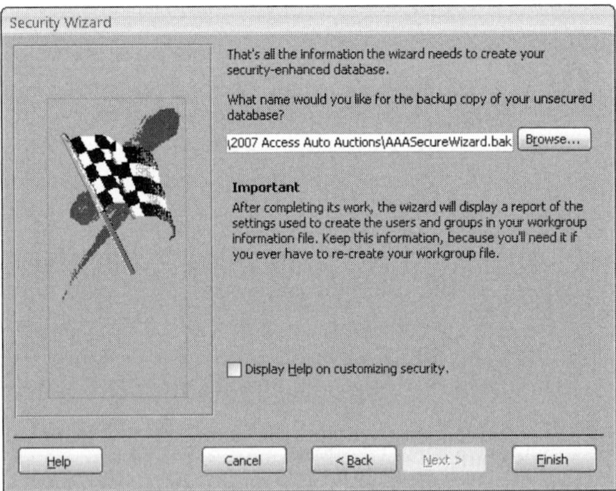

Technically, the Security Wizard doesn't make any modifications to the current database; rather, it makes a back-up copy by using the name that you specify and creates an entirely new database with secured objects. However, the new database is given the name of the original database.

When you distribute your secured application, be sure to distribute the database that the Security Wizard created for you.

When the Security Wizard has finished creating the new database, it generates a report called One-Step Security Wizard Report, as shown in Figure 29-25. The report contains all of the settings used to create the users and groups in the workgroup information file. You should keep this information. You will need it if you ever have the need to re-create the workgroup file.

FIGURE 29-25

The One-step Security Wizard Report summarizes the choices made while running the Security Wizard.

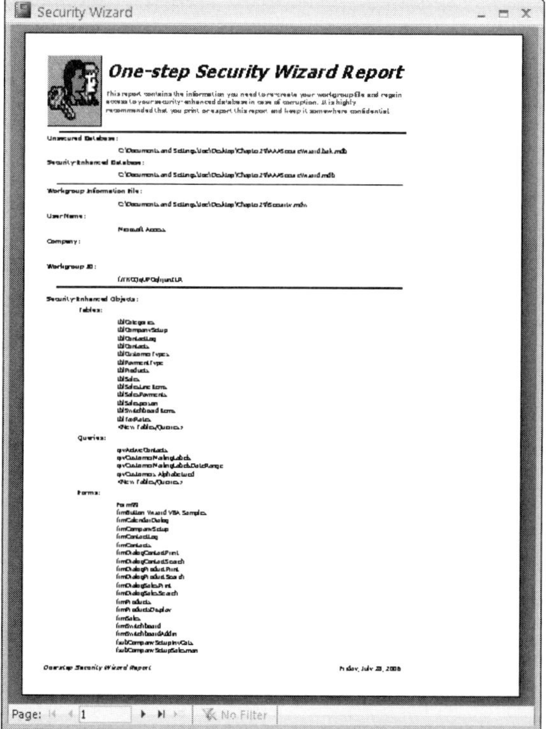

CAUTION **If you click the Finish button and Access finds any problems, it won't create the security database or the backup that you requested. Generally, you get this error if you have created the database and logged on as a user that secured the table and then relogged on as another user to secure it. This wizard works best with databases that have not had any previously defined security.**

Generally, making a copy of the original database and working with the secured database is a good idea. If you make changes to the original database, you need to run the Security Wizard again to create a secured version of the database. In addition, making a copy of the original database and then removing it from development helps prevent accidentally distributing the unsecured database.

Encrypting/Encoding a Database

When security is of utmost importance, one final step that you need to take is to *encrypt* or *encode* the database. Although it takes a great deal of skill (far more than the average computer user — or developer — possesses), it is possible to view the structure of an unencrypted/decoded database. A skilled hacker may use this information to gain full access to your secured database. Microsoft improved the encryption for the `.accdb` file format but still uses the old technique for the `.mdb` file format (and refers to it as encoding rather than encrypting.)

To encrypt an Access 2007 database (`.accdb`), follow these steps:

1. **Open an existing `.accdb` database (for example, `Chapter26.accdb`) exclusively.**
2. **Select the Encrypt with Password command from the Database Tools group on the Database Tools ribbon.**
3. **In the Password field, type the password that you want to use to secure the database (see Figure 29-3). For this example, use the password** bible.

   Access does *not* display the password; rather, it shows an asterisk (*) for each letter.
4. **Retype the same password in the Verify field and click OK.**

Encoding an Access 2003 or earlier database makes using hacker tools to gain any useful information about the database more difficult. Only the database owner or a member of the Admins group can encode or decode an `.mdb` file.

To encode an `.mdb` file, follow these steps:

1. **Open an existing `.mdb` database (for example, `Chapter29.mdb`) exclusively.**
2. **Select the Encode/Decode Database command from the Database Tools group on the Database Tools ribbon.**
3. **Enter a new name for the encoded database (for example, `Chapter29_Encoded.mdb`) in the Encode Database As dialog box (shown in Figure 29-26), and click Save.**

Access doesn't modify the original database when it encodes it. Rather, Access creates a copy of the database and encodes the copy. Just like when using the Security Wizard, you should make a backup copy of the original database and store it somewhere safe to prevent accidentally distributing the decoded database. Remember that in a world of rapidly changing data, your backup will rapidly become out of date.

FIGURE 29-26

Encoding an `.mdb` file requires you to save it with a new name.

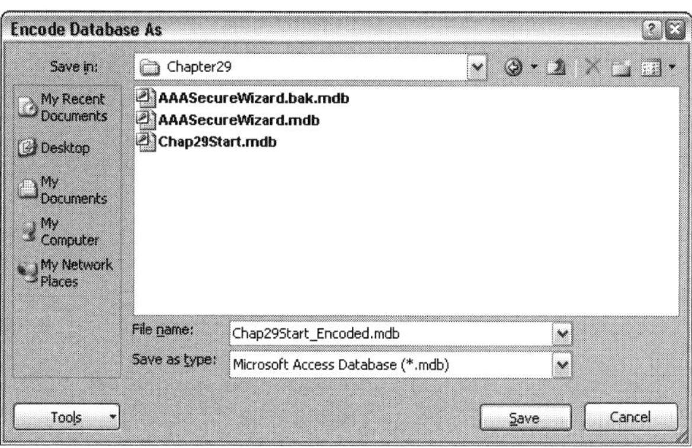

When encrypting a database, however, be aware of the following drawbacks:

- Encrypted/Encoded databases don't compress from their original size when used with compression programs, such as WinZip or sending it to a compressed (zipped) folder. Encryption modifies the way that the data is stored on the hard drive so compression utilities have little or no effect.
- Encrypted/Encoded databases suffer some performance degradation (up to 15 percent). Depending on the size of your database and the speed of your computer, this degradation may be imperceptible.

NOTE **Encoding is performed in addition to securing an `.mdb` database. A secure database is one that is secured using users, groups, and permissions. Simply encoding a database does nothing to secure the database for general Access users.**

Decrypting/Decoding a Database

You can decrypt a previously encrypted database. To decrypt an Access 2007 database (`.accdb`), simply follow these steps (which are similar to the encrypting process):

1. **Open an encrypted `.accdb` database (for example, `Chapter26.accdb`) exclusively.**
2. **Select the Remove Database Password and Encryption command from the Database Tools group on the Database Tools ribbon.**
3. **Type the database password in the Unset Database Password dialog box and click OK.**

To decode an .mdb file, follow these steps:

1. **Open an encoded .mdb database (for example, Chapter29_Encoded.mdb) exclusively.**
2. **Select the Encode/Decode Database command from the Database Tools group on the Database Tools ribbon.**
3. **Enter a new name for the decoded database (for example, Chapter29.mdb) in the Decode Database As dialog box and click Save.**

Protecting Visual Basic Code

Although setting user-level security enables you to restrict access to tables, forms, and reports in your database, it does not prevent access to the Visual Basic code stored in modules. You control access to the Visual Basic code in your application by creating a password for the Visual Basic project that you want to protect. When you set a database password for a project, users are prompted to enter the password each time they attempt to view the Visual Basic code in the database.

A Visual Basic project refers to the set of standard and class modules (the code behind forms and reports) that are part of your Access database.

1. **Open any standard module in the database. For this example, open the basSalesFunctions modules in Chapter29.mdb.**

   When you open the basSalesFunctions module, the Visual Basic Editor displays.
2. **In the Visual Basic Editor, select Tools ➪ Access Auto Auctions Properties.**

   The Access Auto Auctions — Project Properties dialog box displays.
3. **Select the Protection tab in the Project Properties dialog box. Check Lock project for viewing option.**
4. **In the Password field, type the password that you want to use to secure the project (see Figure 29-27). For this example, use the password** bible.

   Access does *not* display the password; rather, it shows an asterisk (*) for each letter.
5. **In the Confirm Password field, type the password again.**

   This security measure ensures that you don't mistype the password (because you can't see the characters that you type) and mistakenly prevent everyone, including you, from accessing the database.
6. **Click OK to save the password.**

FIGURE 29-27

Creating a project password restricts users from viewing the application's Visual Basic code.

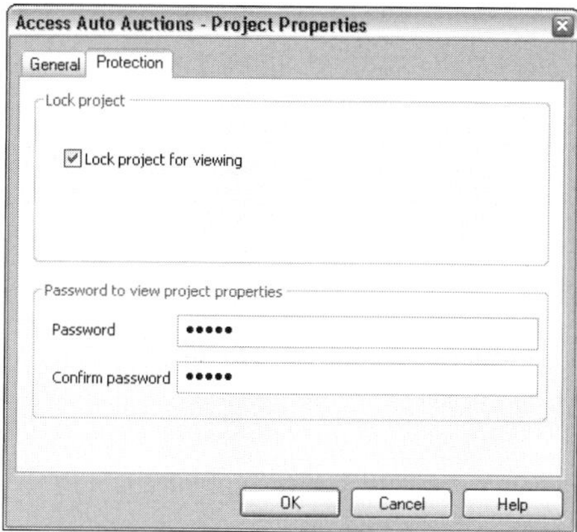

After you save and close the project, any user who attempts to view the application's Visual Basic code must enter the password. Access prompts for the project password only once per session.

A more secure method of securing your application's code, forms, and reports is to distribute your database as an `.accde` file. When you save your database as an `.accde` file, Access compiles all code modules (including form modules), removes all editable source code, and compacts the database. The new `.accde` file contains no source code but continues to work because it contains a compiled copy of all of your code. Not only is this a great way to secure your source code, it also enables you to distribute databases that are smaller (because they contain no source code) and always keep their modules in a compiled state.

See Chapter 26 to learn how to create an `.accde` file. You can also distribute older `.mdb` files as `.mde` files.

Preventing Virus Infections

Implementing a good user-level security scheme protects your database from unauthorized access to the information or objects in your database. User-level security does not, however, protect the physical database file from malicious macro virus attacks.

You probably have had experience at some point with a virus attack on your computer. Or most likely, you know someone who has. It goes without saying that it is imperative to install and run a virus scanning utility on your workstation. Even though you may be religious about keeping your virus scanner up to date, new viruses crop up all the time. Therefore, you have to be proactive about protecting your applications and sensitive data from exposure to these kinds of attacks.

When you run forms, reports, queries, macros, data access pages, and Visual Basic code in your application, Microsoft Office Access 2007 uses the *Trust Center* to determine which commands may be unsafe and which unsafe commands you wish to run. Unsafe commands could allow a malicious user to hack into your hard drive or other resource in your environment. A malicious user could possibly delete files from your hard drive, alter the computer's configuration, or generally create all kinds of havoc in your workstation or even throughout your network environment.

Access 2007 checks its list of unsafe commands. When Access encounters one of the unsafe commands, it can block the command from execution. By default, Access 2007 blocks unsafe commands. To tell Access to block these potentially unsafe commands, you must enable *sandbox mode*.

Enabling sandbox mode

Sandbox mode allows Access to block any of the commands in the unsafe list it encounters when running forms, reports, queries, macros, data access pages, and Visual Basic code. To enable sandbox mode, follow these steps:

1. **Open Access and click the Microsoft Office Button; then click Access Options.**
2. **Select Trust Settings in the left pane; then click Trust Center Settings.**
3. **Select Macro Settings in the left pane; then select either the Disable all macros without notification or Disable all macros with notification options (shown in Figure 29-28).**

FIGURE 29-28

Enabling sandbox mode

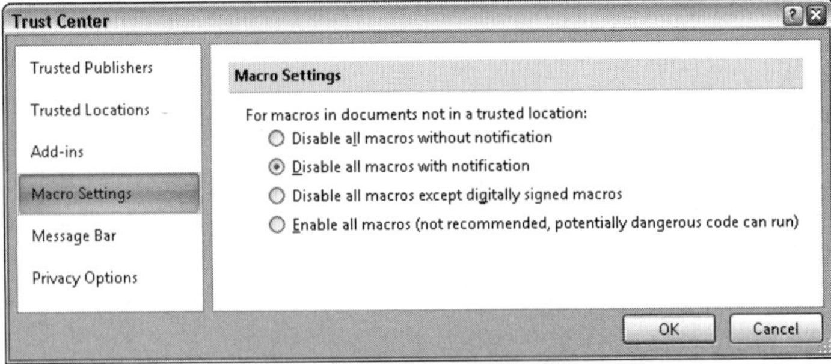

4. **Restart Access to apply the security change.**

Macro Settings provides four levels of macro security:

- **Disable all macros without notification:** All macros are disabled and the user isn't prompted to enable them.
- **Disable all macros with notification:** All macros are disabled and the user is prompted to enable them.
- **Disable all macros except digitally signed macros:** The status of the macro's digital signature is validated for digitally signed macros. For unsigned macros, a prompt displays advising the user to enable the macro or to cancel opening the database.
- **Enable all macros (not recommended, potentially dangerous code can be run):** Macros are not checked for digital signatures and no warning displays for unsigned macros.

A digital signature is an encrypted secure file that accompanies a macro or document. It confirms that the author is a trusted source for the macro or document. A digital signature is contained in a digital certificate. You, or your organization's IT department, can obtain a digital certificate through a commercial certification authority, like VeriSign, Inc. Search `www.msdn.com` for "Microsoft Root Certificate Program Members" to obtain information on how to obtain a digital certificate.

If you are sure of the integrity of your database, you can select the Enable all macros security setting. Digital signatures are generally implemented within large organizations that are willing to fund the added expense of purchasing and keeping digital signatures up to date. For most applications, however, you will probably use the Enable all macros setting.

If you or your organization has acquired a digital certificate, you can use it to digitally sign your Access project. To digitally sign your Access project, follow these steps:

1. **Open the Access database to digitally sign; then open any module to display the Visual Basic Editor.**
2. **Select Tools ➪ Digital Signature from the Visual Basic Editor menu.**

   The Digital Signature dialog box displays, as shown in Figure 29-29.

FIGURE 29-29

Digitally signing an Access project

3. Click Choose to display the Select Certificate dialog box, as shown in Figure 29-30.

FIGURE 29-30

Choosing a digital certificate

4. Select the certificate to add to the Access project. Then click OK to close the Select Certificate dialog box.
5. Click OK to close the Digital Signature dialog box and save the security setting.

NOTE Do not sign your Access project until the application has been thoroughly tested and you do not expect to make any further changes to it. Modifying any of the code in the project invalidates the digital signature.

TIP To prevent users from making unauthorized changes to the code in your project, be sure to lock the project and apply a project password.

The Trust Center

The *Trust Center* is where you can find security and privacy settings for Access 2007. The Trust Center replaces the Security dialog box in previous versions of Access. To display the trust center, click the Microsoft Office Button, click Access Options, click Trust Center; then click Trust Center Settings. The following describes each section and what it controls:

- **Trusted Publishers**: Displays a list of trusted publishers — publishers where you clicked Trust all documents from this publisher when encountering a potentially unsafe macro — for Microsoft Office. To remove a publisher from this list, select the publisher; then click Remove. Trusted publishers must have a valid digital signature that hasn't expired.
- **Trusted Locations**: Displays the list of trusted locations on your computer or network. From this section, you can add, remove, or modify folders on your computer that will always contain trusted files. Any file in a trusted location can be opened without being checked by the Trust Center. You can also choose not to allow network locations and to disable all Trusted Locations and accept signed files.

- **Add-ins**: Lets you to set up how Access handles add-ins. You can choose whether add-ins need to be digitally signed from a trusted source and whether to display a notification for unsigned add-ins. You can also choose to disable all add-ins, which may impair functionality.
- **Macro Settings**: Lets you set the security setting for macros not in a trusted location. For more information on Macro Settings, see the previous section on sandbox mode.
- **Message Bar**: Lets you set whether to display the message bar that warns you about blocked content, or to never show information about blocked content.
- **Privacy Options**: Lets you choose how Microsoft Office Online communicates with your computer. You can set options to use Microsoft Office Online for help, show featured links at startup, download files to determine system problems, and sign up for the Customer Experience Improvement Program.

Summary

In this chapter, you learned about securing both `.accdb` and `.mdb` files. You learned how to set a database password and encrypt (or encode) these files. You learned how to run a database application in runtime mode and how to distribute the database as an `.accde` (or `.mde`) file. You learned how to create users and groups and how to set permissions for the different database objects in `.mdb` files. User-level security has been removed from the Access 2007 file format.

You also learned about the new Trust Center, which replaces the Security dialog box in previous versions of Access. You learned which settings enable sandbox mode and where to set up trusted publishers and locations, how to manage add-ins and other items that may contain malicious code. When securing a database — in any database version — the Trust Center gives you more flexibility.

Chapter 30

Using the Windows API

Access and Visual Basic for Applications (VBA) help you develop powerful applications. Using the Windows application program interface (API), you can take full advantage of the Windows graphical user interface (GUI) to create your own windows (forms), dialog boxes (message boxes), list boxes, combo boxes, command buttons, and so on. These objects make your application a *Windows* application. And that's what this chapter is all about.

Although this chapter concentrates on the API included with Windows, the concepts are applicable to other APIs as well, such as the Open Database Connectivity (ODBC) API, the Messaging Application Programming Interface (MAPI), and the Telephony Application Programming Interface (TAPI).

IN THIS CHAPTER

- **Understanding what the Windows API is**
- **Learning when you'll use the Windows API**
- **Looking at API documentation sources**
- **Knowing the data types used in API calls**
- **Writing API function declarations**
- **Writing API wrapper procedures**
- **Identifying useful API functions for Access developers**

What Is the Windows API?

The Windows API is a set of built-in code libraries extending the Windows interface. Access makes these code libraries available to you and simplifies their use. The API libraries include functions that allow you to create windows, check systems resources, work with communications ports, send messages to applications, control `.ini` files, and access the Registry, among other things.

These functions hook directly into the internal workings of Windows. Although Access and VBA let you reach a great many of these hooks transparently, there are still some you can't get to without writing your application in the C programming language or referencing the Windows API directly. Access and VBA give you everything you need to tap into this collection of hundreds of functions. You only need to know how they work and what to look for.

The API functions are written in libraries that can be dynamically linked to Windows applications. Typically, they are contained in dynamic link libraries (DLLs, or `.dll` files), but they can also be in `.exe`, `.drv`, and `.ocx` files.

Dynamic linking

Dynamic linking is a method of making functions available to your applications without hard-coding them into the executable. In many compiled languages, the code referenced by an application during development is included in the final product when the executable (`.exe`) is produced. Binding a library into an application's executable file is called *static linking* (another common term is *early binding*, because the libraries are bound into the executable early in the executable's life). Static linking makes for tightly integrated code, but it can also be difficult to manage. The same type of function may be included in several applications, which can take up space on your user's hard drive. In addition, if you need to update or enhance your application, you have to replace the entire `.exe`, making those enhancements more difficult to execute.

Dynamic linking, on the other hand, allows you to store a library of code in one place (a dynamically linked library) and reference functions from that library only when they're needed at runtime (dynamic linking is sometimes called *late binding*, because the library routines are bound to the executable "late" in the executable's life).

Using DLLs has several advantages:

- **It keeps unneeded code out of memory.** When calling a function from a dynamic link library, the code takes up memory only when it is being used. Afterward, the memory is reclaimed when the called function is unloaded.
- **As a developer, you may create a host of applications.** Rather than include the same code in each application, you can include only one copy of the DLL, and call the functions from all your applications. This gives your applications a smaller footprint.
- **It allows you to update or enhance just the DLL, without replacing all the applications that use its code.**

As you'll see in the "How to Use the Windows API" section, later in this chapter, calling functions stored in the Windows DLLs involves following certain rules. Generally speaking you must declare a Windows API call before using it in your code, and most API functions are rather fussy about the parameters used in the VBA statements calling them. But overall, the benefits to be gained from using the API functions greatly outweigh the relatively short learning curve necessary to master them.

Why Use the Windows API?

There are many reasons why you should consider using the Windows API (and other application programming interfaces). Here are a few, in addition to the ones listed in the preceding section.

Common codebase

Microsoft has done a lot for programmers. In establishing the Windows API, Microsoft has made a common library of code available to your Access and Visual Basic applications. You can count on the fact that if Windows is installed, the Windows API and its 500-plus functions are available. You don't have to distribute or check for these code modules because they exist on every Windows machine. You also know that any time Microsoft adds functionality to one of its DLLs, that functionality is available to all your applications.

Tested and proven code

If you develop applications professionally, then you know that time is everything. Getting your application to market before a competitor or getting an application up and running in your own installation can give your company the competitive edge. Every module of code you or your programmers produce takes time to develop and time to test. The functions included in the API libraries are already tested and proven. They exist on hundreds of thousands, even millions, of machines all over the world.

A good example is the `GetPrivateProfileString` function. This function retrieves an entry from an application's `.ini` file. Yes, Access VBA has tremendous string manipulation and file I/O capabilities, but why waste time writing and testing a function to do what `GetPrivateProfileString` already does? Let the API take some of the burden off of your programming staff and allow them to concentrate on more important business issues. As you'll see in the "GetPrivateProfileStringA" section, later in this chapter, `GetPrivateProfileString` is easy to use — much easier than writing an equivalent function in Access VBA.

Cross-platform compatibility

Microsoft's strategy for the future of its operating systems includes the convergence of its code base. All editions of Microsoft Windows use the Win32 API, which makes the applications you write for one platform portable to others. Almost all Win32 API declarations are available across all platforms, which gives you an extended user base and keeps you from rewriting much of your code to fit each kind of installation.

Smaller application footprint

Making use of the dynamic link libraries included with Windows keeps you from distributing the same code within your applications. This, in turn, keeps the size of your applications smaller. Users appreciate the consideration you put into helping them manage their hardware resources.

DLL Documentation

Most DLLs are composed of C functions. Windows ships with a fairly large number of DLLs, and most application vendors distribute their own DLLs with their applications. Microsoft has documented its core DLLs so that developers can experience the advantages listed earlier in this chapter. Of course, this strategy has benefited Microsoft as well. By making it easier for programmers to write applications for Windows, Microsoft has made Windows the most popular development platform.

Not every vendor documents its DLLs, however. Many consider the DLLs distributed with their applications as proprietary property and do not make the interfaces for those applications available to the public. If a vendor does not formally release documentation for its libraries, it is usually not good practice to use them, even if some outside documentation exists. A vendor could remove or change functions within a library without notification, making any applications you have based on them unreliable at best, unusable at worst.

Where to find documentation

Microsoft has released Software Development Kits (SDKs) for many of its products, including ODBC, MAPI, and of course Win32. These kits contain not only general product information but also documentation for the core DLLs included in the products. They comprise a wealth of resources, documenting each function, argument, return value, data type, and so on. You can purchase them directly from Microsoft, or if you're a Microsoft Developer Network Member, you can get them with the MSDN library, where they're included.

Deciphering the documentation

The good news is, Microsoft releases documentation of its APIs. The bad news is, the Windows API documentation is pretty cryptic and designed primarily to be used by C and C++ programmers. Most of Microsoft's high-level product documentation assumes you're already an experienced developer. The "official" API documentation from Microsoft is not for the faint of heart, but hopefully the following hints will help you understand what you find. The end of this chapter will also document several useful functions and give you examples of how they're used.

Data types

The hardest part of understanding API documentation is deciphering data types. Many books, articles, and the Microsoft documentation have standards for referring to data types. When you know what kind of data type is being referred to, and how that type translates to Access, the battle is mostly over.

C contains several data types, most of which have Access VBA equivalents, and some of which do not. Occasionally, the arguments included with API functions are structures composed of several different data types. Table 30-1 shows each C data type, its size, and its Access VBA equivalent.

TABLE 30-1

Comparing C and VBA Data Types

C Type	Size	VBA Data Type
char	8 bits	String * 1
short	16 bits	Integer
int	32 bits	Long
long	32 bits	Long
float	32 bits	Single
double	64 bits	Double
UINT	32 bits	Long
ULONG	32 bits	Long
USHORT	16 bits	Integer
UCHAR	8 bits	String * 1
DWORD	32 bits	Long
BOOL	32 bits	Boolean
BYTE	8 bits	Byte
WORD	16 bits	Integer
HANDLE	32 bits	Long
LPTSTR	32 bits	No equivalent
LPCTSTR	32 bits	No equivalent

These all become important when examining both the SDKs and other API references for Visual Basic. You'll have to know what kind of data type the function is expecting, and match it with a compatible type in your Access applications. Listing 30-1 shows how the `GetPrivateProfileString` function is declared in the API reference of the Win32 SDK and how to decipher each argument declared.

LISTING 30-1

SDK Reference for GetPrivateProfileString

```
DWORD GetPrivateProfileString(
  LPCTSTR  lpszSection,       // points to section name
  LPCTSTR  lpszKey,           // points to key name
  LPCTSTR  lpszDefault,       // points to default string
```

continued

LISTING 30-1 *(continued)*

```
  LPTSTR   lpszReturnBuffer, // points to destination buffer
  DWORD    cchReturnBuffer,  // size of destination buffer
  LPCTSTR  lpszFile          // initialization file name
);
```

Listing 30-2 shows the same declaration using Basic syntax instead of C syntax. Notice how the C data types are converted to their VBA equivalents.

LISTING 30-2

Visual Basic Declaration for GetPrivateProfileString

```
Declare Function GetPrivateProfileStringA lib "Kernel32"( _
    ByVal lpszSection as string, ByVal lpszKey as string, _
    ByVal lpszDefault as string, _
    ByVal dwReturnBuffer as long, _
    ByVal cchReturnBuffer as long, _
    ByVal lpszFile as string) as long
```

CAUTION **You must declare the correct data types in your applications. Failure to do so can result in the dreaded General Protection Fault. If you don't declare variables of the proper size, your function calls might try to overwrite memory locations allocated by other applications. Using inappropriate data types as parameters to API functions is the most common cause of problems when using the Windows API.**

In the previous example, notice the prefix attached to each argument passed to the functions. These are standard prefixes used throughout most of the API documentation you'll find. Some of the more common prefixes are shown in Table 30-2.

TABLE 30-2

Common Windows API Argument Prefixes

Prefix	C Data Type	VBA Data Type
lpsz	Long pointer to a null terminated string	String
dw	DWORD	Long
w	WORD	Integer
hwnd	HANDLE	Long
b	BOOL	Long
l	LONG	Long

Sometimes you'll encounter situations where a function uses a data type you aren't familiar with or may not have even heard of. Most likely, the parameter being passed is a *data structure,* which is a fancy term for "user-defined data type." If that term sounds familiar, then you're probably thinking about the Access VBA `Type` statement. Data structures are usually a collection of fields allocated contiguously (next to each other in memory). The `Type` statement in Access VBA is compatible with its `Struct` counterpart from C, as long as the fields declared within the structure are compatible. Listing 30-3 shows the data structure passed in the `GetVersionEx` API and its Access VBA equivalent.

LISTING 30-3

OSVERSIONINFO Structure

```
'C-type OSVERSIONINFO structure syntax
typedef struct _OSVERSIONINFO{
    DWORD dwOSVersionInfoSize;
    DWORD dwMajorVersion;
    DWORD dwMinorVersion;
    DWORD dwBuildNumber;
    DWORD dwPlatformId;
    TCHAR szCSDVersion[ 128 ];
} OSVERSIONINFO;

'VBA-typedef for OSVERSIONINFO
Private Type OSVERSIONINFO
    dwVersionInfo As Long
    dwMajorVersion As Long
    dwMinorVersion As Long
    dwBuildNumber As Long
    dwplatformID As Long
    szVersion As String * 128
End Type
```

What you can't do with the API

We hesitate to place anything in this paragraph, because as soon as we do, someone will find a way to prove us wrong. Programmers are an inventive bunch. But there are a few things that are difficult to do when converting APIs to VBA. One is converting APIs that make use of a `Callback` function. Sometimes APIs make calls to other functions that process messages and then return values back to the calling API. To do this, you must be able to pass the address of the entry point of the function. Access does not provide a way to handle this situation. However, some people have developed their own DLLs that specifically handle these types of situations. Never say never.

How to Use the Windows API

If you've made it this far, congratulations! The concept of APIs can be a little intimidating. Once you understand the concepts, however, using them is as easy as calling any other function or subroutine from Access VBA.

The Declare statement

In order to use an API in your Access application, you must first tell Access the name of the API function and where to find it. You do this within the declarations section of a module using the `Declare` statement. The `Declare` keyword notifies VBA that what follows is not part of VBA but exists outside of the current application. A prototype `Declare` statement is shown here. The `Declare` statement has several parts, all of which are discussed in the following sections.

```
Declare [Function|Sub] FunctionName Lib "LibraryName" _
    Alias "AliasName" (ArgumentList) As DataType
```

The declaration statement is sometimes referred to as an API *function prototype* because it serves as the *prototype* for all calls to the API function.

Function or Sub

APIs can be in the form of a function or a subroutine, just like Access VBA procedures. A function returns a value back to the calling code; a subroutine does not. When an API function returns a value, good programming practices require the calling procedure to check the return value to verify that the function completed as expected. The vast majority of Windows API calls are functions, so you rarely have to deal with the distinction between functions and subs.

Function name

The function name you specify can be one of two things:

- **The actual name of the API function you will be using as declared in the library:** For instance, if you were going to use `GetPrivateProfileString`, listed previously, you would declare `FunctionName` as `GetPrivateProfileStringA`.
- **The name of the function as you would like to use it within your code**

TIP **`GetPrivateProfileStringA` is a long function name, especially if you're going to be using the function frequently within your code. You might want to shorten its name to `GetString` instead. You can do this by using the `Alias` parameter discussed in the "Alias 'AliasName'" section, later in this chapter.**

Lib "LibraryName"

The library name is simply the name of the DLL that contains the API function or subroutine that you're declaring. This parameter tells Access where to find the function. If the DLL is not one of the standard Win32 DLLs, or it has been moved to another location, then you'll have to specify the complete path of the DLL. The `LibraryName` parameter must be enclosed in quotations, but it is not case-sensitive.

Most Windows DLLs are located in the System32 folder within the main Windows folder (usually `C:\Windows` or `C:\WINNT`). The VBA interpreter first looks for the DLL in the System32 folder, then in the Windows folder. In the rare event that you're using a DLL located anywhere else on your computer, you should specify the path to the DLL as part of the `LibraryName` clause in the API function's declare statement.

Alias "AliasName"

If you wanted to call an API function by another name in your Access VBA program, you could. In such a case, the `FunctionName` parameter would be the new name you assigned to the function. However, you still have to tell Access the real name of the function as it exists within the library. The `GetPrivateProfileString` example has been used several times in this chapter. In the following examples, each of the `Declare` prototypes has been prefixed with `api` to indicate that it is an API function call, and not the usual VBA function name.

Here is an example of using a prefix naming convention for API function prototypes:

```
Declare Function apiGetPrivateProfileString _
    lib "Kernel32" Alias "GetPrivateProfileStringA"
```

In some situations, you must use an alias within your Access VBA modules. Occasionally, you'll encounter API functions that begin with an underscore, such as `_lopen` or `_lread`. Access VBA procedures cannot begin with an underscore, so these functions must be aliased. Another reason to alias your function names is to avoid the possibility of declaring a function using a name that already exists in your Access application or in its libraries. If you try to declare a function with a name that already exists, you'll receive an error: `Ambiguous Name Detected: FunctionName.`

TIP **Like library names, the alias reference (`GetPrivateProfileStringA`, in this example) must always be enclosed in quotations. The alias reference is *always* case-sensitive and must be spelled *exactly* like the function name it references in the DLL.**

ArgumentList

The `ArgumentList` is composed of the elements that the function expects to receive from you in order to do its job. When you declare a function, you must declare the same number of arguments in the function declaration that its documentation specifies. If you don't, you'll receive a runtime error 49: `Bad DLL calling convention.` The same error will occur if you pass an API function arguments that are incompatible with what it is expecting. That's a best-case scenario — you could end up with a General Protection Fault that crashes the application, crashes Access, and may even crash Windows.

It's important to realize that the arguments in the argument list are only placeholders. It doesn't matter what you name them, although most developers assign them the same name that the SDK documentation does. The argument list simply tells Access what to expect when the function is called, so that it can type-check and argument-check. In other words, it's for your own good. Access does not, however, check the type declarations against the actual library, so it's up to you to assign the correct data types to your arguments.

ByVal or ByRef?

When you assign arguments to a declaration statement, you must decide how the API expects to receive the arguments. By default, when Access passes an argument it does so by reference, or `ByRef`. This means that Access passes the memory *address* of the variable to the function it is calling. When a function receives the address of an argument, it can change the value stored at that address, which may or may not be desirable. When you pass an argument by value, or `ByVal`, you're telling Access to pass only the *value* of what's in the variable to the function. When a function receives only the value of an argument, it can use only that value to do its job. Passing an argument by value is usually desirable because it ensures that the variables used in your application keep a stable value.

Here is an example of using the `ByVal` keyword.

```
Declare Function apiGetTempPath Lib "Kernel32" _
    Alias "GetTempPathA" (ByVal BufferSize As Long, _
    ByVal lpszReturnBuffer As String) As Long
```

There is always an exception to the rule, and the exception in this case is string variables. Access VBA and C handle strings differently. C expects to receive pointers to strings that are terminated with a null value; Access VBA does not. In order to format a string in the method expected by most API functions, you must pass the string by value (`ByVal`). As we said earlier, passing an argument by value passes the data stored in the variable instead of the memory address — except when you pass strings. When you pass a string using the `ByVal` option, you pass the address of the variable, which means the function can change the value passed to it by manipulating what's stored at the memory address.

In the case of API calls, it's a good thing that strings are always passed with the ByVal qualifier. An API function can't return a string value, so you must give the function permission to alter a memory location in order to retrieve a string value from an API. You do this by specifying that the argument is to be passed by value. Notice that `lpszReturnBuffer` is a pointer to a string that `GetTempPath` uses to place the path that Windows uses for temp files. It is being passed as an address. `BufferSize`, on the other hand, is only passing the value of a variable that contains the length of the string being passed in `lpszReturnBuffer`.

A final note on passing strings: many API functions expect to receive addresses to string values. Most of the time, these functions expect a minimum number of bytes to be allocated for the string value. In order to fulfill these requirements, you must know in advance how many bytes the function expects the string to be, and you must expand your string variables to that length before passing the string. You can do this using the `String$()` function in Access VBA. The `String` function fills a string variable with a fixed number of characters. In the following example, the `strMyString` variable is filled with 20 spaces:

```
Dim strMyString As String
strMyString = String$(20," ")
```

The preceding code fills the fixed-width string variable `strMyString` with 20 spaces. You can achieve the same result by declaring the string with the number of characters already allocated:

```
Dim strMyString * 20
```

If you do not allocate enough space for an API function to write a string, it could end up writing over another application's data, causing a General Protection Fault (GPF). It's very difficult to know how many characters an API will accept, so a safe way to declare your string variables is to allocate 255 characters to them. Most functions will not pass a string any larger than 255 characters. It is, however, inefficient to always pass 255 characters because you're probably using more memory than necessary. If you can, try to find the exact string length that your function expects.

As DataType

Any API call that is a function returns a value. A subroutine does not. Therefore, a subroutine does not need a return value data type specified. The value returned by a function is usually a value you expect to use in your application, or it is an error number. For instance, many functions return zero, or `ERROR_SUCCESS` if the function completes successfully. If the value returned is a non-zero value (indicating that the API call failed to execute properly), you should provide an error-handling routine to deal with the function's failure.

Other functions, such as `GetPrivateProfileString`, return a numeric value indicating the number of characters copied into a string buffer. Therefore, if `GetPrivateProfileString` completes successfully, you use its return value and the `Left$()` function to extract the returned string from a string buffer:

```
StringVar = Left$(StringBuffer, ReturnValue)
```

If the value returned by `GetProfileString` is `0`, of course, it means that no string was found in the `.ini` file.

The data type specified for the return value must be compatible with the data type specified in the API function's documentation.

Using wrapper functions

You rarely directly program API functions. As you'll soon see, API calls frequently require complicated arguments, and the values returned by API functions most often require interpretation before they can be used.

Most developers use wrapper functions to resolve these issues. Generally speaking, a *wrapper function* is a simple VBA function that provides the API call with all the parameters it needs, as well as converting the values returned by the API function to information that an application can use. Your VBA code calls the wrapper function, which, in turn, calls the API function. The wrapper function returns the transformed value provided by the API function.

The sections under the "API Examples" heading provide typical wrapper functions for the API calls documented in this chapter. All that's needed to utilize an API call is to include the API function's `Declare` statement, as well as the VBA wrapper function accompanying the API declaration. Then call the VBA wrapper function as you would any function such as `Format()` or `Now()`. VBA wrappers protect your application from the sometimes-ugly and tedious code needed to properly process API calls.

What is this "hwnd" thing?

You'll notice that many Windows API functions use a parameter named `hwnd`. `Hwnd` is a long integer value that Windows uses to keep track of graphical objects on the computer's screen. Every object on the screen (windows, buttons, text boxes, and so on) has an `hwnd` value, and many API calls require this value before they can operate on the object.

Microsoft has made the `hwnd` very easy to get for most Access objects. Many Access objects include `hwnd` among their properties. You won't see `hwnd` in the property window, but it's there just the same. Use `Me.hwnd` to pass the `hwnd` of an Access form, or `MyControl.hwnd` (example: `txtLastName.hwnd`) to pass the `hwnd` of a control to an API call requiring this important value.

API Examples

Here comes the fun part. At the beginning of the chapter, we reviewed several different uses for the Windows API. From here to the end of the chapter, you'll see some examples of different types of APIs, how to declare them, what you would use them for, error messages you may encounter, and so on.

ON the CD-ROM **All the examples are included on the companion CD-ROM in the `Chapter30.accdb` example database. The code examples in `Chapter30.accdb` are contained in a module named `basAPIFunctions`. This module contains all the raw declarations and working functions you see described in this chapter.**

The System Info dialog box (shown in Figure 30-1) that you open from the Access About box contains useful information. The code in `basAPIFunctions` can be used to construct a form similar to the API Demo form (`frmAPIDemo`) included in the `Chapter30.accdb` example database (see Figure 30-2).

CAUTION **Whenever you're working with API functions you should save your work frequently. Because you're working deep within the Windows system, application errors can occur, especially when you're first learning how to make these calls.**

FIGURE 30-1

The System Info form

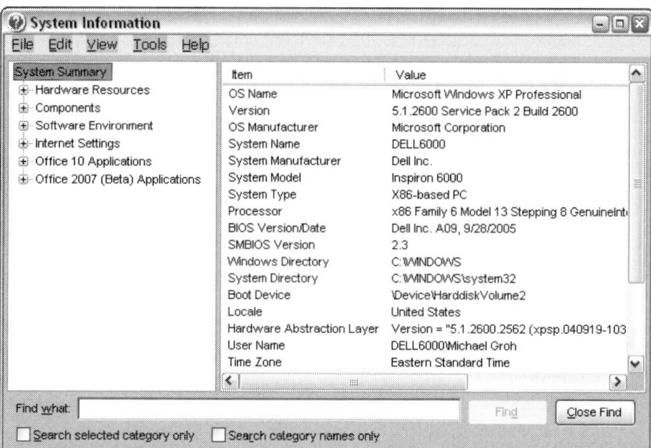

FIGURE 30-2

The API Demo form from `Chapter30.accdb` on the Companion CD-ROM

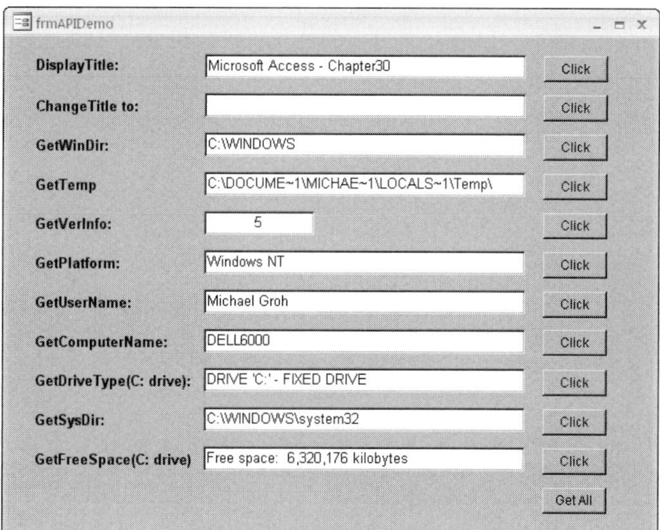

Retrieving system information

The Windows API provides a number of functions you'll find useful for retrieving information about the Windows system, the hardware, and other software that may be running on the computer. This information is often useful for avoiding problems like running out of disk space or trying to write data to a CD-ROM drive. These functions also provide handy information, like the location of the Windows and temporary directories.

GetCommandLineA

`GetCommandLine` returns the command line used to start up the current application. This may be useful if you need to know whether the shortcut used to start an Access application included references to a macro or VBA procedure:

```
Declare Function apiGetCommandLine _
    Lib "Kernel32" _
    Alias "GetCommandLineA" () As String
```

When run from the immediate window in Access VBA, the function returns the full path, including the executable name, for Microsoft Access. The command line is returned in quotation marks.

The following function provides a wrapper around `GetCommandLineA`:

```
Function GetCommandLine() As String
    Dim ReturnVal As String
    ReturnVal = apiGetCommandLine()
    GetCommandLine = Trim$(ReturnVal)
End Function
```

Although not entirely necessary, the `GetCommandLine` wrapper trims leading and trailing spaces from the string returned by the `apiGetCommandLine` declaration. Very often API functions return strings that are padded with extra characters, and the extra characters should be trimmed off of the wrapper's return value.

In `Chapter30.accdb`, `GetCommandLine` is used to retrieve the path for Access. The path is then used when `.ini` files are created and read with other API calls. An application-specific `.ini` file should be stored in the same directory as its application.

GetWindowsDirectoryA

`GetWindowsDirectory` retrieves the path to Windows and stores it in a string buffer.

```
Declare Function apiGetWindowsDirectory _
    Lib "Kernel32" _
    Alias "GetWindowsDirectoryA"( _
    ByVal lpszReturnBuffer As String, _
    ByVal lpszBuffSize As Long) As Long
```

The return value is the length of the string copied into the buffer. If the buffer isn't long enough, the return value is the length required. But if the function fails, the return value is zero.

Here is a function wrapper that uses the `GetWindowsDirectoryA` API function:

```
Function GetWindowsDirectory() As String
    Dim WinDir As String * 255
    Dim WinDirSize As Long
    Dim ErrNumber As Long

    WinDirSize = Len(WinDir)
    ErrNumber = apiGetWindowsDirectory(WinDir, WinDirSize)
    If ErrNumber > 0 Then
      GetWindowsDirectory = Left$(WinDir, ErrNumber)
    Else
      GetWindowsDirectory = vbNullString
    End If
End Function
```

In the `GetWindowsDirectory` wrapper, notice that the API function's return value (`ErrNumber`) is used as an argument to the `Left$` function to extract the Windows folder name from the WinDir string. If `ErrNumber` is zero, and empty string (`vbNullString`) is returned instead.

GetTempPathA

The `GetTempPathA` function retrieves the path to the directory where temp files are stored and places it in a string buffer.

```
Declare Function apiGetTempPath _
   Lib "Kernel32" _
   Alias "GetTempPathA"( _
   ByVal BufferSize As Long, _
   ByVal lpszReturnBuffer As String) As Long
```

The return value is the length of the returned string. Like `GetWindowsDirectory`, if the buffer isn't long enough, the return value is the length required. But if the function fails, the return value is zero.

The wrapper function for `GetTempPathA` properly interprets the return values when the API function is called:

```
Function GetTempDir() As String
    Dim Buffer As String * 255
    Dim BufferSize As Long
    Dim ErrNumber As Long

    BufferSize = Len(Buffer)
    ErrNumber = apiGetTempPath(BufferSize, Buffer)
    If ErrNumber > 0 Then
```

```
        GetTempDir = Left$(Buffer, ErrNumber)
      Else
        GetTempDir = vbNullString
      End If
    End Function
```

GetVersionExA

GetVersionEx returns the version number of the Windows installation on the user's computer.

```
    Declare Function apiGetVersion _
        Lib "Kernel32" _
        Alias "GetVersionExA"( _
        ByRef osVer As OSVERSIONINFO) As Long
```

Notice that the GetVersionExA API function uses a data structure named OSVERSIONINFO as one of its arguments. Notice that OSVERSIONINFO is passed by reference, which means that the API function changes the contents of the data structure. GetVersionExA returns much of its data by setting the members of OSVERSIONINFO to the values returned by Windows. Here is the definition of OSVERSIONINFO:

```
    Private Type OSVERSIONINFO
        dwVersionInfo As Long
        dwMajorVersion As Long
        dwMinorVersion As Long
        dwBuildNumber As Long
        dwplatformID As Long
        szVersion As String * 128
    End Type
```

The OSVERSIONINFO can be interpreted like this: dwVersionInfo is the length, in bytes, of the data structure. dwMajorVersion would be 5 for Windows 2000 or XP, and 6 for Windows Vista. The build number is a value that is mostly used by Microsoft internally.

dwPlatformID is a long integer representing the platform the application is running on. Windows 2000 and XP are both 2, while Windows Me, 98, and 95 are 1. The dwPlatformID constants are declared as follows:

```
    Const VER_PLATFORM_WIN32S = 0
    Const VER_PLATFORM_WIN32_Windows = 1
    Const VER_PLATFORM_WIN32_NT = 2
```

Chapter30.accdb on the CD-ROM uses the GetVersionEx function to display the current version of Windows in the system information using the following two functions. One retrieves the platform number; the other, the major and minor versions:

```
    Function GetVersion() As Long
        Dim RetVal As Long
        Dim VersionNo As OSVERSIONINFO
```

```
        Dim lngVer As Long
        Dim Version As String

        VersionNo.dwVersionInfo = 148
        RetVal = apiGetVersion(VersionNo)
        Version = VersionNo.dwMajorVersion & "." _
            & VersionNo.dwMinorVersion
        lngVer = CLng(Version)
        GetVersion= lngVer
    End Function
```

The `GetPlatform` wrapper function calls the same API declaration, but uses the values returned in `OSVERSIONINFO` to compose a string indicating the Windows version installed on the computer:

```
    Function GetPlatform()
        Dim RetVal As Long
        Dim VersionNo As OSVERSIONINFO
        Dim Platform As String

        VersionNo.dwVersionInfo = 148
        RetVal = apiGetVersion(VersionNo)
        Select Case VersionNo.dwPlatformID
            Case VER_PLATFORM_WIN32S
                Platform = "Windows 3.x"
            Case VER_PLATFORM_WIN32_Windows
                Platform = "Windows 98 or Lower"
            Case VER_PLATFORM_WIN32_NT
                Platform = "Windows NT or Higher"
            Case Else
                Platform = "Unknown"
        End Select
        GetPlatform = Platform
    End Function
```

GetUserNameA

The `GetUserNameA` function retrieves the name of the user currently logged on to the system and places it in a string buffer:

```
    Declare Function apiGetUserName _
        Lib "Advapi32" _
        Alias "GetUserNameA"( _
        ByVal Buffer As String, _
        BufferSize As Long) As Long
```

If the function is successful, it returns a `TRUE` value, and the length of the returned string is placed in the `BufferSize` variable.

The user name returned by the `GetUserName` API function has nothing to do with the user logged into Access — Windows does not know anything about the Access users or groups and does not monitor who's logged into a database. The following wrapper function tells you exactly who logged into the computer:

```
Function GetUserName() As String
    Dim UserName As String * 255
    Dim NameSize As Long
    Dim ErrNumber As Long

    NameSize = Len(UserName)
    ErrNumber = apiGetUserName(UserName, NameSize)
    GetUserName = Left$(UserName, NameSize - 1)
End Function
```

GetComputerNameA

The `GetComputerNameA` function is very similar to `GetUserNameA`. It returns the network name of the local computer:

```
Declare Function apiGetComputerName _
    Lib "Kernel32" _
    Alias "GetComputerNameA" ( _
    ByVal Buffer As String, _
    BufferSize As Long) As Long
```

`GetComputerNameA` retrieves the name of the current computer system. If the function fails, its return value is zero; otherwise the return value is 1, and the `BufferSize` argument returns the number of characters copied to its string variable. The `GetComputerName` function is a wrapper for the `GetComputerNameA`, declaration and returns a string containing the name of the computer:

```
Function GetComputerName() As String
    Dim ComputerName As String * 255
    Dim NameSize As Long
    Dim ErrNumber As Long

    NameSize = Len(ComputerName)
    ErrNumber = _
        apiGetComputerName(ComputerName, NameSize)
    If ErrNumber = True Then
      GetComputerName = Left$(ComputerName, NameSize)
    Else
      GetComputerName = vbNullString
    End IF
End Function
```

GetDriveTypeA

From time to time, you may need to know what types of drives are installed on a user's computer. You wouldn't want to, for instance, try writing to an optical drive on the user's computer unless you knew it was capable of read/write operations. The `GetDriveTypeA` API function returns a value indicating the type of drive specified by the `lpszPath` parameter:

```
Declare Function apiGetDriveType Lib "Kernel32" _
    Alias "GetDriveTypeA"( _
    ByVal lpszPath As String) As Long
```

You pass the function the path to the drive you want to test, and `GetDriveType` returns a long integer value representing the drive type. The following constants can be used to determine the drive type:

```
Const DRIVE_UNKNOWN = 0
Const DRIVE_NOT_AVAILABLE = 1
Const DRIVE_REMOVABLE = 2
Const DRIVE_FIXED = 3
Const DRIVE_REMOTE = 4
Const DRIVE_CDROM = 5
Const DRIVE_RAMDISK = 6
```

Read/write optical drives (such as a CD-RW or DVD-RW drive) and USB "thumb drives" are reported as `DRIVE_REMOVABLE`.

The following function cycles through each drive possibility and prints its type in the debug window using the constants listed above and GetDriveType:

```
Sub GetAllDriveTypes() As String
    Dim DriveInfo As String
    Dim PathName As String
    Dim intChar As Integer
    Dim ErrNumber As Long
    Dim DriveType As String

    For intChar = 65 To 90
        'The backward slash is not required,
        'but does not interfere with this API call:
        PathName = Chr$(intChar) & ":\"
        ErrNumber = apiGetDriveType(PathName)
        Select Case ErrNumber
            Case DRIVE_UNKNOWN
                DriveType = "DRIVE '" & PathName & _
                    "' - UNKNOWN"
            Case DRIVE_NOT_AVAILABLE
                DriveType = "DRIVE '" & PathName & _
                    "' - NOT AVAILABLE"
            Case DRIVE_REMOVABLE
                DriveType = "DRIVE '" & PathName & _
                    "' - REMOVEABLE DRIVE"
            Case DRIVE_FIXED
                DriveType = "DRIVE '" & PathName & _
                    "' - FIXED DRIVE"
            Case DRIVE_REMOTE
                DriveType = "DRIVE '" & PathName & _
```

```
                        "' - NETWORK DRIVE"
                Case DRIVE_CDROM
                    DriveType = "DRIVE '" & PathName & _
                        "' - CDROM; DRIVE"
                Case DRIVE_RAMDISK
                    DriveType = "DRIVE '" & PathName & _
                        "' - RAM DRIVE"
                Case Else
                    ErrNumber = 0
            End Select
            Debug.Print DriveType
            ErrNumber = 1
        Next intChar
    End Sub
```

GetDiskFreeSpaceA

Many database errors occur because the computer simply runs out of disk space. `GetDiskFreeSpaceA` tells you exactly how much space (in KB) is available on a particular drive:

```
Declare Function apiGetDiskFreeSpace _
    Lib "Kernel32" _
    Alias "GetDiskFreeSpaceA"( _
    ByVal lpszPath As String, _
    lpSectors As Long, _
    lpBytes As Long, _
    lpFreeClusters As Long, _
    lpClusters As Long) As Long
```

`GetDiskFreeSpace` uses the `lpszPath` argument to determine the amount of disk space available. If the path argument is `Null`, the function returns the amount of free space remaining in the current path. The number of sectors per cluster, bytes per sector, total clusters, and clusters remaining are all returned, allowing you to determine free and used space for a particular drive. The `GetDiskFreeSpaceA` API function returns `1` if successful, and `0` (zero) if it fails.

The function shown in Listing 30-4 accepts a valid path name as an argument and returns the amount of free space (in KB) available for that path.

LISTING 30-4

Getting Free Disk Space with the `GetDiskFreeSpaceA` API Function

```
Function GetFreeSpace(PathName As String) As String
    Dim ErrNumber As Integer
    Dim Sectors As Long
    Dim Bytes As Long
    Dim FreeClusters As Long
    Dim TotalClusters As Long
```

```
    ErrNumber = apiGetDiskFreeSpace(PathName, Sectors, _
        Bytes / 1024, FreeClusters, TotalClusters)
    GetFreeSpace = "Free space (kilobytes): " _
        & Format(((Bytes * Sectors) / 1024) _
            * FreeClusters, "#,###,##0")
End Function
```

GetVolumeInformationA

The `GetVolumeInformationA` function returns information about the file system and volume information for a valid path.

```
Declare Function apiGetVolumeInformation _
    Lib "Kernel32" _
    Alias "GetVolumeInformationA"( _
    ByVal lpszPath As String, _
    ByVal lpVolNameBuffer As String, _
    ByVal lpVolumeNameSize As Long, _
    lpVolSerialNo As Long, _
    lpMaxFileLen As Long, _
    lpSystemFlags As Long, _
    ByVal lpSysNamebuffer As String, _
    ByVal lpSysNameBufSize As Long) As Long
```

`lpMaxFileLen` is the maximum number of characters allowed for a filename on the particular file system. `lpSystemFlags` indicates whether the volume is compressed, whether filenames are case-sensitive, and whether the volume supports file-based compression. The return value is `1` if successful, `0` if not.

The `GetVolumeInformation` wrapper function accepts a valid path name and a `1` or `2` indicating whether to return the volume name or file system information, respectively:

```
Function GetVolumeInformation(PathName As String, _
    Selection As Integer) As String
    Dim VolName As String * 255
    Dim BufferSize As Long
    Dim VolSerNo As Long
    Dim MaxFileLen As Long
    Dim SysFlags As Long
    Dim SysName As String * 255
    Dim SysBufSize As Long
    Dim ErrNumber As Long
    Const Get_Volume_Name = 1
    Const Get_File_System = 2
    BufferSize = Len(VolName)
    SysBufSize = Len(SysName)
    ErrNumber = apiGetVolumeInformation(PathName, _
```

```
        VolName, BufferSize, VolSerNo, MaxFileLen, _
            SysFlags, SysName, SysBufSize)
    If Selection = 1 Then
        GetVolumeInfo = "Volume Name: " & Trim(VolName)
    Else
        If Selection = 2 Then
            GetVolumeInfo = "File System: " & Trim(SysName)
        End If
    End If
End Function
```

GetSystemDirectoryA

`GetSystemDirectoryA` returns the Windows system directory for the current machine:

```
Declare Function apiGetSystemDirectory _
    Lib "Kernel32" _
    Alias "GetSystemDirectoryA"( _
    ByVal ReturnBuffer As String, _
    uiBufferSize As Long) As Long
```

Upon success, the function returns the number of characters contained in the `ReturnBuffer` argument. `GetSystemDirectoryA` returns zero if unsuccessful. Here is a wrapper utilizing `GetSystemDirectory` to return the Windows installation folder:

```
Function GetSystemDirectory() As String
    Dim ReturnBuffer As String * 255
    Dim BufferSize As Long
    BufferSize = Len(ReturnBuffer)
    Dim ErrNumber As Long
    ErrNumber = _
        apiGetSystemDirectory(ReturnBuffer, BufferSize)
    GetSystemDirectory = _
        Left$(ReturnBuffer, ErrNumber)
End Function
```

General-purpose Windows API functions

Win32 has many functions to manipulate individual windows within applications like Access. A few of these functions are discussed in the following section. The `DisplayTitle()` function section under Listings 30-5 and 30-6 use several of the API functions as an example.

GetParent

The `GetParent` function returns a handle to a window's parent. You might use this call to get a handle on an Access application's parent window:

```
Declare Function apiGetParent _
    Lib "User32" Alias GetParent( _
    ByVal hWnd As Long) As Long
```

When passed a valid window handle, GetParent retrieves the handle of the child window's parent. The function returns a Null value if it is unsuccessful.

GetWindowTextA

GetWindowText returns the title bar text of a window, given its hwnd property:

```
Declare Function apiGetWindowText _
    Lib "User32" _
    Alias "GetWindowTextA"( _
    ByVal hwnd As Long, _
    ByVal lpszCaption As String, _
    ByVal CaptionSize As Long) As Long
```

Occasionally, you may want to capture the text that appears in the title bar of a particular window or the text displayed on a control. GetWindowText captures the text of the handle of the window or control that has been passed and places it in the lpszCaption argument.

GetClassNameA

GetClassName returns the class of the specified window:

```
Declare Function apiGetClassName _
    Lib "User32" _
    Alias "GetClassNameA"( _
    ByVal hwnd As Long, _
    ByVal lpClassName As String, _
    ByVal ClassSize As Long) As Long
```

The window's handle is passed as an argument, and the function places the window's class name in the string lpClassName. The function returns the number of characters copied to the string buffer if it is successful, zero if not.

The DisplayTitle wrapper function (see Listing 30-5) uses GetParent and GetClassNameA to cycle through the windows and controls of an open Access form until the Access application form (class Omain) is located. It then captures the text displayed in the title bar using GetWindowTextA and displays the text in a message box.

LISTING 30-5

Returning the Caption Bar Text for a Window

```
Function DisplayTitle()
    Dim ErrNumber As Long
    Dim Parent As Long
    Dim lngRet As Long
    Dim Caption As String * 128
```

continued

LISTING 30-5 *(continued)*

```
    Dim CaptionSize As Long
    Dim WinHwnd As Long
    Dim Class As String * 6
    Dim ClassSize As Long

    CaptionSize = Len(caption)
    ClassSize = Len(class)
    WinHwnd = Me.hwnd
    Do Until Trim(class) = "OMain"
        Parent = apiGetParent(WinHwnd)
        lngRet = apiGetClassName(Parent, Class, ClassSize)
        WinHwnd = Parent
    Loop
    ErrNumber = apiGetWindowText( _
        Parent, Caption, CaptionSize)
    MsgBox Left$(Caption, ErrNumber)
End Function
```

Notice that the `Do...Loop` in the middle of `DisplayTitle` searches for a window with a class name of `OMain`. The very first version of Microsoft's desktop database project was named Omega. This very early precursor to Microsoft Access lives on to this day in the class name applied to the Access main window.

SetWindowTextA

Use `SetWindowTextA` to change the caption displayed in a window's title bar.

```
Declare Function apiSetWindowText _
    Lib "User32" _
    Alias "SetWindowTextA"( _
    ByVal hwnd As Long, _
    ByVal lpszCaption As String) As Long
```

`SetWindowTextA` is much like altering the `Caption` property of a form. Many people find they want to change the caption of the Access main window to make their applications look more professional. The following function cycles through the windows and controls of an Access application until it finds the Access application form (class `Omain`), and then it changes the title bar caption.

LISTING 30-6

Changing the Caption Bar Text for a Window

```
Function ChangeTitle()
    Dim ErrNumber As Long
    Dim Parent As Long
```

```
    Dim lngRet As Long
    Dim Caption As String * 128
    Dim CaptionSize As Long
    Dim NewCaption As String
    Dim WinHwnd As Long
    Dim Class As String * 6
    Dim ClassSize As Long

    NewCaption = "My New Application Title"
    CaptionSize = Len(caption)
    ClassSize = Len(class)
    WinHwnd = Me.hwnd
    Do Until Trim(class) = "OMain"
        Parent = GetParent(WinHwnd)
        lngRet = apiGetClassName(Parent, Class, ClassSize)
        WinHwnd = Parent
    Loop
    ErrNumber = apiSetWindowText(Parent, NewCaption)
End Function
```

`SetWindowTextA` returns `1` when successful, `0` when it fails.

Manipulating application settings with the Windows API

In the past, software vendors and Microsoft alike have used `.ini` files to control the settings of their applications. The `system.ini` and `win.ini` files controlled almost everything in older versions of Windows. Back then, each application had an `.ini` file, containing sections, string values, key names, and integer values that related to everything from screen color to network protocols.

Although many vendors still use application-specific `.ini` files for their applications, more recent versions of Windows use the System Registry for most settings. The Win32 API comes with all you need to control System Registry settings.

However, you may find it much simpler to use `.ini` files for storing persistent information needed by your applications. One huge advantage that `.ini` files have over the System Registry is that a user can use Notepad or Word to change the contents of an `.ini` file, and changing an application's `.ini` file will not affect any other application on the computer.

This section demonstrates the use of `.ini` functions for Win32. After reviewing these functions, the chapter ends with a demonstration and overview of how to achieve the same results using the Registry.

GetPrivateProfileStringA

`GetPrivateProfileStringA` function retrieves a value from a private (application-specific) `.ini` file.

```
Declare Function apiGetPrivateProfileString _
    Lib "Kernel32" _
    Alias "GetPrivateProfileStringA"( _
    ByVal lpszSection As String, _
    ByVal lpszKey As String, _
    ByVal lpszDefault As String, _
    ByVal lpszReturnString As String, _
    ByVal dwReturnSize As Long, _
    ByVal lpszFilename As String) As Long
```

It is passed the section, key, and `.ini` filename and retrieves the value for the key. If a `Null` value is passed as a key, all the entries for the section are retrieved. If a specified key is not found, the value passed as `lpszDefault` is returned. If the function is successful, it returns the number of characters copied into the string buffer `lpszReturnString`. Sections, keys, and values are illustrated below.

```
[section]
key=string
```

The next example uses the `GetCommandLine` wrapper function to retrieve the path for Access, and uses it as the path for the `test.ini` file. It then uses the `GetPrivateProfileStringA` API function to retrieve a string value for the `AppTitle` key.

```
Function GetPrivateProfileString() As String
    Dim Section As String
    Dim KeyName As String
    Dim default As String
    Dim ReturnBuffer As String
    Dim filename As String
    Dim BufferSize As Long
    Dim ErrNumber As Long
    Dim PathName As String
    Dim lenPath As Integer
    Dim IniPath As String

    'Call the GetCommandLine wrapper function:
    PathName = GetCommandLine()
    lenPath = Len(PathName)
    lenPath = lenPath - 15
    IniPath = Left$(PathName, lenPath)
    IniPath = Right$(IniPath, Len(IniPath) - 1)
    filename = IniPath & "TEST.INI"
    Section = "Settings"
    KeyName = "AppTitle"
```

```
        default = "Not Found"
        ReturnBuffer = String$(128, 0)
        BufferSize = Len(ReturnBuffer)
        ErrNumber = apiGetPrivateProfileString(Section, _
            KeyName, default, ReturnBuffer, _
            BufferSize, filename)
        GetPrivateProfileString = ReturnBuffer
    End Function
```

GetPrivateProfileIntA

The `GetPrivateProfileIntA` function returns an integer value from an application-specific `.ini` file:

```
    Declare Function apiGetPrivateProfileInt _
        Lib "Kernel32" _
        Alias "GetPrivateProfileIntA"( _
        ByVal lpSection As String, _
        ByVal lpszKey As String, _
        ByVal dwDefault As Long, _
        ByVal lpszFilename As String) As Long
```

`GetPrivateProfileInt` accepts a `Section`, `KeyName`, `default`, and `filename` like `GetPrivateProfileString` but does not accept a string buffer. If the function is successful, it returns the integer value. `GetTitleSetting` shows how to use `GetPrivateProfileIntA`:

```
    Function GetTitleSetting() As Long
        Dim Section As String
        Dim KeyName As String
        Dim default As Long
        Dim filename As String
        Dim ErrNumber As Long
        Dim PathName As String
        Dim lenPath As Integer
        Dim IniPath As String

        'Call the GetCommandLine wrapper function:
        PathName = GetCommandLine()
        'The next line extracts "msaccess.exe"
        'from the command line.
        lenPath = Len(PathName)
        lenPath = lenPath - 15
        IniPath = Left$(PathName, lenPath)
        'The next line extracts the quotations
        'from the command line.
        IniPath = Right$(IniPath, Len(IniPath) - 1)
        filename = IniPath & "TEST.INI"
        Section = "Settings"
        KeyName = "TitleBar"
```

```
        default = 1
        ErrNumber = apiGetPrivateProfileInt( _
            Section, KeyName, default, filename)
        GetTitleSetting = ErrNumber
    End Function
```

GetProfileStringA

GetProfileStringA is very much like GetPrivateProfileString:

```
    Declare Function apiGetProfileString _
        Lib "Kernel32" _
        Alias "GetProfileStringA"( _
        ByVal lpszSection As String, _
        ByVal lpszKey As String, _
        ByVal lpszDefault As String, _
        ByVal lpszReturnString As String, _
        ByVal dwReturnSize As Long) As Long
```

This function behaves like GetPrivateProfileString, except it does not accept a filename as an argument. GetProfileString only works with the win.ini file, located in the Windows installation folder. Notice that you do not have to tell GetProfileStringA where Windows is installed. Apparently, GetProfileStringA is able to find the Windows installation folder without any help.

WritePrivateProfileStringA

WritePrivateProfileStringA writes information to a private (application-specific .ini file):

```
    Declare Function apiWritePrivateProfileString _
        Lib "Kernel32" _
        Alias "WritePrivateProfileStringA"( _
        ByVal lpszSection As String, _
        ByVal lpszKey As String, _
        ByVal lpszSetting As String, _
        ByVal lpszFilename As String) As Long
```

Like GetPrivateProfileStringA, this function receives a section, key, default, and filename as arguments. But it also accepts the value you want to place in the .ini file in the lpszSetting argument. If the function is successful, it returns a True value; otherwise, it returns a False value.

The WritePrivateString() function writes a new title bar caption to a specified .ini file by using the GetCommandLine wrapper function and using the returned command line, plus the filename, as the full path to the .ini file:

```
    Function WritePrivateString()
        Dim Section As String
        Dim KeyName As String
        Dim Value As String
```

```
    Dim FileName As String
    Dim ErrNumber As Long
    Dim Setting As Long
    Dim PathName As String
    Dim lenPath As Integer
    Dim IniPath As String

    'Call the GetCommandLine wrapper function:
    PathName = GetCommandLine()
    lenPath = Len(PathName)
    lenPath = lenPath - 15
    IniPath = Left$(PathName, lenPath)
    IniPath = Right$(IniPath, Len(IniPath) - 1)
    filename = IniPath & "TEST.INI"
    Section = "Settings"
    Setting = GetTitleSetting()
    Select Case Setting
        Case 1
            KeyName = "AppTitle"
            Value = "Microsoft Access - " & GetUser()
            ErrNumber = apiWritePrivateProfileString( _
                Section, KeyName, Value, FileName)
            Value = "2"
            KeyName = "TitleBar"
            ErrNumber = apiWritePrivateProfileString( _
                Section, KeyName, Value, FileName)

        Case 2
            KeyName = "AppTitle"
            Value = "My Access Application"
            ErrNumber = apiWritePrivateProfileString(_
                Section, KeyName, Value, FileName)
            KeyName = "TitleBar"
            Value = "1"
            ErrNumber = apiWritePrivateProfileString(_
                Section, KeyName, Value, FileName)
        Case Else

    End Select
End Function
```

WriteProfileStringA

`WriteProfileStringA` behaves much like `WritePrivateProfileStringA`, except it does not accept a filename as a parameter:

```
Declare Function apiWriteProfileString _
    Lib "Kernel32" _
    Alias "WriteProfileStringA"( _
```

```
        ByVal lpszSection As String, _
        ByVal lpszKey As String, _
        ByVal lpszSetting As String) As Long
```

Like GetProfileStringA, this function only works on the win.ini file. If the function completes successfully, the return value is True; if not, it returns False.

Controlling applications with the Registry

All 32-bit versions of Windows store just about everything about your PC in the System Registry. Your hardware settings — user preferences (color, desktop, background), the software you have installed on your PC — all have entries in the Registry. If you open the Windows Registry with Regedit.exe, you'll see that it looks a lot like the Windows Explorer. There are folders representing top-level keys like HKEY_LOCAL_MACHINE and HKEY_CURRENT_USER, and then folders representing subkeys, like SOFTWARE, and then even *more* subkeys to represent specific information. Finally, there are values that contain settings important to your applications and hardware.

When you're manipulating the Registry, there are some standards you should follow:

- **Your application's entry should follow a pattern.** It's a hierarchy that starts with the HKEY_LOCAL_MACHINE key, then moves to SOFTWARE, then to the software vendor's name, then the application name, followed by the current version entry, and then any setting you wish to make. HKEY_LOCAL_MACHINE is the key that tracks what software is installed on the machine. If you wanted to make any user-specific settings, you would also add an entry to the HKEY_CURRENT_USER key.
- **If you place a key in the Registry, make plans to remove it.** In other words, plan an "uninstall" program that removes any traces of your software from the Registry. The System Registry is just a database of information about a computer. It doesn't need to be cluttered with information that isn't relevant anymore.

The next section details all the API calls you need to make to create a Registry entry, set the value of a subkey, query the subkey, and then remove it from the Registry. The basAPIFunctions module contains all the examples.

RegCreateKeyEx

RegCreateKeyEx creates a key in the Registry:

```
Declare Function apiRegCreateKeyEx _
    Lib "Advapi32" _
    Alias "RegCreateKeyExA"( _
    ByVal hKey As Long, _
    ByVal lpszSubKey As String, _
    ByVal dwReserved As Long, _
    ByVal lpszClass As String, _
    ByVal dwOptions As Long, _
    ByVal samDesired As Long, _
```

```
        lpSecurityAttributes As Long, _
        phkResult As Long, _
        lpdwDisposition As Long) As Long
```

If the key already exists, then `RegCreateKeyEx` opens it. This allows you to use only one function to produce both results. You can use `RegOpenKeyEx` if you merely want to open an existing key. However, if you use only `RegOpenKeyEx`, you must do error-checking to see if the key doesn't exist.

`hKey` is a top-level key, such as `HKEY_LOCAL_MACHINE`, and can be represented using one of the following constants:

```
Const HKEY_CLASSES_ROOT = &H80000000
Const HKEY_CURRENT_USER = &H80000001
Const HKEY_LOCAL_MACHINE = &H80000002
Const HKEY_USERS = &H80000003
Const HKEY_CURRENT_CONFIG = &H80000005
Const HKEY_DYN_DATA = &H80000006
```

`lpszSubKey` is a string containing the complete path of the subkey below the top-level key. `dwReserved` is reserved, so it is set to zero. `lpszClass` is a string value that contains a class name (if you are using one). `dwOptions` can be used to specify whether the key is volatile (kept in between sessions) or nonvolatile (the key is not saved in the Registry between sessions). `samDesired` pertains to security access for the key. Security access can be represented using the following constants:

```
Const KEY_QUERY_VALUE = &H1&

Const KEY_SET_VALUE = &H2&

Const KEY_CREATE_SUB_KEY = &H4&

Const KEY_ENUMERATE_SUB_KEYS = &H8&

Const KEY_NOTIFY = &H10&

Const KEY_CREATE_LINK = &H20&

Const READ_CONTROL = &H20000

Const KEY_READ = READ_CONTROL Or KEY_QUERY_VALUE Or _
     KEY_ENUMERATE_SUB_KEYS Or KEY_NOTIFY

Const KEY_WRITE = READ_CONTROL Or KEY_SET_VALUE Or _
     KEY_CREATE_SUB_KEY

Const KEY_EXECUTE = KEY_READ

Const KEY_ALL_ACCESS = KEY_QUERY_VALUE And _
     KEY_ENUMERATE_SUB_KEYS And KEY_NOTIFY And _
     KEY_CREATE_SUB_KEY And KEY_CREATE_LINK And _
     KEY_SET_VALUE
```

lpSecurityAttributes is the address of a security structure, which is an optional parameter. If you aren't using the structure, pass this argument a zero. phkResult is a long integer buffer that contains the handle of the new or opened key if the function is successful. lpdwDisposition is a long value that receives the disposition of the value buffer.

RegCreateKeyEx returns zero if successful.

The OpenKey API wrapper creates (or opens) a key in which an application's title setting is stored.

```
Function OpenKey() As Long
    Dim SubKey As String
    Dim Class As String
    Dim Options As Long
    Dim RegSam As Long
    Dim Sec_Attrib As Long
    Dim Result As Long
    Dim Disposition As Long
    Dim RetVal As Long
    SubKey = _
        "SOFTWARE\MyCompany\MyApp\MySection\SomeValue"
    Options = 1
    RegSam = KEY_ALL_ACCESS
    Sec_Attrib = 0
    RetVal = apiRegCreateKeyEx(HKEY_LOCAL_MACHINE, _
        SubKey, 0, 0, Options, RegSam, Sec_Attrib, _
            Result, Disposition)
    OpenKey = Result
End Function
```

RegSetValueExA

RegSetValueExA sets the value of a registry key:

```
Declare Function apiRegSetValueEx _
    Lib "Advapi32" _
    Alias "RegSetValueExA"( _
    ByVal hKey As Long, _
    ByVal lpszValueName As String, _
    ByVal dwReserved As Long, _
    ByVal dwType As Long, _
    ByVal lpbData As String, _
    ByVal cbdata As Long) As Long
```

hKey is the address of an open key. lpszValueName is a string containing the name of the value you want to set. In an .ini file, this would be the key name. dwReserved should be set to zero. dwType is a flag telling the Registry what type of data value to create. The following constants can be used as symbolic constants for dwType:

```
Const REG_NONE = 0&
Const REG_SZ = 1&
```

```
Const REG_EXPAND_SZ = 2&
Const REG_BINARY = 3&
Const REG_DWORD = 4&
Const REG_DWORD_LITTLE_ENDIAN = 4&
Const REG_DWORD_BIG_ENDIAN = 5&
Const REG_LINK = 6&
Const REG_MULTI_SZ = 7&
Const REG_RESOURCE_LIST = 8&
Const REG_FULL_RESOURCE_DESCRIPTOR = 9&
Const REG_RESOURCE_REQUIREMENTS_LIST = 10&
```

`lpbData` is the value for the key you are setting, and `cbData` is the length (`Len(lpbData)`) of the value. The `SetAppTitleReg` function below sets the value for the application title (`AppTitle`) and the title bar (`TitleBar`) for the System Information form.

`RegSetValueEx` returns zero if successful.

The `SetAppTitleReg` wrapper function shows you how to use the different Registry API calls to write a value into the System Registry:

```
Function SetAppTitleReg() As Long
    Dim Value As String
    Dim Data As String
    Dim DataSize As Long
    Dim ErrNumber As Long
    Dim Setting As Long
    Dim hKey As Long
    hKey = OpenKey()
    Setting = GetTitleSettingReg(hKey)
    Select Case Setting
        Case 1
            Value = "AppTitle"
            Data = "Microsoft Access - " & GetUser()
            DataSize = Len(Data)
            ErrNumber = apiRegSetValueEx(hKey, Value, 0, _
                REG_SZ, Data, DataSize)
            Value = "TitleBar"
            Data = "2"
            DataSize = Len(Data)
            ErrNumber = apiRegSetValueEx(hKey, Value, 0, _
                REG_SZ, Data, DataSize)
        Case 2
            Value = "AppTitle"
            Data = "Access Auto Auctions"
            DataSize = Len(Data)
            ErrNumber = apiRegSetValueEx(hKey, Value, 0, _
                REG_SZ, Data, DataSize)
            Value = "TitleBar"
            Data = "1"
```

```
                DataSize = Len(Data)
                ErrNumber = apiRegSetValueEx(hKey, Value, 0, _
                    REG_SZ, Data, DataSize)
            Case Else
        End Select
        ErrNumber = RegFlushKey(hKey)
        ErrNumber = RegCloseKey(hKey)
    End Function
```

RegFlushKey

When a Registry key is created or altered, the changes can be cached in memory. To force the changes to be written immediately to the Registry, *flush* the key using `RegFlushKey`:

```
Declare Function apiRegFlushKey _
    Lib "Advapi32" _
    Alias RegFlushKey( _
    ByVal hKey As Long) As Long
```

`RegFlushKey` accepts the handle of an open key as an argument and returns zero if successful. `SetAppTitleReg()` from the previous section uses `RegFlushKey` to commit changes made to the title bar settings it has made.

RegQueryValueEx

The `RegQueryValueEx` function returns the value of a registry key opened with the `RegCreateKeyEx` API call.

```
Declare Function apiRegQueryValueEx _
    Lib "Advapi32" _
    Alias "RegQueryValueExA"( _
    ByVal hKey As Long, _
    ByVal lpszValueName As String, _
    ByVal lpdwReserved As Long, _
    lpdwType As Long, _
    ByVal lpbData As String, _
    lpcbSize As Long) As Long
```

`hKey` is the handle of an opened key. `lpszValueName` is a string containing the key of the value you want to retrieve. `lpdwReserved` should be set to zero. `lpdwType` is a buffer containing one of the symbolic constants listed earlier, which tells the function what kind of data it should expect to receive. `lpbData` is a buffer to receive the data, and `lpcbSize` is a buffer to receive the size of the returned value.

`RegQueryValueEx` returns zero if successful.

The `GetTitleSettingReg` wrapper function accepts the handle of an open key and returns the value for the `TitleBar` key in our System Information form:

```
Function GetTitleSettingReg(hKey As Long) As Long
    Dim Value As String
    Dim Reserved As Long
    Dim Data As String * 128
    Dim DataSize As Long
    Dim DataType As Long
    Dim RetVal As Long
    Value = "TitleBar"
    Reserved = 0
    DataSize = Len(Data)
    RetVal = apiRegQueryValueEx( _
        hKey, Value, Reserved, DataType, Data, DataSize)
    If DataType = 0 Then
        Data = 1
        RetVal = apiRegSetValueEx( _
            hKey, Value, 0, REG_SZ, Data, DataSize)
    End If
    GetTitleSettingReg = Left$(Data, DataSize - 1)
End Function
```

RegCloseKey

`RegCloseKey` closes an open Registry key:

```
Declare Function apiRegCloseKey _
    Lib "Advapi32" _
    Alias RegCloseKey( _
    ByVal hKey As Long) As Long
```

Whenever you access a Registry key—whether you open it, query it, set the value, or remove it—you must close the handle of the key when you're finished with it. `RegCloseKey` accepts the handle of an open key as an argument and returns zero if successful.

RegDeleteKey

`RegDeleteKeyA` removes a key from the registry:

```
Declare Function apiRegDeleteKey _
    Lib "Advapi32" _
    Alias "RegDeleteKeyA"( _
    ByVal hKey As Long, _
    ByVal lpszValue As String) As Long
```

Whenever you alter the Registry, you should provide a way to remove the changes you've made. For instance, you should provide a plan for "uninstalling" your application should the user choose to do so (perish the thought!). `RegDeleteKey` removes a subkey from the specified parent key. It accepts a pointer to the top-level key (such as `HKEY_CURRENT_USER`) and the path of the subkey. It returns zero value if it is successful.

The sample form in `Chapter30.accdb` creates a Registry key and assigns two values to the key. Figure 30-3 shows the structure of the keys created in the application as viewed through `regedit.exe`. The `On Close` event of the form calls `RegDeleteKey` to remove the keys. If you check the Registry while the form is up and after the form has been closed, you will see that the structure changes.

FIGURE 30-3

Keys created by the System Information form

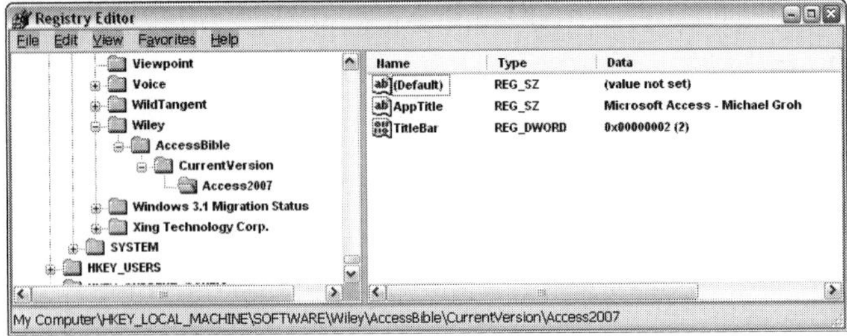

Summary

In this chapter, you've gotten a look at how you can go beyond Access's limits by digging into the interior of Windows. The Windows API is a great way to add extra functionality to your applications. There are close to 1,000 different functions built into Windows that allow you to control your application settings, communications, Registry settings, and network functions.

In this chapter, you learned:

- What the API is and how you use it
- How to write Windows function `Declare` prototypes
- How to write function wrappers to make using the API functions easier
- A number of practical API calls that work well for Access applications

The next chapter sheds light on the complex subject of using Access's replication features. There, you'll see how replication can help your data be more secure while helping you distribute application updates to users, no matter where they're located.

Chapter 31

Using the Access Replication Features

IN THIS CHAPTER

- Understanding database replication
- Creating a replication Design Master
- Creating replica databases
- Synchronizing data between replicas
- Synchronizing design changes between replicas
- Studying VBA code to perform replication operations

In most up-to-date offices, Access database users are working on a number of different computer systems, but their computers are connected in a local area network (LAN). Because of the network users can share a single copy of an Access `.mdb` file located on a file server. In this kind of setup, problems arising from out-of-date data and simultaneous changing of data by multiple users are rare. As long as the appropriate locking scheme has been implemented by the developer and all users are trained in what to do in the event of locked records, little can go wrong.

However, the situation is not so simple in companies where some people need to run Access applications on portable computers, or in company offices so geographically distributed that it's impossible to link all copies of an Access database with a LAN. In these situations, synchronizing the data managed by the "roving" Access applications with the "stationary" copies in the main office can be a daunting task. A laptop user virtually always has a complete copy of the database on their computer and makes changes directly to the mobile database. Later on, these changes have to be synchronized with the stationary database located on the company's network.

A frequently requested feature in Microsoft Access is an easy way to synchronize data changes among multiple copies of the same database. Many developers have implemented complex — and often inefficient — schemes whereby data are exchanged between Access database files. With very few exceptions, these schemes fail to take into account all the issues involved with data synchronization, such as resolving the conflict that occurs when multiple users change the same record between synchronization events. Which record (roving or stationary) should win and be updated on the network? There is no easy way to establish rules that accommodate all contingencies in a home-grown replication scheme.

There are many other problems with such schemes. Most often the newest record is selected as the winner and updated in the network copy of the database. Time zone differences and other time dependencies quickly ruin such a plan.

Access 2007 provides a solution: *database replication*, a feature designed to permit flawless updates and synchronization of changes to data performed at any number of remote sites. As a developer, you have a number of techniques at your disposal when it comes to implementing database replication. In this chapter you see how the replication engine in Access 2007 accommodates all but the most stringent requirements for data coordination between local and remote sites.

ON the CD-ROM **The companion CD-ROM contains two sample databases for this chapter. `MyDM.mdb` is a fully replicable design master, and `Chapter31.mdb` is a typical Access database before being converted to a design master. Feel free to experiment with these databases as you explore Access 2007 replication, and be sure you understand the principles involved (including the need to backup the database) before converting your production applications to a replica set.**

It is important to note that the `.accdb` file format does not support replication. The example database on this books CD is actually an Access 2000 database file. Access 2007 does support replication when working with `.mdb` format files. The discussions in this chapter are applicable to all 32-bit versions of Access except for the `.accdb` file format.

Understanding Replication

Replication is the process of copying and sharing information between copies of the same database, so that the data and designs of the copies remain consistent. Properly implemented replication ensures that no copy of a database will have data that is inconsistent with the same records in any other existing copy of that database.

In the Microsoft Access replication scheme, the original copy of the database is called the *Design Master;* each copy of the Design Master is called a *replica*. The Design Master and its replicas comprise a *replica set* and share many elements in common. The Design Master and each replica may contain other elements that are not shared with the other members of the replica set, however.

Data changes can be made to any member of the replica set (Design Master or replicas). New data can be added, and existing data can be changed in any member of the replica set. Periodically the members of the replica set are *synchronized* to ensure that the data are consistent across all members of the set. Synchronization does not have to happen to all members simultaneously. Any replica set member can synchronize with any other replica set member at any time.

Only the Design Master, however, supports changes to the existing database's structure (table, query, and form design, for instance). If changes to the database structure are needed, the changes are made to the Design Master and are propagated to the other members of the replica set during synchronization. For the purposes of data replication, the Design Master behaves just as any other replica in the replica set.

In addition to the replicable objects in a database, a member of a replica set can contain a number of *local* objects that are not replicable. Local tables, for instance, might protect private or sensitive information that should not be shared with other replicas in the set. As you'll soon see, database objects have a number of properties that either make them part of the replication scheme or keep them local to the database in which they reside.

Database replication almost (but not quite) eliminates the problems that arise when multiple users are making changes to different copies of the same database. On rare occasions, users working with different replicas from a replica set still make changes to the same record in the same table, but the Access 2007 replication engine catches these *synchronization conflicts* and permits manual resolution of these instances.

The normal sequence of events in a replication scheme is as follows (Figure 31-1 diagrams the process step by step):

1. **Administrator builds and tests an Access database.**
2. **When the database development is complete, the database is converted to a replication Design Master.**
3. **Multiple replica copies of the Design Master are made and sent to multiple locations. Each copy initially contains an identical set of data.**
4. **Data updates are made at each location.**
5. **Periodically, each replica is synchronized with some other replica in the replica set. For instance, each replica may be synchronized with the Design Master copy, or with another "designated" replica.**
6. **As changes to the database structure are needed, the Design Master is modified and synchronized with each member of the replica set.**

FIGURE 31-1

Replication is a multistep process that ensures consistent databases.

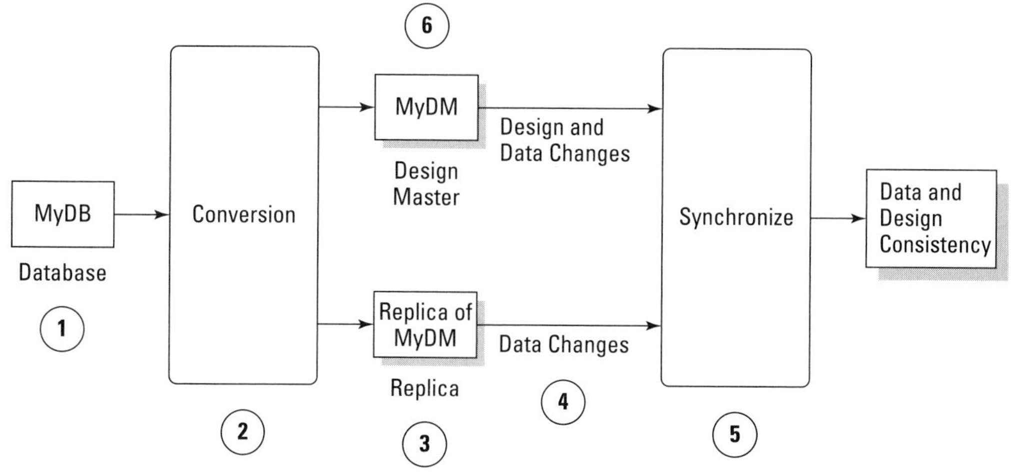

It is important to note that the Access replication feature applies to record-level data changes. Changes to individual fields within records are not tracked. A change to any field within a record is tracked as a change to the record, and the entire record will be exchanged at the next synchronization.

A Replication Demonstration

Perhaps the best way to demonstrate how replication works is to build a simple Access database, convert it to its replicable form (by default, a Design Master replica), create a replica from the Design Master, and make a few changes to the Design Master's data and structure. You then synchronize the replica with the Design Master's new data and structure.

Creating the database

Follow these steps to create the database to use in this example:

1. **To begin, create a new, empty Access database and call it `MyDM.mdb` (for "My Design Master"). Be sure to select either the Access 2000 or Access 2002–2003 format. Next, import the Employees and Categories tables from the Northwind Traders sample database. Then select the Replication Options button in the Administrator group in the Database Tools ribbon tab (see Figure 31-2) to access the Create Replica command.**

FIGURE 31-2

The Administrator ➪ Replication Options menu showing the Create Replica command.

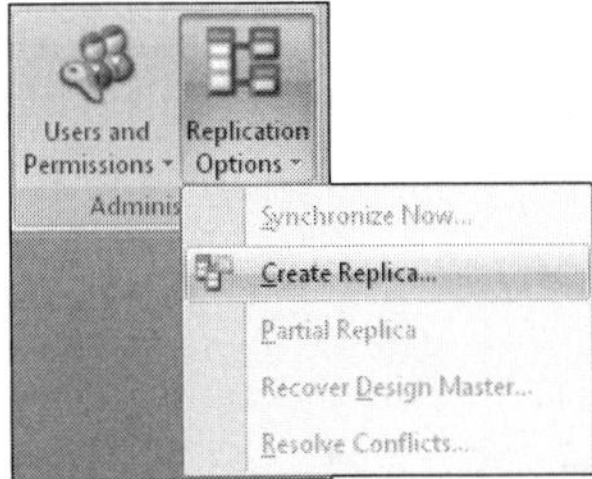

2. **When you select the Create Replica command, a dialog box appears asking whether to proceed with the process of creating a Design Master replica. Click Yes to complete the conversion.**
3. **Before the conversion occurs, Access asks whether you want a backup of the original `.mdb` file (Figure 31-3). In most cases (disk space permitting, of course) you want to keep a backup of the database on hand in case the conversion to Design**

Master fails or is incomplete. As you'll see later in this chapter, converting a replica back to nonreplicable form can be a tedious and time-consuming process.

FIGURE 31-3

In most cases, you want to let Access make a backup of the original `.mdb` file.

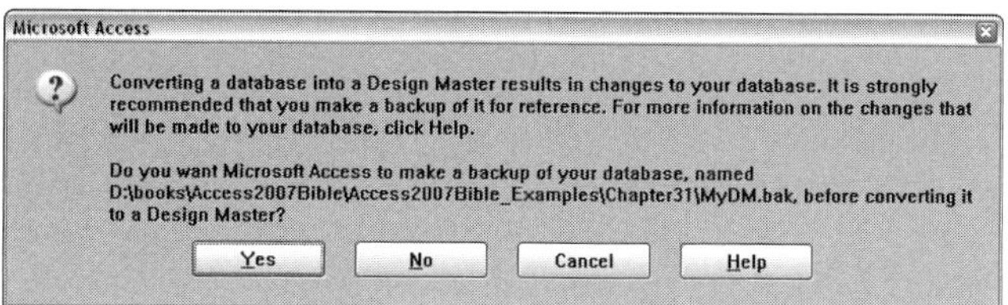

TIP **Be watchful of disk space when you request a backup, however. The backup produced by Access during the conversion process is a *complete* copy of the existing database, including all tables, forms, and other bulky database objects. And the dialog in Figure 31-4 does not permit you to put the backup copy on another disk on your system. So be sure you have adequate disk space to accommodate the copy and the converted `.mdb` file. If you're working with a large `.mdb` file, you may want to compact it before converting to Design Master to reduce the file to the smallest possible size.**

Just in case you're wondering, you can certainly make a replica of the front-end database of a split database system, but there's probably no reason to do so. One of the major advantages of replication is that each user works with a complete copy of the Access application. Replication enables users to synchronize their data changes periodically. Also, replication allows database developers to replicate database design changes, including tables, queries, forms, reports, and code, and make those changes available to users working with replica databases.

On such a small database as our example, the conversion to Design Master takes only a few seconds. As part of the conversion process, Access builds the first replica of the Design Master. Just as the conversion finishes, the dialog you see in Figure 31-5 pops up to ask where you want the replica put on your system. The path you specify for the replica is recorded in the Design Master, so put it where you need it on your system. For our demonstration we'll drop the replica in the My Documents folder along with the MyDM Design Master.

At the conclusion of the process, the new Design Master opens and a message box tells you the conversion is complete. In Figure 31-5, notice that the title bar of the Access window shows that MyDM is now a Design Master. The message box tells you that only MyDM can accept design changes for the new replica set. Also notice the replication icons next to the Categories and Employees tables, which indicate that these tables are involved in the database's replication events.

FIGURE 31-4

Access builds the first Design Master replica as part of the conversion process.

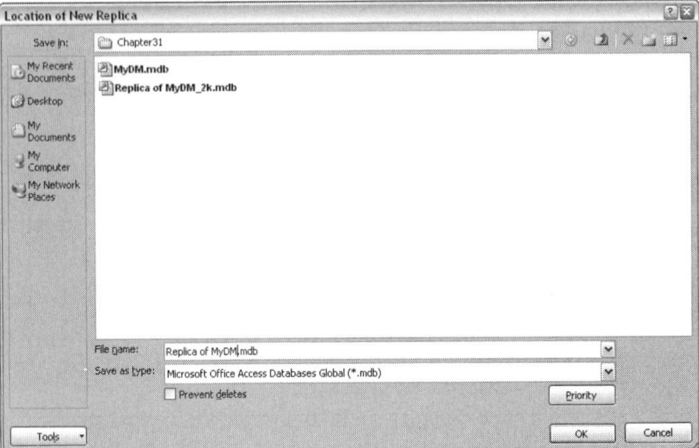

FIGURE 31-5

The conversion is complete. Notice the title bar in the MyDM Database window.

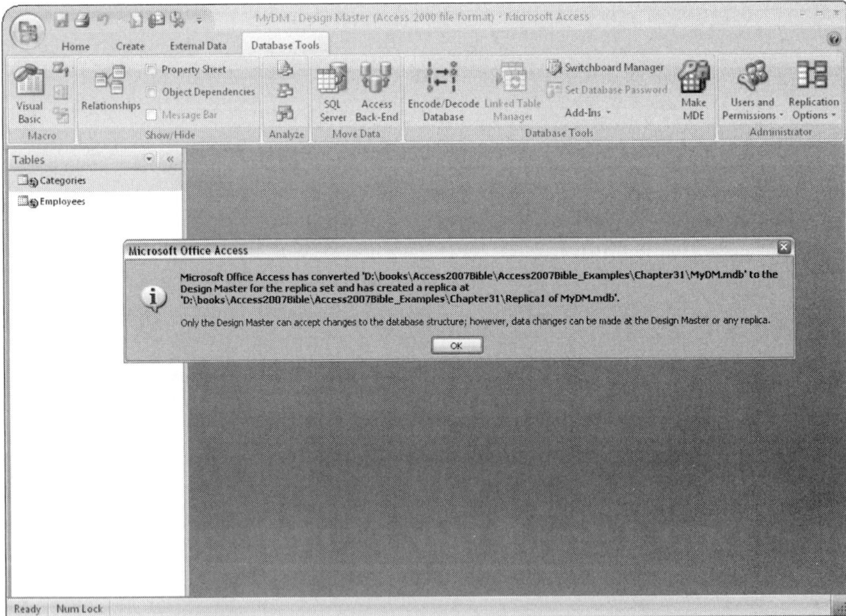

Changing the replica

Close MyDM and open `Replica of MyDM.mdb`. Figure 31-6 shows the Database window for `Replica of MyDM.mdb`. Notice the title bar text in the Database window. The table objects you see in Figure 31-6 are identical to the table objects in Figure 31-5, with the exception that all tables and other database objects in a replica are read-only, because you cannot make changes to the *design* of database objects in a replica. You can, of course, make changes to the *data* contained in a replica's tables; follow these steps to see how that works:

FIGURE 31-6

A replica looks a lot like a Design Master. Notice the text in the Access title bar.

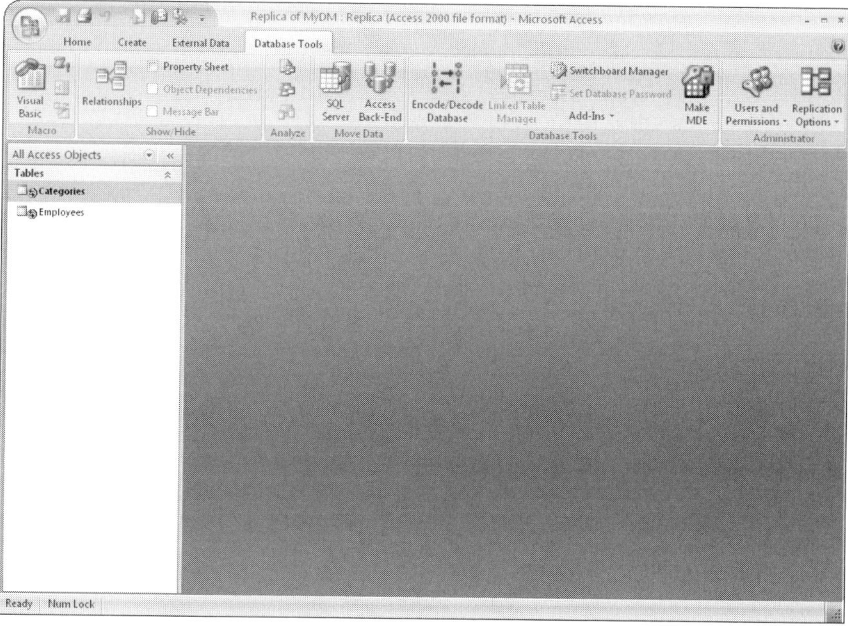

1. **In `Replica of MyDM`, open the `Employees` table and change Nancy Davolio's name to Betty Merrill.**
2. **Close the `Employees` table and select Tools ➪ Replication ➪ Synchronize Now to initiate data synchronization with MyDM. Notice also that you now have a full complement of replication tasks available to you.**

   As soon as you select the Synchronize Now command, the confirmation dialog in Figure 31-7 opens. As you learn later in this chapter, the location of the replica's Design Master is stored in a hidden system table within the replica. If you move either the Design Master or a replica, you have to use the Browse button in the Synchronize Database dialog to locate the moved file.

FIGURE 31-7

Jet remembers where the replica's Design Master is located.

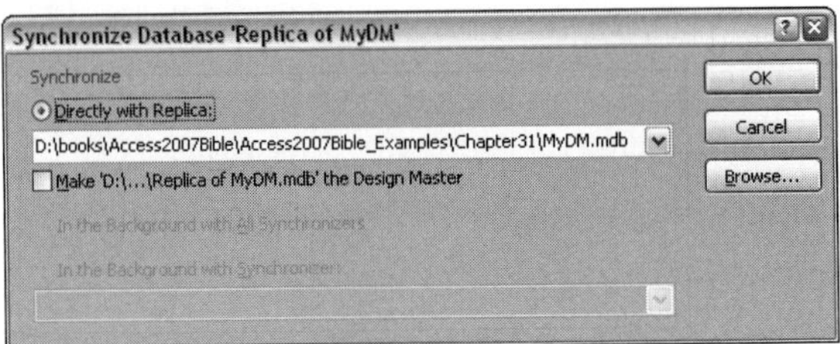

Synchronization is straightforward and should take just a few seconds to complete. It is important to note that the replication direction demonstrated here (replica-to-Design Master) is unimportant. A replica can synchronize with any other replica in its replica set.

In this small example you are exchanging only a little data with the Design Master replica. In a real-world situation you may exchange many other objects, including tables, forms, and other items. The best way to ensure that you're seeing all of the structural changes wrought by the synchronization is to close and reopen the database.

Close the `Replica of MyDM` database; then open `MyDM` and view the `Employees` table. Notice that Nancy Davolio has been replaced with Betty Merrill. Close the `Employees` table when you're done admiring your work.

Now, change the database design by deleting the `Categories` table. If Access refuses to delete the `Categories` table, make sure you're in the Design Master (`MyDM.mdb`). (Remember, you cannot make design changes in any replica other than the Design Master.) Then click Tools ➪ Replication ➪ Synchronize Now to synchronize the design change with `Replica of MyDM.mdb`. When you close `MyDM` and open `Replica of MyDM`, the `Categories` table should be gone.

The principles illustrated by this demonstration apply to all Jet replication installations. The major difference between our demonstration and replication in practice is that most real-world situations involve more than a Design Master and one replica, and, of course, most databases contain more than a single table.

To summarize the important principles illustrated by this demonstration:

- Converting a database with the Access menus results in a Design Master and one replica. Additional replicas can be made from the Design Master or *any replica* by selecting Tools ➪ Replication ➪ Create Replica.
- Information about the replica set (for instance, the location of the Design Master) is stored in hidden system tables. You can view these tables by selecting Tools ➪ Options ➪ View ➪ System Objects. Each of the replication system tables is described later in this chapter.

- Synchronization proceeds in any direction (replica-to-Design Master, Design Master-to-replica, or replica-to-replica). The only stipulation is that the databases being synchronized must not be involved in another synchronization event at the same time.
- The changes exchanged by the synchronization event include *data* and *design*. Only the Design Master supports design changes. All objects in a replica are read-only.

As you read this chapter, keep in mind that it's actually the Jet engine that implements replication and synchronization. The Access menus simply provide an interface to the Jet replication features. Later in this chapter you learn how to create your own replication interface with Access VBA and DAO code.

Replication Pros and Cons

Replication has many benefits for Access database users:

- **Simplifies sharing of data with traveling users.** As in the scenario described in the previous section, roving copies of a database can be synchronized with a stationary copy. The synchronization is not done in real time, but is a good fit where "real-time enough" is adequate.
- **Facilitates data-sharing with remote offices.** Replicas of the Design Master can be produced and sent to geographically distant satellite offices. Periodically, each office synchronizes with the central office or a replica in the replica set at another satellite office. Each office can maintain a number of local tables to maintain sensitive information.
- **Prevents database demand overload.** The Microsoft Jet engine does not support true client-server database access. Instead, each user in a shared environment places demands on the Jet engine to process queries, sometimes resulting in overloaded systems when a large number of simultaneous users are hitting the same `.mdb` file. In situations where immediate updates to the data are not critical, the shared `.mdb` file can be broken into a number of replicas, even though they exist on the same network system. Each copy services a number of different users at high-demand times, reducing the number of users on any one copy of the database. Periodically the replicas are synchronized to bring the data contained in each up to date with the other members of the replica set.
- **Distributes updates to the application.** Because Jet replication involves more than just the data contained in the database, you can use replication to distribute updates to forms, reports, and other database components. You may want to reserve the Design Master just for producing application updates, rather than using it as a normal member of the replica set.
- **Serves as a backup for data.** Because the data in a recently synchronized replica is guaranteed to be up to date, you have a robust back-up system built into every replica set. Microsoft has made it easy to designate any replica as the Design Master for the replica set in the event that the current Design Master is lost due to equipment failure, so it is not necessary to maintain the Design Master on back-up media. In fact, as you read later in

this chapter, certain problems are associated with performing traditional backups of replicated databases — in particular, it's easy for data to be lost if you restore a backed-up copy of a replica that has missed one or more synchronization events and therefore contains out-of-date data.

In each of these cases, it isn't necessary for the remote copy of the Access database to be connected permanently to the central copy by a local area network (LAN). Windows offers a several connectivity solutions, including the built-in Windows peer-to-peer network, dial-up networking (in which a remote computer obtains network services through a modem), and direct-connect networking (the remote computer is connected through a serial or parallel cable to a desktop computer). Each of these networking solutions offers a convenient way to synchronize large amounts of data across connections between the desktop computers.

Another solution is to use a CD-ROM to transfer the replica database to the desktop computer for synchronization. If the remote computer can't be physically connected to the desktop machine, sometimes this is your best approach to synchronization.

Jet replication is not appropriate in several situations. For example, the unavoidable delay between data acquisition and synchronization may be too long to provide a good solution to the user's needs. Replication is not an ideal solution under the following circumstances:

- **When data consistency is critical:** Many industries (banking, airline reservations, point-of-sale inventory management, and so on) demand instant updates to the data managed by the database. Because of the unavoidable delays in communicating data changes to the other users in a Jet replica set, real-time data updates are often impossible when using replication. Traditional transaction processing is a better approach when real-time data updates are necessary.
- **When large numbers of updates to many different records are required:** Replication works best when the usual database update is simply a matter of adding new records to the underlying tables or making relatively few changes to existing records. In these cases, replication is mostly a question of distributing the new records to each member of the replica set. In situations where large numbers of existing records are being changed at several different sites, the same records may be simultaneously changed by a number of users, resulting in an unacceptably high number of record conflicts which must be manually resolved.

Introducing the Access Replication Tools

Access 2007 provides a number of tools for working with replication. These tools let you convert existing Access 2007 databases into replica Design Masters as well as synchronize replicas with other replicas and the Design Master in a replica set.

Using Access menus

The Access 2007 menu system includes all commands necessary to convert existing databases to Design Masters or produce individual replicas. These menu options work only when replication was selected during the Access 2007 installation process. If you have trouble getting the replication menu commands to work, you may have to run the Access 2007 installation again, making sure replication is selected as an option.

The demonstration earlier in this chapter showed you how the Access menu interface to Jet replication works. The Replication menu you saw in Figure 31-2 contains all actions required to create and maintain a replica set.

You can't go too far with the Access replication menus, however. For instance, there's no easy way to verify that the synchronization has been successful (other than the error messages that might occur in the event of a failure), nor is there any way to schedule synchronization for low-demand times. For these features you have to use VBA to program the feature yourself.

Replicating through VBA and DAO

The Access 2007 data access objects (DAO) contain a number of new replication-specific properties and methods. As you'll see in the section titled "Programming Replication," it's possible to build a complete interface to replication through these properties and methods, including creating Design Masters and replicas, synchronizing replicas, and changing the replica status of members of replica sets. The programmatic replication interface is ideal for relatively untrained or unskilled users and provides the developer with a way to protect a replicable database from tampering.

The DAO replication extensions in the Jet database engine are sufficient to convert existing Access `.mdb` files to replicable form (by default, the conversion results in a Design Master replica, but any replica in a replica set can be designated as the Design master for the set). They also allow you to create replicas from the Design Master and synchronize replicas in a replica set.

There are also a number of properties available at runtime to help you programmatically identify the Design Master and replicas in a replica set. Each object within a replicable database also has a number of properties that enable you to identify the replicable objects in the database.

Creating a Replica Set

The process of creating a replica set is straightforward and includes the following steps:

1. **Make a database replicable: Convert an existing database to Design Master status.**
2. **Create replicas: Copy the Design Master to a number of replicas.**
3. **Make data changes: Roll the replica set out to users and let them make changes to the data.**

4. **Synchronize: Periodically synchronize replicas with one another. Design changes made to the Design Master will be propagated to each replica during synchronization.**
5. **Resolve conflicts and replication errors.**

The following sections describe each of these steps (although not necessarily in this exact sequence) using the Access menus, and VBA programming.

Using Access replication menus

Using the Access replication menus was thoroughly discussed in the section "A Replication Demonstration" earlier in this chapter. The Access menu interface is well suited for users with sufficient training and understanding of the replication process. If your application hides the Access menus, you can use the `DoMenuItem` method of the `DoCmd` object to provide some access to the menu commands. Otherwise, you should plan on using the replication DAO alternative.

Programmatic replication

Controlling replication through VBA code and DAO requires a thorough understanding of the objects, properties, and methods employed during replication. Using VBA programming to control replication has many advantages:

- You can provide replication services to users with minimal training. If you properly construct your VBA code, you can effectively hide all the nastiness of synchronizing changes with other replicas yet still provide robust synchronization services to each replica. Users do not have to learn the intricacies of the Access menu system nor do they have to understand replication principles.
- Your VBA code can use the information in the replication system tables to prepare reports or inform users that replication has occurred and that their data are up to date.
- A custom replication interface can provide a lot more scheduling flexibility. Users can choose which replicas to synchronize with and when to perform the synchronization.

Using VBA and DAO to implement replication is described in the section titled "Programming Replication" later in this chapter.

Understanding Database Security in Replication Sets

Jet preserves the current security settings when it converts a database to replicable form. Any permissions a user had before conversion are in place in the new replica or Design Master. This means that the `System.mdw` file, which contains the user and group security information for your Access installation, must be distributed along with each copy of a database replica. New users and groups can be added at any replica, but permission changes can be made only to the Design Master (because they are design changes).

The `System.mdw` file is not part of a replica set and must be manually copied around the system.

Certain permissions are required to perform some replication activities. For instance, a user must have administrator permission to perform the following actions:

- Convert a database to replicable form.
- Make a local object replicable or make a replicable object local.
- Designate a replica as the Design Master for the replica set. (Be sure not to have multiple Design Masters in the replica set!)

Be sure you fully understand the Access security system before distributing replicable databases containing sensitive information to its users. By default, all members of the users group (which means all users) have administrative permissions. If security is an issue, modify the default permissions at design time.

At least one user at each replica site should have administration privileges. In the event that a catastrophic failure wipes out the Design Master and its associated `System.mdw` file, you need to be able to designate another replica as Design Master. This can only be done if the `System.mdw` file at the replica site recognizes a valid administrative user.

The Importance of Local Objects

Not every database object needs to be included in a replication scheme. Each replica in a replica set (including the Design Master) can contain any number of objects that are not exchanged with other members of the replica set. By default, when you convert an Access database to replicable format, all objects in the `.mdb` file are marked for replication.

If, after the Design Master is created, you wish to reserve some objects to be used only within the Design Master, you must set the Replicable property of each one to `F` (or False). The easiest way to do this is to right-click the object's name in the Design Master's Database window to open the object's Property Sheet (see Figure 31-8).

Simply uncheck the Replicated check box in the lower-right corner of the Property Sheet, and Jet keeps the object local during future synchronizations.

FIGURE 31-8

It's easy to make an object local in the Design Master by unchecking the Replicated check box in the object's Property Sheet.

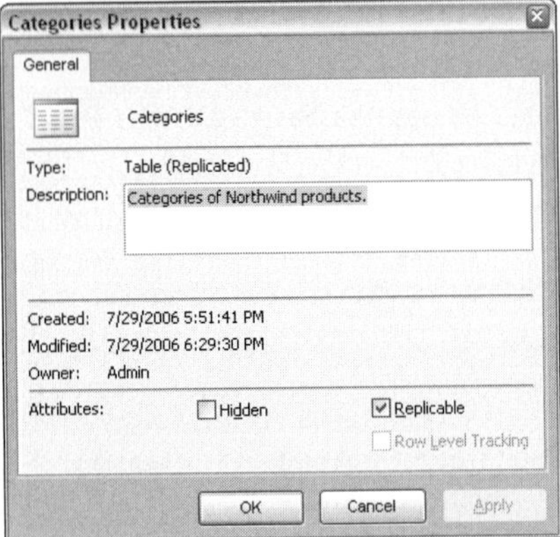

Resolving Replication Conflicts

Replication can generate a number of different types of conflicts and errors. These problems may cause the data in replicas to become unsynchronized, depending on the root cause of the error.

Design errors

True design errors are relatively rare. Because the structure of tables and other database objects can be changed only in the Design Master, opportunities for design problems are greatly reduced.

Design changes made to the Design Master can cause design errors at synchronization, however. For instance, assume that the structure of a table is modified to make a particular field a primary key. At the next synchronization a primary key violation will occur if a user has entered a duplicate value in the field that is now designated as the primary key. Jet detects this conflict as a design error because a structural change has been made to the table.

Another example: You create a new replicable table in the Design Master that just happens to have the same name as a local table maintained in a replica in the set. Jet will be unable to add the new replicable table to that replica because of the name conflict.

Design errors are reported in the `MSysSchemaProb` table in each replica. This table is local to each replica and contains the following information:

- The design change that failed (Create Index, Create Table, and so on)
- The text of the design change error message

- The Design Master design version that triggered the error
- Other information such as the name of the local table with the conflict, the names of fields involved in the conflict, and so on

`MSysSchemaProb` is present only when a design conflict has occurred. Its presence indicates there has been a problem synchronizing design changes between replicas.

Resolving design errors is straightforward. Review the `MSysSchemaProb` table for the nature of the problem; then rename the table, field, or other object generating the error or resolve the primary key conflict. Most often you end up removing or renaming some object in the replica database.

Synchronization conflicts

A synchronization conflict occurs when two or more users make changes to the same record in different replicas between synchronizations. There is no way for Jet to know which record change takes precedence over another. Because changes are tracked only at the record level, a change in almost any field causes the entire record to be exchanged. (The exceptions are OLE and memo fields — changes in these fields are tracked separately and they are exchanged only when the OLE or memo data has changed.)

True synchronization errors may occur with relative frequency, depending on many factors:

- The number of replicas in the replica set
- The number of changes to existing records made by each user
- How often synchronization events occur

Very often you can minimize future conflicts by modifying the parameters (synchronization frequency, for instance) that lead to these conflicts).

When a synchronization conflict occurs, Jet determines a winner by looking at the version numbers of the records. You'll recall that the `s_Generation` field is incremented each time there is a change to the record. Given two conflicting fields with differing `s_Generation` values, Jet chooses the record with the most changes (and therefore the highest version number) since the last synchronization, on the assumption that the data in that record is the most recent.

In the case where both version numbers are the same (for instance, each record has been changed only once), Jet chooses a winner based on the replica's ID number. Admittedly, this is an entirely arbitrary way to choose a conflict winner, but it does provide for a consistent selection between conflict pairs.

In any case, Jet records the synchronization conflict in a *conflict table* (sometimes called a *side table*) that is local to the replica that lost the conflict resolution. The conflict table is named `TableName_Conflict`, where `TableName` is the name of the table with the conflicting records. Conflict tables are not replicated.

At the conclusion of the conflict resolution, the tables in the replicas with the conflicting records are consistent because Jet exchanges the winning record with both replicas.

Manual conflict resolution

You should look for conflict tables after synchronizing two replicas. The presence of a conflict table indicates that Jet encountered a synchronization conflict that it resolved by declaring a winner and placing the loser in the conflict table. Examine the conflict table to identify the record(s) that caused the conflict. Very often there's nothing more to do than simply delete the losing record from the conflict table. Other times you need to dig down deeper to find out what happened.

You could, for instance, run a routine that looks at each table's `ConflictTable` property to see if a conflict occurred. This property contains the name of the conflict table containing the conflicting records. If `ConflictTable` is a null string, no conflict occurred.

Microsoft suggests using the following subroutine (Listing 31-1) to test for the presence of conflicts and display the conflict records stored in the conflict table:

LISTING 31-1

Programmatic Conflict Resolution

```
Sub Resolve (db As Database)
  Dim tdfTest As DAO.TableDef
  Dim rsConflict As DAO.Recordset

  'The For Each...Next loop looks at each
  'ConflictTable property for each table in the
  'replica. If the ConflictTable is not a null
  'string, run through the records in the conflict
  'table and perform some action on them:
  For Each tdfTest In db.TableDefs

    If (tdfTest.ConflictTable <> "") Then
      'Conflict occurred:
      Set rsConflict = _
        db.OpenRecordset(tdfTest.ConflictTable)

      'Process each record:
      rsConflict.MoveFirst

      Do While Not rsConflict.EOF

        '<<<
        'Perform conflict resolution in this loop.
        'Perhaps display or report each record,
        'or email a message to the replica's owner.
```

```
            '>>>

            rsConflict.Delete

            'Remove conflicting record when finished:
            rsConflict.MoveNext

          Loop

          rsConflict.Close

        End If

      'Move to next table in replica:
      Next tdfTest

    End Sub
```

Short-term conflict resolutions include the following:

- Manually entering the data from the conflict table into the database
- Accepting the conflict resolution proposed by Jet and deleting the conflict record from the conflict table

If you notice an unacceptable number of conflicts, possible long-term resolutions include developing a custom conflict resolution into the VBA routines implementing your synchronization activity. The routine may incorporate business rules such as "Marketing always wins" or "The changes input by order entry have lowest priority." You can even store such business rules in a replicable table within the database and keep it updated as business objectives change.

You may also encounter a high level of conflicts for simple procedural reasons. For instance, maybe due to poor planning the same customer records are being entered by more than one department or clerk. Perhaps the inventory figures are being updated in the field as well as at the home office. If you find situations such as these, do your best to make the necessary procedural changes required to eliminate the redundancy.

Synchronization errors

Synchronization errors occur when the data are incorrectly replicated or the wrong data are replicated. For instance, a table-level validation rule causes Jet to reject an otherwise valid entry into a table — or two users insert different records using the same primary key value. Jet isn't able to insert both records into the same table at synchronization time, causing a primary key violation.

Synchronization errors are records in the `MSysErrors` replication system table. `MSysErrors` is exchanged with all replicas, so the same errors are available to all replicas. `MSysErrors` contains the following information:

- The name of the table involved
- The incoming record that generated the error
- The replica(s) where the error was detected (One reason `MSysErrors` is replicated is so that all replicas can report the same error, if it occurs in multiple locations.)
- The replica that most recently changed the record
- The operation (insert, append, change) that failed
- The reason the operation failed (duplicate primary key, and so on)

You should rectify replication errors as soon as possible. They normally don't simply go away, and they indicate situations (such as inappropriate table design or restrictive validation rules) that are much more serious than simple synchronization conflicts.

A few types of errors that do self-correct, however. A simple record lock prevents a record update, generating an error that is not present at the next synchronization event.

Replication Topologies

A number of different arrangements can be used to synchronize the members of a replica set. Because each member of a replica set can synchronize with any other member of the same set at any time, chaos can ensue if synchronizations don't follow an organized pattern. Synchronization should proceed in an orderly fashion to ensure that all members of the replica set receive updates in a timely fashion.

The order in which replicas are synchronized is called the *replication topology*. As you schedule synchronization between replicas, keep in mind how the update exchanges flow from one replica to another. You should choose the topology that is best suited to your users and how they are working with their Access applications.

Make sure you are actually synchronizing with all members of a replica set. Use the information in the replication system tables to verify synchronization events and that the synchronizations occurred when expected. You can use this information to notify users that synchronization conflicts have occurred or when it's time to manually initiate synchronizations.

At first glance, it may appear there is one and only one valid replication topology (the star arrangement) for all replication environments. In this scenario, each replica connects to a single replica and synchronizes with it. But, as you'll soon see, there are equally valid arrangements that are even better suited in some situations.

Although this section describes three different topologies, other arrangements are possible. As you build your replication scheme, be sure to consider alternatives if it appears the chosen design is too inefficient or adds too much traffic to the network.

Replication from the Developer's Perspective

Replication presents many interesting and intriguing challenges for you as an Access developer. Not only do you have to understand how replication works; you have to design a replication scheme that is best suited for your users and their work flow. Then you have to decide whether to train users how to use the Access menus, or whether it is better to build a custom routine using VBA and DAO. No matter which system you design, you have to test and debug it after you build it.

A properly implemented replication scheme can save users thousands of hours a year merging and updating changes in multiple databases. Because replication eliminates the possibility of transcription errors, the accuracy of the data contained in multiple databases is ensured. And, a great deal of time backing up individual databases is saved because replicas represent a built-in redundant backup system.

The following sections discuss some global issues that you should be aware of as you begin working with replication. These topics round out your initial exposure to this fascinating technology.

Understanding the Changes to Database Objects

A number of structural changes are made to a database as it is converted to a Design Master or replica. These changes enable the replica engine to track changes to the data and synchronize data between replicas. Specifically, new tables are added to the `.mdb` file, new fields are added to each record in replicable tables, and new properties are added to all database objects (tables, queries, forms, and so on).

In addition, the behavior of AutoNumber fields changes, and the overall size of the `.mdb` file increases because of the new objects added to the database.

Globally unique ID

Many changes to a replica database involve the addition of globally unique IDs (GUID) to tables and other parts of the database. The Jet engine creates GUIDs to ensure that each object tracked by the replication mechanism has a unique handle the replicator can recognize. The GUID fields are special system fields in the replicable tables and cannot be seen unless you select Tools ➪ Options ➪ View ➪ System Objects.

A GUID is a combination of bits of information Jet gathers from the computer that was used to create the Design Master. This information includes the network node ID, the time on the computer's system clock, a sequence identifier, and a version number for the replica. If the computer does not have a network card installed, a 47-bit random number is generated and used instead. The random number itself is a combination of bits of information, including the node name, the amount of free space on the computer's hard drive, and the system's free memory status.

The combination of values used to produce GUIDs is almost guaranteed to be unique on every computer. It is *highly* unlikely that any other computer exactly duplicates the conditions used to produce the GUIDs on a given machine.

New system tables

Jet adds a fairly large number of tables to a database as it converts the database to replicable format. Figures 31-9 and 31-10 show the same database before and after conversion. In both these figures the View System Objects option has been selected in the Tools ➪ Options dialog.

FIGURE 31-9

Every Access database contains these system tables.

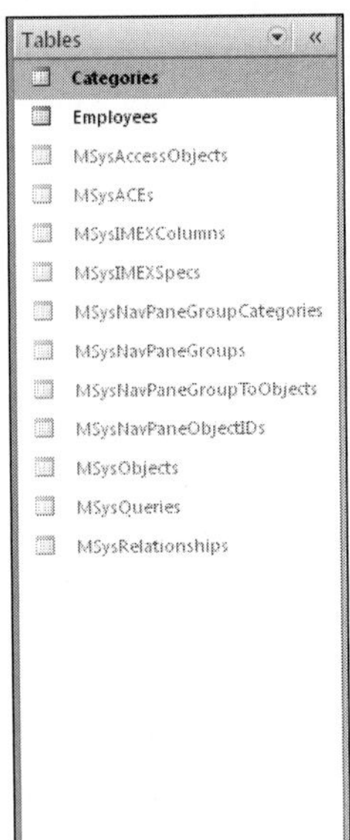

FIGURE 31-10

Not all of these system tables are present in every replicable database.

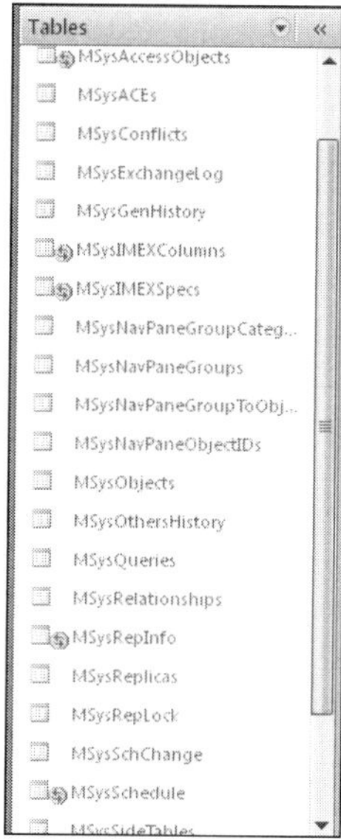

The following list describes each of the new system tables created during a database's conversion to replicable format. Unlike the usual system tables in an Access database, each of these tables contains relatively straightforward information that is easy to read and understand.

To help you manage your installation, you could, as part of your replication design, build forms and reports into your applications to display the information contained in these tables. You might want to make these forms and reports local to the Design Master replica or another replica that you designate as the administration replica.

Several of these tables grow every time a synchronization occurs. As the replica set administrator, you should monitor the size of these system tables. When it appears that the information stored in a shared table is no longer useful, you can delete old records from the table. The deletions are replicated to other members of the replica set at the next synchronization. Keep in mind that simply deleting records doesn't reduce the size of the `.mdb` on each member of a replica set. You may also have to compact each `.mdb` to free up the space made available by the deletion.

- `MSysRepInfo`: This table stores information pertaining to the entire replica set, including things like the GUID that identifies the Design Master. This table contains only one record and is found in every member of a replica set.

- `MSysReplicas`: This table contains information about each replica in the replica set, such as the path of each replica, the GUID that identifies each replica, and so on. Every member of the replica set has a copy of `MSysReplicas`.
- `MSysTableGuids`: Each original table in a replica (including system tables) is assigned a GUID. This table contains the GUID information for each original table. During replication, tables are processed efficiently so that referential integrity and design features are maintained. This table is maintained by the Design Master and is changed each time the database design is modified.
- `MSysSchemaProb`: The `MSysSchemaProb` table stores design synchronization errors. You'll see this table only when there was a problem synchronizing changes to the database structure between replicas in the replica set. In a well-managed replica set, this error should never occur because design changes occur only at the Design Master and are exchanged with the other replicas only during synchronization.
- `MSysErrors`: The `MSysErrors` table records synchronization errors; it is included in every member of the replica set. Use `MSysErrors` to help identify problems that have occurred. This table includes plain text fields, object GUIDs, and other information to help you resolve synchronization conflicts.
- `MSysExchangeLog`: The `MSysExchangeLog` (included in every replica in the replica set) contains 26 fields that report everything you need to know about every synchronization event the replica has performed, such as the synchronization date, the number of rows inserted, deleted, or modified, and other information concerning the synchronization events. This table can grow rapidly when replications frequently occur. This is a local table and is not exchanged with other replicas.
- `MSysSidetables`: This table appears only when a synchronization conflict has occurred between records in a replica set. It shows the name of the conflict table containing the conflict details. View the data in the referenced conflict table for details about the conflict.
- `MSysSchChange`: The `MSysSchChange` table is a local table that records schema changes seen by the replica. Compare this table with the same table in other replicas if it appears that a replica is not properly synchronizing database design changes with the Design Master.
- `MSysTombstone`: This table (included in all replicas in a replica set) tracks records that have been deleted during synchronizations. A deleted record's `s_GUID` and `s_Generation` fields are recorded here, as well as the deleted record's table GUID. Obviously, this table will continue to grow as records are deleted in any replica.
- `MSysTranspAddress`: This table appears in every member of a replica set and contains information about all synchronizers known by the replica. You'll find things like the synchronizer description and ID, and other information you can use to make sure each replica is using the appropriate synchronizer.
- `MSysSchedule`: `MSysSchedule` contains scheduling information used by the synchronizers for implementing synchronization events. This table is replicated with every synchronization.

- MSysGenHistory: This table stores the generation history for the replica. Each replica may have a somewhat different version of MSysGenHistory because not all replicas take part in every synchronization. The information in MSysGenHistory is useful when you need to track the generation information for a single replica and compare it with another replica. This information is useful if it appears replicas are out of sync. This is one of the tables that continues to grow as replication proceeds.
- MSysOthersHistory: This table contains generation information from *other* replicas in the replica set. The generation information in this table should correspond to the information given in MSysGenHistory. You may see entries on replicas that the replica doesn't synchronize with very often. This table also continues to grow with each synchronization.

Although none of these system tables are very large to begin with, several grow as the data in the replica changes and the replica is synchronized with other replicas. Be sure that all host computers have sufficient room for future growth.

New fields

Three new fields are added to each record in a replicable table: The Gen_Notes and Gen_Photo fields are used to track a memo field named Notes and an OLE field named Photo, respectively (see Figure 31-11). Jet first looks at a table to see if any field contains an AutoNumber field with the ReplicationID field size (the FieldSize property of AutoNumber fields can be set to either Long Integer or ReplicationID). If no field in the replicable table matches these characteristics, Jet adds a new field, s_GUID, that holds the ReplicationID AutoNumber (a 31-byte GUID) that uniquely identifies each record in the table. Jet uses the s_GUID field to track changes to each record so that data updates can be synchronized with the same record in other members of a replica set.

FIGURE 31-11

Jet adds a number of hidden system fields to replicable tables.

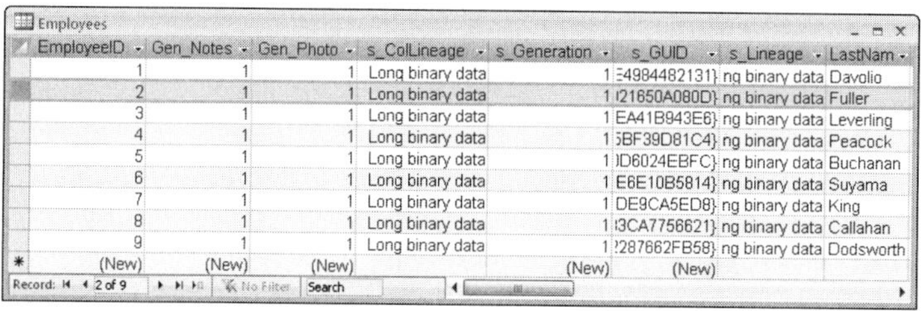

The Gen_Notes and Gen_Photo fields keep track of large data types (memo fields and OLE data types, for instance) that may be included in the replicated table. Because these fields can be very large, the replication process transfers data in these fields only if the data has actually been changed.

The new fields added to tables reduce the space available for data. Jet permits only 2,048 bytes per record in tables, not including Memo or OLE fields. Adding the three fields, plus other overhead, adds at least 54 bytes to each record in a replicable table. Each memo and OLE field, for instance, requires an additional 4 bytes to replicate. In a table with many thousands of fields, the additional space demands can be considerable.

The new fields also take away from the total number of fields available to Jet tables. Jet supports a maximum of 255 columns in any table. The three additional system fields can be a problem in rare cases. Properly designed Access databases rarely approach the 255-column limit imposed by Jet. If it appears that the number of tables in your database may exceed the 255-column limit, consider overhauling the database's basic structure.

The other system fields added to each replicable table are `s_Generation` and `s_Lineage`.

s_Generation

Each record in the replicable table contains an `s_Generation` field. This field is set to `0` when any data contained in the record is modified. At synchronization, all records containing 0 in the `s_Generation` field are exchanged with other replicas and the `s_Generation` field is incremented by 1. Because only records with `s_Generation` values equal to 0 are exchanged, unchanged records are not involved in synchronization exchanges, reducing the amount of traffic.

During synchronization Jet checks the generation number of the sending and receiving replicas and makes sure that data are not exchanged out of sequence.

An extra generation field is added for each memo and OLE field in a record. This generation field specifically records changes to its associated memo or OLE field to prevent these large fields from being exchanged if some other field has been changed in the record while the OLE or memo field has remained consistent.

The extra memo or OLE field is named `Gen_xxx` where `xxx` is the name of the associated memo or OLE field. In all other respects, these extra fields are identical to `s_Generation`.

s_Lineage

Each record also contains an `s_Lineage` field. This field contains the "nicknames" of replicas that have updated that particular record and the version number produced by that replica. Jet uses `s_Lineage` to monitor which replicas are responsible for changes to the record and the version number of each change.

Changes to AutoNumber fields

Many developers use AutoNumber fields as primary keys in tables. AutoNumber fields are automatically generated as new records are added to tables, and they are guaranteed to be unique within a table. The problem with AutoNumber fields in replication schemes is that if they are incremental, they are incremented in the same sequence in each replica that adds records to the table. Therefore, many primary key conflicts develop as the tables are updated during synchronization.

During conversion to replicable form, Jet modifies incremental AutoNumber fields to random AutoNumbers. The values of existing AutoNumber fields are not changed, so that primary and foreign keys that rely on the AutoNumber values are not disturbed; but all new records contain random AutoNumber values.

Primary key conflicts still are possible with random AutoNumber fields. If you determine that using random Autonumber primary keys introduces too many conflicts and errors, consider changing the primary key fields to the `s_GUID` field in each replicable table. Jet goes to a great deal of trouble to ensure that the `s_GUID` field value is unique in every record.

Because the random AutoNumber fields result in randomly arranged records in the tables (by default, of course, the records in an Access table are ordered in ascending order by the primary key value), an application that relies on the sequential nature of an incremental AutoNumber field may fail. In this situation, Microsoft recommends that you add a Date/Time field to provide the sequence information needed by your application.

Changes to the Design Master Structure

As described elsewhere in this chapter, the design changes you make to the Design Master propagate throughout the replica set. Each change you make to the Design Master is recorded and tracked in `MSysSchChange`, enabling you to "back out" of bad design decisions.

When changes are made to the Design Master's structure, those changes are exchanged before data exchange during synchronization. This sequence ensures that important structural changes that affect the way data are stored and used in the database occur before new data are added.

Always limit access to the Design Master. You shouldn't permit users to make their own design changes to the Design Master — one silly mistake could be disastrous as the change is exchanged throughout the replica set.

Changes to data

Changes to the data managed by the replica set can occur at any replica. Any replica can synchronize with any other replica, making the replica set's topography important in some situations.

Remember that replication always exchanges entire rows of data (except for memo and OLE fields, which are exchanged only when necessary). The Jet database engine cannot detect or exchange field-level changes in Access tables.

Controlling replica creation

Any user who has permission to open a database can use the Access menus to create replicas from any member of a replica set. In most cases you won't want users making personal replica copies or experimenting with the replication options in the Access menus. This is especially true if you are using DAO to manage replication. Because the names of the members of a replica set are usually hard-coded into the subroutines and functions, the copies created by unauthorized users aren't included in synchronization events and will quickly contain invalid data.

Your best bet for controlling replication is simply to grant Open permissions only when a user has invoked the database application, and revoke the permission when the user exits the application. This scheme gives users access to the application as if they had full permissions but prevents them from opening the database file when they're not using the application.

The following function (Listing 31-2) grants permission on the database as the application starts.

LISTING 31-2

Temporarily Assigning Open Permissions to a Database

```
Function SetDBAccess (db As Database, _
     intGrantAccess As Integer) As Integer

  Dim MyCon As Container
  Dim MyDoc As Document

On Error GoTo HandleError

  Set MyCon = db.Containers("Databases")

  'Documents(0) is the document
  'representing the entire database:
  Set MyDoc = MyCon.Documents(0)
  '
  'Get the current user's name:
  MyDoc.Username = CurrentUser()

  If intGrantAccess = True then
    'Grant full access permissions:
    MyDoc.Permissions = dbSecFullAccess
  Else
    'Revoke all permissions:
    MyDoc.Permissions = dbSecNoAccess
  End If

  'Refresh the Containers collection to make
  'sure the new permissions are seen by Access:
  db.Containers.Refresh

 ExitHere:
  Exit Function
```

```
HandleError:
  'Return the error value as this function's value:
  SetDBAccess = Err
  Resume ExitHere

End Function 'SetDBAccess()
```

Invoke `SetDBAccess( )` with the name of the database and either `True` or `False` as arguments. If you insert this function in the `Open` event of the application's startup form, you can effectively control permissions on the application's database file.

Things to avoid

There are a number of situations you should avoid as you plan and implement a replication scheme. Because replication fundamentally alters the way people use their databases and data, carefully consider the impact that replication will have on the way your users work and your practices as a database professional.

Avoid making backups of replicas

It is a mistake to back up replica databases. Even though we've all been taught that backups are an important part of managing a database installation, backing up a replica removes the backup from the data and design synchronization cycle.

Keep in mind that each replica in a replica set contains a complete copy of the replicable data from each of the other replicas in the set. The only unique information managed by a replica consists of the local tables and other database objects that may be present in each replica. You may want to create some scheme for providing backups of those particular objects (perhaps an import/export utility that copies the local objects to an offline database that is backed up in a traditional fashion), leaving the replicable data alone.

If the backup is restored at a later date, the backup's out-of-date data and design may be propagated through the replica set, and that could cause a great deal of consternation and confusion as the out-of-date information is exchanged.

Avoid high-volume updates

As you learned when reading about replication topology, several replication designs lead to a large number of synchronization events. If your users are changing or adding large amounts of data to their replicas between synchronizations (particularly when computers are connected through dialup solutions), consider a ring or linear topology that minimizes the number of exchanges between replicas.

Replication housekeeping tasks

Keep in mind that several of the replication system tables continue to grow as replicas synchronize. Keep watch on the size of the replicable database on users' computers. Particularly when working with laptops and other small computers, the space requirements added by the system tables can overwhelm the available disk space.

You may need to purge records periodically from the replication system tables. Although you can't alter the design of these tables, you can delete records as needed. Your deletions will be propagated through the replica set at the next synchronization.

Simply deleting records will not reduce the size of databases on the users' desktops. You must also compact the `.mdb` files to free up the unused space.

Programming Replication

All replication tasks can be handled with VBA code. Making a database into a Design Master or creating a replica from a Design Master is mostly a question of setting certain properties or running certain methods on the database and its tables.

The major advantages of programming replication into your Access applications are as follows:

- Hiding the replication user interface
- Providing a simplified user interface for unskilled or untrained users
- Controlling permissions and access to data and replication commands

As with manually implemented techniques, the steps required to build replication into applications with VBA code are as follows:

- Convert a database to replicable Design Master form
- Create replicas from the Design Master
- Synchronize replicas as data and design updates occur

TIP

The DAO required to implement replication programmatically is built into the Jet database engine. Therefore, the same code is shared among Access, Word, Excel, and Visual Basic 6.0 (not Visual Basic.NET).

The following sections describe the VBA code required to perform each step of the replication process.

Keeping objects local

Earlier in this chapter (in the section titled "The Importance of Local Objects"), several reasons were given for not replicating every object in a database. For instance, you may have specific tables, forms, or reports that you'd rather not share with every user of a replica in the replica set.

Before you convert the database to a Design Master replica, you may want to set the `KeepLocal` property of these objects to "`T`" to keep them from becoming part of the replicable objects in the Design Master. Listing 31-3 shows how to check on this.

LISTING 31-3

Checking to See if KeepLocal Is Set on a Table

```
Function IsLocal( _
    TableName As String, _
    DatabaseName As String) As Boolean

  Dim MyTable As DAO.TableDef
  Dim MyDB As DAO.Database
   Dim ws as DAO.Workspace
 Dim intMatch As Integer
  Dim i As Integer

On Error GoTo HandleError

  Set ws = DBEngine(0)
  Set MyDB = ws.OpenDatabase(DatabaseName, False)
  Set MyTable = MyDB.TableDefs(TableName)

  'Check to see if the KeepLocal
  'property exists on the table:
  For i = 0 To MyTable.Properties.Count - 1
    If MyTable.Properties(i).Name = "KeepLocal" Then
      intMatch = True
    End If
  Next i

  'If KeepLocal property wasn't found,
  'set the function's value and exit:
  If intMatch = False Then
    IsLocal = False
    Exit Function
  End If

  'If KeepLocal is found and its value is "T",
  'set the function's value to True and exit.
  'Otherwise, set function's value to False and exit.
  If MyTable.Properties("KeepLocal") = "T" Then
    IsLocal = True
    Exit Function
```

continued

LISTING 31.3 *(continued)*

```
  Else
    IsLocal = False
    Exit Function
  End If

ExitHere:

  Exit Function

HandleError:

  Select Case Err

    Case 0
      IsLocal = False
      Resume ExitHere

    Case Else
      IsLocal = False
      MsgBox "ERROR " & Err & ": " & Error
      Resume ExitHere

  End Select

End Function
```

The `IsLocal()` function returns `False` if the `KeepLocal` property isn't found or if its value is set to anything other than `T`. `IsLocal()` will be `True` only if `KeepLocal` is found and its value is `T`. When the `KeepLocal` property is set to `T`, the object will not be made replicable when the database is converted to a Design Master.

You'll recall from earlier chapters that not all objects in a database are managed by Jet. Only Database, `TableDef`, and `QueryDef` objects are managed by Jet—everything else (forms, reports, macros, and modules) are owned by the Access application. You can append the `KeepLocal` property directly to Jet objects and set its value. You must append the `KeepLocal` property to the documents collection holding Access objects. The code in Listing 31-4 shows how to create and append the `KeepLocal` property to the forms document collection in an Access database.

LISTING 31-4

Setting the KeepLocal Property on an Object

```
Sub SetKeepLocal(db as Database)
  Dim MyDoc as Document
  Dim pKeepLocal as property
  set MyDoc = db.Containers!Forms.Documents![frmMyForm]
  set pKeepLocal = _
       MyDoc.CreateProperty("KeepLocal", dbText, "T")
  MyDoc.Properties.Append pKeepLocal
End Sub
```

As with the other replication properties, you must create and append the `KeepLocal` property to the database object (table, form, report, and so on) before setting its value. Once the `KeepLocal` property is appended and set, Jet considers its value when converting the database to a replicable format.

You cannot apply the `KeepLocal` property to objects after the database has been made replicable. If you already converted the database and made its objects replicable, you can set the object's `Replicable` property to `False` to prevent it from being included in future synchronization events.

To complicate things even further, if two tables are involved in a relationship, you must set the `KeepLocal` property the same way in both tables. Jet replicates related tables only in pairs. You cannot have one table with `KeepLocal` set to `True` and the other table's `KeepLocal` set to `False`.

Also, you cannot set `KeepLocal` on related tables while the relationship is in effect. You must remove the relationship, set `KeepLocal` on both tables, and then reestablish the relationship between the tables. If your attempt to set `KeepLocal` on a table fails, check to see if the table is involved in a relationship with another table before proceeding.

Converting a database to a Design Master

Converting an existing database file to replicable format is actually quite easy. The conversion itself occurs when you set the database's `Replicable` property to `T`, and Jet does the rest.

Before setting the `Replicable` property, however, you should probably check to make sure the database is not already replicable. The function in Listing 31-5 shows how to conduct this check:

LISTING 31-5

Checking to See if an Object Is Replicable

```
Public Function IsReplicable( _
    MyDBName As String) As Boolean

  Dim intMatch As Integer
  Dim i As Integer
  Dim MyDB As DAO.Database
  Dim ws as DAO.Workspace

On Error GoTo HandleError

  Set ws = DBEngine(0)
  'No need to open the database exclusively,
  'so second argument is False:
  Set MyDB = ws.OpenDatabase(MyDBName, False)

  'First, check to see if Replicable property has
  'been added to this database's Properties collection:
  For i = 0 To MyDB.Properties.Count - 1
    If MyDB.Properties(i).Name = "Replicable" Then
      intMatch = True
    End If
  Next i

  'We didn't find the Replicable property,
  'so we're sure this database is not replicable:
  'Therefore, set the function's value and exit.
  If intMatch = False Then
    IsReplicable = False
    Exit Function
  End If

  'We found the Replicable property,
  'so check its value:
  If MyDB.Properties("Replicable") = "T" Then
    IsReplicable = True
    Exit Function
  Else
    IsReplicable = False
    Exit Function
  End If

 ExitHere:

  Exit Function

 HandleError:
```

```
   Select Case Err

     Case 0
       IsReplicable = False
       Resume ExitHere

     Case Else
       IsReplicable = False
       MsgBox "ERROR " & Err & ": " & Error
       Resume ExitHere

   End Select

 End Function
```

If you determine that the database is not currently replicable, you can create and append the `Replicable` property, then set its value to `T`, as shown in Listing 31-6.

LISTING 31-6

Setting the Replicable Property on an Object

```
Public Function SetReplicable(MyDBName As String) As Boolean

  Dim pRep As DAO.Property
  Dim MyDB As DAO.Database
  Dim ws as DAO.Workspace

On Error GoTo HandleError

  Set ws = DBEngine(0)

  'The database must be opened exclusively to change
  'Replicable property, so second argument is True.
  Set MyDB = ws.OpenDatabase(MyDBName, True)

  'If the Replicable property doesn't exist, create it.
  'Turn off error handling in case the property already
  'exists:

On Error Resume Next

  Set pRep = MyDB.CreateProperty("Replicable", dbText, "T")
  MyDB.Properties.Append pRep
```

continued

LISTING 31-6 *(continued)*

```
    MyDB.Properties("Replicable") = "T"

    SetReplicable = True

ExitHere:

    Exit Function

HandleError:

    Select Case Err

        Case 0
            SetReplicable= False
            Resume ExitHere

        Case Else
            SetReplicable= False
            MsgBox "ERROR " & Err & ": " & Error
            Resume ExitHere

    End Select

End Function
```

This very simple function forces the `Replicable` property into the database's Properties collection. The `On Error GoTo Next` jumps over the error that is generated if the `Replicable` property already exists.

TIP **As mentioned elsewhere in this chapter, once the `Replicable` property has been set to `T`, you can't return the database to nonreplicable status by setting the `Replicable` property to `F`. If you try to do this, an error is raised.**

When using VBA to convert a database to replicable format, all you get is the Design Master. Unlike the equivalent Access menu commands, this method does not produce a replica at the same time. You must explicitly create a replica using the replicable database object's `MakeReplica` method.

By default, a replica set Design Master is created when you set the `Replicable` property to `T`. All of other database properties that existed at conversion time are preserved in the new Design Master. Jet automatically adds all hidden system tables, system fields, and other properties and objects required to support replication on the new Design Master.

Making new replicas

Replicas can be made from any member of the replica set. Immediately after conversion, however, the only member of the replica set is the Design Master. All future members of a replica set are created from existing members of the replica set. There is no way to add another database to a replica set — for instance, you can't add a new member to a replica set by running the conversion routine on the copy of the original database.

New replicas are created by running the `MakeReplica` method of a replicable database. The following subroutine (Listing 31-7) shows how to use the `MakeReplica` method.

LISTING 31-7

Creating a New Replica Database

```
Sub MakeAdditionalReplica(ReplicaDB As String, _
     NewReplica As String)

  Dim db As DAO.Database
  Dim ws as DAO.Workspace

  Set ws = DBEngine(0)

  'Open the existing replica database as db.
  'The database must be opened in exclusive mode
  '(2nd argument is True):
  Set db = ws.OpenDatabase(ReplicaDB, True)

  'Run the MakeReplica method to create the new replica:
  db.MakeReplica strNewReplica, "First Replica of" & _
       ReplicaDB, dbRepMakeReadOnly

  db.Close

End Sub
```

As the replica is created, all properties of the existing replicable database are applied to the new replica, including all table relationships, indexes, and permissions.

If the source database includes attached tables, you should verify that the attachment path is correct in the new replica. It's possible the path will be invalid, particularly if the new replica is placed on another computer in the network.

Synchronizing replicas

Perhaps the easiest task to implement in VBA is actually synchronizing two databases. The `Synchronize` method of the database object invokes the replication facility in Jet and processes the entire synchronization event. The syntax of `Synchronize` is:

```
db.Exchange TagetDBPathName, intExchType
```

Where `db` is one of the database objects involved in the exchange, `TargetDBPathName` is the path to the target database, and `intExchType` specifies what type of exchange to perform between the databases.

The permissible values of `intExchType` are the following:

- `dbRepImpExpChanges`: Performs a bidirectional change between the replicas
- `dbRepExportChanges`: Changes only the flow from the current database to the target

If you leave out the `intExchType` argument, Jet assumes a bidirectional exchange and performs a complete synchronization.

The following subroutine (Listing 31-8) demonstrates the `Synchronize` method.

LISTING 31-8

Using the Synchronize Method

```
Sub SynchronizeDB(db1Name, db2Name)
  Dim db As DAO.Database
  Dim ws as DAO.Workspace
  Set ws = DBEngine(0)
  Set db = ws.OpenDatabase(dbName1)
  'Perform a bidirectional synchronization:
  db.Synchronize db2Name, dbRepImpExpChanges
  db.Close
End Sub
```

As the synchronization proceeds, Jet always updates design changes before exchanging data. Because changes to table structures alter the way the data are used in the tables, it makes sense that the design changes must occur first. The `intExchType` argument affects only data synchronization. If the structure of the Design Master has changed, those design changes are propagated to the replica.

Replication properties

The Jet database engine adds several new properties to a database as it is converted to a replicable format (by default, this conversion results in a replication Design Master). These properties are the following:

- `Replicable`: (Boolean) Indicates that the database is replicable (`value = "T"` or `True`). Once set to `T`, this value cannot be changed to make the database nonreplicable.
- `ReplicaID`: The `ReplicaID` is a GUID that uniquely identifies the Design Master. Each replica made from the Design Master will use this GUID to identify the Design Master, and each replica in a replica set is assigned its own `ReplicaID`.
- `DesignMasterID`: The `DesignMasterID` property is stored in the `MSysReplicas` system table and contains the `ReplicaID` of the Design Master in the replica set. Change this property only when you want to change the replica that is designated as the Design Master for the replica set. When you change this property on one of the replicas, you must set the `DesignMasterID` in the original Design Master to point at the new Design Master.

  The only time you might change the `DesignMasterID` in a replica without resetting the `DesignMasterID` in the original Design Master replica is when the original Design Master has been lost due to disk or other hardware failure. Under most circumstances you won't need to change this property at all. See the following section, "Moving the Design Master," to see the VBA code associated with changing the `DesignMasterID` property.

CAUTION **Never designate two different replicas as Design Masters within the same replica set. Doing so may split the design set into two separate replica sets that can no longer replicate with each other.**

Moving the Design Master

If the Design Master of a replica set is lost because of a hardware failure or user error, you may need to designate another replica as the set's Design Master. Switching the `DesignMasterID` between the old Design Master and the new Design Master is sufficient to reassign the Design Master status. The changes will be propagated at the next synchronization.

The following code (Listing 31-9) performs such an action.

LISTING 31-9

Transferring the Design Master Status to Another Database in the Replica Set

```
Sub SetNewDesignMaster(OldDMName As String, _
     NewDMName As String)

  'Points to existing Design Master:
```

continued

LISTING 31-9 *(continued)*

```
    Dim OldDM as DAO.Database

    'The replica to become new DM:
    Dim NewDM as DAO.Database

    Dim ws as DAO.Workspace

    Set ws = DBEngine(0)

    'Open old Design Master in exclusive mode:
    Set OldDM = ws.OpenDatabase(OldDMName, True)

    'Open database that will become the new Design Master.
    'Because we're changing the ReplicaID of the new Design
    'Master, it must be opened exclusively as well:
    Set NewDM = ws.OpenDatabase(NewDMName, True)

    'Change the DesignMasterID in the old Design Master
    'to point to the ReplicaID in the new Design Master:
    OldDM.DesignMasterID = NewDM.ReplicaID

    'Now synchronize the changes with the new Design Master:
    OldDM.Synchronize NewDM, dbRepImpExpChanges

    OldDM.Close
    NewDM.Close

End Sub
```

The current Design Master (if there is one!) must be open before you can change the designated Design Master. (If the Design Master has been lost through a system failure — perhaps a hard drive has gone bad — the soon-to-be Design Master must be opened in read/write mode so that its status can be changed.) The Design Master must be read/write to accept design changes. As the database `DesignMasterID` is changed, the old Design Master becomes read-only and the new Design Master becomes read/write.

Scheduling synchronization events

When using DAO to conduct replica synchronization events, you have to program synchronization schedules and topology into your VBA code explicitly. In many cases, you use a single replica (the *controlling replica*) to initiate and control replication with the other replicas in the set.

For instance, in a star topology, the controlling replica might be the star's hub replica. This replica synchronizes with each satellite replica in turn and then resynchronizes with each to ensure that all data are up to date on all replicas.

Whatever design you implement for your synchronization scheme, make sure you provided enough protection against synchronization failure. In many situations, failure to update all records from all replicas is a serious issue. Your code should be able to handle situations when a particular replica is not available or when synchronization conflicts occur. Use the information provided in the replication system tables to determine the success or failure of synchronization events.

In fact, your replication design should respond to the situation in which the controlling replica is not available. For instance, if you normally run synchronization at midnight, you might have each replica in a replica set check the synchronization log tables to see if synchronization is complete by 3:00 a.m. If synchronization has not occurred, a second replica should assume the role of controlling replica and initiate replication with the other replica set members. Obviously, these complicated designs are easiest to implement when all replicas in the replica set exist on the same network and only a few replicas are involved in synchronization.

Keep in mind that there is no problem with running redundant synchronizations. Even if two replicas have already had their updates, no error occurs if the replicas rerun the synchronization. If time permits, you may decide to run all synchronizations twice, once from each of two controlling replicas, to increase the probability that synchronization was successful.

If you decide to use multiple controlling replicas in your design, be sure not to simultaneously run the synchronizations on each controlling replica. Not only can a replica not service synchronization demands with two other replicas, but you defeat the purpose of redundant synchronization events. You really want them to proceed sequentially.

Partial Replicas

So far, all of the replication examples we've looked at have exchanged entire sets of data. All of the changed data in the tables in a replica member are exchanged with other members of the replica set. However, some times you would rather exchange only part of the data contained within a replica member. For instance, assume the data includes sales figures for different regions. You may not want to exchange all the sales data with all regions. Instead, you may want to exchange only data relevant for each sales region, and need some way to filter the data appropriately.

It is possible to replicate only a select portion of the records in a replica set. This process is called partial replication, and is implemented as the Partial Replica Wizard, described in the next section. Partial replication is very useful when large sets of data are included in the replica members. When thousands (or even millions) of records have to be considered, the replication process can consume considerable amounts of time, even if only a small number of records are actually updated.

The partial replication implemented in Access 2007 does not replicate individual fields within records. Instead, you construct a `WHERE` clause that tells the replica master which records to consider during the replication process. Each member of a replica set can have its own `WHERE` clause, which means that the records exchanged during replication can be site-specific. Furthermore, a member of a partial replica set can replicate only with the set's Design Master and not another member of the partial replica set.

A partial replica can be produced only with the Partial Replica Wizard or through VBA code.

Using the Partial Replica Wizard

You invoke the Partial Replica Wizard by selecting Partial Replica from the Replication Options button in the Administrator group on the Database Tools ribbon tab.

The Partial Replica Wizard works against an existing replicable database, so use the procedures described earlier in this chapter to establish a replica set. Open any replica set member (other than the Design Master), and follow these steps to set up partial replication on this replica:

1. **Select the Partial Replica Wizard command from the Replication Options menu on the Database Tools ribbon tab.**
2. **The next dialog (Figure 31-12) asks for the location of the partial replica. Normally this location is a folder on the local computer.**

FIGURE 31-12

Specifying the location of the partial replica

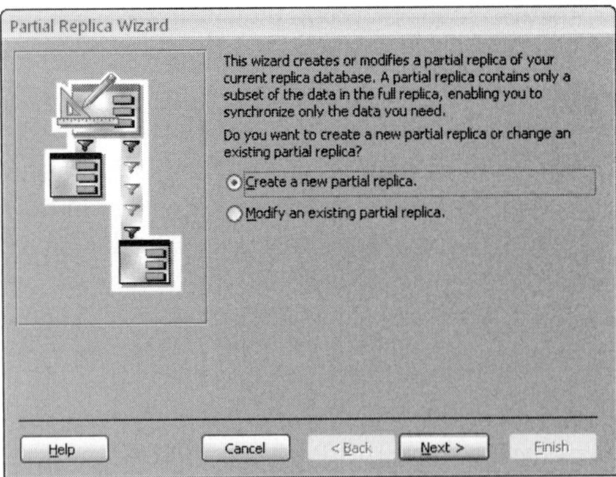

3. **The second dialog of the Partial Replica Wizard (Figure 31-13) asks which specific type of partial replica you wish to create. The three options are Global, Local, and Anonymous. These options are explained in detail later in this section.**

FIGURE 31-13

Specifying the type to apply to the new partial replica

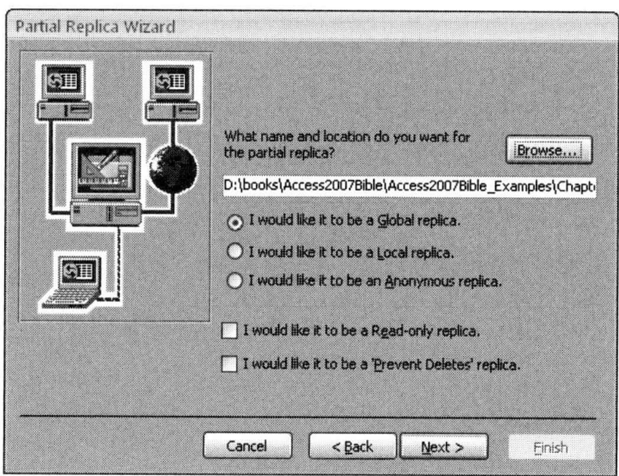

4. The Partial Replica Wizard needs to know how to select records for the replication event. You specify the selection criteria on the next wizard dialog (Figure 31-14). First select the table from the drop-down list at the top; then select the field for the selection expression from the list below the table drop-down list. Click the Paste button to paste the field name into the Filter Expression text box. If necessary, use the comparison operators on the left side of the dialog to build the selection expression. Alternatively, of course, you might simply type an expression into the Filter Expression text box instead of using the operator controls.

FIGURE 31-14

Create the filter expression the wizard will use to select records.

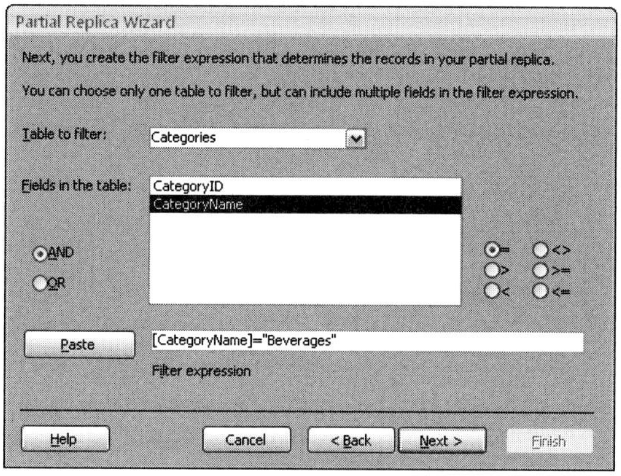

Partial Replica Wizard

Next, you create the filter expression that determines the records in your partial replica.

You can choose only one table to filter, but can include multiple fields in the filter expression.

Table to filter: Categories

Fields in the table: CategoryID, CategoryName

AND / OR

= <> > >= < <=

Paste [CategoryName]="Beverages"

Filter expression

Help Cancel < Back Next > Finish

The selection criteria can include more than one field, if necessary. For instance, valid selection criteria include the following:

```
[BranchID] = "NY" And [Location] = "Albany"
[Location] = "Syracuse" Or [ManagerID] = 12
```

5. **The next dialog (Figure 31-15) shows which tables in the database are related to the table you have used for the replica's selection expression. Use this dialog to specify which tables should be entirely or partially included in the replica. If it's important that the replica include all records from certain tables, make sure these tables are checked in this dialog. Only the records directly related to the selection criteria are selected from the unchecked tables in Figure 31-24. In this particular example, all the customer, product, and inventory data are included in each replication event, while only the order and order details information directly related to the New York regional office will be replicated.**

FIGURE 31-15

Tell the wizard which tables should be entirely included in replication events.

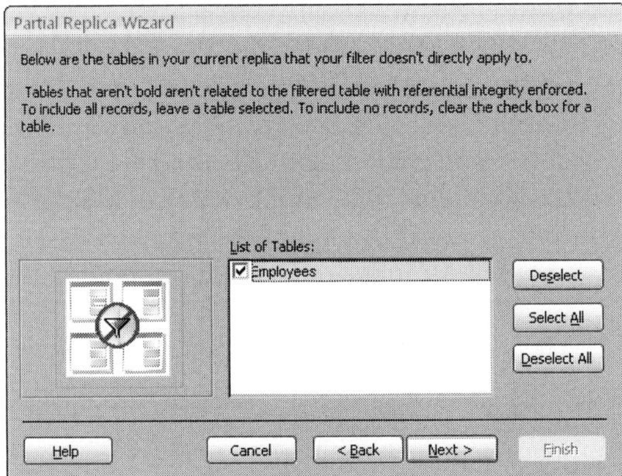

6. **The last dialog of the Partial Replica Wizard asks you if you want a report of the wizard's configuration. Normally, a report isn't necessary, unless you'll be working with dozens of partial replicas. (Remember that each partial replica is independent of all other replicas in the replica set.)**

After you set up a partial replica, the tables in the replica will contain only the records you specified. If you have successfully filtered the data available in the Design Master to a smaller subset, replication events occur much more quickly than when working with full sets of data.

Choosing the type of replica

The second dialog of the Partial Replica Wizard asks which type of partial replica you wish to create. The three options are:

- **Global:** The changes in a global partial replica are fully tracked and are available for synchronization with any other global replica in the replica set. A global partial replica is also able to synchronize with local and anonymous replicas, as long as the global replica is that the center of the replica set.
- **Local:** A local replica member is able to exchange data with a global replica member that serves as the hub of a replica set, but cannot arbitrarily exchange data with other members of the replica set.
- **Anonymous:** An anonymous replica member does not track the names or locations of replica members during synchronization operations. This means that an anonymous replica is able to exchange data with virtually any other replica set member, without generating a lot of conflict errors. Anonymous members are particularly useful in situations where many, many different users are synchronizing data and there is a significant chance of conflict errors.

Programming partial replication with VBA

Earlier in this chapter you read about using VBA and DAO syntax to control replication. The benefits of using VBA are clear: more control over replication events, ability to modify replication parameters at runtime, ability to create a customized user interface to replication information, and so on. The same benefits apply to using VBA to establish and conduct partial replication events.

Creating the partial replica

Earlier in this chapter (in Listing 31-7) you saw how to use the `MakeReplica` method to create a new replica from an existing replica master. Use the `dbRepMakePartial` parameter to specify that the new replica is a partial replica of a full replica database. The code in Listing 31-10 illustrates this process.

LISTING 31-10

Using the dbRepMakePartial Parameter to Create a Partial Replica

```
Public Function CreatePartial() As Boolean

  Dim db As DAO.Database

On Error GoTo HandleError

  'In the following statement, MyDM.mdb has already
```

continued

LISTING 31-10 *(continued)*

```
  'been designated as a Design Master database:
  Set db = OpenDatabase ("C:\My Documents\MyDM.mdb")

  'Use the MakeReplica method to create the
  'partial replica. Notice the use of the
  'dbRepMakePartial parameter:
  db.MakeReplica "C:\My Documents\MyDMP.mdb", _
      "Partial Replica of MyDM", dbRepMakePartial

  CreatePartial = True

ExitHere:

  db.Close
  Exit Function

HandleError:

  CreatePartial = False
  MsgBox Err.Number & ": " & Err.Description
  Resume ExitHere

End Function
```

As you can see in this function, the code is not very involved. Access knows to create the partial replica when you pass `dbRepMakePartial` to the `CreateReplica` method. The other statements in this function open the replica master and handle errors that might occur as the partial replica is created.

The `ReplicaFilter` property of the new partial replica is set to `False` by the `MakeReplica` method, indicating the replica contains no data (`ReplicaFilter` is described in the next section). You can use the `ReplicaFilter` property to test whether data has been added to the partial replica.

Setting the partial replica's filter criteria

So far all you've created is an empty replicable database with no tables, queries, forms, or other data. The next step is to specify the filter criteria Jet will use to populate the partial replica with data. You apply the filter by setting the `ReplicaFilter` property of relevant tables in the partial replica. Use a `WHERE`-type expression to specify the filter criteria. Listing 31-11 sets the expression "`[BranchID]='NY'`" on the `tblBranchOffices` table:

LISTING 31-11

Setting the Filter Criteria on tblBranchOffices

```
Public Function CreateFilter() As Boolean

  Dim db As DAO.Database
  Dim td As DAO.TableDef

On Error GoTo HandleError

  'MyDMP.mdb must be opened in exclusive mode so
  'that we can manipulate its tables. Use the True
  'parameter to tell Jet to open the table exclusively:
  Set db = _
      OpenDatabase("C:\My Documents\MyDMP.mdb", True)

  'Set the filter on tblBranchOffices
  Set td = db.TableDefs("tblBranchOffices")
  td.ReplicaFilter = "BranchID = 'NY'"

  CreateFilter = True

ExitHere:

  db.Close
  Exit Function

HandleError:

  CreateFilter = False
  MsgBox Err.Number & ": " & Err.Description
  Resume ExitHere

End Function
```

Again, the code is quite simple. Most of the statements in this function involve opening the database and handling errors. The `ReplicaFilter` property can be set only on an open `tabledef` object, so you must trap the error that occurs if the `tabledef` is not available. Also, the `On Error` statement at the top of the `CreateFilter( )` function traps the error that will occur if the database cannot be opened exclusively.

You cannot use aggregate expressions, user-defined functions, or subqueries as part of the filter expression. You should keep the filter expression as simple as possible to avoid possible errors during the replication events.

Creating table relationships in the partial replica

Next you need to establish the relationship between the primary table and its related tables in the partial replica. Jet uses this relationship to find records related to the partially replicated records in the primary table. The function in Listing 31-12 creates a relationship between the `tblBranchOffices` and `tblOrders` tables so that only the orders taken by the specified branch office will be included in replication events.

LISTING 31-12

Setting the Relationship between Tables in the Partial Replica

```
Public Function SetRelationship() As Boolean
  Dim db As Database
  Dim Rel As Relation

On Error GoTo HandleError

  Set db = _
       OpenDatabase("C:\My Documents\MyDMP.mdb", True)

  'Walk through Relations collection in MyDMP.mdb and
  'set the PartialReplica property to True for the
  'relation between tblBranchOffices and tblOrders:
  For Each Rel In db.Relations
    If Rel.Table = "tblBranchOffices" _
         And Rel.ForeignTable = "tblOrders" Then
      Rel.PartialReplica = True
      Exit For
    End If
  Next Rel

  SetPartialRelationship = True

ExitHere:

  db.Close
  Exit Function

SetPartial_Err:

  SetPartialRelationship = False
  MsgBox Err.Number & ": " & Err.Description
  Resume ExitHere

End Function
```

Each relation object in a replicable Access 2007 database has a `PartialReplica` property. This property tells Jet that the tables on either end of the relation are involved in the partial replica.

Filling the partial replica with data

The last step is to actually add data to the partial replica. `PopulatePartial`, a new method of the Access 2007 Database object, fills the partial replica with data from a full replica in the replica set (the full replica does not have to be the replica set's Design Master). The `PopulatePartial` method requires the name of the full replica to be used. (See Listing 31-13.)

LISTING 31-13

Filling the Partial Replica with Data from MyDM.mdb

```
Public Function FillPartial() As Boolean
  Dim db As Database
  Dim sReplica As String

On Error GoTo HandleError

  'Set sReplica to MyDM.mdb (the parent database):
  sReplica = ("C:\My Documents\MyDM.mdb")

  'Open MyDMP.mdb (the partial replica) in exclusive mode:
  Set db = _
       OpenDatabase("C:\My Documents\MyDMP.mdb", True)

  'Fill the partial replica with data from MyDM.mdb.
  'The data source does not have to be
  'the Design Master of the replica set:
  db.PopulatePartial sReplica

  FillPartial = True

ExitHere:

  db.Close
  Exit Function

HandleError:

  FillPartial = False
  MsgBox Err.Number & ": " & Err.Description
  Resume ExitHere

End Function
```

Although the `PopulatePartial` method conducts a one-way synchronization between the Design Master and partial replica, you should not routinely use `PopulatePartial` to trigger synchronization events. Because `PopulatePartial` does not perform a full two-way synchronization, you should continue to use the `Synchronize` method for routine replication events. `PopulatePartial` is meant to be run only to establish the initial data set in the partial replica and then run anytime the filter criteria changes. Furthermore, `PopulatePartial` cannot be run from within the partial replica.

The `PopulatePartial` method removes any "orphaned" records in the partial replica. For instance, if the filter criteria for a partial replica is changed, the `PopulatePartial` method (which must be run anytime the filter is modified) removes records left over from the previous filter criteria. Or if a synchronize event has been run on the partial replica before the filter criteria is established, the partial replica contains all records in the full replica. Running `PopulatePartial` removes unneeded records from the partial replica.

Replicating partial replicas

A partial replica can be replicated only against a full replica in its replica set, not against another partial replica in the set. For obvious reasons, another partial replica won't contain all the records that may be required for synchronization.

Also, compound filters are *unioned* instead of OR'ed together. This means the data returned by a compound filter contains all records returned by either part of the expression, instead of the intersection of the filters. For instance, if you filter for `"BranchID = 'NY'"` and `"OrderDate > 6/1/2007"` you get *all* records where `BranchID = 'NY'` and *all* records with order dates after 6/1/2007.

Also, the `PopulateReplica` method can be run only as part of a direct replication event. Indirect replication is possible only when both replicas are available on a network and no drop box is used. Once the partial replica has been established, replication events proceed normally.

Maintaining referential integrity in partial replicas

It's easy to produce a partial replica that violates the referential integrity rules established in its parent replica. For instance, assume that `tblOrders` must contain only records with valid Customer ID numbers. In other words, you do not want orders to appear in `tblOrders` that are not matched with corresponding records in `tblCustomers`. Unless you include both `tblCustomers` and `tblOrders` in the partial replica, Jet won't let you add records to `tblOrders` in the partial replica.

As a general rule, always include all tables involved in referential integrity in the partial replica. Also, make sure the filter criteria will return all records required to maintain referential integrity.

The Partial Replica Wizard automatically includes all dependent tables in the partial replica. Make sure you include all records necessary to avoid violations of the referential integrity rules. In the example described earlier in this chapter, the entire customers and products tables were included in the partial replica to ensure that dependent records in `tblOrders`, `tblOrderDetails`, and `tblInventory` could be updated without error.

Advanced Replication Considerations

As you plan a replication design, there are several considerations to keep in mind as you create the Design Master and its replicas. Although none of these suggestions are mandatory, you may avoid some problems if you always follow these guidelines:

- **Compact before synchronizing.** It only makes sense to compact replicas before synchronizing, particularly after making design changes that will propagate through the replica set. Compacting the replicas ensures that all unwanted objects have been removed from each replica, including the old versions of structural objects, and that they won't be involved in the replica exchange.
- **Synchronize before making design changes.** Jet always updates design changes before synchronizing the data in a replica set. If you synchronize before making design changes, you reduce the amount of time and data exchanged during the synchronization because the data elements will be up to date before the design changes are exchanged.
- **Remove the database password before making a database replicable.** Because the database password blocks synchronization attempts by other replicas, always remove an existing database password before you convert the database to a Design Master. You should also enforce a prohibition against assigning a database password to any replica in a replica set. User permissions do not interfere with synchronization.
- **Do not put a Synchronize Now button on an open form.** An interesting Catch-22 occurs if you include a Synchronize Now button on a form that is part of the replication user interface you build using VBA and DAO. This button, of course, would initiate synchronization between the currently open local replica and some other replica within the replica set.

  Because the database being synchronized must be opened exclusively by Jet, the first synchronization will fail: Jet won't be able to exclusively open the current database because it's already in use. The best that can be done is that the Synchronize Now button will actually trigger synchronization between some other replicas in the set, or it will simply open a new database that initiates the dialogue between the current database and another. A bit confusing, perhaps, but easy enough to work around.
- **Keep View System Objects turned off.** As you've already learned, the Jet replication engine adds several system fields to replicable tables. If you allow users to turn on the View System Objects option, the system fields may become visible in list boxes, combo boxes, and other controls that display data in the replicable tables. Obviously, this information will be confusing to your users.

You may find it necessary to make a replica nonreplicable. Perhaps the needs of its users have changed making it unnecessary to exchange data with other replicas, or a project or activity that formerly required a distributed replica set is no longer under way.

Unfortunately, you cannot simply convert a replicable database by resetting its `Replicable` property. As you learned earlier in this chapter, once the `Replicable` property is set to `T` or `True`, an error occurs if you try to reset it to `F` or `False`.

The only way to revert a replicable database to nonreplicable status is by building an entirely new database containing the same data elements as the replicable version. Follow these steps:

1. **Create a new, empty database and open it.**
2. **Import the queries, forms, reports, macros, and modules from the replicable database.**

   Keep in mind that you'll need Administrator permission on the replica before you can import objects from it.
3. **Create a make-table query for each table in the replicable database.**

   Include all of the original table's fields except for the system fields (`s_Generation`, `s_GUID`, and `s_Lineage`). Run the query to build the same tables in the new database. Obviously, you should not import the replication system tables from the replica.
4. **Re-create the indexes and relationships that exist in the original database.**

TIP **Each replica in a replica set is read-only. You cannot make design changes to a replica, so you can't simply remove the system fields from a replica to convert it back to a non-replicable database. Furthermore, you can't open the Design Master and delete the system fields from each replicable table and then import the tables into your new database. Jet protects the replication system fields and will not allow you to remove them, even from the Design Master.**

Summary

This rather lengthy chapter focused on the fascinating topic of database replication with the Jet database and Access 2007. Replication is a significant feature for many organizations using Access as a workgroup or enterprise database system. Although this chapter did not explore replicating changes to database objects in detail, a replication operation sends updates to forms, reports, and other database objects to replica members just as it does data.

Although the `.accdb` file format does not support replication, you may be able to design a hybrid system in which the user interface (the front-end database) is an Access 2007 `.accdb` file, and the replicated back-end is an Access 2000 `.mdb` file with tables linked to the `.accdb`. The Jet database engine does not care how data are consumed in an Access application as long as the replicated database is of the proper type.

Chapter 32

Object-Oriented Programming with VBA

A major incentive in all modern application development is to produce robust, reusable code. Microsoft Access provides a number of ways to make code more reusable, beginning with simple import or export of code modules on through building runtime code libraries.

This chapter covers one approach to creating code modules you can reuse from any Access database. The code modules we describe in this chapter define new types of objects for your Access applications. These objects include properties and methods, and you can copy the objects into other Access applications or add them to Access code libraries.

The objects you create enforce modular, object-based programming. You've likely noticed how Access is based on objects. Microsoft defines just about everything in an Access application as some kind of object. All the forms, the controls on the forms, the reports, and other visible parts of your programs are objects.

In addition, there are any number of hidden objects (such as table relationships) lurking in your program. These objects are one of the ways Access is modular in nature. Each built-in Access object (such as a table, query, or form) performs some task in the application.

In this chapter, we dive into the important topic of object-oriented programming (OOP) in Access. Here you'll learn what objects are and how to use them in your programs. You'll also learn how to build your own objects using Access VBA code. Although this chapter discusses objects such as forms and controls as examples, the emphasis is on the technology of creating and using custom objects in your Access applications.

IN THIS CHAPTER

You create the custom objects in your applications by adding code to a special class module. In the lexicon of object-oriented programming, a *class* is a code element that defines an object. A good analogy for a class module is the engineering specification that defines a car or airplane. You create an object using the class as its specification. You add code to the class module to define the object's properties and methods. Modifying the code in a class module modifies how the object defined by the class module behaves.

This chapter uses the database named `Chapter32.accdb`. If you haven't already copied it onto your machine from the CD, you'll need to do so now.

Benefits of Object-Oriented Programming

You might be wondering why it's important to bother with objects. What are the advantages of Access object-oriented programming? Why complicate things by introducing the complexity of building and maintaining custom objects when traditional procedural programming techniques have worked so well in your Access applications?

You've already seen how Access's object-based programming benefits database developers. You do all the Access data access through Data Access Objects (DAO) or ActiveX Data Objects (ADO) recognized by the Jet database engine. Other built-in Access objects such as forms and controls include properties you can easily manipulate at design time. As the application runs, these properties determine the object's behavior. Creating a form or report requires nothing more than dropping control objects on the form or report's surface and setting properties to bind the control to data and establish the control's appearance.

The greatest benefit from using objects is *encapsulation,* which is the ability to wrap all aspects of the object's functionality into an entity. For example, dropping a text box onto an Access form adds several new properties, methods, and events to the form. The text box control encapsulates all the relevant properties (for example, `ForeColor`, `BackColor`, and so on), methods (for example, `SetFocus`), and events (for example, `BeforeUpdate`, `LostFocus`, and so on) required to support a text box type of object. Although you add these new items to the form, you can access the new properties, methods, and events through the new text box control.

The textbox control encapsulates everything a text data-entry control requires to do its job. In addition, Access text box controls incorporate a lot of hidden capabilities, such as binding to a data source, applying validation rules, and so on. In other words, there's a lot going on in the humble text box control that you probably seldom recognize or appreciate.

A custom Access object lets you encapsulate complex activities and tasks as a simple, compact entity you can use in any other Access database. An encapsulated object is often much easier to maintain than a traditional module or VBA procedure. Because the object contains all its functionality as a single entity, there's just one module for you to modify or maintain as you make improvements to the program.

Although you can't create new form controls using the Access object-oriented development tools, you can add many capabilities to your applications through class modules alone.

For instance, most applications include extensive data-validation routines. Depending on the type of data the user enters, data validation ranges from one line of code to extensive modules containing dozens or hundreds of lines of code. Using Access's OOP features, you can wrap all data-validation routines into a single object you can use by setting its properties and invoking its methods.

Custom objects, therefore, provide a simplified interface to complex operations. When properly designed and implemented, you can use the custom objects you create in Access in virtually any compatible VBA programming system, exposing the same properties and methods you work with when incorporating the objects in your Access databases.

Object basics

Our world is filled with objects. The car you drive, the computer you use, and the radio you listen to are all examples of objects. Some objects, such as a desk lamp, are relatively simple, while other objects, such as a stealth bomber, are considerably more complex.

In addition to physical objects, our world is filled with objects you can't feel or touch. Electricity, sound, and light are all examples of objects people can produce, measure, and use, but you can't sense them as physical entities. An object's visible characteristics have little to do with its value to people. The electricity coursing through your computer's circuitry can be as valuable as the car you drive, under the right conditions.

You'll find any number of visible and invisible objects in most Access databases. And, just as with the objects that make up our environment, the invisible objects in an Access database can be as valuable as the forms, menus, and ribbons the user sees.

An Access object is a programmable entity of one sort or another. The `Err` object is an example of an invisible, but valuable, object built into Access. You use the `Err` object's properties (`Number`, `Description`, and so on) to determine which error has occurred. The `Clear` method resets the `Err` object, preparing it for the next error to occur. Even though the `Err` object never appears on an Access form or report, it has an important role in every professional Access application.

What's an object?

Although there's an endless variety of objects, all objects have a number of features in common. An object is a programmable entity; most objects contain a number of properties you can read or set at runtime. In addition, most objects include methods you can execute to perform tasks. An object's properties and methods define the object's interface to the rest of the program.

You can write custom objects to adapt to changing environments and user requirements. Most often you can exploit an object's programmable nature by changing its properties and invoking its methods. But you can engineer a custom object in such a way that the object automatically adapts to differing conditions by running different internal routines.

You can create most object types multiple times in an application. Each time you create the object, Access assigns it a unique name to distinguish it from other instances of the object. In other words, a single Access program can host more than one instance of the object, each object operating independently of the others (possibly even cooperating with the other objects), and maintaining its own set of properties and other data.

For example, say the Northwind Traders database (included with Microsoft Access) contains a `Product` object. The class module supporting the `Product` object defines the `Name`, `Supplier`, `UnitPrice`, and other properties of the product. There are any number of `Product` objects in the Northwind Traders database, each with its own name, price, and supplier.

To carry the analogy further, another class module might define a `ProductInventory` collection object that contains a number of `Product` objects. The `ProductInventory` class would feature a `Count` property that tells you how many `Product` objects are in the collection. The `ProductInventory` class module might contain a `Sell` method that deducts a certain `Product` item from the `ProductInventory`.

Using objects in applications

Every time you've written code setting a label's `Caption` property or returning the contents of a text box's `Value`, you've worked with objects. Although a label or text box control is a simple type of object, the principles behind these objects are the same as using more complex and intelligent objects you create yourself.

The following Access VBA code shows a series of statements that are typical of how you'd use objects in Access applications.

```
Dim ObjectName As ObjectClass
Set ObjectName = New ObjectClass
'Setting a property of the object:
ObjectName.SomeProperty = SomeValue
'Invoking a method of the object:
ObjectName.SomeMethod
```

In this code, the name of the object is `ObjectName` and its object class (described in the next section) is `ObjectClass`. You declare the object in the `Dim` statement and the `New` keyword instantiates (creates) it. `SomeProperty` is a property of the object, and `SomeMethod` is a method of the object.

Class module basics

You define an object by the code in a class module. You must add a class module to your Access application, and then add the property and method code to the module before using the object the class module defines. The name of the class module is the name of the object's class.

A class module is a special type of code module. Access recognizes the module as an object's definition and lets you create new instances of the object from the code in the module. Any of the object's special features — including properties, methods, and events — are exposed as procedures tagged with the `Public` keyword in the class module. You should declare any code in the class module you intend for only the object to use, and won't expose to the outside world, with the `Private` keyword.

Each object you create from the class module is an instance of an object class. For example, the Nissan Sentra is a particular class of automobile. The Nissan Sentra that your Uncle Joe owns is a particular instance of the Nissan Sentra class of automobile. Even though Uncle Joe's car looks pretty much like every other Nissan Sentra, certain attributes of his car set it apart from all the other Nissan Sentras on the road.

Carrying the car analogy a bit further, consider the properties and methods of the automobile object class. A car has a color property that defines the color of the car's exterior. It's likely that the color of any car matches the color applied to other cars produced by the car's manufacturer. A car also has a vehicle identification number (VIN) that isn't shared with any other car anywhere in the world.

An object's property values, therefore, are a combination of values shared with other objects of the same class and values unique to the particular instance of the class. In fact, there must be a property or some other attribute of the object that sets it apart from all other instances of the same type of object in the application. Otherwise, Access can't know which instance you're referring to in your code.

If you were to construct a `Product` class module, you'd include properties such as `Name` (a string), `UnitPrice` (a currency data type), `UnitsInStock` (an integer or long integer), `ReorderLevel` (also an integer or long integer), and `Discontinued` (a Boolean value). Depending on how you'll use the product object in the application, you may add properties to contain the quantity per unit, the category ID, and other information relevant to the application. You'll also want to add the `ProductID` property to uniquely identify each instance of the product object.

You may have noticed that all the properties we mention in the preceding paragraph correspond to the fields in the `Products` table in the Northwind Traders database. In fact, often each instance of the object represents a record contained in a database table.

Because you're constructing the class in VBA code, you can add any properties necessary to support the application and the data you're constructing. When you build Access classes, you have access to all the power and utility available through the Access data types and features. Adding new public procedures to the class module extends the properties and methods available to the object. You can, therefore, define new data types to accommodate whatever peculiarities your application requires.

In the class module, private variables handle property values. As you can see in the "Persisting property values" section, later in this chapter, the mechanism for implementing properties is part of the special attributes of class modules. You must follow certain rules and coding conventions to successfully implement properties in Access class modules.

In addition to properties, most objects support a number of methods, which are the actions that the class performs. An airplane has a number of rather obvious methods: ascend, descend, and land, among others. The classes you construct in Access implement whatever functionality you want the class's objects to support. The `Product` object we describe earlier might have `Sell` or `Discount` methods not shared with a `Customer` object in the same database.

The methods of a custom object exist as public procedures (functions and subroutines) in the class module. And, just as with properties, you have the full power and flexibility of VBA at your disposal as you write the methods of your custom classes.

A simple class module

Most often, the classes in your applications will model some real-world object, such as customers, contacts, employees, and products. Your knowledge and understanding of the physical object translate directly into Access VBA code and become the properties and methods of the Access objects you create from the class module's code.

This chapter's database (`Chapter32.accdb`) implements a `Product` class similar to the one we describe in the previous sections. The product class module (`clsProduct1`) in `Chapter32.accdb` includes the properties and methods in Table 32-1 and Table 32-2, respectively.

TABLE 32-1

Example Properties in the Chapter32.accdb Database

Name	Data Type	Description
`ProductID`	Long integer	The product's ID
`Name`	String	The name of the product
`Supplier`	String	Name of company supplying the product
`UnitPrice`	Currency	Customary selling price of product
`UnitsInStock`	Integer	Current stocking level of product
`ReorderLevel`	Integer	Minimum stocking level before reordering
`Discontinued`	Boolean	True if product has been discontinued

TABLE 32-2

Product Class Methods Used in the Example Database

Name	Purpose
`Sell`	Sells a quantity of the product
`Discount`	Reduces the selling price of the product instance

The `Product` class object in `Chapter32.accdb` doesn't completely model a real product. You can add many other properties and methods to this class to more effectively model a real product, but this simple class does show you how to approach modeling a physical object in Access.

You can describe the product you'd create from the class like this: A product `Name` and `ProductID` identify the product. A certain manufacturer (the `Supplier`) produces the product, and it is intended to be sold for a certain `UnitPrice`. Northwind Traders keeps track of the number of units in stock (`UnitsInStock`) and has determined the minimum number of units to keep in stock (`ReorderLevel`). The manufacturer may discontinue a product, in which case its `ReorderLevel` is set to zero and the `UnitsInStock` is allowed to decrease to zero as items are sold. Periodically, a product may be sold (the `Sell` method) and may also be discounted through the `Discount` method.

Adding a class module to a database

Choose Insert ➪ Class Module to open a new class module in the editor window, or select the Macro drop-down list in the Other group of the Access Create ribbon tab, and choose Class Module.

It's a good idea to click on the Save button on the Code Editor toolbar and assign a name to the class module early in its development cycle. The name you provide for the class module becomes the name of the object's class when creating objects from the class module (see Figure 32-1). The name you provide for class module is similar to the names you've given other objects in your databases.

FIGURE 32-1

You'll use the name you provide for the class module as the object's class name.

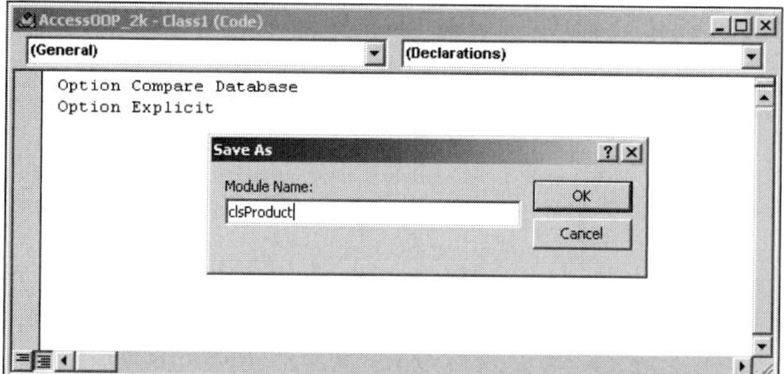

The class name should be descriptive but not excessively long. Furthermore, the name should be meaningful to you. Users never see the name of the class, so use a name that means something to you or another developer.

The class module is in the code editor window in Figure 32-1. Notice the class module looks just like any other module in the editor window. Your only indication that it isn't a normal module is the tiny icon in the left corner of the module as it appears in the code editor. It's a little box icon, rather than the "tinkertoy" icon you see in standard modules.

Creating simple product properties

The easiest way to establish the properties of a class, and the technique you'll use in your first class example, is to simply declare each of the properties as a public variable in the `clsProduct1` class module. Adding a public variable to a class module creates a new property for the class. The variable's public scope makes it accessible to other routines in the database. Later in this chapter, in the "Using Property Procedures" section, you'll see an alternate way to create properties for your class modules.

```
Public ProductID As Long
Public Name As String
Public Supplier As String
Public UnitPrice As Currency
Public UnitsInStock As Integer
Public ReorderLevel As Integer
Public Discontinued As Boolean
```

Figure 32-2 shows the class module after you've added the public variables.

FIGURE 32-2

Public variables in a class module become properties.

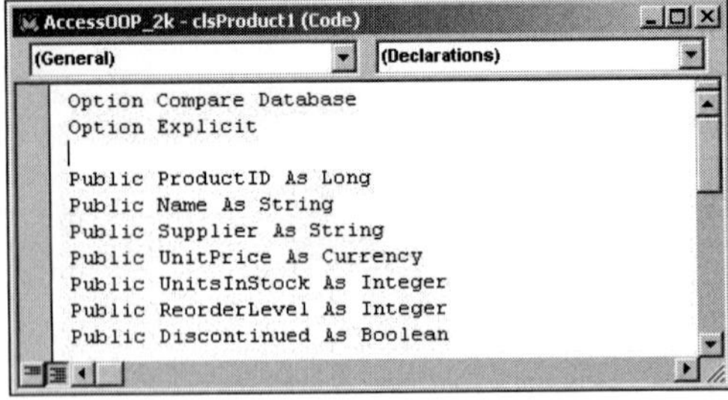

Access treats each public variable in a class module as a property of the objects created from the class. Because you declare the public variables in a class module, Access uses the variables as properties of the class's objects without further work on your part. Figure 32-3 shows how IntelliSense displays the properties in the Auto List Members drop-down list in a module using an object created from the class.

FIGURE 32-3

IntelliSense shows you the properties and methods created for the new object class.

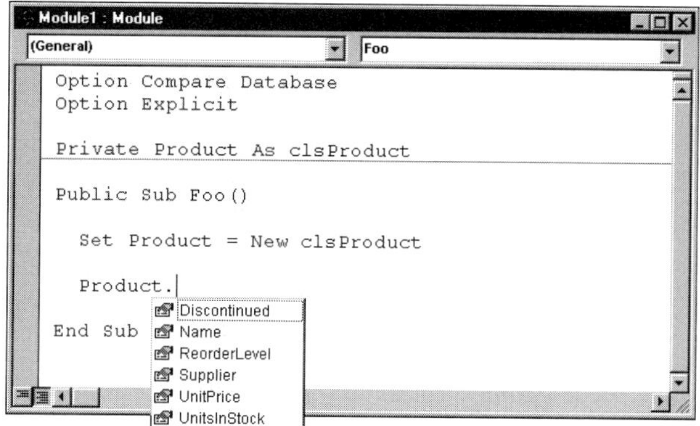

The names you provide for an object's properties and methods should be descriptive and easy to recognize. Because the class's properties are variables in the class module, the names you assign to these items must conform to VBA's variable naming requirements. That is, property names should be 64 or fewer characters and contain only alphanumeric characters and the underscore character. Property names must begin with an alphabetic character and should never begin with the underscore character or a number.

Creating methods

The `clsProduct1` class includes two methods. These methods, like all object methods, define actions supported by the objects created from the class. Each method is nothing more than a public procedure in the object's class module.

The following code example shows the procedure implementing the `Sell` method. Because all procedures in a class module are public by default, the `Public` keyword is optional and you add it to the `Sell` method to clarify the status of the procedure.

```
Public Sub Sell(UnitsSold As Integer)
  Me.UnitsInStock = Me.UnitsInStock - UnitsSold
End Sub
```

Notice there's nothing special about the `Sell` method. There's no special declaration for this procedure, nor is there reference to its status as a method of the class. Methods are an example of how Access treats class modules differently from simple code modules. As long as you haven't declared the procedure (sub or function) with the `Private` keyword (remember the `Public` is the default!), Access treats the procedure as a method of the objects created from the class module.

Because it's a subroutine, the `Sell` method doesn't return a value. If you had declared it as a function, it could return any valid Access data type. The `Sell` procedure requires an argument specifying how many items were sold.

Notice the use of the Me keyword in the previous code example. In this context, Me refers to the object instance created from the class module.

You may have noticed an obvious bug in the Sell method. If the UnitsSold is larger than the UnitsInStock, the UnitsInStock value will be a negative number after the method runs. To fix this bug, you must add a couple of lines of code to the method:

```
Public Sub Sell(UnitsSold As Integer)
  If UnitsSold > Me.UnitsInStock Then
    Exit Sub
  End If
  Me.UnitsInStock = Me.UnitsInStock - UnitsSold
End Sub
```

This change causes the Sell method to simply exit and not deduct any units when the UnitsSold value would result in a negative value for the UnitsInStock.

Obviously, there's much more you could add to the product class. I've included the complete class module in the Chapter32.accdb example database as the clsProduct1 module in the Modules tab of this database.

The Discount method is similar to Sell (see the following code example). In this case, the method ends immediately if the Percent is less than 1 or larger than 99. Otherwise, the object's UnitPrice property is discounted by an expression derived from the Percent and current UnitPrice.

```
Public Sub Discount(Percent As Integer)
  If Percent < 1 _
  Or Percent > 99 Then
    Exit Sub
  End If
  Me.UnitPrice = _
    Me.UnitPrice - ((Percent / 100) * Me.UnitPrice)
End Sub
```

Eventually, with enough work and attention to detail, you can refine the product class to the point where it would support all the features and requirements of a real product sold by Northwind Traders. Other classes could model other data in the Northwind database such as customers, employees, and orders. Later in this chapter, you'll see some of the advantages of using class modules in your Access applications.

Using the product object

After you've assembled the class module from properties and methods, you can create new objects from the class. Figure 32-4 shows frmProductUnbound, a form included in Chapter32.accdb, the database accompanying this chapter. The text boxes along the left side of this form display the object's properties. The buttons to the right side of this form invoke the object's methods.

FIGURE 32-4

`frmProductUnbound` creates an object from `clsProduct1` and provides an interface to its properties and methods.

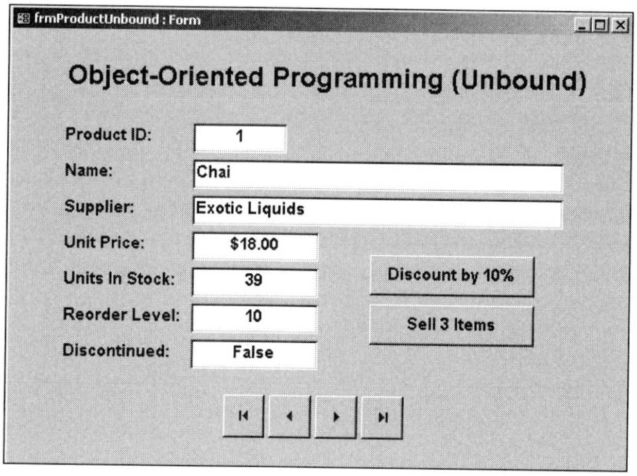

The code behind `frmProductUnbound` is quite simple.

Creating a new product object requires you to use the `New` keyword. This statement is one way to create a new instance of a product object from the `clsProduct1` class module:

```
Private Product As New clsProduct1
```

Alternatively, you can first declare the `Product` object, then instantiate as separate statements. For instance, place this statement in the module's `Declarations` section to establish the `clsProduct1` object:

```
Private Product As clsProduct1
```

The object instantiates in the form's `Load` event procedure:

```
Set Product = New clsProduct1
```

We prefer using separate statements for declaration and instantiation. It isn't possible to trap errors when declaration and instantiation are processed as a single statement, which means your application may exhibit instability in some situations.

In either case, the code creates the new `Product` object instance at the instant the `New` keyword executes. The code behind `frmProductUnbound` uses the two-statement approach to creating the `Product` object: In `frmProductUnbound`, you declare the product in the form's `Declarations` section as a module-level variable, and then the object instantiates during the form's `Load` event. Therefore, the `Product` object is available as soon as the form opens on the screen, and it's accessible to all the code behind the form.

The code in the form's Load event procedure also fills a recordset object with records from tblProducts. You then use this recordset to set the Product object's properties. A private subroutine named SetObjectProperties retrieves values from the recordset and sets the object's properties to those values:

```
Private Sub SetObjectProperties()
  'Set the product object's properties:
  With Product
    .ProductID = rs.Fields("ProductID").Value
    .Name = rsFields("ProductName").Value
    .Supplier = rsFields("Supplier").Value
    .UnitPrice = rsFields("UnitPrice").Value
    .UnitsInStock = rsFields("UnitsInStock").Value
    .ReorderLevel = rsFields("ReorderLevel").Value
    .Discontinued = rsFields("Discontinued").Value
  End With
End Sub
```

After you create the product, you can reference its properties and methods. References to the product object's properties are similar to property references anywhere else in VBA. This statement retrieves the current value of the product's UnitPrice property and assigns it to the text box named txtUnitPrice on frmProductUnbound:

```
txtUnitPrice.Value = Product.UnitPrice
```

You can find a number of similar statements in the form's FillForm procedure:

```
Private Sub FillForm()
  'Fill the form with the product's properties:
  txtID.Value = Product.ProductID
  txtName.Value = Product.Name
  txtSupplier.Value = Product.Supplier
  txtUnitPrice.Value = Product.UnitPrice
  txtUnitsInStock.Value = Product.UnitsInStock
  txtReorderLevel.Value = Product.ReorderLevel
  txtDiscontinued.Value = Product.Discontinued
End Sub
```

frmProductUnbound makes several property assignments from the form's Load event procedure. The following code listing shows the entire Form_Load sub from frmProductUnbound. Notice how the code builds the recordset, makes the property assignments, and fills the text boxes on the form through the SetObjectProperties and FillForm procedures.

```
Private Sub Form_Load()
  Set Product = New clsProduct1
  Set rs = CurrentDb.OpenRecordset("tblProducts")
  If rs.RecordCount > 0 Then
    Call SetObjectProperties
    Call FillForm
```

```
    End If
  End Sub
```

Similarly, selling a product involves using the object's `Sell` method. The code below shows how a form might use the `Sell` method. Notice the code passes a parameter (`txtNumberToSell`). The user has entered the number of items to sell into a text box named "`txtNumberToSell`. That value becomes the `UnitsSold` argument for the `Sell` method we discuss earlier in this chapter.

```
Private Sub cmdSell_Click()
  Product.Sell txtNumberToSell
  Call FllForm
End Sub 'cmdSell_Click
```

The `FillForm` procedure is called to refresh the form's contents after the `Sell` method executes.

Create bulletproof property procedures

In many cases, assigning an invalid value to a property results in a runtime error or other bug. If you're lucky, the invalid value causes the application to halt and display an error message to the user. It's much worse to have the application continue operating as if nothing is wrong when, in fact, the class module is working with invalid data. The best situation is when the class module itself validates property values as they're assigned, instead of waiting until the properties are used by forms, reports, and code in the application.

For instance, consider a banking application that calculates exchange rates for foreign currency deposited in the bank's vault. A class module is the ideal vehicle for handling foreign currency exchange calculations. Keeping these calculations in a class module isolates these complicated routines from the rest of the application and makes it easy to maintain the calculations as currency values fluctuate. And, because class modules support IntelliSense, it's much easier to work with objects defined by class modules than public procedures stored in standard modules.

Ideally, the exchange rate class module wouldn't accept invalid exchange ratios or would check the exchange ratios that the user inputs at runtime. Perhaps the class module could check online sources such as *The Wall Street Journal* or other financial publications to verify that the data the user input is correct.

Property errors might occur if the code passes a string when a numeric value is required or when a property value is less than zero. The following methods help bulletproof properties and avoid run-time errors:

- Set default property values if the code passes an inappropriate data type. Use a conversion routine to correct the value, if possible.
- Use private procedures in the class module to validate data types. These data-validation routines are often class-specific.
- Use error trapping everywhere in the class module, especially on the class's properties and methods. The property procedures and methods (the public procedures in the class) are where most unexpected behaviors occur.

Keep in mind that a basic principle of using object-oriented programming is encapsulating functionality. Whenever possible, you should include anything that affects how the class operates in the class module. Keeping the property validation, method error handling, and other features in the class module makes the class more portable and reusable.

Encapsulation isn't well implemented in the clsProduct1 example presented in this section. For instance, the form's code retrieves the data, and assigns values to the product object's properties. A better approach would be to have all the data management performed by the class itself, isolating the form from the data-management operations. A form using a properly-constructed class shouldn't have to know which database table contains the product data; instead, the form should be a strict consumer of the product data.

Other Advantages of Object-Oriented Programming Techniques

The simplest way to add properties to a class is to include public variables within the class module. In fact, anything declared with the `Public` keyword is exposed by the class as either a property or a method. In the "Creating simple product properties" section, earlier in this chapter, you can see public variables used to define properties. The following sections explain using property procedures, a more robust and sophisticated way to define properties, and explain in detail the requirements and rules governing the properties in a class.

The mix of properties (and their data types), methods (and the arguments accepted or returned by the methods), and the events supported by a class are referred to as the class's *interface*. A developer working with an object created from a class module is typically unable to access the class's interface, and not the code within the class (unless, of course, the class's creator and the developer working with the class are the same person). Very often, class modules are bundled as Access libraries, or distributed as `.mde` or `.accde` files, and the interface is the only hint a developer has of the operations supported by the class (unless printed or online documentation accompanies the class).

A class's interface is revealed by the Object Browser (press F2 with the Code Editor window open). Figure 32-5 shows the Object Browser open to the `Product2` class, revealing the properties, methods, and events supported by this class.

At the bottom of the Object Browser, you'll see that `ProductName` is defined as a public property and is a string data type. This area is where you'd see that a property is read-only or write-only. Also, all private elements are identified accordingly. Finally, notice how all the property variables are sorted together because of the m_ prefix. You can read about property variables in the "Using Property Procedures" section, later in this chapter.

FIGURE 32-5

The Object Browser reveals a class's interface.

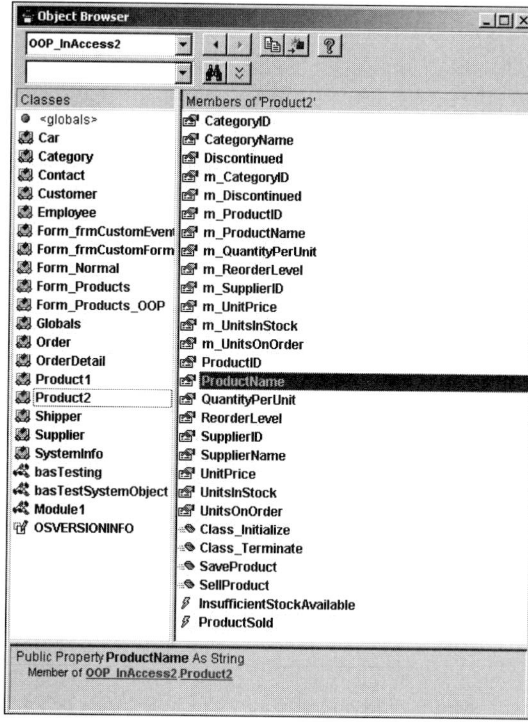

Figure 32-6 illustrates one of the most valuable aspects of object-oriented programming. Notice how the IntelliSense Auto List Members drop-down list shows you all of the appropriate interface elements as soon as the object is identified and the dot is typed. This is a huge benefit to anyone working with your class module.

FIGURE 32-6

The Auto List Members drop-down list makes it easy to select an object's properties or methods.

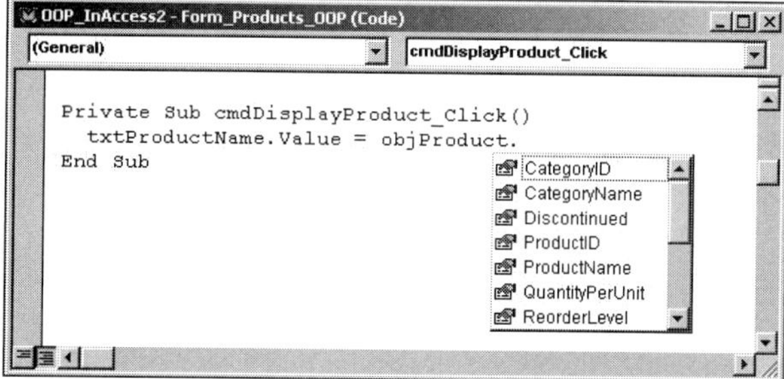

Furthermore, if you position the input cursor anywhere within the property name (such as `ProductName`) and press Shift+F2, the class module opens, showing you the code associated with the property (see Figure 32-7).

FIGURE 32-7

Shift+F2 shows you the code associated with an object's property.

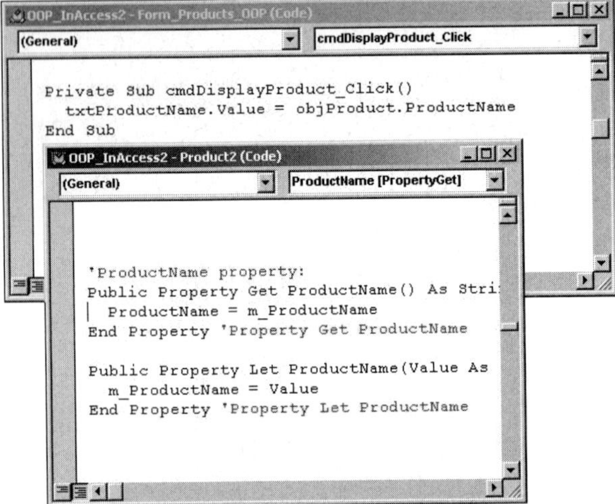

The class module's VBA code must be available for the Shift+F2 shortcut to work, of course. If the class has been bundled as an `.mde` or `.accde` file or is otherwise unavailable, Shift+F2 will not work.

Generally speaking, object-oriented programming techniques are most often applied to unbound applications. Although it is possible to build an Access application with a mix of bound, unbound, and object-oriented techniques, using bound forms misses one of the main advantages of object-oriented programming. Most developers turn to object-oriented programming techniques because they want more control over how the data are used by their applications. Using bound forms negates many of the considerable advantages of using object-oriented programming techniques without really adding anything of value to the project.

Also, most developers using object-oriented programming techniques are fairly advanced and are comfortable building unbound applications. The extra code involved in building classes containing properties and methods is not a hindrance to the majority of advanced Access developers.

Object-Oriented Programming Rules

There are two cardinal rules that you must obey when applying object-oriented programming techniques. We didn't make up these rules, but we know from personal experience that you're asking for trouble when you fail to pay adequate attention to them.

Never reveal a user interface component, such as a message box, from a class module

This rule is perhaps less important in Access applications than in other systems, but ignoring this rule may cause problems later on.

Here's why this is important: Consider a class that opens a message box to the user, indicating that a problem has arisen. Although this works fine in Access environments, this practice may cause problems if the class is ported to other environments.

All Access applications run locally on the user's computer. Therefore, opening a dialog box from an Access class module is guaranteed to open on the user's computer. In an Access application, there's no way to cause a message box to appear on another computer.

However, other development platforms support the notion of *remoting*, which means running code on an application server. Most often, the remoted component is implemented as a set of compiled classes, and if one of those classes opens a dialog box, the dialog box opens on the remote application server.

In this case, the application freezes in front of the user, and the user has no idea what happened. All the user knows is that the code stopped running. The code on the remote machine has stopped running, waiting for a response to the dialog box that has opened on the application server.

For obvious reasons, you're not going to make many friends if your application causes an application server to stop running!

Preserve the class's interface as the class is updated

You can add to the interface by introducing new properties, methods, and events, but you should never alter the data type of existing properties or method arguments, or remove an event from a class module.

It is very difficult to know where a class may be used, and once a class has been distributed, any changes to the class may break code in many different places without warning.

Sometimes it's impossible not to change a property's value or modify a method's arguments. As an example, users may require an additional argument to be passed to the `SellProduct` method so that shipping charges can be accurately calculated. Unless you take care to preserve backward compatibility, the consumer code referencing the original version of the `SellProduct` method is sure to fail.

One technique I've seen used to ensure backward compatibility is to duplicate the property or method, suffixing a numeric value to its name. For example, you might add `SellProduct1` to the class module, leaving the unchanged, original `SellProduct` for older code. New code will use the updated `SellProduct1` to take advantage of the shipping charges calculation.

Using Property Procedures

The concept of property procedures is fundamental to object-oriented programming. As the name implies, a property procedure is a VBA procedure that defines a property for a class. Most classes contain several to many property procedures.

There are three types of property procedures:

- `Property Get`: Retrieves the value of a property. A `Property Get` works very much like any function, and follows the same pattern as any VBA function.
- `Property Let`: Assigns a new value to the property. `Property Let` works only for simple data types such as numeric, strings, and date properties.
- `Property Set`: Assigns a value to an object property. You would use a `Property Set` for a property defined as a recordset or other object data type.

The concepts behind property procedures are illustrated in Figure 32-8. Each type of property is detailed a bit later in this chapter. In the meantime, be aware that each time your code references a property, the class module responds by running the appropriate property procedure.

FIGURE 32-8

Each time you read or write an object's properties, the class module runs a property procedure.

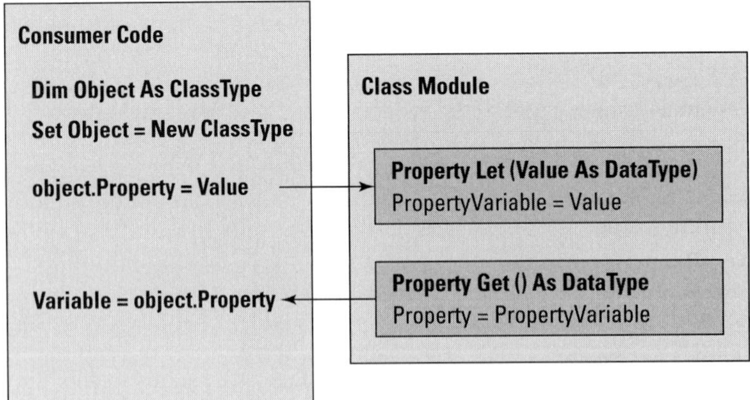

Property procedures are always public by default. Even if you omit the `Public` keyword, your property procedures is exposed to the other elements of your applications. You should, however, always use the `Public` keyword to clarify the property procedure's scope. It never hurts to be very explicit in your code.

The properties you add to your classes can be read/write, read-only, or write-only, depending on how you expect the property to be used. Omitting either the `Property Get` or `Property Let` (or `Property Set`, for that matter) makes the property read-only or write-only, respectively.

Omitting the `Property Let` (or `Property Set` for object properties) makes a property read-only. A consumer can read the property's value through the `Property Get` procedure, but cannot assign a new value to the property.

Obviously, because there is no way to assign a value to a read-only property, the class must provide the read-only property's value. This is often done by extracting a value from a database, or from the System Registry, or by reading a value from an `.ini` file or the operating system. Because a `Property Get` is a procedure, you can add any logic your class requires to obtain the property's value.

Omitting a `Property Get` makes a property write-only. You may decide to use a write-only property for sensitive information such as passwords and login identities. Making a write-only property is an excellent way to preserve the security of sensitive data. Write-only properties are also used to provide a class with information that it needs to support its activities, such as a connection string or database name.

Persisting property values

At this point, we know that properties can be read/write, read-only, or write-only. What hasn't been explained is where the property persists the value when the property is written, and where the property gets its value when the property is read.

In a VBA project, property value persistence is mediated through private variables contained within the class module. Generally speaking, each property is accompanied by a private variable that is the same data type as the property. This means that a property that reads or writes a string value will be accompanied by a private string variable, and each date property will be accompanied by a private date variable.

As you'll see in the next sections, the property variables are either assigned or returned by the property procedures. A property variable should be given a name that indicates which property owns the variable. In the examples accompanying this chapter, each property variable has exactly the same name as its property, and is tagged with an m_ prefix. For example, the property variable for the `CustomerID` property is named `m_CustomerID`. Furthermore, because the `CustomerID` property is a string, `m_CustomerID` is also a string.

There are cases, of course, where a property is not accompanied by a variable. For instance, a read-only property may extract the value from a database file or retrieve it from the operating system. Or, the property might be write-only, in which case the property may act immediately on the value passed to the property procedure, and no storage is necessary.

Property Let syntax

As described earlier, the Property Let procedure assigns a value to a property. The property's value is passed into the procedure as an argument, and the value is then assigned to the class module's private variable that stores the property's value.

The following example is a prototype for any `Property Let` procedure:

```
Public Property Let <PropertyName>(Value As <DataType>)
  <PrivateVariable> = Value
End Property
```

The property's argument can be named anything you want. We always use `Value` as the argument name. Consistently using `Value` is simpler than assigning a meaningful name to the argument, and is consistent with how property values are assigned to built-in Access properties.

The following example is from the `Employee` class module:

```
Public Property Let LastName(Value As String)
  m_LastName = Left$(Value, 20)
End Property
```

This small example hints at the power of property procedures. Notice that the `Value` argument is a string. The statement within the property procedure assigns only the 20 leftmost characters of the `Value` argument to the `m_LastName` variable. This is because the `LastName` field in the Northwind Employees table only accepts 20 characters. Many database systems generate errors if more characters are sent to a field than the field can hold. Adding a little bit of logic to a property procedure can go a long way toward bulletproofing an application.

Property Set syntax

The syntax of `Property Set` is parallel to the `Property Let` procedure. The only difference is that the argument is an object data type, and the VBA `Set` keyword is used for the assignment within the body of the `Property Set`. The following is an example of hypothetical `Property Set` procedure that accepts a recordset object and assigns it to a private variable named `m_Products`:

```
Public Property Set Products(Value As ADO.Recordset)
  If Not Value Is Nothing Then
    Set m_Products = Value
  End If
End Property
```

In this small example, the argument is validated before it is assigned to the private variable.

Property Get syntax

This is the basic syntax of the `Property Get`:

```
Public Property Get <PropertyName>() As <DataType>
  <PropertyName> = <PrivateVariable>
End Property
```

Notice the similarities between a `Property Get` and a VBA function. The `Property Get` is declared as a particular data type, and the property is assigned a value within the body of the property. The syntax is identical to any VBA function.

This is the `Property Get` from the `Employee` class module in the example application accompanying this chapter:

```
Public Property Get LastName() As String
  LastName = m_LastName
End Property
```

The `Property Get` executes whenever the property's value is assigned to a variable or otherwise used by the application. For instance, the following VBA statement executes a `Property Get` named `LastName` in the `Employee` class module (`objEmployee` has been declared and instantiated from the `Employee` class):

```
strLastName = objEmployee.LastName
```

Notice that this statement does not directly reference the `Property Get`. Because the `objEmployee` object was created from the `Employee` class, the VBA engine knows to run the `Property Get` because a variable is assigned the value of the `LastName` property. In other words, the VBA engine gets the `LastName` property value from the class.

In this example, the `Property Get` is very simple and only returns the value of the private variable. However, you could have a much more complex `Property Get` that performs data transformation on the value or retrieves the value from a database file, an `.ini` file, the operating system, or some other source.

This example also illustrates the simplified programming possible with object-oriented techniques. A single VBA statement in the application's consumer code is enough to run whatever complex operation is necessary to retrieve the value of the property. The consumer is never aware of the logic supporting the property.

Property procedure rules

There are just a few rules that apply to property procedures. First of all, the name assigned to a property procedure is the name of the property. Therefore, you should use a descriptive, helpful name for all of your properties. Typically, a developer using objects created from a class you create does not have access to the VBA code in the class and has to rely on the names you've assigned to its properties and methods for guidance.

Also, the data type of the `Property Let`, `Property Get`, and the private variable must coincide. For example, if the property is defined as a string, the private variable must be a string. Figure 32-9 illustrates this concept.

FIGURE 32-9

The property variable data type must coincide with the property's data type.

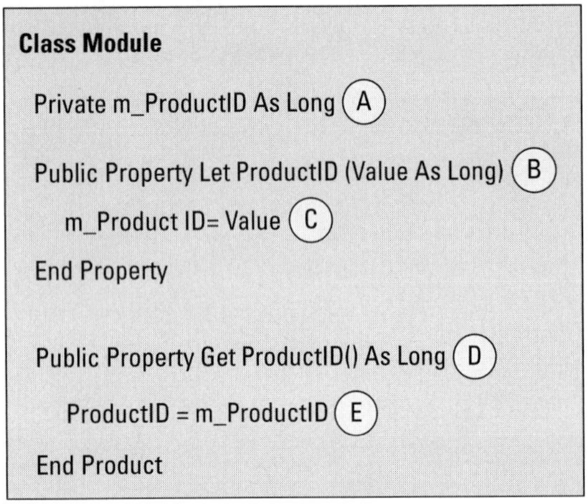

```
Class Module
  Private m_ProductID As Long (A)
  Public Property Let ProductID (Value As Long) (B)
     m_Product ID= Value (C)
  End Property

  Public Property Get ProductID() As Long (D)
     ProductID = m_ProductID (E)
  End Product
```

Note the following points in Figure 32-9:

- The property variable is declared as some data type (labeled "A" in Figure 32-9).
- The argument to the `Property Let` procedure is the same data type as the property variable ("B" in Figure 32-9).
- The property variable is assigned its value in the body of the `Property Let` ("C" in Figure 32-9).
- The `Property Get` procedure returns the same data type as the property variable ("D" in Figure 32-9).
- The `Property Get` is assigned the value of the property variable ("E" in Figure 32-9).

You'll get the following error if the data type assigned by the property procedures does not coincide:

> Definitions of property procedures for the same property are inconsistent, or property procedure has an optional parameter, a ParamArray, or an invalid Set final parameter.

Although you can use an incorrectly typed private variable for your property procedures, you'll encounter side-effect bugs if the variable does not match the data type used for the property procedures.

Extending the Product Class

Earlier in this chapter, we built a simple product class representing a Northwind product. The initial class is included in the Access .accdb file accompanying this chapter as the clsProduct1 class module. In this section, we extend the initial class (as the clsProduct2 class module) by making its properties more intelligent and useful.

Specifically, this section extends the property procedures within the Product class module, and adds methods to the module. We also expand the basic application by adding a few other classes needed to support the Northwind Traders application.

The example application accompanying this chapter includes a form named Products_OOP, which is based on the Products form included with Northwind Traders (see Figure 32-10). This form utilizes the majority of OOP techniques described in this chapter and can serve as a model for your OOP endeavors.

FIGURE 32-10

The Products_OOP form demonstrates unbound object-oriented techniques.

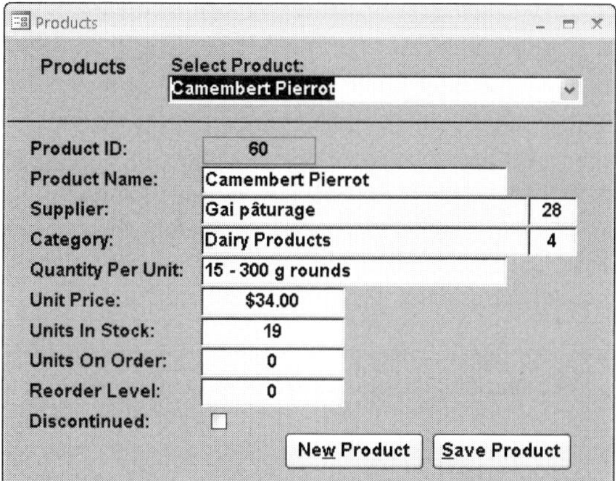

Retrieving product details

The first enhancement to the Product class is to update the process of retrieving product details, given a particular ProductID. In the initial example, the user selected a product from a combo box, and the form used an inline SQL statement to extract the details for the selected product.

The problem with having the form directly manage data are that the form (which is the consumer of the product data) has to know a great deal about how the product data are stored. The form holds a hard-coded SQL statement, creates a recordset with product data, then assigns the recordset's data to the product object's properties. This is far too much to entrust to the user interface.

Consider an application with perhaps hundreds of forms. Using the design described in the previous paragraph, each form in the application has to manage its own data. Changing anything in the database means many different changes have to be made to the user interface, greatly complicating maintenance.

Two of the primary objectives of object-oriented programming are code-reuse and data abstraction. We all know and understand code reuse: Write the code once, and use it many different places. Data abstraction is a bit more complex, but it's based on the notion that each layer of an application (data management, business logic, and user interface) should do what it does best, and not have to worry about other parts of the application. The data layer should concern itself with getting data into and out of the data source. The business logic should concern itself with the rules that drive the application, and the user interface presents data from the user and manages the application's interaction with the user.

Bundling all of those operations behind or within a form violates the notion of data abstraction. Every form in a bound application knows everything about the data managed by the form. Although this works well in small applications where complete control over the data are relatively unimportant, larger, more ambitious applications generally require significant control over the data.

The new ProductID property

The `ProductID` property enhancement is quite simple, even though the implementation requires a bit of code. The `Property Get` procedure simply returns the value of `m_ProductID`, as described earlier in this document. The real change comes with the `Property Let`.

The enhancements works like this: If a value greater than zero is assigned to the `ProductID` property, the class retrieves all of the product details matching the assigned `ProductID`. Each product detail selected from the database is assigned to the corresponding product property. If a value zero or less is assigned, the class assumes the product entity is a new product, and default values are assigned to each property.

The updated `Product` class is utilized behind a form named `Products_OOP`.

The code contained in the `ProductID Property Let` is fairly extensive. It begins by opening a recordset against the `ProductID` value, and then determines whether any data was selected. A small bit of logic then either assigns the found data to the property variables, or sets the property variables to default values:

```
Public Property Let ProductID(Value As Long)

  Dim db As DAO.Database
  Dim rs As DAO.Recordset

  m_ProductID = Value

  If m_ProductID <= 0 Then
    Exit Property
```

```
    End If

    Set db = CurrentDb()

    Set rs = db.OpenRecordset( _
      "Products", dbOpenTable)

    rs.Index = "PrimaryKey"

    'Seek the Product record matching
    'the m_ProductID value.
    rs.Seek "=", m_ProductID

    If Not rs.NoMatch Then

      'Assign database data to object properties:
      If IsNull(rs.Fields("ProductName").Value) Then
        m_ProductName = vbNullString
      Else
        m_ProductName = rs.Fields("ProductName").Value
      End If

      <This pattern is repeated for each property>

    Else 'Product not found!

      'Assign default values to
      'each property variable:
      m_ProductName = vbNullString
      m_SupplierID = -1
      m_CategoryID = -1
      m_QuantityPerUnit = vbNullString
      m_UnitPrice = -1
      m_UnitsInStock = -1
      m_UnitsOnOrder = -1
      m_ReorderLevel = -1
      m_Discontinued = False

      'Also assign default value to ProductID.
      'This will serve as a signal to the consumer
      'that an product was not found:
      m_ProductID = -1


      'An alternate approach would be to raise an
      'event telling the consumer that the product
      'could not be found.

    End If

End Property 'Property Let ProductID
```

This is a good example of encapsulation. Instead of requiring a consumer of the `Product` class to select the product data, the `Product` class easily supplies the data through the `ProductID` setting.

This small example also illustrates one of the major benefits of object-oriented programming. In a well-designed application, the only way to retrieve product data should be through the `Product` class. No other portion of the application needs to know anything about where the product data are stored, how to select or insert product data, and so on. In the future, should the need arise to change the product data source, only the `Product` class is updated, and all other portions of the application continue to function as before, without any changes.

Consider the time savings in a large application where the product data are used in dozens or even hundreds of different places. Good object-oriented design enforces modular programming and provides significant efficiencies when maintaining medium to large applications.

A new property

One of the things that bothers me about the Northwind Traders application is that it relies very heavily on Access-only constructs. In particular, most of the tables, when viewed in datasheet view, display related data. For instance, opening the `Products` table in datasheet view shows the product category and supplier information, and not the ID values associated with each of these items. For instance, the supplier name is shown in the `Products` table because the lookup properties of the `SupplierID` field are set to display a combo box containing the supplier names.

We've found these constructs to be confusing to users, especially people new to Access. Most people, when they see the supplier's name in the `Products` table, expect to find the supplier name among the data stored in the table. However, the only type of supplier information in the `Products` table is the `SupplierID`. If the supplier name is required, you must extract it the from the `Suppliers` table, using the `SupplierID` as the criterion.

An enhancement to the `Product` class is to make the supplier and category names accessible as read-only properties. You probably can guess how this is done: Simply extract this information from the respective tables, using the property variables for the `SupplierID` and `CategoryID` properties.

Here is the `Property Get` procedure for the new `SupplierName` property. The `Property Get` for the `CategoryName` property is virtually identical:

```
Public Property Get SupplierName() As String

  Dim varTemp As Variant

  If m_SupplierID <= 0 Then
    SupplierName = vbNullString
    Exit Property
  End If
```

```
    varTemp = DLookup("CompanyName", "Suppliers", _
      "SupplierID = " & m_SupplierID)

    If Not IsNull(varTemp) Then
      SupplierName = CStr(varTemp)
    Else
      SupplierName = vbNullString
    End If

  End Property
```

The Property Get uses DLookup to retrieve the CompanyName from the Suppliers table that matches the m_SupplierID property variable. The property variable is first checked to make sure its value is greater than zero, and the property ends if this condition is not met.

The SupplierName property is an example of how a class module can be enhanced by introducing new properties — either read-only, write-only, or read/write — that provide functionality not otherwise available. Again, the consumer of the class needn't know anything about the underlying data structures, and all of the data management is handled through the class module.

Product Methods

Another major advantage of encapsulation is that, because all data operations required by the entity are contained within the class, it's quite easy to update business logic.

Earlier in this chapter, you read about a hypothetical SellProduct method that had to be updated to accommodate a new sales tax. Whichever technique you use to update the method, the end result is the same. Because the method is an integral part of the class, there is only one update needed to update all uses of the SellProduct method in the application.

The previous section dealt with an update to the ProductID property. In the new ProductID Property Let, the property variable was assigned –1 when it appeared that the product was a new product. Here's how the SaveProduct method would handle the various values of the m_ProductID variable:

```
Public Function SaveProduct() As Boolean
  Dim db As DAO.Database
  Dim strSQL As String

On Error GoTo HandleError

  Set db = CurrentDb()
  If m_ProductID > 0 Then
   'Update existing record:
```

```
    strSQL = _
        "UPDATE Products SET " _
      & "ProductName = '" & m_ProductName & "'" _
      & "SupplierID = " & m_SupplierID _
      & "CategoryID = " & m_CategoryID _
      & "QuantityPerUnit = '" _
      & m_QuantityPerUnit & "'" _
      & "UnitPrice = " & m_UnitPrice _
      & "UnitsInStock = " & m_UnitsInStock _
      & "UnitsOnOrder = " & m_UnitsOnOrder _
      & "ReorderLevel = " & m_ReorderLevel _
      & "Discontinued = " & m_Discontinued _
      & "WHERE ProductID = " & m_ProductID
  Else
    'Insert new record:
    strSQL = _
        "INSERT INTO Products (" _
      & "ProductName," _
      & "SupplierID, " _
      & "CategoryID," _
      & "QuantityPerUnit, " _
      & "UnitPrice," _
      & "UnitsInStock, " _
      & "UnitsOnOrder," _
      & "ReorderLevel, " _
      & "Discontinued, " _
      & ")VALUES(" _
      & m_ProductName & ", " _
      & m_SupplierID & ", " _
      & m_CategoryID & ", " _
      & m_QuantityPerUnit & ", " _
      & m_UnitPrice & ", " _
      & m_UnitsInStock & ", " _
      & m_UnitsOnOrder & ", " _
      & m_ReorderLevel & ", " _
      & m_Discontinued & ")"
  End If
  SaveProduct = True
ExitHere:
   Exit Function
HandleError:
   SaveProduct = False
   Resume ExitHere
End Function
```

The code in the SaveProduct method is straightforward. If the m_ProductID variable is larger than zero, the record in the Products table matching the ProductID is updated. Otherwise, a new record is inserted into the Products table.

Class Events

There are two very important built-in events that accompany every Access class module. These are the Initialize and Terminate events. As you'll soon see, these two events provide invaluable assistance in many object-oriented programming projects.

Using class events is one of the things that is completely different from using standard code modules. Not only do class modules maintain their own data states, they provide events that provide a great deal of control over how the data are initialized and cleaned up within the class.

The Class_Initialize event procedure

Very often the property variables or other resources used by a class need to be initialized or set to some beginning state. Other than adding a method to trigger initialization, it may not seem obvious how to add initialization operations to your classes.

For instance, let's say you create a class module that needs to have a recordset open the entire time the class is used. Perhaps it's a class where the data needs to be frequently selected from a database. Frequently opening and closing connections and recordsets can be a unnecessary drain on performance. This is especially true when the selected data set doesn't change from operation to operation. It'd be much more efficient to open the recordset one time, leave it open while the class is being used, and then close it at the conclusion of the session.

That's where the class's Initialize event comes in. The Initialize event fires whenever an object is instantiated from the class module. In the following consumer code example, the Class_Initialize event procedure runs when the object is set to a new instance of the class:

```
Dim objProduct As Product
Set objProduct = New Product
```

Select Class from the object drop-down list in the upper-left corner of the VBA editor, then select the Initialize event from the Events drop-down list in the upper-right corner. There's nothing else you must do other than add the code you want to run when an object is instantiated from your class module. Figure 32-11 shows an example of a Class_Initialize event procedure in the Product class.

FIGURE 32-11

The `Class_Initialize` event procedure runs whenever an object is instantiated from the class module.

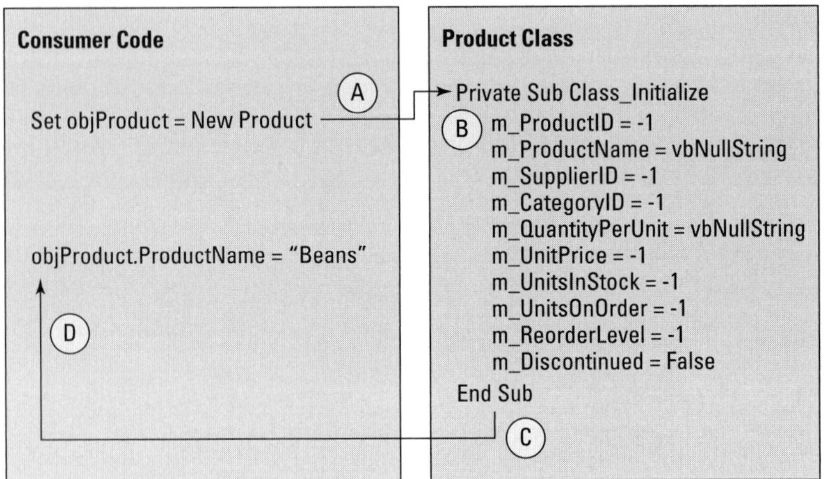

The sequence indicated by the numbers in Figure 32-11 is:

- The object is instantiated (A). Before this statement is completed by the VBA engine, the `Class_Initialize` event is invoked.
- Notice that `Class_Initialize` (B) is a private subroutine. It is owned by the class, and executes independently of the consumer code. No arguments are passed to `Class_Initialize`.
- Execution is passed back to the consumer code when `Class_Initialize` ends (C).
- Execute recommences in the consumer code at the statement following the object instantiation (D).

In this small example, you'll notice that numeric property variables are set to –1, rather than VBA's default of zero for numeric variables. This is because certain logic in the class module uses –1 to determine when certain states, such as when the user is entering a new product, are in effect.

The Class_Terminate event procedure

The opposite of the `Initialize` event is the `Terminate` event. The `Terminate` event fires whenever an object created from the class is set to `Nothing`, or goes out of scope. In the following code fragment, the `Class_Terminate` event procedure runs when the object is set to `Nothing`:

```
Set objProduct = Nothing
```

Use the Terminate event to clean up your class module. For instance, if a Database or Recordset object has been opened, but hasn't been closed by the class, use the Terminate event to perform these operations.

The Terminate event fires as the statement dismissing the object runs, not after. VBA processes one statement at a time, no matter where the statement takes the execution point. Therefore, when the Set objProduct = Nothing executes, the Class_Terminate event procedure runs before the statement ends. This sequence ensures that the class is cleaned up before execution is returned to the code using the class. This process is illustrated in Figure 32-12.

FIGURE 32-12

The Class_Terminate event procedure passes control back to the consumer code when it ends.

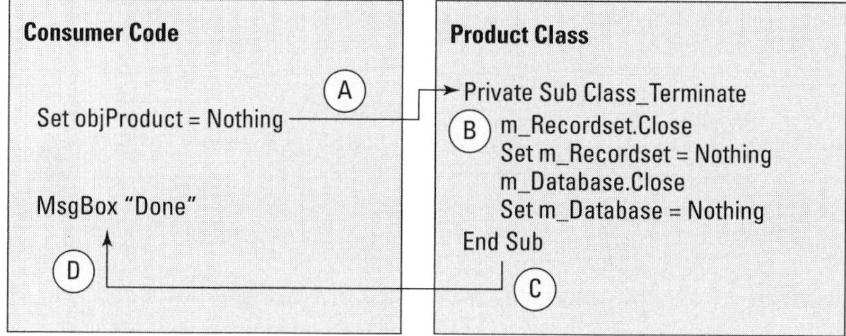

Just as with the Class_Initialize event procedure, the sequence of Class_Terminate's execution is important:

- The object is set to Nothing, or goes out of scope (A). Before the statement causing these states executes, control is passed to Class_Terminate.
- Just as you saw with Class_Initialize, notice that Class_Terminate (B) is a private subroutine. It is owned by the class, and executes independently of the consumer code. No arguments are passed to Class_Terminate.
- Execution is passed back to the consumer code (C) when Class_Terminate ends.
- Execution recommences in the consumer code at the statement following the object's dismissal (D).

Adding Events to Class Modules

We're all familiar with the interfaces supported by the objects built into Microsoft Access. A TextBox object, for example, supports ForeColor and BackColor as properties. The DoCmd object provides a wide variety of methods (such as OpenForm) that perform a number of essential actions in Access applications.

Beginning with Access 2000, developers have been able to add events to the class modules in their applications. (Although Access 97 supported class modules with properties and methods, Access 97 did not provide for custom events in class modules.) Adding events to your class modules is an excellent way to enhance and strengthen the object-oriented elements you add to your applications.

An Access events primer

Events are a bit more complex than properties or methods. Even though we constantly use events in our applications, you never see an event (because events do not exhibit a use interface), and under most circumstances, you don't deliberately invoke an event through your code. Events just sort of happen when a user clicks on a command button or tabs off of a control. Events are just there, and we use them as needed.

A reasonable analogy for events is the ringer on your cell phone. Your phone rings whenever someone wants to talk to you. The ring alerts you to the incoming call, and you decide whether to respond to the ring or ignore it.

From an object-oriented perspective, you add events to your objects so that the object has some way of notifying its consumer that something has happened within the object or has happened to the object. For instance, consider a data management object that reads and writes data from a data source. The properties are easy to understand and may include the path to the data source, the name of a table, and an ID value to use when extracting or saving data.

In this case, you may add an event to the data management object that is triggered when the data source is unavailable, or when a record matching the ID value cannot be found. Using events is much cleaner and more direct than relying on errors to be thrown when the data management object fails to complete its task.

The need for events

To my knowledge, there is no limit on the number of events you can add to a class module. You declare events in a class module's header, and invoke the events within the class's properties and methods.

This process may make more sense if we consider a property procedure built earlier in this chapter:

```
Public Property Get SupplierName() As String

  Dim varTemp As Variant

  If m_SupplierID <= 0 Then
    Exit Property
  End If

  varTemp = DLookup("CompanyName", "Suppliers", _
    "SupplierID = " & m_SupplierID)
```

```
    If Not IsNull(varTemp) Then
      SupplierName = CStr(varTemp)
    End If

End Property
```

This property procedure returns the name of a product supplier, given the SupplierID (notice that the SupplierID is obtained through the class-level m_SupplierID variable). The SupplierName property assumes that the m_SupplierID property variable has already been set through the SupplierID Property Let procedure. The If..End If at the top of this procedure handles cases where the m_SupplierID variable has not been properly set to a value greater than zero.

So far, so good. But, what happens if the SupplierID cannot be found in the supplier table? The only way the class's consumer can determine that the supplier does not exist is by examining the value of the SupplierName property. If the SupplierName property is an empty string, the consumer can assume the supplier cannot be found in the supplier table, and notify the user accordingly.

The problem with this scheme is that a lot of work is left up to the consumer. The consumer must first set the SupplierID property, then ask for the SupplierName property, and then finally examine SupplierName to see if a non-zero-length string was returned by the SupplierName Property Get.

One of the basic tenets of object-oriented programming is that a class module should encapsulate most, if not all, of the processing required by the entity represented by the class. In the case of our Product class, a consumer should not be required to examine a property's return value to verify its validity. The class should notify the consumer when a problem (such as missing or invalid data) arises within the class.

And, that's one of the primary purposes of events. The InvalidSupplierID event is invoked whenever the class determines that a problem exists with the SupplierID value supplied by the consumer code.

Creating custom events

Events must be declared within a class module. Although an event declaration may occur anywhere within a VBA module, it only makes sense to position event declarations near the top of the module where they are easily seen by other developers. An event declaration is actually quite simple:

```
Public Event InvalidSupplierID()
```

That's all there is to an event declaration. The Public keyword is needed, of course, to expose the event to the class's consumers. In effect, the Public keyword adds the event to the class's interface. The Event keyword, of course, specifies that the declaration's identifier (InvalidSupplierID) is an event, and should be managed by VBA's class module hosting mechanism.

You may recall that I've asserted that class modules were special in a number of regards. Events are clearly one of the special characteristics of VBA class modules.

A quick look through the Object Browser at the class module (see Figure 32-13) shows that the class's interface does, indeed, include the `InvalidSupplierID` event.

FIGURE 32-13

The `InvalidSupplierID` event appears in the Object Browser.

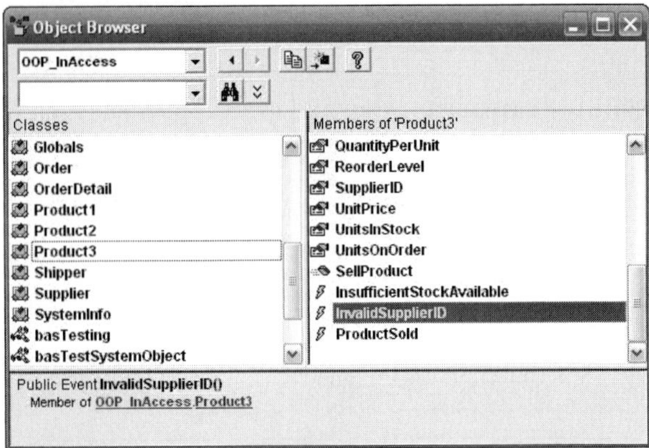

You'll notice a couple other events (`InsufficientStockAvailable` and `ProductSold`) in the `Product` class module. We've added the other events in exactly the same manner as the `InvalidSupplierID` event. An event declaration is all that is required to add an event to a class's interface. The class module never even has to trigger an event shown in the Object Browser.

Raising events

It should be obvious that an event that is never invoked by a class module's code isn't much use to anybody. Events are typically triggered (or raised) whenever circumstances indicate that the consumer should be notified.

Raising an event requires a single line of code:

```
RaiseEvent <EventName>(<Arguments>)
```

We'll discuss event arguments in the "Passing data through events" section, later in this chapter. In the meantime, take a look at raising the `InvalidSupplierID` event from the `SupplierName` `Property Get`:

```
Public Property Get SupplierName() As String

  Dim varTemp As Variant
```

```
    If m_SupplierID <= 0 Then
      RaiseEvent InvalidSupplierID()
      Exit Property
    End If

    varTemp = DLookup("CompanyName", "Suppliers", _
      "SupplierID = " & m_SupplierID)

    If Not IsNull(varTemp) Then
      SupplierName = CStr(varTemp)
    Else
      RaiseEvent InvalidSupplierID()
    End If

  End Property
```

The `SupplierName` property raises the `InvalidSupplierID` under two different situations: when the `SupplierID` is zero or a negative number, and when the `DLookup` function fails to locate a record in the `Suppliers` table.

There is no requirement that consumer code respond to events raised by class modules. In fact, events are very often ignored in application code. We doubt you've ever written code for every single event raised by an Access `TextBox` control, and custom events raised from class modules are no different.

But, again, that's one of the nice things about object-oriented programming. You can add as many events as needed by your classes. Consumer code working with your classes can ignore irrelevant events and trap only those events that are important to the application.

Trapping custom events

About the only place where event-driven programming with Access classes becomes tricky is when it's time to capture events (also called "sinking" events) in consumer code. There are a number of rules governing event consumption:

- The class hosting events must be declared within another class module.
- The object variable created from the class must be module-level and cannot be declared within a procedure.
- The object variable declaration must include the `WithEvents` keyword.

Let's examine these requirements. It shouldn't be surprising that events can only be captured by code within class modules. After all, class modules are special critters and have capabilities beyond simple code modules. You've never seen a stand-alone VBA code module directly respond to events raised by controls on an Access form, so there's no reason to expect a plain code module to be able to consume events raised by the classes you add to an application.

However, a plain code module can very well create and use objects derived from class modules. It's just that VBA code modules cannot capture events raised from class modules.

This requirement is not quite as onerous as it first appears. After all, every form and report module is a class module. That means that forms and reports are ready-built for consuming the events thrown by your class modules.

Similarly, the second requirement (the object variable must be module-level) also makes sense. There's no way to capture an event from within a procedure. Procedures know nothing about objects, and there's no provision for hooking a locally declared object variable to its events.

When you look at the class module behind a form, it becomes obvious why object variables must be module-level before their events can be sunk by consumer code. You've seen the typical Access form module, as shown in Figure 32-14. Notice what appears in the code module's event list when an object variable has been declared with the `WithEvents` keyword.

FIGURE 32-14

The `WithEvents` keyword instructs VBA to watch for events raised from the object's class module.

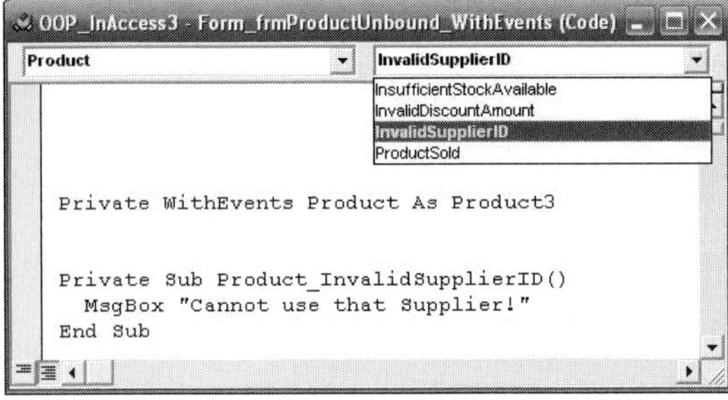

As you'd expect, selecting an event from the `Product` object's event list opens a new event procedure, enabling you to write code in response to the event. The `Product_InvalidSupplierID` event procedure notifies the user whenever the `Product` class determines that the `SupplierID` value cannot be used by the class.

Obviously, the code in the event procedure runs whenever the corresponding event is raised from the object's class module. The consumer does not have to explicitly check the value returned by the `SupplierName` property. Instead, the event procedure linked to the `InvalidSupplierID` handles the event and takes appropriate action.

Also, because the same event can be raised from multiple places within the class module, a single event procedure may handle many different situations related to a single problem within the class module.

We suspect that, behind the scenes, Access does exactly the same thing for built-in objects such as text boxes and command buttons. As soon as you add a control to an Access form, you're able to add code to event procedures hooked into the control's events.

Passing data through events

You probably noticed that the event declaration example given earlier in this chapter included a set of empty parentheses:

```
Public Event InvalidSupplierID()
```

What may not be obvious is that event arguments may be added within the parentheses:

```
Public Event ProductSold(Quantity As Integer)
```

The `RaiseEvent` statement includes a value for the event argument:

```
RaiseEvent ProductSold(UnitsSold)
```

Event declarations may include multiple arguments, and (to our knowledge) can pass any valid VBA data type, including complex data such as recordsets and other objects.

The ability to pass data through event arguments is an incredibly powerful tool for developers. A class module can directly communicate with its consumers, passing whatever data and information is necessary for the consumer to benefit from the class's resources.

Exploiting Access class module events

It is possible to add custom events to Access forms and to raise those events from code within the form. Custom events are declared with exactly the same syntax as declaring events within any class module and are raised with the `RaiseEvent` statement. The only tricky part is sinking custom events raised by a form in another form's module.

Custom events can be exploited as a way to convey messages and data between forms. Recently, we responded to a reader's question about dialog boxes with a relatively lengthy explanation of modally opening the dialog box, hiding the dialog box when the user was ready to return to the main form, and then reading a custom property from the hidden dialog box. Although this technique works well, it requires quite a bit of planning and preparation.

The dialog box operation can be more simply implemented by adding a custom event to the dialog form that is raised by the dialog and sunk by the main form. Information entered by the user on the dialog form is passed to the main form as an event argument. The event is raised when the user closes the dialog form and the information passed as the event argument is captured by the main form. There is no need for the main form to close or otherwise manage the dialog form.

Let's start with the dialog form that raises a custom event. The dialog form is shown in Figure 32-15.

FIGURE 32-15

This form uses a custom event to pass data back to the main form.

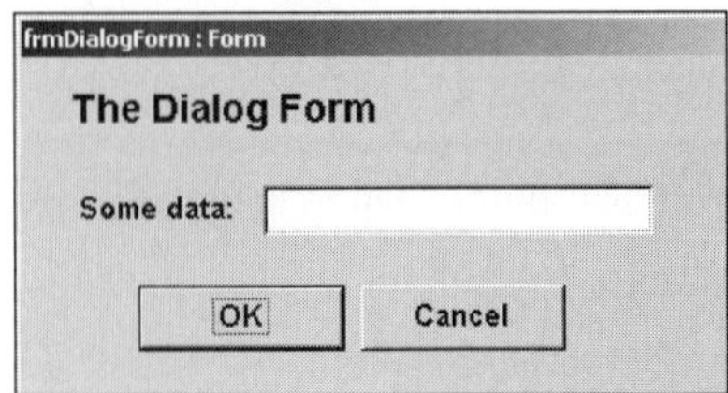

The user types something into the text box and clicks either OK or Cancel. The OK button passes the text box's contents to the main form, while the Cancel button passes a `"No Data` message, indicating that the user dismissed the dialog box without entering any data.

Here's all of the code behind this simple dialog box:

```
Public Event FormClosing(Message As String)

Private Sub cmdOK_Click()
  DoCmd.Close acForm, Me.Name
End Sub

Private Sub cmdCancel_Click()
  txtSomeData.Value = Null
  DoCmd.Close acForm, Me.Name
End Sub

Private Sub Form_Close()
  If Not IsNull(txtSomeData.Value) Then
    RaiseEvent FormClosing(txtSomeData.Value)
  Else
    RaiseEvent FormClosing("No data")
  End If
End Sub
```

A public event named `FormClosing` is declared at the top of the dialog form's module. This event returns a single argument named `Message`. The `cmdOK_Click` event procedure closes the form, while the `cmdCancel_Click` event clears the contents of the text box named `txtSomeData` before closing the form.

The `FormClosing` event is raised by the dialog form's `Close` event procedure, ensuring that the event is raised whenever the form is closed. If the `txtSomeData` is not `Null`, the value of the text box is passed by the `FormClosing` event, while a default message is passed if the text box's value is `Null`.

No other code is needed by the dialog form, and the form is allowed to close normally because the `FormClosing` event fires just before the form disappears from the screen.

The main form is shown in Figure 32-16.

FIGURE 32-16

The main form sinks the custom event raised by the dialog form.

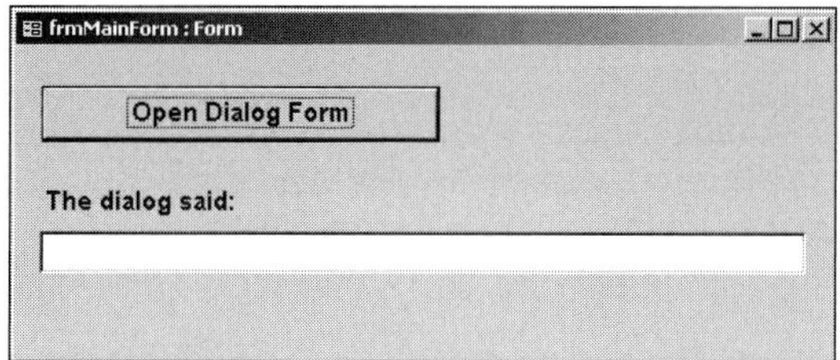

The code behind the main form is also quite simple. Notice the `WithEvents` keyword applied to the form object's declaration:

```
Private WithEvents frm As Form_frmDialogForm

Private Sub cmdOpenDialogForm_Click()
  Set frm = New Form_frmDialogForm
  With frm.Visible = True
End Sub

Private Sub frm_FormClosing(Message As String)
  txtDialogMessage.Value = Message
End Sub
```

The dialog form must be declared as a module-level variable behind the main form. The `WithEvents` keyword notifies the VBA engine that you want the main form to capture (or sink) events raised by the `frm` object.

Also notice that the form's class name is `Form_frmDialogForm`. This is the name of the class module behind `frmDialogForm`, and is the entity that actually raises the event. From the perspective of the VBA project driving the application, the form's surface is just a graphic interface and has nothing to do with the class module that supplies the logic driving the form.

The `WithEvents` keyword is almost magical. Once you've qualified an object declaration with `WithEvents`, the name of the object appears in the drop-down list at the top of the class module, and the object's events appear in the right drop-down list (see Figure 32-17).

FIGURE 32-17

The `WithEvents` keyword enables the main form's class module to capture events raised by the object.

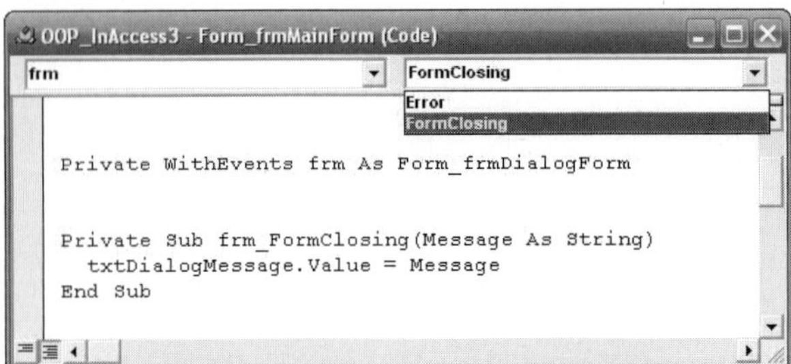

All Access developers are familiar with how the object drop-down list shows all of the controls placed on the surface of an Access form, as well as an entry for the form itself. In this case, the object drop-down list shows the form object declared with the `WithEvents` keyword in addition to controls on the form's surface.

In this case, the form object named `frm` is declared and instantiated and is completely controlled by the main form. The main form captures the dialog form's events, and uses the data passed through the `FormClosing` event. The main form could just as easily reference other properties of the dialog form.

Notice that this technique eliminates the infamous bang-dot notation that Access developers have suffered with for so many years. Treating a form as an OOP object eliminates a lot of overhead from the code behind the main form.

Access forms are objects

It's important to understand that every Access form is actually an object created from a class and is not a physical entity stored within the `.accdb` file. Most of us think of forms as a UI object that is maintained somewhere within the `.accdb` file and used as needed. In reality, each form is stored as a class, and Access instantiates a form object and displays the form on the screen whenever we work with the form's class. In design view, Access presents us with an editable interface to the form's class, and we work with the form's properties.

Interestingly enough, the code behind an Access form is nothing more than a property of the form's class. The code behind an Access form is, itself, a class. There is nothing in the object-oriented paradigm supported by Access that prohibits a class from containing another class.

Summary

This chapter has taken on the important topic of creating and using object classes. Access's object-oriented features are a powerful way to encapsulate functionality, letting you design modular applications that are easy to create and maintain. Breaking complex features into discrete objects is a powerful way to incrementally build applications from a series of components, each of which performs a single job in the application.

Property procedures and class events are at the core of any OOP project. Object-oriented programming enforces modular programming, and the only access a consumer has to an entity's data are through a class's interface. Assigning a value to an object's property can run hundreds of lines of code in the class module, greatly simplifying programming tasks on the consumer side.

Also, because encapsulation means that all of an object's logic is contained within its class module, maintenance is much simpler than with traditional linear programming practices.

There's a lot to think about and learn when you begin using object-oriented programming in database applications. Sometimes the rewards are a bit difficult to see at first, but once you begin using OOP in your applications, you'll wonder how you got along without it!

In case you're wondering, class modules, properties, methods, and events are very similar in .NET applications. The major difference is that the .NET framework adds many, many capabilities that are not possible in VBA classes. However, the OOP code you write in Access would be quite comfortable in a .NET application.

Chapter 33

Reusing VBA Code with Libraries

You'll use many of the techniques described in this book in most of the Access applications you prepare. Common features such as splash screens, data validation, logging, and progress indicators will be used over and over again in different applications. You may be discouraged at the thought of having to program each of these techniques into every Access application you build. After all, some of the techniques described in the Access 2007 Bible require considerable programming and implementation.

A primary objective in most application-development projects is to reuse as much of your programming as possible. People simply cannot afford to write everything from scratch in every project. You'll be happy to know that Access provides a handy method of reusing not only code, but also forms and other database objects. In fact, when you use Access libraries, the improvements you make to a library's contents are shared by all applications using the library.

Access also provides a way to share the more sophisticated aspects of the user interfaces you build among applications. For instance, let's assume you've built a multiform dialog box that allows users to customize the user interface. Using this dialog box, they can choose such things as the background color of forms, title bar color, fonts to use in labels, and so on. Changing the colors on the other forms in the application, displaying samples to the user, and other such options may require a great deal of code behind the dialog box. It would be a shame to be able to use such a sophisticated feature in only one application.

This chapter explores the concepts of reusing code and other database objects as Access libraries, and describes how to use custom libraries in your Access applications. You'll also learn how to add these database objects to virtually any Access application.

IN THIS CHAPTER

Understanding Access libraries

Comparing libraries with traditional code-sharing techniques

Building Access libraries

Establishing library references

Debugging library databases

Packaging libraries as `.accde` files

ON the CD-ROM This chapter uses the database named `Chapter33.accdb`. If you haven't already copied it onto your machine from the CD, you'll need to do so now. The Chapter 33 folder on the CD also includes an `.accde` file created from `Chapter33.accdb`. You may want to examine the `.accde` to see how converting an `.accdb` file to `.accde` format affects an application's objects.

What Are Libraries?

Access users often work with libraries without even being aware that they're using anything other than the basic Access product. In fact, many of the most sophisticated Access features don't even exist in the `msaccess.exe` executable file. Instead, these features exist as special *libraries* that are loaded into the Access environment at startup or whenever the user asks for a feature that is supported by a library.

Because it was created with the capability to be extended through library components added at runtime, Access gives almost unlimited power to the advanced developer. Libraries give you powerful tools that allow you to reuse your carefully developed forms and code.

The library database is the basis of all other types of Access add-ins. A library database contains Access VBA code, forms, queries, and other database objects that can be called from any Access database application. Once referenced, an Access application can use any of the resources provided by a library as if the resource existed in the current database.

You use library databases to store code such as data validation and error messaging that you frequently add to your applications. Putting this code into a library database saves you from having to add the routines to every application you create. Putting code into an external library database also means that improvements and enhancements you make to the code will be shared by all applications using the library. Library databases are also a valuable way to distribute new features and changes to your users.

Also, tables, queries, forms, and even reports contained in the library database file are accessible to the Access application using the library. Access has no trouble opening a form or report contained within a library. In fact, this is exactly how the built-in Access wizards work. When you open the Linked Table Manager, for instance, you're actually opening a complex form stored in an Access library. The Linked Table Manager is not built into the `msaccess.exe` executable.

The Access wizards and other add-ins are contained in several Access libraries with extensions such as `.accde`, `.accdu`, and `.accda` in the Office 2007 installation folder. Although you can open these files in Access 2007, all the database objects are secured against changes, and you won't be able to modify the built-in Access wizards.

Traditional Access programming

In most applications, the code and objects you add to the database work only within that application and aren't shared with other databases. This is how the Access product documentation and most books and other training materials describe creating Access applications. You create the tables, queries, forms, reports, and code within the `.accdb` or `.mdb` file that you make available to your users. If necessary, you import code modules and forms from other `.accdb` or `.mdb` files to use in the new application.

This approach is completely appropriate when the objects and code won't be used by other Access applications. If a code module is highly specific to an application, there is no reason to consider using the same code in other databases. But there are many instances in which the VBA routines, forms, or reports you've carefully constructed in an application might be used within another database. Using a library is a simpler technique than physically importing database objects from another database.

Sharing code between applications

It is likely that you'll eventually seek more efficient ways to share application elements between databases. Even though Access allows you to import any database object from another database with complete fidelity, you import a *copy* of the object. If you change the original object later on, the changes are not reflected in any database using a copy of the original object. Therefore, improvements and enhancements to the shared code, forms, and other database objects are not shared with the other databases.

As an example, consider the situation where the user has asked for business rules to be added to a database. These rules determine how the data is to be validated, displayed, calculated, and so on. If the user needs a number of different databases, you could simply copy the business rules module among the databases. Later, however, if the business rules are modified because of changes in tax laws, policies, or company strategy, each of the databases would have to be individually updated with the new business-rules module.

A more efficient technique is to encapsulate the business rules in a single library database (located on a file server, if the databases are used by many different users) that is loaded by each of the databases at runtime. When changes are made to the library database, the changes are seen in each of the relevant databases the next time that database is used.

It is important to keep in mind that library databases can contain much more than just code. Although a code module is an obvious example of a database object that may be periodically updated, there are many other examples as well. For instance, a company may use a table in a library database to share employee phone numbers and contact information. A particular style of report may be used to output information from a number of different databases, particularly if the databases work with similar data.

Access library basics

A library database is identical in all regards to any other Access database. In fact, you create library databases by building a normal database, adding to it all of the components and code you want to have available to other databases, and converting it to the special `.accde` file format. As you'll see in the next section, Access 2007 automatically recognizes an Access database file with an `.accde` extension as a library database.

The `.accde` file format is special. Most of the objects in an `.accde` file are read-only and cannot be changed by the user. The only exceptions are tables and queries, which remain read/write so that new tables and queries can be added or modified, if needed. You cannot export to or export from an `.accde` file.

Because of its (mostly) read-only nature, the `.accde` file format is the ideal library database. You can distribute code and other database objects without worrying whether users will try to make changes to the `.accde`'s contents. Also, because certain elements have been stripped out of an `.accde`, the size of the file is somewhat smaller than the equivalent `.accdb`.

When it's time to use the library database, Access references the library database directly and opens it for you. You don't need to include any special code or calling routines in an application in order to use the contents of a library database.

Access 2007 library database references

Most Access 2007 wizards and add-ins are loaded on demand, which means they're read from their respective library databases only when a user requests their features. You may have noticed that there's a significant delay the first time you invoke a Form or Table Wizard in Access 2007, and a much smaller delay when you subsequently invoke the same wizard during the same session.

Knowing how to reference library database contents from your Access applications is important. Admittedly, this is not a simple subject, but there are many benefits derived from the various referencing options. As you'll see in the following sections, references range from simple and direct (but limited) to complex and powerful.

Under Windows you have a number of options when it comes to setting references to your add-ins. Access 2007 doesn't support the notion of global modules in libraries, which means that loading library databases involves more than simply pointing at a library name at startup and letting Access find the add-in references within the library. When working with Access 2007, you have the following options for referencing library database contents:

- Using explicit references
- Using a runtime reference

Explicit library references

A library reference creates a "link" between an application and a specific library database. You must manually create library references in each application before you can use the code contained in the library database.

You create the library reference in the References dialog box (see Figure 33-1). You open this dialog box by choosing Tools ➪ References with any VBA code module open for editing in Design view.

FIGURE 33-1

You use the References dialog box to create connections to library databases.

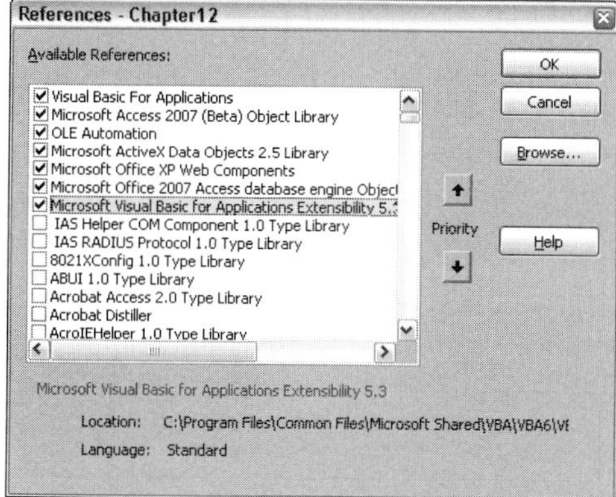

Use the Browse button to locate the library database with the Add Reference dialog box (see Figure 33-2). By default, the `.accde` file type is not shown in the Add Reference dialog box. You must use the Files of Type drop-down list to select `.accde` and `.accdb` files (this list is open in Figure 33-2).

Notice that the drop-down list in Figure 33-2 includes older Access file types, such as `.mdb`, `.mde`, and `.mda`. Access 2007 makes no distinction when it comes to the database file referenced as a library. This means that, if you have existing Access library files, you can reference them from Access 2007 without changing anything.

When you've located the library, click OK to accept the library database and return to the References dialog box. The selected library database will be added as shown in Figure 33-1.

Once you've connected to a library database, all of the code and other database objects contained in the library are available to the application you're building. When the application is opened by a user, the library objects are still be available — you don't have to reconnect each time the application is opened. Other applications have access to the library database as well — the library database will appear in the Available References list you see in Figure 33-1 but will not be selected.

FIGURE 33-2

The Browse button makes it easy to locate library databases.

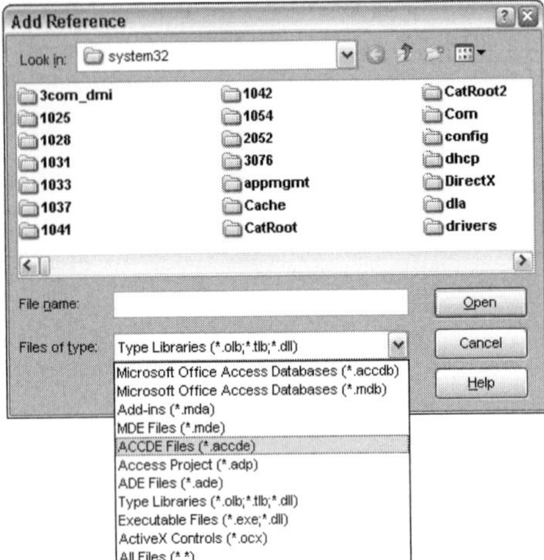

Using the References dialog box to make library database references has several drawbacks. You must manually perform the connection operation on each and every database needing access to the library database. The library reference is stored within the Access database file and should not have to be reset unless the location of the library file changes.

Also, the exact path to the library database is stored in the application database. This means that if the library database is moved, renamed, or unavailable at runtime, calls to functions and objects in the library database will fail. Be sure to adequately trap and handle such errors.

Programming references

Perhaps the easiest way to add references, or at least ensure that references are included in your Access applications at runtime, is to add a little bit of code that adds the reference to the current database:

```
Public Sub AddLibraryReference()
  On Error Resume Next
  References.AddFromFile("<Path To Library File>")
End Sub
```

The `On Error Resume Next` is a little bit of a cheat. Access raises an error if you add a reference that already exists in the database. Putting `On Error Resume Next` above the statement that adds the reference instructs Access to ignore this error. However, this technique works fine and causes no problems in Access applications. Access will not allow you to add the same reference to an application more than once, so there is no danger that your users will end up with multiple references to the same library database.

The library database path could be stored as a configuration item in a hidden Access table, or hard-coded into the application as a constant or other value.

Creating Library Databases

It should be clear that there are certain advantages to using library databases. First and foremost, adding VBA routines and database objects to library databases makes them available to all applications needing those routines and objects. The objects in a library database are easily maintained. Changes to a library database are seen in all applications using the library. You don't need to make multiple maintenance changes to a number of different databases as you would if no libraries were used. Finally, your users will benefit from consistency across all applications. Because you can put tables containing message text, dialog boxes, and other user interface components into library databases, your users will see the same interface components in all of the applications using the library.

Any time you need to share database components among a number of different applications, you should consider adding them to a library database. In contrast to the complexity of library database references, creating libraries is actually quite easy:

1. **Create the objects and write the functions in a new Access .accdb file.**
2. **Save the `.accdb` as an `.accde` data file.**
3. **Load the database as a library.**

We expand on these steps in the following sections.

Create the objects and write the functions

As mentioned earlier in this chapter, a library database is simply an Access database used as a library. Therefore, the first step in creating a new library is to start with an empty `.accdb` file and add to it the objects and code needed to support the wizards and builders. In many cases, you'll simply import database objects from existing databases rather than create new ones.

Make sure, of course, that the library database is fully debugged. Any errors in the code or user interface in the library database will be seen in every application using the library. Because you specify the entry points into the library, you can include routines and other components such as dialog boxes needed to test the library functions.

All of the library's entry points must be functions. You cannot call a subroutine from a control or menu option, so be sure to code the starting point for each wizard and builder as a function.

Keep in mind that library databases can also contain tables, queries, and other database components. You might, for instance, use a library database to store message text (a valuable aid to internationalizing applications), commonly used message boxes, and tables containing data of interest to the user.

CROSS-REF **Library databases can be part of a replica set. *Replication* (the process of distributing changes to Access databases) is fully discussed in Chapter 31. The Access 2007 replication feature makes it easy to distribute changes you make to your libraries to all users of your applications.**

When all development on the library database is complete, choose Run ➪ Compile (you see the Run menu only when you have a module open for editing, of course). After compilation, compact the library database.

Save as .accde

Saving the new library database as an `.accde` file is very easy. Simply select the Make ACCDE button in the Database Tools ribbon group, and you'll see the familiar Windows Save As dialog box. Notice that ACCDE File is selected as the default format for the save as operation (see Figure 33-3).

FIGURE 33-3

Saving an Access `.accdb` file as an `.accde` library.

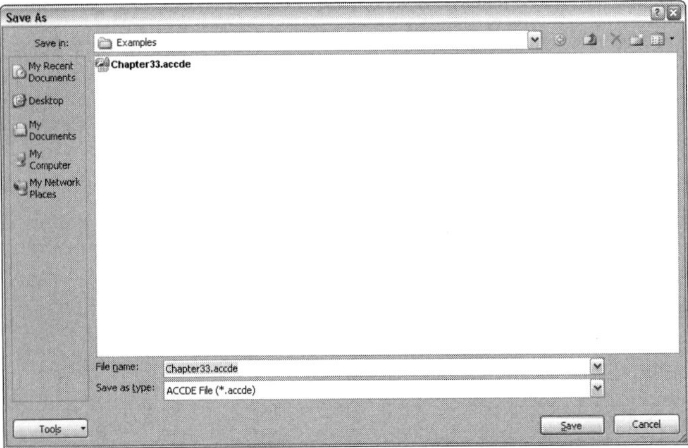

That's all there is to it. The `.accde` file contains all of the objects that were in the `.accdb` file, with the forms, reports, macros, and modules made read-only. The `.accde` file can be placed on a file server, making it simultaneously accessible to multiple users.

Converting the `.accdb` to `.accde` format is not a requirement of Access libraries. In fact, any Access `.accdb` file can be used as a library; the main advantage of using the .accde format is that no one is able to change the code, forms, and other objects in an `.accde` file.

Load the database as a library

Once you've created and tested the library database, you simply reference it using one of the reference techniques described earlier in this chapter. There is no special process for converting an application database to a library.

You'll want to give the database an `.accde` filename extension to indicate that it's a library and not a normal database file. By default, the Access Open dialog box won't show files with the `.accde` extension, so there is little chance a user will accidentally open a library database.

If you find it necessary to disguise the identity of your Access library files, you can provide an alternate filename extension for your libraries. There is no requirement that all Access libraries have the `.accde` extension. You could, for instance use a filename extension such as `.sys` or `.dat` to infer that the file contains nothing of interest to users. Just be sure to use the proper filename extension when you create the reference to the library database.

Debugging Library Databases

You debug a library database as you would any other Access database application. You simply test all of the functions and other code, forms, queries, and database objects against the conditions expected when the application is used in real life. The only difference is that you must make sure the library database operates well when referenced as a library.

This means you must build a "test bench" application database, create the references to the library database, and use the library database as a library. You may have to make some changes to the library code (particularly to object names in the library) to ensure there are no conflicts with existing code or objects in the application database.

A good convention to follow is to use a special prefix for function and object names in the library database. For instance, you may use your initials or `lib` as a prefix to make sure all objects in the library have unique names. If, by coincidence, a library function or library object has the same name as a function or object included in an application, an error occurs.

Library Database Object References

Perhaps the most common problem associated with library databases is keeping object references straight. For instance, if a function in a library database refers to a table, is the table found in the application database or in the library database?

Access follows these rules when referring to objects in library databases:

- **Bound controls, forms, and reports are always bound to record sources (tables and queries) in the library database.** Access always searches the library database when trying to resolve a record-source reference. If the record source cannot be found, an error occurs. If necessary, you may have to use unbound controls and use DAO code to connect to a record source in the application database at runtime.

- **Access will first search the library database for a macro reference, then the application database for the macro.** If the macro cannot be found in either database, an error occurs.
- **Domain aggregate functions such as `Dlookup`, `DMin`, and `Dmax` always refer to the data in the current database, not the library database.**
- **When using DAO, use `CurrentDB()` or `DBEngine(0)(0)` to refer to objects in the application database, or `CodeDB()` to refer to objects in the library database.**

In any case, it's important to keep in mind which database is referenced by the code and objects in a library database. If you encounter errors when working with library databases, be sure to check the record source and other object references in the library.

Because multiple users may need access to the information stored in library databases, Access always opens add-ins for shared access.

Summary

This chapter has reviewed the process of creating library databases as a way to reuse your Access code. You may find it very efficient to take your frequently used code, add it to an `.accdb` file, and save the `.accdb` file in the `.accde` format. Then, load the `.accde` as a library in any Access application that needs the resources provided by the library.

Keep in mind that Access does not care what extension is applied to the library file. There are many situations in which you might want to disguise the identity of a library file by given it an uninteresting extension such as `.sys` or `.dll`. Most users are quite familiar with these extensions, and have no reason to use Access to explore a file with a `.sys` or `.dll` extension. However, to some people, a file with an extension that makes it look like an Access data file of some kind is too tempting to ignore.

The library file can be located on a file server, making it accessible to all users on the network. Access does not care if it has to go across the network to retrieve a library file reference. It's all the same to Access if the file is located on the user's local computer or somewhere else on the network.

Chapter 34

Customizing Access Ribbons

Perhaps the greatest surprise in Access 2007 for experienced Access developers is the ribbon — the new control that replaces the Access toolbars and menus. Many Access developers and users have long had a love-hate relationship with the Access toolbars and menus. Toolbars and menus are an effective user interface component when users need to get to a variety of different tasks and operations. However, the CommandBars model used in previous versions of Access was quite complex and sometimes difficult to program.

Microsoft has replaced toolbars and menus in Access 2007 with the ribbon, a large horizontally oriented object at the top of the main Access 2007 screen. The ribbon is quite unlike any toolbar or menu that you may have seen before and supports features not possible with toolbars and menus. As you will soon see, customizing Access 2007 ribbons is a very different process than using CommandBars to compose toolbars and menus in previous versions of Access.

IN THIS CHAPTER

- Learning about the new Access ribbon
- Working with the default ribbon
- Examining ribbon architecture
- Studying ribbon controls
- Learning the XML necessary to construct ribbons
- Adding VBA callbacks

ON the CD-ROM In the `Chapter34.accdb` database, you will find several database objects needed to support the techniques described in this chapter. You will not be able to see the `USysRibbons` table until you right-click the Navigation Pane, select Navigation Options and select the Show System Objects check box in the Navigation Options dialog.

Why Replace Toolbars and Menus?

Unlike previous version of Access where developers used CommandBar objects to build toolbars and menus, Access 2007 developers work with the Ribbon construct. The Ribbon is the large, horizontal control that stretches across the top of the main Access 2007 window. A ribbon is a complex entity, consisting of a number of nested controls that support the functions previously provided by toolbars and menus.

The older CommandBars model (see Figure 34-1), although complex and somewhat difficult to work with, featured a complete object model that included several different object types, with properties, methods, and events. Although a considerable amount of work was involved building CommandBar-based toolbars and menus, a developer working with CommandBar objects benefited from IntelliSense and online help that documented each type of CommandBar control.

FIGURE 34-1

CommandBars were difficult to produce and sometimes confused users.

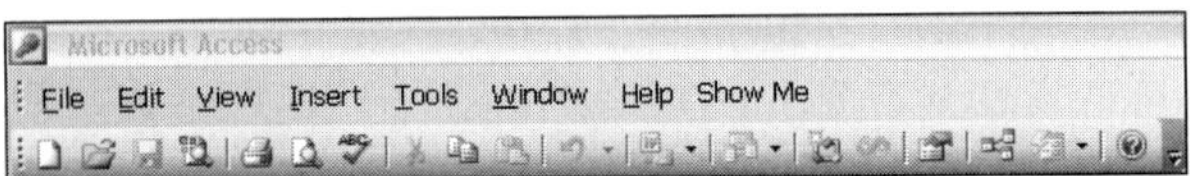

In addition to the difficulty programming the complex CommandBar model, CommandBar-based toolbars and menus were somewhat limited in their abilities. Because of their rather "flat" construction, many developers had to resort to deeply nested menus, and toolbars buttons that didn't do much more than open dialogs that actually performed the task the user required. Many users complained about the difficulty learning how to use custom menus, especially if they were not particularly well planned and constructed.

As a final issue, some users had tremendous trouble with movable toolbars and menus. By default, the CommandBar objects in previous versions of Access were not only movable, they could be docked at the top, bottom, or either side of the main Access screen. Users often complained that, after accidentally moving a toolbar or menu, it'd "stick" to one side or the other of the main Access screen, and they couldn't figure out how to move it back to its original location. Also, even though the convention was to always place a menu CommandBar above a toolbar CommandBar, it was easy to swap these positions, contributing to a user's confusion.

The Access 2007 ribbon (see Figure 34-2), which is shared by all of the Office 2007 applications, is an innovative approach to dealing with the problem of flat toolbars and menus. Perhaps the first thing a new users notices about the ribbon is how large it is, being considerably taller than the toolbar/menu combination common in previous versions of Access. However, when you take a closer look at the ribbon, its differences from earlier user interface tools quickly become apparent.

FIGURE 34-2

The ribbon is a new paradigm for Access developers and users.

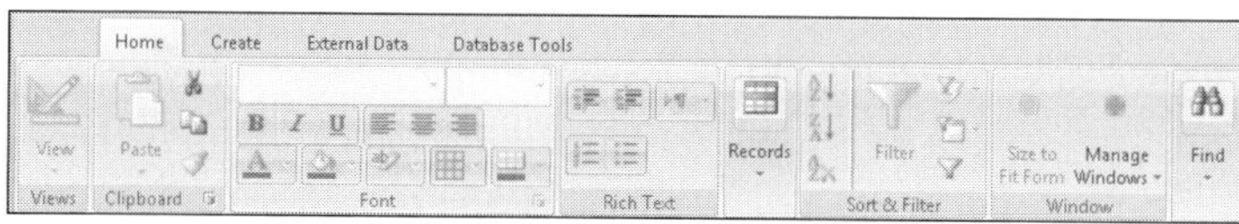

First of all, the Access ribbon supports tabs that separate categories of tasks into logical groupings. Each tab may contain a number of groups that further define task categories. Within a group many different types of controls — both large and small — that actually perform tasks required by the user might appear.

Microsoft's objectives for introducing ribbons in Office 2007 included simplifying the user interface by eliminating overly complex menus, with their fly-outs, drop-down lists, and other conventions made necessary by the limitations of toolbars and menus.

Another benefit of the 2007 ribbons is that you can use different size controls within a group. This means that you can use a large icon for frequently-performed operations, and smaller icons for less common tasks.

One final benefit of the ribbon to developers is that you compose the XML for ribbons in any qualified text editor. In this chapter we use the Microsoft Web Developer 2005 Express, a free download from Microsoft at `http://msdn.microsoft.com/vstudio/express/vwd/`. This tool has several advantages over using a plain text editor such as Windows Notepad. In the Web Developer editor, XML is displayed with different colors signifying XML tags, keywords, and identifiers. Also, Web Developer is smart about XML, and flags poorly formed XML statements with the familiar red squiggles Microsoft Word places under misspelled words.

Although a complete explanation of Microsoft Web Developer 2005 Express is beyond the scope of this chapter, because Access does not support a qualified XML editor, you need access to an external tools such as Web Developer for composing your ribbon XML. Because Web Developer is a free download, and because it does such a fine job composing XML statements, it is the ideal tool for Access developers to use when developing ribbon XML.

Because the XML syntax is used to create and customize Access 2007 ribbons, the exact same XML code can be used in any of the Office 2007 applications. Also, because the XML exists in a file outside of Access, it is possible to work on a ribbon without disturbing users working with the application. As you will soon see, updating the XML driving an Access 2007 ribbon is a simple process, and does not require importing or exporting database objects.

At some point, it is inevitable that Microsoft will provide a developer interface for creating and customizing Access ribbons. It is safe to assume that this tool will be made available as an Access add-in and will provide the same or similar functionality as Microsoft Web Developer 2005 Express. Therefore, the sections of this chapter describing how to compose the XML for Access 2007 ribbons will be applicable even after a ribbon customization tool becomes available from Microsoft.

New controls for Access ribbons

The Access 2007 ribbon supports many more types of controls then the older command bars. In previous versions of Access, the type and variety of controls you could add to menus and toolbars were severely limited. Most toolbars included buttons, and if you had drop-down lists, and menus could be nested menus within them, but there were very few options for adding complex or sophisticated controls to command bars.

Access 2007 ribbons can contain text boxes, labels, separators, check boxes, document controls, with buttons, toggle buttons, edit boxes, and even nested menus. This chapter has only enough room to explore a few of these controls, but examples, showing how to utilize virtually every type of ribbon control in Access 2007, exist on the Microsoft Office Web site (`http://office.microsoft.com`).

Access 2007 features some very interesting new controls to use on your custom ribbons. These controls are used in the default Access 2007 ribbon and are accessible to the custom ribbons you add to your applications. These controls have no analogues in older versions of Access, and are completely new or Access 2007.

SplitButton

The *SplitButton* is similar to a traditional button in an Access interface. What makes the SplitButton different is that it is, quite literally, split vertically into two different controls. The left side of the control works as any other button, and responds to a single click. The right side of the button includes a right-pointing arrow that, when clicked, reveals a selection list of single-select options. SplitButtons can also be split horizontally, into upper and lower portions.

The best example of a SplitButton is the Save As button in the File menu. Clicking the left side of the Save As button opens the Save As dialog, whereas clicking the right side of the button reveals the selection list you see in Figure 34-3.

Only one option in the SplitButton list can be selected. As soon as an item in the list is selected, the SplitButton closes and the action selected by the user is performed.

DropDown

The *DropDown* is shown in Figure 34-4. Although the DropDown looks very much like a combo box, they are not the same type of object. Notice that the items in the drop-down list in Figure 34-4 include not only text (Macro, Module, Class Module) but also an image and ToolTip help associated with each item.

Each item in the list can be selected only once, providing an easy-to-understand interface for your users, when a limited number of options exist.

FIGURE 34-3

The SplitButton is new to Access 2007.

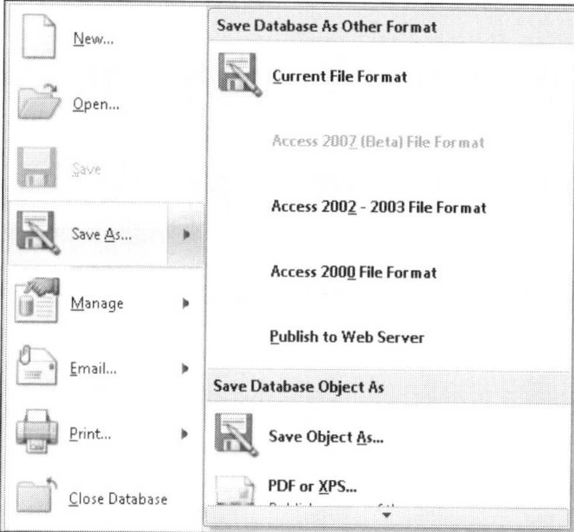

FIGURE 34-4

The DropDown control simplifies user's selections.

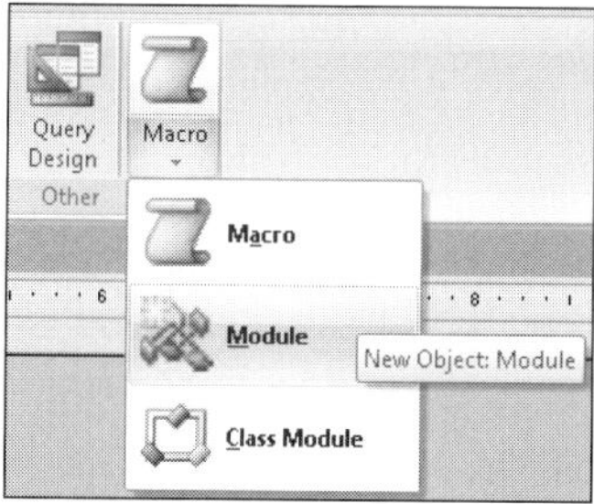

The SplitButton and DropDown are very similar in many ways. They both expose a list when clicked, and present a list of single-select items. The main difference is that a SplitButton is, literally, split into two portions (horizontal or vertical), while the DropDown simply drops down the list when clicked.

Gallery

The *Gallery* presents the user with an abbreviated view of different options for formatting and other tasks. Figure 34-5 shows the Gallery of the Auto Format options in Access 2007. The premise of the Gallery is that the user can actually see the results of selecting any of the options displayed in the control.

FIGURE 34-5

The Gallery provides the user with a preview of the options.

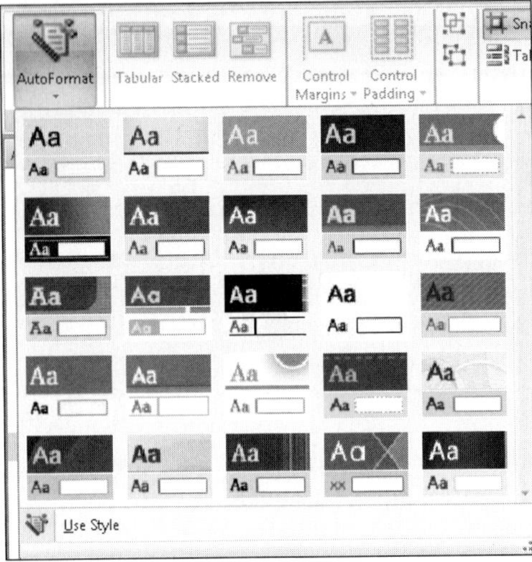

Gallery controls are used extensively in Access 2007 for displaying options such as ForeColor, BackColor, and font selections.

SuperTips

One last new Access 2007 ribbon control is the *SuperTip*. The SuperTip is very similar to the ToolTip used in previous versions of Access. A SuperTip is relatively large and contains text that you specify, helping the user understand the purpose of a control. The SuperTip, shown in Figure 34-6, appears as the user hovers the mouse over a control on the ribbon.

FIGURE 34-6

The SuperTip provides helpful information to the user.

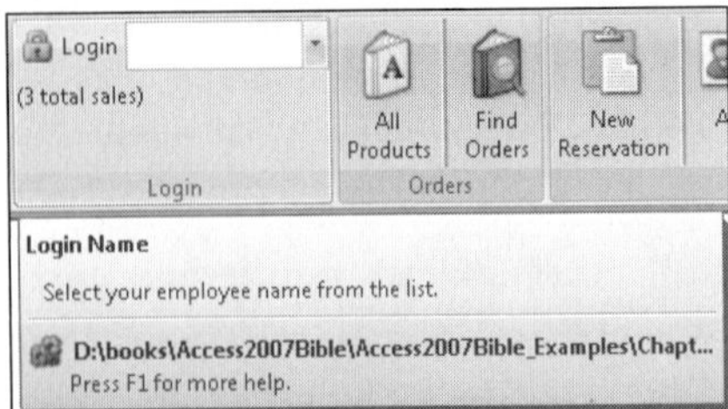

You see examples of creating each of these controls in the following sections of this chapter. The Access Auto Options database accompanying this chapter (`Chapter34.accdb`) includes several other examples that are not discussed in this chapter. You are encouraged to take a look at these examples and to use them in your own Access ribbons if you find them useful.

Working with the Access 2007 Ribbon

We begin our discussion of the Access 2007 ribbons by briefly touring a custom ribbon built for the Access Auto Auctions (shown in Figure 34-7). Later in this chapter you see how this ribbon was constructed, but in the meantime just tour the ribbon, its controls, and its behaviors.

FIGURE 34-7

The custom ribbon built for the Access Auto Auctions

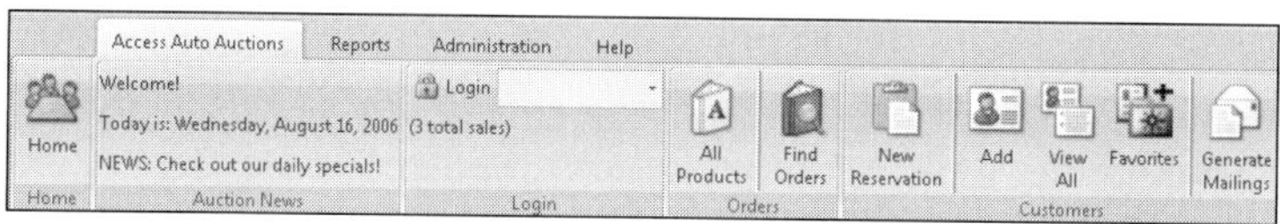

The Access Auto Auctions ribbon was constructed by modifying an example ribbon distributed by Microsoft during the Access 2007 beta. As you'll soon see, you are almost always better off starting with a good example ribbon than constructing a ribbon entire from scratch. You will find numerous examples of ribbons on the Microsoft Office web site (`http://office.microsoft.com`) to serve as starting points for your custom ribbons.

Oddly enough, the default Access ribbon is inaccessible to developers. You cannot easily customize the default Access ribbon. Instead, you have to build an identical ribbon from scratch, and customize your hand-built ribbon. At some point Microsoft will probably publish an example ribbon that mirrors the default Access ribbon, but such an example was not available during the Access 2007 beta.

Tabs

The Access Auto Auctions ribbon contains four tabs: Access Auto Auctions, Reports, Administration, and Help. The main tab (Access Auto Auctions) contains the operations most frequently conducted by the Access Auto Auctions application users, while the other tabs contain less frequently used controls.

Groups

Each tab in the Access Auto Auctions ribbon includes a number of groups. Figure 34-7 shows the Access Auto Auctions tab which contains the Home, Auction News, Login, Orders, and Customer groups. A tab can contain numerous groups, but take care not to overload a tab with too many groups. It's much better to add additional tabs as needed, rather than add so many groups that a user is confused.

Controls

In Figure 34-7, each group contains a variety of controls. For instance, the Home group contains a single large button labeled Home, whereas the Customers group contains three different buttons. A DropDown control is located within the Login group, and the Auction News group includes only label controls.

Managing the ribbon

By default, the ribbon is always open on the screen. However, the ribbon, with all its controls, and tabs, is quite large, and may be in the way while users work with an application. The ribbon is easy collapsed by double-clicking any tab. Single clicking any tab brings the ribbon back again.

Any forms or reports that are open as the ribbon is collapsed and expanded are moved up or down so that their positions (relative to the ribbon) remain the same. For instance, a form that is open right below the ribbon jumps up to occupy exactly the same position below the collapsed ribbon (see Figure 34-8).

FIGURE 34-8

Objects move up or down to accommodate the ribbon as it is opened and closed.

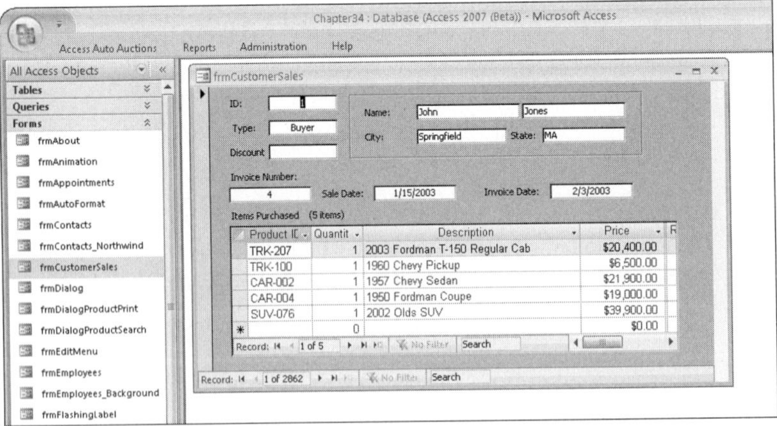

Working with the Quick Access Toolbar

You may have noticed the new Quick Access Toolbar (QAT) in the upper-left corner of the main Access screen (see Figure 34-9), just to the right of the File button. The QAT remains visible at all times in Access and provides a handy way to give your users quick access to commonly performed tasks such as opening a database file, or sending an object to a printer.

FIGURE 34-9

The Quick Access Toolbar remains on the screen at all times.

The QAT is fully customizable. You can quickly and easily add any of a large number of operations to the QAT. Also, the controls you add to the QAT are applicable either to the current database, or to all Access databases.

Open the Customization dialog by clicking the large, round File button in the upper-left corner of the main Access screen, and clicking the Access Options button near the bottom of the Office dialog. Then, select the Customization item from the Access Options list to open the Customize dialog box.

The list on the left side of the screen contains items representing every command available in the Office 2007 applications, even if the command is not relevant to Access. Above the list is a drop-down containing the many, many different categories of Office commands (File, Home, External Data, and so on). Selecting an item from this drop-down list reveals the commands within that category.

Keep in mind that the candidate list on the left contains commands that are not applicable to Access. Be sure to choose commands appropriate to your application. The QAT is intended to replace the Microsoft Office commands that are available in the Office (or File) menu you see when you click the large round button in the upper-left corner of the main Access screen. Normally, end users do not need to access these commands, and the QAT provides a handy way for you to control which commands the users access as they work with your Access applications.

The tasks available to the QAT include operations such as backing up the current database, converting the current database to another Access data format, viewing database properties, and linking tables.

Because the QAT is visible to all users, be sure not to include commands (such as Design View) that may be harmful to your applications, or confusing to users. Because the QAT is easy to customize, it's not difficult to add the commands you need at the time you need them, instead of leaving them visible to all users all of the time.

Use the right- and left-pointing arrows to move an item from the list on the left to the list on the right. The Customization dialog is quite smart. Once a command has been added to the QAT, the command is no longer available, so there is no chance you'll add the same command more than once.

The Customization dialog also contains up and down arrows to the right of the selected list that enable you to reorder the left-to-right appearance of the QAT commands.

Be warned that you can add virtually any number of commands to the QAT. When more commands are contained than the QAT can display, scroll arrows appear at the far right side of the QAT. However, because the whole idea of the QAT is to make commands quickly available to users, there is no point in loading up the QAT with dozens of commands that only make it more difficult for the user.

Access 2007 Ribbons: The Developer's Perspective

Ribbons are not represented by a programmable object model in Access 2007. Each ribbon is defined by XML statements contained in a special table named `USysRibbons`. Access uses the information it finds in the XML to compose and render the ribbon on the screen.

The ribbon creation process

Briefly, creating custom ribbons is a five-step process:

1. **Design the ribbon and compose the XML that defines the ribbon.**
2. **Write callback (described in the following section) routines that support the ribbon's operations.**
3. **Create the USysRibbons table.**
4. **Add XML to USysRibbons table.**
5. **Specify the custom ribbon property in the Access configuration screen.**

None of these steps is particularly intuitive, especially when it comes to composing the XML and writing callback routines. Your best bet is to find an example that is reasonably close to your desired end-product, and customize its XML to suit your purposes.

Using VBA callbacks

A *callback* is code that is passed to another entity for processing. Each procedure you write to support operations on a ribbon is passed to the "ribbon processor" in Access that actually performs the ribbon's actions. This is very unlike the event-driven code you've been working with in Access. Clicking a button on a form directly triggers the code in the button's `Click` event procedure. A ribbon's callback procedure is linked to the ribbon, but is internally processed by Access and does not directly run in response to the click on the ribbon.

To fully understand this process, imagine that Access contains a process that constantly monitors activity on the ribbon. As soon as the user clicks a ribbon control, the ribbon processor springs into action, retrieving the callback procedure associated with the control, and performing the actions specified in the callback.

This means that there are no `Click` or `GotFocus` events associated with Access 2007 ribbons. Instead, you bind a callback to a ribbon control through the XML that defines the ribbon. Each ribbon control includes a number of action attributes that can be attached to callbacks, and the ribbon processor takes over when the user invokes a control's action.

Here is an example. The following XML statements define a button control on a ribbon:

```
<button id="cmdFindOrders" label="Find Orders" size="large"
imageMso="GalInsertFnLookupReference"
onAction="onOpenFormEdit" tag="frmFindOrders"/>
```

(These lines appear as a single statement in the XML code behind the Access Auto Auctions ribbon. Also, this XML is explained in detail later in this chapter.)

Notice the `onAction` attribute in the last line of this XML code. Notice also that the `onAction` attribute is set to `onOpenFormEdit`. The `onAction` attribute is similar to the events associated with a form's controls. Each interactive ribbon control (buttons, SplitButtons, and so on) includes the `onAction` attribute. The callback procedure (`onOpenFormEdit`, in this example) assigned to the `onAction` attribute is passed to the ribbon processor when the control's action occurs.

Notice that the button control does not contain a "click" event. Instead, each interactive control's `onAction` attribute handles whatever action is expected by the control. In the case of a button, the action is a user clicking the button, whereas for a text box, the action is the user typing into the text box. Both of these controls include the `onAction` attribute.

Ribbon controls have several other important attributes, described later in this chapter.

TIP **You probably want to see errors generated by your custom ribbon during development. By default, ribbon error reporting is disabled, and you must enable before you see error messages thrown by the ribbon. Click the Office button in the upper-left corner of the main Access screen, and choose the Access Options button at the bottom. Next, select the Advanced tab in the Options dialog and scroll down to the General section. Make sure the Show add-in user interface errors option is selected; then click OK at the bottom of the dialog. The error messages generated by the ribbon are invaluable debugging aids (see Figure 34-10). Without these messages you have no idea what has failed in your custom ribbons.**

FIGURE 34-10

An error message thrown by a custom Access 2007 ribbon

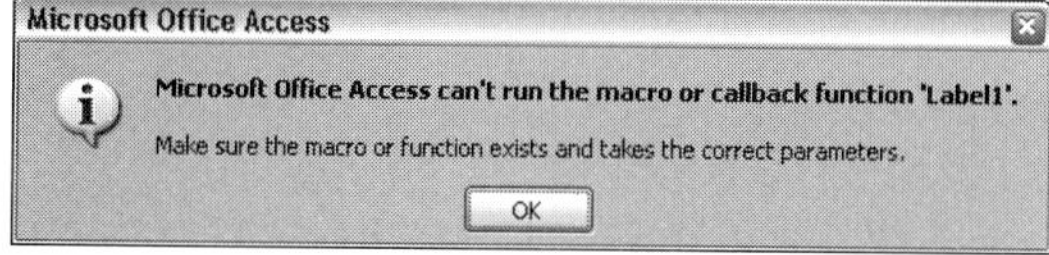

The Ribbon Hierarchy

The ribbon itself is a fairly complex structure and is hierarchical in nature. At the top-most level are the tabs you see along the top of the ribbon. Each tab contains one or more groups, each containing one or more controls.

- **Tabs:** The top-level object in the ribbon hierarchy. You use tabs to separate the most fundamental operations into logical groups. For instance, the default Access 2007 ribbon contains four tabs: Home, Create, External Data, and Database Tools.
- **Groups:** The second highest object in the ribbon hierarchy. Groups contain any of the number of different types of controls, and are used to logically separate operations supported by a ribbon tab. In Figure 34-11, the Home tab contains eight groups: Views, Clipboard, Font, Rich Text, Records, Sort & Filter, Window, and Find.
- **Controls:** In Figure 34-11, notice the variety of controls within each group on the Home tab. The View group contains a single control, while the Font group contains 13 different controls. Normally, the controls within a group are related to one another, but this is not a hard and fast rule.

FIGURE 34-11

The default Access 2007 ribbon

As you design your custom Access ribbons, you should keep the basic ribbon hierarchy in mind. Microsoft has spent a great deal of time experimenting with and testing the Office 12 ribbon paradigm, and it works well for a wide variety of applications.

One of the principles employed in Access 2007 ribbons is that there is virtually no limit to the number of objects at each level of the ribbon hierarchy. This means that you can add virtually any number of tabs to a custom ribbon. Obviously, too many tabs or too many groups can become a real problem for your users. Generally speaking, you should design your ribbons in a conservative manner, including only the items at each level that your users actually need.

Getting Started with Access 2007 Ribbons

As mentioned before, creating and customizing ribbons is somewhat more complicated than working with CommandBars in earlier versions of Access. Creating Access 2007 ribbons is, at a minimum, a five-step process. Each of these steps is described in detail in the following sections. Later you'll see many more examples of these steps.

Step 1: Design the ribbon and build the XML

As with most database objects, the first step to creating a new Access ribbon is to design it carefully on paper. If you are converting an existing toolbar or menu to an Access 2007 ribbon, you have a pretty good idea of the controls and other items to add to the ribbon.

The XML document you create for your ribbon mirrors the design you've laid out. Perhaps the most challenging aspect of composing the ribbons XML is visualizing how the ribbon will look, based on the XML behind it. There are no visual cues in a ribbon XML document that hints at the ribbon's appearance when rendered in Access 2007. Experience will be your best guide as you work with ribbon customization, and sometimes trial and error is the only way to achieve a desired objective.

As a final point, Access is extremely fussy about the XML used to compose ribbons. There appears to be no "parser" in Access that validates the XML as a ribbon is rendered. If an error exists in the XML document, Access refuses to render the ribbon, or the ribbon will be missing elements defined in the XML.

Inevitably, ribbon development in Access 2007 requires a number of back-and-forth cycles in which you modify the XML, transfer it to Access, and view the results. Until a graphical development tool is available, you have no way of really knowing how well your XML will work as a ribbon specification.

The section titled, "The Basic Ribbon XML," later in this chapter, describes the fundamental XML statements required by Access 2007 ribbons.

See the section "Using Visual Web Developer 2005" later in this chapter to see how to use the Express edition to compose the XML driving your Access 2007 ribbons. Also, several sections later in this chapter discuss the XML necessary to define ribbons, tabs, groups, and controls.

Step 2: Write the callback routines

Before writing any callback code for Access 2007 ribbon controls, you must reference the Microsoft Office 12.0 Object Library in the References dialog (select Tools ➪ References, and select the check box next to Microsoft Office 12.0 Object Library). Otherwise, the VBA interpreter will have no idea how to handle references to ribbon controls.

As described earlier in this chapter, callback routines are similar to event procedures but do not directly run in response to control events. Each type of callback routine has a specific "signature" that must be followed in order for the ribbon processor to locate and use the callback. For instance, the `onAction` callback signature for a button control is:

```
Public Sub OnAction(control as IRibbonControl)
```

The `onAction` callback for a check box is:

```
Public Sub OnAction(control As IRibbonControl, _
    pressed As Boolean)
```

Even though these callbacks support the same onAction control attribute, because the controls are different, the signatures are different. Clicking a button is just that — a simple click, and the action is done. In the case of a check box, a click either selects (pressed = True) or deselects (pressed = False) the control. Therefore, an additional parameter is required for check boxes.

The complete callback procedure for a simple button might be:

```
Public Sub OnAction(control As IRibbonControl)
    DoCmd.OpenForm "frmMyForm", , , , acNormal
End Sub
```

The callback procedure for the check box uses the pressed parameter to determine which path to take through the procedure:

```
Public Sub OnAction(control As IRibbonControl, _
    pressed As Boolean)

    If pressed = True Then
        DoCmd.OpenForm "frmHelp"
    Else
        DoCmd.Close acForm, "frmHelp"
    End If

End Sub
```

We've been focusing on the onAction callback, but many other callbacks exist. Here is the XML definition of a simple Label control:

```
<labelControl id="lblTodaysDate" getLabel="onGetLabel"/>
```

Notice the getLabel attribute. The callback signature of the getLabel attribute is:

```
Public Sub onGetLabel(control as IRibbonControl, ByRef label)
```

The Label control is passed as the IRibbonControl parameter, and the label's contents are passed as the (variant) label parameter. Notice that the label parameter is passed by reference, allowing the callback to modify the parameter's value. The complete procedure for filling a label with the current date is:

```
Public Sub onGetLabel(control as IRibbonControl, ByRef label)
    label = "Today is: " & FormatDateTime(Date, vbLongDate)
End Sub
```

The attribute linked to this callback is getLabel, which designates the procedure that fills the label's text at runtime. The name of the callback (onGetLabel) can be anything, but it makes good sense to provide it with a name that links it to the control's getLabel attribute.

Notice that none of these callback procedures discussed so far reference the control by name. This means that you have to write a uniquely named callback for each control, or use a single callback for multiple similar controls. Several of the Access Auto Auctions callbacks use the control's `id` property to determine which control has triggered the callback:

```
Public Sub onGetLabel(control As IRibbonControl, ByRef label)

  Select Case control.id

    Case "lblWelcome"
      label = GetWelcomeMessage()

    Case "lblToday"
      label = "Today is: " & FormatDateTime(Date, vbLongDate)

    Case "lblOrderCount"
      label = GetSalesCountString()

    Case "lblCompany"
      label = "Name: " & DLookup("Company", "tblContacts")

    Case "lblCompanyLocation"
      label = "Location: " & DLookup("City", "tblContacts") _
        & ", " & DLookup("State", "tblContacts")

  End Select
End Sub
```

A control's `id` property, of course, is the name assigned to the control in the XML:

```
<labelControl id="lblCompanyName" getLabel="onGetLabel"/>
<labelControl id="lblCompanyLocation" getLabel="onGetLabel"/>
```

Because the `id` properties are different, both of these Label controls use the same callback procedure. The callback uses the `id` to determine which label has triggered the callback.

Because the `getLabel` attribute specifies where the control gets its text, the `getLabel` attribute could be just as easily written as follows:

```
<labelControl id="lblHello" label="Hello!"/>
```

In this case, no callback is used, and the label is filled with a literal text string.

Step 3: Create the USysRibbons table

Access 2007 looks for a table named `USysRibbons` to see whether there are any custom ribbons in the current database application. This table does not exist by default and, if present, contains the XML that defines the custom ribbons in the application.

`USysRibbons` is very simple and contains only three fields, shown in Table 34-1.

TABLE 34-1

The USysRibbons Table Design

Field	Data Type
ID	AutoNumber
RibbonName	Text 255
RibbonXML	Memo

The ID field just keeps track of the ribbons in the table. The `RibbonName` is used to specify which ribbon Access should load at startup (described in Step 5 later in this chapter), whereas `RibbonXML` is a memo field (maximum size = 65,000 characters) containing the XML that defines the ribbon.

Because `USysRibbons` is a table, your Access database may actually include the definitions of many different custom ribbons. However, only one custom ribbon can be active at a time. In the section titled "Managing Ribbons," later in this chapter, you'll read how to invalidate an existing ribbon and load a new ribbon in its place.

Step 4: Add XML to USysRibbons

Figure 34-12 shows the XML, in a Microsoft Visual Web Developer window, for a very simple Access ribbon.

FIGURE 34-12

The XML required for a very simple Access 2007 ribbon

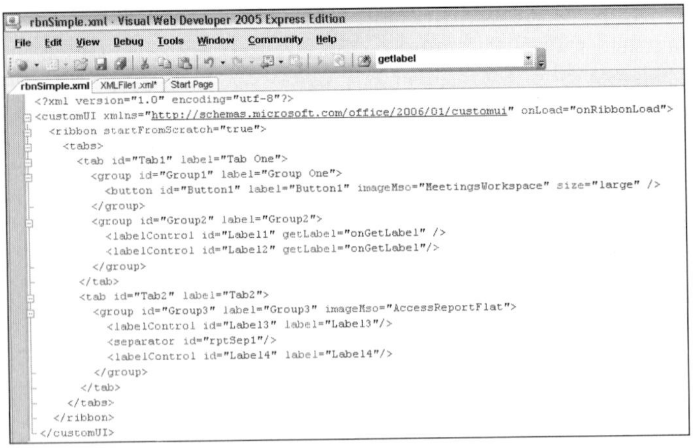

rbnSimple.xml - Visual Web Developer 2005 Express Edition

File Edit View Debug Tools Window Community Help

getlabel

rbnSimple.xml | XMLFile1.xml* | Start Page

```
<?xml version="1.0" encoding="utf-8"?>
<customUI xmlns="http://schemas.microsoft.com/office/2006/01/customui" onLoad="onRibbonLoad">
  <ribbon startFromScratch="true">
    <tabs>
      <tab id="Tab1" label="Tab One">
        <group id="Group1" label="Group One">
          <button id="Button1" label="Button1" imageMso="MeetingsWorkspace" size="large" />
        </group>
        <group id="Group2" label="Group2">
          <labelControl id="Label1" getLabel="onGetLabel" />
          <labelControl id="Label2" getLabel="onGetLabel"/>
        </group>
      </tab>
      <tab id="Tab2" label="Tab2">
        <group id="Group3" label="Group3" imageMso="AccessReportFlat">
          <labelControl id="Label3" label="Label3"/>
          <separator id="rptSep1"/>
          <labelControl id="Label4" label="Label4"/>
        </group>
      </tab>
    </tabs>
  </ribbon>
</customUI>
```

The ribbon produced with this XML is shown in Figure 34-13.

FIGURE 34-13

The simple Access 2007 ribbon created with the XML in Figure 34-12

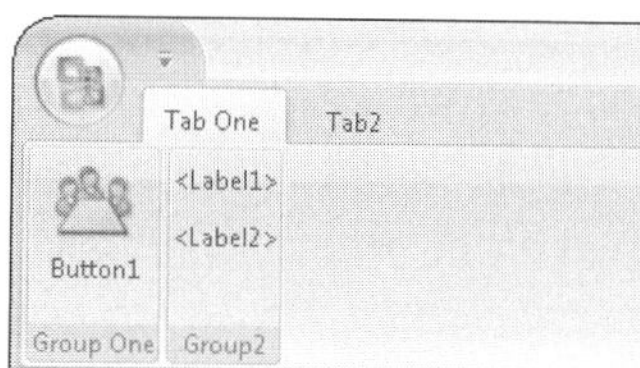

The XML for the Simple ribbon is included in the USysRibbons table in Chapter34.accdb. To use this ribbon, set the Custom Ribbon Id value in the Current Database options to Simple and restart the application.

In Figure 34-12, notice the absence of red squiggles, indicating improperly formed XML. Visual Web Developer flags any obvious XML errors (such as unmatched tags) by underlining suspicious passages with red squiggles.

Keep in mind that the Visual Web Developer locates syntax errors but cannot detect problems with the XML's logic. Incorrect references, misplaced or missing attributes, and other problems with the XML's content can still prevent your XML code from working as expected.

Notice the very top line of XML (<?xml version="1.0" encoding="utf-8"?>) in Figure 34-12. This line is automatically added to every XML document created with Visual Web Developer and is not really needed by Access ribbons. However, no harm is caused if this line is copied into the USysRibbons table.

Copying the XML from an editor such as Visual Web Developer to USysRibbons is a simple process. Highlight the XML, making sure to include the very top (<customUI...) and bottom (</customUI>) tags. Then, switch to Access, open the USysRibbons table, and paste the XML into the RibbonXML column of a new row. Finally, provide a RibbonName for the new ribbon (see Figure 34-14).

FIGURE 34-14

Copying the XML to USysRibbons and naming the new ribbon

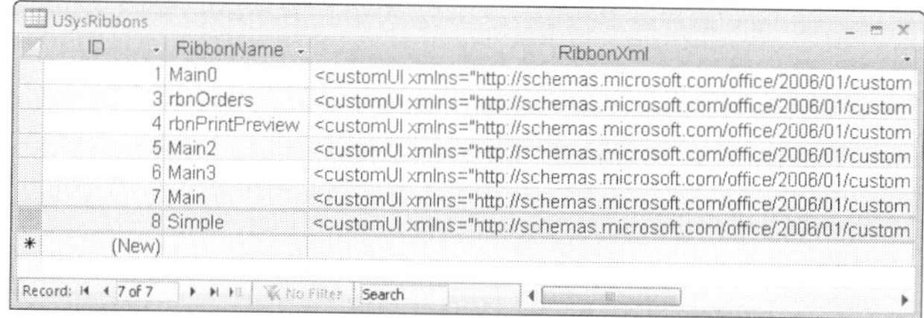

ID	RibbonName	RibbonXml
1	Main0	<customUI xmlns="http://schemas.microsoft.com/office/2006/01/custom
3	rbnOrders	<customUI xmlns="http://schemas.microsoft.com/office/2006/01/custom
4	rbnPrintPreview	<customUI xmlns="http://schemas.microsoft.com/office/2006/01/custom
5	Main2	<customUI xmlns="http://schemas.microsoft.com/office/2006/01/custom
6	Main3	<customUI xmlns="http://schemas.microsoft.com/office/2006/01/custom
7	Main	<customUI xmlns="http://schemas.microsoft.com/office/2006/01/custom
8	Simple	<customUI xmlns="http://schemas.microsoft.com/office/2006/01/custom
(New)		

Step 5: Specify the custom ribbon property

The last step, before restarting the application, is to open the Current Database properties (Office Button ➪ Access Options ➪ Current Database), scroll to the Toolbar Options section, and enter the name of the new ribbon in the `Custom Ribbon Id` combo box (see Figure 34-15). The combo box's list contains only the names of custom ribbons in `USysRibbons` that were in the table as Access started, so it does not contain the name of the new ribbon. You'll have to type the ribbon's name into the combo box or restart the application and let Access find the new ribbon in `USysRibbons`.

FIGURE 34-15

Specifying the new custom ribbon in the Current Database options dialog

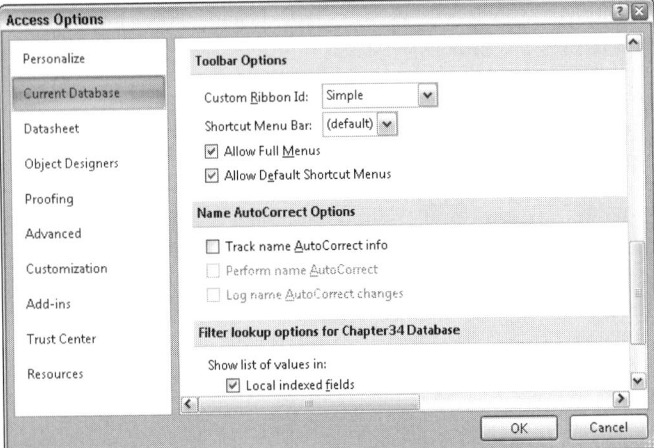

The Basic Ribbon XML

Let's take a closer look at the basic XML required by Access ribbons. The following XML represents a prototype ribbon (line numbers have been added to make the discussion following this XML easier to understand):

```
1 <?xml version="1.0" encoding="utf-8"?>
2 <customUI xmlns="http://schemas.microsoft.com/office
    /2006/01/customui" onLoad="onRibbonLoad">
3   <ribbon startFromScratch="true">
4     <tabs>
5       <tab id="tab1" ...
6         <group id="group1" ... >
7          ... Controls go here ...
8         </group>
9       </tab>
```

```
10        <tab id="tab2" ...
11          <group id="group2" ... >
12           ... Controls go here ...
13          </group>
14          ... Repeat Groups ...
15        </tab>
16        ... Repeat Tabs ...
17      </tabs>
18    </ribbon>
19 </customUI>
```

The first statement (`<?xml version="1.0" encoding="utf-8"?>`), as discussed before, is added by Visual Web Developer and does not affect Access 2007 ribbons.

The following statement (beginning with `<customUI...`) specifies an XML *namespace* (`xmlns`), an XML document that predefines acceptable tags for the XML statements that follow. The Office 12 namespace defines the Office 12 ribbon constructs (tabs, groups, controls, and so on) and enables IntelliSense in the Visual Web Developer editor.

The statement (3) that includes the `startFromScratch` directive is rather important. This directive notifies Access that we are building an entire ribbon from scratch, rather than starting with the default Access ribbon and taking things away. Generally speaking, the majority of your custom ribbons will be built from scratch because the default Access ribbon knows nothing about the forms, reports, and other objects and operations in your database.

The `<tabs>` (line 4) and `</tabs>` (line 17) tags indicate the beginning and end of the tabs on the ribbon. You'll recall that ribbons are very hierarchical, with tabs containing groups which contain controls. The tabs, therefore, are the highest-level objects within a ribbon and enclose all other ribbon objects.

Line 5 defines the left-most tab on the ribbon. In this example the tab's name is `"tab1"`. The other attributes for this tab are not shown but are implied by the ellipsis (...). The ending tag for `tab1` is located on line 9.

Line 6 begins the definition of the first group on `tab1`, and line 8 ends this group. Within the group are the controls displayed by the group.

The rest of this prototype ribbon is simple repetition of the first few items.

It bears repeating that XML is case-sensitive. Be careful to use exactly the same case and spelling for all references in your XML as well as in the callback code driving the ribbon.

Adding Ribbon Controls

The previous section presented a simple prototype ribbon. In this example, the controls were indicated by `"... Controls go here ..."` on lines 7 and 12. Take a moment and look at the actual XML construction of a few common ribbon controls.

NOTE In the following examples, you may be wondering where we got the image references (look for the `imageMso` tag) we used in our examples. The truth is, we guessed, based on a few example ribbons provided by Microsoft. At the time this book was written, Microsoft had not yet published a comprehensive list of built-in ribbon object names and image references to use on ribbons. By the time you read this chapter, undoubtedly Microsoft will have published a comprehensive guide to ribbon objects, the object tags and attributes, and the built-in images you can use in your custom ribbons. Furthermore, Microsoft had mentioned that it is possible to programmatically assign images to ribbon controls to modify a ribbon's appearance at runtime. Unfortunately, these examples are not yet available.

We suggest you search the Microsoft Office Web site (`http://office.microsoft.com`) for comprehensive ribbon examples and documentation to use as you build your custom ribbons. Also, check back at this book's page on the Wiley Web site. As soon as we have good examples, we'll post them there.

Label control

The Label control is, by far, the simplest and easiest to add to a ribbon. A ribbon label is completely analogous to a label you add to an Access form. It contains either hard-coded text or text that is generated by a callback procedure.

Here is an example label definition:

```
<group id="grpFonts" label="Settings">
  <labelControl id="lbl1" label="Font Things" />
  <separator id="s1"/>
  <labelControl id="lc2" label="Choose Font Settings" />
  <checkBox id="chk1" label="Bold" onAction="SetBold"/>
  <checkBox id="chk2" label="Italics" onAction="SetItalics"/>
</group>
```

This XML contains three labels, a separator, and two check boxes. The text in each of these labels is hard-coded, rather than returned by a back procedure. Earlier you read how to use the `getLabel` attribute to specify a callback that returns a label's text.

Separator

A separator is a graphical element that divides items in a group, as shown in Figure 34-16. Separators contain no text and appear as a vertical line within a group. By themselves, they're not very interesting, but they graphically separate controls that would otherwise be too close within a group.

FIGURE 34-16

Separators provide a way to divide controls within a group.

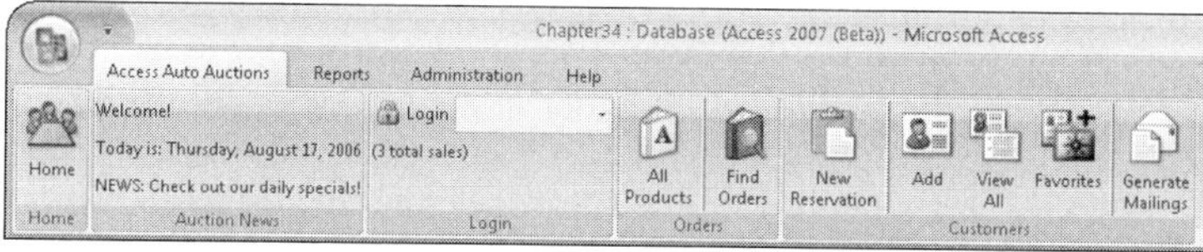

The XML code for the separators in Figure 34-16 is:

```
<group id="grpOrders" label="Orders">
  <button id="cmdNewOrder" label="Place Order" .../>
  <button id="cmdViewOrders" label="All Orders" .../>
  <separator id="sep4"/>
  <button id="cmdFindOrders" label="Find Orders".../>
</group>
<group id="grpCustomers" label="Customers">
  <button id="cmdNewReservation" label="New Reservation".../>
  <separator id="sep2"/>
  <button id="cmdAddCustomer" label="Add" .../>
  <button id="cmdViewCustomers" label="View All".../>
  <button id="cmdFavorites" label="Favorites" .../>
  <separator id="sep3"/>
  <button id="cmdMailings" label="Generate Mailings"..,/>
</group>
```

The previous XML statements have been shortened to make it easier to see the separator placement. `grpOrders` contains a single separator, whereas `grpCustomers` contains two.

The only requirement of separators is that each be assigned a unique ID value.

Check boxes

Check boxes are effective for selecting any of a number of different options. Check boxes are not mutually exclusive, so the user can choose any of the check boxes within a group without affecting other selections.

Check boxes are established as any other ribbon control is:

```
<tab id="tabOutdoor" label="Outdoor">
  <group id="grpSports" label="Sports" ...>
    <checkBox id="chk04" label="Baseball" .../>
    <checkBox id="chk05" label="Basketball" .../>
    <separator id="Sep1"/>
    <checkBox id="chk06" label="Tennis" .../>
    <checkBox id="chk07" label="Water Polo" .../>
  </group>
```

```
    <group id="grpCamping" label="Camping Supplies">
      <checkBox id="chk08" label="Tent" .../>
      <checkBox id="chk09" label="Granola" .../>
      <checkBox id="chk10" label="Lantern" .../>
      <separator id="Sep2"/>
      <button id="btn" imageMso="DaVinciQuerySelect"
        size="large" label="A Big Button" />
    </group>
  </tab>
```

As before, code has been removed and replaced with ellipsis characters to improve clarity of this example XML.

The tab produced by this XML code is shown in Figure 34-17.

FIGURE 34-17

Check boxes are a good choice when the user can select among a number of options.

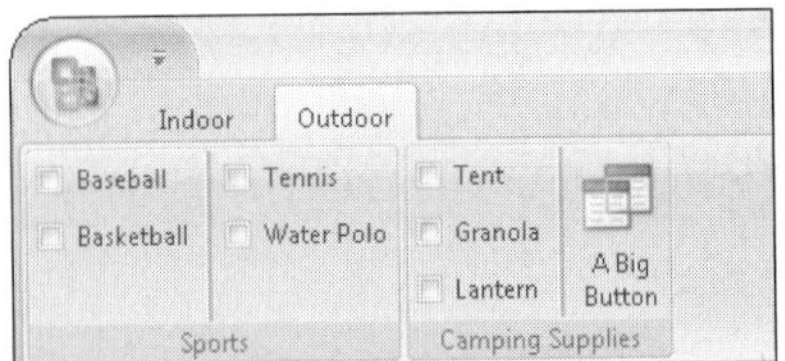

DropDown control

The DropDown control is more complex than the other examples you've seen. It includes a list of items for the user to choose from. Therefore, a DropDown has a number of attributes that define its appearance, as well as callbacks that populate its list:

```
<dropDown
  id="ddLogin"
  label="Login" supertip="Select your employee name...
  screentip="Login Name"
  getItemCount="onGetLoginCount"
  getItemLabel="onGetLogins"
  imageMso="Private"
  onAction="onLogin">
</dropDown>
```

The `id`, `label`, `screentip`, and `imageMso` attributes define the DropDown control's appearance. The `getItemCount` and `getItemLabel` populate the DropDown's list. The `onAction` specifies the callback that handles the control's action.

The VBA callbacks for a typical DropDown are shown in the following code. Two primary callbacks are required for a DropDown. The first sets the count of items to appear in the list, and the second actually populates the list.

```
Public Sub onGetLoginCount( _
    control As IRibbonControl, ByRef count)
    count = Nz(DCount("*", "tblSalesPerson"), 0)
End Sub

Public Sub onGetLogins( _
    control As IRibbonControl, index As Integer, ByRef label)

    Dim strName  As String

    strName = Nz(DLookup("SalespersonName", _
        "tblSalesPerson", "SalesPersonID = " & index + 1), "")

    label = strName

End Sub
```

The first callback (`onGetLoginCount`) gets the count of items to be placed on the DropDown's list. Notice the `ByRef count` parameter. This parameter tells the DropDown how many items to accommodate on its list.

The second procedure (`onGetLogins`) actually retrieves the items for the list. In this case, the procedure pulls the SalesPerson name field from `tblSalesPerson` using `DLookup`. `onGetLogins` is called by the DropDown multiple times; the exact number of calls is determined by the count value established by `onGetLoginCount`.

The `onGetLogins` routine cheats a little bit to supply this information. Notice the index parameter passed to this routine. Index tells the procedure which slot on the drop-down list is being filled when the procedure is called. The `DLookup` adds 1 to this value and extracts the name of the sales person whose ID matches this value. This means that the `SalesPersonID` values have to be sequential, starting with 1, or this procedure will fail.

Extracting data with nonsequential ID values, or where the ID value is non-numeric, requires a bit more work. You could, for instance, create a sorted recordset of the values you want on the list. Then, using the index parameter, advance through the recordset to the record requested by the DropDown.

An accurate count of values to add to the DropDown is important. The DropDown has no way, other than the count parameter, to know how many items to expect. Setting a count too low means that not all items will be added, while setting the count too high means that list contains blank spaces. If, for instance, you set the count to 10 items, but only 5 are available, the DropDown's list contains the 5 items, but also 5 blank spaces.

Using Visual Web Developer 2005

Visual Web Developer 2005 Express (VWD) is a freely downloadable tool provided by Microsoft to aid your efforts to build Web sites. Visual Web Developer is used to produce entire Web sites, and individual files. The XML code you see in this chapter was written and modified using Visual Web Developer's XML editor.

Begin by downloading VWD from `http://msdn.microsoft.com/vstudio/express/vwd/` and installing it on your computer. When started, VWD presents a rather intimidating opening screen (see Figure 34-18).

FIGURE 34-18

Visual Web Developer's opening screen

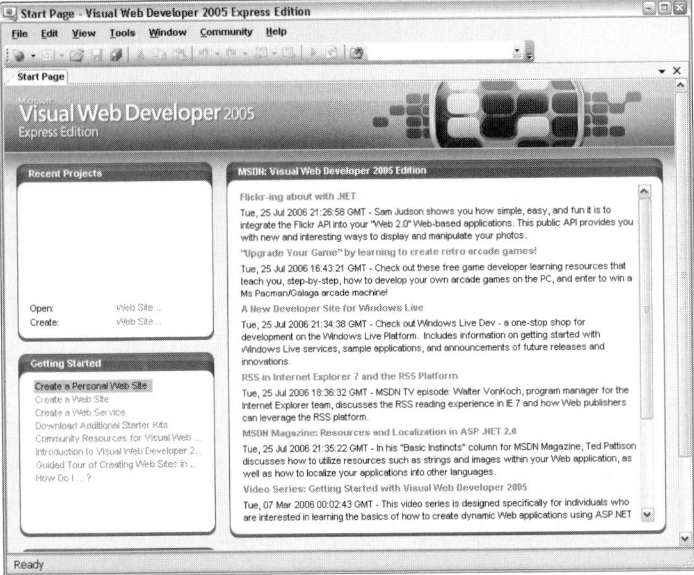

The opening screen contains links to Web sites and pages related to using VWD, as well as navigation aids to help you organize and manage Web sites created with VWD.

For this demonstration, choose File ➪ New File to open the New File dialog (see Figure 34-19).

Notice that VWD is proficient at creating any of a number of different file types, including XML. Selecting the XML option opens the XML editor (Figure 34-20), ready for your Access ribbon XML code.

FIGURE 34-19

VWD's New File dialog

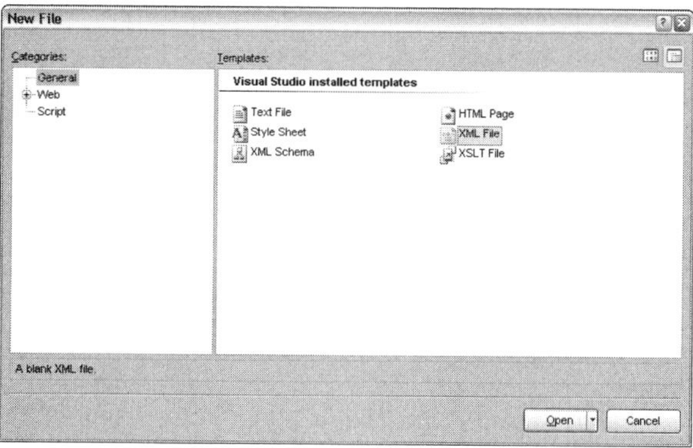

FIGURE 34-20

The XML editor in Visual Web Developer 2005

XMLFile2.xml* - Visual Web Developer 2005 Express Edition

File Edit View Debug Tools Window Community Help

dropdown

XMLFile2.xml* rbnSimple2.xml XMLFile1.xml*

```
<?xml version="1.0" encoding="utf-8"?>
<customUI xmlns="http://schemas.microsoft.com/office/2006/01/customui" onLoad="onRibbonLoad">
  <ribbon startFromScratch="true">
    <fileMenu>
      <button idMso="OpenDatabase" visible="false"/>
      <button idMso="NewDatabase" visible="false"/>
      <splitButton idMso="AccessSaveAsMenu" visible="false"/>
    </fileMenu>
    <tabs>
      <tab id="tabMain" label="Access Auto Auctions">
        <group id="grpHome" label="Home">
          <button id="cmdHome" label="Home" imageMso="MeetingsWorkspace" size="large" onAction="onOpenFormEdit"
        </group>
        <group id="grpNews" label="Auction News">
          <labelControl id="lblWelcome" supertip="Hello" getLabel="onGetLabel"/>
          <labelControl id="lblToday" getLabel="onGetLabel"/>
          <!-- You might have a callback function here to display this text dynamically -->
          <labelControl id="lblNews" label="NEWS: Check out our daily specials!"/>
        </group>
        <group id="grpLogin" label="Login">
          <dropDown id="ddLogin" label="Login" supertip="Select your employee name from the list."
                    screentip="Login Name" getItemCount="onGetLoginCount" getItemLabel="onGetLogins" imageMso="P
          <box id="boxOrderData" boxStyle="horizontal">
            <labelControl id="lblOrderCount" getLabel="onGetLabel" screentip="Number of orders" supertip="My Sup
            <labelControl id="lblSpaces1" label="    "/>
          </box>
        </group>
        <group id="grpOrders" label="Orders">
          <button id="cmdViewProducts" label="All Products" size="large" imageMso="GalInsertFnText"
                  onAction="onOpenFormEdit" tag="frmProductsDisplay"/>
          <separator id="sep4"/>
```

Ready Ln 136 Col 12 Ch 12 INS

And, that's about all there is to VWD as far as working with XML. The primary advantage of using a tool such as VWD is that it understands XML and performs basic syntax checking to help you compose valid XML. Also, VWD supports multiple open documents at one time, making it quite easy to copy XML from one window and paste into another. And, although you can't tell from the figures in this book, the XML code in Figure 34-20 is color-coded to indicate which words are keywords, which are identifiers, and which are XML tags.

Together, these features make VWD a compelling addition to any developer's toolkit.

Managing Ribbons

From time to time you may find it necessary to replace a ribbon with another one while the user works with an application. So far all the examples you've seen are loaded as Access starts, and stay on the screen as long as the user works with the application. You have not yet examined the steps involved in closing one ribbon and opening another.

You don't really close a ribbon. Instead, you *invalidate* it, causing Access to discontinue managing the ribbon. The syntax for invalidating a ribbon is:

```
Ribbon.Invalidate
```

The problem is knowing which ribbon to invalidate. Microsoft suggests you cache a reference to a ribbon each time it is opened, and then use that reference to invalidate the ribbon should the need arise. You may have noticed the `onLoad` attribute of the prototype ribbon in the section titled, "The Basic Ribbon XML," earlier in this chapter:

```
<customUI xmlns="http://schemas...." onLoad="onRibbonLoad">
```

(Some text has been removed from this statement for clarity's sake.)

The `onLoad` attribute specifies a callback that supports the ribbon's startup activities. You can use the `onLoad` callback to cache a reference to the ribbon.

Begin by establishing a public object variable that will point to the ribbon:

```
Public gobjRibbon As IRibbonUI
```

Next, use the object variable to store a reference to the ribbon during startup:

```
Public Sub onRibbonLoad(ribbon As IRibbonUI)
  'Cache a copy of the Ribbon:
  Set gobjRibbon = ribbon
End Sub
```

The `gobjRibbon` object variable remains in scope while the application is used. Should the need arise to invalidate the ribbon, simply invoke the `Invalidate` method:

```
gobjRibbon.Invalidate
```

Of course, after you invalidate a ribbon, you want to replace it with another. Invalidating a ribbon does not remove it from the screen. Unless you overwrite it with another ribbon it stays on the screen, taking up space, but not really doing anything.

Use the Access Application object's `LoadCustomUI` method (new in Access 2007) to load a different custom ribbon:

```
Application.LoadCustomUI( _
    CustomUI_Name As String, CustomUI_XML As String)
```

The `CustomUI_Name` and `CustomUI_XML` are extracted from the `USysRibbons` table:

```
Public Function LoadRibbons(strName As String)

  Dim strXML As String

  strXML = DLookup("RibbonXML", "USysRibbons", _
    "RibbonName= '" & strName & "'")

  Call Access.Application.LoadCustomUI(strName, strXML)

End Function
```

Access should instantly replace the invalidated ribbon with the ribbon specified by the `strName` and `strXML` values passed to `LoadCustomUI`.

Completely Removing the Access 2007 Ribbon

Let's assume, for a moment, that there are perfectly legitimate reasons why you don't want to use the Access ribbons in your applications. Perhaps you've developed a set of effective switchboard forms, or have mimicked the old style toolbars and menus with borderless forms. Or, your applications are entirely forms-driven and don't need the flexibility provided by toolbars and ribbons.

Here's how you can completely remove ribbons from the Access 2007 interface:

1. **Create a new table called USysRibbons.**
2. **Add two fields RibbonName (text) and RibbonXML (Memo).**
3. **Create a new record with the RibbonName set to `"Blank"`.**

   It doesn't really matter what you call it.
4. **Then add the following XML to the RibbonXML column:**

   ```
   <CustomUI xmlns="http://schemas.microsoft.com/office/2006
   /01/CustomUI">
    <Ribbon startFromScratch="true"/>
   </CustomUI>
   ```

5. **Restart the database.**
6. **Click the Office button and select the Access Options button.**
7. **Click the Current Database tab and scroll to the Toolbars area.**
8. **In the Toolbars option set the `Custom Ribbon Id` to `Blank` (the same name you specified for the RibbonName column in Step 3).**
9. **Restart the database.**

This process sets up a dummy ribbon named `Blank` that contains no tabs, no groups, and no controls. In effect, you're telling Access to put up an empty ribbon, which simply removes the ribbon from the Access user interface.

Summary

This chapter documented the process of creating custom ribbons in Access 2007. At the time this chapter was prepared, Access did not include a developer tool for customizing ribbons. Therefore, this chapter describes building ribbons from scratch, using an XML editor to compose the XML that defines a custom ribbon, adding the `USysRibbons` table to Access, and copying the XML into `USysRibbons`.

This chapter has also reviewed several of the most common Access 2007 ribbon controls. You saw how to add controls such as labels, buttons, check boxes, and separators to Access ribbons. Access 2007 supports many other types of ribbon controls, and you are encouraged to investigate the wide variety of available controls.

Chapter 35

Distributing Access Applications

IN THIS CHAPTER

Defining Current Database options

Testing the application

Polishing the application

Bulletproofing the application

Separating tables from the application

Documenting the application

You're lucky if you have the luxury of developing only single-user, in-house applications and you never have to worry about distributing an application within a company or across the country. Most developers have to worry about application distribution sooner or later. You don't even have to develop commercial software to be concerned with distribution; for example, when you develop an application to be run on a dozen workstations in one organization, you need to distribute your application in some form or other.

This chapter covers all the preceding points to some degree. However, because some of the listed items, such as error handling and splitting tables, are covered in detail in other chapters, this chapter focuses primarily on setting database options when preparing your application for distribution.

You need to be concerned with many issues when preparing an Access application for distribution. Distributing your application properly not only makes installing and using the application easier for the end user, but it also makes updating and maintaining the application easier for you. In addition, the support required for an application is greatly decreased by properly preparing and packaging the database and associated files for distribution.

ON the CD-ROM This chapter uses the database named `Chapter35.accdb`. If you haven't already copied it onto your machine from the CD, you'll need to do so now.

Defining the Current Database Options

An Access database has a number of options that can greatly simplify the process of distributing your database (see Figure 35-1). You can access these options for a database by selecting clicking the Microsoft Office Button, selecting Access Options, and clicking the Current Database tab. You can still use an Autoexec macro to execute initialization code, but the Current Database options enable you to set up certain aspects of your application, thus reducing the amount of startup code that you have to write. It is extremely important to correctly structure these options before distributing your Access application.

FIGURE 35-1

The Current Database options enable you to take control of your application from the moment a user starts it.

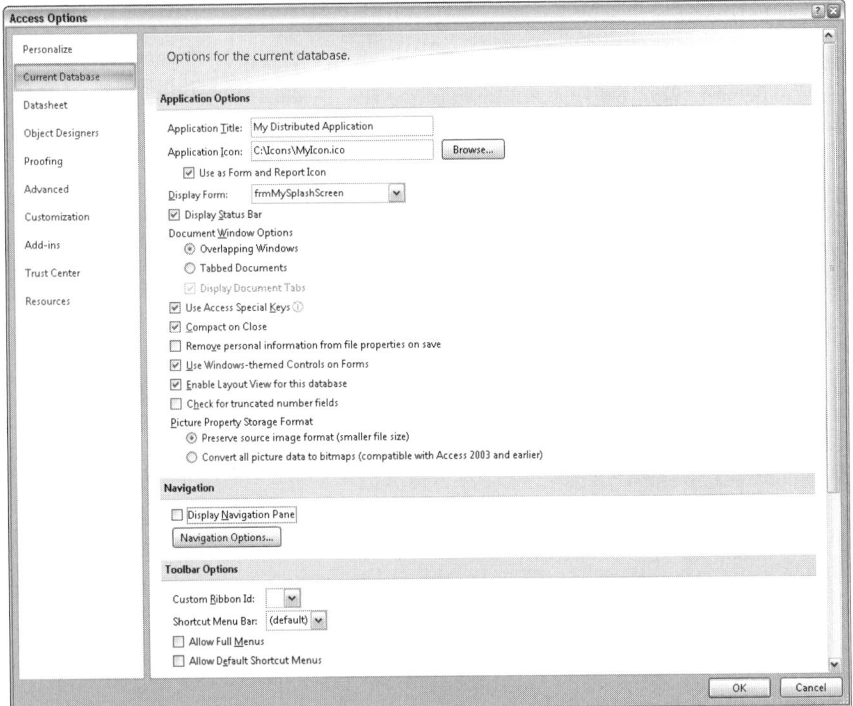

NEW FEATURE The Current Database options replace the Startup dialog box from previous versions of Access.

Application Options

The settings in the Application Options section let you define parameters for your database as an application:

- **Application Title:** The text that you provide in the Application Title field displays on the main Access window's title bar. You should always specify an application title for your distributed applications. If you don't, the database name and Access 2007 appear on the title bar of your application. The Application Title is also the text that is displayed in the Windows task bar when the application is open and running.
- **Application Icon:** The icon that you specify in the Application Icon field displays on the title bar of your application and in the task switcher (Alt+Tab) of Windows. Checking the box "Use as Form and Report Icon" also displays this icon when a form or report is minimized. If you don't specify your own icon, Access displays the default Access icon; therefore, you may want to provide an application-specific icon for your application. Using special program icons helps your users distinguish between different Access applications. You can create small bitmaps in Windows Paint and use available conversion tools to convert a `.bmp` file to an `.ico` file format. You can also create icons using other graphics programs or search for application icons in your favorite search engine.
- **Display Form:** The form you select in the Display Form field automatically displays when the application opens in Access. When the form loads, the Form Load event of the Display form fires (if it contains any code), eliminating the need to use an Autoexec macro. You should consider using a splash screen (which is discussed later in this chapter) as your startup Display Form.
- **Display Status Bar:** Deselect the Display Status Bar option to completely remove the status bar from the screen (this option is selected by default). Keep in mind that the status bar is an incredibly informative and easy-to-use tool because it automatically displays various key-states (such as Caps Lock and Scroll Lock), as well as the Status Bar Text property for the active control. Instead of hiding the status bar, you should make full use of it and disable only it if you have a very good reason to do so.
- **Document Window Options:** Choose Overlapping Windows or Tabbed Documents to display how the forms and reports look in your distributed application. Overlapping Windows retains the look of previous versions of Access, letting you look at multiple screens at once, while Tabbed Documents uses a single-document interface, which is new to Access 2007 (shown in Figure 35-2). You must close and reopen the current database for the changes to take effect.

  The Display Document Tabs option is only available when you select Tabbed Documents; it turns on or off the tabs that appear at the top of any open database object. This setting turns off only the tabs and does not close tabbed objects themselves.

FIGURE 35-2

A database with the Tabbed Documents option selected. The tabs let you select which Access object to work with.

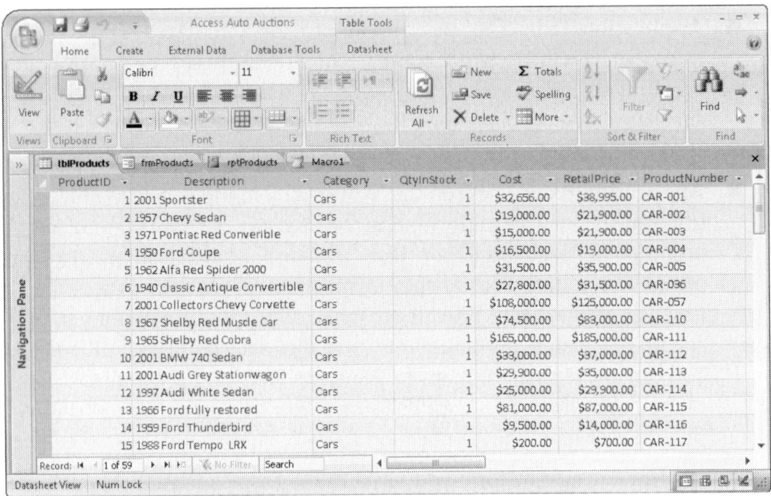

- **Use Access Special Keys:** If you select this option, users of your application can use accelerator keys that are specific to the Access environment in order to circumvent some security measures, such as unhiding the Navigation Pane. If you deselect this option, the following keys are disabled:
  - **F11:** Use this key to show the Navigation Pane (if hidden).
  - **Ctrl+G:** Use this key to display the Immediate window in the Visual Basic Editor.
  - **Ctrl+Break:** In Access projects, use this key to stop Access from retrieving records from the server database.
  - **Alt+F11:** Use this key to start the VBA Editor.

  You should probably deselect this option when distributing the application to prevent users from circumventing the options you select. Otherwise, users may inadvertently reveal the Navigation Pane or VBA code edition, leading to confusion and other problems.

- **Compact on Close:** Checking the Compact on Close option tells Access to automatically compact and repair your database when you close it. You must close and reopen the current database in order for this change to take effect.

CROSS-REF **For more information on the benefits of compacting and repairing a database, see Chapter 26.**

Keep in mind that compacting a large database may take a considerable amount of time. Furthermore, Compact on Close only affects the front-end database. Unless your application uses the front end for temporary tables or other operations that cause the front end to bloat, the Compact and Repair option may be of minimal benefit to users.

- **Remove Personal Information from File Properties on Save:** Checking this option automatically removes the personal information from the file properties when you save the file. You must close and reopen the current database for this change to take effect.
- **Use Windows-Themed Controls on Forms:** Checking this option uses your system's Windows theme on the form/report controls. This setting only applies when you use a Windows theme other than the standard theme.
- **Enable Layout View for This Database:** The Enable Layout View option shows or hides the Layout View button on the Access status bar and in the shortcut menus that appear when you right-click on an object tab. Remember that you can disable the Layout View for individual objects, so even when you enable this option, it might not always be available.
- **Check for truncated number fields:** Checking this option makes numbers appear as "#####" when the column is too narrow to display the entire value. Unchecking this option truncates values that are too wide to be displayed in the datasheet. This means that users see only a part of the column's values when the column is too narrow.
- **Picture Property Storage Format:** This option lets you choose how graphic files are stored in the database. Choose Preserve Source Image Format (Smaller File Size) to store the image in the original format, which also reduces the database size. Choose Convert All Picture Data to Bitmaps to store all images as bitmaps, which increases the database size but keeps it compatible with previous versions of Access (Access 2003 and earlier).

  Earlier versions of Access always stored images twice within the database. The first copy was the original format (such as `.jpg`) of the image file, while the second copy was a bitmap used only to display the image on Access forms and reports. Because images were stored twice, Access databases before 2007 were prone to severe bloating when a lot of image data was stored in the MDB.

  Beginning with Access 2007, you have the option to Preserve Source Image Format to conserve disk space by reducing the database file's size (this option is only available in the `.accdb` file format). When using this option, Access only stores one copy of an image (in its original format) and dynamically generates a bitmap when the image is displayed on a form or report.

Navigation Options

The settings in the Navigation Options section let you define parameters when navigating your database as an application.

- **Display Navigation Pane:** With most distributed applications, you may never want your users to have direct access to any of your tables, queries, forms, or other database objects. It's far too tempting for a user to try to "improve" a form or report, or to make some minor modification to a table or query. Rarely are users really qualified to make such changes to an Access database. Deselecting the Display Navigation Pane option hides the Navigation Pane from the user at startup.

  But unless you also deselect the Use Access Special Keys option (described earlier in this chapter), users can press F11 to unhide the Navigation Pane. You must close and reopen the current database for this change to take effect.

- **Navigation Options:** One nice addition to Access 2007 is the ability to select which database options are exposed to users when the Navigation Pane is visible at startup. The Navigation Options button displays the Navigation Options dialog box (shown in Figure 35-3), which you use to change the categories and groups that appear in the Navigation Pane.

FIGURE 35-3

The Navigation Options dialog box

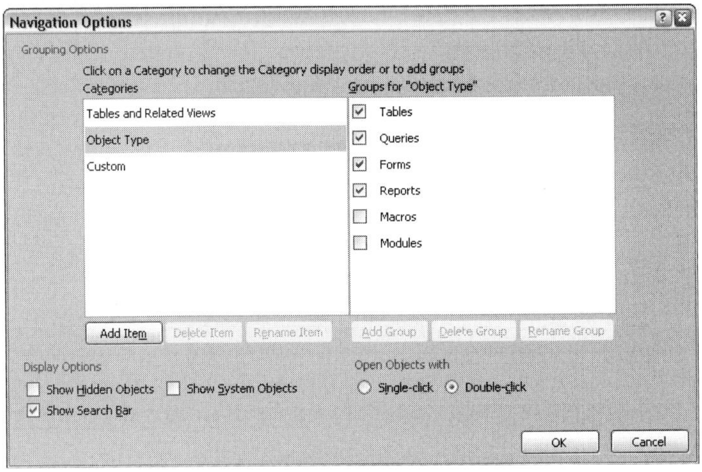

In the Grouping Options, click on a Category on the left side of the dialog box to change the category display order or to add groups to the right side of the dialog box. Click on the Object Type category to disable viewing of certain Access objects (Tables, Queries, Forms, Reports, Macros, and Modules).

Check the Display Options to Show Hidden Objects, Show System Objects, and Show Search Bar. It's usually a good idea to hide the hidden and system objects, which you normally don't want to modify (they're hidden for a reason!).

The Search Bar (see Figure 35-4) is useful in the Navigation Pane when you have a lot of objects and want to narrow the list to avoid excessive scrolling. For example, if you wanted to see the forms that had the word *Customer* in them, you'd type **Customer** in the Search Bar to limit the tables shown in the Navigation Pane.

FIGURE 35-4

The Search Bar appears at the top of the Navigation Pane.

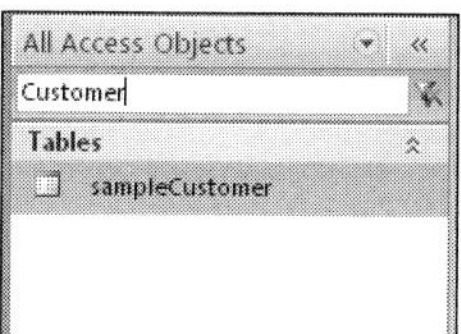

In the Open Objects With section, select Single-Click or Double-Click to choose how you open a database object. Double-Click is the default option and is most likely familiar to all of your users.

Toolbar Options

The settings in the Toolbar Options section let you define custom ribbons and toolbars when using your database as an application. Custom ribbon creation is explained in Chapter 34.

- **Custom Ribbon Id:** The Custom Ribbon Id option lets you specify a customized (usually trimmed-down) version of the Access ribbon. If you don't supply a Custom Ribbon Id, Access uses its built-in ribbon, which may be inappropriate for your application. The default ribbon contains many controls for modifying database objects, which may lead to problems with your users.

  You must close and reopen the current database for this change to take effect.
- **Shortcut Menu Bar:** Setting the Shortcut Menu Bar changes the default menu for shortcut menus (right-click menus) to a menu bar that you specify. Using custom shortcut menus that have functionality specific to your application is always preferable. You must close and reopen the current database for this change to take effect.
- **Allow Full Menus:** Checking the Allow Full Menus option determines whether Access displays all the commands in its menus or just the frequently used commands. If you supply custom menus for all of your forms and reports and set the Menu Bar property to a custom menu bar, this setting has no effect. You must close and reopen the current database for this change to take effect.
- **Allow Default Shortcut Menus:** The Allow Default Shortcut Menus setting determines whether Access displays its own default shortcut menus when a user right-clicks an object in the Navigation Pane or a control on a form or report. You must close and reopen the current database for this change to take effect.
- **Name AutoCorrect Options:** Several chapters in this book have mentioned the problems associated with changing the names of fundamental database objects such as tables and fields within tables. For example, if you change the name of a table, everywhere you refer to that table (a query, a control's ControlSource property, VBA code, a macro, and so on) becomes invalid, causing the application to function improperly.

Microsoft added the Name AutoCorrect feature to Access 2000 as a way of mitigating the problems that inevitably occur when database objects are renamed. Unfortunately, this feature has never worked quite as well as Microsoft had hoped. Primarily, Name AutoCorrect is a major drag on performance. Because Access must constantly monitor activity while Access is used, a database with this option selected runs noticeably slower than when the option is turned off. Secondly, there are far too many places where an object's name may appear for an AutoCorrect feature to effectively capture every instance when the object is renamed. This is especially true of object names appearing in VBA code. Many applications contain hundreds of thousands of lines of VBA code, making it virtually impossible to find and update every object reference.

The Name AutoCorrect option is turned *on* by default in Access 2007 applications. Unless you find this option useful in your projects, you should consider turning it off, as it has been in the `Chapter35.accdb` example accompanying this chapter.

Setting the Current Database options saves you many lines of code that you would ordinarily need in order to perform the same functions and enables you to control your application's interface from the moment the user starts it. Always verify the Current Database options before distributing your application.

Testing the Application before Distribution

After you finish adding features and have everything in place within your application, you should take some time to thoroughly test the application. Testing may seem obvious, but this step is often overlooked by many developers, evidenced by the amount of buggy software appearing on the shelves of your local software stores. If you don't believe this to be true, check out the software support forums on the Internet — almost every major commercial software application has some patch available or known bugs that need to be addressed.

Distributing an application that is 100-percent bug-free is almost impossible. The nature of the software development beast is that, if you write a program, someone can — and will — find an unanticipated way to break it. Certain individuals seem to have a black cloud above their heads and can break an application (in other words, hit a critical bug) within minutes of using it. If you know of such people, hire them, if you can! They can be a great asset when you're testing an application.

While working through the debugging process of an application, categorize your bugs into one of three categories:

- **Category 1: Major ship-sinking bugs:** These bugs are absolutely unacceptable — for example, numbers in an accounting application that don't add up the way they should or a routine that consistently causes the application to terminate unexpectedly. If you ship an application with known Category 1 bugs, prepare for a lynching party organized by your users!

- **Category 2: Major bugs that have a workaround:** Category 2 bugs are fairly major bugs, but they don't stop users from performing their tasks because some workaround exists in the application. For example, a button that doesn't call a procedure correctly is a bug. If the button is the only way to run the procedure, this bug is a Category 1 bug. If, however, a corresponding ribbon command calls the procedure correctly, the bug is a Category 2 bug. Shipping an application with a Category 2 bug is sometimes necessary. Although shipping a bug is officially a no-no, deadlines sometimes dictate that exceptions need to be made. Category 2 bugs will annoy users but shouldn't send them into fits.

  If you ship an application with known Category 2 bugs, document them! Some developers have a don't-say-anything-and-act-surprised attitude regarding Category 2 bugs. This attitude can frustrate users and waste considerable amounts of their time by forcing them to discover not only the problem but also the solution. For example, if you were to ship an application with the Category 2 bug just described, you should include a statement in your application's README file that reads something like this: "The button on the XYZ form does not correctly call feature such-and-such. Please use the corresponding command such-and-such found on the ribbon. A patch will be made available as soon as possible."
- **Category 3: Small bugs and minor nits:** Category 3 bugs are small issues that don't affect the operation of your application. They may be caption or label misspellings or incorrect text box colors. Category 3 bugs should be fixed soon, but should not take precedence over Category 1 bugs. They should take precedence over Category 2 bugs only when they're so extreme that the application looks completely unacceptable or when they cause enough trouble for users that a fix is quickly needed.

Categorizing bugs and approaching them systematically, helps you create a program that looks and behaves the way its users think it should. Sometimes you may feel like you'll never finish your Category 1 list, but you will. You'll be smiling the day you check your bug sheet and realize that you're down to a few Category 2s and a dozen or so Category 3s! Although you may be tempted to skip this beta-testing phase of development, don't. You'll only pay for it in the long run.

TIP Not all Access features are available when an application is run within the Access runtime environment You can operate in the runtime environment and use the full version of Access to test for problems with your code and with the runtime environment by using the `/Runtime` command line option when starting your Access application. Click Run on the Windows Start menu or create a shortcut. The following command-line example starts Access and opens the Invoices database (if it is located at `D:\MYAPPS\`) in the runtime environment (all of this text appears as a single line in a shortcut's `Target` property):

```
D:\OFFICE2007\ACCESS\MSACCESS.EXE /RUNTIME
D:\MYAPPS\INVOICES.ACCDB
```

You should always test and debug your application in the runtime environment if you plan to distribute the application.

NEW FEATURE Access contains a new extension — `.accdr` — that automatically puts your database in the runtime environment when it's opened. Change your database file's extension from `.accdb` to `.accdr` to create a "locked-down" version of your Access 2007 database. Change the extension back to `.accdb` to restore full functionality.

Polishing Your Application

When your application has been thoroughly tested and appears ready for distribution, spend some time polishing your application. Polishing your application consists of the following:

- Giving your application a consistent look and feel
- Adding common, professional components
- Adding clear and concise pictures to buttons
- Using common, understandable field labels and button captions

Giving your application a consistent look and feel

First and foremost, you should decide on some design standards and apply them to your application. This is incredibly important if you want a professional "look and feel" to your applications. Figure 35-5 shows a form with samples of different styles of controls.

FIGURE 35-5

You can decide on any interface style that you like for your application. However, after you decide on a style, use it consistently.

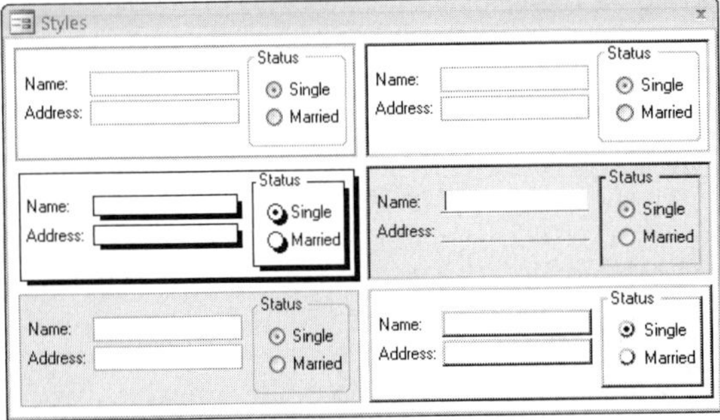

Your design decisions may include the following:

- Will text boxes be sunken, flat with a border, flat without a border, chiseled, or raised?
- What back color should text boxes be?
- What color will the forms be?
- Will you use chiseled borders to separate related items or select a sunken or raised border?
- What size will buttons on forms be?
- For forms that have similar buttons, such as Close and Help, in what order will the buttons appear?
- Which accelerator keys will you use on commonly used buttons, such as Close and Help?

Making your application look and work in a consistent manner is the single most important way to make it appear professional. For ideas on design standards to implement in your applications, spend some time working with some of your favorite programs and see what standards they use. In the area of look and feel, copying from another developer is generally not considered plagiarism but is instead often looked upon as a compliment. Copying does *not* extend, however, to making use of another application's icons or directly copying the look and feel of a competitor's product; this is a very bad practice. For an example of a good look-and-feel environment, see the Microsoft Office Compatible program.

An application may be certified Office Compatible by meeting certain user-interface requirements specified by Microsoft. An Office-Compatible application uses the same menu structures as all the Office applications. In addition, ribbons are similar and, where applicable, have the same button image that Microsoft uses. Making an application look like an Office application saves the developer time by giving clear and concise guidelines for interface features, and it helps end users by reducing the learning curve of the application.

Although you may not want to have your application independently tested and certified Office Compatible, you may want to check out the specifications and use some of the ideas presented to help you get started designing your own consistent application interfaces.

Adding common professional components

Most commercial/professional applications have some similar components. The most common components are the splash screen, About box, and switchboard. Be aware that the splash screen (see Figure 35-6 for a good example) not only aids in increasing perceived speed of an application but also gives the application a polished, professional appearance from the moment a user runs the program. Figure 35-7 shows a skeleton splash screen that can be used with any system. You simply change the content to what you want.

FIGURE 35-6

A splash screen not only increases perceived speed of your application, but it also gives your application a professional appearance.

NOTE Figure 35-7 shows the design window for a splash screen template that you can use when building your own applications. This form is included in the `Chapter35.accdb` database. It is named `SplashScreenTemplateSimple`. Import this form into your application and use it as a template for creating your own splash screen.

FIGURE 35-7

Use this form as a template to create your own splash screens for your applications.

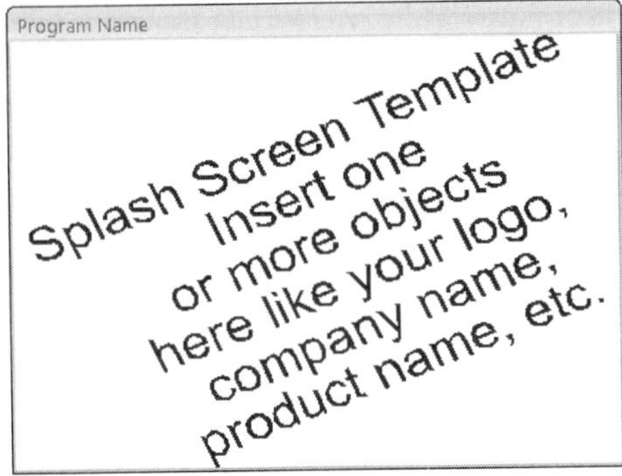

Your splash screen should contain the following items:

- The application's title
- The application's version number
- Your company information
- A copyright notice (© Copyright)

In addition, you may want to include the licensee information and/or a picture on the splash screen. If you use a picture on your splash screen, make it relevant to your application's function. For example, some coins and an image of a check could be used for a check-writing application. If you want, you can also use clipart for your splash screen — just be sure that the picture is clear and concise and doesn't interfere with the text information presented on your splash screen.

To implement the splash screen, have your application load the splash form before it does anything else (consider making your splash screen the Display Form in the Application Options, described earlier in this chapter). When your application finishes all of its initialization procedures, close the form. Make the splash form a light form and be sure to convert any bitmaps that you place on your splash screen to pictures in order to decrease the splash form's load time.

The second component that you should implement is an application switchboard. The switchboard is essentially a steering wheel for users to find their way through the functions and forms that are available in the application. Use the switchboard itself as a navigation form, using buttons to display other forms, as shown in the switchboard example in Figure 35-8. This is the switchboard named `frmSwitchboard` created for the Access Auto Auctions systems in this book.

FIGURE 35-8

The switchboard provides a handy way to navigate throughout the application.

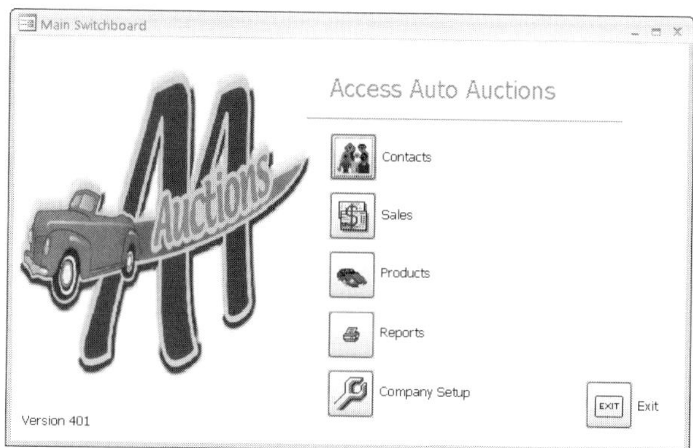

Make sure that the switchboard redisplays whenever the user closes a form. The switchboard provides a familiar place where users can be assured that they won't get lost in the application.

The third component that you should implement is an About box (see Figure 35-9). The About box contains your company and copyright information, as well as the application name and current version. Including your application's licensee information (if you keep such information) in the About box is also a good idea. The About box serves as legal notice of ownership and makes your application easier to support by giving your users easy access to the version information. Some advanced About boxes call other forms that display system information (Figure 35-9 has an additional button — System Info). You can make the About box as fancy as you want, but usually a simple one works just fine.

FIGURE 35-9

The implementation of an About box is a polishing technique that also provides useful information to the user and protects your legal interests.

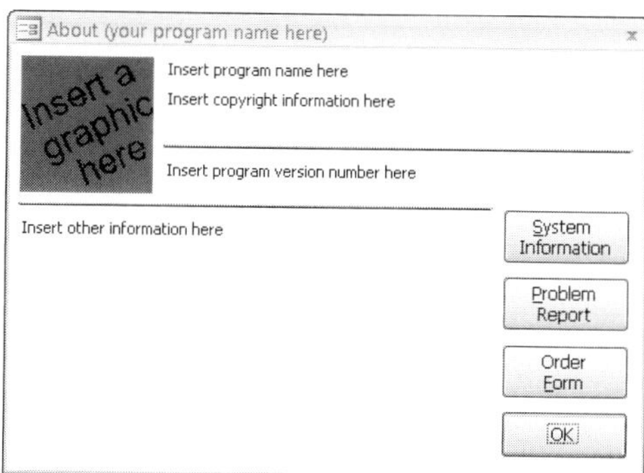

NOTE Figure 35-9 shows an About box template form that you can use when building your own applications. This form is included in the `Chapter35.accdb` database. It is named `AboutTemplateA`. Import this form into your application and use it as a template for creating your own About box.

TIP Most users love pictures, and most developers love to use pictures on buttons. Studies have shown that clear and concise pictures are more intuitive and are more easily recognized than textual captions. Most developers, however, are not graphic artists and usually slap together buttons made from any clipart images that are handy. These ugly buttons make an application look clumsy and unprofessional. In addition, pictures that don't clearly show the function of the button make the application harder to use.

Select or create pictures that end users will easily recognize. Avoid abstract pictures or pictures that require specific knowledge to understand them. If your budget permits, consider hiring a professional design firm to create your button pictures. A number of professional image galleries and tools to create and edit buttons are available.

Picture buttons that are well thought out can really make your application look outstanding, as well as make it easier to use.

The About box should be accessible from a Help menu or from a button on your switchboard form. The submenu title should be About My Application. Of course, substitute *Your program name here* with your application's actual name.

The splash screen, About box, and switchboard may seem like trivial features, but they can greatly enhance your application's appeal. They take little time to implement and should be included in all of your distributed applications.

Bulletproofing an Application

Bulletproofing an application is the process of making the application idiot-proof. It involves trapping errors that can be caused by users, such as invalid data entry, attempting to run a function when the application is not ready to run the function, and allowing users to click a Calculate button before all necessary data has been entered. Bulletproofing your application is an additional stage that should be completed in parallel with debugging, and should be performed again after the application is working and debugged.

CROSS-REF Chapter 28 discusses many bulletproofing techniques in addition to those discussed here.

Using error trapping on all Visual Basic procedures

An error-handling routine gives you a chance to display a friendly message to the user, rather than some unintuitive default message box; Figure 35-10 shows a message box with a runtime error "2102," which is unintuitive; however, it also shows a more-detailed message of a form missing or misspelled. The user will not know the name of the form or if it's misspelled or missing. An error-handling routine is needed to provide the user with a more informative and meaningful error message than what is shown in Figure 35-10.

FIGURE 35-10

An error message resulting from a procedure with no error-handling routine

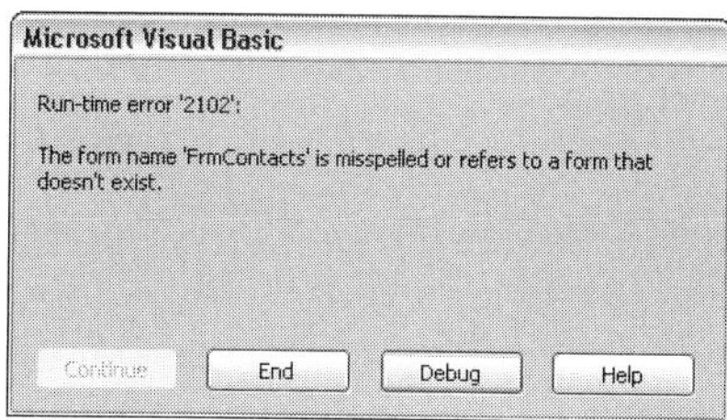

One of the most important elements of bulletproofing an application is making sure that the application never *crashes* — that is, never ceases operation completely and unexpectedly. Although Access provides built-in error processing for most data-entry errors (for example, characters entered into a currency field), automatic processing doesn't exist for VBA code errors. You should include error-handling routines in every VBA procedure, even if you use just the following error line in your code:

```
On Error Resume Next
```

When running an application at runtime, any untrapped error encountered in your code causes the program to terminate completely. Your users can't recover from such a crash, and serious data loss may occur. Your users have to restart the application after such an application error.

CROSS-REF **For more information on error handling and bulletproofing an application, see Chapter 25 and Chapter 28.**

Separating the tables from the rest of the application

You should separate your code objects (forms, reports, queries, modules, and macros) from your table objects. Many benefits are gained from distributing these objects in separate `.accdb` files:

- Network users benefit from speed increases by running the code `.accdb` (the database containing the queries, forms, macros, reports, and modules) locally and accessing only the shared data on the network.
- Updates can easily be distributed to users.
- Data can be backed up more efficiently because only one file is needed, and disk space and time aren't used to continuously back up the code objects.

All professionally distributed applications — especially those intended for network use — should have separate code and data database (`.accdb`) files.

Documenting the application

Most developers don't like to write documentation; it's simply no fun and can be quite frustrating and time-consuming. Also, every time a change is made to the application, the application's documentation needs updating. Taking the time and effort now to prepare thorough documentation, however, can save hours of technical support time down the road. Even if you don't plan to distribute a full user's manual, take time to document how to perform the most common functions in your application. If you've created shortcuts, make sure to share them with the users.

Creating a Help system

Although documentation is extremely important for getting users started on your application, a Help system that is well-written, thorough, and context-sensitive is just as important. A Help system puts pertinent information at users' disposal with just a click of the mouse or a push of a button.

Implementing a security structure

The final item that you need to consider before distributing your application is the level at which you want to secure your application. You can secure specific individual objects, or you can secure your entire application. If it's important to you to secure design permissions for all of your objects in order to protect your source code, you need to be aware that you can't rely solely on Microsoft's word that the security in Access works. For example, Microsoft touted the security model of Access 2.0 as being the most secure available. It was discovered, however, that an average Access developer can unsecure an Access 2.0 database in about five minutes, with only minimum coding! Although no method for unsecuring a secured Access 2007 application has yet been discovered, a method may be uncovered in the future. You must understand and accept this risk when you distribute a secured Access application.

CROSS-REF **For more information on securing Access applications, see Chapter 29.**

Summary

In this chapter, you learned how to set up the Current Database options, which make your application professional looking and more difficult for the nosey user to poke around in. You learned how to restrict components users can interact with as well as how to simulate the runtime environment with the `/runtime` switch or the `.accdr` extension.

You also reviewed testing and polishing procedures that make your application less likely to break after you distribute it. You revisited error handling and bulletproofing as additional methods to make a solid application. Preparing your database for distribution may take a bit more time, but you'll be thankful after the deployment goes smoothly.

Chapter 36

Using Access Macros

Macros have been a part of Access since the beginning. As Access became more of a development tool, the Visual Basic for Applications (VBA) programming language became the standard in automating database applications. Macros in previous versions of Access lacked variables and error handling, which caused many developers to abandon macros altogether. Access 2007 adds these capabilities, as well and a few others, which makes macros a better alternative to VBA than in previous versions. If it's a slow day and you don't feel like writing VBA code, or if you aren't a VBA guru but still want to customize the actions that your application executes, then building structured macros is the answer.

ON the CD-ROM This chapter uses a database named `Chapter36.accdb`. If you have not already copied them onto your machine from the CD, you'll need to do so now. This database contains the tables, forms, reports, and macros used in this chapter.

IN THIS CHAPTER

- Understanding macros
- Looking at the Hello World macro
- Working with multiaction macros
- Using macro names
- Making decisions with conditions
- Using temporary Variables
- Handling errors
- Debugging macros
- Understanding Embedded macros
- Comparing Macros to VBA
- Converting macros to modules

Understanding Macros

A *macro* is a tool that allows you to automate tasks in Access. It's different from Word's Macro Recorder (described in Chapter 22), which lets you record a series of actions and play them back later. Access macros let you perform defined actions and add functionality to your forms and reports. Think of macros as a simplified programming language; you build a list of actions to perform and decide when you want those actions to occur.

CROSS-REF For more information on the Access event model, see Chapter 12.

Building macros consists of selecting actions from a drop-down list, and then filling in the action's *arguments* (values that provide information to the action). Macros let you choose actions without writing a single line of VBA code. These actions are a subset of commands VBA provides, and most people find it easier to build a macro than writing VBA code. If you're not familiar with VBA, building macros is a great stepping-stone to learning some of the commands available to you.

Suppose you want to build a main screen with buttons that open the other screens in your application. You can add a button to the form, build a macro that opens another form in your application, and then assign this macro to the button's `OnClick` event. The macro can be a standalone object — which appears in the Navigation Pane — or an embedded object that is part of the event itself.

The Hello World macro

A simple way to demonstrate how to create macros is to build one that displays a message box that says `Hello World!` To create a new standalone macro, click the Macro command on the far right of the Create ribbon's Other group (shown in Figure 36-1).

FIGURE 36-1

Use the Create ribbon to build a new standalone macro.

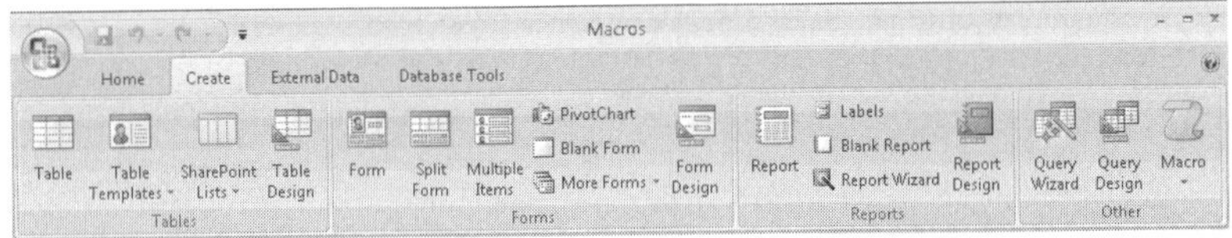

The Macro command opens the macro design window and displays the Macro Tools Design ribbon (shown in Figure 36-2). By default, the macro design window displays the Action, Arguments, and Comments columns. The Action column contains a list of actions from which you select. The Arguments column is read-only and displays the arguments for the selected action. The Comments column lets you give the action a description telling you what that action does. The lower section of the window is where you enter each action's arguments.

NEW FEATURE **The Arguments column in Access 2007 lets you see each action's arguments without clicking on each row and looking at the Action Arguments section in the lower section of the window. To hide this column, click the Arguments command in the Design ribbon's Show/Hide group.**

FIGURE 36-2

The macro design window displaying the Action, Arguments, and Comments columns

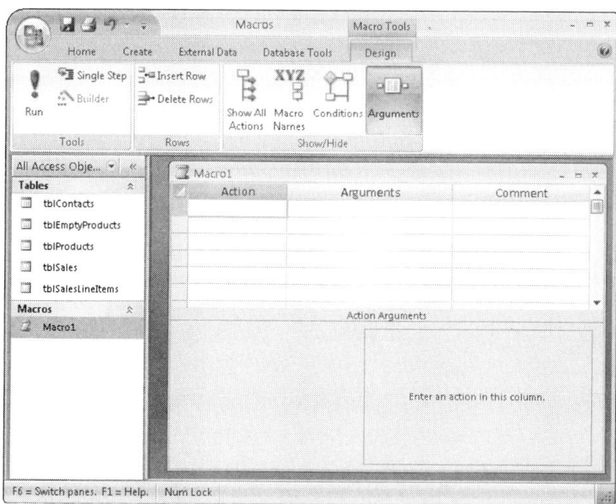

Select the `MsgBox` action from the drop-down list in the Action column; the `MsgBox` action displays a message box. In the lower section of the window, the Action Arguments appear for the `MsgBox` action. They also appear in the Arguments column in the top section of the screen. Set the arguments in the lower section as follows:

- **Message:** Hello World!
- **Beep:** No
- **Type:** Information
- **Title:** My First Macro

Your screen should look similar to the one shown in Figure 36-3. The `Message` argument defines the text that appears in the message box. The `Beep` argument determines whether a beep is heard when the message box appears. The `Type` argument sets which icon appears in the message box: None, Critical, Warning?, Warning!, or Information. The `Title` argument defines the text that appears in the message box's title bar.

FIGURE 36-3

The Hello World macro uses the `MsgBox` action to display a message.

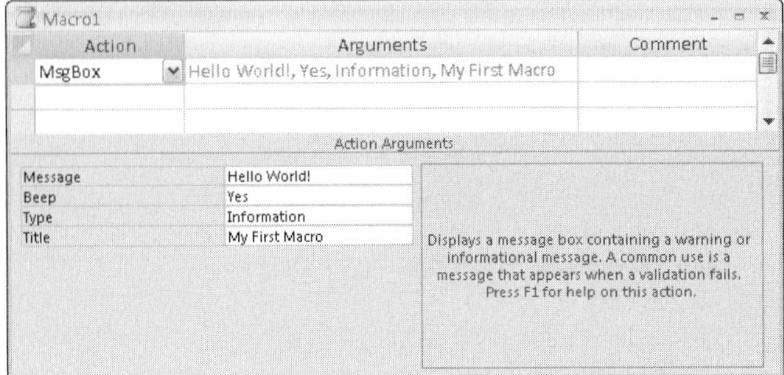

To run the macro, click the Run command in the Design ribbon's Tools group. When you create a new macro, or change an existing macro, you'll be prompted to save the macro. When prompted, click yes to save it, change the name to `mcrHelloWorld`, and click OK. The macro runs and displays a message box with the arguments you specified (shown in Figure 36-4).

FIGURE 36-4

Running the Hello World macro displays a message box with the arguments you specify.

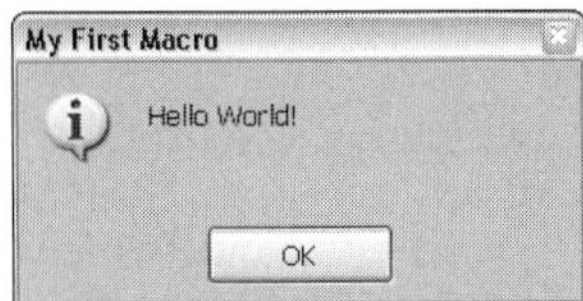

You can also run the macro from the Navigation Pane. Close the macro design window and display the Macros group in the Navigation Pane. Double-click on the `mcrHelloWorld` macro to run it. You'll see the same message box that displayed when you ran the macro from the design window.

Assign a macro to an event

When creating macros, you probably don't want end users using the Navigation Pane to run them — or worse, running them from the macro design window. Macros are intended for you to automate your application without writing VBA code. In order to make an application easy to use, assign your macros to an object's event. The most common event to assign a macro is a button's `OnClick` event. Follow these steps to create a form with a button that runs `mcrHelloWorld`:

1. **Click the Create tab on the ribbon, and click on the Form Design command in the Forms group.**
2. **In the form's Design ribbon, unselect the Use Control Wizards option in the Controls group.**

   For this example, you don't want to use a wizard to decide what this button does.
3. **Click the Button control and draw a button on the form.**
4. **Set the button's `Name` property to `cmdHelloWorld`.**
5. **Set the button's `Caption` property to `Hello World`.**
6. **Click the drop-down list in the button's `On Click` event property, and select `mcrHelloWorld` from the list (shown in Figure 36-5).**

FIGURE 36-5

Set any object's event property to the macro to trigger that macro when that event occurs.

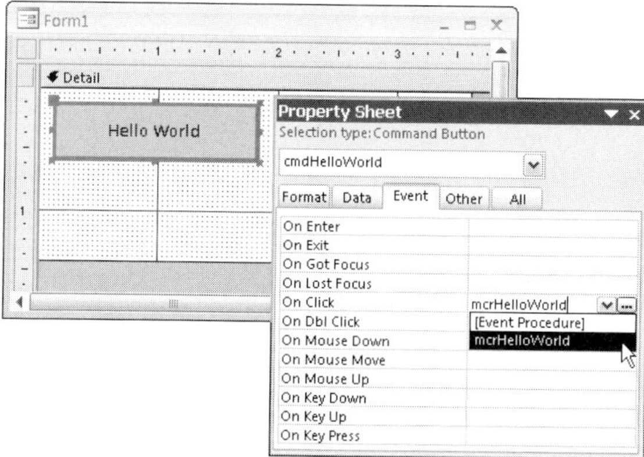

That's all there is to creating and running a macro. Just select the action, set the action arguments, and assign the macro to an event property. ***Remember:*** You aren't limited to the button's `OnClick` event. If you want a macro to run when a form loads, set the `On Load` event property of the form to the macro's name. Use the Event tab on any object's property sheet to see the available events.

Multiaction Macros

The true power of macros comes from performing multiple actions at the click of a button. Creating a macro that runs a series of action queries is better than double-clicking each action query in the Navigation Pane. You might forget to run one or you may run them out of sequence.

Running multiple action queries

For this next example, the Chapter36.accdb contains two delete queries that delete data from two tables — tblContacts_Backup and tblProducts_Backup — and two append queries that copy records from tblContacts and tblProducts to the backup tables. Table 36-1 shows the macro actions and action arguments for mcrBackupContactsAndProducts (shown in Figure 36-6).

NOTE **If all the actions don't appear in the Action drop-down list, click on the Show All Actions command in the Show/Hide group of the macro's Design ribbon. By default, Access only displays trusted macro actions that run regardless of the security settings. Some macro actions require a trusted database or enabling macros through your security settings.**

TABLE 36-1

mcrBackupContactsAndProducts

Action	Action Argument	Action Argument Setting
Hourglass	Hourglass On	Yes
SetWarnings	Warnings On	No
Echo	Echo On	No
	Status Bar Text	Step 1: Deleting Data
OpenQuery	Query Name	qryDeleteContactsBackup
	View	Datasheet
	Data Mode	Edit
OpenQuery	Query Name	qryDeleteProductsBackup
	View	Datasheet
	Data Mode	Edit
Echo	Echo On	No
	Status Bar Text	Step 2: Appending Data
OpenQuery	Query Name	qryAppendContactsBackup
	View	Datasheet
	Data Mode	Edit
OpenQuery	Query Name	qryAppendProductsBackup
	View	Datasheet
	Data Mode	Edit
Echo	Echo On	Yes
	Status Bar Text	<Leave Blank>

Action	Action Argument	Action Argument Setting
SetWarnings	Warnings On	Yes
Hourglass	Hourglass On	No
MsgBox	Message	Contacts and Products have been archived.
	Beep	Yes
	Type	Information
	Title	Finished Archiving

FIGURE 36-6

`mcrBackupContactsAndProducts` archives data from the live tables into the backup tables.

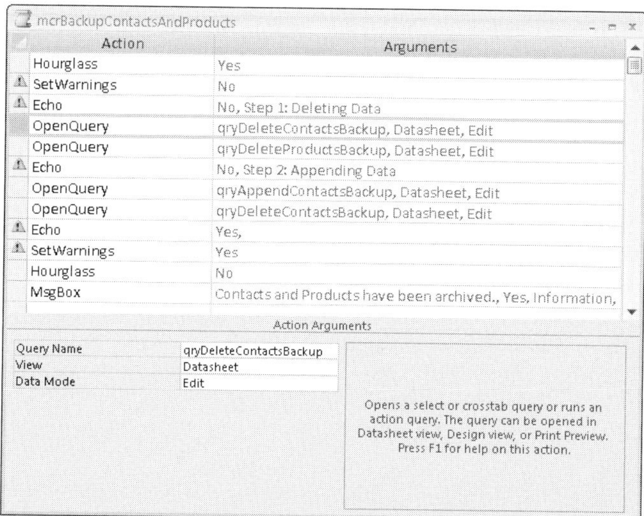

Let's take a look at the actions this macro performs:

- **Hourglass:** This action changes the cursor to an hourglass or a pointer using the `Hourglass On` argument. For macros that may take a while to run, set this argument to `Yes` at the beginning of the macro and to `No` at the end of the macro.
- **SetWarnings:** This action turns the system messages on or off using the `Warnings On` argument. When running action queries, you'll be prompted to make sure you want to run the action query, asked if it's okay to delete these 58 records, and then asked again for the next action query. Set `Warnings On` to `No` at the beginning of the macro to turn these messages off — assuming you'll click OK or Yes in each message box. Set it back to `Yes` at the end of the macro.

- **Echo:** This action shows or hides the results of a macro while it runs using the `Echo On` argument. Set it to `No` to hide the results of the macro or `Yes` to show the results. Set the `Status Bar Text` argument to give the user an indication of what's happening. This is useful in longer-running macros to know where in the process the macro is.
- **OpenQuery:** This action opens a select or crosstab query or runs an action query. The `Query Name` argument contains the name of the query to open or run. The `View` argument lets you pick the view — Datasheet, Design, Print Preview, PivotTable, or PivotChart — that a select or crosstab query opens in. The `Data Mode` argument lets you choose from Add, Edit, or Read Only to limit what users can do in a select query. The `View` and `Data Mode` arguments are ignored for action queries.

The heart of the macro is the four `OpenQuery` actions that run the four action queries. `qryDeleteContactsBackup` and `qryDeleteProductsBackup` clear the contents of `tblContacts_Backup` and `tblProducts_Backup`, so the current data can be copied into them. `qryAppendContactsBackup` and `qryAppendProductsBackup` append data from `tblContacts` and `tblProducts` into the backup tables.

You could easily build this macro just using the four `OpenQuery` actions, but running it would be cumbersome, especially if one of the queries took a few minutes — or hours — to run. Use the `Hourglass`, `SetWarnings`, `Echo`, and `MsgBox` actions to eliminate the need for user interaction and to let the user know what's happening and when it's done happening.

Macro Names

When automating your application with macros, you might easily get carried away filling the Navigation Pane for opening every form and every report. *Macro names* let you create one macro object that contains more than one macro. Click the Macro Names command in the Show/Hide group on the macro's Design ribbon to display the Macro Names column in the macro window.

Opening forms

Without using macro names, you'd have to create three separate macros to automate a main menu form with three buttons that open `frmContacts`, `frmProducts`, and `frmSales`. Using macro names, just create one macro that opens each form individually. Table 36-2 shows the macro names, actions, and action arguments for `mcrMainMenu` (shown in Figure 36-7), which opens one of three forms.

TABLE 36-2

mcrMainMenu

Macro Name	Action	Action Argument	Action Argument Setting
OpenContacts	OpenForm	Form Name	frmContacts
		View	Form
		Filter Name	<Leave Blank>
		Where Condition	<Leave Blank>
		Data Mode	<Leave Blank>
		Window Mode	Normal
OpenProducts	OpenForm	Form Name	frmProducts
		View	Form
		Filter Name	<Leave Blank>
		Where Condition	[ProductID]=3
		Data Mode	Read Only
		Window Mode	Dialog
OpenSales	OpenForm	Form Name	frmSales
		View	Layout
		Filter Name	qrySales2008
		Where Condition	<Leave Blank>
		Data Mode	Edit
		Window Mode	Icon

FIGURE 36-7

`mcrMainMenu` uses macro names to open three forms individually.

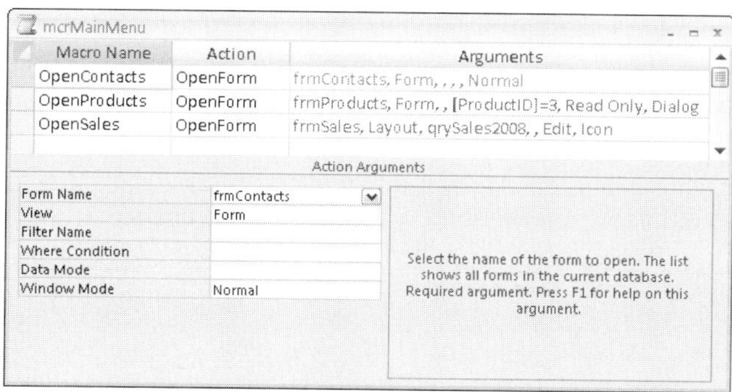

To implement a macro using macro names, create a form (`frmMainMenu`) with three buttons — in this case, `cmdContacts`, `cmdProducts`, and `cmdSales`. Then set the `On Click` event properties of these buttons as follows (see Figure 36-8):

Button name	On Click event property
cmdContacts	mcrMainMenu.OpenContacts
cmdProducts	mcrMainMenu.OpenProducts
cmdSales	mcrMainMenu.OpenSales

FIGURE 36-8

The macro names appear after the macro object in the event property drop-down list.

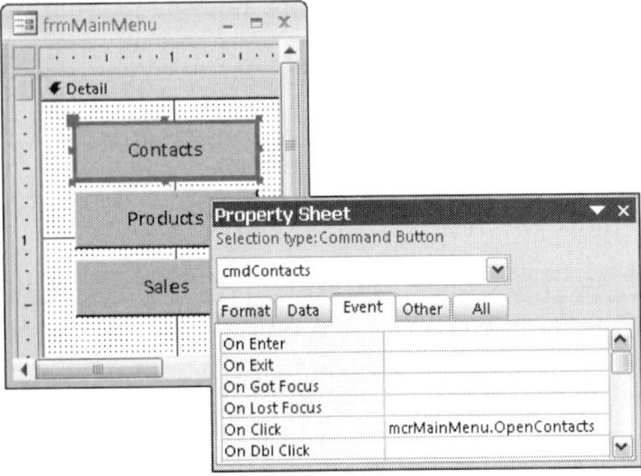

Open `frmMainMenu` in Form View and click on the Contacts button; `frmContacts` opens and displays all the records. Click the Products button to display `frmProducts`, which only displays one record. Click the Sales button to display `frmSales` in a minimized state, which displays the sales made in 2008. To see why these forms open differently, let's take a look at the action arguments for the `OpenForm` action:

- **Form Name:** This argument is the name of the form you want the macro to open.
- **View:** This argument lets you select which view to open the form: Form View, Design View, Print Preview, Datasheet View, PivotTable View, PivotChart View, or Layout View. For this example, `frmContacts` and `frmProducts` open in Form View, while `frmSales` opens in Layout View.
- **Filter Name:** This argument lets you select a query or a filter saved as a query to restrict and/or sort the records for the form. For this example, this argument is set to `qrySales2008` for the `OpenSales` macro name. `qrySales2008` is a query that outputs all the fields in the table and only displays sales between 1/1/2008 and 12/31/2008. This query also sorts the records by `SaleDate`.

- **Where Condition:** This argument lets you enter a SQL Where clause or expression that selects records for the form from its underlying table or query. For this example, this argument is set to `[ProductID]=3` for the `OpenProducts` macro name, which only shows one record when you open `frmProducts`.
- **Data Mode:** This argument lets you choose the data-entry mode for the form. Select Add to only allow users to add new records, Edit to allow adding and editing of records, or Read Only to only allow viewing of records. This setting only applies to forms opened in Form View or Datasheet View, and overrides settings of the form's `AllowEdits`, `AllowDeletions`, `AllowAdditions`, and `DataEntry` properties. To use the form's setting for these properties, leave this argument blank. For this example, `frmProducts` opens in read-only mode while `frmContacts` and `frmSales` allow editing.
- **Window Mode:** This argument lets you choose the window mode for the form. Select Normal to use the form's properties. Select Hidden to open the form with its `Visible` property set to No. Select Icon to open the form minimized. Select Dialog to open the form with its `Modal` and `PopUp` properties set to Yes and `Border Style` property set to Dialog. For this example, `frmContacts` opens normally, `frmProducts` opens as a dialog box, and `frmSales` opens minimized.

CROSS-REF **For more information on form properties, see Chapter 8.**

NOTE **When you run a macro with macro names from the Navigation Pane, only the first macro name executes.**

If you're careful in planning your macros, you can create one macro object for each form or report, and use macro names for each action in the form or report you want to perform. Macro names let you limit the number of macros that appear in the Navigation Pane and make managing a lot of macros much easier.

Using Conditions

While macro names let you put multiple groups of actions in a single macro object, a *condition* specifies certain criteria that must be met before the macro performs the action. You can enter any expression in the macro's condition column that evaluates to True/False or Yes/No. If the expression evaluates to False, No, or 0 (zero), the action will not execute. If the expression evaluates to any other value, the action is performed. Click the Conditions command in the Show/Hide group on the macro's Design ribbon to display the Condition column in the macro window.

Opening reports using conditions

To demonstrate conditions, use `frmReportMenu` (shown in Figure 36-9), which contains three buttons and a frame (`fraView`) with two option buttons: Print and Print Preview. Clicking Print sets the frame's value to 1; clicking Print Preview sets the frame's value to 2.

FIGURE 36-9

`frmReportMenu` uses a frame to select the view in which to open the Contacts, Products, and Sales reports.

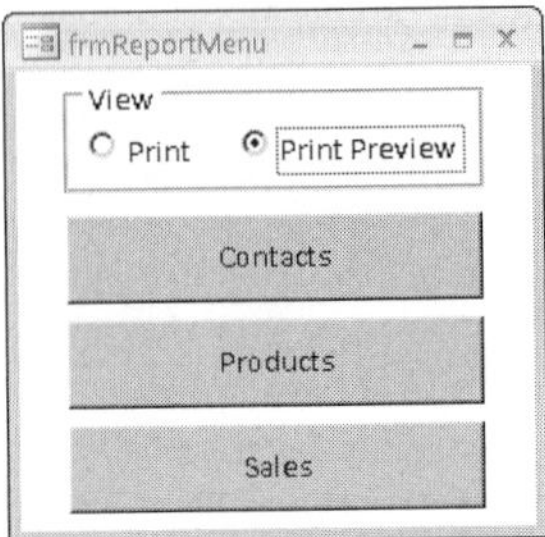

The macro that opens the reports uses the Macro Names column, as well as the Condition column. Table 36-3 shows the macro names, conditions, actions, and action arguments for `mcrReportMenu` (shown in Figure 36-10), which opens one of three reports. The `Filter Name` and `Where Condition` arguments are blank for each `OpenReport` action.

TABLE 36-3

mcrReportMenu

Macro Name	Condition	Action	Action Argument	Action Argument Setting
OpenContacts	[Forms]![frmReportMenu]![fraView]=1	OpenReport	Report Name	rptContacts
			View	Print
			Window Mode	Normal
	[Forms]![frmReportMenu]![fraView]=2	OpenReport	Report Name	rptContacts
			View	Print
Preview				
			Window Mode	Normal
OpenProducts	[Forms]![frmReportMenu]![fraView]=1	OpenReport	Report Name	rptProducts
			View	Print
			Window Mode	Normal
	[Forms]![frmReportMenu]![fraView]=2	OpenReport	Report Name	rptProducts
			View	Print Preview
			Window Mode	Normal

Macro Name	Condition	Action	Action Argument	Action Argument Setting
OpenSales	[Forms]![frmReportMenu]![fraView]=1	OpenReport	Report Name	rptSales
			View	Print
			Window Mode	Normal
	[Forms]![frmReportMenu]![fraView]=2	OpenReport	Report Name	rptSales
			View	Print Preview
			Window Mode	Normal

FIGURE 36-10

`mcrReportMenu` uses the Condition column to open the reports in Print or Print Preview view.

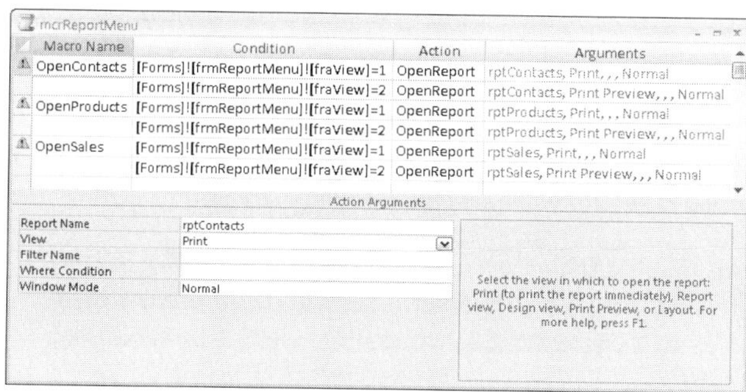

To implement this macro, set the `On Click` event properties of the buttons (`cmdContacts`, `cmdProducts`, and `cmdSales`) on `frmReportMenu` as follows:

Button name	On Click event property
cmdContacts	mcrReportMenu.OpenContacts
cmdProducts	mcrReportMenu.OpenProducts
cmdSales	mcrReportMenu.OpenSales

The Condition column of `mcrReportMenu` has two expressions that look at `fraView` on `frmReportMenu` to determine if Print or Print Preview is selected:

- `[Forms]![frmReportMenu]![fraView]=1`: Print view selected
- `[Forms]![frmReportMenu]![fraView]=2`: Print Preview view selected

If Print is selected on `frmReportMenu`, the `OpenReport` action with the `View` arguments set to Print executes; if Print Preview is selected on `frmReportMenu`, the `OpenReport` action with the `View` arguments set to Print Preview executes. This structure is set up for each macro name.

CROSS-REF **For more information referring to a control on a form using `Forms!expression`, see Chapter 13.**

Multiple actions in conditions

If you want to run multiple actions for a condition, enter ellipses (`...`) in the Condition column directly under the expression being tested. If the expression evaluates to a nonzero value (True, Yes, and so on), the expressions containing the ellipses execute. Set up the macro as follows:

Condition	Action
[Expression 1]	[Action 1a]
... [Action 1b]	
... [Action 1c]	
[Expression 2]	[Action 2a]
... [Action 2b]	
... [Action 2c]	

To temporarily skip an action in a macro, enter False in the Condition column. Temporarily skipping an action is helpful when troubleshooting macros.

Conditions let you selectively run actions based on other values in your application. Use the Condition column to reference forms, reports, controls, and other objects and determine which actions to execute. Think of a condition as an `If` statement — without the word `If` — and the actions as the `Then` portion.

Using Temporary Variables

Before Access 2007, you could only use variables in VBA code; macros were limited to performing a series of actions without remembering anything from a previous action. Three new macro actions — `SetTempVar`, `RemoveTempVar`, and `RemoveAllTempVars` — let you create and use temporary variables in your macros. You can use these variables in conditional expressions to control which actions execute, or to pass data to and from forms or reports. You can even access these variables in VBA to communicate data to and from modules.

Enhanced Hello World macro

A simple way to demonstrate how to use variables in macros is to enhance the Hello World example created earlier in this chapter. Table 36-4 shows the macro actions and action arguments for `mcrHelloWorldEnhanced` (shown in Figure 36-11).

TABLE 36-4

mcrHelloWorldEnhanced

Action	Action Argument	Action Argument Setting
SetTempVar	Name	MyName
	Expression	InputBox("Enter your name.")
MsgBox	Message	="Hello " & [TempVars]![MyName] & "."
	Beep	Yes
	Type	Information
	Title	Using Variables
RemoveTempVar	Name	MyName

FIGURE 36-11

`mcrHelloWorldEnhanced` uses the `SetTempVar` action to get a value from the user and display it in a message box.

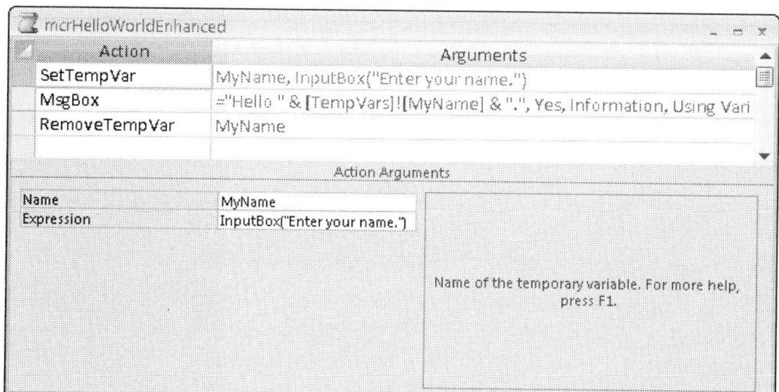

The `SetTempVar` action has two arguments: `Name` and `Expression`. The `Name` argument is simply the name of the temporary variable. The `Expression` argument is what you want the value of the variable to be. In this example, the `InputBox()` function prompts the user for his name.

The MsgBox action's Message argument contains the following expression:

```
="Hello " & [TempVars]![MyName] & "."
```

This expression concatenates the word Hello with the temporary variable MyName, created in the SetTempVar action of the macro. When referring to a temporary variable created with the SetTempVar action, use the following syntax:

```
[TempVars]![VariableName]
```

CROSS-REF **For more information on string concatenation using the ampersand (&), see Chapter 5.**

The RemoveTempVar action removes a single temporary variable from memory — in this example, MyName. You can only have 255 temporary variables defined at one time. These variables stay in memory until you close the database, unless you remove them with RemoveTempVar or RemoveAllTempVars. It's a good practice to remove temporary variables when you're finished using them.

CAUTION **Using the RemoveAllTempVars action removes all temporary variables created with the SetTempVar action. Unless you're sure you want to do this, use the RemoveTempVar action instead.**

Temporary variables are global. Once you create a temporary variable, you can use it in VBA procedures, queries, macros, or object properties. For example, if you remove the RemoveTempVar action from mcrHelloWorldEnhanced, you can create a text box on a form and set its Control Source property as follows to display the name the user entered:

```
=[TempVars]![MyName]
```

Enhanced reporting macro

Using temporary variables, you can eliminate steps from the macro. You can get the form or report name from another control on a form. With a temporary variable, you eliminate the need for creating a structure of many OpenForm or OpenReport actions. You can also use more than one variable in a macro.

For this example, use frmReportMenuEnhanced (shown in Figure 36-12), which contains the same fraView shown in Figure 36-9, but adds a combo box (cboReport), which contains a list of reports to run. The Run Command button executes mcrReportMenuEnhanced, which doesn't use macro names to decide which report to open.

FIGURE 36-12

`frmReportMenuEnhanced` uses a combo box to select which report to open.

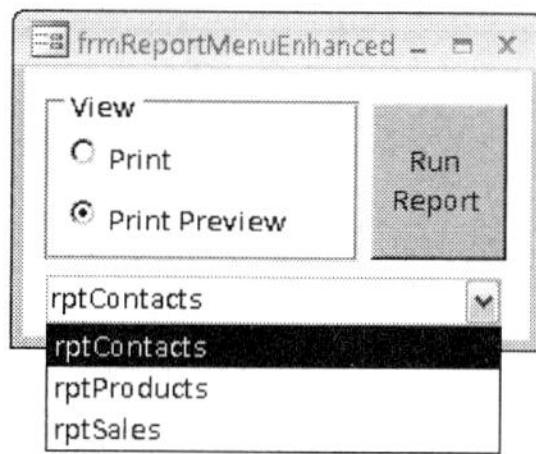

Table 36-5 shows the conditions, actions, and action arguments for `mcrReportMenuEnhanced` (shown in Figure 36-13), which opens one of three reports.

TABLE 36-5

mcrReportMenuEnhanced

Condition	Action	Action Argument	Action Argument Setting
	SetTempVar	Name	ReportName
		Expression	[Forms]![frmReportMenuEnhanced]![cboReport]
	SetTempVar	Name	ReportView
		Expression	[Forms]![frmReportMenuEnhanced]![fraView]
[TempVars]![ReportView]=1	OpenReport	Report Name	=[TempVars]![ReportName]
		View	Print
		Window Mode	Normal
[TempVars]![ReportView]=2	OpenReport	Report Name	=[TempVars]![ReportName]
		View	Print Preview
		Window Mode	Normal
	RemoveTempVar	Name	ReportName
	RemoveTempVar	Name	ReportView

FIGURE 36-13

mcrReportMenuEnhanced uses temporary variables to open the desired report in Print or Print Preview view.

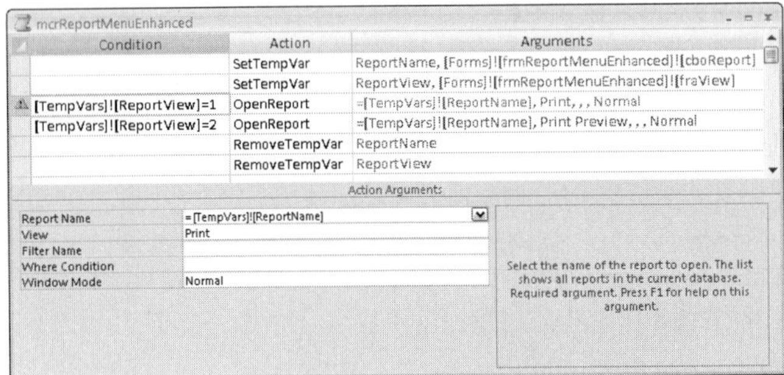

The first two SetTempVar actions in mcrReportMenuEnhanced set the values of the temporary variables — ReportName and ReportView — from cboReport and fraView on frmReportMenuEnhanced. The OpenReport actions use the temporary variables in the Condition column and for the Report Name argument. When using temporary variables as a setting for an argument, you must use an equal (=) sign in front of the expression:

```
=[TempVars]![ReportName]
```

There are still two OpenReport actions in this macro. Certain arguments — such as View — don't allow the use of temporary variables in expressions. Because one of your variables is a setting for the report's view, you still have to use the Condition column to decide which view to open the report.

The last two RemoveTempVar lines remove the temporary variables — ReportName and ReportView — from memory. Because these variables probably won't be used later on in the application, it's important to remove them.

Using temporary variables in macros gives you far more flexibility in Access 2007 than in previous versions of Access. You can use these variables to store values to use later on in the macro, or anywhere in the application. Just remember, you only have 255 of them, so don't forget to clean up after yourself by removing temporary variables from memory once you're finished using them.

Using temporary variables in VBA

You may start out using macros to automate your application, but over time, you'll begin using VBA code to automate and add functionality to other areas. What do you do with the temporary variables you've already implemented with macros? Well, you don't have to abandon them; instead, you can use them directly in your VBA code.

To access a temporary variable in VBA, use the same syntax used in macros:

```
X = [TempVars]![VariableName]
```

If you don't use spaces in your variable names, you can omit the brackets:

```
X = TempVars!VariableName
```

Use the same syntax as above to assign a new value to an existing temporary variable. The only difference is to put the temporary variable on the left side of the equation:

```
TempVars!VariableName = NewValue
```

Use the `TempVars` object to create and remove temporary variables in VBA. The `TempVars` object — new to Access 2007 — contains three methods: `Add`, `Remove`, and `RemoveAll`. To create a new temporary variable and set it's value, use the `Add` method of the `TempVars` object as follows:

```
TempVars.Add "VariableName", Value
```

Use the `Remove` method of the `TempVars` object to remove a single temporary variable from memory:

```
TempVars.Remove "VariableName"
```

When adding or removing temporary variables in VBA, remember to put the variable name in quotation marks.

To remove all the temporary variables from memory, use the `RemoveAll` method of the `TempVars` object as follows:

```
TempVars.RemoveAll
```

Any VBA variables you create are available to use in your macros, and vice versa. Any variables you remove in VBA are no longer available to use in your macros, and vice versa. Using temporary variables, your macros and VBA code no longer have to be independent from each other.

Handling Errors and Debugging Macros

In previous versions of Access, if an error occurred in a macro, the macro stopped execution, and your users saw an ugly dialog box (shown in Figure 36-14) that didn't really explain what was going on. If they were unfamiliar with Access, they quickly became disgruntled using the application. The lack of error handing in macros is one main reason many developers use VBA instead of macros to automate their application.

FIGURE 36-14

Errors in macros cause the macro to cease operation, without running further actions.

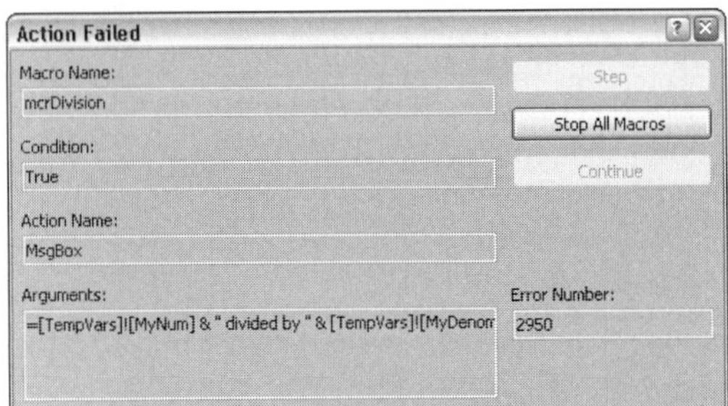

A common error that's easy to demonstrate is the divide-by-zero error. For the next example, `mcrDivision` (shown in Figure 36-15) contains two temporary variables — `MyNum` and `MyDenom` — set with the `InputBox()` function asking for a numerator and denominator. The `MsgBox` action shows the result (`[TempVars]![MyNum]/[TempVars]![MyDenom]`)in a message box and the `RemoveTempVar` actions remove the variables from memory.

FIGURE 36-15

`mcrDivision` divides the numerator by the denominator and generates an error when the denominator is zero.

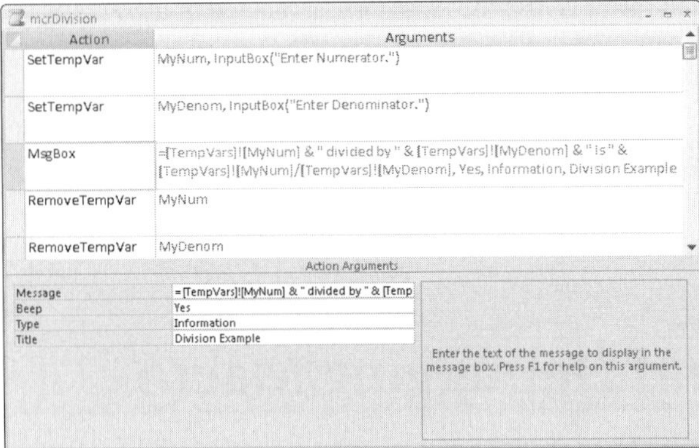

Run the macro and enter **1** for the numerator and **2** for the denominator; the macro runs and displays a message box saying `1 divided by 2 is 0.5`. Run the macro again and enter **0** in the denominator; a divide-by-zero error occurs and the macro stops running. Without error handling, the two `RemoveTempVar` actions won't run and won't remove the temporary variables from memory.

If an error occurs in another macro — such as a string of action queries — any queries after an error occurs won't run. Adding error handling to your macros allows you to choose what to do when an error occurs while a macro's running.

The OnError action

The `OnError` action lets you decide what happens when an error occurs in your macro. This action has two arguments: `Go to` and `Macro Name`. The `Go to` argument has three settings and the `Macro Name` argument is only used with one of these settings, described as follows:

- **Next:** This setting records the details of the error in the `MacroError` object but does not stop the macro. The macro continues with the next action.
- **Macro Name:** This setting stops the current macro and runs the macro in the `Macro Name` argument of the `OnError` action.
- **Fail:** This setting stops the current macro and displays an error message. This is the same as not having error handling in the macro.

The VBA equivalents of these settings are as follows:

```
On Error Resume Next         'Next
On Error Goto LABELNAME      'Macro Name
On Error Resume 0            'Fail
```

The simplest way to add error handling to a macro is to make `OnError` the first action and set the `Go to` argument to `Next`. This will cause your macro to run without stopping, but you won't have any clue which actions ran and which ones didn't.

Instead, create an error-handling structure. Table 36-6 shows the macro names, actions, and action arguments for `mcrDivisionErrorHandling` (shown in Figure 36-16).

TABLE 36-6

mcrDivisionErrorHandling

Macro Name	Action	Action Argument	Action Argument Setting
	OnError	Go to	Macro Name
		Macro Name	ErrorHandler
	SetTempVar	Name	MyNum
		Expression	InputBox("Enter Numerator.")
	SetTempVar	Name	MyDenom
		Expression	InputBox("Enter Denominator.")

continued

TABLE 36-6 *(continued)*

Macro Name	Action	Action Argument	Action Argument Setting
	MsgBox	Message	=[TempVars]![MyNum] & " divided by " & [TempVars]![MyDenom] & " is " & [TempVars]![MyNum]/[TempVars]![MyDenom]
		Beep	Yes
		Type	Information
		Title	Division Example
	RunMacro	Macro Name	mcrDivisionErrorHandling.Cleanup
ErrorHandler	MsgBox	Message	="The following error occurred: " & [MacroError].[Description]
		Beep	Yes
		Type	Warning?
		Title	="Error Number: " & [MacroError].[Number]
	ClearMacroError		
	RunMacro	Macro Name	mcrDivisionErrorHandling.Cleanup
Cleanup	RemoveTempVar	Name	MyNum
	RemoveTempVar	Name	MyDenom

FIGURE 36-16

`mcrDivisionErrorHandling` uses the `OnError` action to display a user-friendly error message and remove the temporary variables.

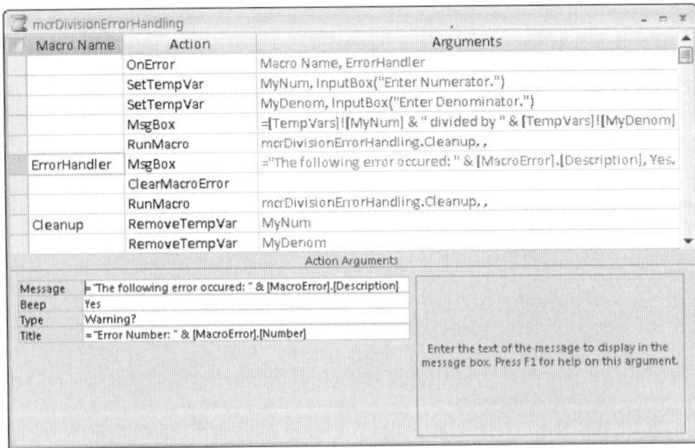

The first OnError action in the macro lets Access know to move to the macro name ErrorHandler when an error occurs. If an error occurs (by entering 0 as the denominator), the macro stops and moves to the ErrorHandler macro name. The ErrorHandler displays a message box — using the MacroError object (described in the next section) to display the error's description in the Message and the error's number in the Title, using the following expressions:

```
[MacroError].[Description]
[MacroError].[Number]
```

After the error handler's message box, the ClearMacroError action clears the MacroError object. The RunMacro action moves the execution to the macro's Cleanup macro name. The Cleanup section of the macro removes the temporary variables.

NOTE **There's no Resume functionality in macro error handling. If you want to run additional code after the error-handling actions, you must use the RunMacro action to run another macro or place the actions in the error-handling section of the macro.**

The RunMacro action also appears after the MsgBox action in the main section of the macro. Because you're using macro names, the macro stops after it reaches the ErrorHandler macro name. In order to force the cleanup of the temporary variables, use the RunMacro action to run the Cleanup macro name. Otherwise, you'd have to put the RemoveTempVar actions in the main section and in the ErrorHandler section of the macro.

The MacroError object

The MacroError object — new to Access 2007 — contains information about the last macro error that occurred. It retains this information until a new error occurs or you clear it with the ClearMacroError action. This object contains a number of read-only properties you can access from the macro itself or from VBA. These properties are as follows:

- **ActionName:** This property contains the name of the macro action that was running when the error occurred.
- **Arguments:** This property contains the arguments for the macro action that was running when the error occurred.
- **Condition:** This property contains the condition for the macro action that was running when the error occurred.
- **Description:** This property contains the text representing the current error message — for example, Divide by Zero or Type Mismatch.
- **MacroName:** This property contains the name of the macro that was running when the error occurred.
- **Number:** This property contains current error number — for example, 11 or 13.

Use the MacroError object as a debugging tool or to display messages to the user, who can then relay that information to you. You can even write these properties to a table to track the errors that occur in your macros. Use this object in the Condition column to customize what actions execute based on the error that occurs. When used in combination with the `OnError` action, it gives you additional functionality by handling errors, displaying useful messages, and providing information to you and the user.

Debugging macros

Trying to figure out what's going on in a macro can be difficult. The new `OnError` action and `MacroError` object make debugging in Access 2007 easier than previous versions. There are other tools and techniques that are useful when debugging macros. Use the following list as a guideline for troubleshooting macros.

- **Single Step:** Click the Single Step command in the macro design ribbon's Tools group to turn on Single Step mode. The Macro Single Step dialog box (shown in Figure 36-17) lets you see the macro name, condition, action name, arguments, and error number before the action executes. From this dialog box, click Step to execute the action, Stop All Macros to stop the macro from running, or Continue to finish the macro with Single Step mode turned off.

FIGURE 36-17

Use the Macro Single Step dialog box to step through a macro.

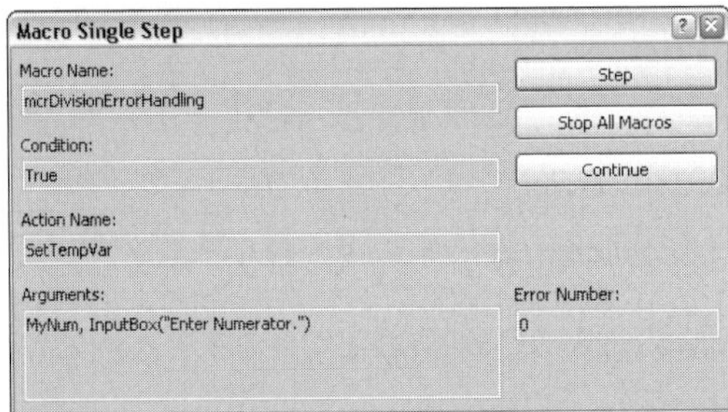

- **MsgBox:** Use the `MsgBox` action to display values of variables, error messages, control settings, or whatever else you want to see while the macro is running. To see the value of a combo box on a form, set the `Message` argument as follows:

  ```
  [Forms]![frmReportMenuEnhanced]![cboReport]
  ```

- **StopMacro:** Use the `StopMacro` action to stop the macro from executing. Insert this action at any point in the macro to stop it at that point. Use this in conjunction with the debug window to check values.
- **Debug window.** Use the Debug window to look at any values, temporary variables, or properties of the `MacroError` object after you stop the macro. Press Ctrl+G to display the code window after you stop the macro. Just type a question mark (?) and the variable

or expression you want to check the value of, and press Enter. Some examples of expressions to display in the Debug window are:

```
? TempVars!MyNum
? MacroError!Description
? [Forms]![frmReportMenuEnhanced]![cboReport]
```

These techniques are similar to ones you'd use when debugging VBA code. You can step through sections of code, pause the code and look at values in the debug window, and display message boxes to display variables or errors that occur. Granted, you don't have all the tools available — such as watching variables and `Debug.Print` — but at least you have the new `MacroError` object to provide the information you need to figure out what's going wrong.

For more information on error handling, see Chapter 25. Debugging VBA code is covered in Chapter 15.

Embedded Macros

An *embedded macro* is stored in an event property and is part of the object to which it belongs. When you modify an embedded macro, you don't have to worry about other controls that might use the macro; each embedded macro is independent. Embedded macros aren't visible in the Navigation Pane and are only accessible from the Property Sheet.

Embedded macros are trusted. They run even if your security settings prevent the running of code. Using embedded macros allows you to distribute your application as a trusted application because they are automatically prevented from performing unsafe operations.

One big change to Access 2007 is when you use a wizard to create a button, it no longer creates an event procedure — it creates an embedded macro. So if you're used to running a wizard and stealing the code, you'll have to abandon that technique. Using embedded macros instead of code accomplishes two things:

- It allows you to quickly create an application that's distributable.
- It allows users not familiar with VBA code to customize buttons created with wizards.

Follow these steps to create an embedded macro that opens `frmContacts`:

1. **Click the Create tab on the ribbon, and then click on the Form Design command in the Forms group.**
2. **In the form's Design ribbon, unselect the *Use Control Wizards* option in the Controls group.**

   For this example, you don't want to use a wizard to decide what this button does.
3. **Click the Button control and draw a button on the form.**
4. **Set the button's `Name` property to `cmdContacts` and the `Caption` property to `Contacts`.**

5. Display the Property Sheet for `cmdContacts`, click the Event tab, and then click on the `On Click` event property.
6. Click the builder button — the button with the ellipsis (...) — to display the Choose Builder dialog box (shown in Figure 36-18).

FIGURE 36-18

Use the builder button in the event property to display the Choose Builder dialog box to create an embedded macro.

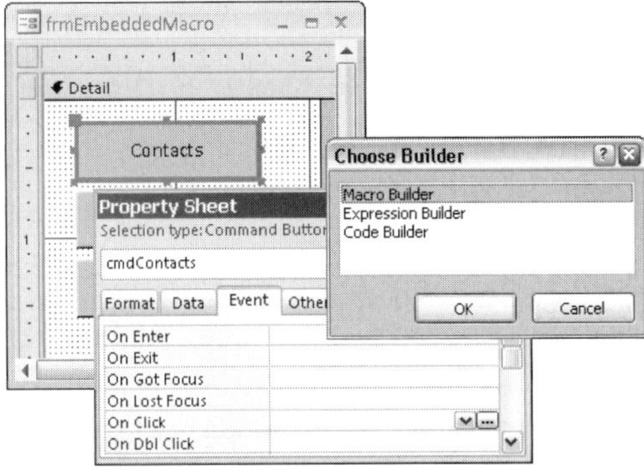

7. Choose Macro Builder and click OK to display the macro window (shown in Figure 36-19).

FIGURE 36-19

An embedded macro doesn't have a name. The title bar displays the control and the event which the macro is embedded.

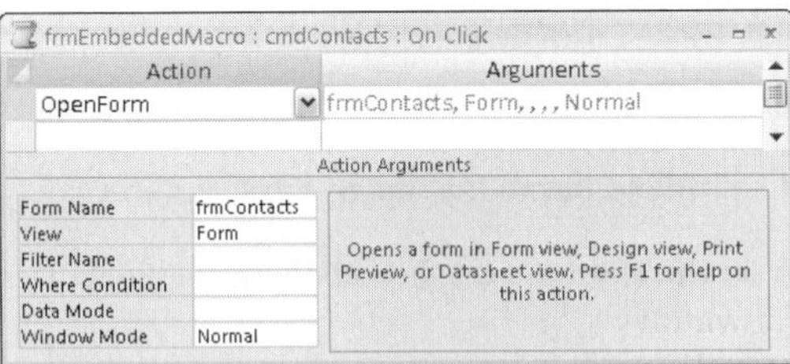

8. Add the `OpenForm` action to the macro, and then set the `Form Name` argument to `frmContacts`.
9. Close the embedded macro, and click OK when you're prompted to save the changes and update the property.

   The `On Click` event property of `cmdContacts` now displays `[Embedded Macro]`.

Using an embedded macro has some advantages over using an event procedure containing VBA code. If you copy the button and paste it on another form, the embedded macro goes with it. You don't have to copy the code and paste it as a separate operation. Similarly, if you cut and paste the button on the same form (for example, moving it onto a Tab control), you don't have to reattach the code to the button.

Embedded macros offer another improvement to macros in previous versions. If you automate your application with embedded macros, and import a form or report into another database, you don't have to worry about importing the associated macros into the database as well. By using embedded macros, all the automation moves with the form or report. This makes maintaining and building applications easier.

Macros versus VBA Statements

In Access, macros often offer an ideal way to take care of many details, such as running reports and forms. You can develop applications and assign actions faster using a macro because the arguments for the macro actions are displayed with the macro (in the bottom portion of the macro window). You don't have to remember complex or difficult syntax.

Several actions you can accomplish with VBA statements are better suited for macros. The following actions tend to be more efficient when they're run from macros:

- Using macros against an entire set of records with action queries — for example, to manipulate multiple records in a table or across tables (such as updating field values or deleting records)
- Opening and closing forms
- Running reports

NOTE **The VBA language supplies a `DoCmd` object that accomplishes many macro actions. Under the surface, `DoCmd` runs a macro task to accomplish the same result provided by a macro action. You could, for example, specify `DoCmd.Close` to run the `Close` macro action and close the currently active form.**

Although macros sometimes prove to be the solution of choice, VBA is the tool of choice at other times. You probably will want to use VBA rather than macros when you want to perform any of the following tasks:

- **Create and use your own functions.** In addition to using the built-in functions in Access, you can create and work with your own functions by using VBA code.
- **Use Automation to communicate with other Windows applications or to run system-level actions.** You can write code to see whether a file exists before you take some action, or you can communicate with another Windows application (such as a spreadsheet), passing data back and forth.

- **Use existing functions in external Windows DLLs.** Macros don't enable you to call functions in other Windows Dynamic Link Libraries.
- **Work with records one at a time.** If you need to step through records or move values from a record to variables for manipulation, code is the answer.
- **Create or manipulate objects.** In most cases, you'll find that it's easiest to create and modify an object in that object's Design View. In some situations, however, you may want to manipulate the definition of an object in code. With a few VBA statements, you can manipulate virtually any and all objects in a database, including the database itself.
- **Display a progress meter on the status bar.** If you need to display a progress meter to communicate progress to the user, VBA code is the answer.

Converting existing macros to VBA

After you become comfortable with writing VBA code, you may want to rewrite some of your application macros as VBA procedures. As you begin this process, you quickly realize how mentally challenging the effort can be as you review every macro in your various macro libraries. You cannot merely cut the macro from the macro window and paste it into a module window. For each condition, action, and action argument for a macro, you must analyze the task it accomplishes and then write the equivalent statements of VBA code in your procedure.

Fortunately, Access provides a feature that converts macros to VBA code automatically. One of the options in the Save As dialog box is Save As Module. You can use this option when a macro file is highlighted in the Macros object window of the Database window. This option enables you to convert an entire macro group to a module in seconds.

To try the conversion process, convert the `mcrHelloWorldEnhanced` macro used earlier in this chapter. Follow these steps to run the conversion process:

1. **Click the Macros group in the Navigation Pane.**
2. **Select** `mcrHelloWorldEnhanced`**.**
3. **Click the Microsoft Office button, and then click Save As to display the Save As dialog box (shown in Figure 36-20).**

FIGURE 36-20

Saving a macro as a module

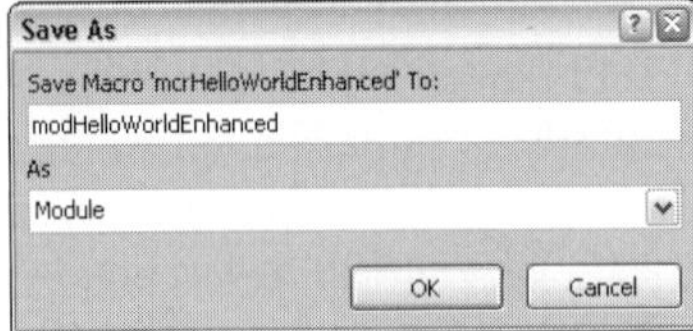

Access assigns a default name for the new module as "Copy of" followed by the macro name.

4. **Enter a name for the new module and select Module for the As option.**
5. **Click OK to display the Convert Macro dialog box (shown in Figure 36-21).**

FIGURE 36-21

The Convert Macro dialog box

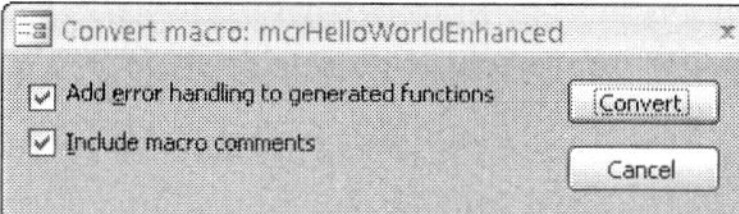

6. **Select the options that include error handling and macro comments, and click Convert.**

   Access briefly displays each new procedure as it is converted. When the conversion process completes, the `Conversion Finished!` message box appears.

7. **Click OK to display the new module in the VBA Editor (shown in Figure 36-22).**

   Access names the new module `Converted Macro- mcrHelloWorldEnhanced`.

FIGURE 36-22

The newly converted module

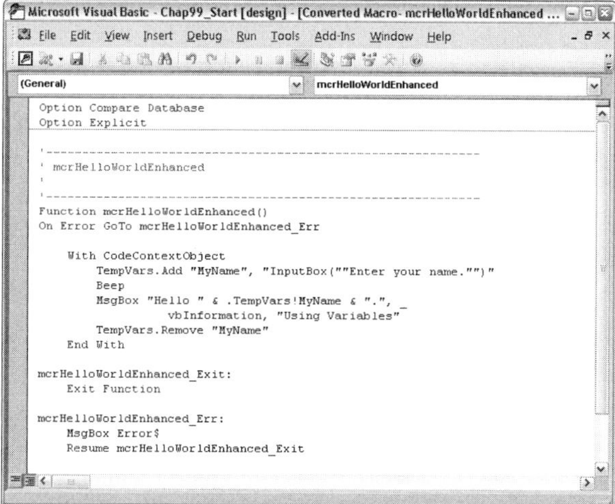

When you open the VBA Editor for the new module, you can view the procedure created from the macro. Figure 36-22 shows the `mcrHelloWorldEnhanced` function that Access created from the `mcrHelloWorldEnhanced` macro.

At the top of the function, Access inserts four comment lines for the name of the function. The `Function` statement follows the comment lines. Access names the function, using the macro library's name (`mcrHelloWorldEnhanced`).

When you specify that you want Access to include error processing for the conversion, Access automatically inserts the `On Error` statement as the first command in the procedure. The `On Error` statement tells Access to branch to other statements that display an appropriate message and then exit the function.

The statement beginning with `DoCmd` is the actual code that Access created from the macro. The `DoCmd` methods run Access actions from VBA. An action performs important tasks, such as closing windows, opening forms, and setting the value of controls.

If you're new to VBA and want to learn code, a good starting point is converting your macros to modules. Just save your macros and modules, and then look at the VBA code to become familiar with the syntax. With the new features available in Access 2007 macros, it becomes harder to decide whether to use macros or VBA.

Summary

In this chapter, you learned how to create a variety of different macros, from simple macros with one action to complex macros containing many different actions that only run under certain conditions. Using macro names, you saw how one macro object can hold many macros. You also compared macros to VBA and converted a macro to a VBA module.

You also learned the new macro features in Access 2007. The addition of temporary variables allows you to store values for use anywhere in your application, including VBA code. The new error-handling actions let you gracefully stop a macro when an error occurs. These new features also make troubleshooting macros easier. You also created a trusted embedded macro, which is stored in the control and moves around with the control.

Part V

Access as an Enterprise Platform

Access continues to grow as an integral part of enterprise data management. Important capabilities have been added with each new release of Microsoft Access. Even though Access is not a strong tool for creating or driving Web sites, Access 2007 includes outstanding capabilities for integrating with data sources located anywhere on the Internet.

This part begins by examining extensible markup language (XML), the lingua franca of Internet data sharing. XML is a native data format recognized and used by Access 2007, and all communication with SharePoint is through XML exchange.

The most significant of these new capabilities is integration with Microsoft SharePoint Services. Access 2007 seamlessly integrates with SharePoint, using SharePoint Lists as linked tables. This means that your Access 2007 applications can share data with SharePoint users anywhere in the world. SharePoint data linked to Access databases is completely updatable and can be displayed on Access forms and reports.

Access is able to share data with SQL Server, Oracle, and other enterprise database engines. For obvious reasons, Access works best with Microsoft SQL Server, and we cover this topic in the following chapters. You'll learn how to extract static data from a SQL Server database and use it in Access forms and reports. You'll also figure out how to connect to SQL Server and seamlessly share dynamic data with this powerful database engine.

IN THIS PART

You'll learn the basics of client-server computing and how to upsize your Access 2007 applications to SQL Server 2005. Server database engines such as SQL Server provide fast and virtually unlimited access to enormous amounts of data. Because of Access's superior user interface tools and strong reporting capabilities, your Access application is the ideal companion to data managed by SQL Server.

Chapter 37

Using XML in Access 2007

Over the past several years, XML has grown in importance as a data storage format, as well as a reliable technology for sharing data among multiple applications. XML is a native data format recognized by all of the Microsoft Office 2007 applications. XML is the technology wave of the future in the computer industry. Earlier in this book you saw how easy it is to link to XML files and how to seamlessly import XML data into an Access 2007 application.

This chapter continues the discussion on XML by explaining XML and using XML in some detail. Also, this chapter includes a significant amount of VBA code demonstrating how to automate XML data import into Access applications. Earlier chapters explained the manual, interactive processes of linking, importing, and exporting XML data, but this chapter shows you how to automate some of these operations with VBA code.

IN THIS CHAPTER

ON the CD-ROM This chapter uses the database named `Chapter37.accdb` on the book's CD. If you haven't already copied the file onto your machine from the CD, you'll need to do so now.

Introducing HTML and XML

Getting an introduction, however brief, to HTML, XML, and XSL is important. These terms are easily confused, and taking the time now to get acquainted with the terminology used when working with XML data sources is well spent. You'll encounter these terms over and over again as you begin working with XML, and a working knowledge of the technologies underlying XML is an important asset to your applications.

What is HTML?

HTML, short for Hypertext Markup Language, is the language commonly used to define Web pages. HTML is restricted to a specific number of tags. In fact, Web browsers such as Internet Explorer closely conform to well-recognized standards controlling HTML tags. A tag in HTML is a language element that defines the appearance of data on a Web page and is appropriately interpreted by a Web browser.

The left and right arrows (often called "pointy brackets") delimit HTML tags. Without these characters, a Web browser is unable to properly interpret HTML markup. For example, the text `<BR>` is recognized by a browser as an HTML tag indicating a line break, whereas the similar string `BR` is not interpreted at all, because it isn't enclosed within the < and > characters.

Here's the script for a very simple HTML page:

```
<HTML>
   <HEAD>
      <TITLE>Contact Details</TITLE>
   </HEAD>
   <BODY>
      <P>Name: Joe Soap</P>
      <P>Address: 1234 Something Way<BR>
         Some Place Somewhere<BR>
         A Country
      </P>
   </BODY>
</HTML>
```

The execution of this HTML script in a Web browser is shown in Figure 37-1.

FIGURE 37-1

A simple HTML script

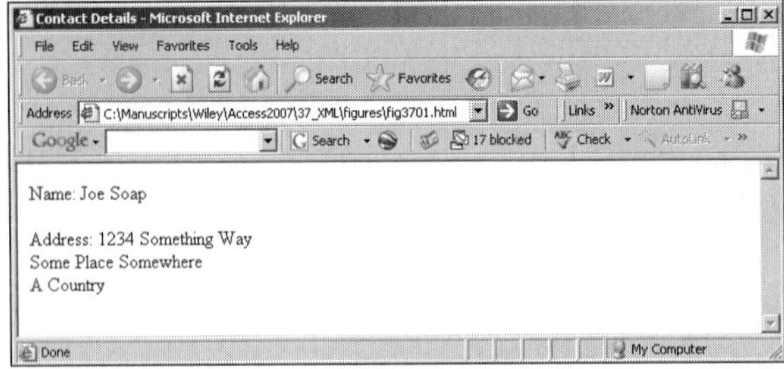

Figure 37-2 shows a somewhat more complex example, which happens to be an HTML export of a `Join` query executed from the Access 2007 database for this chapter (`Chapter37.accdb`).

FIGURE 37-2

A more complex HTML example

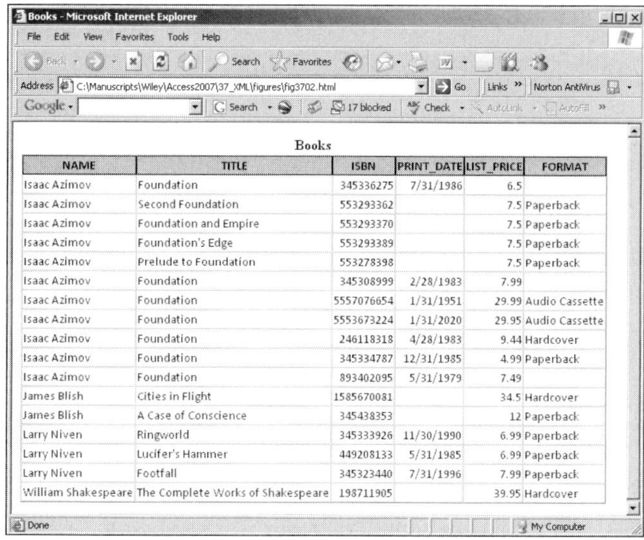

Books

NAME	TITLE	ISBN	PRINT_DATE	LIST_PRICE	FORMAT
Isaac Azimov	Foundation	345336275	7/31/1986	6.5	
Isaac Azimov	Second Foundation	553293362		7.5	Paperback
Isaac Azimov	Foundation and Empire	553293370		7.5	Paperback
Isaac Azimov	Foundation's Edge	553293389		7.5	Paperback
Isaac Azimov	Prelude to Foundation	553278398		7.5	Paperback
Isaac Azimov	Foundation	345308999	2/28/1983	7.99	
Isaac Azimov	Foundation	5557076654	1/31/1951	29.99	Audio Cassette
Isaac Azimov	Foundation	5553673224	1/31/2020	29.95	Audio Cassette
Isaac Azimov	Foundation	246118318	4/28/1983	9.44	Hardcover
Isaac Azimov	Foundation	345334787	12/31/1985	4.99	Paperback
Isaac Azimov	Foundation	893402095	5/31/1979	7.49	
James Blish	Cities in Flight	1585670081		34.5	Hardcover
James Blish	A Case of Conscience	345438353		12	Paperback
Larry Niven	Ringworld	345333926	11/30/1990	6.99	Paperback
Larry Niven	Lucifer's Hammer	449208133	5/31/1985	6.99	Paperback
Larry Niven	Footfall	345323440	7/31/1996	7.99	Paperback
William Shakespeare	The Complete Works of Shakespeare	198711905		39.95	Hardcover

HTML is not central to the subject matter of this book, but if you want more information on it, check out *HTML, XHTML, and CSS Bible*, 3rd Edition, by Bryan Pfaffenberger, Bill Karow, Chuck White, Steven M. Schafer (published by Wiley) or *HTML 4 For Dummies*, 5th Edition, by Ed Tittel and Mary Burmeister (published by Wiley).

What is XML?

HTML has a fixed set of predefined tags — there are many different tags but ultimately the number of variations is limited. XML, short for *eXtensible Markup Language*, can be extended by the addition of *new* tags whenever needed. Tags can be created at any time in XML. Essentially, XML is a scripting language that can have features changed and added to it by any developer for any purpose. XML can be customized such that every XML document can have its own unique tags. The result is a browser-based language, where both the data and the language (the tags) are variable. In other words, XML provides dynamism to both data and metadata.

NOTE **An XML tag is also known as an *element*.**

NOTE ***Data* are information describing something, such as a person's name. *Metadata* describes data, such as how long a person's name can be, and that it must be a string and not a numeric value. In an Access application, the metadata associated with a field in a table include the name applied to the field, its data type, and the maximum length applied to the field. Data, of course, are the values stored within the field.**

One thing that is relatively difficult for some people to understand is that an XML document includes very few predefined tags. Unlike HTML, where every tag is defined by a specification, XML tags are completely variable. There are one or two exceptions, such as the `<XML>` tag. Otherwise, almost anything goes, as long as the tags follow a few basic rules. The only restrictions applying to XML are as follows:

- Every opening tag must have a corresponding closing tag. Therefore, this XML statement works (notice that the data within the `<name>` and `</name>` tags are not enclosed in quotes):

  ```
  <root><name>Jack Jones</name></root>
  ```

  But, this statement causes an error because the closing `</name>` tag is missing:

  ```
  <root><name>Jack Jones</root>
  ```

  The combination of an opening and a closing tag is often referred to as a *node*. Nodes may contain data (`Jack Jones`) or other nodes.

NOTE **An opening tag in both HTML and XML is of the format `<tag>`. A closing tag is of the format `</tag>`. A combination open-closing tag is written as `<tag/>`, but this only applies when no data are contained with in the `<tag>` element.**

- Opening and closing tags must be properly sequenced and positioned in the hierarchy of an XML document. This statement causes an error because the `</name>` tag appears after the `</root>` closing tag:

  ```
  <root><name>Jack Jones</root></name>
  ```

NOTE **HTML doesn't care about the sequence of opening and closing tags. HTML allows `<P><PRE>My name is Jack Jones</P></PRE>`.**

- An XML document must have a single root node, and every other node in the XML document must be a descendant of the root node. In other words, XML nodes must be properly nested within the root node that begins the document.
- XML is case sensitive. So, this will work:

  ```
  <root><name>Jack Jones</name></root>
  ```

  This example returns an error because `<root>` and `</Root>` are different tags because of the case-sensitive nature of XML:

  ```
  <root><name>Jack Jones</name></Root>
  ```

NOTE **The preceding points are generally known as XML being "properly formed," except for processing instructions, such as `<XML . . . ?>`, which do not have the same restrictions. These rules apply in general to XML and not to HTML.**

XML can have its tags defined and is thus flexible depending on the content of its data. In fact, the content of an XML document can be represented by three things:

- **The data or textual values between the tags:** Textual values are strings, numbers, dates, and so on. In this example, Joe is the data:

  ```
  <name>Joe</name>
  ```

- **The tags representing the meaning or semantics of what's between the tags:** So, in the above example, `<name>` and `</name>` describes that Joe is actually somebody's name.

- **The tag hierarchy:** In the following example, the hierarchy describes that regions contain countries, countries contain cities, and some counties contain states that include cities. You can also tell that cities are a part of countries or states:

  ```
  <?xml version="1.0"?>
  <Locations>
     <northamerica>
        <california>
           <losangeles/>
           <sanfrancisco/>
        </california>
        <texas>
           <dallas/>
           <houston/>
        </texas>
     </northamerica>
     <southamerica>
        <peru>
           <lima/>
        </peru>
        <brazil>
           <riodejaneiro/>
           <brasilia/>
           <saopaulo/>
       </brazil>
     </southamerica>
  </Locations>
  ```

All of the countries in this XML script contain states. Sometimes they're called provinces, counties, regions, and so on. Just because they exist doesn't mean they have to be included in the XML document. The execution of the Locations XML document is shown in Figure 37-3.

FIGURE 37-3

A simple XML document

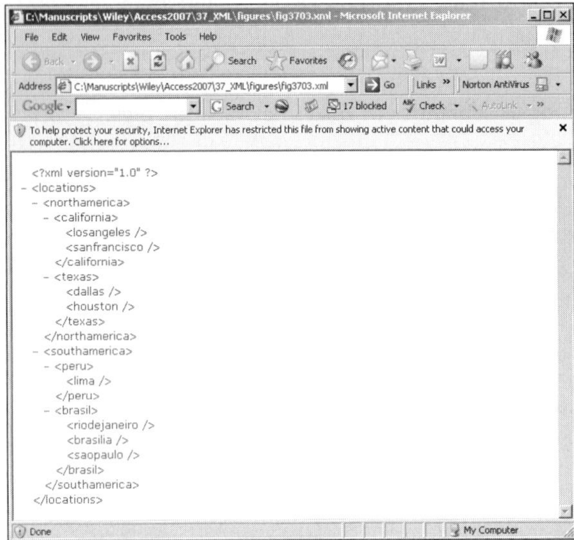

Figure 37-4 shows a more complex example, which is an XML export of a `Join` query executed from the Access 2007 database for this chapter (`Chapter37.accdb`).

FIGURE 37-4

A more complex XML example

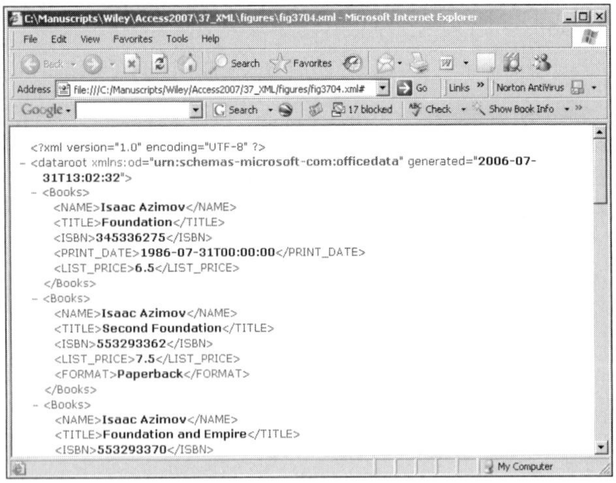

```
<?xml version="1.0" encoding="UTF-8" ?>
- <dataroot xmlns:od="urn:schemas-microsoft-com:officedata" generated="2006-07-
  31T13:02:32">
  - <Books>
      <NAME>Isaac Azimov</NAME>
      <TITLE>Foundation</TITLE>
      <ISBN>345336275</ISBN>
      <PRINT_DATE>1986-07-31T00:00:00</PRINT_DATE>
      <LIST_PRICE>6.5</LIST_PRICE>
    </Books>
  - <Books>
      <NAME>Isaac Azimov</NAME>
      <TITLE>Second Foundation</TITLE>
      <ISBN>553293362</ISBN>
      <LIST_PRICE>7.5</LIST_PRICE>
      <FORMAT>Paperback</FORMAT>
    </Books>
  - <Books>
      <NAME>Isaac Azimov</NAME>
      <TITLE>Foundation and Empire</TITLE>
      <ISBN>553293370</ISBN>
```

Again, as for HTML, XML is not central to the subject matter of this book. But you do need to have some idea of what XML actually is. You can find more information on XML in *Beginning XML,* 3rd Edition, by David Hunter, Andrew Watt, Jeff Rafter, Jon Duckett, Danny Ayers, Nicholas Chase, Joe Fawcett, Tom Gaven, and Bill Patterson; *Beginning XML Databases,* by Gavin Powell; and *XML For Dummies,* 4th Edition, by Lucinda Dykes and Ed Tittel (all three published by Wiley), among other books.

What is a DOM?

A DOM is an acronym for *Document Object Model.* A DOM, as applied to both HTML and XML, allows you to get at the contents of an HTML or XML document when it's running in a browser, using a scripting or programming language.

The DOM allows you to program changes into XML and HTML documents in real-time, while they're running in a browser. For example, you could write a JavaScript script to parse the internal structure behind an HTML document, and extract one or more tags, attributes, or values. Essentially, the HTML DOM and XML DOM, allow you to write programs that can enhance and change the behavior of Web pages during their execution within a browser.

A very general object structure of the HTML DOM is shown in Figure 37-5. A very general structure of the XML DOM is shown in Figure 37-6.

Formatting and transforming XSL(T)

XSL stands for eXtensible Style Sheet language. The HTML equivalent is called Cascading Style Sheets (CSS). A style-sheet language is generally used to apply consistency across the format display and manipulation of things like HTML and XML Web page content.

XSLT is the transformation aspect of XSL; XML-FO encompasses the formatting aspect of XSL.

In short, XSL formats XML documents by applying templates to repetitive sections of data in XML documents. For example, Figure 37-7 shows an example of XML data, displayed in an HTML document but formatted using XSL.

FIGURE 37-5

The HTML DOM hierarchical structure

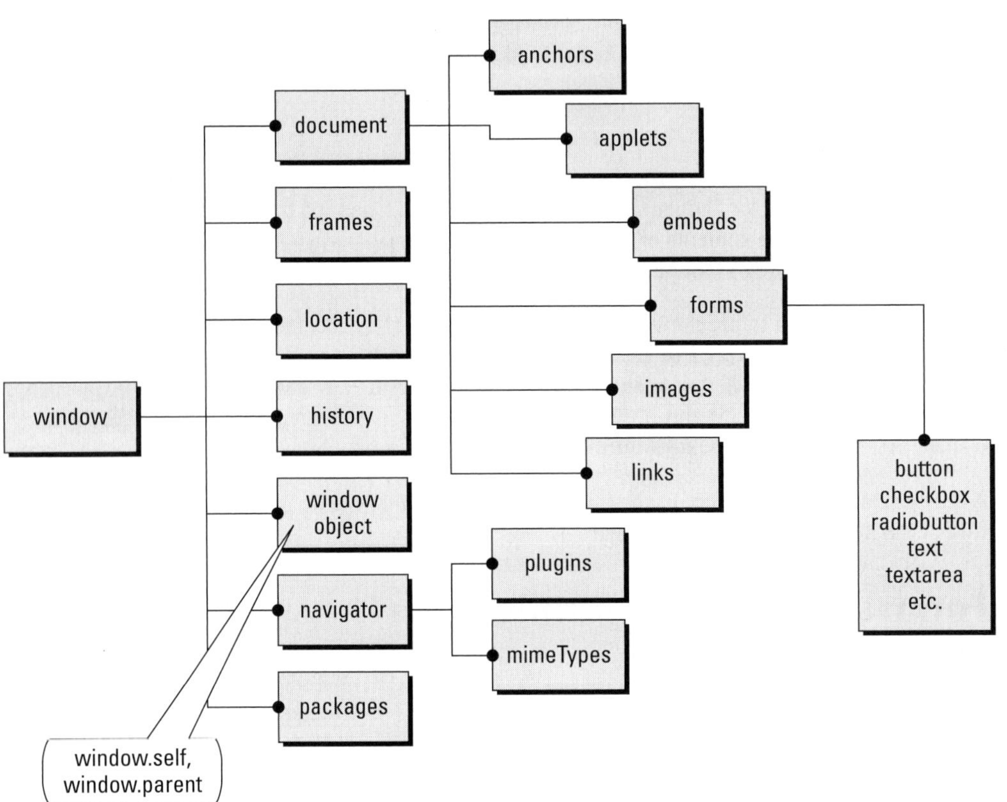

FIGURE 37-6

The XML DOM object hierarchical structure

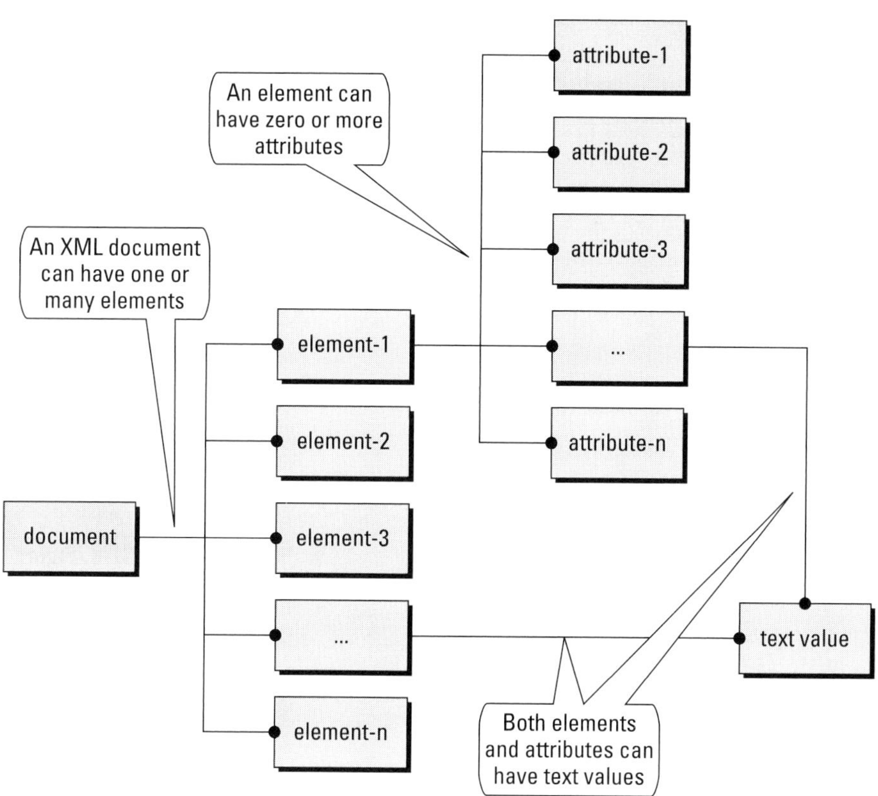

FIGURE 37-7

XSL applies beautification to XML data.

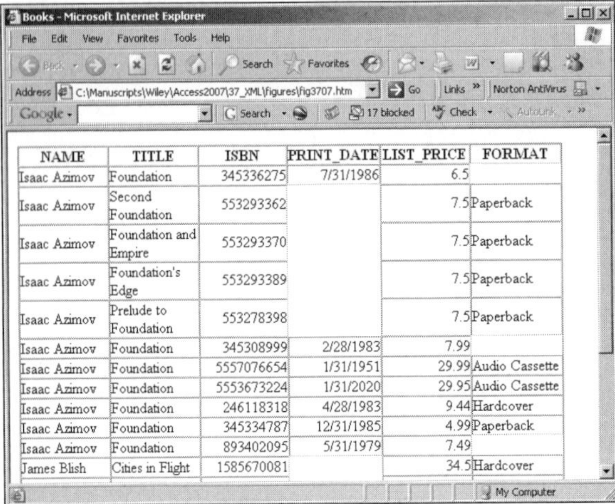

NAME	TITLE	ISBN	PRINT_DATE	LIST_PRICE	FORMAT
Isaac Azimov	Foundation	345336275	7/31/1986	6.5	
Isaac Azimov	Second Foundation	553293362		7.5	Paperback
Isaac Azimov	Foundation and Empire	553293370		7.5	Paperback
Isaac Azimov	Foundation's Edge	553293389		7.5	Paperback
Isaac Azimov	Prelude to Foundation	553278398		7.5	Paperback
Isaac Azimov	Foundation	345308999	2/28/1983	7.99	
Isaac Azimov	Foundation	5557076654	1/31/1951	29.99	Audio Cassette
Isaac Azimov	Foundation	5553673224	1/31/2020	29.95	Audio Cassette
Isaac Azimov	Foundation	246118318	4/28/1983	9.44	Hardcover
Isaac Azimov	Foundation	345334787	12/31/1985	4.99	Paperback
Isaac Azimov	Foundation	893402095	5/31/1979	7.49	
James Blish	Cities in Flight	1585670081		34.5	Hardcover

You've already seen the XML document equivalent of Figure 37-7, as shown in Figure 37-4. Figure 37-8 shows a picture of a small section of the XSL script coding applied in Figure 37-7.

FIGURE 37-8

The XSL formatting applied to the XML data in Figure 37-7

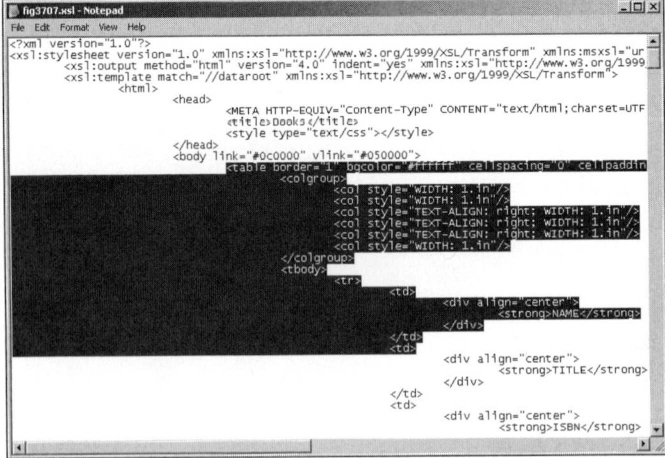

```
<?xml version="1.0"?>
<xsl:stylesheet version="1.0" xmlns:xsl="http://www.w3.org/1999/XSL/Transform" xmlns:msxsl="ur
        <xsl:output method="html" version="4.0" indent="yes" xmlns:xsl="http://www.w3.org/1999
        <xsl:template match="//dataroot" xmlns:xsl="http://www.w3.org/1999/XSL/Transform">
                <html>
                        <head>
                                <META HTTP-EQUIV="Content-Type" CONTENT="text/html;charset=UTF
                                <title>Books</title>
                                <style type="text/css"></style>
                        </head>
                        <body link="#0c0000" vlink="#050000">
                                <table border="1" bgcolor="#ffffff" cellspacing="0" cellpaddin
                                        <colgroup>
                                                <col style="WIDTH: 1.1in"/>
                                                <col style="WIDTH: 1.1in"/>
                                                <col style="TEXT-ALIGN: right; WIDTH: 1.1in"/>
                                                <col style="TEXT-ALIGN: right; WIDTH: 1.1in"/>
                                                <col style="TEXT-ALIGN: right; WIDTH: 1.1in"/>
                                                <col style="WIDTH: 1.1in"/>
                                        </colgroup>
                                        <tbody>
                                                <tr>
                                                        <td>
                                                                <div align="center">
                                                                        <strong>NAME</strong>
                                                                </div>
                                                        </td>
                                                        <td>
                                                                <div align="center">
                                                                        <strong>TITLE</strong>
                                                                </div>
                                                        </td>
                                                        <td>
                                                                <div align="center">
                                                                        <strong>ISBN</strong>
```

Some of the XSL tag elements for creating the table field, as shown in Figure 37-7, are highlighted in Figure 37-8. And of course, XSL is actually written in XML as well. XML is really flexible — it can be used to describe a different type of scripting language, in a file other than an XML document. And that XSL script can reformat the display of the XML data.

The XML, XSL, and HTM (HTML) files used for the example shown in Figure 37-7 and Figure 37-8 are direct exports of data from the `Chapter37.accdb` database. Normally, the XSL scripting commands apply formatting in the XML document itself. You execute the XML document in the browser to apply the XSL formatting.

The example in this section is a direct XML export from the Access database `Chapter37.accdb`. This particular export format applies the XSL scripting formatting in the XSL file, to the XML file, as a sequence of VBScript language commands.

VBScript is a Microsoft browser scripting language used to build both client-side scripts and server-side scripts.

The result is an HTML file (`.htm` extension), shown in Figure 37-7, generated from the combination of the XML and XSL files.

Sharing data using XML

Sharing of data is one of the common current commercial applications of XML. XML has standards established by the World Wide Web Consortium. The result is a highly standardized and consistent structure and syntax in XML documents. The real end result is that any person, computer, operating system, and programming or scripting language can understand XML documents. This is because XML documents all have the same standardized structure.

Therefore, it follows that a set of data from one company, transferred to another company as XML data, is easily understood by both organizations.

Transmitting data between businesses is called B2B or "Business-to-Business" data transfer.

The overall result is data connections established between both consistent and disparate environments, plus across both homogenous and heterogeneous environments and networks. And the more XML comes into general commercial use, the more software tools such as database engines and SDKs have value-added XML features included within them.

Access 2007 has some quite extensive XML capabilities, which you've seen in previous chapters (and this chapter as output XML examples), particularly in the realm of importing XML documents into Access and exporting Access data as XML documents.

Additionally, because XML standards are so open and flexible, software vendors can no longer continue capitalizing on markets by forcing customers to use specific software products for transferring data. As XML comes more and more into commercial use, software vendors have no choice but to adopt XML, without altering the internal structures and mechanism inherent within the universal standards encouraged by the use of XML.

RSS feeds are one of the really incredible spinoffs from sharing of XML data, and the increase in use of XML. Rich Site Summary, Really Simple Syndication, or just RSS, is a specialized formatting language written in XML, which is used to feed information over the Internet. Some RSS feeds are even free. Web sites such as Yahoo! and MSN.com are richly populated with lots and lots of free RSS feeds, including subject matter such as news, sports results, weather reports, daily comic strips, stock quotes — generally anything and everything fun and interesting you might be able to think of.

RSS feeds can be embedded into Web pages. Access can generate pages from ADO recordsets, as you will see later in this chapter. Thus, including RSS feeds into Access database automatically generated Web pages is not currently possible.

Some really advanced XML stuff

There are some advanced features of XML including XPath, XQuery, XLink, XPointer, XForms, XInclude, XML-FO. These features can be described briefly as follows:

- **XPath:** XPath is an expression language used to parse XML documents. XPath treats an XML document as a node hierarchy. XPath expressions return chunks of data from XML documents. XPath finds data by scanning an XML document for a pattern matching a specified XPath expression. An XPath expression can be absolute (searching from the root node) or relative (searching from a node somewhere within an XML document). An absolute XPath expression looks something like this: `/root/nodeX/nodeY`. A relative XPath expression looks something like this: `nodeX/nodeY`.
- **XQuery:** XQuery is used to execute queries against XML documents. XQuery is constructed largely with XPath expressions. Where Structured Query Language (SQL) reads information from relational databases, XQuery reads data from XML documents. XQuery uses specialized tools (such as Saxon) to execute XQuery queries against an XML document.

NOTE **XQuery can be used to query XML documents stored as XML native structure inside XML data types, in relational databases such as SQL Server, Oracle, and to a certain extent DB2 Database using the DB2 Extender.**

- **XLink and XPointer:** These standards are used to create hyperlinks in Web pages using XML. These links are similar to HTML `<A HREF>` tags. The difference is that XLink and XPointer hyperlinks are dynamic, in that they are generated at runtime, based solely on the content of an XML document. More specifically, the difference between XLink and XPointer is that XLink creates links pointing to a complete XML document, and thus the root of an XML document. XPointer, on the other hand, points to a specific fragment within an XML document.

NOTE **The term fragment is used to describe a subset node of an XML document, which includes all that node's descendant nodes. All descendant nodes are the child nodes, the children of the children, and so on. An XML fragment must be properly formed XML and must be a descendant node of the root node. Thus, a fragment cannot be an entire XML document (it cannot begin with the root node of an XML document).**

- **XForms:** XForms is a generic XML standard and is used to dynamically create Web-page entry forms, based on the dynamic content of an XML document.
- **XInclude:** This standard allows embedding or inclusion of one XML document within another, and executed as a single XML document at runtime.
- **XML-FO:** This standard is the display formatting part of XSL, as opposed to XSLT (XSL Transformations).

NOTE **With the exception of XQuery, all of the advanced XML features are consistent with XML standards by being written in XML. However, there is a new XML standard called XQueryX, under development, which is written in XML.**

XML as a database

A special type of a database is known as a Native XML database, of which there are many available and in existence, some in use, and some even freely available. However, as mentioned previously in this chapter: an XML document is made up of data, metadata, and intra-relationships inherent in its hierarchical structure. Based on these three facts, any XML document is, essentially, a self-contained database all by itself.

Various standards are used to help refine XML structure, and map structure between relational tables and XML document structure. This mapping is required because relational databases are relational structures, while XML documents are hierarchical. The differences between relational and object structures are considerable.

NOTE **Comparing relational and object structures has been described as trying to force square pegs into round holes, or visa versa. The effect is the same: difficult!**

There are three XML standards used to create directly programmable mappings between relational database tables and XML documents:

- **Document Type Definition (DTD):** Defines the building blocks of an XML document. A DTD is a separate document (also written in XML of course), containing the relationally understandable structural definition for the data in an XML document. The resulting DTD definition can be used as a mapping structure between metadata and relationships, across relational and XML objects. DTD is not written in XML.

  When generating an XML structure as an export from an Access 2007 database, you'll see an option to generate a DTD file structure as shown in Figure 37-9.

  Figure 39-10 shows a small snippet of the script generated by the export from Access 2007, as shown in Figure 37-9.

FIGURE 37-9

Generating DTDs with Access 2007 XML document exports

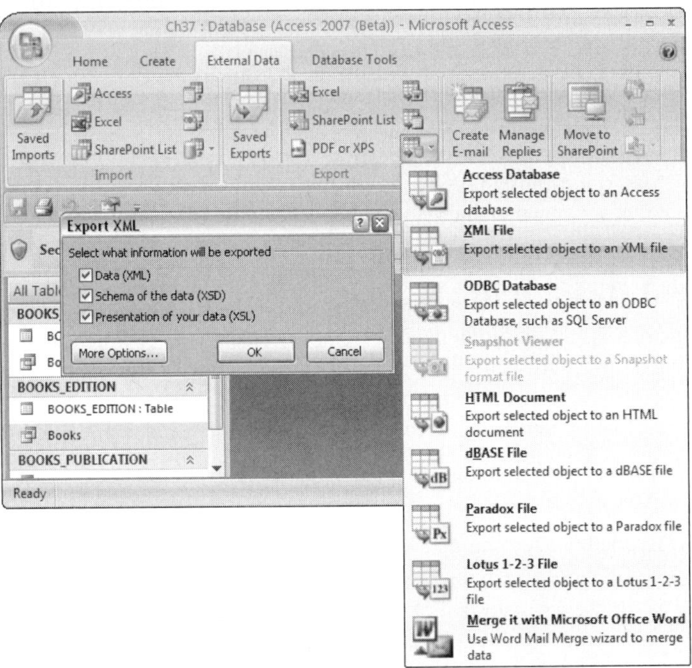

FIGURE 37-10

An Access 2007 generated XSD file

fig3709.xsd - Notepad

File Edit Format View Help


```
<?xml version="1.0" encoding="UTF-8"?>
<xsd:schema xmlns:xsd="http://www.w3.org/2001/XMLSchema" xmlns:od="urn:schemas-m
<xsd:element name="dataroot">
<xsd:complexType>
<xsd:sequence>
<xsd:element ref="Books" minOccurs="0" maxOccurs="unbounded"/>
</xsd:sequence>
<xsd:attribute name="generated" type="xsd:dateTime"/>
</xsd:complexType>
</xsd:element>
<xsd:element name="Books">
<xsd:annotation>
<xsd:appinfo>
<od:tableProperty name="RecordLocks" type="2" value="0"/>
<od:tableProperty name="ODBCTimeout" type="3" value="60"/>
<od:tableProperty name="RecordsetType" type="2" value="0"/>
<od:tableProperty name="OrderByOn" type="1" value="0"/>
<od:tableProperty name="Orientation" type="2" value="0"/>
<od:tableProperty name="DefaultView" type="2" value="2"/>
<od:tableProperty name="GUID" type="9" value="XREqsbttTOOeoVnX/5YRcg==
"/>
<od:tableProperty name="FilterOnLoad" type="1" value="0"/>
<od:tableProperty name="OrderByOnLoad" type="1" value="1"/>
<od:tableProperty name="TotalsRow" type="1" value="0"/>
<od:tableProperty name="DOL" type="11" value="CswOVQAAAACiw/FGdyOuQ7pbT5b/PGy5AA
TwBLAFMAXwBBAFUAVABIAE8AUgAAAAEAAAAYCNr74QDlSY72XB3WH85NAAAAANSq
JZIrAUNAAQAAAIF+IDRCAE8ATwBLAFMAXwBQAFUAQgBMAEkAQwBBAFQASQBPAE4A
AAABAAAAKZJhZdINC06nPshHGMNozgAAAADbKiWSKwLjQAEAAACBfiA0QgBPAE8A
SwBTAF8ARQBEAEkAVABJAE8ATgAAAAAAAABq8yvpn61CR6ds3t0ekUtwBwAAAKLD
8UZ3I65DultPlv88bLlOAEEATQBFAAAATbSACCvEIPHP4tJJuTzVkCJSD7AHAAAA
GHDa++EA5Um09lwd1h/OTVQASQBUAEwARQAAAE20gAhhnX0ld0FgRp2IxS11C8ur
BwAAACmSYWXSDQtOpz7IRxjDaM5JAFMAQgBOAAAATbSACHIwyWLxVyRDqRHZcdtM
```

- **XML Schema Definition (XSD):** This is a newer and more sophisticated form of DTD. XML Schemas apply logical structure to XML data, much like defining a mapping between XML data and relational table structures in a relational database. Unlike DTDs, XML Schemas can be used with other XML technologies, such as XPath and XQuery. The other important improvement of XSD over that of DTD is that XSD is written in XML.
- **XML data type:** One of the most significant XML features in modern relational databases is that of the XML data type. The objective of an XML data type is to store not only the actual text of an XML document into a relational database, but also the programmability of that XML data. The result is that other XML standards such as XPath and XQuery can be executed directly against XML data type XML documents, even when the XML is stored within a relational database.

NOTE **Unfortunately, Access 2007 does not include the capability of an XML data type. As already mentioned earlier in this chapter, XML documents can be stored as directly executable XML data types in high-end relational databases such as SQL Server, Oracle, and to a certain extent DB2 Database using the DB2 Extender.**

DAO, ADO, ADO.Net, Access 2007, and XML

Traditionally, in many Microsoft products, including Office and Visual Studio products, XML is generated using ActiveX Data Objects (ADO) and Recordsets. Essentially, ADO is simply a Data Definition Language (DLL) file containing a set of routines used for reading data sources, such as an Access database, and then creating arrays of records. A recordset is the result of a query against a database. ADO is an ActiveX object, and can, generally speaking, be embedded into any Microsoft-developed system, as an object with executable methods. ADO recordsets can be created in VBA programs, Web pages, and many other interfaces and executables.

And there are multiple versions of ADO. There is "traditional" ADO, found in Access. And there is, of course, ADO.NET, a more sophisticated version of ADO. Microsoft .NET products are technically black-boxable objects that can be consumed by a wide variety of application types. As a result, ADO.NET components can be plugged into anything and used somewhat more easily than ADO.

NOTE **MSXML is a Microsoft XML Parser with a fully function XML DOM. The latest version includes recently introduced standards such as XPath and XQuery (using something called SAX2). MSXML is available in SQL Server 2005 but does not appear to be available in Access 2007. This book is about Access and not SQL Server, so we don't have room to cover MSXML.**

Data Access Objects (DAO) functions in Access 2007. DAO is somewhat faster and less complicated than ADO for certain operations. With this in mind, using DAO to handle XML data in Access 2007 is a simple operation. The `Chapter37.accdb` database contains a query (`qryBooks`) that looks like this:

```
SELECT BOOKS_AUTHOR.NAME, BOOKS_PUBLICATION.TITLE,
BOOKS_EDITION.ISBN, BOOKS_EDITION.PRINT_DATE,
BOOKS_EDITION.LIST_PRICE, BOOKS_EDITION.FORMAT
FROM (BOOKS_AUTHOR
INNER JOIN BOOKS_PUBLICATION
ON BOOKS_AUTHOR.AUTHOR_ID=BOOKS_PUBLICATION.AUTHOR_ID)
INNER JOIN BOOKS_EDITION ON
BOOKS_PUBLICATION.PUBLICATION_ID=BOOKS_EDITION.PUBLICATION_ID
ORDER BY BOOKS_AUTHOR.NAME;
```

`qryBooks` produces the data shown in Figure 37-11.

FIGURE 37-11

The Books query finds records joined from three tables.

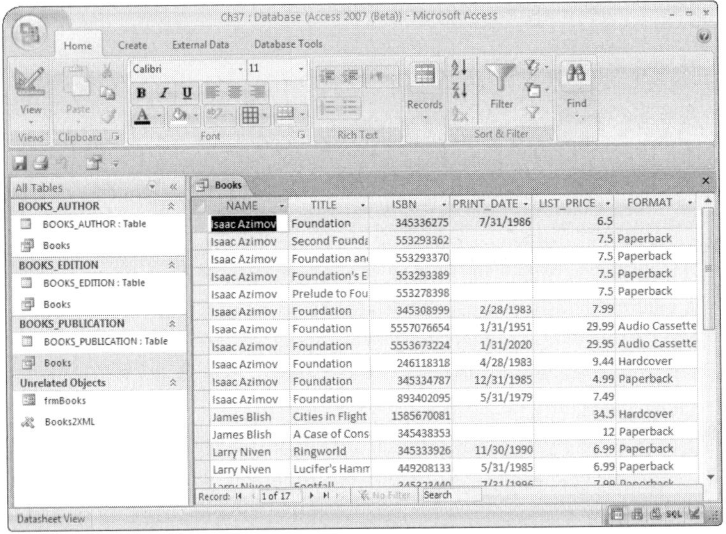

In order to code the example shown in Figure 37-11, you can use DAO in a code module that looks something like this:

```
Public Sub GenerateXML1()
  Dim rs As DAO.Recordset
  Dim strsql As String
  Dim strOut As String

  strsql = "SELECT * FROM Books;"
  Set rs = CurrentDb.OpenRecordset(strsql)
  Do Until rs.EOF
    'The following statement is too long to
    'reproduce here, but includes the names
```

```
      'of all fields returned by the query:
      strOut = strOut & rs.Fields("NAME") & ...
      rs.MoveNext
    Loop
    MsgBox strOut
  End Sub
```

All that remains is to create properly formatted XML using a script like that above. So, we change the script for the generateXML function as follows:

```
Public Sub GenerateXML2()

  'Declare variables:
  Dim rs As DAO.Recordset
  Dim strsql As String
  Dim strOut As String
  Dim fs As Object
  Dim xmlFile As Object

  'Create and execute the query:
  strsql = "SELECT * FROM Books;"
  Set rs = CurrentDb.OpenRecordset(strsql)

  'Build a basic XML document:
  strOut = "<?xml version='1.0'?>" _
    & vbCrLf & "<books>" & vbCrLf

  Do Until rs.EOF
    strOut = strOut & vbTab & "<book author=""" _
      & rs.Fields("NAME") & """ _
      & " title=""" & rs.Fields("TITLE") & """" _
      & " isbn=""" & rs.Fields("ISBN") & """" _
      & " print_date=""" & rs.Fields("PRINT_DATE") & """" _
      & " list_price=""" & rs.Fields("LIST_PRICE") & """" _
      & " format=""" & rs.Fields("FORMAT") & """>" _
      & "</book>" & vbCrLf
    rs.MoveNext
  Loop
  'Clean up by shutting down the recordset:
  rs.Close
  strOut = strOut & "</books>" & vbCrLf

  'write out the XML document
  Set fs = CreateObject("Scripting.FileSystemObject")
  Set xmlFile = fs.CreateTextFile("c:\Books.xml", True)
  xmlFile.Write (strOut)
  xmlFile.Close

End Sub
```

This VBA procedure creates a file named `Books.xml`. The result is shown in Figure 37-12.

FIGURE 37-12

Generating XML from scratch using DAO, a string, and an I/O stream.

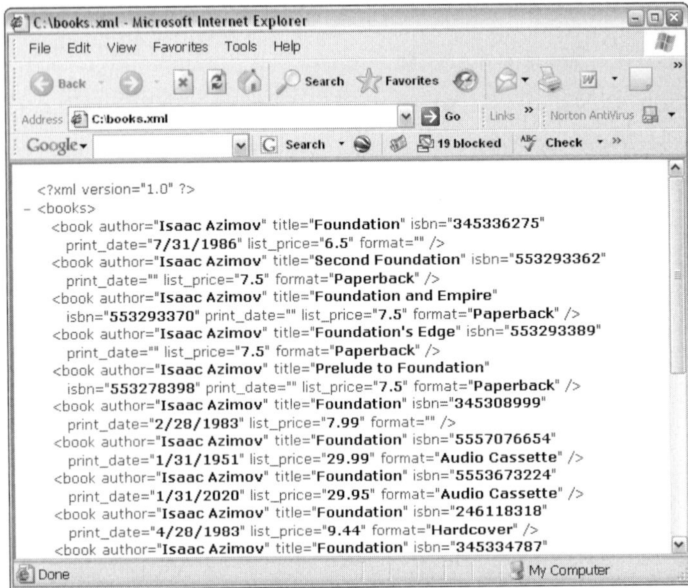

The result in Figure 37-12 doesn't look very good because it has a single-layer hierarchy where all fields are expressed as attributes of the <book> tag. It could be a lot better. The first step is to create a separate tag for each entry as in the following script:

```
Function GetTab(n As Integer) As String
  Dim i As Integer
  Dim str As String
  For i = 1 To n
    str = str & vbTab
  Next
  GetTab = str
End Function

Public Sub GenerateXML3()

  'declare variables
  Dim rs As DAO.Recordset
  Dim strsql As String
  Dim strOut As String
  Dim fs As Object
  Dim xmlFile As Object

  'create and execute the query
```

```
    strsql = ""SELECT * FROM Books;"
    Set rs = CurrentDb.OpenRecordset(strsql)

    'build a basic XML document
    strOut = "<?xml version='1.0'?>" _
      & vbCrLf & "<books>" & vbCrLf

    Do Until rs.EOF
      strOut = strOut & GetTab(1) & "<book>" & vbCrLf
      strOut = strOut & GetTab(2) & "<author>" _
        & rs.Fields("NAME") & "</author>" & vbCrLf
      strOut = strOut & GetTab(2) & "<title>" _
        & rs.Fields("TITLE") & "</title>" & vbCrLf
      strOut = strOut & GetTab(2) & "<isbn>" _
        & rs.Fields("ISBN") & "</isbn>" & vbCrLf
      strOut = strOut & GetTab(2) & "<printed>" _
        & rs.Fields("PRINT_DATE") & "</printed>" & vbCrLf
      strOut = strOut & GetTab(2) & "<list>" _
        & rs.Fields("LIST_PRICE") & "</list>" & vbCrLf
      strOut = strOut & GetTab(2) & "<format>" _
        & rs.Fields("FORMAT") & "</format>" & vbCrLf
      strOut = strOut & GetTab(1) & "</book>" & vbCrLf
      rs.MoveNext
    Loop

    'Clean up by shutting down the recordset:
    rs.Close
    Set rs =Nothing

    'Add the closing XML tag:
    strOut = strOut & "</books>" & vbCrLf

    'Write out the XML document:
    Set fs = CreateObject("Scripting.FileSystemObject")

    Set xmlFile = fs.CreateTextFile("c:\books.xml", True)

    xmlFile.Write (strOut)
    xmlFile.Close

End Sub
```

The preceding script writes out a file called `Books.xml` again. The result looks like what you see in Figure 37-13.

The only problem with these XML examples so far is that the proper relational table structural hierarchy is not properly represented. The first thing to do is to alter the underlying `Books` query in Access 2007, as shown in Figure 37-14.

FIGURE 37-13

Generating XML from scratch using DAO, a string, and an I/O stream

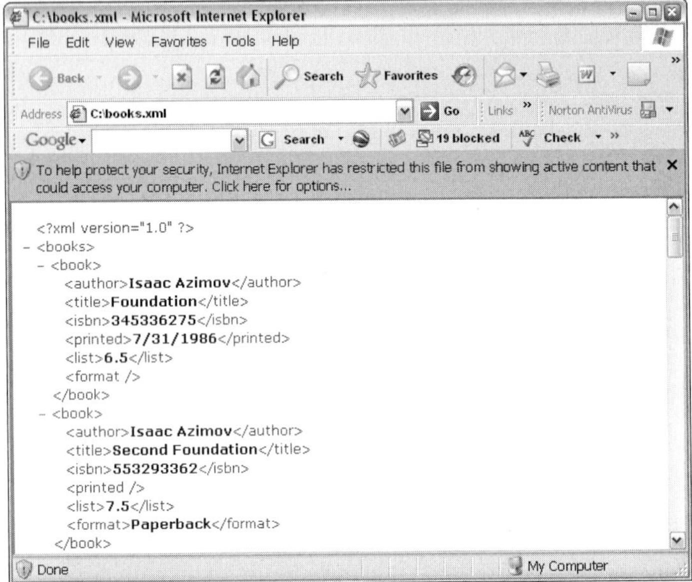

FIGURE 37-14

Sorting the Access query to match the XML hierarchy

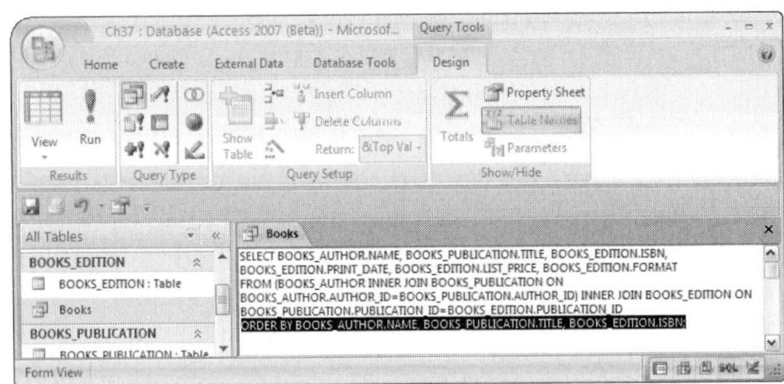

The hierarchical issue is remedied in the following script:

```
Function GetIndent(n As Integer) As String
  Dim i As Integer
  Dim str As String
```

```
  For i = 1 To n
    str = str & Chr(32) & Chr(32) & Chr(32)
  Next
  GetIndent = str
End Function

Public Sub GenerateXML4()

  'declare variables
  Dim rs As DAO.Recordset
  Dim strsql As String
  Dim strOut As String
  Dim fs As Object
  Dim xmlFile As Object
  Dim author As String
  Dim title As String

  'create and execute the query
  strsql = ""SELECT * FROM Books ;"
  Set rs = CurrentDb.OpenRecordset(strsql)

  'build a basic XML document
  strOut = "<?xml version='1.0'?>" & vbCrLf _
    & "<books>" & vbCrLf

  Do Until rs.EOF

    'Could use multiple recordsets for this but
    'in Access it is better to "just code it!"

    If author <> rs.Fields("NAME") Then
      strOut = strOut & GetIndent(1) & "<author name=""" _
        & rs.Fields("NAME") & """>" & vbCrLf
      author = rs.Fields("NAME")
    End If

    If title <> rs.Fields("TITLE") Then
      strOut = strOut & GetIndent(2) & "<title name=""" _
        & rs.Fields("TITLE") & """>" & vbCrLf
      title = rs.Fields("TITLE")
    End If

    'this is the lowest level of the hierarchy
    strOut = strOut & GetIndent(3) & "<edition>" & vbCrLf
    strOut = strOut & GetIndent(4) _
      & "<isbn>" & rs.Fields("ISBN") & "</isbn>" & vbCrLf
    strOut = strOut & GetIndent(4) & "<printed>" _
      & rs.Fields("PRINT_DATE") & "</printed>" & vbCrLf
    strOut = strOut & GetIndent(4) & "<list>" _
```

```
      & rs.Fields("LIST_PRICE") & "</list>" & vbCrLf
    strOut = strOut & GetIndent(4) & "<format>" _
      & rs.Fields("FORMAT") & "</format>" & vbCrLf
    strOut = strOut & GetIndent(3) & "</edition>" & vbCrLf

    rs.MoveNext

    If rs.EOF Then
      strOut = strOut & GetIndent(2) & "</title>" & vbCrLf
    Else
      If title <> rs.Fields("TITLE") Then
        strOut = strOut & GetIndent(2) & "</title>" & vbCrLf
      End If
    End If

    If rs.EOF Then
      strOut = strOut & GetIndent(1) _
          & "</author>" & vbCrLf
    Else
      If author <> rs.Fields("NAME") Then
        strOut = strOut & GetIndent(1) _
          & "</author>" & vbCrLf
      End If
    End If

  Loop

  'Clean up by shutting down the recordset:
  rs.Close
  Set rs = Nothing

  strOut = strOut & "</books>" & vbCrLf

  'write out the XML document
  Set fs = CreateObject("Scripting.FileSystemObject")
  Set xmlFile = fs.CreateTextFile("c:\Books.xml", True)
  xmlFile.Write (strOut)
  xmlFile.Close

End Sub
```

The preceding script once again writes out a file called `Books.xml`. The result looks like what you see in Figure 37-15.

FIGURE 37-15

A properly structured XML hierarchy from a relational table structure

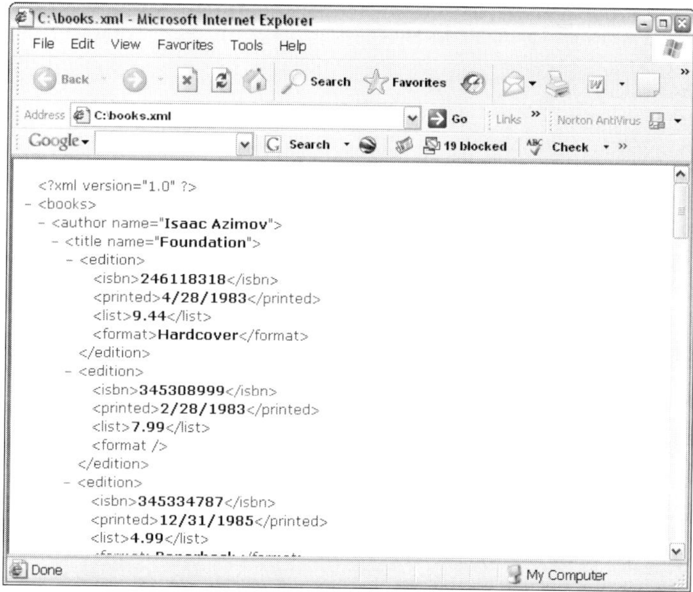

The actual Books.xml document looks like this:

```
<?xml version='1.0'?>
<books>
   <author name="Isaac Azimov">
      <title name="Foundation">
         <edition>
            <isbn>246118318</isbn>
            <printed>4/28/1983</printed>
            <list>9.44</list>
            <format>Hardcover</format>
         </edition>
         <edition>
            <isbn>345308999</isbn>
            <printed>2/28/1983</printed>
            <list>7.99</list>
            <format></format>
         </edition>
         <edition>
            <isbn>345334787</isbn>
            <printed>12/31/1985</printed>
            <list>4.99</list>
```

```
        <format>Paperback</format>
    </edition>
    <edition>
        <isbn>345336275</isbn>
        <printed>7/31/1986</printed>
        <list>6.5</list>
        <format></format>
    </edition>
    <edition>
        <isbn>893402095</isbn>
        <printed>5/31/1979</printed>
        <list>7.49</list>
        <format></format>
    </edition>
    <edition>
        <isbn>5553673224</isbn>
        <printed>1/31/2020</printed>
        <list>29.95</list>
        <format>Audio Cassette</format>
    </edition>
    <edition>
        <isbn>5557076654</isbn>
        <printed>1/31/1951</printed>
        <list>29.99</list>
        <format>Audio Cassette</format>
    </edition>
</title>
<title name="Foundation and Empire">
    <edition>
        <isbn>553293370</isbn>
        <printed></printed>
        <list>7.5</list>
        <format>Paperback</format>
    </edition>
</title>
<title name="Foundation's Edge">
    <edition>
        <isbn>553293389</isbn>
        <printed></printed>
        <list>7.5</list>
        <format>Paperback</format>
    </edition>
</title>
<title name="Prelude to Foundation">
    <edition>
        <isbn>553278398</isbn>
        <printed></printed>
        <list>7.5</list>
        <format>Paperback</format>
```

```
         </edition>
      </title>
      <title name="Second Foundation">
         <edition>
            <isbn>553293362</isbn>
            <printed></printed>
            <list>7.5</list>
            <format>Paperback</format>
         </edition>
      </title>
   </author>
   <author name="James Blish">
      <title name="A Case of Conscience">
         <edition>
            <isbn>345438353</isbn>
            <printed></printed>
            <list>12</list>
            <format>Paperback</format>
         </edition>
      </title>
      <title name="Cities in Flight">
         <edition>
            <isbn>1585670081</isbn>
            <printed></printed>
            <list>34.5</list>
            <format>Hardcover</format>
         </edition>
      </title>
   </author>
   <author name="Larry Niven">
      <title name="Footfall">
         <edition>
            <isbn>345323440</isbn>
            <printed>7/31/1996</printed>
            <list>7.99</list>
            <format>Paperback</format>
         </edition>
      </title>
      <title name="Lucifer's Hammer">
         <edition>
            <isbn>449208133</isbn>
            <printed>5/31/1985</printed>
            <list>6.99</list>
            <format>Paperback</format>
         </edition>
      </title>
      <title name="Ringworld">
         <edition>
            <isbn>345333926</isbn>
```

```
            <printed>11/30/1990</printed>
            <list>6.99</list>
            <format>Paperback</format>
         </edition>
      </title>
   </author>
   <author name="William Shakespeare">
      <title name="The Complete Works of Shakespeare">
         <edition>
            <isbn>198711905</isbn>
            <printed></printed>
            <list>39.95</list>
            <format>Hardcover</format>
         </edition>
      </title>
   </author>
</books>
```

It appears that in Access 2007, XML is only available through the wizards, which handle XML files, such as importing and exporting, as described in Chapter 17.

NOTE **SQL Server can use ADO and ADO.NET to manage XML document. However, with the inclusion of XML data types, and all sorts of other bells and whistles in SQL Server 2005, ADO and even ADO.NET are primitive by comparison.**

Summary

XML is, arguably, one of the most important technologies to emerge in recent years. XML is now a native data format recognized by all of the Microsoft Office applications; it is increasingly finding acceptance as a format for transferring data from application to application. Because of XML's unique ability to support new tags at any time, there are very few types of data that cannot be conveyed in an XML file.

This chapter has barely touched on the capabilities possible when using VBA to directly access XML data. An entire book could be written on just this one topic. This chapter has shown you the basic VBA code required to read and write XML files, but there is much more that can be done in your applications once you've mastered XML. As with so many other things, it's impossible to tell when you'll need to incorporate XML into your Access 2007 applications.

Chapter 38

SharePoint as a Data Source

IN THIS CHAPTER

Considering SharePoint as a data source

Understanding SharePoint and Access interfaces

Using SharePoint data on Access forms

Displaying SharePoint data in Access reports

Using a SharePoint tracking application

Looking at SharePoint collaborative applications

Understanding Microsoft SharePoint Designer

Several of the previous chapters of this book have touched on different data sources for Access 2007. You've seen how Access 2007 supports importing, linking, and exporting data. Access 2007 has no equal when it comes to sharing data with other applications.

This chapter explains how to use Microsoft SharePoint as a data source for Access applications. Microsoft has taken great pains to ensure that Access and SharePoint interoperate seamlessly, providing Access developers with a rich source of data accessible from anywhere on the Internet.

SharePoint data are stored as lists. SharePoint lists can be exported from, and imported into, Access applications. SharePoint lists are available from any SharePoint site, sharing data across the Internet. In earlier chapters, you read about the SharePoint basics, about the services provided by SharePoint Services, and how various types of applications can be implemented using SharePoint. Additionally, you've read about how a SharePoint Web site and Access can integrate with each other. Linking to SharePoint lists make data stored on a SharePoint Web site appear as linked tables in Access.

Essentially, SharePoint is a way of sharing data over the Internet. Quite literally, a point or address on the Internet from which data can be shared between multiple applications. Those applications can be virtually anywhere on the Internet. This chapter takes a more generic look at using SharePoint data than previous chapters. The intent of this chapter is to show how to use SharePoint as a reliable and valuable source of data for Access applications.

Introducing SharePoint as a Data Source

This chapter builds on previous chapters covering importing and exporting SharePoint lists, and includes close integration between Access and SharePoint Web sites. This chapter demonstrates the power and flexibility of using SharePoint data within Access applications. The data in a SharePoint Web site is live and real-time to its users. That same SharePoint data are also live and real-time when data are linked directly to an Access 2007 application.

In reality, SharePoint integration is one of the big stories (from Microsoft's perspective) in Access 2007. Microsoft is busily moving all kinds of features out of Access, expecting SharePoint functionality to take over these capabilities. SharePoint services can be both local to a specific company, and even rented or leased from service providers.

Note: You can find a commercial site, perhaps even a free demonstration service to experiment with. This book uses a Microsoft beta SharePoint Web site, which will not be available in the future. When it comes to Access using SharePoint-available data, you can create links to SharePoint data. The result is views in Access (which are actually Access tables) linked to SharePoint data. Then Access applications can build front-end forms and reports from that SharePoint data.

When hooked into an Access application, SharePoint data are available to all other users of that SharePoint site. This means that the data input by users at their workstations may be viewed and updated by other users around the world. Also, you can consider Access 2007 as a *consumer* of SharePoint data. Access becomes a feature-rich front-end application, using remote SharePoint data as if the data were located locally. The user notices nothing out of the ordinary. For all the world, a SharePoint-hosted Access application looks like any other Access application and contains the same data-entry screens and reports as any other Access database.

NOTE **SharePoint technology is still in its infancy and is not really capable of the performance requirements needed for servicing the Internet community. SharePoint is commonly used for intranet applications running on local area networks (LANs), rather than across the Internet.**

ON the CD-ROM **This chapter uses the database named `Chapter38.accdb`. If you haven't already copied this file onto your machine from the CD, you'll need to do so now.**

Building Access Interfaces with SharePoint

Building Access interfaces with SharePoint simply means going in to Access, hooking up with links to SharePoint Web-site-based data, and then writing forms and reports off those linked tables.

Copying from Access to SharePoint

Let's begin with adding something to a SharePoint Web site:

1. **Open the `Chapter38.accdb` Access 2007 database for this chapter.**
2. **Open the `BOOKS_Author` table.**

   When you open the table the Access ribbon changes.
3. **Under the Table Tools tab, select the Move to SharePoint option (shown in Figure 38-1).**

FIGURE 38-1

Moving data from Access to SharePoint

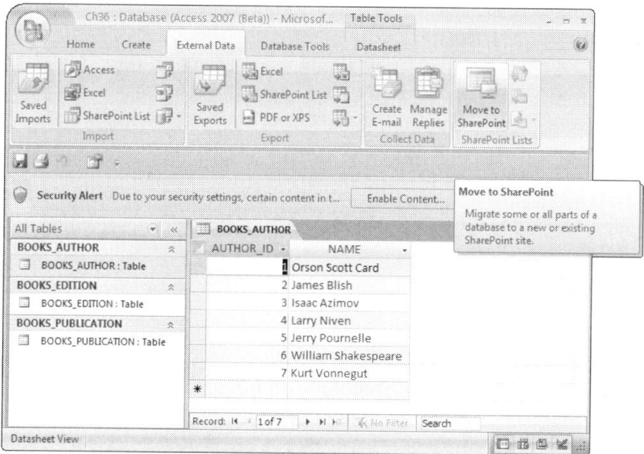

The SharePoint Site Wizard starts.

4. **Enter the SharePoint site URL.**

   The site used in this chapter is shown in Figure 38-2.

NOTE **You can use another active site when reading this book, if you have one available. The site used here (in Figure 38-2) may not be available when reading this book.**

The objective is to create a SharePoint list for each table in your Access database. A SharePoint list is the SharePoint Services equivalent of a table.

5. **Uncheck the Save a Copy of My Database check box.**

6. Click Next.

FIGURE 38-2

Selecting a SharePoint site

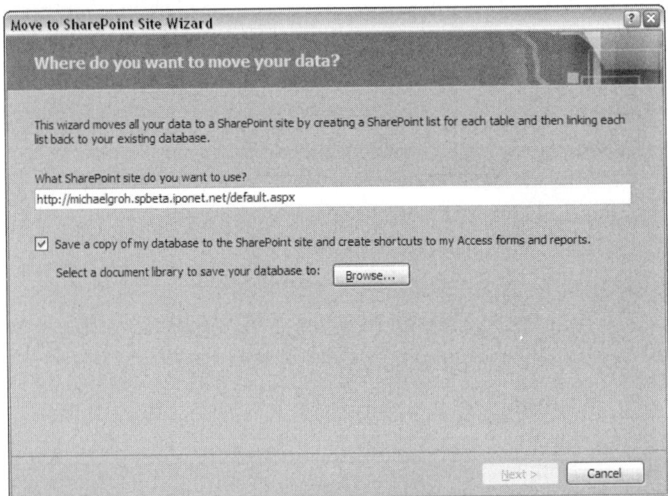

7. **When prompted for a login, enter a valid username and password.**

   As the wizard progresses, you'll notice some things happening on your screen indicating that tables are being copied and converted. The final screen should be as shown in Figure 38-3.

8. **If you receive any errors or warnings, check the Show Details box and read the information as displayed.**

9. **Click the Finish button when you're done.**

   The result should show the tables linked to and stored at the SharePoint Web site, and not just in Access any longer. You can see this by rolling over the table name with the mouse in Access, as shown in Figure 38-4.

FIGURE 38-3

The results of connecting to a SharePoint site

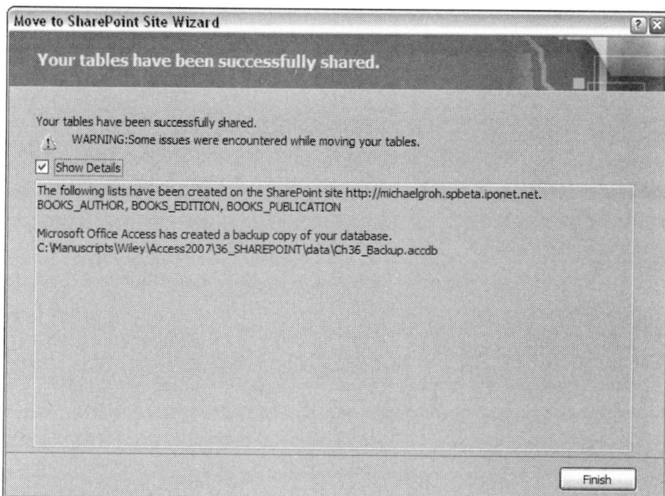

FIGURE 38-4

After executing the SharePoint Site Wizard, tables are shown linked from Access to SharePoint.

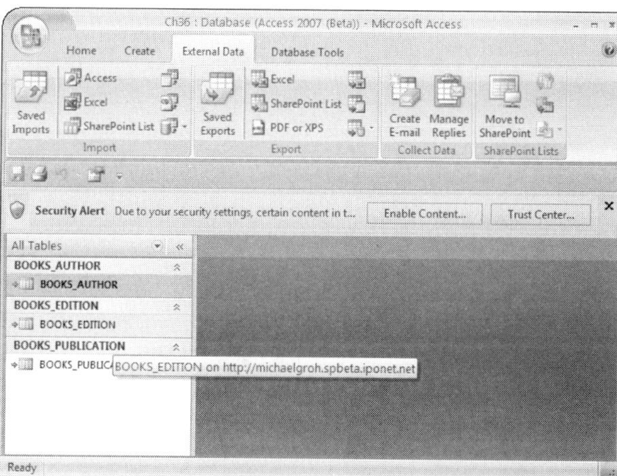

Notice also that the icon next to the table name has changed to indicate that the table is now linked, and not contained locally.

Figure 38-5 shows the three tables copied from Access to the SharePoint site. The tables and their data are now stored and managed by SharePoint Services. All that is left in the Access database are logical links to the SharePoint Web site. The tables and data are no longer stored in the Access database.

FIGURE 38-5

Tables added from Access to SharePoint are highlighted.

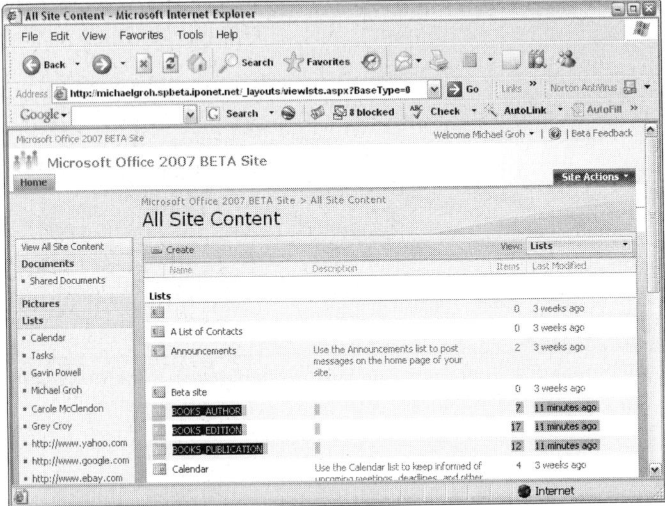

Building an Access form using SharePoint data

Now you can create a form in your Access application front end, hooking to data managed by the SharePoint Web site through the linked tables in the Access database. For this example, we create a simple form from the linked SharePoint data:

1. **Highlight the `BOOKS_EDITION` table.**
2. **On the Access ribbon, select the Create tab and then select the Form icon.**

   Access 2007 builds the form shown in Figure 38-6.

   Now let's use the data in the form.
3. **On the top-left side of the Access ribbon, select the View icon and select the Form View option.**

   The Form's view changes, as shown in Figure 38-7.

FIGURE 38-6

Select a table, and a form creation generates a simple-format form.

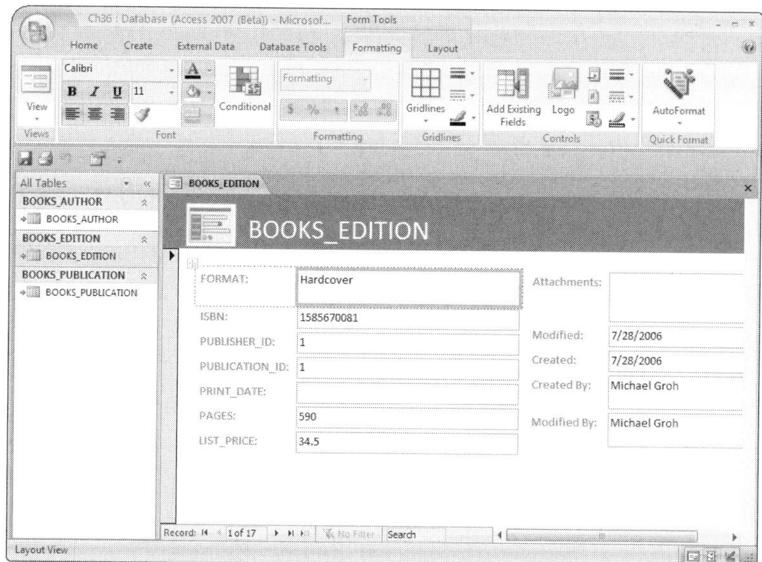

FIGURE 38-7

Executing a form in Access against SharePoint-site-based data

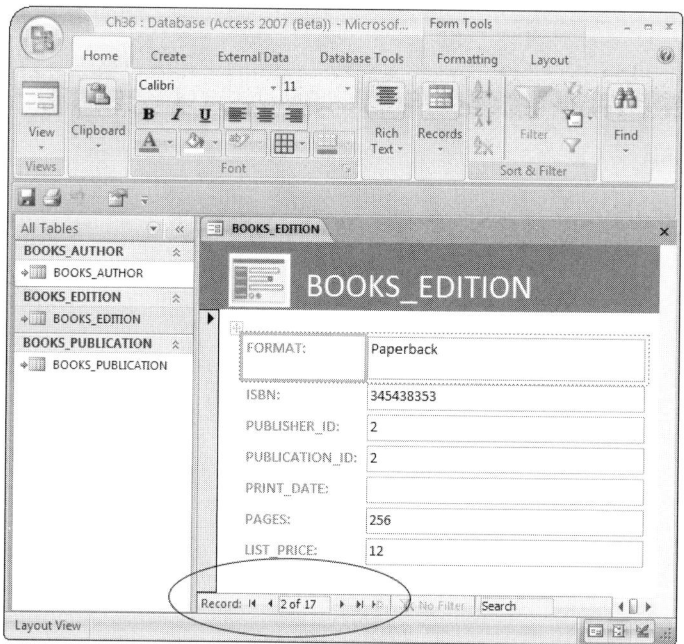

As you can see in Figure 38-7, the Navigation Buttons at the bottom of the form are used to move to the second record in the SharePoint data. (The data displayed in Figure 38-8 is different from the data in Figure 38-7.)

4. **Exit the form and save it as shown in Figure 38-8.**

FIGURE 38-8

Saving the simple form you created

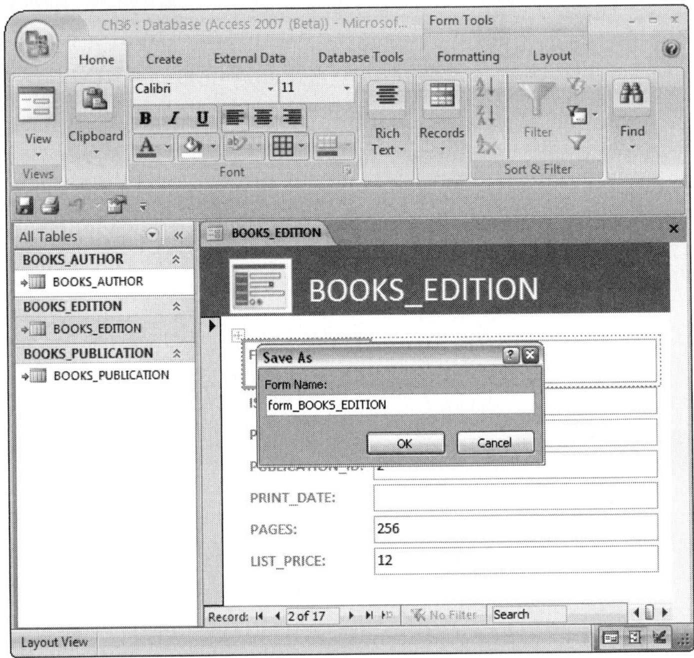

Building an Access report using SharePoint data

Now you can also create a very simple Access report using data source from the SharePoint Web site:

1. **Select a linked SharePoint table.**
2. **On the Access ribbon, select the Create tab and click on the Report icon.**

   The Report wizard appears as shown in Figure 38-9. It may take some time for a response. Remember that Access has to go out across the Internet to find SharePoint data.

FIGURE 38-9

Creating a report from a SharePoint data source

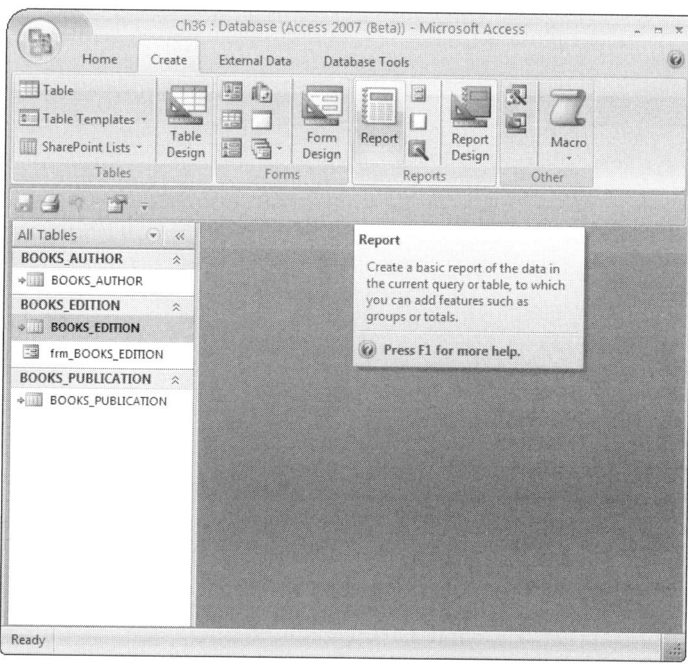

The result is the report shown in Figure 38-10. You've now executed the report and displayed a number of records located anywhere on the Internet in an Access report.

At this point, you've created and executed both a form and a report built from SharePoint data using the Access interface. What you've done in the last two sections is use the Access interface as an application front-end tool. The SharePoint site has been used as a remote data source for an Access 2007 application.

This chapter doesn't need to be more complex than it is so far in order to demonstrate this simple concept. You've already managed to achieve what the title of this chapter states: using SharePoint as a data source (in this case, using Access as an application front-end tool).

FIGURE 38-10

Executing a report from a SharePoint data source

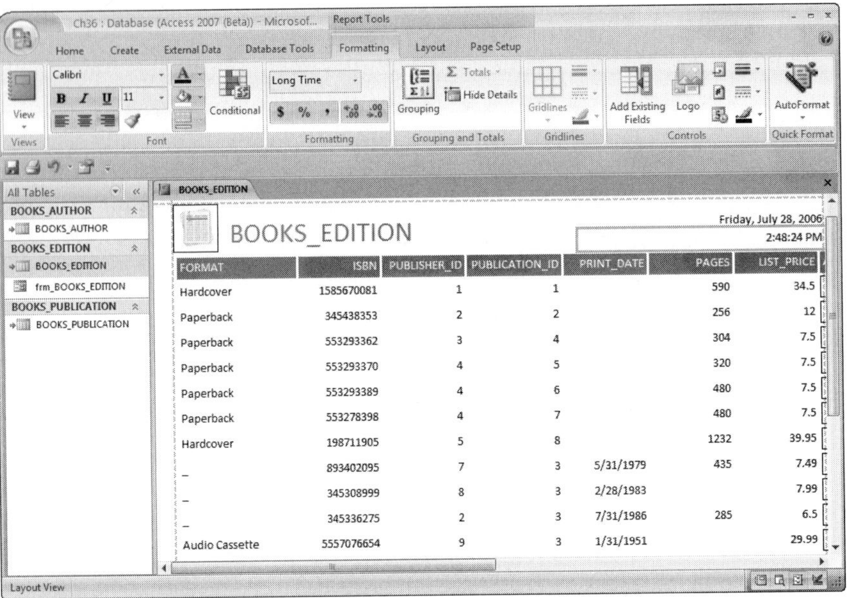

SharePoint Application Types

SharePoint is an online data source. Access can be used to build extremely rich client-side application graphical interfaces. Many collaborative and tracking applications use a SharePoint Services Web site as a store for data, consuming data stored as SharePoint lists.

The simple fact that a SharePoint Services Web site makes data available online over the Internet (or over an intranet) makes SharePoint list data simultaneously available to many users. The result is what's called a *collaborative database* or a *collaborative application*. The word *collaborative* implies that data can be simultaneously shared among many users. For example, a company could share data with its clients, or with employees located at remote offices.

Tracking applications

A tracking application provides simple lists of data elements, which can be combined into richer data sets. Many such applications combine both static and dynamic data. *Static data* in a sales application describe the customers you sell to and the suppliers you buy from. *Dynamic data* consist of day-to-day transactions, such as sales orders and notes issued against customers and invoices from suppliers. In this kind of arrangement, SharePoint lists constitute the tables of a relational database. The data are stored online and shared across an intranet (or the Internet). Then rich GUI interfaces can be built for many different clients, or for specific, individual clients, tailored to specific needs.

Access also ships with templates used to create various common types of applications. Templates for tables are as shown in Figure 38-11.

FIGURE 38-11

Table templates available in Access 2007

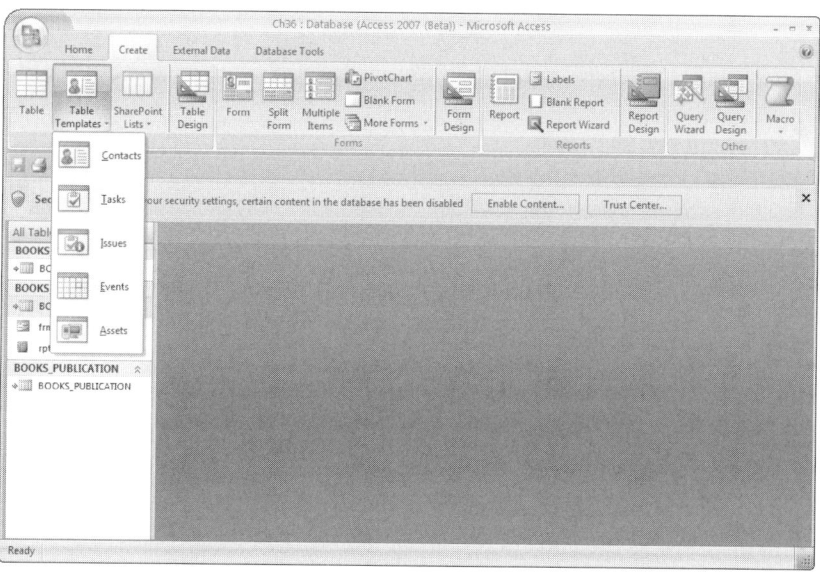

Figure 38-12 shows a number of different templates for SharePoint list data.

FIGURE 38-12

SharePoint list templates available in Access 2007

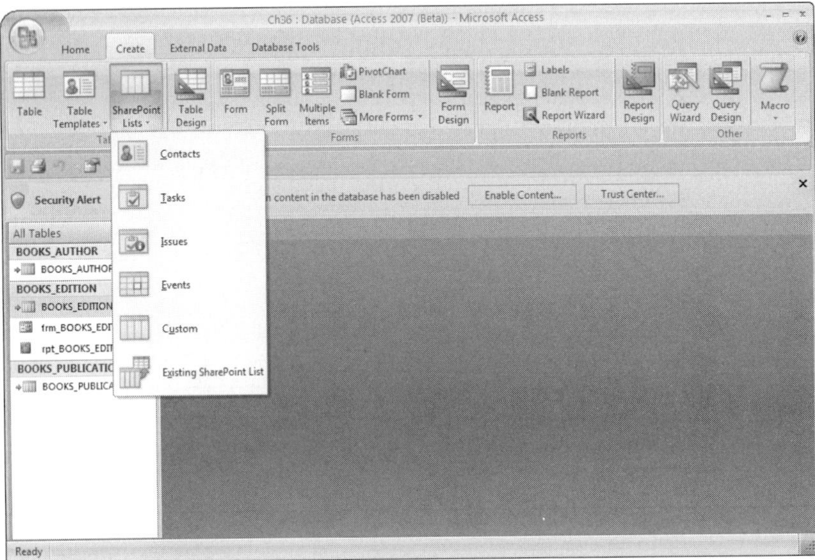

With the available templates, skilled programming is not required to use SharePoint data in an Access 2007 application. Anyone can build Access applications that work with SharePoint data, and data maintenance becomes the responsibility of the company providing the SharePoint Web site. Examine the templates available in Access 2007 with tables and SharePoint lists by following these steps:

1. **Open the `Chapter38.accdb` database for this chapter.**

   Under the Create tab, you should see the Tables icon, the Table Templates icon, and the SharePoint Lists icon.

2. **Click the Table Templates icon.**

   You see the picture shown in Figure 38-13.

3. **Examine the structure of the table.**

4. **Select the Table Templates icon, and click the Contacts option.**

   You get a new contacts table, much like a the contacts list inside Outlook Express or Outlook. The new table is displayed in Datasheet View, making it difficult to understand the design of the table.

5. **Right-click the name of table, and then click the Design View option (both commands are shown in Figure 38-13).**

   You're prompted to save the table.

6. **Name it Contacts and click OK.**

   This assumes, of course, that you don't already have a table called Contacts.

FIGURE 38-13

Creating a table from a table template in Access 2007

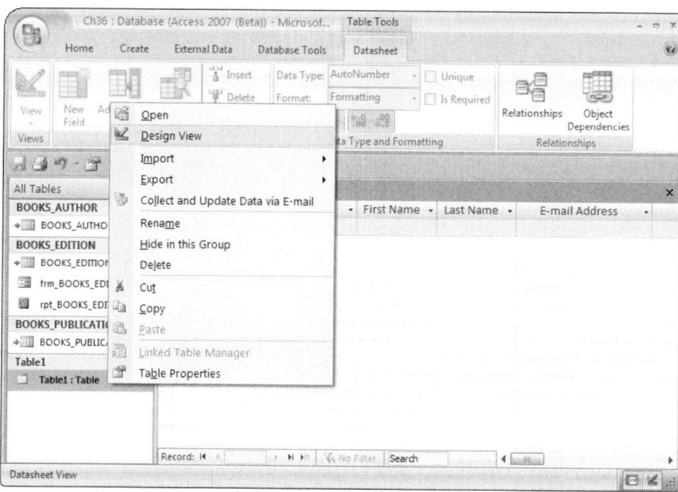

7. **With the table open in Design View, click the View icon, and click the PivotTable View option.**

   No, you're not going to create a PivotTable — we just want you to see the PivotTable Field List window that pops up (shown in Figure 38-14).

FIGURE 38-14

A Contacts table template in Access 2007

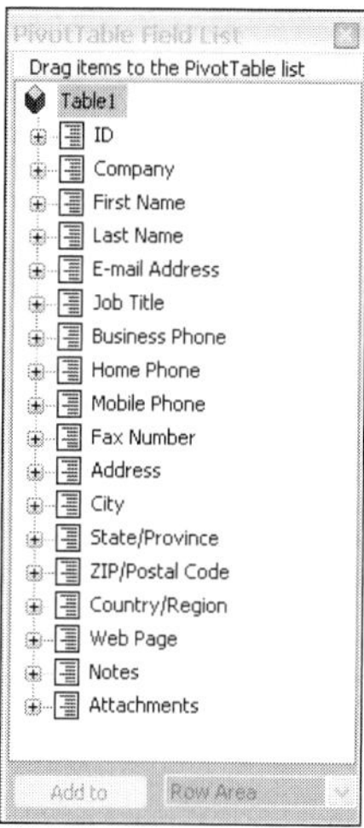

As you can see in Figure 38-14, the Contacts table template has typical contact information, such as names, e-mail addresses, phone numbers, fax numbers, addresses, and so on.

You don't have to go through the steps of examining the table structure in each of the templates, but you can, if you want. That way, you'll get a good picture of what's available from the Access 2007 templates. Figure 38-15 shows the field lists for the tasks, issues, events, and assets table templates.

FIGURE 38-15

Table templates for tasks, issues, events, and assets in Access 2007

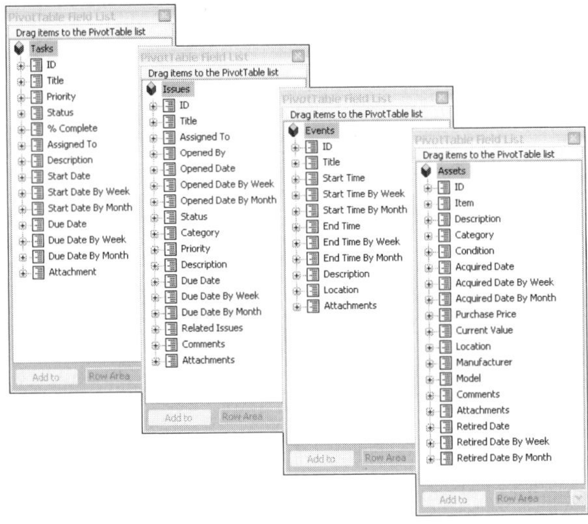

Figure 38-16 shows the field lists for the SharePoint table templates.

TIP **SharePoint list templates actually allow you to create a simple schema in Access using a default template structure. The schema is the table created, as shown by the example SharePoint list templates in Figure 38-16.**

Figure 38-17 shows an example SharePoint Services Web site. With the Existing SharePoint List option template, you can create a template in the Access GUI for any list (table of data) on a SharePoint Services Web site.

FIGURE 38-16

SharePoint list templates in Access 2007

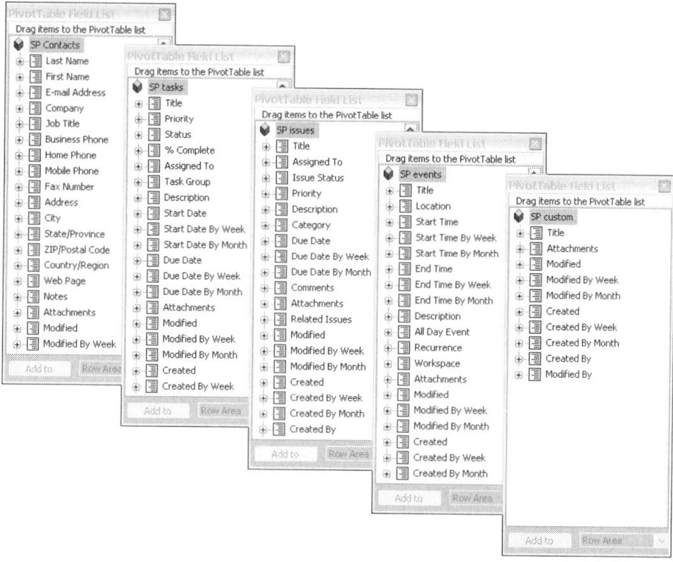

FIGURE 38-17

A template can be created for an existing SharePoint list

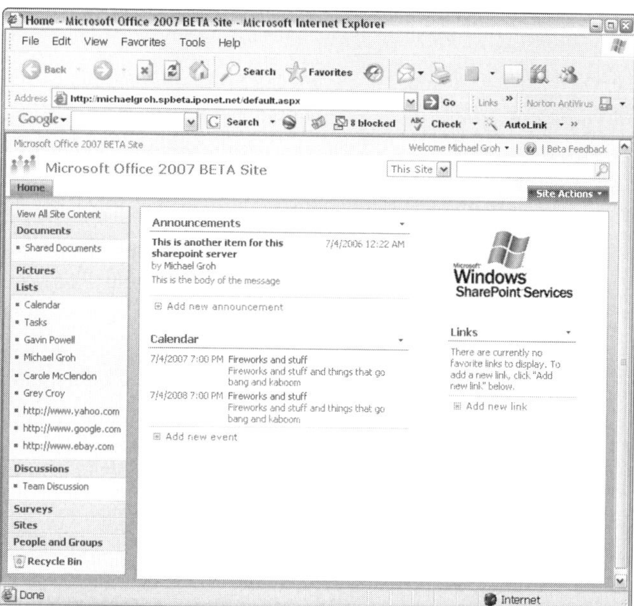

The same type of results can be obtained when using Access to generate reports as for creating form table templates.

In the future, numerous other application templates for Access 2007 might become available. Potential tracking application templates include customer service, projects and project management, marketing, sales channels and pipelines, student management, school and college student management, and others.

Collaborative applications and databases

SharePoint Services Web sites also allow for collaborative, or shared, applications. Companies can even share application implementations, and even share SharePoint source data with their clientele. In these situations, *collaboration* means collaboration between the source of data production (the company producing data) and their clients (also potentially producing data, but likely consuming as a priority).

The result is the sharing of data where the combination of SharePoint Portal Server and SharePoint Services data source, becomes a multiuser database. SharePoint is still emerging as a collaborative resource, and the capabilities provided by SharePoint lists will surely increase over time. The components of a collaborative architecture would be comprised of a database (on a SharePoint Services site), and perhaps applications could also be shared — but that is not strictly a requirement. Different organizations could require a different application look and feel, and perhaps even varying data content. And there is also the issue of data security where you don't want all your clients seeing each other's data. That would be like allowing all the employees in a company to see the salaries for another company's employees.

A collaborative application consists of the following general architectural pieces:

- **Tracking applications:** Used to store and track data changes on a daily basis by storing the data produced by an operating business.
- **Schema free:** A customer using a company's SharePoint data would need to define schema structures for their application, as with a relational database. This is because the structure is already defined in the SharePoint Services data. Also, the template capabilities in tools such as Access and Excel create forms and reports automatically.
- **E-Mail updates:** Data can be collected and automated using e-mail. All Microsoft Office products are integrated using forms, and then updated automatically into what is effectively a SharePoint Services database (this is also available for tables linked into SQL Server database).
- **New Office interface:** Most importantly, the new Microsoft Office interface is responsible for much of the look and feel, and ease of use, of new capabilities and collaborative aspects of Office tools such as Access and Excel.

Microsoft SharePoint Designer 2007

SharePoint Designer is a part of Office 2007 and is interesting enough to mention briefly in this book. Figure 38-18 shows a simple screen of the primary development window in SharePoint Designer.

FIGURE 38-18

Microsoft Office SharePoint Designer 2007

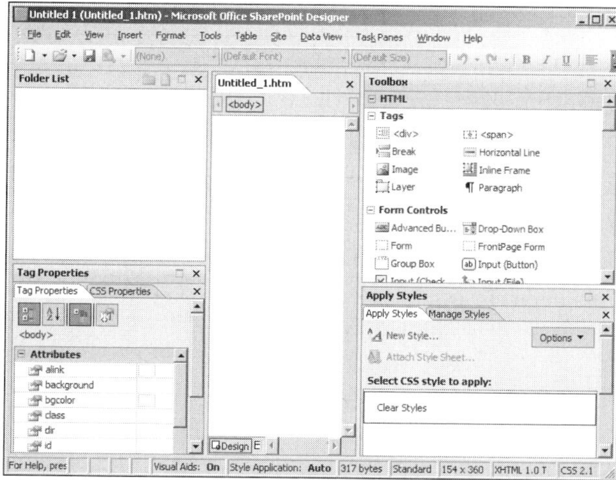

Figure 38-18 shows HTML tags, and Cascading Style Sheet (CSS) settings. Figure 38-18 looks a little like the interface for Visual Studio Designer or a product like Dreamweaver. In this context, SharePoint Designer is a tool used for developing Web pages using basic HTML and CSS elements. This shows that SharePoint is essentially and primarily an Internet (or intranet) source for shared data. SharePoint Designer simply allows for rapid development of browser-driven application interfaces.

SharePoint Designer can also generate ASP.NET pages for server-driven Web applications. It is more or less code-free (most of the objective behind tools like this), and like much of Access itself, heavily wizard-driven. In other words, you don't have to be a highly skilled programmer to produce usable applications.

You can find more information on SharePoint Designer at `http://msdn2.microsoft.com/en-us/library/ms454098.aspx`.

Summary

This chapter has taken a quick look at the potential benefits of combining data stored in SharePoint 2007 with Access 2007 forms and reports. Access 2007 enables you to seamlessly integrate with SharePoint Services, across the Internet or more locally on an intranet. The SharePoint data are available to any SharePoint user with the appropriate credentials (username and password), and data security is provided by SharePoint Services.

Microsoft is aggressively and rapidly improving the performance in capability of SharePoint Services. The ability to share Access data with remote users through SharePoint will only increase over time.

Several unresolved issues will, in the short term, inhibit using SharePoint for mission-critical data. Paramount among these concerns is adequately securing SharePoint data from different categories of SharePoint users.

Chapter 39

Client/Server Concepts

Historically, the term *client/server* has been applied to two-tier, localized computer systems. A client/server environment is typically used to service a single company, using a local area network (LAN), or sometimes a wide area network (WAN), where a multitude of client computers are connected to a single server computer. The server computer quite literally serves up information. The client computer consumes information provided by the server computer. Of course, there is a two-way interaction between the client computer and server computer, such that client computers can also send information back to server computers.

In an Access environment, client/server architecture is not applied only as a historical term; it includes environments where an Access database communicates with a server database engine running on the same computer, as well as server databases running on other computers.

ON the CD-ROM This chapter uses the database named `Chapter39.accdb`. If you have not already copied it onto your machine from the CD, you'll need to do so now.

IN THIS CHAPTER

- Looking at a client/server setup
- Identifying the difference between application and back office (server)
- Understanding multitiered computer systems
- Understanding what an OLTP database is
- Looking at what a data warehouse is
- Knowing where Access 2007 fits
- Seeing where Access 2007 excels and shines

The Parts of Client/Server Architecture

A client/server setup is essentially one or more client computers (workstations) running some kind of application. That client application is connected (usually through a network) to a server computer. The application's features, such as input screens and reports, provide an interface to the data that the application uses. The data is stored on the server computer, not the client computer. In many client/server environments, the only activity that occurs on the client computer is the interaction between the user and the application.

The ideal example of client/server architecture is the Internet. The Internet is really nothing more than a wide area network that connects computers using the TCP/IP networking protocol. Each computer running a Web browser is a client that connects to resources provided by Web servers. Very little data is stored on the client computers, while vast amounts of data may be kept on the Web servers. The primary purpose of the Web browser application running on the client computers is to provide an interface to the data provided by the Web server computers.

Examine the diagram shown in Figure 39-1. Everything is connected to the central server computer. All of the client computers, the Internet browsers shown in the cloud, and even the printer are effectively client applications of one form or another.

FIGURE 39-1

A client/server computer system layout

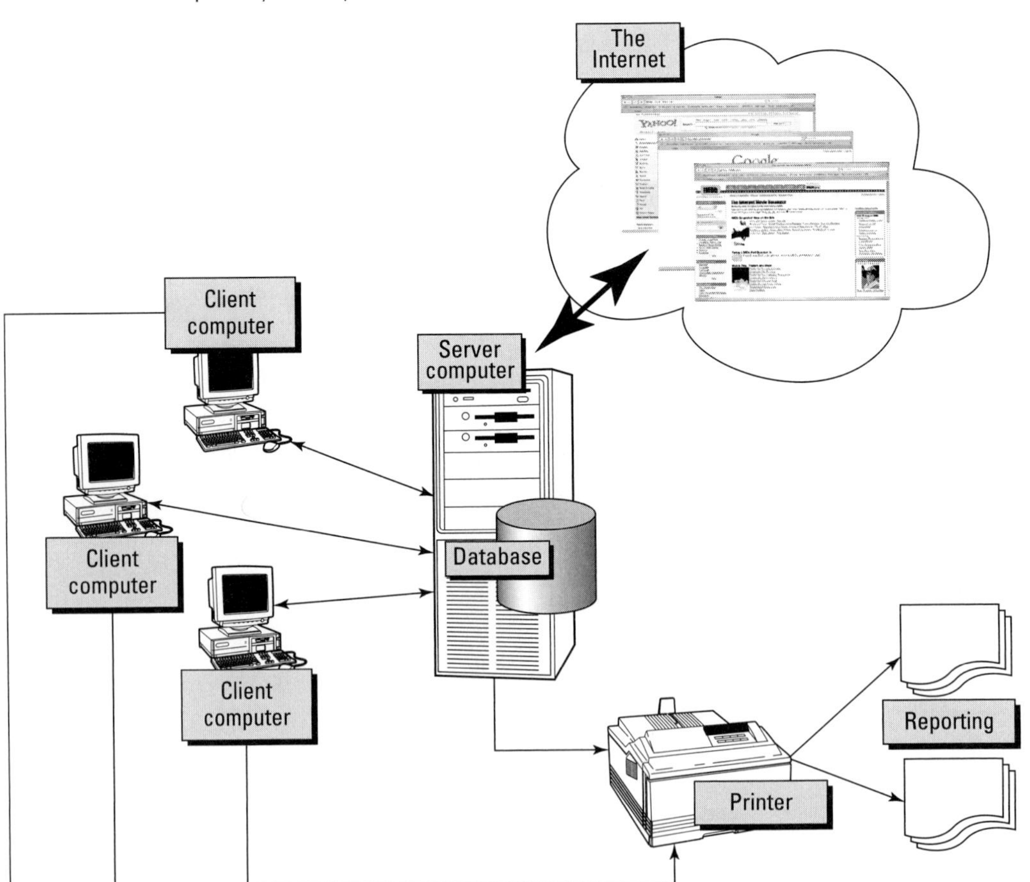

NOTE The printer shown in Figure 39-1 produces reports and is connected to both client computers and the server computer. In this case, a printer is both a client to the server computer, as well as a resource provided by the server.

Applications

From looking at Figure 39-1, you now know how the terms *client* and *server* are used when considering a computer system as a whole. The next thing to explore is what exactly runs on the different computers. In Figure 39-1, you can see that a large cloud is used to represent the Internet in general. Within that large cloud, you can see web browsers connected to various well-known Web sites. Every time you go to Yahoo! on your computer at home, your home computer becomes a client computer connected to the Yahoo! Web site. The combination of your browser program plus the software running from Yahoo! computers (servers) into your browser on your computer is a client/server application.

An *application* is a program running locally on a client computer. The application performs the operation of connecting the client computer to a server computer. The server computer can be somewhere on the local network or located on the Internet. Figure 39-2 and Figure 39-3 show two different applications. Both of these are Access 2007 entry forms found in the Chapter39.accdb example database.

FIGURE 39-2

An automobile products application entry screen (an Access 2007 form)

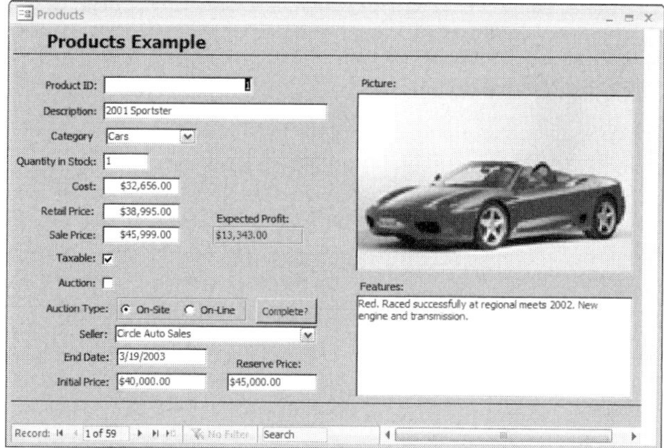

FIGURE 39-3

A contacts application entry screen (an Access 2007 form)

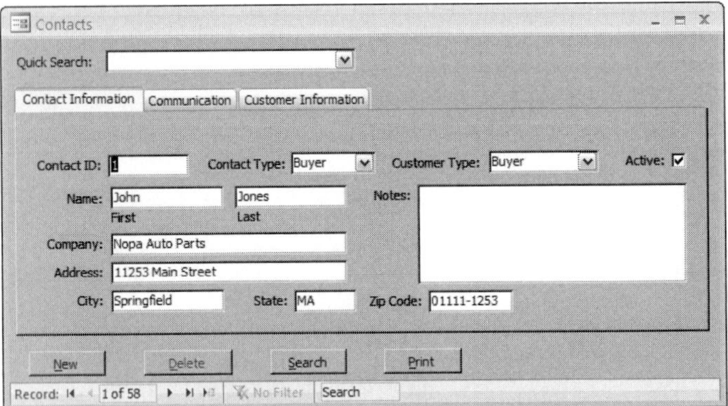

The back office

You may have heard of the expression *back office,* referring to the computers that store a company's data. The back-office section of a client/server computer system is normally unseen by the users of client computers. More than one server computer can be involved in a single application. Server computers can be running databases, such as SQL Server or Oracle. Server computers can be used to form a performance funneling structure and data between database servers and client applications. These funneling-type computers include functions such as acting as Web servers and application servers.

Back-office computers perform the function of providing data to client applications. Back-office computers, such as database servers and Web servers, are almost always invisible to end users. The operation and existence of database and Web server computers is transparent to application users because users do not interact directly with the server computers.

The database

A database is used primarily to store data. In general, larger and more scalable database engines like SQL Server provide features well beyond the capabilities of Microsoft Access. One particular difference between a server database engine like SQL Server and Access is with respect to specialized database objects supported by server database engines. These specialized database objects are *stored procedures, user-defined functions,* and *triggers.*

A *stored procedure* is a block of commands that operates against data in the database. A *user-defined function* is similar to a stored procedure except that it returns a single value. A *trigger* is an event detector, which executes a sequence of commands when a specific event occurs with the database. These objects add intelligence and logic that determines how data stored in the database is handled by the database server.

Access has its equivalent of stored procedures, functions, and triggers, in the form of macros, modules, and class modules (see Figure 39-4).

FIGURE 39-4

Access uses macros, modules, and class modules for coded functionality.

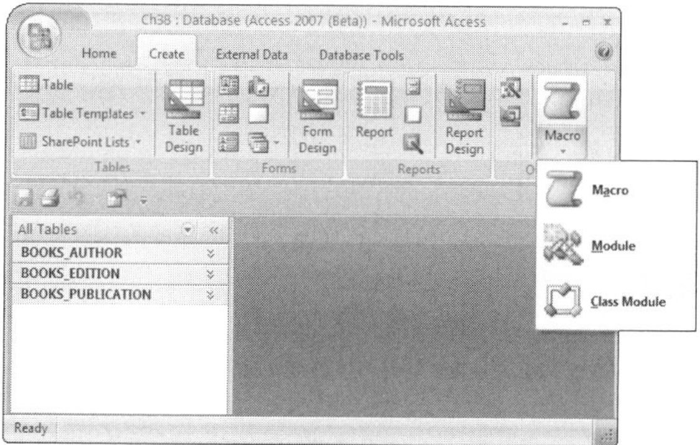

In general, a macro stores a sequence of commands and parameters for later automated repetition. Modules and class modules can be used to create blocks of code, which are stored in an Access database. These three objects all perform a similar function to that of stored procedures in a server database, in that they execute sequences of commands. Those commands typically act on data stored within an Access database, but they can do much more, such as modify the user interface or interact with the user.

In reality, an Access database is not suitable for the extreme processing power that requires a server-based database computer system. This role is more suited to database engines like SQL Server and Oracle Database. Microsoft intends for Access to be used primarily as a single-user or workgroup database system, not to drive Web sites or to support applications used by hundreds or thousands of simultaneous users. Access processes its data locally, on the user's computer. When an Access database is split, and the back-end `.accdb` resides on a file server, Access pulls data from the back-end database and processes it on the user's computer.

In contrast, server database engines like SQL Server and Oracle, process data on the server computer, and only deliver requested data to the client application. The client-side application is responsible for supporting the user interface, and responding to user input. This division of operations is the primary difference between a file-oriented database system like Access and a server database engine like SQL Server.

NOTE **Concurrency is a measure of how many users a computer system can service simultaneously. Scalability is a measure of how much concurrency, processing and physical throughput a computer system can handle. Performance is a measure of how fast a computer system responds to user requests. Generally speaking, a fast response is better than a slow response.**

However, Access also fulfills the dual role of both database and application development. Also, Access 2007 uses its own database engine (called the Access Database Engine), which does not provide the multiuser/multitasking capabilities of SQL Server. For example, in addition to coding in stored procedures, databases like SQL Server and Oracle also support highly specialized database objects as in the following:

- **View:** A stored query definition containing no data. A view is not a physical copy of data. The data are extracted when the view is requested by a client application.
- **Cluster:** Physical copies of entire columnar sections of heavily accessed tables, especially in SQL joins. Clusters do not automatically refresh.
- **Clustered index**: A special type of index that the physical order of records in a table matches the table's primary index.
- **Identity fields**: Maintains sequential index counters. Typically used to generate surrogate primary keys for creation of new records in a table in a relational database. Access does allow auto counters.

NOTE **A surrogate key is where an integer identifier is used to replace a primary key in a table.**

- **Temporary table**: Used to temporarily store data, usually for intermediary steps in larger operations.
- **Partitioning and Parallel Processing:** Physical splitting of tables into separate partitions, including parallel processing on multiple partitions, or individual operations performed on individual partitions. Querying a small portion of a table is called *partition pruning*.

All of the objects described above generally have very specific tasks, roles, or functions. Access 2007 (Access Database Engine) and Access 2003 and before (Jet database engine) do not have objects of the capacity and scope listed above. Server-based database engines such as SQL Server and Oracle Database are much more powerful than Access 2007 and can simultaneously service hundreds or even thousands of users. Furthermore, SQL Server and Oracle databases often contain millions and millions of records that must be made available to a user within seconds.

On the other hand, Access a supports sophisticated forms-and-reports packages. SQL Server and Oracle Database do not have built-in application tools, and you must use other tools to build interfaces to SQL Server or Oracle data.

A huge improvement of the Access Database Engine over the Jet database engine is that the Access 2007 database engine has built-in integration with SharePoint Services capabilities (see Chapter 23). The Access Database Engine handles all of the complexity of communicating with SharePoint operating on a remote server located across the Internet.

Web servers and application servers

These types of servers perform a very specific function and usually were not present in historical, single-company-LAN, client/server environments. On a most basic level, a Web server and an application server perform exactly the same function. They both form a kind of a processing and pooling funnel between application computers and back-end server computers.

Figure 39-5 illustrates that the difference between the computers shown in Figure 39-1 and those shown in Figure 39-5 is a difference of scale and scalability. In Figure 39-5, there is much more interrogation and direct access to the database on the single-server computer. That single-server computer is limited as to how much load it can manage and continue to not irritate users by running too slowly.

FIGURE 39-5

A database server can be overloaded by too many users.

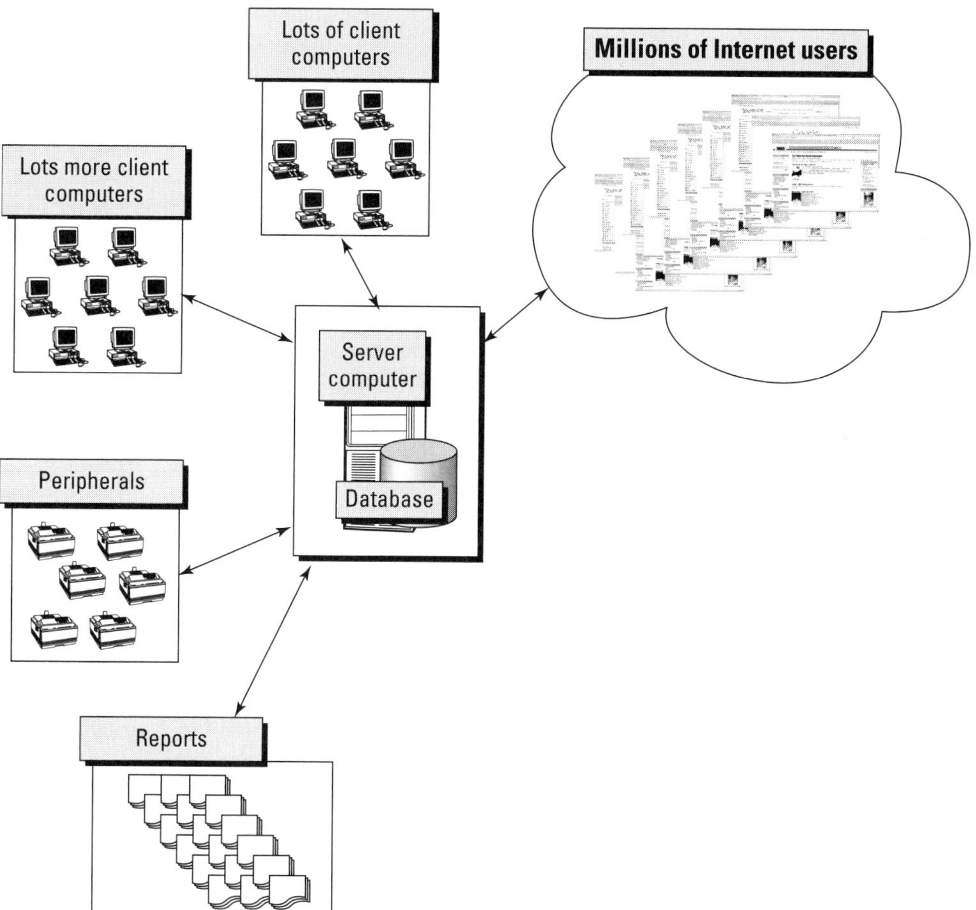

Overloading a database server can be prevented by using an intermediary server of some kind. This intermediary can be a Web server or an application server, as shown in Figure 39-6.

An application server is typically used to serve applications in a largescale client/server environment. Application servers often perform "load balancing" by directing user requests to server computers that are less busy than heavily used servers. A Web server is used to serve applications in an Internet environment, and may simultaneously service many hundreds of users. A Web server is generally focused on the management of connections, by sharing database server connections among many Internet connections, switching between each end user. The Web server uses connection pooling to share the resources of the database among all the concurrent user connections.

FIGURE 39-6

Web and application server computers manage back-end server access.

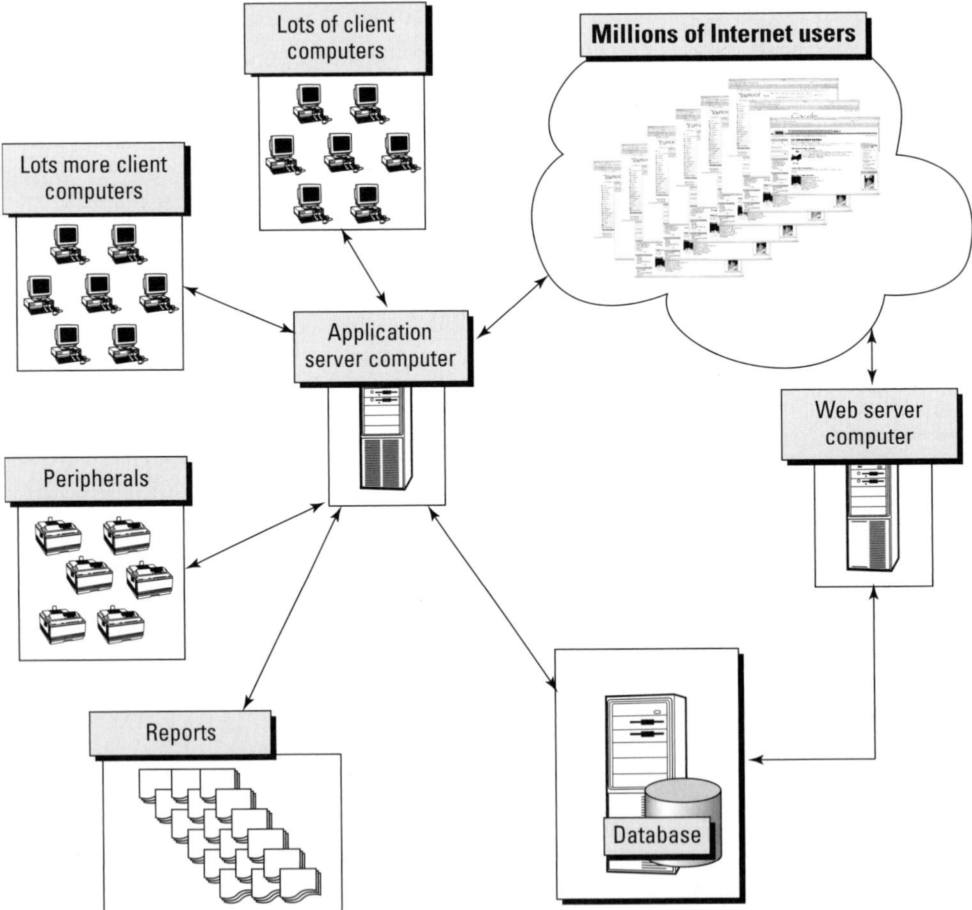

An application server is less often used for connection pooling than Web servers because the scale of the number of connections is much reduced. An application server is better suited to maintain frequently used data in a dedicated computer, as well as performing load balancing.

Multitier Architecture

So, what is a multitier computer system? Database systems can be thought of as consisting of three major components: the data, the business logic that determines how data are handled by the application, and a user interface that interacts with the user. Each of these three components is a *tier* of a multitier system.

A tier is a logical construct. It's a way of segregating an application's activities. Very often, the tier is physical as well as logical, but physical separation of tiers is not a requirement of client/server applications.

Other database architectures involve two tiers, and sometimes only a single tier. Most Access applications are, quite frankly, written as single-tier database applications. Access forms are most often bound directly to a data source, and very often the specification for extracting the data is contained within the `ControlSource` properties of the forms, reports, and controls in these applications.

An Access application that uses VBA code to extract data and populate forms can be considered a two-tier database application, but even then, reports are almost always directly bound to a record source in the database.

Two-tier systems

Most client/server database systems have been built as two-tier systems. This type of architecture is typical of a company running one or only a few applications, against a database across a LAN.

In case you're wondering, splitting an Access database into front and back ends is *not* considered client/server. One of the fundamental characteristics of client/server databases is that processing takes place on both the client end and the server end of the application. The front-end processing is primarily involved with managing and maintaining the user interface, which involves interacting with the user, validating the user's input, and preparing the data for delivery to the database engine. The server-side processing includes extracting and manipulating data before sending to the client side, as well as receiving data sent from the client and storing that data in the database tables.

When an Access database has been split into two pieces and the portion containing the tables has been moved to another computer, no processing ever takes place on the back-end computer. You don't have to install software on the "server" computer in order to place the back-end database on it. Access is, and has always been, a file-based database system. The `.accdb` file used by an Access 2007 application is really nothing more than a data file, much as a Word document is contained within a file. No processing is required on the part of the computer holding the file in order for Access to use the data stored within the `.accdb` file.

Three-tier systems

A three-tier computer system is where the Web servers and application servers come in to use. In this case, the resulting architecture is the same as that shown in Figure 39-6, and for all the same reasons described previously.

Many client/server databases are written as three-tier systems. The data-management tier runs on the server computer, while the user interface is managed on the client-side workstation. The business logic is often split between the client and server computers. Data validation, user notification, and data transformation often take place within the user interface, usually in the programming code under the forms and reports. The server computer may also implement business logic in the form of user-defined functions and stored procedures that validate and verify data before storing it in the database's tables.

What Is an OLTP Database?

Historically a client/server database served clients in one company over a small-scale LAN. Online Transaction Processing (OLTP) is a term used to describe a scaled-up client/server database. The primary difference is that the OLTP-type database is intended to service a much greater number of users, usually over the Internet. The result of OLTP databases for the Internet was the introduction of Web servers and specialized functionality inside relational databases to cater to enormously increased capacity requirements of the Internet.

An OLTP database is also a transaction-processing database. A transaction is change (adding, updating, or deleting a record, or changing a table) to the database. So, OLTP databases are built for large capacity operations (like the Internet) and are primarily used to change data. In other words, the primary purpose of an OLTP database is to allow access to small amounts of data (at any one time) to large numbers of users.

An OLTP database provides rapid access to small amounts of data and large numbers of users at the same. An OLTP database is built with these purposes in mind. Access can be used as a very small scale Internet database. Many Internet databases contain terabytes of data. Additionally, these very large Internet OLTP databases are extremely complex from a hardware architectural perspective and support advanced operations such as:

- **Replication:** A process of copying database changes, in real-time, to one or more computers, typically across a WAN but sometimes across a LAN. The most complex form of replication is master-to-master replication, where data changes are gradually propagated and, thus, equally distributed, both to and from many equivalent master databases across a network of fully integrated databases. The WAN could be global or in the same company.
- **Standby failover:** This is specialized database that continually copies changes made in a primary database, in real-time. If an error situation occurs on the primary database, the standby database fails over and becomes the primary database. Some companies could

have multiple standby databases, distributed all over the world. There could even be standbys of standbys.

- **Clusters and grids:** This is a term used to describe gluing one or more computers together, such that many computers behave as a single, far-more-powerful computer.

Advanced features such as replication, failover, and clustering are requirements of high-performance, high-capacity database systems. These features require the specialized capabilities of server database engines like SQL Server and Oracle and are simply not possible with a desktop database system like Microsoft Access.

Access, Client/Server, and Multiple Tiers

Access is really a combination of an application development system, plus a database engine. The target market for Access as a database development system is not large-scale operations.

Most often, client-side applications that use server-provided data are built with tools like Visual Studio.NET or the Java programming language. These development systems provide no database capabilities themselves, yet, they support all the features needed by client-side database applications. A relatively simple application written in Visual Basic .NET or Microsoft Access is able to work with terabytes of data stored in SQL Server, without having to support all of the database operations supported by a server database engine.

Where does Access 2007 fit?

Now just imagine a scenario with an Access 2007 database on a single desktop computer. Then add an application or two, or maybe 10 or 20 different applications. These applications are all written in that same Access database. Next, imagine that the single computer, with the Access database supports hundreds of simultaneous users. If you've had any experience with Access, or a similar tool, such as dBase or Paradox, you'll know that this kind of scaled-up scenario is likely to drive the programmer to another job.

Microsoft has never represented Access as a strong candidate for an application servicing thousands of simultaneous users. Instead, Microsoft has always primarily represented Access as a single-user database system, or, at most, a workgroup database. Over time, of course, the capabilities built into Access have improved to the point that Access is now a valid tool for building client-side applications that hook into server-provided data. As mentioned earlier in this chapter, Access 2007 seamlessly uses data provided by SharePoint Services, no matter where that data is located. Similarly, Access is also able to use data provided by Microsoft SQL Server or Oracle, located on the local network or anywhere on the Internet.

Access has severe limitations in client/server environments and, realistically, cannot be used to drive an Internet site. Even in large-scale computer systems, a tool like Access has a place as a front-end development tool.

Access as a database repository

Access is used as a database repository throughout this book. The basic relational database consists of the ability to create tables containing fields and records, the ability to establish and enforce relationships between those tables. The application layer of an Access database adds commands allowing changes to data and commands allowing reading of data. Access has all this and then some. However, as a database repository (a thing to shove data into and change the data), Access has all that it needs. Figure 39-7 shows a picture of data stored in records (sometimes called *rows*) in a table in an Access database.

FIGURE 39-7

A database repository stores fields into records and into tables.

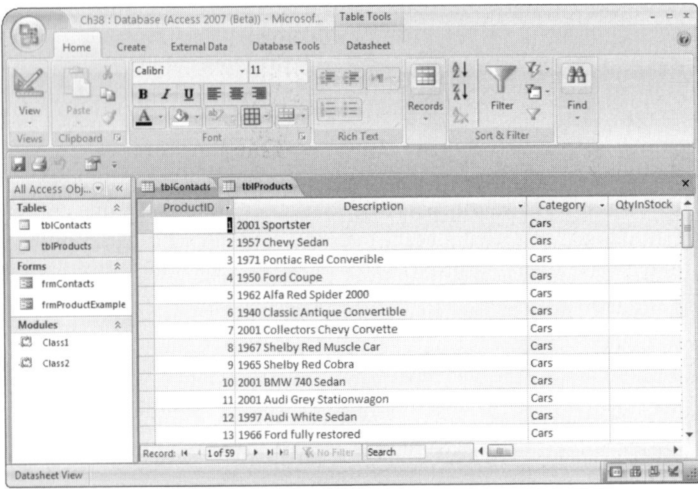

Figure 39-8 shows a table structure in Access, detailing the table's fields, data types, and specifications for each field.

Figure 39-9 shows relationships established and enforced between various tables inside an Access database.

FIGURE 39-8

A database repository stores data into tables with field and data-type definitions.

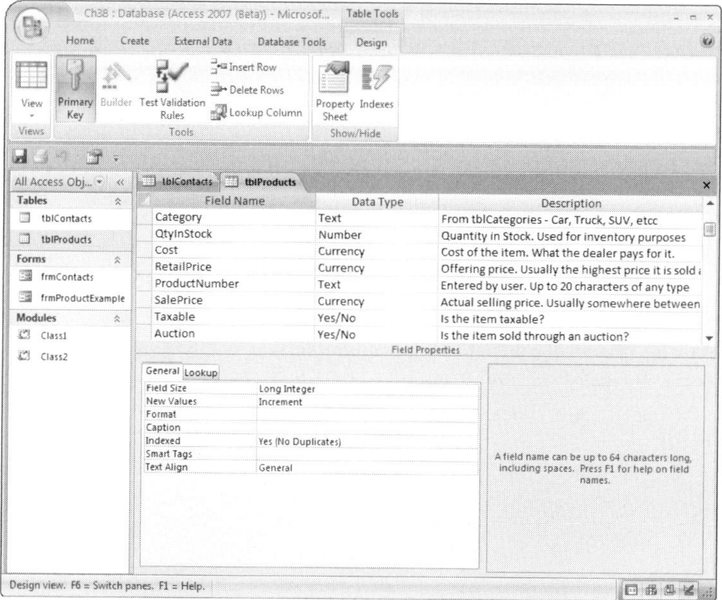

FIGURE 39-9

A relational database allows relationships between related tables.

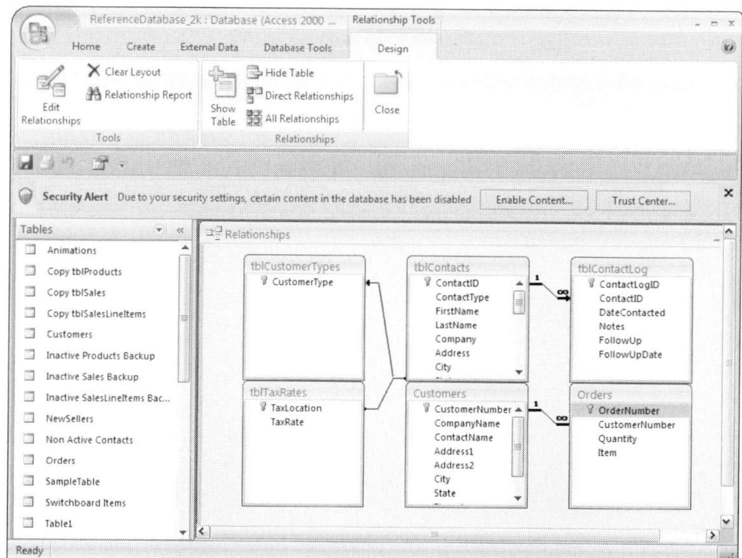

Access as both database and application

The real beauty and value of Access 2007 can be summarized in the following points:

- **Versatile:** Access is a highly versatile tool.
- **Multifunctional:** Access can be used as a database or an application SDK, or both.
- **Very easy to use**: Most importantly, Access is very easy to use. The interfaces are all graphical and all intuitive with end users in mind.

So, scalability, Internet databases, data warehouses are really not the target user population of Access, except in smaller organizations. So all those things are unimportant with respect to Access as a database and an application SDK.

Access as an Internet database

Although an Access database can be used to drive an Internet site, this practice is not recommended. The Access database engine just can't hold up to hundreds or thousands of simultaneous requests. Performance is sure to suffer, and database corruption is virtually guaranteed in such an environment. For any measure of scalability something like SQL Server is best. And SharePoint is increasingly a viable data repository for Access applications, or, at the very least, portions of the data provided by an Access 2007 application. Utilizing SharePoint Services and Access in tandem might allow adequate servicing of a small-scale Internet database, or perhaps a localized company or educational intranet.

Summary

This chapter has provided the basis for understanding the differences between an Access desktop application and a full-blown client/server database produced with a database engine such as SQL Server. Access 2007 is a fine development tool for producing client-side user interfaces to server-provided data. Access's excellent report writer, its superior forms designer, and VBA code combined to produce powerful and useful front ends for SQL Server and Oracle database data.

Microsoft SharePoint Services represents the future of client/server computing. Access 2007 seamlessly integrates SharePoint data. The user is unaware whether the data he sees on an Access form or report resides on his desktop computer, on the local network, or across the Internet. This level of remote data integration was simply not practical with previous versions of Access but is made possible by the new features in Access 2007.

Chapter 40

SQL Server as an Access Companion

Access projects are used to create and maintain SQL Server 2005 Express edition databases, or "full" SQL Server 2005 databases (from here on usually referred simply as SQL Server). You can also use an Access project to create the user-interface objects and forms, reports, macros, and modules, which get their data from SQL Server. The database window for a project looks very similar to the Access database window you are already accustomed to. In fact, creating the user-interface objects is virtually the same as creating them in Access.

ON the CD-ROM This chapter uses a database named `Chapter40.accdb`. If you have not already copied it onto your machine from the CD, you'll need to do so now.

CAUTION In general, SQL Server Express edition automatically installs as if it is to be executed on the same computer you're working on. In other words, even though SQL Server is a server database, the default for SQL Server Express is to execute on the same computer as a client environment such as Access or Excel.

NOTE SQL Server 2005 Express edition is free. You can download it from (`http://msdn.microsoft.com/vstudio/express/sql/`) and use it as a development and deployment database server. Chapter 41 discusses SQL Server 2005 Express Edition in more detail.

Before beginning this chapter, keep in mind that the intention when using SQL Server is to use SQL Server to store data and Access to host and present an application's screens (forms and reports).

IN THIS CHAPTER

- Learning about SQL Server connections
- Understanding Listener process
- Building Connection strings
- Comparing SQL Server and Access 2007 security
- Accessing SQL Server tables from Access 2007
- Using SQL Server stored procedures and views in Access 2007 applications
- Understanding SQL Server procedures, functions, and triggers

Downloading SQL Server 2005 Express Edition

Microsoft is vitally interested in developers learning and using SQL Server 2005. But, the truth is that acquiring and installing the "full" versions of SQL Server can be daunting tasks. As a server application, SQL Server is relatively expensive to license, and its hardware requirements are rather extensive. Not to worry! Microsoft has a wonderful gift available to you, free for the downloading.

SQL Server 2005 Express Edition is a somewhat stripped-down version of SQL Server intended to be used as a database engine for smallish workgroup applications, and as a test platform for developers working on SQL Server front-end applications. You may freely download and install SQL Server 2005 Express, install and use it on your computer, and even bundle it with applications you distribute to users.

SQL Server Express works and behaves exactly like SQL Server Enterprise, its much bigger brother. SQL Server Express supports all of the data types, stored procedures, triggers, and other database objects used in SQL Server Enterprise. In fact, migrating a SQL Server Express database to SQL Server Enterprise involves nothing more than disconnecting from SQL Server Express and connecting the database files to SQL Server Enterprise.

The primary differences between the standard editions of SQL Server 2005 and SQL Server Express is that SQL Server Express databases are limited to 4 GB in size (twice that of Access 2007!), and SQL Server Express does not support some of the more advanced features of SQL Server Standard and Enterprise Editions. Otherwise, the database engines in all SQL Server 2005 editions are identical.

You really owe it to yourself and your users to take a look at SQL Server 2005 Express. At the time of publication, the official home of SQL Server 2005 Express Edition can be found at `http://msdn.microsoft.com/vstudio/express/sql`, or do a Web search for "SQL Server Express download."

This chapter examines a number of different ways to access SQL Server data from Access 2007. Although there are no SQL Server object designers (tables, stored procedures, views, and so on) in the `.accdb` file format, you can use Open Database Connectivity (ODBC) to link to SQL Server data objects. However, if you choose to use the Access 2000 ADP data file format you still have access to the full range of SQL Server object designers (as in earlier versions of Access). You can edit existing or create new tables, stored procedures, and views when using the ADP file format.

Be aware, however, that when you create an ADP file in Access 2007 (File ➪ New ➪ Browse, then select ADP from the Save as Type drop-down list), you're actually creating an Access 2000–format data file. This isn't a big issue for most developers, but you may encounter situations where Access 2007 features cannot be supported in an application because the file is not an `.accdb`.

Connecting to SQL Server

One of the most fundamental operations with any large-scale multiuser database engine, such as SQL Server, is connecting to the database. Connecting directly to SQL Server, using SQL Server front-end tools is quite easy. The most basic connection to a database engine such as SQL Server, or even Oracle Database, is called just that: a connection. A connection is made by routing to that database on a specific computer, using a username and password (for security), usually using some type of network protocol such as TCP/IP.

What is a listener?

In SQL Server 2005 Enterprise Edition, a Windows service called SQL Browser is designated as the SQL Server database listening process. A listening process (or listener) quite literally listens over a network for requests to connect to a database. Computers on an Ethernet network place messages onto the network pipeline. Those messages are continually passed around the pipeline, where a message is routed to by routers, based on an IP address, and sent to the computer having the matching IP address.

A listener listens on a network for messages with an IP address matching its own. When the listener hears a network message directed to its IP address, the listener removes the message packet from the network and services the message. The listener asks the server for a database connection to use for processing the message. When the server grants a connection to the database, the listener hands the connection over to a database server process (server database engines like SQL Server are *multi-threaded*, and can simultaneously process many, many requests). The database server processes the request (perhaps a query), and then passes the result back to the sender. Because the server process assumes responsibility for servicing the user's request, the listener is able to continue listening for new database connection requests.

The interaction between the listener process and the database server means that the database engine does not have to spend time listening for messages directed its way. Instead, the highly specialized listener serves as a "traffic controller" for the database engine, enabling the engine to continue working at top-speed on user requests. Once the database engine allocates an execution thread to process the message handed to it by the listener, the listener returns to its primary task of listening for the appropriate types of messages on the network.

What is a connection string?

The specification that is used to communicate with a database is called a *connection string*. A connection string is made up of a number of things:

- **Hostname:** The host is the computer where the database server resides.
- **Database name:** The name of a database on a specific server. SQL Server allows for multiple databases in a single installation, as well as multiple SQL Server installations on a single computer. Now and then, a SQL Server installation services a single database for each database server.

- **Authentication:** A username and password are used for security. Only authorized users will have usernames and passwords; thus, only people with usernames and passwords have access. In some environments, the username and password can use an operating system username and password. In other cases, a username and password can be part of the database software itself.

The easiest way to connect to a SQL Server database may be to use a command-line shell utility called SQLCMD that comes with both SQL Server and SQL Server Express (look in the `C:\Program Files\Microsoft SQL Server\90\Tools\Binn` folder). SQLCMD provides a simple, command-driven interface to SQL Server. Although not practical for managing complex databases, SQLCMD provides a simple way to verify a SQL Server installation.

The options for SQLCMD are shown in Figure 40-1.

FIGURE 40-1

The SQLCMD utility has numerous options.

```
Select Command Prompt
Copyright (c) Microsoft Corporation.  All rights reserved.

usage: Sqlcmd            [-U login id]          [-P password]
  [-S server]            [-H hostname]          [-E trusted connection]
  [-d use database name] [-l login timeout]     [-t query timeout]
  [-h headers]           [-s colseparator]      [-w screen width]
  [-a packetsize]        [-e echo input]        [-I Enable Quoted Identifiers]
  [-c cmdend]            [-L[c] list servers[clean output]]
  [-q "cmdline query"]   [-Q "cmdline query" and exit]
  [-m errorlevel]        [-V severitylevel]     [-W remove trailing spaces]
  [-u unicode output]    [-r[0|1] msgs to stderr]
  [-i inputfile]         [-o outputfile]        [-z new password]
  [-f <codepage> | i:<codepage>[,o:<codepage>]] [-Z new password and exit]
  [-k[1|2] remove[replace] control characters]
  [-y variable length type display width]
  [-Y fixed length type display width]
  [-p[1] print statistics[colon format]]
  [-R use client regional setting]
  [-b On error batch abort]
  [-v var = "value"...]  [-A dedicated admin connection]
  [-X[1] disable commands, startup script, enviroment variables [and exit]]
  [-x disable variable substitution]
  [-? show syntax summary]

C:\Documents and Settings\Gavin Powell>_
```

Highlighted in Figure 40-1 are the two most significant options, which are `-S server` (the computer on which SQL Server is running) and `-d use database name` (the name of a database within the SQL Server installation).

NOTE **The name of the server in Figure 40-1 (`-S server`) is in reality a SQL Server *instance* name, not the name of a computer. Figure 40-1 shows a hostname which is the name of a computer on a network. When installing SQL Server, the default name applied to the SQL Server instance is the name of the host computer. Also, by default, SQL Server security is set to use the user's login name and password as authentication. In other words, SQL Server uses Windows security and the name of the machine on the network.**

When using the SQLCMD utility, the easiest way to communicate with a SQL Server database is with the following command to get to a specific SQL Server installation:

```
sqlcmd -S mycomputer
```

And the following more refined command to connect to a specific database, within a specific SQL Server installation:

```
sqlcmd -S mycomputer -d mydatabase
```

Figure 40-2 shows two connection screens for a tool called SQL Server Management Studio (SQL Server Management Studio can be downloaded from the same site as SQL Server Express). The screen on the left is connecting to a SQL Server on a remote computer called P450, using a SQL Server stored username and password to authenticate. The screen on the right side of Figure 40-2 is on the local computer, using the Windows username to authenticate.

FIGURE 40-2

Connecting to a SQL Server in the Management Studio

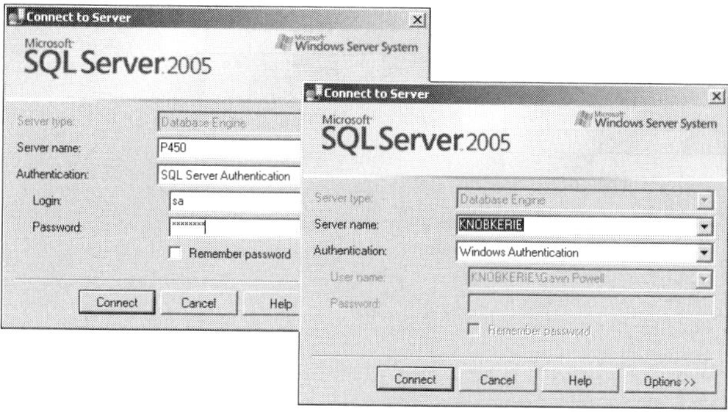

As you can see, the connection parameters (making up the connection string) are the same for both the command-line shell SQLCMD utility and for the windows GUI Management Studio connection to a SQL Server.

Connecting to SQL Server from Access

Creating a connection between Access and SQL Server environments requires a little something extra, as opposed to just a simple database connection, because both Access and SQL Server are essentially autonomous environments that must work together. As with many relational databases running under Windows, drivers are used to allow tools such as SQL Server and Access to communicate. As is common with many Microsoft software tools and toys, special drivers are created to facilitate communication between different software products. These drivers can be used to connect tools such as Excel and Access to an Oracle or DB2 database or, in this case, an Access database connected to SQL Server.

The drivers in question fall into a number of categories and include Object Database Connectivity (ODBC), Object Linked Embedding (OLE), and native drivers. Native drivers are often the best and fastest way to connect to server database engines, but they tend to be less generic and adaptable, and likely to apply to one specific product or database. Many of these drivers are produced by Microsoft because they all run under Windows operating systems. Some individual vendors do produce their own ODBC and OLE drivers. Microsoft drivers are often said to be more reliable, but that is an issue open to debate.

Let's focus on an ODBC driver allowing Access to communicate with a SQL Server. How does one deal with an ODBC driver? You have to create an ODBC data source, then the reference the ODBC data source from within Access. First, you create an instance of an ODBC driver, on your client computer, provide the ODBC driver a name (Access associates with that name). Then Access talks to the data source name (DSN), which is hooked to the ODBC drive. The ODBC driver in turn contains the connection string to the SQL Server, which talks to the SQL Server database either on your local computer or remotely, to another computer, across a network.

Create a data source as follows:

1. **Go to Windows Start menu, and choose Settings ➪ Control Panel.**
2. **In the Control Panel, double-click the Administrative Tools option, and select Data Sources (ODBC).**

   The three ODBC configuration options are

   - User DSN: A User DSN applies to a specific user on the client computer on which the User DSN is created.
   - System DSN: A System DSN is similar to a User DSN except it applies over a network (to a certain extent).
   - File DSN: A File DSN creates a connection configuration (a connection string), for a database, into a file on your client computer.

Of these three options, perhaps the File DSN is most useful in most situations. Because the connection information is stored in a file (the default location for DSN files is `C:\Program Files\Common Files\ODBC\Data Sources`), it is easy for you to share a DSN configuration with other users. Sharing a File DSN is easy: simply locate the DSN on your machine and attach it to an email, or move it to a common location on the network. User DSNs and System DSNs are actually stored in the computer's registry and must be manually set up on each computer needing access to a data source.

Essentially, what you are doing in this situation is creating a link from Access to data that is stored in SQL Server. Therefore, tables are maintained in SQL Server, and the front-end application (queries, forms, reports, VBA code, and so on) is maintained in Access. In Chapter 17, you examined importing tables into Access, making copies of metadata and data, from something like a SQL Server or an Oracle database, creating complete copies of data in an Access database. In this case, you want to simply link between Access and SQL Server because data are maintained in SQL Server, and not copied in their entirety in Access. How can you do this?

1. **In Figure 40-3, you can see that you select the `External Data` tab, the Import section, and the `More` drop-down control from the Access user interface.**

FIGURE 40-3

Linking to an ODBC data source

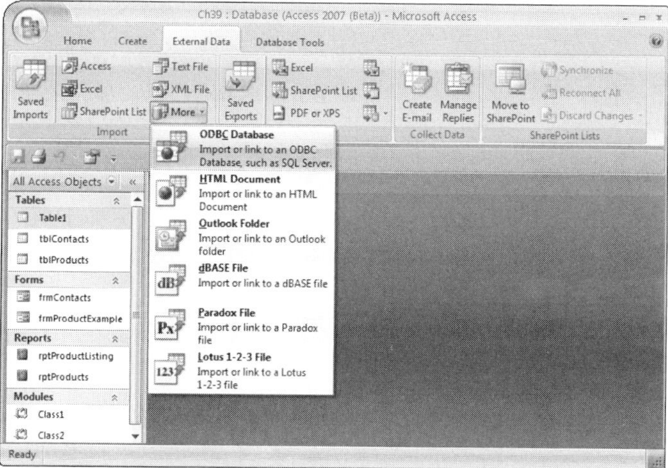

2. **From the `More` drop-down control select `ODBC Database` as a source to link to. As shown in Figure 40-4, select to link to a table in an external database. Click `OK` to continue.**

FIGURE 40-4

Linking to a table stored externally to Access

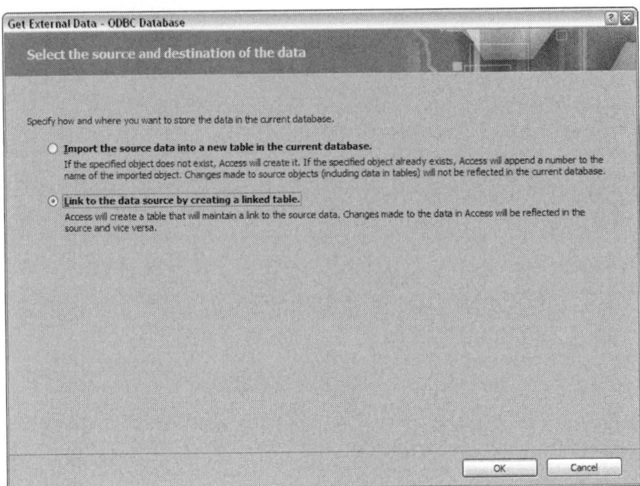

The screen you get is as shown in Figure 40-5.

FIGURE 40-5

Selecting a data source type

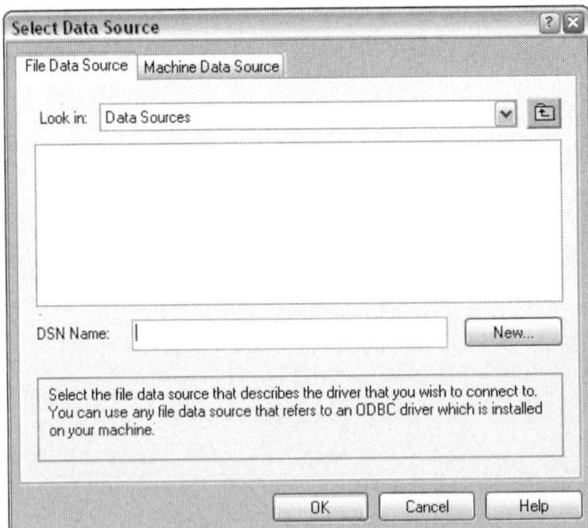

The options are to link to a File Data Source, a User Data Source, or (possibly) a System DSN to communicate between Access and SQL Server. You will see a System Data Source tab in the `Select Data Source` dialog box when a System DSN is already available on your computer.

3. **Type `LocalSQLServer` into the DSN Name box and click `New`.**
4. **Scroll all the way down the list of drivers and select the `SQL Server driver` (ignore the `SQL Native Client driver` for now), and click Next.**
5. **When asked where to store the File DSN file, click the `Browser` button, enter `LocalSQLServer` in the `File Name` box, click Save, and click `Next` when back at the screen with the Browse button.**

   You should have a screen entitled Create New Data Source.
6. **Click Finish.**

   Your next screen is shown in Figure 40-6.
7. **Note how the File DSN filename you created is now shown in the data source name box in Figure 40-6. Enter that, as shown in Figure 40-6, into the other two entry fields.**

   The description is not essential. The name of the SQL Server shown in Figure 40-6 is necessary and should obviously be a SQL Server you can actually get to, if you have access to one.

FIGURE 40-6

Creating a new data source connection to a SQL Server

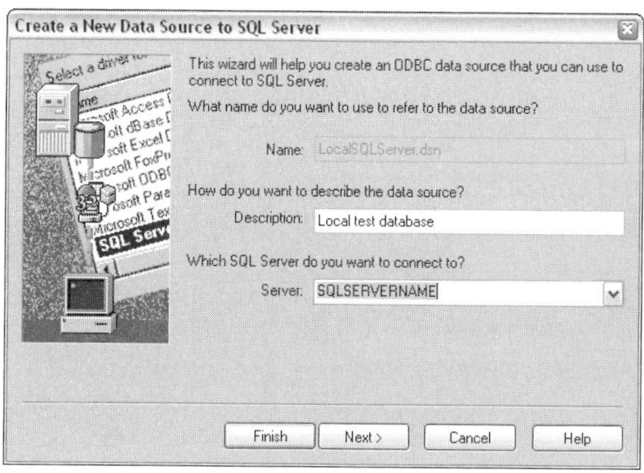

8. Click Next.
9. As you can see in Figure 40-7, you can change all sorts of things.

FIGURE 40-7

Authentication of data source connection to a SQL Server

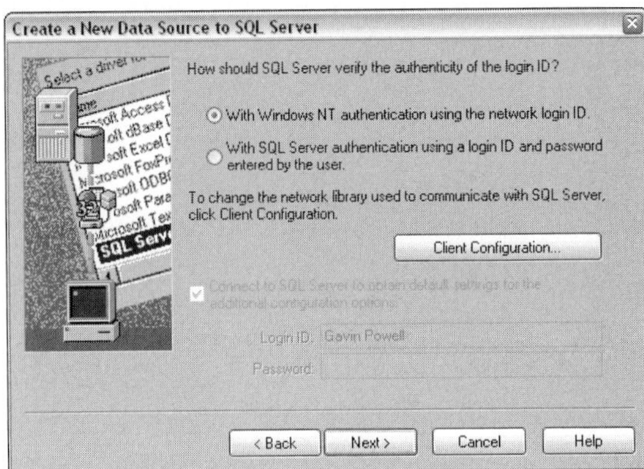

The default settings shown in Figure 40-7 assume you have a SQL Server with operating system authentication (SQL Server uses your Windows login name and password to authenticate you and grant permission to its databases).

10. Click Next.

The next screen, shown in Figure 40-8, shows that my SQL Server installation contains a database called test.

FIGURE 40-8

Changing the name of the default database to access

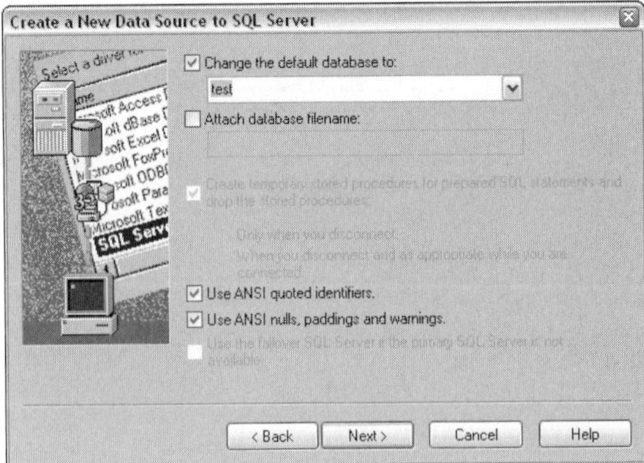

In Figure 40-8, I have checked the `Change the Default Database To` checkbox, and changed the text of the database name from master to that of test.

11. **Click Next.**
12. **The following screen you don't need to worry about. Just click the `Finish` button on it. The screen after that you should worry about. Figure 40-9 shows the last dialog box of the SQL Server Setup wizard after clicking the Test Data Source button.**

    If the connection fails, go back over these steps again. If that doesn't help, you might want to consider talking to a database administrator or a network administrator.

TIP SQL Server is rather fussy about its name. Prior to SQL Server 2000, SQL Server assumed the same name as its host computer because only one instance of SQL Server could be installed on a computer. However, beginning with SQL Server 2000, a single computer can host multiple SQL Sever installations, so the name you use to reference a SQL Server instance is a bit more complex. The syntax used to reference a SQL Server instance is `MyComputer\MySQLServerInstance`, where `MyComputer` is the name of the host computer, and `MySQLServerInstance` is the instance you wish to reference.

If only a single SQL Server instance is installed on the local computer, you may be able to, quite simply, specify `(local)` as the name of server. Otherwise, you'll have to provide the name of the computer and the SQL Server instance name as described in the previous paragraph.

FIGURE 40-9

Ensuring a successful Access to ODBC to SQL Server connection

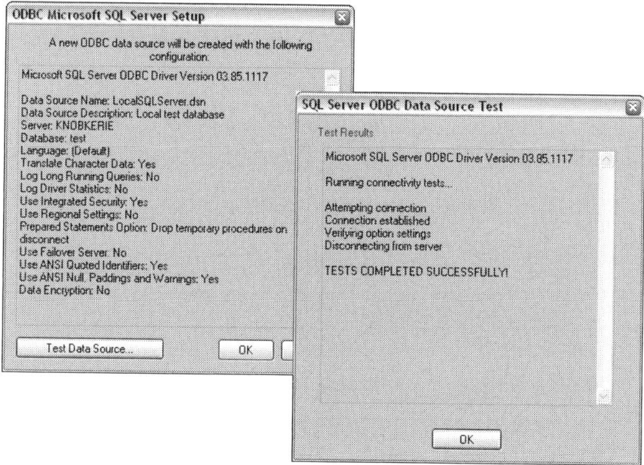

13. **Click OK on the first screen, and then click OK again on the second screen.**

    The resulting screen should look like what you see in Figure 40-10.

FIGURE 40-10

Using an ODBC connection to link to SQL Server using a File DSN

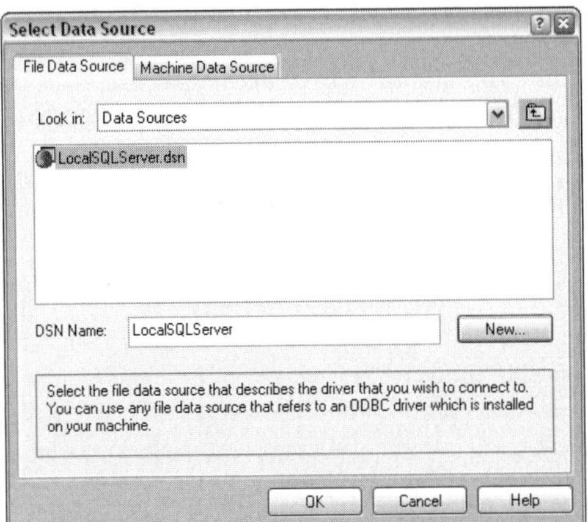

14. **If you want to create a User DSN, a System DSN, or both, go ahead and do so. You'll simply be creating multiple data sources to the same SQL Server database. Click `OK` to save the new DSN.**

    Ignore all the system tables (prefixed with `sys.`) and tables prefixed with `INFORMATION_SCHEMA` in the Link Tables dialog box. The tables you're interested in are generally at the top of the list in the Link Tables dialog box.

15. **Next select tables from the Link Tables dialog box shown in Figure 40-11.**

    In Figure 40-11, a single table has been created in the test database. The table is named `dbo.Table_1`, as highlighted in Figure 40-11. Click the OK button to close the `Link Tables` dialog box.

NOTE **`dbo` is shorthand for *database owner* and is the default prefix for all objects within a SQL Server database. A full explanation of SQL Server authentication, security, and ownership is well beyond the scope of this chapter. For the meantime, it's enough to understand that SQL Server supports multiple users, each of whom is identified by a name. When a user creates a SQL Server object, he creates the object with either his own name prefix, or with the default `dbo` prefix, depending on how SQL Server security is configured.**

16. Click OK.

    The next screen shows the fields to select from the table called `Table_1`. We've selected both fields, which are highlighted as shown in Figure 40-12.

FIGURE 40-11

Selecting tables from a SQL Server database

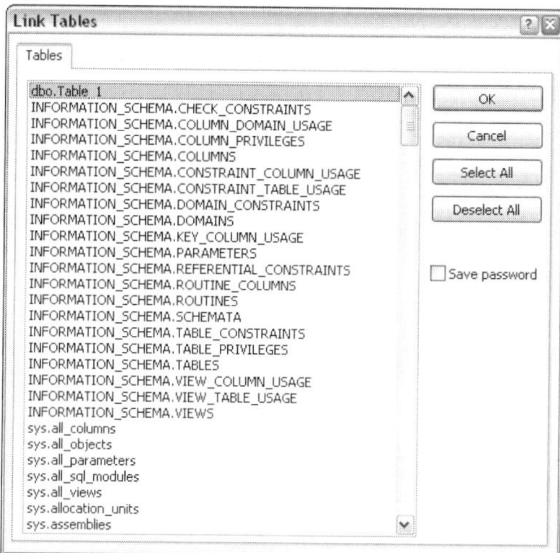

FIGURE 40-12

Selecting fields from a table, from a SQL Server database

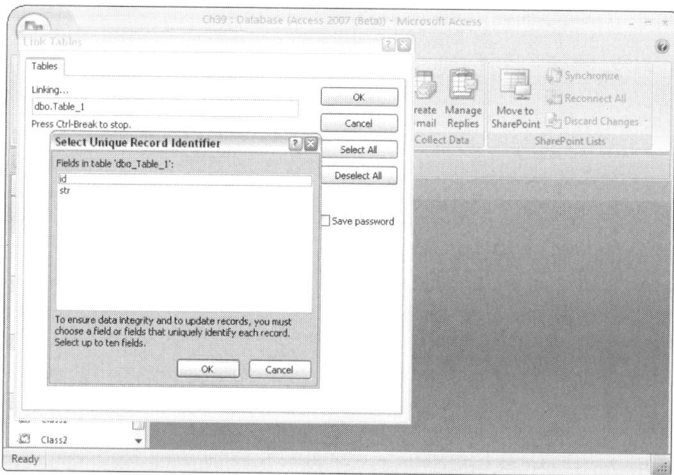

17. Click OK.

The result is a table linked from Access, into a SQL Server database. That data is shown in Figure 40-13, listing the contents of the table from within the Access 2007 graphical user interface (GUI).

FIGURE 40-13

A table linked from Access 2007 to SQL Server is entitled dba_<tablename> by default.

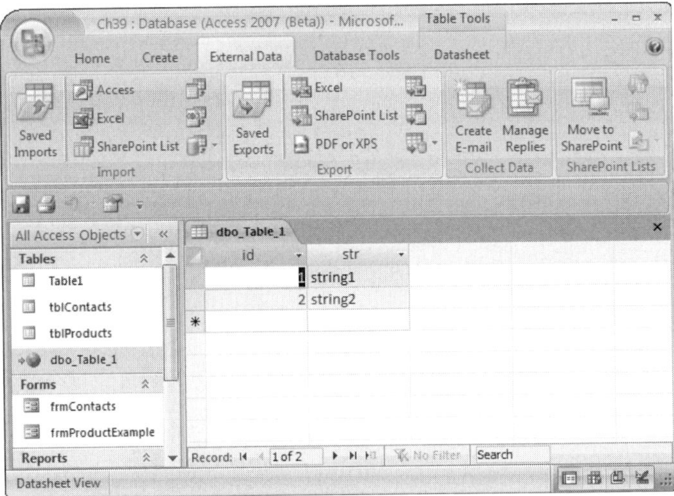

As you can see, connecting from Access 2007 to a SQL Server database is really quite simple, even if quite a number of steps are involved.

SQL Server security

SQL Server security works as many other large scale relational database do, with one small additional difference. Many relational databases such as Oracle Database authenticate by validating usernames and passwords, which are stored in the Oracle database as separate user definitions.

SQL Server can also validate in this manner, allowing a connection to a SQL Server database using a SQL Server username and password, stored within a SQL Server database. The additional factor with SQL Server is that it can authenticate a connection to a SQL Server with a local or even a network Windows username and password. Thus, if you've already logged in to Windows using a network username and password, you're essentially already connected in both the operating system and the SQL Server installation. In other words, when connecting to SQL Server using Windows authentication, the connection tool automatically uses the Windows username and password to connect to SQL Server, without any need to enter a username and password. This is perhaps the easiest and least obtrusive approach to connecting Access databases to SQL Server.

Oracle also supports connections through an operating-system-level username and password, but the process is not quite as seamless and transparent as with SQL Server and Windows. The obvious reason for that is because SQL Server and the Windows operating system are both produced by the same company — Microsoft. Oracle, on the other hand, operates on a variety of operating systems and does not benefit from a homogenous environment as SQL Server does. One of the major benefits of Microsoft software is its inherent integration with all types of software tools and kits.

Comparing Access 2007 and SQL Server Security

How is security in Access 2007 comparable with SQL Server? There is much in the way of security within Access. This includes security features such as trusted zones, trusted Web sites, trusted objects, and restrictions on who can view or change specific documents. When using the `.mdb` file format, Access allows creation of users, plus granting and revoking of a minimum number of privileges to those users. Access users and privilege details are added to a workgroup information file (`.mdw` filename extension), where workgroups are groups of users.

An Access workgroup is much the same as a role in SQL Server. And an Access user is much the same as a SQL Server user. Access allows authentication of users with passwords. SQL Server does the same.

The only real difference is that the privileges allowed for allocation to users in Access are few. Privileges in relational databases such as SQL Server and Oracle Database number in the hundreds and are divided into system and object privileges. A *system privilege* allows access to metadata, such as creating a new table. An *object privilege* allows access to data, such as adding new records to a table.

Access (when using the `.mdb` format with workgroup security configured) pretty much parallels Oracle and SQL Server security. Unlike Access, however, SQL Server and Oracle security is generally applied to data, while Access workgroup security applies to data and the user interface. Data security restricts or allows access to data. From the perspective of data in a SQL Server database, you secure the content of applications, rather than the actual objects or front-end customer facing parts of an application.

SQL Server security is very comprehensive. Data stored in SQL Server is secured not only by the SQL Server database engine, but also by the Windows operating system, as well is whatever security has been applied to the network system on which SQL Server operates. In addition, because a SQL Server database is normally located on a dedicated server computer, the database itself is inaccessible to users. There is very little chance that a user would be able to download a SQL Server database and carry it away on a removable disk.

When it comes to object security, there is some crossover between Access and SQL Server with the advent of object-relational databases (including objects into relational databases). For example, the types of objects that can be stored in a database include things like Word documents, XML documents, images, audio files, and so on. At the data level, SQL Server security can restrict access to specific objects.

With respect to Access being also an application tool, something like an XML document can be executed from within a browser. So, you can effectively secure something like an XML document in both a database and an application, or even both. Even for the scenario of combined features between Access and SQL Server, there is still a distinct difference between database-level security and application security, because a database stores data and an application consumes that data. Again, there is crossover, such as with stored procedures in SQL Server, because stored procedures in a relational database can operate functionally on data. An application operates functionally on data.

Access DDL Security Commands

Access 2007 allows execution of the following Data Definition Language (DDL) commands within Access. These commands cannot be executed from within Access onto another database such as SQL Server. Similar DDL commands can be executed in SQL Server directly, regardless of any communicating Access 2007 database. These DDL commands are allowed in Access 2007:

- CREATE USER: Create one or more users with username and password:

  ```
  CREATE USER <user> <password> [, ... ]
  ```

- ALTER USER: Change an existing Access user's password:

  ```
  ALTER USER <user> PASSWORD <new> <old>
  ```

- CREATE GROUP: Create one or more groups with group name and personal identifier for a person or group of persons (a person is an Access user):

  ```
  CREATE GROUP <group> <pid> [, ... ]
  ```

  A group allows you to group privileges together (like a role in SQL Server). Then you can subsequently add users to that group, granting all the privileges assigned to the group to any user added to that group.

- ADD USER: Add one or more existing Access users into an existing group:

  ```
  ADD USER <user> [, ... ]
  ```

- ALTER DATABASE PASSWORD: Change the password for an entire Access database:

  ```
  ALTER DATBASE PASSWORD <new> <old>
  ```

- GRANT **and** REVOKE: Grant privileges to, and revoke privileges from, a user or a group:

  ```
  GRANT <privilege> [,...] ON {TABLE <table>|OBJECT <object>}
       TO <user>|<group>
  REVOKE <privilege> [,...] ON {TABLE <table>|OBJECT <object>}
       FROM <user>|<group>
  ```

  Some of the more interesting allowed privileges are as follows:

  - SELECT: Read data from a table.
  - INSERT: Add new records into a table.
  - DELETE: Delete records from a table.
  - UPDATE: Change existing records in a table.
  - CREATE **and** DROP: Create or drop an object, respectively, such as creating a new table.
  - SELECTSECURITY **and** UPDATESECURITY: Read and change security, respectively, such as user and password changes.
  - DBPASSWORD: Change the password for an entire Access database.

- DROP: The DROP command has different variations allowing dropping of users and groups:

```
DROP USER <user> [, ...]
DROP USER <user> [,... ] FROM GROUP
DROP GROUP <group> [, ...]
```

Working with SQL Server Objects from Access

SQL Server contains all sorts of things that Access does not, in addition to standard relational tables.

The term *relational tables* implies that both Access and SQL Server contain tables and indexes, as well as primary and foreign keys with enforced referential integrity.

SQL Server also supports database objects such as stored procedures, functions, and triggers. Whatever is linked from SQL Server (not imported) can be utilized from Access tables linked to the underlying SQL Server objects.

Everything is SQL Server–based because Access 2007 can do one of two things:

- **Import tables (with data) from SQL Server as a copy of the SQL Server table.** Any changes to the copy in Access will not be reflected in SQL Server. And any changes to the same tables in SQL Server will require a refresh in Access, which in this case means a full and complete re-import of an entire table.
- **Link to tables that remain within SQL Server.** Linked Access tables can update SQL Server data because the table and data actually reside in SQL Server, not in Access. In fact, the interaction between an Access table linked to SQL Server is so seamless that most users are unaware that they're working with remote data.

CROSS-REF **Data types and a comparison between Access 2007 and SQL Server data types are covered in Chapter 41. The precise meshing of tables between Access and SQL Server is more relevant there. The chapter covers upsizing, which is essentially converting from Access and SQL Server. The data types in SQL Server are much more comprehensive. This chapter deals with top-level objects, such as tables and views, not the structure of those objects (the fields within tables). The real task of this chapter at this point, in explaining SQL Server as an Access 2007 companion, is to show which SQL Server objects can be accessed from Access 2007.**

Using SQL Server tables from Access

The Access 2007 `.accdb` database looks as shown in Figure 40-14.

FIGURE 40-14

The Access 2007 tables in the `Chapter40.accdb` database

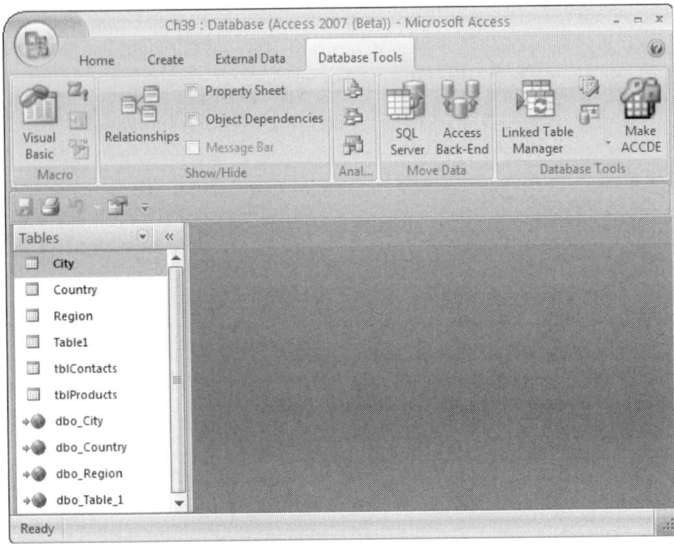

As shown in Figure 40-14, some tables have been imported from SQL Server, and some tables are linked. The Region table is an imported table, which means the table and its data reside in Access. The data of the Region table are shown in Figure 40-15.

As you can see in Figure 40-15, a new record is being added, for the region of The Planet Mars. Obviously, the population is 0. The area is set to 1,000 just for fun. Some points need to be made here:

- The copied Region table has had a new record added in Access as soon as the record is entered and the focus of the Access interface is moved off the row.
- The new record is not present in the SQL Server database because the table resides within Access.
- There is no way to copy the new record into the SQL Server database. Refresh can only be performed by copying from SQL Server to Access once again, thus removing the new record because it is added in Access.

FIGURE 40-15

Adding a new record to an Access 2007 copied table

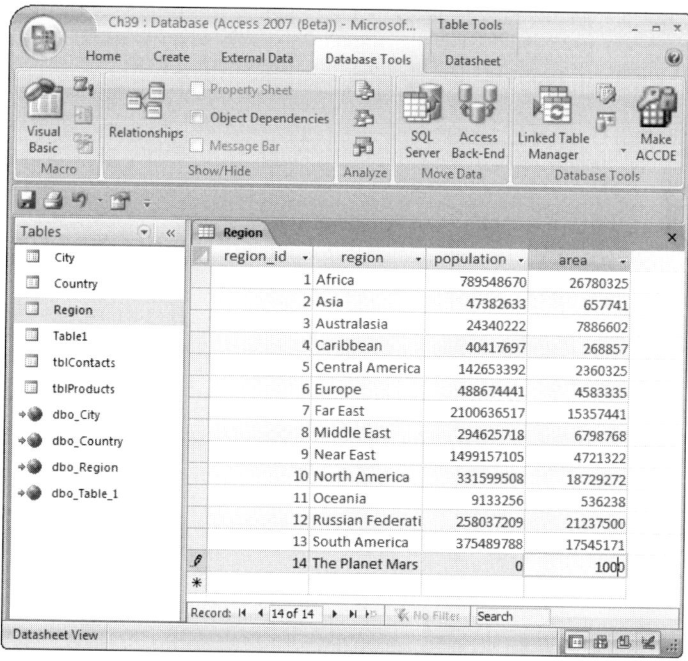

There is no refresh for imported tables in either direction.

Linked tables allow data refresh because the data is maintained in one place. The way that changes are sent back into SQL Server are as shown in Figure 40-16.

As shown in Figure 40-16, changes to tables linked to Access do not appear to be real-time refreshed into SQL Server. Changes are refreshed on command. This method actually makes sense with respect to the difference in the functionality and purposes of Access 2007, as compared with SQL Server 2005.

You could, of course, refresh the other way around and execute a command like this in the SQL Server database. Figure 40-17 shows a script executed in the query window of the SQL Server management studio tool, adding a new record, and then displaying it on the screen.

FIGURE 40-16

Access e-mails changes to SQL Server

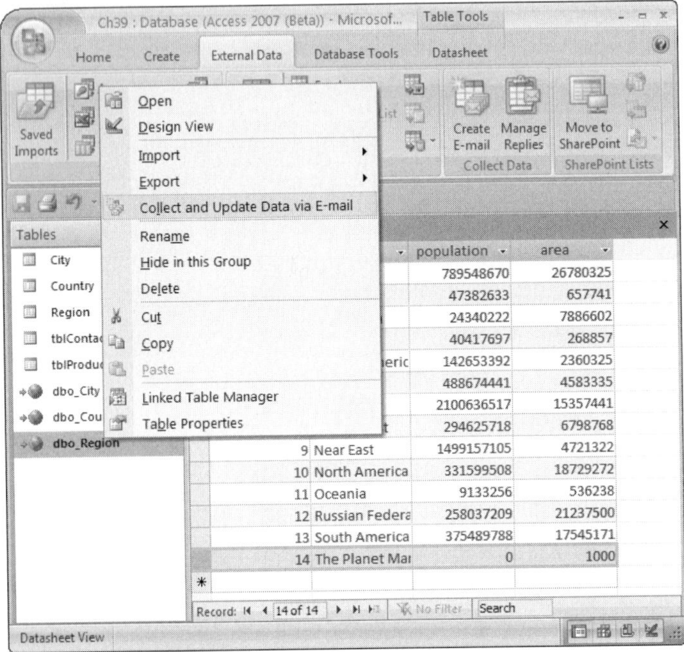

FIGURE 40-17

Making changes directly into SQL Server tables

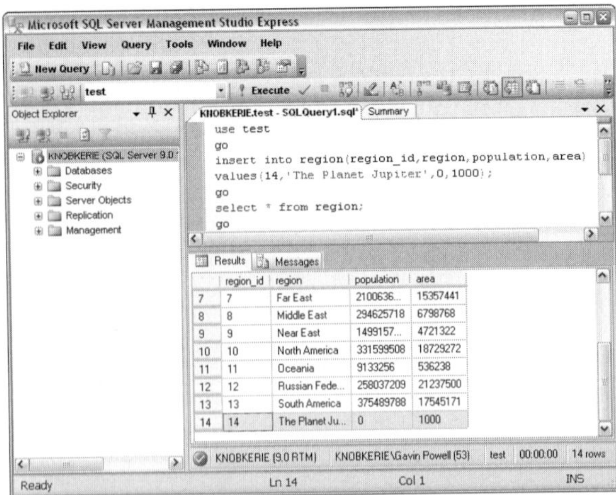

This is the script used in Figure 40-17:

```
use test
go
insert into region(region_id,region,population,area)
values(14,'The Planet Jupiter',0,1000);
go
select * from region;
go
```

After running this short script and reopening the Access 2007 database, the linked table (dbo_Region) contains the record just added in SQL Server (see Figure 40-18).

In Figure 40-18, the imported table (Region) does not contain the new record added to SQL Server, because the copied table has not been recopied.

FIGURE 40-18

SQL Server changes are automatically reflected only in linked Access tables.

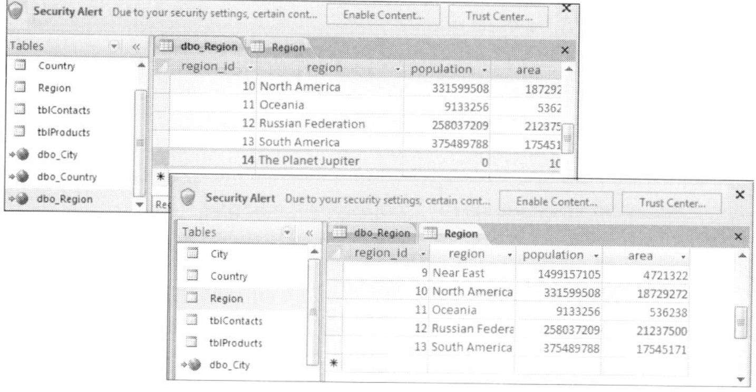

Views in SQL Server

Another object used in larger relational databases such as SQL Server and Oracle is called a *view*. A view is really a stored query that joins tables and filters data. Essentially, when you create a form in Access, you're creating a query behind that form. A SQL Server view object creates a query which exists only as a chunk of SQL code. When a client application references the view, SQL Server executes the SQL statements, producing a table-like view of the data.

The result is that an Access query can be executed against a SQL Server view, as if the view were a table. When the view is accessed in a SELECT command, the records are retrieved from tables underlying the view and the records returned to the client. The view itself can include query command adjustments such as filtering and re-sorting.

Figure 40-19 shows the creation of a view object in SQL Server. This view object is a join of regions and countries, returning only the region and country names, all in alphabetical order by the name of the country, showing a resort of the data by jumbling up the regions. The query and result are both shown in Figure 40-19.

The code used for the view creation in Figure 40-19 is as follows:

```
use test
go
create view countries as
select r.region, c.country from region r join
   country c on(c.region_id = r.region_id)
go
select * from countries order by country;
go
```

The view appears as any other SQL Server table when you ask Access 2007 to link to SQL Server data, as shown in Figure 40-20.

FIGURE 40-19

Creating a view in SQL Server

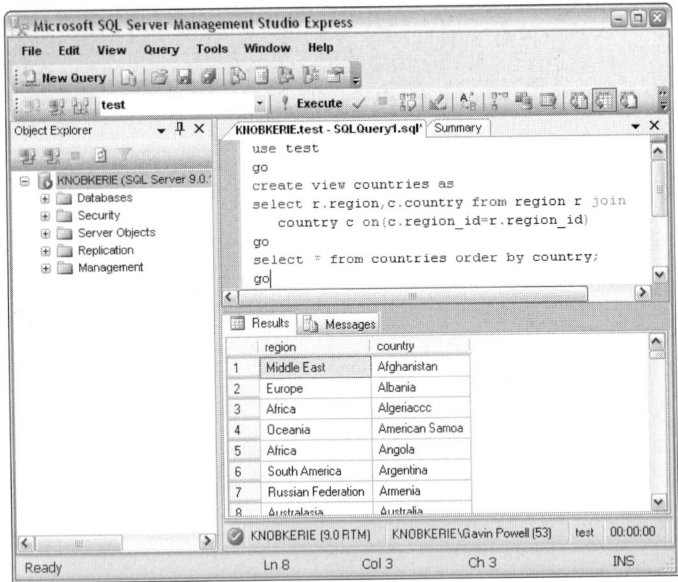

FIGURE 40-20

A view is the same as a table with respect to Access 2007.

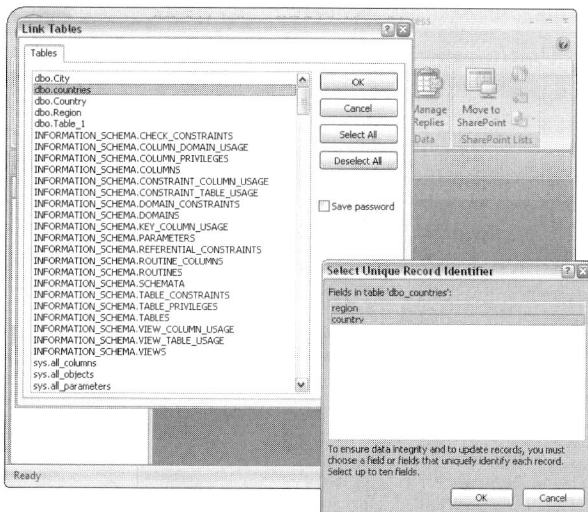

Also, shown in the bottom-right corner is an extra window brought up by Access when linking to the SQL Server view, requesting a unique identifier (what amounts to a primary key), to identify each record. This is obviously the combination of, or composite of, the region and country names.

The unique identifier is needed so that, when data in the view is changed in Access, Access can tell SQL Server which row has been updated. Without a unique identifier, it would be impossible for Access to reliably update SQL Server data.

Stored procedures, functions, and triggers

Traditionally, a stored procedure is an addition to the relational database model, allowing for some processing inside a relational database. The original intention of stored procedures was as a chunk of SQL code acting solely on data in a database. In recent years, some relational databases have made stored procedure languages powerful enough that they can perform number-crunching processing and calculations, often performing tasks that have nothing to do with data stored in a database.

NOTE **Stored procedures, functions, and triggers are not queries. A stored procedure is a block of SQL statements that are executed as a single entity.**

One use of stored procedures is as a handy container for storing all of the SQL statements that you use throughout an application. Instead of writing SQL statements in your application code, you can store them in the database as stored procedures, calling them from your code in much the same way that you call a function stored in an Access module. Some of the many benefits of stored procedures are as follows:

- **They can contain multiple SQL statements.**
- **They can call another stored procedure.**
- **They can receive parameters and return a value or a result set.**
- **They're stored in a semi-compiled, interpretive state on the database server, so they execute faster than if they were embedded in your code.** In other words, stored procedures are typically not compiled into a relational database as binary code, but they are usually pre-parsed, and partially pre-executed, making for faster execution.
- **They're stored in a common container in your application so that others can maintain them more easily because there is less database access code.**
- **After a stored procedure has been added to a SQL Server database, it is accessible to any client application using that database.** This means that an Access 2007 desktop database application will execute the exact same logic as a Web application written with Visual Studio .NET, if they both use the same stored procedure to access data.

Some disadvantages of stored procedures are as follows:

- **Overuse of stored procedures tends to place too much business logic into a database.** This can sometimes make number-crunching-type business logic execute in a database very slowly. Some types of processing are best left to application coding, which is often much better suited to intense calculations.
- **Overuse of stored procedures for data access can sometimes cause serious issues with network performance.**

Let's begin by creating a stored procedure in an Access `.accdb` file (not connected to SQL Server), and then execute that same stored procedure in Access. Follow these steps:

1. **Open the Access `.accdb` database for this chapter.**
2. **Click the `Create` ribbon tab and select `Query Design` from the Other group on the Access ribbon.**
3. **When you see the Show Table dialog box, click Close because you're going to create the query by writing SQL statements, not by using existing tables in the database.**
4. **At the top-left, click `SQL View` icon at the left side of the Access ribbon.**

   This gets you into the query text editor. Experiment by running a query such as this:

   ```
   SELECT * FROM REGION;
   ```
5. **Click the `Run` icon in the `Results` group at the left end of the Access ribbon.**
6. **Click the view icon at the top-left, and click the `SQL View` option.**

   This returns you to the text editor.

7. **Type in the following** `CREATE PROCEDURE` **command:**

```
CREATE PROCEDURE JumbledCountries () AS
SELECT r.region,c.country
FROM region r JOIN country c
ON(c.region_id=r.region_id);
```

NOTE **Unfortunately, the preceding statement cannot be verified because Access 2007 refuses to recognize the `CREATE PROCEDURE` statement. A `CREATE TABLE` error is also produced when attempting to execute the preceding `CREATE PROCEDURE` statement.**

Parameters can be passed to a stored procedure by including them in the procedure's definition as follows:

```
CREATE PROCEDURE (<parameter> [,... ]) AS ...
```

An Access 2007 stored procedure can be executed using the `EXECUTE` command:

```
EXECUTE <procedure> [<parameter> [, ... ] ]
```

You cannot create a function or a trigger in Access 2007. You also cannot access SQL Server procedures, functions, or triggers from an Access 2007 `.accdb`, but they can be useful in SQL Server. (These SQL Server objects can be accessed from the `.adp` file format.)

Now let's create the same two stored procedures in SQL Server, but directly in SQL Server, and see if we can execute them through a link with Access. This is the same procedure used previously, but this time it's created in SQL Server:

```
use test
go
CREATE PROCEDURE JumbledCountries () AS
SELECT r.region,c.country FROM region r JOIN country c
ON(c.region_id=r.region_id);
go
```

A function is an expression because it returns a value, and an expression can be part of another expression. So, a function can call another function, and so on. The following is a function:

```
use test
go
CREATE FUNCTION Density(@population AS INT, @area AS INT)
RETURNS INT
AS
BEGIN
  RETURN @population/@area;
END;
go
```

A trigger is a bit of SQL code that executes when some action occurs on a table in a database. Typically, triggers execute as before (`FOR` in SQL Server), after (`AFTER` in SQL Server), and as instead of (`INSTEAD OF` in SQL Server) triggers. As the name implies, a before trigger fires before data is changed in the table, while an after trigger fires after the data has changed.

Another important point about triggers is that they cannot contain transaction termination commands such as `COMMIT` and `ROLLBACK`, because other `INSERT`, `UPDATE`, `DELETE` commands, which are changing data, cause the trigger to execute. Allowing a transaction to terminate inside a trigger (triggered by a part of a calling transaction) is completely pointless because it negates the transactional aspect of the calling transaction. The biggest danger with triggers is that they can call themselves over and over, sometimes recursively, such that serious performance problems result with what can amount to an extremely large uncommitted transaction (a trigger can't contain a `COMMIT` or `ROLLBACK` command).

CAUTION **Using triggers to implement and enforce referential integrity is not a recommended practice for reasons mentioned earlier.**

Creating a trigger is very similar to a procedure or a function. This one creates an entry in a log file every time new product is added:

```
use test
go
CREATE TRIGGER LogEntries ON Products
  FOR INSERT
    INSERT INTO LogFile(id,event)
    VALUES(<autocounter>,'New Product added');
go
```

Summary

This chapter has taken a look at some of the capabilities possible when Access is partnered with SQL Server. Although some of the techniques used to access SQL Server have changed in Access 2007 the same capabilities are available as in previous versions of Access. Many features require you to use the Access 2000 `.adp` format instead of the Access 2007 `.accdb` file type.

In many ways, Access is the ideal interface tool for SQL Server data. SQL Server provides a high level of data security, the ability to service thousands of simultaneous users, and advanced data management tools such as stored procedures, views, and triggers. Also, the storage capacity of SQL Server installations is practically unlimited. Many SQL Server installations manage billions of records, making that data available to qualified client applications such as Access 2007.

Chapter 41

Upsizing Access Databases to SQL Server

IN THIS CHAPTER

Understanding the Access ADP data file type

Working with the Access 2007 Upsizing Wizard

Upsizing an Access application to SQL Server

Comparing Access and SQL Server data types

The Access 2007 Upsizing Wizard provides a quick and easy way to upsize Access data to a SQL Server database. Either SQL Server 2005 Express or full SQL Server can be the target of an Access upsizing process. The SQL Server database file is exactly the same, regardless of which edition of SQL Server is used.

NOTE SQL Server 2005 Express is a free download from the Microsoft MSDN Web site (`http://msdn.microsoft.com/vstudio/express/sql/`). SQL Server 2005 Express is a somewhat downsized version of SQL Server Enterprise and contains exactly the same core code as all SQL Server editions. The data file format, Transact-SQL syntax, security architecture, and other specifications are the same in SQL Server 2005 Express and SQL Server 2005 Enterprise. The primary differences between these database engines is that SQL Server 2005 Express does not include several of the more advanced features (such as full text searches) that SQL Server Enterprise includes. Also, SQL Server 2005 Express supports databases up to 4GB in size (SQL Server Enterprise supports terabyte databases). However, SQL Server Express includes SQL Server Management Studio and SQL Server Reporting Services. Furthermore, unlike the Microsoft Database Engine (MSDE) that preceded SQL Server Express, the Express edition does not contain the performance throttle that inhibited more than a few connections to MSDE. Consult the SQL Server 2005 Express pages on the Microsoft Web site for more details. SQL Server 2005 Express is the ideal database engine for small workgroups and individuals wanting to make the leap into client-server architecture. And the price is definitely right.

The Upsizing Wizard automatically creates an *Access Data Project* (a special type of Access data file that allows you to work directly with a SQL Server database). In Chapters 16 and 40 you saw the simplest and quickest method of upsizing Access data to SQL Server: simply linking SQL Server data to an existing Access application (presumably, the SQL Server data was imported into SQL Server using SQL Server Integration Services [SSIS]). Although this option moves your data to a client-server architecture, it takes you only part of the way. Even though the data now resides in a client-server database, the linked tables in the existing *Access front end* (the forms, reports, and data-access pages) continue to use the Microsoft Jet database engine to retrieve information from the database.

Access Data Projects (ADPs) are frequently used to create and maintain SQL Server 2005 databases (from here on usually referred to simply as SQL Server). You can also use an Access Data Project to create the user-interface objects and forms, reports, macros, and modules, which get their data from SQL Server. The ADP user interface looks very much like the standard Access database window you are already accustomed to. In fact, creating the user-interface objects is virtually the same as creating them in Access.

ON the CD-ROM **This chapter uses the database named `Chapter41.accdb` on this book's CD. If you haven't already copied it onto your machine from the CD, you'll need to do so now. You'll also need access to some version of SQL Server (Standard, Enterprise, or Express) if you intend to practice upsizing Access databases to SQL Server.**

Before beginning this chapter in earnest, you need to keep in mind a few things about transferring data to SQL Server. When upsizing an Access database to SQL Server, SQL Server takes over data-management tasks. All of the tables, queries, and other data-oriented objects are contained within the SQL Server database. An Access `.adp` file is not much more than an interface to the SQL Server database and contains the forms, reports, VBA code, and other user-interface components.

The good news is that if you're moving from an existing Access front end to SQL Server, you don't have to build these objects from scratch. The Access Upsizing Wizard does most of the work for you, preserving the work you've already invested in the user interface of your Access application.

Using linked SQL Server tables in an Access front end can be an acceptable solution for many small-workgroup environments. However, for environments with large numbers of users or where large volumes of data are processed, you need a solution that utilizes client-server architecture in both the front-end and back-end databases.

NOTE **Although this chapter focuses on upsizing an Access database to SQL Server, a very common technique for using SQL Server data in an Access application is to use ODBC to link to SQL Server tables. Chapter 40 discusses this process and shows how to access SQL Server data from a standard Access 2007 `.accdb` file. The `.adp` file created by the Upsizing Wizard is actually an Access 2000 format data file, but it features all of the user-interface enhancements seen in the `.accdb` data file type.**

Upsizing Access and the Upsizing Wizard

Today, many organizations are becoming more and more dependent on their database applications to manage everyday business operations, and these applications are growing both in volume of data and number of users. Applications that you may have developed using Microsoft Access even in the past year or two may be starting to strain the organization's network. At the same time, client-server databases like SQL Server are becoming more popular, even with smaller businesses, because these databases become easier to install, use, and maintain.

You may be among those who have been recently advised of a new mandate that all new applications must conform to client-server technology only: No file-server database management allowed. Having already invested a significant amount of your budget into the Access applications that you've developed, you're naturally concerned that the move to client-server architecture may require a major rewrite.

Fortunately, with Access 2007 and its Upsizing Wizard, you can provide a relatively simple and inexpensive solution that retains a significant amount of the original development effort while providing a database that conforms to client-server methodology.

You can automatically convert the tables stored in an existing Microsoft Access database (`.accdb` or `mdb`) to a client-server database using the Microsoft Access Upsizing Wizard. The Upsizing Wizard takes an Access Database Engine (formerly called Microsoft Jet database engine), and creates an equivalent SQL Server database with the same table structures, data, and many other attributes of the original database. The Upsizing Wizard re-creates table structures, indexes, validation rules, defaults, autonumbers, and relationships, and takes advantage of the latest SQL Server functionality wherever possible.

Before upsizing an application

You should perform these steps prior to converting an application using the Upsizing Wizard:

- **Back up your database.** Although the Upsizing Wizard doesn't remove any data or database objects from your Access database, it's a good idea to create a backup copy of your Access database before you upsize it.
- **Ensure that you have adequate hard-drive space.** At a minimum, you must have enough hard-drive space to store the new SQL Server database. Plan to allow at least twice the size of your Access database to allow room for future growth. If you expect to add a lot of data to the database, make the multiple larger.
- **Set a default printer.** You must have a default printer assigned, because the Upsizing Wizard creates a report snapshot as it completes the conversion.

SQL Server should be started automatically by the SQL Server Express installation. If SQL Server is not currently running, use the SQL Server Management Studio Express that was installed along with SQL Server Express to start SQL Server. The upsizing process needs a running SQL Server installation.

If, on the other hand, you're using a SQL Server instance running on another computer on the network, it is almost surely up and running, and there is nothing more for you to do.

Running the Upsizing Wizard

After you've completed the steps to prepare for the conversion, you' re ready to upsize your application. First, open the Microsoft Access database that you want to convert. This example upsizes the database for this chapter (`Chapter41.accdb`—make sure you use the original copy). Keep in mind that the result of the upsizing wizard is a brand-new Access `.adp` file already linked to the SQL Server database created by the Upsizing Wizard. Your original `.accdb` file remains unchanged:

1. **Open the Access database for this chapter** (`Chapter41.accdb`).
2. **Select the Database Tools tab.**
3. **Select the SQL Server option from the Move Data section.**

   The first dialog box of the Upsizing Wizard is shown in Figure 41-1.

   FIGURE 41-1

   Upsizing from Access 2007 to SQL Server 2005

   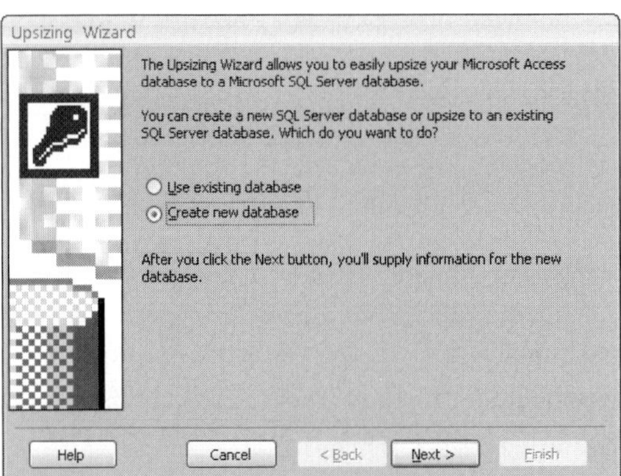

   Notice that the Create New Database option has been selected in this dialog box. Selecting the Use Existing Database option requires an existing SQL Server database as the target of the upsizing process. For the purposes of this demonstration, the assumption is that you're upsizing an Access database to take advantage of the features provided by SQL Server, and you're creating a brand-new SQL Server database to use as the data source for an existing Access application.

4. **The second dialog box of the Upsizing Wizard asks for the location of the SQL Server installation you want to use.**

   In Figure 41-2, a SQL Server 2005 Express database has been selected running on a computer named "DELL6000." The Upsizing Wizard create a new database on the selected server, containing replicates of all of the database objects (except for forms, reports, modules, and macros) in the current database.

FIGURE 41-2

Specifying the SQL Server installation to receive the new database

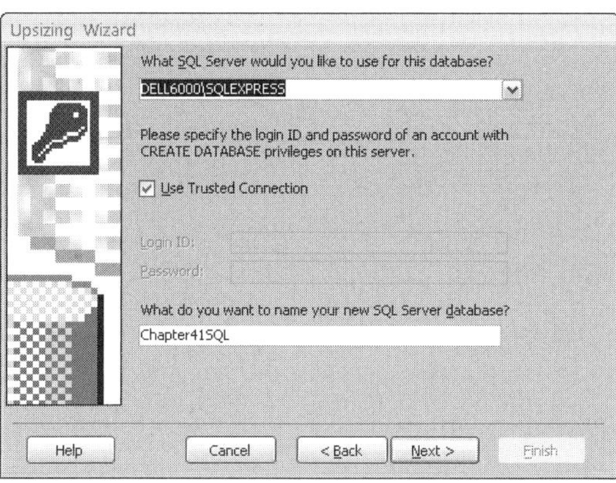

5. **The third dialog box (shown in Figure 41-3) allows you to select which tables to export to the SQL Server database.**

   Again, our scenario is to completely upsize an Access application to SQL Server, so all tables have been selected in this dialog box.

FIGURE 41-3

Selecting tables for the upsizing operation

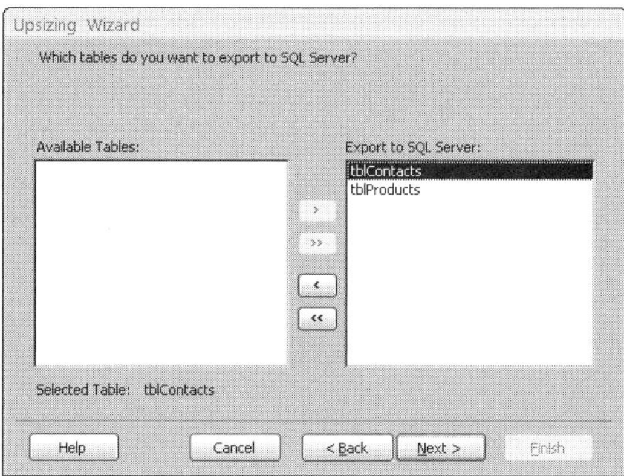

6. **The next screen (shown in Figure 41-4) asks for a lot of details on the table attributes that you want to upsize.**

Generally speaking, if you've added an index or validation rule to an Access table, you want the same attributes in a corresponding SQL Server table. Therefore, all of the options are selected on this dialog box by default.

FIGURE 41-4

Specifying the table details for the upsizing process

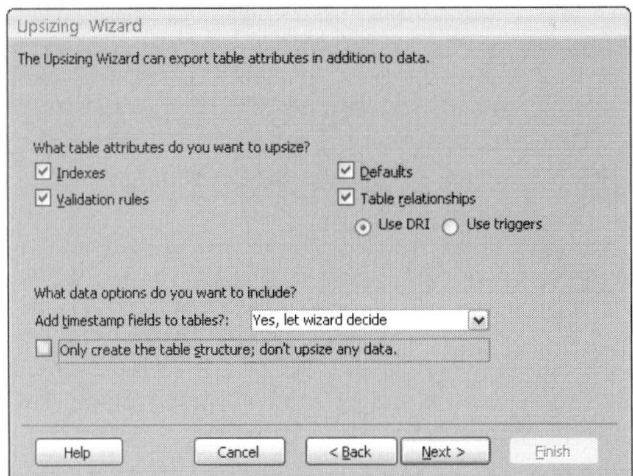

7. **The next screen (shown in Figure 41-5) allows you to either specify a new Access `.adp` file, or simply link the upsize SQL Server tables to the current database.**

   Because our scenario is to completely upsize an Access application to SQL Server, and because we want to use the SQL Server application for managing the tables and other database objects on SQL Server, Figure 41-5 shows the Creating New Access Client/Server Application option selected. The default name for the upsized `.adp` file is the same as the current Access database with a `CS` suffixed.

   You could just as easily have decided to simply upsize the tables without making any changes to the current Access database file. This might be a good option if the intent is to create copies of the Access tables in SQL Server so that other users, working with other SQL Server client-side applications can use the same data. However, because the data is copied to SQL Server, there will be no connection between the data remaining in the Access application and the data seen by other users.

   The SQL Server database created by the Upsizing Wizard is accessible to any qualified SQL Server user. Just because the data came from Access does not mean that the data can only be used in an Access context. Other users will be able to access the upsized Access data using applications written in Visual Studio .NET, Web pages built with ASP .NET, and any other application able to consume SQL Server data (like SharePoint).

FIGURE 41-5

Choosing how you want your Access application upsized

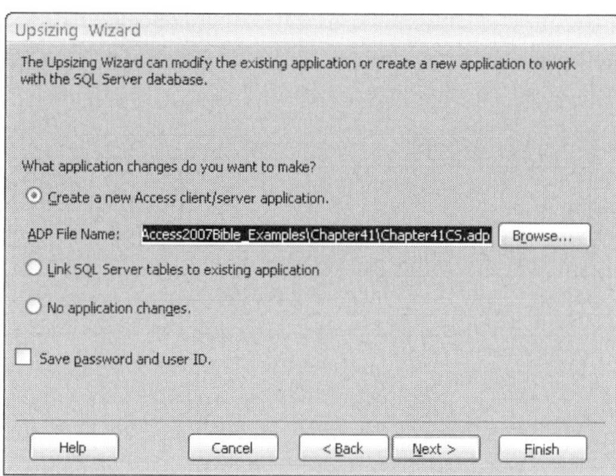

8. **The final dialog box of the Upsizing Wizard (shown in Figure 41-6) asks whether you want to (in this case, at least) open the new `.adp` file.**

   If, instead of upsizing and creating a new `.adp` file, we had chosen to upsize the tables and link them back to the current database, we would be returned to the database. But, for the purposes of this demonstration, we will go ahead and open the new `.adp` file.

FIGURE 41-6

The final Access Upsizing Wizard dialog box

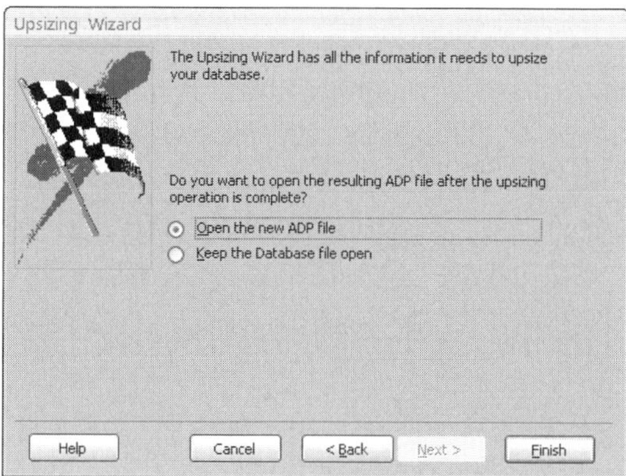

If, instead of upsizing all of the Access tables to SQL Server, you had chosen Link SQL Server Tables to Existing Application, the Upsizing Wizard would have modified your Access database to work with the new SQL Server database. Queries, forms, reports, and data-access pages are automatically linked to the data in the new Microsoft SQL Server database. The Upsizing Wizard renames the tables to be upsized with the suffix `_local` and leaves them intact. For example, if you upsize a table called `Customers`, the table is renamed `Customers_local` in your Access database. Then, the Upsizing Wizard creates a linked SQL Server table named `Customers`.

Upsizing the entire Access application to an Access project connected to a SQL Server database converts your application to a true client-server implementation. However, if you've been developing only Access databases until this point, you'll find client-server development is quite different. The Upsizing Wizard takes you only part of the way. The Upsizing Wizard doesn't make any changes to modules and macros. You may also need to make changes to your tables and queries to reach full functionality in the new architecture.

The conversion process itself should take no more than a few minutes to complete. A message box displays the progress of the conversion, as shown in Figure 41-7

FIGURE 41-7

Waiting for the Upsizing Wizard to complete the conversion process

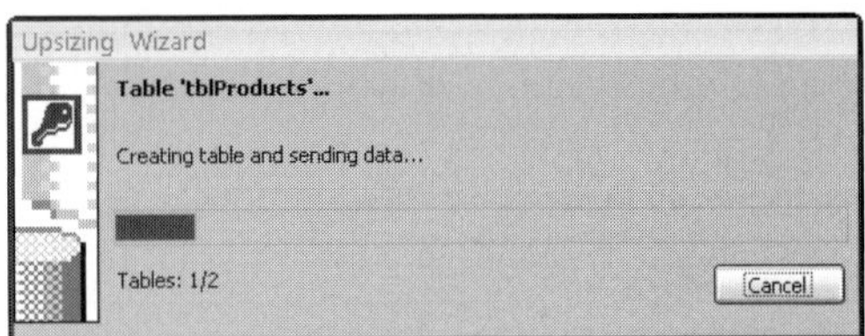

NOTE **An error message will be displayed if the Upsizing Wizard encounters referential integrity errors during the conversion process. You can click Yes to proceed with the conversion if you encounter an error message. Any problem data is not converted to the new database. If you don't want to omit the problem data, you must click No to cancel the conversion process.**

When the conversion process completes, the Upsizing Wizard automatically displays a report snapshot of the upsizing process. An example of the report snapshot is shown in Figure 41-8. The report snapshot includes information about each step of the conversion process for your application. The Upsizing Wizard report contains information about the following:

- Database details, including database size
- Upsizing parameters, including what table attributes you chose to upsize and how you upsized

- Table information, including a comparison of Access and SQL Server values for names, data types, indexes, validation rules, defaults, triggers, and whether or not timestamps were added

FIGURE 41-8

The Upsizing Wizard report

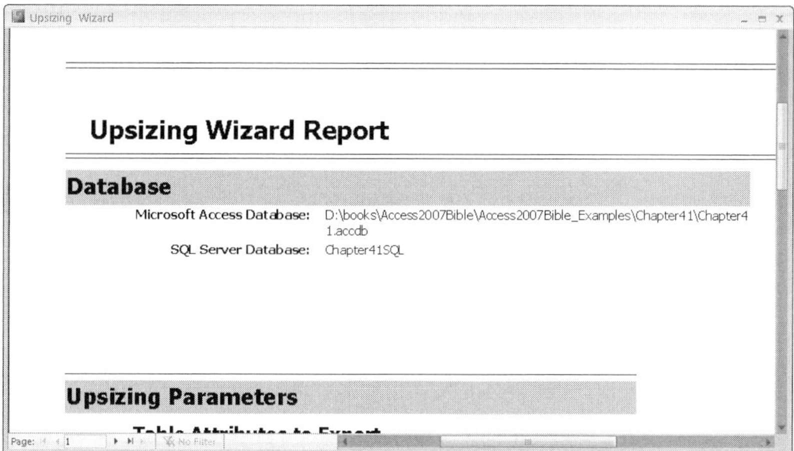

- Any errors, including database or transaction log full; inadequate permissions; device or database not created; table, default, or validation rule skipped; relationship not enforced; query skipped (because it can't be translated to SQL Server syntax); and control and record source conversion errors in forms and reports

The report snapshot is stored in the same folder as your application so that you can refer to it later.

Working with an Access ADP file

After you're finished reviewing the report, close it. When you close the report, the Upsizing Wizard automatically loads the new Access project. The Access Upsizing Wizard migrates the native Access objects into their corresponding objects in the new Access project. Although Access projects are organized into the same object groupings (tables, queries, forms, reports, and so on), Access Data Project objects differ significantly in how they work compared to native Access. The similarities and differences are outlined below:

- **Tables:** Individual tables are converted to SQL Server tables. Data types are converted to their corresponding SQL Server data types.

CROSS-REF **Refer to the next section, "Comparing Access 2007 to SQL Server data types," for a listing of SQL Server data types and how they compare to native Access data types.**

- **Queries:** Queries are converted into views, stored procedures, and functions according to the following rules:
  - Select queries that don't have an ORDER BY clause or parameters are converted to views.
  - Action queries are converted to stored procedure action queries. Access adds SET NOCOUNT ON after the parameter declaration code to make sure the stored procedure runs.
  - Select queries that use either parameters or an ORDER BY clause are converted to user-defined functions. If necessary, the TOP 100 PERCENT clause is added to a query that contains an ORDER BY clause.
  - Parameter queries that use named parameters maintain the original text name used in the Access database and are converted either to stored procedures or inline user-defined functions.
- **Forms and Reports:** Converted with no changes.
- **Data Access Pages:** The Upsizing Wizard changes the OLE DB connection and the data binding information in the Microsoft Office data source control to work with the new SQL Server database, and it copies the page's corresponding HTML file to the same location as the Access project, renaming the HTML file with a _CS suffix. The new pages in the Access project retain the original name, so that hyperlinks between the Access project pages continue to work.
- **Command Bars:** Converted with no changes.
- **Macros and Modules:** Converted with no changes.

To take full advantage of SQL Server and an Access project, you need to make some fairly significant changes to your newly converted application. Although the Upsizing Wizard tries to make its best guess as to the most efficient conversion approach, you should review the table and query designs and revise them as necessary. Record sources and control sources for forms and reports are converted without any changes. In an implementation with a large number of users, you don't want to bind forms and reports directly to a table or even a query.

NOTE **If you're converting an application created in an earlier version of Access, you may also need to manually convert code from Data Access Objects (DAO) to ActiveX Data Objects (ADO) in your modules.**

It is important understand that an Access .adp file does not contain linked tables. The tables in an Access .adp file are equivalent to any Access table. The only difference is that the table's data are provided by SQL Server and not by the Access Database Engine. And, because the tables are hosted by SQL Server, the data types available to you are somewhat different than in a native Access database. Figure 41-9 shows the user interface of the Access ADP created earlier in this chapter. Notice how similar it is to any Access 2007 application.

FIGURE 41-9

An Access 2007 ADP looks like any other Access 2000 application.

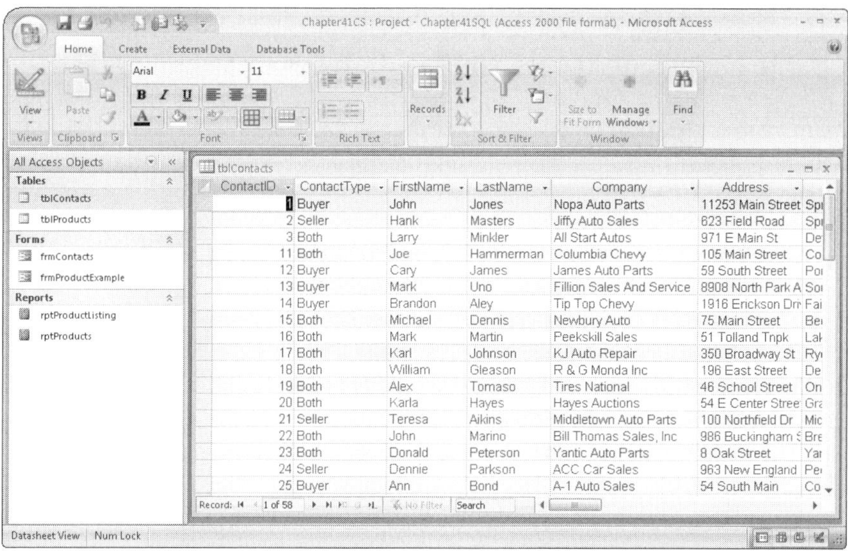

Comparing Access 2007 to SQL Server data types

Opening an upsized `.adp` table in Design View quickly reveals a significant difference between Access and SQL Server. In Figure 41-10, the `Contacts` table has been open in Design View. Notice that SQL Server provides many more different field data types and that the properties at the bottom of the table designer include items such as `Precision`, `Scale`, and `Identity`. These are all SQL Server constructs, yet they're accessible from within the Access user interface.

FIGURE 41-10

SQL Server field data types are considerably different than in Access.

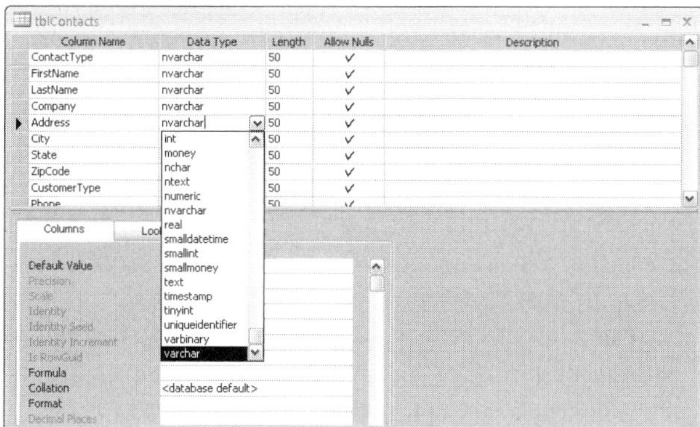

The data types available in Access 2007 are described as in Table 41-1.

TABLE 41-1

The Details of Access 2007 Data Types

Data Type	Used to Store	Limitations/Restrictions
Text	Alphanumeric data (text and numbers)	Stores up to 255 characters.
Memo	Alphanumeric data (text and numbers)	Stores up to 2GB of data (the size limit for all Access databases), if you fill the field programmatically. Remember that adding 2GB of data causes your database to operate slowly. If you enter data manually, you can enter and view a maximum of 65,535 characters in the table field and in any controls that you bind to the field. When you create databases in the Access 2007 file format, Memo fields also support rich-text editing.
Number	Numeric data	Number fields use a Field Size setting that controls the size of the value that the field can contain. You can set the field size to 1, 2, 4, 8, or 16 bytes.
Date/Time	Dates and times	Access stores all dates as 8-byte double-precision integers.
Currency	Monetary data	Stores data as 8-byte numbers with precision to four decimal places. Use this data type to store financial data and when you don't want Access to round values.
AutoNumber	Unique values created by Access when you create a new record	Stores data as 4-byte values; typically used in primary keys.
Yes/No	Boolean (true or false) data	Access uses –1 for all Yes values and 0 for all No values.
OLE Object	Images, documents, graphs, and other objects from Office and Windows-based programs	Stores up to 2GB of data (the size limit for all Access databases). Remember that adding 2GB of data causes your database to operate slowly. OLE Object fields create bitmap images of the original document or other object, and then display that bitmap in the table fields and form or report controls in your database. For Access to render those images, you must have an OLE server (a program that supports that file type) registered on the computer that runs your database. If you don't have an OLE server registered for a given file type, Access displays a broken image icon. This is a known problem for some image types, most notably JPEG images. As a rule, you should use Attachment fields for your `.accdb` files instead of OLE Object fields. Attachment fields use storage space more efficiently and are not limited by a lack of registered OLE servers.

Data Type	Used to Store	Limitations/Restrictions
Hyperlink	Web addresses	Stores up to 1GB of data. You can store links to Web sites, sites or files on an intranet or local area network (LAN), and sites or files on your computer.
Attachment	Any supported type of file	New to Access 2007 `.accdb` files. You can attach images, spreadsheet files, documents, charts, and other types of supported files to the records in your database, much like you attach files to e-mail messages. You can also view and edit attached files, depending on how the database designer sets up the Attachment field. Attachment fields provide greater flexibility than OLE Object fields, and they use storage space more efficiently because they don't create a bitmap image of the original file.

Table 41-2 shows the equivalent SQL Server data type for each Access data type.

TABLE 41-2

Comparison of Access 2007 and SQL Server Data Types

Microsoft Access Data Type	SQL Server Data Type
Yes/No	Bit
Number	tinyint, smallint, int, bigint: Very small integers up to very large integers. Smaller data types use less bytes and occupy less physical space. real, float: Real numbers and floating-point numbers are the same thing. decimal[(18,0)]: A decimal defaults to 2 decimal places but can be sized up to 18 bytes with no decimals. numeric[(18,0)]: Can be a specified length as for decimal.
Currency	money, smallmoney
Date/Time	datetime, smalldatetime, timestamp
AutoNumber	int (with identity property defined)
Text	char(10), varchar(50), varchar(n), varchar(MAX): ASCII character set string variables. nchar(10), nvarchar(50), nvarchar(n), nvarchar(MAX): Unicode character set string variables. char: Fixed-length string, usually short and known sizes, where string is padded up to fixed length regardless of value. varchar(50-n): Variable length strings where no padding added for shorter strings. MAX: Used for extremely large values.

continued

TABLE 41-2 *(continued)*

Microsoft Access Data Type	SQL Server Data Type
Memo	text and ntext: Large variable text strings stored in binary form. ntext stores unicode character set.
OLE Object	Image: Intended specifically for storing images in binary form.
Attachment	No equivalent.
Hyperlink	No equivalent.
Lookup Wizard...: based on a query or multiple literal values	No equivalent.
(no equivalent)	binary(50), varbinary, varbinary(50), varbinary(MAX)
(no equivalent, used for replication before Access 2007)	uniqueidentifier
(no equivalent)	xml: XML data type for storing both content and functionality of XML documents.
(no equivalent)	sql_variant: A variable data type except does not allow text, ntext, image, or timestamp.

Although the Upsizing Wizard maps Access data types to SQL Server data types, there are other conversion issues you'll need to be aware of. If the Upsizing Wizard Report indicates that a table has been skipped, examine the field names in each of the Access tables to ensure that they adhere to the following constraints:

- The first character must be a letter or the @ sign.
- The remaining characters may be numbers, letters, the dollar sign ($), the number sign (#), or the underscore (_).
- Spaces are allowed, but the Upsizing Wizard will insert brackets ([ ]) around the field name.
- The name must not be a Transact-SQL keyword. SQL Server reserves both the uppercase and lowercase versions of keywords.

ON the CD-ROM **To verify SQL Server reserved words, go to `http://msdn.microsoft.com`, and search for Transact-SQL Reference and SQL-Server Language Reference. Be aware that both content and location of these Web pages may change from the time of writing this book.**

If any field name in an Access table fails to follow these guidelines, the Upsizing Wizard is not able to upsize the table. The Upsizing Wizard Report informs you that the table has been skipped. However, the wizard does not always provide the reason the table was skipped. When you review the report, you can refer back to this section to review the field naming rules.

In addition to field-name constraints, the Upsizing Wizard also fails to upsize a table if it encounters any of these situations:

- If the field size between two fields participating in an Access relationship are not exactly the same for both fields.
- No unique index.
- A unique index on a field and Required property is set to No.
- More than two foreign keys defined on a single table.
- Invalid values for a date/time field values must be >=1/1/1753.

After you're finished reviewing the report, close it. When you close the report, the Upsizing Wizard displays the modified Access application.

NOTE **You may notice that all Access text data types are upsized to SQL Server nvarchar columns. This may cause a problem in some situations. The nvarchar data type supports Unicode (16-bit) character sets (as does Access 2007), which means every character requires 16 bits (2 bytes) of data storage, instead of 8 bits (1 byte). Upsizing very large Access tables containing lots of text fields could, conceivably, overwhelm the 4GB limit on the SQL Server 2005 Express database file. However, because an Access 2007 database is limited to 2GB, this is, at best, a remote possibility.**

Figure 41-11 shows the upsized SQL Server database open in Management Studio Express. The column properties of the `Contacts` table are displayed in the Summary tab of the Management Studio interface, showing the data types the Upsizing Wizard selected for each field in the original `Contacts` table.

FIGURE 41-11

Viewing the tables in the upsized database from within SQL Server Management Studio Express

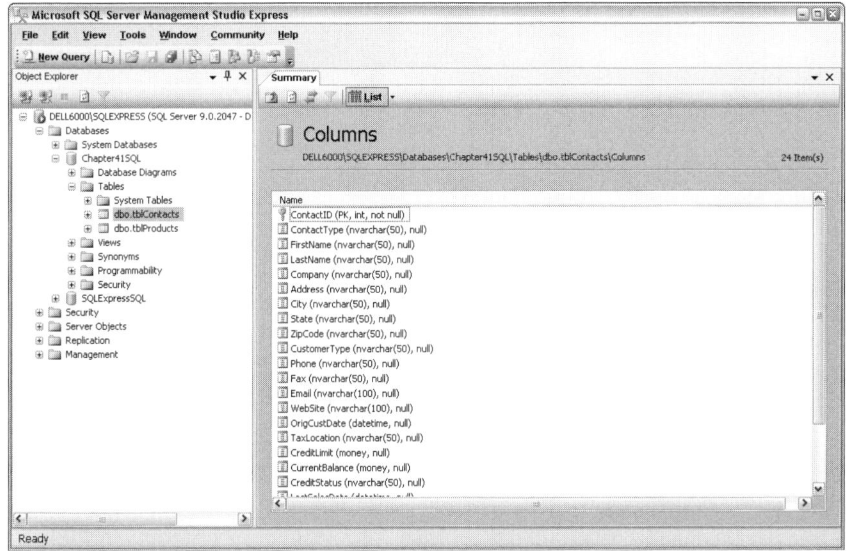

Summary

This chapter has surveyed the process of upsizing Access 2007 applications to SQL Server, using the Access `.adp` data file format as upsized database output. SQL Server alleviates many issues that have long vexed Access developers, such as database corruption, record lock contention, and poor performance when more than a few users make simultaneous updates.

Furthermore, upsizing to SQL Server immediately makes Access data accessible to any application connecting to SQL Server, including Web sites and Microsoft SharePoint Services. It's hard to overemphasize how important this aspect of the upsizing process is to Access developers. The data that your users input into their desktop Access applications is instantly accessible anywhere in the world, to anyone with access to SharePoint or another application connected to the SQL Server database.

This chapter also discussed the SQL Server 2005 Express Edition. SQL Server 2005 Express is a free download from Microsoft's Web site and, outside minimal registration requirements, can be used by anyone wanting to take advantage of the SQL Server database architecture and features. Unlike MSDE, which preceded SQL Server 2005 Express, the Express edition does not include the performance throttle that inhibited more than five or six connections to MSDE. This means that SQL Server 2005 Express is the ideal upgrade path for workgroup applications that have outgrown the Access Database Engine's capabilities.

Part VI

Appendixes

We conclude the *Access 2007 Bible* with several appendixes to serve as reference material as you work with Microsoft Access 2007. These appendixes cover information such as the limits (database size, number of database objects, maximum number of rows in an Access table, and so on), and a description of the contents of the book's CD.

The last appendix is an analysis of the new features in Access 2007. This version of Access includes more changes than any other previous version of Microsoft Access, both in the user interface and in challenges facing developers, and we analyze many of these changes for you in Appendix C.

IN THIS PART

Appendix A

Access 2007 Specifications

This appendix shows the limits of Microsoft Access database files, tables, queries, forms, reports, and macros.

IN THIS APPENDIX

Identifying the Access 2007 specifications and limits

Looking at limits for Access 2007 tables, queries, forms, and reports

Reviewing limits for SQL Server 2005 Standard Edition and SQL Server 2005 64-bit Standard Edition

Microsoft Access Database Specifications

TABLE A-1

Databases

Attribute	Maximum
ACCDB or MDB file size, including all database objects and data.	2GB, minus space needed for system objects (Because your database can include attached tables in multiple files, its total size is limited only by available storage capacity.)
Total number of objects in a database (tables, queries, forms, reports, and so on)	32,768
Number of modules, including modules attached to forms and reports	1,000
Number of characters in object names	64
Number of characters in a database password	14
Number of characters in a username or group name	20
Number of concurrent users	255

TABLE A-2

Tables

Attribute	Maximum
Number of characters in a table name	64
Number of characters in a field name	64
Number of fields in a record or table	255
Number of open tables	2,048, including system tables opened by Microsoft Access internally
Table size	2GB (minus space needed for system objects)
Number of characters in a Text field	255
Number of characters in a Memo field	65,535 when entering data through the user interface; 1GB when entering data programmatically
Size of OLE object field	1GB
Number of indexes in a record or table (including composite indexes, primary key indexes, and other indexes)	32
Number of fields in an index	10
Number of characters in a validation message	255

Attribute	Maximum
Number of characters in a validation rule (including punctuation and operators)	2,048
Number of characters in a table or field description	255
Number of characters in a record	4,000 (excludes Memo and OLE Object fields)
Number of characters in a field property setting	255

TABLE A-3

Queries

Attribute	Maximum
Number of tables in a query	32
Number of enforced relationships	32 per table, minus indexes that are on the table for the fields or combinations of fields that are not involved in the relationship
Number of fields in a record set	255
Dynaset size	1GB
Sort limit	255 characters in one or more fields
Number of levels of nested queries	50
Number of characters in a cell of the design grid	1,024
Number of characters in a parameter name for a parameterized query	255
Number of ANDs in a WHERE or HAVING clause	99
Number of characters in a SQL statement	64,000 (approximately)

TABLE A-4

Forms and Reports

Attribute	Maximum
Number of characters in a label	2,048
Number of characters in a text box	65,535
Form or report width	22 inches (55.87 cm)
Section height	22 inches (55.87 cm)

continued

TABLE A-4 *(continued)*

Attribute	Maximum
Height of all sections plus section headers in design view	200 inches (508 cm)
Number of levels of nested forms or reports	7 (form-subform-subform)
Number of fields/expressions you can sort or group on (reports only)	10
Number of headers and footers in a report	1 report header/footer, 1 page header/footer, 10 group headers/footers
Number of printed pages in a report	65,536
Number of characters in a SQL statement that is the `Recordsource` or `Rowsource` property of a form, report, or control (both `.mdb` and `.adp`)	32,750
Number of controls or sections you can add over the lifetime of the form or report	754
Number of characters in a SQL statement that serves as the `RowSource` property of a form or report, or the `ControlSource` property of a control	32,750

TABLE A-5

Macros

Attribute	Maximum
Number of actions in a macro	999
Number of characters in a condition	255
Number of characters in a comment	255
Number of characters in an action argument	255
Number of modules (including all forms and reports with `HasModule` property set to True)	1,0000

Access Data Projects (ADP) Specifications

TABLE A-6

Access Project

Attribute	Maximum
Number of objects in a Microsoft Access project (`.adp`)	32,768
Modules (including forms and report modules)	1,000
Number of characters in an object name	64
Number of columns in a table	1,024 (MS SQL Server 2000 and 2005)

TABLE A-7

Forms and Reports

Attribute	Maximum
Number of characters in a label	2,048
Number of characters in a text box	65,535
Form or report width	22 inches (56 cm)
Section height	22 inches (56 cm)
Height of all sections plus section headers in design view	200 inches (508 cm)
Number of levels of nested forms or reports	7 (form-subform-subform)
Number of fields/expressions you can sort or group on	10 (reports only)
Number of headers and footers in a report	1 report header/footer, 1 page header/footer, 10 group headers/footers
Number of printed pages in a report	65,536
Number of characters in a SQL statement that is the `Recordsource` or `Rowsource` property of a form, report, or control (both `.mdb` and `.adp`)	32,750
Number of controls or sections you can add over the lifetime of the form or report	754

TABLE A-8

Macros

Attribute	Maximum
Number of actions in a macro	999
Number of characters in a condition	255
Number of characters in a comment	255
Number of characters in an action argument	255

Microsoft SQL Server 2005 Database Specifications

The capacities of SQL Server 2000 databases are the same as SQL Server 2005. With the exception of database size, the values in this table apply equally to Microsoft SQL Server 2005 Express Edition. The maximum size of a SQL Server 2005 Express database is 4GB.

The maximum size of data managed by SQL Server 2005 is practically unlimited because of SQL Server's ability to be configured as *clustered* database servers.

TABLE A-9

Microsoft SQL Sever 2005 Capacities

SQL Server 2005 Database Engine Object	Maximum Sizes/Numbers for SQL Server 2005 (32-bit)	Maximum Sizes/Numbers for SQL Server 2005 (64-bit)
Batch size	65,536 × Network Packet Size	65,536 × Network Packet Size
Bytes per short string column	8,000	8,000
Bytes per GROUP BY, ORDER BY	8,060	8,060
Bytes per index key	900	900
Bytes per foreign key	900	900
Bytes per primary key	900	900
Bytes per row	8,060	8,060
Bytes in source text of a stored procedure	Lesser of batch size or 250MB	Lesser of batch size or 250MB
Bytes per `varchar(max)`, `varbinary(max)`, `xml`, `text`, or `image` column	1,073,741,823	1,073,741,823

SQL Server 2005 Database Engine Object	Maximum Sizes/Numbers for SQL Server 2005 (32-bit)	Maximum Sizes/Numbers for SQL Server 2005 (64-bit)
Characters per `ntext` or `nvarchar(max)` column	536,870,910	536,870,910
Clustered indexes per table	1	1
Columns in GROUP BY, ORDER BY	Limited only by number of bytes	Limited only by number of bytes
Columns or expressions in a GROUP BY WITH CUBE or WITH ROLLUP statement	10	10
Columns per index key	16	16
Columns per foreign key	16	16
Columns per primary key	16	16
Columns per base table	1,024	1,024
Columns per SELECT statement	4,096	4,096
Columns per INSERT statement	1,024	1,024
Connections per client	Maximum value of configured connections	Maximum value of configured connections
Database size	1,048,516TB	1,048,516TB
Databases per instance of SQL Server	32,767	32,767
File groups per database	32,767	32,767
Files per database	32,767	32,767
File size (data)	16TB	16TB
File size (log)	2TB	2TB
Foreign key table references per table	253	253
Identifier length (in characters)	128	128
Instances per computer	16	16
Length of a string containing SQL statements (batch size)	65,536 × Network packet size	65,536 × Network packet size
Locks per connection	Maximum locks per server	Maximum locks per server
Locks per instance of SQL Server	Up to 2,147,483,647	Limited only by memory
Nested stored procedure levels	32	32
Nested subqueries	32	32
Nested trigger levels	32	32

continued

TABLE A-9 *(continued)*

SQL Server 2005 Database Engine Object	Maximum Sizes/Numbers for SQL Server 2005 (32-bit)	Maximum Sizes/Numbers for SQL Server 2005 (64-bit)
Nonclustered indexes per table	249	249
Parameters per stored procedure	2,100	2,100
Parameters per user-defined function	2,100	2,100
REFERENCES per table	253	253
Rows per table	Limited by available storage	Limited by available storage
Tables per database	Limited by number of objects in a database	Limited by number of objects in a database
Partitions per partitioned table or index	1,000	1,000
Statistics on nonindexed columns	2,000	2,000
Tables per `SELECT` statement	256	256
Triggers per table	Limited by number of objects in a database	Limited by number of objects in a database
`UNIQUE` indexes or constraints per table	249 nonclustered and 1 clustered	249 nonclustered and 1 clustered
User connections	32,767	32,767
XML indexes	249	249

Appendix B

What's on the CD-ROM

This appendix provides you with information on the contents of the CD that accompanies this book. For the latest and greatest information, please refer to the ReadMe file located at the root of the CD.

IN THIS APPENDIX

Using the CD-ROM

Knowing what's included on the CD

Solving common problems

This appendix provides information on the following topics:

- System Requirements
- Using the CD
- Files and software on the CD
- Troubleshooting

System Requirements

Make sure that your computer meets the minimum system requirements listed in this section. If your computer doesn't match up to most of these requirements, you may have a problem using the contents of the CD.

- Windows Vista, Windows XP, or Windows 2000 or later. Microsoft Office 2007only works with these operating systems.
- A PC with a fast processor running at 500 MHz or faster (800 MHz for Windows Vista).
- At least 256MB of total RAM installed on your computer (512MB RAM for Windows Vista). For best performance, we recommend a minimum of 512MB for all versions of Windows.
- 2GB of free disk space (for installation of Microsoft Office 2007).
- A CD-ROM drive.

Using the CD

To install the items from the CD to your hard drive, follow these steps:

1. **Insert the CD into your computer's CD-ROM drive.**

   A window appears displaying the License Agreement.

2. **Press Accept to continue.**

Files and Software on the CD

The following sections provide more details about the software and other materials available on the CD.

The Complete Access Auto Auctions Example

The CD includes a completed Access Auto Auctions database in two formats:

- **Split Database:** Consisting of two different files: `AccessAutoAuctions.accdb` and `AccessAutoAuctionsData.accdb`. Both of these files should be installed to the `C:\Access 2007 Bible` folder on your computer.
- **Single File Database:** The entire Access Auto Auctions example (user interface, queries, code, and data) may be found in `AccessAutoAuctions_SingleFile.accdb`. You may find it somewhat simpler to use this example, particularly when working with table design issues. Because the tables are contained within the same file as the rest of the application, Access allows you to make whatever changes you wish to the tables and other data structures without opening an additional database file.

In the event that you encounter problems with the split database examples, it is possible that the table linkages are broken. The table links can be broken by moving either the `AccessAutoAuctions.accdb` file or the `AccessAutoAuctionsData.accdb` file to a different location than the `Access 2007 Bible` folder on your C: drive.

If the table linkages appear to be broken, please consult the "Viewing or changing information for linked tables" section in Chapter 16 for instructions on using the Linked Table Manager to restore the broken linkages.

Example files for the Access 2007 Bible

These files will be installed into a directory named `Access 2007 Bible`, or you can choose any directory in which to install these files. Below this directory will be 41 subdirectories named Chapter_01, Chapter_02, and so on through Chapter_41. Each subdirectory contains all of the files necessary to follow the examples in the corresponding chapter.

A few chapters have no examples, and do not have a corresponding folder on the book's CD. Most chapters contain a single Access 2007 database file with an `.accdb` extension, such as `Chapter30.accdb`, while some folders contain multiple Access database files and auxiliary files used for the chapter's examples.

Also, a few chapters include Access 2000–format `.mdb` data files to demonstrate Access 2007 features that are only supported in the older database file formats.

Many chapters also use additional database files, graphics, document files, or help files as found in each chapter subdirectory and explained at the beginning of each chapter.

eBook version of *Access 2007 Bible*

The complete text of the book you hold in your hands is provided on the CD in Adobe's Portable Document Format (PDF). You can read and quickly search the content of this PDF file by using Adobe's Acrobat Reader, also included on the CD.

Troubleshooting

If you have difficulty installing or using any of the materials on the companion CD, try the following solutions:

- **Turn off any antivirus software that you may have running.** Installers sometimes mimic virus activity and can make your computer incorrectly believe that it is being infected by a virus. (Be sure to turn the antivirus software back on later.)
- **Close all running programs.** The more programs you're running, the less memory is available to other programs. Installers also typically update files and programs; if you keep other programs running, installation may not work properly.
- **Reference the ReadMe:** Please refer to the ReadMe file located at the root of the CD-ROM for the latest product information at the time of publication.

If you still have trouble with the CD, please call the Customer Care phone number: 800-762-2974. Outside the United States, call 1-317-572-3994. You can also contact Customer Service via the Web at `www.wiley.com/techsupport`. Wiley Publishing, Inc., will provide technical support only for installation and other general quality-control items; for technical support on an application, consult the program's vendor.

Appendix C

What's New in Access 2007

When we first opened Access 2007, we spent the first ten minutes looking for a "Switch to Classic View" button and never found it. The user interface is a radical departure from previous versions. You'll find a completely new interface that eventually proves faster and somewhat easier but most definitely has a learning curve. Many additional features have also been added that make the developer's job easier and more enjoyable than ever. Some changes however are not as welcome.

IN THIS APPENDIX

- Reviewing the changes and enhancements for the developer in Access 2007
- Looking at what's new in table design
- Understanding the new form and report options
- Learning the importance of SharePoint integration

The User Interface

Microsoft has gone to great length to change the look and feel of Access 2007. To get an idea of how great these changes are, take a look at Figure C-1.

FIGURE C-1

The Access interface is completely revamped for 2007.

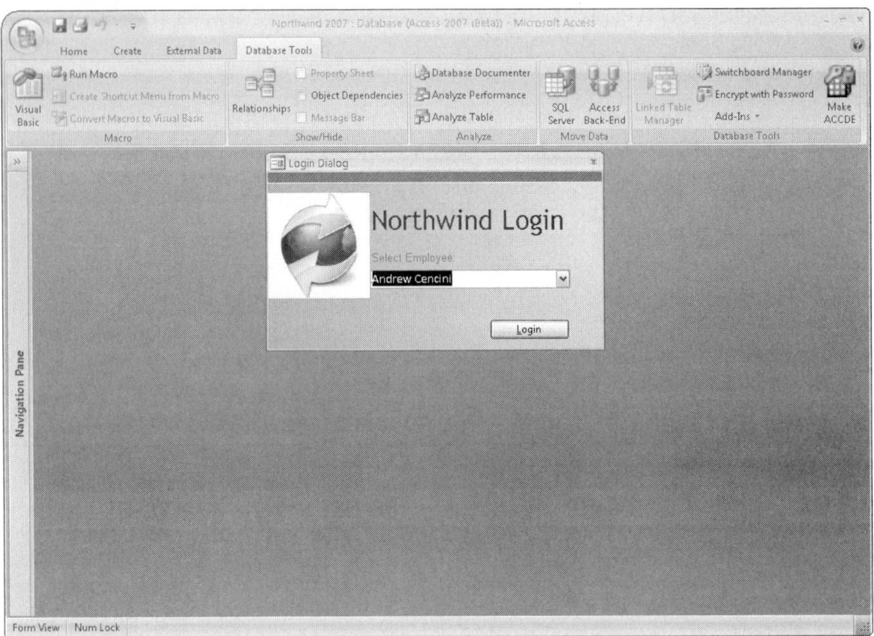

As you can see, our old friend Northwind has an entirely new look. The biggest of the changes to the interface itself is the removal of the traditional nested menus in favor of a more tabular, everything-in-front-of-you, system called the *ribbon*. The hardest part of the ribbon is finding the file menu! After you locate it (it's the circle in the top left with the Microsoft Office logo), you'll be pleasantly surprised with its location as well as its easy jump-to Options and general database utilities like Backup or Compact and Compare. The vastly improved File menu (which Microsoft has renamed the Office menu!) is shown in Figure C-2.

The ribbon is designed to be contextual so that everything you need is there when you need it. Functions such as Font, Records, and Sort & Filter are grouped together and make the ribbon a welcome change. The downside of the ribbon is that creating a custom one requires external XML code as well as a somewhat-strange "callback" model for the VBA procedures that provide the ribbon with its intelligence. The lack of a simpler method within Access itself to create and work with ribbons is a real drawback.

FIGURE C-2

The complicated set of nested menus and dialog boxes is greatly simplified.

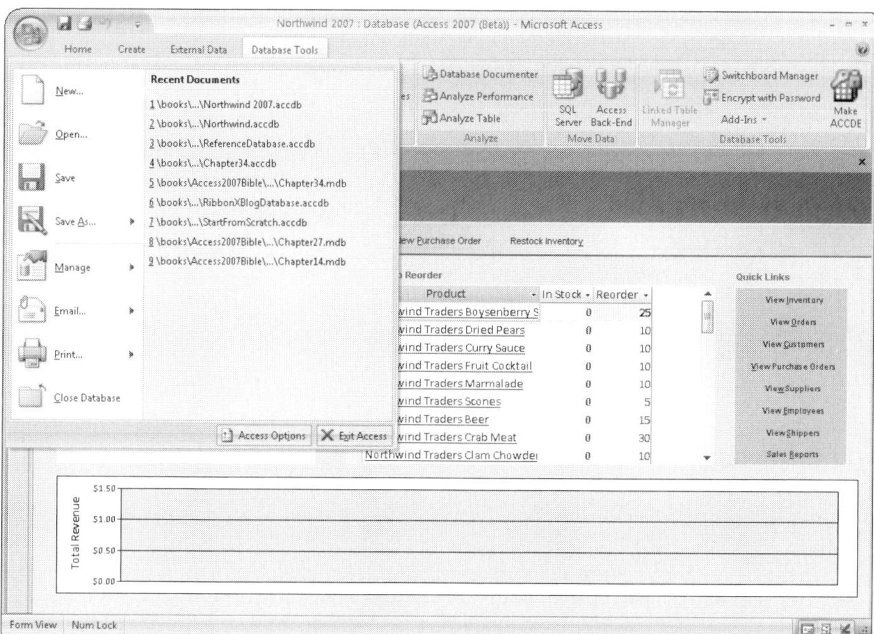

Another organizational feature for the user interface is the use of a tab system for open objects (tables, forms, queries, and so on) instead of independent, floating windows. No more looking for an object through various task bar and menu items. Each open object occupies a tab for easy reference. Figure C-3 shows four different objects open in the tabbed workspace. Even though the Customer List form is currently displayed in the tabbed area, any of the other open objects (Home, Order list, and Customer Address Book) is quickly access through its corresponding tab.

The Navigation Pane has also been enhanced to allow the user to view objects by create date, modified date, dependencies, or custom groups. The Navigation Pane docks at the left side of the screen so that you have more room to work. You can also collapse the Navigation Pane by clicking on the left-pointing arrows in the upper-right corner, if you need more room to work on a form or report. Figure C-4 shows some of the options available for viewing database objects in the Access 2007 Navigation Pane.

FIGURE C-3

The new tabbed interface is a welcome change.

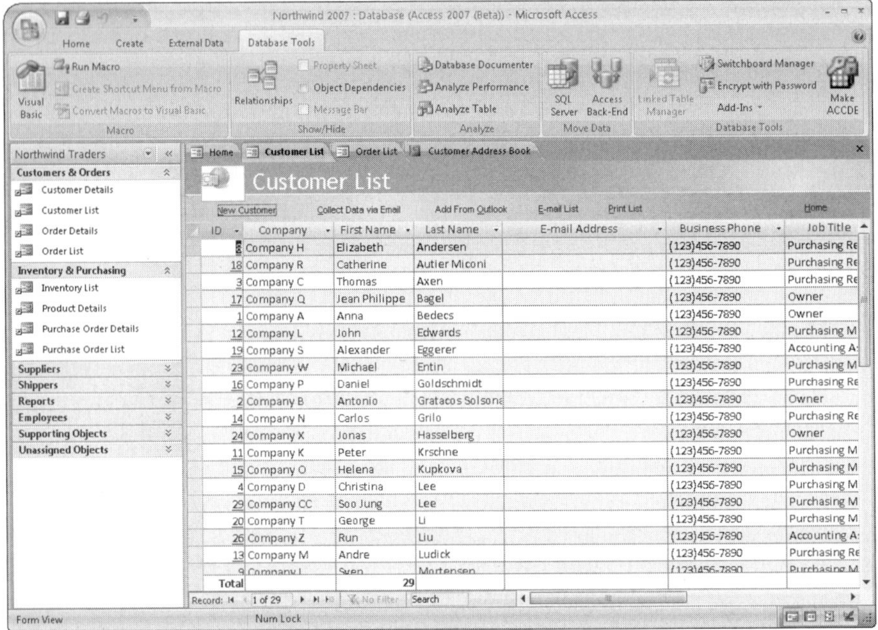

FIGURE C-4

The new Navigation Pane replaces the old Database window.

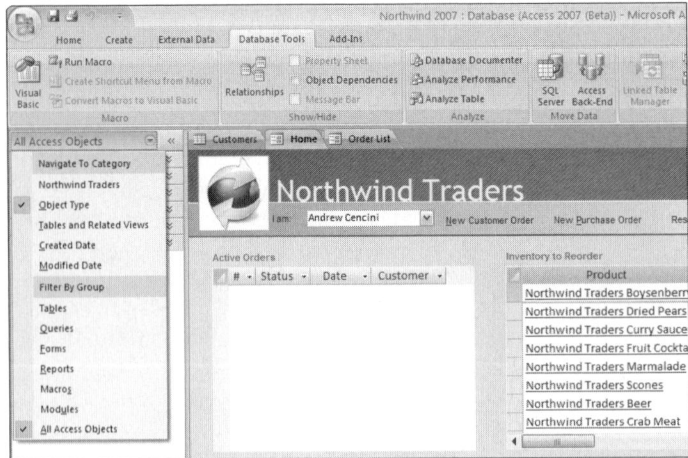

Tables

A table is a table is a table, but new features make life easier and faster. Tables now support rich-text formatting in memo fields, multivalue fields, and automatic formatting of data pasted from Excel. If you paste an Excel date field into a new table, Access recognizes it and formats the field as the Date/Time data type. It's a simple change but it really does help with initial table design.

Another welcome addition is the alternating color option. Creating a "green bar" look for your datasheets is now a snap and makes reviewing data and forms that much easier and appealing for the end user. Another welcome addition to tables is the Attachment data type. Now all types of documents and binary files can be included in your application without database bloat.

Datasheet View

Datasheet view is now an excellent tool to review, modify, or verify your data. The new enhancements embed filtering and simple math as part of the view itself.

Filtering is now contextual to the field type you choose and many new point-and-click sorts are available. Figure C-5 shows the filters Access supports for date fields. Similar filters are available for numeric and text data, as well.

FIGURE C-5

Datasheet view supports a number of powerful filtering and sorting options.

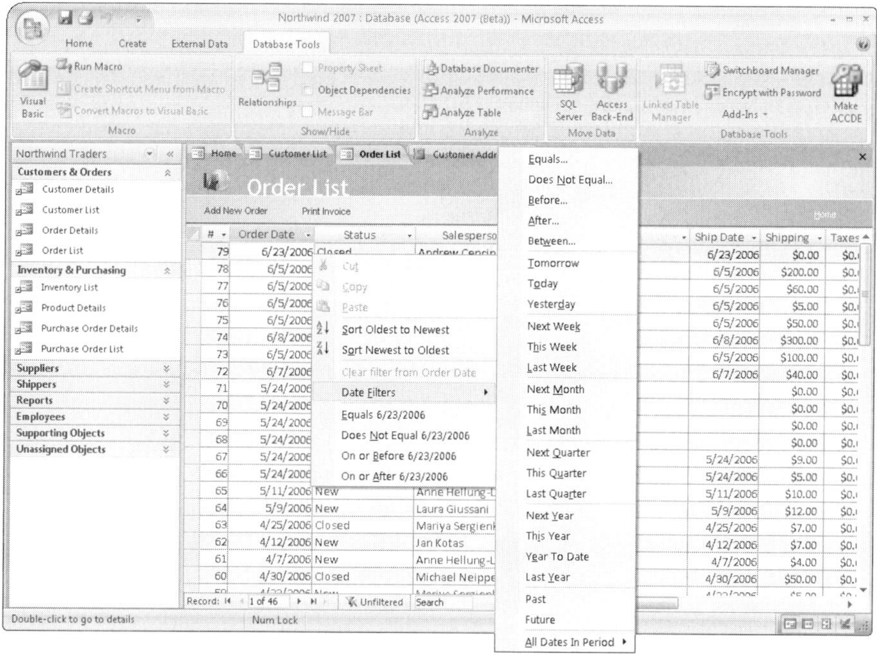

You can also click on the field name itself and get additional sort-and-filter options based on the field content. Figure C-6 shows a few of the filtering options for text data.

Along with filtering, you can now get totals for a column right from Datasheet view. These totals will also apply as you filter down through the records — *very* cool! Figure C-7 shows the Totals row added to the bottom of a datasheet. Notice that the Totals row appears below the data contained within the datasheet, and does not interfere with the datasheet's data.

Fields can easily be added from Datasheet view and there is now a Field Template pane from which you can choose a field complete with name, data type, length, and prepopulated properties. You can also set up your own field templates and standard definitions to share with a workgroup or department.

FIGURE C-6

The Datasheet view's right-click menu contains additional filtering options.

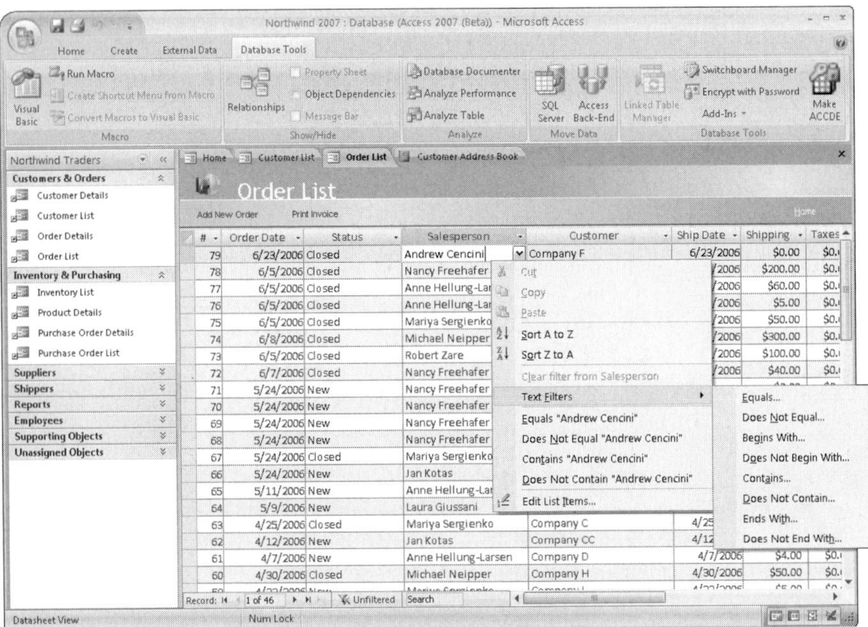

FIGURE C-7

Clicking on the Totals ribbon button adds a Totals row to Datasheet view.

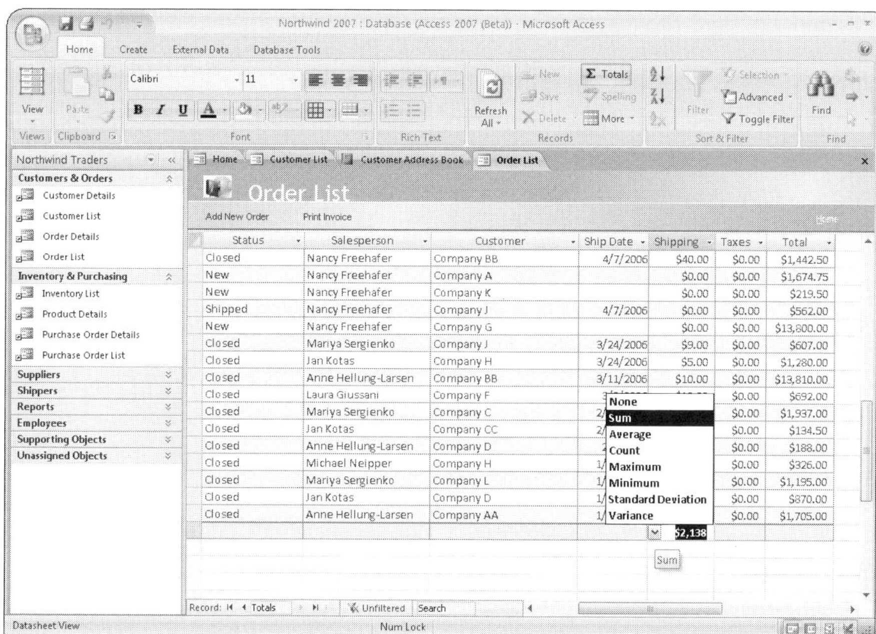

Forms

With the expanded field list task pane, you can now add fields that are part of the recordset, as well as fields from other tables that are not. Access will automatically set up any relationships that are required as you drag the field onto the form. A new split view is available to show both the Form view and Datasheet view on the same form. The datasheet can be placed top, bottom, left, or right side of a split form. Form design has been greatly enhanced with a new view called Layout view. With Layout view, you can perform many of the most common form edit tasks while looking at the data on the form itself as opposed to the standard form design option, which does not display the recordset.

If you're tired of the same old colors and options, you'll really enjoy the new format and color options. Access now has 25 standard color option templates and also includes the ability to create your own style options. The color palettes supported by Access 2007 are shown in Figure C-8.

FIGURE C-8

Access 2007 comes with a wide variety of built-in color and font styles for forms and reports.

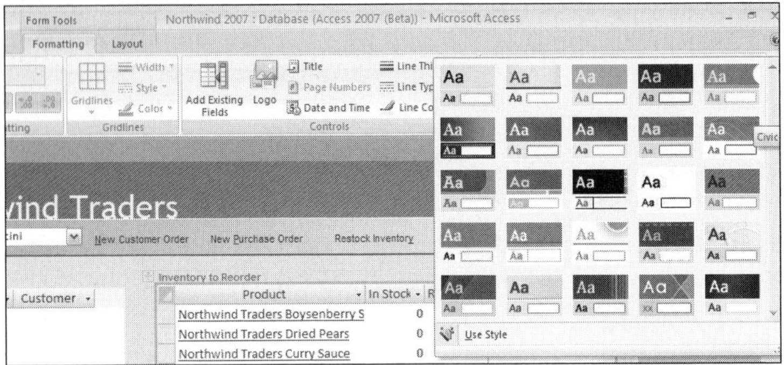

If that is not enough, there is a new updated color selector as well as the old blend box. Figure C-9 shows the new color selector added to Access 2007.

FIGURE C-9

Access finally supports a full color palette for controls, forms, and reports.

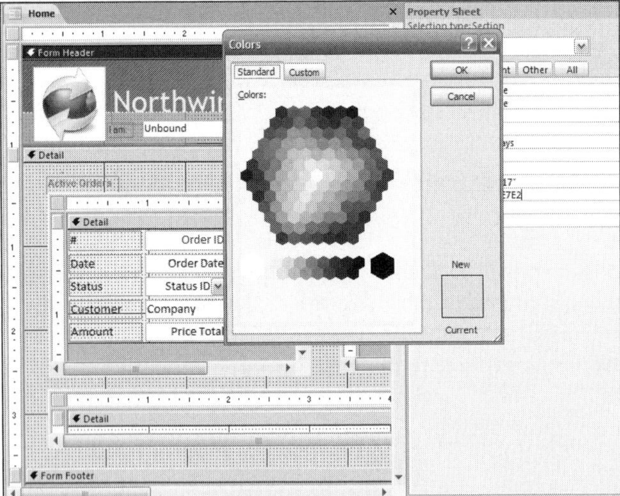

A completely new option on forms is the ability to embed macros within forms and controls. These are traditional Access macros that become part of the form, report, or control object just like a form's module. Embedded macros are somewhat limited in their functionality but are trusted by the new security features of Access. Interestingly enough, macros are now being encouraged more than in the past.

Also added is a calendar date selector for all date/ time formats.

Reports

Reports offer all the new features of forms but also include additional group, sort, and total features. Sorting and grouping can be applied and automatically viewed in Report view. Simple group totals and sums can be added to a section by selecting the section and selecting a Sum Field option. No need to create a calculated control. Figure C-10 shows the new sorting and grouping area, and how you set up a report group in Access 2007.

FIGURE C-10

Access 2007 reports come with a number of built-in summary and other totals controls.

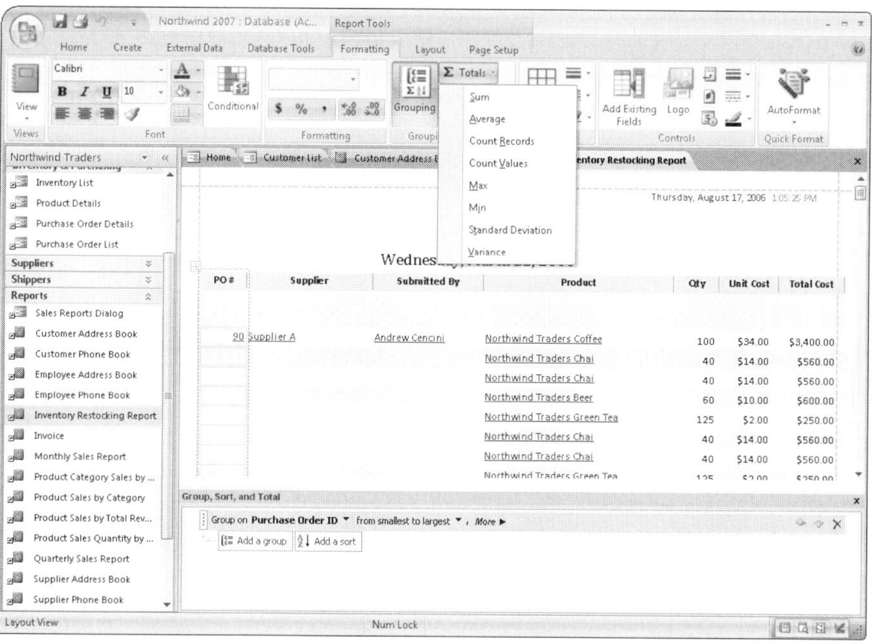

Macros

Microsoft is placing a large emphasis on macros in Access 2007. Much of this has to do with the new security model. Certain macro actions, such as opening forms and reports, are considered "safe" and are permitted to run without any adjustments to the default Access security settings. These macros may be embedded in forms, reports, and controls to automate many common database operations. Macros now include error handling, better debugging, and the ability to assign values to the variables. This is a big change over previous versions of Access and may be difficult for many advanced developers to embrace. One neat feature of the new macros is the ability to schedule them to run through Outlook. This is a neat feature for automatic imports, exports, or report generation.

Security

User-level security has been removed from this version of Access in favor of the new trusted security model that relies on trusted folders and sandbox mode for any other applications. The enhanced macro functionality is further designed to allow users most functionality through it. In a nutshell, the plan is to implement most or all of your application's logic as the new embedded macro so that the application will be trusted and run under the new model. This may prove difficult to implement in certain environments.

For users who require user-level security, Access 2007 works with older-format `.mdb` files without conversion or enabling. This means you can continue to use an Access 2000, 2002, or 2003 `.mdb` file, complete with user-level security, in Access 2007 without changes.

SharePoint

SharePoint Services are being used to provide functionality to enterprise applications over a SharePoint Server for functionality such as revision history, permission setting, and recovery of deleted records. SharePoint data residing on distant Web servers is available to local Access applications with no special requirements other than a fast Internet connection. Access users (with the appropriate security credentials) are able to view, update, and add to SharePoint data as if the data resided on their desktop computer, no matter where the SharePoint server is hosted.

SharePoint is sure to grow in importance and prominence in environments where instant access to remote data is a high priority.

Summary

Access 2007 represents a large number of new and changed features, all of which present challenges for Access developers. The new interface requires some adjustments to your way of thinking, but it's considerably more efficient for many common tasks.

In spite of the new features, the loss of user-level security, replication, and the fact that ribbons completely replace toolbars and menus prove to be an obstacle for some developers. Ribbons are considerably more difficult to build than previous toolbars and menus, and — at least, at the time of this writing — there were not a lot of examples of ribbons available to guide development efforts.

Overall, though, the new interface and new features are welcome changes in Access 2007. We hope you'll find Access 2007 as interesting and productive as we have.

Index

Symbols and Numerics

A

B

C

D

E

F

H

M

O

P

Q

R

S

T

U

V

W

X

Y

Z

Wiley Publishing, Inc.
End-User License Agreement

READ THIS. You should carefully read these terms and conditions before opening the software packet(s) included with this book "Book". This is a license agreement "Agreement" between you and Wiley Publishing, Inc. "WPI". By opening the accompanying software packet(s), you acknowledge that you have read and accept the following terms and conditions. If you do not agree and do not want to be bound by such terms and conditions, promptly return the Book and the unopened software packet(s) to the place you obtained them for a full refund.

1. **License Grant.** WPI grants to you (either an individual or entity) a nonexclusive license to use one copy of the enclosed software program(s) (collectively, the "Software") solely for your own personal or business purposes on a single computer (whether a standard computer or a workstation component of a multi-user network). The Software is in use on a computer when it is loaded into temporary memory (RAM) or installed into permanent memory (hard disk, CD-ROM, or other storage device). WPI reserves all rights not expressly granted herein.
2. **Ownership.** WPI is the owner of all right, title, and interest, including copyright, in and to the compilation of the Software recorded on the physical packet included with this Book "Software Media". Copyright to the individual programs recorded on the Software Media is owned by the author or other authorized copyright owner of each program. Ownership of the Software and all proprietary rights relating thereto remain with WPI and its licensers.
3. **Restrictions on Use and Transfer.**

   (a) You may only (i) make one copy of the Software for backup or archival purposes, or (ii) transfer the Software to a single hard disk, provided that you keep the original for backup or archival purposes. You may not (i) rent or lease the Software, (ii) copy or reproduce the Software through a LAN or other network system or through any computer subscriber system or bulletin-board system, or (iii) modify, adapt, or create derivative works based on the Software.

   (b) You may not reverse engineer, decompile, or disassemble the Software. You may transfer the Software and user documentation on a permanent basis, provided that the transferee agrees to accept the terms and conditions of this Agreement and you retain no copies. If the Software is an update or has been updated, any transfer must include the most recent update and all prior versions.
4. **Restrictions on Use of Individual Programs.** You must follow the individual requirements and restrictions detailed for each individual program in the "What's on the CD-ROM" appendix of this Book or on the Software Media. These limitations are also contained in the individual license agreements recorded on the Software Media. These limitations may include a requirement that after using the program for a specified period of time, the user must pay a registration fee or discontinue use. By opening the Software packet(s), you agree to abide by the licenses and restrictions for these individual programs that are detailed in the "What's on the CD-ROM" appendix and/or on the Software Media. None of the material on this Software Media or listed in this Book may ever be redistributed, in original or modified form, for commercial purposes.

5. **Limited Warranty.**

   (a) WPI warrants that the Software and Software Media are free from defects in materials and workmanship under normal use for a period of sixty (60) days from the date of purchase of this Book. If WPI receives notification within the warranty period of defects in materials or workmanship, WPI will replace the defective Software Media.

   (b) WPI AND THE AUTHOR(S) OF THE BOOK DISCLAIM ALL OTHER WARRANTIES, EXPRESS OR IMPLIED, INCLUDING WITHOUT LIMITATION IMPLIED WARRANTIES OF MERCHANTABILITY AND FITNESS FOR A PARTICULAR PURPOSE, WITH RESPECT TO THE SOFTWARE, THE PROGRAMS, THE SOURCE CODE CONTAINED THEREIN, AND/OR THE TECHNIQUES DESCRIBED IN THIS BOOK. WPI DOES NOT WARRANT THAT THE FUNCTIONS CONTAINED IN THE SOFTWARE WILL MEET YOUR REQUIREMENTS OR THAT THE OPERATION OF THE SOFTWARE WILL BE ERROR FREE.

   (c) This limited warranty gives you specific legal rights, and you may have other rights that vary from jurisdiction to jurisdiction.

6. **Remedies.**

   (a) WPI's entire liability and your exclusive remedy for defects in materials and workmanship shall be limited to replacement of the Software Media, which may be returned to WPI with a copy of your receipt at the following address: Software Media Fulfillment Department, Attn.: *Access 2007 Bible*, Wiley Publishing, Inc., 10475 Crosspoint Blvd., Indianapolis, IN 46256, or call 1-800-762-2974. Please allow four to six weeks for delivery. This Limited Warranty is void if failure of the Software Media has resulted from accident, abuse, or misapplication. Any replacement Software Media will be warranted for the remainder of the original warranty period or thirty (30) days, whichever is longer.

   (b) In no event shall WPI or the author be liable for any damages whatsoever (including without limitation damages for loss of business profits, business interruption, loss of business information, or any other pecuniary loss) arising from the use of or inability to use the Book or the Software, even if WPI has been advised of the possibility of such damages.

   (c) Because some jurisdictions do not allow the exclusion or limitation of liability for consequential or incidental damages, the above limitation or exclusion may not apply to you.

7. **U.S. Government Restricted Rights.** Use, duplication, or disclosure of the Software for or on behalf of the United States of America, its agencies and/or instrumentalities "U.S. Government" is subject to restrictions as stated in paragraph (c)(1)(ii) of the Rights in Technical Data and Computer Software clause of DFARS 252.227-7013, or subparagraphs (c) (1) and (2) of the Commercial Computer Software - Restricted Rights clause at FAR 52.227-19, and in similar clauses in the NASA FAR supplement, as applicable.

8. **General.** This Agreement constitutes the entire understanding of the parties and revokes and supersedes all prior agreements, oral or written, between them and may not be modified or amended except in a writing signed by both parties hereto that specifically refers to this Agreement. This Agreement shall take precedence over any other documents that may be in conflict herewith. If any one or more provisions contained in this Agreement are held by any court or tribunal to be invalid, illegal, or otherwise unenforceable, each and every other provision shall remain in full force and effect.